Studies in Federalism

STUDIES IN FEDERALISM

Directed and Edited by

ROBERT R. BOWIE
and
CARL J. FRIEDRICH

LITTLE, BROWN AND COMPANY
Boston · Toronto
1954

Published simultaneously in Canada
by Little, Brown & Company (Canada) Limited

PRINTED IN THE UNITED STATES OF AMERICA

Preface

The present volume is essentially a record or *documentation*. It reproduces the several studies as they were actually furnished to the European Movement and printed by them, after being translated into French. Only very minor revisions, correcting obvious errors, have been allowed. The studies show the inevitable defects of work done under great pressure. Most of it had to be accomplished between July and October, 1952. The associates listed all worked as hard as circumstances allowed. As is usual in cooperative enterprises, it is difficult to make fully clear who contributed what. It was decided to acknowledge special authorship of the junior associates only where a major portion of the work was done by one of these. Their work was divided between the analytical studies and the appendices. As far as the analytical studies are concerned, it is happily acknowledged that a substantial amount of work was done by Richard Green on the study dealing with the Federal Legislature, by Gustave Hauser and M. Magdelena Schoch on the Judiciary, by A. Bickell on the Defense, by Jack A. Hauer and Hugo Joseph Hahn on the study on Commerce, Transportation, and Customs and by S. Rothman, R. von Pachelbel, T. S. Baer and R. Hirschfield on the Defense of the Constitutional Order, by L. Fuchs and F. Gross on the Admission of New States, and by T. Reuber on the study on Agriculture. Others not specifically mentioned who also contributed are W. C. Baum, Milton Cikins, Richard Dosik, Henry K. Heuser, Franz Jacob and W. S. Rothschild.

For the appendices dealing with particular countries, largely for purposes of documentation, an effort was made to have them either written or reviewed by a "native": in the case of Australia, by Professor McWhinney; Canada, by Mrs. Judith Shklar; Germany, by Dr. G. Dietze and Mr. von Pachelbel; and Switzerland, by Dr. D. Schindler. No such specialized assignment was, of course, attempted in the case of the United States. A draft bibliography was prepared with the help of Dr. G. Dietze, and this draft has been augmented by suggestions from the *Europa-Archiv*, as well as by special references for individual studies.

It might be added here that due to R. R. Bowie's being called to Washington as Director of the State Department's Policy Planning Staff, the editorial work has had to be handled by the undersigned alone; in this he has, however, enjoyed the constant encouragement and help of Arthur E. Sutherland. The editorial assistance of Miss Roberta G. Hill was invaluable.

None of this work could have been done without the financial assistance provided by a grant from the Ford Foundation, secured for the Federalism

Project by the American Committee on United Europe. Needless to say, neither the Foundation nor the Committee assumed any responsibility for the results of this research and the findings based upon it. In keeping with sound academic tradition, this was an enterprise of independent scholars, working to bring knowledge to bear upon a concrete and difficult problem.

As mentioned before, all these studies, with appendices but without the Bibliography, have appeared in French. They were published by the *Mouvement Européen* Headquarters in Brussels during 1953, in seven volumes. A much abbreviated version of them was published in German by *Europa-Archiv* in their two issues of December, 1953.

In his preface to these European editions, M. Paul-Henri Spaak, the President of the Movement and of the Common Assembly of the European Coal and Steel Authority, said:

> The "Studies in Federalism" represent the contribution of American friends to the chief legal work which it is hoped to realize. The American Committee on United Europe, directed by the authority and devotion of William J. Donovan, after obtaining the generous support of the Ford Foundation, and being informed of the work going on in Europe, organized . . . a very important center of research. . . . At the moment when we are engaged in discussions relative to a projected treaty leading to a statute for the European Community, the work of the American jurists is of immense interest. If it is true that it is necessary for Europe to find completely new solutions to the problems presented, it is also very evident that the study of precedents is of very great importance.

Whether the Draft Treaty embodying a Statute of a European (Political) Community adopted by the enlarged Common Assembly of the European Coal and Steel Authority, known as the *Assemblée Ad Hoc,* and presided over by M. Spaak, becomes law, is modified or is superseded, only the future can tell. But that this draft represents a culmination of the efforts to unify Europe politically and economically, few who study the work attentively will doubt. One can only hope that it will not share the fate of the Frankfort Constituent Assembly of 1848 whose imaginative proposals for uniting Germany in peace and freedom were cast aside and eventually superseded by the work of men who believed in "blood and iron." There is still good reason to believe that the counsels of reason and common sense will prevail against bureaucrats and vested interests.

CARL J. FRIEDRICH

Harvard University
February 8, 1954

Directors of Research

Robert R. Bowie
Carl J. Friedrich

Associates

Ayers Brinser
H. van Buren Cleveland
Paul A. Freund
Robert G. McCloskey

Edward McWhinney
Louis B. Sohn
Arthur E. Sutherland

Research Assistants

Theodore S. Baer
Warren C. Baum
Alexander M. Bickel
Milton Cikins
Gottfried Dietze
Richard Dosik
Lawrence H. Fuchs
Richard A. Green
Franz Gross
Robert H. Guttman
Hugo Hahn
Jack A. Haner
Gustave Hauser
Henry K. Heuser

R. G. Hirschfield
Franz Jacob
Alexis E. Lachman
Albert A. Mavrinac
W. R. von Pachelbel
Guy J. Pauker
Stanley Rothman
Walter S. Rothschild
Dietrich Schindler
M. Magdalena Schoch
William J. Schrenk
Paul C. Shafer
Judith N. Shklar
Herbert Spiro

Summary of Contents

Appendices

Table of Contents

STUDY 1

THE FEDERAL LEGISLATURE

STUDY 2

THE FEDERAL EXECUTIVE

STUDY 3

THE FEDERAL JUDICIARY

STUDY 4
DEFENSE

STUDY 5

FOREIGN AFFAIRS

STUDY 6

COMMERCE, TRANSPORTATION, AND CUSTOMS

STUDY 7

PUBLIC FINANCE

STUDY 8

FEDERAL POWERS OVER CURRENCY, BANKING,
CREDIT, AND FOREIGN EXCHANGE

STUDY 9

AGRICULTURE

STUDY 10

LABOR AND SOCIAL SECURITY

STUDY 15

ADMISSION OF NEW STATES, TERRITORIAL ADJUSTMENTS,
AND SECESSION

STUDY 16

AMENDMENT OF THE CONSTITUTION

Appendices

Introduction

The Background of These Studies and the
Development of the Draft Constitution

The *Studies in Federalism* were prepared at the request of the *Comité pour la Constitution Européenne* of the *Mouvement Européen,* whose consultant the undersigned had become in March, 1952. The President of the *Mouvement Européen,* M. Paul-Henri Spaak, in presenting them to the European parliamentarians of the constitutional assembly (*Assemblée Ad Hoc*) described their purpose as follows:

> These studies are a tool of incontrovertible utility which the European Movement is placing at the disposal of all those who participate in the legal work which is now going on. The documentation which is thus furnished is considerable and will limit to a minimum the long and difficult inquiries to which they [the drafters] will have to address themselves. The comparison of the solutions adopted in the different countries where there exists a federal constitution will facilitate making the decisions which must be chosen.

The purpose of this study was to provide detailed comparative material for the deliberations on the European constitution; unfortunately some of the later studies were available only in draft form by the fall of 1952.

It may be worth while to recall briefly the series of events into which these research studies were supposed to fit. During the fall and early winter of 1951, as the negotiations for a European Defense Community were drawing to a close, leaders of the European Movement became increasingly convinced that the most serious difficulties in the way of securing parliamentary approval for the Defense Treaty would arise from the fact that no organized European political community exists. This fact not only makes one ask such questions as: whose foreign policy does this proposed army stand back of? but it also raises the deeper issues of loyalty essential for the morale of any successful fighting force. European leaders therefore insisted more vigorously upon the need for establishing an effective constitutional, i.e., political, framework for the Defense Community which would also comprise the economic community implied by the establishment of the Coal and Steel Authority. While ratification of the treaty establishing this Authority was still being vigorously debated at that time, it was taken for granted that this ratification would occur presently, as indeed it did in May, 1952.

During a visit of M. Frenay and Herr Kogon of the Union of European Federalists to the United States in November, 1951, the possibility of some sort of research cooperation in the preparation of constitutional proposals was broached by Frenay. General William J. Donovan, as chairman of the American Committee on United Europe, expressed strong interest in such cooperation, as did M. Spaak for the *Mouvement Européen*. When Bowie returned, in January, 1952, from his work as Legal Counsel to the United States High Commissioner in Germany, which had brought him into close contact with the negotiations for both the Coal and Steel and the Defense Communities, he joined me in actively interesting himself in the proposed work for the European constitution.

In March, 1952, the European Movement established the *Comité des Juristes*, which later became the *Comité d'Etudes pour la Constitution Européenne*, mentioned above.[1] It consisted of the following members:

Max Becker, Lawyer and Member of the Bundestag, Germany
Lodovico Benvenuti, Deputy, Under Secretary for Foreign Trade, Italy
Piero Calamandrei, Professor at the University of Florence, Deputy
Arthur Calteux, Councilor of the High Court of Justice of Luxembourg
Pierre de Felice, Lawyer and Deputy, France
Henri Frenay, former Minister of State, France
Hans Nawiasky, Professor at the University of Munich and at the Graduate
   School of Commerce at Saint-Gall
Hermann Pünder, Lawyer and Member of the Bundestag, Germany
Altiero Spinelli, General Secretary of the Italian Federalist Movement
Cornelis van Rij, Lawyer, Netherlands
(M. J. H. W. Verzijl, Professor at the Universities of Utrecht and Leyden
   (Netherlands), gave technical assistance to the committee.)

This committee of experts was charged with the task of preparing a number of draft resolutions (see Appendix I, pages 819–827). Its first meeting, attended by Bowie, was held from April 26 to 29, 1952 in Paris. Other extended meetings followed during the summer, for which various materials were prepared, including more particularly critical evaluations of some of the work of the Committee. The basic concept of these consultations, as agreed upon with M. Spaak in early April, 1952, when he was visiting the United States, was that it would be our task and that of our associates to furnish comparative material and analysis as to how federal systems have worked elsewhere, but that we would not undertake to argue for or against particular solutions of the specific problems facing the Committee in connection with a constitution for a European political community. As a matter of fact, a number of earlier draft proposals for such a constitution had been prepared by various organizations participating in the European Move-

---

[1] The work of this group was reported in a publication giving summaries of the discussions of the various meetings entitled *Projet de Statut de la Communauté Politique Européenne: Travaux Préparatoires*, Brussels, Nov. 1952. In this volume the original text of the resolutions eventually proposed is given on pages 216–229.

ment[2] which provided useful starting points for the work of the Committee. Several members of the Committee had been involved in preparing some of these drafts, among them the Secretary General of the Committee, the Belgian Senator Dehousse, Professor of Law at the University of Liége, whose contribution was outstanding. It fell to Dehousse actively to direct the Committee's work under the general chairmanship of Spaak.

Senator Dehousse was in a strategic position for another reason. The Council of Europe decided at Strasbourg in May, 1952, to establish a *Comité des Juristes* of its own to survey various proposals for a European constitution and to make a report thereon as soon as possible. Senator Dehousse was chosen to be chairman of this committee also. He made a report for his committee to the Consultative Assembly at Strasbourg on September 13, 1952.[3] It would be leading too far afield to go into the complex political situation which occasioned this initiative of the Council of Europe. Obviously it is closely related to the general problems confronting the "Community of the Six" vis-à-vis the broader and looser general European community organized in the Council of Europe and including Great Britain.[4]

If it was clear that the only really effective assistance which two American consultants could give a European team of experts working on a constitution was a broad comparative survey of federal practice in the leading federal states, it was equally clear that the lack of such studies called for a broad research program which would have to be organized in the shortest possible time to gather, digest and analyze the material for such comparative studies.[5] Fortunately, both the Graduate School of Public Administration and the Law School at Harvard were ready to sponsor such research work, if adequate support could be found. Such support was provided by the Ford Foundation, upon a request from the American Committee on United Europe. Consequently, it became possible to enlist the cooperation of the Associates and Assistants whose names appear on the page following the Preface. The work was done under great pressure during July, August and

[2] For the text of some of these proposals see De Russett, *Strengthening the Framework of Peace,* Chapter V, Royal Institute of International Affairs (London, 1950). Some of these proposals have been evaluated, e.g., by L. C. Klausner in "Proposed Constitution for the United States of Europe," 20 *World Affairs Interpreter* 241–255 (1949), and by Ernst B. Hass in "The United States of Europe: Four Approaches to the Purpose and Form of a European Federation, 63 *Political Science Quarterly* 528–550 (1948). There were also a number of earlier plans, among them Mackay, *Peace Aims and the New Order* (1941); Weinfeld, *Towards a United States of Europe* (1942); Jennings, *A Federation of Western Europe* (1940); and a summary in Maddox, *European Plans for World Order,* James, Patten-Roe Pamphlet Series No. 8, Philadelphia, March, 1940. Note also the discriminating discussion by R. G. Hawtrey in *Western European Unity* (1950).

[3] Conseil de L'Europe, Assemblée Consultative, Quatrième Session Ordinaire (SG (52)2): Rapport Introductif du Comité des Juristes sur le Problème d'une Communauté Politique Européenne, Strasbourg, September, 1952.

[4] F. L. Schuman, "The Council of Europe," 45 *American Political Science Review* 724 (1951); K. Löwenstein, "Union of Western Europe, 52 *Columbia Law Review* 55–59, 200–240 (1952).

Lowenstein, "Union of Western Europe, 52 *Columbia Law Review* 55–59, 200–240 (1952).

[5] The useful comparative study by K. C. Wheare, *Federal Government* (2d ed. 1951), is largely concerned with governmental structure.

September, 1952, in order that draft reports might be at the disposal of the Committee for their decisive sessions in September, 1952.

These sessions were scheduled for the end of September, because the official program had moved ahead rather rapidly in the meantime. In May, 1952, the Coal and Steel Community Treaty was ratified, and on May 27, 1952, the Defense Community Treaty was signed. Into this latter Treaty, there had been inserted, at the suggestion of Signor de Gasperi, an Article 38 which provided as follows:

1. Within the period provided for in Section 2 of this Article the Assembly shall study:
    (a) The creation of an Assembly of the European Defense Community elected on a democratic basis;
    (b) The powers which might be granted to such an Assembly; and
    (c) The modifications which should be made in the provisions of the present Treaty relating to the other institutions of the Community, particularly with a view to safeguarding an appropriate representation of the States.

    In its work, the Assembly will particularly bear in mind the following principles:

    The definitive organization which will take the place of the present transitional organization should be conceived so as to be capable of constituting one of the elements of an ultimate federal or confederal structure, based upon the principle of the separation of powers and including, particularly, a bicameral representative system.

    The Assembly shall also study problems to which the coexistence of different organizations for European cooperation, now in being or to be created in the future, give rise, in order to ensure that these organizations are coordinated within the framework of the federal or confederal structure.
2. The proposals of the Assembly shall be submitted to the Council within six months from the date on which the Assembly shall have assumed its functions. These proposals will then be forwarded, together with the opinion of the Council, by the President of the Assembly to the Governments of the member States, which within three months from the date of the receipt of these proposals, shall call a conference for the purpose of examining them.[6]

M. Spaak and other leaders of the European Movement, as soon as the Defense Treaty was signed, took the view that it might be desirable to have the Foreign Ministers of the six nations of the Coal and Steel Community request that the Common Assembly of the Coal and Steel Authority — if need be, augmented by the additional members which the European Defense

[6] Senate, 82nd Cong., 2d Sess., Convention on Relations with the Federal Republic of Germany and a Protocol to the North Atlantic Treaty, p. 178. U.S. Government Printing Office, Washington, D.C. (1952).

Community Treaty provided for[7] — undertake the task of drafting a constitution. Such a proposal was natural for two reasons: (1) the ratification of the European Defense Community Treaty would be facilitated by the development of plans for a political community, and (2) the two assemblies were composed largely of the same parliamentarians, designated for this purpose by their respective parliaments. The proposal found favor with several of the Foreign Ministers, notably M. Schuman, and consequently, such a request was in fact made on September 10, 1952, and was favorably acted upon on September 13. As a result, the *Assemblée Ad Hoc* (largely identical with the Common Assembly of the Coal and Steel Community) came into being; only the German Social Democrats refused to participate.

Within this general setting, the Working Committee of the *Comité d'Etudes* undertook to review the draft resolutions submitted to it by one of its most active and effective members, Signor Altiero Spinelli, who has been associated with the European federal movement since the beginning. Spinelli had received a number of drafts from different members of the Committee,[8] which he had organized into nine resolutions, dealing with (1) preamble and General Provisions, (2) executive of the Community, (3) parliament of the Community, (4) judicial power of the Community, (5) jurisdiction of the Community in matters of coal and steel, (6) jurisdiction of the Community in matters of defense, (7) jurisdiction of the Community in matters of foreign policy, (8) jurisdiction of the Community in matters of finance, (9) constitutional amendment. Under the chairmanship of Senator Dehousse, these drafts were subjected to exacting scrutiny and criticism, in which I was able to participate, during a series of sessions from September 12 to 14, 1952, at Strasbourg. At the opening meeting, M. Spaak emphasized the urgency of arriving at solutions which could be of real help to the Constitutional Assembly which was certain to begin its work by the end of that month. It was decided by this working committee not to concern itself with the formal questions, such as whether the Community was to be a federation or a confederation — the article in the European Defense Community Treaty had also left this question open — but to address itself to the concrete issues. Among these the organizational questions loomed large, because according to M. Spaak's instructions, it was of primary importance to devise a sound structure; the problems of what powers to attribute to the Community were for the time being settled by the two treaties on coal and steel and on defense, and their extension could be considered later. Among the issues causing greatest difficulty at the time were, however, certain general questions such as the right of secession, the relations with other states — members of the Council of Europe and more especially to Great Britain — and the admission of new states. In the organizational field, the problems

[7] Article 33. *Id.* at 176.
[8] See for this Comité d'Etudes pour la Constitution Européenne; Projet de Statut de la Communauté Politique Européenne: Travaux Préparatoires. Mouvement Européen, Brussels, November, 1952.

were centered on the issue of whether to propose a dependent executive
of the parliamentary type familiar to Europe, or whether to adopt a more
stable system such as that of the United States or Switzerland. A modified
Swiss system with a strengthened chief executive was tentatively agreed upon.
Closely related to this problem was that of the structure of the legislature.
That it should be bicameral had been settled by the European Defense Community Treaty and the Foreign Ministers, but what should be the nature of
the second chamber had not been decided. At least one German member
of the Committee favored the German type of federal council which would
represent the governments of the member states, whereas others inclined
toward the senate type which would represent the parliaments of the component states (as does the Consultative Assembly of the Council of Europe
and as did the United States Senate under the original Constitution). The
Committee decided to propose a senate, but even this decision still left the
difficult issue of how to provide for this representation. Should every member state have the same number of senators, or should there be some sort of
proportionality? The smallness of Luxembourg with its 70,000 inhabitants,
as against the over forty millions each of France, Germany and Italy, seemed
perplexing. Still, the Committee decided to recommend equality, in order
to be able to maintain complete proportionality of the popular chamber
which was to be based upon general elections.

The draft resolutions[9] developed by the Working Committee in these sessions were submitted to the whole Committee during its sessions at Brussels,
from September 27 to 30, 1952. Spinelli acted as rapporteur. As such, he
reviewed the findings of the Working Committee during the intervening two
weeks. At the first meeting of the Committee, the draft reports of the Fed-
ralism Project at Harvard were submitted and were received with great appreciation by the chairman of the meetings, Senator Dehousse. The preliminary findings of these reports became an integral part of the deliberations
of the Committee, serving as source material on the practice of federal states.

The discussions during the sessions at Brussels were dominated by a spirit
of moderation. Perhaps it would have been preferable that the conclusions
had been more radically federalist in nature, but most of the Committee
members felt that it was necessary to produce resolutions that would recommend themselves to the Ad Hoc Assembly.[10] Thus, the Committee did not
adopt the rule of equality for the representation of the member states in the
Senate, but it did recommend equality of the citizens in elections for the
Peoples' Chamber — 500,000 votes were to elect one deputy.

The major areas of disagreement among Committee members were the following: whether to organize the executive on the parliamentary or the presidential model, whether to have a senate or a council to represent the states,

---

[9] See Appendix I, Draft Resolutions, page 819.
[10] See for the record *Projet de Statut de la Communauté Politique Européenne: Travaux
Préparatoires* as cited at note 8 above, pp. 133–214.

whether this body should be based upon the principle of the equality of member states (as in most existing federations), the problems of judicial appeal, the defense of colonial territories, the treaty power of the Community and the component states, the direct taxation of individuals versus contributions by the member states, amendments, and ratification. It became evident during the discussions that some members were more inclined toward a strong supranational authority than others. But even the more reluctant members of the committee were sufficiently convinced of the importance of establishing a supranational government to avoid altogether the recommending of a body of national ministers, such as was included by the Ad Hoc Assembly in their Draft Treaty, in keeping with the precedent of both the Coal and Steel Community Treaty and the Defense Community Treaty. The Resolutions (see below, page 819) show that the Committee agreed on a simple structure, composed of a largely independent executive, a bicameral legislature composed of a popular house and a federal senate, and an independent high court, and that it was prepared to invest this government with broad powers of defense, limited powers in foreign affairs and finance, and an expanding authority in the development of a common market. It was inclined to make constitutional amendments dependent upon the assent of all the national parliaments for a limited period, but prepared thereafter to subject them only to the requirement of a two-thirds majority.

Having completed its labors, it entrusted its Chairman, Senator Dehousse, with presenting the Resolutions to the Ad Hoc Assembly, and decided, upon M. Dehousse's own motion, to continue in existence for the duration of the Ad Hoc Assembly. As a matter of fact, the Committee was called in January, 1953, at the time of the Ad Hoc Assembly and undertook to consider the recommendations of its Constitutional Committee, which it subjected to a critical examination. It has not met since that time. There is no indication in the record of the Ad Hoc Assembly itself that the Resolutions of the Committee were ever introduced formally either to the Assembly or its committees. However, an analytical comparison of the Assembly's Draft Treaty with the Committee's Resolutions, prepared in April, 1953,[11] shows a substantial amount of agreement, though also some very sharp divergencies. A brief consideration of the work of the Ad Hoc Assembly may therefore be in order.

The Assembly itself, being a rather large body, decided upon establishing a Working Party (Comité de Travail) and a Constitutional Committee (Commission Constitutionelle), the latter again dividing itself into a Committee on Powers and Competence (Comité des Attributions), a Committee on institutions (Comité des Institutions), a Committee on Liaisons, and a Committee on Judicial Institutions (Comité des Pouvoirs Judiciaires). The proceedings of these committees, as well as those of the Assembly, have not

[11] Mouvement Européen. Comité d'Etudes, Parallèle entre le Projet de Traité adopté par l'Assemblée Ad Hoc et le Projet de Statut établi par le Comité.

yet been published, but are available in mimeographed form, partly in English. Unfortunately, the reports are much abbreviated and often do no more than indicate the point at issue.[12]

It is, however, clear from all this material that the disagreements to a considerable extent parallel those which occurred in the Preparatory Committee. It stands to reason, moreover, that in an assembly in which quite a few members are included on the basis of an indirect election (the members were nominated by the respective parliaments as provided for under the Coal and Steel Community Treaty for its Common Assembly), some sentiment sharply antagonistic to the proposed constitution would make itself felt. Indeed, the German Social Democrats, as noted, refused to participate in the deliberations of the Ad Hoc Assembly altogether, and the RFP (Gaullist) members (as well as some others) rejected the Draft Treaty. It is, as a matter of fact, remarkable that so large a measure of agreement was achieved and that the proposed Draft Treaty was adopted by a large majority. Incidentally, a novel feature in the history of federalism was the participation in the Assembly's deliberations of representatives of European powers not members of the Coal and Steel Community, who had a voice but not a vote. The record shows that their cooperation was valuable.

The sharpest conflicts arose over the following questions: whether the executives of the Coal and Steel Community and of the Defense Community should be merged in the Political Community's executive or should be kept separate; the function and role of the Council of National Ministers and whether it should vote unanimously or by qualified majority — and in this connection the question of the balance of power between the supranational community and that of the component national communities; the problem of proportionality in both Senate and Peoples' Chamber; the relation between the executive and the legislative bodies and the status of their members; the extent of powers and more especially those in the economic sphere (common market); the admission of new states and the problem of associated members of the European Community who are not ready to enter into the federation; the general problem of the European Community's foreign relations, including the juridical status of the Community under international law; the problems of overseas territories, of the Saar and of Eastern Germany (on these two issues no solution was finally arrived at); the relation of the European Political Community to the Council of Europe; the matter of amendments, and finally the problem of a common citizenship.

It would be fascinating to trace the debates on these several issues, but such an undertaking would lead much too far afield. Suffice it to say that as the Draft Treaty itself clearly shows, the answers adopted by the Ad Hoc Assembly tended to be quite moderate. In the words of Paul-Henri Spaak, the President of the Assembly, spoken when he presented the Draft Treaty

---

[12] The story in formal outline may be gathered from the Introductory Material given in Ad Hoc Assembly, Information and Official Documents of the Constitutional Committee, October, 1952 — April, 1953, published by the Secretariat.

to the Council of Foreign Ministers at Strasbourg on March 10, 1953, the proposed constitution was "partly federal and partly confederal." [13]   Thus the Assembly avoided making a choice between the federal and the confederal alternatives, suggested by Article 38 of the Defense Community Treaty. It would seem that the Assembly was wise to disregard this artificial dichotomy and to proceed on the assumption that federating Europe is a process which commenced as soon as a limited supranational sphere was recognized and appropriately organized, as in the Coal and Steel Community.

Events since the adoption of the Draft Treaty have greatly disappointed its drafters.   Their moderation has not been rewarded by swift action on the part of the governments concerned.   Various uncertainties, such as the shifts in Soviet policy, the German elections, the Italian and French governmental crises, prevented agreement among the governments, and by the end of 1953 the drafts had not been presented to the parliaments of the several states.   Perhaps the President of the Ad Hoc Assembly should have proceeded in accordance with the provisions of Article 38 of the EDC Treaty, cited above, but no doubt he hesitated to do so, in view of the fact that the Ad Hoc Assembly was called by the Foreign Ministers without reference to the suggested power of the President to forward the draft of the Treaty to the several governments which were to act on it within three months.   Indeed, at a meeting in Rome, in September and October, 1953, the deputies of the six Foreign Ministers proceeded to consider the questions which the Draft Treaty was intended to resolve almost as if no Draft Treaty existed. As a consequence, a wide variety of views were put forward by the diplomatic representatives of the six states.   Against this studied disregard of the work of the elected representatives of the parliaments of the six nations, a solemn protest was entered by the Second Hague Congress, convened by the European Movement from October 8 to 10, which formulated a series of resolutions urging the governments to proceed on the basis of the Draft Treaty, but insisting that the Draft Treaty ought to be amended in a number of vital respects, especially the matters of amendments and of economic powers.[14]

It may be well to conclude this review of the events which led to these *Studies in Federalism* by a brief exposition of the Draft Treaty for a European Community.[15]   Our treatment will have to be highly selective, and can deal only with the major aspects.

The character and scope of the proposed Community can best be ex-

[13] See *Draft Treaty Embodying the Statute of a European Community* (as published by the Ad Hoc Assembly as Doc. 15R, without date, but presumably in late March, 1953), p. 150.

[14] See Mouvement Européen, Comité d'Action, Deuxième Congrès de la Haye, Resolutions, Rapport Politique, Rapport sur les Institutions, Rapport sur le Marché Commun.

[15] This analysis appeared under the title "The Statute of the European Community" in 3 *European Union* 221 (1953), American Committee on United Europe, over the names of R. R. Bowie and C. J. Friedrich.   See also the valuable analysis by Herbert W. Briggs, "The Proposed European Political Community," 48 *American Journal of International Law* 110–122 (1954).   It appeared after this Introduction was written.

plored by examining (1) its proposed institutions, including the amending power, (2) its functions and powers, and (3) the participation in the proposed community.

In submitting the Draft Treaty to the Assembly in March, 1953, the President of the Constitutional Committee which had prepared it stated that the Community was neither a federation nor a confederation but combined diverse elements. The Draft Treaty itself states that it creates a "supranational community" founded on the union of peoples and of states, and that the Community is indissoluble. The objective was clearly to create a European government which could effectively perform the delegated tasks.

The Treaty seeks to build primarily on the earlier treaties for the Coal and Steel Community and the European Defense Community. This is true both for its institutions and for its functions. But in converting them into a political community the Draft Treaty makes certain significant changes and additions.

The Draft Treaty adopts for the Community Part I of the Convention for the Protection of Human Rights and Fundamental Freedoms of 1950, as amended in 1952 (Art. 3).

Taking up first the institutions, the proposed Statute appears to be partly based upon the idea that its institutions should be those familiar to Continental European governmental practice: parliamentary government, proportional representation and legislative power to amend the constitution. But there are included also significant concessions to the presidential pattern of executive leadership, to majority representation and to judicial review of legislation on questions of constitutionality. At the same time, the drafters of the Statute seem very much concerned with protecting the states in every possible way — a tendency which gives the constitution a distinctly cumbersome quality. The following discussion will be centered upon a brief consideration of these two major aspects in their interrelations.

Every federal constitution will embody arrangements through which the component units (states) can effectively participate in the shaping of federal policy. But if this federal fragmentation of power is carried too far, the process of government will break down, as occurred under the Articles of Confederation in the United States, and under the Swiss Confederation before 1848. What are the arrangements in the proposed Statute? The Statute lays out five institutions: namely, a parliament; an executive council of national ministers; a court of justice, and an economic and a social council. In each one of these institutions the states as states participate in a significant way.

The Parliament is composed of two houses of nearly equal powers. The first (or lower) house, called the Peoples' Chamber, "shall be composed of deputies representing the peoples united in the community." (Art. 11; all quotations hereafter are based upon the official translation issued by the Ad Hoc Assembly in March, 1953. This translation is printed in part, in Appendix II.) The second (or upper) chamber, called the Senate, "shall be composed of senators representing the people of each state." By the latter formula, a possibly significant desire of getting away from representing the states as such may be indicated, but designating the first chamber as the Peoples' Chamber confuses the issue. While the Peoples' Chamber is based upon popular election of the deputies, the Senate is elected by the several national parliaments. Strangely, however, both houses are based upon a weighted representation, with equality for France, Germany and Italy on one side, Belgium and the Netherlands on the other, and a smaller special vote for Luxembourg.

	Senate	*Peoples' Chamber*
France	30	63 (plus 7 for France's
Germany	30	63 Overseas Territories)
Italy	30	63
Belgium	10	30
Netherlands	10	30
Luxembourg	4	12
	114	$261 + 7 = 268$

If one assumes that the national parliaments represent the popular vote, this arrangement would mean that the two houses will very closely resemble each other in party composition — a doubtful arrangement, at best.

The Senate, besides participating on an equal basis in the usual parliamentary business of legislation, fiscal control and investigation, is assigned the crucial role of electing the President of the Executive Council. Since this President appoints the other members of the Council (no more than two of any one nationality), it can be seen that the Senate has a predominant role in the parliamentary setup. To be sure, the Executive Council as a whole has to be confirmed by an affirmative vote of confidence in both houses, but the initiative is clearly the Senate's. Furthermore, while the Chamber may overthrow the President and his Council by a vote of no confidence or a refusal of a vote of confidence (when adopted by three-fifths of its members), the Senate may do so by electing a new President. The President and Council cannot protect themselves by dissolution of the Peoples' Chamber against either of these votes; only in cases where the Peoples' Chamber has voted no confidence by less than a three-fifths majority may a dissolution take place, and even this very limited right lapses if the Senate should vote for a new President. It is clear that the system closely resembles the weak French executive, with the house representing the several states having the dominant position.

This weakness of the Executive is reinforced by the establishment of a Council of National Ministers, which is provided with a veto power in a great many decisive situations, in most of which it is required to take action by unanimous vote. Such a Council of Ministers is part of the Coal and Steel and the Defense Community organizations, and the new Council takes over their functions (Arts. 60–62). Coordination of the foreign policy of

member states (Arts. 69, 70), concurrence in all tax measures (Art. 78), determination of the contributions of member states (Art. 80) and important economic steps (Arts. 84, 87) are among the crucial functions in which the
Council of National Ministers participates. It may be possible, but it seems
at the moment difficult to envisage how effective action can be expected of
the Executive Council, when thus hemmed in between the Parliament on
one side and the Council of National Ministers on the other, but maybe the
experience to date of the High Authority for Coal and Steel offers some
encouragement.[16]

In any case, the provisions regarding the Court (Arts. 38 *et seq*.) clearly
indicate that a kind of constitutional government would come into existence
under the Statute. After absorbing the courts of the Coal and Steel Community and those of the Defense Community, this Court is to ensure that
"the rule of law in the interpretation and application of the Statute and of
the laws and regulations of the Community" will prevail. The Court of the
Community has exclusive jurisdiction to hear and decide disputes between
the Member States or one of them and the Community as to the interpretation of the Treaty (Art. 41). States' rights are carefully protected in connection with the Court, both in its procedure and in the appointment of the
judges (subject to the approval of the Senate), since each state may put forward three candidates. What is more — and it seems a questionable provision at that — decisions of the state courts do not appear to be subject
to appeal to this European Court, even if the decision involves federal law.
In the matter of basic rights, on the other hand, the Court will be subject
to the judicial organs of the Council of Europe, when established, at least
in matters involving a question of principle.

Whenever a constitutional document is carefully protected by judicial authority, the problem of amending it must be given great weight. The proposed Statute is no exception. Elaborate provisions (Arts. 109–114) set
forth three different modes of formal amendment. Amendment is very difficult, requiring the assent of all national parliaments, when it involves "a
modification of the powers and competence of the Community vis-à-vis the
Member States" or a modification of the definition of human rights. The
first of these demonstrates once more the extreme solicitude for the states'
rights, the second an almost equal concern for the Council of Europe and
those states not members of the proposed Community. Amendments are
somewhat less difficult if they involve the relations between the institutions,
their competence and the division of powers between them, or if such an
amendment would "affect the guarantees provided for the States in the
composition and working procedure of these institutions." But in both
these cases unanimous consent of the Council of National Ministers is required. All other amendments are made quite easy; in the European tradition they are acted upon like legislation. One wonders whether this un-

[16] Bebr, "The European Coal and Steel Commission: A Political and Legal Innovation,"
63 *Yale Law Journal* (1953).

wieldy system for amendments will turn out to be a wise one. A single method which would be cognizant of the states without surrendering all initiative would have brought the proposed Statute more nearly in line with established practice in other working federal systems. One might wish that the compromise worked out by the study committee, namely a transitional period, might have been adopted.

Turning now to the powers or functions, under the Draft Treaty, the Community will take over the functions of the Coal and Steel Community and the European Defense Community progressively, during a transitional period of two years (Arts. 56, 57, 59). These three will constitute a single legal entity (Art. 5). Thus, the new Community will derive the major part of its powers from the existing provisions of the Coal and Steel Community and from those of the Defense Community when ratified. In the case of coal and steel, these include extensive powers to create and maintain the common market in these products and to protect it from public or private restraints, or from serious economic crises. The Defense Treaty confers substantial authority to train and equip the common army, but under it the measures to finance and to use the forces, and to control foreign policy affecting defense, require unanimous approval of the Council of National Ministers. The Draft Treaty largely retains these limitations.

In international affairs, the Community has authority to conclude treaties within the limits of its other powers (Art. 67). These will be negotiated by the Executive Council, subject to approval of other institutions of the Community where so provided (Art. 68). But in foreign policy generally, the Community has to "coordinate" the policies of the Member States, and apparently may represent them only when so empowered by unanimous decision of the Council of National Ministers (Art. 69). The Executive Council or the Parliament may make proposals to the Council of National Ministers on matters affecting the Community (Art. 70). On the other hand, the Member States are not to conclude treaties which conflict with commitments of the Community (Art. 72). Moreover, the Executive Council must be advised by the Member States of proposed treaties affecting the Community, and may object if a treaty appears likely to interfere with the Statute or the interests of the Community. In case of dispute, the issue shall be settled by arbitration (Art. 73). The Community, also, is entitled to accredit and receive diplomatic representatives within the limits of its powers (Art. 74).

The financial powers of the Community likewise depend primarily on unanimous agreement of the Council of National Ministers as noted above. The Executive Council proposes the annual budget, which is to be voted by Parliament but may not be increased by it (Art. 76). For its revenues, the Community will depend on taxes and loans voted by the Parliament, and on contributions, but neither can become effective without the unanimous approval of the Council of National Ministers (Arts. 78, 80). Under the existing Coal and Steel Community, the High Authority now has power to levy taxes on the industries under its control, within specified limits, without such approval. If, as appears, the Draft Treaty cuts off this authority, it is to that extent a step backward (see Art. 64).

One new and important grant of authority is in the economic field. Here the Community is directed to establish "progressively a common market among the Member States based on the free movement of goods, capital and persons," consistent with the basic principles of the Coal and Steel Community (Art. 82). The Community may take no action for this purpose during its first year, and may act during the next five years only with the unanimous approval of the Council of National Ministers. But after this period, such measures may be proposed by the Executive Council with the approval of the Council of National Ministers and become effective by a vote of a simple majority of the Peoples' Chamber and two-thirds of the Senate (Art. 84). To facilitate the creation of the common market, the Statute provides for a re-adaptation fund to assist enterprises and workers injured by the widening of the market (Art. 84). This economic authority is limited, however, by the right of any Member State to appeal to the Court or Arbitration Tribunal against any such measures which it fears "might cause fundamental and persistent disturbance of their economy." If the Court or Tribunal sustains this view, the measure must be suspended until the Community has taken appropriate steps to eliminate the disturbances (Art. 86). Obviously the scope and effectiveness of these economic powers will turn largely on the interpretation given to this limitation by the Court or Arbitration Tribunal.

One other provision is a significant step toward freer movement of people. Those who serve in the European Defense forces and those born after the effective date of the Treaty are entitled to move freely within the Community, and to choose their domicile in its territory, under the same conditions as nationals of the State (Art. 83).

The Community also has a limited authority to assist in maintaining constitutional order and democratic institutions within the Member States. Any Member State may request such assistance. In addition, with the unanimous concurrence of the Council of National Ministers, the Community, by law, will lay down the conditions under which it may intervene for such purposes on its own initiative (Art. 104).

All of these grants of power must be considered in the light of Article 6. This provides that the functions (*competences*) conferred on the Community by this Treaty "shall be restrictively [limitativement] interpreted." If this is applied to mean that the Community shall enjoy only those powers delegated by the Treaty it should cause no difficulty. But if it is applied to narrow or restrict the powers granted, it may be a source of weakness. Much will depend upon the Court in this connection.

Various provisions deal with the effect of Community action. Decisions of the Executive Council and of the Court have executive force within the Member States and are to be enforced by the judicial organs of each State. The national authorities are only to verify the authenticity of the decision. Moreover, the Member States pledge themselves to take all measures necessary to implement the laws and other actions of the Community, and to assist it in its mission. They specifically undertake to refrain from any measure incompatible with the Statute (Art. 105).

Some of the most difficult issues which confronted the drafters of the Statute were presented by the questions: who beyond the original founders of the Community should participate in the Community, and how should such participation be organized? Into this range of questions belong such hotly contested issues as the association with the Community of other Member States of the Council of Europe, especially Great Britain, the problem of the Saar, the accession of Eastern Germany in connection with the eventual unification of that country, and the role of the overseas territories. All but the issue of the Saar found some solution, and even the latter had been compromised between the French and German members of the Constitutional Committee, but the compromise did not pass the Consultative Assembly. Other European states, according to Articles 115 and 116, may join the Community by formal act, requiring a majority decision by the Executive Council, the Council of National Ministers and the Parliament; a protocol shall in each case be annexed to the Statute, containing such amendments to the Statute as may be involved, e.g., in the matter of representation in the Parliament. Any European state which guarantees the protection of human rights and fundamental freedoms may thus accede.

The problem of Eastern Germany was solved by making the Statute applicable upon the Federal Republic's regaining jurisdiction over this territory; presumably it could also join as an additional state. If it becomes part of the Federal Republic, the latter's representation in the Peoples' Chamber may be enlarged by special amendment, requiring, however, the unanimous assent of the Council of National Ministers (as provided in Art. 112).

Similarly, the Statute will apply to all overseas territories, unless a Member State makes a declaration exempting the particular territory from the Statute. By this provision the entry of all of France is assured. At the same time, it is provided that laws, as well as other decisions of the Community, shall not apply to non-European territories except after having been "adopted" by the Member States. This rather paradoxical compromise of making the Constitution, but not the laws, automatically applicable, actually finds a precedent in the constitutional position of the Commonwealth of Puerto Rico within the American federation.[17] Satisfactory arrangements for partial links may thus be developed.

Finally, the Statute in a special set of provisions (Arts. 90–93) establishes the possibility of looser association than actual membership for such European states as may wish to cooperate closely with the community. Such "association" would be based upon special treaties or agreements in those special fields which warrant it. Such treaties may provide for participation in the Council of National Ministers or in the Senate, that is to say, they may

[17] See "Puerto Rico: A Study in Democratic Development," 285 Annals (Jan. 1953), especially pp. 23 et seq., pp. 42 et seq., and pp. 9 et seq.

assign a positive role to such an associated state in the Community. In accord with this conception the Court may also be assigned a role in settling controversies arising under such treaties or agreements. It is evident (and was clearly so stated in the lengthy discussions on this part of the Statute) that it is the hope of the framers of the document that Great Britain and the Scandinavian countries may by these arrangements be induced into closer and closer *af-federation* with the Community. Reasonable provisions were included for the Statute's coming into effect. These are implemented by provisions (in a separate protocol) for the association of the Community with the Council of Europe; but since they involve changes in the Statute of the Council, they may be long delayed.

What are the major criticisms of the Draft Treaty, when viewed in the light of past federal experience? Among the most objectionable articles are those for constitutional interpretation (Art. 6), non-equality in the election of the Peoples' Chamber (Art. 15), proportional representation (Art. 95), instability of the executive by making it dependent upon a vote of no confidence by the Peoples' Chamber (Art. 31), weakness of the Community in regard to foreign relations (Arts. 67–74), failure to provide for defense power and consequent dependence upon ratification of the Defense Community Treaty for this power (Arts. 5 and 56 *et seq.*), subjection of all tax legislation to unanimous consent of the Council of National Ministers (Art. 78), too large a dependence of the Community upon national administrations for the execution of their "decisions" (Art. 106), and too cumbersome a machinery for amendment of the statute (Arts. 111 and 112). We shall omit here, because of its complicated political aspects, the question of the non-equality of the European voter in the election of the Peoples' Chamber and that of proportional representation. For the others we shall follow the order in which they have been mentioned, except that the first and the last will be grouped together.

In view of the fact that for a considerable period of time there will not exist any firm party organization for the European Community, it seems doubtful that the provisions of Article 31, Sections 2 and 3, will work out very satisfactorily, particularly when the elections of the Peoples' Chamber are based on proportional representation. Even the safeguard of a three-fifths majority requirement (following the French precedent) is not likely to be of much help. Considering the complex process involved in establishing a new government, the European Community may be for long periods of time without an executive, other than one "conducting current business." To be sure, the provisions for election of a new president by the Senate which would supersede the vote of a lack of confidence might be of some help, but in the event of a conflict between Senate and Peoples' Chamber (which is certainly a distinct possibility), this safeguard would not necessarily work. The basic error of principle in the present construction is to give the Peoples' Chamber the power to overthrow the government without any corresponding responsibility for establishing a new one.

In regard to foreign relations, one major objection is the broad phrasing of the second section of Article 68. A detailed check of all the articles providing for participation of the Council of National Ministers (Arts. 24, 2; 44; 60,2; 69,2; 70,2; 70,3; 78; 80; 84,2; 84,3; 87; 91,1; 93; 99; 104; 111,2; 112,2; 116,2; 116,3; 117,5) makes it clear that the European Executive would not only be in no position to make any kind of foreign policy, but would not even be able to move with any dispatch in those fields which are properly assigned to it, due to the unanimity rule in the Council of National Ministers. It is hard to see how an executive thus hamstrung could possibly carry out the provision of Article 69, namely to coordinate the foreign policies of the Member States or those of Article 71.

In regard to defense, the central objection is that the present Statute is completely built upon the previous ratification of the Defense Community Treaty. Since this ratification may never occur or may be long delayed, this tie-in prevents the use of the Statute as a way out of the difficulties which have arisen in connection with the Defense Treaty.

Another decisive defect of the Statute is that of making all tax legislation subject to the unanimous concurrence of the Council of National Ministers (Art. 78). This places the power of the purse in their hands and deprives the Community of all genuine autonomy, as it is generally recognized that this power establishes dependence of one authority upon another. There is, therefore, serious objection to this provision, unless it were counterbalanced by a comparable requirement of consent on the part of the European Executive to all national tax legislation. There is also no adequate provision for the administration of the collection of such revenues. Presumably, like all other federal legislation, it will be dependent upon the execution by national administrations (Art. 106; see next paragraph). No indication is given as to what is to happen if one of the national administrations fails to collect taxes properly (there are wide divergencies between the several states in this respect at present).

Article 106 of the Statute fails to provide for the development of federal administrative services, in case the national administrations are not giving the service required, although in both the Coal and Steel Community Treaty and in the Defense Community Treaty such supranational administrative services are provided. It may also be noted that Article 7 suggests that the Community "shall carry out its functions in close cooperation with the national civil services." It is not clear what is to be understood by this "cooperation," especially when read in the light of Article 106.

Finally, the provisions for amendment of the Statute appear to be much too complicated as far as "the powers and competence of the Community vis-à-vis the Member States" are concerned. When one takes into account that Article 6 further provides that "the provisions defining the powers and competence conferred upon the Community by the present Treaty shall be restrictively interpreted" (in itself a rather unfortunate provision), it becomes clear that the Statute definitely is calculated to prevent that process of "federalizing" governmental activities which has been a characteristic of existing federations and has been a most helpful factor in their steady development and growth. Thus the "Commerce Clause" of the United States Constitution has provided an opportunity for adjustment to the rapid changes associated with industrialization and the expansion of a common market, without having to wait for formal amendment. In the present Statute that healthy principle of growth through sound judicial interpretation is gainsaid and, to make matters worse, formal amendment is made extremely difficult by requiring consent of all the states, and of their parliaments. How many constitutional amendments would the United States have been able to make if such a provision had existed? In my humble opinion, none. Now it may well be that the extreme pressure of necessity will force such amendments in the European case, but it seems unreasonable to make this process depend upon so wide a consent as this provision calls for.

If the necessary changes were made, the Statute might become the basis of a sound constitutional development of the European Community. The Executive would be able to function with reasonable effectiveness, some form of common defense would be possible, the fiscal and administrative services could develop, though slowly, into workable patterns of effective government, and the adaptive growth of the constitution itself would at least be possible, even if by no means assured. There are numerous other improvements that could be made, but these six changes constitute the absolute minimum which is required if the European Community is not to suffer the same fate as the Council of Europe, namely, to disillusion the people of Europe about the possibility of effective joint action. Unfortunately, the trend has been the other way. The Foreign Ministers, acting through their permanent staff, have been emasculating even the project of the Draft Treaty, according to recent reports.

Even so, it is possible to consider the proposed Statute as a significant step forward on the road toward a united Europe. Not only are the functions envisaged rather narrow, but there is a lack of simplicity, clarity and effectiveness in the institutions proposed. If it were not for the cumbersome provisions for constitutional amendment, such defects might readily be remedied by revisions of the Statute. As it is, much will depend upon the wisdom and the political know-how of the men to whom the institutions created under the Statute would be entrusted. Even more important will be the extent of popular support which the Statute when adopted will enjoy. For ultimately it is the people who "make a constitution."

CARL J. FRIEDRICH

Studies in Federalism

S T U D Y   1

The Federal Legislature

I. Outline of the Issues

The structure of the legislature and its role in the government pose difficult problems in establishing a federal state. The five such states chosen for study (Australia, Canada, Germany, Switzerland, and the United States) display the wide variety possible in both form and functions. On the basis of their experience, this study seeks to clarify the available alternatives and to indicate their advantages and disadvantages.

A. *The Role of the Federal Legislature*

A federal legislature must be so constituted as to combine two objectives:

(1) The first is to ensure that the federation can carry out effectively the functions assigned to it. The formation of a federation is a recognition that certain governmental tasks can no longer be performed adequately by the separate States and require handling on a broader basis. This makes it essential that the federal government be able to act to meet the needs of the larger community. In particular, the federal legislature must provide an effective means for mediating conflicts of interests and formulating basic policy within the areas of federal competence.

(2) At the same time, in performing its own functions, the federation must take due account of the interests of the various sections of the new community and of the continuing responsibility of the member States for important fields of government. So far as possible, the federation should exercise its powers so as not unnecessarily to burden or impede the exercise by the member States of their retained powers. Within its competence, the needs and interests of the federation must normally prevail over separate interests of individual States, where it is necessary to make the choice. But it is important to ensure that local interests and problems are adequately presented when the federation reaches decisions for the exercise of its powers.

In combining these two aims, the constitution must not, of course, enable single states or small minorities to block necessary action. Moreover, in view of deep-seated, historic loyalties and antagonisms, it should foster the growth of sentiment for the federation rather than divisive attitudes.

The effort to balance these various objectives directly affects the structure of the federal legislature. Thus, it has led all federal states studied to adopt a legislature with two houses. As in a unitary state, the lower house is typically elected by direct popular vote, with seats allotted according to population, and is designed to give expression to the popular will. The upper house is more specifically federal in character. In a unitary state it serves only the limited purpose of revising chamber: its task is to improve legislation passed by the lower house and sometimes to suspend or delay its adoption for a limited period to prevent precipitous action. But the center of the legislative power in a unitary state is almost always the lower house; the upper house cannot compete with it in either power or standing.

In most federal states, however, the upper house has traditionally had a further role. In various forms, it has been designed to reflect the interests or views of the constituent States, either as regions or as political entities. This influence on the legislation of the federation and on the exercise of its powers has been intended to provide a means of protecting the States or their inhabitants against improper or injurious federal measures. Federal action might be objectionable because: (1) it exceeds the competence conferred by the constitution; or (2) it is harmful to the inhabitants of one or more States; or (3) it is prejudicial to one or more States as political entities. The upper chamber was designed as a bulwark against such threats, especially for the smaller States with limited representation in the lower house.

In evaluating this role of the upper house, however, it is vital to keep in mind that it is not the only protection for the States against the abuse of federal power. The primary safeguard against improper extension of federal authority is the constitution itself, which confines the federation to specific delegated powers. The constitution can also include express guarantees against improper use of the delegated federal powers to the prejudice of a particular state or its residents. For example, it may require equal treatment for all citizens in federal legislation or may prohibit the imposition of burdens or penalties or taxes which discriminate among the states or their inhabitants. When backed by judicial review of federal action, these are strong safeguards against improper measures by the federal government.

Moreover, there are other practical checks on the abuse of federal power. After all, the members of the federal lower house depend on electorates in the states. In a developed federation, the parties themselves become federal in scope with adherents in most or all states, and generally temper or compromise actions likely to antagonize substantial sections of opinion in even a single state. Finally, the executive Cabinet or Council, either by law or custom, tends to draw its members from the various sections of the federation, and thereby to ensure the reflection of their points of view in its day-to-day activities.

Consequently, the upper house should be considered as only one of the devices for bridging the gap between the member states and the federation. It does, however, often serve the smaller states by giving them greater influence in federal affairs, through representation in the upper house, than their population alone would justify.

B. *Basic Issues of Structure and Function*

As will appear, the legislatures of existing federal states exhibit a variety of alternatives, and their experience reveals the effects and significance of such variations sufficiently to provide some guidance for choosing among them. The features which seem most important can be classified in three main categories:

(1) Composition of the legislature: Here the main choice is between two basic types of upper chamber, one of which may be called the Senate-type and the other the Council-type. The Senate-type, illustrated in the United States and Switzerland, is composed of representatives free to act according to their own judgment; the Council-type, found in Germany, is composed of instructed delegates of each member State government. Within the Senate-type, in turn, there are variations as to tenure, selection, and other respects. With either type, seats or votes may be divided among the large and small States in various ways.

(2) Relation between the executive and the legislature: Here the choice is primarily between continuous responsibility of the executive to the legislature, as under Cabinet government, and relative independence of the executive and legislature. The first is found in Australia and Canada, with a variant in Germany; while the United States and Switzerland have adopted different forms of the second system.

(3) The relative roles of the two houses: Here the choice is largely between a system where the upper house enjoys actual powers as great as those of the lower house, as in the United States and Switzerland; one where the lower house is in fact dominant, as in Australia and Canada; or one where the upper house is subordinate for some purposes and equal for others, as in Germany. A related issue involves the procedure for the resolution of deadlocks between the two houses of the legislature.

These various aspects are, of course, closely related to one another. Thus, the functions of the legislature, especially of the upper house, inevitably influence its structure. Similarly, the relation of the two houses to the executive greatly affects their relative standing. Consequently, one of the main objects of this study is to examine how the decisions regarding one issue will affect other aspects of the legislature.

In the initial analysis, however, it seems desirable to take up these several aspects separately. This will facilitate the later discussion and will assist the reader to judge for himself the validity of the conclusions. On each issue, federal practice and experience is analyzed to determine the advantages and weaknesses of various solutions. The analysis will also seek to indicate the political and other conditions necessary for the successful operation of the various systems.

II. STRUCTURE AND COMPOSITION OF THE LEGISLATURE

The legislatures under study, which are all composed of two chambers, show marked similarities in the lower chamber and greater differences in the upper chamber. Accordingly this section will examine separately the structure and composition of the two houses.

A. *The Lower House*

1. BASIS OF REPRESENTATION

In all five federal systems the lower house is elected by direct popular vote and is the organ of government which most clearly represents the views of the people. The seats in the lower house are assigned among the States according to population, but the method of election within the State varies among the federations. In Australia, Canada, and the United States, members are elected from single-member electoral districts of about the same size throughout the federation. Germany uses a system combining single-member districts for part of the seats with Land lists and proportional representation for the remainder. In Switzerland, members are elected by proportional representation, from the canton as a whole.

All the constitutions studied authorize the federal government to regulate the elections for the members of the lower house, and, except for the United States, to determine the qualifications of electors. Such elections are now governed entirely by federal law in all these states except the United States. Under most of these constitutions, however, some or all aspects of such elections were to be regulated by state law until the adoption of federal laws. In the United States alone, the federal government still leaves many electoral matters to state regulation, such as the redefining of electoral districts after each census. The Constitution forbids denial of the right to vote on grounds of sex, race, or color.

The electoral system can contribute to the stability of the federal government. A system based on proportional representation is likely to foster many parties. Single-member districts, on the other hand, tend to encourage the growth of larger and fewer parties, combining various interests and sections, and crossing state boundaries. A new federation would therefore do well to follow the example of the existing federal states in allowing federal regulation of elections for the lower house. It may be necessary to leave the regulation of election to the member States, until the federal law can be adopted, but the federation should have authority to regulate federal elections by its own laws.

2. TENURE AND QUALIFICATIONS OF MEMBERS

The length of the term for members of the lower house varies among the several federations. The shortest term is two years in the United States, followed by Australia where the term is three years. The longest term is in Canada, with five years. In Switzerland and Germany, members are elected for a four-year term. Under the Australian, Canadian, and German constitutions, the actual term may be shortened by dissolution, as described in Section III.

For a European federation, a term of three or four years would seem most appropriate. A shorter term would require elections too often, and a five-year term seems somewhat too long for reflection of changes in popular attitudes.

Qualifications for membership are prescribed either by the constitutions or by federal law. In the United States they are fixed by the Constitution, and may not be altered by law. A member must be at least 25 years old, a citizen for at least seven years, and an inhabitant of the State in which elected. In Switzerland, the Constitution makes eligible any lay citizen entitled to vote, i.e., every male Swiss at least 20 years old except the clergy and those few who are denied suffrage. The provisions in the Australian Constitution are subject to change by federal law, and principally stipulate an age limit of 21 years, eligibility to vote, and residence of three years in the Commonwealth. Under the German Basic Law the age limit is fixed at 25, but all other qualifications are determined by federal law, which largely makes them the same as the qualifications to vote. Canada originally adopted state laws, and now determines qualifications by federal law. These are: an age of 21, being a British subject, and eligibility to vote, which includes a requirement of one year's residence in Canada.

None of these federations permits a member to hold simultaneously any other federal offices, except for Ministers in the Cabinet-system countries and members of the Federal Tribunal in Switzerland.

Despite the use of single-member districts in Australia, Canada and the United States, there is no constitutional or legal requirement that members reside among their constituents. Such residence has been strictly decreed by custom in the United States. In the other two federations, where the Cabinet system requires party leaders to be members of the lower house, they will occasionally choose their districts according to certainty of election rather than residence; but political realities to a large extent make residence necessary. The salaries of the members of all federal lower houses are paid from the federal treasury.

B. *The Upper House*

Typically, the structure of the upper house in federal systems has been shaped in response to two fears: (1) the fear of the smaller States that the larger and more populous States would use their majorities in the lower house to injure them; and (2) the fear of both large and small States that the federation might encroach unduly on their interests and authority. The effort to satisfy both these fears has inevitably caused some of the most serious disputes in the formation of federal states. These disputes have revolved around two primary issues: (1) how votes in the upper house should be allocated between large and small States; and (2) whether the upper house should consist of instructed delegates of the State governments, or of uninstructed members.

1. ALLOCATION OF VOTES AMONG STATES

In the allocation of votes in the upper house, the smaller States have generally claimed a share larger than their proportion of the federal population. At the Philadelphia Convention, their insistence on the same number of votes in the upper house as the larger States threatened to disrupt the Convention, until settled by allowing each State two votes regardless of size or population. In the framing of the Swiss Constitution of 1848, the same dispute arose and was compromised in the same way. Each canton received two members in the upper chamber, and each half-canton one member, even though the disparity in size among the cantons was greater than among the American colonies. Similarly, in Australia, the thinly populated agricultural States, concerned about the domination of the larger commercial States, insisted on an upper chamber patterned on the American model with six Senators for each State.

In Canada and Germany, however, the allotment of votes varied among the States although favoring the smaller States compared with their population. In Canada, the allotment ranged from twenty-four Senators for Ontario and Quebec to six each for the Western Provinces, and four for Prince Edward Island, but as sections, the Western Provinces and Maritime Provinces did receive a total of twenty-four Senators each. In Germany, under the Imperial and Weimar Constitutions, Prussia and other large States received many more votes than the small States, though fewer than if based on their respective populations. Under the Basic Law of the Federal Republic, the number of delegates is also adjusted somewhat for population, ranging from three delegates for the smallest, to not more than five for the largest State.

As this brief summary indicates, the actual distribution of votes has depended on practical compromises rather than abstract theory. Where the disparity among the States was not too great, the tendency has been to grant them equal votes. But where the disparity has been extreme, the allocation of seats has taken account of these differences though still favoring the smaller States with votes more than proportionate to their populations.

2. THE COUNCIL AND SENATE TYPES OF UPPER CHAMBER

Under the Council system, the State governments have a direct voice in the affairs of the federation, through delegates in the upper chamber acting under their instructions. Similar councils of ambassadors have been common in various leagues and loose confederations, including those which preceded certain of the existing federal States, such as the American colonies under the Articles of Confederation, the Swiss Bundesvertrag, and the earlier German Confederations. In the United States and Switzerland, these earlier forms of Council were considered to be unsatisfactory and inadequate for the new federal systems. They were therefore abandoned in favor of a Senate-type structure, which was also adopted in Australia and Canada.

In Germany, however, the older form was carried over into the new federal state under the Constitution of 1871, and continued in 1919 and 1949. The adoption of the Council-type of upper house in Germany was related to the fact that in 1871 State power was largely centered in the executive or monarchs and the bureaucracy responsible to them, and to the necessity of tying the States into the federal structure, especially under the system of administration of federal law relied on under these Constitutions. Since federal law was to be carried out partly through the State bureaucracies, the Council was thought desirable as a forum for the State governments to advance their views regarding administrative questions. In the framing of the Weimar Constitution, however, it was proposed to create a Senate-type of upper house selected by State legislatures, and a separate administrative body. The State governments resisted this change and insisted on the Council system.

The Council and Senate systems differ in the method of voting, selection, and tenure of the members or delegates.

Method of Voting: the crucial difference is in the voting procedure. Under the Council system, the delegates of each State cast their votes as a unit according to direct instructions from their State government. Unit voting was required under the Constitutions of the German Empire and Federal Republic, and was the practice, because of uniform instructions, under the Weimar Constitution. On the other hand, in the Senate the member is not instructed and votes according to his own decisions, whether they represent his own views, those of his party, or those of his constituents.

Selection and Tenure: the method of selection and tenure reinforces the dependence of the Council member. As the delegate of the State government, he is designated by the executive to serve at its pleasure. The member of a Senate is usually elected either by the State legislature (as formerly done in the United States and Switzerland), or by popular vote (as in Australia and, today, in the United States and most of the Swiss cantons); but in Canada Senators are appointed, nominally by the Governor-General, though actually by the federal Prime Minister.

The member of a Senate is named for a fixed term (which may be six years, as in the United States and Australia, or four years, as in most of the Swiss cantons), or for life, as in Canada. In the United States and Australia, terms are staggered so that part of the Senate faces election at the same time as the lower house (one third every two years in the United States; one half every three years in Australia). While nearly all Swiss seats are voted upon at the same time as the lower house, several cantons still provide for shorter terms, so that the upper chamber is in effect a continuous body.

Qualifications: in three federal states the qualifications for Senator are prescribed by the constitution or federal law. In the United States a Senator must be at least 30 years old (five years older than a Representative), a resident of the state from which chosen, and a citizen for at least nine years. In Canada the main constitutional requirements are a minimum age of 30, a specified amount of property, and residence in the appropriate Province. Under the Australian Constitution, the principal qualifications for the Senate, as for the lower house, are a minimum age of 21, eligibility to vote in the elections for the House, and residence within the Commonwealth. These are subject to change by federal law.

In contrast, both Switzerland and Germany, despite their different types of upper chamber, leave it to the cantons or Länder to fix the qualifications for members of the upper house. The Swiss Constitution requires only that they not also be members of the lower chamber or federal executive. The qualifications set by the cantons are similar to those for the lower house. Today in Germany the only requirement is that they be members (Cabinet Ministers) of the State government they represent, but in practice officials serve as alternates.

These differences between the Senate and Council types, especially the voting in the Council by instructed State blocs, cause marked differences in their operation and roles. In order to avoid repetition, however, comparison of the advantages of the two systems is postponed until the concluding section of this study. This course also permits the discussion there to take account of their factors affecting the role of the upper chambers, which are considered in Sections III and IV.

III. Relation Between Legislature and Executive

Under all of the federal systems studied, the relation between the legislature and the executive[1] has many facets, as will appear below. But coloring each of them is the underlying factor of whether the executive is independent of the legislature or is responsible to it.

The American presidential system and the Swiss collegial system reflect the choice of an independent executive. In both systems the executive and legislature are constituted as separate organs and, in general, are intended to perform different functions. The chief characteristics of this form of government are that the executive is elected for a fixed term, is not subject to removal by the legislature, and has no power to dissolve the legislature. One of its most notable achievements is the stability of the executive.

[1] This term is used to cover the various forms of executive, including the American President, the Swiss Executive Council, and the Cabinet as used in Canada and Australia, as well as the modified form under the German Basic Law. For this discussion, it does not seem necessary to distinguish the roles of "Head of State" and executive. For detailed consideration of these matters, see the report on the Federal Executive.

The Cabinet systems of Australia and Canada, and the German variant, reflect the choice of an executive responsible to the legislature. In all cases, this responsibility runs to the lower house alone for several reasons. In part it appears to rest on tradition, derived from British Parliamentary practice, in part on the practical complexity of operating the Cabinet system with responsibility to two houses, and in part on the fact that ordinarily the upper house has not been popularly elected. But the situation is the same even when the upper house is popularly elected as in Australia. The principle behind this system is that the governing powers should constantly reside in the popular assembly. Consequently the executive is composed of the leaders of the lower house, and exercises both executive and legislative functions as a sort of managing committee of that body. Distinctive features of this system are the right of the lower house to depose the Cabinet at its pleasure (limited in practice by the Cabinet's control of the majority party), and the right of the Cabinet to dissolve the lower house. Its main achievement is coordination of the executive and legislative functions.

The successes of both systems have rested in large measure on the existence of appropriate political conditions. In choosing among the alternatives, attention must be given to the political and other conditions in Europe, and to certain special difficulties under which a European federation will have to operate for some time. These will be mentioned in Section V of this study in seeking to apply the experience of other federal states to a new federation

This experience on the relation between the executive and the legislature will be considered under three topics: (1) the role of the legislature in the election and removal of the executive; (2) the participation of the executive in proposing and enacting legislation; and (3) the control by the legislature over the activities of the executive.

A. *Election and Removal of Executive*

In all federations studied, except the United States, the federal legislature or the lower house normally selects the executive or controls its election; and even in the United States it may do so under special conditions. In all except the United States and Switzerland, the lower house may depose the executive for political reasons by some procedure.

The American President was intended to be elected indirectly by a special college chosen for that purpose only. With the rise of parties, this has become only a form for election by popular majorities in a majority of States. If no candidate receives the required majority, the lower house, voting by States, chooses among the three highest candidates; this procedure has been used several times, but not for more than one hundred years.

This American system produces a strong and stable executive, but may be unsuited to European conditions for reasons developed more fully in Study 2, The Federal Executive. Even if the principle of the single executive were acceptable, the absence of well-known public figures, strong inter-state parties, and a European public opinion would all tend to make it extremely difficult to obtain the necessary majorities for popular election of a single individual. If a plural executive were established, its election by popular vote would be even more complicated. Moreover, the American experience indicates that an indirect method of election by a special college or council, chosen for that purpose only, is not likely to be an effective institution where active parties exist.

The Cabinet system of Canada and Australia also has produced relatively stable governments and the necessary leadership. Its success appears to depend to a large degree on strong parties exercising strict discipline over their members. In practice the Cabinet Ministers, as the leaders of the majority party, have a very strong hold on the members through the party machinery and the power to dissolve. If the legislature is composed of many small groups and parties it is extremely difficult to build a stable Cabinet government. Instead, the government is likely to fall constantly as a result of disagreements among members of successive coalitions. Under such conditions, the power of dissolution by the executive is not likely to create the necessary discipline for effective government. For that device to work, the parties must be able to elect or defeat candidates according to their support of or opposition to the party program. But this in turn requires the existence of a few strong parties.

The German variant on the Cabinet system is partly designed to meet this situation. Although the lower house elects the Chancellor, it can remove him only by electing his successor. Thus the government does not fall merely because a proposed bill is rejected; and its opponents can force it to resign only by agreeing on a new Chancellor. This system has the effect of protecting a moderate government against the combination of the extremes to bring it down. Consequently, it should contribute to greater stability; but experience with the actual operation of this system is too limited to reach firm conclusions.

The Swiss system, in which the executive is chosen by the legislature but not responsible to it, has much to recommend it. It separates completely the task of choosing the executive from the task of legislation. This makes it feasible for both houses to join in electing an executive, and thus gives the State chamber a voice in the selection. Moreover, the fact that the legislature has chosen the executive appears to facilitate cooperation between them on legislation. Stability is assured by the fact that the executive is elected for a fixed term and can be removed only for misconduct. Since the executive does not depend for its tenure of office on the continued support of specific delegates or parties, the executive may be able to obtain support for different legislative measures from shifting majorities where the party situation has not crystallized.

B. *Respective Roles in Law-making*

1. GENERAL LEGISLATION

In practice, if not in theory, the independent executive, as well as a responsible one, exercises leadership in developing a federal legislative program.

Under the Cabinet system, the Ministers, heading the executive departments, are entrusted with the task of initiating and drafting all important bills, and steering them through the legislature. The function of the legislature is to debate issues of general policy and then vote the bills into law, unless it is prepared to bring down the government. Where the Cabinet is supported by a single, well-disciplined party, as is usual in Australia and Canada, bills are rarely opposed by the party members although occasionally concessions are made to the opposition. Thus, in examining and revising the Cabinet's proposals, the standing legislative committees, which are organized along party lines and under the control of the Cabinet, limit themselves to making minor corrections in detail, not involving open conflict with the executive. Indeed, strong legislative committees are likely to be incompatible with the strict Cabinet system, especially when the legislature is composed of many parties. The possible rivalry between the committees and the Cabinet may create conflicts and instability.

In the United States, despite his separation from Congress, the President exercises great influence on legislation. In part he does so through his constitutional right to propose legislation by messages to Congress, and to veto legislation passed by Congress, and in part through the members of his party in the legislature. Thus, many of the important bills are drafted in the executive departments. But the President's leadership is much looser than under the Cabinet system. The legislative committees play a major part in the shaping and course of legislation, by holding public hearings on all important bills, by suppressing bills in committee, and by their reports which are ordinarily followed by the houses. Since party discipline is much weaker than in Australia or Canada, the members of Congress can exercise considerable freedom in opposing or supporting particular pieces of legislation even though part of the President's program. Important too is the pressure of organized groups and of public opinion on specific measures. Moreover, the veto of the President can be overridden by the vote of two thirds of both houses, and is weakened by the fact that it cannot be addressed to only part of a bill. The President and his department heads cannot participate in legislative deliberations.

The Swiss experience is especially suggestive on this point. There, the executive also provides legislative leadership, despite its collegial form and its weaker political and party authority. The Constitution lodges full legislative power in the legislature, and confers no veto power on the Executive Council. The Executive Council is authorized, however, to propose bills and submit them to the legislature, and to participate in their discussion, even though its members are not allowed to be members of the legislature. In practice, the legislature tends to rely on the Executive Council to draft nearly all federal measures, and initiate most of them as well. When the legislature wishes to initiate legislation, it often adopts a motion setting out the general principles, to be referred to the Executive Council for formulation. At the same time, the independence of the legislature has resulted in a committee system which is useful but by no means as strong as the American system. For the most part, the committees and the chambers follow the Council's proposals, but do not hesitate to amend if they see fit. This Swiss system appears well adapted for the situation where the legislature is composed of many parties, none of which commands a majority. Under such conditions, the executive can hardly attain the requisite control over the legislature to force its acceptance of a complete program. Instead, the effort must be to obtain support for specific measures by majorities which may differ from proposal to proposal.

The German system under the Basic Law of the Federal Republic seeks to thread a middle course on legislation between the Cabinet and Swiss systems. But when the Chancellor depends on a coalition, the threat to withdraw support may still give small minority parties an undue influence on legislation. Moreover, the possibility of deposing the Chancellor, though limited, still leads to a division of parties into supporters and opposition, as under the strict Cabinet system. The legislature has more freedom in accepting or rejecting particular bills than under the Cabinet system, but, as under that system, the central issue is the control of the government and this determines the position on specific legislation.

2. FISCAL LEGISLATION

The extent of the executive's power over the federal budget and taxes differs between the Cabinet and independent executive systems.

In Australia, Canada, and Germany the constitutions contain specific provisions to strengthen the general authority of the executive on such fiscal matters. The Canadian Constitution prohibits the legislature from enacting any tax or appropriation measure unless recommended by the executive. In Australia, the legislature is forbidden to appropriate funds for any purpose not recommended by the executive. The German Basic Law requires the approval of the Chancellor and Cabinet for any increases or additions to their budget proposals. These provisions reinforce the general authority of the Cabinet over legislation. In view of the complex and voluminous nature of appropriation measures, the ability of the legislature to modify their provisions is limited in fact by the practice of examining them before the full chamber, which can obviously adopt only general policy.

The Swiss and American constitutions contain no such restrictions on the ultimate authority of the legislature over all appropriations and revenue measures. In the United States, the President is required by law to submit a comprehensive annual budget, but the committees of both the House and Senate examine it in detail and hold hearings on the appropriations for the various departments and agencies. The President has the same veto as on other legislation, but the inability to veto specific items without disapproving the entire law limits its effectiveness in this field. In Switzerland, the Constitution assigns to the federal executive the preparation of the budget but reserves to the legislature full powers over its enactment. The Swiss legislative committees also scrutinize the budget of the executive but, in practice, seldom make changes.

Not Read

3. DISSOLUTION BY THE EXECUTIVE

The American and Swiss constitutions provide no method for settling disputes between the legislature and the executive, even on basic policy issues.

Under the Cabinet system such disagreements are resolved either by deposing the Cabinet and organizing another enjoying Parliamentary support, or by dissolving the legislature and holding new elections. By its power to dissolve the lower house and submit the issue to the electorate, the executive can exercise a substantial check on frivolous disagreements by its own party members or even by the opposition. This power is an essential counterweight to the power of the legislature to force resignation of the Cabinet. But this system requires special conditions for successful operation. The power of dissolution cannot be effective in ensuring the support needed for stable Cabinet government unless the party leaders have sufficient control over their party and its members to prevent nomination or re-election of a recalcitrant member. Moreover, new elections can work best only in a two-party system which can present the issues sharply and settle them by the outcome, either by returning the party in power or by replacing it with the opposition party. Such elections obviously cannot have a similar clarifying effect in a multiparty context.

In Germany, the Basic Law provides not only for dissolution at the request of the executive but also an alternative method for handling such disputes between the executive and the legislature. In such cases, where the lower house fails to pass urgent legislation the federal President, at the request of the government and with the approval of the upper house, may declare a state of legislative emergency. If the lower house again rejects the bill or fails to pass it within four weeks, it is considered enacted insofar as approved by the upper house; and the same procedure may be followed for other bills for a period of six months. Such bills may not modify the Constitution and the federal Chancellor may have resort to this procedure only once during his term of office. Since this procedure has not yet been invoked there is no experience as to its effect; clearly, it tends to strengthen the hand of the federal government in dealing with the legislature on urgent legislation.

C. *Legislative Controls over the Executive*

Theory and practice diverge sharply with respect to the extent of legislative control over the executive. In principle, under the Cabinet system, as in Canada and Australia, the executive is held constantly responsible for all its actions to the lower house through power to depose the Cabinet. In the German Federal Republic, the more limited power of removal modifies this nominal position somewhat. On the other hand, in theory, the American President and the Swiss Executive Council are independent of the legislature and largely free from its control.

Actually, the situations are not nearly so distinct. Composed of the leaders of the majority party, the Cabinet can control individual members through the party machinery and party discipline. The power of dissolution reinforces this authority and can be used, to some extent, to coerce the opposition. Thus the Cabinet may often dominate Parliament rather than the reverse.

On the other hand, the American and Swiss executives are subject to important legislative controls despite their independence. Thus the ability of the legislature to withhold appropriations or taxes, or to pass legislation restricting the power or discretion of the executive, or abolishing or curtailing particular agencies may be a strong weapon against an unpopular executive. The American Congress has also made inroads on executive authority in some areas by creating independent commissions to administer its laws.

Furthermore, both the United States and Swiss constitutions give the legislature some special checks over administration. Thus, in the United States, all important federal officials appointed by the President require confirmation by the Senate before taking office. The Congress also has constitutional power to impeach the President and other officials, and to remove them from office for certain serious offenses; actually, this power has been used in recent times only against flagrant misconduct by judges. Under the Swiss system, the federal legislature directly elects certain important officials (in addition to the executive itself) such as the commanding general of the armed forces, the members of the supreme court, and other officers specified by law. The fact that members of the Swiss Executive Council come up for re-election by the legislature at four-year intervals is a further general check on them. Moreover, under both systems, treaties negotiated by the executive must be approved by the Senate in the United States, or by the legislature in Switzerland.

Finally, in the United States, the Congress makes extensive use of its committees to investigate the work of the executive branch and the administration of the laws. Such investigations are an effective device for bringing to light defaults or improper actions and requiring their correction by public censure or the threat of legislation. For the same purpose, Congress has created a Comptroller General responsible only to it for auditing and accounting of public funds.

In the German Federal Republic, in addition to the general supervision of administration by the lower house usual under the Cabinet system, the upper house has more specific power with respect to the execution of federal laws, especially where carried out through Land agencies. It is also entitled to be kept currently informed by the federal government regarding federal affairs. Since this role is directly related to its character as a council, it is discussed below in Section IV.

IV. RESPECTIVE FUNCTIONS OF THE TWO CHAMBERS

The question of the respective roles of the two chambers is closely allied with the matters already considered. The division of powers between them will be affected, for example, by whether the upper chamber is of the Council or Senate type. Moreover, the actual role of the upper chamber directly depends not only on its nominal authority but also on whether the executive is responsible to the legislature or is independent. The fact that, under the Cabinet system, the executive is responsible to the more popular lower house alone and not to the upper house has important consequences on this issue.

This section will examine the formal and actual positions of the two chambers in relation to: (1) the initiation and enactment of legislation; (2) the ratification of treaties and constitutional amendments; and (3) the supervision of administration and appointments.

A. *Roles in Law-making*

In four of the federations studied, the constitutions confer on both houses substantially the same powers to initiate and enact legislation with some exceptions as to fiscal matters which have proved unimportant. In the United States the exception applies only to revenue measures, which must originate in the lower house, but may be amended in the Senate and must be passed by it to become law. In Canada and Australia, the Senate may not initiate appropriation or revenue measures and, in Australia, may not amend them but merely request the lower house to amend. In view of the power to reject, however, this distinction has become ineffective. In Switzerland both chambers have the same powers even for fiscal legislation. The German Constitution has, however, conferred different powers on the two houses, as explained below.

In federations where the executive is independent of both chambers, the actual powers of each chamber correspond substantially to their constitutional authority. In Switzerland and the United States both chambers share about equally in the initiation and passage of legislation; neither dominates, and both must consent for a bill to become law. In Switzerland, a member of the federal executive may not be a member of either chamber, but may and does take part in the deliberations of both chambers, and on request drafts bills proposed in the legislature. In the United States, the President works with leaders of both houses of Congress in proposing and shaping legislation, and both chambers share about equally in the drafting and revision of bills in their course through the legislature. If there is a difference in the actual power of the Senate and House, the Senate may play a more vital role because of the greater independence of its members, fostered by its smaller size and their greater prestige and longer terms.

Under the Cabinet system the actual authority of the two chambers departs sharply from their constitutional equality. In both Australia and Canada, the lower house has almost always been dominant, and the upper house, when not giving automatic assent, has become primarily a revising and checking chamber. On rare occasions, usually when its majority party is different from that of the lower house, it may force amendments not desired by the Cabinet by the threat of a deadlock, or may block bills passed by the lower house until public opinion has crystallized. But if a measure clearly enjoys popular support, the upper house virtually never will prevent its passage. For this situation there are two main reasons:

(1) Most basic is the nature of Cabinet government. The Cabinet is responsible to the lower house and the Ministers are generally members of that house. In presenting their legislative program, they will submit their bills first to that chamber. Inevitably, the principal debates on bills take place at that stage, and when they reach the upper chamber, the policy questions have already been thrashed out.

(2) The second important factor is the strength of the parties. Since the same party has generally controlled both houses, and since party discipline is extremely strict, the party members in the upper house are seldom in a position to oppose legislation approved by the majority caucus and passed by the lower house. Thus, the strong parties requisite for the smooth operation of Cabinet government also militate against a strong upper house. The Australian and Canadian experience suggests that a strong upper house is incompatible with the operation of Cabinet government and the conditions essential for its success.

Under the German constitutions, the situation is further complicated by the presence of the Council-type of upper house. Neither the Weimar Constitution nor the Basic Law of the Federal Republic conferred on the upper house powers over legislation equal to those of the popular house. Under the Weimar Constitution, on legislation approved by the lower chamber, the upper house could impose only a veto which the lower house could override by a two-thirds vote, unless the President chose to order a popular referendum on the bill. Since he acted mainly on the advice of the Chancellor, this power was never invoked. The Basic Law divides federal legislation into two classes: on specified kinds of measures of special interest to the States, the upper chamber must approve for the bill to be enacted; but for most legislation, a rejection by the upper chamber may be overridden by the lower house, by a simple majority or by two thirds, depending on the size of the vote in the upper chamber. This scheme inevitably raises disputes between the houses on whether particular laws fall into one category or the other. Both constitutions have sought to redress the balance slightly in favor of the upper chamber by requiring the government to present proposed bills first to it for criticism, though not necessarily for approval, before submitting them to the lower chamber. This ensures that, in its discussion of the bill, the lower house will have before it the views of the upper chamber. Too little experience is available under the Basic Law to know what the effect of this arrangement will be on the actual positions of the two houses.

B. *Approval of Treaties and Constitutional Amendments*

1. APPROVAL OF TREATIES

With respect to treaties, the position of the two chambers in most federal states is the same as on legislation, except in the United States. In Australia and Canada, the executive is responsible to the lower house in the conduct of foreign affairs as for other matters. The Cabinet is not required to obtain specific approval of treaties unless legislation is required to give them effect. In that case, the roles of the two chambers are the same as for other types of legislation. The Basic Law of the German Federal Republic requires that all treaties be approved by a federal law, for which the authority of the upper chamber depends on the same rules applicable to legislation generally. As on legislation, the Swiss Constitution confers on both chambers the same powers with respect to foreign relations and treaties.

Under the United States Constitution, however, treaties made by the President become effective only when approved by a two-thirds majority of the Senate members voting. The Senate, as the smaller and more stable chamber, was considered better suited for discussion of foreign affairs. Since treaties become the supreme law of the land, this provision has been criticized to some extent because of the exclusion of the lower house from the process of approval.

2. APPROVAL OF CONSTITUTIONAL AMENDMENTS

In the initiation and passage of constitutional amendments the roles of the two houses are usually governed by special provisions of the constitution, but approximate their relative positions on legislation. In the United States and Switzerland, the two chambers share the same authority in the proposal of amendments for ratification, although two-thirds vote of each chamber is required in the United States. In Australia, while amendments normally require approval of both chambers for submission to the people, the approval of one house may be dispensed with under certain conditions if the Governor-General, acting on the advice of the Cabinet, so orders. Under the Weimar Constitution, the veto of the upper chamber on amendments could be overridden by the lower chamber subject to a demand by the upper chamber for popular referendum. Under the Basic Law of the Federal Republic the legislature alone can adopt amendments by the two-thirds vote of both houses. The Canadian amending process, which is now under revision, has called for legislation of the British Parliament, which acts, however, only on request of the Canadian legislature. In practice, this means that the Canadian Cabinet and lower chamber enjoy the same predominance as on legislation.

Thus, in general, the same pattern of equality or inequality between the houses seems to apply to the amending process as to legislation, despite the difference in procedure.

C. *Supervision of Administration*

In the legislative supervision of administration by the executive, the two chambers tend to occupy about the same positions as on legislation in all federal states except the United States and Germany. Under the Cabinet system of Australia and Canada, the executive is responsible to the lower chamber for the conduct of administration as on other matters, and for serious default could be removed by a vote of no confidence. In Switzerland the two chambers share equally a wide authority over administration and appointments to the higher offices of the federal government.

In the United States the situation is somewhat different. Insofar as Congress exercises controls over the executive by legislation, appropriations, and investigating committees, the two houses have the same authority. The Constitution assigns to the Senate alone, however, the power to confirm or reject persons nominated by the President for important federal offices. In practice, since this gives the members of the Senate a share in control over patronage, it is a source of substantial political power for them.

As already mentioned in Section III, the Basic Law of the German Federal Republic, like the Imperial and Weimar Constitutions, confers special powers on the upper chamber with respect to administration. For example, the upper chamber must approve all administrative regulations and other measures by the federal government regarding the administration of federal laws by the States. These provisions are based on the fact that the upper chamber represents the State governments which are charged with the administration of many federal laws. In Switzerland, however, similar reliance on the canton bureaucracies to execute federal laws has not required an upper chamber of the Council-type or any distinction between the chambers.

D. *Resolution of Deadlocks*

Whenever the approval of both houses is required for enactment, legislation may fail of passage because of their disagreement on its terms. The risk of such deadlocks, which depends upon the relative standing of the two houses, has led to creation of various procedures for resolving them.

This risk is greatest in the United States and Switzerland where the legislature and executive are independent and both houses enjoy equal legislative authority in law and fact. In both cases, however, the constitution contains no provisions for resolution of such deadlocks. In Switzerland, in cases of disagreement, the houses act on the bill in turn, passing it back and forth between them as modified until both agree on the same provisions. Apparently, this system has worked without serious difficulty under Swiss conditions.

In the United States, Congress has developed a definite procedure for handling cases when the houses pass a bill in a different form and each refuses to accept the version of the other house. Each house then appoints several of its members to a joint Conference Committee charged with arriving at a single compromise version. This compromise bill is then submitted to both houses for acceptance or rejection, but is not subject to amendment in either house. Like other legislation, it is enacted only if passed by both houses. This system works remarkably well. The Conference Committee is almost always able to arrive at an agreed draft, which often may improve on both of the disagreed versions. Likewise, the two houses ordinarily accept the compromise bill. The success of the method depends partly on the habit of compromise, partly on the fact that the same party is likely to have a majority in both houses (although party discipline is not strong), and partly on the pressure of public opinion where the legislation is urgently needed or strongly supported.

In Germany, the Basic Law has adopted the Conference Committee as part of the legislative procedure. Strictly speaking, deadlock can occur only on legislation requiring the approval of the upper chamber, since a protest by the upper house on other measures can be overridden by the lower house. Yet the Basic Law provides for a Joint Conference Committee for both types: at the request of the upper house on bills subject only to its protest and at the request of the lower house, or government as well, on bills requiring upper house approval. The upper house members of this Committee are not bound by instructions, contrary to their usual situation. If the Conference Committee proposes amendments, the bill is resubmitted to the lower house for another vote, but apparently it can adopt the original or the revised form as it chooses before transmitting it again to the upper house.

The Canadian and Australian experience on disputes between the houses is relevant only under the Cabinet system. Despite the legislative equality of the two houses in law, the actual dominance of the lower house and the strong party control of both houses sharply reduce the frequency of such disputes. They are likely to occur only in the unusual case where different parties hold the majorities in the two houses. Nevertheless, the Australian Constitution has elaborate provisions for resolving such deadlocks by dissolution of both houses and new elections. This can be ordered by the Governor-General, on advice of the Cabinet, when the same bill has been twice passed and rejected. Double dissolution has been resorted to on only two occasions and in both the election settled the issue. Had deadlock persisted, however, it would have been finally resolved by a vote in a joint session of the two houses. The British method of appointing new members to the upper house to break a deadlock is available to a limited extent under the Canadian Constitution, but has never been used. It is obviously feasible only where the upper house is appointed by the central government. Both Australia and Canada have occasionally used a Conference Committee to avoid resort to their elaborate deadlock procedures.

V. Conclusions

From the experience reviewed in this study, it is apparent that federal states can and do operate under legislative systems differing widely in composition, structure, and relation to the executive. But it would be a serious misreading of this experience to conclude that all of these systems are therefore equally adaptable for a new federation. On the contrary, the available evidence indicates that the success of each of these systems depends in varying degrees on the existence of suitable political and other conditions. Accordingly, in seeking to derive guidance from this material, it will be essential to analyze carefully the political environment within which the institutions would have to function and any special difficulties they would be forced to surmount.

Any comprehensive examination of these questions is beyond the scope of this study. But it is possible to foresee certain aspects of the situation which are likely to have great bearing on the workability of some of these alternatives in a European federation. Two seem especially important:

(1) In its formative period the new federation will immediately face tasks more complex and more novel than any of its component States now face. In an existing state, a new government inherits both its problems and the machinery for handling them. The new federal government will largely lack both of these assets:

(a) In an established state, the many processes for sorting out issues have already defined most of the problems which a new government is expected to tackle, and orders of priority for their solution. Thus its tasks are largely formulated. In a new state, such as a European federation, this still has to be done in many areas. Its leaders in the executive and legislature have a much harder task to isolate the problems and settle their relative priority, in terms of need, feasibility and public opinion.

(b) It is the same with the tools for solving them. The existing state has its organized bureaucracy, a mass of accumulated data and methods for keeping it up to date, established procedures for conducting the executive and legislature, and for their cooperation, etc. All this machinery the new state must create. Within a community of six states using at least four languages and each with its own governmental traditions, the task of recruiting officials and employees and molding them into a working administration will be time-consuming and difficult.

These conditions clearly call for an executive which enjoys reasonable tenure and stability, and the cooperation of the legislative body.

(2) These requisites must be achieved in an unstable political context. At present, all parties are national; and the growth of strong parties across state lines will undoubtedly take considerable time and effort in order to form the personal ties and agree on common programs. Thus numerous minority parties can be expected in the federal legislature for some period to come. Moreover, the federal community lacks adequate means for forming a strong federal public opinion. The language barrier, plus the absence of publications circulating generally throughout the federation, will make it difficult to create sufficient organs to form such opinion. Very few public figures are known in more than one country, and virtually none have any following outside their own state.

All these factors suggest that the legislature cannot be organized on clear lines in the first period. The many minority parties are likely to form shifting alliances. They may be able to agree more easily on specific legislation than on general programs. Thus, majorities for different measures may be made up from a varying group of parties. In this situation, if measures can be submitted and adopted on their individual merits rather than as parts of a broader program, they will be more likely to enable effective action on the initial problems which will have to be explored and solved by trial and error and experiment.

A. *Relation Between Legislature and Executive*

The necessary stability can hardly be obtained under these circumstances if the executive must rely on the continuous support of a specific coalition of minority parties in the legislature. Moreover, the executive is more likely to succeed in working out acceptable solutions if it can propose them for acceptance or rejection individually on their merits, and can seek support for different measures from different groups.

These conditions would seem to narrow substantially the field of choice. In particular they appear to rule out the adoption of a Cabinet system like that in Australia and Canada. Experience there and elsewhere seems to show that it will produce the requisite stability only if the parties are limited in number, well organized and strictly disciplined. For the reasons already discussed, these requirements seem unlikely to be fulfilled in a European federation in the near future. Without a few disciplined parties, the Cabinet is constantly at the mercy of minority elements in the coalition, and cannot exercise sufficient control in the legislature to provide the necessary leadership. Under these circumstances, the threat of dissolution is a very weak deterrent, and, even if used, would seldom operate (as in Britain and the Dominions) to settle the disputed issue. The modified form of Cabinet government adopted in Germany under the 1949 Basic Law attempts to meet this problem and assure greater stability, but experience with the operation of this system is too limited to allow conclusions as to its effect under various conditions.

The alternative is an independent executive not subject to removal by the legislature, as in the United States and Switzerland. Both seem to meet the need for stability. The American system of electing the President by popular vote results in strong individual leadership, but might be difficult to operate or unacceptable in Europe for reasons already discussed, and for others set out in Study 2, The Federal Executive, which need not be repeated here.

The Swiss experience therefore seems to offer the best guidance for stable and effective government under the conditions likely to be faced. Its main strength comes from three advantages:

(1) It separates the election of the executive from the acceptance of a legislative program. The collegial executive can be composed of members chosen from various parties for their general competence without thereby approving of their political views. At the same time, their selection by the legislature should facilitate cooperation between the two branches on later legislation.

(2) The fact that the members of the executive hold office for a fixed term, which cannot be ended by the legislature, provides the stability of the executive necessary to organize the federal administration and to tackle its problems in an orderly, systematic way.

(3) The fact that the executive does not depend upon a specific coalition for its continued tenure enables it to submit measures separately for acceptance or rejection by the legislature. Such measures can be enacted by the support of majorities drawn from different party groupings. In other words, one measure may be able to attract support from certain members of the legislature who will not support proposals of the executive on other matters.

The Swiss structure, like the American, does, of course, entail risks of delay and possible deadlock between the executive and the legislature. But these risks are inherent in the situation until the federation develops more effective public opinion and stronger and fewer parties as a means of organizing political views and programs. Until then, compromises of opinions and interests necessary for governing the community will have to be made mainly by means of the federal institutions, and especially the executive and the legislature. Thus, agreement on specific measures will have to be obtained largely by "give and take" within the collegial executive and within the legislature, as well as between these two. It therefore seems wise to adopt a legislative system which focuses attention directly on the need for such cooperation and compromise.

To establish Cabinet government, which presupposes a high degree of political organization and unity and a well-developed tradition of discipline, may increase the inherent difficulties. The effort to make these institutions operate in an unsuitable context is likely to divert attention from the substantive problems requiring solution, and to disillusion popular opinion. It seems better to create a system which stresses the fact that its successful working demands active cooperation and good will between the legislature and the executive and between the two houses of the legislature. As it develops, public opinion can then put pressure on these organs to work together for the solution of problems.

The experience in the United States and Switzerland also suggests that the dangers of legislative deadlocks are much less serious in practice than might be assumed theoretically. The fact that under the proposed system the legislature will elect the executive should also facilitate cooperation. Undoubtedly, some legislation will fail to pass because of inability to agree, but this has seldom been of a character to interfere with the ability to govern. Ordinarily, when the need for legislation is really urgent, some form of compromise can be worked out.

The Swiss and American systems have operated without special provisions for deadlocks, such as dissolution of the legislature by the executive, or automatic extension of a preceding budget. Indeed, the inclusion of such provisions under this system seems more likely to impair its operation than to improve it. Its success depends ultimately on a sense of responsibility of the legislature and the executive, and on their efforts to find compromise solutions. The danger is that such expedients will encourage extreme positions on one side or the other, and reduce efforts to compromise. It seems better to place on the members of the legislature a clear political responsibility for its actions and for any failure to enact necessary legislation.

At the same time, to encourage necessary leadership, the executive should have authority to propose legislation for enactment, and should be required, by the constitution or by law, to submit an annual budget for revision and enactment. Further executive participation might be provided by permitting its members to support their proposals before committees and in the legislature. In addition, an executive veto might be considered, but the legislature should have the authority to override it by a qualified majority or by a simple majority after a certain period of time.

If Swiss and American practice is followed, the legislature would have to approve treaties and would be given a voice in appointments of major

officials. The American method of having such officials nominated by the
executive, subject to confirmation by the legislature, seems preferable to
their election by the legislature.

B. *Composition of the Two Houses*

The accepted federal tradition of a legislature with two houses would presumably be followed in a new federation.

Lower House. The lower house has always been elected by popular vote,
with seats distributed by population, and can be expected to be similarly
constituted in a new federation. In this connection, the experience of the
various federal states emphasizes the influence of the electoral systems for
the lower house or the composition of parties and especially on their number and character. In the Anglo-American countries, for example, the
two-party system, which has certainly contributed to the working of a federal structure, has been fostered by the use of single-member constituencies.
In Europe, parties uniting similar interest groups across State lines would
clearly promote the development of European attitudes and ideas. Thus,
in order to ensure an electoral system which will encourage a sound party
structure the federation should have the power under the constitution to
regulate the methods and procedures for federal elections. For practical
reasons, it may be necessary at the start, however, to adopt State practices
or allow the States to regulate such elections, including suffrage, until a federal law can be worked out and put into effect.

Upper House. As stated in Section I, the crucial question regarding the
legislative structure is whether the upper house should be a Senate or a
Council, that is, whether its members should be representatives elected by
the State legislatures and free to vote according to their own views or party
affiliations, or should be instructed delegates appointed by the member
State governments, and voting by State blocs. Here, the experience of the
existing federal States strongly indicates that the Senate-type of upper chamber has important advantages over the Council-type for a federal system
under European conditions. For this there are several reasons.

(1) The adoption of the Council form in Germany, the only federal state
using it, had its origin in special conditions not duplicated in Europe today. In 1871, power in the German States was vested primarily in the
monarchs and their bureaucracies, and the essential problem was to federate
and draw together these centers of executive power. The Council was assigned to solve this problem. In Europe today, the Parliament is universally accepted as the central democratic organ in the state. It is therefore
only appropriate that the State representatives in a federal upper chamber
should be designated by the Parliament rather than by the executives of
the States.

The Council form is not required to enable the federal government
to delegate to the States the administration of federal laws where that is de-

sirable. The necessary cooperation for this purpose can be worked out by devices such as administrative committees or councils composed of State and federal officials, and by giving State officials a voice in the making of administrative regulations necessary for those purposes, through consultation or issuance by joint boards of federal and State officials. This problem should not be allowed to confuse the more basic issue of the structure of the legislature.

(2) The Senate provides sufficient safeguards to the States and regions. The actual experience of the federations studied has shown that the fear that the larger States would combine to impose on the smaller ones has not been realized.[2] From the very start, the groupings are almost certain to be formed on other bases. Under either a Senate or a Council system, the members will reflect State interests, but not from precisely the same standpoint. The Senator may not place the same emphasis on preserving the prerogatives of the States as political entities as would a Council member. But he will be at least as alert as the Council member in protecting the cultural, commercial, agricultural or labor interests of his State when they may be jeopardized or benefited by proposed federal measures.

(3) An upper chamber of the Council-type, composed of delegates of State governments, would tend to be divisive and disruptive of the federation. Since the delegates in a Council vote as instructed State blocs, every issue would involve dividing the States into groups against each other. The efforts to obtain majorities by combining such blocs is likely to perpetuate old national rivalries, antagonisms and distrust.

The Senate-type, on the other hand, will meet the need for integrating forces in the federation. Under this system, majorities can be formed by individual members on the basis of common views or interests, or party affiliation, which will cut across national allegiances, and often align members from the same State into different groups. This will tend to foster wider loyalties on a federal basis, including various sections and States. Thus, every vote in the Senate would serve to underscore the deeper unity of economic and social interests among groups in different States.

Moreover, the Senate facilitates the balancing of the responsibilities and interests of the federation and of the States. Discussion among the members is more likely to influence decision and to foster compromise of disputed issues. In a Council, instructed voting tends greatly to reduce the value of debate and the opportunity for compromise. This seriously impedes the role of the legislature as a forum for focusing conflicts of interests and for resolving them or compromising them. Accordingly, the Senate form has shown itself better able to evolve in step with the growth of the community itself.

All of these factors suggest the advisability of the Senate system under European conditions. If it should be adopted, it would seem wise to pro-

---

[2] The dominance of Prussia in the earlier German federations was clearly due to special factors and conditions not comparable to the present circumstances.

vide for election of members by the legislatures of the member States or by their lower houses. This would allow the choice of Senators cognizant of the needs and attitudes of the member States without subjecting them to a direct control of the State governments themselves. The Senators should be named for a fixed term and should, of course, be free to vote without instructions from the governments or legislatures. The term of office should be long enough to give members of the Senate an opportunity to learn to work together and to assure reasonable stability, and might be between four and six years. The system of staggered terms, so arranged that part expire at the end of each two-year period, would facilitate continuity while still enabling each State legislature to name some Senators often enough to ensure that the Senate reflected the party strength and popular views in the member States.

A Senate so constituted can take account of the interests both of the States and of the federation in reaching its conclusions.

C. *Respective Functions of the Two Houses*

Experience in the federations studied indicates that the actual role and influence of the two houses depend as much on their basic structure as on their formal powers.

(1) The Australian and Canadian experience shows clearly that under a Cabinet system, the popular house, to which the Cabinet is responsible, soon becomes dominant and the upper house becomes mainly a revising body, even though the nominal powers of the two houses are equal. This tendency, inherent in the Cabinet system itself, is reinforced by the strong party discipline necessary for its successful operation. Consequently, it seems clear that a system with the two houses relatively equal in actual authority is not likely to be achieved with the Cabinet form of executive responsible to the popularly elected house. Conceivably, a Cabinet system could be responsible to both houses jointly, but this would raise serious practical problems when the two houses did not agree. In such cases, dissolution would not be an effective way to solve the difficulty unless both houses were elected by popular vote. Even then such a system would be too complicated to be feasible without a few strong parties and strict party discipline. Neither of these conditions seems likely in a European federation in the near future.

(2) Under the Council system, other forces tend to erode the powers of the Council so as to ensure that the federation can function effectively. The fact that the States have the controlling voice in such a chamber inevitably leads to pressure to reduce its role in legislation. Both the Weimar Constitution and the Basic Law of the Federal Republic show this tendency. The upper chamber may be restricted to a veto, which can be overruled by the lower house, except possibly on matters of special concern to the States.

(3) The Swiss and American experience shows that approximate equality between the two houses can be maintained under suitable conditions. If the executive is independent of both houses, the factors favoring the lower chamber in the Cabinet system are largely removed. Moreover, if the upper chamber is of the Senate-type, there will not be the same popular pressure to cut down its powers even though it is initially elected by the State legislatures. Instead, as the federal sentiment grows, public opinion may lead to election by popular vote instead of by legislatures, but this change can be made without seriously affecting the standing or operation of the legislature.

On the basis of this analysis, the experience of the federations studied appears to support the conclusion that a legislature of the Swiss or American type, with an independent executive, offers the most practical solution for a new federation.

Both houses of the legislature should then share equal authority in the election of the federal executive, the enactment of legislation, the initiation of constitutional amendments, and the approval of treaties, and should enjoy equal power to investigate the administration of the laws by the executive. For practical reasons it may be desirable to confer any power to confirm appointments on the smaller upper house.

Judging by Swiss and American experience, the allocation of functions suggested in this study should enable the executive to exert the necessary leadership in legislation and administration, and the legislature to maintain the necessary controls over the executive and the administration of the laws, without undermining the independence and responsibility of either the executive or the legislature, or impairing the equality of both houses of the legislature.

APPENDIX I

Australia

The legislature of Australia, called the Parliament, is composed of a Senate and a House of Commons. In the House, representation is based on population. In the Senate, however, each State has the same number of Senators, regardless of size or population, although the two largest States, New South Wales and Victoria, contain about three times the population of the four smallest.

I. COMPOSITION AND STRUCTURE

A. *Members and Tenure*

Currently the Senate is composed of ten members from each of the six states. The Constitution fixed the original number of Senators from each

State at six, but granted Parliament the power to increase that figure by federal law so long as equal representation was maintained (Commonwealth of Australia Constitution Act, §7). The term of office of a Senator is six years, half of the membership being elected every three years (§§7, 13). The Senate is not affected by the fall of a Cabinet and election of a new House but may be dissolved to resolve a Parliamentary deadlock, as explained below (§57). In that case, a full new Senate is elected along with a new House. This "double dissolution" has occurred only twice and is quite distinct from the fall of a Cabinet.

The Constitution fixes the House membership at double that of the Senate (§24): it is now one hundred and twenty-three, of whom all but two are voting members. Seats are distributed among the States according to population, with a minimum to five to each. The tenure of the House members is three years, unless shortened either by a dissolution on the fall of a Cabinet or by a "double dissolution" (§§28, 57).

The salary of members of Parliament is controlled by them (§48).

B. *Method of Election*

Australian federal elections are conducted by the federal authorities according to a uniform method of voting determined by Parliament (§9). Under the Constitution, the State legislatures were allowed to prescribe the method of election, until the federal Parliament provided otherwise (§§9, 29). Also subject to change by federal law, qualifications for electors and regulations for elections were to conform to the laws of the States applying to elections for their more numerous houses (§§8, 10, 30, 31). In all cases, however, federal law now governs elections uniformly.

In fixing the qualifications of electors, Parliament cannot disenfranchise a person entitled to vote for the lower chamber in his own State (§41). It has, in fact, given the vote to all citizens without disabilities, male or female, married or unmarried, and made voting compulsory. Suffrage is the same for both houses.

Senate members are all elected on a State-wide basis (§7). These elections have been conducted in three ways. Initially, each elector voted for the number of vacancies to be filled, the candidates with the highest totals being elected. Approximately twenty years later, preferential voting was adopted (Commonwealth Electoral Act of 1918), which had the effect in Australia of giving all contested seats to the party with a majority of popular votes in the state. In 1948, proportional representation was adopted for Senate elections (Commonwealth Electoral Act of 1948); it is expected to make Senate membership correspond to party popularity. Casual vacancies in the Senate are filled temporarily by the Parliament of the State affected and permanently by the electorate at the next regular election (§15).

Members of the House are elected from approximately equal, single-member constituencies by preferential vote (Commonwealth Electoral Act of 1918). Casual vacancies are filled by special election (§33). The districts are redefined periodically, according to shifts in population, by an independent commission.

C. *Qualifications*

Qualifications for membership in Parliament are the same for both houses (§16), and are subject to change by federal law (§34). The principal requirements are a minimum age of 21, eligibility to vote in the elections for the House, and three years' residence within the Commonwealth. There are express constitutional prohibitions, however, against simultaneous membership in both federal houses (§43), and against seating a foreign citizen, a criminal, an undischarged bankrupt, a Crown officeholder other than Cabinet Ministers of the federal or State governments and military personnel, or a party to contracts with the federal Public Service (§44). Members of State Parliaments are forbidden by State law to sit simultaneously in the federal Parliament.

D. *Rules and Organization*

Each house is constitutionally enabled to make its own rules (§50). They are allowed to expel a member for non-attendance of two months' duration (§§20, 38). Each has its own majority leader and opposition leader, though they may be of different parties in the two houses.

Senators and Representatives are free of libel and defamation actions arising out of speeches in Parliament (§49). Parliamentary debates in Australia are broadcast.

II. POWERS OF THE HOUSE AND SENATE
A. *Relation to the Executive*

The Australian government resembles the British Cabinet system, in which the executive is responsible to the lower house. The Prime Minister and his colleagues in the Cabinet are nominally appointed by the Governor-General, who is mainly a symbol of the British monarch. In fact, the Cabinet is chosen on the basis of support by the majority party or coalition in the House and consists of the House party leaders, although some minor members are from the Senate. The Ministers will automatically resign at the end of the House's tenure every three years, and may be forced to resign at any time upon a vote of no confidence by a majority of the House. This vote may be indicated by the defeat of the Cabinet on an important measure or may be explicitly called for. Adverse votes arise when the Ministers fail to unite their party in a caucus, which seldom occurs on anything but a major issue of general policy. In that situation the Cabinet will usually request the Governor-General to dissolve the lower house so that the issue may be put to the electorate for decision, by returning the Cabinet to power or by giving victory to the opposition party. As a result, when the Cabinet is forced to step down, so must the House, a factor which promotes party cohesion and generally assures the Cabinet of cooperation.

Since the Cabinet proposes and frames most public legislation, Parliament provides a forum in which party decisions are turned into law, where party policy is subject to criticism, and where it is publicized to the electorate. House control of administration is limited to open questioning of the Ministers, unless it is prepared to force a Cabinet crisis. The well-organized opposition party, however, maintains a close scrutiny of executive conduct.

B. *General Legislative Authority of the Two Houses*

Under the Constitution the Senate has the same power as the House on all proposed laws except those imposing taxation or appropriating revenues (§52). In principle, either house may initiate such legislation and amend it, and the assent of both houses is required before any bill can become law.

In practice, however, the operation of Cabinet government and the party system affects the relative standing of the two houses in important ways. Thus, most legislation is initiated in the House because of the practice of having bills introduced by the appropriate Cabinet member, who is usually a member of the House rather than the Senate. Consequently, the crucial debates take place in the House, and the Senate debates tend to be more perfunctory and to receive less public attention. Furthermore, the practice of the House in adopting much of its legislation toward the end of its session severely limits the opportunity of the Senate to revise it and thus to perform the traditional task of an upper house. Finally, where the same party controls both House and Senate, rigorous party discipline ensures Senate approval of major measures adopted by the House. In consequence, the standing of the Senate in actual power or public position is much lower in relation to the House than its powers under the Constitution would suggest. This tendency may also be accentuated by the British tradition of the relative position of the House of Commons and the House of Lords.

There are very few standing committees in either house and those which exist are dominated by the Cabinet and generally ineffective. Bills are almost always considered by the House as a Committee of the Whole.

C. *Authority over Taxation and Appropriations*

The assent of the Senate is required for appropriations and tax measures as for other legislation, but it may not initiate money bills (§53). It may not amend tax laws or appropriations for the regular operating expenses of government, or amend any other law so as to increase any proposed charge or burden upon the people. In such matters, however, the Senate may return the law to the House requesting omission or amendment of any items or provisions therein, and the House may adopt them or not as it sees fit.

In practice, however, the Senate's power to reject money bills and submit requests now seems almost equivalent to the power to amend, since the House, when faced with rejection of a money bill accompanied by requests, has generally accepted them. Although constitutional doubt exists whether the Senate has the power to reject a money bill more than once, it has in fact done so. Under the Constitution, bills which provide for the ordinary annual services of the government or for taxation may concern those subjects only (§§54, 55). This prevention of "tacking" protects the Seante's power of initiation and amendment of ordinary legislation.

As in other matters, the Cabinet usually has its way with fiscal measures. This dominance is buttressed by two other factors. One is the practice of each house to consider fiscal measures as a Committee of the Whole, rather than through smaller, more expert standing committees. Since these bills tend to be bulky and complex, this precludes detailed study and understanding. The conditions for tax bills are somewhat more favorable because of the constitutional requirement that laws imposing taxation shall deal with one subject of taxation only (§55). Another reason for executive control of appropriations is the requirement that no appropriation may be passed unless its purpose has been recommended by the Governor-General who, in practice, will act only on the advice of the Cabinet (§56).

D. *Treaty Power*

The treaty power, in Australia, is vested in the executive, except where legislation may be required to carry out a treaty. In order, however, to ensure necessary implementation of the treaty, Parliament is frequently consulted prior to executive action. Alternatively, the executive may sign a treaty, "subject to the approval and acceptance by the Government of the Commonwealth of Australia" as in the case of the treaty creating the World Health Organization. When the legislature gives its approval, the pattern is similar to that for ordinary legislation.

E. *Authority on Constitutional Amendments*

The Senate's powers on amendments of the Constitution are the same as those of the House, except in one situation. Under Section 128, a proposed law to amend the Constitution must ordinarily be passed by both houses of Parliament and then submitted by the Governor-General to the electors for ratification or rejection.

However, where the two houses deadlock on a proposed amendment, the Governor-General may still submit the amendment to the electors if the initiating house has passed it twice, with an interval of at least three months between votes, and the other house has twice rejected or amended it unacceptably. Since the Governor-General, in exercising his authority, acts on the advice of his Ministers, the House of Commons can bring such a proposal before the electorate while the Senate cannot. Ultimately, therefore, the power of the Senate is only to postpone submission of any amendment to the people; but this may give an opportunity for more adequate public discussion of the amendment.

III. Resolution of Deadlocks

When the Senate and House disagree on legislation, Section 57 of the Constitution provides:

> If the House of Commons passes any proposed law, and the Senate rejects or fails to pass it or passes it with amendments to which the House of Commons will not agree, and if after an interval of three months the House of Commons in the same or the next session, again passes the proposed law with or without any amendments which have been made, suggested, or agreed to by the Senate, and the Senate rejects or fails to pass it, or passes it with amendments to which the House of Commons will not agree, the Governor-General may dissolve the Senate and the House of Commons simultaneously. But such dissolution shall not take place within six months before the date of the expiry of the House of Commons by effluxion of time.
>
> If after such dissolution the House of Commons again passes the proposed law, with or without any amendments which have been made, suggested or agreed to by the Senate and the Senate rejects or fails to pass it, or passes it with amendments to which the House of Commons will not agree, the Governor-General may convene a joint sitting of the members of the Senate and the House of Commons.
>
> The members present at the joint sitting may deliberate and shall vote together upon the proposed law as last proposed by the House of Commons, and upon amendments, if any which have been made therein by one House, and not agreed to by the other, and any amendments which are affirmed by an absolute majority of the total number of the members of the Senate and the House of Commons shall be taken to have been carried, and if the proposed law, with the amendments, if any, so carried is affirmed by an absolute majority of members of the Senate and House of Commons, it shall be taken to have been duly passed by both Houses of Parliament, and shall be presented to the Governor-General for the Queen's assent.

Under Section 57 an election does not automatically follow a deadlock between the two houses. The Governor-General will dissolve the Parliament and call for an election only on the advice of his Cabinet. The Senate's power is, therefore, limited to blocking House legislation or forcing amendments by threat of stalemate and dissolution.

Due to strict party discipline, deadlocks on controversial measures occur only when the House and Senate are controlled by different parties. The dissolution of the entire Parliament has occurred only twice, in 1913 and 1951: in both cases the ensuing elections resulted in control of the houses by the same party and no joint sitting was necessary. In any joint sitting, since the House has twice the membership and votes of the Senate, a strong House majority would be able to enact legislation despite Senate opposition.

Conference Committees have occasionally been formed to iron out differences without resort to dissolution.

IV. EVALUATION

At the time of federation, the small States insisted on equal representation in a strong Senate, expecting it to protect them from the large States and from the federal government. While no single State could veto legislation in the Senate, the four smaller States as a group, which held two thirds of the votes in the Senate, were in a position to block any legislation discriminating against the smaller States.

In practice, the Senate has not primarily played this role for various reasons. The issues in Australia have not ordinarily arisen in the form of conflicts of interest between the larger and smaller States. The rise of strong national parties has cut across State loyalties so that the Senate has tended to reflect party views rather than State prerogatives. Occasionally, State loyalties have controlled the attitudes of some Senators. During the depression, the agricultural States so strongly opposed the protective tariff that Western Australia demanded the right to secede from the federation; at this time, its Senators supported its sectional interests. After this issue was compromised, the divisions based on party lines again became dominant.

The Senate has failed to check the growth in the powers of the federation, and has been blamed by some on this ground. This tendency, however, appears to result from more basic forces, such as the revenue needs of the States and the increasing economic interdependence of Australia.

The experience with the Senate and its functioning have led to various suggestions for its reform. These fall into three main groups:

(1) Some propose the complete abolition of the Senate. These people strongly favor a unitary state, feeling that Australia has outgrown a federal structure. They accordingly conclude that the Senate serves no useful purpose: They consider that the States should no longer be treated as separate political entities, and that the Senate is not useful as a check on the lower House.

(2) Others wish to retain the Senate but to overhaul it extensively, though in divergent directions. One view would provide for election of Senators by the State Parliaments in order to make its members more adequately reflect the views of the States. Others would reduce the power of

the Senate on legislation to merely a suspensive veto on House action, with the additional power to force a popular referendum on ordinary legislation. Still another proposal (Mr. Ashworth) advocates a Senate patterned on the German Federal Economic Council, which would be appointed so as to be representative of vocational and professional groups.

(3) The third type of proposal consists of more moderate suggestions for reform. These would include provisions for questioning of Cabinet Ministers in the Senate, for raising the minimum age of electors, for providing for election of Senators from single-member districts, and for promoting more effective committee work. It is recognized, however, that the committees should not rival the Cabinet.

There appears to be no strong sentiment for making the Senate a real equal of the House. Since the principle of Cabinet government, responsible primarily to the House, is generally accepted, it seems clear that the House will continue to exercise the major legislative power even if reforms were adopted to strengthen the Senate.

The major proposals for changes in the House would extend the term of office because some consider the three-year term to be too short and to disrupt the working of the federal government.

APPENDIX II

Canada

I. COMPOSITION AND STRUCTURE

The Canadian legislature, called the Parliament, is composed of a House of Commons and a Senate. Representation in the House of Commons is based on provincial population; but each Province is assigned a fixed, although unequal, number of Senators.

A. *Membership in Senate*

Quebec and Ontario each received twenty-four Senators, while twelve were allotted to New Brunswick and Nova Scotia. When Prince Edward Island later joined the federation, it received four Senators, and the other two Maritime Provinces lost two Senate seats. Subsequently, four Western Provinces were allotted six Senators each on admission to the federation. Thus, Quebec, Ontario, the Maritime Provinces as a group, and the Western Provinces as a group, had the same Senate representation (24 members) in a Senate totaling 96 members, until the admission in 1949 of Newfoundland with six Senators brought Senate membership to 102. There has thus been regional, rather than provincial, equality in the upper house, favoring the Provinces with smaller population.

Members of the Senate are appointed for a life tenure. These appointments are controlled by the Cabinet and, more particularly, by the Prime Minister, although made by the Governor-General (British North America Act of 1867, §24). Appointments to the Senate have consistently been made along party lines, in order to ensure Senate approval of the government program. The life tenure and not ungenerous salary, coupled with a desire of the Prime Minister to retain effective legislative power in the House, have led to use of the appointments as rewards to loyal party members toward the end of an active political life. There has been a tendency also to recognize racial and religious minorities in distributing such appointments. The overall composition of the Senate is largely traceable to these factors.

B. *Method of Election to the House of Commons*

Seats in the lower chamber are assigned to the Provinces according to population, with the exception that no Province shall have fewer members in Commons than in the Senate (§51; British North America Act of 1946, §1). This exception creates an advantage for the smaller Provinces, reflecting to some extent the inability of a strong federal upper house to exist in a Cabinet system of government. Membership is now fixed at 262. Within each Province, there are single-member districts, except for two which have double-membership, of approximately equal size. The districts have always been defined by federal authority, originally in the Constitution and currently by a standing committee of the House after each decennial census. Under the Constitution, all other matters relating to the elections, including their regulation and the qualifications of electors, were to be governed by the provincial laws applying to elections to their popular chambers, until otherwise provided by federal law (§43). Parliament has since enacted such federal laws, granting universal suffrage.

The term of the Commons is five years, unless it is sooner dissolved (§50). Vacancies in it are filled through by-elections called at the discretion and convenience of the government. The Cabinet usually takes advantage of its power of dissolution to call general elections at a political propitious moment a short time prior to the legal end of a term.

C. *Qualifications for Membership*

Qualifications for appointment to the Senate are prescribed by the Constitution. The principal requirements are a minimum age of 30, ownership of land worth $4000 above encumbrances, ownership of real and personal property worth $4000 above debts and liabilities, and residency in the Province for which appointed (§23). Senators from Quebec must reside in certain districts. The Senate has authority to judge the satisfaction of these requirements (§33). Except for the prohibition on simultaneous

membership in the two chambers (§39), the qualifications for election to
Commons were originally governed by provincial law in the same manner
as other election matters.   Today this matter is also covered by the uniform
federal law (Dominion Elections Act of 1938).   A member need only be a
British subject over 21 and a qualified elector, which includes the requirement of one year's residence in Canada.   Federal officeholders (except
Cabinet Ministers) and contractors with the federal government are disqualified.   Most members reside in the districts in which they are elected;
but as many as ten per cent, usually party leaders who must be assured of
getting a seat, do not meet this political (rather than legal) requirement.
The Commons may refuse to seat any candidate or expel any member.

D. *Rules and Organization*

The Parliament determines its own privileges and immunities but they
cannot exceed those of the contemporary British Commons (B.N.A. Act of
1875, §1).   Members of Parliament are excused from jury duty, cannot be
compelled to appear as witnesses nor can they be sued or prosecuted for
statements made in Parliament (Senate and House of Commons Act, R.S.
1927, c. 147).

Speeches in the Parliament may be delivered in either French or English
(§133).   The Speaker of Commons is elected by each Parliament and
French- and English-speaking Speakers alternate.   By Standing Order No.
56 of the House, the Deputy Speaker never belongs to the same language
group as the Speaker.   The Speaker of the Senate is chosen by the Prime
Minister, acting through the Governor-General (§34).   The salary of members of Parliament is $4000 plus a $2000 allowance which is tax free in the
case of the Commons.

II. POWERS OF THE HOUSE AND SENATE

A. *Relation to the Executive*

Canada, like Australia, has a British-type Cabinet system, and the relationship between the legislature and executive is the same in most respects
(see Appendix on Australia).   An adverse vote in the Senate does not affect
the tenure of the Cabinet.   Since the same party usually retains its majority
in Commons for many years, the executive has proved quite stable.

All Cabinet Ministers are members of Parliament and, except for a Minister Without Portfolio who is a Senator, all have been, during recent years,
members of Commons.   For political reasons, the practice has developed of
having each Province represented in the Cabinet by at least one Minister.
The one Senator in the Cabinet acts as a general caretaker of legislation in
the Senate.   Most important legislation is introduced in the House by the

Minister concerned and the most important and publicized debates occur there. The executive and the Commons are, therefore, well integrated while the Senate has much less contact with the executive.

The executive makes use of the Senate by elevating to it those who have become "deadwood" in the Cabinet but cannot be otherwise conveniently eliminated. Party harmony is thus retained without reducing executive efficiency.

Due to the rather strict party discipline operating through caucus, the private member's influence over the executive by means of his vote is more theoretical than practical. The possibility of a vote of no confidence may, however, encourage compromise within the Cabinet. The private member can question members of the Cabinet in Commons during periods set aside weekly for that purpose. Ministers are obliged to defend their policy and to supply information on their Departments. Private members of the majority are not loath to question the Cabinet on matters of interest to themselves or their constituents, and the opposition party is constantly critical.

B. *General Legislative Authority of the Two Houses*

The houses were given equal power over non-fiscal legislation: either may initiate, amend or reject any such bill. Commons was to wield greater legislative power but the Senate was expected to perform three tasks: to represent sectional interest, to represent property interest, to revise legislation passed by the House.

Despite its great nominal powers, the Senate has not completely fulfilled expectations for it. Sectional interests have not always been upheld, yielding to party loyalty. In fact, those interests have received greater protection from members of Commons who are responsible and responsive to the electorate. Property interests have received some protection from the Senate especially where legislation might have operated to harm unfairly the rights of a few individuals. The Senate is further credited with blocking "pressure group" legislation and laws which would have had a retroactive effect. But the Senate, following the precedents of the House of Lords, has acquiesced in reform when it was certain that a measure had popular support. The Senate's opportunity to revise bills coming from Commons is curtailed by the latter's practice of adopting much legislation toward the close of a session. The Senate does reshape some bills.

The Senate has been given the function of initiating most private bills. Senate committees gather information and prepare the way for future legislative action. The Commons, however, performs the vast majority of legislative tasks and exercises, in practice, the legislative power.

The Commons has a number of permanent standing committees covering broad fields of public interest. They have become quite inactive legislatively due largely to the dominance of the Cabinet. More useful are special committees formed to consider or investigate topics of immediate concern and which may endure over a number of sessions. Most important measures are considered in a Committee of the Whole, and the smaller committees limit themselves to study and investigation of detail.

C. *Authority over Taxation and Appropriations*

The Constitution gives Commons the exclusive power to initiate tax and appropriation measures (§53). Section 54 prohibits the passage of either a tax or appropriation bill unless recommended by the Governor-General by message during the current session. The Governor-General's recommendations are, in practice, those of the Cabinet. The traditional control of the lower house over the public purse, combined with the overall docility of the Senate, virtually ensures the latter's approval, without important amendment, of money bills passed by the Commons. Effective control over the budget, therefore, lies with the Cabinet, the House majority and the leadership of the party in power.

D. *Authority on Treaties*

The power to bind Canada internationally lies with the Cabinet. Most treaties, however, require financial or other implementation which must come from Parliament. The Cabinet will, therefore, almost always present a proposed treaty to Parliament for discussion. The federal government's power to bind Canada internationally, however, is limited to those fields over which it is competent to legislate internally (*Attorney-General of Canada v. Attorney-General of Ontario,* [1937] A.C. 326 (P.C.)). As with ordinary measures, actual power is enjoyed by the lower house.

E. *Authority on Constitutional Amendments*

The Canadian Constitution was originally enacted by the British Parliament; the power to amend the Constitution remained in that body. In practice, the British Parliament made amendments only on the request of the Canadian government and Parliament. Protests by the Provinces against this federal power have led to the provision that the Canadian Parliament could amend the Constitution "except as regards matters coming within the classes of subjects . . . assigned exclusively to the Legislatures of the provinces . . ." and certain other basic matters (B.N.A. Act of 1949). The method of amendment in these excepted areas has not yet been decided. In any event, to the extent Parliament may amend, the roles of the two chambers are the same as in legislation, with formal power equally divided but actual power held by the Cabinet and the House of Commons.

III. RESOLUTION OF DEADLOCKS

The provisions of the Constitution for breaking deadlocks between the houses have never been exercised, since the Senate has usually bowed to the wishes of the House. In case of deadlock, however, the executive may name four or eight new Senators (§26; B.N.A. Act of 1915, §1). The Senate's compliant attitude is, perhaps, fortunate, since the power to add eight Senators to a body of 102 is a lesser one than the corresponding power of the British Cabinet to name an unlimited number of new Lords. It might, by itself, prove inadequate to break a stubborn deadlock between the houses. Occasionally, Conference Committees, composed of managers from each house, have been formed.

IV. EVALUATION

Many Canadians are dissatisfied with the operation of the Senate. Its failure to protect regional interests, the political nature of appointments and its overall lassitude are contrasted, in many Canadian minds, with the powerful United States Senate and the dignified House of Lords. It would seem, however, that the Canadian upper house was fated for its lowly role. The British tradition of lower house control was accepted by the Canadians. Beginning with the assumption that the Senate was definitely a secondary as well as a second chamber and with appointments controlled by the executive, it was rapidly assimilated to the party system. The nature of the appointments caused a further reduction in the effective legislative power.

The Senate is, however, sheltered from reform. Quebec still considers it to be a safeguard of her minority group. The party in power is always reluctant to jeopardize such a lucrative field for patronage. Few responsible people wish to elevate the Senate to a position comparable in power to the House. Consequently, the effective suggestions for change are somewhat limited: partial or total popular election, limited tenure, permission for Ministers to introduce bills in either house. Whether any of these would make the Senate a useful legislative body is questionable.

The House has been criticized for the inactivity of its legislative committees. Some are almost inert, others sporadically active; they could be used to revise hasty legislative proposals and, possibly, to provide continuity of policy in relatively noncontroversial areas.

A P P E N D I X   I I I

Germany

I. COMPOSITION AND STRUCTURE

Each of the three German federal constitutions established two chambers to participate in federal legislation, but they have been considered to some extent as separate organs, rather than together as a Congress or Parliament or Federal Assembly. One chamber, which corresponds to other lower houses, has always been a deliberative assembly representing the people. The other body has always been a council of emissaries from the State governments. Under the Imperial Constitution of 1871, they were called, respectively, the Reichstag and the Bundesrat: under the Weimar Constitution of 1919, the Reichstag and the Reichsrat; and under the Basic Law of 1949, the Bundestag and the Bundesrat.

A. *Voting and Representation*

These upper chambers of the federations continued the principle of representation which had existed in the preceding confederations, where emphasis was on the autonomy of the member States. The upper chamber has been designed expressly for the purpose of giving the member States a role in federal legislation and administration (Imperial, Art. 6; Weimar, Art. 60; Basic Law, Art. 50). Like the diplomatic representatives in the German Confederations and in contrast to the Senators in other federations, the members of the German Councils have been merely delegates appointed by their respective State governments, subject to binding instructions and to recall at any time. In fact, members of the Imperial Bundesrat were to be given "diplomatic protection" by the Kaiser (Art. 10). The first draft of the Weimar Constitution intended to create a Staatenhaus or Senate-type of upper chamber, uninstructed and elected by the State parliaments; but the proposal was rejected in later drafts on objection by the States, especially those of medium or small size and importance.

The Imperial Constitution provided that votes which were not instructed would not be counted (Art. 7), but the Bundesrat would not inquire into whether an instruction had been violated, leaving this matter to the States. The succeeding constitutions omit such a provision as presumably not necessary; the States continue to bind their delegates, and are considered unable by law to divest themselves of this right.

State representation was further secured by provisions in the Imperial Constitution and the Basic Law which required each State's delegates to cast their votes as a unit (Imperial, Art. 6; Basic Law, Art. 51 (3)). Such a provision was omitted from the Weimar Constitution as part of the plan to allot half the Prussian votes to its provincial administrations (Art. 63) in an effort to avoid repetition of the Prussian hegemony in the Empire. In fact the other States did cast their votes as a unit under uniform instructions. In the Empire the States did not need to have as many members present as they had votes; but under the Basic Law votes can be cast only by the members present or their alternates (Art. 51 (3)).

Under the three constitutions, the lower chambers have been like other popular assemblies, with express provisions stating that the members shall not be bound by instructions (Imperial, Art. 29; Weimar, Art. 21; Basic

Law, Art. 31 (1)). Furthermore, federal law has determined their payment (Imperial, Art. 32; Weimar, Art. 40; Basic Law, Art. 48 (3)).

B. *Distribution of Votes and Seats*

Votes in the upper chamber have been distributed among the member States so as to give greater strength to the smaller States than they would have if votes were based on population alone. But in recognition of the different importance of the States, the quotas have not been equal. Under the Imperial Constitution, Prussia had seventeen, Bavaria six, Saxony four, Württemberg four, Baden three, Mecklenburg-Schwerin two, Brunswick two, and all the other States, including the free cities, one vote each (Art. 6). Under the Weimar Constitution each member State received at least one vote. The larger States received one vote for every 700,000 inhabitants, but none could have more than two fifths of the total vote (Art. 61). Under the Basic Law each Land has at least three votes. Länder with more than two million inhabitants have four, and with more than six million inhabitants, five (Art. 51 (2)).

For the lower houses, seats were allotted according to population to the member States or, as in the Weimar Republic, to large artificial divisions.

C. *Method of Selection and Tenure*

The delegates to the upper house have always been appointed by and responsible to the person or body in each State exercising the executive power. Under the Imperial Constitution it was the State prince or the senate of the free cities; in the Weimar and Federal Republics, generally, an executive cabinet. The popular house of the State has had no right to participate in their appointment or instruction and could not be vested with it by State law. In practice, the executive often consulted or informed the lower house as to its acts. Tenure has not been fixed and has been solely at the State government's discretion.

Under the Imperial Constitution, the details of elections for the lower house, including franchise and constituencies, were regulated by federal law. Constituencies were single-member districts within the States. To be elected, a candidate had to receive an absolute majority of the votes, which might require a second election balloting between the two top candidates. Every male citizen at least 25 years old had the right to vote, except for a few minor disqualifications. The term of office was five years, subject to earlier dissolution of the chamber.

The lower house under the Weimar Constitution was selected on the principle of proportional representation (Art. 22). Details were also regulated by federal law. To carry this out, the country was divided into thirty-five constituencies, regardless of State boundaries. In each division votes were cast for a party list, and the total was divided by 60,000 to deter-

mine the number of its seats. Surplus votes were carried over in some instances to the lists of other divisions, and finally to a national list. The system tended to encourage the formation of small parties and to separate the
delegate from his constituents. Suffrage, also determined by the Constitution and federal law, was granted to every citizen, male or female, over 20
years old, with very few minor disqualifications (Art. 22). Except in the
event of dissolution, the term of office was four years (Art. 23).

Under the Basic Law details of lower house elections, including the basis
of representation, are determined by federal law (Art. 38 (3)). The present method of election combines single-member districts of approximately
equal size with proportional representation over an entire Land. Seats
are distributed among the Länder according to population, then divided by
the Land government between the electoral districts and supplementary
Land party lists in an approximate proportion of 60 to 40. This system is
currently under modification by federal law. The principal qualification
for the franchise is a minimum age of 21 years (Art. 38 (2)). The term
of office is four years, subject to earlier dissolution (Art. 39 (1)).

D. Qualifications of Members

Since upper house members have been State delegates, their qualifications have not been prescribed in the Constitution, or federal law. In Imperial Germany they were usually the Ministers or civil servants of the
States. Under the Weimar Constitution the State delegates were to be
members of their respective governments (Art. 63): normally the delegates were high officials. The Basic Law appears to continue this policy. It
states that the Bundesrat shall consist of members of the Länder governments, but appears to contemplate alternates (Art. 51 (1), (3)).

In all the federations eligibility for the lower house has been determined
by the Constitution and federal law. In general, anyone qualified to vote
could be elected. Although the voting age was lowered in the Weimar and
Federal Republics, the minimum age for membership remained at 25 (Basic
Law, Art. 38 (2)).

II. Functions and Powers of the Chambers
A. Relation to Executive

The executive of the German Empire consisted of the Kaiser and a Chancellor whom the Kaiser appointed and removed. Neither was responsible
to the people or the legislature, although the Chancellor had the duty of
giving an account of his work to the Reichstag. If the Reichstag disagreed
with the policy of the executive, the Kaiser could dissolve it. In practice
the Kaiser also exerted authority over the Bundesrat through the Prussian
representatives whom he controlled.

The Weimar Constitution adopted the Cabinet system of government, in which the Cabinet was responsible to the lower chamber. The Chancellor and upon his recommendation, the Ministers were appointed and dismissed by the federal President (Art. 53); they did not have to be members of the lower chamber. However, they were required to resign if the Reichstag withdrew its confidence by an express resolution (Art. 54). Thus, in practice, the President conformed to the wishes of a majority of the lower chamber, who usually favored a coalition of their leaders. The power of removal, coupled with the splintering of parties by proportional representation, enabled minorities to combine to immobilize the executive to suit their different purposes. Day-to-day control was exercised through a Committee of Inquiry (Art. 34), and by interpellations and questions to the Ministers.

In the Federal Republic the executive is also a Cabinet responsible to the lower chamber, and is chosen substantially as under the Weimar Constitution. It is specifically provided, however, that, before appointment by the President, the Chancellor is to be elected by the Bundestag (Art. 63). The remainder of the Cabinet is appointed by the President on recommendations by the Chancellor (Art. 64). In practice these appointments are controlled by the Bundestag when it elects the Chancellor. To avoid the paralysis of government present in the Weimar Republic, the Basic Law permits the Bundestag to remove the Chancellor only by electing a successor by a majority of its members (Art. 67). The Bundestag and its committees may demand the presence of Cabinet members for questioning (Art. 43 (1)), and may set up an investigating committee (Art. 44). Either chamber may impeach the President before the Federal Constitutional Court for willful violation of the Basic Law or federal law (Art. 61 (1)).

Although in the Weimar and Federal Republics general control over the government has been entrusted to the lower chamber, their constitutions, as well as the Imperial Constitution, assigned special administrative functions to the upper chambers, as discussed below.

B. Legislation

Under the Imperial Constitution both chambers had the right of initiative and both had to approve all federal laws (Art. 5). The more important legislative role was actually played by the Bundesrat. Most of the bills originated in that chamber, largely because executive measures were prepared and initiated by the Prussian Ministers, who were the Kaiser's delegates. In addition, even if the bills were passed by the Reichstag, they had to be returned to the Bundesrat for final consideration (Art. 7). Members or appointees of the Bundesrat represented it in the Reichstag's deliberations. A Bundesrat delegate with a minority view could also defend it before the Reichstag. The Kaiser could resolve disputes between the two houses and between himself and the Reichstag by dissolving the latter, but only with the consent of the Bundesrat (Art. 24).

In the Weimar and Federal Republics, the Cabinet system has tended to concentrate legislative authority in the lower chamber. Under the Weimar Constitution all federal laws were enacted by the Reichstag (Art. 68). Bills were introduced by the Cabinet or originated in the Reichstag itself. If introduced by the Cabinet, they first had to be presented to the Reichsrat, whose criticism had to be taken with the bills to the Reichstag (Art. 69). There was no time limitation on the Reichsrat's deliberations, but, of course, the same bills could also be initiated by the Reichstag. The Reichsrat had a suspensive veto over bills passed by the Reichstag. If an overriding vote (two thirds) was not obtained in the Reichstag, the President could submit the bill to popular referendum (Art. 74). A popular vote on legislation was also required if called for by the President or, in certain situations, by popular petition. In practice, these initiative and referendum powers were dormant.

To resolve disgreements between the Cabinet and Reichstag the President could dissolve the latter, but only once on the same ground (Art. 25).

Under the Basic Law some matters require approval of the upper chamber, while on much legislation it has only a protest or veto which can be overridden by a simple majority or two thirds of the Bundestag, depending on the size of the Bundesrat vote (Art. 77 (3)). Bills are initiated substantially as in the Weimar Republic, except that the Bundesrat is limited to holding Cabinet bills for only three weeks (Art. 76 (2)). In addition, all laws, however initiated, must be submitted to the Bundesrat after having passed the Bundestag (Art. 77 (1)). If it disagrees, the Bundesrat may demand that a committee composed of members of both chambers (who shall not be bound by instructions) be convoked to consider the bill jointly. Should the committee propose amendments to the adopted bill, a new vote must be taken by the Bundestag (Art. 77 (2)). A law adopted by the Bundestag is enacted if the Bundesrat approves it, or, where its approval is not required, if it does not impose a veto or withdraws its veto or if the veto is overridden by the Bundestag (Art. 78). Although the cabinet has no veto on ordinary legislation, additions to the budget which it has proposed require its approval (Art. 113).

Normally the Bundestag will accept the Cabinet's leadership; but if there is dispute on a general policy issue the Chancellor may, through the President, dissolve the lower chamber unless another Chancellor is chosen shortly after a vote of no confidence (Art. 68). As an alternate to dissolution, where the Bundestag rejects urgent legislation, the President is empowered, at the request of the Cabinet and with the approval of the Bundesrat, to declare a state of legislative emergency (Art. 81). If, on resubmission of the disputed bill, the Bundestag again rejects it, makes changes unacceptable to the Cabinet, or fails to pass it within four weeks, the bill is adopted to the extent approved by the Bundesrat. This procedure may be repeated for any other bill rejected by the Bundestag during a period of six months after the emergency has been declared. But a Chancellor may have only one such period during his term of office.

The laws requiring the approval of the Bundesrat are specified in the Basic Law. They fall primarily into four classes: (a) laws affecting the rights of the Länder over their administrative agencies or procedures in the execution of federal law, or establishing federal field agencies for new activities (Arts. 84 (1), (5), 85 (1), and 87 (3)); (b) laws regarding taxes shared with the Länder or assigned to finance grants to the Länder, or regulating Länder finance agencies (Arts. 105 (3), 106 (3), (4), 107, 108 (3)); (c) laws affecting Länder territory or property or the distribution of Reich property (Arts. 29 (7), 134 (4), and 135 (5)); and (d) amendments to the Basic Law (Art. 79 (2)).

C. Constitutional Amendments

In all three federations amendments to the Constitution have been made in substantially the same manner as legislation. Under the Imperial Constitution, however, an amendment could be defeated in the Bundesrat by 14 negative votes out of a total of 58 (Art. 78), and rights granted to an individual member State could not be changed without its consent. Under the Weimar Constitution, if the Reichstag overrode the Reichsrat's veto of a proposed amendment, the latter could demand a popular referendum within two weeks (Art. 76). Under the Basic Law an amendment requires the approval of two thirds of both houses (Art. 79 (2)), and certain amendments, such as those affecting the basic cooperation of the Länder in legislation, are inadmissible (Art. 79 (3)).

D. Ratification of Treaties

Under the Imperial Constitution, the executive concluded and ratified treaties, but the two chambers had to give their consent, in the manner in which they legislated, to make a treaty the law of the land. In the Weimar Republic the treaties were concluded by the executive, nominally the President, but treaties referring to matters of federal legislation required the consent of the Reichstag (Art. 45). The Reichsrat was altogether excluded. The Basic Law has a similar provision, except that the Bundesrat must also consent to treaties on matters where its approval would be required for federal legislation (Art. 59). In addition, executive agreements must be approved under the same requirements applying to ordinary administrative matters.

E. Administrative Role of the Upper House

Because much of the federal law was carried out through the State governments, the upper house has always had substantial authority over administrative matters. In the Empire, the administration was divided between the Kaiser and the Bundesrat. The latter had the power to lay down statutory rules and pass on their defects (Art. 7), while the former, through his Chancellor, was responsible for their specific execution (Art. 16). Furthermore, although formally the Kaiser alone appointed Reich officials (Art. 18), the fact that he could make an appointment only after having heard the opinion of the Bundesrat (Art. 36, 56) gave it great practical power. The Bundesrat also decided whether supervision by the Reich was necessary (Art. 17), and if members of the federation did not fulfill their constitutional federal duties, they could be held thereto by measures decided upon by the Bundesrat and carried out by the Kaiser (Art. 19).

Under the Weimar Constitution and the Basic Law, the administrative functions of the upper chamber have not been so broad as those of the imperial Bundesrat, but have nevertheless been important. It has had the right to approve general administrative regulations issued by the federal government for execution of federal laws by the Länder (Weimar, Art. 77; Basic Law, Arts. 84 (2), 85 (2)); orders (*Rechtsverordnungen*) concerning standards and fees for the federal communication services and, under the Basic Law, railroads (Weimar, Art. 88; Basic Law, Art. 80 (2)); and orders concerning the construction and operation of the railroads (Weimar, Art. 91; Basic Law, Art. 80 (2)). Under the Basic Law, the upper chamber has the additional right to approve orders (*Rechtsverordnungen*) issued under federal laws to which its consent is required or which are executed by the Länder; but all its rights as to orders (including those above) are subject to change by federal law (Art. 80 (2)). Furthermore, the upper chamber has had the right, in both federations, to be kept informed by the Cabinet on the conduct of federal affairs and, in the Weimar Republic, to be consulted by the Cabinet on important matters (Weimar, Art. 67; Basic Law, Art. 53). Under the Basic Law, the upper chamber has a further role in assuring proper execution of the laws by the Länder, serving as an intermediate tribunal to determine whether the Land has conformed to federal law (Art. 84 (4)), and approving measures taken by the executive to compel the Land to fulfill its duties (Art. 37).

F. *Judicial Functions*

Under the Imperial Constitution several high judicial functions were settled on the Bundesrat (Arts. 76, 77). They principally concerned administrative matters, but also included deciding disputes between the member States, particularly on interpretations of the Constitution. The Bundesrat could also force a State to render justice to an individual. These functions, however, invited partiality, especially in a dispute between a large and a small State, and there were strong efforts to transfer all judical powers to a separate court. This was done under the Weimar Constitution and the Basic Law, where neither chamber was granted judicial functions.

III. Evaluation

The German legislatures have differed from those of other federations in the fact that the upper chambers have all been of the Council type. The distinctive features of the upper chambers were instructed and bloc voting and tenure of delegates at the discretion of the State executive authorities. Since it was the State executive which appointed, instructed, and recalled the delegate, the State as a body politic was represented rather than the people of the States. These features have prevented adapting the upper chamber to conform to popular federal sentiment. At the same time, because of the extreme State participation in federal affairs, it has been considered necessary in the later federations to deny the upper chamber a role in legislation equal to the lower. Thus the people of the States have been deprived of minority influence as in the upper chambers of Switzerland and the United States.

One of the reasons for clinging to the Council form, however, has been the fact that much of the federal administration has been carried out through the State bureaucracies of which the upper chamber delegates have been members. The premise has been that this is the best way of achieving State participation in these matters. The question thus arises whether some other method might be successfully employed without sacrificing the advantages of a fully coordinate and vital second chamber.

There has been general satisfaction with unequal representation in the upper chamber, so long as the smaller States are given a weighted vote sufficient to prevent voting dominance by one or two large states.

APPENDIX IV

Switzerland

The federal legislature, called the Bundesversammlung (or Federal Assembly), consists of the Ständerat, which represents the cantons, and the Nationalrat, which is the lower chamber. In theory and largely in practice, these two houses share equally in the exercise of the "supreme authority" of the federation (Swiss Federal Constitution, Art. 71).

I. Composition and Structure

A. Composition

Seats in the lower house are allocated among the cantons, primarily according to population, one for every 24,000 persons and a minimum of one for each canton or half-canton (Art. 72). The upper chamber, on the other hand, was modeled on the Senate of the United States, and its members are divided equally among the cantons, each canton appointing two deputies and each half-canton one (Art. 80). Small cantons, having had equal powers in the loose alliance of the Bundesvertrag, wanted the principle of equality continued as some measure of protection against the large cantons' majorities in the lower house. Moreover, most cantons saw in state representation a better protection of their reserved powers.

B. *Tenure*

The lower house is elected for four years (a recent change from three years), and is completely renewed at each election (Art. 76). Tenure for the upper house is not prescribed by the Constitution and has been fixed by the cantonal legislatures. Most cantons set the term at four years to coincide with elections for the lower house, but a few prescribe three- or one-year terms. Because of this system, there is never complete renewal of the upper house, except in certain situations involving a total revision of the Constitution. In that event the entire Bundesversammlung must be renewed (Art. 120). New members then finish the unexpired portion of the terms of their predecessors. Neither house can be dissolved by the executive.

C. *Method of Election*

Election procedures for the lower house are regulated by the Constitution and federal laws, and provide for direct elections on the principle of proportional representation (Art. 73). Members are chosen on the basis of the number of votes given to a party list of candidates, with the entire canton or half-canton forming the electoral constituency. This method tends to support the existence of many parties. Every male Swiss of the age of 20 or over was given the right to vote, subject to cantonal exclusions or, at the option of the Bundesversammlung, uniform federal regulations. Federal laws now prescribe most of the grounds for denying suffrage, mainly for conviction of crime and the like.

Regulation of all aspects of Ständerat elections has been left to the cantons. At first members were usually selected by the cantonal legislature, but only four cantons now cling to this method. The remainder of the cantons provide for direct election by the people of the entire canton. In the undivided cantons the two delegates are chosen at the same time, but both on the basis of plurality, rather than proportional or preferential, vote. In contrast to the Nationalrat elections, a party with a majority of the vote, no matter how small the margin, will usually obtain both seats. This difference in elections invariably leads to differences in party composition between the two houses. For example, the Catholic Conservative Party controls 22 per cent (or 44 members) of the Nationalrat and 43 per cent (or 19 members) of the Ständerat. Although the qualifications for voting may be fixed exclusively by the cantons, they are generally the same as for the Nationalrat elections.

D. Qualifications of Members

Every lay citizen entitled to vote is eligible for membership in the Nationalrat (Art. 75), thus excluding the clergy. Other restrictions, mostly minor, are determined by cantonal suffrage laws, or the federal laws which supersede them. Members of the Nationalrat may not simultaneously hold other federal offices (Art. 77).

The cantons set their own qualifications for membership in the Ständerat. In practice the qualifications for membership tend to coincide with the qualifications for voting. Members of the Ständerat are excluded from simultaneous membership in the Nationalrat and Executive Council (Art. 81).

E. Independence of Members

Members of the Nationalrat are paid by the federal government, members of the Ständerat by the cantons. The Ständerat, however, is as independent of the electorate or cantons as the Nationalrat, under the express constitutional provision that the members of both houses are to vote without instructions (Art. 91). Despite this provision, some cantons in the past would recall their delegates. Nevertheless, this general freedom from the cantonal governments has fostered the change to direct election by the people and permitted voting in the upper house by federal party lines rather than state blocs. Members of both houses are exempt from prosecution under certain criminal laws and from military training.

II. POWERS AND FUNCTIONS OF THE BUNDESVERSAMMLUNG

A. Election of the Executive

The Bundesversammlung appoints the federal executive, which consists of a collegial body of seven department heads, called collectively the Bundesrat or Federal Council (Art. 96). This election is made for each office by a majority vote of the two chambers in joint session (Art. 92). The term of office is fixed at four years, and there is complete renewal of the Council after Nationalrat elections. There is no interim power of removal by the Bundesversammlung, either by direct procedure or the custom of forced resignations. In fact, members of the Council are ordinarily re-elected, and enjoy considerable personal respect and authority. In addition, they may not also have a seat in the legislature. Thus, despite election by the legislature, the Council is an independent organ of the government.

Since there is no power of dissolution, complete agreement between the Council and the legislature is not the basis for government. The Council tends to be more nonpartisan than political, and must seek shifting majorities on specific proposals, rather than a continual and disciplined majority on an entire program.

B. *Legislation*

All federal laws and decrees must be approved by both houses of the Bundesversammlung. They may be rejected, however, by a popular referendum to be called upon petition by 30,000 people or eight cantons. On measures requiring immediate enactment, the Bundesversammlung may suspend the power to demand a referendum by a declaration of urgency requiring approval of a majority of all the members of both houses (Art. 89).

The members of the Bundesversammlung share with the Executive Council the function of initiating federal measures (Arts. 93, 101, 102 (4)). Neither house has special powers or plays a dominant role. Cantons have the right of initiative by correspondence (Art. 93).

In the process of law-making, the Bundesversammlung mainly limits itself to deliberating over bills while the Council has the task of drafting them (Art. 102 (4)). If a measure originates in the Bundesversammlung, it is usually in the form of a motion on general principles, which, upon passing both houses, becomes a binding instruction to the Council. When a bill is returned or proposed by the Council, it goes first to the appropriate committees of the respective houses for study and possible revision. Because of party, as well as constitutional, independence from the Council, the committees are conscientious and quite active, particularly in the Ständerat. Parties are represented on a committee in proportion to their numbers in the chamber. When a committee is finished with a bill, it is reported to the chamber, which then deliberates over it and puts it to a vote. Each chamber may question members of the Council.

In practice, both the committees and chambers tend to follow the Council's proposals. This is perhaps due to the following reasons: (1) the Bundesversammlung selects the Council; (2) the members of the Council, partly because of extensive governmental experience prior to election and partly because of their long periods in office, enjoy considerable prestige, and are allowed to support their views on the floor of either chamber (Art. 101); and (3) legislators view their jobs as part-time work and therefore tend to rely on the Council. But if the Council's proposals are amended, it has no power to veto them.

There is no provision or well-established machinery for resolving deadlocks between the houses. A bill approved with amendments by one house will be returned to the other, and continue to go back and forth between them until it is adopted by each in identical form or it becomes evident that their views are irreconcilable. A conference committee, chosen from the committees in charge of the bill in the respective houses, will occasionally try to iron out their differences. This system seems to work effectively under Swiss conditions.

C. *Constitutional Amendments*

The Bundesversammlung may, by a law, propose either amendments or total revision of the Constitution (Arts. 119, 121). It may be requested by popular petition to do so, but may, if it disagrees with such request, first submit the question to popular vote. If such a popular vote is necessary on the question of total revision, the two houses must be completely renewed (Art. 120). An amendment, if in the form of a completed draft, may also be proposed directly by popular petition; the Bundesversammlung may, at the same time, propose a counterdraft or express its objections to the proposed draft.

In all cases, an amendment or a total revision is effective only upon approval by popular majority in the country as a whole and in a majority of the cantons (Art. 123).

D. *Ratification of Treaties*

The Executive Council has general charge of foreign affairs (Art. 102 (8)), but federal treaties and alliances are within the authority of the Bundesversammlung (Art. 85 (5)), and its approval is necessary to make them legally binding. The Bundesversammlung limits itself to acceptance or rejection of treaties concluded by the Council. The Bundesversammlung must also approve treaties between the cantons and foreign states whenever made, and treaties between the cantons themselves in the event the Council or another canton raises objection. International treaties of indefinite duration, or for more than fifteen years, are, like federal laws, subject to rejection by the people through a referendum (Art. 89).

E. *Administrative Supervision*

Most of the powers and duties assigned to the Council constitute the administrative side of the powers conferred on the Bundesversammlung (Art. 102). The extent of its independent authority in administration is not clear, largely because the issue never arises. One reason is that, in addition to the other executive powers, the Bundesversammlung is granted general supervision of federal administration (Art. 85 (11)). This is viewed as making the executive subject to binding administrative instructions by the legislature, so long as they are not too specific. Generally, the Bundesversammlung is content to control current administrative matters by asking questions of the Council or making recommendations known as postulates. The Council is also required to make detailed reports (Art. 102 (16)), which are carefully studied. In practice, however, the Council has great influence, and enjoys wide discretion in the conduct of federal business and in execution of the laws.

Beside the treaty power, the following matters are specified in Article 85 as within the competence of the two houses:

(1) The election of the Federal Council, the Federal Tribunal, the Chancellor, and the general-in-chief of the federal army. Other rights of election or confirmation may be vested in the Federal Assembly by federal legislation (cl. 4).

(2) Measures to ensure external safety and the preservation of the independence and neutrality of Switzerland; the declaration of war and the conclusion of peace (cl. 6).

(3) The guarantee of the constitutions and territory of the cantons; intervention in consequence of this guarantee; measures for the internal security of Switzerland and for the maintenance of peace and order; amnesties and pardons (cl. 7).

(4) Measures necessary to ensure the observance of the federal constitution and the guarantee of cantonal constitutions, and measures whose object is to secure the fulfillment of federal obligations (cl. 8).

(5) The control of the federal army (cl. 9).

F. *Judicial Functions*

Under Article 85, the Bundesversammlung may hear appeals against decisions of the Federal Council relating to administrative disputes (cl. 12), may decide conflicts of jurisdiction between federal authorities (cl. 13), and may grant pardons (cl. 7). The first two functions inevitably affect the balance of power between the legislature and executive on close questions of their respective authority. When exercising the right of pardon or of decision on a conflict or jurisdiction, the two chambers meet in joint session (Art. 92).

III. EVALUATION

Although the Swiss legislature has considerable constitutional power over the executive, the Council's structural independence has permitted it to become both a stable and an influential organ of the government. At the same time, its formal participation in the law-making process has promoted remarkable cooperation between it and the Bundesversammlung. Moreover, the independence of the organs and their procedure for working together have been constituted in such a way as to preserve approximate equality of the two legislative houses as intended by the framers of the Constitution.

While the Nationalrat tends to have greater influence than the upper chamber, at least in those matters handled in joint session, the Ständerat has maintained its strength and vigor. As community sentiment has grown, proposals have been made to abolish the Ständerat or to change its basis of representation to correspond to population. To the extent its original function is no longer necessary, defenders of the Ständerat can point to the continuing utility of having variety between the houses in a bicameral system and the definite contribution made by the smaller assembly to Swiss government. In addition, while having proved adaptable to popular election and to party voting, the Ständerat has recently shown itself yet capable of representing the interests of the cantons, as in the matter of the *lex splugensis* (a revision of the *Wasserrechtsgesetz* of 1947) and in the reunification of Basel-Stadt and Baselland in 1947.

APPENDIX V

United States

The legislature of the United States has two chambers, known together as the Congress and separately as the House of Representatives and the Senate. The House is typical of lower bodies, being the larger assembly. The Senate, like other second chambers, is much smaller and was intended as a check on the popular House. In its strength, however, the Senate is unique, for it is an equal, if not dominant, partner of the lower chamber.

I. COMPOSITION AND STRUCTURE

A. *Composition*

One of the chief differences between the two chambers is the basis of representation. Seats in the lower house are apportioned among the States according to population, with a minimum of one to a State (United States Constitution, Art. I, §2), but Senators are divided equally among the States, regardless of size (Art. I, §3). This "partly federal, partly national" character of Congress resulted from the dispute at the Constitutional Convention of 1787 between the small and large States. The small States, fearing that they would be overwhelmed by their larger neighbors, were reluctant to depend solely upon a written constitution for defense of their rights, and insisted also upon equal voices in the enactment of federal legislation. The large States, for their part, saw in equal State suffrage the possibility of dominance by a minority of the population and a perpetuation of the weaknesses of the existing Articles of Confederation. The final solution reflected a practical compromise. It was made permanent by a provision in the amendment article that no State could be deprived of its equal suffrage without its consent (Art. V).

The number of Senators from each State is two, in order to make the

Senate large enough for its legislative functions, and small enough for its special executive functions. The Senate today has 96 members in contrast to 435 members in the House. Total membership in the House, which for years increased with the growth of population, is now fixed by federal law. This disparity makes the Senate a better forum and has enabled it to maintain the tradition of unlimited debate, under the Constitutional provision permitting each chamber to fix its own rules of proceedings (Art. I, §5).

B. *Tenure*

The term of office of a Senator is six years (Art. I, §3), and of a Representative two (Art. I, §2). Terms of Senators are staggered, with one-third expiring every two years, so that elections for this number of seats, of which not more than one is from each State, take place at the same time as the election of Representatives. This system of elections makes the Senate the only continuous political organ in the federal government and more in tune with public opinion as a body than the length of individual terms would indicate.

C. *Method of Election*

Originally Senators were chosen by the State legislatures (Art. I, §3), while Representatives were elected directly by the people (Art. I, §2). The Convention believed that the indirect election of Senators, by refining the popular choice, would ensure a higher grade of member for the upper chamber. Some States chose their Senators as they enacted legislation, each house voting separately; but others conducted their elections in a joint session. Congress finally passed a law requiring initial use of the first method and then, in case of deadlock, a joint session. Lengthy deadlocks still occurred, however, because a clear majority, rather than plurality, was necessary for election.

In 1913, however, this method of selection was ended by the Seventeenth Amendment, which provides that the Senate shall also be elected directly by the people. The change largely recognized the fact that the members of the Senate now reflect party and sectional interests more than those of the States as political entities. But the change has served the purpose of making Senators more responsive to the voters, whose views are primarily influenced by factors other than State loyalty. The Senate today is, like the House, a popular body, distinct because of its unequal and generally larger constituencies.

The two Senators from each State are elected on a State-wide basis; but since only one is chosen at a time, his election is determined by a majority vote. Members of the House are elected from approximately equal electoral districts, each of which selects its member by majority vote. This method of election, determined by federal law, has contributed to the development of a federal two-party system.

The States are permitted by the Constitution to regulate federal elections, but Congress has the authority to make or alter such regulations (Art. I, §4). It appears that Congress, if it wishes, may control the procedure for selection (in "primary" elections) of a political party's candidate for federal office, although this has long been subject to State regulation. In practice, Congress has left to the States the defining of electoral districts and most regulation of federal elections.

The Constitution enables the States to fix the qualifications of electors by providing that they be the same as those requisite for electors of the most numerous branch of the State legislatures (Art. I, §2; Amend. XVII). Constitutional amendments, however, forbid exclusion from voting on grounds of sex, race, color, or previous condition of servitude (Amends. XV and XIX). Congress may reduce a State's representation in the House in accordance with the number of "male inhabitants of such state, being twenty-one years of age, and citizens of the United States" whose right to vote is denied or abridged "except for participation in rebellion, or other crime," but such a reduction has never been made.

D. *Qualifications of Members*

The higher caliber of the average Senator has resulted from other reasons than the method of election. It is due rather to factors such as the longer term of office, the smaller size, the larger area of representation, and the special powers of the Senate. They give the individual Senator much greater prestige and influence in national affairs than a member of the House. The Senator's role is thus more demanding and more attractive, with the result that candidates are frequently men of proved ability and experience, such as outstanding members of the lower chamber and governors of the States. The somewhat greater standing and ability of its members enables the Senate, in practice, to overshadow the House to some extent.

The Constitution sets up few qualifications for the members of Congress: age, citizenship, and residence. A Senator must be at least 30 years old, a citizen of the United States at least nine years, and a resident of the State in which he is chosen (Art. I, §3). A Representative must be at least 25 years old, a citizen at least seven years, and also a resident of the State in which he is chosen (Art. 1, §2), although custom limits him to residence in his electoral district. The stricter requirements for the upper chamber were part of the design to make it a more elite body. Neither federal nor State law can add to the qualifications prescribed for members of Congress.

Each chamber is the sole judge of whether its own members should be seated, deciding on the validity of elections, returns, and qualifications. Each chamber also has the sole power of expulsion (Art. I, §5).

E. *Independence of Members*

Senators, like Representatives, vote individually and not by State blocs (Art. I, §3). The Convention recognized that this principle would tend to contravene the strict State representation. The provision makes it easier for the Senate to vote and to organize its work along party lines.

Control of members of Congress by the electorate is distinctly limited. Members are elected for fixed terms and paid out of the federal treasury (Art. I, §6). Moreover, there is no provision in the Constitution for recall or for binding instruction of the Representative or Senator by his constituency. This is more important in the Senate, where the term is six years, than in the House, where the term is so short that it has been criticized for diverting the members from legislating to campaigning for re-election. Occasionally some State legislatures have attempted to instruct Senators or to require a pledge by a candidate to submit to a "recall election." Such restrictions have been ineffective and their validity has not been tested but seems doubtful.

Members of Congress are free from arrest for all but serious crimes while attending and going to and from a session, and they are immune from all consequences of what they say on the floor of their chambers (Art. I, §6).

II. FUNCTIONS AND POWERS OF CONGRESS

A. *Relation to Executive*

Under the Constitution, the legislature and executive are constituted as independent organs of government. The President is elected in fact by the people, though nominally indirectly by an Electoral College. If no candidate obtains a majority in the Electoral College, the House of Representatives chooses from among the top three candidates, each State then having but a single vote (Amend. XII). This method has not been resorted to for more than a hundred years, ever since the two-party system solidified.

The President's term is fixed at four years. Although Congress may remove him by impeachment for serious offenses, such a removal has never occurred. Congress, on the other hand, cannot be dissolved.

In practice, Congress may exercise a great deal of control over the President. By virtue of its powers over legislation and appropriations, it may restrict the President's power and discretion in most areas, withhold fiscal support, and abolish or curtail executive agencies. In recent times, to administer certain laws, it has created commissions largely independent of Presidential control. Congressional committees also frequently undertake investigations into the conduct of the executive departments, thereby exposing them to public criticism and the possibility of corrective legislation.

This permits considerable day-to-day, informal control over the executive. Moreover, the Senate must confirm the President's appointments to major offices, as discussed below.

B. *Legislation*

The legislative powers conferred on Congress by the Constitution are shared equally by both chambers (Art. I, §1). To become law, a bill must be approved by a majority of both the Senate and the House (Art. I, §7).

In general, bills may also be initiated in either chamber. The one exception is that only the House may originate bills for raising revenue (Art. I, §7). This provision was mainly a concession to the more populous and heavier-taxed states as part of the compromise on equal state suffrage in the Senate; but it was also dictated by the fear of giving the upper chamber too much power. After much dispute, the Senate was expressly granted the right to alter and amend revenue bills, like other bills, and now exercises it freely to revise revenue bills in all respects. The Senate has power to initiate appropriation bills, but as a matter of custom leaves this function to the House. By virtue of the separation of the executive from the legislature, bills sponsored by the President must be introduced in one chamber or the other by a member of that body. Which chamber is chosen depends merely on which happens to be the more suitable at the time.

Congress frames, as well as debates and approves, federal bills. The President, of course, has great influence in legislation by virtue of his position, his political standing, and his leadership of the majority party. In addition, the Constitution provides for annual and special messages recommending legislation (Art. II, §3) and federal law requires him to submit an annual budget.

Legislation is shaped largely through strong committees of each house. Each chamber has several standing committees devoted to perennial topics of legislation, and, when the occasion demands, will create special committees. Membership on committees is decided by party caucuses, the balance of power in a committee going to the majority party in the chamber. The chairman is chosen from the majority party on the basis of seniority. When a bill is introduced on the floor, it is referred to the appropriate committee to be tailored into proper shape, usually after public hearings. It is then reported back to the full chamber for discussion and a vote.

After passage by both houses, a bill ordinarily must be approved by the President to become effective (Art. I, §7). But if the President vetoes the bill and sends it back to Congress, it may still become law without his approval upon passage by two thirds of each chamber. Most vetoes are upheld; but since they may be applied only to an entire bill, Congress has sometimes forestalled their use by attaching matters likely to be vetoed to necessary measures, such as appropriations.

C. *Resolution of Deadlocks*

Although a bill must pass both chambers in identical form, the Constitution makes no provision for adjusting the divergencies between the two houses which inevitably arise under the bicameral system. To fill the void, the device of the Committee of Conference was established by the First Congress, and has become one of the deeply entrenched institutions of the federal government.

When one chamber alters or amends the proposal of the other, each appoints several members to represent it in a joint meeting to work out a compromise measure. Generally each house names three conferees, selected by the presiding officer; by usage they are usually the chairman of the committee in charge of the bill, the next-ranking committee member from the majority party, and the top-ranking committee member from the minority party. Conferees are restricted by the rules and precedents of their respective chambers, such as those which forbid introducing new matter into the bills. In the Conference Committee, the representatives of each chamber vote en bloc rather than individually to present a united front. If a deadlock occurs, the conferees may go back to their chambers for instructions. If the conferees fail to reach agreement, or the Conference report is not accepted by either chamber, the bill is dead unless a new conference is called. Under the rules of both chambers, the report of a Conference Committee is not open to amendment and must be accepted or rejected in its entirety. The Conference Committee is used for about ten per cent of all bills, and for almost all important ones. The two houses sometimes appoint joint committees to prepare or consider legislation, and several have become standing committees.

D. *Constitutional Amendments*

Two methods have been provided for proposing amendments to the Constitution (Art. V), under one of which Congress plays an essential role. If two thirds of each chamber "shall deem it necessary," Congress may propose an amendment to the States for ratification. The alternative method of proposal, which has never been used, imposes on Congress the duty of calling a constitutional convention upon request by the legislatures of two thirds of the States. Regardless of how it is proposed, an amendment must be ratified by three fourths of the States, either by conventions or by their legislatures.

E. *Approval of Treaties*

The Senate was given a share with the executive in the exercise of the federal treaty power. The President has "power, by and with the Advice and Consent of the Senate, to make treaties, providing two thirds of the

Senators present concur" (Art. II, §2). The Senate may consent with conditions or with reservations.

Its share in the treaty power greatly increases the strength and power of the Senate. The Constitution makes a treaty "the supreme law of the land" without the necessity of further legislation (Art. VI). The power has been construed by the Supreme Court as authorizing treaties regulating matters which are within the State sphere of authority, or which might be settled by Acts of Congress. In concurring with the President in ratifying such treaties, the Senate in effect legislates as the sole chamber. In practice, however, some limit arises on this power where the execution of the treaty will necessitate any appropriations which will require approval of the House. But when a treaty has been ratified by the Senate, it becomes binding in international law, and the House has never yet refused to cooperate in carrying it out. In addition many treaties, such as those which purport to fix legal rights only, are self-executing under the Constitution.

F. *Approval of Appointments*

The Constitution provides that the President "shall nominate, and by and with the Advice and Consent of the Senate, shall appoint" important federal officers, such as ambassadors and judges (Art. II, §2). Here, the President has an unqualified power of nomination. The role of the Senate is either to confirm or reject, but not directly to determine the President's choice. Under a cherished usage, known as "senatorial courtesy," nominations from a given State are not ordinarily confirmed unless approved by the Senators of the President's party from that State, if there are any. Although it is rarely necessary, the Senator may disapprove solely on the ground that the nominee is "personally obnoxious" to him, and needs no other reasons to secure the cooperation of his colleagues. As a consequence the Senator has a federal patronage power not enjoyed by a member of the House.

While the issue is not yet entirely settled, it appears that the President need not get the consent of the Senate to remove an official appointed with its consent. The law creating certain offices, however, has defined the grounds for removal, and such provisions have been sustained by the courts for some types of functions.

G. *Trial of Impeachments*

The Senate has the sole power to try all federal impeachments (Art. I, §3) upon initiation of proceedings by the House (Art. I, §2). The authority is sparingly invoked, partly because only extreme grounds will lead to conviction and partly because the Senate will refuse to try the impeached official if he has resigned or been dismissed and no longer holds civil office. Only federal judges, who are appointed for life or good behavior, have been removed by impeachment.   One President has been impeached, but was not convicted.

The Constitutional Convention considered giving the Senate the judicial function of deciding disputes between the States but abandoned the idea upon the decision to create the Supreme Court.

III. EVALUATION

The House and Senate have maintained equality on legislation, largely because the executive is separate from both chambers and is not responsible to the lower house, as in the Cabinet system.   Any difference in the standing of the two houses is in favor of the Senate due to its special powers on treaties and appointments and the greater prestige and caliber of many of its individual members.   Its small size and longer tenure enable some of its members to become national figures, with great influence on legislation and public policy.

The character of the Senate has gradually tended to change in keeping with the integration of the nation.   Its original role as guardian of the interests of the States as political units has largely disappeared.   This evolution has led to some objections to the continuance of equal representation of the States in the Senate, in view of the wide differences in populations. Actually, the Senate has long reflected informal groupings of regional interests, which may also represent similar interests in the minority in other areas.

More recently, some proposals have been directed toward cutting down the role of the Senate in treaty-making by requiring approval of treaties by both houses of Congress, to ensure the passage of any necessary appropriations and because the treaty, when ratified, becomes domestic law.   Another view objects that the two-thirds majority required for Senate approval allows a veto by a small minority, who may represent an even smaller percentage of the population.   Such critics suggest reducing the required vote to a majority of the Senate.

The Federal Executive

I. INTRODUCTION

Existing federal systems operate under a variety of executive systems, ranging all the way from the Parliamentary type employed in Australia and Canada through the Presidential system of the United States to the collegial or Council system of Switzerland. Each of the existing systems is rooted in established tradition and operates fairly successfully. Even the modified Parliamentary system of the Federal Republic of Germany seems to be working reasonably well, although it is too early to be very certain about it. Each of these systems was adopted at a particular time as the one most suitable for the government to be established; each was the result of a careful review of past, present, and future activities, failures, and needs. The review of executive systems suggests that there are various ways to organize a federal government so that it can act with efficacy and dispatch.

In the light of the historical record, it is not possible to assert with any degree of assurance that one rather than another executive system is clearly and demonstrably right for the European Community. However, those federal states which have a Parliamentary system have found it necessary to provide for a separate Head of State. This Head of State exercises certain ceremonial and formal functions, but largely with the required consent of the executive Cabinet or Council. Still, a separate Head of State seems to be necessary in a Parliamentary system because a neutral ceremonial official is needed to bridge the gap between the outgoing and the incoming Ministry, not by taking over the government, but by providing the decisions involved in getting a new one. If therefore a Parliamentary system were to be adopted, existing experience would definitely point toward the conclusion that a separate Head of State must be provided. This raises a number of difficulties to be dealt with below.

The executive, no matter how structured, has proved to be a centralizing force in all existing federal systems. The increasingly dominant role which the executive tends to play in all modern states is no doubt connected with this centralizing role of the executive. But there are specific issues involved in federal systems which are peculiarly the result of federalism itself. For while it is possible to accommodate the representative bodies to the requirements of local representation, the same is not very easily possible in the organization of the executive. True, a certain regionalism may be enforced in connection with appointments to the civil service, but the fact that officials come in fairly even proportion from the several regions or component States does not necessarily ensure their remaining concerned with these local units; they may identify themselves with the federal government and join in centralizing power in its hands. One method, widely practiced in certain existing federal states (though hardly at all in the United States) is therefore that of delegating much administration to the component units, leaving to the federal authorities merely the task of supervising these activities (see below). But even when such delegation of administration is an accepted principle, as in Switzerland, Germany, and Austria, the federal government continually extends its control.

In view of this inherent propensity to centralize, a federal system which is being organized with a view to keeping it on a fairly stable basis for some time ought to avoid too centralized a pattern of leadership. Both the Presidential and the Cabinet form of government have shown a pronounced tendency in that direction. The American President as well as the British Prime Minister are decidedly more powerful today than they were a hundred years ago. The plebiscitary character of mass elections, the need for effective coordination, the recurrence of crisis, both economic and military — these and a number of other factors contribute to the emergence of a central human pivot as the decisive wielder of actual leadership in these systems. Only the collegial or Council system of Switzerland (also practiced in some American States) seems calculated to escape from these difficulties. At the same time, such a Council appears to be capable of operating effectively, where it has been tried. The obvious objection that only Switzerland with its unique and long democratic tradition can hope to operate such a system seems ill founded, because it is precisely the multilingual character of the Swiss population which has led to the development of this system. Why? Because this system enables one to maintain a measure of regional balance even within the executive establishment. If no more than two Ministers were to belong to any one nationality (supposing the ministry to be composed of seven in all, as in Switzerland), and if these were to be chosen by the two houses of the federal legislative assembly acting jointly (as provided for now in Switzerland, as well as for the presidential elections in both France and Germany), a fair balance would probably be struck and steady leadership would be provided, even if these councilors did not hold office for such extended periods as in Switzerland. Moreover, the collegial or Council form has been adopted for the established Coal and Steel Community and is proposed for the European Defense Community (see Articles 19–32 of the EDC Treaty). Therefore, a degree of continuity would also be provided by the adoption of this system.

If it be asked whether sufficient coherence is achieved under such an executive council, the answer can probably not be given except in terms of actual experience. Since all federal systems must strive to achieve a balance between unity and diversity, between coordination and divergence, and since this balance is bound to be especially difficult in a multinational community, it is probably wise to follow the experience of the one system which has had to cope with this very problem. But a more detailed analysis of the actual experience in existing federal states will be undertaken to test this working hypothesis.

II. The Structure of the Executive

Under this heading will be considered: the questions of political composition of the executive; variations of tenure and relation to the legislature; methods of selection; and problems of organizing the non-political executive, i.e., the civil service.

A. *Composition*
1. SINGLE AND PLURAL

The supreme executive power of the federal government may be vested either in a single individual or else in a group acting with joint responsibility. It is, of course, axiomatic that the actual direction of executive affairs must be diffused among a number of men directing the departments and supervising the varied activities of the executive — the distinction that we are making here is only between the various modes of composing the highest decision-making authority. A small group, as well as a single man, will need assistance and advice in executing the affairs of a federation but it is nonetheless possible to isolate that body with which rests the political responsibility as well as the final authority for making executive decisions.

Successful experience with a single executive in a federal system is practically confined to the United States. The executive power of the federal government is vested in the President. He has, it is true, a Cabinet whose members head the various executive departments and advise the President on policy, but the President has ultimate power of decision and therefore the complete political responsibility for all executive action. The Cabinet is not a device for sharing responsibility among a group; it is a necessary result of the President's inability to supervise all affairs directly.

The basic argument for the concentration of the executive power in a single man is that it ensures a vigorous executive unhampered by internal deadlocks. The framers of the American Constitution felt this to be a peculiar necessity in a federal government which would tend to be weak in any case; they feared that a plural executive would be weakened by internal dissensions based on sectional loyalties. The effect of the system has been that "the Presidency has become essentially and pre-eminently the unique unitary and unifying institution in the general government of the United States" (Wheare, *Federal Government* 90 (1947)). The President has become the spokesman of the nation as a whole and is often in direct conflict with the legislature in which the sectional interests have more direct representation.

The imposition of a greater degree of unity in the institutional structure than exists in the political reality creates the danger of the withdrawal of consent by disaffected sections. If the heterogeneity of the union is too great, there is the danger that the single executive will represent not a compromise among the sectional interests, but rather the domination of one section over another, and the minority section will then lose any safeguard for its interests within the executive branch. The situation just prior to the Civil War in the United States is illustrative. The divisions in the country were too deep and hence candidates for the Presidency tended to be rival sectional candidates: the losing section was unwilling to consent to the selection of Lincoln because this concentrated too much power in an authority in which it had no share. In short, the single executive leaves the protection of sectional interests exclusively to the legislature and if these interests are felt too strongly, such protection is not sufficient.

The plural executive, whether of the conciliar (Swiss) or Cabinet type, obviates this difficulty. It enables executive power to be vested in a group and suitable provisions can ensure that representatives from all sections will be included within that group. Thus in Switzerland the Constitution requires that all the members of the Executive Council be citizens of different cantons and this constitutional provision has been supplemented by a convention that allocates a minimum number of seats to the French-speaking cantons. In Canada, though there is no constitutional provision, seats in the Cabinet have always been assigned with rigid observance of all sectional claims. There is always one member from each Province, and at least four go to both Ontario and Quebec, the two largest Provinces. In both countries decision is taken by the members of the executive jointly and members are expected to speak for their sections as well as for the departments with which they are specifically concerned.

In other words, the plural executive may consist of a coalition of regional representatives with joint responsibility while the single executive is necessarily an agent of the nation as a whole. The former represents a coalition of the sections, the latter at best a compromise. It would appear that the single executive is expedient only in federations in which regional diversities are not too great — its unifying tendency and the exclusion of sectional representatives from executive decision-making power means that only the legislature is available as an institution for preserving the sectional diversities. In federations with deep political, linguistic, religious, or traditional differences this has been felt to be insufficient. Although it has been objected that the plural executive may be too weak because it does contain within itself sectional differences of opinion, this weakness (when it does exist) is only a reflection of the limits of unity on which the federation is based.

In deciding between the single and plural executive, the essential point is whether the representation of regional differences is to be confined to the legislature or whether the executive itself shall also be so composed as to reflect these interests. Two other points must be mentioned. First, the plural executive is based on a similar constituency to the legislature, i.e., the nation taken as a grouping of sections and subject to the same type of pressures, and is therefore more likely to work in harmony with the legislature. On the other hand, the single executive is based on the national constituency and is therefore more likely to be in conflict with the legislature based on the sectional constituency. This fact is quite independent of the separation of powers as a comparison of the relation of the Swiss and American executives to their legislature indicates. However, as a corollary, should there be a sectional deadlock in the legislature the plural, unlike the single, executive is not in a superior position to resolve it.

As a second point, there are certain difficulties arising from the selection of a single executive. These are discussed below under the method of selection, page 79 *et seq.*

2. SEPARATION OF HEAD OF STATE FROM EXECUTIVE AND FUSION

Besides single versus plural there is a second major issue to be decided in regard to the composition of the executive: Should the functions of the Head of State be separated from those of the political executive, or should the two functions be given to the same authority? The functions of the Head of State may be divided into two main categories. (a) In all states he serves a ceremonial and symbolic function as the representative of the state in both internal and external affairs. This function may be of particular importance in a federal system as an aid to developing a sense of unity among the constituent States. (b) The Head of State is usually also entrusted with some political functions although the extent of these varies considerably from an importance almost equivalent to the Chancellor in Weimar Germany to the practically nonexistent role of the Austrian President of the 1920 Constitution. In general such political powers as the Head of State is given to exercise on his own initiative are intended either to be a residuary defense for the constitutional order or else to simplify the working of the Parliamentary system.

For the exercise of both of these functions it is eminently desirable that the Head of State be as little identified with the political or sectional differences as possible because he is supposed to be a representative of the federation as a whole. For this reason the separation of the offices of Head of State and political executive has a strong claim to consideration in any system because any political action necessarily implies that it is not supported by the whole population. The only way for the Head of State to carry out his symbolic function is not to be politically identified; if he engages in political action he must cease to be an adequate symbol for the whole federation. Thus in the United States, where the two offices are combined, the symbolic function of the President is minimal. He is the leader of a party and as such is not acceptable to the opposition as a symbol of the federation. Rather the nation uses the inanimate symbols of flag and Constitution.

The argument for separation of the offices applies as much to the Head of State in carrying out his political functions, for these are generally designed to be carried out by a "neutral" figure in a Parliamentary system. If the offices are combined and the Head of State has the partisan affiliation that adheres to the political executive, the neutrality of his actions must be placed in doubt. Not only the neutrality, but, even more, the general belief in the neutrality of the Head of State, have been essential to the proper performance of his functions, as can be seen in the untenable situations in which Dominion Governors-General have been placed when their actions have been politically criticized.

There is another argument, based on antithetical assumptions, for the separation of the offices of political executive and Head of State, especially in a Parliamentary system. Instead of being based on the desire of removing the Head of State from political controversy, this argument stresses the need for a second executive agency with political backing to serve either as a check or else as a stabilizing agency on the normal political executive. It was such a consideration which led the framers of the Weimar Constitution to give the Head of State a strong political position as well as extensive powers. The separation of President and Ministry was not designed to remove the President from political affiliation; it was to provide a balance between the executive agencies. Similarly the Austrian Head of State's position was strengthened in 1929 in order to provide a stabilizing influence on the Parliamentary political executive.

Both these arguments provide grounds for separating the executive and the Head of State. The offices have, however, been united both in the United States and in Switzerland. In the United States the fusion is due to the practical difficulties of separating the offices in a unitary executive system. We indicated above that the unitary executive becomes the spokesman of the federation as a whole as opposed to the sectional divergencies — but this is the very role that the Head of State is supposed to fill in his ceremonial function. A separate Head of State would therefore be a duplication. There are likewise few noncontroversial political functions that a Head of State could perform under the separation of powers.

The reason for the fusion of the offices in Switzerland is a different one. It is, in fact, not completely accurate to say that the offices are fused. The political executive is a plural one and one of the members of the Executive Council performs the functions of the Head of State as well. The President of the Confederation is primarily the chairman of the Executive Council but he also performs the traditional functions of the Head of State, i.e., representing the federation in internal and external affairs. He has almost no special political powers and such as he does have are his in virtue of his chairmanship of the Executive Council (i.e., as a member of the political executive). The fusion may thus be rather regarded as a practical abolition of the office of Head of State than as a precedent for the fusing of the offices. This is particularly true as the symbolic functions of the President of the Confederation are peculiarly small; the office is minimized in importance by the practice of having it rotate among the members of the Executive Council. Nor is the Head of State needed for any but these ceremonial functions.

B. *Tenure and Relation to Legislature*

There are two basic alternatives in this category. The executive may hold office for a fixed period or else at the discretion of the legislature. Corresponding to these two alternatives are two basic types of executive-legislative relations; in the case of the fixed-tenure executive, executive and legislature are constitutionally independent, while in the other form the executive is constitutionally dependent on the legislature. These basic alternatives are illustrated in the American and Parliamentary types of government. In the United States the President is elected for a period of four years and is irremovable during that period except for the special process of impeachment and conviction for crime. During his period of office, he is not accountable to the legislature and may be in conflict with it.

In the Parliamentary system on the other hand tenure of the executive is not for any specific term, but depends on the retention of the Parliament's confidence. Correspondingly, executive and legislature are not independent of one another and conflict between them must result either in the resignation of the executive or else in the dissolution of the legislature. The constitutional relation is usually nominally one of executive dependence on the legislature although in point of practice the relation may be the reverse. But in either case, the two bodies are interdependent.

Before examining the advantages of these two systems, the Swiss variant of the independent executive must be noted. The Swiss executive is elected for a fixed term and is not removable by the legislature during this period by a withdrawal of its confidence. The distinction from the American type therefore lies not in the tenure of the executive but in its relation with the legislature. Unlike the American President, the Swiss executive is elected by the legislature and formally subordinate to it. This in any case might be the impression of one merely reading the constitutional document. In actual practice one or another of the councilors may perform the role of political leadership, and the Council as a whole is increasingly prepotent in the formulation as well as the execution of policy. There is a separation of powers but these powers are not constitutionally coordinate. Because the executive is only quasi-independent of the legislature, being bound by its directives, deadlock between the two branches does not arise even though there are no provisions either for removal of the executive or for dissolution of the legislature. This constitutional relationship tends to make the executive more of an administrative than a political body. This development is facilitated by the frequent use of the referendum which provides a ready and final solution even if there should be policy differences between executive and legislature.

Without reviewing all the arguments about the relative advantages of the separation of powers (fixed tenure of the executive) and the dependence of the executive on the legislature for its tenure, it is possible to indicate the main general considerations and then turn more fully to those peculiarly related to the federal organization of government. The constitutional independence of the executive from the legislature has been advocated on two main grounds. First, by a system of independent authorities it is hoped to prevent the encroachment of government into unauthorized fields. Second, fixed tenure of the executive provides an assurance of stability in the executive especially in systems where firm majorities do not exist in the legislative branch. It is a matter of historical record that in systems in which the executive has a fixed tenure no such governmental "crises" have occurred as come about with more or less frequency in Cabinets based on unstable Parliamentary coalitions.

On the other hand the Parliamentary-Cabinet executive ensures the absence of deadlock between executive and legislature; however, such deadlocks occur infrequently in the American system. As indicated above, this is not necessarily a result of the fixed tenure of the executive as the Swiss experience indicates. The Cabinet system is also advocated because of the greater likelihood of coordinated legislative programs following from both the confidence of the legislature in the executive and the joint responsibility of the Cabinet for all policy.

Beyond these general considerations, there are some particular problems arising from the federal nature of the state and of the bicameral form of legislature associated with it. In any bicameral system the possibility of disagreement between the two houses is always present; it may be either simply accepted or else provision can be made for overcoming it by a differentiation between the powers of the two houses. The nature of the legislative-executive relation is intimately associated with this question. In every system of responsible (Parliamentary) government the Ministry has always, either in law or in practice, become responsible to one house alone. The reason for this is obvious: should there be disagreement between the two houses and either could turn out the Ministry, it might well be impossible to establish any executive at all. The support of the Ministry has therefore consistently become the prerogative of the lower house alone.

As a consequence, in all federal systems that have adopted the parliamentary form of the executive, the second chamber has become of subsidiary importance. This has occurred not only in systems in which the second chamber is explicitly given a subsidiary role in the Constitution such as in the case of the German Republic, but also in Canada and Australia where the upper house is given constitutionally coordinate functions with the lower. The Australian experience is most conclusive on this point. Not only is the second chamber given equivalent powers in the Constitution (except for the origination of money bills) but it is also popularly elected and could therefore, unlike the appointed Canadian upper house, be expected to have important political influence. However, the responsibility of the Cabinet to the lower house alone, resulted in a very short time in a considerable decline of its political importance. The Cabinet system requires that there be a mode of overcoming differences between the two chambers so that an executive having the confidence of the legislature may be constituted. The universal result has been that the popular chamber has become of far greater importance than the upper house.

The importance of this point for federal systems is clear. The upper chamber in a federal system is traditionally instituted in order to protect sectional interests. As it declines in importance with the Cabinet system it loses the ability to perform this function effectively. In both Canada and Australia the upper chambers were expected to perform this function and in neither have they done so. Instead sectional interests have been protected by the regional distribution of seats in the Cabinet, as well as by certain extraparliamentary devices such as the Premier's conference in Australia. Although the second chamber necessarily loses its general function of protecting sectional interests in the Cabinet system, it may be assigned certain more moderate functions, particularly in the control over federal administration and its impact on the States. (See page 78 below, and Study 1, The Federal Legislature, Appendix III.)

It is one of the great advantages of the fixed-tenure executive that it does not require this differentiation of political importance between the two houses of the legislature. In both Switzerland and the United States the two houses were given equivalent status by the Constitution (actually the American Senate received certain important powers in relation to the executive as well as its equivalent position in legislation) and have maintained this equivalent situation since. These second chambers are therefore suitable agencies for the protection of the regional interests and though in Switzerland this function is also performed within the executive, they can perform the function for which the second chamber is instituted in federal systems.

In the Cabinet system there can neither be deadlocks between the executive and the legislature nor between the two houses of the legislature. Either through constitutional provisions limiting the power of the second chamber, the political predominance of one chamber, or through special provisions such as the Australian double dissolution, serious differences between the houses are overcome, normally by the preponderance of the lower chamber. These differences must be overcome in order that an executive power may be constituted. On the other hand in the independent-executive system not only may there be unreconciled differences between legislature and executive but also between the two houses of the legislature. As the executive power is continuous, such disagreements do not produce governmental "crises" although they do of course tend to frustrate coordinated legislative and executive programs. The essential point is that in the independent executive the two houses of the legislature can also be independent of one another. In both Switzerland and the United States there are no constitutional means of overcoming differences between the houses and though informal means such as joint committees of both houses have been used to overcome minor differences in draft bills, it is not essential to the governmental system that these deadlocks be resolved.

The greater possibilities of dissension between the governmental agencies that exist under the independent executive may be seen as disadvantages; it is, however, quite as justifiable to regard them as essential in preserving the balance between centralization and autonomy, and to argue that it is the essence of the federal idea that government requires a greater degree of consent than that of the majority represented in a single chamber. The independent executive, both of the Swiss and the American type, enables the legislature to consist of two houses of equivalent powers although based on different constituencies. If it is desired that the second chamber be an efficient means for protecting sectional interests, the possibility of sustained differences of opinion with the lower house is a necessary consequence.

The nature of the second chamber desired is thus intimately connected with the choice between independent and responsible executives. It was argued in the Australian Constitutional Convention that responsible government was incompatible with the maintenance of the federal balance because of the necessary decline of the second chamber. That is an overstatement; but it can be said that if Parliamentary government is adopted in a federation there must be a means other than the second chamber by which regional interests are protected. As shown above, this has occurred in Canada where regional representation in the executive fulfills the function which was originally supposed to be performed by the second chamber.

C. *Method of Selection*

The method of selection of the executive is directly associated with its composition and tenure and relation to the legislature but certain significant alternatives and their effects can be noted.

1. SELECTION OF THE POLITICAL EXECUTIVE

a. *Election by popular vote.* This mode of selection is necessarily confined to the independent executive and in practice to its single form. Although the chief executive is not directly elected in any of the federations here considered, the American experience has shown that indirect election by bodies having no other function than electing the executive readily becomes equivalent to direct election. Direct election of the executive is both a highly centralizing force and a system that creates strong pressure towards a two-party system on the federal level. Should this not develop, it presents the great danger of purely sectional candidates whose election may not be acceptable to one or more of the other sections. Popular election of the executive may thus require a greater degree of homogeneity within the federation than is likely to be found in the European situation.

Direct election of a plural (independent) executive is, however, not unknown. It exists to a varying extent in many American States as also in several Swiss cantons. Direct election of the Swiss Federal Council has been proposed on several occasions but has been consistently rejected and the reasons for this rejection appear conclusive: (a) direct election would tend to upset the sectional distribution of the executive (one of the main reasons for the plural executive in federal systems); (b) it would tend to destroy the concept of collegial action by giving each councilor an independent basis of support; and (c) it would emphasize even further the dominance of the Council over the assembly.

b. *Election by legislature.* Both houses can be associated in the election of an independent executive. Federal experience has been limited to the Swiss Executive Council in which the constitutional provision of election of the Council for the fixed duration of the legislature has been supplemented by the convention of the indefinite re-election of the councilors. Although elected by the legislature, the party composition of the Council reflects that of the assembly only very roughly and a considerable time lag exists between the growth of a party in the electorate and its representation on the Council. Conflict between assembly and Council is avoided more by the Councilors' conception of their office than by constitutional provisions. The Council acts as a managing committee for the legislature and though exercising considerable political leadership as well as exerting great influence because of the weight of experience gained through long tenure of office, the Council is more of an administrative than a political organization.

c. *Other forms of indirect election.* Another form of indirect election is that used for the High Authority of the Schuman Plan. The members of the Authority are appointed by the joint action of the participating governments, the object being to secure sufficient influence of those governments and yet, by making the appointments joint, to prevent members from being (or considering themselves) delegates of individual governments. Although appointed for a fixed term, the Authority is responsible to the Assembly which can by a two-thirds vote remove the Authority as a whole although no action can be taken against individual members of it.

d. *Appointment by head of state plus confirmation by legislature.* This has been the universal form under Parliamentary systems (although the confirmation may only be implicit — in British countries) except for the Austrian Constitution before its amendment in 1929.

2. SELECTION OF HEAD OF STATE

a. *Direct election.* Direct election gives to the Head of State political authority even without express constitutional provision. It also tends to make him a partisan and though the purpose of direct election is to provide an embodiment of the federation, it destroys that air of neutrality that both the ceremonial functions in any federation and the specific powers under a Parliamentary system demand (but compare the contrary arguments above, pp. 65–66).

b. *Various indirect forms.* In the attempt to secure a neutral Head of State acceptable to as wide a body of opinion as possible, various forms of indirect election have been used. Without going into detailed description, the essential possibilities are (1) election by the federal legislature; (2) election by State legislatures, or other State bodies; (3) a combination of 1 and 2. Appointment from outside the federation as formerly practiced in the Dominions is hardly relevant and recent practice of making the appointment on the recommendation of the Dominion Prime Minister has in fact vested the power in the leader of the majority in Parliament and can thus be regarded as essentially equivalent to election by that body.

D. *The Civil Service*

In the federal civil service, as in all aspects of federal government, the central problem is to achieve a balance between the demands of homogeneity imposed by the requirements of efficient action and the need for diversity stemming from the traditional heterogeneity of the member States. In terms of the civil service, this problem has two main aspects: (1) the formulation of a system of appointments and promotion which, while ensuring an efficient service, will not too strongly contravene territorial demands for representation in the service, and (2) the formulation of standards for the federal service that take into account not only the linguistic diversities of the member States but also the differing standards of the State civil services and their educational systems. Though the two are aspects of the same problem, we will deal with the former in terms of the power of appointment and limitations on it while the latter will be considered in terms of the peculiar problems of applying the merit system to a federal service.

1. SOME LIMITATIONS ON THE APPOINTMENT POWER AND POTENTIAL CONFLICT WITH THE MERIT SYSTEM

In federal as in unitary states, the power of appointment to civil offices has been generally accepted as a function of the political executive but, as in unitary states, this power has been limited by either constitutional or statutory provisions. The most important of these limitations have been those that have sought to remove appointments from political considerations and replace them by a system of appointment for merit based on an objective standard and administered by some "non-political" agency such as a Civil Service Commission. The degree to which this depoliticization has occurred varies, but it is a common objective in all the countries considered here except in the appointment of that small group of top civil servants that may be designated as "policy-forming." Some special difficulties arising from the application of the merit system to a federal service will be considered in 2, The Formulation of Standards, below — this section deals with other limitations on the appointment power and their potential conflict with the merit system.

a. *The field service.* By either custom (United States), statute (Canada), or constitutional provision (Weimar), federal systems have usually provided that civil servants administering federal affairs within a State shall be citizens of that State and/or members of the linguistic group dominant within their jurisdiction. Though this could be considered a deviation from the strict standard of objective appointment the patent advantages of local familiarity and acceptance would seem to more than counterbalance any purely theoretical disadvantages. It is of course possible that too strict an observance of such a rule might engender difficulties in the filling of very specialized positions but on the whole such a rule appears as a reasonable adjunct to the merit system. For instance, it was introduced in Canada only after the change from patronage to merit systems.

b. *The central service.* Within the central service four distinct categories can be recognized: the small top layer of policy-forming officials, the larger skilled administrative group, the professionally qualified (doctors, engineers, etc.) and the clerical. The demand for "equality of treatment" by apportioning appointments among the member States is encountered in nearly all federations and if granted raises serious implications for the merit system because nationality as well as merit becomes a decisive standard for appointment and promotion. Proportionality and the merit system may be combined in a variety of ways but the basic method is to make the objective test a qualifying rather than eliminating one and then to make appointments from qualified applicants on a proportional basis. This procedure has proved basically satisfactory for filling the clerical and less skilled positions but becomes increasingly less effective for more responsible (highly qualified) appointments, because the fewer the number of qualified applicants the greater the difficulty in finding a proportionate number from each area.

It is because of the difficulty of applying the merit test and at the same time meeting the demands of regional distribution that other forms of appointment are both practiced and advocated. This is particularly true of the "policy-forming" group of officials who are often legally distinguished both in method of appointment and in tenure of office in order to give greater discretion to the political executive's power of appointment and removal. Though political harmony between the executive and its top executing officials is perhaps the primary reason for this distinction, it is also relevant to ensuring the play of political forces to secure proportional representation in this level of the service. It may be added, however, that political discretion does not of itself ensure regional distribution even if this distribution exists in the political executive. Thus in Canada, where the Cabinet is regionally balanced, there was not a single French Canadian deputy minister (the highest rank of civil servant) in 1947. The causes for this disproportionality, not only in the policy-forming but also in the administrative level of the service, are directly traceable to the problem of the formulation of standards for the federal service.

2. THE FORMULATION OF STANDARDS

The merit system has been almost universally accepted for the civil service at least as an ideal, but its implementation in a federal system raises problems even more basic than those directly connected with proportional representation in the service. It is the essence of the system that appointments and promotions be made on the basis of some fairly objective standard — in the case of appointment usually some sort of examination. But these examinations are based on a concept of the qualifications desirable in a civil servant and are usually more or less integrated into the educational system from which candidates are recruited. The specific problem of standards arises in the federal civil service from the fact that the member States may have varying conceptions of the qualifications for the service and different educational standards and therefore any objective standard applied to the federal service may in fact give definite advantages to candidates from those areas that have had a similar criterion for their own services (and whose school systems are integrated to preparing candidates for the given type of examination).

The most obvious aspect of the problem is that of the criterion of linguistic competence. In any federal state possessing more than one official language, facility in these languages is certainly a relevant requirement at least in the higher ranks of the civil service (it is with these ranks that this whole section is primarily concerned). However, in the absence of a sufficient body of men completely fluent in all the official languages, any practical qualification will leave room for interpretation and the consequent weighting of one language at the expense of others. Thus in Canada many positions which ostensibly require binguality are in fact practically limited to the English-speaking because binguality is interpreted as fluent English and passing French; French Canadians having a good knowledge of English are passed over because of the way the requirement is interpreted. A somewhat similar position obtains in Switzerland in regard to Italian.

Language is however only one, and not the most insurmountable, aspect of the problem of the formulation of standards. Any system of standards or examinations is related at least implicitly to an educational system and to a concept of the civil servant. When the educational systems of the member States are different both in quality and in orientation, the products of one will have an advantage over those of the other, and recruiting by the merit standard will not yield an (even roughly) proportional distribution of appointments among the member States. This has been most clearly illustrated in the experience of Canada with its different educational systems in the French- and English-speaking Provinces. The standards of the Canadian Civil Service Commission are implicitly those of the English educational system rather than those of the French (i.e., scientifically rather than legally oriented). Combined with the greater extension of education in the English-speaking Provinces, the change from patronage to merit system has therefore resulted in a large disproportion of English civil servants in the higher categories and a consequent demand from the French for either an open return to the patronage system or the institution of a strict quota system which would nullify the results of the objective recruiting system.

3. CONCLUSIONS

a. Criteria of selection of civil servants vary from State to State and the educational facilities of each State are more or less geared for training students to these criteria.

b. The educational facilities of States differ both in quality and availability to the general population.

c. Therefore if federal civil servants are selected by objective criteria a serious disproportion of State representation in the civil service will arise in those offices having high qualifications, i.e., not enough qualified applicants to enable selection to be made on a proportional basis without a lowering of standards.

d. If the pressure for proportional representation in the federal service is strong enough so that it must be met, there appear to be two basic alternatives: (a) a sufficient retreat from the merit system to allow political pressures to ensure equal distribution of offices, or (b) some federal provisions for (higher) education either in its own institutions or by prescribing standards for the State institutions.

One further aspect of the federal civil service requires consideration — its relation to the State civil services. This issue is of immediate and particular importance in the establishment of the federal service because the State service must be for a considerable time at least the major source of recruits for those offices requiring administrative experience. Even if federal execution is primarily indirect, the federal service will require at least a supervisory staff as well as an executive apparatus for those functions whose (exclusive) execution is vested in the federal government. New federal executive departments can be created either by federalizing those employees who performed these functions within the States (cf. Canada) or else by a system of loans between the State and federal services. In either case some provision for protecting the accumulated rights of the State officers who will be required within the federal establishment is necessary if their adherence is to be assured.

Aside from the imperative needs of the establishment of the federal service it would appear that provisions for access into the federal service from the State services (either permanent or on a loan basis as practiced in Australia) are a useful device not only in recruiting for the higher ranks of the federal service but also for providing a source of understanding between federal and State governments.

III. FUNCTIONS OF THE EXECUTIVE

A. *Sphere of Competence*

It is of the essence of the federal idea that governmental functions be divided between central and State governments. As a result, certain subject matters are assigned to one or the other government or to both jointly as within their sphere of legislative competence; but the division of legislative competence, though it must precede, does not settle the question of the relative executive competences of the two governments. In no federation is the range of executive action greater than its legislative power, but in some it is significantly smaller. The execution of federal legislative policy may be provided for in two ways: (1) it may be assigned exclusively to the federal executive, or (2) it may be given in whole or in part to the State executive authorities. There are both advantages and disadvantages in each course.

1. DIRECT EXECUTION ONLY

Exclusive federal execution of all federal policy has the basic advantage of ensuring uniformity throughout the union. If federal officers are responsible for the carrying out of federal policy it simplifies the problem of responsibility and makes supervision a purely administrative issue. In both the United States and the Dominions, federal legislation has been implemented by the federal executive, the President or Cabinet being responsible and supervising civil officers in the employ of the federation. Though this is not explicitly demanded by the constitutions, and there are in fact a few exceptions to it, the basic pattern is well established.

The advantages of this course are that it ensures that once a federal policy is authorized by the legislature its implementation cannot be frustrated by the State governments; officers carrying it out are federal employees subject to the direct supervision of the political chief of the federal executive authority. Besides the unifying effect achieved through the unity of executive authority throughout the union, direct federal execution has another strong centralizing effect. It necessitates a large-scale federal civil service, and the growth of direct employment by the federal government gives a vested interest to its perpetuation. In Canada in particular the great extent of federal patronage was one of the important forces that served to bind the disparate parts of the Dominion together.

But associated with these advantages are difficulties particularly great in federations formed out of States with an already well-developed administrative apparatus. The most important of these arises from the problem of transforming State into federal administrative services. In the case of powers assigned exclusively to the federation, it involves the abolition of those State executive departments that previously carried out those functions. The procedure in both Canada and Australia was to transfer certain departments from the States to the federation on the formation of the union (or when the federal legislature first exercised its legislative power within the concerned field). Federalization of State executive departments is probably the easiest way in which the federation can acquire a sufficient body of administrators to execute its functions but it is a procedure to which the constituent States, as well as the civil servants concerned, may not be amenable. The transition can be facilitated by a constitutional guarantee to the civil servants that they will lose none of their accrued rights, but this will impose a considerable financial burden on the federation or on the individual States in regard to those officers of the State departments not needed by the federation for its own administrative services. In short, direct federal execution requires a development of federal administrative machinery which is only feasible rapidly by the federalization of the State executive departments but this in turn poses problems not only for the federation but also for the States faced with the loss of some of their major departments. It is significant that this expedient has only been tried in States with fairly rudimentary administrative organs.

Another major disadvantage of exclusive direct federal execution is that it necessarily involves a considerable amount of duplication with already existing State machinery especially in those functions which are performed by both State and central governments. For example, it involves two separate tax-collection authorities which would inevitably overlap considerably.

2. DIRECT AND INDIRECT EXECUTION

The advantages of assigning federal executive authority to the States can be seen from the above. Before discussing the advantages and disadvantages of this system, it must first be more fully described. As practiced in both the German and the Swiss federations, it means that the federal power of execution is divided between the federal executive authority and the separate State governments. This division can be made in the constitution by assigning the execution of some federal functions to the State governments and others to the federal authority or else can be regulated by legislation. The division cannot, however, be only a functional one; it must also be hierarchic, the federal authority being given some form of supervisory power over the State governments in their role of carrying out federal policy.

The advantages of assigning certain federal executive functions to the State governments are mainly two: first, the advantages of decentralization and lack of duplicating machinery, in which can be included the fact that the federal government's impact on the citizen is felt through the medium of familiar agencies and is thus less likely to arouse antagonism; and second, that it obviates the need for a rapid organization of a large-scale federal bureaucracy which would be a matter of great difficulty, as the availability of qualified men not already in the employ of the State governments is very limited. In other words, it enables the federal government to draw directly on the developed administrative services of the member States.

But with its advantages, leaving the execution of federal policy to the States also involves problems of great importance to the keeping of the federal balance. As stated above, it is not possible to make the division between State and federal execution of federal policy a purely functional one; the federal authority must have powers of supervision and ultimately of compulsion to ensure that the States actually execute the federal policy and also to provide for a sufficient degree of uniformity among the various States.

Execution by the States of federal policy means in effect that the States become, in some of their functions, agents of the federation, and safeguards are required to ensure both that the States do not encroach upon the federal jurisdiction and that the federal government's supervision of the States in their aspect as its agents does not undermine the autonomy of the States in their other functions. Although related, these problems can be considered separately. If the States do not execute the federal policies assigned to their jurisdiction or execute them in a manner not in keeping with their intent, they are in fact encroaching upon the federal jurisdiction. Likewise, if the different States execute the policies in too different a manner, the unity of federal policy is lost. It is therefore essential that the federal executive have a means of control over the States in their execution of federal policy.

Effective control requires three broad elements. First, there must be a channel of information by which the federal government can remain aware of the manner of the States' exercise of their powers; second, it must be empowered to give instructions to the States relevant to their proper execution of federal policy; and, finally, it must have a power of compulsion if its directives are not obeyed. These elements are found in both the Swiss and the German cases.

The power of federal supervision supplemented by a coercive power provides an effective safeguard for the federation but implies a danger to the autonomy of the States. The federal executive may use its power of supervision in such a manner as to infringe upon the States' autonomous functions, i.e., under the guise of ensuring that federal policy is carried out by the States, it may seek to impose its own views on the State governments in fields outside the federal jurisdiction. In order to maintain State autonomy while allowing for federal supervision, various devices have been used. Before discussing these devices, it should be mentioned that a basic safeguard exists in any form of the executive that ensures State influence on the federal executive, for instance the Swiss constitutional provision that the Executive Council be composed of members of different cantons. More specific safeguards are found in joining the executive's supervisory power with some other agency. In Germany, the Federal Council Bundesrat (in Weimar, the Reichsrat), consisting of representatives of the State governments, shares, or is permitted to nullify, federal ordinances addressed to the State governments. In Switzerland, the cantons have a right of appeal to the administrative court if they feel that federal supervision is encroaching into their autonomous affairs.

Protection of the States is particularly needed in provisions allowing for federal coercive measures against the States. Such measures therefore usually require the consent either of the assembly as a whole or else of the chamber in which the States are particularly represented. Carefully elaborated rules of procedure that are publicly known and subject to legislative review and criticism are also important.

B. *Functions in Relation to the States*

Besides the division of competence between federal and State executives, two other functions of the executive involve the relation between the federal and State governments.

1. CONTROL OVER LEGISLATURE AND/OR EXECUTIVE OF STATES

Though disallowance of legislative and executive action is usually vested in the courts, it is in Canada also given to the federal executive. The executive's power of disallowance was frequently used in the early years of the federation but has tended to fall into disuse although it still remains as a potential source of control over the provincial governments. It can be used not only to prevent provincial action that is *ultra vires* but also for purely policy reasons. Arguments in favor of such a provision are, first, its far greater speed than court action, and second, that there are forms of State *ultra vires* action that it would be difficult for concerned parties to bring to litigation. An intermediate possibility is to allow the federal executive to bring State action directly to the constitutional court for its opinion.

2. PRESERVATION OF THE PEACE AND MAINTENANCE OF THE CONSTITUTIONS OF THE COMPONENT STATES

By the act of federating, the component States have transferred many of their sources of coercive power to the central government and in return all federal constitutions make provision for federal aid to the State governments in cases where the State governments are not able to enforce their own laws, maintain the peace, or maintain their constitutions. This aid is usually made available on the application of the duly constituted State authorities, but the federal executive may be given two kinds of discretion: (a) to act on its own initiative in certain defined situations such as the inability of the State government to communicate, or if it considers that the situation threatens the general peace of the federation even though the State government has not applied for aid; (b) the federal executive may be granted discretion to refuse the application of the State authority if it considers the situation does not warrant federal action.

Federal intervention in support of the State government is at least in theory to be distinguished from federal execution (above, pp. 79–81) which arises from the States' failing to carry out federal law. The question of constitutional safeguards for both of these compulsive actions within State spheres is however closely related. For a discussion, see Study 13, Defense of the Constitutional Order.

C. *General Problems of Executive Functions Not Specifically Related to Federalism*

1. OF THE POLITICAL EXECUTIVE

Besides the functions ordinarily assigned exclusively to the political executive, there are a number of functions which require mention because they are differently assigned in different political systems, i.e., either not granted at all or shared by the executive with the legislature.

a. *Functions in relation to legislature.* Both the power of vetoing legislative enactments and that of dissolving the legislature are forms of giving the executive a measure of control over the legislature. While the former is associated with the independent and the latter with the responsible executive, neither power is essential to any system. Thus the Swiss independent executive has no veto power and (for practical purposes) the French Cabinet (Third Republic) had no power of dissolution. In federal systems both powers may be considered as operating as centralizing tendencies in that they increase the powers of the executive at the expense of the legislature which is likely to have more particularist tendencies or at least to see issues less in the context of total federal policy and more in terms of impact on the individual regions. Both powers may be qualified in various ways — the veto by provisions for overriding it by special majority, and dissolution by removing it from the complete discretion of the executive.

Legislative initiative is now universally accorded to the executive but both its degree and the ability of the executive to participate in debates of the legislature vary. Essentially this is a problem only in systems having an independent executive as in other cases the executive usually has a seat in one of the houses and is entitled to the privileges thereof. Executive participation in legislative debate has been generally found to be a useful aid to deliberation, and even in the United States, where it is not formally provided for, executive officers do appear before the legislative committees. Besides initiative and participation in debate, certain systems also provide the executive with a monopoly of the right of proposing financial legislation. This is another device for securing coordinated policy and implies a considerable degree of centralization. The same can be said for devices which give to the executive control over the time of the legislature.

b. *Functions in cooperation with legislature.* A number of functions historically in the exclusive province of the executive have in many constitutions required the cooperation or ratification of the legislature. Among such may be mentioned the treaty power, army command and disposal of troops, appointing power to civil offices, pardon and amnesty. As indicated above, the assignment of these functions to the executive exclusively can be viewed roughly as measures making for centralization, and the tendency in federal systems is to make most of these powers dependent on ratification by the legislature or else to define their scope of operation by constitutional or legislative enactment.

2. OF THE HEAD OF STATE

The main functions of the Head of State in all systems are ceremonial and symbolic, the vast majority of his political actions being in fact the actions of his Ministers. Under most systems of responsible government there is, however, a sphere in which he can act on his own initiative. The Head of State is usually entrusted with the selection of the Prime Minister, and while this is a purely formal task in a well-defined two-party system it becomes an actual function when the party situation is not well clarified.

In certain situations the Head of State may refuse to follow the advice of his Cabinet. Thus the signature of the Head of State on legislation is usually an indication that constitutional forms have been complied with and he may refuse his signature if they have not. Also the Head of State may be granted powers in regard to dissolution which usually requires his consent, i.e., he may refuse a dissolution if he considers there is a readily available alternative government.

The Head of State may be granted the right to be present at Cabinet meetings and/or to be consulted on its policy decisions. Such influence as he may exercise through the right to be consulted and to advise is of course primarily a question of personality.

IV. Conclusions

The more detailed review of executive systems appears to confirm the conclusion that some kind of Council system is best adapted to a multinational federated community. It provides an adequate yet stable executive leadership, subordinate to the representative assembly in formal law, but in practice able to guide and lead it. It avoids competition in terms of prestige between the several nationalities, since executive leadership is divided among them. If offers a ready solution for the problem of how to provide a functioning ceremonial Head of State, without requiring the discarding of existing heads in the member States. It remains close to, and indeed definitely identified with, the permanent service, thereby increasing its responsibility. It offers a symbol of stability and businesslike practicality for the several nations federated for limited, practical purposes. It depends less than other systems upon party cohesion which will probably be of slow growth and not be available as a significant determining factor for some time to come, and consequently makes it possible to provide for divergent party participation, without the necessity of close-knit coalition arrangements.

If, in spite of all these advantages, it should be found preferable to discard the Council system and to adopt a Parliamentary type of Cabinet system, it would be desirable to seek to organize it in such a way that it resembles the French Cabinet in its collegial quality, and the German Cabinet in its relative independence from votes of no confidence. Clearly, an executive for a federated Europe ought not to be displaced, except by an agreed-upon new executive. It might be well even to extend the German system and to allow that an individual Minister could be thus replaced by the election of a new one, with proper safeguards so that the new minister does not disrupt the executive organization. Experience would point toward the French, rather than the British type of Cabinet structure, because the British system depends upon firm party support, such as is not likely to exist in the European Parliament for some time to come. There will be *ministrables,* and there will be groupings; but the two-party system will be a far cry from the political dynamics of the assembly, if the political dynamics of the several Parliaments of the member States are any indication.

If such a restricted Parliamentary system were adopted, the problem of the Head of State would have to be faced. Such a Head of State might be a President, elected by the two houses of the European Parliament in a manner similar to that employed in France, Italy, and Germany. Or he could be one of the existing Heads of State, in rotation, so that the King of Belgium, the President of France, and so forth, would fulfill this ceremonial and formal role for a year. He would, for the year he occupied the office, be the titular head of the federation. One might even consider forming the six Heads of State into a college with a rotating chairmanship, leaving it to the group to choose; but this would entail complications in connection with the

Parliamentary systems in the several component States. All things considered, perhaps a fixed system of rotation would be the least troublesome.

Finally, such a restricted Parliamentary system would call for a careful elaboration of the problems of constitutional defense and emergency power, since, as a matter of experience, prolonged periods of difficulty in connection with the succession of Cabinets are definitely part of it. It is doubtful that the ceremonial heads would be suitable repositories of this emergency power, and it would therefore be important to find an adequate solution in terms of practical operation. The problem is dealt with in Study 13, Defense of the Constitutional Order, and will therefore merely be mentioned here.

But a review of these complications, arising in connection with a Parliamentary system for the federated community of Europe, reinforces the conclusion stated at the outset that a Council type of executive seems the least troublesome and objectionable one to adopt.

APPENDIX I

Australia

The articles of the Commonwealth of Australia Constitution Act dealing with the executive[1] give by themselves a very misleading idea of the organization of the executive authority in Australia. It is only as supplemented by the conventions of the Constitution that the real nature of the executive authority can be seen. The main authorities to be considered are the Governor-General and the Federal Executive Council, mentioned in the Constitution, and the Cabinet for which no constitutional provision is made.

I. THE GOVERNOR-GENERAL

The Governor-General is the Head of State. He is appointed by the Commonwealth Prime Minister usually in consultation with his Cabinet, or, to be formally correct, he is appointed by the British Sovereign acting on the advice of his Commonwealth Ministers. Though appointed for a normal term of five years, he is removable at any time by the same authority that appointed him. His main functions are ceremonial and social and he acts as the representative of the Crown, the symbol of unity among the countries of the British Commonwealth. His political actions are all performed on the advice of his Ministers although under certain circumstances he might yet have some occasion for discretionary action. The only likely possibility for such is in the summoning of a Prime Minister and would occur if the party situation in the House of Commons became complex and there were alterna-

[1] The most important portions dealing with the executive are Sections 2–5, 56, 57, 58–70, 84–86, 119, and 126.

tive men who might be able to form governments. In the past the Governor-General has also on occasion refused the Prime Minister's request for a dissolution, but this authority has probably lapsed although it might be revived if a clearly improper demand were made.

II. EXECUTIVE COUNCIL

The constitution associates an Executive Council with the Governor-General. The Executive Council is a purely formal agency that gives legal force to certain executive decisions. Its membership consists of present and past Cabinet members but its only efficient part is a small number of members of the current Cabinet needed to observe the constitutional forms. The Governor-General attends its meetings but its only business is to ratify previous Cabinet decisions (at the making of which the Governor-General was not present).

III. THE CABINET

The Cabinet is the real exerciser of executive authority in Australia. There are no explicit references to such a body in the Constitution, but the basis for the system of responsible government is laid in Section 64 which provides that Ministers of State shall be members of the Parliament and also of the Federal Executive Council. From one point of view the Cabinet is therefore a committee of the Parliament and from another the efficient committee of the Executive Council. It is this exercise of the executive powers by a body of the legislature which is the basis of responsible government. The Cabinet consists of the Prime Minister, the Ministers directing the departments of State, plus some Ministers without portfolio.

IV. THE PRIME MINISTER

The Prime Minister is selected by the Governor-General but in actual fact the latter has no discretion in his choice, being limited to the leader of the majority party in the House of Commons. These leaders are selected by the Parliamentary party with a varying degree of influence by the parties' extraparliamentary bodies.

The remaining members of the Cabinet are appointed by the Governor-General on the advice of the Prime Minister who also has the constitutional authority to advise the Governor-General to dismiss Ministers. There are, however, severe limits on the Prime Minister's discretion in the selection of his colleagues. These limits are imposed by the caucus of the Parliamentary party which, in the Labor Party, has grown to such dimensions that the Ministers are elected by the caucus, the Prime Minister's role being limited to the distribution of offices among the men selected. The choice of Cabinet members is, however, not greatly limited by considerations of sectional representation. Though there is usually one member from each of the States, there is no rigid convention as to the distribution of posts among sectional representatives as is, for example, found in Canada. In fact, members tend to come predominantly from the two large States. The Cabinet, unlike plural executives in most federations, is thus not the primary body for the conciliation of sectional differences even though the second chamber also does not serve this function. To a large extent this is due to the fact that sectional divergences in Australia in matters of policy tend to be minimal; insofar as they do exist their resolution takes place within the parties which are federally organized. (See also Study 7, Public Finance, for the Loan Council as an executive agency that resolves sectional policy differences.)

V. Cabinet-Parliament Relations

The relation between the Cabinet and Parliament follows closely the familiar British usage. The Cabinet is collectively responsible to the House of Commons and as a corollary any Minister disagreeing with government policy is expected to resign before making his disagreement public. In case of an adverse vote in the Commons the Cabinet can either resign or request a dissolution but cannot carry on with a House that it does not control. The Cabinet is responsible to the Commons only; an adverse vote in the Senate does not affect its standing. However, if disagreement between the houses results in a frustration of government policy, the Cabinet may request a simultaneous dissolution of both houses (cf. Australian Legislature, Study I, Appendix I).

The Cabinet enjoys a constitutional monopoly of the right of proposing expenditures from the Treasury and in fact a practical monopoly on the initiation of all legislation, private-member legislation in Australia having been very rare. This dominance over the legislative process is of course due to the fact that the Cabinet consists of the leaders of the majority party and consequently has control over the time of the House.

The Cabinet has control over the armed forces of the Commonwealth and, on the application of the States, may use them to suppress insurrection or violence within the State boundaries.

The Cabinet at present consists of nineteen members administering the following departments: Treasury, Attorney-General's, Postmaster-General's, Defense, Trade and Customs, Prime Minister's, External Affairs, Works and Railways, Repatriation, Health, Home Affairs, Markets and Transport, and Industry. There is a Cabinet secretariat attached to the Prime Minister's department.

VI. Relation of State and Federal Executive Departments

On the establishment of the federation several of the State executive departments were transferred to the federation. Civil servants employed in these departments became federal employees but retained their financial and other rights as if they had remained in the employ of their State governments. Other departments have been established from time to time either by legislation or by executive minute. The constitution vests the right of appointment to civil offices in the Governor in Council, i.e., the Cabinet, until other provision is made by Parliament. Provisions for a merit system for the civil services were made in the very first years of federation and though a number of difficulties arose from the fact that the civil servants transferred from the State services were guaranteed in their different pay and pension scales, the Commonwealth has never had a patronage system of any large extent. Control of recruitment and promotion is now in the hands of a Public Service Commission. The Commonwealth has not had to face the problems of meeting the demand of proportional representation in the service by States because such demands have not been made with any degree of political vigor.

APPENDIX II

Canada

The articles of the British North America Act of 1867, containing provisions for the executive power,[2] give a most imperfect picture of the actual executive. The Cabinet, which is not even mentioned, exercises the real executive power in Canada. The Governor-General, historically a survival from Canada's colonial past, possesses prerogatives which, though more limited, are parallel to those of the British sovereign, whose representative he is. At present he is selected by the Canadian Prime Minister, usually after consultation with the leader of the opposition, and is then merely appointed by the Crown. He holds office at the pleasure of the Canadian government, generally for a five-year term. His main functions are social and ceremonial. All his official acts are performed upon instruction from the Cabinet. Although he is informed of most Cabinet actions, he does not attend Cabinet meetings and his advice need neither be sought nor accepted. His original power to refuse his signature to bills that he considered unconstitutional (B.N.A. Act, §§55–57) has long since lapsed.

I. THE GOVERNOR-GENERAL

Potentially the Governor-General still has some opportunity for independent action, for instance, in deciding which party leader to call on to form a government after an inconclusive election. As recently as 1926 a Governor-General refused the request of a Prime Minister to dissolve a re-

---

[2] The provisions for the executive power in this Constitution are the following: §§ 9–15, 54–57, 90, 93 (3) and (4), 105, and 130–132.

cently elected Parliament, but the action was unpopular, and there have been no public differences of opinion between Governors and Cabinets since. The Chief Justice acts for the Governor-General in the absence of the latter.

The Privy Council consists of all present and past members of the Cabinet as well as a few honorary members. The Privy Council has never met. Its only active part is the Cabinet.

II. The Cabinet

Cabinet government in Canada follows British practices closely. The Cabinet is composed of the leading members of the majority party in the House of Commons to which House it is responsible. All members must be members of Parliament and, in fact, all but one member of the Cabinet have seats in the House of Commons. If a government loses the confidence of the House, it resigns and usually asks the Governor-General for a dissolution. Since throughout most of Canada's history there have been only two large, well-disciplined parties, governments have been very stable and usually stay in power during the entire five-year term of Parliament.

In recent years the Cabinet has consisted of at least twenty members: the heads of most departments and usually a few Ministers without portfolio. There are no junior ministers although during the last war a number of parliamentary assistants were appointed to act on behalf of several Ministers. As in Great Britain, the principle of Cabinet solidarity prevails. A Minister who wishes to disagree with his colleagues in public must first resign. All Ministers give an oath to observe secrecy about all Cabinet proceedings. The choice of Ministers falls to the Prime Minister whose real authority is based on his leadership of the party in power. He may ask the Governor-General to dismiss a Minister, though usually he will ask the incompatible member to resign.

Next to the courts the Cabinet is the most important institution in Canada in the process of maintaining a balance between federal and provincial interests. This can be clearly seen from its composition. In selecting a Cabinet a Prime Minister must not only consider the party standing and personal ability of future Ministers, but also their geographic and religious origins. Every Province has at least one representative on the Cabinet whenever it is possible, who is expected to speak for his Province as well as for his department. Quebec receives traditionally four seats, three of which must go to French-speaking Roman Catholics and one to an English Protestant. Ontario has usually four or five Cabinet Ministers, one of them an English Roman Catholic. Certain departments which are of special interest to specific Provinces will traditionally be headed by a Minister from that Province. The Department of Fisheries, for example, will go to a Minister from the Maritime Provinces, the Department of Justice to one from Quebec. Lastly, if a provincial Premier decides to enter federal politics, and belongs to the party in power, he can generally expect a Cabinet post. Refusals to grant such requests have seriously weakened parties in the past. Obviously all these conditions narrow the Prime Minister's field of selection greatly and may well lower the standards of competence in the Cabinet, but it is well recognized that this is an essential element in the process of integrating federal and provincial political life.

From time to time the Cabinet divides itself into committees for greater efficiency and speed and to coordinate several departments in carrying out policy. Since 1940 there has also been a Cabinet committee on Dominion-Provincial affairs. Besides these *ad hoc* bodies there are also a number of permanent "Privy Council" committees, such as the Treasury Board which is in charge of preparing estimates for annual presentation to Parliament, the Wheat Board, and the Committee on Scientific and Industrial Research.

III. THE PRIME MINISTER

The Prime Minister enjoys a position of considerable pre-eminence in the Cabinet. Not only does he choose the other Ministers, but he is also responsible for the Cabinet's general policies and internal procedures. When he resigns the entire Cabinet follows him. Each new Prime Minister usually issues a Minute-in-Council setting down his personal prerogatives and rules of procedure. Thus in 1934, for example, it was provided that he call Cabinet meetings and that a quorum for naming submissions for the signature of the Governor-General be four Ministers (P.C. 3374, October, 1934). No Minister was to make recommendations about the discipline of another's department, but the Prime Minister was not limited in this way. The Prime Minister can decide on the times for the dissolution and convocation of Parliament. He appoints the Lieutenant-Governors, the Chief Justices of all courts, Senators, the Treasury Board, the deputy heads of all departments, and a number of other officers.

IV. THE CABINET AND THE PROVINCES

In relation to the Provinces the Cabinet exercises several significant powers. Education is a field under the concurrent jurisdiction of the Dominion and provincial governments (B.N.A. Act, §93). The Cabinet may hear complaints from religious groups whose educational rights, as guaranteed by the British North America Act at the time of their joining the federation, have been violated by provincial legislation. The Cabinet can ask a Province to amend such acts, or, if that fails, request Parliament to pass remedial legislation. (These provisions affect only Quebec, Manitoba, Saskatchewan, and Alberta, which had separate Protestant and Catholic school systems at the time of their joining the federation.) Only once did a dispute reach this stage, in the 1890's, on which occasion the Cabinet did introduce a bill providing a remedy for Catholics in Manitoba, but it was not passed (H. of C. Debates 1894, 139; 1895, 11; 1896, 239, 198; 1898, 345, 358). However, most educational conflicts are settled by the courts.

The Cabinet also appoints, recalls, and pays the salary of the Lieutenant-Governors whose relations to provincial governments are much like those of the Governor-General to the Dominion government. (B.N.A. Act, §§56, 58–63, 66, 67, 90). However, unlike the latter, they may still refuse to sign a bill passed by a provincial legislature and "reserve" it for the consideration of the Dominion Cabinet, which can then grant its assent or uphold the Lieutenant-Governor's veto. Moreover, even if the Lieutenant-Governor has signed a provincial Act, the Cabinet may "disallow" it within one year of its enactment (§90). Disallowances were frequent in the first years following Confederation. The Dominion Cabinets tended to consider provincial legislatures irresponsible, and in general entertained strongly centralist policies. With the increasing importance of judicial review and the greater integration of federal and provincial parties, such drastic measures became unnecessary. It is, moreover, an unpopular device, frequently held to be "undemocratic." Recent Cabinets regard it as something to be employed as a last resort. Nevertheless, when in 1938 a number of Alberta Acts were disallowed the Supreme Court of Canada declared that the Cabinet's power of disallowance was unimpaired. *(In Reference Re Disallowance and Reservation Case,* [1938] S.C.R. 71). There are no rules which the Cabinet need follow in accepting or disallowing provincial legislation, except the one-year time limit. In the past, serious infringements upon Imperial policy, a deliberate invasion of a Dominion field of competence, or "unjust and confiscatory" legislation have provoked disallowance. There has been no case of disallowance since 1938.

V. THE CABINET AND PARLIAMENT

Besides these powers, arising from Canada's federal structure, the Cabinet has also considerable powers in its relation to Parliament. The Cabinet alone prepares and introduces financial bills in Parliament (§54). In practice, moreover, most legislation originates in the Cabinet, which also exercises considerable legislative powers, by delegation from Parliament, which is expressed in the numerous orders-in-council issued annually. The Cabinet alone is responsible for negotiating and signing treaties and international agreements, though these are often debated in Parliament, which may also have to pass legislation to make them effective. The power to pardon and reprieve persons sentenced under Dominion law rests with the Cabinet. It also makes a large number of appointments to the judiciary and the civil service, though the Civil Service Commission makes most appointments to the latter. Occasionally the Cabinet appoints eminent citizens to Royal Commissions of Inquiry to study and report on questions that the government holds to be of national interest. The members of the various standing and select committees of the House of Commons are chosen by the Cabinet, after consultation with the leaders of the opposition.

VI. THE EXECUTIVE DEPARTMENTS

Most Ministers are in charge of the administration of a government department and are responsible to Parliament for all its activities. There are at present the following departments: Agriculture, External Affairs, Finance, Fisheries, Justice,[3] Labor, Mines and Resources, National Defense, National Health and Welfare, National Revenue, Post Office, Public Works, Reconstruction and Supply, Trade and Commerce, Transport, and Veterans Affairs.

Attached to these departments, or at least under the supervision of one of the Ministers, are a number of more or less independent boards. These can be divided into three categories — advisory, administrative, and operating boards. Among the advisory boards are such organizations as the Fisheries Research Board and the Tariff Board which provide information for the operating department. Among the administrative boards are agencies that administer a specific Act of Parliament such as the Civil Service Commission or the Unemployment Insurance Board. The tenure of the members of these commissions is secure and their terms of office long to ensure their independence from political influence and control. This applies also to the operating boards such as the Canadian Broadcasting Corporation and the Canadian National Railway Commissions. Although the Minister of Transport is responsible for these to Parliament, his authority over their operations is nominal. The degree of such independence will vary, of course, being emphasized most in such cases as most demand impartiality (e.g., see Civil Service Act, R.C.S. 1919, c.12).

VII. THE CIVIL SERVICE

The British North America Act of 1867 (§130) provided that all civil servants performing duties that came under Dominion jurisdiction after Confederation were to become federal officials until the Canadian Parliament had made other provisions. The Dominion thus inherited the old colonial service with its traditions of patronage, unequal pay for similar work, haphazard promotions, and general lack of competence. While there were several attempts at reform from 1868 on, the "spoils system" lasted unusually long. Not until 1919 (Civil Service Act, R.C.S. 1919, c.12) was the Civil Service Commission in its present form established and given full control over recruitment, examinations, and promotion, as well as classifica-

[3] This department controls the Royal Canadian Mounted Police which not only polices the Northwest Territory but also acts as a provincial police by a special arrangement with all the Provinces except Quebec, Ontario, and British Columbia.

tion of the entire civil service. There is always at least one French-speaking member on the Commission.

The Canadian civil service still faces many general organizational problems, arising from an excessively rigid system of classification, numerous "temporary" employees, conflict between the Treasury Board and the Civil Service Commission in matters of establishment and organization, and a failure to recruit college graduates of high caliber and a lack of in-service training (see Report of the Commission on Administrative Classification in the Public Service, 1946). From the point of view of those interested in the operations of a federal system, however, the most pertinent — and still unsolved — problems are the result of the necessity of building a cohesive civil service with personnel recruited from two very different educational systems, and capable of serving a people of two different languages and diverse cultural attitudes. Some of the inevitable irritations were removed in 1938 (R.S. 1938, c. 7) by an Act providing that civil servants in the field must be able to speak the language of the locality in which they serve.

Recruitment involves special difficulties. In recent years French Canadians have pointed out with some bitterness that the percentage of their number employed in the federal public service has declined, and that they rarely reach the highest positions. English Canadians reply that the French educational system with its almost exclusive emphasis on the classics renders French Canadians unfit for the many jobs demanding technical skills. It has been suggested that entrance examinations designed to test general aptitudes rather than special skills for a given job, followed by a probationary period of rigorous in-service training, might help to alleviate this difficulty. Some French Canadians have demanded a quota proportionate to their number in civil service, but this is clearly incompatible with the merit system and not likely to be accepted. On the other hand, the interpretation given by some departments to the requirement of bilingualism results in their insisting on a perfect knowledge of English with a certain ability to understand French, a system that obviously works against the French Canadians.

It is unlikely that these and related difficulties will be solved in the near future, but such attempts as the opening of a Junior Administrative Class drawn from college graduates, in 1946–1947, are a beginning, though, of course, it is too early to judge at present what results this will bring.

APPENDIX III

Germany

Following the example of the Weimar Constitution with its division of the executive power between the Reichspräsident and Reichsregierung, the Basic Law vests the executive power in the Bundespräsident and the Bundesregierung. The division of powers between the two authorities has, however, been changed by reducing the powers of the Bundespräsident towards those more generally associated with a Head of State in a Parliamentary system. The federal influences on both bodies have also been strengthened. Both of these points will be illustrated in this description.

I. THE BUNDESPRÄSIDENT

Both the decrease in importance and the increase of federal influence can be seen in the method of electing the Bundespräsident. In contrast to the popularly elected Reichspräsident of the Weimar period, the President is now elected by a federal convention consisting of the Bundestag and an equal number of members elected by the popular representative bodies of the Länder according to proportional representation. In other words, the President is elected indirectly by representatives of both the nation as a whole and of the constituent States. Though, to a certain extent, these two types of representatives will not diverge too much as they will be members of the same parties, it must be remembered that there are parties which exist only in a certain Land and also that the parties that exist throughout the federation often have federalistic wings within the Länder.

Federal influence over the President is also established by the provision that he may be impeached before the federal constitutional court by the Bundesrat, which consists of the delegates of the Länder governments.

The functions of the Bundespräsident, as of all Heads of State in Parliamentary systems, are mainly formal and/or ceremonial, but some also leave room for his discretionary decision and are therefore political. Among the first are the traditional functions of the Head of State: he represents the federation in matters of international law, accredits and receives envoys, engrosses and publishes the laws. As the representative of the federation, he promotes unity and harmony between the Länder and the federal government by speeches, personal appearances, etc. The Constitution also assigns him such powers as the conclusion of treaties, appointment and dismissal of federal judges and civil servants, and the right of pardon. These duties must, of course, be seen in the light of the provision that all actions of the President must be validated by the signature of the Chancellor or other competent federal Ministers. They are reflections of the fact that executive action of the state is taken in the name of the Head of State but by the responsible ministry.

The Bundespräsident has, however, some functions in which he may exercise his discretion and act without the countersignature of a Minister, and it is the decline in these powers that shows most clearly the difference from the Reichspräsident of the Weimar period. The Reichspräsident could appoint and dismiss the Chancellor at his discretion: the Bundespräsident is limited to nominating a Chancellor for election by the Bundestag. Though this gives the Bundespräsident a certain measure of influence in the selection of the Chancellor especially in a complex party situation, the sole responsibility of the Chancellor to the Bundestag is clearly established.

The Bundespräsident also has a very clearly and narrowly defined right in regard to dissolution and in the authorization of the state of legislative emergency (cf. Study 1, The Federal Legislature, Appendix III). He lacks the important powers that the Reichspräsident had in relation to emergencies and federal coercive measures against the Länder. Neither has he the right to issue emergency decrees.

II. Bundesregierung

In contrast to the election of the Bundespräsident, the federal principle cannot be seen in the formation of the Bundesregierung. The provision of the Hohen-Chiemsee draft, that the Bundesrat should have the right to appoint the Chancellor in case this could not be done by the Bundestag, was dropped by the Parliamentarian Council. Similarly, there is not, as there is in the case of the Bundespräsident, a right of the Bundesrat or the Bundestag to impeach members of the government, owing to the fact that the government is politically responsible to the Parliament.

The federal government is dependent upon the confidence of the Bundestag. Although this is nowhere stated in the Basic Law, it follows from the fact that the Chancellor is elected by the Bundestag (Art. 63), that the Bundestag may under certain conditions force the Chancellor to resign (Art. 67), and that the Chancellor may ask the Bundestag for a vote of confidence and that, in case of a denial, the Bundestag may be dissolved (Art. 68). It follows further from the fact that for its participation in the legislative process which includes the drafting of the budget (Art. 110)[4] the government is always dependent upon the Bundestag. Even in the case of emergency under Article 81 the government may rule without the Bundestag no longer than six months, and this may happen only once during the term of office of one Chancellor. The relations between the government and the Bundestag are not restricted to a dependence of the former upon the confidence of the latter. The Bundestag may, further, demand the presence of any member of the federal government, just as the members of the government have to be heard by the Bundestag at any time. The Bundestag has further the right to approve the budget (Art. 110) and approve the obtainment and granting of credits by the federal government. It has to discharge *(entlasten)* the federal government with respect to all revenues and expenditures as well as assets and liabilities of the past year (Art. 114). On the other hand, expenditures exceeding the budget and any extraordinary

---

[4] The government has the right of initiative (Art. 76). As a matter of fact, laws are mostly initiated by the government because it alone possesses in its bureaucracy the means to draft laws. Only a few bills introduced by members of the Bundestag or Bundesrat have become law, like, for instance, the Law for the Election of Judges of August 25, 1950, BGBl. p. 368.

expenditures require the approval of the federal Minister of Finance (Art. 112).

The executive functions of the Bundesregierung are of two types. Certain federal laws and functions are executed by federal administrative agencies over which it has organizational and directive powers. More important from the federal point of view, much federal policy is left to the Länder governments to execute. The federal government exercises a supervision over the Länder to ensure that their execution is in accordance with the federal legislation; if it finds that this is not the case, it may request the Bundesrat to determine whether the Land has infringed the law; it may, with Bundesrat approval, issue general administrative provisions; and, by federal legislation requiring Bundesrat approval, it may be granted the right of issuing individual instructions to the States in special cases. The federal government exercises the federal coercive power over the Länder as a final resort for ensuring that their execution of federal law is in harmony with it. Finally, if the democratic order is endangered within a Land which is not prepared to cope with the situation, the federal government may place the police of that Land and of other Länder under its own instructions as long as the Bundesrat does not object.

The federal government thus has supervisory power over the State governments in their role of federal administrative agencies. This supervison is, however, safeguarded by associating the Bundesrat with the federal government in its exercise. The Länder have thus an assurance that the supervision will not be used to impose centralizing policies or to encroach on their internal affairs.

APPENDIX IV

Switzerland[5]

I. THE FEDERAL COUNCIL

The Constitution vests the supreme executive power of the federation in a Federal Council of seven members. The Council is elected at a joint sitting of the two houses of the Federal Assembly for a term of four years, i.e., the same tenure as that of the members of the National Council. A new election of the Federal Council takes place after each renewal of the National Council. In case of vacancies occurring during the four-year period, a new member is elected at the next meeting of the Federal Assembly to fill the unexpired term of the retiring member.

Any Swiss citizen eligible for election to the National Council is eligible

[5] The main constitutional provisions concerning the executive are Articles 10, 16, 32 (as amended October, 1947), 86, and 95–105. But see also Articles 7, 12, 20, 35, 55, 77, and 81. Also of major importance is the *Bundesgesetz über die Organisation der Bundesverwaltung* of March 26, 1914 (as amended), especially Articles 1–28.

for election to the Federal Council subject to the following limitations: (a) no two members of the Federal Council may be citizens of the same canton; (b) no councilor may be related within a stated degree (see note 5 supra) to any other councilor, to the Federal Chancellor, or to the chief civil servants in the department under his jurisdiction.

Membership in the Federal Council is not compatible with any other office in the service of either the cantons or the federation. Members of the Assembly elected to the Council must resign their seats. Councilors are not permitted to carry on a private business or profession nor serve on the board of any corporation.

II. THE FEDERAL PRESIDENT

The Constitution also provides that the Federal Assembly shall each year elect one of the members of the Council as Federal President and one as Vice-President. Each is elected for one year; neither is re-eligible for the same office in the following year nor may the outgoing President be elected Vice-President. As a matter of custom, the Presidency rotates among all the members of the Federal Council. The Vice-President of the previous year is elected President.

III. COUNCIL-ASSEMBLY RELATIONS

Members of the Council may not be members of either house of the Assembly, but they are allowed to participate in debate and to introduce legislation and motions. The constitutional relation of the Assembly and Council is one of master and servant: not only does the Assembly choose the Council, but it is given supervision over the administration and may direct the Council to specific action by resolution. In actual fact, the relation is practically the reverse. The practical dominance of the Council over the Assembly is to be explained by a variety of factors but, before naming these, the constitutional relation between the two bodies must be clarified. Once the Council has been elected it is independent of the Assembly in the sense that neither individually nor collectively are the councilors removable by any action of the Assembly. On the other hand, the Council has also no constitutional authority over the Assembly; in case of disagreement it cannot force new elections or dissolve the Assembly.

IV. RE-ELECTION OF COUNCILORS

Probably the single most important factor that has led to the increase of authority of the Council is the custom that councilors are re-elected at the expiration of their normal term. In other words the Assembly has ceased to make the quadrennial elections to the Council a method of ensuring the Council's political responsibility to it. The custom of re-election of mem-

bers of the Council arose during the long dominance in the Assembly of
the same party, and when the governing party gave way to a new coalition
the custom was retained. Besides relieving the councilors of political responsibility to the Assembly, continuous re-election has increased the authority of the Council for another reason. The tenure of office has tended to
be very long and the councilors have therefore acquired that degree of experience and mastery of technical detail which in other countries has tended
to increase the authority of the civil service. In fact, the long tenure of
members of the Council tends to blur the distinction between the political
and the non-political members of the executive.

This tendency toward the depoliticization of the Council has been aided
by the frequent use of the referendum and initiative. Authoritative political decisions are easily arrived at by this device and the executive is thus
more able to assume the role of impartial administrator. Therefore, though
the Council has been almost completely freed from political responsibility to
the Assembly, the responsibility of its functioning is nevertheless assured.

There is one important qualification to be made to the statement that
councilors are usually re-elected. Their status depends to a large extent on
the fact that they are representatives of their cantons and they must remain
in political contact with their canton and maintain its confidence. If they
lose touch with the prevailing opinion in their home canton, they may not
be re-elected.

The Council is a collegial body but each of the members is given direction
of one department. Before discussing the division of decision-making power
between the Council as a collegial body and each of the members as head
of one department it is necessary to take account of the special position of
the Federal President. Like his colleagues, the President is head of one of
the departments, and since 1914, no particular department has been specially
associated with the President. The President is the closest approximation
that the Swiss have to the office in other countries associated with the title of
Head of State. In this capacity, the President represents the federation in
both internal and external affairs, i.e., he officiates at ceremonial functions,
receives foreign representatives, etc. From this capacity the President derives no political powers and his symbolic role is a very small one. He is,
however, given a few functions which differentiate him from his fellow councilors: (a) he presides at sessions of the Council; (b) he is charged with
the general supervision of the work of the Council and ensures the proper
carrying out of the departmental tasks (under this heading may also be mentioned his right of granting leaves of absence to the other councilors); (c)
in case of tie votes in the Council, he is given a second casting vote; (d) in
situations of urgency, the President may act for the whole Council with the
proviso that such action must immediately be communicated to the whole
Council for its approval; (e) besides his regular department, the President
is responsible for the work of the Chancellery (secretariat); (f) he signs both
laws and ordinances of the Council. Except for his potential role in emer-

gencies, which may be increased by delegation from the Bundesrat, the status of the President is little more than that of Chairman of the Council. He is truly a *primus inter pares*.

V. The Council and Decision-making

According to the original conception of the Constitution each member of the Council was entrusted with the supervision of his department but all decisions had to emanate from the Council as a whole. This has proved impractical and, since 1914, councilors have been granted a large measure of autonomous decision-making power in affairs relating to their own departments exclusively (*Bundesratsbeschluss betreffend die Zuständigkeit der Departmente . . . zur selbständigen Erledigung von Geschäften,* November 17, 1914). However, appeal still lies to the Council as a whole from any decision of one of its members and hence collegial authority is still a fact. The Council acts by majority vote in closed session and, though it is usual for members not to disagree publicly, it is by no means unknown. The fact that members disagree is not, as in Cabinet systems, any cause for resignation of one of the members, as the collegial system does not presuppose the degree of internal solidarity that the Cabinet system does.

Even though the Council has delegated many of its functions to the individual members (and to their department chiefs), the Council is faced with an imposing quantity of work. The chief reason is undoubtedly the constitutional provision that the Council be composed of seven members each heading one department. With the growth of governmental activities this has meant that all new governmental functions have had to be assigned to one of these departments, some of which now deal with an extremely wide variety of subject matter. Though councilors can delegate much of their work in respect to these complex departments to officials, they are nevertheless the only spokesmen for their departmental affairs both in the Council and before the Assembly. They must therefore be familiar with the whole range of work of their departments as well as keeping aware of the major issues in all the departments which are decided at the meetings of the whole Council.

The Constitution makes provision for a Chancellor elected by the Assembly. He is assisted by two Vice-Chancellors and serves as a secretariat for the Council.

VI. The Civil Service

The civil service is recruited on a merit system and there has been no major complaint in regard to distribution of appointments by territorial or linguistic division. For the higher appointments, fluency in two or sometimes three of the national languages is required but on the whole the requirements seem to be interpreted so as to place French and German on an equal plane while regarding Italian as distinctly subsidiary. It may be noted that appointments to the service are for a definite term and not for life although reappointment is so customary that the distinction is perhaps not significant.

VII. FEDERAL AND CANTON EXECUTIVE COMPETENCE

Though the Swiss Constitution defines the area of federal legislative competence it does not mention specifically the area of federal executive competence. Unlike American and Dominion practice, federal executive competence is not coextensive with the legislative area, as the bulk of federal legislation is executed by the cantons. The execution of federal policy by the cantons raises certain problems which require discussion. Is the function of the Council to "supervise" cantonal execution of federal policy to ensure that the administration is within the letter and the spirit of federal law? This supervision is carried on, not directly over the cantonal officials who execute the policy, but rather over the cantonal governments as such which are responsible for carrying it out. This supervision includes not only examination of cantonal ordinances for the carrying out of federal policy, but also the right of giving general directions to the cantonal administrations to guide them in the exercise of their functions.

Certain aspects of federal policy are directly entrusted to the cantons by the Constitution while others are given to the cantons by legislation. In the former, in particular, the Constitution generally provides that cantonal ordinances must be submitted to the Federal Council for its approval before these can have legal effect. The Federal Council is thus given direct authority to pass on the constitutionality of cantonal action and may disallow this action if it sees fit.

Any system of federal supervision of cantonal governments and their administration of federal policy is, however, incomplete unless it contains some form of sanction. These coercive measures are necessary, both to ensure the proper carrying out of functions assigned by the Assembly to the cantons and to ensure that cantonal authorities do not trespass on the competence of the federation. The authority to take coercive measures against cantons that do not carry out their federal obligations is assigned by the Constitution both to the Assembly and to the Council but as a general matter of practice the matter lies with the Council. The Constitution does not specify exactly what measures may be taken to coerce a recalcitrant canton, and it appears to be accepted that the measure must be such as to be reasonably designed to achieve the desired end. Warning must precede action but in the last resort the federation may proceed to the use of military force. The cantons do, however, have a dual protection against encroachments on their own sphere by the federation: (a) all action by the Council is liable to reversal by the Assembly, and military action if it reaches a certain degree requires the positive approval of the Assembly within a given period; (b) the cantons are allowed to appeal to the federal court if they consider that any federal measures taken to enforce the execution trespass on their own sphere of competence.

Besides supervision and execution, the federal executive has one other important function in relation to the cantons. This is federal intervention. Intervention does not, like federal execution, mean simply an extension of direct federal execution at the expense of the indirect federal executive authority assigned to the cantons — it means federal executive action in the sphere expressly reserved to the cantons. Federal intervention occurs when the cantons are not able to enforce *their own* laws or to maintain the peace, and may come about either on the application of the cantonal authority to the Bundesrat or by the autonomous action of the federal authorities. The point to be noted here is that the federal executive is on occasion authorized to participate directly in a cantonal executive action within the cantonal sphere of competence.

The Swiss executive is organized unlike that of any other country. Its peculiar features are its collegial aspects, the fact that the executive, though elected by the legislature, is not thereafter removable by it, and the remarkable stability that is assured by the convention of continuous re-election of the members of the Executive Council. The efficient working of the Swiss system has been attested to by nearly all commentators on Swiss government, but numerous doubts have been raised as to the possibility of imitating such a system. These doubts are based on the following grounds: (a) the Swiss have managed to secure a type of executive that is almost non-political but it is often felt that this is due to factors that are non-reproducible, i.e., the relative paucity of issues on which the electorate is divided (i.e., there is practically complete consensus on the foreign policy of neutrality and therefore one of the main political issues common to other countries is removed from dispute); (b) the size of the country permits the use of the referendum and initiative on a much wider scale than would be generally feasible and hence a large number of issues can be directly decided by the people and removed from the authority of the political bodies; (c) the tradition of re-election and cohesion of the Council depends on specific historical factors and without these a Council based on the Swiss model might find it too difficult a task to reach decisions, and would also lose that stability of the executive which is one of the main features of the Swiss government.

A P P E N D I X   V

United States[6]

I. THE PRESIDENT

The executive power of the federal government is by the constitution vested in the President of the United States. Any natural born citizen of

[6] The important constitutional clauses are Article I, §4, cl. 4, §7, cl. 2, and §8, cl. 18; Article II, and Amendments XII and XXII.

the United States is eligible for election provided he is over thirty-five years old and has been a resident in the States for 14 years. The formal method of election through electors is complex, but the practical effect of the electoral system is that the President is chosen by popular plurality vote, or more accurately, he requires a plurality of votes in as many States as between them have a majority of the population. The Vice-President is chosen in the same way.

The President is chosen for a term of four years and is eligible for re-election only once. In case of death or disability, he is succeeded by the Vice-President who except for this contingency has no executive function. The latter's sole duty is to act as presiding officer of the Senate in which he has a casting vote only. Once elected, the President is irremovable during his term with the exception that he may be impeached by the House of Representatives for crimes and removed from office on conviction by the Senate.

Although the President is the only executive officer specifically provided for in the constitution there are, of course, numerous other executive authorities subsidiary to him.

II. THE CABINET

The Cabinet consists of the heads of the executive departments, i.e., of the Departments of State, Treasury, Defense, Justice, Post Office, Interior, Agriculture, Commerce, and Labor. They are appointed by the President and require the confirmation of the Senate which is practically always given. They are removable by the President. The American Cabinet is not to be confused with the institution of the same name existing in countries with Parliamentary government. The primary duty of the members is to supervise the work of their departments in accordance with the general policy laid down by the President. He may call upon them for advice but the Cabinet is not a collective decision-making organ. Decision is essentially a matter for the President who alone bears the full political responsibility for the whole work of the executive department.

The selection of Cabinet members is a composite of many factors. Usually a few positions go to men of high political standing in the party although these tend to be in a minority. A general bow is made to some regional distribution of appointments and there is also a tendency to have the client agencies headed by men acceptable to the groups with which they deal. However, on the whole, administrative capacity and personal connection seem to be the most important factors leading to the President's selection of his Cabinet members.

III. THE EXECUTIVE OFFICE OF THE PRESIDENT

With the growth of governmental business in the twentieth century, the inability of the President to cope singly with the increasing duties of his office became ever more apparent. The Executive Office has been established in order to provide the President with a staff agency to assist him in the coordination and supervision of the work of the departments. The most important agency within the Executive Office is the Bureau of the Budget which scrutinizes all appropriations requested by the departments and is responsible for drawing up the yearly budget which the President is required to submit to the Congress.

Also technically within the Executive Office are several Cabinet Committees, notably the National Security Council, whose function it is to advise the President on specific aspects of policy. These agencies are established by Act of Congress.

IV. OTHER EXECUTIVE AGENCIES

Besides the executive services grouped under the departments, there are also a large number of executive agencies working outside the departments. The chiefs of these agencies are usually appointed and removed in the same way as the Cabinet members and, in the more important agencies, serve a similar function vis-à-vis the President. Such extradepartmental agencies have been particularly prolific in wartime and were responsible for such functions as price stabilization, war production, etc. All these agencies are more or less directly subordinate to the President and follow policy as laid down by him, within the framework of Congressional enactment.

Congress has also established a large number of executive agencies that are largely divorced from Presidential control. These are the independent regulatory commissions that are charged not only with certain executive but also with legislative and judicial functions as well, within their given field of jurisdiction. These commissions consist of members appointed by the President and confirmed by the Senate but the commissioners are not removable by the President for policy reasons and hold office for a fixed term.

Before passing to a discussion of the powers of the President it must be repeated that, except for the independent regulatory commissions, all the executive officers and departments are agents of the President. They may, and certainly do, advise and influence him, but nonetheless he cannot delegate his political responsibility to them. It is in this sense that the American executive is a unitary one, that ultimate decision and responsibility rest in the President alone.

V. POWERS IN RELATION TO CONGRESS

The President is given certain express legislative powers by the Constitution and has acquired more through his role as party leader. He is given the power to veto bills although these may become law if passed again by both houses of the Congress with a two-thirds majority. The veto power has been used extensively and it has been comparatively rarely overridden.

The effectiveness of the power is somewhat reduced by the fact that it is applicable only to bills *in toto* and Congressional majorities have often "tacked" clauses onto essential Acts which the President is unable to veto because he cannot dissent to any specific clause of a bill.

The constitutional basis for the President's exercise of initiative in legislation is found in the clauses that authorize the President to call special sessions of Congress, and to "give to the Congress Information of the State of the Union, and recommend to their consideration such measures as he shall judge expedient." Neither the President nor his Cabinet members may be members of the Congress nor may they introduce bills or participate in debate on the floor of one of the houses. Presidential legislation must therefore be both introduced and defended by the President's party supporters in the Congress. The role of the President in initiating legislation has increased consistently especially in the last twenty years and can be traced to the fact that Presidential elections have become the focus in the discussion of national issues. As leader of his party, the President is held responsible for all policy during his tenure even though he may have little influence in shaping some of it.

Because of the fixed terms of the President and of the houses of the Congress (all three of which are different), disagreement between President and Congress is usual on at least some issues while on occasion a different party may be in control of Congress than that which holds the Presidency. To the extent that this situation occurs, the President loses his role of legislative leader and may find it impossible to implement his own policies. The independence of Congress and President and the resultant lack of co-operation between them has been a subject for endless discussion and proposals. The effect is undoubtedly that legislation does not fit into a unified policy, especially as Congressional majorities do not consist of disciplined blocs, but rather tend to be composed of shifting groups. The extent to which the President can impose his leadership on the Congress is largely a matter of personality and the degree of support he can muster by periodic direct appeal to the people. He is of course aided by the technical resources and information in the executive departments, and such party discipline as he can command reinforced by the considerable patronage that he has to dispense.

VI. EXECUTIVE POWERS

The scope of the President's powers as chief executive has been the subject of much dispute centering about the question as to whether he has only those specific powers assigned to him by the Consitution and the laws passed by Congress or whether he has also some inherent power by virtue of being chief executive. His main powers arise from three sources: (1) as chief of the administration, (2) as commander-in-chief of the armed forces, and (3) as the conductor of foreign relations.

(1) The President is required by the Constitution to "take care that the laws be faithfully executed" and from this grant stems his supervision over the executive apparatus.   There are, however, limitations on his control. First, certain administrative agencies have been placed by Congress completely outside his control (above, p. 103), and, second, Congress has vested many functions directly in certain inferior officers, whose authority is therefore not based on a delegation from the President but is autonomous of him.

As chief executive the President is given the power of appointing to civil offices with the consent of the Senate.   The Constitution authorizes Congress to vest the appointing power to inferior offices in the President alone or in the heads of the departments.   The great majority of appointments in the civil service are now made on the basis of the merit system but the appointment power still provides the President with a large amount of patronage to dispense.   It might be added that by a practice known as "senatorial courtesy," the President defers to the opinion of the Senators of his own party in making appointments within their State.

The extent of the President's removal power is still a matter of dispute. It appears that he may remove executive officers on his own initiative, but that in the case of officers with quasi-legislative or judicial authority the Congress may prescribe limitations to his power of removal.

(2) The President is the commander-in-chief of the armed forces of the United States.   For the powers that derive from this, see Study 4, Appendix V.   It may be mentioned here that as commander-in-chief the President exercises the power of federal intervention for the preservation of order within the States.

(3) The President is granted the authority to make treaties with the approval of the Senate.

In conclusion, it may be noted that the President is also the Head of State insofar as such an office may be said to exist.   It is in this capacity that his power of pardoning offenses against the federal laws as well as such duties as receiving ambassadors may be mentioned.   He represents the nation in both external and internal affairs even though the latter role is largely confused by the fact that he is also the leader of one of the parties within the state.

STUDY 3

The Federal Judiciary

I. INTRODUCTION

Federal judicial power is essential to resolve issues which cannot appropriately be left to the member States for final decision. Such issues may be characterized as federal because of their subject matter or because of the nature of the parties involved. The federal judiciary will have the function of safeguarding the supremacy of the Constitution by interpreting and applying its provisions in case of asserted conflict with the laws or public acts of the federal government or of a State government. Similarly the federal judiciary will have the function of promoting the uniformity of federal law by interpreting and applying the provisions of federal legislation. In addition, the federal judiciary should serve to adjudicate controversies between member States, controversies to which the federation is a party (as for example disputes over the ownership of property claimed by the federation or over contracts with the federation) and controversies affecting ambassadors, public ministers, and consuls accredited to the federation.

This study will consider these functions of a federal judiciary (Secs. II, III, and IV); it will then discuss the allocation of these functions within the federal judiciary (Sec. V), the relation of the federal Supreme Court to the State courts (Sec. VI), and the appointment and tenure of federal judges (Sec. VII).

II. THE JUDICIAL FUNCTION IN MAINTAINING THE SUPREMACY OF THE CONSTITUTION

Federal government, as Dicey observed in a celebrated passage, is legalistic government. Since the powers of government are by definition allocated, an arbiter is required to determine the limitations imposed by the Constitution, to check power which has not been conferred, and to authenticate power which has been granted. A Supreme Court has been the institution commonly established by federations to perform these functions. Its responsibility involves passing upon the validity of both federal and State laws and decrees when they are subjected to appropriate challenge.

Only in Switzerland, of the federations studied, must this generalization be qualified; cantonal laws but not federal laws are subject to constitutional review by the Federal Court. This limitation in Switzerland should be viewed along with the special position of the members of the Swiss Federal Court as appointees of the Federal Assembly for a limited term of office, subject to re-election. The Swiss pattern has been the object of some criticism in that country,[1] and whatever may be said in its favor as an expression of a democratic spirit, its balancing of the scales in favor of the central government appears less suited to a European federation than does the more usual model of judicial review found in the United States, Australia, Canada, and Western Germany.

It is worth noting that not every one of these constitutions makes explicit provision for judicial review of constitutional questions, and yet the practice has developed and has been accepted. In the United States it was established a hundred and fifty years ago under Chief Justice Marshall. In Canada the practice has been followed despite the constitutional power of the Dominion government to disallow any provincial legislation — a power that might have been regarded as a substitute for judicial review, which is not mentioned in the British North America Act. In order to avoid uncertainty, it would be desirable that a new constitution confer expressly on the federal judiciary the power to determine the constitutional validity of legislation and other public acts of both the central government and the member States.

A more troublesome question relates to the method or procedure by which this function should be carried out. We leave for discussion at a later point the problem of the relation of the federal judiciary to the courts of the member States. Here we shall consider the procedural framework in which judicial review may best be exercised. Specifically, should it be done through the processes of ordinary litigation, through declaratory judgments at the instance of private parties or public officers, or through advisory opinions to the legislative or executive branches of government? This is a problem on which the experience of the major federations is far from uniform.

The advisory opinion is a familiar feature of Canadian practice.[2] The Governor-General may seek the opinion of the Supreme Court on the validity or interpretation of Dominion or provincial legislation, and the Senate or House of Commons may refer to the Supreme Court questions concerning private bills presented in the Parliament. While advisory opinions are not binding, they are reported with the ordinary decisions of the Court and in effect they have virtually the force of such decisions. In Australia, owing to the use of the term "matters" in the Judiciary Articles

[1] See, e.g., Fleiner and Giacometti, *Schweizerisches Bundesstaatsrecht* 933 *et seq.* (1949).
[2] ". . . the typical constitutional reference . . . has become almost the normal method of determining constitutional issues in Canada." Laskin, *Canadian Constitutional Law* 102 (1951).

of the Constitution, the jurisdiction of the High Court is held not to include advisory opinions.[3] Nevertheless the jurisdiction of the High Court to decide suits between the Commonwealth and the States has been construed to permit proceedings to be brought by an attorney general to secure a determination of the validity of national or State legislation after its passage by the legislature, whether before or after it has entered into force.[4] In both Canada and Australia this power in public officers to seek constitutional declarations is in addition to the power of private parties to challenge the validity of legislation in ordinary lawsuits, where the parties are adversely affected in a legally protected interest. The Basic Law of the West German Republic in relation to declaratory judgments seems close to the Australian practice. In Switzerland, on the other hand, not only are advisory opinions precluded, but in general (subject to certain exceptions in case of hardship) the ordinary processes of litigation must be exhausted before a constitutional complaint can be brought, either by a public officer or by a private party. The constitutional issue cannot be raised in the ordinary litigation itself, and of course must relate in any event to a cantonal, not a federal, law.

In the United States the federal courts have no power to render advisory opinions.[5] The theory of constitutional decision is that the power may be exercised when, and only when, the decision in an ordinary lawsuit requires the validity of a law to be considered and adjudged. Normally constitutional questions reach the Supreme Court on appeal from decisions of State courts or of the inferior federal courts. Frequently an officer of the United States or of a State is an original party to the litigation in which a constitutional question is raised, as for example in suits to restrain the execution of a regulatory law or in suits by a taxpayer to recover taxes which have been paid. It sometimes happens, however, that a law is challenged as unconstitutional in litigation to which no public officer is a party. When a federal statute of general importance is challenged in such a case notice must be given to the Attorney General of the United States, who may intervene in the case.[6]

As a formal matter, the lack of power of the federal courts to render advisory opinions is held to stem from the requirement in Article III of the Constitution that the judicial power be exercised in "cases" or "controversies." This requirement is also applied to declaratory judgments where the validity of a law is challenged after its enactment but without a showing of legal injury to the complainant. The declaratory judgment procedure is authorized in the federal courts by federal statute which was not directed particularly to the use of this device for constitutional questions,

[3] In re Judiciary and Navigation Acts, 29 C.L.R. 257 (1921).
[4] Attorney-General for Victoria v. Commonwealth, 71 C.L.R. 237 (1945).
[5] Muskrat v. United States, 219 U.S. 346 (1911).
[6] 28 U.S. Code §2403.

and in fact the Supreme Court has been highly cautious in allowing the declaratory judgment procedure to be employed for that purpose.[7]

Apart from these recitals of actual practice, what are the considerations for and against the use of advisory opinions and declaratory judgments in resolving constitutional questions? The advantages which may be claimed are quite obvious: guidance to the government, and prompt removal of any cloud of uncertainty in the minds of the public regarding the validity of the legislation. The objections are perhaps not so evident. In the United States they go back to the deliberations of the Constitutional Convention of 1787. It was proposed by leading members of the Convention that the judiciary should have a share in a council of revision empowered to veto legislative acts. This proposal was debated at length and defeated. Speaking of this incident, Chief Justice Hughes has observed: "It may be doubted if the Supreme Court would have fared so well, if one of the proposals keenly debated in the Federal Convention had been adopted." [8] In the earliest days of the Republic, President Washington presented a series of questions to the Supreme Court relating to the interpretation of treaties with France. The Court respectfully replied that it would be improper to declare opinions on questions not growing out of a case before it.[9] The policy of deciding constitutional questions only when necessary for the adjudication of legal rights has been reiterated to the present time. Recently the Supreme Court summarized the foundations of the policy in this way:

> The policy's ultimate foundations, some if not all of which also sustain the jurisdictional limitation, lie in all that goes to make up the unique place and character, in our scheme, of judicial review of governmental action for constitutionality. They are found in the delicacy of that function, particularly in view of possible consequences for others stemming also from constitutional roots; the comparative finality of those consequences; the consideration due to the judgment of other repositories of constitutional power concerning the scope of their authority; the necessity, if government is to function constitutionally, for each to keep within its power, including the courts; the inherent limitations of the judicial process, arising especially from its largely negative character and limited resources of enforcement; withal in the paramount importance of constitutional adjudication in our system.

> All these considerations and perhaps others, transcending specific procedures, have united to form and sustain the policy. Its execution has involved a continuous choice between the obvious advantages it produces for the functioning of government in all its coordinate parts and the very real disadvantages, for the assurance of rights, which deferring

---

[7] See, e.g., Ashwander v. TVA, 297 U.S. 288, 324 (1936); Electric Bond & Share Co. v. SEC, 303 U.S. 419, 443 (1938).

[8] *The Supreme Court of the United States* 27 (1928).

[9] *Id.* at 30.

decision very often entails. On the other hand it is not altogether speculative that a contrary policy, of accelerated decision, might do equal or
greater harm for the security of private rights, without attaining any of
the benefits of tolerance and harmony for the functioning of the various
authorities in our scheme. For premature and relatively abstract decisions, which such a policy would be most likely to promote, have
their part too in rendering rights uncertain and insecure.[10]

Thus the objections to advisory opinions and, *mutatis mutandis,* to declaratory judgments are these: (a) the courts would be drawn into the
political processes with the hazards of loss of popular respect and abandonment of truly judicial standards; (b) the responsibility of the legislature for
the formulation of policy would be diluted and weakened; (c) the courts
would be deprived of the benefit of fully developed facts and the light of
experience in assessing the validity of legislation.

The last point deserves emphasis. Constitutional problems of federalism
are likely to present issues of judgment which cannot be solved wisely by
mere examination of verbal texts, but which require the fullest possible understanding of the operation of challenged legislation in the context of social and economic facts. One cannot read the constitutional opinions of
the Canadian and Australian courts, in comparison with those of the
United States Supreme Court, without a sense of abstractness. Doubtless
there are a number of elements entering into the comparison. The
Canadian and Australian Constitutions are technically legislative Acts of
the British Parliament, and their interpretation has tended to follow the
rules of statutory construction, whereas the best tradition of constitutional
decision in the United States has been mindful of Chief Justice Marshall's
admonition that we must never forget it is a Constitution we are expound-
ing. But the habit of rendering advisory and declaratory opinions is surely
responsible in significant measure for the general approach to constitutional problems in those countries as compared with the more concrete appraisal on the basis of the actual operation of legislation in the United
States.

A similar contrast was pointed out by Professor (now Mr. Justice)
Frankfurter between the advisory opinions of a State court and the decisions of the United States Supreme Court on identical constitutional questions:

Advisory opinions are rendered upon sterilized and mutilated issues.
Let any one, for instance, compare the adverse opinions of the Massachusetts Supreme Court upon the constitutionality of municipal coal
and wood yards with the opinion of the Supreme Court sustaining such
legislation; the adverse opinions of the Massachusetts Court on prohibition of trading stamps with the opinion of the Supreme Court sustaining

[10] Rescue Army v. Municipal Court, 331 U.S. 549, 571–572 (1947).

such legislation; the adverse opinion of the Massachusetts Court on
the State's power to provide for dwelling houses with the opinion of
the Supreme Court sustaining such legislation.   These are samples
taken from the court in which, presumably, advisory opinions have been
rendered under the most favorable circumstances.[11]

The requirement of a case or controversy has well been said to reflect a
preference for a judgment from experience as against a judgment from
speculation. If constitutional questions dealt simply with the mechanics of
government, the problem would not be so serious. Questions, for example, presented for advisory opinion to the International Court of Justice concerning the permissible procedures for the admission of new members to the United Nations may not require an appreciation of complex
economic facts such as would be required to decide whether a particular
regulation of trade by a State is an undue burden on interstate commerce.
And in the long run it is the second type of question that will press for solution.

It may be said by way of reply that the kinds of questions which have
proved most perplexing and for which advisory or declaratory opinions
would be least appropriate will be entrusted by the European Constitution
to specialized tribunals such as a Commission on Trade and a Commission
on Human Rights. But it is submitted that the creation of these institutions would not solve the problem. The Supreme Court will presumably
have jurisdiction to consider appeals from these tribunals, and the Court
should have the benefit of the facts as presented to those tribunals in the
first instance. Moreover there will be other fields, not covered by the
competence of the specialized tribunals, where comparable problems of
drawing the line between valid and invalid legislation in a federation must
be faced.

The basic question is how to avoid the dangers of premature and abstract decision on the one hand and avoid the evils of excessive delay on
the other. The question has been well put by Mr. Justice Jackson, speaking of the United States: "Can we not establish a procedure for determination of substantial constitutional questions at the suit of real parties in interest which will avoid prematurity or advisory opinions on the one hand
and also avoid technical doctrines for postponing inevitable decisions?" [12]
The question thus becomes one of devising procedures for expediting decisions of constitutional questions which are inescapably raised in litigation and which ought to be determined promptly in the common interest.
Such procedures are considered in Section VI below, which deals with the
relation of the Supreme Court to the courts of the member States.

[11] "A Note on Advisory Opinions," 37 Harv. L. Rev. 1002, 1006 (1924). One could say of
legislation exposed to advisory opinions what was said in *Hamlet* of the early flowers: "The
canker galls the infants of the spring/Too oft before their buttons are disclosed."
[12] *The Struggle for Judicial Supremacy* 306 (1941).

III. THE JUDICIAL FUNCTION IN PROMOTING THE UNIFORMITY OF LAW

Acts of the national legislature obviously require uniform interpretation, which is traditionally achieved through the role of the Supreme Court
as the ultimate authority in that domain. Occasionally the role of the
Supreme Court in fostering uniformity of law in a federation is broader,
notably in Canada, where the Supreme Court has authority to review the
decisions of provincial courts on non-federal as well as federal questions.
But in Canada the important provincial courts are appointed and maintained by the Dominion, so that in a substantial sense the Supreme Court
of the Dominion is a court of appeal in a unified judicial system.   More
commonly the Supreme Court is not a court of review for the State courts
on questions of State law. The importance of the Supreme Court in promoting uniformity of law thus varies with the extent of national legislation
in the field of private law. Probably the outstanding example of the expansion of such national legislation is Switzerland. In a European federation it seems quite clear that the Supreme Court would properly be limited
to questions of federal, as distinguished from State, law.

There are, however, some intermediate areas. Thus compacts between
the member States should be regarded as giving rise to a federal question in
their interpretation. In the United States this result is reached the more
easily because such compacts require the approval of Congress. Again,
where several member States have adopted uniform State laws, the objective of uniformity tends to be defeated unless there is a central tribunal
charged with ultimate interpretation. This defect persists in the United
States. In Australia and Canada, on the other hand, the Supreme Court
has authority to interpret state legislation. It would be desirable to give
the Supreme Court jurisdiction to resolve conflicting interpretations of uniform State laws; perhaps such jurisdiction should be made conditional on
the assent of the interested States expressed through legislation.

The field of private international law or conflict of laws presents greater
difficulty. The problem is minimized in Australia and Canada, where
the Supreme Court has general jurisdiction over decisions of the State
courts, and in Switzerland, where the important branches of private law
have been codified on a national scale. In the United States questions of
conflict of laws are regarded for the most part as matters of State law and
hence great diversity prevails. In cases which seem to present extreme
misapplications of State law from a territorial standpoint the Supreme
Court, however, has taken jurisdiction of appeals under either the due
process clause of the Fourteenth Amendment or the full faith and credit
clause of Article IV of the Constitution. It should be remarked, incidentally, that there are other forces at work in the United States toward uniformity, notably law schools drawing their students from all parts of the
country, academic treatises, and restatements of various branches of the

law, which are the product of lawyers, judges, and professors, and which, though not authoritative, have an important persuasive effect.

Jurisdiction in a Supreme Court to review conflict of laws questions is not a main essential of a federation, and the differences which have existed in this subject among the European states would probably make it premature to confer such authority immediately on the Court. It would be desirable, nevertheless, to empower the federal legislature to enact rules regarding private international law for conflicts both within the federation and between members of the federation and foreign states and to confer on the Supreme Court authority to decide questions of private international law. What has just been said is not meant to deny the power of the Supreme Court, without special authority, to determine questions of conflict of laws as they may arise in the delimitation of federal legislation. Such a function should accompany the authority to interpret that legislation.

The legislature might well be given the power to enact laws for the registration of judgments of a member State in the courts of another member State. Such a constitutional provision should carry with it a grant of power to the Supreme Court to review questions arising in the enforcement of such legislation; the competence, in the international sense, of the tribunal rendering the judgment would be open to challenge. Moreover, legislative power on the subject of judicial assistance might well be conferred. Pending such legislation, the States having mutual conventions for judicial assistance might be authorized to accept the jurisdiction of the Supreme Court in disputes arising out of the enforcement of these conventions.

IV. The Judicial Function in Determining Controversies Between Certain Classes of Parties

A. Controversies Between States, and Between the Federation and Member States

The constitutions of federations characteristically give power to the Supreme Court to adjudicate controversies between member States or between the federation and member States. Such a grant of jurisdiction is interpreted to constitute a waiver of immunity by the states. In the United States it has been said that this jurisdiction of the Supreme Court is "a substitute for the diplomatic settlement of controversies between sovereigns and a possible resort to force." [13] It should be emphasized, however, that the authority of the United States Supreme Court does not extend to the decision of "political" questions arising between States or between the United States and a State. The controversies which may be brought to the Supreme Court are those which involve an assertion of rights comparable to justiciable interests of private parties. Thus the subject matter of such cases commonly relates to disputes over boundaries, the

[13] North Dakota v. Minnesota, 263 U.S. 365, 372–373 (1923).

utilization of interstate waters, the maintenance of nuisances, the payment of debts, and the like. More than sixty-five cases brought by one State against another have been heard in the United States Supreme Court. A somewhat smaller number brought by the United States against a State have also been heard.

In a European federation it seems advisable to provide a suprastate authority for the adjudication of such disputes, limiting its authority to the adjudication of justiciable controversies as contrasted with merely political issues. It is true that resort may be had to the International Court of Justice. Nevertheless it would be useful if a body of law were established by a tribunal more familiar with the special background of European conditions. Article 95 of the Charter of the United Nations authorizes agreements by member States to submit disputes to a tribunal other than the International Court of Justice.

B. *Controversies to Which the Federation or an Officer Thereof in His Official Capacity Is a Party*

Such cases will usually be covered by one of the other categories, such as the decision of disputes turning on the Constitution or on an interpretation of federal law. There may be cases, however, such as disputes over ownership of property to which the federation lays claim, or over the performance of contracts with the federation, which do not clearly fall within those other provisions. It seems advisable that the federation be allowed recourse to its own judiciary for the decision of such matters. It may be enough to authorize this type of jurisdiction and to make it depend on the choice of forum by the federation in a given case, either in bringing the case or in removing it. There will be situations where even this limited choice of forum should probably not be permitted; e.g., cases in which the federation must present a claim in the administration of a decedent's estate or in an insolvency proceeding under the law of a State. Of course, in such instances, if a federal law (such as a federal provision regarding priority of claims) is violated there would arise a federal question for review by the Supreme Court under another head of jurisdiction.

C. *Controversies Between Citizens of Different States*

This type of jurisdiction has been conferred on the federal courts, concurrently with the State courts, in the United States. A similar provision for federal jurisdiction is found in Australia, which here as in many other particulars closely modeled its basic law on the American. In practice this jurisdiction has placed a heavy burden on the federal judiciary without, it seems, any compelling reason for doing so. Historically there was fear that the State courts would be hostile to out-of-state interests. It was not until the adoption of the Fourteenth Amendment in 1868 that a specific equal protection clause was included in the Constitution. Today a case involving discrimination, without rational basis, against a person on the score of residence would be subject to review in the Supreme Court on constitutional grounds. The chief beneficiaries of the diversity of citizenship jurisdiction have been corporations chartered outside the forum state, which are regarded as citizens of the State of incorporation and thus entitled to bring or remove a case to a federal court if a citizen of the forum is an adversary.[14] While a similar jurisdiction obtains in Australia, it is of interest that the Australian High Court has excluded corporations from the definition of nonresidents and has thus avoided one major application of the diversity jurisdiction as it exists in the United States.[15] It is also of interest that in Brazil, where a similar jurisdiction was conferred, it has been abolished.[16]

There seems to be no good reason to follow the American precedent on this point. If a European federation is not prepared to make the conflict of laws a question for the Supreme Court, in the interest of uniformity and the protection of parties against unduly parochial attitudes, it is hard to see how the federation could establish general diversity of citizenship jurisdiction in the federal judiciary. Cases of actual discrimination should, as has been suggested, be referable to the Supreme Court for review on constitutional grounds.

D. *Controversies Affecting Ambassadors, Other Public Ministers, and Consuls Accredited to the Federation*

This sphere of jurisdiction is conferred on the federal courts in the American and Australian constitutions. The purpose is evident: to avoid affronts to the comity of nations through unfortunate exercises of jurisdiction by courts of States which are not in relation with the foreign governments involved. In a European federation, where the member States will retain some diplomatic relations, this consideration is doubtless less weighty. Nevertheless it may be wise to draw a distinction, for purposes of the jurisdiction of courts, between foreign representatives accredited to the member States and those accredited to the federation. Perhaps it would be sufficient to permit such suits, involving diplomats accredited to the federation, to be brought in or removed to a federal court at the instance of the foreign representative involved.

V. ALLOCATION OF FEDERAL JUDICIAL POWER WITHIN THE FEDERAL JUDICIARY

A Supreme Court, it is assumed, will be provided for in the Constitution. The establishment of inferior federal tribunals, it is suggested, may best be

---

[14] See the criticism in Frankfurter, "Distribution of Judicial Power Between United States and State Courts," 13 Cornell L.Q. 499 (1928).

[15] Australasian Temperance Society v. Howe, 31 C.L.R. 290, 339 (1922).

[16] See Riesenfeld and Hazard, "Foreign Courts in Federal Systems," 13 Law & Contemp. Prob. 29, 48 (1948).

left to the legislature, under a grant of power for this purpose in the Constitution. While several federal constitutions have authorized a full system of inferior federal courts, only in the United States has such a parallel system been actually established. In view of the expense involved, as well as possible duplication and confusion of jurisdiction as between these federal courts and the State courts, the burden is on those who would favor such a scheme.

In the United States the inferior federal courts were given jurisdiction from the beginning over controversies between citizens of different States (subject to a minimum amount in controversy, which is now $3000). They were also given jurisdiction of certain federal specialties, such as maritime cases, federal criminal cases, and federal tax cases. Beginning in 1875 the inferior federal courts have had jurisdiction over all cases arising under the laws or Constitution of the United States. Only in the federal specialties, however, has the jurisdiction of the inferior federal courts been made exclusive. Authority to hear cases between citizens of different States and those arising under the Constitution or laws of the United States (save for the special categories) is vested also in the State courts. It rests with the complainant to choose the forum (assuming the minimum amount in controversy) or with the defendant to remove a case from a State court to a federal court before it has proceeded to a hearing. If the case is brought in a State court and is not removed it must proceed by way of appeal to the highest State court before it can be reviewed in the Supreme Court of the United States on the ground that the decision turns on a question of federal constitutional or statutory law.

If, as seems advisable, a European federation rejects the American plan of parallel State and federal courts, it will still be necessary to provide for original federal jurisdiction in limited classes of cases. Special tribunals for the decision of questions relating to interstate trade and to human rights have already been mentioned. In addition, original federal jurisdiction should probably be authorized for federal revenue and federal criminal cases, for actions brought to restrain federal officers in the peformance of their duties, and for actions between States or between the federation and a State.

These are matters which will call for amendment from time to time and are therefore best left for statutory treatment. It should be sufficient for the Constitution to authorize special federal tribunals, whose decisions may be reviewed by the Supreme Court, and to authorize the Supreme Court to take original jurisdiction over such categories of the federal judicial power as may be designated by the legislature.

The last suggestion carries with it a corollary: the division of the Supreme Court into an appellate and an original chamber. The details of a division into chambers may best be put on a non-constitutional basis. It should be sufficient if the Constitution authorizes the Court to establish divisions.

It seems unwise to contemplate a division of the Supreme Court into a constitutional chamber and a general appellate chamber. The function of deciding constitutional questions cannot realistically be divorced from the function of interpreting federal laws and considering other non-constitutional grounds of decision. Constitutional decisions may be avoided or precipitated depending on the interpretation given to a statute, and conversely the interpretation of a statute may be affected by constitutional doubts which a particular construction would produce. It seems unwise to separate functions which are so closely interrelated. Judges are given more scope for resourcefulness in reaching wise accommodations if such an artificial division is not imposed. Furthermore, in the decision of highly charged constitutional issues it would be advisable that all the judges of the Supreme Court participate, lest the decision be thought to turn on the particular panel serving in the case. At the least, it would seem unsound for the Constitution itself to require a division into a constitutional and a non-constitutional chamber.

VI. Relation of the Supreme Court to the State Courts

To what extent should the State courts share in the responsibility of deciding constitutional questions, subject to review in the Supreme Court? To this question a wide variety of answers can be found in the practice of the major federations.

In Canada the advisory opinion or constitutional reference in the Supreme Court has become almost the normal procedure for raising constitutional questions. But such questions can and do arise in the courts of the Provinces and come to the Supreme Court on appeal from the decisions of the highest court of a Province. Also, under the authority of a provincial law and in the discretion of the provincial judge a constitutional case may be removed to the Supreme Court. In Switzerland, generally speaking, a constitutional complaint brought in the federal court must await the exhaustion of remedies in the cantonal courts.

The other federations make provision in one form or another for the removal of a case or a constitutional question to the Supreme Court prior to the exhaustion of State judicial remedies. In Australia a case involving a question of the distribution of constitutional powers between the Commonwealth and the States must be removed to the High Court from a State supreme court. Cases involving other constitutional questions may be removed in the discretion of the High Court or may be appealed by a party to the High Court from an inferior State court.

A variation of the removal device is found in the practice of the West German Republic. There a case must be removed to the Constitutional Court if a State court in which it is pending is of the opinion that a challenged law is unconstitutional. If the State court is of opinion that a law is constitutional the defeated party may, after exhausting his ordinary appellate remedies, appeal to the Constitutional Court by the process of constitutional complaint. In addition, a constitutional complaint may be brought in the Constitutional Court for violation of basic rights as defined in the Basic Law. The distinction between compulsory removal and the right of appeal, turning on whether the State court regards a law as unconstitutional or constitutional, does not appear to be satisfactory. If it were limited to the validity or invalidity of federal legislation the distinction in procedures would have obvious support. But where a State court is of opinion that a State law is constitutional, in the face of an objection that it conflicts with the federal Constitution or a federal law, there is even greater reason for expediting review in the Constitutional Court than where the State court regards a State law as unconstitutional. It may be remarked, in passing, that in the United States account is taken of this need, in the distinction between obligatory review on appeal and discretionary review on certiorari. Where the highest court of a State holds a federal law unconstitutional or a State law constitutional there is a remedy by appeal; the opposite decisions are reviewable only by certiorari.[17]

The device of removal is employed also in the treaty constituting the European Coal and Steel Community. Article 41 provides: "When the validity of acts of the High Authority or the Council is contested in litigation before a national tribunal, such issue shall be certified to the Court, which shall have exclusive jurisdiction to rule thereon."

In the United States, as has already been indicated, cases arising under the Constitution or federal laws may be removed at the outset from a State to a federal court. If not so removed, the case must proceed through the courts of the State to a final decision, at which time review may be sought in the Supreme Court by appeal or certiorari. Thus many important constitutional questions, particularly those involving the validity of State laws, are decided in the first instance by a State court. As was stated by Chief Justice Hughes: "Upon the state courts, equally with the courts of the Union, rests the obligation to guard and enforce every right secured by the Constitution and laws of the United States whenever those rights are involved in any suit or proceedings before them." [18]

The disadvantage of requiring exhaustion of State remedies is, of course, the consequent delay in the final settlement of the question. On the other hand, this procedure permits the issues to be sifted so that a controversy which at first sight may have appeared to present a grave constitutional question may be turned off on a non-constitutional ground and may never have to be entertained by the Supreme Court. What is needed is a system which will preserve, so far as possible, the merit of expedition while not sacrificing the value of preliminary screening.

None of the federations appears to have devised an ideally balanced solution for this problem. The Swiss system may be thought to lean too heavily

[17] 28 U.S. Code §1257.
[18] United States v. Bank of New York Co., 296 U.S. 463, 479 (1936).

on the side of exhaustion of State remedies; the Australian and German, to make removal unduly mandatory in constitutional cases involving the distribution of powers; the Canadian, to place undue emphasis on the discretion of the provincial judge; the American, to confer too much discretion on private parties. The Coal and Steel Community, which employs mandatory removal when the validity of acts of the High Authority or the Council is challenged in a national tribunal, is hardly comparable in this respect because of the limited range of its activities.

The necessary flexibility could be provided by vesting in the federal attorney general the discretionary authority to remove a case from a State court to the Supreme Court when such a course appeared appropriate in the light of the importance of the constitutional question and the interest of the community in a prompt decision. Notice and an opportunity to be heard should be given in any event to the federal attorney general when a constitutional question is raised in a State court. It is felt that compulsory removal might burden the Supreme Court with unsubstantial constitutional questions as well as depriving it of the sifting process whereby constitutional questions may prove to be unnecessary to the decision. On the other hand, to require exhaustion of State remedies in all cases might delay unduly the final decision of urgent constitutional issues. If it be objected that the attorney general of a State should have equal discretion with the federal attorney general, the answer can be given that a State attorney general has no real standing to complain when a constitutional question is tried in the courts of his own State.

A word may be added on the experience in the United States with respect to the time elapsing between the bringing of a constitutional case and its decision by the Supreme Court. If the case is brought in a State court and not removed to a federal court, the total elapsed time may be a year or two, largely depending on the progress of the case in the State courts. If the case is brought in a federal court or removed thereto, there are procedures for expediting appeal to the Supreme Court. A decision of a federal court holding a federal statute unconstitutional may be appealed directly to the Supreme Court without recourse to the intermediate federal Court of Appeals. Moreover, whatever the decision in the lower court, certiorari can be applied for and may be granted by the Supreme Court before the case is heard in the Court of Appeals.[19] Thus although there is no authority to bring a case originally in the Supreme Court (save in controversies between States or between a State and the United States or affecting foreign representatives), prompt decisions can be and have been secured. In the Social Security litigation, only a little more than four months elapsed between the commencement of the case in the district court and the decision of the Supreme Court.[20] In the recent litigation over the President's order taking possession of steel plants, the decision of the Supreme Court was

[19] 28 U.S. Code §§1252, 1254.
[20] Helvering v. Davis, 301 U.S. 619 (1937).

rendered less than two months after the case was brought in the district court.[21] These are examples of expedition where a prompt authoritative decision was obviously of great public importance. At the other end of the scale, certain controversies may wend their way through the courts without ever coming to a decision on constitutional grounds. For example, although there was long-drawn-out litigation challenging the validity of the electric power program of the Tennessee Valley Authority, the Supreme Court finally held that the complainants, private utility companies, had no standing to attack the constitutionality of TVA.[22] The successful operation of the TVA program is some evidence that the community can accommodate itself to the absence of an authoritative pronouncement on constitutionality in an important public enterprise. The public may then be led to consider the enterprise in terms of its wisdom — a question which is too often confused with constitutional validity.

VII. Appointment and Tenure of the Judges

The independence of the judiciary is safeguarded in the federations (though Switzerland and to some extent Germany are exceptions) by life tenure. Two limitations on life tenure are appropriate for inclusion. The first is a provision that a judge may be removed from office for misconduct or incapacity. In the United States removal may be based only on high crimes and misdemeanors and can be effected only by impeachment, which requires action by the Senate and House of Representatives. It may be more desirable to vest the power of removal, which would be exercised only in extraordinary circumstances, in the Supreme Court itself. The second limitation is a provision for compulsory retirement at a fixed age, which might be placed at 75. In the United States no such provision was made in the Constitution, though voluntary retirement at 70, with compensation, after at least ten years of service, is made possible by statute. In Australia, where likewise no provision for compulsory retirement is contained in the Constitution, the Royal Commission in 1929 recommended a compulsory retiring age for future justices at 72 years.[23] While the services of judges who retain their intellectual vigor after the age of 75 would regrettably be lost by a provision such as that suggested above, it is felt that this circumstance is outweighted by the embarrassment surrounding questions of voluntary retirement and by the virtue of securing an infusion of new talent at intervals. Writing in 1928, Mr. (later Chief Justice) Hughes had this to say on the subject:

> Under present conditions of living, and in view of the increased facility of maintaining health and vigor, the age of seventy may well be thought too early for compulsory retirement. Such retirement is too

[21] Youngstown Sheet & Tube Co. v. Sawyer, 343 U.S. 579 (1952).
[22] Tennessee Electric Power Co. v. TVA, 306 U.S. 118 (1939).
[23] Report of the Royal Commission on the Constitution 251–252 (1929).

often the community's loss. A compulsory retirement at seventy-five could more easily be defended. I agree that the importance in the Supreme Court of avoiding the risk of having judges who are unable properly to do their work and yet insist on remaining on the bench, is too great to permit chances to be taken, and any age selected must be somewhat arbitrary as the time of the failing in mental power differs widely. The exigency to be thought of is not illness but decrepitude.[24]

The requirement of life tenure is hardly appropriate for members of specialized tribunals which may perform some adjudicatory functions but which are also part of the administrative process. Difficulties have been caused in Australia owing to the requirement of life tenure for judges and a broad construction of judicial power which has encompassed certain administrative commissions.[25]

The appointment of federal judges, it is everywhere recognized, should be in the hands of the federal government. At the same time the wishes of the member States might well be consulted. In the United States the voice of the States is expressed through the power of the Senate to confirm the nominations made by the President. There are various other ways to provide safeguards on such appointments by the federal government. Thus it could be required that judges be selected from lists presented by specified agencies, such as law faculties, the supreme courts of the member States, or even by the members of the Supreme Court itself. Nomination by the Court itself, however, is open to the serious objection that the Court would to that extent be made a self-perpetuating body, more removed from the currents of popular sentiment than is necessary to assure its independence from outside intervention.

The compensation of the judges would be left, of course, to be fixed by the legislature. But the Constitution should provide that the compensation of a judge shall not be diminished during his continuance in office. This is a characteristic provision associated with the independence of the judiciary.

Similarly the number of judges on the Court should be left to legislation. There may well be occasion to increase the number of judges if the business of the Court requires it. There is, to be sure, a danger that the legislature might provide for additional judges in order to affect the outcome of a matter brought before the Court. Presumably with this danger in mind the treaty constituting the European Coal and Steel Community provides: "the number of judges may be increased by unanimous vote of the Council on proposal by the Court." The requirement that a change be initiated by the Court seems unnecessarily restrictive for the Supreme Court of a federation, since the Court may not be prepared itself to recognize the desirability of additional members. It would probably be sufficient to re-

[24] *The Supreme Court of The United States* 76–77 (1928).
[25] Report of the Royal Commission on the Constitution 251 (1929).

quire that an increase in membership be authorized by a two-thirds vote of the legislature.

It is a corollary of the separation of powers and the independence of the judiciary that the federal judges should not hold any other public office during the period of their judgeship. If a provision to this effect is placed in the Constitution, it should be drawn in terms which would not preclude a judge from accepting an extrajudicial assignment of a temporary character not incompatible with his duties. This is a matter which is best left to the good judgment of the judge himself.

VIII. Conclusions

Suggestions have been made at various points in this study and will not be repeated here. Perhaps it need only be said that a basic problem of constitutional draftsmanship in the field of the judiciary, as in other fields, is the degree to which specific provisions should be included or left to the more flexible process of legislation. Because of the technical questions that are bound to arise in matters of procedure, particularly in the relation of State to federal courts, it would be wise not to encumber the Constitution with the details of the system of judicial review, but to include the essentials and authorize the legislature to prescribe the particulars.

The essentials are: an independent judiciary, resting on definite guarantees of tenure and non-diminished compensation and on a fixed method of appointment; and a Supreme Court with the power to declare legislative or executive acts of the federal or State governments to be in conflict with the federal Constitution, as well as the power to interpret and apply federal legislation. A further point that ought to be settled is whether advisory opinions shall be permitted, or whether the function of passing on constitutionality shall be preserved for actual juridical controversies.

Beyond these provisions, it is suggested that the Constitution should empower the legislature to establish inferior federal courts, and to apportion the original and appellate jurisdiction of the Supreme Court.

Having assured that constitutional questions and the interpretation and application of federal law shall be within the jurisdiction of the Supreme Court, the Constitution should empower the legislature to confer additional jurisdiction on the federal judiciary over controversies between States, those to which the federation or its officers in their official capacity are parties, and those affecting foreign representatives accredited to the federation. The legislature should have power to determine the extent to which any such jurisdiction shall be exclusively conferred on the federal courts, and the manner in which cases may be appealed or removed from a State court to a federal court, including the Supreme Court.

The legislature should also be empowered to provide for judicial assistance among the States, for the recognition and enforcement of judgments of the States, and for the formulation of rules of private international law.

APPENDIX I

Australia

I. Constitutional Provisions

51. The Parliament shall, subject to this Constitution, have power to make laws for the peace, order, and good government of the Commonwealth with respect to: —

(xvii) Bankruptcy and insolvency:

(xxiv) The service and execution throughout the Commonwealth of the civil and criminal process and the judgments of the courts of the States:

(xxv) The recognition throughout the Commonwealth of the laws, the public Acts and records, and the judicial proceedings of the States:

(xxxv) Conciliation and arbitration for the prevention and settlement of industrial disputes extending beyond the limits of any one State:

(xxxix) Matters incidental to the execution of any power vested by this Constitution in the Parliament or in either House thereof, or in the Government of the Commonwealth, or in the Federal Judicature, or in any department or officer of the Commonwealth.

71. The judicial power of the Commonwealth shall be vested in a Federal Supreme Court, to be called the High Court of Australia, and in such other federal courts as the Parliament creates, and in such other courts as it invests with federal jurisdiction. The High Court shall consist of a Chief Justice, and so many other Justices, not less than two, as the Parliament prescribes.

72. The Justices of the High Court and of the other Courts created by the Parliament —

(i) Shall be appointed by the Governor-General in Council:

(ii) Shall not be removed except by the Governor-General in Council, on an address from both Houses of the Parliament in the same session, praying for such removal on the ground of proved misbehaviour or incapacity:

(iii) Shall receive such remunerations as the Parliament may fix; but the remuneration shall not be diminished during their continuance in office.

73. The High Court shall have jurisdiction, with such exception and subject to such regulations as the Parliament prescribes, to hear and determine appeals from all judgments, decrees, orders, and sentences —

(i) Of any Justice or Justices exercising the original jurisdiction of the High Court:

(ii) Of any other federal court, or court exercising federal jurisdiction; or of the Supreme Court of any State, or of any other court of any State from which at the establishment of the Commonwealth an appeal lies to the Queen in Council:

(iii) Of the Inter-State Commission, but as to questions of law only:

and the judgment of the High Court in all such cases shall be final and conclusive.

But no exception or regulation prescribed by the Parliament shall prevent the High Court from hearing and determining any appeal from the Supreme Court of a State in any matter in which at the establishment of the Commonwealth an appeal lies from such Supreme Court to the Queen in Council.

Until the Parliament otherwise provides, the conditions of and restrictions on appeals to the Queen in Council from the Supreme Courts of the several States shall be applicable to appeals from them to the High Court.

74. No appeal shall be permitted to the Queen in Council from a decision of the High Court upon any question, howsoever arising, as to the limits inter se of the Constitutional powers of the Commonwealth and those of any State or States, or as to the limits inter se of the Constitutional powers of any two or more States, unless the High Court shall certify that the question is one which ought to be determined by Her Majesty in Council.

The High Court may so certify if satisfied that for any special reason the certificate should be granted, and thereupon an appeal shall lie to Her Majesty in Council on the question without further leave.

Except as provided in this section, this Constitution shall not impair any right which the Queen may be pleased to exercise by virtue of Her Royal prerogative to grant special leave of appeal from the High Court to Her Majesty in Council. The Parliament may make laws limiting the matters in which such leave may be asked, but proposed laws containing any such limitation shall be reserved by the Governor-General for Her Majesty's pleasure.

75. In all matters —

(i) Arising under any treaty:

(ii) Affecting consuls or other representatives of other countries:

(iii) In which the Commonwealth, or a person suing or being sued on behalf of the Commonwealth, is a party:

(iv) Between States, or between residents of different States, or between a State and a resident of another State:

(v) In which a writ of Mandamus or prohibition or an injunction is sought against an officer of the Commonwealth:

the High Court shall have original jurisdiction.

76. The Parliament may make laws conferring original jurisdiction on the High Court in any matter —

(i) Arising under this Constitution, or involving its interpretation:

(ii) Arising under any laws made by the Parliament:

(iii) Of Admiralty and maritime jurisdiction:

(iv) Relating to the same subject-matter claimed under the laws of different States.

77. With respect to any of the matters mentioned in the last two sections the Parliament may make laws —

(i) Defining the jurisdiction of any federal court other than the High Court:

(ii) Defining the extent to which the jurisdiction of any federal court shall be exclusive of that which belongs to or is invested in the courts of the States:

(iii) Investing any court of a State with federal jurisdiction.

78. The Parliament may make laws conferring rights to proceed against the Commonwealth or a State in respect of matters within the limits of the judicial power.

79. The federal jurisdiction of any court may be exercised by such number of judges as the Parliament prescribes.

80. The trial on indictment of any offence against any law of the Commonwealth shall be by jury, and every such trial shall be held in the State where the offence was committed, and if the offence was not committed within any State the trial shall be held at such place or places as the Parliament prescribes.

118. Full faith and credit shall be given, throughout the Commonwealth, to the laws, the public Acts and records, and the judicial proceedings of every State.

II. Types of Courts

Despite a Constitution which contemplates the existence of parallel hierarchies of courts on both the local and national levels, the Australian Parliament has never found it expedient to bifurcate the present unitary judicial structure in which State courts administer local law and much of the law of the Commonwealth. Justice in Australia has been left to a considerable extent in the hands of the dual-functioning judicial systems of the six States.

Federal questions are dealt with exclusively or concurrently by three separate tribunals. Original jurisdiction in such matters may be exercised by the so-called High Court established by Section 75 of the Constitution, two specialized federal courts created by Parliament, pursuant to Sections 71 and 77 (ii), or by such State courts as Parliament invests with federal jurisdiction in accord with Section 77 (iii) of the Constitution. The High Court, in addition, is a final appellate tribunal for all Australian courts.

The colonial link with Britain is maintained by Section 74 of the Constitution which preserves the possibility of appeal from the High Court to the Judicial Committee of the Privy Council in all State and some federal matters. The Committee may also in principle exercise its traditional prerogative to hear appeals direct from the State courts if a non-federal question is in issue.

III. JUDICIAL POWER OF THE COMMONWEALTH

The Constitution of the Commonwealth of Australia, like that of the United States, makes separate provision for each of the three departments of government. The constitutional inference has been drawn that none but the judiciary may exercise judicial power and that the judiciary itself may not be empowered to exercise anything but judicial power. In practice as well as in principle this amounts to a rather definite separation of powers; the judicial power of the Commonwealth is exercisable only by courts duly created in accord with constitutional requirements.

The content of the federal judicial power is defined and broadly limited by the word "matters" within Sections 75 and 76 of the Constitution; the federal judiciary with regard to such matters may perform only traditional judicial functions. Thus, Parliament could not compel the federal courts to deliver opinions on abstract questions as it had attempted to do in the original Judiciary Act, for the word "matters" implies only disputes of the sort ordinarily brought before courts.

IV. APPOINTMENT AND TENURE OF JUDGES

Section 72 postulates the rules governing the appointment of judges and their tenure of office. Although the Constitution does not indicate that the judges of the High Court or of any other federal courts must be appointed for life, it was held by the High Court in the famous *Alexander* case[26] that life tenure for judges was an essential and mandatory characteristic of courts exercising the judicial power of the Commonwealth (except State courts invested with federal jurisdiction), and that any federal tribunal not so constituted may not validly be called a court and so cannot exercise judicial powers.

This doctrine has made the definition of judicial power a matter of considerable importance in Australian law, and the practical results of the interpretation of Section 72 have proved most troublesome. It is not possible to compel a federal judge to retire at any specified age; the Commonwealth has sought to escape senility on the bench by offering a pension to judges after fifteen years of service, but there have been few takers. Moreover, by insisting that federal judicial power be vested only in tribunals whose membership complies with Section 72 as interpreted, the High

[26] Waterside Workers Federation of Australia v. J. W. Alexander Ltd., [1918] 25 C.L.R. 434.

Court has made it certain that all federal tribunals not strictly courts will exercise only non-judicial powers.

The federal government in the past thirty years has resorted increasingly to administrative practice, and the legislation creating administrative tribunals whose members do not enjoy life tenure is frequently subject to challenge on the ground that there has been an unconstitutional attempt to confer judicial power. Administrative efficiency suffers from the excessive caution of administrators who fear the interruption of frequent challenges if not the complete invalidation of some segment of their authority.

V. Relation of National and State Courts
A. *Distribution of Original Jurisdiction*

The pattern of original jurisdiction in the Australian judicial system is exceedingly complex.

Section 75 specifies five subjects which are unalterably within the High Court's original jurisdiction. Just as Parliament may not deprive the High Court of original jurisdiction in these matters, so it is not free to confer an unlimited additional jurisdiction on the Court. Section 76 authorizes Parliament to confer original jurisdiction on the High Court under four other headings. Effect is given to these provisions in the Commonwealth Judiciary Act[27] which vests in the High Court original jurisdiction:

(a) in all matters arising under the Constitution or involving its interpretation
(b) in all matters of admiralty or maritime jurisdiction
(c) in trials of indictable offenses against the laws of the Commonwealth.

The Court may also have original jurisdiction in matters arising under federal legislation where the particular law so provides.

Any one justice of the High Court, though there is nothing to prevent more than one from sitting, can and usually does exercise the High Court's original jurisdiction in all matters not confined to the full court by the Judiciary Act. Thus, original jurisdiction, when exercised, is handled by a single judge sitting in the State in which the cause of action arose or in whatever locale the court chooses.

Two federal courts, the Bankruptcy Court and the Court of Conciliation and Arbitration, enjoy a limited original jurisdiction, the former exercising its jurisdiction concurrent with, the latter exclusive of, the State courts.

State courts pursuant to Section 77 (iii) have been invested with plenary power to hear all federal questions in the first instance unless Parliament in accord with Section 77 (ii) reserves the subject matter for exclusive determination by the High Court or another federally created tribunal. Section 38 of the Judiciary Act does reserve to the High Court exclusive original jurisdiction in:

[27] 1903, §48.

(a) matters arising directly under any treaty
(b) suits between States
(c) suits by the Commonwealth against States or by States against the
    Commonwealth
(d) matters in which a writ of mandamus is sought against an officer
    of the Commonwealth or a federal court.

Section 38A postulates, further, that in matters involving any question as to
the limits *inter se* of the constitutional powers of the Commonwealth and
those of any State, or of the powers of two or more States, the original jurisdiction of the High Court is rendered exclusive. When such a constitutional question arises in a proceeding in a state court, the Judiciary
Act provides (§40 (1)) for an immediate and mandatory removal of the
case to the High Court.

Thus, the High Court original jurisdiction is exercised exclusive of or
concurrent with that enjoyed by federally invested State courts; and in federal matters over which no federal court has been given original jurisdiction (e.g., matters arising under laws made by Parliament), State courts
by default are the only forums where proceedings may be begun.

B. *Distribution of Appellate Jurisdiction*

1. STATE QUESTIONS

The defeated litigant in a State court proceeding involving a matter of
only local import has a choice of appealing to the High Court or to the
Judicial Committee of the Privy Council. If the High Court is chosen, a
further appeal lies to the Judicial Committee from the High Court decision. In practice, the invocation of the Judicial Committee's authority to
settle matters of common law or local legislation is an important but sparingly used recourse. Prohibitive financial preconditions, and the reluctance of the Judicial Committee to grant leave to appeal, leave the High
Court as an equally significant arbiter of State common and statutory law, a
position anticipated by Section 73 of the Constitution.

An appeal of right lies to the Judicial Committee direct from a State
court exercising State jurisdiction if the case involves at least £500. The
High Court imposes only a £300 minimum. All other appeals, including
appeals from the High Court to the Judicial Committee, are by leave of the
court appealed to.

2. FEDERAL QUESTIONS

Appeals in federal matters, regardless of where the case is begun, must be
channeled through the High Court. From a State court acting under invested federal jurisdiction an appeal lies only to the High Court. The
right of appeal is absolute from decisions of the High Court sitting in its
original jurisdiction (usually a single judge), but leave must be granted

in cases below the £300 minimum, coming from State courts invested with federal jurisdiction. Where federal questions are involved, further appeals from the High Court to the Judicial Committee fall into two categories, those involving *inter se* constitutional questions and those raising other federal problems. Section 74 of the Constitution expressly eliminates the appeal to the Judicial Committee in *inter se* cases unless the High Court itself refers such a question to the Committee for an opinion. Where no such question is involved, the special leave of the Committee creates an appeal without the consent of the High Court. But judicial interpretation has imparted such a broad meaning to the words *inter se* that they operate to include nearly every federal issue. In the past fifty years — since the inception of the Australian federation — only a handful of cases involving the interpretation of the Constitution or of federal law have passed beyond the High Court and been settled by the Committee.

VI. Judicial Function in Maintaining the Supremacy of the Constitution

The constitutional definition of judicial power in terms of "matters" precludes the High Court from giving advisory opinions or performing other tasks which fall outside the federal jurisdiction described in Section III. Abstract declarations of law or advisory opinions have been held not to be "matters" within the meaning of Section 75 or Section 76 of the Constitution where the federal judicial power is defined. The Court may not act unless there is some immediate right, duty, or liability to be established by its determination.[28]

The restrictive effect of this rule has been mitigated to some extent by the readiness with which the High Court has permitted the States and Commonwealth to sue each other for declarations as to the constitutional validity of each other's legislation, pursuant to Sections 75 and 78 of the Constitution. Section 75 has been read as conferring a substantive right of action against the States and the Commonwealth in addition to High Court jurisdiction. Though an individual may not challenge legislation unless he is able to show special damage to himself as an individual, any citizen may question the validity of legislation simply by inducing his State attorney general to lend his name to an attack.

If an individual is able to show a personal interest, however, he may avail himself of the provisions of the Judiciary Act which provide for individual citizens a right of action against the Commonwealth or the States although the governmental unit being sued has not consented to the proceeding. In order that an individual may bring an action to have legislation declared invalid it is necessary that his legal rights be affected thereby. But it has been the practice of the High Court to apply this rule non-technically, and to allow interested persons seeking only a declaration

[28] In re Judiciary and Navigations Acts, 29 C.L.R. 257 (1921).

of invalidity to challenge the constitutionality of statutes and regulations. There are, thus, three routes available to the Australian citizen for upsetting legislation: the direct controversy, the suit for a declaration of invalidity, or an attack by a State attorney general. Where an interest is touched on by offending legislation, it is no objection to a suit by an attorney general or by an individual that the legislation is not yet operative at the time it is brought.

Power to declare statutes unconstitutional is possessed by virtually all Australian courts, and this power applies to both State and federal legislation as affected by either or both the federal and State constitutions. Although the power of judicial review is not conferred either explicitly or implicitly by the Constitution, the judiciary has clothed itself with this power on the theory that it is a logical and necessary adjunct of the judicial function, and has construed the Constitution to mean that the High Court (subject to a modicum of interference by the Judicial Committee) has the sole responsibility of constitutional interpretation, the duty to determine the validity of the exercise of legislative power.

Because the Australian Constitution does not attempt any comprehensive guarantee of individual rights or liberties the role of the courts in judicial review has been narrower and somewhat less dramatic than in the United States. Most of the constitutional prohibitions are directed at the distribution of legislative powers between the Commonwealth and the States, and the primary task of the courts is to define and enforce this division of legislative authority.

VII. Judicial Function in Determining Disputes Between States

The exclusive original jurisdiction of the High Court extends to disputes between States; under the provisions of the Judiciary Act, one State may sue another in the High Court without the consent of the State being sued, on the theory that Section 75 of the Constitution provides not only jurisdiction for the High Court, but substantive rights for litigants in the disputes specified therein.

VIII. Judicial Function in Determining Disputes Between Citizens of Different States

A resident of one State may sue another State or a resident of another State in the High Court or in a State court exercising federal jurisdiction. In practice, however, this choice has not really been open, since the High Court has narrowly construed its power, and has been reluctant to exercise even the bare unavoidable residue. It has, in fact, taken several overt steps to check the public's resort to its original jurisdiction in such matters. For example, the word "residents" as used in Section 75 (iv) of the Constitution has been held not to include artificial persons such as corporations.

Such a rule effectively eliminates a large segment of litigation from the field of federal jurisdiction.

IX. JUDICIAL FUNCTION IN PROMOTING AND MAINTAINING UNIFORMITY OF LAW

A. *Accommodation of Diverse State Laws*

Section 118 of the Constitution provides for the giving throughout the Commonwealth of full faith and credit to the laws and judicial proceedings of every State. This provision is supplemented by two placita of Section 51 of the Constitution. Placitum xxiv gives to the Commonwealth Parliament a right to legislate with respect to the service and execution of process throughout the Commonwealth and the judgments of the courts of the States. Placitum xxv adds an important power to regulate the recognition of laws and judicial proceedings throughout the Commonwealth. Pursuant to these sections, Parliament has enacted two statutes which modify to a considerable extent the English principles of private international law in force in the States before the establishment of the federation. The various States are considered as foreign jurisdictions to each other, and apart from the modifications imposed by these statutes, the common law rules governing the enforcement of foreign judgments apply as between one State and another.

In the Service and Execution of Process Act, Parliament has provided for the summary registration in any State of all judgments obtained in any other State to become directly executive in the registering State. Once registered, a judgment must be accorded the same force and effect as it would have if rendered by the State where it is registered.

The State and Territorial Laws and Records Recognition Act provides, furthermore, that the judicial proceedings of any State shall have such faith and credit given to them in every court as they have by law and usage in the court of the State where judgment is given.

Another important effect of Commonwealth legislation in this field is the freedom with which Australian State courts may make service on parties to a suit. The Service and Execution of Process Act enables the process of any one State to run throughout the Commonwealth. Jurisdiction is made to depend primarily on the character of the litigation and not on whether the defendant lives, or does business, or owns property in the summoning State.

B. *Interpretation of National and State Law*

In its dual role as both a federal and national court of appeals, the High Court is able to exercise a considerable but not controlling influence over the interpretation of national and State laws. Interference by the Judicial Committee with this High Court function is technically possible but in practice its authority is manifested only in the most important cases involving local law. It may be said by way of generalization that the High Court is the most active court of last resort for Australia and as such it is in a position to synchronize not only the judicial interpretation of Commonwealth law, but also any divergencies which may exist in the common law in force in the States.

Commonwealth legislation enjoys a single uniform interpretation throughout Australia. Appeals from all courts empowered to hear federal questions must be channeled to the High Court. Cases not deemed to involve *inter se* questions have the further possibility of being appealed through the High Court to the Judicial Committee, but for reasons already suggested the latter is not an effective competitor for the High Court's position as the final interpreter of federal legislation and of the Constitution.

The system of judicial precedent in Australia and the position of the High Court and the Judicial Committee as ultimate interpreters of State common law insure that, insofar as the statutes and common law inherited from England have not been modified by subsequent legislation, they remain uniform throughout the Commonwealth. A broad common law is in force throughout Australia, and it is administered by the courts as a general law of the land independent of its source. It is not a federal common law as distinct from that of the States, for the possibility of appealing State decisions on common law matters is a guarantee against a permanent deviation by any State from the accepted common law standards. State legislation, on the other hand, is a confused tangle of heterogeneous laws which often results in a different treatment of the same subject in the various jurisdictions. Such legislation has often interfered with the basic uniformity of Australian common law, but of course it is beyond the power of any court to bring uniformity by way of interpretation to any but uniform statutes.

X. Difficulties in the Australian Judicial System

Apart from the difficulties already mentioned posed by the judicial interpretation of Section 72, impeding the creation of administrative tribunals, there have been other points of criticism. In 1929 the basic provisions of the Commonwealth Constitution Act were investigated by the Royal Commission on the Constitution. With regard to the jurisdiction of the High Court, the following criticism was made by the Commission.

The Commission recommended that subsections (i), (ii), and (iv) of Section 75 of the Constitution be deleted. Subsection (i) is useless, it was said, for no one really knows what is meant by a matter "arising under a treaty." No treaty signed by an executive creates a right or duty in any citizen which may be the subject "matter" of a claim. And if a treaty is adopted by the legislature and so converted into a statute, it is then the statute and not the treaty which affects the right of litigants.

Section 75 (ii) is equally nebulous. When does a matter affect a consul as described in that section? The logical assumption is that the paragraph refers to a consul's official activities only, but the Constitution is vague and leaves the matter open to interpretation.

Finally, the Commission could find no compelling necessity for the provisions of Section 75 (iv) relating to the High Court's original jurisdiction in diversity suits — a responsibility which it has sought to avoid. Justice Dixon criticized the apparent assumption on the part of the founders that diverse parties cannot be expected to receive fair treatment in State courts. The possibility of appeal to the High Court, it was felt, makes the special federal jurisdiction of diversity suits an unnecessary complication in an already intricate jurisdictional pattern.

APPENDIX II

Canada

I. CONSTITUTIONAL PROVISIONS

91. It shall be lawful for the Queen, by and with the Advice and Consent of the Senate and House of Commons, to make Laws for the Peace, Order, and good Government of Canada, in relation to all Matters not coming within the Classes of Subjects by this Act assigned exclusively to the Legislatures of the Provinces, and for greater Certainty, but not so as to restrict the Generality of the foregoing Terms of this Section, it is hereby declared that (notwithstanding anything in this Act) the exclusive Legislative Authority of the Parliament of Canada extends to all Matters coming within the Classes of Subjects next hereinafter enumerated; that is to say: —

27. The Criminal Law, except the Constitution of Courts of Criminal Jurisdiction, but including the Procedure in Criminal Matters.

92. In each Province the Legislature may exclusively make Laws in relation to Matters coming within the Classes of Subjects next hereinafter enumerated; that is to say: —

14. The Administration of Justice in the Province, including the Constitution, Maintenance, and Organization of Provincial Courts, both of Civil and of Criminal Jurisdiction, and including Procedure in Civil Matters in those Courts.

15. The Imposition of Punishment by Fine, Penalty, or Imprisonment for enforcing any Law of the Province made in relation to any Matter coming within any of the Classes of Subjects enumerated in this Section.

94. Notwithstanding anything in this Act, the Parliament of Canada may make Provision for the Uniformity of all or any of the Laws relative to Property and Civil Rights in Ontario, Nova Scotia, and New Brunswick, and of the Procedure of all or any of any of the Courts in those Three Provinces, and from and after the passing of any Act in that Behalf the Power

of the Parliament of Canada to make Laws in relation to any Matter comprised in any such Act shall, notwithstanding anything in this Act, be unrestricted; but any Act of the Parliament of Canada making Provision for such Uniformity shall not have effect in any Province unless and until it is adopted and enacted as Law by the Legislature thereof.

96. The Governor General shall appoint the Judges of the Superior, District, and County Courts in each Province, except those of the Courts of Probate in Nova Scotia and New Brunswick.

97. Until the Laws relative to Property and Civil Rights in Ontario, Nova Scotia, and New Brunswick, and the Procedure of the Courts in those Provinces, are made uniform, the Judges of the Courts of those Provinces appointed by the Governor General shall be selected from the respective Bars of those Provinces.

98. The Judges of the Courts of Quebec shall be selected from the Bar of that Province.

99. The Judges of the Superior Courts shall hold office during good Behaviour, but shall be removable by the Governor General on Address of the Senate and House of Commons.

100. The Salaries, Allowances, and Pensions of the Judges of the Superior, District, and County Courts (except the Courts of Probate in Nova Scotia and New Brunswick) and of the Admiralty Courts in Cases where the Judges thereof are for the Time being paid by Salary, shall be fixed and provided by the Parliament of Canada.

101. The Parliament of Canada may, notwithstanding anything in this Act, from Time to Time, provide for the Constitution, Maintenance, and Organization of a General Court of Appeal for Canada, and for the Establishment of any additional Courts for the Better Administration of the Laws of Canada.

129. Except as otherwise provided by this Act, all Laws in force in Canada, Nova Scotia, or New Brunswick at the Union, and all Courts of Civil and Criminal Jurisdiction, and all legal Commissions, Powers, and Authorities, and all Officers, Judicial, Administrative, and Ministerial, existing therein at the Union, shall continue in Ontario, Quebec, Nova Scotia, and New Brunswick respectively, as if the Union had not been made; subject nevertheless (except with respect to such as are enacted by or exist under Acts of the Parliament of Great Britain or of the Parliament of the United Kingdom of Great Britain and Ireland) to be repealed, abolished, or altered by the Parliament of Canada, or by the Legislature of the respective Province, according to the Authority of the Parliament or of that Legislature under this Act.

II. TYPES OF COURTS

Canada is divided into ten separate Provinces, each a distinct jurisdiction maintaining and following its own body of law implemented through its own hierarchy of courts headed by a provincial Court of Appeals or a Supreme Court. The federal government exercises an important control over these systems of provincial courts through its power (found in Section 96 of the British North America Act) to appoint and pay the judges of provincial superior, county, and district courts and to impose procedural rules on such local courts effective when they adjudicate federal questions. While the legislative authority granted the Dominion Parliament in Section 101 of the British North America Act is broad enough to allow for the creation of a distinct system of federal courts with a comprehensive jurisdiction of federal matters, Parliament has never chosen to utilize this power. Instead, it has preferred a unitary judicial system in which a single set of provincial courts adjudicates questions of both federal and local import arising between any and all parties. Federal legislation, because there are no specialized courts to implement it, is treated as a part of the law in force in the Provinces and is given effect as such by the provincial courts.

All courts extant at the time of confederation were provincial and were continued intact by virtue of Section 129 of the British North America Act. General authority to regulate and provide the machinery for the administration of justice was left to the Provinces under Section 92 (14) subject only to the federal appointment power. Under Section 92 (14) the Provinces have exclusive authority to make laws with regard to the administration of justice in the Provinces including the constitution, maintenance, and organization of provincial courts both of civil and criminal jurisdiction and including procedure on civil matters in those courts. Only Section 96 subtracts from what amounts to a plenary power in the local legislatures to deal with the judiciary.

Federal courts number only two, the result of Parliamentary enactment under Section 101 of the Constitution. The only important federal court of first instance is the Exchequer Court. It has exclusive original jurisdiction in admiralty, patent, copyright, and trade-mark cases, and in claims against the government for tortious acts or property taken for a public use. In addition, it exercises a concurrent jurisdiction with the provincial judiciaries in all cases in which the Dominion government is a plaintiff, in revenue matters, and in suits against an officer of the federal government. Special jurisdiction may be conferred on the Exchequer Court by the separate Provinces to enable it to hear suits between a Province and the Dominion or between two Provinces which have consented to its jurisdiction. All other Canadian litigation must be commenced in the provincial courts.

The Federal Supreme Court created in 1875 by Parliament is primarily an appellate tribunal and as such exercises over both federal and local matters a decisive and final power which is difficult to overestimate. Its original jurisdiction extends only to the issuance of writs of habeas corpus in connection with commitments under Dominion criminal legislation and to the non-judicial task of giving advisory opinions.

III. THE FEDERAL JUDICIAL POWER

Only Sections 96–101 of the Constitution, labeled "Judicature," deal specifically with federal control of the courts and then only to the extent of outlining a procedure for the appointment and tenure of the judges of certain courts and authorizing the Dominion Parliament to create a separate federal system. No court is created by the Constitution and vested with power to deal with a class of cases.

In practice, a separation of powers is achieved, and the judiciary is prevented from becoming a subordinate branch of the government. The Dominion power (§96) to appoint and pay the officers of certain courts has been interpreted to mean that the functions performed by such courts in 1867, the date of confederation, may not be assumed by any Canadian tribunal which has not been constituted in conformance with the rules of Section 96. The authority to appoint judges has been equated to an exclusive exercise of most judicial powers by the judges of those courts specified in Section 96; provincial legislatures can grant their own appointees (administrative boards are a prime example) little more than administrative duties. In this manner, a rather rigid if ill-defined separation of powers has been effected and the courts provided with a handy tool for invalidating legislation.

Judicial power for lack of specific constitutional provisions is largely a matter of implication either from traditional concepts of judicial activity or from practice which over a period of time becomes controlling. The federal Parliament may broaden or narrow its scope, even impose non-judicial powers on the federal courts such as the duty to render opinions on abstract questions submitted to the Supreme Court for its consideration.

IV. APPOINTMENT AND TENURE OF JUDGES

The judges of the Supreme Court, the Exchequer Court, and the superior, county, or district courts of each Province are appointed by the Dominion Governor-General. All other judicial officers owe their appointments to the Provinces responsible for the courts over which they preside. Sections 97 to 100 of the Constitution impose a set of special rules relative to the exercise of the federal appointment power in certain Provinces and provide for the tenure of judges of Superior Courts during good behavior. The Constitution goes no further. Other provisions for the appointment or tenure of judicial officers are to be found in the statutory enactments of the federal and local governments.

The Supreme Court of Canada, which has varied in size, now consists of nine members. By statute three are required to be appointed from Quebec, in recognition of the special legal and cultural position of that Province. As a matter of custom Ontario enjoys equal representation, so that the remaining eight Provinces furnish in practice only three members of the Court.

V. The Relation of National and State Courts in Practice

A. *Distribution of Original Jurisdiction*

There is little complexity in the Canadian pattern of original jurisdiction. Of the two federal courts, only the Exchequer Court possesses sufficient original jurisdiction (described in Section III above) to detract from the general power of provincial courts to hear cases in the first instance. The only basic limitations on this power are the territorial boundaries of the jurisdiction in which they sit. Cases may arise in the provincial courts in either of two ways: at the instigation of a private party or by a direct proposal — a reference — from the Lieutenant Governor of the Province (this procedure is discussed below). There are no qualifications, constitutional or otherwise, as to the identity of parties, or the matter in controversy, or the amount of money involved which may be deemed preconditions of judicial action.

Where a constitutional question (national or local) is raised in the course of ordinary litigation most Provinces have statutes calling for a delay in proceedings until notice is given to the Attorney General of Canada or of the Province, as the case demands, and the Attorney General accepts or declines the right to intervene. Many provincial statutes also provide for a carefully restricted removal procedure as contemplated by the Supreme Court Act. A judge of a court in a Province with such a statute may at his discretion order any case involving the invalidity of Dominion or provincial legislation removed to the Supreme Court regardless of the amount of money in controversy.

Not all the jurisdiction exercised by provincial courts has as its source the act of a provincial legislature. The Dominion Parliament may confer and has from time to time conferred on provincial tribunals jurisdiction to deal with matters over which the Parliament of Canada by virtue of Section 91 has exclusive authority. In the absence of any special federal provisions for the enforcement of national legislation, the provincial courts have been held to possess an automatic jurisdiction, for the existence of a law presupposes that it will be enforceable in some court. Such jurisdiction may be withdrawn, if Parliament sees fit, and vested exclusively in federal tribunals.

Provincial courts enforcing claims arising under valid Dominion legislation are normally, as a matter of convenience, left free to follow their own rules of procedure. But if the Dominion chooses not to accept provincial rules it may make applicable to any federal matter a special procedure which must then govern the action of the local court.

All criminal prosecutions are brought in the Province where the offense is alleged to have been committed. Section 91 (27) of the Constitution relegates all aspects — substantive and procedural — of the criminal law to the exclusive legislative authority of the Dominion Parliament. This includes both statutory and common law crimes. The provincial courts exercise an exclusive original jurisdiction, but may not interfere with the procedural or substantive rules prescribed by the Federal Criminal Code. A body of separate provincial penal law, it should be noted, has grown up pursuant to Section 92 (15) of the Constitution in connection with the enforcement of provincial legislation. This is distinct from the criminal law of Canada and wholly subject to local regulation.

B. *Distribution of Appellate Jurisdiction*

The matter of appellate jurisdiction in the provincial courts is, like most other jurisdictional matters, subject to the legislative authority of two governmental bodies. In civil matters of local import only, the provincial legislatures have power to adjust the right of appeal in the provincial courts as discretion commands, subject only to the immutable right of the Supreme Court to utter the final word in all cases whether they involve local or national law. The appellate procedure for federal questions and prosecutions under the criminal law of Canada, on the other hand, may be prescribed by the Dominion government.

The Canadian Supreme Court is the final court of appeal for Canada in all matters, federal or provincial. Until 1950, when its authority was abolished by Parliamentary legislation, the Judicial Committee of the British Privy Council was the court of final appeal for Canada. But the Supreme Court has now been raised to paramountcy in the judicial system.

The Supreme Court Act provides for three types of appeals from the courts of the various provinces. Appeals as of right may be taken from a final judgment of the highest court of final resort of a Province where the amount in controversy exceeds $2000. Such a provincial court of final resort may also grant its own leave to appeal where in its opinion the question is one which ought to be submitted to the Supreme Court. A third and most important type of appeal is made possible by Section 41 of the Supreme Court Act which enables the Supreme Court to grant leave to appeal "from any final or any other judgment of the highest court of final resort in a province in which judgment can be had in the particular case." The Supreme Court is, thus, able to hear an appeal from any court the judgment of which represents an exhaustion of the appellant's remedies. Thus the Court is enabled to bring about a substantial uniformity of law in Canada.

VI. JUDICIAL FUNCTION IN MAINTAINING THE SUPREMACY OF THE CONSTITUTION

Individual citizens may challenge legislation only in the ordinary course of litigation; their suits are subject to the normal preconditions of actionability such as the need for a legal interest and a case in controversy. A more direct method, however, is available to the Governor-General of Canada or the Lieutenant-Governors of the Provinces. The Supreme Court Act imposes a duty on the Supreme Court to hear, consider, and answer questions referred to it by the Governor-General in council. Analogous provincial legislation imposes similar duties in favor of provincial officers on the courts of the local jurisdictions. Virtually any matter deemed important may be referred, including questions concerning the constitutionality or interpretation of both Dominion and provincial legislation and abstract questions of legislative power. Opinions rendered in the performance of this duty are purely advisory; they have no binding effect on any party or court. But they are reported along with other court decisions and in practice have nearly the same effect. The Supreme Court may hear appeals from the advisory opinions of a provincial court where the Province has indicated that such an opinion is to be considered a judgment and accorded a similar effect. The practice of submitting references to the courts, even in anticipation of legislation, has become a common and extremely important phase of federal government in Canada.

VII. Judicial Function in Determining Disputes Between Provinces

Section 31 of the Exchequer Court Act confers on that court a special jurisdiction to adjudicate disputes arising between Provinces or between the Dominion and a Province. But the exercise of this jurisdiction is contingent upon the express consent of every Province which may be a party to such a suit. The provincial legislatures are required to pass special acts bestowing jurisdiction on the Exchequer Court before it may regard them as proper parties, plaintiff or defendant. The alternative is a suit in one of the provincial courts from which, as in the case of a suit in the Exchequer Court, an appeal lies to the Supreme Court for final adjudication.

VIII. Judicial Function in Determining Disputes Between Citizens of Different Provinces

No special federal jurisdiction exists for the adjudication of disputes between the citizens of different Provinces or between one Province and the citizens of another. There has not, apparently, been any reason to doubt that a fair and impartial hearing may be had, whatever the provincial court in which the case is brought. Furthermore, the possibility of appeal to the Supreme Court lends assurance that insofar as federal legislation or provincial common law is involved, litigants will have the benefit of the same law applied in the same way regardless of where their suit is begun.

IX. Judicial Function in Promoting and Maintaining Uniformity of Law

Because every Province is a distinct legal personality, each treats the others as foreign jurisdictions. Nothing in the British North America Act commands that full faith and credit be given the judgments and the law of one Province in the courts of another. In two Provinces such judgments must be sued on, and in Nova Scotia the defendant may even resist on the merits. Seven other Provinces have agreed to a Uniform Reciprocal Enforcement of Judgments Act requiring only the registration of judgments as a precondition of enforcement. However, not all judgments are reciprocally effectuated. Criminal decisions are valid only in the Province where the offense is alleged to have been committed.

The presence of a common appeal court for all jurisdictions in Canada in all matters howsoever arising guarantees a uniformity of interpretation to national and uniform provincial legislation as well as the existence of a broad common law in force throughout the Dominion. Any divergence of viewpoints with regard to the proper interpretation of uniform legislation or common law principles can only be temporary, that is, such divergencies may exist only until the Supreme Court has had an opportunity to decide the point in controversy. Aside from its function as guardian of the Constitution, the work of the Supreme Court has been primarily directed at securing uniform law in matters affecting the whole of Canada, rather than the mere correction of errors by the provincial courts. In criminal matters the Court has even regarded provincial appeal court decisions as final unless the judgments of two provincial courts of appeal differed on the same question.

APPENDIX III

Germany

I. BASIC LAW FOR THE FEDERAL REPUBLIC OF GERMANY[29]

I. BASIC RIGHTS

Article 19. (1) Insofar as, under this Basic Law, a basic right may be restricted by legislation or on the basis of a law, this law must be of general

---

[29] Adopted by the Parliamentary Council on May 8, 1949. Finally agreed Anglo-American translation, published in the Monthly Report of the Military Governor, No. 50 (Final Issue), pp. 133 *et seq.*

The following abbreviations are employed:

Basic Law	Basic Law (Constitution) for the Federal Republic of Germany, of May 8, 1949
BGBl.	Bundesgesetzblatt (Official Law Gazette)
BGH	Bundesgerichtshof, High Federal Court
BVG	Bundesverfassungsgericht, Federal Constitutional Court
BVGG	Gesetz über das Bundesverfassungsgericht, Law Concerning the Federal Constitutional Court, of March 12, 1951, BGBl. 1951, I, 243
GVG	Gerichtsverfassungsgesetz, Law Concerning Judicial Administration, in the Version of September 12, 1950, BGBl. 1950, 515
ZPO	Zivilprozessordnung, Code of Civil Procedure, in the Version of September 12, 1950, BGBl. 1950.

application and not applicable solely to an individual case. Furthermore, the law must specify the basic right and indicate the Article (concerned).

(2) In no case may a basic right be infringed upon in its essential content.

(3) The basic rights also apply to domestic juridical persons insofar as the former, according to their nature, are applicable to the latter.

(4) Should any person's rights be infringed by public authority, he shall have recourse to the courts. Insofar as there is no other jurisdiction, the recourse shall be to the ordinary courts.

II. THE FEDERATION AND THE LÄNDER

Article 34. If any person, in exercising a public office entrusted to him, violates his official duty to a third party, responsibility (liability) rests in principle with the state or the public body which employs that person. In a case of willful intent or gross negligence, the (employing body's) right of recourse (against the civil servant or employee) is reserved. With respect to the claim for compensation of damages and to the right of recourse, the jurisdiction of the ordinary courts must not be excluded.

Article 35. All Federal and Land authorities render each other mutual legal and administrative assistance.

IX. THE ADMINISTRATION OF JUSTICE

Article 92. Judicial authority is vested in the judges; it is exercised by the Federal Constitutional Court, by the Supreme Federal Court, by the federal courts provided for in this Basic Law, and by the courts of the Länder.

Article 93. (1) The Federal Constitutional Court decides:

1. on the interpretation of this Basic Law in the event of disputes concerning the extent of the rights and duties of any of the highest federal agencies or of other parties granted independent rights by this Basic Law or by Rules of Procedure of the highest federal agencies;
2. in case of differences of opinion or doubts as to the formal and material compatibility of federal law or Land law with this Basic Law or on the compatibility of Land law with other federal law, at the request of the Federal Government, of a Land Government, or of one third of the Bundestag members;
3. in case of differences of opinion on the rights and duties of the Federation and the Länder, particularly in the execution of federal law by the Länder, and in the exercise of federal supervision;
4. on other public law disputes between the Federation and the Länder, between different Länder or within a Land, insofar as recourse to another court is not provided for;
5. in all other cases provided for in this Basic Law.

(2) Furthermore, the Federal Constitutional Court shall act in such cases as are otherwise assigned to it by federal legislation.

Article 94. (1) The Federal Constitutional Court consists of federal judges and other members. Half of the members of the Federal Constitutional Court are elected by the Bundestag and half by the Bundesrat. They may not belong to the Bundestag, the Bundesrat, the Federal Government, or corresponding agencies of a Land.

(2) A federal law determines the constitution and procedure of the Federal Constitutional Court and specifies in what cases its decisions shall have the force of law.

Article 95. (1) A Supreme Federal Court is established for the maintenance of the unity of federal law.

(2) The Supreme Federal Court decides cases in which the decision is of fundamental importance for the uniformity of the administration of justice by the high federal courts.

(3) The appointment of the judges of the Supreme Federal Court is decided jointly by the Federal Minister of Justice and a committee for the selection of judges consisting of the Land Ministers of Justice and an equal number of members elected by the Bundestag.

(4) In other respects, the constitution of the Supreme Federal Court and its procedures are regulated by federal legislation.

Article 96. (1) High federal courts shall be established in the spheres of ordinary, administrative, finance, labor, and social jurisdiction.

(2) Article 95, paragraph (3), applies to the judges of the high federal courts with the proviso that the place of the Federal Minister of Justice and the Land Ministers of Justice shall be taken by the Ministers competent in the particular matter. Their service status must be regulated by a special federal law.

(3) The Federation may establish federal disciplinary courts for disciplinary proceedings against federal civil servants and federal judges.

Article 97. (1) Judges are independent and subject only to the law.

(2) Judges definitively appointed on a full-time basis to established court offices may, against their will, be dismissed before the expiration of their term of office, or permanently or temporarily suspended from office, or transferred to another position or placed on the retired list, only by the decision of a court and only on grounds and according to the procedures provided for by law. Legislation may set age limits for the retirement of judges who have been appointed for life. In the case of changes in the structure of the courts or their area of jurisdiction, judges may be transferred to another court or suspended from office with the retention, however, of their full salary.

Article 98. (1) The legal status of the federal judges is to be regulated by a special federal law.

(2) If a federal judge, in his official capacity or unofficially, infringes on the principles of the Basic Law or the constitutional order of a Land,

the Federal Constitutional Court may, upon request of the Bundestag, rule, with a two-thirds majority, that the judge be transferred to another office or placed on the retired list. In a case of willful infringement, dismissal may also be ordered.

(3) The legal status of the judges in the Länder is to be regulated by special Land legislation. The Federation may issue general provisions.

(4) The Länder may determine that the Land Minister of Justice shall, together with a committee for the selection of judges, decide on the appointment of judges in the Länder.

(5) The Länder may, in conformity with paragraph (2), provide a regulation for Land judges. Land constitutional law in force remains unaffected. The decision concerning a case of impeachment of a judge rests with the Federal Constitutional Court.

Article 99. The decision on constitutional disputes within a Land may be assigned by Land legislation to the Federal Constitutional Court, and the decision of last instance, on such matters as involve the application of Land law, to the high federal courts.

Article 100. (1) If a court considers unconstitutional a law, the validity of which is pertinent to its decision, proceedings must be stayed and, if a violation of the Constitution of a Land is at issue the decision of a Land court competent for constitutional disputes shall be obtained and, if a violation of this Basic Law is at issue, the decision of the Federal Constitutional Court shall be obtained. This also applies if the violation of this Basic Law by Land law or the incompatibility of a Land law with a federal law is at issue.

(2) If, in litigation, it is doubtful whether a rule of international law forms part of federal law and whether it directly creates rights and duties for the individual (Article 25), the court has to obtain the decision of the Federal Constitutional Court.

(3) If the constitutional court of a Land, in interpreting the Basic Law, intends to deviate from a decision of the Federal Constitutional Court or of the constitutional court of another Land, the (said) constitutional court must obtain the decision of the Federal Constitutional Court. If, in interpreting other federal law, it intends to deviate from the decision of the Supreme Federal Court or a high federal court, it must obtain the decision of the Supreme Federal Court.

Article 101. (1) Extraordinary courts are inadmissible. No one may be removed from the jurisdiction of the lawful judge.

(2) Courts dealing with matters in special fields may be established only by law.

II. Courts of Ordinary (Non-constitutional) Jurisdiction

A. *State Courts*

The basis of the court system is the local courts (*Amtsgerichte*), which have original jurisdiction over minor civil suits and minor criminal offenses. Original jurisdiction in the more important civil and criminal matters is exercised by the district courts (*Landgerichte*); these courts also hear appeals from decisions of the local courts. The principal appellate courts are the district Courts of Appeal (*Oberlandesgerichte*).

Beside these courts of general jurisdiction there exist or will exist *special courts* for specialized fields of the law. The labor courts, which were created under the Weimar regime to handle individual controversies between employees and employers, will be restored, according to a bill submitted by the federal government, on the local and district level, with a Federal Labor Court as the last instance (see B, Federal Courts, below). Administrative courts are established in every State by State legislation, with extensive jurisdiction to review administrative action including the exercise of administrative discretion. Special tax courts regulated by federal legislation (Art. 108 (5), Basic Law) entertain appeals against decisions of the tax authorities.

B. *Federal Courts*

When the German Reich was established in 1871, it was not feared that the application of federal law by State courts would give rise to difficulties. Previous experience with uniform laws such as the Bills of Exchange Act and the Commercial Law in the North German Federation warranted the conclusion that the uniform application of federal law would be sufficiently safeguarded by a federal court superimposed upon the State courts as a tribunal of last instance. In addition, national legislation on the organization of the State courts and on procedure, both civil and criminal, was contemplated at the outset, and, in fact, achieved as early as 1879. Also there was no reason to fear that citizens of one State would be discriminated against in the courts of another State.

These considerations were confirmed by the experience of decades, and hence the Weimar Constitution of 1919 retained the organizational pattern of State courts subject to the reviewing powers of a federal Supreme Court. The Basic Law of 1949 followed this tradition, with modifications which will be discussed presently. It added a Supreme Constitutional Court to which it assigned the role of "guardian of the Constitution."

C. *High Federal Courts*

The Basic Law provides for a "high federal court" each in the spheres of ordinary, administrative, finance, labor, and social jurisdiction (Art. 96).

The most important of these is the High Federal Court (*Bundesgerichts-hof*), which has jurisdiction to determine appeals on questions of law from the lower civil and criminal courts. It was established in 1951, by virtue of the Law to Re-establish Uniformity of Law, of September 12, 1950 (BGBl. 1950, I, 455). This Court is practically the successor of the *Reichs-gericht*, the former German Supreme Court. Its main function is to secure uniform interpretation and application of federal law in civil and criminal matters. In addition it serves as a court of first and last instance in cases of treason (§§134 *et seq.* GVG).

1. THE HIGH FEDERAL COURT AS A SAFEGUARD FOR UNIFORMITY OF THE LAW

The appeal (*Revision*) which is brought before the High Federal Court is a complaint that the Court of Appeal erred in applying a statutory or code provision or in failing to apply the proper provision (§§549 and 550 ZPO). In matters involving a monetary claim the appeal is restricted to cases involving a sum of money exceeding 6000 DM, except where the Court of Appeal grants leave to appeal in its decision. Such leave must be granted whenever an important principle of law is involved, regardless of the value of the claim; it must be granted if the decision of the Court of Appeal is contrary to a prior decision of the High Federal Court (§546 ZPO). In this manner uniformity of interpretation is secured in a system which does not accord binding force to precedents. In criminal matters, where the Courts of Appeal decide as the last instance in minor crimes, they must nevertheless submit the case to the High Federal Court for review if they intend to decide a question of law contrary to a decision of another OLG rendered after April 1, 1950, or contrary to a decision of the High Federal Court.

The High Federal Court is subdivided into "senates" for civil and for criminal matters. There exists a "Great Senate" for each of the two main branches of the law (civil and criminal), each composed of a President and eight associate judges. Detailed provisions are made to prevent contradictory opinions by different senates (§§136, 137 GVG).

2. OTHER HIGH FEDERAL COURTS

The other federal courts are designed for the same purpose of uniformity of law within specialized fields. The Federal Administrative Court (*Bundesverwaltungsgericht*) has not yet been established. The Federal Tax Court (*Bundesfinanzhof*), which continues the tradition of the Reich Tax Court (established by law of June 29, 1950, BGBl. 1950, 257), has jurisdiction to review decisions of the State tax courts. The Federal Labor Court (*Bundesarbeitsgericht*), which is the successor to the Reich Labor Court of the Weimar Republic, is planned as the last instance in labor disputes which are heard by labor courts.

3. THE SUPREME FEDERAL COURT (OBERSTES BUNDESGERICHT)

The Supreme Federal Court which is to be established "for the maintenance of the unity of federal law" (Art. 95 Basic Law) has not yet come
into being. This Court would have the sole task of coordinating the decisions of the high federal courts on "fundamental" questions of law. Since
the specialized federal courts exercise jurisdiction in fields which have long
developed as specialized branches of the law, with statutes and legal concepts
shaped and elaborated for their specific purposes, there may be no real need
for a superimposed coordinating court. The critics of this provision of the
Basic Law point out that there were few conflicts among the decisions of
the independent federal courts of the Weimar Republic, and that if a serious
conflict should arise it could be handled by some simple arrangement such
as a panel composed of representatives of each of the five courts.

D. *Full Faith and Credit and "Judicial Assistance"*

In a federal State with a great diversity of State laws and court jurisdictions a constitutional provision securing recognition and enforcement of
judgments of one State in all other States is imperative. In Germany this
has not proved necessary. Ever since the creation of the German Reich it
was tacitly assumed that as far as the effect of judgments was concerned
Germany was regarded as one territory. Neither the Constitution of the
Empire nor the Weimar Constitution contained any rule comparable to
the full faith and credit clause of the American Constitution. Nor does the
federal Constitution as laid down in the Basic Law. It is likewise predicated upon the unspoken principle that the acts of a State court, whether
a court of general jurisdiction or a specialized court, are effective throughout the territory of the Federal Republic. This principle is reflected in
procedural rules which provide, e.g., that any German court may refer a
pending case to another court if it does not have jurisdiction (§§276, 506,
697 ZPO) or that a court may carry out executions, service of process, and
subpoenas not only within the State but in any other State (§160 GVG).

Where the law permits the taking of evidence outside the trial, the courts
are bound to execute the letters rogatory addressed to them by another
court, or, to use the Continental term, to render one another judicial assistance (Art. 35 Basic Law, §§156 *et seq.* GVG). If the requesting court
is a court on a higher level than the requested court, the latter must comply
with the request under all circumstances; if the request comes from a court
on the same level it may be declined only on the grounds that the requested
court lacks local jurisdiction, or that the judicial act to be carried out is
prohibited under the law of the requested court (highly improbable in
view of the far-reaching uniformity of procedural law), or that it is not
sufficiently specified in the letters rogatory.

E. *The Judiciary*

Judges in the State courts are appointed by the State governments in a manner to be determined by State law (see Art. 98, pars. 3 and 4, Basic Law), and they are subject to the supervision of the State government through the State Ministry of Justice. The federal judges are appointed by the federal government, in accordance with a federal law, which will be discussed presently.

A homogeneous judiciary throughout Germany is achieved by federal rules laying down the qualifications to be met by all candidates for judicial office, whether federal or State. These minimum requirements as defined in the Federal Law Concerning Administration of Justice are: three years' study in the law faculty of a German university, followed by the first examination; probationary period (interne training) of three and a half years, followed by the final examination (§2 GVG). Details are left to the States. Full professorship in a law faculty qualifies for judicial office, regardless of training (§4 GVG). Qualification obtained in one State is recognized in any other State (§5 GVG). Any one who has passed the first examination in one State may be admitted in another State for the probationary period and the final examination (§3 GVG).

F. *Status of Judges Under the Basic Law*

The Basic Law guarantees the independence of judges and their life tenure (Art. 97). They may be removed from office, suspended from office, or retired before the retirement age only by the decision of a disciplinary court in accordance with established legal procedures.

The above guarantee of tenure is in the case of federal judges limited by the impeachment provided for in Article 98, paragraph 2. This is one of the more controversial provisions in this part of the Basic Law. It was obviously believed necessary in order to prevent what had happened under the Weimar regime, where the majority of judges were not staunch supporters of the Constitution. The wording of paragraph 2 may permit the removal of judges on grounds of political conviction. Critics point out that while a judge must be amenable to disciplinary action for certain political activities he should not be punished for his political ideas and in particular not by the Federal Constitutional Court which is basically a political tribunal.

G. *Selection of Federal Judges*

Under the Weimar regime, as under the Emperor, the judges of the Supreme Court were proposed by the Federal Council (*Reichsrat*), which was the body representing the interests of the States in legislative and administrative matters. By custom rather than by law the judgeships were distributed among the States in proportion to their representation in the Federal Council.[30]   Whenever a vacancy occurred, the State from which the holder of the office had come was entitled to suggest a successor, who would, if acceptable, be proposed by the Federal Council and appointed by the head of the executive.

The Basic Law contemplates a more formalized mode of selection.   A committee composed of the State Ministries of Justice and an equal number of members of the federal Parliament is to decide jointly with the federal Minister of Justice; in the case of the specialized High Federal Courts (Federal Administrative Court, Federal Tax Court, Federal Labor Courts, and Federal Social Court) the Ministers responsible for each respective field are substituted for the Ministers of Justice (Arts. 95, 96, Basic Law). The Federal Law Concerning Selection of Judges (*Richterwahlgesetz*) of August 25, 1950 (BGBl. 1950, 368) furnished rules on the manner in which the Parliament (Bundestag) is to elect the members of the Selection Committee who are to counterbalance the State Ministers who are ex officio members of the Committee.   Each party may nominate a candidate, who must be qualified for membership in the federal Parliament and "experienced in the law."   Election is by a specified system of proportional representation. Every newly elected Parliament elects new members to the Committee.   The Committee decides by simple majority in secret ballot.   The federal Ministry concerned then submits the names to the Federal President, who makes the appointment.

III. The Federal Constitutional Court [31]

A. *Jurisdiction in General*

The function of maintaining the supremacy of the Constitution has been assigned to a separate court, the Federal Constitutional Court (*Bundesverfassungsgericht*, Art. 93, 94 Basic Law).   This Court has a very extensive jurisdiction, which actually exceeds that of any other federal Supreme Court. Its jurisdiction is outlined in the Basic Law and specified in the Law Concerning the Federal Constitutional Court (BVGG) of April 16, 1951 (BGBl. 1951, I, 243).   It includes the following:[32]

(1) disputes between the highest federal organs regarding their rights and duties, e.g., conflicts between the President and the Parliament, or between the government and the Parliament;

(2) disputes between the federal government and the States regarding the constitutionality of federal or State legislation in the administration of federal and State law;

---

[30] The votes which each State had were determined by the number of its inhabitants; a State had to have at least one vote.

[31] See von Mehren, "Constitutionalism in Germany: The First Decision of the New Constitutional Court," 1 Am. J. Comp. Law, 70 (1952).   The article deals mainly with problems of judicial review of legislation but contains also valuable general materials on the Court.

[32] See §§13 and 90 BVGG.

(3) disputes between the federal government and the States arising out of the execution of federal law by the States and the exercise of federal supervision;

(4) disputes between States in cases for which no other jurisdiction is provided;

(5) constitutional disputes within a State if State legislation so provides;

(6) disputes over the constitutionality of federal or State law arising in ordinary litigation;

(7) complaints by any person who asserts that his constitutional rights were violated by a public authority (§§90 *et seq.* BVGG);

(8) determination of unconstitutionality of political parties (Art. 21, par. 2, Basic Law) and forfeiture of certain constitutional rights by subversive individuals (Art. 18 Basic Law);

(9) impeachment of the Federal President (Art. 61 Basic Law) and of federal judges (Art. 98, par. 2, Basic Law).

As can be seen from this list alone, the function of the Court goes far beyond that of deciding the constitutionality of governmental acts or of legislation in individual cases. In many respects the Court is entrusted with the final decision of conflicts which are of a political nature and may defy solution by judicial means. Thoughtful critics in Germany point out that while it is inevitable that the Court's decisions have important political consequences, yet it should have been restricted to legal questions proper; the present provisions, it is argued, reflect an overestimation of the potentialities of court action, especially in a country where the judicial power does not have the traditional prestige which it enjoys in the Anglo-Saxon world.

The Federal Constitutional Court is also intended to serve the government in an *advisory capacity* (§97 BVGG). The Parliament, the Federal Council, and the federal government may jointly request the Court to render a legal opinion on a specific question of constitutional law; the same right is granted to the Federal President. Such legal opinions are rendered by the full bench of the Court, while for the purpose of litigation the Court is divided into two senates.

B. *Power to Set Aside Federal and State Legislation*

The power of judicial review comes into play not only as a result of an attack by a party in the course of ordinary litigation but also upon the initiative of governmental organs, of courts, and of individuals.

(a) It is sufficient that there are "differences of opinion or doubts" as to whether a federal law or a State law is compatible with the Basic Law or whether a State law is compatible with federal law (Art. 93, par. 1, subs. 2, Basic Law). Then the case can be brought before the Court by the federal government, a State government, or one third of the members of the federal Parliament (*ibid.*).

The question whether a *proposed* law can be declared unconstitutional *before* it has been passed by the legislature was raised recently when the Social-Democratic members of the *Bundestag* filed a suit in the First Senate of the court asking for a determination whether the Parliament could enact the legislation necessary to carry out Germany's obligations as a member of the European Defense Community without an amendment to the Constitution. The situation was rendered more difficult by the fact that the Federal President requested the Federal Court to furnish him a legal opinion on the same question. The decision held the suit in the First Senate to be premature, and the request for an advisory opinion from the full court was withdrawn.

(b) Whenever a court in a pending case comes to the conclusion that a law which is pertinent to the adjudication of the case violates the Basic Law, it must stay the proceeding and refer the constitutional question to the Constitutional Court.[33] This the Court must do ex officio, independent of whether a party makes a motion to that effect. The same rule applies whenever a court holds that a State law is incompatible with federal law (and hence violates the constitutional distribution of legislative powers between the federation and the States) (Art. 100, Basic Law). The Constitutional Court must give the Parliament, the Federal Council, and the federal government, as well as the parties in the case, an opportunity to be heard (§82 BVGG).

(c) If a party challenges the constitutionality of a law pertinent to the case and the court holds against him, he may carry an appeal to the final appellate court (High Federal Court). Every appellate court will refer the constitutional question to the Constitutional Court if it is of the opinion that the particular law violates the Constitution. If, however, the party gets an adverse decision from the final court of appeal he may carry the case to the Constitutional Court on the ground that the law in question violates one of his basic rights. This remedy, which is known as "constitutional complaint" (*Verfassungsbeschwerde*), was introduced by the Law Concerning the Federal Constitutional Court. Section 90 of that law provides as follows:

Any one claiming that he has been injured by public authority in one of his basic rights[34] or in one of the rights established in Articles 33,[35] 38,[36] 101,[37] 103,[38] or 104[39] may file a constitutional complaint with the Federal Constitutional Court.

[33] In a case where the court holds a law violative of a State constitution, it must refer the question to the State Constitutional Court.

[34] Art. 1–19 of the Basic Law.

[35] Equality of civil rights.

[36] Right to vote.

[37] Prohibition of extraordinary courts.

[38] Due process in court.

[39] Personal liberty.

If recourse to the courts is admissible with regard to the injury alleged, the constitutional complaint may not be filed until the ordinary remedies are exhausted. The Federal Constitutional Court may, however, immediately decide upon a constitutional complaint before the ordinary remedies are exhausted, if the complaint concerns a question of general interest or if the complainant would suffer a serious and irremediable disadvantage by pursuing the regular course of appeal.

The right to file a constitutional complaint in a State Constitutional Court under the law of a State Constitution shall not be affected hereby.

If the Constitutional Court renders a decision favorable to the claimant it declares the law in question null and void and sets aside the decision of the lower court. If the party has exhausted the ordinary appeal, the Constitutional Court remands the case to a competent court (§95, pars. 2, 3, BVGG).

(d) A constitutional complaint against legislation may also be directed by *anyone,* that is, a person who is not a party in a concrete lawsuit, who shows that such legislation violates one of his basic rights mentioned in Section 90, paragraph 1. In that case the complaint must be brought within one year after the law has become effective (§93, par. 2, BVGG). Thus, e.g., if a law were enacted limiting the rights of women to vote or to hold public office, any woman could file a constitutional complaint within one year after the effective date.

C. Power to Set Aside Court Decisions and Governmental Acts

Any court decision and any governmental act may be attacked by way of constitutional complaint, i.e., on the ground that it violates a basic right of the party concerned (§90 BVGG, see above). Where there is a right to appeal in the courts (courts of general jurisdiction or administrative courts) the appeal must first be exhausted. In the case of a governmental act which cannot be challenged in a court, the constitutional complaint must be brought within one year after the act has occurred (§93, par. 2 BVGG).

D. Enforcement of the Decisions of the Court

"The decisions of the Federal Constitutional Court are binding on all constitutional agencies of the Federation and the States as well as all courts and public authorities" (§31, par. 1, BVGG). In cases where the Court declares a law unconstitutional the decision has the formal effect of legislation and its tenor must be published in the Official Law Gazette (§31, par. 2, BVGG).

How can the Court enforce its decisions? This question hardly arises in countries that have a tradition of constitutional adjudication; there the recognized authority of the Court has sufficient weight to assure compliance.

In the Weimar Constitution the execution of the decisions of the *Staatsge-richthof* was assigned to the President of the Reich; and it was argued by the constitutional lawyers — as a matter of theory, which was never put to the test — that there could never be an execution against the Reich itself and even that the Reich President had the right to deny the binding force of a decision and to refuse execution. The government draft of the Law Concerning the Federal Constitutional Court likewise provided for execution by the Federal President. But that was not acceptable to the constituent assembly. The Law gives the Federal Constitutional Court discretion to determine in its decision the person or body that shall be responsible for the execution of the decision; it may also order details concerning the manner of execution (§35).

E. *Selection and Status of Judges of the Constitutional Court*

The Federal Constitutional Court is comprised of twenty-four judges, who are elected by the Federal Council and the federal Parliament in equal numbers (Art. 94 Basic Law; §2 BVGG). Eight of the judges must be taken from one of the High Federal Courts, with the same tenure to which they are entitled there (i.e., as a rule, for life); the remainder are elected for eight years (§4 BVGG).[40] Candidates must be 40 years old, they must have the qualifications required for members of the federal Parliament, the qualifications for judicial office or for the higher administrative service, and in addition "distinguish themselves by special knowledge of public law and be experienced in public life" (§3, pars. 1, 2).

The election by the federal Parliament is made by an indirect method similar to that prescribed by the Law for the Selection of Judges (see above). The Parliament elects twelve electors according to a specified proportional system; a candidate for judicial office who obtains nine electoral votes is elected. (§6). The Federal Council elects its quota of judges with a majority of two thirds (§7). The Chief Justice and his deputy are alternately elected by the Federal Council and the federal Parliament (§9). The elected judges are appointed by the Federal President (§10).

This system is an attempt to combine permanency with change. The eight permanent judges selected from the High Federal Courts form a core which is not subject to political change; the other sixteen reflect the Parliamentary party constellation at a given time and are liable to be replaced after eight years (although re-election is permissible). Yet under the rule that a candidate must obtain nine electoral votes it is highly probable that as a rule he will be elected by a coalition of parties. Should one party succeed in electing nine electors, then it is true that it could man the Court with eight judges of its choice at one election. Yet that would leave the eight permanent members and the eight members remaining from the preceding election (under the staggered system) as a counterpoise. The ex-

---

[40] In the first election, half of the judges are elected for four years only (§4 BVGG).

perience with the first election showed that while the State governments represented in the Federal Council on the one hand and the political parties in the Parliament on the other strove to elect judges whose political attitude was close to theirs, yet in the debates less stress was placed on party affiliation than on the question whether a candidate was a "federalist" or a "centralist." Some critics maintain that the Court in order to gain the full confidence of the people and greater prestige should be made less dependent on political fluctuations. One suggestion is to have a gradually increasing number of judges elected for life.

APPENDIX IV

Switzerland[41]

INTRODUCTION

Under the Swiss Constitution and the amendments thereto[42] the federal legislative power extends over a large area of substantive law, including civil, commercial, criminal, and labor law, patent and copyright law, as well as the law of bankruptcy and execution. A federal Code of Obligations (containing also the commercial and corporation law) was adopted in 1881 and revised in 1911 and 1936. A federal Civil Code was enacted in 1907 and a Criminal Code in 1937 (it entered into effect on January 1, 1942). On the other hand, the organization of courts, civil and criminal procedure, and the administration of justice were generally reserved to the cantons (Art. 64. last par. BV). A Federal Court was established for purposes of a limited federal jurisdiction. This jurisdiction is roughly sketched in Articles 110, 112, 113 and 114-bis, with a general clause authorizing federal legislation to enlarge the powers of the Federal Court (Art. 114) and a provision leaving the organization of the Court to federal legislation (Art. 107, par. 2). In order to gain a complete picture of the powers and the functioning of the Court one must read these constitutional provisions together with the Fed-

---

[41] The following abbreviations are used:

AS   Amtliche Sammlung der Bundesgesetze, Official Gazette of Federal Laws
BG   Bundesgericht, Federal Court
BStPO   Bundesstrafprozessordnung, Code of Federal Criminal Procedure, of June 15, 1934
BV   Bundesverfassung, Federal Constitution of 1874, as amended
OG   Bundesgesetz über die Organisation der Bundesrechtspflege (Organisationsgesetz), Federal Law on the Organization of the Federal Administration of Justice, in effect since January 1, 1945

The following authoritative works will be referred to by the name of the authors:

Burckhardt, *Schweizerisches Bundesrecht* (5 vols. 1930–1931)
Fleiner-Giacometti, *Schweizerisches Bundesstaatsrecht* (1949)
[42] See especially Articles 64 and 64-bis.

eral Law on the Organization of the Federal Administration of Justice
(briefly referred to as Organizational Law, *Organisationsgesetz,* or OG) in
the amended version of December 16, 1943 (in effect since January 1, 1945).

I. Federal Constitution of the Swiss Confederation of May 29, 1874, as Amended[43]

First Part: General Provisions

Article 58. No one may be withdrawn from his natural judge. Consequently, there may not be established any extraordinary tribunals.

Ecclesiastical jurisdiction is herewith abolished.

Article 59. Any solvent debtor having his permanent residence in Switzerland may be sued for personal claims in the courts of his residence only;
consequently his property may not be attached outside the canton of his
residence for the satisfaction of his debts.

With regard to foreigners the provisions of applicable treaties are
reserved.

Imprisonment for debt is herewith abolished.

Article 60. All cantons are obligated to treat all Swiss citzens in the same
manner as they treat their own citizens in legislation as well as in judicial
procedure.

Article 61. Final judgments in civil matters rendered in one canton shall
be executory in the whole of Switzerland.

Article 67. Federal legislation shall make the necessary provisions for the
extradition of accused persons from one canton to another; however, extradition may not be rendered compulsory for political and press offenses.

Second Part: Federal Authorities

IV. ORGANIZATION AND POWERS OF THE FEDERAL COURT

Article 106. A Federal Court shall be established for the administration of
justice in federal matters.

Juries shall be formed for deciding criminal matters (Art. 112).

Article 107. The members and deputy members of the Federal Court
shall be elected by the Federal Assembly. In the election the Federal Assembly shall see to it that all three official languages of the Confederation
are represented in the Court.

Legislation shall determine the organization of the Federal Court and its
sections, the number of its members and deputy members, their term of
office and their salary.

Article 108. Every Swiss citizen eligible for the National Council may be
elected to the Federal Court.

The members of the Federal Assembly and of the Federal Council and

---

[43] The translation has been specially prepared by Miss M. Magdalena Schoch for the purpose of this study. It follows in part the translation found in Rappard and others, *Source
Book on European Governments* 1–2 *et seq.* (1937).

the officials elected by these authorities cannot at the same time be members of the Federal Court.

The members of the Federal Court may not hold any other public office, whether in the federal or in the cantonal service, nor pursue any other career or exercise any other trade or profession.

Article 109. The Federal Court organizes its own chancery.

Article 110. The Federal Court has jurisdiction in civil-law disputes:

1. between the Confederation and the cantons;
2. between the Confederation on the one hand and corporations or individuals on the other, when such corporations or individuals are plaintiffs and when the dispute reaches a degree of importance to be determined by federal legislation;
3. between cantons;
4. between cantons on the one hand and corporations or individuals on the other, when one of the parties demands it and when the dispute reaches a degree of importance to be determined by federal legislation.

The Federal Court also has jurisdiction in disputes concerning statelessness, as well as those which arise between communes of different cantons over the right of citizenship [in a commune].

Article 111. The Federal Court is obligated to take jurisdiction in other cases when the parties agree to submit such cases to it and when the dispute reaches a degree of importance to be determined by federal legislation.

Article 112. The Federal Court, sitting with a jury which shall decide on the facts, has jurisdiction in the following criminal matters:

1. cases of high treason concerning the Confederation, of revolt and violence against federal authorities;
2. crimes and offenses against international law;
3. political crimes and offenses which are the cause or the consequence of disorders calling for armed federal intervention;
4. charges which a federal authority prefers against officials appointed by it.

Article 113. The Federal Court has furthermore jurisdiction

1. over conflicts of jurisdiction between federal authorities on the one hand and cantonal authorities on the other;
2. over conflicts between cantons which involve questions of public law;
3. over complaints concerning violations of constitutional rights of citizens, as well as complaints of individuals concerning violations of intercantonal compacts and international treaties.

Administrative disputes as determined by federal legislation are reserved.

In all the above-mentioned cases the Federal Court shall apply the laws enacted by the Federal Assembly and those ordinances of the Federal Assembly which are of a general nature, as well as the treaties which the Federal Assembly has ratified.

Article 114. Aside from the cases mentioned in Articles 110, 112, and 113, federal legislation may assign other matters to the jurisdiction of the Federal Court; in particular it may define the powers that are to be given to the Court for the purpose of securing uniform application of the federal laws contemplated in Article 64.[44]

IV-*bis*. FEDERAL JURISDICTION IN ADMINISTRATIVE AND DISCIPLINARY MATTERS

Article 114-*bis*. The Federal Administrative Tribunal shall have jurisdiction over all federal administrative disputes which may be referred to it by federal legislation.

It has also jurisdiction over disciplinary matters of the federal administration which may be referred to it by federal legislation, insofar as these matters have not been referred to a special jurisdiction.

The Administrative Tribunal shall apply the federal legislation and the treaties approved by the Federal Assembly.

The cantons have the right, subject to the approval of the Federal Assembly, to confer upon the Federal Administrative Tribunal jurisdiction over cantonal administrative disputes.

The organization of the federal administrative and disciplinary jurisdiction as well as the procedure to be applied therein shall be determined by law.

II. THE SWISS FEDERAL COURT: FUNCTIONS AND ORGANIZATION

The two main functions of the Federal Court may briefly be defined as (1) maintaining the supremacy of the Constitution vis-à-vis the cantons, and (2) safeguarding the uniform application of federal law in the cantonal courts.

The Federal Court serves the enforcement of the Constitution in two important ways: it determines the dividing line between federal and cantonal powers in conflicts between federal authorities on the one side and cantonal authorities on the other (Art. 113, subs. 1, BV), and it safeguards the constitutional rights of individuals (Art. 113, subs. 3). It is, however, limited in the exercise of this function by the unassailable position which the Constitution has assigned to the federal legislature: no federal law can be tested by the Court for its constitutionality. This limitation was written into Article 113 of the Constitution, which defines the constitutional jurisdiction of the Federal Court but adds that in all such cases the Court is bound to apply the laws and general ordinances enacted by the Federal Assembly. This supremacy of the legislature is to be explained by the general attitude of the makers of the Constitution, who thought more highly of the legislative body than of a court whose members were to be elected by that

---

[44] I.e., the legislation on civil and commercial law, copyrights and patents, bankruptcy and execution.

body; to permit the judiciary to review laws passed by the representatives of the people seemed contrary to the democratic principle.

There is a good deal of criticism among the Swiss on this point.[45] Advocates of judicial review of federal legislation point out that the field of national legislation is constantly widening and that the Federal Assembly, largely relying on its "urgency" powers, has in recent years frequently enacted laws in violation of the Constitution. It is true that the referendum procedure, by which eight cantons or 30,000 voters can demand a direct popular vote on any law or general ordinance passed by the Federal Assembly (Art. 89 BV), offers a certain protection against federal encroachments on the rights of the cantons and the constitutional rights of citizens — provided the people feel strongly enough about it. But this device has been greatly weakened by increasing use of the "urgency clause," i.e., a clause by which the Federal Assembly designates certain general ordinances as "urgent," whereupon they cannot be subjected to a referendum. Therefore the need for judicial review appears more obvious today than it may have been in 1874.

In 1874, when the Federal Court first became a fully independent judicial body, the number of judges was fixed at nine. Under the pressure of constantly increasing business, largely due to the broadening of national legislation, the number was steadily increased. Today it is between 26 and 28, with between 11 and 13 substitutes (Art. 1 OG). The Court is subdivided into divisions and chambers according to subject matter (Art. 12 OG); the quorum in each is 5, in certain constitutional cases 7 (Art. 15 OG). Uniformity of adjudication among the several divisions is secured by the rule that if one division wishes to decide a question contrary to a previous decision of another division, it must obtain the consent of that division or a joint decision of the divisions concerned or a decision of the full bench (Art. 16 OG).

Since the Constitution declares that German, French, and Italian are the official languages in Switzerland (Art. 116 BV)[46] provisions are made for the equality of the three languages: where the Court has original jurisdiction, the language to be used is the language of the parties or, where they have different languages, that of the defendant; in that case the decision is rendered in the two languages (Art. 19, par. 2 of the Rules of the BG); in criminal matters the language of the accused is used (Art. 97 BStPO); in appeal cases and cases of constitutional complaint, the Court employs the language in which the challenged decision or act was rendered (Art. 37, par. 3, OG).

The Federal Constitution does not expressly proclaim the separation of powers but the principle is implicit in the structure of the government. The independence of the judiciary is, however, declared in Article 21, paragraph 3 of the Organization Law. Organizationally, however, the Federal

---

[45] See, e.g., Fleiner-Giacometti, 933 *et seq.*

[46] "Romansch" is recognized as a fourth "national language" (*ibid.*).

Court is not an autonomous body. It is under the administrative super-vision of the Federal Assembly (Art. 21, par. 1, OG), to which it has to render an annual report (Art. 21, par. 2). The report is to be examined only from the point of view of administrative efficiency in the handling of the Court's business, personnel administration, and other technical matters; the Parliament is not supposed to interfere in any way with the decisions of the Court. Nevertheless, the potentiality exists, and there are occasional reports that the Court has been criticized in the debates for its interpretation of the law (for an illustration, see 2 Burckhardt, No. 625 I). If one bears in mind that the legislature elects the judges, this state of affairs is apt "to keep awake a feeling that to some degree the Federal Court is de-pendent on the federal legislature" (Fleiner-Giacometti, 633).

III. The Jurisdiction of the Federal Court

The Court has original and appellate jurisdiction. Its original jurisdic-tion comprises the following "private-law disputes" (Arts. 110, 111 BV; Arts. 41, 42 OG):

(a) disputes between the federal government and the cantons; claims of individuals or corporations against the federal government pro-vided at least frs. 4000 are involved (excepting claims against the Swiss Railway and some other claims); other disputes which may be referred to the Court by cantonal constitutions or laws with the consent of the Federal Assembly;

(b) disputes between private parties which may be referred to the Court by agreement of the parties, provided a minimum of frs. 10,000 is involved;

(c) disputes between a canton on one side and a private party or corporation on the other, if one party requests it and a minimum of frs. 4000 is involved.

In the field of administrative law it exercises original jurisdiction over the following (Art. 114-*bis* BV; Arts. 110–112 OG):

(a) monetary claims by the Confederation or against the Confedera-tion based upon federal public law, in particular claims arising from civil service status, and disputes between the federal govern-ment and cantons over their respective share in tax proceeds;

(b) other disputes of an administrative character specifically enumer-ated (Art. 111) and those that may be assigned to the Court by legislation;

(c) all other administrative disputes referred to it by agreement of the parties, if at least frs. 10,000 are involved;

(d) disputes within the jurisdiction of a canton which the canton has referred to the Court with the approval of the Federal Assembly.

The Federal Council may provide that defined suits against the federal

government may not be filed with the Court until after a specified administrative agency has ruled on the matter (Art. 113 OG).

In criminal matters the Court functions as a trial court in cases specified
in Article 112 of the Constitution.

By far the more important functions of the Federal Court lie in the area
of judicial review and appeal. These cover the following:

(a) conflicts of jurisdiction between the federal government and cantonal authorities (Art. 114, subs. 1, BV);

(b) disputes of a public-law nature between cantons (Art. 113, subs.
2);

(c) complaints of individuals regarding violation of their constitutional rights by acts of a cantonal government as well as violation
of an intercantonal compact or an international treaty by such
government (Art. 113, subs. 3);

(d) appeals against decisions of federal departments and federal agencies on the ground that they are in violation of federal law, in the
cases specifically enumerated in the Organizational Law (Arts. 97–
99) (administrative appeal);

(e) appeals against decisions of the corresponding cantonal bodies in
the same type of cases;

(f) appeals against the highest cantonal courts in civil and criminal
matters, on the ground of violation of federal law (Arts. 43–50
OG) (civil and criminal appeal);

(g) appeals against cantonal decisions in matters relating to prosecution for debt and bankruptcy (Arts. 75–82 OG).

IV. Relation of Federal Court and Cantonal Courts

The cantonal courts, organized under cantonal law, have jurisdiction in
all matters which are not expressly assigned to the jurisdiction of the Federal
Court either in the Constitution or by federal legislation. As there are no
federal courts on the lower level, there is no concurrent jurisdiction, except
in the rare instances where jurisdiction may be conferred upon the Federal
Court by agreement of the parties (see p. 155 above). The Federal Court
functions as an appellate court which reviews cantonal decisions with regard
to their compliance with the Federal Constitution or federal law, as a rule
after the cantonal remedies have been exhausted.

V. Limitations of Cantonal Judicial Power by the Federal Constitution and by Federal Law

Cantonal procedure may not discriminate against citizens of other cantons (equality before the law, Art. 60 BV). Ecclesiastical courts, extraordinary courts, imprisonment for debt, and physical punishment are sup-

pressed (Art. 58, par. 2; Art. 58, par. 1; Art. 59, par. 3; Art. 62, par. 2). The rule that a solvent debtor must be sued for personal claims (i.e., claims arising from contract or tort) in the courts of his residence and that his property may not be attached outside that canton (Art. 59 BV) is designed to delimit the jurisdiction of courts of different cantons. The full faith and credit clause of Article 61 of the Constitution requires the cantonal courts to recognize and enforce civil judgments rendered in another canton, and their duty to render mutual judicial assistance prior to judgment is implied from that clause. In criminal matters such judicial assistance is made mandatory by statute (Arts. 352, 354 StPO). Moreover, federal legislation has established certain jurisdictional and procedural rules in the interest of uniform application of substantive law, which are binding on the cantons; thus, for instance, the Civil Code contains rules determining which is the proper court, within a canton, for matters of family law and succession, rules relating to the burden of proof, rules on evidence in divorce and paternity suits, and the like.[47] And in connection with appeals from cantonal courts to the Federal Court, the Organizational Law imposes certain uniform standards of procedure on the cantonal courts (Art. 51 OG (pp. 163–164 below)).

VI. Deciding Conflicts of Jurisdiction Between Federal and Cantonal Authorities
(Art. 113, subs. 1, BV; Art. 83a OG)

Any federal authority may complain that in an actual case an administrative or legislative or judicial act of a canton conflicts with the delimitation of jurisdiction as laid down in the Constitution. A cantonal authority may complain against federal administrative acts and simple ordinances of the Federal Assembly, but not against federal laws and general ordinances which it believes interfere with its jurisdiction over the subject matter. Thus the cantons have no judicial protection against federal legislation infringing upon their jurisdiction.

The complaint may not be brought unless the ordinary remedies have been exhausted, and it is not admissible in cases where another remedy has been provided, e.g., where an administrative complaint is expressly sanctioned in the Organizational Law.

VII. Safeguarding Civil Rights
(Art. 113, subs. 3, BV; Art. 84 OG)

This function of the Court is in practice far more important than the adjudication of conflicts of jurisdiction discussed above. It is designed to

---

[47] For a detailed discussion, see Schoch, "Conflict of Laws in a Federal State: The Experience of Switzerland," 55 Harv. L. Rev. 738, 758 *et seq.* (1942).

protect the citizens against cantonal acts which violate one of the individual rights guaranteed in the Federal Constitution and the cantonal constitutions (many cantonal constitutions exceed the guarantees established in the Federal Constitution). The remedy, which is known as "constitutional complaint," may be asserted by individual citizens, by non-citizens to the extent that the Constitution grants them protection, and by corporations (Art. 88 OG). As a rule the complainant must first exhaust the cantonal remedies, except in specified cases where this requirement would work a serious hardship (see Art. 86, par. 2, OG). The decision of the Court is declaratory in nature: it either denies or affirms the alleged violation. The result of the latter decision is that the disputed act is set aside.

A constitutional complaint is furthermore admissible on the ground that a cantonal act violates an intercantonal or international treaty (Art. 113 BV). In the case of international treaties, violations of private-law or criminal-law provisions by a cantonal court cannot be alleged in a constitutional complaint (Art. 84c OG), since such decisions can be appealed in the ordinary procedure as violations of federal law.

VIII. How the Function of Safeguarding the Constitution Is Performed

As has been indicated in the foregoing, the Federal Court performs its functions in safeguarding the Constitution only on the initiative of the parties actually affected by the act which they challenge. It does not decide questions of constitutionality *in abstracto;* nor does it render advisory opinions. In this respect it can be compared to the United States Supreme Court. In contrast, however, to the latter system, federal laws and decrees of general importance enacted by the Federal Assembly are not reviewable (Art. 113 BV). Although the Constitution does not also exclude acts of the Federal Council and of federal administrative authorities from judicial review, the Organizational Law has limited the constitutional complaint to the challenge of cantonal acts (Art. 84 OG). However, the issue of constitutionality or legality of acts of the Federal Council or of federal as well as cantonal agencies can be raised preliminarily in the course of ordinary litigation in any cantonal court and in the Federal Court. This right (called *akzessorisches richterliches Prüfungsrecht*) is stated in no provision but is generally executed by the courts.[48] Its effects, however, are small. For the review of all acts of the Federal Council which are based upon federal laws (i.e., a delegation of power in a federal law) is in fact limited to a test of conformity with the laws. There is not also a test of conformity with the Constitution because such a test would in reality be the same as a review of constitutionality of the law itself — and the law is not reviewable.

[48] For details, see Fleiner-Giacometti, 935 *et seq.*

IX. JUDICIAL FUNCTION IN REVIEWING ADMINISTRATIVE ACTS OF FEDERAL AGENCIES (ADMINISTRATIVE APPEAL)

Switzerland does not have a full-fledged system of administrative adjudication. Until 1929, complaints by individuals against acts of federal administrative agencies were, with few exceptions, handled by the administrative hierarchy itself, in the last resort by the Federal Council. After an amendment to the Constitution (Art. 114-*bis*) had authorized the establishment of a federal administrative court, a federal law in 1928 (AS 44, 779) designated the Federal Court as such tribunal and assigned to it jurisdiction to review specifically enumerated acts of specified federal and cantonal agencies (Arts. 97–99 OG). Where a cantonal agency is involved, the cantonal remedies must first be exhausted (Art. 102b OG). The appeal can only be based on the ground that the disputed act violated federal law (Art. 104 OG). If the Federal Court sets the act aside, it may either render its own decision or remand the case (Art. 109 OG).

In order to decide finally conflicts arising out of questions of federal social insurance (sickness and accident insurance, old age and surviving dependents insurance, military insurance) the Federal Insurance Court, a special court not incorporated in the Federal Court, was founded in 1917. Its members are elected also by the Federal Assembly and have nearly the same position and privileges as the members of the Federal Court.

All other disputes over the legality of administrative action continue to be decided by the administrative hierarchy, topped by the Federal Council. As a result a large portion of the activities of federal authorities and agencies is not amenable to independent adjudication — a state of affairs which arouses a good deal of criticism, especially in view of the increasing rule-making powers of the administration.[49]

X. DETERMINATION OF DISPUTES BETWEEN STATES

The Court has original civil jurisdiction over disputes between cantons in matters involving private law (Art. 110c BV; Art. 41a OG), regardless of the value of the object. In its capacity as constitutional court it decides "public law" disputes between cantons (Art. 113, subs. 2, BV) if the government of one canton invokes this jurisdiction and provided that the matter does not belong to the jurisdiction of the Federal Council (Art. 83b OG). Such disputes are mainly concerned with the delimitation of the powers of the cantons *inter se,* as for instance questions of court jurisdiction and conflicts of jurisdiction between guardianship authorities in different cantons. Other cases are border disputes, conflicts arising out of intercan-

---

[49] Cf. Fleiner-Giacometti 908: "The idea of government by law [*Rechtsstaat*] in the Confederation is not fully realized as long as there exists no comprehensive judicial control over the legality of administrative action, i.e., as long as the federal administrative branch is party and judge in one person in administrative disputes."

tonal compacts, or disputes over intercantonal judicial assistance. The highly important intercantonal conflicts over jurisdiction to tax are brought into the Court not as disputes between cantons, but through the constitutional complaint of taxpayers affected by double taxation.[50]

XI. Disputes Between Citizens of Different Cantons

Diversity of citizenship is not a basis of federal jurisdiction in Switzerland. The Constitution makes it the duty of the cantonal courts to mete out equal treatment to all citizens (Art. 60 BV), and cantonal laws or court decisions may be attacked in the Federal Court on the ground that they violate this guarantee.

Parties who do not wish to have their case tried in a cantonal court may, by agreement, refer the matter to the Federal Court if it involves a defined minimum amount (Art. 111 BV; Art. 41c OG).

XII. The Function of the Federal Court in Maintaining Uniformity of Law

The Court performs this function in its capacity as final court of appeal in civil and criminal matters and in matters of prosecution for debt and bankruptcy which are governed by federal law. This jurisdiction of the Court is authorized in Article 114 of the Constitution and implemented by the Organizational Law and other laws.

In civil matters (Arts. 43 *et seq.* OG), some of which are limited by the amount involved (Art. 46 OG), the Court hears appeals against decisions of cantonal courts on the ground that the decision violates federal law or an international treaty (Art. 43, par. 1, OG).[51] The Court reverses the decision of the lower court if the lower court applied cantonal or foreign law in a case where federal law should have been applied, or if the lower court gave an erroneous interpretation to the applicable federal law; it remands the case to the cantonal court if that court applied federal law in a case where cantonal or foreign law governed (Art. 60c OG).

The appeal is as a rule admissible only after the remedies which cantonal law offers have been exhausted, that is, against decisions of the final court of appeal of the canton (Art. 48 OG), with certain exceptions (Arts. 48– 50 OG).

The Organizational Law reiterates the general rule that the procedure in the cantonal courts is governed by cantonal law, but sets up certain uniform

---

[50] The Court proceeded on the strength of Article 46, paragraph 2 of the Constitution, which gives the federal legislature power to enact provisions against double taxation; it interpreted this provision as a prohibition of double taxation which it must enforce even in the absence of a law to that effect. See 1 Blumenstein, *Schweizerisches Steuerrecht* 131 *et seq.*

[51] If violation of a constitutional right is alleged, the proper remedy is the "constitutional complaint" discussed earlier.

standards which must be met (Art. 51 OG) so that the Court has a proper record before it. This is an indirect means of securing some degree of uniformity among the diverse procedural laws of the cantons.

A limited remedy, the so-called "nullity complaint," is granted in cases which are not appealable, if the lower court applied cantonal or foreign law instead of the applicable federal law or if it violated federal rules of court jurisdiction (Arts. 68 *et seq.* OG).

In criminal matters the appellate jurisdiction of the Court has the purpose of securing uniform application of the Federal Criminal Code (Arts. 268 *et seq.* StPO). An appeal against the conclusions of law of the cantonal court may be filed not only by the accused and the public prosecutor of the canton but also, in specified cases, by the federal attorney, who is the federal public prosecutor (Art. 279 StPO). If the Court sets the decision of the lower court aside, it remands the case to that court.

XIII. UNIFORMITY OF CONFLICT OF LAWS RULES

Intercantonal conflicts of law have been practically eliminated by the adoption of national substantive law. But questions of choice of law between Swiss law and foreign law play a fairly important part in the civil jurisdiction of the Federal Court. The Court determines questions of choice of law not only in cases covered by the Federal Law on Conflict of Laws (AS 1892, 369) but also in matters for which no legislative provisions exist, as in the fields of contract, tort, and property. It has deduced its power to do so from the theory that all substantive law includes implicit rules as to its territorial purview.[52] In this way choice of law between federal law and foreign law became a "federal question," and on this basis the Court has developed a considerable body of conflicts rules.

XIV. SELECTION AND STATUS OF JUDGES

The Constitution provides that the judges and substitute judges of the Federal Court shall be elected by the Federal Assembly, and that care shall be taken that all three languages are represented on the bench (Art. 107 BV). Any Swiss citizen who is eligible for the National Council (the lower house of the Federal Assembly) can be elected (Art. 108 BV). Neither the Constitution nor the Organizational Law requires any legal qualifications or training for the office; as a matter of custom, however, only lawyers are selected. The judicial office is an exclusive one: no judge may hold a political office or engage in any other professional or business activities (Art. 108 BV).

Nominations are made by the political parties in the Federal Assembly, and election is performed by the Joint Federal Assembly, i.e., in a joint

---

[52] For details, see Schoch, "Conflict of Laws in a Federal State: The Experience of Switzerland," 55 Harv. L. Rev. 738, 754 *et seq.* (1942).

session of the two houses. The judges are elected for a term of six years (Art. 5 OG) but they can be — and in fact nearly always are — re-elected, so that their appointment is practically for life. The Joint Federal Assembly likewise elects from among the members of the Court the Chief Justice and his Deputy for two years (Art. 6 OG). It is customary that after two years' service the Deputy is elected Chief Justice, and a new Deputy takes his place.

Swiss federal judges have been accorded certain privileges which remove them from the local jurisdiction of the canton where the Court sits (Lausanne in the canton of Vaud) (Art. 9 of the Law Concerning Political and Police Guarantees in Favor of the Confederation, the so-called Guarantee Law, of March 26, 1934, AS 50, 509).

XV. ENFORCEMENT OF THE DECISIONS OF THE FEDERAL COURT

The Confederation does not have its own machinery for the execution of the judgments of the Federal Court. This function is assigned to the cantons. The cantons have a duty to carry out federal judgments in the same manner as they execute final judgments of their own courts (Art. 39 OG). If a canton fails in this duty, a complaint may be filed with the Federal Council, which will then take the "appropriate action" (Art. 39 OG) under Article 102, subs. 2 of the Constitution. It is usually sufficient for the Federal Council (through the federal Department of Justice) to contact the cantonal government and "invite" it to initiate the necessary measures. As a last resort, the Federal Council may set aside a decision of the cantonal agency or court handling the matter (see 3 Burckhardt, Nos. 975 et seq.).

APPENDIX V

United States

I. CONSTITUTIONAL PROVISIONS [53]

ARTICLE III

Section 1. The judicial Power of the United States, shall be vested in one supreme Court, and in such inferior Courts as the Congress may from time to time ordain and establish. The Judges, both of the supreme and inferior Courts, shall hold their Offices during good Behavior, and shall, at stated Times, receive for their Services a Compensation which shall not be diminished during their Continuance in Office.

Section 2. The judicial Power shall extend to all Cases, in Law and Equity, arising under this Constitution, the Laws of the United States, and

[53] These are implemented by Title 28 (Judiciary) of the United States Code, and by the Rules of the Supreme Court.

Treaties made, or which shall be made, under their Authority; — to all Cases affecting Ambassadors, other public Ministers and Consuls; — to all Cases of admiralty and maritime Jurisdiction; — to Controversies to which the United States shall be a Party; — to Controversies between two or more States; — between a State and Citizens of another State; — between Citizens of different States; — between Citizens of the same State claiming Lands under Grants of different States, and between a State, or the Citizens thereof, and foreign States, Citizens or Subjects.

In all Cases affecting Ambassadors, other public Ministers and Consuls, and those in which a State shall be Party, the supreme Court shall have original Jurisdiction. In all the other Cases before mentioned, the supreme Court shall have appellate Jurisdiction, both as to Law and Fact, with such Exceptions, and under such Regulations as the Congress shall make.

The trial of all Crimes, except in Cases of Impeachment, shall be by Jury; and such Trial shall be held in the State where the said Crimes shall have been committed; but when not committed within any State, the Trial shall be at such Place or Places as the Congress may by Law have directed.

Section 3. Treason against the United States, shall consist only in levying War against them, or, in adhering to their Enemies, giving them Aid and Comfort. No Person shall be convicted of Treason unless on the Testimony of two Witnesses to the same overt Act, or on Confession in open Court.

The Congress shall have power to declare the Punishment of Treason, but no Attainder of Treason shall work Corruption of Blood, or Forfeiture except during the Life of the Person attainted.

ARTICLE IV

Section 1. Full Faith and Credit shall be given in each State to the public Acts, Records, and judicial Proceedings of every other State. And the Congress may by general Laws prescribe the Manner in which such Acts, Records and Proceedings shall be proved, and the Effect thereof.

Section 2. The Citizens of each State shall be entitled to all Privileges and Immunities of Citizens in the several States.

A Person charged in any State with Treason, Felony, or other Crime, who shall flee from Justice, and be found in another State, shall on demand of the executive Authority of the State from which he fled, be delivered up, to be removed to the State having Jurisdiction of the Crime.

ARTICLE VI

This Constitution, and the Laws of the United States which shall be made in Pursuance thereof; and all Treaties made, or which shall be made, under the Authority of the United States, shall be the supreme Law of the Land; and the Judges in every State shall be bound thereby, any Thing in the Constitution or Laws of any State to the Contrary notwithstanding.

The Senators and Representatives before mentioned, and the Members of the several State Legislatures, and all executive and judicial Officers, both of the United States and of the several States, shall be bound by Oath or Affirmation, to support this Constitution; but no religious Test shall ever be required as a Qualification to any Office or public Trust under the United States.

AMENDMENT XIV

Section 1. All persons born or naturalized in the United States, and subject to the jurisdiction thereof, are citizens of the United States and of the State wherein they reside. No State shall make or enforce any law which shall abridge the privileges or immunities of citizens of the United States; nor shall any State deprive any person of life, liberty, or property, without due process of law; nor deny to any person within its jurisdiction the equal protection of the laws.

II. JUDICIAL REVIEW IN CONSTITUTIONAL CASES

The authority of the Supreme Court to pass on the validity of federal and State legislation under the federal Constitution is not expressly conferred in the document itself. The authority was asserted by the Supreme Court under Chief Justice Marshall in 1803, with respect to Acts of Congress.[54] Marshall drew largely on the arguments of Hamilton in Numbers 78 and 80 of *The Federalist*, maintaining that a court must necessarily apply the law and in case of conflict between a higher and a subordinate law the former must prevail. Some years later a similar power was asserted with respect to review of decisions of State courts.[55] Although these exercises of power were bitterly challenged at the time, the practice has become a settled one, and it is generally acknowledged that, at least in respect of review of State legislation, the authority is one of the great unifying forces in the United States. Mr. Justice Holmes observed: "I do not think the United States would come to an end if we lost our power to declare an Act of Congress void. I do think the Union would be imperiled if we could not make that declaration as to the laws of the several states." [56]

It was also established at an early date that the power could be exercised in the federal courts only as part of the process of deciding disputes between litigants in what are termed in Article III of the Constitution "cases" or "controversies." Thus advisory opinions cannot be given; so-called political questions, not raising issues which are conventionally justiciable, will not be decided, and States may secure constitutional decisions only as ordinary litigants.[57] When, for example, the State of Massachusetts sought to challenge and restrain the grant of federal funds to the States for maternity ben-

[54] Marbury v. Madison, 1 Cranch 137 (1803).
[55] Martin v. Hunter's Lessee, 1 Wheat. 304 (1816).
[56] "Law and the Court," *Collected Legal Papers* 295 (1920).
[57] See Muskrat v. United States, 219 U.S. 346 (1911).

efits, as an invasion of the reserved powers of the States, the Supreme Court dismissed the suit as non-justiciable.[58]

It should be pointed out, at the same time, that various devices have been employed, sometimes with success, to mitigate the severity of these limits on judicial review. Suits for injunctive relief brought promptly after a law has gone into effect may bring the constitutional question into the federal courts at a very early stage. But the Court has adhered in principle, and generally in practice, to the requirement that one who attacks a statute as unconstitutional must show that his legally protected interests are threatened by the feature of the statute about which he complains.

III. DISTRIBUTION OF FEDERAL JUDICIAL POWER WITHIN THE FEDERAL JUDICIARY

Article III confers certain categories of jurisdiction on the federal courts, defined in terms of subject matter and in terms of parties. The former category includes cases arising under the Constitution, laws, or treaties of the United States. The second includes cases between citizens of different States, cases between two or more States, cases in which the United States is a party, cases of maritime jurisdiction, and cases affecting ambassadors, other public ministers, and consuls.

The *original* jurisdiction of the Supreme Court is relatively restricted by Article III. Such jurisdiction comprises only cases in which a State is a party and those affecting ambassadors, public ministers, and consuls. Article III has been interpreted to permit such cases to be brought in the lower federal courts so long as an option is given to bring them originally in the Supreme Court. Section 1251 of the Judicial Code thus defines the original jurisdiction of the Supreme Court:

(a) The Supreme Court shall have original and exclusive jurisdiction of:

(1) All controversies between two or more states;

(2) All actions or proceedings against ambassadors or other public ministers of foreign states or their domestics or domestic servants, not inconsistent with the law of nations.

(b) The Supreme Court shall have original but not exclusive jurisdiction of:

(1) All actions or proceedings brought by ambassadors or other public ministers of foreign states or to which consuls or vice consuls of foreign states are parties;

(2) All controversies between the United States and a State;

(3) All actions or proceedings by a State against the citizens of another State or against aliens.

The great bulk of cases falling within federal jurisdiction are brought in the federal district courts, of which there is at least one in every state, and

---

[58] Massachusetts v. Mellon, 262 U.S. 447 (1923).

reach the Supreme Court in its *appellate* jurisdiction. The territorial jurisdiction of a district court extends, with certain exceptions, only within the boundaries of the State in which it is situated. The principal heads of jurisdiction in the district courts are diversity of citizenship cases and cases arising under the Constitution, laws, or treaties of the United States. In diversity of citizenship cases there must be involved at least $3000. The same is true of cases arising under the Constitution, laws, or treaties, with certain important exceptions. Among these exceptions are cases to redress the deprivation of civil rights by any act done under color of State law (28 U.S. Code §1343).

Between the district courts and the Supreme Court stand the federal Courts of Appeals, of which there is one for each of ten judicial circuits, as well as one for the District of Columbia. Normally appeals from district courts must be taken to the Court of Appeals for the appropriate circuit. Review by the Supreme Court of decisions of the Court of Appeals is largely discretionary, depending on the general importance of the question or the need to resolve a conflict of decisions among the circuits.[59]

A limited but important group of cases may be appealed directly from a district court to the Supreme Court. This group includes decisions holding an Act of Congress unconstitutional and decisions in suits to restrain the enforcement of a Federal or State law on the ground of unconstitutionality. In the latter type of case, the district court must be composed of three (instead of the usual one) judges.

It will thus be seen that the function of the Supreme Court in the federal hierarchy is chiefly appellate, and that it has a large degree of control over its own docket by reason of discretionary review (save in direct appeals from the district courts).

The Supreme Court has for many years consisted of nine members. It does not sit in panels or divisions. Every Justice who is not disqualified participates in the hearing and decision of every case, whether it be original or appellate. One of the objections raised against President Roosevelt's plan in 1937 to increase the size of the Supreme Court to a maximum of fifteen was that the Court would be less able to act upon full consultation and discussion among its members or would be forced to divide itself into panels. This objection was in fact pointed out by Chief Justice Hughes in a statement signed also by Justices Van Devanter and Brandeis, addressed to Senator Wheeler upon the latter's request for an expression of views regarding the effect of the proposal on the efficiency of the Court.

IV. RELATION OF FEDERAL AND STATE COURTS

The State courts, presenting their own hierarchy of original and appellate tribunals, are established and maintained entirely under the authority of the respective States. The federal district courts are vested with juris-

[59] See Rule 38 of the Rules of the Supreme Court.

diction exclusive of that of State courts over a few federal specialties, such as maritime, bankruptcy, patent and copyright cases, and prosecutions under federal criminal law. In the residue of cases arising under the Constitution or laws of the United States the jurisdiction of the two sets of courts is concurrent. That is, the party plaintiff may choose to bring the case in either court. If it is brought in a federal court it cannot be removed to a State court. But if it is brought in a State court the defendant has an election to remove it to a federal court before the time for a hearing. The same is true of suits between citizens of different States; removal to a federal court is there, however, the privilege only of defendants who are non-residents of the forum state, on the principle that they alone need the protection of a federal tribunal.

A case must proceed in the States courts to the highest State court having jurisdiction over it, as a prerequisite to appeal to the Supreme Court of the United States. Moreover, such appeal is permitted only where the decision of the highest State court has actually depended on a question of federal constitutional or statutory law. The federal Supreme Court has no authority to pass upon questions of the interpretation of the State law or the validity of State law under a State constitution. On such questions the decision of the State court is final and binding. The requirement of a case or controversy obtains in the review of State decisions; thus an advisory opinion of a State court is not reviewable by the federal Supreme Court.

V. PROMOTION OF UNIFORMITY OF LAW

Federal legislation receives a uniform interpretation through the authority of the Supreme Court to review decisions of the federal Courts of Appeals or of the State supreme courts which turn on the meaning or application of federal statutes.

Uniformity of another sort was for many years an objective of the federal courts. A so-called federal common law, where neither State legislation nor federal legislation was relevant, was developed by the federal courts in diversity of citizenship cases, under the rule of *Swift v. Tyson*.[60] This practice came to an end in 1938, with a series of decisions of the Supreme Court holding that where no federal question is involved the federal courts must follow the decisions in the State where the federal court is sitting (including the decisions on conflict of laws).[61] This renunciation of a federal common law has caused some critics, for example the late Professor Lambert of France, to speak of a Balkanization of American law and to regret the loss of the impetus to uniformity which had been furnished by *Swift v. Tyson*. But in truth the problem was not so simple. Two kinds

[60] 16 Peters 1 (1842).
[61] Erie R.R. v. Tompkins, 304 U.S. 64 (1938); Klaxon Co. v. Stentor Co., 313 U.S. 487 (1941); see R. H. Jackson, "The Rise and Fall of Swift v. Tyson," 24 A.B.A.J. 609 (1938).

of uniformity were in competition: uniformity among federal courts and uniformity between State and federal courts within a single State. The former, in conjunction with the system of parallel courts, had produced many abuses of "forum shopping" for a State or federal tribunal, with the result that the outcome of a controversy over a contract or a tort might depend on the accident of diversity of citizenship. Today there is uniformity of common law rules within a State, though there remains the hazard of divergence between the decisions of courts in the several States which may be empowered to adjudicate a given case. The latter problem is, of course, a function of a system of conflict of laws.

Thus far the Supreme Court has been quite cautious in reviewing questions of conflict of laws. When arising in federal courts in diversity of citizenship cases these questions are treated as matters of State law. When arising in State courts these questions are reviewable in the Supreme Court only if they present constitutional issues. Two clauses of the Constitution are available to support such review: the full faith and credit clause of Article IV and the due process clause of the Fourteenth Amendment. But these clauses have been held to limit State courts in their choice of law only in extreme cases, as where the State court applies its own law to a transaction having no contact with the State except as forum, or where the by-laws of certain benevolent associations have been disregarded by the forum State.[62] While some commentators have urged that the scope of review over conflict of laws be more inclusive, such an exercise of jurisdiction would obviously involve the Supreme Court in a complex and pervasive field of law. Moreover, it is generally assumed that Congress, under the grant of power in Article IV, could deal with conflict of laws problems through legislation.

The full faith and credit clause does, however, have important applications. (a) The judgments of one State must be recognized by sister States, except where jurisdiction to render the judgment was lacking and there was no prior opportunity to contest it. Even judgments for taxes in favor of one State must be recognized and enforced in another.[63] (b) A State may not refuse to entertain a cause of action on the ground that it arises under the law of another State. Although a doctrine of *forum non conveniens* is permitted, the mere out-of-state origin of a cause of action is not sufficient ground for denying access to the courts of a State.[64] Whether this compulsion extends to tax claims of a sister State, not reduced to judgment, is an open question.[65] In fact many States do voluntarily entertain such claims.

[62] Home Insurance Co. v. Dick, 281 U.S. 397 (1930); Order of United Commercial Travelers v. Wolfe, 331 U.S. 586 (1947); cf. Pacific Employers Insurance Co. v. Industrial Accident Commission, 306 U.S. 493 (1939).

[63] Milwaukee County v. White Co., 296 U.S. 268 (1935).

[64] Hughes v. Fetter, 341 U.S. 609 (1951).

[65] Massachusetts v. Missouri, 308 U.S. 1, 19–20 (1939).

VI. Appointment and Tenure of Judges

Federal judges hold office for life and are removable only by impeachment. Their compensation is fixed by law from time to time, but the compensation of a judge may not be diminished during his continuance in office. There is no constitutional basis for compulsory retirement. There is, however, statutory provision for voluntary retirement on full salary after ten years of service and the attainment of the age of seventy.[66] A number of judges, both in the lower federal courts and the Supreme Court, have availed themselves of this privilege, but there is no common practice in this regard, and if retirement is availed of it is generally some time after the age of seventy has been reached.

Appointment is by the President with the consent of the Senate. The Constitutional Convention rejected a proposal that the appointment be vested in the legislature. As one of the delegates put it, he considered that body "as too numerous for that purpose; as subject to cabal; and as devoid of responsibility." On a few occasions the Senate has refused confirmation. There are no formal qualifications required of federal judges. In fact the appointees to the Supreme Court have always been drawn from a wide variety of backgrounds. The great majority of them have held public office, though a majority have not previously been judges. Considerations of party allegiance have on the whole been less important than the general outlook of an appointee: his social and economic philosophy and his conception of a federal system. Geography likewise has not played a major part, although some effort has been made to see that regions of the country are not unrepresented. Since there are eleven judicial circuits and nine members of the Court, it would be fairly easy to follow a practice of giving representation to the various circuits; but no such rigid practice has developed.

---

[66] 28 U.S. Code §371.

Defense

I. INTRODUCTION

The need to provide a strong defense for a group of States has been, along with economic motives, a primary reason for the formation of federations. By combining their manpower, natural resources, and scientific and industrial capacity, the member States of a federation increase their total strength by substantially more than the sum of the parties. Such a pooling of efforts avoids the duplication of facilities which is necessary if each member State maintains its own defense structure, assures standardization of arms and techniques, and permits the most efficient use of the resources of each State.

This motivation would be equally true of the formation of a European federation. The European Defense Community Treaty evidences this joint interest in defense. Its signature by the six member countries before a federation has been established shows the urgency of this problem for the States involved.

This study attempts to bring together the experiences of the federal systems of Australia, Canada, Germany, Switzerland, and the United States, to show how those systems have met the need for a strong defense and to suggest conclusions from those experiences.

II. RESPONSIBILITY FOR DEFENSE OF THE FEDERATION

A. *Allotment of Responsibility*

The practice in all the federal systems studied has been to allot to the federal government exclusively the responsibility for the defense of the federation. To entrust defense to the member States would undermine the security and unity of the federation by subjecting its defense to the disaffection, improvidence, or inability of each member. Moreover, conflicts between the member States would be inevitable as to the burden of defense, and as to foreign policies, economic policies, and other matters related to defense. Separate forces would lead the member States to compete in their armaments, and would enable the stronger States to dominate the federation or to withdraw from it with impunity.

This allotment of responsibility to the federal government has usually been made by express constitutional provision. Thus, the Australian Constitution gives the Commonwealth the duty "to protect every State against invasion"; the Weimar Constitution stated that "The defense of the Reich is a matter of the Reich"; the Swiss Constitution imposes upon the Confederation the duty to guarantee "to the Cantons their territory [and] their sovereignty"; and the United States Constitution provides that "The United States shall protect them [every state] against invasion."

B. *Territorial Extent of Federal Responsibility for Defense*

The federal responsibility, in all the federal systems studied, extends not only to the territories of the member States themselves but also to any dependencies and protectorates. Indeed, in those systems, relations with dependencies and protectorates are regulated by the federation rather than its member States, and the question of responsibility for defense has therefore not been singled out. If the member States of a federation were to retain responsibility for the defense of any such territory, the States might tend, to that extent, to pursue foreign policies, to incur financial obligations and to use their industrial and manpower facilities in a manner conflicting with the programs of the federation as a whole.[1]

C. *Responsibility for Internal Security of the Federation* [2]

Ordinarily the member States are charged with maintaining internal order. The existing federal systems have, however, granted ultimate responsibility to the federation, since a threat to the constitutional order in any State may be a threat to the entire federal structure or may give assistance to the external enemies of the federation. Under the American Constitution, for example, the United States guarantees to every State a "republican" form of government. The Swiss Constitution gives the Confederation the duty to guarantee to the cantons "their constitutions [and] the liberty and rights of their people." The Australian Constitution requires the Commonwealth to "protect every State . . . against domestic violence."

The ultimate form of internal disturbance is the secession of a member State from the federation. No effective federation has permitted to its member States a right of secession. Some (the Australian Constitution, the Weimar Constitution) have provided against it, and the American Civil War was fought to carry out the federal responsibility for preservation of the Union. By forming a federation, the member States become dependent upon its continuance for their security and economic order. Although this fact itself is a substantial deterrent to defections by member States, it also emphasizes the necessity for permanence of the federal relationship.

III. POWER TO ESTABLISH DEFENSE POLICIES OF THE FEDERATION

The defense policies of a federation are established by three principal means: control of the necessary aspects of foreign affairs; control of the

---

[1] The subject of overseas territories is examined in Study 14.
[2] The maintenance of constitutional order is treated more fully in Study 13.

strength and composition of the armed forces; and control of the disposition and use of those forces.

A. *Control of the Necessary Aspects of Foreign Affairs*

The existing federal systems have recognized the necessity for conferring on the federal government exclusive control of foreign affairs at least as related to defense. The federation thus makes all alliances and other treaties related to defense. These constitutions usually forbid the member States to enter into treaties, alliances, or agreements with foreign powers (except in some cases with the consent of the federal government). Where the member States have been permitted to enter into international agreements on certain subjects (as in Switzerland or under the German Imperial Constitution), this power has not extended to matters related to defense. In all instances the regular foreign affairs of the federation are carried on by a foreign service representing the federal government.

B. *Control of the Strength and Composition of the Armed Forces*

The second element of the federal government's power to establish the defense policies of the federation is control of the strength of the armed forces, including reserves, and of the distribution of that strength among the various principal branches of the forces. This power has usually stemmed from the general federal power to provide for defense and to raise armed forces and provide for their organization. Under the German Imperial Constitution, however, where organization of the armed forces into *Kontingente* of the member States might have created a possible doubt as to federal powers in this field, the Constitution expressly granted to the Emperor and the Imperial legislature the power to determine the strength and composition of the *Kontingente*.

The member States of a federation are likely to have different views as to the strength and type of armed forces which should be maintained, according to the special requirements of their own defense. In none of the federal systems studied, however, do the member States have constitutional power to control these decisions (except through their participation in the federal legislature), either directly or indirectly by controlling defense funds or the location of military installations within their territories.

C. *Control of the Disposition and Use of the Armed Forces*

In all the federal systems studied, the federal government (in most cases the federal legislature) exercises the power to declare war and make peace. Otherwise the very purpose of the unified defense system could be defeated by individual members. Likewise, the federal governments in these systems control the command, use, and deployment of the armed forces. This power flows mainly from the general federal power with respect to defense, fortified, in the case of the United States, Canada, Australia, and the Weimar Republic, by constitutional assignment to the Head of State of the powers of commander-in-chief. In some cases, further specification has been included, as in the Swiss Constitution, which provides that "the control of the army and of war material . . . is vested in the Confederation," and that "in case of danger the Confederation has also the right of exclusive and immediate control."

The early experience of the United States shows the danger of any divided authority in this field. Under its Constitution, the federal government was authorized either to raise and maintain troops itself or to rely on State militia organized under federal law but trained and officered by the States. For the first two decades of its history the federal government depended on the State militia. In the War of 1812 two States illegally refused to call up their militia, and a third refused to permit use of its troops outside the United States. Since then the federal government has relied on its authority to raise forces directly.

In addition to use of the armed forces against external enemies, constitutional provision is customarily made for their use in the event of insurrections and other domestic disturbances. Here also a controlling federal power has proved necessary. Thus the United States Constitution authorizes the federal legislature to call forth the militia to "execute the laws of the Union [and] suppress insurrections." (Under the general defense powers the federal armed forces may also be used for this purpose.) The Australian and Canadian organic acts authorize the federal legislature to provide for the "peace, order and good government" of the federation; and the Australian Constitution empowers the Commonwealth legislature to make laws for "the control of the forces to execute and maintain the laws of the Commonwealth." The Weimar Constitution authorized the President to use the armed forces to maintain order within the Länder.

In some cases the States themselves have been given constitutional power to employ the armed forces to protect internal security. The Swiss Constitution provides for the calling up of troops by the cantons to maintain constitutional order. This is also the case in the United States with respect to units of the National Guard, and was true under the German Imperial Constitution. Under the Weimar Constitution the German Länder were also given the right to call on the armed forces in domestic emergencies, and this right was a source of considerable conflict between the federal and Bavarian governments. In all these cases, however, the powers of the member States have been subject to control by the federations.

IV. GENERAL POWERS TO EXECUTE DEFENSE POLICIES

The defense policies established by the federal government require for their execution certain further powers if the responsibility for defense is to be effective. These are the power to raise armed forces, to administer them, to support and equip them, and to finance these and all other activities related to defense.

A. *Power to Raise Armed Forces*

All the federal systems studied give to the federal government the power to raise armed forces — army, navy, and air force — permanent forces and reserves, by conscription or enlistment. In some cases (e.g., Switzerland) this power has been reinforced by express constitutional provision that every male member of the population shall perform military service. In addition, the power to raise forces is prohibited to the member States under the Canadian and Australian organic acts, except with the consent of the federal legislature. The United States Constitution forbids the States to raise troops without federal consent except in time of war, and even then State measures are subject to control by the overriding federal defense power as well as the specific federal power over State militia. However the American States may, within this framework, recruit "home guard" units in times of emergency, as they did during both World Wars. The Swiss cantons likewise possess a very limited power to maintain troops, which is also subject to federal control. Some administratiive functions with respect to raising armed forces, such as maintenance of manpower registers, are also exercised by the Swiss cantons subject to federal supervision. In all systems, of course, the member States have retained the power to maintain police forces for their internal security.

Dependence by the federal government upon armed forces raised by the member States is one of the most serious handicaps under which a unified defense system can labor. Prior to establishment of the American Constitution, the member States were united in a form of Confederation under an organic act giving to the central government the power to raise troops only by making requisitions upon the States for quotas of men. This practice had caused so much inefficiency and inequity during the American Revolution, through competitive recruiting and unequal distribution of burdens, that the Constitution assured, in specific terms, the power of the federal government to raise forces directly. The difficulties faced by the United States during the War of 1812, through reliance on the armed forces raised by member States, have been mentioned above.

It is also the practice of the existing federal states studied that the armed forces raised by the federation are unified in organization and owe their allegiance to the federation as a whole. They are integrated, not as a coalition force, but in such a fashion that units identified in any way with the member States cannot mount an effective operation alone. Switzerland and the United States do retain vestiges of regional formations in their cantonal corps and National Guard units, but these formations are subject to such extensive federal control that they cannot be regarded as exceptions to the general practice. Germany, under both the Constitution of 1871 and the Weimar Constitution, organized its army on a Land basis. The system under the Constitution of 1871 gave some of the member States considerable power; however, the constitutional system was greatly qualified in practice by the influence of the central government.

B. *Power to Administer the Armed Forces*

The power to command and administer the armed forces is vital to control of their disposition and use. For this reason, in the United States, Canada, and Australia, and in the Weimar Republic, the organic acts constitute the Head of State the commander-in-chief of the armed forces (which also has the desirable result of strengthening civilian supremacy). Federal power in this field arises also from the general grant of power to provide for defense.

In addition to these general grants of power, specific federal powers concerning the administration of the armed forces are found in a number of constitutions. The American Constitution gives to Congress the power to make rules for the government of the armed forces; the Swiss Constitution specifies that the Confederation shall enact the laws on the organization of the army and has the right of "exclusive and immediate control over the armed forces"; the Canadian and Australian organic acts give to the federal legislature exclusive power with regard to militia, military and naval service; and the Weimar Constitution gave the federal government exclusive legislative power with respect to laws relating to the military establishment. As a consequence of these powers the federal governments may, through action either of the legislature or of the executive as commander-in-chief, provide for the organization of the forces, act on behalf of their security and welfare, enact codes of military justice and withdraw members of the forces as necessary from civilian jurisdiction, and provide for pay, pensions, and veterans' privileges. The appointment of officers is also of first importance in maintaining federal control of the armed forces, and this is recognized in present American practice as to officers of the National Guard and in Switzerland as to officers of the cantonal troops.

The member States may, as in Canada and Switzerland, exercise certain jurisdiction over the members of the armed forces within their territory (as, for certain tax purposes), but this jurisdiction has not been permitted to interfere with the mission or security of those forces. Likewise certain powers in this area may be delegated to the member States, as, in Australia during World War II, the States were given the power to maintain order in areas of troop concentration.

C. *Power to Support and Equip the Armed Forces*

Federal defense powers with respect to the strength, composition, disposition, and use of the armed forces cannot be executed unless the federal government has also the power to support and equip those forces. Federal control in this field is necessary to ensure efficient and standardized equipment and to obtain the benefits of specialized production. Moreover, to grant the States any control of supply and procurement for the armed forces would entail many of the same risks which would accompany maintenance of separate armed forces. This necessity for federal control of arms is recognized by the provision of the Basic Law of the German Federal Republic requiring federal consent to the manufacture, transport, or marketing of armaments; and likewise by the Swiss Constitution which provides for federal regulation of such activities.

In all the federal systems studied, the federal government has the power to procure armaments and materials necessary for the armed forces from any sources, including foreign sources. It has also the authority to construct, acquire, own, and operate such installations as airports, military reservations, arsenals, and shipyards, and to exercise the power of eminent domain for these purposes. Acquisition of such properties by the federal government, however, makes it necessary to settle the relation between federal and State jurisdiction over them. The American Constitution, for example, permits the States to continue to exercise jurisdiction in such cases, unless they agree otherwise; but such jurisdiction may not interfere with federal ownership or use.

These powers to supply the forces stem from the general defense powers, reinforced in some cases by specific grants of power regarding the support of the armed forces. In addition, both the Australian and Weimar Constitutions include provisions dealing expressly with use of the railroads for defense purposes.

The federal government may at times find it necessary to take special measures for equipping and supplying the armed forces. These may include, for example, the allocation of strategic materials to permit stockpiling, or the maintenance of war production capacity by assuring that such capacity is kept busy in time of peace. Power to take such measures as these has been held also to flow from the general defense power under the Australian Constitution, and has been exercised by the United States government on the same theory. The exercise of further federal powers in time of actual or apprehended war, through economic and manpower mobilization, is discussed below.

The federal defense procurement will, of course, have an impact on the economies of the member States, but none of the constitutions of the federal systems studied contains any restrictions on the federal power on that account. In practice this type of problem has often been handled by informal federal-state consultations, such as the annual Federal and State Premiers Conferences in Australia, or by the regional distribution of membership in plural executives. The federal upper chamber is also alert to ensure that the exercise of such federal power does not unfairly injure any State or region.

D. *Power to Finance Federal Defense Activities*

The constitutions of all contemporary federal systems studied, except the Swiss, appear to have given the federal government adequate powers to levy taxes for defense financing, and all these constitutions give to the federal government the power to borrow. The limitation on tax sources of the Swiss Confederation has been a cause of difficulty in carrying out a postwar legislative policy of strengthening and modernizing defense, and has led to various transitory constitutional amendments extending the federal tax sources.

As in the case of measures to supply the forces, State interests in federal defense financing measures have customarily been protected through federal-state conferences and State representation in the federal upper chamber and in the federal executive body.[3] In some instances, however, the federation has had to assert constitutional powers to act without State cooperation. Thus, under the Australian Constitution the Commonwealth has felt required to exercise its defense powers so as, in effect, to exclude the member States from the field of income taxation, by assigning priority to payment of federal as against State income taxes and by authorizing the federal government to take over the use of the income-tax-collecting officials and facilities of the States. These measures were employed, however, only after the Commonwealth found it impossible to obtain agreement of the States to a voluntary arrangement of fiscal problems.

Any arrangement for financing federal defense expenses by quotas requisitioned from the States seriously weakens the defense program by requiring the federal government to rely on sources of funds which it cannot control. Under the American Articles of Confederation (in force prior to the Constitution) such arrangements resulted in persistent defaults by the States and disputes among them as to their quotas. In view of this experience, the United States Constitution grants to the federal government a general power to levy taxes.

V. SPECIAL POWERS TO EXECUTE DEFENSE POLICIES IN EXTRAORDINARY PERIODS

The responsibility of the federal government to provide for the federation's security is constant. However its defense activities will vary according to the nature and extent of the dangers threatening it. Thus a period of apprehended war, actual war, or post-hostilities must bring about both an expansion of the normal federal defense powers and the development of certain new powers.

---

[3] The subjects of federal tax powers and their relation to State tax authority are discussed in Study 7, Public Finance.

A. *Economic Mobilization and Postwar Adjustment*

When a federation apprehends that a state of war may develop in the foreseeable future, it acts to increase its armed forces, dispose them to best effect, and attempt to secure strategic foreign alliances. These efforts will of course be even greater if war begins. To meet these demands the federal government must recruit more men, provide more equipment and supplies, and raise greater funds. These needs may in turn require economic and manpower mobilization to channel the resources of the federation into necessary production and to protect against inflation.

Even federal constitutions written before the period of modern war have generally been interpreted to permit the federal government to conduct the necessary economic activities. These activities have included the fixing of prices and wages, the allocation of housing and materials, the assignment of priorities for government contracts, the construction and commandeering of manufacturing facilities, the arbitration of labor disputes, and the close regulation of the labor supply. In the case of the United States, Canada, and Australia (and in Germany during World War I under the Constitution of 1871), the general defense powers of the federal government have been broadly interpreted to permit these activities where they have been necessary.

Under the Swiss Constitution a commander-in-chief may be elected by the Federal Assembly who may, by law, claim for service all personal and material forces in time of emergency. In Switzerland, however, the general defense powers of the federal civil authorities have not been as broadly interpreted as in the other systems studied, and during both World Wars the federal government resorted to measures outside the Constitution. As a result, the Swiss Constitution was amended after World War II to permit the Federal Assembly to enact, for periods up to a year, emergency legislation not based on the Constitution; and to enact economic measures to ensure preparedness in time of war, which are not limited by the general constitutional guarantee of the freedom of trade and industry.

In order to demobilize the wartime economy, many controls must be continued temporarily into the postwar period. The federal powers to continue such controls have been supported in the United States, Canada, and Australia as a part of the general defense powers. In these federal systems, the duration and extent of these postwar powers are fixed by the courts, as interpreters of the constitution, and they have shown a disposition to examine postwar measures much more closely than wartime acts to determine their necessity for economic adjustment. In Switzerland many of the wartime economic measures were also continued for a period after the recent war.

The member States of the federal systems carry on some of the economic regulations necessary for defense purposes. These may be based either on delegation by the federal government or on normal State powers for regulation of economic matters. However, basic control has been retained by the federal governments in order to ensure maximum effort and a fair distribution of burdens, and since most of these matters involve inter-State relationships. In addition, many federal defense measures are administered by State agencies. In the United States, Australia, and Canada, where States do not generally administer federal laws, the success of this method has depended principally on federal-state cooperation, which has on occasion broken down where important State interests were involved. In Australia, failure to obtain State cooperation led, in one instance, to federal legislation commandeering the services of certain State officials and the use of certain State equipment.

B. *Internal Security as Related to Defense*

The power to protect the security of the armed forces, defense installations, and the like is a part of the general power to maintain and administer the armed forces, discussed above. Apart from this, the federal governments exercise powers with respect to internal security which principally come into being with the apprehension or existence of hostilities. These federal powers have included, for example, the power to proclaim and administer martial law, and to use elements of the armed forces for this purpose, and to control subversive groups. Such powers will need to be exercised to deal with internal disturbances which interfere with the mission of the armed forces or furnish assistance to enemies or potential enemies, and also with enemy aliens or other groups sympathetic to an enemy. Thus both Canada and the United States removed from their West Coasts during World War II persons of Japanese descent. The Canadian War Measures Act of 1914 authorized the executive to exercise the powers of censorship and of arrest, detention and deportation. In both the Civil War and World War II the United States government proclaimed martial law in sensitive areas. All these actions were based largely on the general defense powers. Article I, Section 9, Clause 2 of the United States Constitution provides: "The privilege of the Writ of Habeas Corpus shall not be suspended, unless when in Cases of Rebellion or Invasion the public Safety may require it." The Imperial German Constitution also provided expressly for the declaration of martial law by the Emperor, and the Weimar Constitution authorized the President to suspend the fundamental rights and employ the armed forces in the event of a threat to peace or public order.

The defense power has been likewise, in large part, the constitutional basis for the prosecution of leaders of the Communist Party in the United States in the past few years. The defense powers granted by the Australian Constitution have, however, been held not to permit the outlawing of the Communist Party during the "cold war" period.

The powers to protect internal security in the interest of defense through

measures not involving the use of the armed forces may also be exercised
by the member States, although the federal power is dominant and overrides
inconsistent State regulations.   (Use of the armed forces by the States to
protect internal security was discussed above in connection with the disposition and use of the armed forces.)   As in economic matters, the federal
governments have also, on occasion, relied on the States for enforcement
of federal legislation in this field.

C. *Civil Defense*

Even in normal times certain civil defense measures must be carried on
or planned to provide for protection of the civil population against enemy
action in case of war.   These activities may be left primarily to the member
States, with the federal government providing coordination, advice, and financial help, as is being done in the United States.   In times of actual or
apprehended hostilities, however, the federal government would possess a
controlling authority in this field, in order to carry out its responsibility for
defense (e.g., State inability could not be permitted to expose the working
population of an important industrial center to unnecessary injury).   Moreover, civil defense measures must be closely coordinated with activities of
the armed forces in such matters as troop movements and the location of
air raid warning centers.

D. *Special Constitutional Provisions for Emergency Powers*

Of the federal systems considered here, only the Weimar Constitution
and the Swiss Constitution have included provisions for formal declaration of emergencies, with consequential expansion of federal powers (although the German Basic Law includes an emergency provision of a sort,
permitting enactment of legislation in crises without approval of the lower
chamber).[4]   The absence of any such provisions in the constitutions of
Australia, Canada, and the United States has not produced difficulties.

In the Weimar Republic, the President was empowered by the Constitution, in the event of a serious threat to public safety and peace, to take any
"necessary measures" including use of the armed forces and temporary suspension of fundamental constitutional rights.   Such measures were, however, subject to disapproval by the lower legislative chamber.   There was
no occasion to use this power in time of war or apprehended war.   However, it was frequently exercised to protect internal security and, although
it was eventually one of the media of the downfall of the Republic, it had
earlier been an important source of strength to deal with rebellious groups.

In Switzerland, by a recent constitutional amendment, the Federal Assembly is authorized to enact emergency legislation which is not based on

---

[4] Provisions on emergency powers are also discussed in several other studies of this series,
particularly Study 13, Defense of the Constitutional Order.

the Constitution and which is not subject to a referendum (as is ordinary legislation); but such laws may not have a duration of more than one year. In addition, the Swiss Constitution provides for election by the Federal Assembly, in time of defense crisis, of a commander-in-chief of the armed forces, with powers to provide for economic and manpower mobilization. Ambiguity as to the relation between the commander-in-chief and the federal executive has caused some conflict, however.

VI. ALLOCATION OF FEDERAL DEFENSE POWERS

The federal defense powers are exercised either by the legislature or by the executive or, more commonly, by some combination of the two. The legislature, as a body representing both the people and the member States, has been given a predominant role in the establishment of defense policies and in laying down the basic principles for their execution. However, legislative control of the executive diminishes considerably in wartime, as a result of the increase in the delegation of powers to the executive.

A. *Powers of the Legislature*

In the exercise of federal defense powers during wartime the legislature has usually prescribed at most the general policies, such as those relating to conscription, economic mobilization, control of subversive organizations, the proclamation of martial law, and the procurement of supplies for the forces. In all these matters the federal legislatures have found it necessary to delegate to the executive broad authority to carry out legislative policy, relying for control on the legislative power to control funds, investigate, and if necessary, to enact restrictions; and, under Cabinet government, on its power to question and depose the executive. This legislative control has been exercised with special vigilance in periods of postwar adjustment, in response to public demand for rapid termination of wartime measures.

The Canadian and Australian legislatures, in times of war or apprehended war, have delegated to the executive extremely wide powers to mobilize the economy and control subversive activities. Similar delegations of power were made by the Swiss Federal Assembly in both World Wars. In the United States, although the President has been given great power by Congress in time of war or near-war, the basic policies of federal defense measures have been laid down by statute. The danger of excessive delegation of powers to the executive has been recognized in some cases by specific constitutional provisions. Thus, the Swiss Constitution limits emergency legislation (and any extensive delegation of powers would have to be made by emergency legislation) to a duration of one year; and the United States Constitution limits to two years the period for which certain defense appropriations can be made.

The legislatures, through their power to approve the federal budget, have controlled the size and composition of the armed forces, and exerted a powerful influence over their disposition and general strategic planning. To strengthen this control the United States Constitution expressly requires that all withdrawals from the federal treasury be authorized by legislation.

Under the United States and Swiss constitutions, and under the Weimar Constitution, war is declared only by the legislature. The Canadian and Australian organic acts provide for declaration of war by the Head of State. Even where war must be declared by or with the consent of the legislature, however, the executive is not necessarily excluded from using the armed forces against aggression by foreign powers, as is discussed in more detail below. In such cases, the legislative power to declare war is more a formal than a real control.

The legislature may participate in the establishment of defense policies through requirements for its approval for ratification of treaties,[5] or for the appointment of high civil and military officials. In most federal systems studied, heads of the Ministries are either appointed by or approved by the legislature. In the United States, other high officials, including military officers of high rank, must be approved by the Senate and are subject to impeachment by the legislature. Under the Swiss Constitution, the legislature itself elects the commander-in-chief of the army.

In addition to these more general legislative powers with respect to defense matters, other specific provisions are present in the constitutions of some federations. Thus the United States Constitution expressly grants to Congress the power to make rules for the government of those forces and concerning captured enemy property, and to provide for the organization and use of the State militia units.

B. *Powers of the Executive or Head of State*

The constitutions of the United States, Australia, and Canada, and of the Weimar Republic, constitute the Head of State the commander-in-chief of the armed forces. As such he administers, trains, and otherwise prepares the armed forces, exercises disciplinary authority over them, and ensures their security, subject to the provisions of legislation. In addition the Weimar Constitution expressly authorized the President to use the armed forces if the public safety and peace were seriously threatened.

In the United States, the powers of the President, as commander-in-chief, are quite broad, although their extent is not entirely settled. He has relied on this power to use the armed forces to carry on military operations in advance of declaration of war or approval of hostilities by Congress; to deploy the forces within or without the federal territory to provide the most effective defense; and, in certain instances, to provide for their supply. Thus, he relied on this power to send additional troops to Europe in

[5] See Study 5, Foreign Affairs.

1951, to use the forces to protect Atlantic shipping prior to American entry into World War II, and to intervene in Korea in 1950. He has also commandeered railroads, factories, and shipyards to supply the armed forces. The President may not act contrary to legislation, however. Moreover, Congress can review and often control such actions in passing on requests for necessary funds or other supporting legislation.

The executive, as such, also has powers with respect to the conduct of foreign affairs and the appointment of officers and officials which give him a strong voice in the establishment and execution of defense policies. He also receives, by delegation from the legislature, authority to carry out and fill in gaps in all aspects of legislative defense policies. As discussed above, these delegated powers have been very wide under all federal systems, but especially under the Parliamentary systems of Canada and Australia and in Switzerland. The general questions of the powers of the executive, and its relation to the legislature, are discussed in other reports.[6]

VII. SPECIAL CONSTITUTIONAL LIMITATIONS ON THE DEFENSE POWER

A. *Limitations for the Protection of Personal Liberties*

Under the constitutions of the United States, Switzerland, and the German Republics, federal defense powers have been limited by constitutional safeguards protecting such personal civil and economic liberties as freedom of movement, freedom of press, speech, and political organization, freedom of trade and industry, and freedom of the use of property. The Australian Constitution guarantees freedom of religion and of interstate trade and commerce. The German Basic Law contains, in addition, a unique limitation, providing that "No one may be compelled against his conscience to render military service as an armed combatant." The Weimar Constitution, however, permitted the President to suspend the fundamental liberties upon his declaration of an emergency, and the Swiss Constitution permits federal legislation to disregard the constitutional guarantee of freedom of trade and industry where necessary for defense preparedness.

The effectiveness of these limitations depends primarily upon the power of the courts to review governmental action, discussed below. In a system such as Switzerland, having no judicial review of action of the federal government, these limitations have less force. It does not appear, however, that even in those countries with the strongest traditions of judicial control these constitutional limitations have been permitted to hamper necessary defense efforts. Thus, both the United States and Canada, in World War II, were able to remove from their West Coasts all persons of Japanese ancestry, and martial law was imposed by the United States throughout the territory of Hawaii during most of the war. Likewise regulation of the

---

[6] See Study 2, The Federal Executive, and Study 1, The Federal Legislature.

labor supply was carried out to a point little short of conscription of labor, without meeting constitutional difficulties.

Neither Australia nor Canada includes in its organic act a general "bill of rights," but, in Australia at least, the courts seem to have extended a certain protection to civil liberties by restricting the defense powers. They have generally had to do this in a manner which tends to reduce the scope of the defense powers as a whole, since their decisions could not rest on any constitutional protection of liberties. The presence of a constitutional bill of rights, on the other hand, permits the restriction of defense powers in only certain directions, leaving their other aspects (e.g., economic and military) undiminished.

B. *Other Constitutional Limitations*

Some constitutions have included other express limitations on the federal defense power. For example, the United States Constitution restricts the period for which funds may be appropriated for the armed forces, thus requiring periodic legislative review of defense requirements. Another type of limitation was contained in the Weimar Constitution, which provided that "the military organization of the German people shall be regulated . . . with consideration for the peculiar local characteristics of the people."

The referendum provisions of the Swiss Constitution are a form of limitation on federal powers. On the request of 30,000 voters or eight cantons, all legislation must be submitted to popular referendum. Under a recent amendment to the Constitution, however, the referendum may be suspended by the Federal Assembly in urgent cases for not more than one year.

VIII. Judicial Enforcement of Constitutional Provisions Concerning Defense

The courts play an important role in the enforcement of constitutional provisions and limitations in all countries except Switzerland where, as noted above, they have no power to pass on the validity of measures of the federal legislature or executive.

The general authority of the federal and State judiciaries in interpreting the constitution is dealt with elsewhere.[7] Certain aspects of judicial review are peculiar, or nearly so, to the enforcement of constitutional provisions regarding federal defense. For example, the courts cannot be expected to act rapidly enough in all cases to regulate effectively, by their decisions, the governmental action which they consider. Thus, in the important cases involving the relation between civil rights and defense powers during the Civil War and World War II, the United States courts did

[7] See Study 3, The Federal Judiciary, Section II.

not render their decisions until about two years after hostilities had ceased and the governmental action in question had run its course. These decisions were therefore chiefly valuable as precedents.

The courts also lack the physical power to enforce their judgments against military authorities if a showdown occurs. In the American Civil War, the military, with the support of the President, successfully defied an order of the Chief Justice of the Supreme Court invalidating the President's establishment of martial law.

In cases involving basic judgments of defense policy, the courts have given great weight to determinations of the executive or legislature as to the necessity for the measures taken. This attitude appears in the decisions of the courts of the United States, Canada, and Australia passing on the validity of various wartime measures of their governments, such as relocation of Japanese persons in Canada and the United States or the imposition of price and wage controls. Moreover, there are certain questions which the courts, especially in the United States, have refused to decide as being inherently non-justiciable and political in nature.

In Australia, Canada, and the United States, judicial review provides a principal mechanism for adjusting the defense powers to the different circumstances of peace and war. This system enables the constitutional power to be adapted to the requirements of emergency periods, while keeping it in bounds by stricter construction in normal times. Thus, general constitutional provisions interpreted by a strong and independent judiciary give to the defense powers a desirable flexibility and reduce to some extent the chance of abuse of the emergency power. This method also avoids the need for special provisions for the declaration of an emergency.

IX. Conclusions

All of the federal systems considered in this study have granted to the federal government the exclusive responsibility for the defense of the federation and of all overseas territories, accompanied by powers necessary to carry out that responsibility. Experience has shown that the following federal defense powers are essential:

a. To establish defense policies through control of certain aspects of foreign affairs, of the strength and composition of the armed forces, and of their use and deployment;

b. To raise armed forces;

c. To supply and equip these forces;

d. To administer and command the forces;

e. To finance, by taxation or borrowing, the cost of defense activities;

f. To provide for economic and manpower mobilization in times of actual or apprehended war, and for postwar adjustment of the economy;

g. To take measures to protect the internal security of the federation; and

h. To provide for defense of the civil population.

These powers have been derived in most instances from a general grant of power to provide for defense, usually accompanied by specific powers to raise armed forces, to provide for their regulation, to acquire military installations, and so on. Other general constitutional grants of federal power, such as with regard to taxation, borrowing, and foreign affairs, have also been of great use in the carrying on of defense activities.

The general grant of federal power with respect to defense has usually been interpreted broadly in response to increasing defense requirements, notably to permit economic mobilization in time of actual or apprehended war (and economic adjustment in postwar periods). In Switzerland, where this sort of interpretation has not been made, the federal defense effort has suffered and the federal authorities have on occasion (prior to recent amendments of the Constitution) been forced to adopt extraconstitutional measures.

Only the Swiss and Weimar Constitutions have provided expressly for the exercise of special powers in defense emergencies. In the United States, Australia, and Canada this expansion of power has generally been made possible by constitutional interpretation which responds to the needs of defense. Where courts are strong and independent, this practice has given desirable flexibility to the defense powers and has tended to prevent their abuse. The practice of providing expressly for federal emergency powers to come into being upon a declaration which is not closely circumscribed by legislative and judicial control has had unfortunate consequences where it has been attempted.

The States have generally been severely limited in the maintenance of armed forces and in their participation in the establishment of defense policies, as through powers in regard to foreign affairs. They have, however, exercised certain power for the support of defense activities, either by delegation from the federal government (as in the administration of federal laws) or on the basis of their own separate powers (as in the case of civil defense measures). But it has proved desirable to subject these State powers to federal control. Where reliance has been placed on the exercise of State powers or on State cooperation with the federation, the likelihood of serious conflicts exists, as shown by the American experience with reliance on State militia for defense of the federation.

Under most federal systems the Head of State (who usually acts on the advice of the executive) has been constituted the commander-in-chief of the armed forces. This has helped to maintain civilian supremacy over the military and has given to the executive those powers of command and deployment of the forces which are essential for effective defense. At the same time the legislatures have possessed fundamental control of defense policies and their execution. This includes in many cases a power to review the actions of the executive as commander-in-chief. The legislatures have generally found it necessary to delegate extensive powers to the executive to administer legislative defense policies and fill in their details, relying for control on their powers over the budget, and of investigation, as well as legislation.

All the constitutions include, in varying degrees, specific limitations on the defense powers. These include in most cases limitations for the protection of personal liberties. In addition, further safeguards have sometimes been included to help assure close legislative supervision of defense policies, to help protect local interests, and for other reasons. The effectiveness of these limitations has depended in large part upon the powers of the federal judiciary in reviewing defense activities for constitutional defects. While this review is not appropriate for some activities, and has proved ineffective for others, the experiences of the federations seem to show that this form of control is the best protection consistent with the necessary governmental freedom.

Many of the problems involved in a common defense were examined in connection with the drafting of the European Defense Community Treaty, the major provisions of which are summarized in an Appendix VI to this study. The basic principle of entrusting to the institutions of the community as a whole the responsibility for the defense of all its members, which is a feature of all the federal systems discussed above, also underlies that Treaty. Likewise, the EDC Treaty recognizes the necessity for homogeneous armed forces. The acceptance of these principles by the member States of the EDC should go far toward providing an effective foundation for the defense aspects of a European federation.

By a comparison with the constitutional provisions and experiences of the several federal systems discussed above, it appears clearly, however, that the EDC Treaty is inadequate in many respects for the purposes of a European federation. For this, the underlying reason is the fact that the community lacks a politically responsible government. This fact has two consequences:

(a) The Treaty inevitably confers on the member States, which are politically responsible agencies, many of the powers and duties which must be performed by a federation if it is to be permanent and effective in conducting the common defense.

(b) The Treaty relies heavily on the fact that the member States now follow a common foreign policy coordinated through NATO.

A permanent federation must have the power to adopt and carry out a foreign policy by its own institutions, although it would presumably join, through NATO, with other nations having the same basic policies. The EDC Treaty recognizes this situation by its inclusion of Article 38, calling for an extensive revision of the structure and authority of the various institutions of the Community. Thus, the Treaty should be looked on as an effort to form a common army while the steps are being taken for the creation of the requisite political authorities. When those authorities are created, the terms and provisions of the EDC Treaty must be modified, in many respects, to make them adequate for the common defense. For these reasons it is inappropriate to regard the EDC Treaty as more than a starting point in developing the federal structure with regard to defense.

APPENDIX I

Australia

I. FEDERAL RESPONSIBILITY FOR DEFENSE

The Constitution of Australia places on the federal government the responsibility for providing for the defense of the Commonwealth. Under Section 119, the Commonwealth has the duty to "protect every State against invasion and, on the application of the Executive Government of the State, against domestic violence." The command of the naval and military forces of the Commonwealth is vested in the Governor-General (§68), who acts only on advice of the Cabinet. The Governor-General, acting also on advice of the Cabinet, has power to declare war.

The Commonwealth is also entrusted by the Constitution with the control of external affairs. The executive handles relations with foreign countries and makes treaties which, however, require approval by Parliament in order to become effective in domestic law. The Constitution empowers Parliament to legislate with respect to external affairs (§51 (xxix)).

Under the Constitution, the duty to ensure the internal security of the States depends on the request of the State government. Since the States have no right to secede, however, the Commonwealth would also appear to have the right to take action to prevent such secession. Even when a request is made by a State, the federal government has the right to decide whether its aid is needed by a State to suppress domestic violence; in 1913 it refused to send forces at the request of the State of Queensland. Moreover, in implementing this section, the federal Parliament in 1914 prescribed that the armed forces should not be used in industrial disputes.

The Constitution also withdraws from the States the authority for defense, which had formerly belonged to them at least in part before federation. Thus, a State may not, without the consent of the federal Parliament, "raise or maintain any naval or military force" (§114). On the formation of the federation, the naval and military defense departments of the States were transferred to the Commonwealth (§69), and the authority of the Commonwealth is made exclusive by Section 52 as to "matters relating to any [such] department of the public service."

II. Federal Authority for Defense

The federal responsibility for defense is matched by a broad grant of power to Parliament to make laws "for the peace, order and good government of the Commonwealth with respect to . . . the naval and military defense of the Commonwealth and of the several States, and the control of the forces to execute and maintain the laws of the Commonwealth" (§51 (vi)). In addition, the Commonwealth is given "control of railways with respect to transport for the naval and military purposes of the Commonwealth" (§51(xxxii)).

A. *Peacetime Defense Power*

Under its defense power, the Commonwealth is able in normal times of peace to take measures directly related to immediate military needs and make the usual preparations for the possibility of armed conflict. The government may recruit, train, and equip men, of course, build fortifications, and manufacture munitions. It may also closely regulate civilian production of strategic materials in short supply which have a direct military use as well as a civilian use. Such regulation may be undertaken with a view to stockpiling.[8] The government also has the power, in order to maintain capacity for producing war materials, to put industrial facilities acquired by it for defense purposes to civilian production in time of peace.[9]

It is too early to say with any precision how far the federal defense power can go in a period of "ostensible peace" or "cold war." A Defense Preparations Act was enacted in the summer of 1951 authorizing measures to expand production capacity with a view to meeting future war needs, to divert and control materials and credit for defense purposes, and to control inflation. The Act does not confer power to impose compulsory direction of labor or compulsory military service. The constitutionality of this Act has not been determined, but doubts have been raised[10] because of the language used by the High Court in invalidating the government's effort in 1950 to deal with the subversive activities of the Australian Communist Party in the cold war period.[11]

The peacetime defense powers of the Commonwealth are complemented by other powers assigned to it by the Constitution, powers which, although they are directed primarily to meet peacetime non-military needs, contribute to the government's ability to prepare its defenses. Among these are the Commonwealth's power to levy taxes, to borrow money, to acquire property on just terms from any State or person, to engage in railroad construction with the consent of the State concerned, to arbitrate labor dis-

[8] Jenkins v. Commonwealth, 74 C.L.R. 400 (1947).
[9] Attorney General for Victoria v. Commonwealth, 52 C.L.R. 533 (1935).
[10] See Ellicott, "The Defense Preparations Act, 1951," 25 Aust. L.J. 162 (1951).
[11] "Australian Communist Party v. The Commonwealth," 24 Aust. L.J. 485 (1950).

putes extending beyond the limits of any single State, and to legislate concerning matters incidental to the exercise of powers expressly granted.[12]

B. *Wartime Defense Power*

In wartime the Commonwealth is, under the defense power, a strong central government capable of mobilizing all essential aspects of national life.[13] The separation between the federal legislative and executive powers is not sharp, especially in time of war, and wartime government by regulation has been the rule under delegation from Parliament to the executive.[14] Under the National Security Act, which was the enabling legislation during the Second World War, the executive was even authorized to amend or render inoperative previous Acts of Parliament.

The Commonwealth is able to fix wages in defense industries.[15] It can determine conditions of work and arbitrate all industrial disputes, although its peacetime, specific constitutional power to do so (§51 (xxxv)) applies only to disputes "extending beyond the limits of any one State."[16] It can regulate, restrict, or prohibit the production, movement, sale, and purchase of any articles appearing to the government to be essential to defense or in order to conserve manpower.[17] It can fix prices,[18] and a divided Court has held that it can control profits directly.[19] As will be seen, fairly drastic measures to ensure internal security can be taken.

In time of war the Commonwealth has also extended greatly the exercise of its fiscal powers, and correspondingly reduced those of the States. During World War II, the Commonwealth enacted legislation levying an income tax and requiring taxpayers to discharge their federal tax obligations before paying any income taxes imposed by the member States. At the same time the Commonwealth undertook to pay to any States not levying an income tax a grant based on that State's usual income tax revenue. In addition, the legislation authorized the Commonwealth to take over certain State officials, premises, and equipment for the collection of income taxes. This legislation was enacted only after the States refused to agree with the Commonwealth upon a voluntary settlement of the problem. It was upheld by the High Court as a valid exercise of the Commonwealth's defense power.[20]

[12] §§51 (11) (iv), (xxxi), (xxxiv), (xxxv), and (xxxix).

[13] See Report of the Royal Commission on the Constitution 120 (1929).

[14] Wishart v. Fraser, 64 C.L.R. 470 (1941).

[15] Australian Woollen Mills Ltd. v. Commonwealth, 69 C.L.R. 476 (1944); and H. V. McKay Massey Harris Ltd. v. Commonwealth, 69 C.L.R. 501 (1944).

[16] Pidoto v. State of Victoria, 68 C.L.R. 87 (1943). See also Rex v. Commonwealth Court of Conciliation and Arbitration, 66 C.L.R. 488 (1942).

[17] Stenhouse v. Coleman, 69 C.L.R. 457 (1944).

[18] Farey v. Burvett, 21 C.L.R. 433 (1916); see Shrimpton v. Commonwealth, 69 C.L.R. 613 (1945).

[19] Rex v. Bromhead, 73 C.L.R. 237 (1947).

[20] South Australia et al. v. Commonwealth, 65 C.L.R. 373 (1942). Dicta of the Court suggest, however, that these measures might also be sustained under other constitutional powers of the Commonwealth.

C. *Power in Postwar Period of Readjustment*

The defense power extends beyond its normal peace time scope, not only in wartime, but also during a postwar period of readjustment. The High Court has said that the

> defense power does not cease instantaneously to be available as a source of legislative authority . . . with the end of the war . . . [It] includes not only a power to prepare for war and to prosecute war, but also a power to wind up after a war . . . gradually if that is thought wise. . . .[21]

Consequently, the Court upheld, against a series of attacks following immediately upon the conclusion of the last war, price controls and wage controls.[22] Other controls were also continued through the end of 1946, and the Court has further indicated that some specific and immediate consequences of war are within the power of the federal government to deal with as such while they persist. Thus the federal government may see to the housing of returning soldiers; it can arrange for loans to them, and otherwise attend to their rehabilitation, and see as well to the reconstruction of physical war damage.[23] It may even continue close regulation of an industry in order to fulfill, in the postwar period, a wartime agreement to supply an ally.[24] Controls over black marketing and prices were held still valid through 1947.[25]

Eventually, however, most of these special aspects of the defense power will be cut off. In the important case of *Rex v. Foster,* 79 C.L.R. 43, decided in 1949, the Court held that time had run out on certain war-derived powers.[26] The entire life of the nation had in some way been affected by the war, the Court said; that, however, did not mean that for a generation or so after a war the federal government could continue to control the entire life of the nation. The Court invalidated a measure of manpower control; it threw out gas rationing, which was defended on the ground of a war-produced dollar shortage, saying that the government could use what normal power it had to control imports. It even invalidated eviction controls applicable to homes occupied by veterans; there was still a housing shortage, the Court said, but veterans were, in respect of eviction, at this late date no longer a special class in the position of wards of the federal government.

Despite some earlier language looking the other way, the formal existence

---

[21] Dawson v. Commonwealth, 73 C.L.R. 157, 176 (1946).

[22] *Ibid.;* Miller v. Commonwealth, 73 C.L.R. 187 (1946); Australian Textiles Ltd. v. Commonwealth, 71 C.L.R. 161 (1946).

[23] Real Estate Institute v. Blair, 73 C.L.R. 213 (1946); Attorney General v. Balding, 27 C.L.R. 395 (1920); Rex v. Foster, 79 C.L.R. 43, 82–83 (1949).

[24] Sloan v. Pollard, 75 C.L.R. 445 (1948).

[25] Hume v. Higgins, 78 C.L.R. 116 (1949); Rex v. Regos, 74 C.L.R. 613 (1947).

[26] See also "Queensland Newspapers Ltd. v. McTavish," 25 Aust. L.J. 491 (1951).

of a state of war seems to make no difference in determining the duration of these extraordinary defense powers.[27] Following the Second World War the Australian government had a period of two to three years to use these powers to deal with postwar adjustment; its powers then reverted to normal.

III. LIMITATIONS ON DEFENSE POWER

A. *Role of High Court in Interpreting Defense Power*

As has been seen, the constitutional grant of defense power expands and contracts according to conditions. This expansion and contraction is accomplished under the control of the High Court. The Court performs this function in the light of its conception of the proper boundaries of judicial review and of the degree of deference it should show for the judgment of the legislative and executive branches concerning the necessity, wisdom and expediency of any given measure.

In the leading case of *Farey v. Burvett,* 21 C.L.R. 433 (1916), which upheld price-fixing by the Commonwealth in the First World War, Chief Justice Griffith and Justices Isaacs and Barton stated that, in reviewing measures purporting to carry out the defense power, the function of the Court is a limited one. The Court is to determine whether the measure in question can be thought even incidentally "to conduce to the successful prosecution of war and defeat of the enemy" in wartime, or whether it related to "preparation for war" in time of peace. Issues of the wisdom, expediency, or necessity of any given measure are not for the Court, but are within the discretion of Parliament and the executive, which "alone have the information, the knowledge and the experience . . . to judge the situation."

The Court has since held that it will not question legislative motives and hidden purposes so long as legislative power exists,[28] and it has, as the expansion of the defense power in wartime illustrates, implemented the view of its function stated in *Farey v. Burvett* with considerable consistency.[29] However, the Court seems to have undertaken to control somewhat more closely the implementation by administrative bodies of defense legislation and regulations. It has, at times, looked into the motives of such bodies, and, on the ground that they were not motivated by defense purposes, has invalidated specific administrative actions taken under laws or regulations which the Court agreed were valid.[30]

---

[27] Compare Jerger v. Pearce, 28 C.L.R. 588 (1920), with Rex v. Foster, 79 C.L.R. 43, 83 (1949).

[28] Australian Textiles Ltd. v. Commonwealth, 71 C.L.R. 161, 170 (1945).

[29] See Andrews v. Howell, 65 C.L.R. 255, 263 (1941); Rex v. Regos, 75 C.L.R. 613, 625–626 (1947); and Bailey, "Fifty Years of the Australian Constitution," 25 Aust. L.J. 314, 318–319 (1951).

[30] Arthur Yates & Co. v. The Vegetable Seeds Committee, 72 C.L.R. 37 (1945); Shrimpton v. Commonwealth, 69 C.L.R. 613 (1945). Cf. Little v. Commonwealth, 75 C.L.R. 94 (1947).

B. *Constitutional Limitations on the Exercise of Federal Powers*

The defense power, like all other powers granted to the federal government by the Australian Constitution, is subject to certain limitations and safeguards. Thus, the Constitution decrees, in Section 92, that "trade, commerce, and intercourse among the States, whether by means of internal carriage or ocean navigation, shall be absolutely free." Many wartime controls closely regulating the movement of goods did not run afoul of this provision. However, the High Court did invoke Section 92 to strike down a federal regulation which specifically prohibited inter-State railroad and other travel except as licensed, under a system of priorities, by federal authorities.[31]

The High Court has enforced as a limitation on the defense power the separation between the judicial function on the one hand and administrative and legislative ones on the other, which is embodied in Sections 71 and 72 of the Australian Constitution. These sections vest the judicial power of the Commonwealth in federal courts staffed by judges with life tenure. Under them the Court has sometimes invalidated administrative actions on the ground that they were judicial in character, yet taken by officials without life tenure.[32] The Court has, however, declared courts-martial constitutional under the defense power, although they do not meet the constitutional requirements for the judiciary.[33]

Section 116 of the Constitution forbids the making by the Parliament of "any laws for establishing any religion, or for imposing any religious observance, or for prohibiting the free exercise of any religion. . . ." Nevertheless, in *Adelaide Company of Jehovah's Witnesses, Inc. v. Commonwealth,* 67 C.L.R. 116 (1943), where the High Court considered the government's action, under the defense power, against the Witnesses as a subversive organization advocating refusal to bear arms, the Court said that the government was moving against subversive, not religious, activities. The fact that a religious sect was engaged in them could not serve to invoke the protection of Section 116.

Aside from Section 116, the Australian federal Constitution contains no detailed guarantee of civil rights. These rights are, it is said, safeguarded by the good sense of a Parliament which must go to the country every three years, and by the common law.[34] This condition has, it would seem, enabled the Australian Parliament and executive at times to go a bit farther in restricting personal liberty on grounds of disloyalty or suspected sub-

[31] Gratwick v. Johnson, 70 C.L.R. 1 (1945).

[32] Silk Bros. Ltd. v. State Electricity Commission, 67 C.L.R. 1 (1943); Victorian Chamber of Manufacturers v. Commonwealth, 67 C.L.R. 413, 416–417 (1943). Cf. Lloyd v. Wallach, 20 C.L.R. 299 (1915); Little v. Commonwealth, 75 C.L.R. 94 (1947). See Cowen, "The Separation of Judicial Power and the Exercise of Defense Powers in Australia," 26 Can. B. Rev. 829, 842–843 (1948).

[33] Rex v. Cox, 71 C.L.R. 1 (1945); Rex. v. Bevan, 66 C.L.R. 452 (1942).

[34] Bailey, "Fifty Years of the Australian Constitution," 25 Aust. L.J. 314, 325–326 (1951).

version than might have been the case under a written bill of rights.[35] However, in a few cases involving personal liberties the Court has seemed to exercise a wider and less modest power of review than it deemed advisable in *Farey v. Burvett*. Thus, in the *Jehovah's Witnesses* case the Court seemed to construe the regulations more strictly than it did many regulations dealing with economic controls, and held that at least parts of the regulations went beyond the defense power. Recently, the Court held that an Act of Parliament outlawing the Communist Party went, at least in this time of "ostensible peace," beyond the defense power.[36] Unlike the *Jehovah's Witnesses* case, the *Communist* case did not come up while the defense power was expanded to its full wartime extent. It may nevertheless form a part of an emerging trend to treat civil rights cases arising under the defense power somewhat differently from other cases. A third example of what may be such a trend, this time in the field of academic freedom, is a holding by the Court that a wartime attempt to set quotas for admissions to certain university graduate schools was invalid,[37] although it had upheld the widest forms of manpower control.

The absence of written civil rights provisions in the Australian Constitution has thus not left the government's powers over individuals entirely untrammeled in this respect. However, in invalidating measures involving civil rights, the High Court has had to base its decision on a lack of defense power; ostensibly it must apply the same criteria it would to a case involving economic controls, since there is no separate constitutional ground to rest on. As a result such cases have the effect of narrowing the government's general defense power rather than merely limiting it in a specific and well-defined direction. A demonstration of this fact is the weight assigned by at least one commentator to the *Communist* case, in examining the constitutionality of federal powers of economic control in a cold war period.[38]

IV. ROLE OF STATES IN DEFENSE

Although there is an early case looking the other way,[39] it is clear now that the broad power to take social and economic measures related to defense is not the exclusive province of the federal government. Subject to the primacy of federal law in the case of conflict between State and federal law (§109 of the Constitution), the States may exercise concurrent powers with those of federal government which are not expressly declared to

[35] See Lloyd v. Wallach, 20 C.L.R. 299 (1915), and Little v. Commonwealth, 75 C.L.R. 94 (1947). Section 13 of the National Security Act of 1939–1940 authorized the arrest without warrant and detention without arraignment for ten days of any person suspected of having violated any of the Act's provisions.
[36] See "Australian Communist Party v. The Commonwealth," 24 Aust. L.J. 485 (1950).
[37] Rex v. The University of Sydney, 67 C.L.R. 95 (1943).
[38] See Ellicott, "The Defense Preparations Act, 1951," 25 Aust. L.J. 162 (1951).
[39] Joseph v. Colonial Treasurer of New South Wales, 25 C.L.R. 32 (1918).

be exclusively federal. Furthermore, inconsistency between State and federal legislation in a field of concurrent powers must be fairly clear before it will invalidate the former. The mere fact that the federal government has legislated in an area is not sufficient. The federal legislation must declare or clearly indicate the intention to occupy the field exclusively.[40]

This doctrine concerning concurrence of powers opens up a potentially valuable area for state-federal cooperation. The institutional framework for such cooperation has existed for some time in the form of the Federal and State Premier's Conference, which takes place at least once a year. A number of defense problems have been handled by cooperative state-federal action. Thus, the federal government delegated to State Premiers during the Second World War power to maintain order in areas of troop concentrations. Settlement of veterans on land and veterans' housing and slum clearance were undertaken as joint state-federal projects. In administering a number of wartime regulations, the federal government made use of State government employees. Reliance on federal-state cooperation proved unsuccessful, however, in the case of the fiscal arrangements during the Second World War discussed above.

APPENDIX II

Canada

I. FEDERAL RESPONSIBILITY FOR DEFENSE

The federal government alone is responsible for the defense of Canada. Section 91 (7) of the British North America Act of 1867 provides expressly that

> . . . the exclusive Legislative Authority of the Parliament of Canada extends to all Matters coming within the Classes of Subjects next hereinafter enumerated, that is to say: —
> 7. *Militia, Military and Naval Service and Defence.* [emphasis added]

Thus, federal legislation (Militia Act, R.S.C., c. 132) provides for assistance to the Provinces by the armed forces in the event of internal disturbances which the Provinces are unable to deal with.

In addition, Section 15 of the organic act states:

> The Command-in-Chief of the Land and Naval Militia and of all Naval and Military Forces, of and in Canada, is hereby declared to continue vested in the Queen. [The Crown acts only at the request of the Canadian Cabinet.]

Formal declaration of war is made by the Crown, as Head of State. However, Great Britain and the Dominions associated with it are "equal

---

[40] Carter v. Egg and Egg Pulp Marketing Board, 66 C.L.R. 557 (1942).

in status, in no way subordinate to one another in any respect of their domestic or external affairs, though united by a common allegiance to the Crown." [41] Accordingly, war was declared by the King to exist between Canada and Germany in 1939 only after he had received the advice of the Canadian Cabinet which had formally consulted Parliament. Moreover, under the Letters Patent issued in 1947, the Governor-General, as the King's representative in Canada, was delegated all the prerogative powers of the Crown, including the formal power to declare war.

In foreign affairs, as in the declaration of war, the federal government has complete sovereignty, although in the making of treaties it also acts through the Crown or its representative, the Governor-General. The Provinces have been inactive in the field of foreign affairs, although they have concluded agreements with foreign countries on minor matters. They would, however, lack power to conclude any agreements with foreign countries relating to defense.

II. Federal Defense Powers

A. *Peacetime Defense Powers*

In addition to its competence with respect to the armed forces and defense, the federal Parliament has jurisdiction with respect to "the raising of money by any mode or system of taxation" and "the borrowing of money on the public credit" (§91 (3), (4)). One of the principal reasons for granting such unlimited tax powers to the Parliament was to enable it to finance defense activities. These defense and finance powers give to the federal government competence, even in peacetime, to provide for Canada's ordinary defense requirements and, apparently, for any necessary abnormal program of defense. For its current defense program, however, the federal government has relied on its general authority under Section 91 to make laws for the "peace, order and good government of Canada, in relation to all matters not coming within the Classes of Subjects . . . assigned exclusively to the Legislatures of the Provinces." This clause has been interpreted to give it extensive powers in time of special emergency. But applicability has been circumscribed: in several instances where the federal government has sought to rely on it to take economic measures (as during the depression of the 1930's), the courts have not permitted what they considered to be an invasion of the Provinces' constitutional powers over "property and civil rights."[42] It is not certain what interpretation would be made, however, where federal defense measures were involved.

Nevertheless, the defense preparations which the federation has undertaken in the last few years have not been opposed by the courts. Under the National Defense Act (C.S. 1950, c. 43) the federal government may

---

[41] Declaration of Imperial Conference of 1926.

[42] Toronto Electric Commissioners v. Snider, [1925] A.C. 396; Attorney-General of Canada v. Attorney-General of Ontario, [1937] A.C. 326, 355.

take control of property, including transportation and communications facilities, for defense purposes during an emergency. The courts have upheld such appropriation of property in other instances when it was incidental to the exercise of a power held by the federal government under Section 91 of the British North America Act and reasonable compensation was paid.

Under its unlimited powers of taxation, the federal Parliament may impose "direct taxes," the only form of taxes which the Provinces may levy (§92 (2)). Exercise of both federal and provincial powers has therefore resulted in exceptionally high income taxes and succession duties in some Provinces. As discussed further below, the federal government has called several "Dominion-Provincial Conferences," both during and since the war, to resolve these fiscal problems. As a result, Quebec is the only Province which does not now have a taxation agreement with the Canadian government. Thus, the constitutional arrangement of taxing powers has been modified, in times of heavy defense expenditures, by agreement between the federal government and the Provinces permitting greater federal control.

B. *Wartime Defense Powers*

Since formation of the federal government there has been in force a statute making all males between the ages of 18 and 60 liable for service in the militia at the order of the Governor-General.[43] It was not until 1917, however, that compulsory military service was first enforced. The majority of French Canadians resisted this measure energetically. However, the federal government's power to conscript troops was not successfully challenged. Similar difficulties arose in the Second World War. At the outbreak of the war the government, recalling its earlier difficulties, formally committed itself to limit compulsory military service to Canadian territory (National Resources Mobilization Act, C.S. 1939, c. 13). In 1942, however, it became evident that more men might be required for overseas service. A referendum was therefore called on whether the Act should be amended. As a result, 72 per cent of the voters of Quebec replied No, and 80 per cent of the voters of the other Provinces replied Yes. Parliament thereupon altered the Act. The Cabinet did not use this new power until late in 1944, however, and by the end of the war only 13,000 men had been compelled to go overseas.

As discussed further below, in time of war the federal Parliament's control of taxation has been extended by agreements with the Provinces whereby the latter withdrew from many fields of taxation in return for compensation by the federal government. No less extensive has been the federal power for economic and manpower mobilization in time of war. Under the National Resources Mobilization Act (C.S. 1940, c. 13), the ex-

[43] Militia Act, R.S. 1927, c. 132, §8. This Act is subject to repeal by proclamation of the Governor-General under the National Defense Act, C.S. 1950, c. 43, §250.

ecutive was given power to "make from time to time such orders and regulations requiring persons to so place themselves, their services and their property, at the disposal of His Majesty in the right of Canada, as may be deemed necessary and expedient for securing the public safety, or the efficient prosecution of the war, or for the maintaining of supplies or services essential to the life of the community." Under this broad authority an order was issued providing for the arbitration of all labor disputes (P.C. 2685 June 1940). A permanent basic wage was set for all industries and firms, as well as a compulsory cost of living bonus to be paid at the determination of the federal government (P.C. 7440, December 6, 1941). Some two hundred National Selective Service Bureaus were set up throughout the country at which all unemployed men and women between the ages of 20 and 24 had to register. No job transfer could be undertaken without a permit from the Board, and in 1943 compulsory transfers of workers and "freezing" of workers in high priority jobs were ordered. Wage and salary stabilization, when the danger of inflation began in 1943, was similarly enforced by an order-in-council (P.C. 9384, December 9, 1943).

The great powers that accrue to the federal government in time of war are, in fact, exercised by the Cabinet, not by Parliament. Cabinet leadership is strong in Canada at all times, but in war it becomes much greater. In addition, very broad powers are delegated to the Cabinet. The chief grant of power by Parliament to the Cabinet is the War Measures Act of 1914 (R.S.C. 1927, c. 206). Under it, a proclamation by the Governor-in-Council or by the Crown is taken as conclusive evidence of the existence of war. Thereupon the Governor-in-Council (i.e., the Cabinet) may, "by reason of the existence of real or apprehended war, invasion or insurrection," do and authorize such acts and things as he deems necessary "for the security, defense, peace, order and welfare of Canada." Beside this sweeping grant of power are listed six special categories of executive power, including (1) censorship of all written or published material, (2) arrest, detention, and deportation, (3) control of harbors and shipping, (4) control of transportation, (5) control of trade, manufacture, production, importing and exporting, (6) control, appropriation, and forfeiture of property and the use thereof. The Cabinet may prescribe the penalties to be imposed for violation of any of its orders issued under this Act.

The government relied on the War Measures Act when it announced a "state of apprehended war" to exist on September 1, 1939, and, even before Parliament had met, issued several important orders, including the Defense of Canada Regulations which curtailed drastically the liberties of individuals, both aliens and citizens, for the duration of the war. Until revoked in August and September, 1945 (P.C. 4136), these Regulations provided for the censorship of the mails, the suppression of all writing likely to harm the war effort, the prohibition of subversive organizations, and the arrest, punishment, or internment of persons who made prejudicial remarks about the war on recruitment. Enemy aliens were subject to indefinite detention or deportation. The federal government also exercised extensive controls over persons of Japanese ancestry, both citizens and aliens, especially by its order for their evacuation from the western part of the Province of British Columbia. The Supreme Court upheld these and the deportation orders, issued to both aliens and citizens of Japanese ancestry, in its interpretation of the government's wartime powers.[44]

Restrictions on civil liberties were not the only measures challenged unsuccessfully before the courts. The orders-in-council imposing rent controls, and the wide discretionary powers of the Minister of National Revenue under the War Income Tax Act (R.S.C. 1927, c. 97) were both upheld.[45]

C. *Power in Postwar Period of Readjustment*

In the years following the Second World War no Act of Parliament has been held to exceed the federal government's emergency powers. The Supreme Court seems to be basing its decisions on an opinion of the Privy Council, which declared that "[very] clear evidence that the crisis had wholly passed away would be required to justify the judiciary . . . in overturning the decision of the Government that exceptional measures were still requisite." [46] The Court has held, however, in one instance that an order issued by the Cabinet purporting to be based on authority delegated to it by a postwar enabling Act, providing for appropriation and control of wheat and barley, exceeded the power delegated to the executive by the statute.[47] This follows the precedent set by the judiciary after the First World War, when the Cabinet's orders-in-council based on the War Measures Act were scrutinized with far greater severity after the termination of hostilities.

In view of the extraordinary difficulties of postwar reconstruction and the combination of international tensions, the Canadian Parliament has passed three successive enabling Acts since the end of the Second World War. These Acts supersede, but do not repeal, the War Measures Act. The latter Act comes into force as soon as war is declared, at which time the current enabling Act passes out of effect. All three of the postwar Acts display a progressively narrower scope. The first, The National Emergency Transitional Powers Act (C.S. 1945, c. 25), provided a statutory basis for the continuation of many wartime controls on rents, wages, prices, and transportation. It also allowed the executive to provide relief for foreign countries and maintain armies in occupied territory, as well as to arrange for demobilization and rehabilitation of the returning armed forces. Its main difference from the War Measures Act lay in its require-

[44] Co-operative Committee of Japanese Canadians v. Attorney-General of Canada, [1947] D.L.R. 577.

[45] See Pure Spring Co. v. Minister of National Revenue, [1946] Ex. C.R. 471; and In re Wartime Leasehold Regulations, [1950] S.C.R. 124.

[46] Fort Francis Pulp and Paper Co. Ltd. v. Manitoba Free Press, [1923] A.C. 695.

[47] Canada Wheat Board v. Nolan, [1951] S.C.R. 81.

ment that all orders be presented to Parliament within fifteen days. When the Act expired in May, 1945, it was extended for another year (The Continuation of Transitional Measures Act, C.S. 1947, c. 16), with the added requirement that all orders be published in *The Canada Gazette* immediately.

One of the factors in Parliament's increased wariness in adding this requirement was the Cabinet's conduct of the postwar spy investigation, in which a Royal Commission on Espionage was set up by a secret order-in-council in February, 1945 (P.C. 411). The Council's procedures were received unfavorably by elements of press and public when they became known. The effect of this reaction can also be seen in the preamble and provisions of the current enabling statute, the Emergency Powers Act (S.C. 1195, c. 5). This Act resembles the two previous postwar statutes in most respects, giving the executive continued power over defense preparation, but it explicitly denies authority to the executive to "arrest or detain or deport anyone," except pending judicial trial, or to undertake any "censorship, control or suppression" of written and published materials. The preamble also states that the Act is not to limit "the fundamental liberties of the individual."

The federal defense powers also include full competence over all legislation affecting veterans, including their pensions, allowances for education, medical help, and some conditions of employment upon their return to civilian life.[48]

III. Constitutional Limitations on Federal Defense Power

From the foregoing account it appears that in time of war the continued existence of the Provinces as political entities and hence of opposition to the federal government provides the principal restraint on the latter's powers. The legal limitations of the federal powers, as enforced by the judiciary, remain another source of restriction. However, during periods of active warfare the judiciary has shown great self-restraint in considering the actions of the federal government. The courts have repeatedly refused to review the wisdom of Acts of Parliament or orders-in-council. In discussing regulations made necessary by war conditions, Lord Haldane said:

> The question of the extent to which provisions for circumstances such as these may be maintained is one on which a Court of law is loath to enter. No authority other than the central Government is in a position to deal with a problem that is essentially one of statesmanship. [*Fort Francis Pulp and Paper Co. Ltd. v. Manitoba Free Press Co. Ltd.*, [1923] A.C. 695.]

The separation of legislative and executive powers is a principal constitutional limitation on the exercise of federal powers. However, exten-

[48] Fry v. W. H. Schwartz & Sons Ltd., [1951] D.L.R. 198.

sive powers with respect to defense have been delegated to the executive by Parliament, especially in critical times. These delegations have been upheld by the courts, as in the *Gray* case ([1918] S.C.R. 158), where the Chief Justice said:

> Parliament cannot "abdicate" its functions, but within reasonable limitations it can delegate its powers to the executive government. It seems obvious that Parliament intended . . . to clothe the executive with the widest powers .in time of danger. Taken literally . . . unlimited powers . . . [and it is for Parliament] to put any limitations on the power conferred.

IV. THE ROLE OF THE PROVINCES IN DEFENSE AND IN TIME OF WAR

The Provinces are excluded by the British North America Act from maintaining any military forces of their own, and, in fact, only two of the Provinces maintain police forces, the rest depending entirely upon the federal police. The power of the Provinces to enact legislation affecting members of the armed forces is, moreover, limited. A soldier driving a military vehicle on official duty cannot be required to obtain a provincial driver's license, but the Provinces may enforce speed rules.[49] The Provinces have also the power to tax the pay of members of the armed forces (and federal civil servants) within their territory.[50]

As mentioned above, however, the main burden of political opposition falls to the Provinces in time of war. Members of the opposition in the federal Parliament are too close to the center of the war effort, and share in its responsibility too much, to be enthusiastic in criticism of the government. This was noticeable during the Second World War, even though, unlike during the First World War, no coalition government was set up. Moreover, the vast powers that Parliament delegates to the Cabinet reduce its activity. The burden of criticism thus shifts to the Provinces which have, in the past, exercised this right energetically. Between 1939 and 1945 the government was berated in Quebec for excessive aggressiveness, and in Ontario for lagging in its war efforts.

Members of the provincial governments are also drawn into cooperative activities by the federal government. Thus, between 1939 and 1944 the federal Department of Agriculture called twelve conferences between federal and provincial officials to plan agricultural production, labor distribution, and subsidy needs. Members of producers' organizations were also represented. Again, in 1948, the Minister of Defense appointed a coordinator of Civil Defense, whose functions are mostly of a planning nature, and who consults provincial officials in periodic conferences.

---

[49] See Rex v. Rhodes, [1934] O.R. 44; Rex v. Anderson, [1930] 39 M.A.R. 84; and Rex v. McLeod, [1934] 4 D.L.R. 226.

[50] Attorney-General of Manitoba v. Worthington, [1936] S.C.R. 40.

Cooperation between the federal and provincial governments has sometimes been difficult, however. The extent of federal taxation presented occasion for one such disagreement among the Provinces, and between the
Provinces and the federal government. At the outbreak of the Second
World War it became evident that the federal government would have to
tax every available field, including some which the Provinces were already
taxing. Accordingly, Prime Minister King called a Dominion-Provincial
Conference for January 14, 1941, to discuss the recommendations on taxation made by the Rowell-Sirois Report, to the effect that the Provinces
should give up certain fields of taxation in exchange for grants from the
federal government. The conference lasted only two days, and ended in
total failure, since three Provinces refused to consider the Report as a basis
of discussion. The 1941 federal budget, consequently, left no source un-
tapped, including such provincial fields of taxation as gasoline and succession duties. The federal government again made an offer to the Provinces to come to terms, and one by one they signed agreements based on
the recommendations of the Rowell-Sirois Report (Bk. II, pp. 75–130).
After the end of the war the federal government tried to continue these
arrangements, and most of the Provinces accepted. However, Quebec has
refused and now imposes its own income and corporation taxes.

APPENDIX III

Germany

I. IMPERIAL CONSTITUTION OF 1871

A. *Responsibility for Defense and Defense Powers of the Reich*

The Imperial Constitution contained no provisions expressly assigning
responsibility for defense of the Reich. It follows, however, from the constitutional grants of extensive defense powers to the federation that corresponding responsibility for defense was likewise transferred to it.

The Emperor had authority to declare war in case of an attack upon
the territory of the Empire or its coasts; in the absence of attack he could
declare war with the approval of the Bundesrat (whose members were appointed by the governments of the member States) (Art. 11). Article 11
also authorized the Emperor to conclude foreign alliances, although the
approval of the Bundesrat was necessary if the alliance related to matters
within the competence of Imperial legislation, and also of the Reichstag if
it was to be valid as internal law. Treaties of peace also required the approval of the Imperial legislature so far as they changed internal law or
required financial appropriations.[51]

---

[51] This Article was amended in 1918 to require the consent of both legislative chambers
for all declarations of war and treaties of peace, as well as all treaties relating to matters of
Imperial legislation.

Article 4 of the Constitution made subject to Imperial legislation "the military system of the Empire and the Navy"; and "the establishment of roads and waterways in the interest of the defense of the country." The Constitution also provided that all Germans were liable for military service (Art. 57) and that all who were capable of bearing arms should serve with the regular and reserve forces for specified periods (Art. 59). The navy was an Imperial domain, subject exclusively to the command of the Emperor, and its budget was met out of the Reich treasury (Art. 53). The navy was completely unified in structure and command, and until 1898 had no statutory basis (other than legislative approval of the budgetary laws) and rested entirely upon ordinances of the Emperor.

The status of the Reich military forces was somewhat different from that of the navy. They were, under the Constitution, composed of the armies (*Kontingente*) of the several States. However, the Imperial legislature had the power to determine the strength of these armies (Art. 60) and to determine the military budget (Art. 62). The military budget was fixed by Imperial statute, with contributions from the member States according to a formula provided in the Constitution. Article 61 of the Constitution provided for introduction of all Prussian military legislation without delay throughout the entire Reich. The Emperor was, under Article 63, commander-in-chief of the Kontingente, and could determine "the strength, composition and the division of the Kontingente . . . designate the garrisons . . . and provide for the war-ready array of every part of the Imperial Army"; his determination of armed strength was, however, subject to determinations by the legislature under Article 60. His commands were directly operative on the forces and did not require the mediacy of the State governments (Art. 64). All important military commanders, including the princes of the member States in command of their Kontingente, were subordinate to him and appointed by him. The appointments of all other general officers serving with the Kontingente were subject to his approval (Art. 64, §2). (Some of the statements in this paragraph are subject to exceptions in the case of Bavaria, as discussed below.)

An exception to the organization of the military forces into Kontingente of the member States was made in the case of troops in the German colonies. These were exclusively forces of the Reich, likewise under the command-in-chief of the Emperor.

The Emperor's wide constitutional powers also included the power to declare martial law in case of a threat to the public safety, although the manner and consequences of his declaration were regulated by statute (Art. 68). Moreover, in case of disagreement on military or naval matters in the Bundesrat, the Prussian votes, controlled by the Emperor as King of Prussia, were decisive (Art. 5, §2), giving him a veto against the votes of the other member States in such matters. His extensive powers also made it possible for him to create an unofficial cabinet of military advisers. His consultation with this group was considered to be an Imperial prerogative and was free from control by the civil authorities. Through its influence with the Emperor this military group, especially during the First World War, gradually became predominant, its influence culminating in control of the removal and appointment of Ministers during 1917 and 1918.[52]

Although the Constitution made no provision for economic mobilization of the Reich, measures of this nature were necessary during the First World War. These measures were provided by enactments of the Bundesrat but were subject to approval by the Reichstag. In many cases broad powers were delegated to the executive.

B. *Role of the Member States*

Through their appointment of the members of the Bundesrat the governments of the member States of course played a large part in all matters regulated by Imperial legislation, including defense matters.

As discussed above, the German military forces under the Imperial Constitution did not consist of one unit but of Kontingente of the member States. The States had certain rights with respect to these formations. They could appoint officers, other than those appointed by the Emperor, although all officers were subject to the Emperor's command. They could use their troops (as well as those of other Kontingente stationed in their territory) for police purposes (Art. 66), subject to the overriding commands of the Emperor. The States were also competent for the administration of military justice, and could provide for the regulation of their units so far as consistent with federal regulations.

The position of the member States with regard to their Kontingente was regulated by treaties concluded between the various States, on the one hand, and Prussia or the Reich on the other hand, as well as by the provisions of the Constitution. Two of these treaties, those of Bavaria and Württemberg with the Reich, were incorporated by reference into the Constitution (closing provision of Division XI) thus making them qualifications of the constitutional provisions described above. The treaty between the Reich and Bavaria gave to the King of Bavaria considerable autonomy with regard to the Bavarian Kontingente. He was its commander-in-chief in peacetime and, although the Imperial decision for mobilization was binding upon him, had the power to issue the formal mobilization order in his own name. Moreover, the Bavarian Kontingente retained considerable independence from Prussian military administration. The agreements of Württemberg and Saxony with the Reich served principally to give those States certain additional powers with respect to the appointment of officers and the regulation of their Kontingente, but did not greatly

[52] Several constitutional amendments were adopted in October, 1918, for the purpose of introducing a Parliamentary system, and these subjected the entire military system, including administration and command, to ministerial authority and thereby to responsibility to the Reichstag.

modify Imperial control. The special privileges of these three States disappeared in time of war, however, when their forces came under the direct control of the Reich. All three States were also given a special voice in the military councils of the Reich through permanent seats on Bundesrat committees. The treaties of the other German States were concluded with the King of Prussia, and, in general, merged the forces of those States with the Prussian army, so that there were in fact only four Kontingente.

The economic measures provided in wartime by legislation of the Bundesrat were addressed to the governments of the member States which were charged with administration of the laws. In this activity they were, in principle, subject to Imperial supervision, although the States retained, in fact, a high degree of administrative autonomy.

II. THE WEIMAR CONSTITUTION

A. *Responsibility for Defense and Defense Powers*

Under the Weimar Constitution responsibility for defense of the Reich was given to the central government by Article 79 which provided: "The defense of the Reich is a matter of the Reich. The military organization of the German people shall be regulated uniformly by a statute of the Reich, with consideration for the peculiar local characteristics of the people."

Corresponding to this responsibility, the Reich was given "exclusive legislative power concerning . . . military organization" (Art. 6). Similarly, "declaration of war and conclusion of peace" were to be made through "a statute of the Reich" (Art. 45).

The President held "the supreme command over all the armed forces of the Reich" (Art. 47). He "appoints and dismisses the Reich officials and the military officers, in so far as is not otherwise provided by statute." He also concluded "alliances and other treaties with foreign powers" although any of these "which relate to the competence of the legislation of the Reich, need the approval of the Reichstag" (Art. 45).

Article 48 conferred on the Reich, and especially the President, other very important powers, as follows:

> If a Land does not fulfill the duties laid upon it by the constitution or statutes of the Reich, the Reichspräsident can hold it thereto with the aid of the armed forces.
>
> The Reichspräsident can, if in the German Reich the public safety and peace are seriously disturbed or threatened, take the necessary measures for the restoration of the public safety and peace, and, in case of necessity, intervene with the aid of the armed forces. For this purpose he may temporarily, in whole or in part, suspend from operation the Fundamental Rights enumerated in Articles 114, 115, 117, 118, 123, 124, and 153.

Of all the measures taken in accordance with paragraph 1 or paragraph 2 of this article the Reichspräsident must immediately inform the Reichstag. The measures are to be revoked upon demand made by the Reichstag.

In case of danger from delay a Land Government can take for its territory temporary measures of the nature mentioned in paragraph 2. The measures are to be revoked upon demand made by the Reichspräsident or by the Reichstag.

A statute of the Reich shall provide the details.

The most important of these provisions was that giving the President "dictatorship" powers to suspend the basic rights and take all necessary measures including use of the armed forces in the event of emergency. Although the exercise of this power was subject to review by the Reichstag, the President also had power to dissolve the Reichstag.

Legislative control of defense policies was also exercised through control of finances. Article 85 required the federal budget to "be determined by statute before the beginning of the fiscal year." Expenditures could not be added or increased without the consent of the Reichsrat (the second chamber), suggesting a remainder of the influential position of the Bundesrat under the Imperial Constitution.

Other powers with respect to defense were defined by Article 96, which provided that all railroads "must meet the demands of the Reich . . . for the defense of the country"; and by Article 106 which abolished the jurisdiction of military courts "except for times of war and on board warships."

The defense powers under the Weimar Constitution were thus centralized in the Reichstag and, especially, the President. The Constitution permitted the use of the army by him as a means of compulsion and, although this power was rarely used, it was the actual basis of the "Presidential" Cabinets of the last period before January 30, 1933.

B. *Role of the Member States*

The Länder retained some symbols of their former military autonomy under the Reichswehr Statute (§§12, 14, 16, and 17) which provided for formation of units within the Länder which were, as far as possible, made up of citizens of one Land. In the conduct of their local administration the military authorities were required to consult the Land government and to pay due regard to the economic interests of the Land concerned. Bavaria was again given a special position, and the Bavarian military unit was always to be a separate organization under one commander, with the Land government having greater control over the selection of the commander of that unit than did the other Länder. In the case of the other Länder, although their governments might propose commanders of the local military forces, appointment was made only with the approval of the President (§12 of the Reichswehr Statute).

The most important power of the Länder was, however, conferred by Article 48, Section 4, of the Constitution (quoted above), giving the Land governments the right to use the "dictatorship" powers described in Article 48, in the case of an immediate threat to public safety and peace. Similarly, the Reichswehr Statute (§17) required that, in case of public emergencies or of a threat to public order, the armed forces give assistance to Land governments upon their request. These provisions led to conflict between the Reich and the Länder, notably when the Bavarian government, in October, 1923, invoked its powers to requisition army units stationed within its territory and to give those units orders inconsistent with ordinances of the Reich government. The difficulty was finally settled by negotiations.

Notwithstanding these powers of the Länder under Article 48, that Article gave to the President the power to call to order a Land, with the assistance of the armed forces if necessary. This provision was made use of several times, even to the point of delegating the executive power over certain Länder to the competent military commander. Likewise, Article 48, Section 2, authorized the President to intervene with the armed forces in the case of public disorders, even though a Land government was proceeding against the unrest. Intervention by the President in these cases was subject to review by the Staatsgerichthof, but was upheld in all instances.

III. BASIC LAW OF THE FEDERAL REPUBLIC

In contrast to the Imperial and Weimar Constitutions, the Basic Law of the German Federal Republic has only very limited provisions relating to defense powers, and contains no provision for emergency powers in the nature of Article 48 of the Weimar Constitution. The power to provide for defense does not appear among the powers of the federation set forth in Article 73. There are, however, several provisions relating to defense. Article 4, Section 3, provides: "No one may be compelled against his conscience to render military service as an armed combatant. Details will be regulated by a Federal law." Article 26, Section 2, states: "Weapons designed for warfare may be manufactured, transported or marketed only with the permission of the Federal Government." Most important, under Article 24, Section 2, the federation may join "For the maintenance of peace . . . a system of mutual security; in so doing it will consent to limitations upon its sovereign powers apt to bring about and secure a peaceful and lasting order in Europe and among the nations of the world." And, under Article 24, Section 1, "The Federation may by legislation transfer sovereign powers to international institutions."

APPENDIX IV

Switzerland

I. Federal Responsibility for Defense and Defense Powers

A. *Principal Constitutional Provisions*

Under the Swiss federal Constitution, the responsibility of providing for the defense of the federal territory is placed upon the Confederation. Article 5 imposes upon the Confederation the duty to guarantee "to the Cantons their territory, their sovereignty within the limits fixed by Article 3, their constitutions, the liberty and rights of their people, the constitutional rights of the citizens, and the rights and power conferred by the people on the authorities."

Article 8 states that "the Confederation has the sole right to declare war and conclude peace, and to make alliances with foreign states." Article 19, paragraph 3, provides that "the control of the army and of the war material prescribed by law is vested in the Confederation," and that "in case of danger, the Confederation has also the right of exclusive and immediate control (*Verfügungsrecht*) over all troops."

Article 20 provides that "laws on the organization of the army are enacted by the Confederation." It further states that "military instruction is entirely vested in the Confederation; the same also applies to arming." Based on this power the Confederation enacted in 1907 a law on *Militärorganisation,* which it has amended several times since. This law contains the main provisions on the organization and the instruction of the army, and defines the distribution of military powers between the Confederation and the cantons. Article 85, paragraph 4, of the Constitution provides that the commander-in-chief of the armed forces is to be elected by the Assembly.

Under the Constitution, the Federal Assembly is given competence concerning defense of the independence and neutrality of Switzerland, and alliances and treaties with foreign states. The Assembly also declares war and concludes peace, and has power to take measures for the internal security of Switzerland and for the maintenance of peace and order (Art. 85, pars. 5–7). The federal Executive Council is given responsibility to administer federal military activities and to protect external and internal security, and "has general charge of foreign affairs" (Art. 102).

B. *General Defense Powers*

1. RAISING ARMED FORCES

Since the Constitution forbids the Confederation to maintain standing troops (Art. 13), the Swiss army is, with few exceptions, entirely an army

of militiamen. The Constitution states that every male Swiss shall perform military service (Art. 18), and the *Militärorganisation* provides the
details of military service. The only exceptions to the constitutional prohibition of standing troops are instructors, corps and division commanders, and special corps which guard the Swiss fortresses.

2. SUPPORT OF THE ARMED FORCES

Article 22 of the Constitution provides: "In return for a reasonable
compensation, the Confederation has the right to make use of or to acquire
drill grounds and buildings used for military purposes, together with their
accessories, in the Cantons." The Confederation also is entitled to ex-
propriate lands for fortifications or other installations for the general welfare (Art. 23). According to the same Article the Confederation may
order the construction at its own expense of public works (e.g., highways
and railways), or may encourage the same by granting subsidies to the
cantons. The Confederation also may prohibit the establishment of public
works which would endanger its military interests, but this power has
never been exercised.

The Constitution further states in Article 41 that the manufacture,
purchase, trade, and distribution of gunpowder as well as of arms, munitions, and other war materials fall within the competence of the Confederation. The Confederation has built factories for the manufacture of
arms and munitions, and has also granted concessions for this purpose to
private manufacturers.

During the present "cold war" period, there has been an increase in
defense activities. The Confederation has provided for the modernization
of arms and, in 1951, enacted a special program for armament. There has
been, however, some difficulty in carrying out this program for reasons explained below.

3. FINANCING DEFENSE COSTS

The Federal Assembly has the power to levy only certain taxes specified in the Constitution. The revenues of the Confederation, as provided
for in Article 42 of the Constitution, have been insufficient since World War
I. They have been increased by several transitory financial programs, but
every attempt at a permanent increase in the grant of taxation powers to
the Confederation has failed. The latest of these transitory programs was
adopted in 1950 and has been added as an appendix to the Constitution.
It will remain in force until the end of 1954, but does not provide sufficient funds for the armament program of 1951. A bill initiated by the
Socialist Party providing a capital levy on large properties was rejected
by the people and the cantons in May, 1952. Also, a proposal of the
Federal Assembly for a supplementary income and property tax and a tax

on beverages had no success. The Federal Assembly has, however, the right to borrow money (Art. 85, par. 10).

4. INTERNAL SECURITY

The Confederation and the cantons have power to take measures for internal security. Thus, they may forbid meetings which are dangerous for the state. The Swiss Penal Code provides for punishment of all actions dangerous to the state, and a new amendment to the Code, of October 5, 1950, provides in particular that all subversive propaganda and all participation in associations dangerous to the state will be prosecuted (Arts. 275-*bis, -ter*).

C. *Emergency Defense Powers and Powers in Post-emergency Periods*

1. MOBILIZATION AND COMMAND OF THE ARMED FORCES

The power to call up the armed forces for active service is conferred on the Federal Council by the *Militärorganisation* (Art. 198). After a large number of troops has been called up, a commander-in-chief of the armed forces is elected by the Assembly pursuant to its constitutional authority. Under Article 208 of the *Militärorganisation,* this commander-in-chief may claim all personnel and material forces of Switzerland. The relation between this power of the commander-in-chief and that of the Federal Council to call up the armed forces is not quite clear and this circumstance led to some conflict during World War II regarding the levying of troops. In general, however, the commander-in-chief is limited to strictly military functions.

2. ECONOMIC MOBILIZATION

The constitutional powers of the legislature increase considerably in time of emergency. Under Article 80-*bis,* added by amendment in 1949, the Assembly may enact urgent decrees which need not be based on the Constitution or submitted to referendum; however such decrees become invalid in one year unless they are accepted by the people and the cantons. Further powers of a general economic nature have recently been granted to the Confederation, which are particularly useful in critical times. Article 31-*bis,* which was added to the Constitution by amendment in 1947, authorizes the Confederation "to enact regulations concerning the exercise of trade and industry and to take measures for the promotion of branches of the economy"; and, under Article 31-*bis,* III, these measures are not limited by the principle of freedom of trade and industry (otherwise guaranteed by Article 31) where the Confederation enacts "regulations on measures for insuring preparedness in time of war."

Prior to adoption of the two amendments discussed above, however, during both World Wars, constitutional limitations were overcome by extra-constitutional emergency measures. In 1914 and 1939 the Federal Assembly empowered the Federal Council to take all measures necessary for the security, independence, neutrality, and economic interests of Switzerland, although such legislation was not provided for by the Constitution. Based on this emergency power, the Federal Council regulated the rationing of nearly all food, fixed prices and wages, controlled a great part of industrial production, and granted subsidies for the construction of houses, for the maintenance and development of industries, and for social aid. It also levied taxes not provided for in the Constitution. The Federal Council's power was subject only to control by the Federal Assembly. Since the Swiss Federal Court is entitled only to invalidate cantonal laws and acts, it has no power to examine the constitutionality of the federal emergency measures. Both the recent amendments to the Constitution appear to be attempts to regularize the exercise of emergency powers by the Confederation.

3. POST-EMERGENCY ADJUSTMENT

After the end of both World Wars the Federal Assembly, which had granted broad powers to the Federal Council, regulated their termination. In a federal decree of December 6, 1945, it stated that the Federal Council was no longer authorized to exercise emergency powers except in urgent cases. On December 18, 1950, the Federal Assembly provided that after 1952 all acts based on the emergency power were annulled. The few provisions of this kind which were still in force in 1952 were concerned mainly with the control of rents. Many provisions which were introduced by emergency law have, however, been taken over in regular legislation. Moreover, in 1947, the constitutional power of the Confederation in the economic area was, as already mentioned, largely extended.

II. CONSTITUTIONAL LIMITATIONS ON THE FEDERAL DEFENSE POWER

The fact that federal law prevails over cantonal law (Transitory Provisions of the Constitution, Art. 2), and that there is no judicial power to invalidate federal acts, has meant that the constitutional limitations on defense powers are not strictly settled. Nevertheless, the popular rights and liberties represent fundamental limitations on federal power. There is, in the first place, the right of initiative and referendum. While the constitutional and legislative referendum may be suspended in urgent cases for one year (Art. 89-*bis*), the initiative is never restricted. Further, the following freedoms are guaranteed by the federal Constitution: equality before the law (Art. 4), freedom of trade and industry (Art. 31), freedom of establishment (Art. 45), freedom of conscience and religion (Art. 49), freedom of the press (Art. 55), right to form associations (Art. 56) and of petition (Art. 57).

The right to form associations is, however, guaranteed only on the condition "that the objects and methods of such associations are not unlawful or dangerous to the state. Cantonal laws will make the necessary provisions for the prevention of abuses." Under this authority several cantons prohibited the Communist Party in the years before 1939. The Federal Court, entitled to invalidate cantonal acts, declared such prohibitions constitutional in view of Article 56, on the ground that Communist activity constituted a danger to the state at that time (*Entscheidungen des Bundesgerichts* 63 I 281). In 1940, the Confederation dissolved the Communist Party throughout Switzerland.

Under emergency measures during the two World Wars some civil rights, especially the freedom of trade and industry, the freedom of establishment, and the freedom of the press, were considerably restricted. Since there is no fixed limitation of the federal emergency power provided in the new Article 89-*bis* of the Constitution, the popular rights do not constitute such a limitation either.

III. Role of the Cantons in Defense

Article 3 of the Constitution provides that the cantons exercise all the rights which are not delegated to the federal authorities. However, all essential defense powers are delegated to the Confederation. The Constitution contains a number of provisions dealing with the rights of the cantons in the military field. Article 19 states: "The Federal army consists of: (a) the Cantonal corps of troops; (b) all Swiss who, not being members of these corps, are, nevertheless, liable for military service." This reference to cantonal corps is a relic of old times and is of subordinate importance. In fact, although the cantons may maintain their own corps of troops, the Confederation prescribes the number and the equipment of these troops and provides for their instruction. The only differences between cantonal and federal troops are that each cantonal corps is recruited from the same canton, and that the officers of the cantonal troops are nominated and promoted by the cantonal government. But the cantonal government must observe the federal requirements for promotion and the officers must have been declared suitable for their rank in federal instruction courses.

Article 20 of the Constitution states that "the execution of military laws within the Cantons is undertaken by the Cantonal authorities within the limits prescribed by federal legislation and under the supervision of the Confederation." One of the main functions of the cantons in executing the military laws is to keep registers of all Swiss liable for military service. The cantons also maintain registers of all their residents and of all members of federal and cantonal troops.

Article 20 further provides that "the supply and maintenance of clothing and equipment are within the competence of the Cantons, but the cost thereof shall be reimbursed by the Confederation to the Cantons in a manner to be prescribed by Federal law." In executing this duty the cantons must observe federal requirements.

Article 19, IV, states: "The Cantons exercise control (*verfügen,* dispose) over the military forces in their territory, except when this right is limited by the Federal Constitution or laws." On the basis of this power the cantons may call up their cantonal troops, as well as the federal troops within their territory, but only to maintain order within their borders. Moreover, they have this right only if the Confederation itself does not claim the troops (Art. 19, par. 3).

Finally, there are other Articles in the Constitution which refer to the cantonal military power. Article 13, II, states: "No Canton or half-Canton may have more than three hundred permanent troops without permission of the Federal power; the police are not included in this number." Further, Article 15 provides: "In case of sudden danger from without, the government of the Canton threatened must invoke the assistance of the confederated states and immediately notify the Federal authority, all without prejudice to the measures which the latter will take. The Cantons so called upon are bound to give their assistance. The cost shall be borne by the Confederation." This Article, too, is no more than a historical remainder, since the Confederation has both responsibility and the powers to provide for defense.

APPENDIX V

United States

I. FEDERAL RESPONSIBILITY AND CONSTITUTIONAL POWERS FOR DEFENSE

A. *Principal Constitutional Provisions*

The United States Constitution places on the federal government the responsibility of providing for defense. Article IV, Section 4, thus provides:

> The United States shall guarantee to every State in this Union a Republican Form of Government and shall protect them against Invasion, and on Application of the Legislature or of the Executive (when the Legislature cannot be convened) against domestic Violence.

The Constitution grants to Congress the power to declare war (Art. I, §8, cl. 11), to raise and maintain a navy and armies, and other powers relating to defense discussed below, along with the general power "to make all laws which shall be necessary and proper" to carry out its specific powers (cl. 18).

The powers of the President in regard to defense are laid down in Article II, Section 2, paragraph 1, which provides:

> The President shall be Commander in Chief of the Army and Navy of the United States, and of the Militia of the several States, when called into the actual Service of the United States . . .

In addition, the executive power is vested in the President (Art. II, §1), and (Art. II, §2, par. 2) he is given the power

> . . . by and with the Advice and Consent of the Senate to make Treaties, provided two thirds of the Senators present concur; and he shall nominate, and by and with the Advice and Consent of the Senate, shall appoint Ambassadors, . . . and all other Officers of the United States. . . .

The defense powers are further concentrated in the federal government by express constitutional provisions prohibiting in large part the exercise of such powers by the States. Thus Article I, Section 10, provides:

> No State shall enter into any Treaty, Alliance or Confederation; grant letters of Marque and Reprisal . . .
> . . . No State shall, without the Consent of Congress, . . . keep troops, or Ships of War in time of Peace, enter into any Agreement or Compact with another State, or with a foreign Power, or engage in War unless actually invaded, or in such imminent Danger as will not admit of delay.

B. *General Defense Powers*

1. RAISING AND USE OF THE ARMED FORCES

The Constitution sought to avoid the disability imposed on the central government by the Articles of Confederation, in force prior to the adoption of the Constitution, which provided that the central government could raise troops only by requisitioning them from the States. This practice had caused great inefficiency and inequity during the American Revolution, through competitive recruiting and unequal distribution of burdens. Accordingly, the Constitution grants to Congress the power "to raise and support armies" and "to provide and maintain a navy"; in addition, Congress may "make rules for the government and regulation of the land and naval forces." (Art. I, §8, cl. 12, 13, and 14). The powers of Congress and those of the President as commander-in-chief have been interpreted to give to the federal government (i.e., the legislature and executive) an authority to raise and employ the armed forces which is constitutionally unlimited by any rights of the States to maintain forces.[53]

A strong popular sentiment against maintenance of a standing army, and

[53] Selective Draft Law Cases, 245 U.S. 366 (1918).

a long tradition of the maintenance of militia by each State, resulted, how-ever, in the following provisions of the Constitution (Art. I, §8, cl. 15 and 16) which contemplated the maintenance of armed forces (militia) by the individual States:

> The Congress shall have power . . .
> To provide for calling forth the Militia to execute the Laws of the Union, suppress Insurrections, and repel Invasions;
> To provide for organizing, arming, and disciplining the Militia, and for governing such Part of them as may be employed in the Service of the United States, reserving to the States respectively, the Appoint-ment of the Officers, and the Authority of training the Militia accord-ing to the discipline prescribed by Congress;

The maintenance of militia by the States, it was expected, would make un-necessary a large standing army. The militia were, however, expressly sub-jected to certain federal controls by clauses 15 and 16, and by Article I, Section 10, clause 2, prohibiting the maintenance of troops by the States in time of peace except with the consent of Congress.

During its early history the United States relied for its defense prin-cipally upon the State militia. Because of State control of training the militia and of their officers, and limitation of the right of the federal gov-ernment to use them, this reliance led to some of the misadventures which the writers of the Constitution had hoped to avoid. In the War of 1812 with Great Britain, the governors of Massachusetts and Connecticut, who opposed the war, refused to provide their militia which the federal gov-ernment had called for, and the government was unable to enforce its constitutional power. In the same war the militia of New York refused to fight in Canada on the ground that such fighting was not for the purpose of repelling invasion, and thus could not be required of the militia by the federal government; for this reason no effort was made to use militia in the subsequent wars with Mexico and Spain which were carried on outside the United States. In all these instances the federal government was required to raise a large, untrained army of volunteers and conscripts upon the commencement of the war.

In the early 1900's, however, Congress decided, by the use of its un-restricted power to raise armies, to give to these militia the character of a federal army, as well as that of State troops. Thus, the federal govern-ment could override, through the use of its constitutional power, the States' privileges with respect to the use, training, and leadership of the militia. This concept has been developed until today the militia (now called the "National Guard of the United States") have been thoroughly federalized and have in fact a dual status — as part of the federal army, subject to regulation by Congress and control by the President, and as State militia. Although their capacity as federal troops is controlling, and the federal government provides funds for their support and controls the appointment of officers, the National Guard is still organized into divisions made up of citizens of a State or adjacent States and the States participate in the selection of officers. In addition, these troops are available to the State governments for use in emergencies, so far as not inconsistent with federal policies. Any use of troops by the States is also subject to the constitutional limitation (Art. I, §10, cl. 3) which prohibits the States, without Congressional approval, from engaging in war unless invaded or immediately threatened with invasion.

2. SUPPORT OF THE·ARMED FORCES

The federal government may provide for the support of the armed forces, pursuant to the powers of Congress described above and to the powers of the President as commander-in-chief. Their respective powers are discussed below in connection with the allocation of federal powers.

In addition, Article I, Section 8, clause 17, of the Constitution empowers Congress "to exercise exclusive Legislation . . . over all Places purchased by the Consent of the Legislature of the State in which the Same shall be, for the Erection of Forts, Magazines, Arsenals, dock-Yards, and other needful Buildings." This does not inhibit the federal government's acquisition of property within State boundaries by purchase, or by the exercise of eminent domain, or by other means. Although the State's jurisdiction continues in such cases unless it has otherwise agreed, that jurisdiction cannot be exercised to deprive the federal government of title or embarrass it in its use of the property.[54]

3. FINANCING DEFENSE COSTS

Congress is given the power, by Article I, Section 8, clause 1, of the Constitution, "to lay and collect Taxes, Duties, Imposts and Excises; to . . . provide for the common Defence and general Welfare . . ." Clause 2 empowers Congress "to borrow money on the credit of the United States." Thus the federal government is given complete authority to finance defense costs.

Under the Articles of Confederation, the expenses of the federal government were financed by quotas requisitioned from the States. This arrangement required the federal government to rely on sources of funds which it could not control, and resulted in serious defaults by the States and disputes among them as to fixing quotas. It was recognized as a fundamental error by the writers of the Constitution.

C. *Special Defense Powers in Extraordinary Periods*

The United States Constitution makes no provision for emergency powers as such. Instead, the defense powers increase greatly in time of

[54] James v. Dravo Contracting Co., 302 U.S. 134 (1936).

war and trail off with the end of hostilities and their consequences, but, unlike express emergency powers, they do not come into being or terminate upon any specified event but can be exercised in a degree corresponding to the need.

1. ECONOMIC MOBILIZATION AND POSTWAR ADJUSTMENT

The constitutional powers of Congress to provide general economic controls in the interest of supporting a national defense effort in time of war are very great. They include power to fix prices and wages, to impose rent controls, to prevent abnormal profits, to regulate labor disputes, and to allocate materials; and they spring from the specific powers granted to Congress in Article I, Section 8, of the Constitution, and the general power there granted to do all things "necessary and proper" to carry out the specific powers. Legislation of this sort has been upheld by the courts against contentions that it violated constitutional provisions against deprivation of liberty or property without due process of law (Fifth Amendment) or against taking property for public purposes without compensation.[55] Nevertheless, these constitutional provisions set standards of reasonableness for both the substance and procedures of these economic measures.

The federal defense power "carries with it inherently the power to guard against the immediate renewal of the conflict, and to remedy the evils which have arisen from its rise and progress." [56] Thus Supreme Court opinions have upheld economic controls imposed by Congress in a posthostilities period. These opinions nonetheless in most cases have carefully examined the necessity of the measure in question for postwar recovery, and often have been accompanied by dissenting opinions that such necessity did not exist.[57] However, the terminal point for the exercise of these powers has no necessary relation to the formal termination of hostilities or of the state of war.

Although the Congressional measures discussed here have been upheld by the courts on the ground that they were necessary to deal with conditions created by an existing or recently concluded war, there is no reason to doubt that they would equally be sustained where they were necessary to meet conditions arising from defense efforts to meet an apprehended need for use of the armed forces.

The question of Congress's power to conscript labor in the interest of national defense requires special consideration, for here a further potential limitation on Congressional action is presented, i.e., the Thirteenth Amendment, which provides: "Neither slavery nor involuntary servitude,

[55] See Legal Tender Cases, 12 Wall. 457 (1870); Yakus v. United States, 321 U.S. 414 (1944); Bowles v. Willingham, 321 U.S. 503 (1944).

[56] Stewart v. Kahn, 11 Wall. 493, 507 (1870).

[57] Ruppert v. Caffey, 251 U.S. 264, 304 (1923); Ludecke v. Watkins, 335 U.S. 160, 173 (1948). See also Woods v. Miller, 333 U.S. 138, 146 (1948).

except as a punishment for crime whereof the party shall have been duly convicted, shall exist within the United States, or any place subject to their jurisdiction." Strong persuasive controls on labor have been exercised in both World Wars through use of the military conscription laws, and through allocation of materials so as to reduce the labor requirements of unessential industries. From here it would not be far to conscription of labor, should that become necessary.[58]

2. PROTECTION OF INTERNAL SECURITY AS RELATED TO DEFENSE

Under its defense powers the federal government is authorized to take measures to protect internal security. Special constitutional limitations are concerned here, however. These are the limitations of the first ten Amendments (the Bill of Rights, protecting freedom of speech, religion, press, assembly, the right against unreasonable searches and seizures, the right to jury trial, etc.; and Article I, Section 9 ("The privilege of the Writ of Habeas Corpus shall not be suspended, unless when in Cases of Rebellion or Invasion the public Safety may require it"). This latter provision makes clear that the Constitution contemplates the taking of extraordinary measures, such as the imposition of martial law, by the government in certain circumstances. It is an unsettled constitutional question whether, under Article I, Section 9, the President may suspend the writ of habeas corpus, or whether only Congress may do so. The Supreme Court has refused to approve, however, measures taken by the President, acting without Congress, to close the civil courts and subject the civil population to trial by military tribunal, or suspend the writ of habeas corpus, so long as the civil courts are able to function normally. President Lincoln took such action during the Civil War in the case of persons in areas removed from the hostilities who assisted the rebellion, and similar measures were taken in Hawaii in the early days of World War War II; in both instances the Court held the action to be invalid.[59]

Another question of this type is the extent to which the government may restrict ostensibly political activities to protect the country's security. Government employees who are believed to be unreliable are subject to dismissal at the President's discretion, in the absence of Congressional regulation.[60] With regard to the public generally, the Supreme Court has upheld the constitutionality of a law making it a crime to conspire to "willfully advocate, abet, advise or teach the duty, necessity, desirability or propriety of overthrowing any government in the United States by force or violence," as applied in the prosecution of leaders of the Communist Party.[61] In up-

[58] See Butler v. Perry, 240 U.S. 328 (1916).

[59] Ex parte Milligan, 4 Wall. 2 (1866); Duncan v. Kahanamoku, 327 U.S. 304 (1945). See also Ex parte Quirin, 317 U.S. 1 (1942).

[60] Bailey v. Richardson, 182 F.(2d) 46 (D.C. Cir. 1950), affirmed by an equally divided Court, 341 U.S. 918 (1951).

[61] Dennis v. United States, 341 U.S. 494 (1951).

holding this law the Court relied heavily on the relation between the external threat to national security and the domestic activities of the Communist Party. Recent federal legislation has gone even further in restricting organizations which follow, in one or more respects, the Communist line, but this has not yet come before the Court.

In World War II the President and Congress, acting together (i.e., through an executive order issued by the President, followed by an Act of Congress providing penalties for violation of that order), authorized the military to restrict and remove from the West Coast of the United States all persons of Japanese ancestry, whether United States citizens or not. This action was upheld by the Supreme Court in two cases, the first concerning a curfew order applied only to Japanese inhabitants, the second concerning the exclusion order.[62] Notwithstanding the impact of the government's action on civil liberties protected by the Constitution, the Court was of the opinion that the executive and legislative judgment of the necessities of the situation was sufficiently reasonable that it could not be questioned by a judicial body. In a third case, however, the military's action in detaining in a camp outside the prohibited area a Japanese of acknowledged loyalty, pursuant to a policy of reducing the burden of these displaced persons on the inland communities, was annulled as having no relation to national defense or to the purpose of the government's action which could justify its interference with liberties protected by the Bill of Rights.[63]

3. CIVIL DEFENSE

Civil Defense is a concurrent federal-state power, with the federal power supreme because of the constitutional responsibility of the federal government for national defense. In practice the principal action in this field has so far been taken by the States, with the federal government contributing funds and advice and providing the necessary coordination with the military authorities. Should it be necessary, however, the federal government would have the power to take the steps which it considered essential for proper defense of the civilian population.

II. ALLOCATION OF POWERS BETWEEN EXECUTIVE AND LEGISLATURE

A. *Disposition and Use of the Forces*

In a government such as the United States, with a President who is not dependent for his tenure on the legislature, the demarcation of the legislative and executive powers is of great importance. Because of apprehensions about placing too much power in the hands of the federal executive,

---

[62] Hirabayashi v. United States, 320 U.S. 81 (1943); Korematsu v. United States, 323 U.S. 214 (1944).

[63] Ex parte Endo, 323 U.S. 283 (1944).

the Constitution granted to the President only the powers of commander-in-chief of the army and navy (in addition to his powers as chief executive and with respect to foreign affairs and the appointment of officials). The President was intended to have "nothing more than supreme command and direction of the military forces," and his powers were contrasted with those of the British king which extended to "the declaring of war and to the raising and regulating of fleets and armies — all of which, by the Constitution under consideration, would appertain to the legislature." [64]

In practice, however, it has been necessary for the President, in time of emergency, to exercise powers on his own authority (i.e., without their being delegated to him by Congress) which resemble the powers granted to Congress by the Constitution. For example, after the first shots of the Civil War were fired, President Lincoln increased the army and navy and declared a blockade of Southern ports before Congress had authorized this action or taken cognizance of the hostilities. The validity of such acts is based on recognition that war can exist although not declared by Congress, and the President, as commander-in-chief, may act in the case of war without waiting for Congress.[65] Prior to World War II President Roosevelt employed the navy for convoy duty and otherwise disposed the armed forces in the manner he deemed best suited to defense of the nation.[66] Thus, the commander-in-chief may influence greatly the federal defense policies by his deployment of the forces.[67] In addition, Congress has found it necessary to delegate to the President, as chief executive, broad additional powers over the recruiting and use of armed forces pursuant to laws passed by it.

To the President's power as commander-in-chief are added his powers in the field of foreign affairs, either alone or with the support of the Senate, to make international commitments which deeply affect national defense policies. These foreign affairs powers are discussed at length elsewhere;[68] it may be enough to note here that the President has made commitments (e.g., the guarantees of Berlin and Western Germany) which amount to undertakings to make war in the event of attack on a foreign country.

For full effectiveness if not for constitutional reasons, however, such actions as those described above require in almost all cases the approval of Congress in the form of appropriation of funds or other supporting legislation. This Congressional power of review is fortified by the constitutional provision that "No money shall be drawn from the treasury, but in consequence of a law . . ." (Art. 1, §9, cl. 6).

In addition, there has, on occasion, been claimed for Congress a right directly to participate in, or approve, fundamental decisions of strategy re-

[64] Hamilton, *The Federalist*, No. 69.
[65] Prize Cases, 2 Black 635 (1862).
[66] Corwin, *Total War and the Constitution* 22 *et seq.* (1947).
[67] The use of United States forces in Nicaragua during the 1920's and their initial employment in Korea in 1950 are other examples.
[68] See Study 5, Foreign Affairs.

garding deployment of forces. For example, when additional American forces were sent to Europe in 1951, the Senate adopted a resolution approving this action and stating that "no [further] ground troops . . . should be sent to Western Europe . . . without further Congressional approval."

The Constitution gives to Congress the power "to make rules for the government and regulation of the land and naval forces" (Art. I, §8, cl. 14). The commander-in-chief also has power to act in this regard, but is governed by the procedures and substantive rules which are laid down by Congress. The commander-in-chief may also provide for the government of territories occupied by the United States armed forces.[69] However, if such territory is annexed to the United States its government then becomes a power of Congress pursuant to Article IV, Section 3, of the Constitution. ("The Congress shall have power to dispose of and make all needful rules and regulations respecting the territory or other property belonging to the United States. . . .")

B. *Support of the Forces and Economic Measures*

In its legislation providing for the support of the armed forces Congress has delegated to the President, as executive, wide power to carry out the legislative policy, often leaving him great discretion.[70] Frequently, enabling legislation of this sort enacted in time of war is left dormant in the statute books after the war, making it possible for the President to call upon the powers thereby delegated to him when he considers that some subsequent emergency so requires.

In addition to these delegated powers, the President, as commander-in-chief, has exercised certain undefined powers to commandeer private property necessary for the maintenance of the armed forces. During the Civil War the President seized and operated a railroad, important in supplying troops, which passed through territory whose inhabitants were sympathetic to the South; and immediately prior to World War II the President seized and operated factories producing aircraft and ships for the armed forces where, because of labor disputes or for other reasons, private operation had broken down.

The Supreme Court has recently rejected a claim by the President of a broad power relating to defense, by annulling his seizure of the steel industry.[71] The seizure was made, at a time when an industry-wide strike was impending, on the ground that continuous production of steel was vital to the support of armed forces in Korea and to the defense program generally. The President immediately notified Congress of his action, requested that Congress act, and stated his understanding that Congress could reject his action; thus seeking to justify the seizure as an emergency act pending Con-

---

[69] Madsden v. Kinsella, 343 U.S. 341 (1951).
[70] See Steuart & Brothers v. Bowles, 322 U.S. 398 (1944).
[71] Youngstown Sheet & Tube Co. v. Sawyer, 343 U.S. 579 (1952).

gressional consideration. The Court found that no Act of Congress authorized the seizure, and annulled the President's action on the ground that it constituted an act of legislation and was beyond the competence of the commander-in-chief. The Court also relied on the fact that Congress had earlier rejected proposals for legislation authorizing governmental seizure of strike-bound industries in emergencies.

III. Constitutional Limitations of the Defense Power

The principal constitutional limitations of the defense power are those protecting personal liberties. These have been discussed above, principally in connection with the defense powers relating to internal security.

In addition, however, the Constitution places two express limitations on the federal defense powers. First, the Third Amendment provides that "No Soldier shall, in time of peace be quartered in any house, without the consent of the Owner, nor in time of war, but in a manner to be prescribed by law." Second, Article I, Section 8, clause 12, empowering Congress to raise and support armies, states that ". . . no Appropriation of Money to that Use shall be for a longer Term than two years."

The restriction imposed by the Third Amendment was intended to prevent certain abuses suffered by the American colonials before the Revolution. The prohibition of the appropriation of money to raise and support armies for more than two years was intended to prevent Congress from granting to the President funds for such purposes for an indefinite period, reflecting the fear of a standing army and of concentration of power in the executive. This limitation was not imposed upon the maintenance of navies, however, and Congress is therefore free to provide for long-range naval building programs.

Another limitation is contained in the Fifth Amendment, which provides that no "private property [shall] be taken for public use without just compensation."

IV. Role of the States in Defense

The basic source of State power is the residue of powers left after the specific grants to the federal government. This is expressed in the Tenth Amendment to the Constitution which provides: "The powers not delegated to the United States by the Constitution, nor prohibited by it to the States, are reserved to the States respectively, or to the people."

The specific constitutional limitations of the powers of the States with respect to defense have been set forth in Section I, A above. The States' powers to maintain armed forces have also been dealt with at page 217. It should be noted, however, that since the Constitution (Art. I, §10) only forbids the States to keep troops "in time of peace" without Congressional approval, there is no constitutional obstacle to the maintenance of "home guard" or similar units by the States in time of war, as was done in both World Wars. However, such measures may not interfere with any exercise of its defense power by the federal government, and any troops so maintained would be subject to the federal government's constitutional powers with respect to State militia.

Although the federal powers in the field of economic mobilization are supreme and prevail over State action, the States are free, in the absence of inconsistent federal policy, to provide necessary economic controls.[72] Where Congress has deemed it necessary to apply economic controls to State activities, however, no doctrine of intergovernmental immunities has been invoked.[73]

The enforcement of federal economic controls has often been dependent for its effectiveness upon the cooperation of State enforcement officials. In addition, Congress has on occasion delegated to the States substantial powers with respect to the administration of federal laws, going so far as (in the Housing and Rent Act of 1949) to authorize the States to cancel the application of federal rent controls when they consider them no longer necessary.[74]

The States also have power to deal with insurrections and disturbances within their borders, and to use the National Guard for this purpose (so long as consistent with federal policies). However the federal courts have inquired closely into the existence and seriousness of the unrest and the necessity for the action which the State has taken. Where the court has doubted the State's judgment on this point, it has annulled the action.[75] The constitutional standard for State action impinging upon civil rights in order to deal with local disorders is probably the same as that applied to federal action in the interest of national defense. Here, however, the courts have been more willing to assert their own judgment in deciding this question, with the result that a much clearer need must exist to support State action.

V. Role of the Courts in Interpreting Defense Powers

The Supreme Court and the other federal courts have the authority to interpret and enforce the Constitution against unlawful governmental action, including action pursuant to the defense powers. In the field of defense, however, the Court has recognized that the basic judgments must be made by Congress or the President and that the Court should restrain itself in inquiring into those judgments. The principle of judicial restraint in this field was declared by the Supreme Court in an early case where it

---

[72] See Crowley v. Allen, 52 F. Supp. 850 (N.D. Cal. 1943); Clark v. Allen, 331 U.S. 503 (1947).

[73] Case v. Bowles, 327 U.S. 52 (1945).

[74] United States v. Shoreline Cooperative Apartments, 84 F. Supp. 660 N.D. Ill. (1949) 338 U.S. 897 (1949).

[75] Sterling v. Constantin, 287 U.S. 378 (1932).

held that the President, having received general authority from Congress to call up troops in an emergency, was the sole judge of when such an emergency existed and the only restriction on his judgment was that imposed by the political influence of the electorate and Congress.[76] This principle has, however, been limited to matters which are inherently nonjusticiable or involve basic policy decisions; in other sorts of cases the federal courts have been willing to form their judgment and impose it on the official concerned.[77]

The courts have exercised special vigilance with respect to the protection of civil liberties. Here again they have recognized that the question of what is necessary for preservation of the country is primarily for determination by Congress and the President. However, the courts have reviewed and, on occasion, annulled defense measures restricting civil liberties, and the existence of this power to review and annul has had a tempering effect on both the legislature and the executive.

The courts in the United States have also been a principal instrument for controlling the expansion of defense powers in times of crisis and their contraction with the return of normal periods. This function is reflected in the courts' deference to legislative and executive judgments as to defense requirements in time of war, and their greater willingness to review such judgments in postwar periods.

Two inherent limitations on the powers of the courts in interpreting the defense powers should be pointed out. The first is the delay involved in bringing a case through the court system to the Supreme Court. The important civil rights cases of both the Civil War and World War II (see notes 59, 62, and 63 above) were decided several years after the action in question had run its full course. They were, therefore, of limited practical effect in enforcing the interpretation of the Constitution which they pronounced.

The second limitation is the physical inability of a court to enforce its judgment against unwilling military authorities. For example, during the Civil War President Lincoln, on his own authority, ordered the suspension of the writ of habeas corpus in the vicinity of a military line of communication running through an area dominated by persons of doubtful loyalty. Although the Chief Justice of the Supreme Court found that the President's action was unconstitutional,[78] his decision was disregarded by the President whose order continued to be enforced.

[76] Martin v. Mott, 12 Wheat. 19 (1827); also Luther v. Borden, 7 How. 1 (1849).

[77] Wilcox v. Emmons, 67 F. Supp. 339 (S.D. Cal. 1946) reversed sub. nom. Dewitt v. Wilcox, 161 F.2d 785 (9th Cir. 1947), cert. denied, 332 U.S. 763 (1947); Little Barreme, 2 Cranch 169 (1804).

[78] Ex parte Merryman, 17 Fed. Cas. 144 (1861).

A P P E N D I X   V I

The European Defense Community Treaty

I. INTRODUCTION

The European Defense Community Treaty would establish a supranational organization and entrust to it the responsibility of defending against all aggression the European territories of the member States, and of participating on their behalf in the defense efforts which have been undertaken by the North Atlantic Treaty Organization. The member States would divest themselves of the responsibility so transferred to the EDC and of the means to carry it out alone. They would pledge themselves not to raise or maintain any national armed forces for the purpose of defending their European territories and not to engage on an independent national basis in the production of armaments. The armed forces of the EDC are not to be coalition forces, but are to be integrated in such a fashion that units of homogeneous nationality would be unable to mount an effective operation alone.

The member States which organized the EDC have not, however, transferred to the Community all the powers necessary for it to discharge completely the responsibility which they entrusted to it. Under the Treaty, unanimous agreement of the member States is required to raise EDC forces, decide upon their size and nature, raise the finances necessary for their support, command them, or decide where they should be stationed or how and when they should be used.

Some assurance of a coincidence in the defense and foreign policies of the six member States, which is necessary to enable the EDC to operate, exists for the immediate future. It is provided by the North Atlantic Treaty alliance and the organization through which it is given effect. Although the German Federal Republic is not a party to the North Atlantic Treaty, Germany would participate in making crucial decisions in NATO through joint NATO and EDC Council meetings (provided for in Section 1 of The Protocol Concerning Relations Between the EDC and NATO, which is annexed to the EDC Treaty).

II. EDC AND STATE RESPONSIBILITIES FOR DEFENSE

Article 2 of the Treaty declares the Community's objectives to be exclusively defensive and states that the Community shall consequently ensure the security of the member States against any aggression. The Article then provides that any attack directed against any one of the member States in Europe or against the defense forces of the Community will be considered an attack against all the member States, and that the member

States and the forces of the Community shall furnish to the State or forces attacked all military and other aid and assistance in their power.

A Treaty between the United Kingdom and the EDC member States extends the guarantee recited above to the United Kingdom and its forces in Europe, in return for a like guarantee running from the United Kingdom to the member States and to the latter's forces in Europe. An Additional Protocol annexed to the EDC Treaty provides that any armed attack on the territory of a party to the North Atlantic Treaty in the area defined in Article 6 (i) of that Treaty, or any armed attack on the forces of any such party in the area defined in Article 6 (ii) of that Treaty, shall be considered an armed attack on the members of the EDC and on the latter's forces.

This defense mission is limited, insofar as attacks on the member States are concerned, to Europe. But it extends, insofar as the forces themselves are concerned, to attacks anywhere; and, under Article 120, the forces may be sent anywhere in the world, although it takes unanimous agreement among the member States to do so. Furthermore, the responsibility which rests on the forces of the Community is not restricted to defense against external aggression. European forces will protect the member States against internal disturbances as well, under Article 12.

The member States may not, under Articles 9 and 10 of the Treaty, recruit or maintain any armed forces except for a series of specific tasks defined in the Treaty. Under Article 10, these State tasks are the defense of their non-European territories, the maintenance of forces in Austria and Berlin, and in areas in which the States undertake a mission on behalf of the United Nations. The States also retain authority to maintain such navies as they may need.

III. Use of Forces

The Treaty and related treaties contain various provisions relating to the use of EDC forces. The principal provisions are in Article 2 of the Treaty, and of the Treaty with the United Kingdom, and Article 1 of the Additional Protocol regarding NATO.

(1) The Additional Protocol regarding NATO, after stating that a specified attack on NATO will be considered an attack on EDC members and forces, goes on to provide that, in the event of such an attack, "the member States of the European Defense Community, in respect of themselves and of the European Defense Forces," shall have the obligations undertaken by the parties to the North Atlantic Treaty in Article 5 of that Treaty; that is, they shall take such action as they "deem necessary." The Community's forces would thus go into action in this case only upon unanimous agreement of the member States.

(2) Under Article 2 of the EDC Treaty, and Article 2 of the Treaty with the United Kingdom, the member States and the EDC forces are

obliged to furnish "all military and other aid and assistance in their power" in the event of an attack on the EDC forces, or an attack in Europe on any of the member States or on the United Kingdom or its forces. The question of how these obligations are to be fulfilled appears to be answered by implication in Article 18 of the Treaty and in Article 1 of the Protocol, annexed to the Treaty, concerning relations between the European Defense Community and NATO; and by the fact that, in the scheme of this Treaty, any powers and functions not granted to the Community are retained and to be exercised by the States.

Article 18 of the Treaty places the European Defense Forces "at the disposal" of the competent NATO Supreme Commander, who is authorized in peace and war to exercise with respect to them such powers as are or may be conferred upon him by NATO. Article 1 of the above-mentioned Protocol provides for joint meetings of the NATO and EDC Councils of Ministers, for the purpose of consultations concerning common objectives, and especially for the purpose of deciding upon measures to be taken whenever the territorial integrity, political independence, or security of a member State is threatened. The NATO Supreme Commander is an agent of the States which allocate forces to him, and is authorized to exercise certain powers on their behalf. The sense of these provisions is that the EDC member States retain power by unanimous agreement to order the use or other disposition of the European Defense Forces and will employ the NATO Supreme Commander as their agent in the exercise of this power.

In exercising the power to order the use of the European Defense Forces through the NATO Commander or otherwise, at least some of the member States may do so only with the agreement of their Parliaments. Article 131 of the Treaty states that the provisions of the Treaty shall be "applied in accordance with the constitutional rules of such member State." Each member State must, therefore, decide whether, before agreeing to the use of the European Defense Forces in implementation of Article 2 or of the Treaty with the United Kingdom or the guarantee to NATO, it need seek the approval of its Parliament.

(3) The question arises whether the Community's senior commanders may exercise the power, which usually accrues to commanders in the field, to take, without reference to civilian authority, limited measures to ensure the immediate security of their troops against an armed attack. It is made clear in the Treaty that Community commanders can take no action in the event of internal violence or disturbances in the area in which they are stationed, for, as will be seen, other provisions are made to cover this case. But nothing is said about taking urgent necessary measures against an armed attack by organized forces. Possibly this authority may be held to be implicit.

(4) The Treaty's other provisions concerning the use of the forces do not

vest significant power in the Community, other than Section 2 of Article 12 of the Treaty. This section reads: "In case of disaster or calamity requiring immediate aid [i.e. floods and other acts of God], elements of the European Defense Forces which are in a position to be of use shall give their aid without regard to their national origins." No special command provision is made in Section 2 of Article 12, but the Community's military commander on the scene may well have the authority to implement this Section.

(5) The eventuality of internal violence is covered by Section 1 of Article 12. In case of disturbances or threatened disturbances within the territory in Europe of a member State, the Community, at the request of the State, shall place at its disposal such part of the contingents supplied by that State to the Community forces as is necessary to meet the situation. The released contingents are to be employed by the government of the State concerned under its laws.

(6) Another and similar provision for the use of Community forces is made by Article 13. In the event of a serious emergency affecting a non-European territory for which a member State assumes responsibilities of defense, it is mandatory for the Community to release to such State, on request, the necessary part of contingents of its nationality, which upon their release "cease to be subject to the authority of the Community." Under this Article, unlike Article 12, the agreement of the competent NATO Supreme Commander is required before the Community may release the contingents requested.

(7) Article 14 is similar to the two just discussed, but here discretion is assigned to the Community. Before contingents from a member State are released to it, as provided by this Article, for the purpose of carrying out an international mission outside the European territories of the member States, the consent of the Community, given by a two-thirds vote of the Council of Ministers, is required.

(8) The other definite provisions for the use of the Community forces are those of Article 120. This Article requires the unanimous agreement of the member States for the use of the forces anywhere outside Europe, except as provided in Articles 13 and 14 and except as such use may be authorized through the NATO Commander in implementation of the defense guarantee extended to NATO.

IV. POWER TO RAISE THE FORCES

The Community does not have power to raise forces. Under Article 73 of the Treaty, the European Defense Forces are, until such time as the member States may agree to vest this power in the Community, to be recruited by the member States under their own laws. Recruiting will proceed under policies established in Articles 12, 13, and 14 of the Military Protocol attached to the Treaty, compliance with which may be enforced by the Community. These policies include setting the period of 18 months as a minimum length of active service (which may be changed only by unanimous decision). Some authority is given the Community to make policy on deferments, by providing that deferments must not impair the effectiveness of a country's contingents.

The policy decision on the total size of the forces requires unanimous agreement of the member States, including both their governments and their Parliaments. Article 71 of the Treaty provides that the Council of Ministers must unanimously approve "the plan for the organization of the Forces," and the Treaty also requires that the Community fill its financial requirements largely through action of the Parliaments of the member States.

V. Power to Supply, Equip, and Support the Forces

The Community has authority, in general, to execute a given armament and equipment program. It is not rigidly bound to the terms of detailed budgetary appropriations (Art. 90). It has no power of eminent domain, but it can acquire and transfer property and sue and be sued (Art. 7). However, the Community can acquire the use of, or build, infrastructure and public services without the agreement of the State concerned only upon a two-thirds vote in the Council of Ministers (Arts. 21 and 18 of Status Convention). It has the power to award the necessary contracts (Art. 104), and if it meets production or procurement difficulties through lack of raw materials, high prices, or other circumstances requiring the exercise of economic controls, it can require the State concerned to take remedial action, provided such action has not already been taken by unanimous vote of the Council (Art. 105). Above all, the Community has the power to prohibit production, import, and export of war materials as well as all military research in the member States, except as licensed by it (Art. 107). It is thus able at least to ensure that such defense production as exists in member States which do not have heavy overseas responsibilities of their own will be for its benefit. The Community can obtain foreign aid with which it may freely purchase foreign equipment, and can obtain foreign end-item aid directly as well (Art. 99).

The Community's supply, armament, equipment, and infrastructure program, as well as its program for scientific and technical military research, forms part of the budget which is subject to approval by the member States (Art. 106). In addition, the Community must respect the general commitments taken by member States with NATO (Art. 91). The Community may not, without the agreement of each member government, spend less than 85 per cent, or more than 115 per cent, of a State's financial contribution in the monetary zone of that State (Arts. 29 and 30 of the Financial Protocol).

VI. Power to Finance Community's Activities

The Community's yearly budget is a statement of all Community receipts, broken down into contributions from the several States, and all expenditures. It is prepared by the Commissariat, but the Council of Ministers must by unanimous vote approve "the total volume of the budget as expressed in authorizations for cash outlays and contracting authorizations"; it must also, by unanimous agreement, approve "the amount of the contribution of each member State." Approval of the expenditures side of the budget requires a two-thirds weighted vote only, and, until the Council agrees on another equitable method, contributions of the member States are to be calculated in accordance with the burden-sharing procedure adopted in NATO. This NATO procedure is to be informally extended to the German Federal Republic (Arts. 87, 88, and 94 of the Treaty).

Agreement on the budget having been reached, it is "incumbent," under Section 2 (a) of Article 87, "upon the government of each member State to ensure the inclusion of the amount determined as its contribution in its budget, in accordance with its constitutional rules." In each member State, the appropriation of funds depends upon action by the national Parliament.

The Community may, under Article 99 of the Treaty, receive foreign aid under agreements negotiated by the Commissariat. The Council may, by a two-thirds weighted vote, issue general directives to the Commissariat to ensure that "the latter's action concerning foreign aid does not endanger the economic, financial and social stability of one or more of the member States." But aside from these general directives, an aid agreement needs only approval by a majority vote of the Council to become valid with respect to receipt of currency and its expenditure outside the monetary areas of the member States. If a foreign aid agreement provides for the exchange of dollars or other freely convertible currency into the currency of one or more of the member States (that is, if the aid is to be spent within the Community), unanimous agreement of the Council of Ministers is required under Articles 32 and 37 of the Financial Protocol attached to the Treaty.

Article 15 of the Financial Protocol provides that "every decision of the Commissariat which entails the acknowledgment of a debt by the Community" must have the unanimous approval of the Council of Ministers.

VII. Power to Command, Administer, and Train the Forces

Under Article 18 of the Treaty the competent Supreme Commander responsible to NATO (meaning, presumably, the Supreme Commander whose area of responsibility comprises the territories of the EDC member States) is empowered "to satisfy himself" that the forces are "organized, equipped, trained and prepared for use in a satisfactory manner." However, the organization of the forces must be agreed to unanimously by the member States (Art. 71). The Community's considerable powers with regard to equipment have been discussed in detail. Some authority for administration, schooling, and training of the forces also rests in the Community (Arts. 74, 76, and 78 of the Treaty, and Art. 27 of the Military Protocol).

Appointments to the rank of commander of a unit higher than the basic unit of homogeneous nationality require unanimous agreement of the member States; that is, the rank of a general officer commanding an operational unit, since basic units will be part of integrated corps. Appointments to the rank of basic unit commander, as well as appointments to all other ranks, are made, at the option of the member State concerned, either by itself on recommendation of the Community, or by the Community "after consultation with national authorities." But *assignments* of officers to the command of basic units, to any higher command, or to a post involving the exercise of authority over elements of more than one nationality, can be made only with the consent of the member States. Appointments of civilian officials of high rank also require the consent of all the governments (Art. 31).

The Community does not have a Code of Military Justice, and can get one only by observing the constitutional processes of the member States. Until there is a Community Code of Military Justice, the law of his State of origin, and, in some cases, the law of the State in which he is stationed, is applicable to a member of the forces (Art. 26 of the Jurisdictional Protocol). A member of the European forces is to be tried, at the option of the State of origin, either in the courts of that State, or in so-called European courts operating in all respects, including procedure, under the laws of such State and staffed by nationals of that State (Arts. 22, 23, and 24 of the Jurisdictional Protocol). The right to pardon remains in the State of origin, as does the function of carrying out sentences (Arts. 27 and 28 of the Jurisdictional Protocol). By unanimous agreement of the governments, the Community may take jurisdiction over a class of cases involving "grave injury to the interests of the Community" (Arts. 22, §1 (c), and 30 of the Jurisdictional Protocol).

The Community is not entirely free to order the forces to be stationed where it wishes. It must follow, in this respect, recommendations made by the competent NATO Supreme Commander, unless it can obtain the agreement of all six governments to override them. In the absence of a NATO recommendation, or in the event that the NATO Supreme Commander should no longer be authorized under NATO policies and procedures to issue recommendations concerning the deployment of troops, the Community is not authorized to act. In such an event, it would presumably be for the member States to decide concerning the stationing of troops.

VIII. Other War and Emergency Powers

The Treaty assigns to the Community the function of drawing up manpower and economic mobilization plans (Arts. 75 and 111). However, it states that "the decision to proceed with mobilization shall be made by the member States" (Art. 75). The member States may employ the Community to execute mobilization measures, under Article 75. In addition, in time of war or "urgent necessity," more extensive powers may be delegated to the Community by agreement of the member States; the additional powers must, however, fall "within the limits of the general mission of the Community" (Art. 123; see also Arts. 124 and 125). Since the provisions of the Treaty are to be applied "in accordance with the Constitutional rules of each member State," each government, where its consent is required, must decide whether it must go to its Parliament.

S T U D Y 5

Foreign Affairs

I. INTRODUCTION

In all federations foreign relations are controlled by the federal government, and it is generally recognized that no federation can properly function without adequate power to control the basic aspects of foreign relations. The extent of control can vary, however, in different types of federations, and in almost all federations there are areas in this field in which the component States have retained a certain amount of jurisdiction.

Constitutions of federations usually contain both provisions allocating the powers in the field of foreign relations to various organs of the federal government, and provisions circumscribing the exercise of such powers by the component units. Most of them deal, in particular, with the following powers:

   (1) to conduct relations with foreign states (and international organizations),

   (2) to appoint diplomatic and consular officials and to receive foreign diplomatic and consular officials,

   (3) to conclude, ratify, and implement treaties and other international agreements, and

   (4) to assure the supremacy of a treaty over the laws of the federation and of the component units.

In addition, some constitutions deal explicitly with other problems connected with, but really separable from, general conduct of foreign relations, e.g., foreign trade, immigration, aliens, foreign corporations, extradition of criminals, crimes against international law, declaration of war, cession and acquisition of territory. These subjects will be treated here only incidentally, in so far as their treatment throws light upon a more general problem.

II. RELATIONS WITH FOREIGN STATES AND INTERNATIONAL ORGANIZATIONS

A. *General Division of Powers*

Some constitutions provide explicitly that "the maintenance of relations with foreign states shall be the concern of the federation" (Germany, Basic

Law, Art. 32).[1] In other federations this general power can easily be deduced from other provisions on the subject. For instance, in the United States the vesting of the treaty power and the power to appoint and receive ambassadors and public ministers in the federal government implies the concomitant power to maintain relations with foreign states. In Switzerland, the general power to conduct foreign relations can be easily deduced from the provision that the Federal Council has general charge of foreign affairs, and that even the intercourse between the cantons and foreign governments shall take place through the Federal Council. In Australia and Canada the situation is different, for both constitutions were drafted at times when neither of these countries was regarded as independent in the conduct of foreign relations. However, the gradual decentralization of the British Commonwealth led to devolution of the power to maintain relations with foreign states from the United Kingdom to the Dominions. Though this transfer of power was not accomplished by amendments in the written constitutions of these countries, it is generally agreed that the federal governments, and not the States or Provinces, are in charge of foreign affairs. In Australia the power given to the federal government to legislate with regard to "external affairs" serves as the basis for the general power to maintain relations with foreign states. In Canada an obsolete treaty provision of narrow scope would seem to limit also the power of the federal government to conduct foreign relations, but in practice the federal government exercises broad powers in this field and determines the foreign policy of the nation; only its power to implement treaties continues to be severely limited.

The principal issue in federal states is whether the power to conduct foreign relations should be lodged in the federation exclusively or whether the component units retain some powers in this field. In most federations this question has been resolved to the advantage of the federation but the component units are often allowed to maintain some relations with foreign states, subject to proper supervision by federal authorities.

Even where a constitution provides that "the conduct of foreign affairs is the exclusive concern" of the federation, component units have been permitted to conclude agreements with foreign states with respect to matters over which they have been given legislative jurisdiction (Germany, Weimar Constitution, Art. 78). It seems wrong to speak in such instances of "exclusive" federal power, and may be desirable to indicate instead that this power may be exercised by the component units under certain conditions (e.g., subject to approval by a federal authority).

In order to establish a basic principle for the interpretation of other provisions on the subject, it would seem desirable to state in any new federal constitution that the federal government shall determine the foreign policy of the federation and that its power over foreign relations shall ex-

[1] The Brazilian Constitution of 1946 provides similarly that "it is the prerogative of the Union to maintain relations with foreign powers" (Art. 5).

tend to all matters transferred to the jurisdiction of the federation. In addition, there should be a provision limiting the power of component units to matters left within their jurisdiction. To assure that these powers are exercised by the component units in a uniform way, the federal government may be given power to establish general procedures for the coordination of relations between the component units and foreign states. Such power may be general, or it may be limited to matters of common concern to the federation and the component units. Further coordination may be achieved by requiring the component units to supply the federation with information concerning their international activities. Opportunity should be provided in such a case for the federation to make a statement with respect to its interest in the matter, which should be taken into account by the component unit in further negotiations.[2]

B. *Authorities in Charge of Representation*

Once it is decided that power over foreign affairs is to be lodged in the federation, exclusively or partially, a further decision is necessary with respect to the federal organ in which the power to represent the federation in foreign affairs should be vested. The Basic Law for the Federal Republic of Germany of 1949 provides, for instance, that "the Federal President represents the Federation in matters concerning international law (*völkerrechtlich*)" (Art. 59).[3] The Austrian Constitution of 1929 provides similarly that "the Federal President represents the Republic in external matters (*nach aussen*)" (Art. 65).[4] Though there is no express provision in the United States Constitution on the subject, the President undoubtedly has broad powers over the conduct of foreign affairs. Congress can validly delegate powers to him which it would be unconstitutional to delegate to him in purely domestic affairs. The Supreme Court in describing the constitutional position of the President has said that he is the sole organ of the federal government in the field of foreign relations and possesses a power which does not require for its exercise an Act of Congress but which is still subject to the limitations of the Constitution. The Court felt that it is necessary to give the President a degree of discre-

[2] Such procedures have been put into practice by the members of the British Commonwealth and have been codified by several Commonwealth Conferences. For instance, a resolution of the 1930 Imperial Conference provided that: " (1) Any of His Majesty's Governments conducting negotiations should inform the other Governments of His Majesty in case they should be interested and give them opportunity of expressing their views, if they think that their interests may be affected. (2) Any of His Majesty's Governments on receiving such information should, if it desires to express any view, do so with reasonable promptitude. (3) None of His Majesty's Governments can take any steps which might involve the other Governments of His Majesty in any active obligations without their definite assent."

[3] Similar provisions were contained in the German Constitutions of 1871 and 1919.

[4] The Brazilian Constitution of 1946 provides that the President of the Republic shall have the exclusive power "to maintain relations with foreign states" (Art. 87). See also Article 198 (2) of the Venezuelan Constitution.

tion and freedom from statutory restriction not proper if domestic affairs alone are involved, if in the maintenance of international relations serious embarrassment is to be avoided and success for the nation's aims achieved.

In addition to this source of power the President of the United States also has those stemming from his constitutional role as commander-in-chief of the army and navy. While the Constitution states that the power of declaring war is reserved to Congress, the President may still commit the armed forces to combat by his unilateral action. It is the established constitutional practice that the power of recognition of a new regime resides in the President. Presidents have used this broad discretionary power as a political and legal instrument, e.g., in relations with Mexico, the Soviet Union, and Communist China. However strong the President's constitutional position may be, it is erroneous to view him as an entirely free agent, for he is not independent of Congress; Congressional possession of the appropriation power and the Senate veto power over treaties demand that Presidential formulation of foreign policy must have Congressional approval if it is to be effective. The bipartisan foreign policy of the post-World War II period has been a product of close executive-Congressional cooperation.

Where the highest state authority is not an individual but a collective body, the power to represent the state is usually lodged in that body. Thus, the Constitution of Switzerland provides that the Federal Council "watches over the interests of the Confederation abroad, paying particular notice to its international relations, and has general charge of foreign affairs" (Art. 102). In practice, the formal functions of a Head of State are exercised by the President of the Federal Council. If the proposed European executive authority is collective, these provisions may easily be followed.

Actually, only the President of the United States takes an active part in the conduct of negotiations with foreign states. In other federations, the Head of State represents the state only in a formal sense, signing documents and granting audiences to foreign diplomats. International negotiations are usually conducted by, or under the supervision of, the Ministers for Foreign Affairs or the Prime Ministers. This development is recognized, for instance, in the French Constitution of 1946 which provides merely that "the President of the Republic shall be kept informed of the progress of international negotiations" (Art. 31).[5]

To the extent that component units may be allowed to conduct such relations with foreign states, they may be allowed to conduct such relations directly, through their own organs. The proper organ should in such a

[5] The Venezuelan Constitution of 1947 supplements the provision that the President of the Republic represents the nation in its relations with other nations, with the more accurate statement that he shall also have the power "to direct, by means of the corresponding ministry, the foreign relations of the Republic and the diplomatic negotiations and to enter into treaties, contracts, and agreements with other nations through the plenipotentiaries whom he may designate in council of ministers."

case be designated not in the constitution of the federation, but in the constitution of each component unit.

On the other hand, if the component units are not permitted to enter directly into relations with foreign states, they would have to proceed through appropriate organs of the federation. Thus the Swiss Constitution provides that "official intercourse between the cantons and foreign governments or their representatives shall take place through the Federal Council" (Art. 10). With respect to questions of public economy, border traffic, and police, the cantons may, however, "enter into direct relations with subordinate authorities and officers of a foreign state."[6] In the United States the State Department has rejected proposals by American States to negotiate with foreign states for the formulation of an agreement. Where cooperation between member States and foreign states is desirable (e.g., in the allocation of water rights to an international river), the usual procedure is for the State Department to conclude a treaty with the foreign government and for the States to implement it by a compact among themselves, approved by Congress. Only once in American history, in a dispute involving State claims for compensation arising from changes in the American-Canadian boundary, did the federal government authorize State agents to negotiate directly with foreign representatives.

If in the proposed European federation the component States would retain large powers over a variety of matters and commensurate powers over foreign affairs, it would seem advisable to permit them to conduct their foreign relations directly in accordance with their own constitutional processes. They should be encouraged, however, to use the federal facilities and, after a while, at least some of them may find it no longer necessary to maintain direct relations with many foreign states.

C. *International Personality*

The right to maintain relations with foreign states is closely related to the question of international personality of the federation and of the component units. As long as the component units retain a general right to enter into direct relations with foreign states, their international personality will continue to exist. On the other hand, if they entirely surrender to the federation their power over external affairs, they may lose thereby their international status.

The treaties constituting the European Coal and Steel Community and the European Defense Community provide explicitly that each of these Communities shall have "juridical personality" and shall enjoy, in its international relationships, "the juridical capacity necessary to the exercise of its functions and the attainment of its ends." They do not contain any

---

[6] It may be noted also that in those federations in which the component units have the power to appoint their own representatives to foreign states (see page 245 below), they can conduct through them direct negotiations with foreign states.

express provisions depriving their member States of their separate international personalities, or limiting directly their juridical capacities in the fields assigned to the two Communities. It seems desirable to deal with this matter more clearly in any future treaty, especially if it is contemplated that the component units should retain international personality to the extent necessary to enable them to continue their membership in various international organizations. Such a provision will have not only theoretical importance in solving a long-standing dispute on the subject among writers on federalism, but also will have important practical consequences, e.g., with respect to their representation in international organizations, their privileges and immunities in other states, and their international responsibility.

D. Representation in International Organizations

Older federal constitutions naturally contain no special provisions on representation of the federation in international organizations, as the flowering of international organizations is an entirely modern phenomenon. Several recent constitutions provide explicitly for federal membership in international organizations. For instance, the Constitution of the United Kingdom of Libya, adopted in 1951, provides that the federal government shall exercise legislative and executive powers in connection with the "affairs of the United Nations and specialized agencies," and with "participation in international conferences and bodies." [7]

Ordinarily, only fully sovereign states are entitled to become members of general international organizations, but in both the League of Nations and the United Nations certain exceptions have been permitted. British Dominions and India exercised only limited powers with respect to foreign relations when they became members of the League of Nations in 1919; India and the Philippines were still in a transition stage, when they obtained membership in the United Nations. While the Byelorussian S.S.R. and the Ukrainian S.S.R. were allowed to become members of the United Nations for political rather than legal reasons, the fact that constitutionally they had the right to conduct foreign relations made it easier for the San Francisco Conference to accept their claim to membership.

In many other international organizations, including several of the specialized agencies of the United Nations, a few non-self-governing territories have participated as full members for a long time. For instance, various colonies have been members of the Universal Postal Union since 1878 and of the International Telegraphic Union since 1885. [8]

[7] The phrasing of this provision is similar to that of List I of the 7th Schedule of the Indian Constitution of 1949, which grants to the federal Parliament exclusive legislative power with respect to "United Nations Organization" and "participation in international conferences, associations and other bodies."

[8] In a few recently established organizations, and in regional Commissions of the United Nations Economic and Social Council, a special category of associate members has been devised for such territories.

Such special treatment of some non-self-governing territories was usually defended on the ground that they enjoyed complete independence with respect to the relevant matters (e.g., postal communications), and that their interests were often incompatible with those of the mother country and could not be defended properly by her representatives.

Similarly, when the interests of the component units of a federation differ, it is difficult for a representative of the federation to present adequately their views at a meeting of an international organization or to vote there on important decisions. This becomes particularly important when the execution of these international decisions is entirely within the jurisdiction of the component units. Assuming, for instance, that all labor questions are within the jurisdiction of component units, it would be desirable to give to those units direct representation in an international organization dealing with labor matters. The United States delegation to the Paris Peace Conference in 1919 proposed in fact that "the several states of a federation of states where the states have reserved in whole or in part their autonomy in respect to labor legislation shall have the same rights and obligations" as other members of the International Labour Organization, and shall be entitled to proper representation at the conferences of the organization. This proposal was, however, almost unanimously rejected, and in consequence almost all federal states have run into difficulties in trying to fulfill their obligations under the ILO Constitution. In recognition of this fact, the federal clause in that Constitution was amended extensively in 1946 (see page 252 below). No provision was made there, however, with respect to direct representation of component units of federations, though it permitted the appointment of "representatives of non-metropolitan territories" as advisers to delegates "in regard to matters within the self-governing powers of that territory." [9]

The question of international representation of component members of a federation arose also in several international organizations after World War II as the result of the incorporation of Estonia, Latvia, and Lithuania into the Union of Soviet Socialist Republics. For instance, at the 1947 Congress of the Universal Postal Union, the Soviet delegation claimed that these States have not lost their membership in the Union because of that incorporation, particularly in view of their constitutional right to conduct foreign affairs. That contention was rejected by a vote of 28 to 11, but 32 delegations found it necessary to abstain.

This history seems to indicate that, in general, component units of a fed-

[9] Though not obliged to do so by the ILO Constitution, the Canadian government has frequently included in its delegation at least one provincial labor official; similar appointments have been made regularly by the United States, and recently also by Australia. The Standing Orders of the International Labour Conference provide, in addition, that apart from delegates and advisers "representatives of a State or province of a federal State who have been appointed to accompany a delegation by the Government of a Member of the Organization" shall be permitted to enter the Conference hall. They may not take part in the discussion, however, unless they have the status of delegates or advisers.

eration are not entitled to separate membership in international organizations. On the other hand, in none of the previous cases was the situation of the component units really identical with that of the members of the proposed European federation. These states have a tradition of direct representation in international organizations and have made important contributions to the development of these organizations. In view of the prevalence of the one-state-one-vote rule in international organizations it may be desirable, not only for the member States but also for the federation, to continue to have six votes rather than one in these organizations, even if in some instances not all of them would vote on the same side. The situation is different, of course, where, as in the consultative Assembly of the Council of Europe, representation is based on population (or other factors), because the delegation of the Community to such a body would be able to retain a proper number of delegates from each member State. Until that system is adopted in other organizations, it may be important to retain the extra votes now possessed by member States. The coordination of policies in such a case can be achieved by other means, for instance by frequent conferences between officials of the federation and the delegates of member States both before and during important international conferences and meetings of international organizations.

While it might be theoretically possible to substitute the European federation for France as a permanent member of the Security Council of the United Nations, such a step would require an amendment of the Charter. No amendment of the Charter can come into force, however, without the consent of all permanent members, including the Soviet Union; it may be doubted that she would agree to such an amendment. Similarly, if the federation were to apply for membership in the United Nations, a Soviet veto could prevent the approval of such an application. On the other hand, there is no veto in the specialized agencies of the United Nations, and the federation may acquire membership in them without any difficulty. In such a case, however, the member States of the federation would probably lose their membership in those agencies, though in some of them the Ukrainian S.S.R. and the Byelorussian S.S.R. are members alongside the Soviet Union.

The question may arise, however, whether in international organizations dealing with problems within the exclusive jurisdiction of the federation, and in organizations in which the unanimity rule prevails, it may not be desirable to have a single delegation, representing the federation as a whole. There may also be other occasions on which a single representation may be more appropriate. It seems, therefore, that no too strict rule should be adopted here, but that a large amount of flexibility would be desirable.

III. Appointment of Diplomatic and Consular Officials and Reception of Foreign Diplomatic and Consular Officials

A. *Federal Powers*

Foreign affairs are conducted principally through diplomatic officials; personal contacts between Foreign Ministers are not frequent. The usual procedure is to maintain direct contacts between the legation or embassy of one country and the Ministry of Foreign Affairs of the other country. Even most written communications are delivered through these channels.

If a federation wishes to maintain control over the conduct of foreign affairs, it must have control over the selection and appointment of diplomatic agents representing the federation abroad. It needs also to exercise the right, possessed by each state under international law, to accept, or refuse to accept, a particular diplomatic agent of a foreign country.

The federation should also have power to decide the basic question whether diplomatic relations should be maintained with any particular state, or whether they should be discontinued. This question is of special importance when a new state comes into being or a revolutionary government comes into power in a foreign state. The difficult problem of "recognition" is closely connected with this question, and may require a constitutional solution forestalling divergencies in recognition policies of the federation and of some of the component units.

Under the Constitution of the United States the President "shall nominate, and, by and with the advice and consent of the Senate, shall appoint ambassadors, other public ministers and consuls." He also "shall receive ambassadors and other public ministers" (Art. II, §2). In practice, some Presidents have avoided the approval of the Senate by appointing "personal representatives," whose influence on the conduct of foreign affairs was often larger than that of regular ambassadors.

The Austrian Constitution empowers the federal authorities to enact and execute legislation with respect to "political and economic representation abroad." It provides further that the Federal President "receives and accredits ministers, approves the appointment of foreign consuls, appoints the consular representatives of the Republic abroad" (Arts. 10 and 65). Similarly, the German Constitution of 1949 provides that the Federal President "accredits and receives envoys" (Art. 59).

In states where the highest executive organ is a collective body, it usually exercises similar functions. Thus, though there is no express provision in the Swiss Constitution on the subject, the Federal Council has always exercised the power of appointing diplomatic envoys and consuls.

Similar provisions may be embodied in the Constitution of the proposed European federation. If the executive organ of that federation is a collective one, the interests of the various member States will be sufficiently represented in it and there seems to be no necessity to safeguard them further by requiring the consent of the upper house of the legislature. Such a consent is desirable only where, as in the United States, large executive powers are granted to an individual rather than a group.

The powers of the executive body of the federation in this field should embrace: the appointment and recall of its own diplomatic representatives; the appointment and recall of its own consuls; acceptance (*agrément*) of diplomatic representatives of foreign states accredited to the federal government; right to request that a foreign state recall a diplomatic representative who has become *persona non grata;* admission of, and granting of *exequatur* to, foreign consuls appointed to exercise their functions in consular districts which are under direct control of the federal government; and withdrawal of its consent to the exercise of consular functions (revocation of *exequatur*).

B. *Powers of Member States*

If component units of a federation are allowed to maintain direct relations with foreign states, they may be permitted to retain their own diplomatic and consular service and to receive diplomatic and consular agents of foreign states.

The German Constitution of 1871 did not take away the right of member States to maintain direct relations with foreign States. It was necessary, therefore, to coordinate the activities of the federal and State diplomatic missions. For instance, an agreement with Bavaria provided that the Bavarian ambassadors should be granted by the federal government full powers "to represent, in cases of hindrance, the Federal Ambassadors at the Courts to which they are accredited." On the other hand, "the Bavarian Ambassadors will be instructed to give their aid to the Federal Ambassadors in all cases wherein it should be necessary or advantageous for the promotion of general German interests." In consideration of this cooperation and of the fact that "in those places at which Bavaria will maintain her own legations, the Federal envoys will not have to attend to Bavarian affairs," the federal government agreed that "in fixing the expenses for its diplomatic service it will make a suitable allowance to the Bavarian Government."

A different solution was provided for the consular service in the German Constitution of 1871. The whole consular service of the Empire was put under the supervision of the federal government, and arrangements were made for a transition from the old system to the new one. In foreign districts for which consuls had been appointed by the federal government "no new consulates for separate states may be erected." Federal consuls were empowered to exercise consular functions for any State not having its own consuls in their districts. All separate State consulates were to be abolished upon the completion of the organization of the federal consular service, and upon certification by the Federal Council that the representation of the interests of all member States was satisfactorily secured by the federal consulates (Art. 56). In addition, assurance was given to member States that "federal consuls will be appointed at foreign places if it should appear desirable that this should be done even for the interest of one member State only." These rules applied only to consuls in foreign countries; no restrictions were placed on member States with respect to the continuance of consulates in other member States. The supplementary agreement with Bavaria made it clear, also, that member States retained the right "of receiving foreign consuls and of providing them with an *exequatur* for their territory."

The Weimar Constitution of 1919 took away the right of member States to diplomatic and consular representation in foreign states and the right to receive foreign diplomats and consuls; they retained only the right to send diplomatic and consular agents to other member States and to receive such agents sent by other member States. In addition, the Constitution provided that "in order to safeguard the representation of interests arising for certain States from their special economic relations with, or their proximity to, foreign States, the Federal Government undertakes to adopt the necessary arrangements and measures in agreement with the States concerned" (Art. 78). No such guarantee is contained in the Basic Law of 1949.

At the time the Australian federation was formed, the member States had their own representatives in London. They are still represented there by agents-general, in addition to a federal High Commissioner. The Conferences of Commonwealth and State Ministers in Australia in 1930 and 1931 discussed the question of amalgamation of these London offices, but the States refused to accept the recommendations of the federal government. Some Canadian Provinces also maintain agents-general in London, whose status was for a long time in dispute between the Provinces and the Canadian and British governments. In the 1930's most Provinces stopped sending such representatives, as their activities did not seem to justify the expense, but some of them were reappointed in the 1940's. From time to time, Quebec had agents-general also in France, Belgium, and New York.

In the United States and Switzerland the component units have not exercised an independent right of legation, whether active or passive. While the States of the United States also play no role in the appointment and acceptance of consuls, the Federal Council of Switzerland at one time agreed to consult the cantons before granting *exequatur* to foreign consuls. But the Confederation is not really obliged to do this, nor to comply with a cantonal opinion.

The Constitution of the proposed European federation may follow any one of these patterns, but the solution adopted by Germany in 1871 seems best fitted to the requirements of that federation. During a transition period, when the diplomatic and consular service of the federation is being built up, the federal services may exist side by side with the services of the member States. When confidence in the efficiency and impartiality of the federal service is established, the member States, or at least some of them, may agree to transfer to the federation their diplomatic representation in most of the countries of the world. They may also agree later to transfer to the federation their financially burdensome consular services, with the exception probably of the consulates in the principal economic centers of the world.

Similarly, it does not seem necessary to impose constitutional limitations on the right of member States to receive foreign diplomatic and consular agents. Actually, with the increase of the powers of the federal government in the political, military, and economic field, there will come a gradual concentration of foreign representatives in the federal capital, and foreign governments will find it unnecessary to maintain costly missions in centers of declining power. On the other hand, consular agents are more interested in local conditions and deal more often with local authorities than with the federal government. Their situation on the spot may be better if they obtain their *exequatur* from a member State rather than the federation.

IV. Conclusion, Ratification, and Implementation of Treaties and Other International Agreements

A. *Federal Treaties*

1. CONCLUSION OF FEDERAL TREATIES

The power to conclude treaties is usually coextensive with the general power over foreign relations. If the federal government possesses broad powers over the conduct of foreign relations, it also possesses a general power to conclude treaties. But if the power of the federal government with respect to foreign relations is limited to matters which by other provisions of the constitution have been made federal, similar restrictions need to be imposed on the power to conclude treaties.

Some federal constitutions provide explicitly for the conclusion of treaties by the federation; in others a similar rule can be deduced from provisions conferring on various organs of the federal government the power to conclude and ratify treaties.

The treaty-making power is usually vested in the executive organ of the federal government. In the United States, the Constitution provides that the President "shall have power, by and with the advice of the Senate, to make treaties, provided two-thirds of the Senators present concur." In the beginning this provision was interpreted as requiring the President to seek advice from the Senate during negotiations, but the first President found it difficult to follow this procedure, and since then the Presidents have limited themselves to asking for the consent of the Senate to the ratification of a treaty. While the Senate as a whole no longer is consulted, there is a growing practice of consulting leading members of the Senate during important negotiations. To facilitate Congressional execution of treaties the President very often appoints Senators, and sometimes even members of the House of Representatives, as members of delegations charged with negotiation and conclusion of important treaties or of delegations to international conferences and organizations. Similar procedures have developed in some other federations, even where there is no requirement of Parliamentary participation in the negotiation and conclusion of treaties.

The Constitution of the German Empire of 1871 (Art. 11) empowered the German Emperor "to enter into alliances and other treaties with foreign powers," but the consent of the Council of the Confederation was required for the conclusion of treaties with foreign states in so far as these treaties referred to matters within imperial legislative jurisdiction. (In addition, the approval of the Reichstag was required for the coming into force of the treaties.) The German Constitution of 1919 provided that the President of the Federation "concludes alliances and other treaties with foreign powers in the name of the Federation" (Art. 45). Similarly, under the 1949 Constitution, the Federal President "concludes treaties with foreign states on behalf of the Federation" (Art. 59). The Swiss Confederation has the sole right "to make alliances and treaties, particularly customs and commercial treaties" (Art. 8).

A new federal constitution may simply empower the federation to conclude treaties on certain subjects. It may also provide that such treaties should be concluded and signed in the name of the federation by plenipotentiaries properly authorized by the executive branch of the government.

2. RATIFICATION OF FEDERAL TREATIES

Very few international agreements come into force upon conclusion and signature. A treaty provides, usually, for its ratification or approval by the proper authorities of the signatory states. A formal acceptance is also required when a non-signatory state accedes to a treaty.

In practice, the same organ of a federation which concludes treaties also ratifies them, and some provisions on conclusion of treaties have been interpreted as extending not only to the process of negotiation and signature but also to the preparation and deposit of the instruments of ratification and accession.

Some confusion has been caused by the fact that a few constitutions provide that the President shall conclude international treaties subject to ratification by the legislature (e.g., Brazilian Constitution of 1946, Art. 87 (vii)).

Other constitutions seem to distinguish more clearly between the act of ratification by the executive and the approval of a treaty by the Parliament prior to its ratification by the executive. In some countries such Parliamentary concurrence is required with respect to all treaties, in others only with respect to certain types of treaties.

The Constitution of Germany of 1949 provides, e.g., that "treaties which regulate the political relations of the Federation or refer to matters of Federal legislature require, in the form of a federal law, the appoval or participation of the respective bodies competent for federal legislation." [10]   On the other hand, "for administrative agreements the provisions concerning the federal administration apply accordingly" (Art. 59).   Similarly, the Austrian Constitution of 1929 provides that "all political treaties, and other treaties in so far as they contain provisions involving changes in the law, require the approval of the National Council for their validity" (Art. 50).

In the United States, the consent of two thirds of the Senate is required for "making" treaties.   This provision has customarily been interpreted to mean that the consent of the Senate should be obtained prior to Presidential ratification.   The two-thirds requirement is an unusual feature in a constitution and was inserted to pacify sectional groups which feared that their interests would be endangered by a treaty requiring only a majority vote for its approval.   Compared to the number of treaties it has considered, the number of treaties rejected by the Senate is small.

There have, however, been many proposals to amend the two-thirds rule. Some proposals would keep the power of approval in the Senate, but would require only a majority vote of the Senators present.   More frequent are the proposals which would require a majority vote of a quorum of both Houses of Congress for approval.   A Joint Resolution embodying such a proposal was passed by the House of Representatives in 1945, but there has been no further action on it.

In Australia and Canada, there is no constitutional obligation to submit treaties to the Parliament for approval, but in practice prior approval is sought, especially when legislation may be necessary to implement the treaty.

In Switzerland, in addition to the requirement of approval by the legislature, the Constitution has required since 1921 that a treaty be submitted to a popular referendum, if it is concluded for more than 15 years or a period of indeterminate duration, and if a demand to that effect is made by 30,000 citizens or by eight cantons (Art. 89).

In the various member States of the proposed European federation, the necessity of Parliamentary participation in treaty approval is also recognized.   The Belgian Constitution, for instance, provides that "treaties of commerce and treaties which may burden the state, or bind Belgians individually, shall take effect only after having received the approval of the two houses" (Art. 68).   Similarly, under the Italian Constitution "the Chambers authorize by law the ratification of those international treaties which are of a political nature, which involve arbitration or judicial settle-

[10] This provision has been interpreted by the German Constitutional Tribunal as not applicable to a French-German "economic" agreement which could be executed by administrative action on the basis of prior general laws.

ment, or which involve changes in the national territory, financial burdens, or modification of laws" (Art. 80). The French Constitution is even more detailed; it provides that "treaties relative to international organization, peace treaties, commercial treaties, treaties that involve national finances, treaties relative to the personal status and property rights of French citizens abroad, those that modify French internal legislation, as well as those that involve the cession, exchange or addition of territories, shall not become final until they have been ratified by an act of the legislature" (Art. 27).

The federal practice in this field, and the constitutional provisions in the Western European nations, lead to the conclusion that in the ratification process participation by the legislative body cannot be avoided. While in almost every country such participation has caused rejection of important treaties, it is necessary to provide a check on the power of the executive in this field. In federations, in particular, the legislature is more responsive than the executive to sectional interests and is more likely to assure the member States that the treaty power will not be abused to their detriment. It may be argued that, for that reason, the control over the executive in this field may be vested in the Senate rather than in both houses, and this course was followed by the United States and Mexico. On the other hand, the fact that many treaties require legislative implementation makes it desirable to have treaties approved by the same body which has the power of implementing them, and this road has been followed by the national constitutions of Western Europe.

3. EXECUTIVE AGREEMENTS

The provision in the United States Constitution which relates to the making of "treaties" has been interpreted as applying also to other international agreements, conventions, acts, etc. However, from the earliest days of the independence of the United States, many "executive agreements" have been concluded by the President, or under his authority, without reference to the Senate, and with no express constitutional provision sanctioning them. Such agreements are particularly frequent in the preparation for and conduct of hostilities. The validity of such agreements rests not only on the inherent executive control over foreign affairs, but also on the Presidential power as commander-in-chief of the army and navy.

In a growing number of cases, especially in recent years, international agreements have been sent for approval not to the Senate, acting under the two-thirds rule, but to both houses of Congress, acting by joint resolution which requires only a majority of each house. Another group of international agreements, including important tariff arrangements and trade agreements, has been entered into on the basis of prior Acts of Congress authorizing such agreements, without the necessity of obtaining further consent of the Senate after conclusion of these agreements.

The line of demarcation between treaties and executive agreements is a thin one, and the growth of Presidential power to make such agreements has encountered strong opposition. An amendment to the Constitution of the United States proposed by a group of Senators in 1951 would forbid conclusion of executive agreements "in lieu of treaties," thus restricting the use of such agreements to areas other than those reserved for treaties.[11] But in view of the difficulty of defining such areas, some other approach to this problem may have to be devised.

The same proposed amendment also suggested that "executive agreements shall, if not sooner terminated, expire automatically one year after the end of the term of office for which the President making the agreement shall have been elected, but the Congress may, at the request of any President, extend for the duration of the term of such President the life of any such agreement made or extended during the next preceding Presidential term. The President shall publish all executive agreements except that those which in his judgment require secrecy shall be submitted to appropriate committees of the Congress in lieu of publication." [12]

It seems too difficult to try to define in a constitution the respective spheres of treaties and executive agreements, though it is possible to do it indirectly, by enumerating the kinds of treaties which cannot be concluded without legislative approval (see page 248 above). Some constitutions contain, e.g., the requirement that treaties involving modification of laws or affecting rights or obligations of citizens must be approved by the legislature. Such provisions limit considerably the sphere of the executive agreements. The practice in the United States, though not entirely clear, seems to be in partial agreement with these provisions; at least, an executive agreement may not modify a law, though, in the absence of a federal law, it may modify individual rights.

In any case it may prove useful to require the executive body to submit executive agreements to the legislative body as soon as possible after their conclusion. In order to safeguard the powers of the Parliament, it may be

[11] Such a provision is embodied in Article 66 of the Constitution of Austria, which provides that the Federal President may empower the federal government or the competent members thereof to conclude certain categories of international treaties provided they do not belong to the group covered by requirement of approval by the National Council (i.e., political treaties and treaties involving changes in the law). Under this provision, the President of Austria empowered various agencies of government to conclude agreements, provided that such agreements may not be expressly called "international treaties" (*Staatsverträge*), or require an exchange of ratifications (Presidential Proclamation of December 31, 1920).

[12] The Constitution of Venezuela makes specific provision for executive agreements, providing in Article 105 that all agreements concluded by the executive must be approved by Congress to be valid except those dealing with the "execution of ordinary acts concerning international relations or the exercise of faculties which the law expressly attributes to the executive power." Nevertheless all such executive agreements must be submitted to the legislature for inspection even though Congressional approval is not required for their validity.

further provided that the executive should be obliged to denounce the agreement, if the legislature disapproves it and requests the executive to terminate it.

4. THE LIMITS OF THE FEDERAL TREATY POWER

A few constitutions contain direct limitations on the federal treaty power; in other countries such limitations have been established by constitutional practice. The purpose of these limitations is either to safeguard the rights of citizens against encroachment by the federal government[13] or to prevent an invasion by the federal government of the sphere reserved to member States.

In the United States, the Supreme Court has stated in a much-quoted dictum: "The treaty power, as expressed in the Constitution, is in terms unlimited except by those restraints which are found in that instrument against the action of the government or of its departments, and those arising from the nature of the government itself and of that of the States. It would not be contended that it extends so far as to authorize what the Constitution forbids, or a change in the character of the government or in that of one of the States, or a cession of any portion of the territory of the latter, without its consent." But in no case has a treaty yet been held invalid by the Court. An amendment to the Constitution proposed by a group of Senators in 1951 would provide explicitly that "no treaty or executive agreement shall be made respecting the rights of citizens of the United States protected by this Constitution, or abridging or prohibiting the free exercise thereof." Such a provision seems to be merely an expression of a basic rule of constitutional law that a constitution may not be changed by a treaty and that in case of conflict a constitution prevails over a treaty (see Section V below).[14]

Constitutional provisions do not usually deal with the question whether federal treaties may infringe on the distribution of powers between the federal government and the governments of member States, but in all federations this question has caused considerable difficulties.

In Canada three Acts of the Parliament passed in execution of previously ratified international labor conventions were held in 1937 by the Privy Council to be *ultra vires,* as the field of labor was reserved for the Provinces. The Court emphasized that in the distribution of legislative powers the treaty power is not a specific source of legislative authority, but rather the distribution of powers is based on classes of subjects specifically enumer-

[13] The Constitution of Mexico provides clearly that no treaty or agreement shall be entered into "which restricts or modifies the guarantees and rights which this Constitution grants to the individual and to the citizen" (Art. 15).

[14] Only the Austrian Constitution seems to envisage the possibility of constitutional amendment by treaty, but in such a case it requires that the treaty be approved by the same majority as is required for a constitutional amendment (Art. 50). Such a possibility is, of course, implied in other constitutions.

ated, and the validity of legislation passed to implement a treaty will be ascertained by reference to these classes. The federal government cannot be allowed to undermine by treaty the constitutional safeguards of provincial autonomy. The situation in Australia is not entirely clear, but two decisions in aviation cases seem to indicate the possibility of treaty-based legislation dealing with certain matters within the legislative power of States. It is quite possible, however, that federal powers in such a case would be limited to matters which are a "proper" subject for international negotiations. In view of the vagueness of this concept of "propriety" and the rapid growth of the area covered by international agreements, such restrictions may easily become meaningless.

In the United States, it has also been stated by courts that the treaty power extends to "all proper subjects of negotiation between our government and the governments of other nations." In a case relating to an Act giving effect to a treaty for the protection of migratory birds, the Supreme Court answered in the negative the question whether the treaty and Act were void as an interference with the rights reserved to the States. Previously two lower courts had held a federal statute regulating the shooting of the birds unconstitutional. The Court said that there may be matters of great national exigency which a Congressional Act could not deal with alone but could if it followed a treaty. It felt that a great national interest was involved which could be protected only by national action in concert with another power. A long line of decisions confirmed also the right of the federal government to deal by treaty with questions of private law which usually fall within the control of the States (discharge of debts, land titles, statutes of limitation, inheritance, etc.). On the other hand, the federal government has proceeded rather cautiously in other fields; e.g., despite the broad federal powers in labor matters derived from the commerce clause of the Constitution, it has refused to ratify almost all international labor conventions on the ground that they deal with subjects which belong to an area reserved to States. To safeguard the States against a future change in this practice, an amendment proposed by the American Bar Association in 1952 would limit legislation by Congress under a treaty to matters in which it could enact legislation "under its delegated powers in the absence of such treaty."

The limitations on the power of federal governments to enact legislation in execution of their treaty obligations have been acknowledged in the Constitution of the International Labour Organization when it was revised in 1946, and in the drafts of a federal clause proposed by several states for insertion in the International Covenant of Human Rights which is being prepared by the United Nations. In so far as the implementation of the labor conventions or human rights provisions is within the jurisdiction of the constituent units, the obligation of the federal government is limited to transmitting these international instruments to them and obtaining from them certain information to be sent back to the international organizations.

The ILO Consitution provides, in addition, that the federal governments shall "arrange, subject to the concurrence of the State, provincial or cantonal Governments concerned, for periodical consultations between the federal and the State, provincial or cantonal authorities with a view to promoting within the federal State, coordinated action to give effect to the provisions of such Conventions and Recommendations." Such consultations are customary in Australia, and attempts have been made to develop them in Canada and, to a lesser extent, in the United States.

It seems quite clear that in any federation in which member States retain important legislative powers, provisions will be necessary which would circumscribe the treaty powers of the federal government in such a way as would protect the member States against an invasion of their powers. Experiences with attempts to limit federal powers to matters which are a proper subject for international legislation do not warrant further application of such a test. On the other hand, it may be possible to limit the treaty power to matters with respect to which the federal government has legislative powers under other provisions of the Constitution. This approach would also facilitate the legislative implementation of a treaty, as it would be done by the same body which has approved its ratification and has at the time of such approval already solved the question of its competence to deal with matters contained in the treaty.

5. IMPLEMENTATION OF FEDERAL TREATIES

Once a treaty has been ratified by a state, the question may arise whether any further official act will be necessary to make the treaty a part of the law of the land. The French Constitution makes it clear that "diplomatic treaties duly ratified and published shall have the force of law even when they are contrary to internal French legislation; they shall require for their application no legislative acts other than those necessary to ensure their ratification" (Art. 26). But at the same time it requires that certain treaties, including those which modify French internal legislation, "shall not become final until they have been ratified by an act of the legislature" (Art. 27). In some other countries the same effect is obtained by requiring legislative approval before ratification, and this legislative act usually transforms the treaty into a part of national law. Whenever necessary, that act may also contain such further rules as are needed for the implementation of the treaty.

In Australia and Canada, the British system of treaty enforcement prevails and the performance of a treaty requires legislative action; the stipulations of a duly ratified treaty do not by themselves have the force of law. Even if prior to ratification the executive has obtained approval of the treaty by the Parliament, such approval does not operate as law, and the assenting Parliament or any subsequent Parliament may refuse to give its sanction to any legislative proposals to implement the treaty. In practice, however, in Parliamentary systems of government, the government has sufficient majority in the Parliament to assure legislative implementation of treaties ratified by it. In doubtful cases, the modern tendency is to obtain not only legislative approval but also an implementing law before ratification, the coming into force of the law depending on the actual coming into force of the treaty.

In the United States the question is complicated by the fact that the treaty-making power and the legislative power are vested in different bodies, and it seems that a treaty cannot be directly enforced if it deals with matters within federal jurisdiction but reserved to Congress (e.g., appropriations); in such cases joint action of both houses is necessary. Further difficulties have been caused by a distinction made since the early days of the nineteenth century between self-executing and non-self-executing treaties. Only treaties belonging to the first group become a part of the law of the land, and do not require legislative implementation. The non-self-executing treaties, i.e., treaties which contain a stipulation for legislative execution, require further legislative action before they can be applied by the courts. Quite a few international agreements (on industrial property, submarine cables, tariffs, land titles, prosecution of certain crimes, etc.) have been considered by courts as non-self-executing, though similar treaties, if more precisely worded, have been included in the self-executing group.

When a treaty is held non-self-executing additional political obstacles must be surmounted if it is to be implemented. Not only must it pass the Senate with a two-thirds vote of approval, but it must also in effect be passed again by a majority of both houses of Congress, thus giving those hostile to the treaty a double opportunity to defeat it. Several of the recently proposed amendments to the Constitution would make all treaties non-self-executing; for instance, a group of Senators has proposed that "no treaty or executive agreement shall alter or abridge the laws of the United States . . . unless, and then only to the extent that, Congress shall so provide by act or joint resolution."

This whole question is, of course, simplified if treaties are approved by the legislative organ, which at the time of approval may enact such additional provisions as may be needed to implement the treaty.

B. *Agreements Concluded by Member States*

A few federal constitutions prohibit completely the conclusion of agreements by member States;[15] others prohibit certain types of agreements only;

[15] In Mexico, "under no circumstances may a state enter into alliances, treaties, or coalitions with another state or with foreign powers" (Art. 117). Similar practice prevails in Argentina, Brazil, and Venezuela. While there are no express prohibitions in Australia and Canada, the component units of these federations have not tried to utilize the treaty-making power.

a third group allows the conclusion of agreements relating to certain specified matters.

While the Constitution of the United States contains the prohibition that
"no state shall enter into any treaty, alliance or confederation," it allows
agreements and compacts, subject to the consent of Congress. ("No State
shall, without the consent of Congress, . . . enter into any agreement or
compact with another State, or with a foreign power.")   Though many
compacts have been concluded between States, only recently has the consent of Congress been obtained for a compact with Canadian Provinces
with respect to forest fire prevention.   Some informal arrangements between American States and Canadian Provinces have been made from time
to time, without reference to Congress; one of them, concerning extradition, has been held invalid as the Supreme Court felt that it should have
been made in the form of a compact requiring the consent of Congress.
The lack of development in this field is due to a large extent to an unfavorable attitude by the federal government, which in several instances
rejected proposals by States to develop natural resources by joint action
with neighboring countries; it expressed the view that the interest involved
was national rather than local, and that a federal treaty rather than a compact was required.

The Swiss Constitution contains a double limitation: certain matters are
reserved entirely to the Confederation, in others its approval is required for
cantonal treaties. The federal government possesses the sole right "to
make alliances and treaties, particularly customs and commercial treaties,
with foreign states."   On the other hand, "the cantons retain the right to
conclude treaties with foreign states in respect to matters of public
economy, frontier traffic and police relations; nevertheless, such treaties
must not contain anything prejudicial to the Confederation or the rights of
other cantons" (Arts. 8 and 9).   Treaties concluded under this provision
are subject to approval by the Federal Council; if the Council, or another
canton, raises an objection, the treaty is referred to the Federal Assembly
for final decision.   Cantonal treaties with foreign states are not concluded
by the cantons directly, but by the Federal Council in the name of the particular canton, subject to approval by the proper cantonal authorities.
Despite this complicated procedure, a considerable number of treaties have
been concluded by cantons with neighboring states and a few with other
states. Informal agreements, e.g., by exchange of declarations as to double
taxation, have sometimes been concluded directly by cantonal authorities.

In Germany under the Constitution of 1871, the member States had complete freedom to enter into agreements with foreign states except on subjects which were within the exclusive competence of the Empire. In 1919,
the States retained the right to conclude agreements with foreign states "in
matters the regulation of which belongs to the state legislatures," but that
right was circumscribed by the requirement of obtaining the consent of the

federation, either before or after the conclusion of the agreement (Art. 78). The 1949 Constitution provides similarly that "insofar as legislation falls within the competence of the Länder, these may, with the approval of the Federal Government, conclude treaties with foreign states" (Art. 32).

Current practice seems to show that member States seldom exercise an independent treaty power, even where they possess one. Federal consent is usually required; it has proved useful as a safeguard against possible abuse, and it has not been unduly denied. If it were decided, however, that the federal government should not be entitled to supervise the activities of member States with respect to treaties dealing with subjects under their jurisdiction, the constitution might still provide a judicial remedy where the member States act outside their jurisdiction (see Study 3, The Federal Judiciary). One special problem here is created by the desire to avoid too frequent nullification of agreements with foreign states which have already entered into force, as this will create special international complications, including the need for paying damages to the foreign states for non-fulfillment of the agreement. It may be useful, therefore, to devise procedures for informing the government of the federation of all pending treaty negotiations and for allowing the federation to challenge the validity of agreements with foreign states prior to their entry into force. If proceedings have been begun before the competent tribunal, the member States should be obliged to refrain from ratifying the treaty until their right to do so has been upheld by the tribunal.[16]

Even when the treaty has been ratified, it might still be challenged by any individual or body whose rights have been violated, in accordance with the general provisions for challenging the unconstitutionality of the acts of member States, either under the constitution of the federation or under the constitution of the member State which concluded the treaty.

The question of constitutionality has to be distinguished from the political question of the desirability, in the light of the general foreign policy of a federation, of having a particular treaty concluded by a member State. In any case, the federation should receive an advance notice of all pending treaty negotiations and it might exert pressure on the member State to discontinue any undesirable negotiations. If the matter is very important, the executive authority may seek the advice on the matter of the legislature of the federation. It may be expected that a member State will not ratify a treaty, if the federal government objects to it on valid political grounds, especially if this objection is strongly supported by the legislature of the

---

[16] In a recent German case, the Federal Constitutional Tribunal had to deal with the question when the constitutionality of a treaty may be challenged. It decided that the challenge should be directed against the legislative act approving the treaty rather than the treaty itself, and the case should be brought before the Tribunal not after the signature of the treaty but only after the enactment of the approving statute. It emphasized, however, the desirability of having the issue decided prior to the ratification of the agreement in order to avoid international complications. Though the case related to a federal treaty, similar procedure can be applied to treaties made by member States.

federation. Such a political question has to be solved by political rather than legal means, though it is possible to formulate special procedures for dealing with it. For instance, the Swiss system may be followed and a member State might be prohibited from ratifying a treaty, if objections have been raised by the executive authority of the federation because of the incompatibility of that treaty with the general foreign policy of the federation; but a member State might be allowed to appeal from such a decision to the legislature of the federation.

Each member State can implement treaties validly concluded by it in any way its own constitution may provide. There is no need to deal with this subject in the federal constitution.[17] Adequate provisions on the conclusion, ratification, and execution of treaties are contained at present in all Western European constitutions; they can remain in force, subject to the general limitation that certain types of treaties may no longer be concluded by member States.

V. Supremacy of Treaties over the Law of the Federation and of Member States

A. *Supremacy of Federal Treaties over Federal Law*

The hierarchical position of treaties among the various sources of law has been solved differently in international and national laws. A properly ratified treaty is binding upon the parties to it, irrespective of any contrary provisions of national constitutions. For instance, if a President ratifies a treaty but a Parliament refuses to enact the necessary legislation or a court declares the treaty unconstitutional (as in the Canadian case relating to labor conventions), the state is still bound by the treaty internationally and may have to pay an indemnity to other parties to the treaty for its failure to apply it internally.

Even when a treaty has been properly incorporated into the law of the land, international complications may be caused later by enactment of an inconsistent statute. In the United States, for instance, statutes and treaties are on the same level as sources of law and later statute abrogates such provisions of a prior treaty as are inconsistent with it. (Similarly, later treaties may change a prior statute.) Thus a Chinese citizen, lawfully residing in the United States, was denied the right of re-entry following a visit to China, when Congress passed a statute forbidding re-entry under such

[17] Article 16 of the Austrian Constitution contains, however, an interesting provision on this subject: "Provinces are obliged within the limits of their independent competence to take such measures as are necessary for the execution of international treaties. Should a province fail to comply punctually with this obligation, its competence in the matter and particularly in the enactment of necessary legislation, will pass to the Federation. In the execution of treaties with foreign States the Federation enjoys supervisory rights even in those matters which belong to the independent competence of the provinces. In such matters the Federation has the same rights in relation to the provinces as in matters of indirect Federal administration."

conditions; the Supreme Court applied the statute though it was inconsistent with an earlier treaty with China which guaranteed the right. As such an act cannot really abrogate a treaty internationally, the state will be responsible for any damage suffered by any other state or its citizens as a result of such an abrogation. The position of an executive agreement authorized by Congress is similar to that of a treaty. However, if it does not have Congressional sanction it cannot change a prior statute or treaty and may be abrogated by a subsequent statute or treaty.

A few recent constitutions have made an attempt to remedy this situation. In France, duly ratified treaties have the force of law "even if they are contrary to internal French legislation" and "have an authority superior to that of French internal legislation." Consequently, "their provisions shall not be abrogated, modified, or suspended without previous formal denunciation through diplomatic channels" (Arts. 26 and 28). In case of treaties concluded with the approval of the legislature, such approval is required by the French Constitution for their denunciation as well, except for commercial treaties.

Several constitutions achieve a similar result through provisions making general rules of international law a part of the national law. The German Constitution of 1949 goes a step further and provides that these rules "take precedence over the laws and directly create rights and duties for the inhabitants of the federal territory" (Art. 25). It is not clear whether this provision can be applied to all treaties or only to treaties establishing general rules of international law, but at least some treaties may enjoy under this provision supremacy over ordinary laws.

B. *Supremacy of Federal Treaties over the Law of Member States*

In federal states, the additional question arises whether federal treaties are superior to constitutions and laws of member States. Some federal constitutions provide explicitly that treaties made under federal authority "shall be the supreme law of the land and the judges in every state shall be bound thereby, anything in the constitution or laws of any state to the contrary notwithstanding" (e.g., United States, Argentina, and Mexico). In the United States there are many decisions holding that treaties abrogate inconsistent State laws. The relation of the "Presidential" executive agreement to State law has not been clearly determined; however it is judicially established that such agreements prevail over local State policy. Thus when the President concluded an agreement with Russia providing for the assignment to the United States of Soviet claims against American nationals, it was held to be no defense that the policy of the State of New York did not recognize Soviet nationalization decrees. In other federations similar rules are derived from constitutional provisions or practices relating to the general supremacy of federal law.

C. *Supremacy of Federal Treaties over Treaties of Member States*

Upon the coming into force of a new federation, provision will have to be made with respect to treaties previously concluded by its member States. In order not to create a hiatus in international relations, it may be desirable to maintain temporarily in force all treaties of member States, even if they deal with matters transferred to federal jurisdiction. But when the federation later concludes a treaty with a foreign state on a subject within its competence, that treaty should abolish contrary provisions of prior treaties on the subject concluded by member States with that foreign state.[18] Even prior to that date, member States should terminate their treaties on subjects no longer within their competence as soon as possible in accordance with provisions of such treaties or the general rules of international law.

VI. CONCLUSIONS

The experience of federations with respect to conduct of foreign relations seems to show the need for clear provisions on the subject in future federal constitutions. Such provisions should state, at least, the basic principles of the distribution of powers in this field. The conclusions and suggestions presented here have been designed to cover as many ramifications of the problem as possible. Only some of them need to be embodied in a constitutional text; others may be left to future practice.

While some older constitutions have not found it necessary to include a general provision on the distribution of powers in the field of foreign relations, it is important to make it clear from the outset that the maintenance of relations with foreign states and international organizations with respect to matters within the jurisdiction of the federation (as enumerated in the provisions defining other powers of the federation) shall be the concern of the federation. It is equally important to show at the beginning that, in consequence of the federation, the powers of member States in this field will be considerably limited. They can be allowed to maintain relations with foreign states and international organizations only with respect to matters which remain within the jurisdiction of member States.

If the control over foreign relations is exercised simultaneously, though over different areas, by both the federal government and the governments of member States, it is necessary to devise procedures for the coordination of activites in this field. For instance, the federation may be authorized to establish, after consultation with member States, general procedures

[18] The German Constitution of 1949 deals with the converse situation, the transfer of treaty power from the federation to the States. It provides that "treaties concluded by the German Reich concerning matters for which under this Basic Law, Land legislation is competent, remain in force if they are valid and continue to be valid in accordance with general principles of law, subject to all rights and objections of the interested parties, pending the conclusion of new state treaties by the authorities competent under this Basic Law or until they are otherwise terminated pursuant to the provisions that they contain" (Art. 123).

for the coordination of relations with foreign states and international organizations in matters of common concern to the federation and the member States. Member States may be required to present reports to the federation on their general relations with foreign states. They should keep the federation informed of any international negotiations which might be of special interest to the federation and should give it the opportunity of expressing its views on the subject. It would be desirable for the Ministers for Foreign Affairs of the federation and of the member States to meet at stated intervals in order to exchange information on current problems, to coordinate their activities, and to solve jurisdictional disputes. The policies of member States in international organizations should be coordinated through conferences of their delegates to these organizations with officials of the federation, both before and during the sessions of the principal bodies of these organizations.

The likelihood of continued participation of member States in foreign relations within a prescribed area may make desirable a provision in the constitution defining the international personality to be enjoyed both by the federation and the States. It could state that the federation shall have international juridical personality and shall enjoy the international juridical capacity necessary to the exercise of its functions and the attainment of its ends, and that member States shall retain their present international personality and juridical capacity to the extent necessary to enable them to maintain such relations with foreign states and international organizations as are allowed by the constitution of the federation.

The prominent role of international organizations in the modern world would seem to require that a modern constitution should deal explicitly with the relationship of the federation and member States to such organizations. This is especially true when the member States, prior to their joining the federation, have enjoyed fully autonomous membership in international organizations. To eliminate possible ambiguities with respect to the rights of member States after the surrender of a part of their international personality to the federation, it may be necessary to give permission to member States to retain their membership in some international organizations. On the other hand, member States should not apply for membership in any international organization of which they are not members at present, without the consent of the legislature of the federation, except when the organization in question deals only with matters within the jurisdiction of member States. Besides the problem of State membership in international organizations, there is also the question whether the general limitations on federal activity in foreign relations should apply to federal membership in international organizations. It is clear that the federation may accept membership in any international organization dealing with matters exclusively within the jurisdiction of the federation. However, it may be necessary to put some limits on the acceptance of membership in other international organizations; for instance, such membership may be made dependent on a special arrangement agreed to by the majority of member States possessing membership in a particular organization. Upon the membership of the federation in an international organization becoming effective, the separate membership of any member State in that organization should be discontinued.

A general grant of power to the federal government to maintain foreign relations without an accompanying provision describing the authority which should exercise that power can only invite future controversies. If the past practice is to be followed, the conduct of relations between the federation and foreign states and international organizations should be under the general direction of the executive authority of the federation, which might delegate certain functions in this field to its President and others to the Minister for Foreign Affairs. The executive authority should be kept informed of the progress of all important international negotiations. (There is no need to include in the federal constitution special provisions with respect to conduct of relations between member States and foreign states and international organizations, as they would have to be conducted in accordance with methods provided for in the constitutions of member States.)

In order to avoid the difficulties encountered in Canada, it is desirable to recognize that the distribution of power between federal government and member States in the field of foreign relations is not immutable. It should be possible for member States to transfer to the federation, in whole or in part, their powers with respect to the conduct of foreign relations with all or certain foreign states or international organizations on the basis of an agreement approved by the executive authority of the federation and by the proper authority of the member State. Such an agreement would determine, in particular, the extent of the obligations of the Ministry for Foreign Affairs of the federation to act in accordance with directives from and to present reports to the proper authorities of the member State involved. This procedure would facilitate transfers of power without resort to the cumbersome method of constitutional amendment.

From the general power to conduct foreign relations additional powers may be easily deduced, but most constitutions contain explicit provisions on special subjects. It is customary, for instance, to provide in a federal constitution for the appointment and reception of diplomatic and consular officials by the federal government. In particular, the executive authority of the federation should be given the power to: appoint and recall the diplomatic representatives of the federation; appoint and recall consular officers of the federation; accept diplomatic representatives of foreign states accredited to it, and arrange for their recall when they have become *personae non gratae;* grant *exequatur* to foreign consuls with respect to consular districts which are under the control of the federation and revoke such *exequatur* in proper cases. On the other hand, each member State should retain, at least during a transitional period, the power to: appoint and recall its diplomatic representatives in foreign states; appoint and recall its consular officers; accept diplomatic representatives of foreign states accredited to it, and arrange for their recall when they have become *personae non gratae;* grant *exequatur* to foreign consuls with respect to consular districts in its territory, and revoke such *exequatur* in proper cases.

At formal functions in a foreign country, the diplomatic and consular representatives of the federation in that country should have precedence over the diplomatic and consular representatives of member States accredited there. To safeguard the interests of the federation and to ensure proper coordination, the diplomatic and consular representatives of member States in a foreign country should maintain close contact with the diplomatic and consular representatives of the federation in that country, and should give them all necessary assistance with respect to matters of common concern. As a member State might desire to transfer its diplomatic representation to the federal government, the federation should be authorized to take over diplomatic representation of member States in a particular country upon request. When such authorization has been given by a majority of the member States, the transitional period might end and the federation might be permitted to take over the representation of all member States in that country.

When member States are allowed separate diplomatic representation, the possibility of political embarrassment to the federation is substantial with respect to the question of recognition of foreign states and governments. To prevent such embarrassment, it might be desirable to provide that no member State may establish diplomatic relations with any new state or government which has not been recognized by the executive authority of the federation.

In the field of consular representation questions with respect to the power of the federal consular service in the absence of State representation and the possible unification of federal-State services are likely to arise. To avoid such difficulties, the consulates of the federation might be allowed to exercise consular functions in their districts for any member State which does not have its own consulate there. If a member State should decide to abolish its consulate in a particular district, the consular functions for that State would then be taken over by the consulate of the federation in that district. The legislature of the federation might be given the additional power to provide by law for the complete unification of the consular services of all member States with the consular service of the federation at a certain date (for instance, when the majority of member States have authorized the taking over of their consulates by the federation in the majority of foreign countries). Such a law might, however, authorize arrangements between the federation and member States for their continued consular representation in cities where they have special economic interests.

Questions relating to the conclusion, ratification, and implementation of treaties have been the subject of more constitutional debate in federal systems than any others in the field of foreign relations. It is particularly desirable in this area that a constitution anticipate the issues and make explicit and clear provision for them.

If there are general limitations on the jurisdiction of the federation in the field of foreign relations, a provision limiting the power of federal government to conclude treaties to matters within that jurisdiction may be desirable. Experience in other federations has shown that the lack of a clear provision on the subject has at times allowed the expansion of federal legislative jurisdiction to subjects not expressly delegated to the federal government. In the United States the alleged danger of such an expansion has led to serious proposals for a constitutional amendment prohibiting it. It is clear that the federation would be entitled to conclude treaties with foreign states at least with respect to any matter within the jurisdiction of the federation. If an expansion of this power is desired, there should be an explicit provision in the constitution establishing the boundaries beyond which this power may not be extended.

It is usual to provide in constitutions who can conclude treaties in the name of the federation. For instance, it might be provided that the executive authority of the federation shall be given the power to conclude and ratify treaties with foreign states in the name of the federation; the signing of the necessary documents might be delegated to appropriate officials.

Many constitutions blur the distinction between legislative approval of a treaty and its ratification. Sometimes they fail to make clear the procedure by which treaties are to be implemented. Finally, there should be a designation of the appropriate houses of the legislature which are to give approval and provide for implementation. These problems may be clarified by providing that prior to ratification each federal treaty should be submitted to the legislature of the federation for approval by a legislative act, which should embody the text of the treaty and all provisions necessary for its implementation.

The legislature of the federation might desire to formulate a policy with respect to a given subject matter and delegate to the executive the task of implementing it by making agreements; for instance, in the field of trade and tariffs. When definite standards to guide and limit the discretion of the executive are provided, subsequent review of the executive's act would be unnecessary. Therefore the legislature should be allowed to authorize by law the executive authority to conclude and ratify certain categories of treaties specified in such law without further approval of the legislature. The executive decrees enacting such treaties should have the same force as laws approving treaties.

Experience under various constitutions shows the desirability of the executive agreement as an instrument of national policy. Moreover, it shows that when drafting a provision on executive agreements, it is futile to limit its use by declaring it appropriate only for narrowly specified subjects. The emphasis should be placed on providing checks on its exercise by creating some form of review. Perhaps it might be sufficient to provide that the executive authority might make such administrative agreements with foreign states as may be necessary for the normal conduct of foreign relations or for dealing with emergency situations; such agreements should be submitted to the legislature as soon as possible, and should be terminated by denunciation if disapproved by either chamber of the legislature.

Consistent with provisions allowing member States to maintain foreign relations and diplomatic services, member States should be allowed to conclude treaties with foreign states with respect to any matter within their jurisdiction. The procedure for the approval and ratifications of their treaties would be governed by their respective constitutions rather than by the federal constitution. To facilitate the concentration of treaty-making power in federal hands, a member State might be allowed to delegate to the executive authority of the federation the right to conclude and ratify treaties on its behalf. The transitional period might end when a majority of the member States agrees to such a delegation; from that date the executive authority of the federation should have the power to conclude and ratify treaties for all member States. Such a delegation of the treaty-making power would not affect, however, the necessity of obtaining the approval of the proper authority of a member State prior to ratification, whenever such approval is required by the constitution of the member State.

If both the federation and the member States are allowed to conclude agreements, provision must be made for the coordination of their activities. In addition, proper methods must be devised for the solution of disputes over the exercise of treaty power by States.

Member States should keep the executive authority of the federation informed of all their treaty negotiations, and should transmit to it immediately the texts of all concluded treaties. If the executive authority of the federation should be of the opinion that a treaty concluded by a member State had encroached upon matters reserved to the federation, it should so notify the member State. If the member State should disagree with this opinion, the federation should be entitled to bring the matter before the constitutional tribunal of the federation in accordance with the general provisions for challenging unconstitutional acts of member States. If the particular treaty has not yet been ratified when the case is brought before the court, its ratification should be postponed until the right of the member State to ratify it has been confirmed by the court. While provision for the method of resolving legal questions is important, it can deal only with one aspect of the problem of possible federal-member State friction in this area. Political issues might arise if a member State should insist on concluding agreements which are inconsistent with federal foreign policy. Such an issue would have to be solved not by a court but by political means. For instance if the executive authority of the federation should object to a treaty concluded by a member State not on constitutional grounds, but on the ground that it would violate the basic principles of the foreign policy of the federation, the matter should be submitted to the federal legislature which might be given the power to disallow the treaty and enjoin its ratification. Such an act of the legislature would not be ordinarily subject to judicial review.

It is desirable that the constitution deal explicitly with the hierarchical position of treaties among the various sources of law. If the current constitutional practices are followed, treaties made by the federation should have, at least, the same status as the laws enacted by the federation; they should have an authority inferior only to the constitution of the federation. From this it would follow that the treaties made by the federation should prevail over prior laws of the federation. On the other hand, if treaties and laws are of equal status, then subsequent laws would have the effect of abrogating earlier treaties. Such action would involve the breach of an international obligation, and it might be desirable to provide that a law of the federation should not directly abrogate a prior treaty made by the federation, but that on request of the legislature of the federation the executive authority of the federation should be obliged to terminate a treaty in accordance with the provisions of that treaty or the general rules of international law.

If the federal government is to fulfill the obligation it has contracted by treaty, and nullification by state action is to be avoided, American experience would dictate the necessity of providing that treaties made by the federation should prevail over the constitutions, treaties, and laws of the member States. On the other hand, the States must have the means of protecting themselves against federal encroachment on the fundamental distribution of powers provided in the constitution. Therefore, under the general provisions for challenging the constitutionality of various acts of the federation, procedures should be available both for contesting the validity of federal treaties which encroach on the powers reserved by the constitution of the federation to member States, and for declaring invalid constitutions, treaties, and laws of member States which are in conflict with treaties made by the federation.

A new federation of previously sovereign States will be confronted by the fact that, before their entry into the federation, member States will have concluded treaties on many subjects, some of which would now fall within federal jurisdiction. Some procedures must be established for the orderly termination of those treaties. This could be accomplished, for instance, by providing that treaties made by member States prior to the coming into force of the constitution of the federation should, in so far as they deal with matters transferred to the jurisdiction of the federation, be terminated as soon as possible in accordance with their provisions or the general rules of international law. In any case the provisions of any treaty between a member State and a foreign state which deal with matters within the jurisdiction of the federation should terminate upon conclusion by the federation of a treaty on the subject with that foreign state.

Many modern constitutions expressly provide that international law should be supreme over municipal law. It might be useful to provide explicitly that the general rules of international law should form part of the law of the federation. Without necessity of legislative implementation, they should bind all the authorities of the federation and might directly create rights and duties for individuals. They should prevail over contrary laws and treaties of the federation and of the member States.

APPENDIX I

Australia

I. The Treaty Power and the Commonwealth

The right of the government of Australia to make treaties with foreign states and to participate in international organizations is the same as that of any other sovereign state, and is now subject only to a limited extent to the conditions codified in the resolutions of the Imperial Conferences of 1926 and 1930. These conditions required that any of the Commonwealth governments conducting negotiations should inform the other governments of the Commonwealth in case they should be interested and give them the opportunity of expressing their views, if they think that their interests may be affected. The other governments should express their views with "reasonable promptitude." Finally none of the Commonwealth governments should take any steps "which might involve the other Governments of His Majesty in any active obligation without their definite assent." To implement this point, the Conferences recommended that the instrument of ratification as well as the treaty should list the parts of the Commonwealth which have assumed the obligations of the treaty. If the agreement takes the form of one between governments, then it can be negotiated and concluded without any intervention on the part of the Crown and without the use of the Great Seal of the Realm. However, if it is between Heads of States, then all the documents which are necessary for the negotiation, signature, and ratification of such treaties are issued by the Crown upon the request of the Australian government.

II. Constitutional Provisions

Section 51 of the Australian Constitution in referring to the powers of Parliament says:

The Parliament shall, subject to this Constitution, have power to make laws for the peace, order, and good government of the Commonwealth with respect to:—

    (xix) Naturalization and aliens:
    (xx) Foreign corporations, and trading or financial corporations formed within the limits of the Commonwealth:

(xxvii) Immigration and emigration:
(xxviii) The influx of criminals:
(xxix)   External affairs:
(xxx)   The relations of the Commonwealth with the islands of the Pacific.

Of these powers placitum (xxix) relating to "external affairs" is the most important. While the other clauses are external in their nature, they only serve as a basis of legislation of very limited scope. Placitum (xxix) is couched in very broad terms; it is the recognized basis of the treaty power and of legislation to implement treaties.

Placitum (xxix) was inserted into the Australian Constitution without much debate. In the draft approved by the National Australian Convention of 1891 this clause read "external affairs and treaties" (Official Report of the National Australian Convention Debates 952 (1891). That draft also contained among the covering clauses the following provision (at page 944):

7. The Constitution established by this Act, and all laws made by the Parliament of the Commonwealth in pursuance of the powers conferred by the Constitution, and all treaties made by the Commonwealth, shall, according to their tenor be binding on the Courts, Judges, and people in every State, and of every part of the Commonwealth, anything in the Laws of any State to the contrary notwithstanding: and the Laws and Treaties of the Commonwealth shall be in force on board of all British ships whose last port of clearance or whose port of destination is the Commonwealth.

In the 1897 constitutional debates, proposals were made to omit references to treaties in covering clause 7 (now 5) and in Section 52, placitum (xxvi) (now §51 (xxix)), on the ground that only sovereign states could enter into treaties and the new Dominion was not a sovereign state but a part of the British Empire. While the amendments were adopted in both instances, the discussion made it clear that though the power to make treaties should be retained by the British government, the Australian government might be able to conclude "agreements" or "arrangements," such as trade arrangements. Thus, as in Canada, the framers of the "external affairs" clause did not draft it with a view to the needs of a sovereign Australia conducting her own foreign relations. (See Appendix II.) However, unlike Section 132 of the British North America Act of 1867, the language of placitum (xxix) is not so narrow that it is incapable of interpretation adapting it to such needs.

In Great Britain the treaty-making power in all of its stages, i.e., negotiation, signature, and ratification, is vested in the Crown. In Australia that power is exercisable by the Governor-General, who exercises the executive power for the Crown (§61 of the Constitution). However, it is the custom of Britain and also Australia that while a treaty may bind the state simply by its ratification, it is necessary that Parliament implement it by legislation if it is to confer new or alter existing rights and obligations of individuals. In practice Parliament is not limited to passing enforcing legislation, for it is customarily asked to approve treaties by the executive before ratifications are deposited. Thus Australia signed the Constitution of the World Health Organization "subject to approval and acceptance by the Government of the Commonwealth of Australia." The Government then introduced a bill in Parliament asking approval of Australia's membership in the Organization before it sent its acceptance.

III. Judicial Interpretation of the "External Affairs" Clause

Judicial decisions on the scope of placitum (xxix) have been few and for the most part confined to dictum. No legislation has ever been declared invalid on the strict ground of exceeding the power conferred by the "external affairs" clause. While some of the early cases illustrated possible uses of placitum (xxix), none of them addressed themselves to the fundamental question of the validity of legislation passed to implement a treaty which is not otherwise declared by the Constitution to be within the competence of the federal legislature. The High Court first faced this problem in 1936 in the case of *Rex v. Burgess, Ex parte Henry*, 55 C.L.R. 608 (1936). Section 4 of the Air Navigation Act of 1920 authorized the Governor-General to make regulations for the purpose of giving effect to and carrying out the Air Navigation Convention signed in Paris on October 13, 1919 and ratified June 1, 1922 and to control air navigation in the Commonwealth. The Court unanimously held that the second part of the Act authorizing the making of regulations to control air navigation in the Commonwealth was invalid, for the Commonwealth had no power to control wholly intrastate flights unless in exercise of other powers, e.g., of defense power. The majority of the Court also held that the regulations issued to carry out and give effect to the Air Convention were invalid, as they did not use the language of the Convention and thus the conviction was reversed. However all of the judges expressed the view that if such regulations had followed the Convention there would have been a legitimate exercise of the "external affairs" power.

The proposition seems to have been thus established that placitum (xxix) made permissible legislation which would otherwise be within the powers of the States, but this proposition cannot be stated without limitation, for of five judges only two were able to agree as to the extent of the power. One of them pointed out that the Constitution could not be amended by use of the treaty power, e.g., the provisions of Sections 113 and 116 could not be violated. Another judge felt that legislation was limited to obligations that "the Commonwealth may properly assume in its relations with other Powers or States" and that the subject matter of the treaty should be "of sufficient international significance to make it a legitimate subject for international cooperation and agreement" (*id.* at 658). A third judge, though willing to accept treaties with respect to matters "indisputably international in character," refused to take the "extreme view" that "merely because the Executive Government undertakes with some other country that the conduct of persons in Australia shall be regulated in a particular way, the legislature thereby obtains a power to enact that regulation although it relates to a matter of internal concern, which, apart from the obligation undertaken by the Executive, could not be considered as a matter of external affairs (*id.* at 669)."

The broadest view of the power was taken by the two remaining judges. They took the position that "it is no longer possible to assert that there is any subject matter which must necessarily be excluded from the list of possible subjects of international negotiation, international dispute or international agreement." For instance, "it must now be recognized that the maintenance or improvement of conditions of labour can (as it does) form a proper subject of international agreement, for differences in labour standards may increase the friction between nations which arises even when trade competition takes place under conditions of reasonable equality." Consequently, they expressed the view that "the fact of an international convention having been duly made about a subject brings that subject within the field of international relations so far as the subject is dealt with by agreement (*id.* at 681)."

One only has to contrast this opinion with those of other judges to appreciate the uncertain status of the "external affairs" power. As a minimum it may be assumed that the placitum would support legislation invading what would otherwise be the reserved powers of the States if the treaty concerns a subject which is a proper subject for international negotiation.

In 1939 the High Court had an opportunity to consider the question again. The same defendant was again accused of violating regulations issued by the Governor-General on a wholly intrastate flight (*Rex v. Poole, Ex parte Henry,* 61 **C.L.R.** 634 (1939)). The conviction was sustained as the regulations on this occasion were substantially in accord with the Convention.

The difficulties in the field of aviation may be further illustrated by the two Air Navigation Acts of 1947. Section 5 of the first Air Navigation Act (45 Australian Commonwealth Acts 86) provided that the Governor-General might make regulations to carry out and give effect to the Chicago Convention for the purpose of controlling air navigation: " (a) in relation to trade and commerce with other countries and among the states; (b) in relation to the military and naval defense of the Commonwealth; (c) in relation to postal and other like services; (d) within any territory of the Commonwealth; (e) within any state the Parliament of which has referred to the Parliament of the Commonwealth the matter of the control of air navigation within the state; and (f) for carrying out and giving effect to any other international convention or agreement relating to air navigation to which Australia is or becomes a party."

After more study on the subject the government felt that the list of enumerated powers did not exhaust the power of the Commonwealth to make regulations controlling air navigation, so it introduced a second Air Navigation Bill (45 Australian Commonwealth Acts 416) which repealed Section 5 set forth above and said that the Governor-General could issue regulations to carry out and give effect to the Chicago Convention and to any other international agreement or convention relating to air navigation to which Australia became a party by prescribing all matters " (1) in respect of air navigation which are necessary or to be prescribed in relation to any matter with respect to which the Parliament has power to make laws; or (2) which are necessary or convenient to be prescribed in respect of air navigation within any Territory of the Commonwealth or to or from any such Territory."

IV. Implementation of Labor Conventions

The statement of two judges in the *Burgess* case that the placitum could be used to support legislation pursuant to an international labor convention that the Commonwealth had ratified has not been tested. In 1924 the Prime Minister of the Commonwealth informed the International Labour Office that in Australia it was for the States to determine the extent to which the draft conventions should be ratified or applied.

In 1929, when the subject of ratification of international labor conventions was discussed at a meeting between the Commonwealth and State Ministers, the Commonwealth government said that "it would be prepared to ratify any such conventions to the provisions of which the states had given effect under their domestic legislation, and in the respect to which the states had also given an assurance that they would not modify such legislation so as to make it inconsistent with the provisions of the conventions, without previous discussion with the Commonwealth." Most of the conventions that have been ratified seem to concern subjects that would be in the competence of the Commonwealth apart from the use of the "external affairs" power, but the matter has not been judicially determined. If they were not within the scope of Commonwealth powers then State legislation was first procured on the subject before the ratification was deposited. An illustration of this procedure is found in the treatment of Draft Convention (No. 47) Concerning the Reduction of Hours of Work to Forty a Week, which was discussed at the Premiers Conference in 1936; as it proved impossible to secure any uniformity of State action, the government felt that it was unable to proceed further with the matter. The opposition in Parliament then introduced a motion of censure for the failure of the government to promote the adoption of the work week in accordance with the convention. In the ensuing debate the government admitted that there was a sizable body of legal opinion stating that Parliament could legislate to implement any labor convention because of the "external affairs" power. This opinion was subsequently given some support by the *Burgess* case but no government has ever acted in accordance with it. Of the one hundred conventions approved by the International Labour Office by 1951, Australia ratified only thirteen.

V. REPRESENTATION IN FOREIGN COUNTRIES

The Foreign Service of the Commonwealth has had a slow development. It was not until 1940, when an envoy extraordinary was accredited to the United States, that Australia had representation of diplomatic status ouside of the British Commonwealth. Since then progress has been more rapid but the country still has diplomatic representation in only a small number of nations.

The Australian States perform several functions relating to state external interests. They have separate representation in London in the form of Agents-General who handle the external interests of their States. Their functions relate chiefly to trade, but they serve also as a medium of communication with London on other matters. In 1930 and 1931, despite their precarious financial position, the States rejected a Commonwealth proposal for an amalgamation of these offices, as they felt that the services performed by the Agents-General were important and there was no adequate substitute.

The State governors have the right of direct communication with the United Kingdom government in respect to questions of the allowance and disallowance of Acts passed by the State legislatures. The State Cabinets communicate directly with the British Colonial Office in such questions as the appointment of State governors and changes to State constitutions. If a matter is tinged with a federal color, it is customary for the British Foreign Office to deal through the Commonwealth.

A P P E N D I X   I I

Canada

I. THE TREATY-MAKING POWER

Until the end of the First World War the foreign affairs of Canada were largely controlled by the government of Great Britain, although the Canadian government was, from 1867, represented at negotiations relating to treaties which affected its special interests. However, treaties concluded by Great Britain alone could be binding upon the entire Empire without consent of the Dominion Government, though in practice such consent was usually obtained. Thus, the British North America Act of 1867 envisaged only one form of treaty power, and merely provided that "The Parliament and Government of Canada shall have the Powers necessary or proper for performing the Obligations of Canada or of any Province thereof, as Part of the British Empire, towards Foreign Countries arising under Treaties between the Empire and such Foreign Countries."

The term "Empire treaty" has become rather vague, the courts having refused to define it with any degree of accuracy. Properly, it may be applied only to the series of treaties signed by Great Britain before 1926. Whatever the exact meaning of an Empire treaty may be, it was never doubted that the British government in signing, and the Canadian Parliament in implementing such treaties, were not limited by the division of powers between the Dominion and provincial governments. This is not surprising, since the power to amend the British North America Act also rested with the British government. However, as Canada's role in international affairs became increasingly independent, until, by the Seals Act of 1939 (C.S. 1939, c. 22) complete sovereignty in foreign relations was attained, judicial interpretation made it evident that the treaty powers transferred to the Dominion government were not as extensive as those formerly exercised by the British government. This too is in line with other developments, since the courts consistently favored provincial claims and since the amendment powers of the Dominion government are limited as regards the existing division of powers (see Statute of Westminster, 1931, and B.N.A. (No. 2) Act of 1949). It is not unreasonable to insist that the Dominion government should not, by treaty, be able to achieve that which it cannot do by constitutional amendment. Since, at present, the exact nature of the amending power and the procedure for amendment are unsettled, the treaty power, as well, cannot be precisely defined at this time. At any rate, the powers provided in Section 132 have become meaningless in view of Canada's new status in international affairs, in particular as Empire treaties are no longer concluded. In time of war, however, Canada for all purposes and intents becomes a unitary state, and the treaty power, along with the powers ordinarily reserved to the provincial governments, comes under the full and unhampered control of the Dominion government (see Study 4, Appendix II).

II. Representation in Foreign Countries

Although during the interwar period Canada did have a number of representatives in foreign countries, the British diplomatic service usually attended to Canadian affairs. High Commissioners have for some years been exchanged with Great Britain and other countries of the Commonwealth. Since 1941 Canada has set up a consular service and now has diplomatic representation in all major countries. Ambassadors and High Commissioners are appointed by the Cabinet without Parliamentary consultation. The Department of External Affairs, first set up in 1909, has been entirely independent of the British Colonial Office since 1925, and is now headed by a Cabinet Minister. In spite of the efforts of the Dominion government to discourage the practice, some of the Provinces have at times maintained agents in charge of immigration and trade in foreign countries (see, e.g., Statutes of Quebec, 1940, c. 10). While the provinces have no power over aliens and naturalization (B.N.A. Act, §91 (25)), they have concurrent powers over immigration, although in case of conflict Dominion law prevails (§95). The activities of provincial agents abroad have usually been limited to promoting their Provinces' exports and to encouraging prospective immigrants to settle in their respective Provinces and to circulate information about them. Provincial governments do not have ministries in charge of foreign affairs.

III. Cabinet and Parliament in External Affairs

Formally the responsibility for negotiating and ratifying treaties rests entirely with the Cabinet. By custom, however, proposed treaties are debated in Parliament, and a resolution by both houses in favor of ratification precedes such a step. This custom is a political necessity in a country which, in the past, has been sharply divided on matters affecting foreign policy. As in the United Kingdom, treaties are not "self-enforcing," and legislation must be passed to implement them, before they become binding upon individuals (see *Arrow River and Tributaries Slide and Boom Co. v. Pigeon Timber Co. Ltd.,* [1932] S.C.R. 495). Several times the Cabinet has referred treaties to the Supreme Court to determine whether their terms were within the legislative competence of the Dominion government, but only one proposed treaty was so referred prior to ratification (see, e.g., *In re Legislative Jurisdiction over Hours of Labour,* [1925] S.C.R. 505).

IV. The Treaty-making Power as Limited by Reserved Powers of the Province

Until 1937 no Canadian treaty had been held *ultra vires* by the courts. Indeed, until that year there had been but few occasions on which it was necessary to determine the limits of the Dominion government's power in this field. The regulations imposed by federal legislation enforcing the 1916 Convention on Migratory Birds between the United States and Great Britain were held to deal with a question of national scope and not a provincial matter (*Rex v. Stuart,* [1925] 1 D.L.R. 12)); the extent of the treaty power was not discussed. Similarly, the Japanese Treaty Act of 1913 guaranteeing Japanese residents in Canada conditions of labor equal to those of the "most favored nation" was held to fall within the Dominion government's general orbit of legislative power over questions of national concern, and provincial legislation contrary to its provisions was held invalid (*Attorney-General of British Columbia v. Attorney-General of Can-*

ada, [1924] A.C. 203). Again in 1932 the regulation and control over aeronautics and radio communications imposed by federal legislation, in consequence of Canada's obligations under the International Conventions of 1919 and 1927, respectively, to which it was a signatory, were upheld by the Judicial Committee of the Privy Council (see *In re Regulation and Control of Aeronautics in Canada,* [1932] A.C. 54, and *In re Regulation and Control of Radio Communications in Canada,* [1932] A.C. 304). These decisions, it seemed at the time, were reached both because of the plenary nature of the Dominion's treaty-making powers and because the subject matter of the treaties fell within the fields of exclusive federal legislation set out in Section 91 of the British North America Act. However, in 1937 the Privy Council declared that these decisions had been based entirely on the second ground, and this interpretation has been recently reaffirmed, at least as far as aeronautics is concerned (*Johannerson et al. v. West St. Paul,* [1951] 4 D.L.R. 609)).

The far-reaching decision of 1937 (*Attorney-General of Canada v. Attorney-General of Ontario,* [1937] A.C. 326) concerned three Acts passed by the Canadian Parliament to give effect to its obligations under Part XIII of the Treaty of Versailles, which set up the International Labour Office. The three Acts in substance gave effect to three ILO conventions which Canada had previously ratified and which dealt, respectively, with (a) the limiting of the hours of work in industrial undertakings, (b) the application of weekly rest in industrial undertakings, and (c) the creating of minimum-wage-fixing machinery. The Parliament had passed these Acts in spite of the opinion of the Supreme Court in a reference ([1925] S.C.R. 505) and the reports of the Dominion-Provincial conferences of 1922 and 1923, which had insisted that the treaty power of the Dominion government did not enable it to legislate on conditions of labor, a field reserved entirely to the Provinces. The Privy Council agreed with the provincial point of view. In Lord Atkin's words, "For the purposes of s.91 and 92, i.e., the distribution of legislative powers between the Dominion and the Provinces, there is no such thing as treaty legislation as such. The distribution is based on classes of subjects: and as a treaty deals with a particular class of subjects, so will the legislative power of performing it be ascertained. . . . The Dominion cannot, merely by making promises to foreign countries clothe itself with legislative authority inconsistent with the constitution which gave it birth. . . . While the ship of state now sails on larger ventures and into foreign waters, she still retains the water-tight compartments which are an essential part of her original structure."

After this decision only a few of the one hundred ILO conventions could ever have any force in Canada by Dominion legislation, and the twelve conventions which had been ratified were mostly limited to maritime workers. Even if treaties involving "property and civil rights" form only a small part of the total, Canadian ratification of international treaties cannot be regarded as a reliable indication of ability to execute them, as long

as the Canadian Supreme Court follows closely the decisions of the Privy
Council.

In spite of Lord Atkin's suggestions to that effect, hopes of close
Dominion-Provincial cooperation, and of speedy ratification by almost a
dozen parliaments, are ephemeral. Nor can the provincial legislatures delegate their powers to the Dominion Parliament, which many observers had
felt might offer the simplest solution to the problem (*Attorney-General
of Nova Scotia v. Attorney-General of Canada,* [1951] S.C.R. 31). Informal
attempts at cooperation, too, have been of no avail. The delegations to the
ILO almost always included representatives chosen by the provincial governments, but this seems to have had no attenuating influence on the latter.
At San Francisco and at subsequent meetings of the United Nations the
Provinces as such have not been represented in Canadian delegations. At
present only an amendment of the British North America Act, such as add-
ing the words "or under multilateral international convention" to Section
132 seems to provide an answer to the dilemma (see Angus, "The Canadian
Constitution and the U.N. Charter," 12 Can. J. Econ. & Pol. Sci. 127 (1946)).
Difficulties have become more frequent recently, as the results of the "ILO
Conventions Case" have come to impinge upon Canada's actions as a member
of the United Nations. Teaching the principles of the U.N. Charter, the
Canadian delegate to the General Assembly declared in 1947, could be under-
taken only by provincial governments, while the Dominion government
could do no more than give financial aid to such bodies as the United Nations
Association of Canada. Again in January 1949, while voting in favor of the
Universal Declaration of Human Rights, the Minister of External Affairs,
Mr. Pearson, explicitly disavowed any intention of altering the division of
powers between the Provinces and the Dominion government. Beyond for-
warding relevant declarations and conventions to the Lieutenant-Governors
of the several Provinces there is, at present, little that the Dominion government has done (or could do) to enforce such international obligations.

Indeed the principles of the U.N. Charter have not, as yet, affected
Canadian law or practice to any noticeable extent. In 1945 a restrictive
convenant was declared invalid by an Ontario court because it was contrary to "public policy" as expressed, among several other documents, in
the U.N. Charter (*Re Drummond Wren,* [1945] O.R. 778). However, in
a very similar case the concept of "public policy" expressed in such documents was rejected as a ground for declaring discriminatory covenants
illegal (*Re Noble and Wolf,* [1948] O.R. 579). While the Supreme Court
did finally declare such covenants illegal, it based its decisions on entirely
different reasons (*Noble and Wolf v. Alley,* [1951] S.C.R. 64).

V. THE PROVINCES IN EXTERNAL AFFAIRS

While the clause (§132) of the British North America Act concerned
with the treaty power of the Dominion government has become obsolete,

that Act has no provision at all for or against provincial activity in foreign affairs. In practive the Provinces have not been very active in this field. From time to time some of the Provinces (mainly Quebec and Ontario) have entered into agreements with the United Kingdom and the United States to avoid duplication of succession duties. No such agreements exist at present. There were also attempted administrative agreements between Ontario and the American States bordering on Lake Erie to prevent depletion of fisheries in that lake in 1917. Agreements about tourist advertisements were made between British Columbia and the neighboring states of Oregon and Washington. The Dominion government discourages the making of direct international agreements by the Provinces.

Interferences by provincial governments with the terms of Dominion treaties have been rare. The most serious instance, discriminatory legislation against Orientals in British Columbia, was "disallowed" by the federal government in 1922 as violating the terms of the treaty with Japan of 1913. Not excessive activity by the Provinces, but the inability of the Dominion government to act effectively, is causing at present the gravest difficulties in the conduct of Canada's external relations.

APPENDIX III

Germany

I. THE IMPERIAL CONSTITUTION

Under Article 11 of the Imperial Constitution, the Kaiser as the presiding officer of the federation was the representative of the Reich in matters concerning the law of nations as well as private law. At the same time, the member States, in order to protect their interests in matters which did not fall within the exclusive competence of the federation, retained the power to have relations not only with other member States, but also with foreign countries.

Among the powers the Kaiser possessed as the representative of the federation were those which pertain to diplomatic relations with foreign countries. Under Article 11, I, he had to accredit and to receive ambassadors. To this passive ambassadorial right corresponded an active one: the Kaiser appointed and recalled ambassadors to foreign governments. However, the right to receive and send diplomatic representatives was not exclusively possessed by the supreme authority of the Reich. The individual member States could also send and receive ambassadors. Thus Bavaria and Saxony had ambassadors in Paris and Vienna.[19]

As to consular officials, under Article 56, I, the entire consular system of

---

[19] This was already recognized in the constitutional Reichstag of 1867 and in the Schlussprotokoll to the treaty with Bavaria of November 23, 1870.

the German Reich was under the supervision of the Kaiser, who appointed the consuls after hearing the Committee of the Bundesrat on Trade and Commerce.[20] In contrast to the regulation on ambassadors, in Article 11, the right of the Reich to appoint consuls was intended to become an exclusive one after a transition period necessary to develop a federal consular service. Article 56, II, provided that in the districts of the German consuls new consulates of the member States might not be established, that the German consuls should discharge for the members of the federation not represented in their district the functions of a State consul, and that all existing State consulates should be abolished as soon as the organization of the German consulates was so perfected that the representation of the separate interests of all the members of the federation was recognized by the Bundesrat as secured by the German consulates. On the other hand, there was, with respect to the right to receive consuls from foreign nations, no restriction on the member States; their government could give an *exequatur* to consuls from foreign states.[21]

The Kaiser had the power to enter, in the name of the Reich, into alliances, and other treaties with foreign states (Art. 11, I). The member States, however, had the right to conclude treaties with foreign powers with respect to specific matters, such as, for instance, extradition. On matters that were exclusively within the competence of the Reich (matters concerning the navy, war and peace, customs, commerce, mail and telegraph: see the enumeration in Article 4), the member States were not allowed to conclude treaties with foreign nations. If, however, matters were within the competence of the Reich only facultatively (such as, for instance, the regulation of the courts (*Gerichtswesen*) and the care of the poor), member States could conclude treaties as long as the Reich had not done so. In matters that were neither exclusively nor optionally within the competence of the Reich, the member States could conclude treaties with foreign states, without any restrictions. Of course, none of the treaties concluded by the member States could contain anything that was incompatible with the law of the federation.

Article 11, III, provides that in so far as treaties with foreign states relate to such matters as, according to Article 4, belong in the domain of Reich legislation, the concurrence of the Bundesrat is required for their conclusion; in order that such treaties may not only be internationally binding, but may also become the (municipal) law of the land, the approval of the Reichstag is required for their coming into force. For instance, a treaty on customs and commerce did not create rights and duties for German subjects directly by its mere conclusion, but only after the Reichstag had ap-

[20] Compare Article 4, VII, under which the following questions were subject to supervision by the Reich and to its legislation: the organization of common protection of German trade abroad, of German navigation and its flag upon the sea, and establishment of common consular representation which shall be maintained by the Reich.

[21] See the Schlussprotokoll to the treaty of November 23, 1870, concerning the entry of Bavaria into the German League (RGBl. 1871, p. 25) under Article XII.

proved it. This approval could be given before as well as after the conclusion of the treaty.

Since, through the approval of the Reichstag, a treaty concluded by the Kaiser became a federal law binding on and giving rights to German citizens, it was, under Article 2 which prescribed that Reich statutes supersede State statutes, also binding upon the State governments, i.e., supreme over State laws. Therefore, no specific provision stating that treaties are supreme over the laws of the member States was necessary.

Aside from the powers that were specifically enumerated in Article 11, the Kaiser as the supreme Reich authority had of course all the powers that are in the nature of a "representative" of a nation in its international relations. For instance, the Kaiser could not only conclude treaties, but he could decree, with the approval of the Bundesrat, restrictions with respect to imports and exports (Ein- und Ausfuhrverbote). Further, there were, in the field of posts and telegraph, matters which could under the Constitution be regulated by the Kaiser alone, that is, without a law, although these regulations contained rules which created rights and duties for the people (for instance, regulations concerning the fee for money orders, printed matters, registered mail, etc.). The constitutional provision on the matters requiring approval of the Reichstag was interpreted as allowing the Kaiser to conclude a treaty on matters which he alone could regulate,[22] without the approval of the Bundesrat and the Reichstag.[23]

II. The Weimar Constitution

Article 45, I, of the Weimar Constitution was copied almost verbally from Article 11, I, of the Imperial Constitution: the Reichspräsident represents the federation in matters of international law. The rights of the member States to have relations with foreign countries, which existed under the Imperial Constitution, were considerably restricted through Article 78, I, which provided that the cultivation of relations with foreign states should be exclusively a matter of the Reich. Nevertheless, the fact that the Reich was not a unitary state can be seen in many provisions of the Weimar Constitution which gave to the member States certain rights with respect to the foreign affairs of the federation.

The dilminution of the federal aspect of the Reich is obvious, first of all, in the regulation of diplomatic relations with other countries. Under Article 45, I, the Reichspräsident accredited and received ambassadors,

---

[22] The question was raised whether the Kaiser might delegate his powers in this field. This question was answered in the affirmative in practice: agreements concerning not too important matters could not only be negotiated but also concluded by officials, with a force binding upon the federation.

[23] If, however, a treaty was made on matters enumerated in Article 4 — for instance, on the fee for ordinary letters, on the norms concerning civil and criminal procedure, on naturalization, customs and commerce, etc. — the approval of the Bundesrat and the Reichstag was necessary. See also Article 48, II.

a right which was complemented by his right to appoint ambassadors and to send them abroad. In contrast to the Imperial Constitution, this right was under the Weimar regulation exclusively possessed by the Reich (Art. 78, I), and the State governments had neither the right to send nor to receive ambassadors from foreign states.[24] Similarly, the right to have consulates in foreign countries ceased to exist for the States under the Weimar Constitution.[25]

The Reichspräsident, as the representative of the Reich in matters of international law, also had the power to conclude, in the name of the Reich, alliances and other treaties with foreign powers (Art. 45, I). This was, again, an exclusive right of the Reich (Art. 78, I). However, the following sections of Article 78 demonstrate that in a qualified sense the member States were still allowed to exercise certain powers with respect to international relations. In matters the regulation of which was within the competence of the legislatures of the Länder, a Land could conclude treaties with foreign states. However — and this shows the preponderance of the Reich treaty-making power — such treaties needed the approval of the Reich (Art. 78, II). Matters which fell within the competence of the Land legislation were not only those which were (because of their omission in the enumeration of competences in Arts. 6–11) not within the legislative competence of the Reich, but also matters within the concurrent legislation of the Reich (Arts. 7–11) as long as they were not regulated by Reich legislation. For as long as the Reich had not legislated, the Länder retained the right of legislation (Art. 12, I) and, therefore, of the conclusion of treaties.[26]

In order to safeguard the representation of interests which might arise for individual Länder from their particular economic relations with, or their proximity to, foreign states, the Reich was to adopt the necessary arrangements and measures in agreement with the Land concerned (Art. 78, IV).

Under Article 45, III, alliances and treaties with foreign states, which related to subjects within the legislative competence of the Reich, needed the approval of the Reichstag. Whereas Article 11, III, of the Imperial Constitution was always interpreted to mean that the validity of a treaty in the international sphere was not dependent upon approval by the legislature,

[24] The French ambassador in Munich was accredited under a special provision of the Treaty of Versailles.

[25] However, the member States could have relations with each other and with the Reich through permanent or *ad hoc* appointed representatives, under the title of "ambassador," "envoy," or "consul," since this did not fall within the sphere of international but of national relations. Also the member States contended that they could maintain relations with the Catholic Church, since that church is not "a foreign power" in the sense of Article 45, I.

[26] Examples of matters which under Article 78, II, were within the treaty power of the member States were: regulation of traffic on a common border, questions of improvement of land, exploitation of water power which lay partly abroad, partly within the Land. The Länder might, further, conclude treaties on the status of aliens (*Fremdenpolizei*) as long as this was not regulated according to Article 7(4) by the Reich. On the other hand, treaties on extradition could not be concluded by the Länder, because under Article 6(3) this fell under the exclusive competence of the Reich.

but only its validity as the law of the land, creating rights and duties for individuals, the requirement of approval by the Reichstag was interpreted differently under the Weimar Constitution. In the constitutional convention that drafted Article 45, the majority was of the opinion that treaties, which under Article 45, III, must be approved, were, without such approval, neither law of the land (i.e., binding upon individuals), nor binding upon the Reich in its capacity as a subject of international law, and created no rights for foreign states. (See the statements by Preuss, *Protokoll*, p. 282, and *Ablass*, *id.* p. 283.) Approval by the Reichstag was considered as making an intended ratification legally possible, or, in case that ratification had already taken place, as giving validity to that ratification.[27]

Under Article 13, which provided that Reich law superseded Land law, a treaty bound not only citizens of Germany but also the legislatures of the member States. (Compare, in this connection, also Article 4 of the Weimar Constitution, under which the universally recognized rules of the law of nations — one of which is the rule *pacta sunt servanda* — became binding component parts of German Reich law.)

The powers of the Reichspräsident with respect to foreign relations included not only those specifically enumerated in the Constitution. He had, besides, all those powers which are ordinarily possessed by a Head of State. Thus Article 45, II, according to which declarations of war and conclusion of peace were made by federal law, did not forbid the Reichspräsident to order the troops to fight against an invader without a federal law having been passed. He had also the right to issue regulations (*Verordunngsrecht*).

III. THE BASIC LAW OF THE FEDERAL REPUBLIC

The States have, with respect to foreign policy, greater rights under the Basic Law than under the Weimar Constitution, in spite of the fact that Article 32, I, is nearly a copy of Article 78, I, of the Weimar Constitution. It provides that the maintenance of relations with foreign states shall be the concern of the federation. It may be noted, however, that this article omits the word "exclusively."

As under the Imperial and Weimar Constitutions, under the Basic Law the Bundespräsident represents the federation in matters concerning international law. He has the right of accrediting and receiving diplomats

---

[27] The practice was as follows: a treaty which needed approval was put, together with the draft of a law of approval, by the Reichsregierung before the Reichsrat (Art. 69, I), or the Wirtschaftsrat (Art. 165, IV), i.e., it was treated as any ordinary bill. The Reichstag also decided upon it as if it were an ordinary bill. After the treaty and the law of approval had been approved, there was, if the Reichsrat did not object, promulgated not only the approving law, but also the treaty, in the *Federal Gazette*, Part II (*Reichsgesetzblatt* II). The fact of ratification and the exchange of the ratification documents was thereafter separately announced in the *Federal Gazette*. As in the Imperial Constitution, the Reichspräsident did not need to ratify the treaty personally, but could delegate that power. This power to delegate was affirmed by the German Reichsgericht (RGZ 105, s. 159).

(Art. 59, I), as well as the right to send ambassadors to foreign states. The member States have no right to have diplomatic relations with foreign states, and have no right to have consuls in foreign states (see also Arts. 73 and 87, I).

The federal President has further the power to conclude treaties with foreign states on behalf of the federation, but alliances, which were expressly mentioned in the Weimar Constitution (Art. 45)[28] are not mentioned in this provision. Before the conclusion of a treaty affecting the special interests of a member State, this State must be consulted in good time (Art. 32, II). Furthermore, insofar as legislation falls within the competence of the States, these may, with the approval of the federal government, conclude treaties with foreign states (Art. 32, III). The matters with respect to which the member States may conclude treaties with foreign states are not only those which fall exclusively under the legislative competences of the States (Art. 70, I in connection with Art. 73), but also those where there exists a concurrent legislative power (Art. 74), as long and insofar as the federation has not legislated (Art. 72, I). However, all treaties concluded by States require approval by the federation which in principle should be obtained before the treaty is concluded, although an approval given after the conclusion of the treaty may make the treaty valid, too.[29] The States decide by themselves upon the formalities of the conclusion of treaties with foreign states. They are not obliged to conclude the treaties through organs of the federation.

Under Article 59, II, treaties which regulate the political relations of the federation or refer to matters of federal legislation require, in the form of a federal law, the approval or the participation of the respective bodies competent for federal legislation. Treaties which under Article 59, II, need the approval of the legislature may be ratified by the Bundespräsident only after the approval has been obtained. It is disputed whether treaties which need the approval of the legislature but are concluded by the Bundespräsident without that approval are valid in the international sphere. Of course they have, as long as they are not approved, no binding force upon the citizens, although even this may be disputed in view of the fact that Article 25 prescribes that the general rules of international law form part of federal law (and one rule is without doubt the principle of *pacta sunt servanda*) and that these rules "take precedence over the laws and directly create rights and duties for the inhabitants of the federal territory."

Since Article 31, similar to Article 2 of the Imperial and Article 13 of the Weimar Constitutions, prescribes that federal law overrides Land law, a treaty must be binding as federal law upon the legislatures and govern-

---

[28] The word "alliance" was omitted, perhaps because at the time of the framing of the Basic Law, Western Germany, being occupied by the allies, was in no position to conclude alliances.

[29] It is debatable whether a treaty concluded by a member State with a foreign state is valid under international law without the approval by the federation.

ments of the member States as well as upon the citizens and the government of the federation.

Aside from treaties, the Bundespräsident may make administrative agreements with foreign states. Here the provisions concerning the federal administration apply correspondingly. The German Constitutional Tribunal decided on July 29, 1952 that a French-German "economic agreement" which could be properly executed by administrative action on the basis of prior laws did not require Parliamentary approval.

Though the Basic Law does not differ greatly from the Imperial and Weimar Constitutions with respect to matters concerning international law, there are a few novel provisions in it. Thus Article 24 provides that the federation may, by legislation, transfer sovereign power to international institutions. For the maintenance of peace, the federation may join a system of mutual collective security; in doing so it may consent to those limitations of its sovereign powers which are necessary to bring about and secure a peaceful and lasting order in Europe and among the nations of the world. Also, for the settlement of disputes between nations, the federation shall accede to conventions concerning a general, comprehensive obligatory system of international arbitration. Activities tending to disturb the peaceful relations between nations, and to prepare for an aggressive war, are declared unconstitutional and punishable.

A P P E N D I X   I V

Switzerland

I. CONSTITUTIONAL PROVISIONS

The Federal Constitution contains the following provisions on foreign affairs:

Article 8. The Confederation has the sole right to declare war and conclude peace, and to make alliances and treaties, particularly customs and commercial treaties, with foreign states.

Article 9. Exceptionally, the cantons retain the right to conclude treaties with foreign states in respect of matters of public economy, frontier relations and police; nevertheless, such treaties must not contain anything prejudicial to the Confederation or the rights of other cantons.

Article 10. Official intercourse between the cantons and foreign governments or their representatives shall take place through the Federal Council.

In regard to the matters mentioned in the preceding article, however, the cantons may correspond directly with the subordinate authorities and officers of a foreign state.

Article 85. The following matters in particular are within the competence of the two councils (Federal Assembly):

    5. Alliances and treaties with foreign states, as also the approval of
treaties made by the cantons between themselves or with foreign
states; nevertheless, such treaties of the cantons shall only be
brought before the Federal Assembly when the Federal Council
or another canton raises objection.

Article 89. . . . International treaties concluded for a period of indeterminate duration, or for more than fifteen years, shall be submitted
for acceptance or rejection by the people if a demand to this effect be
made by thirty thousand active citizens or by eight cantons.

Article 102.   The powers and duties of the Federal Council, within
the limits of the present Constitution, are more particularly the following:

    7. It examines treaties of the cantons between themselves or with
foreign states, and gives its approval thereto if it thinks fit.

    8. It watches over the interests of the Confederation abroad, pay-
ing particular notice to its international relations, and has
general charge of foreign affairs.

Finally, it may be mentioned that the basic principle of Swiss foreign
policy, since the early days of the Confederation, has been neutrality. Article 85, paragraph 6, and Article 102, paragraph 9, of the Constitution
provide that the Federal Assembly and the Federal Council shall take measures to preserve the neutrality of Switzerland.

II. The Federal Council and Foreign Affairs

Article 102, paragraph 8, of the Constitution empowers the Federal
Council to conduct the foreign affairs of Switzerland. Thus the Federal
Council maintains relations with foreign states and carries on negotiations
with them. The Federal Council nominates all diplomatic and consular officials of Switzerland and receives all officials of foreign states. As to consuls,
there is a custom that the Federal Council, before giving the *exequatur* to
a foreign consul, consults the governments of the cantons which belong to
his consular district (see Fleiner, *Schweizerisches Bundesstaatsrecht* 732
(1923)). But the Confederation is neither obliged to do this nor has it to
comply with a cantonal opinion.

Although all important decisions are taken by the whole Federal Council,
the conduct of foreign affairs falls within the competence of one particular member, namely, the head of the Political Department. For a while
this department was headed by the President of the Confederation, but as
the President of the Confederation changes every year this solution was not
satisfactory. Since the end of World War I the Political Department has
been permanently conducted by one member of the Federal Council.

III. Federal and Cantonal Powers

Although Article 8 of the Constitution delegates to the Confederation
the sole right to make alliances and treaties with foreign states, opinions

whether the Confederation could conclude treaties on any subject, or only on matters in which it has the legislative power, differed for a long time. Nowadays, however, the opinion which considers the federal treaty power as unlimited is predominant (see Fleiner and Giacometti, *Schweizerisches Bundesstaatsrecht* 810 (1949)). A comparison between Article 8 of the Constitution and Article 9, which deals with the cantonal treaty power, supports this opinion. Regardless of theoretical considerations, the federal government has always exercised this unlimited power and has concluded treaties on many subjects of special interest to the cantons. Sometimes it has asked the cantons for their opinions, but it has done this merely for political reasons, not because it felt obliged to do so. In a similar way, the Federal Council asks private unions and associations interested in special subjects for their opinion.

The federal treaty power is, of course, not completely unlimited. The federal authorities have to observe the Constitution, and especially its provisions on the rights and freedoms of citizens. However, in case of a violation of those rights, there is no possibility of an appeal to a court. The Constitution states expressly that the Federal Court is bound by the federal laws and treaties (Art. 113).

According to Article 9 of the Constitution the cantons retain the right to conclude treaties with foreign states with respect to matters of public economy, frontier relations, and police. This article has always been interpreted as meaning that the cantons should be excluded from concluding political treaties, but no attention is paid to the enumeration therein of subjects within cantonal competence. Thus the cantons have concluded treaties with foreign states (through the intermediary of the Federal Council) on subjects which seem to be outside their competence. On the other hand, the Confederation, without being authorized by the cantons, has made treaties on matters enumerated in Article 9, for instance, treaties dealing with navigation on border waters or the practice of medicine in border districts.

It may thus be said that the Confederation and the cantons have concurrent treaty powers. The Confederation can conclude treaties on any matter it wants, but, as long as it does not exercise this power, the cantons may do so, at least in so far as the treaties do not deal with political matters. However, since the Confederation has to approve all treaties between cantons and foreign states and generally has to conduct the negotiations, there is no danger that the cantons conclude treaties prejudicial to the Confederation.

While the scope of the cantonal treaty power is, with regard to the subject matter of treaties, rather broad, the cantonal power to negotiate with foreign states and to conclude treaties is very narrow. Article 10 of the Constitution states that official intercourse between the cantons and foreign governments or their representatives shall take place through the Federal Council. Only with regard to the matters mentioned in Article 9, the cantons may correspond directly with "subordinate" authorities and officers of foreign states, i.e., they are not authorized to negotiate with a foreign government or with a Minister or other representative of a foreign state in Switzerland. A foreign authority will generally be a subordinate one, if the scope of its activity is limited either to a special local district or to a special matter. Treaties concluded by the cantons directly with foreign states deal, for instance, with the transmission of electric current through a part of foreign territory, protection of river sources, mutual admission of theater groups, etc.

If a canton wants to make a treaty with a foreign government, it has to ask the Federal Council to take the necessary steps. The Federal Council then conducts the negotiations itself or through representatives and concludes the treaty in the name of the canton. The Federal Council often appoints officials of the canton concerned as its representatives. In the first decades of the Swiss federal state, treaties between cantons and foreign states which were concluded by the Confederation in the name of the cantons concerned particularly the construction of railroads, navigation on border waters, and the avoidance of double taxation. In the twentieth century, however, treaties on these matters were exclusively concluded by the Confederation. Cantonal activity in the field of foreign affairs has become less and less important, while the Confederation now exercises its powers more extensively than in the past. Moreover, the general constitutional power of the Confederation has steadily increased through more than forty constitutional amendments. Thus the Confederation has obtained the legislative power with respect to railways and navigation, the power to grant concessions for power stations on watercourses forming the border of Switzerland, extensive powers in the economic and social field, and the right to legislate on the entry, exit, and residence of foreigners.

Treaties made between the cantons and foreign states have to be approved by the Federal Council (Art. 102). If the Federal Council or another canton raises objection against them, the treaties are brought before the Federal Assembly (Art. 85). The federal authority examines whether cantonal treaties contain anything prejudicial to the Confederation or to the rights of other cantons. As the Federal Council has to negotiate for a canton with a foreign state, it may even refuse to begin negotiations. In the first years after the foundation of the Swiss federal state in 1848, the Confederation had to admonish the cantons several times not to negotiate directly with foreign states (see Ullmer, *Die staatsrechtliche Praxis der schweizerischen Bundesbehörden*, 1848–1863, Nos. 723–729). In 1849 it had to invalidate a treaty between the canton of Uri and Naples because it dealt with military matters (see Ullmer, *id.*, No. 39). Ever since, it seems that the Confederation has found it unnecessary to interfere with cantonal treaties. But in 1882 the Federal Council refused to require a reciprocity declaration from the state of Baden for the canton of Schaffhausen (see 4 Salis, *Schweizerisches Bundesrecht*, No. 1778), and in 1903 it rejected a request of the canton of Geneva to negotiate with France. (Geneva wanted to participate in a railroad project in France, but the Confederation had already granted its concession to another railway permitting it to cross Swiss territory, and there was no need for the other project.)

IV. The Powers of the Federal Assembly

Article 102 of the Constitution delegates to the Federal Council the sole right to represent Switzerland in the field of international relations. Accordingly, the Federal Council concludes all treaties between Switzerland and foreign states. Article 85, however, states that alliances and treaties with foreign states have to be approved by the Federal Assembly. Yet in practice the Federal Assembly approves only treaties which contain new international obligations for Switzerland or the abandonment of rights. All other treaties as well as the prolongation of any treaty do not need the approval of the Federal Assembly. Experience has shown that the Federal Council is the predominant authority in foreign affairs. The Federal Assembly has generally approved treaties unconditionally. Only once, in 1865, has it refused approval, and a few times it has proposed amendments. In some cases the Federal Assembly has authorized in advance the Federal Council to conclude treaties on certain subjects. Moreover, the Federal Council has concluded treaties containing some new obligations for Switzerland, without previous or subsequent approval by the Federal Assembly.

Article 89 was amended in 1921 to add the requirement that international treaties concluded for a period of more than fifteen years shall be submitted for acceptance or rejection to the people upon demand by 30,-000 active citizens or eight cantons. The referendum provided for in Article 89 has been asked for only once; in 1923 a treaty with France on border zones was rejected by the people. It may be also mentioned here that the accession of Switzerland to the League of Nations in 1920 was submitted to the constitutional referendum of the people and the cantons because it was an exception to the constitutional principle of neutrality; it was approved by a small majority.

V. Treaties and the Law of the Land

Although the Constitution contains no provisions on the relation between treaties and federal laws, it is an uncontested principle that treaties prevail over federal laws. As to the cantonal laws the principle of the supremacy of treaties results from the provision that federal law prevails over cantonal law (Transitory Provisions, Art. 2); treaties concluded by the Confederation are considered as federal law. Moreover, Article 113 states that federal laws as well as treaties approved by the Federal Assembly cannot be invalidated by the Federal Court.

A P P E N D I X   V

United States

I. THE PRESIDENT AND FOREIGN AFFAIRS

Article II, Section 2, of the Constitution provides that the President "shall have Power, by and with the Advice and Consent of the Senate, to make Treaties, provided two thirds of the Senators present concur." The President is the sole organ of the federal government in meeting the outside world.[30] He has great advantages in the conduct of foreign relations over the members of Congress. He has far superior sources of information, for the diplomatic correspondence of all American representatives abroad is at his disposal. His office has the capacity for secrecy and speed.

Since Washington's second administration it has been the established constitutional practice that the power of recognition of a new regime resides in the President. This broad discretionary power has had great legal and political significance, e.g., in relations with Mexico, the Soviet Union, and Communist China. In addition to his powers as chief executive he also has powers stemming from his constitutional role as commander-in-chief of the army and navy. There are numerous examples in American history when the President by his unilateral action committed the armed forces to combat or conduct very close to it.

[30] A clear description of the constitutional position of the President in foreign affairs is found in *United States v. Curtiss-Wright Export Corporation*, 299 U.S. 304 (1936), where the Court said at pages 319–320: ". . . we are here dealing with . . . the exclusive power of the President as the sole organ of the Federal government in the field of international relations — a power which does not require as a basis for its exercise an act of Congress, but which, of course, like every other governmental power, must be exercised in subordination to the applicable provisions of the Constitution. It is quite apparent, that if, in the maintenance of our international relations, embarrassment — perhaps serious embarrassment — is to be avoided and success for our aims achieved, congressional legislation which is to be made effective through negotiation and inquiry within the international field must often accord to the President a degree of discretion and freedom from statutory restriction which would not be admissible were domestic affairs alone involved." The Court went on to say that the power of the federal government over foreign relations was different from its power over internal affairs because in the latter area the federal government obtained only those powers delegated to it by the States while "the states severally never possessed international powers" and thus "such powers could not have been carved from the mass of state powers but obviously were transmitted to the United States from some other source." The Court explained that "as a result of the separation from Great Britain by the colonies, acting as a unit, the powers of external sovereignty passed from the Crown not to the Colonies severally, but to the Colonies in their collective and corporate capacity as the United States of America. Even before the Declaration, the colonies were a unit in foreign affairs, acting through a common agency, namely, the Continental Congress, composed of delegates from the thirteen colonies (*id.* at 316).

II. THE CONGRESS IN FOREIGN AFFAIRS

While the President may be the government's sole agent in international relations he is not entirely independent from Congress, in particular in view of Congressional possession of the appropriation power. The Constitution envisions the Senate as advising the President in the conclusion of treaties. However, as early as Washington's administration it became the practice to ignore the Senate as a council of advice and submit only the concluded treaty for approval. This practice was rigidly adhered to until the post-World War II period when the need for bipartisan foreign policy led to closer relations with the competent committees of Congress. A more important source of Senate control over foreign relations is the requirement that two thirds of the Senate must approve a treaty before it becomes the law of the land.[31]

A variety of figures may be produced to show approval or disapproval of the Senate's record in the exercise of its veto power. However, the Senate has consistently emasculated only one type of treaty, namely that relating to pacific settlement of disputes. For instance when the President submitted the Olney-Paunceforte Treaty of 1897, providing for arbitration as a means of settling disputes, to the Senate for approval it changed its main part beyond recognition and defeated the remainder. The Hay Arbitration Treaties of 1904 were so amended with reservations that they were arbitration treaties in name only. A minority of the Senate was able to defeat the Treaty of Versailles and prevent American participation in the League of Nations by proposing crippling amendments. When the question of American membership in the World Court arose the Senate introduced reservations to the treaty which were unacceptable to the other members. When the measure was again introduced in 1935, it was rejected in spite of a 52 to 36 vote favoring membershp. Sweeping reservations accompanied the final acceptance of the jurisdiction of the Court in 1946.

Proposals to amend the two-thirds requirement have been numerous. One proposal does not consider the present requirement of Senate approval as a sufficient safeguard, for it would require a two-thirds vote of the entire membership of the Senate rather than two thirds of the Senators present. Other proposals tend in the opposite direction, of which the most extreme one would require approval by only a majority of the Senate. Those which would require a majority vote of a quorum of both houses have more support. In particular the House of Representatives approved in 1945 a resolution proposing that the Constitution be amended to require

---

[31] The two-thirds rule was inserted to protect the sectional interests of the South in the navigation of the Mississippi River and of New England in fishing rights off the Newfoundland Banks. Both groups feared that their interests would be jeopardized by a treaty requiring only a majority vote for approval.

that "hereafter treaties shall be made by the President by and with the advice of both houses of Congress" (91 Cong. Rec. 4368 (1945)).

III. EXECUTIVE AGREEMENTS

Of the nearly 2000 international agreements entered into by the United States between 1789 and 1939 only some 800 of them were concluded by the treaty process, the remainder by executive agreements, i.e., by arrangements with other nations which were not submitted to the Senate for approval. In one type of executive agreements the President acts pursuant to authority conferred by act or joint resolution of Congress, or the action is subsequently sanctioned by Congress; for instance, reciprocal trade agreements have been authorized by the Tariff Act of 1934 (48 Stat. 943 (1934)) and later tariff acts; and agreements for economic and military assistance were authorized by the Economic Cooperation Act of 1948 (62 Stat. 151), the Mutual Defense Assistance Act of 1949 (63 Stat. 714, 715, 717), the Act for International Development of 1950 (64 Stat. 204), and the Mutual Security Act of 1951 (65 Stat. 386). Congress may authorize an agreement on any subject on which it might legislate and can give the President the widest possible discretion in making the agreement without fear of an unconstitutional delegation of power (*United States v. Curtiss-Wright Export Corporation*, 299 U.S. 304, 315 (1936)). A second type of executive agreement is concluded by the President alone, without previous authority or subsequent approval by Congress. His authority proceeds from his constitutional position as the sole agent of the nation in foreign affairs and as commander-in-chief of the armed forces. Thus when the President, as commander-in-chief, sends troops overseas to protect American interests, he may make agreements on the subject.

The executive agreement has even been used as a device to accomplish an act previously prevented by Senate rejection of a treaty. When the treaties proposing annexation of Texas and Hawaii were rejected by the Senate, they were later admitted by joint resolution embodying the terms of the rejected agreements. The executive argument has also been used when emergency action was necessary. A recent example was the arrangement of September, 1940, in which the United States gave Great Britain 50 old destroyers in return for 99-year leases on certain bases.

The number and importance of executive agreements have excited much criticism. A constitutional amendment proposed by Senator Bricker in 1951 would deal with them in the following manner: "Executive agreements shall not be made in lieu of treaties. Executive agreements shall, if not sooner terminated, expire automatically one year after the end of the term of office for which the President making the agreement shall have been elected, but the Congress may, at the request of any President, extend for the duration of the term of such President the life of any such agreement made or extended during the next preceding presidential term. The

President shall publish all executive agreements except that those which in his judgment require secrecy shall be submitted to appropriate committees of the Congress in lieu of publication" (Sen. Jt. Res. 130, 82d Cong., 2d Sess. (1952)). Another proposal would empower Congress "to regulate all executive and other agreements with any foreign power or international organization," and to enforce this provision by appropriate legislation (Sen. Jt. Res. 1, 83d Cong., 1st Sess. (1953)).

IV. Representation in Foreign Countries

Article II, Section 2, of the Constitution provides that the President "shall nominate, and by and with the Advice and Consent of the Senate, shall appoint Ambassadors, other public Ministers and Consuls." In addition Article II, Section 3, states that the President shall "receive Ambassadors and other public Ministers." The Foreign Service Act of August 13, 1946, is the principal act regulating the personnel of the Foreign Service (60 Stat. 999). By the terms of the Act ambassadors, ministers, and Foreign Service officers are appointed by the President with the advice and consent of the Senate. Foreign Service officers may be commissioned as diplomatic or consular officers. Vice consuls and consular agents may be appointed by the Secretary of State. Presidents have frequently appointed their own special representatives without the consent of the Senate; lack of constitutional confirmation has not mitigated their effectiveness and some of them have had unusual influence on foreign relations.

The Constitution is silent on the question of receiving consuls. The procedure is for the sending state to forward the commission of the newly appointed consul to its diplomatic agent in this country who gives it to the Secretary of State for transmission to the President. The commission is recorded at the Department of State and exhibited to the President before *exequatur* will be issued. The *exequatur* is signed by the President, countersigned by the Secretary of State, and bears the seal of the United States.

V. Power of the States in External Affairs

Article I, Section 10, of the Constitution states that "No State shall enter into any Treaty, Alliance, or Confederation." It also provides that "No State shall, without the Consent of Congress, . . . enter into any Agreement or Compact with another State, or with a foreign Power, or engage in War, unless actually invaded, or in such imminent Danger as will not admit of delay."

There is no example in the history of the United States of a compact or agreement between a State and a foreign power that was approved by Congress, but recently Congress has approved several compacts which are open to accession by Canadian provinces, e.g., the Northeastern Forest Fire Protection Compact of 1949 and the Interstate Civil Defense Compact of 1951. A few informal arrangements have been considered by the courts, but in most of them the courts have held that no national interest was involved and the consent of Congress was not required (*McHenry County v. Brady*, 37 N.D. 59 (1917). In one case the Supreme Court held that Vermont had no authority to return fugitives to Canada as the tacit agreement between the two providing for such return was a compact or agreement and it did not have the approval of Congress (*Holmes v. Jennison*, 14 Peters 540 (U.S. 1840)). The distinction between a treaty on one hand and an agreement or compact on the other is not clear, and the distinction has had no importance in practice.

VI. Relation of Treaties to the Law of the Land

Article VI of the Constitution states in part that "This Constitution, and the Laws of the United States which shall be made in pursuance thereof; and all Treaties made, or which shall be made, under the Authority of the United States, shall be the supreme Law of the Land, and the Judges in every State shall be bound thereby, any Thing in the Constitution or Laws of any State to the Contrary notwithstanding."

This clause was due primarily to the State obstruction to the execution of provisions of the treaty of peace of 1783 which ended the Revolutionary War. The treaty attempted to provide a satisfactory solution to the problems of debts owed to British creditors and forbade the future confiscation of Royalist lands. In spite of it, States of the Confederation persisted in passing legislation contrary to these provisions. The Federal Constitutional Convention was in session at a time when the British were protesting against such State action, and the American Minister in London was corresponding with the Continental Congress in an effort to correct it. To avoid further difficulties a special supremacy clause was inserted in the Constitution.

However, Article VI has not been interpreted to mean that all duly made treaties become the supreme law of the land. Chief Justice Marshall said that "when the terms of the stipulation import a contract, when either of the parties engages to perform a particular act, the treaty addresses itself to the political, not the judicial department; and the legislature must execute the contract before it can become a rule for the court" (*Foster v. Neilson*, 2 Peters 253, 314 (U.S. 1829)). In the absence of explicit language in a treaty, the question whether "the terms of the stipulation import a contract" often becomes a difficult problem subject to judicial review. The courts are likely to hold a treaty non-self-executing if it explicitly provides that the parties shall enact legislation of a certain content or if it deals with a subject matter vested solely in the legislature, e.g., criminal penalties or appropriation of money.

As a treaty[32] is the "Law of the Land" of equal force with a statute, it can directly repeal a prior conflicting statute.[33] A desire to change the self-executing feature of treaties, when they have the effect of repealing national or state legislation, has been expressed by Senator Bricker, who in 1951 proposed an amendment to the Constitution reading in part as follows: "No treaty or executive agreement shall alter or abridge the laws of the United States or the Constitutions or laws of the several States unless, and then only to the extent that, Congress shall so provide by act or joint resolution" (Sen. Jt. Res. 130, 82d Cong., 2d Sess. (1952)). Some proposals go further and would eliminate the self-executing feature of treaties altogether. They would require that before any treaty could have internal effect an Act of Congress would be necessary. It has been proposed, for instance, that "a treaty shall become effective as internal law in the United States only through legislation which would be valid in the absence of treaty" (Sen. Jt. Res. 1, 83d Cong., 1st Sess. (1953)).

VII. THE "PROPER SUBJECTS" OF INTERNATIONAL NEGOTIATION

The treaty power of the United States extends to "all proper subjects of international negotiation" (*Geofroy v. Riggs*, 133 U.S. 258, 267 (1890)). The question of what is a proper subject of international negotiation is a difficult one to answer. While no provision of a treaty has ever been held unconstitutional, that does not mean that the Constitution is not a limitation on the treaty power. It has been said, for example, that a treaty could not usurp the appropriation or amending powers nor could it stand if it were repugnant to the Bill of Rights. The most quoted statement of the limitations on the treaty power is found in a dictum of the Supreme Court: "The treaty power, as expressed in the Constitution, is in terms unlimited except by those restraints which are found in that instrument against the action of the government itself and that of the States. It would not be contended that it extends so far as to authorize what the Constitution forbids, or a change in the character of the government or in that of one of the States, or a cession of any portion of the territory of the latter, without its consent" (*Geofroy v. Riggs*, 133 U.S. 258, 267 (1890)). Apparently feeling that the issue is still unresolved, Senator Bricker would amend the Constitution as follows: "No treaty or executive agreement shall be made respecting the rights of citizens of the

---

[32] An executive agreement would not have the same status as a treaty as the supreme law of the land. An executive agreement which Congress did not authorize or ratify could not abridge a prior statute. However two cases have held that they are superior over state public policy (United States v. Belmont, 301 U.S. 324 (1937), United States v. Pink, 315 U.S. 203 (1942)).

[33] On the other hand, a subsequent and contrary statute repeals a treaty (Chae Chan Ping v. United States, 130 U.S. 581 (1888)). This in no way affects the international obligation of the United States, and international claims against the United States may arise from a breach of the obligation caused by contrary legislation.

United States protected by this Constitution, or abridging or prohibiting the free exercise thereof" (Sen. Jt. Res. 130, 82d Cong., 2d Sess. (1952)).

VIII. TREATIES AND THE LAWS OF THE STATES

Article VI of the Constitution provides that treaties shall be supreme over the constitutions and laws of the States. The judicial interpretation of the clause has been faithful to the letter of the Constitution. A Virginia statute declaring that any debtor of a British subject could discharge the debt by payment of the amount to the State was declared invalid as being contrary to Article 4 of the Treaty of Peace of 1783 (*Ware v. Hilton,* 3 Dall. 199 (U.S. 1796)). Later the Supreme Court declared invalid a land title created by a State contrary to Article 6 of the same treaty (*Fairfax v. Hunter,* 7 Cranch 603 (U.S. 1813)). State acts placing impediments on the rights of aliens to take and hold title to land have been held invalid when they were repugnant to treaties guaranteeing removal of such impediments (*Geofroy v. Riggs,* 133 U.S. 258 (1890); *Hauenstein v. Lynham,* 100 U.S. 483 (1880)). Likewise a State's police power is ineffectual to discriminate against a class of aliens when there is a treaty ensuring equality of treatment. The Bricker amendment (quoted above) would require that before a treaty could abridge the laws or constitutions of States, it would be necessary to require an Act or joint resolution of Congress in addition to the present requirement of a two-thirds vote of the Senators present.

In enacting legislation to give effect to treaties, Congress is not limited to the powers specifically delegated to it, but may invade what would otherwise be the reserved powers of the States. In 1913 Congress passed a statute which regulated the shooting of migratory birds. Two lower courts held that the statute was unconstitutional, as it exceeded the legislative authority of Congress. The United States then concluded a treaty with Great Britain in which the parties pledged themselves to pass reciprocal legislation to give the desired protection. When Missouri sought to enjoin a federal game warden from enforcing the statute enacted pursuant to the treaty, the Court upheld its validity (*Missouri v. Holland,* 252 U.S. 416 (1920)). The Court said: "It is obvious that there may be matters of the sharpest exigency for the national well being that an act of Congress could not deal with but that a treaty followed by such an act could, and it is not lightly to be assumed that, in matters requiring national action, 'a power which must belong to and somewhere reside in every civilized government' is not to be found" (*id.* at 433). It added: "Here is a national interest of very nearly the first magnitude involved. It can be protected only by national action in concert with that of another power. The subject matter is only transitorily within the State and has no permanent habitat therein. But for the treaty and the statute there soon might be no birds for any powers to deal with" (*id.* at 435). Some proposals for constitutional change would limit Congress to the delegated powers when legislating pursuant to a treaty.

The expansion of the commerce clause since 1937 would seem to allow the federal government to implement the conventions of the International Labour Organization apart from the use of the treaty power. However, the federal Government continues to refer most conventions to the States for action. Thus in 1950 the Secretary of State, when considering Draft Conventions 89 and 90 concerning night work of women and young people in industry, recommended to the President that federal legislation be enacted with respect to them for the District of Columbia only, and that they be forwarded to the governors of the forty-eight States for further action. The few labor conventions which have been ratified by the United States deal mostly with maritime questions which are clearly within federal jurisdiction.

STUDY 6

Commerce, Transportation, and Customs

I. INTRODUCTION

A. *Scope of the Analysis*

A fundamental question here discussed is the extent to which, in the nations studied — Australia, Canada, Germany, Switzerland, and the United States — power has come to be allotted to the community to control those governmental activities of the component States which detrimentally affect the unitary character of:

(a) Commerce, including not only trade in commodities, but also the production of the subject matter of commerce, and the financial functions necessary to its existence; and

(b) Transport and communications, without which modern economic processes are impossible.

Anti-unitary activities of the States may consist in the imposition of customs duties or similar imposts by whatever name known; or in more direct regulation of production, interchange, and transport, by the imposition of various types of controls.

Also treated here, because inseparable from the question of community power to inhibit State fragmentation, is the correlative question of the power of the community government to regulate private economic processes by central governmental means. If State regulation is prevented, and there is no corresponding community power, a complete absence of government appears in certain areas. To fill such gaps, the necessary community power must be supplied.

There is also included in this analysis a consideration of the agencies by which economic functions of government are performed. Some discussion is devoted to the principles of constitutional formulation. Should grants of power and prohibitions be expressed in simple and inclusive terms, subject to appropriate interpretation to meet situations as they arise, or does the experience of federal nations indicate the desirability of more detailed definitions?

The relevant constitutional provisions of the several federal nations here studied, and some account of their experiences with those provisions, are discussed in the five appendixes which follow this study. The study itself undertakes to analyze and evaluate in more general terms the various constitutional devices used by the five nations to solve economic problems of federalism.

B. *The Importance of These Problems*

The prominence of economic provisions in the constitutions of all successful federations demonstrates the historic importance of economic factors in persuading separate States to unite. The inadequacy of the arrangements for interstate commerce in the Articles of Confederation, under which the United States existed from 1781 to 1789, was a principal cause of the Convention of 1787 where the present Constitution of the United States was drafted. Recurring efforts, successful and otherwise, to establish customs unions among various European states furnish other examples. The Schuman Plan, while treating only of coal and ferrous metal, amply demonstrates the same point.

The achievement of economic union, of a single market, obviously contributes to essential united defense while it improves material peacetime welfare. In any federation, certain member States are necessarily more adapted to some economic specialties than others. The full development of their respective capabilities will benefit the entire community; but the fullest development has been possible, in the nations studied, only because the several States no longer faced the possibility of war among themselves, and no one of them needed to face independent war against an outsider. Industrial specialization with its accompanying efficiency has promoted the capacity of these communities to defend themselves, and in turn has only been possible in communities united for defense.

C. *Relation to Other Federal Functions*

The close connection between battlefield defense and economic mobilization inevitably requires that the military provisions of any constitution take its economic provisions into account. This mutual dependence is peculiarly important in considering the question of any express provisions for changed or extended community powers over the economy in case of war or other emergency.[1]

Constitutional provisions for foreign affairs are likewise related to economic objectives. In Canada and in the United States, instances have occurred in which the central government has made treaties undertaking to subject local economic matters, within the several component States, to controls which in the absence of the treaties would have been beyond the powers delegated to the central government. Because of differences in the fundamental law of the two nations, the results of these international agree-

---

[1] See page 331 below, for a discussion of "emergency powers."

ments were different. In Canada, the treaties (International Labour Organization Conventions) could not extend the competence of the Dominion government to include control of the conditions of employment of labor within the several Provinces;[2] in the United States a treaty providing for the protection of wild fowl became, under Article VI of the Constitution, the "supreme law of the land" and thus permitted federal regulation of what would otherwise have been solely in State control.[3]

The interrelation of the powers of the community to raise revenue with its powers to control economic life is so apparent that demonstration of the relationship is here superfluous.[4] Similarly, constitutional provisions concerning the freedom of movement of peoples and of capital are closely concerned with freedom of other economic processes. The United States Supreme Court has held that a California statute, forbidding any person to bring a known indigent nonresident into that State, is invalid because the statute conflicts with the constitutional grant of power to the federal government to regulate commerce between States; the exclusion of such migrants was an unconstitutional barrier to interstate commerce.[5] Any constitutional provisions facilitating or impeding the flow of labor from member State to member State are intimately related to any provisions governing transport and trade. And what is here true of the free flow of labor appears true of the flow of investment capital. Economic unity despite political diversity — the essence of modern federalism — has, in the nations studied, proved inconsistent with any sort of tight compartments for the member States. Barriers to men, to machines, to money, or to products, all tend to divide the desired single economic unit.

The relation between economic clauses in a constitution and those treating of the powers of the judiciary is also apparent. Throughout the study of this subject there recur examples demonstrating the desirability that constitutional provisions be general in terms. Detailed application of the sweeping language has fallen, in large part, to judicial organs. In several federal countries the judiciary has in effect written a gloss on the economic details of the constitution.

Some constitutions contain specific provisions concerning permissible objects of public expenditure. On the other hand the Constitution of the United States contains, as its only limit on federal spending for economic objectives, the requirement that expenditures be provided by the Congress "for the general welfare," [6] a restriction so nebulous as to leave to the federal Congress almost entirely unlimited power to authorize projects. The power to spend is one form of power to control. Selective aid is often the equivalent of selective restriction — depending on the choice of objects.

[2] Attorney-General of Canada v. Attorney-General of Ontario, [1937] A.C. 326 (P.C.).

[3] Missouri v. Holland, 252 U.S. 416 (1920).

[4] See pages 300 and 320 below, for a discussion of constitutional limitations on the taxing power of community and member States.

[5] Edwards v. California, 314 U.S. 160 (1941).

[6] U.S. Constitution, Art. I, §8, cl. 1.

Generous or restricted powers to spend lead to corresponding powers over the economy of the community.[7]

This list of related constitutional powers could easily be extended. The point is sufficiently clear, however, that the division of a discussion of federalism into economic matters and others is necessarily somewhat arbitrary. All governmental functions have some economic implications.

II. TENDENCIES TO ECONOMIC ISOLATION IN MEMBER STATES, AND CONSTITUTIONAL CORRECTIVES IN COMMUNITY GOVERNMENTS

A. State Tariff Barriers, and Similar Imposts Set Up by Member States Which Impair the Economic Unity of the Community

1. THE TENDENCY TO STATE PROTECTIONISM HAS APPEARED IN ALL FEDERAL NATIONS STUDIED

The elimination of State tariff barriers (by whatever name called) was an impelling motive in the formation of the federal unions of all five nations here considered. Their constitutional history displays the devices used by each community government to prevent a fragmentation, by local customs barriers, of the common national market. James Madison, delegate to the Convention which drafted the present Constitution of the United States, and later President of the Republic, discussed early tariff barriers between the States of the American Union in the draft preface to his report of the debates in the Constitutional Convention. He wrote:

Besides the vain attempts to supply their respective treasuries by imposts, which turned their commerce into neighboring ports, and to co-erce a relaxation of the British monopoly of West-Indian navigation, which was attempted by Virginia, . . . the States having ports for foreign commerce, taxed & irritated the adjoining States, trading thro' them, as New York, Pennsylvania, Virginia and South Carolina. Some of the States, as Connecticut, taxed imports as from Massachusetts higher than imports even from Great Britain, of which Massachusetts complained to Virginia and doubtless to other States . . . In sundry instances as New York, New Jersey, Pennsylvania and Maryland, . . . the navigation laws treated the Citizens of other States as aliens.[8]

One of the strong purposes of the Swiss Federal Constitution of 1848 was the elimination of the intercantonal trade barriers.[9] The long history of German customs unions shows the same considerations. In Canada, the

[7] This influence is recognized in the Australian Constitution which provides (§51 (iii)) that any bounties granted by the Commonwealth Parliament on the production or export of goods shall be uniform throughout the Commonwealth.

[8] Farrand, *The Records of the Federal Convention* 547–547 (1911). See also Hamilton in *The Federalist*, No. 7 and Madison, in No. 13.

[9] Rappard, *La Constitution Fédérale de la Suisse* 42 et seq. (1948).

discouragement of barriers to interprovincial trade was one motive for the establishment of the Dominion government.[10]   Section 92 of the Australian Constitution which provides, in part, that "trade, commerce and intercourse among the States whether by means of internal carriage or ocean navigation shall be absolutely free" was inserted in order that New South Wales, richest and second most populous State and the only free-trade State in Australia, might be sure that protectionism would not be reintroduced.[11]

2. THE FORMS OF CONSTITUTIONAL PROVISIONS INHIBITING LOCAL TARIFFS

Constitutional restrictions on State tariff barriers appear in several forms. In practice, all have demonstrated one common weakness.   The ingenuity of local governments can devise more means of tariff restriction than the most carefully devised constitutional provisions can in explicit terms prohibit.   It has been necessary, wherever the problem has become acute, to assign some agency to interpret the general prohibitions, and to determine whether or not any one of them should apply to a given State measure.

An obvious form of restriction is, of course, an express prohibition.   For example the Constitution of the United States provides:

> No State shall, without the Consent of the Congress, lay any Imposts or Duties on Imports or Exports, except what may be absolutely necessary for executing its inspection Laws: and the net Produce of all Duties and Imposts, laid by any State on Imports or Exports, shall be for the Use of the Treasury of the United States; and all such Laws shall be subject to the Revision and Control of the Congress.[12]

The Canadian Constitution, the British North America Act of 1867, has a comparably explicit restriction in its Section 121, which provides: "All Articles of the Growth, Produce, or Manufacture of any one of the Provinces shall, from and after the Union, be admitted free into each of the other Provinces."

Section 92 of the Australian Constitution, as already pointed out, provides that trade, commerce, and intercourse among the States "shall be absolutely free," a prohibition intended by its draftsmen to apply to State tariff barriers, but given in practice a much wider application.

Another form of prohibition depends upon the principle of *ultra vires*. Thus in Switzerland the entire matter of customs duties is turned over to the federal government by Article 28 of the Constitution.

The Basic Law of the Federal Republic of Germany of May, 1949, similarly by Article 72 gives to the federation exclusive legislative powers over

---

[10] Report of the Royal Commission on Dominion-Provincial Relations   (Rowell-Sirois Report), Bk. II, p. 62   (1940).

[11] Julius Stone, "A Government of Laws and Yet of Men, Being a Survey of Half a Century of the Australian Commerce Power," 25 N.Y.U.L. Rev. 451–462 (1950).

[12] Art. I, §10, cl. 2.

"the unity of the territory as regards customs and commerce, . . . and the exchanges of goods and payments with foreign countries, including customs and frontier control"; except as far as the federation may by express legislation permit the Länder to act in this area.

Due to the fact that the Supreme Court of the United States construed the import-export clause in the federal Constitution[13] to restrict the States only in their attempts at protectionism against imports from foreign countries, or attempts to levy taxes upon exports to foreign countries, other constitutional provisions have been used in the United States to inhibit barriers between States of the Union. These are Article I, Section 8, clause 3, which provides that the Congress shall have power "To regulate Commerce with foreign Nations, and among the several States, and with the Indian Tribes"; and that part of the Fourteenth Amendment which forbids any State to ". . . deprive any person of life, liberty, or property, without due process of law . . ."

While the commerce clause does not in terms restrict State protectionism, it has come in time to be construed to have a restrictive effect on the States in those matters where the Supreme Court has considered that uniformity was necessary to national economic well-being. The due process clause of the Fourteenth Amendment has been used by the Supreme Court to invalidate certain State attempts to make tax exactions predicated on resources outside the State borders: for example, an attempt to tax a domiciliary corporation on the value of its entire fleet of freight cars or river barges, although at all times the major part of the fleet was outside the taxing State.[14] The policy exemplified by such decisions under the Fourteenth Amendment is not exactly to restrict protectionism as much as it is to prevent one State from unreasonably taxing an interstate operation, with consequent risk of similar taxation by other States, and the destruction of the interstate enterprise by cumulative multiple tax burdens.

As is pointed out below, the generality of these clauses, and the necessity that some federal agency prevent State fragmentation and destructive economic localism, has resulted in the performance by the judiciary in the United States of a function of sorting out permissible from nonpermissible State legislation, predicated on considerations which appear primarily economic and political rather than "legal" in the strict sense of the word.

3. JUDICIAL AND OTHER GOVERNMENTAL EXPERIENCE IN ADMINISTERING COMMUNITY CONSTITUTIONAL INHIBITIONS AGAINST STATE TARIFF BARRIERS

The tradition in Australia, Canada, and the United States, that affected individuals may challenge in court the validity of State tax provisions

[13] Art. I, §10, cl. 2, quoted above; Woodruff v. Parham, 8 Wall. 123 (1869).

[14] Union Refrigerator Transit Co. v. Kentucky, 199 U.S. 194 (1905); Standard Oil v. Peck, 342 U.S. 382 (1952. See page 303 below, for a discussion of the use in the United States of the commerce clause to inhibit State tariff barriers.

claimed to conflict with national constitutional limitations, has provided in these three nations a considerable accumulation of experience in the application of community constitutional restrictions to local taxation.

In Canada in 1940 the Royal Commission on Dominion-Provincial Relations commented that a statute of British Columbia, taxing fuel oil in that Province, was protective of coal which British Columbia produces in quantities.[15] Of such measures the Royal Commission said:

> . . . local protectionism does tend to hamper national economic life and thus to reduce the income of the people of Canada upon which the prosperity of the whole Dominion rests. It is probable that there is no single province so situated as to gain on balance by the existence of local protectionism in Canada. In each case the desired objective is sought with such immediacy that the longer view, taking account of secondary results and ultimate consequences, is excluded from consideration. It is obvious that if one province can invoke these expedients to serve or protect a local interest, other provinces can do likewise; and that if a protective provincial tariff can be imposed for the advantage of a particular interest, other interests in the same province will exact the same advantage by the employment of political pressure. With the expansion of these experiments in provincial self-sufficiency, it would be speedily found that the local market obtained at such a cost would be a poor substitute for the lost freedom of trade throughout the Dominion. The damage done by local protectionism takes many forms: among them, the artificial location of industries within the national economy; the wastes of uneconomic competition; the financial burdens involved in supporting uneconomic industries; the uncertainty to business everywhere if markets in other provinces are in danger of being shut off by protectionist devices; the emphasis laid on rivalry and jealousy between the provinces . . .[16]

A similar problem has appeared in Australia. In 1925, the State of South Australia undertook to impose a tax upon the income of vendors of motor spirits. The statute defined a "vendor" as "every person who sells and delivers motor spirits within the State to persons within the State for the first time after the entry of such motor spirit into the State or as the case may be after production refinement manufacture or compounding of such motor spirit within the State . . ." This statute was held invalid the following year by the High Court of Australia on the ground that it violated Section 90 of the Australian Constitution which made exclusive the power of the Commonwealth to impose duties of customs and excise; and on the further ground that it violated the provision in Section 92 of the Constitu-

---

[15] Rev. Stat., B.C., 1936, c. 278, cited in Report of the Royal Commission on Dominion-Provincial Relations, Bk. 2, p. 63, n.52 (1940). (For a re-enactment, see Rev. Stat., B.C., 1948, c. 326.)

[16] Report of the Royal Commission on Dominion-Provincial Relations, Bk. II, p. 64 (1940).

tion that on the imposition of uniform duties of customs, "trade, commerce and intercourse among the States shall be absolutely free." [17]

In the United States, control by the federal Supreme Court of State taxation which tends to break up the national economy has had a number of aspects. Earliest to develop was the judicial construction of the clause of the federal Constitution which forbids a State to tax imports and exports.[18] The phrase "Imposts or Duties on Imports or Exports" did not define itself. Some governmental institution, here the federal judiciary, was required to say how long goods entering the country should retain their character as imports; for certainly their constitutional immunity from taxation would not continue indefinitely, regardless of change of title, of form, and in general of merger with the mass of domestic goods. In 1827, the Supreme Court decided that so long as the import continued in its original package it retained its immunity.[19] Definition of the clause has continued to be difficult for over a century since that time. In 1951 two of the Justices found themselves unable to join in opinions upholding a State tax on the gross revenues of railroad companies derived from operating a marine terminal and other port facilities where imports and exports were handled, and from hauling exports and imports to and from the port.[20] Mr. Justice Jackson, reserving his judgment in those cases, said:

> If the roads to the ports may be obstructed with local regulation and taxes, inland producers may be made to pay tribute to the seaboard for the privilege of exportation, and the longer the road to port, the more localities that may lay burdens on the passing traffic. The evident policy of the Constitution is to avoid these burdens and maintain free and equal access to foreign ports for the inland areas. If the constitutional policy can be avoided by shifting the tax from the exported article itself to some incident such as carriage, unavoidable in the process of exportation, then the policy is a practical nullity. I think prohibition of a tax on exports and imports goes beyond exempting specific articles from direct ad valorem duties — it prohibits taxing exports and imports as a process.
>
> This is a matter of giving the inland farms and factories a fair access to the sea which will enable them to compete in foreign commerce, as well as to make imports as equally available as possible, regardless of distance from port. Ocean rates to a given foreign port are the same from all Atlantic ports, so that any differences in the costs of reaching

[17] The Commonwealth and Commonwealth Oil Refineries Ltd. v. South Australia, 28 C.L.R. 408 (1926).

[18] Art. I, §10, cl. 2: "No State shall, without the Consent of Congress, lay any Imposts or Duties on Imports or Exports, except what may be absolutely necessary for executing its inspection Laws: and the net Produce of all Duties and Imposts, laid by any State on Imports or Exports, shall be for the Use of the Treasury of the United States; and all such Laws shall be subject to the Revision and Control of the Congress."

[19] Brown v. Maryland, 12 Wheat. 419 (1827).

[20] Canton R. Co. v. Rogan, 340 U.S. 511 (1951); Western Maryland R. Co. v. Rogan, 340 U.S. 520 (1951).

the coast from the inland cannot be offset and represent net differences in the costs of reaching foreign markets.[21]

In 1869 the Supreme Court decided that the import-export clause referred only to international traffic, and that it imposed no limit on tax barriers impeding traffic between the States of the United States.[22] The practical necessities of a free national market, however, turned the Court to a search for some other constitutional clause to limit State imposts having the effect of State traffic barriers. This was found in the clause granting to the federal government power over interstate commerce.[23] In 1876 the Supreme Court thus held invalid a State statute imposing a license tax on peddlers of goods not the growth, produce, or manufacture of the taxing State. In its opinion it said:

> The power of the State to exact a license tax of any amount being admitted, no authority would remain in the United States or in this court to control its action, however unreasonable or oppressive. Imposts operating as an absolute exclusion of the goods would be possible, and all the evils of discriminating state legislation, favorable to the interests of one State and injurious to the interests of other States and countries, which existed previous to the adoption of the Constitution, might follow, as the experience of the last fifteen years shows, from the action of some of the states.[24]

Sometimes State authorities have made an effort to conceal the protectionist nature of their taxes by verbally indiscriminate taxation of local as well as foreign commerce, skillfully drawing the statute, however, so as to tax activities which in practice are not engaged in by local traders. The Supreme Court has not considered itself bound to accept such legislation at its face value, but has struck it down, regardless of specious verbal equality, when its operation was protectionist.[25]

Another type of State tax which has been held invalid as an unreasonable impediment to interstate commerce is one which subjects such commerce to the possibility of multiple burdens as it travels through several States, even though in any one State it is taxed equally with local commerce. Thus, where, because of the irregular shape of the State of New York, a highway route between two New York termini crossed parts of Pennsylvania and New Jersey, New York was disallowed the privilege of taxing the gross receipts of a New York omnibus corporation earned in operation over that tri-State route.[26]

The use of the due process clause of the Fourteenth Amendment to strike

[21] 340 U.S. 511, 517 (1951).
[22] Woodruff v. Parham, 8 Wall. 123 (1869).
[23] Art. I, §8, cl. 3: "The Congress shall have Power . . . To regulate Commerce with foreign Nations, and among the several States . . ."
[24] Welton v. Missouri, 91 U.S. 275 (1876).
[25] Best v. Maxwell, 311 U.S. 454 (1940).
[26] Central Greyhound Lines, Inc. v. Mealey, 334 U.S. 653 (1948).

down taxes imposed by a State on parts of a fleet of railway cars or barges circulating outside the taxing State, has been mentioned already.[27]

The disadvantages under which the judiciary labors, in undertaking the duties in the control of State taxation which fall to it in the United States, are particularly apparent when the problem is this allotment among several States of tax resources which transcend the borders of a single State. The Supreme Court of the United States can prohibit the operation of an unconstitutional tax program, but it cannot prescribe a constitutional substitute. Furthermore, it can act only in such cases or controversies as litigants may start — it cannot initiate action. The legislative process is necessary for devising a comprehensive scheme for community control of local taxation.

4. SUMMARY OF THE DISCUSSION OF INTERSTATE TRADE BARRIERS RAISED BY TAXATION

The experience of the nations studied discloses certain persistent features of the subject of State tariff barriers.

(a) Such barriers appear in many different forms, and often are disguised, wearing the outward appearance of innocent taxation for revenue. The sorting of protectionist measures from innocent measures for local revenue presents a difficult problem. The community agency which undertakes to police State antiprotectionist policies must be prepared to engage in subtle economic analysis.

(b) In none of the constitutions studied has there been discovered a verbal formula which will adequately differentiate permissible measures to produce essential local revenue, on the one hand, from protectionist measures, hidden or otherwise, on the other.

(c) While the problem of obnoxious local tax measures could be solved by turning the entire tax function over to the central government, and providing for maintenance of the governments of the component States by payments from the central treasury, such a system goes far in the direction of entirely eliminating the federal structure. Local governments with no powers to raise revenues for their own purposes would tend to become merely administrative subdivisions of a unitary state.

(d) Assuming then that some taxing power is to remain in the member States of such federal nations as those studied, and further assuming the impossibility of devising a differentiating formula in the constitution, to divide permissible from prohibited taxes, some organ of the community government must undertake the function of deciding, case by case, which instances of local taxation may be allowed to stand and which may not. Legislation of the community government may give some guidance to such a body; but the infinitely diverse possibilities of local imposts are such that economic judgments are essential in the case-by-case sifting out of permis-

---

[27] See page 300 above.

sible local taxes from those which are intolerable. Some tribunal, whether called a judicial organ or otherwise, is necessary to determine on economic grounds which local taxes may stand, and which are unconstitutional.

B. *State Limitation of the Volume of Trade: The Form of "Quotas" in Certain Nations*

Perhaps because of the strong impulse to freedom of commerce which was effective in the formation of the federal nations here studied, the history of member State "quotas" as restrictions on the production or marketing of goods in the several States is not extensive. It may be that the obviously restrictive nature of such State-imposed quotas has tended to inhibit their enactment. There have been instances, however, in Australia and in the United States, of a surplus production of some commodity which has seriously affected the market, and has led to an attempt by member States in those nations to restrict production and marketing in order that the price might be stabilized. The State of South Australia, under its Dried Fruits Act of 1924, once attempted to seize a quantity of dried fruit from one James, which he proposed to market in excess of the amounts fixed by the authorities. James sought in the Australian courts a judgment for damages for trespass against the Minister of Agriculture of South Australia for the seizure of the fruit, on the ground that the establishment of the limitation and the seizure under it were void under Section 92 of the Constitution of the Commonwealth of Australia which provides that trade, commerce and intercourse among the States shall be "absolutely free." Although the highest court in Australia denied James his judgment that the quota scheme was unconstitutional, the Privy Council reversed this judgment and gave James the damages he sought, remarking that if the limitation of the proportion of dried fruits produced by James which might be marketed in the Commonwealth of Australia should be sustained "and if it were held that such a limitation still leaves interstate commerce 'absolutely free' the constitutional charter might as well be torn up." [28]

The opposite result was reached in the United States with respect to State restriction on marketing the same commodity, in this instance a crop of raisins. The United States Supreme Court upheld as constitutional the California Agricultural Pro-rate Act, which undertook to keep an excessive quantity of raisins off the market. The Supreme Court found that this program was not an undue restriction on interstate commerce, and thus was not void as in conflict with the commerce clause of the United States Constitution.[29]

In the United States, State statutes have sometimes attempted to limit the export to other States of commodities needed for the domestic market. Naturally this arises in instances where the commodity is in short supply rather

[28] James v. Cowan [1932] A.C. 542.
[29] Art. I, §2, cl. 3; Parker v. Brown, 317 U.S. 341 (1943).

than where there is an oversupply as in the cases of the quotas just considered. The Supreme Court has sustained a State statute restricting the export from the State of potable water.[30]   On the other hand attempts by States to reserve to their own citizens natural gas[31] and milk[32] have both been struck down by the Court. The reason for the distinction is not easy to perceive. Perhaps water is more essential. A statute of the State of Maine[33] prohibiting the export from the State of any electric current generated by water power within the State, unless specially authorized by an act of the Maine legislature, has not been passed upon by the federal courts.

It is worthy of remark that in none of the five constitutions here studied is there a specific prohibition against State marketing or production quotas. The quotas which were declared invalid in the Australian instance and upheld in the California case were treated by the competent courts as controlled by the general clauses of the constitutions in question dealing with trade and commerce.

C. *Protectionism Disguised as Legitimate Police Regulation*

The report of the Royal Commission on Dominion-Provincial Relations[34] stresses the ingenuity of the Canadian provincial Parliaments, and even of municipal governments, in devising what are essentially means of local economic protectionism though disguised as protections of local health, safety, and welfare. In the United States, the device of inspection of merchandise, purportedly for quality, may be so arranged that its operation in practice is protectionist for the local produce. Thus a city ordinance of Madison, in the State of Wisconsin, provided that no milk could be sold in that city unless inspected within twenty-five miles of the city; and none could be sold as pasteurized unless processed and bottled within five miles of Madison. The effect of this ordinance was to bar the importation of milk from adjoining States, and (so the Supreme Court found) alternative methods of inspection were available which would permit the sale of out-of-State milk with safety. The ordinance was held unconstitutional in an action brought by an Illinois distributor, who successfully contended before the Court that the Madison ordinance was invalid because of its interference with interstate commerce.[35]

The same device of disguised protectionism has appeared in a number of other States, and the Supreme Court has been obliged to distinguish, as best it may, the permissible regulation of goods brought in from other States in the interests of protecting the health and safety of local residents from specious measures actually intended for economic discrimination.

[30] Hudson County Water Co. v. McCarter, 209 U.S. 349 (1908).
[31] Pennsylvania v. West Virginia, 262 U.S. 553 (1923).
[32] Hood v. Dumond, 336 U.S. 525 (1949).
[33] Maine Rev. Stat. 1944, c. 46, §1.
[34] Book 2, p. 62 (1940).
[35] Dean Milk Co. v. City of Madison, 340 U.S. 349 (1951).

308   STUDIES IN FEDERALISM

The difficulty of determining what local ordinance should be permitted and what should be disallowed is apparent. In the case of the Madison ordinance, the Supreme Court noticed the oversupply of milk in the Madison area, and also noticed that alternative means of inspection were available which would take care of the health of the people of Madison as effectively as the provision of the ordinance. The Court went through a somewhat similar course of reasoning when in 1945 it declared invalid a statute of the State of Arizona which undertook to limit the length of railroad trains running across the State.[36] When the objecting railroad had demonstrated that accidents would not be diminished by cutting up long trains into short trains, and that the impediments to interstate commerce resulting from the necessary marshaling operations would be severe, the Supreme Court chose the policy of facilitating the movement of commerce since there was no showing that a policing benefit would arise from the measure imposed.

A comparable situation arises out of local attempts to fix prices. Thus, in Australia, the Parliament of the State of Queensland passed the Profiteering Prevention Act of 1920 which fixed maximum prices upon goods to be sold in that State. A merchant doing business in the State of New South Wales, who wished to take his goods into Queensland and sell them regardless of the price there fixed by the Queensland authorities, brought an action to have the Queensland statute declared invalid. The High Court of Australia found the price-fixing statute invalid under Section 92 of the Australian Constitution which provides that ". . . trade, commerce and intercourse among the States, whether by means of internal carriage or ocean navigation, shall be absolutely free." To the contention of the State of Queensland that it might properly prevent the sale of imported goods unless the goods were sold at a price consonant with local policy, three of the justices, in an opinion in which they all joined, said:

If such a contention could be upheld, it would, in our opinion, render Section 92 practically useless. It would be idle in such an event to say that border duties and State bounties are abolished — that would be purely nominal. If the goods themselves can be prohibited, if commercial dealings between the States can be restricted to dealings on the basis of such prices as the State fixes to suit its own special conditions, then there is no practical freedom even from border duties and bounties. It is the old inter-Colonial trade war perpetuated in an outwardly different form.[37]

Protectionism by price fixing is not limited to fixing of maximum prices. It has appeared in the United States in the fixing of minimum prices. When New York provided by statute for the payment to its milk producers of a minimum price for their milk, and then, to protect its market, attempted to forbid the sale in New York of milk produced in other States

[36] Southern Pacific Co. v. Arizona, 325 U.S. 761 (1945).
[37] MacArthur Ltd. v. State of Queensland, 28 C.L.R. 530, 545 (1920).

whose producers were paid less than the minimum price provided for New York producers, the United States Supreme Court held this to be an invalid attempt to create a State protective trade barrier in favor of New York milk producers.[38]

The persistent tendency of the member States in a federal nation to over-look the importance of a fused national economy and to seize some apparent local advantage by means of protectionism appears in many different forms. It frequently appears disguised as a legitimate police measure such, for example as a law apparently designed to protect the health of children by inspection of milk, or to protect the local economy by the regulation of prices. That the incidental effect of a measure to provide for pure milk would be to eliminate competition should not by itself be sufficient to condemn the legislation. On the other hand a balancing of policies becomes necessary to determine which will prevail, the police measure or the policy of economic unity. This balancing of policies is a function traditionally legislative in its nature. But as the ingenuity of local protectionism tends to outrun the speed of legislative enactment, either many such measures must go unchecked or some type of government device other than a legislature, capable of operating more rapidly and of making judgments in a great number of specific instances, must be devised. Such judgments are often made in Australia, in the United States, and in Canada by courts. The Canadian Royal Commission has suggested the possible constitution of a special tribunal containing both judicial and economic personnel, empowered to strike down provincial legislation and administrative practices.[39] Such a new body, with technical qualifications not found in existing courts, which might be termed a Supreme Court of Commerce, might perform the function now performed by ordinary judicial tribunals, without criticism based on lack of the economic and similar qualifications requisite to make the judgment called for.

D. *State Discrimination in Transportation*

Obviously the tendency toward State protectionism which has been noted in other areas could easily appear in the field of transportation. If a member State were to make the intra-State carriage of goods originating within its borders cheaper than the carriage of goods from outside, a very effective form of preference for local merchants would appear. Such an instance arose in the State of Texas in 1911 when the Texas Railroad Commission

---

[38] Baldwin v. Seelig, Inc., 294 U.S. 511 (1935). It is worth noting that when the efforts of the local authorities to protect their milk producers by the fixing of minimum prices thus failed because buyers went to adjoining States where milk was cheaper, federal price regulation ultimately proved necessary. This was sustained in the subsequent leading case of United States v. Rock Royal Co. Operative, Inc., 307 U.S. 533 (1939) and in United States v. Wrightwood Dairy Co., 315 U.S. 110 (1942).

[39] Report of the Royal Commission on Dominion-Provincial Relations, Bk. 2, pp. 65, 66 (1940).

fixed a lower rate per mile for the transportation of certain commodities by
railroad between points in the State of Texas than was fixed by the federal
Interstate Commerce Commission for carriage into Texas from areas adjacent to that State. As a result of these two different rates, goods could be
carried from the distant western part of Texas to markets in the eastern
part of that large State as cheaply as they could be brought from nearer
competing points in Louisiana. The geographical advantage of cities in
the western part of Louisiana for shipping goods into Texas was thus eliminated by the Texas rate-fixing order. The United States Interstate Commerce Commission, after a complaint by the Louisiana authorities, and after
hearing the testimony of shippers and commercial bodies, directed that the
carriers within Texas equalize their charges with those of the carriers moving from outside Texas into the Texas marketing areas. This order, challenged in the federal courts, was approved by the Supreme Court of the
United States in 1914.[40] The episode is interesting not only in demonstrating one more of the protean forms of State protectionism; it also demonstrates the use of a special technical tribunal to strike down the protectionist move. The discriminating Texas rate was not immediately challenged in the federal courts, but in the first instance was attacked before
the Interstate Commerce Commission, a body selected for its expertness in
the field of federal transportation problems. The function of the federal
courts in this instance was limited to a determination that the administrative
body had not exceeded the reasonable bounds of its competence.

A somewhat similar situation has arisen where a State undertakes to require that a carrier, for example a passenger omnibus line, obtain a State
license, known in the United States as "a certificate of convenience and
necessity," before operating from the licensing State into an adjacent State.
Where such a license has been denied by State authorities on the ground
that there are already a sufficient number of carriers operating out of the
licensing State and that the addition of another competing carrier will damage the prior licensees, the effort thus to protect the existing carriers has
been held by the United States Supreme Court to be an undue restriction
on interstate commerce.[41] It is worthy of remark that in 1935 the Congress
found it necessary to provide that the federal Interstate Commerce Commission take over the function of issuing certificates of convenience and
necessity for interstate motor carriers.[42]

[40] Shreveport Rate Case, 234 U.S. 342 (1914). Compare Article 70 of the treaty constituting the European Coal and Steel Community (Schuman Plan) which contemplates measures
making possible "the application of such transport rates for coal and steel as will make
possible comparable price conditions to consumers in comparable positions." It is also
significant that the convention containing transitional conditions, provided for in Article 85
of this treaty, contains in its tenth section a provision that the High Authority shall immediately call into session a commission of experts who shall study the problem of transport within the community and the establishment of direct international rates, which take
into account total distance.
[41] Buck v. Kuykendall, 263 U.S. 307 (1925).
[42] See 49 U.S. Code §§301 et seq.

Essentially there is no difference in the constitutional problems presented by local regulation of transport and the local regulation of other phases of commerce. Obviously some State policing of carriage across a State, in the interests of the safety of the residents, may be entirely necessary, although even here the degree of regulation may rise to the point of practical prohibition. Such an example occurred in the State of Georgia when a statute required so radical a slackening of speed on interstate trains at railroad crossings within the State that the operation of traffic would have been slowed to an intolerable extent. The statute was declared invalid as an unreasonable impediment to interstate commerce.[43] Here, as in the other fields discussed, it appears to be necessary to have some organ of the central government more flexible than the community legislature, to determine instance by instance what local regulation may be permissible in the interests of the economy of the nation as a whole.

E. *Monetary Localism*

The experience of the United States in the short period of independence which preceded the Constitution of 1789 presents a striking example of the evils of competing currencies within a federal nation.

> . . . Until 1785 no national coinage was established, and none was issued until 1793. English, French, Spanish, and German coins, of various and uncertain value, passed from hand to hand. Besides the ninepences and fourpence-ha'-pennies, there were bits and half-bits, pistareens, picayunes, and fips. Of gold pieces there were the johannes, or joe, the doubloon, the moidore, and pistole, with English and French guineas, carolins, ducats, and chequins. Of coppers there were English pence and half-pence and French sous; and pennies were issued at local mints in Vermont, Massachusetts, Connecticut, New Jersey, and Pennsylvania. The English shilling had everywhere degenerated in value, but differently in different localities; and among silver pieces the Spanish dollar, from Louisiana and Cuba, had begun to supersede it as a measure of value. In New England the shilling had sunk from nearly one fourth to one sixth of a dollar; in New York to one eighth; in North Carolina to one tenth. . . . During the period of the Confederation, the chaotic state of the currency was a serious obstacle to trade, and it afforded endless opportunities for fraud and extortion. Clipping and counterfeiting were carried to such lengths that every moderately cautious person, in taking payment in hard cash, felt it necessary to keep a small pair of scales beside him and carefully weigh each coin, after narrowly scrutinizing its stamp and deciphering its legend.[44]

When to the confusion created by this bewildering diversity of metallic currency there was added the difficulty of dealing in half a dozen kinds of

[43] Seaboard Airline Railroad Co. v. Blackwell, 244 U.S. 310 (1917). See also Southern Pacific v. Arizona, 325 U.S. 761 (1945), discussed at page 308 above.
[44] Fiske, *The Critical Period of American History* 165–166 (1888).

paper money issued by several States, there was "created such a labyrinth as no human intellect could explore. No wonder that men were counted wise who preferred to take whiskey and pork instead. Nobody who had a yard of cloth to sell could tell how much it was worth.[45] A result was the prohibition in the Constitution contained in Article I, Section 10, clause 1, forbidding the States to ". . . coin Money; emit Bills of Credit; make any Thing but gold and silver Coin a Tender in Payment of Debts. . . ."

Switzerland, plagued for centuries with monetary disorder which had become proverbial,[46] inserted a prohibition of coinage of money by the cantons, and gave to the Confederation all rights over the monetary system.[47] The British North America Act of 1867 similarly gave to the Dominion government of Canada exclusive powers over currency and coinage and over the issue of paper money.[48] Australia, by Section 51 (xii), (xiii), gave to the Commonwealth government power over currency, coinage, legal tender and the issue of paper money, and then by Section 115 forbade the States to coin money or make anything but gold or silver coin legal tender. The Basic Law for the Federal Republic of Germany, Article 73, gives to the federation the exclusive power to legislate on currency, money, and coinage.

Perhaps because of the clear early recognition of the dangers in local utterance of currency, and these explicit provisions against it in various federal constitutions, little trouble of this nature has arisen in the nations here studied. In the United States, the national government experienced some difficulty with notes, intended to circulate as currency, issued by banks chartered by the States. The Congress met this problem by imposing on such notes a tax so high as to drive them out of circulation. The Supreme Court of the United States, in a leading case,[49] held that the Congress had the power to restrain the circulation as money of any notes not issued under its own authority, and that it might achieve this end by prohibitive taxation.

F. Summary: Constitutional Inhibitions Against State Economic Sectionalism

The problem here considered is economic parochialism. The people of any one State in a federal structure are apt to see their own interests as paramount to those of the community. As a result in all federal nations there tend to appear instances of State legislation or administrative regulation inimical to the economic welfare of the community as a whole. If the community is to thrive, some means must be devised to correct these local aberrations.

State action of this sort appears in many forms, sometimes as tariff bar-

[45] *Id.* at 171.
[46] Rappard, *La Constitution Fédérale de la Suisse* 254 (1948).
[47] Article 36 of the Constitution of 1848; see the present Article 38.
[48] See §91 (14), (15).
[49] Veazie Bank v. Fenno, 8 Wall. 533 (1869).

riers or taxes tantamount to tariff barriers, sometimes in the guise of local police regulations inimical to economic unity.

The choice of a constitutional provision to supply needed correctives is not easy. Any formula general enough to be written in a community constitution will inevitably lack sufficient definition to make it applicable to all instances. Community control necessarily depends on a standard of reasonableness applied, case by case, by some agency in which the people of the community as a whole and the people of the State affected will have confidence. In the United States, where this problem has become acute, the solution, insofar as one has been achieved, is to rely upon constitutional statements of an objective of economic freedom, leaving the more precise definition of this standard to legislative provisions by the central government which can be adopted from time to time, and leaving the application in individual cases which may differ each from the other, in minor but significant details, to a court or other appropriate agency.

The experience of the United States with several different fields of State activity tends to show a uniform pattern of development. State legislation or administrative action is taken which appears harmful to the economic welfare of the nation as a whole, and, under the federal commerce clause, the United States Supreme Court strikes the action down as unconstitutional. Then, whether the subject matter in question be railway transport, or highway transport, or commerce in natural gas, or in milk, or in other agricultural commodities, the combination of the necessity of some regulation, with the demonstrated unconstitutionality of the State regulation, has caused the political forces concerned to bear on the federal Congress, with the result that federal regulation has taken over the area in question.[50]

A prime necessity in any federal government which is to survive is some flexible means of prohibiting the tendency of the member States to go their several economic ways, to the community detriment. The economic field is not the place to hobble a central government; danger to the economy, as shown in the experience of the federal states here studied, comes from fractionalization. In 1913 Justice Holmes said of one function of the court on which he sat:

> I do not think the United States would come to an end if we lost our power to declare an act of Congress void. I do think the Union would be imperiled if we did not make that declaration as to the laws

[50] *Railway transportation:* see Wabash, St. Louis & Pacific Railway Co. v. Illinois, 118 U.S. 557 (1886); Interstate Commerce Act, 49 U.S. Code §§1–40.

Motor carriers by road: Buck v. Kuykendall, 267 U.S. 307 (1925); Federal Motor Carrier Act, 1935, 49 U.S. Code §§301 *et seq.*

Natural gas: State of Missouri v. Kansas Natural Gas Co., 265 U.S. 298 (1924); Natural Gas Act, 1938, 15 U.S. Code §717.

Electric power: Public Utilities Commission v. Attleboro Steam and Electric Co., 273 U.S. 83 (1927); Federal Power Act, 1935, 16 U.S. Code §§824 *et seq.*

Milk: Baldwin v. Seelig, 294 U.S. 511 (1935); Agricultural Marketing Agreement Act, 1937, 7 U.S. Code §601.

of the several States. For one in my place sees how often a local policy prevails with those who are not trained to national views and how often action is taken that embodies what the commerce clause is meant to end.[51]

This is not to suggest that the economy in all of the several States of a federal nation is best controlled from a central point. On the contrary, efficiency appears to lie in the decentralization which is characteristic of the federal structure. What is necessary is that there be some federal power capable of stepping in when economic parochialism asserts itself to an extent which places the national economy in danger of breaking up.

III. COMMUNITY POWERS OVER ECONOMIC MATTERS
A. *Concurrence or Exclusiveness: The Residuary Powers*

Unless there is to be a dead space where no governmental power exists, in any federal nation there must be granted to the community government at least those powers which are prohibited to the member States. As a matter of practice, in the five nations here studied, there is a considerable overlapping of powers, so that some exist both in the central government and in the member States. Two problems of constitution-making immediately arise. One of these is the relative extent of the concurrent and the exclusionary powers. The other is the location of the residual powers — those areas of government competence which are not enumerated specifically as being within the member State or federal powers.

1. CONCURRENCE AND EXCLUSIVENESS OF ECONOMIC POWER

Of the five constitutions here studied, the Basic Law for the Federal Republic of Germany has the most systematic provisions for concurrence and exclusiveness. Certain powers are enumerated as exclusive in the central government under Article 73. The subsections of this article which particularly concern economic matters treat of currency, money and coinage, weights and measures, computation and time, the unity of the territory as regards customs and commerce, freedom of traffic in goods, the exchange of goods and payments with foreign countries, federal railroads and air traffic, postal and telecommunications services, industrial property rights, copyrights and publication rights. Under Article 105 the federal government is further given exclusive power to legislate on customs and fiscal monopolies. However, Article 71 provides that the federation may by law permit the Länder to legislate in these otherwise federal preserves.

On the other hand, Article 74 specifies a number of powers concurrent in the federation and in the Länder, including the law relating to economic matters (mining, industry, supply of power, crafts, trades, commerce, bank-

---

[51] *Collected Legal Papers* 295–296 (1920).

ing and stock exchanges, private insurance); labor law; prevention of the abuse of economic power; promotion of agricultural and forest production, deep sea and coastal fishing; protection with regard to traffic in food and stimulants, and other necessities of life, seeds, etc.; ocean, coastal, and inland shipping, sea and inland waterways; road traffic; motor transport and construction and maintenance of long distance highways; railroads other than federal railroads, except mountain railroads.

The use of these concurrent powers by the federation is limited, at least in form, by Article 72. The federation may legislate in the concurrent field only insofar as need for a federal rule exists because a matter cannot effectively be dealt with by individual Länder, or a Land dealing with a matter might prejudice the interest of other Länder or the entire community or the maintenance of legal or economic unity. The Länder may legislate on any matter only so long as the federation has not pre-empted the field. The breadth of these provisions is such that they appear to give to the federation almost complete power over the national economy.

The United States, by judicial action, has arrived at a somewhat similar arrangement of exclusiveness and concurrence of economic powers. In contrast to the elaboration of the grants of power described in the German Constitution, the grants in the Constitution of the United States to the federal government of power over commerce and economic processes generally were made in the simplest and shortest terms. The principal grant of power is contained in Article 1, Section 8, Clause 3, generally known as the commerce clause: "The Congress shall have Power . . . To regulate Commerce with foreign Nations, and among the several States, and with the Indian Tribes . . ." This clause, under which a vast amount of federal legislation has been enacted in the United States, contains no statement as to whether the powers so granted are to be exclusive in the federal government or concurrent with like powers in the States. However, in 1852, in a famous leading judgment[52] the Supreme Court laid down three propositions which brought the law of the United States to a point much like that of Germany under the present Bonn Constitution. These three propositions were, first, that the commerce clause does not by its own force exclude all State legislation in the field of interstate commerce. In the second place, the Court stated that certain matters "are in their nature national or admit only of one uniform system, or plan of regulation," and that such matters were in the exclusive control of the federal legislature. Thirdly, the Court found that the federal legislature might by statute permit the States to legislate, thus eliminating in such an instance any question of federal exclusiveness. Subsequent decisions, numerous and continuing down to the present time,[53] have held that, when the Congress has acted in such a way as to occupy a given field of legislation, it has impliedly expressed its intention to exclude the State from legislating in the same area, and thus made ex-

[52] Cooley v. Portwardens of Philadelphia, 12 How. 299 (1852).
[53] For example, Cloverleaf Butter Co. v. Patterson, 315 U.S. 148 (1942).

clusive with respect to the subject matter in question its own legislative competence.

The constitutional arrangements of these two different nations — originating so far apart in time, brought about under different circumstances, but arriving at approximately the same end — indicate a constitutional necessity that there not be left a governmental vacuum from which the legislative power of the component States has been removed but which the central government has chosen not to fill. They illustrate another necessity, that the central government must be able to protect the powers granted to it, when necessary, by legislatively or otherwise excluding State lawmaking over any subject which conflicts with and tends to defeat the federal legislation in question.

The Canadian Constitution[54] has adopted a somewhat different plan. Section 91 lists a number of subject matters upon which the Dominion Parliament's legislative authority is stated to be exclusive. Section 92 contains a list of subjects upon which the provincial legislatures are to have exclusive legislative jurisdiction. Finally Section 95, dealing with agriculture and immigration, provides that the Dominion Parliament and the provincial legislatures may both legislate, but that provincial legislation is to have effect only insofar as it is not repugnant to any act of the Parliament of Canada.[55] As in all constitutions, the grants of power in the British North America Act are necessarily rather general, despite the effort to achieve detailed enumeration. As a result, subject matters have appeared in need of legislative action which might reasonably fall into any one of these three inconsistent Sections: 91, 92, or 95. The judicial organs have found themselves charged with the choice of the governing clause. Thus the Dominion Parliament, by a statute of 1927, provided that no person should manufacture, import into Canada, or offer, sell, or have in his possession for sale any oleomargarine. The Supreme Court of Canada, and in its turn the Privy Council, were faced with the argument on behalf of the Dominion authorities that the prohibition of manufacture or sale was within the Dominion powers under any of four provisions; that it was a regulation of trade or commerce and therefore within the Dominion powers under Section 91 (2) of the British North America Act; that as it was enforceable by criminal sanctions it was legislation relating to the criminal law and hence was within the Dominion powers under Section 91 (27); that it was a law in relation to agriculture and hence fell within the Dominion powers under Section 95 of the Act and also that, not being within any of the powers exclusively granted to the provincial legislatures under Section 92, it passed with the residual governmental powers, not otherwise allocated, to the Dominion under Section 91. The Privy Council, however, found that it was a statute dealing with "property and civil rights" and

---

[54] British North America Act, 1867, 30 & 31 Vict., c. 3, as amended.
[55] For a further discussion of the details of the grant of power in the British North America Act, see Appendix II, which deals with the Canadian Constitution.

therefore exclusively in the provincial competence under Section 92 (13). It was thus held *ultra vires* the Dominion of Canada, and invalid.[56]

The provision of a detailed list of mutually exclusive grants of power to the central government and to the member States places a construing tribunal in the embarrassing predicament of making a choice of alternatives; and this embarrassment is accentuated, as the margarine case shows, when the matter *sub judice* falls equally well under both the State and the community headings of power.

Concurrence of powers unless expressly stated to the contrary in the Constitution, with an option in the community legislature to make its exercise of the powers exclusionary as it sees fit, simplifies the federal handling of economic matters.

2. RESIDUAL POWERS

Even where, as in Canada, a fairly exhaustive list of powers is catalogued and allotted respectively to the Dominion and to the provincial legislatures, there will inevitably be a residue which has not been expressly ascribed to either. Under these circumstances it becomes necessary to allot these remaining powers either to the member States or to the community government. Canada, as has been pointed out, chose the Dominion government by Section 91 of her Constitution. On the other hand, Australia,[57] the United States,[58] Switzerland,[59] and Germany[60] place the reserve or residual powers in the governments of the member States.

The decision whether to give such reserved powers to the community government, or to leave them with the several member States, involves questions of political expediency which may reasonably be the subject of differing judgment. Of the five governments studied, four apparently felt that, as fairly complete governmental competence historically resided in the component States,[61] the preferable course was to allot to the community government only those powers specifically delegated, provided these were delegated in terms sufficiently broad to accomplish the wide purpose intended. One might conclude, from the judicial history of Canada and the United States, that the formal allotment of the reserved powers is less important than might appear at first to be the case. The decided cases do not demonstrate that the Canadian arrangement has resulted in a greater concentration of federal power than in the United States. Due perhaps to a difference in judicial attitude, the result has instead been inverse to the constitutional

---

[56] In re A Reference as to the Validity of Section 5 (A) of the Dairy Industry Act, [R.S.C. 1927, c. 45] [1951] A.C. 179.

[57] §107.

[58] Amend. X.

[59] Art. 3.

[60] Art. 70.

[61] While this may not have been true of the German member States immediately prior to the Bonn Constitution, it was true at an earlier stage of national history.

provisions; in the United States the federal government appears to exercise a more complete power over the national economy than is true in Canada.[62]

3. A COMPARISON OF FORMS OF GRANT OF COMMUNITY POWERS

The draftsmen of the constitutions in each of the five nations studied have undertaken to devise a verbal formula to describe those economic matters which are to be within the community cognizance, and those which are to be continued in the competence of the member States. The difficulty of devising a satisfactory formula has proved to lie in the fact that the economic life of a nation is not readily divisible. Whatever formula is devised to describe that economic area which is to be within the federal competence appears inevitably to describe some matters which are essentially local. In no one of the five constitutions here considered has the solution been attempted of turning the entire economic life of the nation over to the central government. Such a move, while ending the difficulties arising out of a federal form of economy, would accomplish this by ending the federal character of the nation. Instead, at least three types of definitions have been attempted to describe the respective community and State spheres.

a. *Definition in terms of interstate character.* The constitutions of Australia and the United States undertook to allot to the community government power over commerce in terms of its interstate or foreign, as distinguished from its intrastate, character.

This formula is not self-defining. The determination of the limits of community and State competence in both nations constitutionally rests with the federal judiciary.

b. *Definition of federal and State power by mutually exclusive lists of functions.* As pointed out in the discussion of the concurrence or exclusiveness of powers, the Canadian Constitution attempts a definition of federal and State powers by mutually exclusive lists of functions.[63] It might have been supposed that, by thus describing grants of power in detail, legal certainty would be achieved and the task of judicial construction would be diminished. It has been found in Canada, however, that the length of the lists of powers has not eliminated duplication, and in an effort to solve such dilemmas the courts in Canada, as elsewhere, have been obliged to make

---

[62] By a statute of March 16, 1950, the United States Congress forbade the sale of colored oleomargarine in a public eating place unless each separate serving is labeled as margarine, or is served in triangular shape. 21 U.S. Code §347A. It is notable that this statute does not appear as yet to have been passed on by the federal courts. The Congress, in passing it, made an express finding and declaration that the sale of unidentified colored margarine would "affect" interstate commerce in butter and clearly identified oleomargarine. Thus locally produced and sold oleomargarine is apparently brought within the scope of the power to control interstate commerce which has been entrusted to the federal government. See, for a discussion of this "affect" power, page 319 below.

[63] See Appendix II.

decisions which depend ultimately upon conceptions of political and economic desirability.[64]

c. *Definition of federal power in terms of the need for uniformity.* The Basic Law for the Federal Republic of Germany adopts a third technique of description of those economic powers allotted to the community government. By Article 74 the federation and the Länder are given extremely broad concurrent powers over the law relating to economic matters.[65] Taken by itself this grant would allot to the federation complete control over the economic life of the nation. However, it is controlled by the language of Article 72 which purports to limit federation action to matters in which national uniformity is essential. Under Section 93 of the Basic Law, a federal constitutional court is granted jurisdiction to decide what federal measures are essential for "the maintenance of legal or economic unity." [66]

Under no one of these three formulas has it been possible to relieve the central constitutional tribunal in the nation in question from the task of making decisions essentially based on economic policy.

B. *Community Powers over Local Transactions Which "Affect" Interstate Commerce*

The courts in the United States have had to face the economic fact that transactions essentially local affect interstate commerce; and that the constitutional mandate given to the federal government to regulate commerce between the several States cannot effectively be carried out unless the federal government also regulates those local transactions which produce disturbances in transactions between the several States. The difficulty with this rationale has been that it leaves no obvious place to stop. During the depression of the 1930's the United States Congress determined to regulate the production of those agricultural commodities of which there then appeared to be an uneconomic surplus. As a practical matter, the production of agricultural surpluses, even when consumed within the borders of the State where grown, was found to have a significant effect upon commerce in those commodities which otherwise would have moved from neighboring States into the State of consumption. Accordingly the federal government by appropriate measures undertook to control the volume of the production of certain crops. These regulations, challenged before the Supreme Court of the United States on the ground that they were entirely local and so *ultra vires* the federal government, were sustained on the ground that the grant of power to regulate interstate commerce carried with

---

[64] See, for example, In re A Reference as to the Validity of Section 5 (A) of the Dairy Industry Act, [1951] A.C. 179, discussed at page 316 above.

[65] For a further description of the extraordinarily broad grants of power in Article 74 over all phases of economic life, see the Appendix III.

[66] In Switzerland federal legislation is beyond challenge in the courts (Art. 113).

it the additional power to regulate intrastate transactions as well, where the one could not be effectively controlled without the other.[67]

This doctrine of the "affect" power has had many applications in the judicial history of the Constitution of the United States. It was applied as early as 1914 to justify federal control of railway rates for carriage exclusively within the confines of a single State;[68] it has been used to justify federal control of the labor relations of a company manufacturing gasoline, whose materials came from the ground in the same State in which the manufacturer disposed of the finished product.[69] Perhaps the most extreme recent application of the "affect" power is found in the statute of March 16, 1950, in which the Congress relied upon this principle to prescribe the form in which unlabeled margarine is sold in a restaurant in the same State in which it is produced.[70] The net result of the "affect" doctrine is to place the Supreme Court of the United States in much the same position in which the Constitutional Court in Germany is placed by Articles 72 and 74 of the Basic Law.[71]

C. *Specific Limitations on Community Powers over the Economy*

In many instances, constitution-makers have not been willing to rely solely upon the principle of *ultra vires* for a limitation of the economic powers entrusted to the community; it has seemed necessary to impose more specific prohibitions. Conspicuous examples have resulted from fear lest a central government exercise its powers so as to favor one member State or group of member States to the disparagement of the others. Section 99 of the Australian Constitution directs that the Commonwealth shall not "by any law or regulation of trade, commerce, or revenue, give preference to one State or any part thereof over another State or any part thereof." Article I, Section 9, of the Constitution of the United States provides in part that "No Preference shall be given by any Regulation of Commerce or Revenue to the Ports of one State over those of another: nor shall Vessels bound to, or from, one State, be obliged to enter, clear, or pay Duties in another." Article I, Section 8, clause 1, of the Constitution of the United States requires that ". . . all Duties, Imposts and Excises shall be uniform throughout the United States." Section 88 of the Australian Constitution likewise provides for "uniform duties of customs." By Section 51 (ii) the Commonwealth is forbidden to discriminate in taxation between States or parts of States. Correlatively, while the Commonwealth may grant boun-

[67] Wickard v. Filburn, 317 U.S. 111 (1942).

[68] Shreveport Rate Case, 234 U.S. 342 (1914), discussed at page 310 above.

[69] National Labor Relations Board v. Mid-Co Gasoline Co., 183 F.2d 451 (5th Cir. 1950).

[70] 21 U.S. Code §347A; see page 318 above, where this statute is described.

[71] Since 1936, the Supreme Court of the United States has not found any federal statute constitutionally invalid on the ground that it exceeded the powers delegated to the federal government to regulate commerce between the several States.

ties on the production or export of goods, the bounties must be uniform throughout the Commonwealth (§51 (iii)).

Since 1936, Section 92 of the Australian Constitution, which provides that "Trade, commerce, and intercourse among the States . . . shall be absolutely free," has been construed to restrict the Commonwealth as well as the several States. In that year the Privy Council declared invalid a Commonwealth statute which required a license for all interstate shipments of dried fruits,[72] and in 1950 the same doctrine was restated in a case which inhibited the nationalization of State Banks.[73] In the Constitution of the United States there are various limitations on the federal power over the economy in addition to the prohibitions on regional favoritism. Of these perhaps the best known is the Fifth Amendment to the Constitution, which provides that "No person shall be . . . deprived of life, liberty, or property, without due process of law; nor shall private property be taken for public use, without just compensation." However, the Supreme Court of the United States has held no important federal statute concerning the national economy to be invalid under any one of these restrictive clauses since 1936.[74] The federal judiciary in the United States has been much more ready to strike down States statutes which conflict with some federal policy than it has been to find federal statutes invalid. At least during the last fifteen years, judicial self-restraint in this respect has brought the United States close to the position of Switzerland with respect to judicial challenges of the validity of federal legislation.

D. Community Powers over Various Economic Fields

If the development of constitutional experience had followed an engineering sequence, a discussion of the specific details of economic control by the community should start with the production of goods, proceed to transportation, and thence to merchandising. Historically, however, in the United States the earliest experience with the use of the federal commerce power was in the field of transportation.

1. TRANSPORTATION AND COMMUNICATION

In the Constitution of the United States, there is no grant in so many words over transport and communications. The nearest thing to any express provision is Article I, Section 8, clause 7 which authorizes the Congress "To Establish Post Offices and post Roads." However, the general grant of power in Article I, Section 8, Clause 3, for the Congress to "regulate Commerce with foreign Nations, and among the several States," was given a wide construction. In 1824 the Supreme Court held that this power

---

[72] James v. Commonwealth of Australia, [1936] A.C. 578.
[73] Bank Nationalization Case, [1950] A.C. 235.
[74] See Appendix V, page 353 below, for a discussion of these limitations and the adjudications under them since 1936.

authorized the United States to enroll and license ships and vessels in the coasting trade and fisheries, and that a vessel so enrolled could not be excluded from a port of the State of New York even by appropriate New York legislation.[75] In addition to the commerce clause, the power of the United States to regulate navigation has been predicted in part upon the jurisdiction over maritime cases entrusted to the federal court system by Article III, Section 2. Article I, Section 8, clause 18, which authorizes the Congress "To make all Laws which shall be necessary and proper for carrying into Execution the foregoing Powers," tends to expand the construction of the other grants of power.

The United States has thus been able to exercise legislative power over all phases of interstate land, water, and air transportation, and over that local transportation which "affects" interstate commerce. Safety devices are prescribed by the federal government upon trains, even though intrastate, moving upon any railroad engaged in interstate commerce.[76] The federal government has utilized the commerce power to enact a complete system of regulation of transportation by aircraft in the United States, including a provision that "there is recognized and declared to exist in behalf of any citizen of the United States a public right of freedom of transit in air commerce through the navigable air space of the United States." [77] The United States has provided a complete national system of registration of liens upon aircraft and of licensing for use.

The commerce clause has likewise authorized the federal Congress to make provisions for community control of transport by gas-pipe line, and by electric transmission line.[78] The same clause has sufficed to grant to the federal government control over telegraph, telephone, and radio communication, which includes broadcasting and television.[79] Telephonic communication, even when between two points in the same State, is in the control of the United States because of the interconnection between local and national telephony.[80]

It should be emphasized that this great comprehensive sweep of federal power over transport and communications, derived from a very few words in the Constitution of the United States, does not make compulsory the full exercise of this power, nor deprive the States of the control they exercise until the federal government chooses to step in. It is, however, a striking example of the fact that a simple and broad clause, if widely construed by the judicial organs competent to do so, will be sufficient to create federal power over the entire area of transport and communications.

Other constitutions here studied have spelled out in considerable detail powers over transport and communications which in the United States are

[75] Gibbons v. Ogden, 9 Wheat. 1 (1824).
[76] Southern Railway Co. v. United States, 222 U.S. 20 (1911).
[77] 49 U.S. Code §403.
[78] See page 313 above.
[79] Federal Communications Act, 47 U.S. Code §151.
[80] Weiss v. United States, 308 U.S. 321 (1939).

derived from the simple language of the commerce clause. For example the Commonwealth legislative powers in Australia are expressed to extend to trade and commerce with other countries and among the States, navigation and shipping, railways, the property of any State, postal, telegraphic, telephonic, and like services.[81] Canada grants to the Dominion, besides regulation of trade and commerce, power over navigation and shipping, railways, canals, telegraphs and other works and undertakings connecting one Province with another Province or extending beyond provincial limits.[82] The German Basic Law specifies, among the exclusive powers of the federation, the unity of the territory as regards commercial and navigation agreements; the freedom of traffic in goods; federal railroads and air traffic; postal and telecommunication services; and it gives to the federal government additional concurrent legislative powers, exercisable where necessary because the matter cannot effectively be dealt with by the legislation of individual Länder. These concurrent powers include ocean and coastal shipping, inland shipping, road traffic, motor transport, and the construction and maintenance of long distance highways and railroads other than federal railroads.[83] The Swiss Constitution gives to the Confederation authority to legislate concerning transportation by water, railroad, highway, and air, and also gives full federal competence over matters of post and telecommunication (Arts. 26, 27-ter, 36, 37-bis, 37-ter).

The matter of community power over transportation and communication might well be summarized by saying that in the United States, by judicial construction of the commerce clause, the federal government has achieved at least as complete a control as is exercised by the other countries under their much more detailed grants of power.

2. TRAFFIC IN GOODS

The commerce clause of the Constitution of the United States[84] has been construed as a sufficient grant of power to permit the federal legislature to engage in an extraordinarily detailed regulation of American traffic in goods even when that traffic would appear at first glance to be entirely local. Under this clause, monopolies or combinations in restraint of interstate commerce or any part thereof are penalized.[85] Price discrimination by any person, in the course of interstate commerce, is forbidden where the discrimination tends to monopoly, and where there is no justification for the differential because of differing methods or quantities concerned.[86] The federal government, through the Secretary of Agriculture, regulates sales of perishable agricultural commodities in "all cases where sale is

[81] See Appendix I.
[82] See Appendix II.
[83] See Appendix III.
[84] Art. I, Sec. 8, cl. 3.
[85] See 15 U.S. Code §§1, 2.
[86] See 15 U.S. Code §13.

either for shipment to another State, or for processing within the State and the shipment outside the State of the products resulting from such processing." [87] The United States has regulated the price of milk sold in the same State where produced on the ground that the sales so made affected commerce between the States.[88] The Federal Congress prohibits the introduction or delivery for introduction into interstate commerce of any food, drug, device, or cosmetic that is adulterated or misbranded.[89] The United States Congress has established a Federal Trade Commission which is charged with the duty of regulating "unfair methods of competition in commerce, and unfair or deceptive acts or practices in commerce," "commerce" being defined as "commerce among the several States or with foreign Nations, or in any territory of the United States, or in the District of Columbia, etc., etc." [90] In brief, the very terse language of the commerce clause of the United States Constitution has been sufficient to furnish a foundation for a searching regulation of interstate commerce, and in some instances of local commerce which affects interstate commerce, even in comparatively minor transactions.[91]

The legislative provisions of Section 51 of the Australian Constitution, and those covering "the regulation of trade and commerce" in Subsection 2 of Section 91 of the British North America Act of 1867, have given to the community governments of Australia and Canada less sweeping powers than the commerce clause has given the United States, apparently because of a more restricted interpretation given to these clauses by the judicial tribunals interpreting them. In the case of Australia, Section 92[92] was held to invalidate a Commonwealth statute requiring a license for all interstate shipments of dried fruit on the ground that this licensing provision, passed in an effort to cope with a surplus of the product, was inconsistent with freedom of trade among the States.[93] Similarly the Privy Council in 1950 held that the Dominion of Canada had no power to prohibit the sales of margarine within a province, on the ground that the sale

---

[87] Perishable Agricultural Commodities Act, 1937, 7 U.S. Code §§499A et seq.

[88] Agricultural Marketing Agreement Act, 1937, 7 U.S. Code §608C; United States v. Wrightwood Dairy Co., 315 U.S. 110 (1942).

[89] Federal Food, Drug and Cosmetic Act, 1938, 21 U.S. Code §§ 301 et seq. See pages 318 and 320 above, for federal regulation of sales of margarine, produced in the same State in which sold.

[90] 15 U.S. Code §§41 et seq.

[91] In a recent celebrated case the Supreme Court of the United States was required to determine whether a manufacturer of a food product labeled "imitation jam" must suffer the seizure of his property because the product did not contain the components which the federal Administrator had prescribed for any preparation to be known as "jam." The Court decided that the Federal Food, Drug and Cosmetic Act had not been violated in the light of the word "imitation" inserted in the label. See 62 Cases of Jam v. United States, 340 U.S. 593 (1951). This decision is, however, not a challenge of federal power to legislate, merely a finding that in a specific instance the statute did not prohibit the branding or labeling in question.

[92] ". . . trade, commerce, and intercourse among the States, whether by means of internal carriage or ocean navigation, shall be absolutely free."

[93] James v. Commonwealth of Australia, [1936] A.C. 578.

related to civil rights within the province and therefore was exclusively within provincial dominion.[94] In the last analysis, the grant of power over traffic in goods will be no broader and no narrower than the construing tribunal chooses to make it.

3. PRODUCTION OF GOODS; LABOR RELATIONS

The difficulty of defining community competence to control the economic processes of a federal nation in terms of what is "interstate," as distinguished from what is local or "intrastate," clearly appears in a consideration of community efforts to control production, and labor relations in the production process. Production, whether it be extractive as in mining, or processing as in manufacture, appears at first glance to be characteristically local, and therefore appropriate for control by the member States, rather than by the community. However, where one or more member States puts in force an advanced program of labor legislation, favoring relatively high wages and superior working conditions, the expense of the program, reflected in heightened costs of production, tends to send the business to a cheaper State. As a result, political pressures arise in the States having the progressive and therefore expensive legislation, urging the central government to take some action which will require the nonconforming State to bring its standards up to those observed by the others. The industries in the nonconforming States, however, may be expected under these circumstances to assert that conditions of production are essentially local matters, and are so outside the scope of the constitutional powers entrusted to the central government.

The process just described has resulted, in the United States, in efforts by those interested in federal legislation concerning labor standards to obtain an expanded construction of the commerce clause. Thus in 1916 the Congress passed a statute forbidding any producer, manufacturer, or dealer to ship in interstate or foreign commerce any article produced by any mine or quarry in the United States in which children under the age of 16 were employed, or any product of any manufacturing establishment in which children under the age of 14 were employed, or in which children between the ages of 14 and 16 were employed more than specified hours per day. In 1918 this statute was held unconstitutional by the Supreme Court on the ground that it attempted regulation of the hours of labor of children in factories and mines, which was exclusively within the constitutional competence of the States.[95]

In 1919, the Congress attempted to circumvent this determination by achieving the same end by taxation. The Constitution gives the Congress the power "to lay and collect Taxes, Duties, Imposts and Excises, to pay the

[94] In re A Reference as to the Validity of Section 5 (A) of the Dairy Industry Act, [1951] A.C. 179.

[95] Hammer v. Dagenhart, 247 U.S. 351 (1918).

Debts and provide for the common Defense and general Welfare of the United States." [96] The statute in question attempted to impose a tax upon persons employing children under specified ages, though excusing the employer if he acted mistakenly and without intention to evade the tax. A company engaged in the manufacture of furniture brought an action against a federal tax collector to recover a tax paid, on the ground that the statute levying it was unconstitutional, and the Supreme Court, in 1922, sustained this claim on the ground that Congress was misusing its power to tax in order to penalize the employment of child labor. This, the Court found, was an effort to do by indirection what had been held in 1918 to be exclusively within the powers of the States. Accordingly the tax was held invalid.[97]

Ineffectual proposals to amend the Constitution in such a way as to extend the competence of the central government over various phases of local economic processes were under discussion for about fifteen years after the decision of the Child Labor Tax Case. In 1936, the Supreme Court held unconstitutional a federal statute which, by an elaborate combination of taxation and federal expenditures for benefits to farmers, was designed to produce a limitation of the overproduction of agricultural produce.[98] A little later, in 1936, a federal statute undertaking to fix hours of labor and wages in the bituminous coal mining industry was similarly held unconstitutional.[99]

However, a strong minority on the Supreme Court had come to feel that these decisions were restricting the federal powers too drastically, and in the spring of 1937 a notable decision of the Court produced a complete reversal of attitude when it held constitutional the National Labor Relations Act as applied to manufacturing.[100] This statute provided a substantial degree of regulation of labor relations by a federal board. It applied both to interstate commerce and to economic activities "affecting commerce"; many matters which appear entirely local have repercussions upon interstate matters, and thus as a practical matter the decision in 1937 extended the federal power to control labor relations throughout the field of production. Since 1937 the Supreme Court has not held any activity of the National Labor Relations Board *ultra vires* the power of the federal government.

Under the Fair Labor Standards Act of 1938, the Congress undertook to prohibit the shipment in interstate commerce of lumber manufactured by employees whose wages are less than a prescribed minimum, or whose weekly hours of labor are greater than a prescribed maximum, and undertook further to prohibit the employment of workmen in the production of goods "for interstate commerce" at other than prescribed wages and hours.

[96] Art. I, §8, cl. 2.
[97] Child Labor Tax Case (Bailey v. Drexel Furniture Co.), 259 U.S. 20 (1922).
[98] United States v. Butler, 297 U.S. 251 (1936).
[99] Carter v. Carter Coal Co., 298 U.S. 238 (1936).
[100] National Labor Relations Board v. Jones & Laughlin Steel Corp., 301 U.S. 1 (1937).

This statute was declared constitutional in 1941 by the Supreme Court,[101] which expressly overruled the precedent of 1918 to the contrary.[102]   In 1945 the federal minimum wage statute was held applicable to porters, night watchmen, and elevator operators in a 24-story building owned and operated as an administrative headquarters for a corporation in interstate manufacture and shipment.[103]   No manufacture or shipment of goods occurred in the building, but the maintenance employees were held to have such a connection with the company executive officers in the building that the maintenance work and operation of the elevators could be said to be "production for interstate commerce."

In Canada there has arisen the same problem of community control of the conditions of production, but the controlling judicial decisions have given to the Dominion government a scope much narrower than in the United States.   In 1935, the Dominion Parliament passed certain statutes known as The Weekly Rest in Industrial Undertakings Act,[104] The Minimum Wages Act,[105] and The Limitation of Hours of Work Act.[106]   All these statutes were enacted in accordance with conventions adopted by the International Labour Organization of the League of Nations, under the labor provisions of the Treaty of Versailles.   When litigation reached the Privy Council challenging the competence of the Dominion Parliament to enact legislation regulating local undertakings, that tribunal declared that the statutes in question were *ultra vires* the national government.   The fact that a treaty was first entered into by the Dominion government, and that the legislation was enacted pursuant to the treaty, did not extend the powers of the Dominion government in such a way as to permit it to legislate in areas constitutionally reserved to the Provinces.[107]

In Australia the Commonwealth government has exercised substantial control over labor matters through Section 51 (xxv) of her Constitution which empowers the Commonwealth to make laws with respect to "conciliation and arbitration for the prevention and settlement of industrial disputes extending beyond the limits of any one State."   The Australian courts have given this clause a wide construction, so that "industrial" includes mining, banking, and insurance.   Sufficient interstate character is found if persons employed in different States join in the same complaint before the Commonwealth's Court of Conciliation and Arbitration, constituted under the Conciliation and Arbitration Act, 1904.[108]

In 1944 the Labor Government of Australia put before the people of the Commonwealth a proposal for a constitutional amendment authorizing

[101] United States v. Darby, 312 U.S. 100 (1941).
[102] Hammer v. Dagenhart, 247 U.S. 251 (1918), discussed above.
[103] Borden Co. v. Borella, 325 U.S. 679 (1945).
[104] 1935, St. Can. 25 & 26 Geo. V, c. 14.
[105] 1935, St. Can. 25 & 26 Geo. V, c. 24.
[106] 1935, St. Can. 25 & 26 Geo. V, c. 63.
[107] Attorney-General of Canada v. Attorney-General of Ontario, [1937] A.C. 326 (P.C.).
[108] See Report of the Royal Commission on the Constitution 160 *et seq.* (1929); Wheare, *Federal Government* 148 (1947).

the Commonwealth government to legislate concerning fourteen specified topics, including employment and unemployment, the organized marketing of commodities, companies, trusts, combines, and monopolies, profiteering, the production and distribution of goods (with the consent of the State concerned in the case of primary products), and uniformity of railway gauges (now differing between States of Australia) and certain other economic matters.[109]   The amendment failed to obtain the requisite popular vote.   In 1946 and 1947, further unsuccessful efforts were made to extend the power of the Australian Commonwealth over economic matters by constitutional amendments.   The proposals of 1946 would have empowered the Parliament to make laws with respect to terms and conditions of employment in industry,[110] and would have authorized the Commonwealth to regulate "organized marketing of primary products." [111]   In 1947 an amendment was proposed to empower the Commonwealth to regulate "rents and prices (including charges)." [112]   Each of these, though passed by the Commonwealth Parliament, failed to obtain the required votes of the electors.

In Switzerland, the abundant powers of the federation government, and the inability of the judiciary to declare federal laws unconstitutional, make the adequacy of federal powers over production much less of a problem than is the case in the other nations here discussed.   Under the Basic Law for Germany, Articles 74 and 72 appear to give to the federation powers over production so complete that the difficulties experienced in other federal nations are unlikely to arise.

In Australia, Canada, and the United States, then, there has clearly appeared a tendency to seek increasing power in the community legislature over the production of goods, and especially over the labor relations involved in their production.   The efforts, at first unsuccessful and then successful, to persuade the United States Supreme Court to give a construction of the commerce power which reaches that objective; the unsuccessful attempts in Canada to attain that end through the use of the treaty-making power; and the efforts of the Australian Parliament to extend its powers over production and labor relations by passing proposals for constitutional alteration, which were rejected by the electors[113] — these may be taken to indicate a substanial opinion that the increasingly close integration of the economic activities of a modern federal nation makes necessary a considerable measure of community control over production and labor relations.

4. EXCHANGE, CURRENCY, AND BANKING

Because of the obvious necessity for central monetary control, the constitutions here studied contain relatively explicit provisions on this subject,

[109] 42 Australian Commonwealth Acts, 1944, p. 185.
[110] 44 Australian Commonwealth Acts, 1946, p. 278.
[111] Id. at 277.
[112] 45 Australian Commonwealth Acts, 1947, p. 458.
[113] 44 Australian Commonwealth Acts, 1946, pp. 277, 278; see 45 id., 1947, p. 458.

and comparatively little difficulty has arisen in determining that the central governments in each case have all necessary power in the financial field. The Australian Constitution not only gives to the Commonwealth power over trade and commerce of an interstate nature but also gives express power over currency, coinage, legal tender, over banking other than State banking, and over that State banking which extends beyond the limits of the States concerned. The Commonwealth has also control of the incorporation of banks and the issue of paper money, over insurance, aside from that conducted by a State within its own boundaries, and over bills of exchange and promissory notes.[114] The British North America Act, besides entrusting to the Dominion government the regulation of trade and commerce, vests in the Dominion Parliament legislative power over the currency and coinage, banking, incorporation of banks, the issue of paper money, savings banks, bills of exchange and promissory notes, interest, and legal tender.[115] Article 39 of the Swiss Constitution gives the federation powers over the currency, and authorization to establish and control a central bank. Article 64 gives to the Confederation power to legislate over "all legal relations pertaining to commerce and to trade in securities," including the law concerning obligations, commercial law, and the law of exchange. The Basic Law for the Federal Republic of Germany, by Article 73, entrusts the federation with exclusive power to legislate on currency, money and coinage; and, by Article 74 (11), with concurrent legislative power over banking, stock exchanges, and private insurance. As Article 72 gives the federation power to exclude the Länder, if it desires, from these concurrent areas, the net effect appears to be to give to the federation ample power over this whole field.

In contrast to these detailed provisions, the Constitution of the United States is much briefer and less explicit in the grants of power under which the federal government controls banking, currency, and exchange. In addition to the power to regulate commerce with foreign nations and among the several States, the United States is simply given, by Article I, Section 8, clause 5, power "to coin Money, regulate the Value thereof, and of foreign Coin," and by the next clause the federal government is authorized to punish counterfeiting.

Despite the comparatively brief form of these grants of power, they were held sufficient as early as 1819 to justify the United States in chartering a bank.[116] Since that time the Congress has enacted a series of comprehensive statutes regulating many phases of financial and banking activities in the United States including the establishment of Federal Reserve Banks,[117] the insurance of banking deposits,[118] the regulation of exchanges where

---

[114] §51 (i), (xii), (xiii), (xvi).
[115] §91 (2), (14), (15), (16), (18), (19), (20).
[116] McCulloch v. Maryland, 4 Wheat. 316 (1819).
[117] 12 U.S. Code §§221 et seq.
[118] 12 U.S. Code §§264 et seq.

securities are bought and sold,[119] and many other pieces of financial legislation.

The subject of exchange, currency, and banking might be summarized by a statement that experience in all the nations studied shows the necessity of community power to control the financial institutions of the nation for the proper conduct of the economic functions of government. This has been explicitly provided for in the constitutions of all the nations studied except the United States; and by construction of more general clauses, the Supreme Court has afforded the same powers to the United States Congress.

E. *Community Tariffs and Taxation*

The power of community governments to prevent the erection of tariff barriers between the member States, and to control that State taxation which impedes the nation's economic unity, has already been discussed.[120] Under the discussion of specific constitutional limitations on community powers,[121] prohibitions of unequal treatment of one area of the nation by discriminatory taxation or customs preferences have been described.

In all the constitutions studied, the power of the community government to levy sufficient taxes to supply the means of supporting government has been clearly recognized,[122] but here, as in other fields, the presence of limiting constitutional phrases can have unexpected and distressing results. The Constitution of the United States requires that "direct Taxes shall be apportioned among the several States which may be included in this Union according to their respective Numbers";[123] it further provides that "no Capitation or other direct Tax shall be laid, unless in proportion to the Census or Enumeration herein before directed to be taken," [124] and that "All Duties, Imposts and Excises shall be uniform throughout the United States." [125]

Because the meaning of the expression "direct Taxes" is not clear, argument on the point has been abundant. In 1895 the Supreme Court decided that a federal income tax law was a "direct" tax, unapportioned, and was therefore unconstitutional.[126] Federal income taxes were accordingly impossible in the United States between 1895 and 1913, when the Sixteenth Amendment to the Constitution was enacted providing that "The Congress shall have power to lay and collect taxes on incomes, from whatever source derived, without apportionment among the several States, and without regard to any census or enumeration."

[119] 15 U.S. Code §§78A *et seq.*
[120] See page 299 above.
[121] See page 309 above.
[122] See appendices below.
[123] Art. I, §2, cl. 3.
[124] Art. I, §9, cl. 4.
[125] Art. I, §8, cl. 1.
[126] Pollock v. Farmers Loan and Trust Co., 157 U.S. 429 (1895).

Another question which has occasionally arisen in the United States involves the determination whether a given federal tax is really a revenue measure, or is actually a fine or penalty intended primarily to inhibit the activity taxed, when a direct prohibition would be *ultra vires* the community. The distinction between a tax and a penalty is difficult to define. The Supreme Court has rarely found a tax invalid on the ground of its essentially penal character.[127]

F. *Constitutional Provisions for Emergency Powers*

In the life of any nation there are inevitable crises, economic as well as military. "War powers" are provided in all constitutions and by force of necessity they cut across peacetime limitations on government. But in drafting a constitution, is it desirable to set up special provisions to apply in economic crises? This question is also referred to in Study 13, Defense of the Constitutional Order.

Such emergency clauses appear neither necessary nor desirable. In at least two federal constitutions, emergency powers have been express — in that of Switzerland[128] and in the German Constitution of 1919. But in Switzerland the emergency clause has not been used in economic dislocations; and the use made of Article 48 of the 1919 German Constitution was not such as to recommend that its example be followed.

The reluctance of British constitutionalists to accept the institution of solely economic crisis powers appeared in the construction given by the Privy Council to Section 91 of the British North America Act which empowered the Dominion Parliament to "make laws for the Peace, Order, and Good Government of Canada, in relation to all Matters not . . . assigned exclusively to the Legislatures of the Provinces." The Privy Council, while recognizing the possibility that wartime emergency would under this general language permit Dominion legislation otherwise *ultra vires,* held that peacetime dislocation was not such a crisis as to authorize legislation otherwise *ultra vires* the Dominion.[129]

The device of "emergency provisions" has not proved necessary in the United States, where the Constitution contains no such special grant of power. The ordinary provisions have been construed by the Supreme Court to permit somewhat more drastic temporary legislation in times of economic emergency than would be approved in normal times, the explanation being that "While emergency does not create power, emergency may

---

[127] See, for examples of invalidity, Bailey v. Drexel Furniture Co., 259 U.S. 20 (1922), which attempted to tax manufacturers using child labor, discussed at pages 325–326 above, and United States v. Constantine, 296 U.S. 287 (1935), in which a federal excise tax of $1000 for dealing in malt liquor contrary to a State law, when the ordinary federal tax was only $25, was held to be an unconstitutional penalty.

[128] Art. 31 *quinquies.*

[129] In re the Board of Commerce Act, [1922] A.C. 191 (P.C.) in which the power discussed was held not to exist.

furnish the occasion for the exercise of power," and "Although an emergency may not call into life a power which has never lived, nevertheless emergency may afford a reason for the exertion of a living power already enjoyed."[130]   To these somewhat cryptic statements of the elastic nature of the United States Constitution, that Court added the observation that the continued existence of an emergency upon which the operation of a statute depends is always open to judicial inquiry.[131]   The Supreme Court has recently prohibited a seizure of the steel industry by the executive branch of the government of the United States, despite a Presidential finding that in the emergency arising out of the military operations in Korea a threatened strike made seizure necessary to assure the continued availability of steel and steel products.[132]

The doctrine of "emergency powers" is a dangerous one.   Military crises appear with increasing frequency.   If, in addition to these defense emergencies, recurrent economic crises also redistribute the allotment of constitutional competence as between the central government and the States and relax other constitutional limitations, the end of a preceding crisis tends to overlap the start of its oncoming successor, the extraordinary becomes normal, and constitutional limitations cease to limit.   Crisis becomes chronic.

There is, to be sure, no organizational remedy for the distortion of constitutional structure caused by crisis government.   It can be inhibited only by the resolute purpose of all branches of the community government to accept the delay and debate of a Parliamentary regime in order to gain its benefits.   Lacking this resolution, continuous crisis government can occur no matter what the form of the constitution.

But the insertion of an express provision for emergency powers is an invitation to use them.   Grants to the community of normal constitutional power should be sufficiently wide to enable it to cope with the normally unexpected.   An unrealistically restricted constitution, with an escape clause for difficult times, is an invitation to trouble.

G. *A Summary of the Question of Community Power over the Economy*

In all the nations studied there appears the same tendency toward integration of the economy without regard to State boundaries.   In each, transactions which at first glance seem local eventually may be expected to call for control by the central government because of a need for national uniformity, and because of discord in State regulation.

But transfer to the community of all economic powers is not a perfect

---

[130] Home Building and Loan Assn. v. Blaisdell, 290 U.S. 398, 426 (1934).
[131] Chastelton v. Sinclair, 264 U.S. 543 (1924), cited in the Home Building case above, at page 442.
[132] Youngstown Sheet & Tube Co. v. Sawyer, 343 U.S. 579 (1952).

formula. It cures the defects of federalism by ending the federalism, substituting a centralized unitary system which brings its own difficulties. Centralization only when essential to national economic unity is the ideal, difficult of attainment, toward which modern constitutions seem to tend.

IV. INTERGOVERNMENTAL IMMUNITIES

Modern states and nations have a tendency to engage in businesses which originally were considered suitable for nongovernmental rather than public activity. Australia has been the scene of a great litigation over the projected nationalization of banks. Canada owns airlines. The State of New York operates a spa with an elaborate hotel, and engages in the mineral-water business; the City of New York operates a busy subway and surface transportation system. Taxation by the central government of such state-owned businesses, or vice versa, is in a way an absurdity, as it means only the shifting of the economic impact of taxation from one private group to another. Nevertheless, as the tendency to public ownership progresses, the taxable corpus in private hands shrinks. In the United States the Supreme Court has been obliged to assume the task of deciding, case by case, on the permissibility of the taxation, by federal statute, of State projects and personnel, and vice versa. These reciprocal immunities do not depend on any particular constitutional clause, but on the general theory that unlimited reciprocal tax power is inconsistent with the independent existence of nation and component States.

Any constitutional provision on this subject must, of necessity, be as vague as those concerning State regulation or taxation of interstate commerce. A statement that neither government shall tax essential governmental operations of the other would leave open to adjudication the question as to what is merely proprietary, and is therefore subject to taxation. Whether the salaries of State and community functionaries are to be taxable by community and State respectively, and whether the bonds of States are to be taxable by the nation, are problems which have occasioned a great deal of debate in the United States. At present, salaries of each class of employees (federal and State) are taxable by the other government, and no evil results have been visible.

As is the case in other conflicts of policy between State and nation, questions of reciprocal tax immunities appear in many diverse forms. In 1940 and 1941 the United States was building large military cantonments in many States, under agreements with contractors by which the United States paid the cost, plus a fixed fee for services. State taxes levied on the sale of lumber to the contractors (which directly added to the costs of the federal government) were upheld by the Supreme Court in 1941.[133]

The tendency of reciprocal tax immunities appears to be in the direction

---

[133] Alabama v. King & Boozer, 314 U.S. 1 (1941).

of diminution.[134] But the question is not solely one of taxation: the State may wish to control the driving of a federal postal vehicle through crowded streets; the community may wish to take State property by eminent domain. An infinite series of such adjustments arises in any federal nation. A solution might be to place in the constitution in question a provision that the community legislature is empowered to determine the respective immunities of the community and State government properties, obligations, activities, and employees from taxation and control by State and community governments respectively.

V. A Summary of This Study of Constitutional Problems Involving Commerce, Transportation, and Customs

An appraisal of economic control in federal nations involves a study of two theories of government affected by one economic fact. The attractive theory of the composite nation, its component States retaining all their individualism save for minimum powers grudgingly surrendered to a community government, comes under the pressure of technological development, population growth, and other factors resulting in the economic interdependence of the whole nation, regardless of political subdivisions. The government of the community, under this pressure, tends to move bit by bit toward the unitary nation, while certain forces in the States, retarding the movement, assert their continued independence.

The line, then, between the economic functions of State and nation is not clear, nor easily defined in a constitutional clause, nor is it fixed. The boundary moves irregularly, depending on an adjustment to the practical needs of the time. The State asserts itself too individualistically and threatens national solidarity. The community undertakes government of wholly local affairs. Some continuing arrangement for reconciling these opposed urges must be devised; and unless the States are to negotiate diplomatically with one another over every local margarine law, reconciliation of State protectionism with community policy must be accomplished by a community agency.

Assuming that the constitution is to lodge this power of adjustment somewhere in the community, is the Parliamentary organ the only place for it? Assuredly such potential legislative control is necessary. When popular demand for change arises, the legislature is the traditional place for the demand to be heard. But is the legislature the only organ to entrust with the function of detailed redefinition of the line between central and local economic control?

Recently one of the Justices of the United States Supreme Court commented, in an opinion concerning State impediments to interstate trade, on the difficulty of reliance on the legislative process alone:

[134] See Powell, "The Waning of Intergovernmental Tax Immunities," 58 Harv. L. Rev. 633 (1945); "The Remnant of Intergovernmental Tax Immunities," 58 id. at 657.

The extent to which state legislation may be allowed to affect the conduct of interstate business in the absence of Congressional action on the subject has long been a vexatious problem. Recently the tendency has been to abandon the earlier limitations and to sustain more freely such state laws on the ground that Congress has power to supersede them with regulation of its own. It is a tempting escape from a difficult question to pass to Congress the responsibility for continued existence of local restraints and obstructions to national commerce. But these restraints are individually too petty, too diversified, and too local to get the attention of a Congress hard pressed with more urgent matters. The practical result is that in default of action by us [the Supreme Court] they will go on suffocating and retarding and Balkanizing American commerce, trade and industry.

I differ basically with my brethren as to whether the inertia of government shall be on the side of restraint of commerce or on the side of freedom of commerce. The sluggishness of government, the multitude of matters that clamor for attention, and the relative ease with which men are persuaded to postpone troublesome decisions, all make inertia one of the most decisive powers in determining the course of our affairs and frequently gives to the established order of things a longevity and vitality much beyond its merits. . . . Our national free intercourse is never in danger of being suddenly stifled by dramatic and sweeping acts of restraint. That would produce its own antidote. Our danger, as the forefathers well knew, is from the aggregate strangling effect of a multiplicity of individually petty and diverse and local regulations. Each may serve some local purpose worthy enough by itself. Congress may very properly take into consideration local policies and dangers when it exercises its power under the commerce clause. But to let each locality conjure up its own dangers and be the judge of the remedial restraints to be clamped onto interstate trade inevitably retards our national economy and disintegrates our national society. It is the movement and exchange of goods that sustain living standards, both of him who produces and of him who consumes. This vital national interest in free commerce among the states must not be jeopardized.[135]

When decision must be made in individual cases, some arbitral organ is necessary. In Australia, Canada, and the United States the courts of law perform the function in most cases, although in a few fields specialized bodies with technical expertness have similar duties, and some criticism of the courts is heard on the ground that they are not equipped to make economic judgments. But the qualities of the judiciary — independence, detachment from political controversy, a habit of scholarly weighing of the contentions of both sides — have made judicial determinations widely re-

[135] Mr. Justice Jackson, concurring in Duckworth v. Arkansas, 314 U.S. 390 (1941) at 400–401. The Court there upheld an Arkansas statute requiring a license for the transport of intoxicants across that State, on a journey from the State of Illinois to the State of Mississippi. Mr. Justice Jackson urged that the Court rest its judgment solely on the Twenty-first Amendment to the Constitution, which grants to the States wide powers to control traffic in intoxicants, as distinguished from commerce in general.

spected and accepted, even in the economic field. If, in this area, a special tribunal were to be created to replace the ordinary courts, its attributes would have to be much the same.

A P P E N D I X   I

Australia

I. GRANTS OF POWER TO THE FEDERAL GOVERNMENT

The Australian Constitution creates a central government of limited powers. The powers of the States, "unless . . . by this Constitution exclusively vested in the Parliament of the Commonwealth or withdrawn from the Parliament of the State, continue as at the establishment of the Commonwealth, or as at the admission or establishment of the State, as the case may be" (§107).

The powers of the Parliament are enumerated in Section 51 in considerable detail. These are not stated as exclusive, and under Section 107 they are therefore concurrent unless a Commonwealth statute and a State statute on the same subject are inconsistent. In that event, Section 109 makes the State statute invalid to the extent of the inconsistency.

The Commonwealth legislative powers under Section 51 extend to " (i) trade and commerce with other countries, and among the States," and this power is stated by Section 98 to extend to "navigation and shipping, and to railways the property of any State." The Commonwealth Parliament is given certain additional regulatory powers by Section 102. Section 51 goes on to grant power over " (ii) taxation; but not so as to discriminate between States or parts of States; . . . (v) Postal, telegraphic, telephonic, and other like services." Besides these three grants of power, which if adequately construed would seem to cover the entire field of commerce, transport, and taxation, there are also in Section 51 subsections granting the Commonwealth powers over navigational aids; fisheries beyond territorial limits; banking (other than State banking) and State banking extending beyond the limits of the State concerned; the incorporation of banks; the issue of paper money; insurance (other than State insurance) and State insurance extending beyond the limits of the State concerned; weights and measures; bills of exchange and promissory notes; bankruptcy and insolvency; copyrights, patents, and trade marks; foreign corporations and trading or financial corporations formed within the limits of the Commonwealth; railway construction and extension in any State with the consent of that State.

There is a final grant under Section 51 (xxxix) covering power over "Matters incidental to the execution of any power vested by this Constitution in the Parliament or in either House thereof, or in the Government of the Commonwealth, or in the Federal judicature, or in any department or officer of the Commonwealth."

The grants of power to the Commonwealth can be characterized as abundant, specific, and detailed in form rather than general, and concurrent with like State powers subject to assumption of exclusive power by the Commonwealth Parliament.

There is no special provision for expanded Commonwealth powers in times of economic crises.

II. LIMITATIONS OF THE POWERS OF THE FEDERAL GOVERNMENT

The constitutional limits on the economic powers of the Commonwealth are of three sorts: the limited nature of the specific grants of power to the Commonwealth, certain detailed limitations respecting specific matters; and a sweeping limitation contained in Section 92.

The history of the *ultra vires* limits on Commonwealth power has been comparable to that in the United States. At first the powers granted to the Commonwealth were somewhat narrowly construed by the Australian courts.[136] In 1920, however, the Commonwealth powers were given the more extended interpretation which an integrated economy makes necessary, even though their exercise began to interfere with what had been considered exclusively State matters.[137]

The specific limitations forbid: taxation which discriminates as between States or parts of States (§51 (ii)); any commercial or revenue preference to a State or part thereof (§99); abridgment of the reasonable use of rivers by a State or its inhabitants (§100); and taxation of State property (§114). (This immunity granted by Section 114 is reciprocal; the same Section exempts Commonwealth property from State taxes.)

However, a more striking limitation on the Commonwealth powers is that contained in the general language of Section 92, a Section which has played a great part in the judicial interpretation of the Australian Constitution. That Section reads (omitting a transitional provision not here significant): ". . . trade, commerce, and intercourse among the States, whether by means of internal carriage or ocean navigation, shall be absolutely free."

This Section, though its historical context shows that it was intended to bar State customs barriers, has, in Australian decisions, come to be a limit both on the Commonwealth and State governments' general legislation. Its limitation on the Commonwealth was announced in 1936 when a Commonwealth statute requiring a licence for all interstate shipments of dried fruits was declared invalid by the Privy Council;[138] and was restated by the same

[136] Kalibia S. S. Owners v. Wilson, 11 C.L.R. 689 (1910).

[137] McArthur's Case, 28 C.L.R. 530, 546–547 (1920); Amalgamated Society of Engineers v. Adelaide Steamship Co., 28 C.L.R. 129 (1920).

[138] James v. Commonwealth of Australia, [1936] A.C. 578.

tribunal, in expressing the opinion that a Commonwealth statute, nationalizing private banks, interfered with the constitutional freedom of trade.[139]

III. Mechanism of Enforcing the Distribution of Powers

As in Canada and in the United States, the judiciary has played the major part in delimiting the permissible spheres of action of federation and State in Australia. While constitutional limitations are, in theory, binding alike on all three branches of the Commonwealth and State governments, the legislatures and executive officials, feeling the pressure of economic events, have tended to respond by enacting and enforcing regulations which strain the seams of constitutionality. An example appears in the *James* litigation, in which State and Commonwealth governments strove to preserve a satisfactory price for dried fruit which had fallen very low in world markets, and in which the courts found both governments had exceeded the limits imposed by Section 92.[140] That these cases apply an express prohibition rather than a principle of *ultra vires* is not a significant distinction here. The point is that the judiciary plays the deciding role in applying constitutional limitations of power.

IV. Powers of the States

The Australian Constitution, predicated on the assumption of originally complete economic power in the States, which has been diminished substantially only to the extent that the Commonwealth Parliament has chosen to pre-empt the field under Sections 51 and 109, presents no problem of original allotment of commerce power to the States. Whether the subject be commerce, transport, and communications, or taxing power, one considers the powers of the State under the Australian Constitution from the position of affirmative restrictions rather than as a study in *ultra vires*.

V. Restrictions on State Powers

These restrictions may be thought of in three classes: those imposed by specific provision in the Constitution, those imposed by the "absolutely free" provision of Section 92, and those imposed under Section 109 because the Commonwealth Parliament has occupied the field and impliedly excluded State legislation.

Limitations on economic legislation imposed by specific provision are very few. The imposition of charges on goods arriving in or leaving the State may only be in such a sum as will pay for executing the inspection charges of the State, and surplus yield must go to the Commonwealth (§112). A State may not tax Commonwealth property (§114).

[139] Bank Nationalization Case, [1950] A.C. 235.
[140] See James v. Cowan, [1932] A.C. 542; James v. Commonwealth, [1936] A.C. 578.

A more significant limitation is Section 92 with its guarantee that trade, commerce and intercourse between the several States shall be absolutely free. This has been used to strike down State economic regulation, much as the commerce clause and the due process clauses have in the United States. See Section III, above, for a discussion of the invalidation by this clause of Commonwealth and State legislation which attempted to stop the fall of the price of dried fruit to the world price level.

VI. SUMMARY

The experience of Australia has shown her need for economic unity, and the impediments to desired Commonwealth legislation caused by originally rather narrow judicial views of the powers incidental to those expressly granted the Commonwealth. It has shown the danger of a clause like the "absolutely free" provision of Section 92, which, inserted to prevent internal tariff barriers, has come to be to some extent an embarrassing guarantee of governmental noninterference in business. It has also shown the inevitability of the judicial function in marking the line between State and Commonwealth. Compared to the Constitution of the United States, the specification of Commonwealth powers in the Australian Constitution is greatly detailed. Yet the decision of specific cases depends, as the Privy Council recognized in the *Bank Nationalization case*,[141] on factors not so much legal as political, social, or economic. Under Australia's Constitution the judiciary has decided these questions of statecraft in a manner sufficiently satisfactory to give that country a workable government.[142]

A P P E N D I X   I I

Canada

I. GRANTS OF POWER TO THE CENTRAL GOVERNMENT

The British North America Act of 1867, as amended, makes complicated and detailed provision for the allotment of economic powers to the Dominion government, but adds a long list of specific powers allotted exclusively to the provincial governments. A recurring difficulty in Canadian constitutional law, which has plagued the judicial organs charged with construction of the British North America Act, has been the inclusion, among the powers stated to be exclusively allotted to the Provinces by Section 92,

---

[141] [1950] A.C. 235.

[142] See, for a recent review of the subject, Stone, "A Government of Laws and Yet of Men, Being a Survey of Half a Century of the Australian Commerce Power," 25 N.Y.U.L. Rev. 451 (1950). For an earlier survey of the Australian constitutional system, see the Report of the Royal Commission on the Constitution (1929).

of matters falling as well within the description of those powers allotted to the Dominion Government by Section 91.

This difficulty of distinction is not a verbal one. It does not result from a lack of attention on the part of the draftsmen to an adequate description of what they wished to allot to the Provinces and what to the Dominion. It derives from the fact that the economic life of a large nation like Canada is not susceptible of fractionalization. The total process by which the material needs of the Canadian people are supplied is not susceptible, by any exercise of verbal ingenuity, of being divided into two categories one of which is placed in the charge of the Provinces and one of which is allotted to the Dominion government. Where either is allotted exclusive power in any part of the economic structure, conflicts of jurisdiction will inevitably arise. Since 1867, when the judiciary was charged with adjudicating the constitutional validity of provincial and Dominion legislation, it has been occupied by the task of determining, case by case, the line between that which is appropriate for the governments of the Provinces.

The two sections of the Canadian Constitution which are most concerned in the economic control of the nation are Section 91, titled "Powers of the Parliament," and Section 92, titled "Exclusive Powers of Provincial Legislatures." The terms of Section 91, taken literally, would appear to be sufficient to give the Dominion Parliament a complete control over the economic life of the country, comparable to that exercised by the Congress of the United States under the commerce clause of its Constitution. Section 91 consists of a preamble, twenty-nine enumerated headings of power, and a concluding paragraph. In the preamble, the Dominion Parliament is authorized ". . . to make Laws for the Peace, Order, and Good Government of Canada, in relation to all Matters not coming within the Classes of Subjects by this Act assigned exclusively to the Legislatures of the Provinces." Thus the Dominion of Canada has the residuary powers, in contrast to the situation in Australia and in the United States where the several States retain the residuary powers not delegated to the central government.

Following this grant of residuary power, occurs this language:

> . . . and for greater Certainty, but not so as to restrict the Generality of the foregoing Terms of this Section, it is hereby declared that (notwithstanding anything in this act) the exclusive Legislative Authority of the Parliament of Canada extends to all Matters coming within the Classes of Subjects next hereinafter enumerated, that is to say: . . .

The exclusive grants then enumerated include the following:

2. The Regulation of Trade and Commerce.
2A. Unemployment Insurance.
3. The Raising of Money by any Mode or System of Taxation.
5. Postal Service.
9. [Various navigation aids.]

10. Navigation and Shipping.
12. Sea Coast and Inland Fisheries.
13. [Interprovincial and foreign ferries.]
14. Currency and Coinage.
15. Banking, Incorporation of Banks, and the Issue of Paper Money.
16. Savings Banks.
17. Weights and Measures.
18. Bills of Exchange and Promissory Notes.
19. Interest.
20. Legal Tender.
21. Bankruptcy and Insolvency.
22. Patents of Invention and Discovery.
23. Copyrights.
27. [The substantive criminal law.]

(Some of these grants might appear not to deal with economic subjects, but they have been utilized by the Dominion, other resources failing, to attempt economic controls over matters otherwise within provincial cognizance.)

Section 91 then goes on to grant exclusive federal legislative authority over: "29. Such Classes of Subjects as are expressly excepted in the Enumeration of the Classes of Subjects by this Act assigned exclusively to the Legislatures of the Provinces."

Section 95 further provides for federal legislative power. This Section gives to each Province the power to make laws in relation to agriculture in the Province and immigration into the Province, but the Parliament of Canada is stated also to have power to make laws in relation to agriculture and immigration and the Dominion legislation is here expressly stated to displace inconsistent provincial legislation.

II. LIMITATIONS ON THE POWER OF THE CENTRAL GOVERNMENT

The Canadian experience has stressed *ultra vires* as the principal limitation on the power of the central government. The inclusion of sixteen headings of exclusive provincial competence has obliged the Privy Council, or other judicial body passing upon the validity of any given piece of Dominion legislation, to decide whether the legislation in question deals for example with "the regulation of trade and commerce" or "property and civil rights in the Province." As it is a practical impossibility to make a Dominion regulation of trade and commerce of any sort which does not to some extent concern property within a Province, it is obviously necessary to choose the one or the other. Judicial construction has thus in Canada retained within the Provinces considerable areas of economic activity which are exempt from Dominion interference. The desirability of this exemption is a matter of policy, involving the choice of the benefits of local autonomy balanced against the benefits of competence in a central government.

III. The Mechanism of Enforcing the Distribution of Power

As in Australia and the United States, the judiciary in Canada has become, by its refusal to enforce invalid legislation, the means of effectuating the constitutional division between the State and federal powers. The complexity of this process under the Canadian Constitution can best be understood by examining a case in which the Privy Council, in 1950, upheld a Dominion statute barring the importation of margarine, and in which it found another part of the same statute, forbidding local transactions in margarine, to be beyond the powers of the Dominion because exclusively within those of the Provinces.[143] The statute in question provided that "no person shall manufacture, import into Canada, or offer, sell or have in his possession for sale, any oleomargarine, margarine, butterine, or other substitutes for butter . . ." The Dominion contended that this Dominion statute was valid as a regulation of trade and commerce, that it was legislation relating to criminal law, that it was a law for the peace, order, good government of Canada, relating to a matter not exclusively within the power of the Provinces under Section 92, that it was a law relating to agriculture in the Provinces within Section 95. The Privy Council felt that the statute related to civil rights within the Provinces, and therefore, insofar as it prohibited manufacture, offer, sale or possession, it was beyond the powers of the Dominion Parliament. The prohibition of importation was within the powers of the Dominion. To the difficult question raised by the Dominion contention that this was a criminal statute and therefore within Dominion powers, the Privy Council answered that the "pith and substance" of the statute was the protection of the dairy industry, not the criminal law. This phrase, recurring in judicial discussions both in Canada and in Australia, is here quoted because it illustrates the impossibility of finding a verbal formula which will solve the question of choice.

IV. Powers of States

Under Section 92 the exclusive powers of the Provinces include:

2. [Direct taxation within the Province in order to raise revenue for provincial purposes.]
9. [The issuing of licenses for various callings in order to raise revenue for provincial or local purposes.]
10. Local Works and Undertakings other than such as are of the following Classes:
    a. Lines of Steam or other Ships, Railways, Canals, Telegraphs, and other Works and Undertakings connecting the Province with any other or others of the Provinces, or extending beyond the Limits of the Province.

[143] In re A Reference as to the Validity of Section 5 (A) of the Dairy Industry Act, [1951] A.C. 179.

   b. Lines of Steam Ships between the Province and any British or
      Foreign Country.
   c. Such Works as, although wholly situate within the Province, are
      before or after their Execution declared by the Parliament of
      Canada to be for the general Advantage of Canada or for the
      Advantage of Two or more of the Provinces.
 11. The Incorporation of Companies with Provincial Objects.
 13. Property and Civil Rights in the Province.
 16. Generally all Matters of a merely local or private Nature in the
     Province.

Section 122 provides that "The Customs and Excise Laws of each Province shall, subject to the Provisions of this Act, continue in force until altered by the Parliament of Canada."

The Provinces in Canada therefore have considerable legislative power over commerce, transportation and communications, and taxation. Difficulty has been created, however, by the fact that the grants of provincial powers, in terms exclusive, are susceptible of interpretation so as to conflict with the grants of Dominion powers.

V. RESTRICTIONS ON STATE POWERS

The principal source of restrictions on provincial power in Canada is the stated exclusiveness of the list of Dominion powers in Section 91. As pointed out above, this has made the judiciary the agency which makes the policy determinations as to which of two overlapping grants of power, that to the Province or that to the Dominion, shall be effective at any given instance.

As in other federal systems, Canada has been troubled by the problem of finding effective means to stop protectionism, the creation of what amount to customs barriers by unacknowledged means, for the benefit of the economic life of one Province at the cost of the Dominion as a whole. This question, and the whole problem of Dominion-Provincial relations, was the subject of a comprehensive study by a royal commission which reported in a three-volume work in 1940. On the protectionism question, the commission reported (in Book 2, pp. 62 ff.) that as the federal Parliament alone was authorized to impose customs and excise taxes and indirect taxation generally, the more obvious forms of customs protection were not possible. But taxation appearing on the surface to be for local revenue purposes could be devised in such a way as to bear more heavily on outside products than on local products. The commission pointed out that in practice it is extremely difficult for a court to disentangle legitimate local measures from those which are indirectly calculated to discriminate against the products of other Provinces. The commission thus questioned as an appropriate remedy for Canada the constitutional practice in the United States under which the courts, on the basis of criteria essentially economic, determine when the State has overstepped the boundaries of permissible taxation.

A commentary on this might be that, in the first place, Canadian courts appear to be in exactly this situation at the present time, and, in the second place, the available alternative is not apparent.

VI. COMMENTARY

The Canadian Constitution, and judicial and economic experience under it, demonstrate the difficulties which arise when a long series of headings of economic power is allotted to the federal government, and another long and detailed series to the governments of the member States, and each is stated to be exclusive. As the economy of the Dominion is not susceptible of such dissection with any measure of success by verbal definition, there remains for some organ the task of determining in each instance whether the allotment of power to the Province or to the Dominion shall give way. Concurrence of power between Dominion and Province, with the Dominion having a pre-emptive power of excluding provincial legislation, as occurs under Section 95 of the Canadian Constitution concerning agriculture and immigration, seems on the whole an easier system to administer. However, it contains possibilities of greater Dominion domination than is possible under the present system in Canada in which "States' rights" are rather strongly protected.[144]

APPENDIX III

Germany

Basic Law for the Federal Republic of Germany

I. GRANTS OF POWER TO FEDERAL GOVERNMENT IN ECONOMIC MATTERS

Powers granted to the federal government are partly exclusive, by constitutional provision; partly concurrent, until the federal government chooses to act and to exclude the Länder from legislative competence in the particular area in question. By Article 70 the residuary powers are left with the Länder. However, in view of the extent of the exclusive and other powers of the federal government, the areas remaining to the Länder in which the federal government cannot legislate are actually very small. See Section II below.

Article 73 gives to the federation exclusive legislative powers over:

[144] Federal-State relations in Canada are discussed in the Report of the Royal Commission on Dominion-Provincial Relations (1940). See also Jennings, "Constitutional Interpretations: The Experience of Canada," 51 Harv. L. Rev. 1 (1937); and McWhinney, "The Role of the Privy Council in Judicial Review of the Canadian Constitution," 5 Vand. L. Rev. 746 (1952).

(3) freedom of movement, passports, immigration and emigration, and extradition;

(4) currency, money and coinage, weights and measures, as well as computation and time;

(5) the unity of the territory as regards customs and commerce, commercial and navigation agreements, the freedom of traffic in goods, and the exchanges of goods and payments with foreign countries, including customs and frontier control;

(6) federal railroads and air traffic;

(7) postal and telecommunication services;

(9) industrial property rights, copyrights and publication rights; . . .

Under Article 105 (1) the federation has the exclusive power to legislate on customs and fiscal monopolies.

It is noteworthy that if the federal legislature finds it convenient, Article 71 authorizes it to pass a law permitting the Länder to legislate to whatever extent the federal legislature chooses in any of these areas.

Article 74 defines the concurrent legislative powers concerning, among other things, economic matters, including the following:

(11) the law relating to economic matters (mining, industry, supply of power, crafts, trades, commerce, banking and stock exchanges, private insurance);

(12) labor law, including labor relations, protection of workers, employment exchanges and agencies, as well as social insurance, including unemployment insurance;

(15) transfer of land, natural resources and means of production into public ownership or other forms of publicly controlled economy;

(16) prevention of the abuse of economic power;

(17) promotion of agricultural and forest production, safeguarding of the supply of food, the import and export of agricultural and forest products, deep sea and coastal fishing, and the preservation of the coasts;

(18) dealings in real estate, land law and matters concerning agricultural leases, housing, settlements and homesteads;

(20) protection with regard to traffic in food and stimulants as well as in necessities of life, in fodder, in agricultural and forest seeds and seedlings, and protection of trees and plants against diseases and pests;

(21) ocean and coastal shipping as well as aids to navigation, inland shipping, meteorological services, sea waterways and inland waterways used for general traffic;

(22) road traffic, motor transport, and construction and maintenance of long distance highways;

(23) railroads other than federal railroads, except mountain railroads.

Under Article 105 (2) the concurrent legislative power also includes:

1. excise taxes and taxes on transactions, with the exception of taxes with localized application, in particular of the taxes on the

acquisition of real estate, on increments in value, and for fire
protection;

2.   taxes on income, on property, on inheritances and on donations;

3.   taxes on real estate and businesses (*Realsteuern*), with the exception of the fixing of the tax rates, if it [the federation] claims the
taxes in whole or in part to cover federal expenditure or if the
conditions laid down in Article 72, paragraph (2), exist.

Article 72 makes provision for those instances in which the federal legislature chooses to act in the area of concurrent powers. As soon as the
federation acts in any given area, the Länder are excluded from legislative
authority to that extent. Article 72 (2) then follows with what is at least
in form a limitation upon the federation authority in the concurrent field.
The federation is given a right to legislate on these matters only to the extent that a need for a federal rule exists because (1) the matter cannot be
effectively dealt with by the legislation of individual Länder, or (2) dealing
with a matter by a Land law might prejudice the interests of other Länder
or of the entire community, or (3) the maintenance of legal or economic
unity, especially the maintenance of uniformity of living conditions beyond
the territory of a Land, necessitates it. These qualifications are necessarily
somewhat indefinite. As is the case in the constitutions of every other federal nation, when an effort is made to define the area in which the policy of
the individual States must give way before the policy of the central government, indefinite expressions must be used. The decision of specific instances
must be left to some organ which will weigh, as best it is able, economic
and social factors to determine whether the interests of the State or the
nation shall predominate in the particular instance.

II. LIMITATIONS ON THE POWER OF THE FEDERAL GOVERNMENT

In the economic field, the powers of the federal government under the
Basic Law seem to be so sweeping that none of the constitutional problems
of *ultra vires* which have appeared in the United States, Canada, and Australia, should trouble the federal government. The flexibility of the grants
of power seems to be complete in that the federal legislature may delegate
legislative competence in the exclusive field if it sees fit, and may withdraw
from the Länder legislative competence in the concurrent areas when the
federal legislature wishes.

There is as yet no accumulation of judicial determinations which would
demonstrate whether the courts may give an expanded construction to any
of the provisions on the basic rights in Articles 1 to 19 of the Constitution
which might tend to restrict the legislative competence of the federation, as
for a time the due process clause did in the United States. The wording of
the provisions on basic rights seems as though it would counter any such
tendency. Nor is there any accumulation of decisions under Article 72 to
indicate how much of a limit it will impose on the central government.

III. The Mechanism of Enforcing the Distribution of Powers

The Basic Law makes explicit what has been proved by experience to be necessary in Canada, Australia, and the United States, that is, the function of a judicial tribunal to define the respective limitations of member State and community powers. However, the form of the grants of power in economic matters to the federal government is such that under Article 72, in almost any case of an assertion of economic control by a Land government which the federal legislature deems undesirable, the federal legislature may displace the Land statute by a federal enactment. In this way the federal legislature serves as a practical engine of enforcing the distribution of powers.

IV. Powers of States

In the economic field, the powers of the Länder are in general those which the federation chooses to allot. The inclusive total of the federation's exclusive and concurrent powers, taken together with the powers of the federation to delegate its exclusive powers and to withdraw concurrent powers, in effect leaves the Federation in a position to utilize the Länder as administrative agencies to handle in a decentralized manner whatever economic functions the federation finds it most expedient thus to delegate. Such concentration of federal power is inconsistent with the economic independence of the Länder; but economic independence is again in its turn inconsistent with the high degree of economic integration characteristic of the modern industrial state.

V. Restrictions on State Powers

In practical effect, the Basic Law restricts the State economic powers to those matters which the federal legislature wishes. The problems which have arisen in Australia, Canada, and the United States, when the several member States have attempted to enforce some local preferential law for the benefit of that State, which operates to fractionalize the community as a whole, need not arise under the German Constitution because of the collective powers vested in the federal legislature. Long experience with customs unions among the several German States may have indicated the wisdom of this course. The exclusive grant of customs and fiscal monopolies to the federation by Article 105 (1), and the concurrent grant of tax power of other sorts under 105 (2), taken in connection with the pre-emptive powers of the federal government under Article 72 (2), give to the federal government a prohibitory competence with respect to local taxation which can eliminate fiscal parochialism no matter what its form.

VI. Conclusions

The life of the Basic Law of the Federal Republic of Germany has not thus far been sufficiently long for mature judgment on its economic qualities. It could be characterized as a constitution of presently and potentially centralized economic power. Its clauses will solve, in favor of the federal government, many of the disputes which have arisen in other federal nations. This resolution depends upon a choice of policy in each case as it arises.

APPENDIX IV

Switzerland

I. Grants of Power to the Confederation

Under Article 3 of the Swiss Constitution, all non-delegated powers are reserved to the cantons. However, the grants of economic power in other sections are so sweeping that the reserve powers are necessarily very limited.

By unusually numerous separate provisions on economic competence, the Swiss Confederation has been given broad powers over commerce, transport, communications, customs, and considerable powers over taxation. Article 64 empowers the Confederation to legislate with respect to "all legal relations pertaining to commerce and to trade in securities (law of obligations, including law relating to commerce and to exchange)". Under Articles 24-*ter,* 26, 37-*bis,* and 37-*ter,* the Confederation is authorized to legislate concerning transportation by water, rail, road, or air. Article 36 gives full federal competence over matters of posts and telecommunications.

The problem which has disturbed other federal states, as to whether federal authority over commerce includes the authority to regulate child labor and other labor conditions in factories, will not arise in Switzerland because Article 34 gives to the Confederation express powers of regulation concerning the utilization of children in factories and the working hours of adult persons in industry. Article 34-*ter* authorizes the Confederation "to promulgate general principles regarding trade." Article 39 gives the Confederation broad banking powers and powers over currency. The powers of federal taxation under Articles 41-*ter* and 42 are somewhat less general than those in other federal states. Article 42 contemplates a system of shared taxation with the cantons.

Notable, in a series of additions to Article 31, are grants of power to the Confederation to take measures to prevent economic crises. Unique among the constitutions of the five nations covered by this study is this express arrangement for unusual economic circumstances.

II. LIMITATIONS ON THE POWERS OF THE CENTRAL GOVERNMENT

Article 31 guarantees the "freedom of commerce and of business . . . throughout the Confederation." This rather wide and indefinite guarantee is, however, qualified by a number of reservations including "e. Regulation of the practice of commerce and business, regarding taxation of business enterprises and regarding the use of highways. Such provisions may, however, not violate the principle of free trade and business." As will be pointed out, the *ultra vires* limitation on the central government which operates in other federal nations is judicially inoperative in Switzerland.

III. THE MECHANISM OF ENFORCING THE DISTRIBUTION OF POWER

Neither absence of grants of power, nor the express prohibition of Section 31, is effective in invalidating through the courts an act of legislation of the federal legislature. The Federal Court set up under Part III of the Constitution is required to treat federal statutes as valid, although it may declare the invalidity of cantonal legislation (Art. 113). Under these circumstances, Switzerland presents no such picture as do Australia, Canada, Germany, and the United States, where the appropriate judicial organ passes upon the validity not only of State but also of community legislation.

IV. THE POWERS OF THE STATES

The sweeping character of the powers entrusted to the federal government in Switzerland, together with the fact that federal legislation cannot be challenged in court, tends in theory to reduce the powers of the cantons to a very small portion of the State power in other federations. While this is true as a constitutional matter, in fact much administration is delegated to the cantons. Centralized power but decentralized administration characterize much of the actual operation of the Swiss Constitution.

V. SUMMARY

Among the five federal systems studied in this analysis, Switzerland is unique in its sweeping federal powers, in its provisions for federal economic legislation in the event of economic crisis, and in the judicially unchallengable nature of its federal legislation. The frequency with which the Swiss Constitution has been amended, providing for additional federal powers, tends to add to the impression of a highly unitary nation so far as economic life is concerned. In Switzerland political control over federal legislation takes the place of the judicial control in the larger federal states studied. Under Article 89, on the demand of 30,000 qualified voters or of eight cantons, a federal legislative resolution of general binding effect must be submitted to popular referendum (except for certain urgent resolutions effective only for a limited time). In this way popular desires concerning unpopular federal laws can have a direct effect. The small size of the country and the relatively small number of qualified voters make this procedure possible in Switzerland, although it would be impractical in a larger state.

A P P E N D I X   V

United States

I. POWERS OF THE FEDERAL GOVERNMENT WITH REGARD TO COMMERCE, TRANSPORTATION AND CUSTOMS

The principal grants of economic power to the federal government in the Constitution of the United States are made in Article I, Section 8:

The Congress shall have Power To lay and collect Taxes, Duties, Imposts and Excises, to pay the Debts and provide for the common Defence and general Welfare of the United States; but all Duties, Imposts and Excises shall be uniform throughout the United States;
To borrow money on the credit of the United States;
To regulate Commerce with foreign Nations, and among the several States, and with the Indian Tribes;
To establish an uniform Rule of Naturalization, and uniform Laws on the subject of Bankruptcies throughout the United States;
To coin Money, regulate the Value thereof, and of foreign Coin, and fix the Standard of Weights and Measures; . . .
To establish Post Offices and post Roads; . . .
To make all Laws which shall be necessary and proper for carrying into Execution the foregoing Powers, and all other Powers vested by this Constitution in the Government of the United States, or in any Department or Officer thereof.

The characteristics of these grants of power are brevity and generality. Under them the federal government exercises power not only over commodities which pass from one State to another but also over the means of interstate carriage. As early as 1819, the power of Congress to incorporate a bank was challenged as *ultra vires* any specific power delegated in the Constitution. The Supreme Court of the United States, in a leading opinion which has greatly influenced the broad construction of the various economic clauses of the Constitution, found that the creation of a federal bank was within the delegated powers.[145] The unsuccessful argument that the creation of a federally chartered bank was beyond the powers of the federal government was substantially rested upon the Tenth Amendment to the Constitution, which reads: "The powers not delegated to the United States by the Constitution, nor prohibited by it to the States, are reserved to the States respectively, or to the people." Chief Justice Marshall, in sustaining

[145] McCulloch v. Maryland, 4 Wheat. 316, 407–411 (1819).

the federal power to create a bank despite the lack of any specific provision in the Constitution, remarked:

> In considering this question, then, we must never forget that it is a *constitution* we are expounding.
>
> Although, among the enumerated powers of government, we do not find the word "bank" or "incorporation," we find the great powers to lay and collect taxes; to borrow money; to regulate commerce; to declare and conduct a war; and to raise and support armies and navies . . . [I]f it may with great reason be contended that a government, entrusted with such ample powers, on the due execution of which the happiness and prosperity of the nation so vitally depends, must also be entrusted with ample means for their execution. . . . But the Constitution of the United States has not left the right of Congress to employ the necessary means for the execution of the powers conferred on the government to general reasoning. To its enumeration of powers is added that of making "all laws which shall be necessary and proper, for carrying into execution the foregoing powers, and all other powers vested by this constitution, in the government of the United States, or in any department thereof."

Upon the broad construction so given by the Court to the aggregate of powers entrusted to the federal government, the United States has effected a wide control over all aspects of the economic life of the nation. For example, through an interstate commerce commission it controls the operations, services, and charges of railroads. Federal legislation also controls highway trucking, airplane services, and inland and foreign shipping. In the field of communications, all radio is federally licensed, and telephone communications, even when the message begins and ends within the borders of a single State, fall within the regulatory power of Congress to the extent that it chooses to exercise it.

The federal government, aside from certain specific restrictions which will be discussed below, and which are limited in their application, has an unrestricted power of taxation. By what has been considered a somewhat technical ruling, the federal power to impose an income tax was declared unconstitutional in 1895.[146] However in 1913 the Constitution was changed, by Amendment Sixteen, to authorize this form of tax. The federal government, either now or in the past, has taxed real property, cigarettes, playing cards and many different articles of luxury, individual and corporate incomes, inheritances, and a great number of other sources.

The grant of power to the Congress to regulate commerce "with foreign nations, and among the several States" appears at first glance to be a limited grant, and to leave outside the federal competence that great mass of extractive, industrial, and commercial activity carried on within the boundaries of a single State. Two factors have tended to eliminate almost completely any limit on the federal powers so granted. One of these is the

---

[146] Pollock v. Farmers' Loan and Trust Co., 157 U.S. 429 (1895).

attitude of the Supreme Court of the United States exemplified by its holding that the meaning of "commerce" is extraordinarily inclusive, covering,
in addition to traffic in goods, such collateral activities as the passage of
individuals from state to state,[147] insurance,[148] and many other activities
not appearing at first to be "commercial" in the strict sense.

The second factor is the Supreme Court's interpretation of what constitutes regulation of commerce "among the several states." The Court has
held that purely local transactions, occurring exclusively within the borders
of a single State, are within the competence of the federal government if
they affect commerce which is truly interstate. Thus, the federal government was able to regulate railway rates for traffic entirely within the borders
of a State. This was because of the adverse effect on commerce of rates
set at different levels by different States; a trip entirely within a state setting low rates was, for example, cheaper than a trip of the same length into
that State from another State imposing higher rates for travel within its borders. This principle, added to the wide construction given to the word
commerce, has given to Congress control over many activities which might
not appear to be covered by the grant of power contained in the commerce
clause. For example, the power of the United States has been sustained
when it was exercised to forbid a farmer growing more than a specified
quota of grain, for his use upon his own farm.[149] The United States has
also issued regulations with regard to the wages of persons engaged in manufacture of goods "for interstate commerce," [150] and with regard to the
wages of elevator operators in a building belonging to a corporation engaged in interstate commerce.[151]

The federal power has increased with the passage of time, the development of new means of transport and communications, and the increased
need for the interchange of commodities. It was greatly accelerated after
the middle of the 1930's by the need for federal control of economic matters
which, as it was found, could not be adequately regulated by diversified state
action.

As pointed out above, under the Tenth Amendment the residual powers
of government remain in the States. However, the effect of this amendment
has been merely to indicate that some powers were intended to be left with
the States, without specifically identifying those powers. Recent constitutional interpretation by the Supreme Court has been such that the residual
powers of the States have not, since 1936, been held to prevent legislation
by the federal government.

In the economic field, the federal powers are to a great extent potentially,
but not necessarily, exclusive of powers of the States over the same matters.
The limitations on the powers of the States will be discussed more fully

[147] Edwards v. California, 314 U.S. 160 (1941).
[148] United States v. Southeastern Underwriters, 322 U.S. 533 (1944).
[149] Wickard v. Filburn, 317 U.S. 111 (1942).
[150] United States v. Darby, 312 U.S. 100 (1941).
[151] Borden v. Borella, 325 U.S. 679 (1945).

below. It should be pointed out here, however, that in practice the States exercise a wide jurisdiction over trade and commerce, transportation and communication, and also a wide taxing power. In a great many fields this is because the federal government has not exercised in full its potential powers, thus leaving the States free to act. Thus, in fields in which the federal government has not acted, the federal powers over economic matters are held by the Supreme Court to be exclusive only when their nature is such that the Court considers they should only be regulated by measures uniform throughout the country.[152] On the other hand, where the federal government has acted in a particular field pursuant to its commerce powers, the Supreme Court has held that Congress may ensure the exclusiveness of its exercise of power in that field by so declaring, either expressly or by implication, in its legislation.[153]

II. LIMITATIONS ON FEDERAL POWER

The express constitutional limitations imposed on the federal government in the economic field are very few. Three clauses of Article I, Section 9, recite the principal limitations:

[Cl. 4] No Capitation, or other direct, Tax shall be laid, unless in Proportion to the Census or Enumeration herein before directed to be taken.

[Cl. 5] No Tax or Duty shall be laid on Articles exported from any State.

[Cl. 6] No Preference shall be given by any Regulation of Commerce or Revenue to the Ports of one State over those of another: nor shall Vessels bound to, or from, one State, be obliged to enter, clear, or pay Duties in another.

The Fifth Amendment to the Constitution provides that "no person shall be . . . deprived of life, liberty or property without due process of law; nor shall private property be taken for public use without just compensation."

The slight employment given to these clauses in recent years is shown by the fact that no important federal statute concerning economic matters has been held unconstitutional on such grounds since 1936.[154]

---

[152] Southern Pacific Co. v. Arizona, 325 U.S. 761 (1945). Here the Supreme Court held invalid, as conflicting with the general delegation of commerce power to the United States, an Arizona law limiting the number of cars in trains operating within the state.

[153] Cloverleaf Butter Co. v. Patterson, 315 U.S. 148 (1942).

[154] In the years 1937–1953 inclusive, the United States Supreme Court has held unconstitutional only the following federal statutes: an act creating a presumption that firearms found on a convict had been shipped in interstate commerce, held invalid under the Fifth Amendment in Tot v. United States, 319 U.S. 463 (1943); an act barring certain named persons from federal employment, held invalid under Art. I, §9, Cl. 3, as a Bill of Attainder in United States v. Lovett, 328 U.S. 303 (1946); an act providing, in vague and self-contradictory terms, for the inspection by federal officers of factory premises, held invalid apparently under the Fifth Amendment in United States v. Cardiff, 394 U.S. 174 (1952).

III. Enforcement of Distribution of Powers

The courts in the United States, both federal and State, pass on the validity under the federal Constitution of federal and State legislation involved in suits which are brought before them. The court of last resort for such constitutional review is the Supreme Court of the United States. Thus it is the judiciary, and especially the Supreme Court, which interprets the Constitution to determine the distribution of economic powers between the State and federal governments.

The judicial criteria in making this interpretation are almost exclusively those of economic policy. In the application of these criteria the Court has shown considerable tactical adaptability, and has permitted the federal commerce power to expand to meet increasing needs, both permanent and temporary, for federal control. Thus, although the Constitution contains no "emergency clause," the Court has upheld federal legislation which is more drastic in economic crises than in ordinary times. It has stated that the existence of an emergency should be a consideration in construing the extent of constitutional grants of federal power and, consequently, in determining the scope of the power of the States.[155]

IV. Powers of the States and Restrictions on Those Powers

The powers of the States with regard to commerce are the residue remaining after the constitutional grants to the federal government and prohibitions to the States. This principle is expressed in the Tenth Amendment to the Constitution, quoted above. Accordingly, to determine the extent of state commerce powers, there must be considered: (a) the constitutional prohibitions relating to those powers; and (b) the impact on State powers of grants of power to the federal government.

A. *Constitutional Prohibitions on State Power*

The principal restrictions of State economic power are contained in Article I, Section 10, of the Constitution, which provides as follows:

[Cl. 1]   No State shall . . . coin Money; emit Bills of Credit; make any Thing but gold and silver Coin a Tender in Payment of Debts; pass any . . . Law impairing the Obligation of Contracts.

[Cl. 2]   No State shall, without the Consent of the Congress lay any Imposts or Duties on Imports or Exports, except what may be absolutely necessary for executing its inspection Laws: and the net Produce of all Duties and Imposts, laid by any State on Imports or Exports, shall be for the Use of the Treasury of the United States; and all such Laws shall be subject to the Revision and Control of the Congress.

[Cl. 3]   No State shall, without the Consent of Congress, lay any

---

[155] Home Building and Loan Assn. v. Blaisdell, 290 U.S. 398 (1934).

duty of Tonnage, . . . enter into any Agreement or Compact with another State, or with a foreign Power. . . .

A more important restriction has developed from the general language of the Fourteenth Amendment, the applicable portion of which reads:

No State shall make or enforce any law which shall abridge the privileges or immunities of citizens of the United States; nor shall any State deprive any person of life, liberty, or property, without due process of law; nor deny to any person within its jurisdiction the equal protection of the laws.

This amendment came into force immediately after the Civil War, with the primary intention of protecting the newly enfranchised Negroes in the Southern States. However, it came to be applied very widely in the economic field, resulting in the Supreme Court's invalidation of many State statutes on the ground that they interfered to an unreasonable degree with the freedom of economic life, and so constituted a deprivation of "liberty or property" without "due process of law." [156] The economic dislocations which began in 1929 and continued through the early 1930's brought a change in the attitude of the Supreme Court toward the due process clause. Many forms of State regulation, including the regulation of sales, prices, wages and hours of labor, which in some cases had previously been declared invalid under that clause, were now found proper. During the last two decades, the States have come to enjoy much more freedom to engage in economic legislation than during the two preceding decades.

B. *Impact of Federal Powers on State Powers*

There are also inhibitions on State action which arise out of the constitutional delegation of commerce powers to the federal government. Soon after the adoption of the Constitution the Supreme Court declared that the commerce clause created a nation-wide area of free trade by removing State lines as impediments to interstate commerce.[157] Not all State laws affecting or even directly regulating interstate commerce are invalid under this principle, but a limitation upon State power has been imposed by the Supreme Court through balancing national against local interest. The great problem has been, however, to draw the line between these interests. In 1852 the Supreme Court announced the doctrine that matters which should be subject only to regulations which are uniform throughout the country are within the exclusive province of the federal government.[158] Later tests applied by the Supreme Court have made the validity of State action depend on whether the State law was a "burden" on commerce, or a "substantial" or

[156] It should be pointed out that the Fourteenth Amendment applies only to State action, while the Fifth Amendment (referred to earlier), which includes identical "due process" language, applies only to federal action.

[157] Gibbons v. Ogden, 9 Wheat. 1 (1824).

[158] By dictum in the case of Colley v. Portwardens, 12 How. 299.

"undue" burden, or whether the effect on commerce was "direct" or "indirect," or whether the regulation was imposed "on" interstate commerce itself. By all these tests the courts have weighed conflicting local and national interests. This has meant that the States' attempts to exclude out-of-state products, or to prevent the removal from their territory of goods produced therein, have been found invalid.[159] State laws limiting the number of railroad cars in a train,[160] or requiring the segregation of passengers in interstate motor busses according to race,[161] have been held to impinge upon commerce in fields where the Court has considered that any regulation should be uniform throughout the country. A State law requiring cabooses to be placed at the end of freight trains has been held to have a lesser impact upon interstate transportation and to be valid.[162]

In addition to applying these standards of interpretation, the Supreme Court has also accepted the findings of Congress as to whether, in the regulation of certain fields, there should be uniformity throughout the country. Where such a finding has been made expressly in a Federal statute, or where the Court has inferred such a finding from the legislative language, it has held any State action in the field concerned to be excluded.[163]

Fundamentally, the same problem presented by State regulation of interstate commerce is presented by State taxation of such commerce. Since a larger part of the economic life of the United States has come to involve more than one State, withdrawal of State power to tax interstate commerce would mean impoverishment of many local governments. On the other hand, the States cannot be permitted to tax interstate commerce as they please, since taxes are a potent form of regulation. In determining when interstate commerce is subject to State taxation, the Supreme Court has adopted various verbalizations, such as that "direct" burdens on interstate commerce by taxation are invalid while "indirect" burdens are permissible. For example, in *McCarroll v. Dixie Greyhound Lines,* 309 U.S. 176 (1940), the Court held invalid a state tax on the gasoline in the tank of a motor bus traveling across the State on an interstate journey.[164]

V. Summary

The provisions contained in the United States Constitution concerning regulation of commerce, transportation, and customs consist of a few broad expressions of principle. They grant to Congress a largely unlimited control over the nation's economic affairs, but permit the States certain regula-

[159] Pennsylvania v. West Virginia, 262 U.S. 553 (1923); Dean Milk Co. v. City of Madison, 340 U.S. 349 (1951).
[160] Southern Pacific Co. v. Arizona, 325 U.S. 761 (1945).
[161] Morgan v. Virginia, 328 U.S. 373 (1946).
[162] Terminal Railroad v. Brotherhood, 318 U.S. 1 (1943).
[163] Cloverleaf Butter Co. v. Patterson, 315 U.S. 148 (1942).
[164] See also Freeman v. Hewitt, 329 U.S. 249 (1946); McGoldrick v. Berwind-White Co. Mining Co., 309 U.S. 33 (1940); General Trading Company v. State Tax Commission, 322 U.S. 335 (1944).

tion and taxation of commerce. Some of these State powers, however, may continue only so long as Congress has not forbidden their exercise.

The determination of the multitude of individual questions as to the respective powers of State and federal governments is left to the judiciary. This has been criticized as a system which allots improper power to the judicial branch.[165] In the nature of things, however, complete definition of the respective spheres is too detailed a function to be performed by legislation, and, all the more, to be written in a constitution. Therefore, this essential function of dividing the realms of federal and State governments, if not performed by the judiciary, must be performed by another federal organ having most of the same attributes. Public confidence in the federal judiciary has led to public acceptance of the rather extraordinary economic function which it performs in the United States. The successful operation of the entire system is dependent upon such confidence as well as upon the ability of the courts.

[165] See, for example, the remarks of Mr. Justice Black and others, dissenting in the McCarroll case, discussed above, page 356.

STUDY 7

Public Finance

I. General Problems of Federal Finance

Among the problems presenting themselves for solution in any federal system one of the most important is that of finances, of the raising of revenues wherewith to pay for the various functions of the several levels of government. The joint impact of wars, depressions, and of an increasingly technologized economy has brought broadened social services and thereby has enlarged the scope of the fiscal system to an extent undreamed of fifty years ago. Far exceeding all the numerous costs of the welfare state, the greatest burden of the modern state is the cost of war. In the United States today, nearly 85 per cent of the federal budget is allocated to providing for the veterans and debts of past wars and to preparation for the possibility of a future one. Debts, pensions, and armaments are likewise crushing the nations of Western Europe, where damage must be repaired, refugees resettled, and the rest. Even neutral Switzerland has three times in a century devoted more than half of her public revenue to mobilization. Since the European Community is to be first of all a community for defense, it is clear that merely the taking over of those expenditures which relate to defense in its various ramifications means that the community of Europe will be a primary factor in the public finance of the nations therein united. The community will be carrying approximately half of the fiscal burden. Hence its tax resources must be very substantial, if the Union is to succeed.

Taxation in federal systems can be organized in different ways, depending upon various circumstances, and the experience of existing federal states is quite varied. Broadly speaking, there are three variants: (1) all taxes are raised by the component States, and a fixed contribution is made to the federal authorities to cover their requirements; (2) all taxes are raised by the federal authorities and fixed contributions are made therefrom to the States, and (3) the power to tax is divided between the federal government and the component States. (The same broad division applies, *ceteris paribus*, to the matter of debts (loans)). Characteristically, most federal systems have opted for the third alternative; it is the alternative most nearly in keeping with the basic outlook of federalism. A certain amount of fiscal autonomy is required to maintain the balance between central and local power.

The third alternative, in turn, allows for some broad divisions. For such a division of the power to tax may be accomplished either by dividing the actual tax resources, such as income for one, property for the other, or by leaving each unit free to raise any kind of tax, or again by "sharing" the taxes, or by a combination of these methods. In actual practice, federal states display the greatest variety of practices, and hence it is not easy to be very certain as to what is best. Speaking generally, experience in the several federal states under examination suggests a broad grant of power to raise taxes (as in the United States Constitution) without qualifications.

When it comes to the problem of collecting these taxes, all federations claim the *right* to organize their own tax-gathering agencies. At times, this appears as a residuary right. This is the case when the established fiscal systems of the component States are fully developed and can be used. This requires, however, that adequate supervisory power be constitutionally provided for the executive.[1] Switzerland and Germany have thus operated in the past, and with adequate results.

This problem is tied in with that of equal taxation throughout the federal territory. It is of course a universally acknowledged principle in all federal systems that no taxes should be adopted discriminating among the citizens of the several States. But if the tax-collecting machinery is markedly less efficient in one State than another, then a delegation of federal authority would actually result in discriminatory treatment and would have to be supplanted by federal administration, unless the defect can be remedied through supervisory efforts.

Another problem of central importance for any tax system is whether there is a federal currency. All existing federations have such a currency. Hence, there is no experience with a tax system based upon several currencies. Whether convertibility would solve the problems involved seems not clear at present. The constitution could restrict itself to the enunciation of a broad negative principle to the effect that the States may not obstruct the transfer of funds belonging to the federal authorities; presumably the legislation could tie in the European Payments Union and utilize its machinery for this purpose.

The auditing of and accounting for federal expenditures also deserve careful attention. In every sound modern government, these have been carefully worked out. What particular institutional arrangements to make — e.g., whether a comptroller or a quasi-judicial body, like the German *Rechnungshof* — depends upon the dependence or independence of the federal executive with respect to the federal legislature. In the case of executive independence, a comptroller operating under strict legislative control has been utilized.

A related problem is that of the budget. One of the great advantages of the system of a dependent executive is that it can afford to centralize budgetary control in the executive, usually the Minister of Finance. In the

[1] See the discussion of delegated administration in Study 2, The Federal Executive.

other system, budgetary matters are more diffuse, offering opportunities to special interests, both bureaucratic and organizational, to assert themselves unduly. Existing experience would suggest that concentration of the responsibility for expenditures and an integrated budget are highly desirable and deserve to be constitutionally fixed.

Mention ought also to be made in this general survey of the problem of grants-in-aid. A major share of federal income may well be — and is, in fact, in existing federal states — reallocated to the component governments. In some cases such funds are a free grant. In other cases they are restricted to specified governmental functions. Sometimes the States are required to "match" grants by the federal authorities. Anyhow, such grants-in-aid can become a powerful weapon in the hands of the federal authorities, and a constitution ought, in the light of American experience, to provide for them. In any case, grants-in-aid are a valuable fiscal aid to federal coordination.

Under modern conditions, and in view of the magnitude of the tax burden, the problem of the incidence of taxation has led to radical changes in outlook on fiscal policy. Taxes are no longer merely viewed as "revenue," but their impact upon the economy is broadly considered a weapon in the hands of policymakers to effect basic readjustments in the economy. Thus full employment, i.e., prosperity, is seen as at least in part the result of the taxing and spending activities of the government; likewise inflation and deflation, the flow of capital, and many other important economic processes are vitally affected by fiscal policies. Older federal systems have encountered serious problems when it comes to meeting the requirements springing from such impacts of taxes upon general economic activity. Their fiscal policy is hampered by the division of authority between the States and the federation. A modern federal constitution should be written so as to leave the door open for later developments in this field.

As the analysis shows, the transitional arrangements by which existing federal states have started their fiscal systems are quite varied. Usually, the problem has been how to protect the component States from becoming "bankrupt" by too large and too sudden a transfer of tax resources to the federal authorities. Generally speaking, to compensate for such losses, new federations have been inclined to take over the debts of the component States in whole or in part at the time of federation. These matters have usually been left to legislation, though Canada has provided for them in the Constitution. The right of a federation to do this would seem to exist in any case, as part of its power to raise taxes and to incur debts. If it is considered desirable, the principle could be embodied in the constitution. Such transfer might well be related to the transfer of tax resources, as that makes the taking over of debts more palatable.

One special problem, previously alluded to, deserves some further general comment. In each of the six federal systems (including Austria), regulation of commerce with foreign nations has been a federal function. This allocation is, broadly speaking, a complete and inclusive one. Together with this, the central government has in all instances received the power to levy customs duties upon imports. Indeed, in the early federations, customs were intended to provide most of the federal revenue. They did for quite some time. For about seventy years, customs in the United States accounted for 99 per cent of all federal income. They did not during the Civil War, of course. But after that and until the end of the century (Spanish-American War) they did again, with slight additions from liquor and tobacco. In Switzerland customs accounted for a similarly high proportion, never falling to 88 per cent until the First World War. In Canada, too, until 1914, customs provided 80 per cent and more of Dominion revenues. All that was changed by the First World War. In the United States, by 1919, customs had fallen to less than 5 per cent and have never since exceeded that figure. In Australia and Canada, customs played a greater role between the two World Wars, but all but disappeared during them and have become less and less important since that time. It is clear from this overall development that on the one hand customs ought probably to become a revenue of the federation, and on the other hand that customs will not become the mainstay of federal finance, and that therefore their transfer to the federation could be made gradual.[2]

Finally, mention should be made of the difficult problem of how to coordinate the exercise of the tax power by the several States. This problem is of central importance in connection with interstate commerce and it is therefore treated at some length in Study 6. Basically, the principle ought to be that a person is taxed where he is resident, and that a thing is taxed where it is located. Federal judicial bodies have struggled with the task of adjusting conflicting claims of the component units of federal systems in this field for many years.

With these general observations in mind, it is now possible to turn to a more detailed examination of the outstanding problems which the constitutional draftsmen must consider in dealing with the fiscal problems of a federal system. No pretense is made that the broader economic issues can be adequately weighed; they are mostly of concern to the legislative authorities, and their bearing need only be considered in order to learn from existing federations what kind of restrictions are out of date and ought to be avoided.

II. The Facts of Federal Finance
A. Concurrent Versus Exclusive Jurisdiction

Wherever two or more taxation authorities operate in the same geographical area, the allocation of taxing power may be more or less fully divided between the federal and the State authorities. For to leave all

[2] Further details are found below in Section III of this study; Study 6, Commerce, Transportation, and Customs, Section III, ought also to be consulted.

taxing power to the component units of a federal system, with the central authority subsisting entirely upon grants from them, is hardly feasible. None of the six existing federations operates in this manner. Its only historical illustration of note, the American Confederation during the War of Independence, was a complete failure. In that period of American history, the Continental Congress found itself at the mercy of independent colonial governments which persistently refused to honor requests for funds. On the other hand, federal predominance is found in a number of systems as shown in the next section.

In point of fact, all federal constitutions allocate some sources of revenue exclusively to the federal government. Generally, restrictions of one sort or another are laid upon the exercise of those taxing powers which the federal authorities exercise concurrently with the component governments. Practice as to the taxing jurisdiction of the latter units varies widely; in some constitutions they are allocated specific sources of tax income, whereas in others they hold unspecified residual powers to invoke all powers of taxation not explicitly and exclusively granted to the federal government. A further range of variation may be found in the presence or absence of deliberate constitutional provision for the supremacy of federal taxation where power is concurrent and conflicts arise. Finally, there is the problem of tax administration, that is, the extent to which federal taxes may be collected by the federation alone, by it in combination with the States or cantons or Provinces, or by the latter units alone on behalf of the central treasury; furthermore, we must look into the converse situation of federal administration, in whole or in part, of State revenues from taxes. In the investigation of all these problems, we shall find that the older documents tend to be shorter and more general, whereas the most recent charters are long and detailed.

In the United States, the statements as to taxation are most concise. Customs are exclusively granted to the federation by the provision that "no state shall . . . lay any imposts or duties on Imports or Exports" except for essential inspection purposes, in which case all such revenues shall accrue to the federal treasury and all such laws "shall be subject to the revision and control of the Congress." In its original form, the document provided further that the federal Congress might "lay and collect taxes, duties, imposts, and excises." This broad power was subjected to four limitations: (1) direct taxes must be apportioned between the several States in accordance with their population; (2) all other taxes must be uniform throughout the United States; (3) Congress may not tax exports from any State; (4) revenue regulations may not give preference to the ports of one State over those of another.

These provisions are worthy of analysis. They served as models in all subsequent federal constitutional conventions. Two classifications of tax types are employed: that between import and export duties on the one hand and "all other" taxes on the other hand, and that between direct taxes and all others (implicitly, between direct and "indirect," the latter term not appearing in the text). The first of these distinctions has been adhered to by every federation since 1789; the second is tending to disappear.

Uniformity of taxation and nondiscrimination as between component units or their parts have been embodied into every federal tax scheme. Usually, the provision is explicit, but where the document itself is silent constitutional courts have asserted that the two principles are inherent in any federal government.

In the original Constitution of the United States, the central government is accorded control over State taxation only in the minor case of inspection fees on exports and imports. Speaking generally, later federal constitutions have departed widely from this narrow grant of federal authority. They allow instead wide powers of federal control if not complete federal domination of the entire tax field.

The provisions of the American Constitution itself have been altered but once with respect to taxation. In 1913, the Sixteenth Amendment was added, empowering the federal Congress "to lay and collect taxes on incomes, from whatever source derived, without apportionment among the several states, and without regard to any census or enumeration." This change was made obligatory by a decision of the Supreme Court. Hence other types of direct taxes still would have to be apportioned.

But, in the modern economy, problems of taxation are not confined to the constitutional provisions directly addressed to the raising of revenue. Other clauses of the constitution, granting other powers to the central government or denying them to the component States or restricting their exercise at either level, may well have an impact upon the taxing attempts of both jurisdictions.

The federal power to tax is in terms conferred only by the taxing provisions themselves, so far as the text of the United States Constitution is concerned. But, beyond the text, one most important limitation upon both federal and State taxation has been developed by judicial interpretation. In one of the earliest of the crucial constitutional decisions, the Court decided that States may not tax the instrumentalities of the federal government, and in 1871 this doctrine was rendered reciprocal by a further ruling that State instrumentalities are similarly exempted from federal taxes. From the date of the latter decision until the late 1930's, the "reciprocal immunity" doctrine had a checkered and confusing career.

The theory of reciprocal immunity, in one form or another, has been incorporated into nearly every federal constitution adopted in the nineteenth and twentieth centuries. In contrast to American practice, however, the bilateral exemption has been stated with tolerable clarity in these constitutions and has been narrowly interpreted by the courts. So much for restrictions on the federal authorities.

The power of the American States to tax has been affected by constitutional construction in two primary ways. The body of the Constitution allocates to Congress the power "to regulate commerce with foreign nations, and among the several states." The Fourteenth Amendment, adopted in 1868, imposes upon the states the "due process" restrictions originally laid upon the federal government by the Fifth Amendment, and adds to them the provision that no State shall "deny to any person the equal protection of the laws." State taxes have been invalidated by the Supreme Court for interfering with interstate and foreign commerce, and for allegedly discriminatory or confiscatory provisions. The history of these judicial interpretations is far too complex to be analyzed here, but it is necessary to record that the law appears to be blind to economic reality in many portions of the field.

The constitutional postition with respect to taxation in the United States may then be summarized as follows. Both authorities, federal and State, are prohibited from levying export duties. Basically, neither may tax the other's instrumentalities. There are, however, limitations placed upon what are instrumentalities. Thus employees, with respect to their salaries, and probably interest on bonds, are not "instrumentalities." Both federal and State levels may tax all other sorts and kinds of taxable objects, with two exceptions. Direct poll and property taxes are constitutionally restricted and administratively prohibited to the federal government; taxes which discriminate against or burden interstate and foreign commerce are forbidden to the States. The States, furthermore, must not levy arbitrary or discriminatory taxes which deny equal protection of the laws.[3]

We may now examine the other five federal systems with respect to customs as well as the problems of concurrent taxation.

All of the five later federal constitutions grant plenary power over customs duties to the federal government. In Switzerland "customs matters are the concern of the Confederation, which may impose import and export duties." The Canadian Constitution does not grant customs powers to the Dominion, but it vests therein exclusive legislative authority for "the raising of money by any mode or system of Taxation," while restricting the provincial legislatures to "direct taxation within the Province in order to the raising of a revenue for provincial purposes." Since customs duties have universally been considered an indirect mode of taxation, these general statements effectively exclude the Provinces from the field. The Australian Constitution required the Commonwealth government to impose uniform customs duties within two years and provided that the power of the Commonwealth Parliament in the field should thereupon become exclusive (§90). In Germany the heritage of the Zollverein was perpetuated in the Constitutions of the Empire and of the Weimar Republic, and an exclusive power reappears in Article 105·(1) of the Basic Law of 1949 for the Federal Republic. Finally, the Austrian Constitutions of both 1920 and 1929 gave exclusive

[3] See also further comments in Study 6, Appendix V.

powers over import and export duties to the Confederation, and these provisions remain in force under the present military occupation.

Reciprocal immunities are provided for explicitly in the Australian and Canadian constitutions. The former document provides that "a state shall not, without the consent of the Parliament of the Commonwealth, . . . impose any tax on property of any kind belonging to the Commonwealth, nor shall the Commonwealth impose any tax on property of any kind belonging to a state." The Canadian Constitution similarly rules that "no lands or Property belonging to Canada or any Province shall be liable to Taxation." It is worth noting that both Dominion charters speak of *property;* the prohibitions do not apply to income, individual or corporate. In the European federal states, no similar restriction is to be found. But the fully developed separation of taxable sources in Switzerland and the fiscal domination of the central authorities in Austria and Germany greatly attenuate the difficulties.

With respect to discriminatory taxation, the record is not so clear. In Australia wide powers of taxation are granted to the Commonwealth Parliament, "but so as not to discriminate between states or parts of states." In Germany, both the Weimar Constitution of 1919 and the Basic Law call for "customs unity" and "uniform execution of federal finance law"; however, the broad constitutional principle of "equality before the law" serves to bar discriminatory taxation. Switzerland and Australia have no explicit constitutional statements on the point, largely for the reason that both federal governments were expected to subsist primarily from customs revenues, with both charters stating that the countries are unitary for purposes of customs assessments. Canada is unique; there, no limitations whatever are placed upon the Dominion's power to levy taxes.

It is in the classification of tax types and their allocation among the different levels of government that later federal constitutions have departed most widely from the precedent of the Constitution of the United States. Neither the Constitution of Switzerland nor those of Australia, Austria, or Germany make use of the distinction between "direct" and "indirect" taxation. Instead, those four constitutions either grant sweeping federal powers over taxation, as in Australia, the two Austrian constitutions, and in Weimar Germany, or they specify in great detail the specific types of taxation to be accorded to the two levels of government (the Swiss model and the German Basic Law).

Switzerland's original Constitution provided only one exclusive federal resource: customs. The Confederation was to receive one half of the military exemption taxes levied by the cantons. The remainder of its income derived from federal property, the posts and telegraphs, and the powder monopoly. Over the years these provisions have proved inadequate, and several amendments have added to the federal tax competence such specific items as tobacco, taxes, stamp duties on legal documents, and income and estate taxes. Some of these taxes are direct, others indirect. In most cases the power to levy the taxes was withdrawn entirely from the cantons, with provision that a fixed part of the revenue from each specific tax should accrue to them in lieu of their former receipts. Switzerland today, as a result of this course of development, has the most fully developed division between federal and cantonal finance to be found. Double taxation, because of these arrangements, is only a minor problem.

The German Basic Law contains the most elaborate of all constitutional allocations of taxing jurisdiction. But, unlike the Swiss charter, with its rigid differentiations, the German document allows for considerable flexibility in the application of the constitutional standards. It recognizes and relies upon the difference between exclusive and concurrent jurisdiction in all governmental fields to an extent unparalleled in modern constitutional regimes. In the area of taxation, the use made of the distinction is most complicated. The federation has exclusive jurisdiction over customs and financial monopolies. It receives the yield of all excise taxes except that on beer, of the transportation tax, of the turnover tax, and of nonrecurrent property taxes. These four types of tax are subject to concurrent legislation, but are administered solely by the federal authorities. All other taxes are for the Länder, with the important proviso that the federation may claim all or part of the yield from income, real estate, property, inheritance, and gift taxes. Insofar as it makes such a claim, it may provide standards for the administration of the taxes, but it may delegate to the States their actual administration. To date, the federal government has received 27 per cent of the yield from income taxes. These taxation provisions, as this brief summary will make clear, are complex indeed. The present German situation results partly from the demands of the military occupying powers, but it also reflects a reaction against the fiscal system under Weimar, which conceded to the Republic full powers to pre-empt any and all types of tax revenue, with a requirement merely that it "must have consideration for the financial requirements of the states."

In only one case — Canada — has the American model of distinguishing "direct" from "indirect" taxes been followed. There, it is provided that the Provinces may levy "direct taxation within the province . . . for provincial purposes." The interpretation of this clause by the courts has, however, been strikingly different from that applied to the direct tax provisions in the United States. In Canada, the courts have held that a tax is direct when it cannot be shifted. This makes it possible for the Canadian Provinces to levy excise taxes to be collected from the final purchaser at the time of final sale, and such taxation has long been a major source of revenue for the Provinces.

The general picture in regard to concurrent taxation, then, is this: In the United States and in Canada, an attempt is made to isolate some few sources of revenue for or from particular levels of government. In Switzerland the process has gone into much greater detail with much greater precision and with a minimum of overlapping. In the Bonn Republic joint taxing jurisdiction is explicitly permitted, but is not required. In the cases of Austria, Australia, and Weimar Germany, the grant of dominant taxing powers to the central government has made unnecessary such divisions between sources of revenue.

B. *The Issue of Tax Supremacy*

In substance, the matters discussed in this section do not diverge sharply from those taken up in the preceding one. But whereas Switzerland, the United States, and the present German Republic separate sources of taxation, with Canada tending in the same direction, the two constitutions of the Austrian Federal Republic, that of Australia, and those of Imperial and Weimar Germany make no such distinctions. The constitutional situation in these is one of complete federal dominance.

The Australian Constitution explicitly conferred full tax powers on the federal government. The charter grants to the Commonwealth Parliament "power to make laws for the peace, order and good government of the Commonwealth with respect to . . . (ii) taxation." There are but two restrictions: the Commonwealth must not discriminate between States or their parts, and it must not tax their property. Beyond this, its power is plenary. There is no mention at any point in the document of taxing powers reserved exclusively to the States, or of tax sources denied to the Commonwealth. Except for the usual monopoly of customs granted to the center, and the federal monopoly on excise taxes, no single specific type of tax is even mentioned. Down to the Second World War, these two sources of income accounted for 80 per cent of all Commonwealth revenue, and the federal income taxes first adopted in World War I were responsible for the remaining fifth.

The costs of World War II obliged the Australian Commonwealth, for the first time, to exploit the coercive possibilities inherent in its constitutional grant of tax power. In 1942, the Commonwealth imposed income taxes sufficiently high to exclude the States, enacted grants to the States in lieu of their former income tax revenues if and only if the State discontinued its own income taxes, and provided that the Commonwealth income tax should be a priority lien on all incomes. These measures were sustained by the High Court in decisions which make it clear that the same procedures would be constitutional with respect to other sorts of taxation so long as the non-discrimination and non-taxation-of-state-property restrictions are honored.

The Australian experience is very recent, but its implications are undeniable. In the Weimar Republic,[4] financial control at the center was pro-

---

[4] It may be worth while to recall briefly the fiscal system of the federated Imperial Reich here. Its Constitution placed not only customs duties, but "such taxes as are to be applied to the uses of the Reich" under "the supervision and legislative control of the Reich." The Reich is also granted four specific excise taxes. All of these taxes, however, were ad-

vided for not only explicitly but in great detail. After the usual grant of exclusive jurisdiction over customs, the Constitution went on to state: "The Reich also has jurisdiction over taxation and other sources of income, in so far as they may be claimed in whole or in part for its purposes. If the Reich claims any source of revenue which formerly belonged to the States, it must have consideration for the financial requirements of the States."

The Reich also was enabled to prescribe by law fundamental principles concerning the validity and mode of collection of State taxes, in order to prevent certain undesirable conditions, including injury to the Reich, double taxation, excessive burdens, discriminations, or in order to protect important social interests. Finally, the Reich was authorized to regulate the State tax administrations.

The Weimar Constitution, furthermore, makes no mention of any specific type or sort of tax except to provide that customs duties and taxes on articles of consumption be administered by the Reich authorities. The concentration of regulatory and administrative powers at the federal level, taken together with the utter absence of any restrictions upon the types of taxes the federation may levy, clearly provides for a degree of centralization fully comparable to that of a unitary state. This result was, at the time, justified by the extraordinary fiscal burdens of the Versailles reparations totals. The ability of the central government to invade formerly local fields and to vary at will the share of the local governments in the fruits left the Länder and Gemeinde completely dependent upon the federal fiscal policies.

The Austrian state of affairs, from 1920 to the Dollfuss "constitution" of 1934, is closely parallel to that of Weimar Germany. The texts of the Constitutions of 1920 and 1929 spelled out in complete detail a scheme for centralizing fiscal power in the hands of the Confederation. Both Austrian Republican constitutions, moreover, contain lengthy articles establishing an "Audit Department," with authority to "supervise the management of all the finances." Its competence was broadened in the Constitution of 1929 to include complete examination of all aspects of provincial finance. As one might well expect, the upshot of these constitutional provisions was a completely standardized fiscal system. The Constitution conceded plenary

---

ministered and collected by the component States. There is in the Constitution no restriction on federal pre-emption of any other sort of tax. Throughout the first four decades of the Reich's history, the central government invaded more and more fields of State and local taxation, frequently with an arrangement guaranteeing to the lower levels of government a fixed percentage of the yield from specific taxes removed from their jurisdiction. By 1913, the Reich had established inheritance taxes, estate increment taxes, levies on automobiles and directors' fees, on tea and coffee, and direct taxes on income, property, and property increments. The treasuries of the Länder and the Gemeinde found themselves more and more dependent upon shares in taxes which they did not impose and in which their participation could be reduced without warning.

This condition of financial dependence upon the center was intensified by the fact that it was possible for the central government to assess the States according to their population. Such State contributions, constitutionally obligatory in nature, were actually levied every year. They prevented Reich deficits, but made efficient fiscal policy at the lower levels utterly impossible.

powers to the central government with no guarantees of fiscal autonomy to the Provinces. The finances of the lower levels of government depended heavily upon their portions of the federal taxes granted to them by the federal government. In 1926, 40 per cent of the Länder revenues and 58 per cent of the Gemeinde incomes were derived from such shared taxes, notably those on incomes, property, and business turnover.

The case of Canada has been left until last, for here federal fiscal dominance is much less certain. Its Constitution, it will be remembered, granted full power to the Dominion to raise money "by any mode or system of taxation." This provision appears more sweeping than the Australian one. But, at the same time, the Provinces are positively granted the power to levy "direct taxation within the province . . . for provincial purposes." These grants of power seem to conflict, and the extent of their inconsistency has exercised Canadian courts and the Privy Council ever since the Dominion was founded. The weight of opinion is in favor of the conclusion that there is, in fact, no conflict, unless the Dominion Parliament attempts to create one. To date, it has refrained from doing so; the constitutional issue is therefore as yet undecided. There are, however, decisions which make it clear that the Dominion debt and its service take precedence over the debts of the Provinces, a precedent which might well entail Dominion priority in taxation too.

The constitutional provisions examined in this section have, in all cases save that of Canada, clearly conceded fiscal dominance to the federal government. In each of the federal regimes which postdate the First World War, the exercise of such federal pre-eminence has been focused upon income taxes, which the central government takes to itself either exclusively or with concessions of a share in their revenue to the component States. In the context of contemporary fiscal practice, it is the income tax which indubitably takes the center of the stage. To the special problems of income taxation in federal states this survey will therefore now turn.

C. *The Special Problems of Income Taxation*

At the present time, each of the six federations here under examination receives revenue from personal and corporate income taxes. The constitutional basis of such taxation may be reviewed summarily, for several of the relevant provisions have already been examined in other contexts.

In Australia, Austria, and Canada, the power of the federal government to levy income taxes proceeds simply from its sweeping general authority over taxation. The same constitutional ground for income taxation existed in Weimar Germany. In none of these cases is there explicit constitutional authority empowering the federal government to impose such taxes.

Two constitutions contain such explicit provisions. One is that of the United States, where a special amendment, the Sixteenth Amendment, has been added, as we have already shown. In contemporary Germany, as we have also seen above, the Constitution provides for federal authority over such taxes insofar as it claims for itself all or part of their yield. The Republic has made such a claim, and its authority has therefore come into effect.

The case of Switzerland is somewhat ambiguous. The Swiss national treasury obtained revenue from income taxes in every year from 1916 through 1931, and from 1940. In the earlier period the taxes were termed "war" levies, and their bases were constitutional amendments adopted in 1915 and 1919. The earlier amendment authorized only a single, nonrecurrent imposition, and the second provided that the revenues so raised were to go toward charging off the capital burden assumed during the First World War. The latter purpose was declared completed in 1931, and the amendment lapsed.

The second period of Swiss income taxation, which began in 1940 and has continued since, has also been grounded upon extraordinary constitutional devices. An amendment adopted in 1939 allowed the promulgation of "urgent federal decrees of general import," provided that they were passed by a majority of all members of both legislative Councils and were of limited duration. Under this authority, the Federal Council or executive adopted and obtained approval for a special defense income tax. It is this emergency justification which underlies the present Swiss federal income tax statute.

Whatever the different constitutional foundations might be, it has long since become evident that income taxes are more and more providing the great bulk of tax revenue for central governments in federal states. In the period since 1946, such direct taxes on corporate and personal income (and on personal property, though these taxes are of minor import) accounted for about 80 to 86 per cent of all central tax revenue in the United States, 60 per cent in Australia, and 55 to 60 per cent in Canada. On the continent of Europe, reliance on such taxes is somewhat less; they provide 45 to 50 per cent of federal tax income in Austria, and just under 30 per cent in Switzerland. The lesser figures for Europe are in part explained by the reliance upon turnover taxes which are easier to collect. In Switzerland and Austria turnover taxes yield sums closely comparable to those derived from income taxes; in Germany, they are to date more fruitful by far than income taxes. But the income taxes are forging ahead. All in all, it is probably safe to say that income taxes may soon hold the predominant importance once held by customs duties; in the United States, this is already the case.

D. *Federal Subventions to Component Units*

Every modern state, federal or unitary, makes use of subventions or grants in one form or another. But our concern here is with the federal practices in the matter, and the variation in the form of grants is very important.

Such grants may or may not be tied to specific forms of revenue (shared taxes) or to specific objects of expenditure (grants-in-aid), and their basis may be either constitutional or legislative. All subventions treated in this section, if they rest on constitutional grounds, are those originally intended to be permanent. Deliberately transitional transfer provisions are discussed at page 381 below. Only one of the constitutional documents is completely silent on the issue. The Constitution of the United States makes no mention of transfers of funds in either direction. All such payments in the United States are, therefore, on a purely legislative basis, subject to Congressional suspension at any time. This, of course, is a statement of legal principle, not of political feasibility. The size of such grants in the United States is currently much less, as a percentage both of federal appropriations and of State revenues, than in any other federation. In the years since the end of World War II, federal payments to the States have run at an average of 10 per cent of all State income and never more than 2½ per cent of federal expenditures.

Switzerland has, as we already mentioned, a system of shared taxes. The present Constitution provides that all customs revenue shall flow into the federal treasury, with four Alpine cantons receiving, perpetually, stated sums of money for the support of international Alpine roads. It also provides that the federal government receives half of the yield from the cantonal military service exemption taxes. Since 1874, virtually every new tax power granted to the Confederation has contained clauses reserving a major share in the yield to the cantons. Thus Article 32-*bis*, first added in 1885 and amended in 1930, divides among the cantons in proportion to their populations one half of the federal gain from taxes on liquor. According to another article, all of the tobacco tax and all federal liquor tax revenues are allocated to old age and survivors insurance, and the article further provides that the cantons must match federal appropriations, with the total public subsidy limited to one half the total cost of the insurance. Since 1917, the federal government has the power to levy stamp taxes; the second section stipulates that one fifth of the net yield must be paid to the cantons. These and similar provisions for other taxes summarize one most significant aspect of the taxation system of Switzerland; almost exclusively, it is one of shared taxes. The system is constitutionally guaranteed. In the past five years, less than one tenth of federal revenues has been derived from taxes which it alone levies. Shared taxes in the same period have provided about 10 per cent of all cantonal revenues.

Section 118 of the Canadian Constitution provided for annual subsidies to New Brunswick, Nova Scotia, Ontario, and Quebec of sums ranging from $50,000 to $80,000, with a further per capita subvention of 80 cents per head. These arrangements were said to be "in full settlement of all future demands on Canada," but the full-settlement clause has been a dead letter since the day it went into effect. The original Section 118 was amended in 1907, changing the basis of subsidy to a sliding grant from $100,000 to $240,-

000 per Province, depending upon its population, plus a further per capita grant of 80 cents up to a population of 2,500,000 and 60 cents per head above that figure. These subsidy provisions have done no more than provide a minimum below which the Dominion Parliament may not reduce its subventions to the Provinces. Ever since 1907, subsidies actually paid have far exceeded the constitutionally obligatory figures. Special grants of a lump-sum sort go to the poorer Provinces, and the Dominion government makes available small sums in support of agricultural research. These Province-by-Province grants, since the end of the Second World War, have varied from $1.20 to $1.30 per capita per annum.

By far the larger federal grants to the Provinces are those which accrue to those areas which have entered into the taxation agreements. The seven Provinces which have accepted the tax-lease arrangements gain around $100,-000,000 each year from this source. These payments to the seven Provinces, together with the regular subsidies which go to all Provinces, have aggregated about 20 per cent of net provincial revenues in the past five years. Of Dominion expenditures, they are of course a smaller part; in the past five years this figure has been dropped downward from about 10 per cent to just under 7 per cent. The Canadian system of subventions is thus seen to be mixed; approximately 15 per cent of the Dominion transfers to Provinces are constitutionally obligatory minima, another 5 per cent are annual legislative grants, and the remaining 80 per cent are payments in lieu of former provincial tax revenues in the income and inheritance fields. This last item is not precisely a shared tax in the technical sense, but it may fairly be regarded as a Canadian substitute for tax sharing in a field where the Dominion's power to force the Provinces into tax sharing is doubtful.

In Australia, the Constitution contained a complicated series of temporary provisions governing grants. These are examined at page 382 below. Of the permissively permanent provisions, only Section 96 is of relevance here. It provided that, "During a period of ten years after the establishment of the Commonwealth and thereafter until the Parliament otherwise provides, the Parliament may grant financial assistance to any State on such terms and conditions as the Parliament thinks fit." This section furnished much of the constitutional basis for the Uniform Tax Program of 1942–1943, and it undergirds most of the grants currently being made in Australia. The combination of special grants authorized by Section 96, and tax reimbursement grants under the Uniform Tax Program which rests in part upon that section, has reached a sum which over the past five years has been about 30 per cent of total state revenues and about 13 to 14 per cent of total Commonwealth expenditure. In effect, these grants are either legislative gifts, grounded on a permissive and in no sense obligatory constitutional provision, or they are an Australian version of tax sharing which was forced through in the face of State resistance and which has completely excluded the States from the tax fields affected.

The situation with respect to grants in contemporary Germany and Austria is confused. The Austrian charters of 1920 and 1929 make no reference to grants in any form, and customary practice in the Republic restricted federal subventions to the sharing of taxes. From the pre-war days Austria has continued the practice of federal reimbursement to the Länder for administrative services which they render to the central government, but these have never bulked larger than 4 per cent of Land revenues and one quarter of 1 per cent of Bund expenditures.

The German Basic Law provides, in Article 106 (4), as follows:

> In order to ensure the working efficiency of the Länder with low revenues and to equalize the differing burden of expenditure of the Länder, the Federation may make grants and take the funds necessary for this purpose from specific taxes of those accruing to the Länder. A federal law, which shall require the approval of the Bundesrat, shall determine which taxes shall be utilized for this purpose and in what amounts and on what basis the grants shall be distributed among the Länder entitled to equalization; the grants must be handed directly to the Länder.

This article is the most forthright equalization provision in any federal constitution at present in force. It explicitly takes the necessary funds from taxes accruing to the Länder, and makes it fully evident that the richer areas are underwriting the poorer ones. The divergence in war damage, burdens from refugees, and the like, made this kind of provision imperative.

The pattern of federal subventions makes it clear that these transfers of funds have complicated severely the whole fabric of finance in federal nations. Increasingly (especially in the two British Dominions and in Switzerland), the penetration of the central government into local financial operations is reaching considerable proportions. It is worth noting that the one country where central tax domination is least evident — the United States — is also the nation where federal grants are least important on a purely proportional basis. But, in the other federation with the best balance between federal and local tax powers — Switzerland — shared taxes and federal subventions bulk larger in cantonal budgets than in those of component States in any other federation.

E. Budgets and Budgetary Procedure

From the more narrowly financial side of public fiscal arrangements it is now necessary to turn to the governmental aspects. In actual practice, virtually all modern governments have organized their financial operations in three phases: (a) preparation of an annual financial plan; (b) enactment of the details of that plan; (c) review and audit of the accounts after the end of each auditing period. In this and the two following sections these functions will be taken up in turn.

Surprisingly enough, it is the federal nation whose constitution is least explicit in this matter, and whose entry into the ranks of those countries practicing budgetary controls is most recent, which has the most complete and complex arrangements. On financial controls the Constitution of the United States provides only that "no money shall be drawn from the treasury but in consequence of appropriations made by law; and a regular statement and account of the receipts and expenditures of all public money shall be published from time to time." Except for the very early years of the Republic, when Alexander Hamilton as Secretary of the Treasury dominated federal fiscal planning, both taxes and appropriations were determined by the Congress as the Founding Fathers had projected. In the early and middle decades of the nineteenth century such arrangements served fairly well, but the coming of industrialism and a huge population made utterly unworkable this system of piecemeal legislation drafted and proposed by as many as thirty different and distinct Congressional committees with no centralized control whatsoever.

After many years of criticism, the traditional procedures were formally abandoned in 1921 with the enactment of a statute establishing the Bureau of the Budget. This agency, originally a part of the Treasury Department, was charged with the task of screening and systematizing the appropriations requests of all parts of the federal government prior to their submission to Congress. At the same time, the two houses of Congress organized specialized committees, each house to have one group with jurisdiction over the raising of revenue and another with authority over its appropriation. Seventeen years later, in 1939, the Bureau of the Budget was separated from all other administrative agencies of the federal government and placed directly under the President. At the present time, its financial functions are exercised primarily in the late autumn of each year, when departmental estimates for the fiscal year to begin the following July are subjected to minutely detailed reviews in which the departments must, theoretically at least, justify every last cent.

The activities of the Bureau of the Budget culminate in the submission to Congress each January of a complete federal financial plan for the fiscal year which commences six months thereafter. This arrangement ensures a unified executive proposal, but it does not by any means guarantee its passage, without extensive alterations, by the legislative branch. As we shall see below, there is no effective bar to Congressional increases in specific items, and the President lacks the power to veto individual appropriations. The existence of the Bureau of the Budget is an effective barrier to excessive demands by particular organs of the executive branch, but the laxity of legislative procedure prevents its ensuring adequate appropriations controls throughout the fiscal process.

In all of the other five federal nations, budgetary planning is the responsibility of the Minister of Finance, or his equivalent with a somewhat different title. Neither Canada nor Australia, Germany, Austria or Switzerland, has found it necessary to adopt the quasi-independent agency utilized in the

United States. In the four federations with Parliamentary institutions, the
budgetary function is considered one of the responsibilities of the Cabinet
as a whole, and the stringent executive control of the fiscally dominant lower
house ensures that government proposals will be adopted unless a serious
Parliamentary crisis ensues. It deserves attention that such concentration
of the budgetary function in the hands of the Cabinet Minister responsible
for financial legislation in the narrower sense has given that office a prestige
second only to that of the Prime Minister (or Chancellor) himself.

The case of Switzerland is unusual, because of the unique nature of the
Swiss executive. In that country, the plural executive as a whole takes a real
part in the planning of budgets, and the annually selected President of the
Confederation finds himself in a strategic role. The rather conservative nature of Swiss public finance, however, makes it risky to draw conclusions
from Swiss practice. In general, the Swiss budget of one year embodies
significant changes from prior years only in the event of an emergency —
particularly wars involving her neighbors — which all parties and politicians consider exceptional.

F. *The Legislative Process in Taxation*

The legislative procedures in fiscal matters require some special attention.
In the United States, financial legislation is subjected to only one peculiar
constitutional requirement. Article I, Section 7, provides that "all Bills for
raising Revenue shall originate in the House of Representatives." To this
it immediately adds "but the Senate may propose or concur with Amendments as on other Bills." Tax measures are usually drafted by Congressional staff experts assisted by experts of the Treasury Department. The
hearings are initiated before the House Committee on Ways and Means.
Tax statutes are not discussed on the floor of the Senate in formal debate
until after the House has sent up a bill on which its action is complete, but
there is no rule to prevent an individual Senator from delivering a speech
on some tax proposal. Usually, the House and Senate versions of a bill
will differ and will go to a conference Committee for compromise, a technique exactly like that applied to other sorts of legislation. The balance of
power between the House and Senate on tax law is fairly even.

There is no constitutional barrier to the attachment of legislative "riders"
to tax laws. Tax legislation has, however, not been very often used in connection with this device, in contrast to appropriation bills. A great handicap of sound fiscal procedures in the United States has proved to be the
weakness of executive leadership in this field, which is the result of the strict
separation of powers.

The Swiss Constitution is completely and utterly silent on the subject.
The powers of the two legislative councils are coordinate in all respects. In
practice, federal tax laws are drafted by the chancellery of the executive
Federal Council and then submitted to the two legislative chambers. They

may be, and frequently are, amended by one or the other of the two legislative houses.

Later federal constitutions have tended to become more and more detailed on these problems. This feature of the charters of Australia, Austria, Canada, and Germany is of course closely connected with the fact that those nations possess executive organs responsible to popularly elected assemblies, and many of the provisions of their constitutions relating to financial legislation are merely codifications of practices which have grown up, notably in Britain, over the course of centuries.

The Canadian Constitution provides that all money bills, both for the raising and for the expenditure of public funds, must originate in the House of Commons. No such measure can be adopted unless the measure is put before the House by the government then in office; private bills affecting the public treasury are excluded. In actual fact, the opposition bench is not completely powerless, but its influence can only be brought to bear through amendments which the government is willing to accept.

The powers of the Canadian Senate in financial matters are most unclear. In actual practice, the Senate has frequently succeeded in proposing amendments subsequently accepted by Commons, but the latter invariably adds a clause stating that its acquiescence flows from a desire not to enforce its sole powers, and that the instant agreement does not constitute a precedent.

The Canadian Constitution clearly displays two of the three practices customary in Parliamentary nations. All tax bills must originate with the government. Implicitly, given governmental control of the proceedings of the House, this requirement effectively bars "riders" so long as the government sees fit to enforce its dominance. The third usual characteristic of Parliamentary finance — the impotence of the upper house — is not decisively settled.

In Australia all of these aspects, and more, are embodied in the written Constitution. Section 53 effectively excludes the Senate from participation in financial legislation. It may not amend either tax or appropriations bills. It may not amend any other law "so as to increase any proposed charge or burden on the people." It may request changes in money bills, but the House of Representatives "may, if it thinks fit, make any of such omissions of amendments, with or without modifications."

Executive pre-eminence in financial matters is guaranteed by provisions which stipulate that appropriations shall not be passed unless recommended by the Governor-General in the same session, and that neither tax nor appropriation bills may originate in the Senate. Since the Governor-General makes recommendations only on the advice of his Ministers, and since those Ministers collectively dominate the House of Representatives, both taxing and spending are controlled by the Cabinet.

"Tacking" is prevented by the Australian Constitution, since appropriation bills may deal only with appropriations and tax bills only with taxation.

The Australian Constitution contains one rather unfortunate provision. It requires that "Laws imposing taxation, except laws imposing duties of customs or of excise, shall deal with one subject of taxation only; but laws imposing duties of customs shall deal with duties of customs only, and laws imposing duties of excise shall deal with duties of excise only." As the Commonwealth has moved into new fields of taxation, this clause has seriously hampered its business. In Australia at present, it is not at all unusual for the government to present fifteen tax measures in the same session, each of which must go individually through the various stages of Parliamentary consideration.

The Austrian Constitutions of 1920 and 1929 have provisions on financial legislation only with respect to the powers of the upper chamber. They provide that the Council of Provinces and Estates may not "raise objection" to the voting of the federal budget or to the passing of the state accounts. "These laws when passed by the National Council shall be authenticated and published without further formalities." On tacking and on executive dominance, the text is silent. With respect to the position of the executive, however, it is worth noting that the lower Austrian house was as fully under its domination in the period between the two World Wars as any legislative chamber in any nation, and this control extended to taxation and appropriation as well as to all other governmental problems.

Contemporary Germany is a most peculiar case, insofar as financial laws are concerned. Scattered throughout the Basic Law, especially in its financial sections, are statements to the effect that certain measures may be undertaken only by means of "a federal law which shall require the approval of the Federal Council." All governmentally sponsored legislation, furthermore, must be submitted first to the upper chamber, which has the right to give its opinion, favorable or unfavorable, on the proposed statutes. On those bills for which its approval is not constitutionally obligatory, the Federal Council's veto may be overridden by the lower house, provided that a two-thirds majority in the upper house be matched by an equal majority in the lower. Generally speaking, differences between the two bodies are arbitrated by joint committees.

It is the financial provisions which do in fact require approval by the Federal Council that concern us here. These provisions taken together make it clear that the Federal Council is an equal partner with the Federal Assembly in all financial matters which impinge upon the distributions of powers and functions between the two levels of government. In the routine issues of finance, on the other hand, the Assembly is predominant. Thus the provisions of the Basic Law more carefully protect the federal system.

The Basic Law also guarantees executive control over expenditure, for it stipulates that neither house of the Parliament may pass appropriations in excess of budgetary estimates, or extraordinary expenditures, without the approval of the federal government.

Tacking is taken care of by the budgetary provisions. All revenues and expenditures must be estimated and included in the budget, and the budget may contain no provisions which do not refer to income and outgo. Nevertheless, the federal legislature has frequently enacted tax statutes outside the budget, but it is noteworthy that these invariably are addressed to tax matters alone.

The general situation, then, as far as legislative procedure is concerned, may be summarized thus: the older constitutions are relatively inexplicit on revenue legislation as a special category. The four more recent constitutions tend to ensure the financial predominance of the lower house, to forbid tacking, and to enhance the control of the executive over both the initiation of financial measures and their alteration during the process of enactment.

G. *Auditing and Accounting*

Formulation, discussion, and enactment of a budget are necessary steps in the fiscal procedures of any government. No less important is the problem of control over the use of funds thus appropriated. In each federal government, a specialized agency exercises such supervision, but the status and nature of the organizations charged with this duty vary considerably.

In the United States, an official known as the Comptroller General is responsible both for the "preaudit" and the "postaudit" functions — in other words, he both authorizes expenditures from funds already appropriated and, after the close of a fiscal year, scrutinizes the accounts of each governmental organ authorized to expend public moneys. The Office of the Comptroller General is completely independent of all branches of the federal government but is directly responsible to the national legislature. He reports solely to that body. He has the power to summon all files and records which bear upon his task of financial control. In the strict sense of the phrase, it is impossible to allocate this agency to any of the three branches of government recognized by the American conception of "the separation of powers." One can only assert that the Comptroller General's Office is a "quasi-judicial investigative agency with some executive powers, created by and subordinate solely to the legislative branch."

In Canada and Australia, the preaudit and postaudit functions have been separated. The two constitutions require that all Dominion revenues go into one consolidated fund, from which the Parliament makes appropriations to the Crown at large, and not to specific departments or agencies. The funds thus appropriated must then be "released," a task which is performed by the Governor-General himself ("under the sign manual") and countersigned by a member of the Treasury. This device makes it possible for the rate at which annual appropriations are drawn down to be controlled. The next step is the actual issue of the funds, an act vested in the Comptroller of the Treasury. Both steps in the process involve officers of the Treasury, not of an independent governmental body.

The postaudit procedures in both Dominions are placed in the hands of an Auditor-General, who holds office during good behavior and can, like members of the judiciary, be removed from office only by an address to the Governor-General by both houses of the federal legislature. The Auditor-General reviews all accounts of the federal government, and, in Australia, may perform the same functions for the States if they so request. In both Dominions he renders annual reports to the Parliament and, if he so desires, to the Cabinet. This officer is completely independent of the executive organs of the government.

Germany, like the two federal Dominions of the British Commonwealth, has divided the preaudit and postaudit phases. The former is vested in the Finance Ministry, the latter in a unique organ known as the Federal Court of Accounts (*Bundesrechnungshof*). The latter quasi-judicial body is a specialized tribunal concerned only with financial control functions. It reviews all governmental accounts and reports on their status to the Minister of Finance, who must lay the report before both houses of the federal legislature and request a motion to discharge the Ministry of responsibility for the accounts to which the Court has taken no exception.

This institution, the Court of Accounts, can trace its history to a special chamber established by Frederick William I of Prussia in 1714. In addition to its essentially financial duties, it has the power to inquire into the economy and efficiency of all governmental administration. It enjoys the immunities of all other judicial bodies; in the words of the statute establishing the present Court of Accounts, it is "one of the highest federal authorities, subject only to the law and independent with respect to the federal administration." And, in the German Federal Republic, the powers of the Court of Accounts have been expanded by constituting a "Senate" of Accounts, consisting of the senior members of the Federal Court and of the analogous officers in the several Länder. This body has authority to exercise the powers of financial audit and administrative review in the case of those Land authorities charged with administration of federal statutes and policies.

The Austrian case is unique, for the reason that the Austrian Constitutions provide the most detailed auditing and accounting procedures of any Federal charters. Close scrutiny of these extensive requirements will reveal, however, that the Austrian Constitutions of 1920 and 1929 merely placed into the basic law a set of arrangements closely similar to those of the United States. Like the American Comptroller General, the head of the Audit Department in Austria is subordinate solely to the federal legislature, and may be removed from office only by its vote. He possesses the powers both of authorizing expenditures and of reviewing accounts, and must report on the latter to the Federal legislature.

Switzerland, too, has established a procedure closely similar to that of the United States. The organ concerned is known as the Federal Finance Control, and it is empowered both to issue public funds and to examine their use by the various federal departments. In addition, like the German Court of Accounts, it can recommend administrative reorganization where it seems advisable on grounds of economy. In recent years, there have been suggestions that Switzerland should adopt the German system of a judicial auditing body, but these proposals have not been adopted.

None of these devices for controlling the use made of public funds can be termed an unqualified success. In no case does responsibility for the shortcomings rest with the accounting agency itself. Instead, the fault appears to lie in the fact that the bodies to whom its reports are made are so intensively concerned with present business that further review of an ex post facto audit of last year's accounts is an unattractive chore. It is significant that no federal legislature has established a committee whose sole business is analysis and inquiry into the annual reports of the auditing and accounting officials.

H. *Tax Administration*

In the area of administration, we may distinguish three types. First is administrative separation, with the federal and State authorities operating revenue departments which do not supervise the collection of any taxes but their own. Second is administrative devolution, with the tax agencies of the lower level of government collecting taxes proper to the central government. Third is administrative concentration, with the federal organs servicing the States by collecting taxes which the latter have enacted.

The nearest approach to complete administrative separation exists in the United States. In a few cases the federal government has collected taxes for the States or permitted them to administer its own revenues. All such instances have involved only small amounts and have been of short duration. But there is now developing an increasingly effective cooperation.

Wherever shared taxes are important — notably on the continent of Europe — administrative devolution is the rule. In Germany and Austria, it was usual during the 1920's for the Länder financial authorities to employ nearly ten times as many civil servants as the number working in the federal Finance Ministry. The duties of the latter were almost exclusively those of supervising the States, of collecting statistical data, and of enforcing administrative uniformity upon the States. The actual work of tax collection was accomplished in the Länder. The same pattern has persisted into the postwar period, though not in the same degree. Despite the change in proportions, however, it remains true that well over two thirds of all public finance officials are employed at the State rather than at the federal level.

In Switzerland the same state of affairs persisted only to the end of the First World War. Since then, as the federation has taken over more and more tax jurisdiction, it has assumed the burden of administration of the shared taxes. In these cases, the central government services the cantons, debiting their shares of the taxes in order to cover the costs of collection.

For the 90 per cent of their revenue which comes from their own taxes, however, the cantons retain their own tax administration bureaus.

The two federal Dominions present a mixed picture. In Australia, the
Constitution permits the federal government to make use of State administrative agencies and the States to employ the agencies of the central government. Down to the time of the Uniform Tax Plan of 1943, both the federal
and the State income taxes were collected by the Commonwealth in five of
the six States. In the sixth — Western Australia — the State employed federal officials for the administration of its entire fiscal system. In Canada,
the two levels of tax administration are almost as separate as in the United
States, a result entailed by the high degree of separation in tax sources. The
Provinces at present tax property and sales almost exclusively, fields which
the Dominion has vacated except for special excise levies.

Tax administration thus varies widely in the six nations. In general, the
duties are devolved or concentrated in accordance with the degree to
which the two levels of tax authority interpenetrate one another. Where
sources are separate, administration also tends to be so. Where taxes are
shared and the central government dominates the field, administration
tends to be shared. But the exceptions — notably Australia and Switzerland
— violate the rule and make the correlation far from perfect.

III. Special Problems

A. *Transitional Arrangements*

The joining together of previously independent or differently associated
States into a new federal state may well impose severe fiscal strains upon
the juristic parties to the new federation. Whatever the concession of financial powers to the central government may in fact amount to, it represents
a net diminution of such powers in the hands of the component areas. Not
infrequently, a constitution will take cognizance of the problems which such
changes create, and will provide for a period of adjustment during which
the full force of the new financial provisions shall be abated. It is these
arrangements which are to be analyzed here.

The Constitution of the United States contains but one unimportant transitional provision. The reason was that the new government was expected
to subsist from customs revenues, and the federating colonies had come during the Revolutionary War to depend more and more exclusively upon
property taxation as international trade disappeared. The fact of federation therefore was no immediate financial threat.

Subsequent federations have faced a different situation. With only occasional exceptions, they have linked together political entities which themselves have lived on customs revenues, and the centralization of this source
of income in federal hands has raised temporary but troublesome difficul-

ties. It is, therefore, not surprising that transitional provisions for gradual centralization of customs administration should be a recurrent feature.

The Swiss Constitution is the earliest example. The revised Constitution, of 1874, having transferred military responsibilities to the Confederation, presented a corresponding need for increased financial resources of the federal government. During the period of a quarter century prior to the revision, the Confederation had been obligated to pay to the cantons subventions in lieu of their customs revenues, but it now appeared highly probable that it would be unable to continue the practice. Similarly, the Constitution of 1848 had required that the federal government pay over to the cantons, from its post office and telegraph profits, a sum equal to average net cantonal revenues from that source in the three years immediately preceding confederation. In 1874, it was evident that these subsidies must also be discontinued. Finally, the Confederation gained in the later charter one half of the cantonal exemption taxes.

The first of six "transitional provisions" placed limitations on the going into effect of the new financial devices. The postal and customs revenues would continue to be divided "on the existing bases" until the Confederation should fully assume its new military obligations, and those particular cantons most seriously embarrassed by the totality of the revised fiscal provisions should be affected "only gradually . . . and after a transitional period of several years."

This Swiss article, it should be noted, contains two types of provisions. One of them, governing the division of customs and postal revenues, is of general application throughout the Confederation. The other, which requires gradualness in the imposition of the new fiscal system, applies only to some of the cantons, provided that they are particularly hampered. The Swiss article does not name specific cantons; instead, it establishes a classification without identifying the members of the class.

The Canadian Constitution contained two transitional financial articles, of which one is of purely administrative significance. It provided that the customs and excise laws of each Province should remain in effect until altered by the Dominion Parliament. This happened in 1867, when the Parliament established national tariff and excise rates.

The second Canadian transitional provision provided that the Province of New Brunswick should receive an additional federal subsidy allowance of $63,000 per annum for ten years. The provision was inserted in order to make federation more attractive to the most reluctant of the North American colonies.

The technique of temporary constitutional provisions reached its fullest development in the Australian Constitution. There is but one temporary provision with a fixed limit of time, providing that Western Australia, if it be an original State, might continue for five years after the enactment of uniform customs to impose its own supplemental customs duties, provided that they be diminished by one fifth each year. This Section was an attempt to make federation more feasible, in the Australian situation, for an area heavily dependent upon imports and revenue from them.

All other temporary financial provisions of the Australian charter are obligatory for a stated period of years, with a provision that they should continue thereafter "until the Parliament should otherwise provide." Thus, one Section requires that at least three fourths of Commonwealth revenue from customs and excise must be paid to the States for at least ten years. Another makes a similar provision for federal subventions to the States for ten years "and thereafter until the Parliament otherwise provides." Another Section contains a provision for temporary suspension of a federal power: "After five years from the imposition of uniform duties of customs, the Parliament may provide . . . for the monthly payment to the several states of all surplus revenue of the Commonwealth."

These provisions clearly anticipated two situations. In the first place, the Australian "founding fathers" expected the States to suffer greatly from loss of their customs revenues. In the second place, they looked forward to a central government so limited in its functions that its revenue from customs and excise would exceed its expenditures. Both predictions held true from 1901 until the onset of the First World War — a period closely corresponding to the ten years provided in most of the temporary provisions.

Similar expectations of temporary exigencies colored the texts of both of the twentieth-century German constitutions. But the special circumstances of their case make them of less significance (see Appendix III).

Through all of these temporary constitutional arrangements with respect to finance there runs a common thread. Whenever the draftsmen of a constitution can anticipate a serious loss of revenue either to all of the States as a group, or to a subclass of them, some sort of transitional provision is inserted. And, if an unusual federal burden of limited duration is foreseen, special articles may be inserted for its financing. In no case have such provisions carried a stated term of longer than ten years, but, it should be noted, some of them either carry no time limitation whatsoever or are to continue until the federal legislative body shall otherwise provide.

B. *Double Taxation*

Double or multiple taxation can, from a jurisdictional viewpoint, occur in either of two situations. Any taxable object or activity which falls under two coordinate taxing authorities will, if both of them levy the relevant taxes, find itself doubly liable. This situation arises internationally, where it is the subject of treaty-like agreements which eliminate or ameliorate the effects. In federal states it occurs most often with respect to activities or objects which are interstate in nature. The second type of double taxation is that which arises when both of two tax jurisdictions applicable to the same area levy the same type of tax. It is more properly called concurrent taxation. The most frequent example in federal states is the income tax, which is often imposed by both the central government and the governments of the component units. In the discussion to follow, these types of double taxation will be distinguished.

This distinction, however, does violence to the texts of the constitutions here under scrutiny. Only three of them — the Weimar German Constitution of 1919, and the two Austrian charters of 1920 and 1929 — mention "double taxation" at all. The subject comes up in those provisions of the three constitutions which provide for federal domination of the tax field. In all of the other federal constitutions relevant to this study, the subject is never mentioned.

But, in all jurisdictions, the problem arises. The complexity of modern economic life is such that many enterprises overlap the borders of single component States, and the mobility of individual human beings makes them frequently liable to taxation by more than one such area. Similarly, the needs of all levels of government for increased revenues have led to more pronounced overlapping of taxation except where the constitution explicitly provides for tax sharing. In general, one is justified in concluding that the issue of double taxation has been "solved" on a constitutional level only where the constitution itself provides for fairly complete federal domination of the entire tax field. This state of affairs obtains in Australia and Austria. In Canada it is probably the case, though the Dominion government has not as yet attempted to exert coercive powers. In Switzerland and Germany, federal domination is by no means so clear, but the provisions for sharing of taxes, with the federal government responsible for the regulations governing their collection, goes far to eliminate the problem of overlapping taxes.

These remarks, however, apply only to the second sort of multiple taxation: that is, to the assessment by two different levels of government of the same sorts of taxes upon the same sources of revenue. Interterritorial double or multiple, i.e., concurrent, taxation, which involves duplicate payments to different jurisdictions at the same governmental level, is an unsolved problem in every federal nation. Interstate agreements have not been exploited in federal countries, even where — as in the United States — the Constitution makes explicit provision for such compacts.

One must conclude that double taxation is hardly as serious an issue as some economists would lead us to believe. There certainly are occasional inequities, and frequent added costs of compliance with tax laws, but from the viewpoint of juristic or governmental analysis one is tempted to remark that such are the inherent and unavoidable costs of federal government. Any attempt to eliminate double taxation by centralizing powers is unquestionably antithetical to the federal principle itself.

C. *Competitive Tax Rates and Tax Exemptions*

Problems of competitive tax rates and tax exemptions are even less clearly reflected in constitutional provisions than are those of multiple taxation. Only one of the six constitutions here under examination makes allowance for the issue, and that allowance is only implicit, in the German Basic Law of 1949.

The possibility of competition between component States in the field of taxation can arise on a large scale only where the regional diversity of a nation is such that the same industries or types of taxable object can be located in any one of two or more areas which fall within the territory of separate States. These situations have arisen most strikingly in the United States. The areas which are tending to lose industries have, however, not asked for federal control. Here, as in the case of multiple taxation, it remains to be shown whether such industrial migration is a net gain or a net loss for either the States concerned or for the federal union as a whole.

In only one field has a federal government adopted legislation intended to reduce the impact of competitive State tax rates. In the early 1920's, several American States attempted to attract wealthy taxpayers by repealing their State inheritance taxes. In 1926, the federal Congress enacted an inheritance tax law with higher rates than those exacted by any State, and with a proviso that receipts for payment of State estate taxes might be used as a credit for a substantial portion of the federal tax. This law made it no advantage at all to reside in a State without an inheritance tax, for the individual would still remain liable to payment of the full federal tax. In the income tax field, deductions are allowed in computing income for federal income tax purposes. Such credits or deductions are devices for reducing the impact of discriminatory tax rates or tax exemptions, but it cannot be said either that any nation has made extensive use of them or that their employment requires special provision in the constitution. The power to tax, inherent in any government, surely involves the power to exempt or to deduct.

D. *Federal Responsibilities for Debts*

In the matter of the transfer of debts, two situations ought to be distinguished: a federal system which is a "successor state" to some other affiliation of all or part of its constituent units, and a federal state which assumes particular responsibilities with respect to the debts of the component entities themselves. The former situation may be disposed of with a sentence. Only the Constitution of the United States of America makes explicit provision for the debts of a predecessor state. That document provides that the debts of the Continental Confederacy be taken over by the new federation — a provision inserted primarily to ensure the support, in the ratification debates, of the holders of Continental bonds. No other federal constitution makes similar allowances.

But with the State debts it is a different matter. In this field the constitutions of the United States, Switzerland, and Austria are silent. There are no explicit provisions in the German Constitution of 1919, but the requirement that the Reich assume ownership of the Länder-owned railroads entailed an assumption as well of the State debts incurred to build them.

Canada and Australia have the most detailed provisions concerning State debts. The Canadian Constitution not only stipulated that the Dominion should assume the debts of the colonies, but also that it should receive the contents of their treasuries. The amount of debt to be assumed, furthermore, was specified, with a provision that provincial debts in excess of the stipulated figure should entail a deduction from Dominion subsidies to the amount necessary to service the excess, or that provincial debts below the agreed ceiling should entitle the Provinces to larger subventions. In Canada, however, only the debts existing as of the date of federation were taken over by the federal government.

Australia has gone much farther. Its Constitution originally provided that State debts "as existing at the establishment of the Commonwealth" might (but need not) be taken over by the Commonwealth. The qualifying clause was stricken out in 1909, making it possible for the Commonwealth to assume State debts incurred after federation. Then, in 1928, a new Section 105A was added to the Constitution, under which the Commonwealth might make agreements with the States not only with respect to their past debts but governing their future borrowings. This article is the most generous constitutional provision for federal fiscal coordination yet adopted anywhere; it is discussed in detail in Section IV below.

Provisions for the assumption of State debts display a clear pattern. Wherever such debts are sizable and have been serviced in the past from revenues which are being conceded to the federal government, the latter usually takes the responsibility for their amortization.

IV. ISSUES IMPLICIT IN CONTEMPORARY FISCAL POLICIES

A. *Flexible Taxation as a Compensatory Device*

Except for incidental mention of regulatory taxes such as excises on liquors and tobacco, taxation has been discussed here as if it had but one function: that of providing the revenues necessary for governmental operations. This is what might be called the "classical" view, and until the mid-1930's it was the only widespread opinion on the proper function of taxation.

Since then, however, an additional function has been imputed to taxation systems. They have been found capable of exerting great influence upon the major economic variables — national income, consumer expenditures, saving, employment, price level, and the like. Generally speaking, taxes which redistribute income from the relatively rich to the relatively poor tend to increase the proportion of income which is expended and to reduce that part which is saved. Excise or sales taxes, on the other hand, tend to inhibit consumer expenditures and to reduce the pressure of consumer demand upon prices.

Beyond the question of the types of taxation and their economic effects there is the problem of the balance between income and outgo. It is widely believed that governments have the duty of spending beyond their revenue in times of economic depression, and of taxing to provide budgetary surpluses in times of high prosperity.

There is no need here to sketch in detail the theoretical considerations which underlie contemporary fiscal policies in most modern Western nations. But we must notice that they pose peculiar problems in federalized nations. In federal countries which do not provide constitutionally for central control of the financial field as a whole, it is frequently difficult to arrange for coordinated changes in tax structures at the two levels of government as economic conditions vary. The task of arranging for parallel policies with respect to deficits and surpluses has also been troublesome. In all federal states today, the powers of the central government in fiscal matters have reached a point sufficient to guarantee that the federal authorities can neutralize fiscally whatever divergent policies are adopted on the local level, but resort to this technique is both wasteful and inexact.

These issues are relatively new, and few federal constitutions take cognizance of them. There is one federal nation, however, in which the Constitution makes provision for such fiscal coordination. The section which follows is an analysis of the terms of the Australian arrangements.

B. *Federal Coordination of Fiscal Policies*

Two sections of the Australian Constitution are relevant in the present context. The Commonwealth is empowered "during a period of ten years . . . and thereafter until the Parliament otherwise provides" to grant financial assistance to the States "on such terms and conditions as the Parliament thinks fit" (§96). As a part of the terms of such grants, the Parliament in 1933 passed an act establishing a Commonwealth Grants Commission of three members to conduct continuing studies of State finances and to recommend extending or denying aid to needy States. The Commission has been concerned primarily with the three poorest Australian States, but its powers include the right to review the taxation systems of all of the States and to make recommendations to their Parliaments, or to the Commonwealth Parliament, concerning financial practices in the States.

The review powers of the Grants Commission, together with the demonstrated ability of the Commonwealth to make its grants dependent upon tax uniformity as among the States, make it clear that the Dominion possesses a plenitude of fiscal powers. It can, within limits, if it so desires, effectively force the six States to adopt whatever tax system the federal government of the moment deems fit.

Central powers in Australia also extend into the second area of fiscal policy — the balance between income and outgo. In 1929, the electorate ratified an amendment providing that the Commonwealth might "make agreements" with the States with respect to their public debts, including the taking over, management, and amortization by the Commonwealth and Commonwealth control over future borrowings (§105A). Two final clauses in the Section exempted agreements made under it from any qualifications stemming from other articles of the Constitution of the Commonwealth or of the constitutions of the States. This amendment "ratified" constitutionally a financial agreement which had been made in 1927 and given legislative status by the Commonwealth Parliament and by all of the State Parliaments. By its terms, all State debts (with minor exceptions) were assumed by the Commonwealth, and future Commonwealth and State borrowings (except for Commonwealth defense loans) were placed under the jurisdiction of a Loan Council of seven members. Six of its members were representatives of the States, and the seventh a Commonwealth Minister who possessed a double vote and a casting vote. Since 1927, all State loans have been cleared by the Council, which has also exercised its right to control the rate at which debt is paid off. The Council is unable to force a single State to run at a budgetary surplus, but it can make most difficult a State's attempts to continue deficit operations. Generally speaking, the States have been most careful to operate their fiscal systems in a manner satisfactory to the Council at large, for fear that divergence from its standards might lead to future difficulties in times of need.

Australia thus possesses ample institutional arrangements for the coordination of fiscal policies between the central government and the six State governments. Some scholars, in fact, are of the opinion that financial coordination has reached a point in Australia which threatens the federal scheme itself. In the major aspects of public financial policy, the States are almost completely at the mercy of the plenary Dominion powers over taxation and grants. Only in the matter of loans is the Commonwealth unable alone to coerce; there each State is subject to the judgment of the Commonwealth plus any two of its five sister states.

In the other five federations fiscal coordination is almost exclusively a matter of informal agreement, usually between the public officials most directly concerned with the problem. In nations with Parliamentary regimes at all levels, such as Canada and Germany, party discipline offers possibilities for effectuating suitable agreements whenever the central and the component governments are controlled by the same party or coalition of parties. But there is no means of assuring that such will be the case at the required moment in the financially crucial areas. In a country such as the United States, agreement on policy among State commissioners of taxation, or between those officials and the officers of the federal Treasury, may be and are thwarted by the national and State legislatures.

One more aspect might be mentioned. It appears entirely feasible so to establish the scheme of federal subventions as to make their continuance dependent upon compliance by the States with overall fiscal policies upon which the central government and a majority — perhaps even a qualified preponderant majority — of the component States are able to agree. This arrangement is closely similar to the Australian Loan Council, but it does not enable a minority of the States, in combination with the federal government, to coerce the remainder. Working out the details of such a scheme would clearly require prior determination of other constitutional provisions. Perhaps through the Administrative Council proposed in Study 2, The Federal Executive, a coordinating program could be achieved, when the federation has achieved sufficient stability and prestige to handle so heavy a responsibility. Whatever the difficulties, it would appear that in the area of fiscal policy we have a problem which requires continuing consultation and the coordination of decisions at both levels of a federal system. Since the European Community will not be able to shoulder such a task at the outset, care should be taken to avoid commitments.

V. CONCLUSIONS

In spite of a great variety in detail, some broad conclusions stand out from the preceding survey of federal public finance. Clearly, any federal system must settle in its constitution the power to tax, and the prevailing tendency has been to grant both federal and State authorities the right to tax, to acquire and own property, and to borrow on their own credit. This tendency to allow both levels of government in a federal system equal access to the tax resources of the community is in keeping with the principle of federalism. A certain amount of fiscal autonomy is, as we saw, required to maintain the balance between central and local authorities; to make either dependent upon the support of the other implies the danger that this fiscal dependence will soon spread to other fields and the federal system thereby be perverted into a unitary one or dissolved into its parts. It is furthermore to be observed that the oldest and most successful federal states, the United States and Switzerland, have been most careful in developing and maintaining this balance. Hence a broad grant of power to the federal authorities, when a new federation is established, would appear sound from an empirical viewpoint.

When it comes to the collecting of the taxes actually adopted by federal legislation, established practice varies to such an extent that hard and fast conclusions are not indicated. However, either a federal administration or the employment of the local administration would seem to be feasible. The decision turns upon very practical considerations of efficiency, availability of trained personnel, and the like. A newly established federation would probably be well advised to adopt, at least at the start, a system of delegated tax administration, if the fiscal burdens to be assumed by the federation are considerable. The United States started with a very limited federal budget, and early estimates of the ultimate sums were far from the mark; hence it did not develop a federal internal revenue service of any size presenting unusual administrative problems until the advent of the income tax. On the other hand, Switzerland and Germany, which started with a relatively large federal budget, adopted a delegated system and managed to develop reasonably sound practices in this field. Certainly a federation worth the name ought to have the right to establish its own tax-gathering agencies; and in one field, namely customs, it probably ought to do so at the outset. Grants-in-aid, which are really tax transfers from the federal to the State level for specific purposes, present special problems. In view of past experience, any new federation ought to provide itself with the right to make such grants.

Older fiscal systems, notably that of the United States, suffer considerably from certain constitutional provisions which were adopted at a time when fiscal policies were not seen in the broader context of developmental economic policies. But with an ever larger part of the community's local product going into governmental channels the incidence of taxation and governmental borrowing has become a major consideration of all policy makers. Money is still the "vital nerve" of defense, but as contrasted with the days of Colbert, money now means a complex pattern of economic considerations related to inflation and deflation, unemployment, and the general business cycle — in short, fiscal policy. Experience in existing federal states would argue for *not* including in the constitution provisions which would hamper the development of sound fiscal policies, and the possible inclusion of provisions which would facilitate the coordination of fiscal policies on the federal and local level.

Existing federal states have, upon their creation, taken over the debts of the component units to a greater or lesser extent. Such a procedure is sound and practical when correlated with the taking over of tax resources. But there is no indication in past experience that this needs to be done by express constitutional provision, and as long as the power exists it has been done effectively, in the United States and elsewhere, by appropriate legislation. The power of borrowing implies this possibility to legislate.

Customs receipts, which as we said constitute in existing federations definitely federal revenue, have ceased to possess the great fiscal importance they once had. Hence, while they ought to be made federal in the interest of the federation's relations with foreign nations, their fiscal significance ought not to be overestimated. The United States, for example, could turn over all its customs revenue to the States (as it does in the case of Puerto Rico) without suffering serious financial embarrassment. Any new federation could therefore, if it were desirable for other than fiscal reasons, leave the customs revenue temporarily in local hands without too much difficulty.

The real mainstay of all federal systems in the age of the welfare state is the income tax, and a uniform system of progressive income taxation appears to be the most important foundation of sound federal finance. For such income taxation can take due account of the diversity in taxable wealth most equitably, and any new federation presumably will want to start in the light of this clear conclusion from past experience. But the effective employment of the income tax presupposes a reasonably stable and uniform means of exchange and is therefore intimately bound up with the problem of establishing a workable federal currency. To this problem, Study 8, Federal Powers over Currency, Banking, Credit, and Foreign Exchange, gives major attention. In any case, the immensely varied experience of established federal systems clearly shows that there are many workable ways for setting up a practical balance between federal and State revenues under which both can effectively finance the various functions which are theirs.

APPENDIX I

Australia
(Financial Provisions in the Text of the Constitution)[5]

I. THE POWER TO TAX AND LIMITATIONS THEREON

51. The Parliament shall, subject to this Constitution, have power to make laws for the peace, order and good government of the Commonwealth with respect to: —

(ii) Taxation; but so as not to discriminate between States or parts of States:

(iii) Bounties on the production or export of goods, but so that such bounties shall be uniform throughout the Commonwealth:

(iv) Borrowing money on the public credit of the Commonwealth:

88. Uniform duties of customs shall be imposed within two years after the establishment of the Commonwealth.

90. On the imposition of uniform duties of customs the power of the Parliament to impose duties of customs and of excise, and to grant bounties on the production or export of goods, shall become exclusive.

On the imposition of uniform duties of customs all laws of the several States imposing duties of customs or of excise, or offering bounties on the production or export of goods, shall cease to have effect . . .

99. The Commonwealth shall not, by any law or regulation of trade, commerce, or revenue, give preference to one State or any part thereof over another State or any part thereof.

[5] The term "Constitution" here includes the Commonwealth of Australia Constitution Act of 1900 together with those subsequent Constitution Alteration Acts which bear on financial matters.

112. After uniform duties of customs have been imposed, a State may levy on imports or exports, or on goods passing into or out of the State, such charges as may be necessary for executing the inspection laws of the State; but the net produce of all charges so levied shall be for the use of the Commonwealth; and any such inspection laws may be annulled by the Parliament of the Commonwealth.

114. A State shall not, without the consent of the Parliament of the Commonwealth . . . , impose any tax on property of any kind belonging to the Commonwealth, nor shall the Commonwealth impose any tax on property of any kind belonging to a State.

II. TAX ADMINISTRATION

69. The departments of customs and of excise in each State shall become transferred to the Commonwealth on its establishment.

85. When any department of the public service of a State is transferred to the Commonwealth:

(i) All property of the State of any kind, used exclusively in connection with the department, shall become vested in the Commonwealth; but, in the case of the departments controlling customs and excise and bounties, for such time only as the Governor-General in Council may declare to be necessary.

86. On the establishment of the Commonwealth, the collection and control of duties of customs and of excise, and the control of the payment of bounties, shall pass to the Executive Government of the Commonwealth.

III. THE LEGISLATIVE PROCESS IN TAXATION

53. Proposed laws appropriating revenue or money, or imposing taxation, shall not originate in the Senate. But a proposed law shall not be taken to appropriate revenue or moneys, or to impose taxation, by reason only of its containing provisions for the imposition or appropriation of fines or other pecuniary penalties, or for the demand or payment or appropriation of fees for licences, or fees for services under the proposed law.

The Senate may not amend proposed laws imposing taxation, or proposed laws appropriating revenue or moneys for the ordinary annual services of the Government.

The Senate may not amend any proposed laws so as to increase any proposed charge or burden on the people.

The Senate may at any stage return to the House of Representatives any proposed law which the Senate may not amend, requesting, by message, the omission or amendment of any items or provisions therein. And the House of Representatives may, if it thinks fit, make any of such omissions or amendments, with or without modifications.

Except as provided in this section, the Senate shall have equal power with the House of Representatives in respect of all proposed laws.

54. The proposed law which appropriates revenue or moneys for the ordinary annual services of the Government shall deal only with such appropriation.

55. Laws imposing taxation shall deal only with the imposition of taxation, and any provisions therein dealing with any other matter shall be of no effect.

Laws imposing taxation, except laws imposing duties of customs or of excise, shall deal with one subject of taxation only; but laws imposing duties of customs shall deal with duties of customs only, and laws imposing duties of excise shall deal with duties of excise only.

56. A vote, resolution, or proposed law for the appropriation of revenue or moneys shall not be passed unless the purpose of the appropriation has in the same session been recommended by message of the Governor-General to the House in which the proposal originated.

IV. Federal Grants to Component Units

96. During a period of ten years after the establishment of the Commonwealth and thereafter until the Parliament otherwise provides, the Parliament may grant financial assistance to any State on such terms and conditions as the Parliament thinks fit.

V. Debts

105. The Parliament may take over from the States their public debts [as existing at the establishment of the Commonwealth,] [6] or a proportion thereof according to the respective numbers of their people as shown by the latest statistics of the Commonwealth, and may convert, renew, or consolidate such debts, or any part thereof; and the State shall indemnify the Commonwealth in respect of the debts taken over, and thereafter the interest payable in respect of the debts shall be deducted and retained from the portions of the surplus revenue of the Commonwealth payable to the several States, or if such surplus is insufficient, or if there is no surplus, then the deficiency or the whole amount shall be paid by the several States.

105A.[7] — (1) The Commonwealth may make agreements with the States with respect to the public debts of the States, including —

(a) the taking over of such debts by the Commonwealth;

(b) the management of such debts;

(c) the payment of interest and the provision and management of sinking funds in respect of such debts;

[6] The words in brackets were stricken by Section 2 of the Constitution Alteration (State Debts) Act of 1909.

[7] This Section was inserted by the Constitution Alteration (State Debts) Act of 1928.

(d) the consolidation, renewal, conversion, and redemption of such debts;

(e) the indemnification of the Commonwealth by the States in respect of debts taken over by the Commonwealth; and

(f) the borrowing of money by the States or by the Commonwealth, or by the Commonwealth for the States.

(2) The Parliament may make laws for validating any such agreement made before the commencement of this section.

(3) The Parliament may make laws for the carrying out by the parties thereto of any such agreement.

(4) Any such agreement may be varied or rescinded by the parties thereto.

(5) Every such agreement and any such variation thereof shall be binding upon the Commonwealth and the States parties thereto notwithstanding anything contained in this Constitution or the Constitution of the several States or in any law of the Parliament of the Commonwealth or of any State.

(6) The powers conferred by this section shall not be construed as being limited in any way by the provisions of Section one hundred and five of this Constitution.

VI. Transitional Provisions

87. During a period of ten years after the establishment of the Commonwealth and thereafter until the Parliament otherwise provides, of the net revenue of the Commonwealth from duties of customs and of excise not more than one-fourth shall be applied annually by the Commonwealth towards its expenditure.

The balance shall, in accordance with this Constitution, be paid to the several States, or applied towards the payment of interest on debts of the several States taken over by the Commonwealth.

89. Until the imposition of uniform duties of customs:

(i) The Commonwealth shall credit to each State the revenues collected therein by the Commonwealth.

(ii) The Commonwealth shall debit to each State:

(a) The expenditure therein of the Commonwealth incurred solely for the maintenance or continuance, as at the time of transfer, of any department transferred from the State to the Commonwealth;

(b) The proportion of the State, according to the number of its people, in the other expenditure of the Commonwealth.

(iii) The Commonwealth shall pay to each State month by month the balance (if any) in favour of the State.

94. After five years from the imposition of uniform duties of customs, the Parliament may provide, on such basis as it deems fair, for the monthly

payments to the several States of all surplus revenue of the Commonwealth.

95. Notwithstanding anything in this Constitution, the Parliament of the State of Western Australia, if that State be an Original State, may, during the first five years after the imposition of uniform duties of customs, impose duties of customs on goods passing into that State and not originally imported from beyond the limits of the Commonwealth; and such duties shall be collected by the Commonwealth.

But any such duty so imposed on any goods shall not exceed during the first of such years the duty chargeable on the goods under the law of Western Australia in force at the imposition of uniform duties, and shall not exceed during the second, third, fourth, and fifth of such years respectively, four-fifths, three-fifths, two-fifths, and one-fifth of such latter duty, and all duties imposed under this section shall cease at the expiration of the fifth year after the imposition of uniform duties.

[See also the text of Section 96, reproduced under IV above.]

A P P E N D I X   I I

Canada

I. FINANCIAL PROVISIONS IN THE TEXT OF THE CONSTITUTION[8]

A. *The Power to Tax and Limitations Thereon*

91. It shall be lawful for the Queen, by and with the Advice and Consent of the Senate and the House of Commons, to make Laws for the Peace, Order, and Good Government of Canada, in relation to all Matters not coming within the Classes of Subjects by this Act assigned exclusively to the Legislatures of the Provinces; and for greater Certainty, but not so as to restrict the Generality of the foregoing Terms in this Section, it is hereby declared that (notwithstanding anything in this Act) the exclusive Legislative Authority of the Parliament of Canada extends to all Matters coming within the Classes of Subjects next hereinafter enumerated, that is to say: —

    1. The Public Debt and Property.

    3. The Raising of Money by any Mode or System of Taxation.

    4. The Borrowing of Money on the Public Credit . . .

And any matter coming within any of the Classes of Subjects enumerated in this Section shall not be deemed to come within the Class of Matters of a local or private Nature comprised in the Enumeration of the Classes of Subjects by this Act assigned exclusively to the Legislatures of the Provinces.

92. In each Province the Legislature may exclusively make Laws in re-

---

[8] For the purpose of this discussion, the term "Constitution" includes the British North America Act of 1867 and those later Acts of the same title which bear on financial matters.

lation to Matters coming within the Classes of Subjects next hereinafter enumerated, that is to say: —

  2. Direct Taxation within the Province in order to the Raising of a Revenue for Provincial Purposes.

  3. The Borrowing of Money on the sole Credit of the Province.

121. All Articles of the Growth, Produce, or Manufacture of any one of the Provinces shall, from and after the Union, be admitted free into each of the other Provinces.

124. Nothing in this Act shall affect the Right of New Brunswick to levy the Lumber Dues . . . but the Lumber of any of the Provinces other than New Brunswick shall not be subject to such Dues.

125. No Lands or Property belonging to Canada or any Province shall be liable to Taxation.

B. *Tax Administration*

No provisions.

C. *The Legislative Process in Taxation*

18.[9] The Privileges, Immunities, and Powers to be held, enjoyed, and exercised by the Senate and by the House of Commons, and by the Members thereof respectively, shall be such as are from Time to Time defined by Act of the Parliament of Canada, but so that any Act of the Parliament of Canada defining such Privileges, Immunities, and Powers shall not confer any Privileges, Immunities or Powers exceeding those at the passing of such Act held, enjoyed, and exercised by the Commons House of Parliament of the United Kingdom of Great Britain and Ireland and by the Members thereof.

53. Bills for appropriating any part of the Public Revenue, or for imposing any Tax or Impost, shall originate in the House of Commons.

54. It shall not be lawful for the House of Commons to adopt or pass any Vote, Resolution, Address, or Bill for the appropriation of any part of the Public Revenue, or of any Tax or Impost, to any purpose, that has not been first recommended to that House by Message of the Governor-General in the Session in which such Vcte, Resolution, Address, or Bill is proposed.

90. The following Provisions of this Act respecting the Parliament of Canada, namely, — the Provisions relating to Appropriation and Tax Bills, the Recommendation of Money Votes . . . shall extend and apply to the Legislatures of the several Provinces as if those Provisions were here re-enacted and made applicable in Terms to the respective Provinces and the Legislatures thereof . . .

91. [See the text of the Section as reproduced under A above.]

  [9] The text here reproduced is a change from that of the original act of 1867. The change was introduced by the British North America Act of 1875.

D. *Federal Grants to Component Units*

This problem was originally dealt with in Section 118 of the British North America Act of 1867, whose provisions were superseded by the British North America Act of 1907. The original Section 118 provided for subsidies to the four Provinces of $80,000 per annum in the case of Ontario, 70,000 for Quebec, 60,000 for Nova Scotia, and 50,000 for New Brunswick. In addition, each Province was to receive a subvention of 80 cents per capita per annum. These sums were stated to be "in full Settlement of all future demands on Canada."

By 1907, five more Provinces had been added to the Dominion, each of them having entered it with a subsidy agreement fixed by an order-in-council. The British North America Act of that year substituted, for the grants summarized above and for the special arrangements for the five new Provinces, a series of grants keyed to provincial populations as follows:

Population	Annual Grant
under 150,000	$100,000
150,000 to 200,000	150,000
200,000 to 400,000	180,000
400,000 to 800,000	190,000
800,000 to 1,500,000	220,000
over 1,500,000	240,000

In addition, British Columbia would receive for ten years an annual grant of $100,000. Each of the nine Provinces would receive, beyond the grants thus far indicated, an annual per capita subsidy of 80 cents up to a population of 2,500,000 and 60 cents per head beyond that figure. Special provisions were inserted to protect British Columbia and Prince Edward Island from subsidy losses in the event of population declines.

E. *Debts*

111. Canada shall be liable for the Debts and Liabilities of each Province existing at the Union.

[Sections 112 through 115, which follow immediately upon the Section just quoted, provide that the Provinces shall be responsible for the principal and service of any amount by which their debts, as of the union, shall exceed a stated fixed sum. The sum ranged from $62,500,000 in the case of Ontario and Quebec jointly to $7,000,000 for New Brunswick. Section 116 further provides that, if the debts of Nova Scotia and New Brunswick are below the stated figures at the time of union, they shall receive annually from the Dominion a payment at the rate of 5 per cent of the difference.]

F. *Transitional Provisions*

119. New Brunswick shall receive . . . from Canada for the Period of Ten years, from the Union an additional Allowance of Sixty-three thousand

Dollars per Annum; but as long as the Public Debt of that Province remains under Seven million Dollars, a Deduction equal to the Interest at Five per Centum per Annum on such Deficiency shall be made from that Allowance of Sixty-three thousand Dollars.

122. The Customs and Excise Laws of each Province shall, subject to the Provisions of this Act, continue in force until altered by the Parliament of Canada.

II. JUDICIAL INTERPRETATIONS OF THESE PROVISIONS

The major problem has been the apparent discrepancy between Section 91 (3) and Section 92 (2) (reproduced in Section I above). Is the specific grant of local direct taxation powers to the Provinces a net decrement from the general power of taxation granted to the Dominion? If so, how may this position be reconciled with the undeniably broad grant of powers in the introductory portion of Section 91?

The Judicial Committee of the Privy Council found itself confronted with this issue early in the history of the Dominion. In 1881, their Lordships decided:

> With regard to certain classes of subjects, therefore, generally described in section 91, legislative power may reside as to some matters falling within the general description of these subjects in the legislatures of the provinces. In these cases it is the duty of the Courts, however difficult it may be, to ascertain in what degree, and to what extent, authority to deal with matters falling within these classes of subjects exists in each legislature, and to define in the particular case before them the limits of their respective powers. It could not have been the intention that a conflict should exist; and in order to prevent such a result, the two sections must be read together, and the language of one interpreted, and, where necessary, modified, by that of the other. [*Citizens' Insurance Co. of Canada v. Parsons,* 7 App. Cas. 96 (1881)]

Several years later this general thesis was applied to the reconciliation of Sections 91 and 92 as they bear on taxation. In *Bank of Toronto v. Lambe,* 12 App. Cas. 575 (1887), the Judicial Committee held the latter article to be a limitation on the former, "as regards direct taxation within the province to raise revenue for provincial purposes, that subject falls wholly within the jurisdiction of the provincial legislatures."

Thus the situation is one which permits of double taxation by the Dominion and the Province only in the sphere of direct taxes, for the former authority retains its power to levy direct taxes for federal purposes, and the latter is excluded from the field of indirect taxation.

The doctrines underlying this state of affairs are clearly a compromise among several possible readings of a constitutional text which is far from clear on its face. Despite the conclusion that the provincial power to levy direct taxes for provincial purposes is a net subtraction from the apparently full power of federal taxation, Canadian and British judges and legal scholars cling almost unanimously to the opinion that neither level of government is constituted by delegation from the other level. Furthermore, neither is held to be constituted as a delegate of the Imperial Parliament in Westminster. The Dominion on the one hand, and the Provinces on the other, are independently established governmental entities both of which have been granted full sovereign powers.

This theory, of course, is dubious in the extreme. The thirty subsections of Section 91 and the sixteen subsections of Section 92 delineate a thoroughgoing division of governmental authority, with occasional overlaps as in the case of taxation. And, beyond the text of the charter, it is difficult to see how one can define "sovereignty" in such a manner as to provide two "sovereign" levels of government in the same geographical area.

Since the 1880's, Canadian tax law has developed under both theories: that Section 92 is a restriction on Section 91, and that both Dominion and Province are "sovereign" independently one of another. Since the ruling in the *Bank of Toronto* case, the issues have turned primarily upon the meaning of "direct tax" and of "provincial purpose."

In defining "direct tax," the Judicial Committee went to John Stuart Mill. "A direct tax is one," Mill wrote, "which is demanded from the very person who it is intended or desired should pay it." Directness or indirectness in taxation thus has two dimensions: the question of economic incidence (i.e., of "shiftability"), and the question of legislators' intent or expectation. The Privy Council has held to Mill's doctrine throughout its review of Canadian tax cases, and has persisted in minute examination of the tax statutes and the tax collection procedures in each set of circumstances. It has insisted that a tax found to be direct in one case at bar may be held indirect in altered circumstances. In general, the line of precedents thus far has held that taxes on real and personal property, on incomes, on estates and inheritances, and on sales when collected from the ultimate purchaser, are all "direct" taxes within the meaning of Section 92.

With respect to the "provincial purpose" limitation, only one point need be made. Very early in the life of the Dominion, the Privy Council ruled in *Dow v. Black*, L.R. 6 P.C. 272 (1875) that the purpose need not be general throughout the Province. A provincial legislature in Canada is free to impose direct taxes within one part of a Province without extending them to the Province at large, and correspondingly the purpose for which the tax is imposed may extend only to a small area of the total Province.

Section 92 (2) contains one further restrictive phrase. It limits the Provinces to "direct taxation *within the province*." The problem of defining "within" has of course arisen. But it raises no questions in Canada or in other federations which do not also arise in taxation by the subdivisions of unitary states. For that reason, and because of its great legal complexity, the problem is omitted here.

Thus far, this discussion of limitations on the tax power has turned almost exclusively upon the restriction of provincial taxation. This emphasis accurately reflects the development of Canadian constitutional law on the subject of taxation. The limitations upon the federal power to tax are almost entirely a matter of its territorial jurisdiction as a member of the British Commonwealth. As in the case of "within the province," these are issues of *situs,* and, although the Canadian and Australian cases present peculiarities due to their Commonwealth memberships, they are not functions of the federal structure of the two Dominions. These matters are therefore also omitted.

III. THE INCOME TAX

The powers of taxation reviewed above make double taxation possible in one crucially important field. Both the Dominion and the Provinces may impose income taxes on individuals and corporations, and both may levy death and succession duties. The pressing need for greatly increased Dominion revenues in the Second World War led to proposals that such taxes be concentrated in the hands of the central government. Because of the constitutional bases of taxation in Canada, the Provinces could not be forced to leave the field, and negotiated agreements appeared to be the only constitutional solution.

All nine Provinces, in 1941, entered into agreements with the Dominion which provided that the Provinces should vacate the personal income tax field and should suspend all corporation taxes, of whatever sort. These Wartime Tax Agreements remained in force until 1946. During the period of five fiscal years each Province received a grant in lieu of the revenues which it would have received had it continued to levy its old taxes at the old rates through the war period.

At the end of the war, several Dominion-Provincial conferences on extension of the Wartime Agreements came to naught. In 1947, the Dominion Parliament enacted the Tax Rental Agreements Act, providing a new basis for negotiations. Under the new law, statute agreements were quickly reached with all of the Provinces, save Ontario and Quebec. Under the terms of the new arrangements, the contracting Provinces agreed to remain out of the fields covered in the Wartime Tax Agreements, and in addition to vacate that of succession duties. The Provinces, under a formula too complicated to be summarized here, were guaranteed minimum annual grants totaling about $89,000,000 for those which entered into the new agreements. The subsidies would increase with population and with per capita gross national product. In 1951, the contracting Provinces agreed to extend the contracts for an additional five-year period, with increases in the grants.

The enabling statute which lies behind these agreements is in no sense coercive: the Provinces are free to accept or reject the terms provided for in the Tax Rental Agreements Act, and two of them have yet to agree. Any

Province which does enter the scheme, however, faces certain terms not open to further negotiation. It must, for example, enact a uniform 5 per cent tax on corporate incomes derived from that part of the corporation's business conducted within the Province. Similarly, the Province may or may not withdraw from the succession duties field, but if it does not withdraw its annual grant is reduced by the amount of the revenue thus lost to the Dominion treasury.

Ontario and Quebec, like all the other Provinces, had suspended their individual income taxes during the war. They have not to date decided to reimpose them, although they remain legally free to do so. The Tax Rental scheme thus has concentrated income taxation in the hands of the federal government for a period of more than a decade. Canada possesses the most powerful of all fiscal weapons on a completely voluntary basis.

APPENDIX III

Germany

(Financial Provisions in the Text of the Basic Law)

I. THE POWER TO TAX

Article 70. (1) The Länder shall have the right of legislation insofar as this Basic Law does not accord legislative powers to the Federation.

(2) The division of competence between the Federation and the Länder shall be determined in accordance with the provisions of this Basic Law concerning exclusive and concurrent legislation.

Article 71. In the field of exclusive legislation of the Federation, the Länder shall have powers of legislation only if, and so far as, they are expressly so empowered in a federal law.

Article 72. (1) In the field of concurrent legislation, the Länder shall have powers of legislation so long and so far as the federation makes no use of its legislative right.

(2) The Federation shall have legislative rights in this field insofar as a necessity for regulation by federal law exists because:

1. a matter cannot be effectively regulated by the legislation of individual Länder, or

2. the regulation of a matter by a Land law would prejudice the interests of other Länder or of the Länder as a whole, or

3. the preservation of legal or economic unity demands it, in particular the preservation of uniformity of living conditions extending beyond the territory of an individual Land.

Article 73. The Federation shall have exclusive legislation on:

5. the unity of customs and commercial territory . . .

Article 105. (1) The Federation shall have exclusive legislation on customs and financial monopolies.

(2) The Federation shall have concurrent legislation on:

1. excise taxes and taxes on transactions, with the exception of taxes with localized application, in particular the taxes on real estate acquisition, incremental value and on fire protection,
2. the Taxes on income, property, inheritance and gifts,
3. (*Realsteuern*) taxes on real estate and on business with the exception of the fixing of tax rates,

if it makes a claim on the taxes in their entirety or in part to cover federal expenditures or if the conditions of Article 72, paragraph (2), apply.

(3) Federal legislation on taxes the yield of which accrues in entirety or in part to the Länder or the Gemeinden shall require the approval of the Bundesrat.

Article 106. (1) Customs, the yield of monopolies, the excise taxes with the exception of the beer tax, the transportation tax, the turnover tax and property taxes serving nonrecurrent purposes shall accrue to the Federation.

(2) The beer tax, the taxes on transactions, with the exception of the transportation tax and turnover tax, the income and corporation taxes, the property tax, the inheritance tax, the Realsteuern, and the taxes with localized application shall accrue to the Länder and, in accordance with Land Legislation, to the Gemeinden.

(3) The Federation may, by means of a federal law which shall require the approval of the Bundesrat, make a claim to a part of the income and corporation taxes to cover its expenditure not covered by other revenues, in particular to cover grants which are to be made to Länder to meet expenditures in the fields of education, public health and welfare.

[For Section (4) of this article, see Section IV below.]

Article 107. The final distribution of the taxes subject to concurrent legislation between the Federation and the Länder shall be effected not later than December 31, 1952 and by means of a federal law which shall require the approval of the Bundesrat. This shall not apply to the Realsteuern and the taxes with localized application. In this distribution, both Federation and Länder shall be given a legal claim to certain taxes or shares in taxes corresponding to their functions.

Article 109. The Federation and the Länder shall be self-supporting and independent of each other in their budget economy.

II. TAX ADMINISTRATION

Article 108. (1) Customs, financial monopolies, the excise taxes subject to concurrent legislation, the transportation tax, the turnover tax and the nonrecurrent property dues shall be administered by the federal finance authorities. The structure of these authorities and the procedure to be applied by them shall be regulated by federal legislation. The heads of the authorities at middle level shall be appointed by agreement with the Land Governments. The Federation may delegate the administration of the nonrecurrent property dues to the Land finance authorities to act on behalf of the Federation.

(2) Insofar as the Federation makes a claim to a part of the income and corporation taxes it shall have the right to administer them. It may, however, delegate the administration to the Land finance authorities to act on behalf of the Federation.

(3) The remaining taxes shall be administered by the Land finance authorities. The Federation may, by means of federal legislation which shall require the approval of the Bundesrat, regulate the structure of these authorities, the procedure to be applied by them and the uniform training of the officials. The heads of the authorities at middle level must be appointed by agreement with the Federal Government. The administration of the taxes accruing to the Gemeinden may be transferred by the Länder in entirety or in part to the Gemeinden.

(4) Insofar as the taxes accrue to the Federation, the Land finance authorities shall act on behalf of the Federation. The Länder shall be liable with their revenues for a regular administration of these taxes; the Federal Minister of Finance may supervise the regular administration through federal plenipotentiaries who shall have the right to give instructions to the authorities at middle and lower levels.

(5) Federal jurisdiction shall be uniformly regulated by federal legislation.

(6) The general administrative provisions shall be issued by the Federal Government and, insofar as the administration is incumbent upon the Land finance authorities, with the approval of the Bundesrat.

III. The Legislative Process in Taxation

Article 76. (1) Bills shall be introduced in the Bundestag by the Federal Government, by members of the Bundestag or by the Bundesrat.

(2) Federal Government bills shall first be submitted to the Bundesrat. The Bundesrat shall have the right to give its opinion on these bills within three weeks.

(3) Bundesrat bills shall be submitted to the Bundestag by the Federal Government, which must add a statement of its own views.

Article 110. (1) All revenues and expenditures of the Federation must be estimated for each fiscal year and included in the budget.

(2) The budget shall be established by law before the commencement of the fiscal year. Revenue and expenditure must be balanced. Expenditures shall as a rule be approved for one year; they may in special cases be approved for a longer period. Otherwise the federal budget law may contain no provisions which extend beyond the fiscal year or which do not

concern the revenues and expenditures of the Federation or its administration.

Article 113. Decisions of the Bundestag and Bundesrat which increase the budget expenditure proposed by the Federal Government or include, or imply for the future, new expenditure, shall require the approval of the Federal Government.

IV. FEDERAL GRANTS TO COMPONENT UNITS

Article 106. (4) In order to ensure the working efficiency even of the Länder with a low taxation potential and to equalize the differing burden of expenditure of the Länder, the Federation may make grants and take the funds necessary for this purpose from specific taxes of those accruing to the Länder. A federal law, which shall require the approval of the Bundesrat, shall determine which taxes shall be utilized for this purpose and in what amounts and on what basis the grants shall be distributed among the Länder entitled to equalization; the grants must be handed directly to the Länder.

V. DEBTS

No provisions.

VI. TRANSITIONAL PROVISIONS

No provisions.

APPENDIX IV

Switzerland
(Financial Provisions in the Text of the Constitution)[10]

I. THE POWER TO TAX

Article 28. Customs matters are the concern of the Confederation, which may impose import and export duties.

Article 29. The collection of the federal customs shall be regulated in accordance with the following principles:

1. Import taxes:
   a. Materials necessary to the industry and agriculture of the country shall be taxed as lightly as possible.

---

[10] The text here used is the one currently in force. No attempt is made to reflect the changes between the document of 1848 and that of 1874, or the development of the text since the latter date.

b. The same principle shall apply to commodities necessary to life.

c. Articles of luxury shall be subjected to the heaviest taxes.

Except where circumstances render it impossible, these principles must also be observed in the conclusion of commercial treaties with foreign countries.

2. Export taxes shall be as moderate as possible.

3. Legislation on customs will contain suitable provisions for guaranteeing frontier and market trading.

Article 30. Revenue from customs duties belongs to the Confederation.

Article 32-*bis.* Specialties obtained by the distillation of kernel fruit, wine, grape and wine dregs, gentian roots and other similar materials are subjected to the payment of a tax. . . . The receipts accruing from duties upon the sale and retail trade [in distilled beverages] within the limits of the cantonal territory remain the property of the cantons.

Article 36. Throughout Switzerland posts and telegraphs are within the domain of the Confederation. The revenues from posts and telegraphs belong to the federal treasury.

Article 41-*bis.* The Confederation may charge stamp duties upon deeds, receipts for insurance premiums, bills of exchange and similar instruments, documents in use in transport and other documents relating to commercial operations; such duties may not be imposed on documents concerning transactions in landed property and mortgages. The cantons may not subject to any stamp or registration duty documents which are liable to federal stamp duty or which have been exempted therefrom by the Confederation.

Article 41-*ter.* The Confederation is authorized to tax raw and manufactured tobacco.

Article 42.[11] The expenses of the Confederation shall be defrayed by:

(a) The revenue from federal property;

(b) The revenue from federal customs collected at the Swiss frontier;

(c) The revenue from posts and telegraphs;

(d) The revenue from the powder monopoly;

(e) Half the gross yield of the military exemption tax collected by the cantons;

(f) Contributions from the cantons, to be determined by federal legislation, having special regard to their wealth and taxable resources;

(g) The revenue from stamp duties.

Article 49. No person may be compelled to pay taxes the proceeds of which are specifically appropriated in payment of the purely religious expenses of any religious community of which he is not a member.

Article 54. No marriage fee or similar tax may be levied on either spouse.

---

[11] The precise purpose and legal status of this article are most unclear. It omits many of the important sources of federal revenue. On the other hand, it is the only constitutional warrant for federal participation in the military exemption tax. It should be noted that paragraph (f) is a dead letter; it came into effect only once in 1849, and has not been used since then.

Article 62. Internal taxes on the transfer of property are abolished throughout Switzerland.

Article 63. Taxes on the transfer of property to foreign countries are abolished, subject to reciprocity.

Article 89. Federal decrees of general import whose entry in force admits of no delay can be declared urgent by a decision of a majority of all the members of each of the two councils.

[This provision is the constitutional basis of contemporary Swiss income taxation.]

II. Tax Administration

No provisions.

III. The Legislative Process in Taxation

No provisions.

IV. Federal Grants to Component Units, and Shared Taxes

Article 27-*bis.* Subventions shall be granted to the cantons to aid them in carrying out their obligations in respect of elementary education.

Article 30. The indemnities hitherto paid to the cantons in respect of the redemption of customs, road and bridge tolls, local dues, and similar revenues, are abolished.

The Cantons of Uri, Grisons, Ticino, and Valais shall receive exceptionally, on account of their international Alpine highways, a yearly allowance fixed as follows:

Uri	Frs.	160,000
Grisons		400,000
Ticino		400,000
Valais		100,000

Article 32-*bis.* Half of the net receipts accruing to the Confederation from the taxation of distilled beverages shall be distributed among the cantons in proportion to their populations ordinarily resident; each canton is bound to expend at least ten per cent of its share in combating the causes and effects of alcoholism. The other half of the receipts remains the property of the Confederation; it shall be set apart for old age and dependents' insurance, and shall be paid into the funds established for the same until the time such insurance is introduced.

Article 34-*quater.* The Confederation shall . . . institute a system of old age and surviving dependents' insurance . . .

The insurance plan shall be carried into effect with the cooperation of the cantons . . .

The financial contributions of the Confederation and the cantons shall not exceed, altogether, one half of the total sum necessary for the insurance.

From January 1, 1926, the Confederation shall set apart for old age and surviving dependents' insurance, the total yield of the tobacco tax.

The Confederation's share of the net receipts accruing from the taxation of spirits shall be set apart for old age and surviving dependents' insurance.

Article 35. The cantonal governments may . . . permit gambling for pleasure as in vogue in *Kursaals* up to the spring of 1925 . . .

One-quarter of the gross receipts from the play shall be paid over to the Confederation, which shall set the same apart, without taking into account its own contributions, for victims of natural catastrophes and works of public utility.

Article 37. The sums due to the cantons specified in Article 30 . . . shall be withheld if these highways are not properly maintained by the cantons.

Article 39. The Confederation may exercise its monopoly of note issue through a state bank . . .

At least two-thirds of the net profits of the bank, after payment of interest or reasonable dividend on the endowment or share capital, and deductions of payments to reserve funds, shall go to the cantons.

The bank and its branches shall be exempt from all cantonal taxation.

Article 41-bis. [This is the article on stamp duties. See Section I above.] One-fifth of the net yield of these provisions shall be paid to the cantons.

V. Debts

No provisions.

VI. Transitional Provisions

TRANSITORY PROVISIONS

1. The Proceeds of the postal and customs services shall be divided on the existing bases until the time when the Confederation assumes the military expenditures heretofore borne by the cantons.

The federal legislation shall moreover provide that the part which might entail modifications resulting from Articles 20,[12] 30, 36 and 42 (e), for the treasuries of certain cantons, shall affect the latter only gradually and shall reach its total figure only after a transitional period of several years.

[These provisions were inserted at the time of the constitutional revision of 1874.]

---

[12] Among the four articles here listed only Article 20 is not reproduced above. It imposed upon the cantons the duty of supplying and arming Swiss troops, subject to later reimbursement by the Confederation.

A P P E N D I X   V

United States

I. FINANCIAL PROVISIONS IN THE TEXT OF THE CONSTITUTION

A. *The Power to Tax and Limitations Thereon*

ARTICLE I, *Section* 8. The Congress shall have Power To lay and collect Taxes, Duties, Imposts and Excises, to pay the Debts and provide for the common Defence and general Welfare of the United States; but all Duties, Imposts, and Excises shall be uniform throughout the United States;

To borrow money on the credit of the United States;

Section 9. . . . No capitation, or other direct, Tax shall be laid, unless in proportion to the Census or Enumeration herein before directed to be taken.

No Tax or Duty shall be laid on Articles exported from any State.

Section 10. . . . No State shall, without the Consent of the Congress, lay any Imposts or Duties on Imports or Exports, except what may be absolutely necessary for executing its inspection Laws: and the net Produce of all Duties and Imposts, laid by any State on Imports or Exports, shall be for the Use of the Treasury of the United States; and all such Laws shall be subject to the Revision and Control of the Congress.

No State shall, without the consent of the Congress, lay any duty of Tonnage . . .

AMENDMENT XVI. The Congress shall have power to lay and collect taxes on incomes, from whatever source derived, without apportionment among the several States, and without regard to any census or enumeration.

B. *Tax Administration*

No provisions.

C. *The Legislative Process in Taxation*

ARTICLE I, *Section* 7. All Bills for raising Revenue shall originate in the House of Representatives; but the Senate may propose or concur with Amendments as on other Bills.

D. *Federal Grants to Component Units*

No provisions.

E. *Debts*

ARTICLE VI. All Debts contracted and Engagements entered into, before the Adoption of this Constitution, shall be as valid against the United States under this Constitution, as under the Confederation.

F. *Transitional Provisions*

ARTICLE I, *Section* 9. The Migration or Importation of such persons as any of the States now existing shall think proper to admit, shall not be prohibited by the Congress prior to the Year one thousand eight hundred and eight, but a tax or duty may be imposed on such Importation, not exceeding ten dollars for each Person.

II. APPARENT TEXTUAL IMPLICATIONS OF LIMITS ON THE POWER TO TAX

A. *Limitations on the Federal Government*

AMENDMENT V. No person shall be . . . deprived of life, liberty, or property, without due process of law; nor shall private property be taken for public use, without just compensation.

AMENDMENT X. The powers not delegated to the United States by the Constitution, nor prohibited by it to the States, are reserved to the States respectively, or to the people.

B. *Limitations on the States*

ARTICLE I, *Section* 8. The Congress shall have Power . . . To regulate Commerce with foreign Nations, and among the several States, and with the Indian Tribes.

AMENDMENT XIV, *Section* 1. . . . No State shall make or enforce any law which shall abridge the privileges or immunities of citizens of the United States; nor shall any State deprive any person of life, liberty, or property, without due process of law; nor deny to any person within its jurisdiction the equal protection of the laws.

III. INTERPRETATIONS OF THE APPARENT LIMITATIONS

A. *Limitations on the Federal Government*

Neither the Fifth nor the Tenth Amendment has so far proved to be a limitation upon the Congressional power to tax. The earliest relevant case is *Veazie Bank v. Fenno*, 8 Wall. 533 (1869), in which a bank chartered by the State of Maine challenged the constitutionality of a federal tax, at prohibitive rates, on the notes issued by such institutions. The Fifth and Tenth Amendment grounds were not raised in terms, but the Court refused to sustain the clearly relevant contentions that the tax was both excessive (and hence a deprivation of property) and an attempt to destroy the bank's State-granted franchise (and hence an invasion of reserved powers).

This general position was spelled out in greater detail in later cases. The leading example is *McCray v. United States*, 195 U.S. 27 (1904), in which a prohibitive federal excise tax of 10 cents per pound on colored oleomargarine was held not to transgress the Fifth or Tenth Amendment for the reason that it would confiscate property without due process of law and thereby destroy the colored oleomargarine industry, a power not granted to the Congress. The same line of reasoning was followed in *United States v. Doremus,* 249 U.S. 86 (1919), where a sharply divided Court sustained a nominal tax of one dollar per annum on the production, distribution, or sale of opium and its derivatives.

Two decisions are exceptions to the general line of precedents. In *Bailey v. Drexel Furniture Co.,* 259 U.S. 20 (1922), the Court invalidated a tax of 10 per cent of net profits on any manufacturing concern in interstate commerce which should employ for any period a child under 14 years of age. The Court held the tax to be a penalty imposed for pursuit of employment practices whose regulation remained wholly in the hands of the States. In 1933, the Congress adopted a statute intended to stabilize the agricultural industry, including provision for a "processing tax" equal to the difference between the current price of the agricultural commodity in question and its "fair exchange value" as determined by reference to relative price levels of the period 1909–1914. The Supreme Court, in *United States v. Butler,* 297 U.S. 1 (1936), declared the taxing provisions to be inseparable from the regulatory ones, and that the tax therefore was void together with the regulations since the latter violated the Tenth Amendment.

It is most doubtful that either of these decisions remains "good law." The *Drexel* case has never been overruled, but the Congress has long since been sustained in levying taxes on payrolls for the purpose of raising revenue to subsidize State-administered unemployment and old age insurance programs, and the federal statutes concerned provide that employers may be granted reductions in the taxes where their record for maintaining steady employment is better than the average. In the field of agricultural policy, the Congress followed the *Butler* decision with the Agricultural Adjustment Act of 1938, which established marketing quotas rather than production ceilings, and provided for penalties of 50 per cent of the value of marketings above those quotas. This law was sustained by the Court in *Mulford v. Smith,* 307 U.S. 38 (1939), on the ground that marketing, unlike production, is a part of interstate commerce.

B. *Limitations on the States*

The impact upon the States of the commerce clause and the Fourteenth Amendment is a most complicated subject. The intent here will be to describe its contemporary status, without examination of its historical development.

It is clear that the States are not entitled to "burden" interstate commerce. Taxes which discriminate against such commerce, levying upon it imposts not similarly assessed against commerce conducted wholly within the taxing

State, are "burdens" in this sense. Thus, in 1935, the State of California imposed a special tax upon automobiles towed into the state for the purpose of sale, without imposing a similar tax upon similar towing for similar purposes wholly within the State. The Supreme Court unanimously declared the tax void as a burden on interstate commerce, stating in the course of its judgment that "to justify the exaction by a state of a money payment burdening interstate commerce, it must affirmatively appear that it is demanded as a reimbursement for the expense of providing facilities, or of enforcing regulations of the commerce which are within its constitutional power" (*Ingels v. Morf,* 300 U.S. 290).

The Fourteenth Amendment contains three clauses which have been interpreted to bear on taxation. The first of these, the so-called privileges and immunities clause, serves to buttress the limitations flowing from the commerce clause and to support the doctrine of nondiscrimination in taxing. The second and third clauses, known usually as due process and equal protection, have much more complicated repercussions on taxation.

As the law now stands, these clauses do not limit the States in the types or amounts of taxes which they may impose. Thus a State, like the federal government, may lay taxes in fact prohibitive upon margarine sales (*Magnano v. Hamilton,* 292 U.S. 40 (1934)). The impact of the two clauses is felt in procedural rather than substantive matters. A State is not permitted to tax assessed values without providing for review of the assessments and an opportunity to challenge them. A State may not establish classifications for purposes of differential taxing which are arbitrary, unreasonable, or capricious. In recent years, the Supreme Court has exercised great restraint in enforcing these limitations; in nearly all cases it has relied upon findings of fact as they have been reached by state administrative agencies and state courts.

IV. LIMITATIONS IMPOSED BY JUDICIAL CONSTRUCTION

Of these, by far the most important is the doctrine of reciprocal immunities. Its beginnings are to be found in *McCulloch v. Maryland,* 4 Wheat. 316 (1819), where Chief Justice John Marshall ruled that "the states have no power, by taxation or otherwise, to retard, impede, burden, or in any manner control, the operations of the constitutional laws enacted by congress to carry into execution the powers vested in the general government." In 1842, this principle was given specific application to the salary of a federal officer, with the Court holding in *Dobbins v. Erie County,* 16 Pet. 435 (1842), that a nondiscriminatory State tax on such income is invalid under Marshall's principle.

This unilateral immunity became reciprocal in 1871, when the Court struck down the federal government's attempt to exact one of the Civil War income taxes from a judge of the State of Massachusetts. The decision in *Collector v. Day*, 11 Wall. 113 (1870), found it a "necessary implication" of a federal form of government that the instrumentalities of both levels should be exempt from taxation by the other.

The general principle stood unimpaired until 1939, but the Court's attempts to spell out its particular applications led to a mass of litigation in the first three decades of the present century. In 1905 a chink was opened in the doctrine with a holding, in *South Carolina v. United States*, 199 U.S. 437 (1905), that the basic rule holds only in the case of "strictly governmental" activities, and not in the case of "proprietary" activities of a business nature. Thus, in the leading case, the federal excise tax on liquor dealers was held fully applicable to State-owned dispensaries in South Carolina. From that date, cases before the Court have turned on the definition of "strictly governmental" activities.

Finally, in *Graves v. New York*, 306 U.S. 466 (1939), the entire line of precedents was overruled "so far as they recognize an implied constitutional immunity from income taxation of the salaries of officers or employees of the national or a state government or their instrumentalities." With respect to other instrumentalities, however, the classic doctrine remains in doubt.

STUDY 8

Federal Powers over Currency, Banking, Credit, and Foreign Exchange

I. INTRODUCTION

In the five existing federal systems on which this study is based, federal powers over currency, banking, credit, and foreign exchange are today both extensive and highly centralized. In every case, these powers are exercised mainly through the agency of a strong central government bank. But — and this is again true in every case — the present situation differs considerably from that prevailing at the time of unification. None of these five federal systems made constitutional provisions for the establishment of a strong central federal bank immediately upon federation. Nor did any one of them, at the time of unification, face problems arising out of the existence of strong State banks closely integrated with State governments. The explanation for this is to be sought in the facts that currency consisted largely of coin at the time of union in the United States, Switzerland, Canada, and Germany, and that the issuance of paper money in these four countries, and in Australia later on, was carried on mainly by private banks. The replacement of hard currency with paper notes occurred slowly during the growth of these federal systems. Questions of federal powers in this area, consequently, became important only gradually and only after union. The control of currency, banking, and credit was not primarily a means for the creation of a single market throughout the area of these federations. Rather it slowly became a means for maintaining and perhaps strengthening the unitary character of the market which had already been established, either prior to unification, or after unification but before the emergence of government note issuance.

This study addresses itself to questions about the nature of federal powers in this sphere, and the process by which they slowly evolved in the five federal systems. For how long were these federal governments able to get along without extensive powers over these matters? At what point did strengthening of these federal powers begin? Through what instruments was it effected? Did the question of these central powers remain a truly "federal" issue after the establishment of central federal government banks?

The proposed statute for a European Political Community provides for the eventual creation of a single market. It is therefore assumed that such a single market will come into existence over the area of a European federal union. Thus, whereas federal powers over currency, banking, credit, and foreign exchange in the existing systems were used mainly in order to maintain an already established single market, these same powers will probably be used by a European community in order to bring such a market into being. This means that the problems arising in connection with these federal powers for the proposed European Community and the existing federal systems will not be the same. Nevertheless, the constitutional questions to be faced in this area by a European federation may be examined to good profit in the perspective provided by the experience with the evolution of these powers of Australia, Canada, Germany, Switzerland, and the United States.

II. Evolution of Federal Powers over Banking, Currency, and Credit

The five federal systems here studied achieved their unification before the time of central national banking as we know it today. As a result, when they later came to establish central banks, they did so on a centralized basis, not having to contend with State central banks which were already more or less well integrated with State governments. Consequently, the federal money power in existing systems is now highly centralized at the federal level. Except in the United States and the German Federal Republic, the currency powers of the national government are essentially the same in federal as in non-federal systems. But even for these two exceptional cases, the problem has never been one of federal control over State authorities which already exercise the full powers of governments and central banks over money, credit, and foreign exchange.

Nevertheless, the experience of the five systems, especially during the period immediately following unification, may throw some light on the kind of constitutional problems which may arise in connection with these powers in Europe today. This experience will therefore be considered first. It will be followed by Section III, which deals with the present set-ups in the United States and Germany. Section IV is concerned with a speculative analytical examination of the question: What are the minimum powers over currency and foreign exchange which a European federal government might today need in order to create a single market over the federal area? An Appendix containing relevant constitutional provisions will conclude the study.

No problems which were both of great importance and of "federal" origins arose in connection with central powers over currency, credit and banking, in either Australia or Canada. The evolution of these powers in both cases differs in few respects from that found in non-federal systems. The lack of difference may, as already stated, be explained in terms of the existence of a uniform coinage and the absence of strong state banks of issue at the time of federation.

A. *Australia*

When the Constitution of the Commonwealth of Australia was adopted in 1900, banknote currency consisted of notes issued by commercial banks. These banks operated under charters granted by the States or in England. State Treasury notes circulated only in Queensland. All the States taxed this note currency. The Constitution gave the Australian Parliament power to legislate with respect to "currency coinage, and legal tender; banking . . . ; [and] bills of exchange and promissory notes." [1] On this constitutional basis, the Australian Bank Notes Act was passed in September, 1910, "Prohibiting banks from issuing or circulating State notes as money, and giving the Governor-General in Council power to authorize the Commonwealth Treasurer to issue Australian notes." [2] A further Act, taxing all other notes, placed complete control over the issue of notes in the hands of the Commonwealth Treasury in the same year. In 1920, this control was transferred to the independent Note Issue Department of the Commonwealth Bank. The Note Issue Department was brought under the authority of the Bank's board in 1924. The Commonwealth Bank itself had been established in 1911, but initially not as a central reserve bank. It handled Commonwealth accounts and eventually those of most of the States as well.

No important truly federal problems occurred in the course of this development. A federal problem did arise out of the financial relations between the States and the Commonwealth, and was settled by the Financial Agreement of December 12, 1927, which resulted in the addition to the Constitution embodied in Section 105A.[3] This Amendment and the Agreement consolidated the public debts of Commonwealth and States, established sinking funds, and regulated government borrowing. The arrangement has already been discussed elsewhere in these studies.[4]

B. *Canada*

Canada established a central government bank even later than Australia. The Bank of Canada was created by Act of Parliament in 1934 — so late in the evolution of the federal system that issues of federalism no longer played any role at all. But even in 1867, when the British North America Act conferred great powers in this field upon the Dominion Parliament, hardly any significant federal issues arose in connection with these pow-

---

[1] See Appendix I.
[2] Report of the Royal Commission on Monetary and Banking Systems 27 (1937).
[3] *Id.* at 19. See also Study 7, Public Finance, Appendix I.
[4] See page 386 above.

ers. At that time, "The new federal government assumed the various provincial issues and amalgamated and enlarged them into one called the Dominion Note Issue which was managed by the Minister of Finance pursuant to the Dominion Notes Act of 1868." [5] Meanwhile, the private banks operating at the time came under federal jurisdiction. There were eighteen chartered by Canada, five by Nova Scotia, four by New Brunswick, and one working in all the colonies under a royal charter.[6] Their operations were regulated by the First Dominion Bank Act of 1871, and each of them was permitted to operate throughout the territory of the Dominion. All of them were permitted to issue notes, but, because of their Dominion-wide operations, questions of provincial versus central powers again failed to arouse any controversy.

C. *The United States*

As the oldest of the five federal constitutions studied, that of the United States of America contains the briefest provisions regarding powers over currency, credit, and banking. But it does go farther on this score than the Articles of Confederation which it replaced. The Articles had provided:

> The United States in Congress assembled shall also have the sole and exclusive right and power of regulating the alloy and value of coin struck by their own authority, or by that of the respective States . . .
> The United States in Congress assembled shall have authority . . . to borrow money, or emit bills on the credit of the United States, transmitting every half-year to the respective States on account of the sums of money so borrowed or emitted . . . [Art. IX]

The Constitution, by contrast, states that "No State shall . . . coin Money [or] emit Bills of Credit . . ." (Art. I, §10). The absence of this prohibition from the Articles of Confederation had helped to bring about the chaotic currency conditions which contributed to the movement on behalf of the Constitution.[7] On the question of banking, however, the Constitution is completely silent. Otherwise, it limits itself to the general statements by which the Congress is given power "To borrow money on the credit of the United States; To coin Money, regulate the Value thereof, and of foreign Coin . . ." (Art. I, §8).

This brevity does not mean, however, that the Founders were unconcerned about the details of these questions. On the contrary, Alexander Hamilton had conceived the idea of a federal bank of issue as early as 1779. His thoughts on the subject were finally compiled when he was the first Secretary of the Treasury, and published in the form of a *Report*

---

[5] Stokes, *The Development and Present Position of Central Banking in Canada* 2 (1938).
[6] Breckenridge, *The History of Banking in Canada* 89 (1910).
[7] See page 311 above.

on the Public Credit on December 13, 1790. Hamilton's *Report* provided the basis for the bill to charter the Bank of the United States, which became law on February 24, 1791.

The question of the constitutionality of this Act was argued out carefully and vigorously in Washington's Cabinet. Hamilton naturally supported his brain child, while Jefferson and his followers attacked the plan. The issue whether the Congress had constitutional power to charter such a bank was to offer the United States Supreme Court its first notable opportunity to construe broadly the powers which the Constitution conferred upon the federal government.[8] For many years thereafter, the dividing line between political parties coincided with the line which separated the supporters from the opponents of the First and Second United States Bank. But the main controversy here revolved around the federal power chartering these two banks, not that of controlling banking. Far from being able to control banking, the federal government could not even control either of the two United States Banks. The charter of the First Bank placed it under private management entirely, a point on which Hamilton apparently followed the example of the Bank of England.[9] In the case of the Second Bank of the United States, in existence from 1816 to 1836, the federal government was represented on the board of directors by only five out of twenty-five directors. Thus both of the two Banks of the United States differed from "banks established under state charters in little save size and enjoyment of a few special privileges." [10]

The main office of the First Bank was located in Philadelphia, and branches were opened in eight other cities. Relations between the Bank of the United States and banks in the several States were friendly throughout its existence. It must be borne in mind, however, that none of the latter banks were agencies of the State governments, though chartered by them. Under the charter, the federal government subscribed one fifth of the Bank's $10,000,000 capital, but sold all of this stock by 1802. By the end of 1795, the federal government had borrowed $6,200,000 from the Bank. Since the notes of the Bank were "to be receivable in all payments to the United States," and because the government made all duties payable in the Bank's notes, they "had far more extensive circulation than those of any other bank." [11] The Bank also handled foreign coin for the United States Treasury. Aside from this, however, it had few advantages over other banks chartered by the States, and little influence on their credit policies. Since even this influence was not wielded at the behest of the federal government, the First Bank of the United States cannot be considered an example of a central federal bank. It died, as the result of Congressional refusal to extend or renew its charter, on March 3, 1811.

[8] McCulloch v. Maryland, 4 Wheat. 316 (1819).
[9] Holdsworth and Dewey, *First and Second Banks of the United States* (1910).
[10] *Id.* at 148.
[11] *Id.* at 50 *et seq.*

The Second Bank of the United States was created mainly in order to help bring about resumption of specie payments by banks chartered in the several States. The federal government held one fifth of its $35,000,000 capital. As the result of President Jackson's opposition to it, and his re-election in 1832, it went out of existence in 1836. The United States was not to have a central federal bank until passage of the Federal Reserve Act in 1913. Thus, while constitutional provisions did indeed bring about establishment of a uniform currency throughout the United States, little federal control over banking and credit was exercised before 1913. The National Bank Acts of 1863 and 1864, produced by borrowing policies of the federal government during the Civil War, created uniformity in cir-culating notes issued by private banks. Through imposition of a 100 per cent tax on notes issued by banks operating under State charters only, such banks were driven out of the note-issuing business. But this did not enable the federal government to control credit policies. Nor was there ever, during the entire period from the achievement of independence, much resemblance between the problems faced in this field by the United States and those which might confront a European federation today. The ab-sence of strong government banks in the States accounts for most of the differences.

D. *Germany*

When the German Empire was founded in 1871, seven different coinage systems existed in the several member States. There were thirty-one private banks of issue, operating under laws of the different States. These laws differed considerably with respect to reserve and other requirements. The preliminary legal conditions for a uniform monetary and banking reform were created by provisions in the Constitution of the North German Federation of July 26, 1867, and of the Constitution of the German Empire of April 16, 1871, which made the regulation of coinage, weights, and meas-ures, the formulation of principles for the emission of funded and unfunded paper money, and the general regulation of banking subject to supervision and legislation by the Confederacy and then by the Empire.[12] On this constitutional foundation, a law establishing a uniform Imperial gold coinage went into effect in December, 1871. The monetary system was finally consolidated by the Coinage Act of July 9, 1873. This Act contained a provision ordering withdrawal of paper money issued by the State govern-ments by the beginning of 1876.

In order to establish a strong central federal bank — as for so many other purposes connected with the strengthening of federal powers — the existing Prussian institution was used. In return for compensation, Prussia ceded the Prussian Bank to the Empire under the Bank Act of March 14, 1875. The Act provided that the right to issue banknotes could be granted only

[12] National Monetary Commission, *The Reichsbank* 14.

by Imperial law. It established uniform regulations governing reserve requirements, except for banks which confined their business to the State under whose laws they had been chartered. Under Section 12 of the Act, the task of the Reichsbank was defined as "regulating the monetary circulation in the entire Empire, of facilitating the settlement of payments, and of utilizing available capital." The Empire itself put up none of the capital, but supervised the Bank through a "Curatorium," consisting of the Chancellor as president and four members, one of them appointed by the Emperor, and the other three by the Federal Council. The Board of Directors was also headed by the Chancellor. Its members were appointed by the Emperor on nomination by the Federal Council. This body could order establishment of branches of the Bank. Neither these branches nor the Bank itself could be taxed anywhere in the Empire. The Reichsbank was the only bank which made use of the right of free coinage; consequently, it was able to exercise control over foreign exchange transactions. Profits of the Bank were divided between the Empire and private shareholders, without participation of the States.

The predominance of Prussia in the Empire, reflected in this case in the conversion of the Prussian into the Imperial Bank, which was headed by the Imperial Chancellor who was also the Prussian Chancellor; the lack of participation by the States in either capital or profits of the Bank; and the slight influence on the Bank's management by the States, which could be exerted only through the Federal Council in which Prussia was again predominant — all combine to make the Imperial German experience with the strengthening of federal powers over money, credit, and banking relatively irrelevant to the problems which a European federation may confront in this field.

E. *Switzerland*

The evolution of these federal powers in the Swiss Confederation, by contrast with the federal systems previously discussed, differs considerably from the course which it might have followed had Switzerland been a non-federal system. This is due to the existence of well-established cantonal banks prior to the period during which this federal power was gradually increased. In 1870, when the first proposal was made for giving the Confederation constitutional power "to proclaim general rules for the issue and redemption of bank notes," [18] several cantonal banks were in operation. The first of these, the Cantonal Bank of Bern, had been established in 1834. Six of the cantons accepted partial responsibility for the liabilities of their banks. But reserve requirements varied widely from one canton to the next, and there was little uniformity in banking legislation, which was left up to the several cantons.

The result was confusion, which became especially marked during the

[18] Landmann, *The Swiss Banking Law* 17 (1910).

Franco-Prussian War of 1870. At this time, there was already some advocacy of creating a federal monopoly of issue. But Article 39 of the Federal Constitution of May 29, 1874, merely provided: "The Confederation is authorized to proclaim by way of legislation general rules for the issue and redemption of banknotes. It shall, however, not set up any monopoly in the issue of banknotes, nor shall it express any legal responsibility for the acceptance of the same." On the basis of this Article, both Ständerat and Nationalrat accepted a banking law which was, however, defeated in a referendum on April 23, 1876. An attempt to remove the prohibition of a federal monopoly of issue from Article 39 was defeated in a referendum on October 31, 1880. A Bank Act was finally passed on March 8, 1881, and went into effect at the beginning of the next year. It laid down uniform reserve requirements and made the notes of any Swiss bank acceptable at full value by other Swiss banks.

The effects of the Act of 1881 turned out to be unsatisfactory, in terms of both the solvency of banks and foreign exchange rates. Agitation on behalf of the creation of a central federal bank of issue was resumed in 1885. Thus began a political battle which was to last until passage of the Federal Act of October 6, 1905, which established the Swiss National Bank. Several bills submitted in the course of this period were defeated in the Ständerat and Nationalrat. Of interest here are only those controversies which arose out of the federal nature of the Swiss system. The first of these concerned the profits derived by the cantons through taxation of banknotes or banks' profits. A compromise on this issue was reached in the revision of Article 39 of the Federal Constitution, which was adopted by referendum on October 18, 1891. The new Article, which provided for a federal monopoly of issue and exempted the central federal bank from cantonal taxation, also stated: "At least two thirds of the net profits of the bank, after payment of interest or reasonable dividend on the endowment or share capital, and deduction of payments to the reserve funds, shall go to the cantons." [14]

Legislation to carry this revised version of Article 39 into effect was not to be passed before 1905. A law to establish a federal bank was passed by the legislature on June 18, 1896, but rejected by the electorate in a referendum on February 28, 1897. Another law was proposed by the Bundesrat in 1899, passed by the Nationalrat in the same year, passed with alterations by the Ständerat in December 1900, and agreed to by the Nationalrat except for the provision regarding the seat of the bank. The Ständerat, in June, 1901, insisted on Zurich rather than Bern as the bank's headquarters and thereby killed the bill. The location of the bank thus became the second mainly federal issue to emerge out of attempts to increase federal powers over banking, currency, and credit in Switzerland.

Ten years after revision of Article 39, therefore,

[14] See Appendix IV.

The exclusive right of issuing bank notes, which according to the constitution belonged solely to the Confederation, was still exercised as before, by the 36 existing cantonal and private institutions; and the abnormal situation was presented that the requirements of the federal constitution and the actual organization of the note-bank system were in direct contradiction with each other.[15]

In these circumstances, the Nationalrat passed a motion inviting the Bundesrat to submit a new bill in execution of Article 39. The major difficulty encountered in drafting this bill was the question of how to determine the amount of the revenues derived by the cantons from their banks, so that they could be equitably reimbursed for losses which would be incurred as a result of establishment of a federal bank. A complicated formula was finally agreed upon, which took into consideration both the size of population of each canton and the intensity of trade within it. Profits of the new bank, after the deductions allowed for by Article 39, were to go two thirds to the cantons, and one third to the Confederation.

Of the capital of the bank, two fifths was to be taken up by the cantons in proportion with their population; one fifth by the banks of issue existing at the end of 1902, in proportion with their circulating notes at that time; and the remaining two fifths by private subscriptions. Of the forty members of the council of the bank, twenty-five were to be nominated by the Federal Council and fifteen by the general meeting of the stockholders. The Bundesrat was also to choose the president, vice-president, managers, directors, and local managers of the bank. These provisions, contained in a bill presented by the Bundesrat on June 13, 1904, underwent no important changes prior to final passage as the Swiss National Bank Act of October 6, 1905.

Regarding the location of the bank, this law merely stated that it was to be "determined by a special resolution of the Confederation." [16] After a vigorous Parliamentary battle, a compromise was reached on this issue in September, 1905, according to which the legal and administrative headquarters of the bank was placed in Bern, while the board of directors was to sit in Zurich. Under Article 4 of the Act,

> The National Bank is authorized to establish branches in Bern and Zurich, and, after having obtained the consent of the cantonal governments, to establish branches also in the other important towns of Switzerland, and to create agencies for the remaining places. In case of disagreement between a Canton and the National Bank concerning the establishment of a branch or agency, the Bundesrat decides the question without appeal.
>
> Any Canton or half Canton that has no branch may request that an agency be established in its territory.

[15] Landmann, *The Swiss Banking Law* 110 *et seq.* (1910).
[16] *Id.* at 157.

At the request of the cantonal governments concerned, the cantonal banks are to be made such agencies.

"The chief function of the National Bank," according to Article 2 of the Law of 1905, "is to regulate the monetary circulation of the country and to facilitate the operations of payment." The creation of a central federal bank in Switzerland for these purposes was not possible until, among other issues, those arising out of the federal nature of Swiss government had been settled through compromise. To the extent that this is true, and despite the lack of important differences between the Swiss National Bank as it operates today and central banks in other contemporary non-federal systems, the history of the evolution of federal powers over banking, currency, and credit in Switzerland may be relevant to the problems to be met in this field by a European federation.

F. *General Observations*

If these brief summaries warrant any conclusions at all, they would be these: Some federal governments managed for a time to get along without any powers over currency, banking, credit, and foreign exchange. None of them in fact get along without wide powers in these fields today. Federal governments functioned without such powers only in the absence of strong State banks. Their absence indicates that the historical period in which government begins to play a decisive role in the national economy had not yet been reached by the countries in question. The beginning of this period has usually coincided roughly with an increase in the importance of paper money. Later in this period existing federations have had to assume greater control over these matters, and new federations have had to control or abolish existing State banks. These are the steps which seem to be necessary for the maintenance or establishment of a single market over the federal area. In the past, the result of these steps has ultimately been always the same: the problem ceased to be a federal one. The scope of these powers, and the manner in which they were wielded, have become very similar to those in non-federal constitutional systems.

In the case of a European Community, strong State government banks will already be in existence. The federal government will presumably be expected to play an important role in the economic life of the Community with the probable ultimate goal of the creation of a single market. If it follows the example of the five systems studied here, it will eventually use a central federal bank as the major instrument for its control over currency, credit, banking, and foreign exchange. Such a central federal bank may operate in a unitary fashion, as do those of Australia, Canada, and Switzerland. In that case, it will not differ greatly from non-federal central government banks. Or it may operate on a decentralized basis, as do the federal banks of the United States and the Federal Republic of Germany.

Even in the latter cases, the federation uses a single currency. And while the organization and administration of the United States and German banking systems are decentralized, policy is centralized in all essentials, if not all details. Furthermore, whatever decentralization there may be has been created by delegation of power by the federal government. In these respects, both systems differ from the five federal governments in the earlier stages of their development. They differ also from the probable shape of things during the early stages of a European federation.

The next Section discusses the American and West German banking and currency systems in terms of the present division of functions between federal and district or State levels with respect to the four powers to be discussed in Section IV. They are the powers (1) to assure liquidity of interstate exchanges, (2) to influence the monetary policies of states, (3) to control the use of foreign exchange, and (4) to determine exchange rates.

III. CONTEMPORARY FEDERAL BANKING SYSTEMS IN THE UNITED STATES AND THE FEDERAL REPUBLIC OF GERMANY

A. *The Federal Reserve System of the United States*

Until 1948 the Federal Reserve System was the sole representative in the world of the federal, as against the unitary, type of central bank. The year 1948 saw the establishment of the German federal central banking system, inspired by the Federal Reserve System. However, it must be stressed that the difference between federal and unitary systems of central banking is one of degree only. Organizationally and administratively the system is decentralized, but policy is made at the center. The Federal Reserve Banks, which are in effect regional central banks, are not the organs of subordinate political jurisdictions. Whatever autonomy they possess is derived by delegation of authority from the federal government.

1. CONSTITUTIONAL AND LEGAL PROVISIONS

The United States Constitution gives Congress the power "to borrow money on the credit of the United States" (Art. I, §8 (2)) and "to coin Money, regulate the Value thereof, and of foreign Coin . . ." (Art. I, §8 (5)). This does not mean that Congress itself can or should administer the monetary affairs of the nation. Acting on the principle of delegation, Congress has entrusted the power and duty of executing its monetary policy to a number of agencies. The principal monetary powers have been delegated to the Federal Reserve System. The Federal Reserve Act of 1913, as amended, is the statutory basis for all the powers exercised by the Federal Reserve System with a few exceptions which will be noted below.

2. THE EVOLUTION OF THE SYSTEM

During the debates on the Federal Reserve Act the idea of a single reserve bank with branches was rejected in favor of a regional type of organization composed of separate reserve banking institutions which would be "individually organized and individually controlled, each holding the fluid funds of the region in which it is organized and each ordinarily dependent upon no other part of the country for assistance." [17]

Thus, in the early years of the Federal Reserve System, emphasis on regional differences in credit requirements and policy made for a certain autonomy given to the twelve Federal Reserve Districts. The improvement in facilities for transferring funds and the increasing interdependence of the various districts, however, brought about a gradual lessening of regional differences and the System's experience led to an increasing awareness of the need for a more unified national credit policy. The present organization of the System, which has evolved from experience, provides for the establishment of central banking policy on a national basis. At the same time it provides the means whereby the policy can be adapted or modified to meet differing regional needs. The procedures now followed in the formulation and administration of Federal Reserve credit policy may be contrasted with those of a unitary system in which determination of policy is wholly centralized, without participation of regional representatives, and in which administration is also centralized.

This framework, which is entirely independent of the individual States, has demonstrated sufficient flexibility to weather the major changes in the economy and the money market as well as in the size of the public debt since 1913. The reason for this adaptibility is that, despite its decentralized organization, the purpose of the Federal Reserve System has been national throughout its history. It seeks to minimize economic fluctuations caused by irregularities in the flow of credit and money, to foster more stable values, and thus to make possible the smooth functioning of monetary machinery so necessary to promote growth of the economy and to improve standards of living. Consequently, the idea of central banking at the federal level which won out in 1913 has, over the past forty years, fortified its hold on the loyalty of the United States financial community. There appears to be little, if any, desire to revise the basic institutional framework.

3. POWER TO ACT AS LENDER OF LAST RESORT

The Federal Reserve System is the lender of last resort to the Federal Reserve Banks. For instance, it has the right to require inter-Reserve Banks rediscounting. However, there has been no need to use this power in twenty years. Most Federal Reserve Banks have had sufficient gold, or rather gold certificates, at their disposal to clear and settle among themselves without any trouble movements of funds resulting in interregional balance of payments surpluses and deficits. The financing of any chronic or *structural* interregional imbalances is not the function of the Federal

---

[17] H.R. Rep. No. 69, 63d Cong., 1st Sess. 18 (1913).

Reserve System but rather a function of the federal government in assisting in the recovery or rehabilitation of depressed areas.

Temporary interdistrict balance of payments difficulties, whenever they lead to a reduction in the holdings of gold certificates of a particular district Federal Reserve Bank to a level approaching the reserve limit, are adjusted by a reallocation within the System of participation by the district banks in the holdings of government debt of the System. The existence of the pool of common United States debt makes it possible, then, to increase or reduce a particular district bank's gold certificate reserve by allocating to such a bank a smaller or greater percentage of United States government debt in exchange for an increase or decrease in gold certificates. This process, in fact, has come to be automatic and alleviates the necessity for monetary contraction or expansion by district banks. This does not mean that there are no interregional adjustments of credit policies in response to outflows and inflows of funds. But within a wide range of fluctuations such adjustments result from the action of individual commercial banks seeing their reserves decline or increase rather than from regional monetary policies of the district Federal Reserve Banks.

4. POWER OVER MONETARY POLICIES OF RESERVE DISTRICTS

As mentioned above, the Federal Reserve System is independent of the States. The question becomes therefore what is the distribution of authority over the instruments of monetary policy as between the Federal Reserve Board and the twelve Federal Reserve Banks. The principal instruments of United States monetary policy and their distribution as between the Board and the Federal Reserve Banks may be summarized as follows:

(a) Reserve Banks discount and advance to member banks, providing a means by which a bank at its own initiative may make necessary shortrun adjustments in its reserve position. Because of the traditional reluctance of banks to show continuous borrowing, an increase in discounting is itself a factor of restraint on the borrowing banks. The level of the discount rate may reinforce or relax this factor of restraint.

When the Federal Reserve Act was enacted in 1913, discount rates were regarded as the principal instrument of credit policy. Since that time, discount rates have come to be supplemented by other instruments of credit policy. Today, it is recognized that the process of influencing bank credit expansion is complex and that the instruments or combination of instruments most appropriate to the task will vary at different times according to the changing factors and forces affecting the growth of bank and other credit. Moreover, since the establishment of the System, the structure of the national credit market has changed from a series of interconnected local and regional markets to a relatively well integrated national market, with borrower rates of interest for financing of a given amount and comparable risk in closer alignment as between various localities and regions.

With these changes, local and regional differences which might be reflected in differences in discount rates have diminished in importance and the rates more and more have come to reflect conditions in the nation as a whole.

The present statutory authority for the fixing of discount rates is substantially the same as it was when the Federal Reserve System was established. Section 14 (d) of the original Federal Reserve Act provided:

> Every Federal Reserve Bank shall have power:
> To establish from time to time, subject to review and determination of the Federal Reserve Board, rates of discount to be charged by the Federal Reserve Bank for each class of paper, which shall be fixed with a view of accommodating commerce and business.

The law clearly contemplates that the establishment of discount rates shall involve joint action by the Federal Reserve Banks and the Board of Governors of the Federal Reserve System. It is also clear that rates established by the Reserve Banks shall not become effective until approved by the Board of Governors. Since prospective changes in rates are ordinarily discussed in advance between the Board and the Reserve Banks, it is only rarely that action taken by a Federal Reserve Bank for the setting of discount rates is not promptly approved by the Board. On occasion, however, the Board may fail to approve or defer its approval pending discussions of System credit and monetary policies and Treasury financing policies with the presidents of all Federal Reserve Banks or with the Federal Open Market Committee. The matter is usually discussed also with the Secretary of the Treasury. Since the Board's authority is not limited to mere approval of rates established by the Reserve Banks, but includes power to review and determine such rates, the Board, as previously noted, has legal authority to initiate discount rates.

(b) Open market operations which are conducted at the initiative of the Federal Reserve for one or both of the following primary purposes: (1) to affect the supply of bank reserves, or (2) to contribute to the maintenance of an orderly money market. Open market operations directed to the first of these objectives have an effect upon the amount of discounts and advances. For this reason, open market operations and discount operations are commonly regarded as companion instruments of System policy. Open market operations directed toward the second objective may modify operations toward the first, depending upon the circumstances prevailing at the time.

Section 14 of the Federal Reserve Act authorizes the Federal Reserve Banks, under rules and regulations prescribed by the Board of Governors, to purchase and sell in the open market (1) bankers' acceptances; (2) obligations of the United States; and (3) certain types of obligations of government agencies and of States and municipalities.

Since establishment of the Federal Reserve System, there has been a considerable increase in the scope and importance of open market operations in the implementation of the credit and monetary policy of the Federal Reserve System. Today open market operations are recognized as the most important single instrument of credit control. Closely related to the increase in the importance of open market operations has been an increase in the degree of centralization and formalization in the procedure by which decisions are made concerning such operations. Originally, such decisions were made by the individual Federal Reserve Banks. They are now made by a statutory committee composed of all the members of the Board of Governors of the Federal Reserve System and five Federal Reserve Bank presidents. This, the Federal Open Market Committee, has the authority to direct all operations without the necessity of consent by the individual Reserve Banks. The Board of Governors of the Federal Reserve System has majority representation on the Committee.

Although it may appear awkward and cumbersome, the fact that the Federal Open Market Committee directs open market operations, the Board of Governors fixes reserve requirements (see (c) below), and the Reserve Banks establish discount rates subject to review and determination of the Board of Governors, has not in practice given rise to any serious difficulties. The explanation of the present System is historical, not logical. It is recognized, however, that in the matter of whether or not federal credit policy has been satisfactorily coordinated under existing arrangements there may be justifiable difference of opinion.

(c) Reserve requirements are percentages of their deposits that banks which are members of the Federal Reserve System (i.e., nearly all commercial banks) are required to hold on deposit with the Federal Reserve Banks. The Board is authorized to change these requirements within prescribed limits. Regulatory changes in reserve requirements may be accompanied by open market or discount operations in order to cushion the adjustments of banks and the money market to the changes.

(d) Selective credit controls operate by affecting the equity margin or maturity terms of credit in particular sectors of the economy but do not directly affect the overall supply of credit available. Selective measures may properly be described as subordinate instruments of policy and in some cases have been authorized by Congress for limited periods only. They may be used concurrently with, and as supplements to, the general measures, for example, when undue or excessive credit expansion is localized in an area to which selective regulations may be applied without invoking general measures affecting all credit. Selective controls include those affecting stock market credit, consumer credit, and real estate credit. The statutory bases for these powers are the Securities Exchange Act of 1934 and the Defense Production Act of 1950, as amended. (In 1952, the Congress did not renew the authority of the Federal Reserve System to regulate consumer credit and limited the conditions under which real estate credit could be regulated.)

(e) So-called "moral suasion" (including voluntary credit restraint) and supervisory admonitions may also be employed to discourage or encourage lending activities — either in general or in particular credit sectors.

5. POWER TO CONTROL THE USE OF FOREIGN EXCHANGE
BY THE STATES

The control of the use of foreign exchange by the States is a problem that does not arise in the United States. Nor is there any such problem as regards the twelve Federal Reserve Banks. Even if foreign exchange controls were established in the United States, the power to control the use of foreign exchange would no doubt be exercised by the federal government through the Federal Reserve System over private individuals, corporations, etc. In other words, the administration of foreign exchange control would not differ essentially from that in a country with a unitary central bank.

6. POWER TO DETERMINE EXCHANGE RATES

Since there is a single currency circulating in the United States, the problem of the power to determine exchange rates of the States, etc., does not arise.

B. *The Central Banking System of the Federal Republic of Germany*

At the end of World War II the German central banking system collapsed and was replaced in the Western zones, in accordance with the Potsdam Agreement, calling for the decentralization of the German economy, by a central banking system organized on a Länder basis using the branches of the former Reichsbank as Land Central Banks. When a federal central bank, the Bank Deutscher Länder (BDL), was created at a later date, its formal organization was also determined by the emphasis on decentralization. The BDL is owned by the Land Central Banks, whose stock is presently held by the Land governments. The BDL's Board of Directors, its policy-making body which also appoints the president and the bank management, is composed of the presidents of the Land Central Banks, appointees of their governments.

Despite the fact that the West German central banking system was thus formally organized on the basis of the exercise of control from the bottom up rather than from the top down, it has not, in practice, functioned in a decentralized manner. The real relationship between the BDL and the Land Central Banks today is best viewed as that between any national central bank and its branches. The powers with which we are here concerned are, in fact, exercised centrally. The four powers in the fields of currency and foreign exchange considered in Section IV below to be essential are exercised in Western Germany by the BDL or by agencies of the federal government itself.[18]

1. POWER TO ACT AS A LENDER OF LAST RESORT TO STATE CENTRAL BANKS

Legal provisions. The power of the federal government of Western Germany to act as a lender of last resort to the State Central Banks was first established by decree of the military governments in Law No. 60 of February 15, 1948. This statute created a federal central bank, the Bank Deutscher Länder, as sole bank of issue, in order to "promote in the common interest the best use of the financial resources of the area served by the member Land Central Banks, to strengthen the currency and credit system, and to coordinate the activities of the said Central Banks." The BDL is limited to transactions with the federal government and with the central banks of the Länder and of foreign countries, and is specifically charged with the function of promoting the solvency and liquidity of the member Land Central Banks (Art. III, §9).

The techniques which may be employed by the BDL in fulfillment of its function of lender of last resort are also specified in the law. It is provided with a capital of 100,000,000 marks subscribed by all Land Central Banks in proportion to the amount of their deposits on March 1, 1948. The BDL is specifically empowered to engage in the following transactions with the Land Central Banks:

(a) Buy and sell foreign exchange and gold.
(b) Accept deposits.
(c) Rediscount bills of exchange.
(d) Grant loans against bills of exchange, treasury bills, securities and registered debt issued by the federal government or the Land, and fixed-interest-bearing securities and registered debt on which any Land Central Bank has made advances or acquired on the open market.

The BDL fixes interest and discount rates for its transactions with the member banks.

The question of a currency acceptable to all in which the BDL may extend loans for the settlement of interstate obligations does not, of course, arise, because the Federal Republic of West Germany does have a single currency.

2. POWER OVER MONETARY POLICIES OF THE LÄNDER

Legal provisions. The law establishing the BDL contains a general provision authorizing it to "establish common policies with respect to banking

[18] The new Basic Law which replaced the Occupation Statute on May 23, 1949 and is today Western Germany's Constitution gives the federal government exclusive right to legislate in the field of currency, money, and coinage (Art. 73, par. 4).

and . . . ensure, as far as possible, the maximum uniformity in banking policies within the several Länder." The means by which the BDL exercises its control over the monetary policies of the States are its power to:

(a) Fix minimum reserve requirements for the member Land Central Banks up to 30 per cent of the total deposits of those banks and to require the deposit of these reserves in its vaults.

(b) Issue directions for the general regulation of bank credit, including the interest and discount rates and open market operations of the member Land Central Banks.[19]

(c) Regulate the establishment of minimum reserve requirements for individual commercial banks through the medium of the Land Central Banks.

(d) Conduct open market operations in treasury bills and government securities and registered debt.

The BDL has used its powers over monetary policy actively. The most important examples of this were the measures taken to meet the crisis in Germany's European Payments Union position in the winter of 1950–1951. A new set of "guiding principles" designed to reduce the overall volume of commercial bank credits was instituted in February, 1951, which required the banks to adjust their balances by applying a series of ratios of capital, cash, and other liquid assets to the amount of credits outstanding. This was supplemented by a sharp rise in interest rates as well as by non-monetary measures, including drastic import restrictions and a generally higher tax program. When these measures proved inadequate, the BDL resorted to a direct reduction in the outstanding volume of commercial bank credit to business through a directive, issued in March, 1951, ordering the banks to reduce the total volume of their credit by one billion marks, i.e., to a level about $7\frac{1}{2}$ per cent below that of January, 1951.

The difficulties of 1951 may have stimulated the efforts of the federal government to increase its authority over monetary policy by obtaining a more direct voice in the policy and management of the BDL. To this end, a Transitional Law was passed in 1951 providing for representation of the Ministers of Finance and Economy at meetings of the BDL's Board of Directors. These representatives have no votes but may submit proposals and may require the suspension of Board decisions for eight days. More permanent efforts by the federal government to gain greater control over BDL policy have centered about Article 88 of the Basic Law, which provides that "the Federation shall establish a bank of currency and issue as a Federal Bank." Proposals to implement this provision have been the source of extended controversy about the degree of government control over the new central bank.

---

[19] Open market operations have, in fact, been of no importance in Germany's monetary policy to date because, as a result of the currency reform of 1948, the existing debt of the federal government consists almost entirely of unmarketable "equalization claims."

3. POWER TO CONTROL THE USE OF FOREIGN EXCHANGE
BY THE STATES

Legal provisions. The Basic Law for the Federal Republic of Germany gives the federal government the exclusive right to legislate concerning "the traffic in goods and payments with foreign countries" (Art. 73, par. 5). The government has implemented its power in this field chiefly by empowering the BDL to regulate foreign exchange transactions, advise the appropriate authorities with respect to foreign exchange policy, and to buy and sell foreign exchange for its own account and the account of others. Citizens of Western Germany may not hold foreign exchange nor engage in foreign exchange transactions except with the express permission of the federal government. The BDL has designated certain banks (*Aussenhandelsbanken,* Foreign Trade Banks) to act as its agent in the handling of foreign exchange transactions. Exporters must surrender their earnings of foreign exchange to these banks, which are, in turn, the source from which the importers must seek foreign currency to finance their transactions. Imports are subject to licensing. In sum, the federal government and the BDL have sole authority over the use of foreign exchange in Western Germany.

4. POWER TO DETERMINE EXCHANGE RATES

The federal government has the power to determine the rates at which the Deutsche Mark shall exchange for foreign currencies by virtue of the provision of the Basic Law, cited above, granting it exclusive authority over the currency and over payments with foreign countries. A change in the exchange rate would be the result of an administrative decision on the part of the BDL and the federal Economics Ministry and would probably not involve prior approval by the legislative branch of the government. The Länder have no voice in determining the exchange rate of the national currency, except through the representation of their Land Central Banks on the Board of Directors of the BDL.

IV. Minimum Federal Powers over Currency, Banking, Credit, and Foreign Exchange

The preceding two sections have demonstrated two things: First, at the inception of the five federal systems studied, federal powers in this area were weak and unimportant. Second, today these powers are both strong and important in the five existing federal systems. These systems were founded before paper money had virtually replaced coins and before governments began to assume major economic responsibilities. The proposed European Political Community, however, will come into being in a world which uses government-issued notes. One of its goals will be the eventual establishment of a single market. And it will consist of States which already have strong central government banks of their own. It is therefore difficult to say just how relevant to the problems of a European federation the preceding material is. For this reason, it may be useful to state the question in a new way. Starting from the contrast between the experience of the existing systems and what may be possible in Europe today, we shall speculate about the powers over currency, banking, credit, and foreign exchange which a European Community may need in order to function properly.

Broadly stated, four such powers may be defined as follows:

(1) Power to assure the liquidity of interstate exchanges;
(2) Power to exert, in case of need, decisive influence on the monetary policies of the member States;
(3) Power to determine the uses to which foreign exchange may be put by the States; and
(4) Power to determine the rates at which State currencies may exchange with each other and with outside currencies.

These seem to be the minimum federal powers necessary to permit a government to assure the freedom of interstate exchanges, to bear final responsibility for the external solvency of the union, and to do equity in these matters among member States. The following paragraphs discuss these four powers in order. There is included also some discussion of instrumentalities through which such powers might be exercised and the methods of their exercise. This discussion is, of course, purely illustrative; its purpose is only to make clear the content of the four powers.

A. *Power to Assure the Liquidity of Interstate Exchanges*

Continuous interconvertibility of member currencies is necessary if unhampered trade and capital movements are to be maintained. If such convertibility is not to confront member States with the choice either of following policies they consider inimical to their interests or of restricting trade, there is required a lender of last resort capable of providing State central banks with the credit needed to maintain the liquidity of payments relations among State central banks. Such credit would have to be in a currency made acceptable under federal law to the central banks of member States in settlement of their claims on each other. The lender of last resort might be a federal central bank or some other form of federal central monetary agency or authority. Credit extended by a federal central bank to a State central bank would serve not only the purpose of providing the latter with means of paying its obligations to other State central banks but, like an international loan, would also expand its assets for domestic purposes.

In what currency or currencies would a federal central bank have to extend credit to State central banks in order to maintain full interconvertibility of State currencies? If there had been established a single federal currency for the union, there would of course be no State currencies and such credit could be made in the federal currency. (At page 437 below, it is argued that a single federal currency, however desirable and perhaps ultimately necessary, is not a minimum requirement for achievement of the economic purposes of the union, and, moreover, could create certain serious economic and political difficulties during the early years of a union.) In the absence of a federal currency, a federal central bank could extend credit in the particular state currency needed by the borrowing State to maintain the liquidity of its interstate exchanges. Much more conveniently, however, a federal bank could lend in the form of a federal "unit of account" with which the various State currencies would have a fixed rate of exchange and which State central banks would be required to accept in settlement of their claims on the central banks of other States.[20]

B. *Power over Monetary Policies of States*

A federal power to extend credit to State central banks in a currency usable for settlement of interstate obligations is a necessary, but not a sufficient, condition of maintaining interconvertibility of State currencies. Unless State monetary policies can be harmonized — and this cannot be brought about merely by agreement at the national level — State governments will be impelled by national interests to maintain or reimpose restrictions on interstate trade and payments.

It might be argued that, if a federal central bank had power to extend credit on terms set by it to State central banks — credit usable for interstate payments as well as for domestic purposes — it would have all the leverage needed to require State governments to follow monetary policies consistent with maintenance of reasonable balance of payments equilibrium while keeping interstate trade and payments free. But this does not appear to be true.

Consider the situation of a State in which powerful domestic political interests support an inflationary monetary policy. In this situation a federal bank would have two choices. On the one hand, the federal bank could extend large credits to the State on easy terms in order that the State might settle the payments deficit with other States which its inflationary policies had caused and thereby avoid restricting its imports from other States. On the other hand, the federal bank might try to bring about a change in the State's monetary policies by granting only small credits on hard terms, or by making further credits conditional on changes in the State's monetary policies.

---

[20] There is, in principle, a third possibility, apart from a single federal currency: the use by the federal bank for its unit of account and for extensions of credit to State central banks of the "leading" or "key" national currency among the currencies of its member States. There is, however, no leading currency among the national currencies of the prospective members of a European federal union.

If the federal bank should make the first choice, it would be accused by the other States of draining off their resources to the first state and of permitting the latter to "export its inflation" to them. If the federal bank should persist in this course, it could create a situation in which the other States would feel obliged, in order to protect their monetary stability or to avoid further economic drain, to take unilateral action to restrict exports. Conversely, if the federal bank should adopt the second course, the State desiring to pursue inflationary policies might prefer to restrict imports. It might indeed have no other option, given the internal balance of political forces. In either event, freedom of interstate exchange would be broken.[21] Or, if that freedom had been established by federal law, serious interstate political crisis would probably ensue. It seems likely that a frequent recurrence of such major conflicts over national economic policies would be damaging to the political cohesion of the union.

This dilemma could be solved by transferring the inconsistencies between State monetary policies which are the source of the difficulty to the federal level, where they can be resolved by executive or legislative decision. To accomplish a harmonization of State monetary policies, however, requires that a federal government have power to influence, and in the last analysis to determine, State monetary policy. A reconciliation of State monetary policies, which can not be obtained by agreement among State governments under the external pressure of a federal bank's credit powers, could be accomplished by more direct federal action because, at the federal level, action could take place without the unanimous agreement of the parties at interest.

A few words may be said on the means by which a federal agency — presumably a federal bank — could influence or control State monetary policies.

There are, broadly, four ways in which such a federal bank might influence the credit policies of State central banks and banking systems.

(1) By establishing and altering reserve requirements legally binding on State central banks and banking systems;
(2) By open market operations conducted by a federal bank, and through the establishment of open market policy for State central banks by a federal bank;
(3) By direct administrative control over State central bank credit policies and regulations;

[21] A similar argument can be made in the case of a State pursuing deflationary policies and accused by others of "exporting unemployment." In either case, a federal bank's leverage through its power to extend credit to the States would be insufficient to bring about the changes in national monetary policies necessary to preserve freedom of interstate exchange. It should be added that these cases are not purely hypothetical. There are cases in which the very limited authority of the managing board has proved insufficient to bring about necessary changes in national economic policies, and members have in consequence resorted to increased trade and payments restrictions to reduce payments imbalances among them.

(4) By means of the rediscount rate which, as lender of last resort, a federal bank would have power to set.

Adequate discussion of the many possibilities and alternatives under these headings would take us far beyond the scope of a memorandum on constitutional issues.

Suffice it to say that powers such as these could give a federal monetary authority substantial control over credit arrangements in the member States and, consequently, over the monetary policies which the States could pursue.

C. *Power to Control the Use of Foreign Exchange*

Federal control over the use of foreign exchange by member States appears to be a prerequisite to creation of a single market. The reasons for this are similar to those already discussed.

If each State were left free to determine its own use of its foreign exchange holdings, problems of the following kind would arise. One State could, in effect, raid the dollar reserves of another by pursuing a more restrictive policy on dollar imports and other dollar payments. If interstate trade were free, its citizens could then import dollar goods through another State which was pursuing a more liberal dollar import policy. To protect its dollar reserves, the second State would soon be forced to tighten its controls over dollar imports beyond the point which it considered to be in its best interests or, alternatively, to restrict interstate trade. It seems probable that an issue of this kind could not normally be settled by agreement between the States to harmonize their policies on external trade and payments.[22] If, however, the issue were raised to a federal level by giving a federal government power to control State policies on external trade and payments, restrictions on interstate trade and payments arising for this reason could probably be avoided. Such control, by channeling conflicts between States into the federal decision-making machinery, could prevent their finding expression in unilateral State action disruptive of interstate trade and exchange freedom.

There are a number of ways in which such federal control might be given. To illustrate:

(1) A federal government might be given authority to set standards governing State exchange controls (including import licensing) on external transactions.

(2) A federal government might be given exclusive administrative responsibility for external exchange control and import licensing for the whole federal area.

[22] Agreement to harmonize external trade policies has not proven feasible under the European Payments Union and the OEEC trade liberalization program. The absence of such agreement has been another cause of the relatively limited success of the trade liberalization program.

(3) A federal government might be given authority to set standards governing State exchange control and, in addition, that authority might be sanctioned by requiring State central banks to deposit all or a large part of their holdings and current receipts of gold and foreign exchange with the federal central bank, for distribution among the States at federal discretion.

The first of these possible arrangements would probably give too loose a control to be effective. The second would follow the example of those existing federal states which have exchange control and import licensing. For a European federal union, however, it would probably be too centralized to be politically acceptable or administratively desirable, particularly during the first years of the federation. The third method amounts to a compromise between the first and the second. It combines a powerful sanction with highly decentralized administration. If a European federal government were also entitled to receive and determine the distribution of foreign exchange credits (loans, aid, etc.) from non-member countries, it would be the more appropriate to require a federal pooling of gold and foreign exchange holdings.

D. *Power to Determine Exchange Rates*

Federal control of the rates at which State currencies exchange with each other and with other currencies appears also to be a prerequisite to creation of a single market, for reasons parallel to those already given for other federal money powers. In the absence of this federal power, a State would be able, for example by unilateral exchange depreciation, to do competitive damage to other States or to "export unemployment." Similarly, a State would, by unilateral appreciation, be able to make it profitable for its citizens to import scarce currency goods through another State, thus using unfairly the foreign exchange reserves of that State. Recent history and the history of the interwar period suggest that the pressure of domestic interests will often prevent international agreement to a pattern of exchange rates which is both economically efficient and equitable from the viewpoint of all the members.

Merely to require federal approval of changes in State exchange rates would not appear to be sufficient, as the experience of the International Monetary Fund has demonstrated. Federal power to act affirmatively would be required. Changes in exchange rates among State currencies would probably be an important instrument of federal action to maintain freedom of interstate exchanges and to supplement federal measures in the monetary area in the early years of the union.

In this connection, it should be recognized that all four of the federal currency and exchange powers would so supplement and reinforce each other as to be, in fact, a single power. The absence of any of them would probably render the others insufficient to maintain freedom of interstate exchanges and to control clashes of national economic interests which could otherwise be damaging to the political cohesion of the union.[28]

E. *A Single Currency?*

In principle, the simplest and the most thoroughgoing way to give the federal government these four currency and foreign exchange powers would be to abolish the national currencies and create a single federal currency. In addition to its value as a symbol of unity, the existence of a single federal currency would solve at a stroke the problem of providing as much centralization of power over money and foreign exchange as might be desired. But there would be certain serious difficulties, political and economic, produced by a single currency which might well outweigh these advantages during the early stages of the union.

In the first place, the preceding discussion suggests that it is not absolutely necessary from an economic, financial, or administrative viewpoint to have a common federal currency in order to create and maintain a single market over the federal area.

Second, and more important, creation of a common currency would deprive federal authorities of a valuable and probably essential tool of economic policy: the power to adjust interstate exchange rates. Without this possibility, which abolition of State currencies would preclude, almost the whole burden of managing interstate imbalances would fall on federal monetary policy. More precisely, imbalances in interstate payments, no matter how large or "structural" in character, would have to be corrected primarily by deflationary action in debtor, or by inflationary action in creditor, States. Given the considerable rigidity of the economic structure of the six European countries and the consequent difficulty of making the economic adjustments necessary to the creation of a single market, sole reliance on monetary policy, without the possibility of supplementary exchange rate adjustments, would tend in the shorter run to throw an unacceptable burden of unemployment or reduced incomes on important economic sectors in debtor countries. Exchange rate adjustments, though they would not alone be sufficient to correct interstate payments imbalances, have the great merit from a political viewpoint of spreading the economic burden of adjustment more evenly over the population of the debtor State and over a longer time period. Without a federal power to alter interstate exchange rates, it would very probably prove impossible, in the circumstances in which the union would find itself in its earlier years, to create or

---

[28] The degree of centralization of control of external financial functions here discussed would imply changes in present relations of member States with international bodies. For example, a federal government with powers such as those discussed above would presumably replace the States as member of the European Payments Union and the International Monetary Fund.

maintain freedom of interstate exchanges. At a later stage, after the major economic adjustments to a regime of free interstate trade had been largely accomplished and a federal government had acquired experience in exercising its monetary powers, it might prove desirable to have a single federal currency for the union.

There are of course possible intermediate stages between that envisaged above and a single federal currency. For example, both State currencies and a federal currency might be allowed to circulate as legal tender throughout the federal area. Alternatively, a federal "unit of account" could be made into a real currency by making it legal tender throughout the federal area, national currencies still circulating only within the States. Once either of these stages had been reached, it would become relatively easy, technically and as a matter of politics and psychology, to create a single federal currency for the union by exchanging federal currency for State currencies.

V. CONCLUSION

In the five existing federal systems, the federal governments exercise wide powers over currency, banking, credit, and foreign exchange. They do so in a highly centralized fashion, but with a somewhat decentralized administration in the United States and Germany. But they have not always done so. They did not have to, in the days of their establishment, because (1) money consisted mainly of coin; (2) the issuance of banknotes was mainly a private business; (3) there were no strong State government banks; and (4) governments did not yet play a very important role in the national economies. The history of the accretion of these powers in the hands of the central governments parallels the history of the changes in these conditions. The process was, in every case, a relatively slow one. In at least one case, that of Switzerland, it was a process which involved important issues of a truly "federal" nature causing some major and prolonged controversies. In no case were these problems susceptible to, nor did they call for, immediate solutions.

It is in this light that the conjectural analysis of minimum federal powers in this field, made in Section IV, should be understood. All that can be said is that each of the five federal constitutions on which this study is based deals with the question of federal powers in these fields. Some do so in detail, others in sweeping brevity. Each constitution leaves room for federal legislation to deal with these problems, or to implement constitutional provisions. Through such provisions, the existing federations were able to maintain or strengthen the unitary character of their markets. Since the proposed statute for a European Political Community envisages the eventual creation of a single market, provisions regarding federal powers over currency, banking, credit, and foreign exchange may be expected to become an important feature of its constitution.

A P P E N D I X   I

Australia

CONSTITUTION OF THE COMMONWEALTH OF AUSTRALIA, 1900

51. The Parliament shall, subject to this Constitution, have power to make laws for the peace, order, and good government of the Commonwealth with respect to: —

(iv) Borrowing money on the public credit of the Commonwealth;

(xii) Currency, coinage, and legal tender;

(xiii) Banking, other than State banking; also State banking extending beyond the limits of the State concerned, the incorporation of banks, and the issue of paper money;

(xvi) Bills of exchange and promissory notes;

105. The Parliament may take over from the States their public debts [as existing at the establishment of the Commonwealth],[24] or a proportion thereof according to the respective number of their people as shown by the latest statistics of the Commonwealth, and may convert, renew, or consolidate such debts, or any part thereof; and the States shall indemnify the Commonwealth in respect of the debts taken over, and thereafter the interest payable in respect of the debts shall be deducted and retained from the portions of the surplus revenue of the Commonwealth payable to the several States, or if such surplus is insufficient, or if there is no surplus, then the deficiency or the whole amount shall be paid by the several States.

105A.[25] — (1) The Commonwealth may make agreements with the States with respect to the public debts of the States, including —

(a) the taking over of such debts by the Commonwealth;

(b) the management of such debts;

(c) the payment of interest and the provision and management of sinking funds in respect of such debts;

(d) the consolidation, renewal, conversion, and redemption of such debts;

(e) the indemnification of the Commonwealth by the States in respect of debts taken over by the Commonwealth; and

(f) the borrowing of money by the States or by the Commonwealth, or by the Commonwealth for the States.

115. A State shall not coin money, or make anything but gold and silver coin a legal tender in payment of debts.

---

[24] Under Section 2 of the Constitution Alteration (State Debts) Act, 1909, the words in brackets are omitted.

[25] Under Section 2 of the Constitution Alteration (State Debts) Act, 1928, the Constitution was amended by insertion of Section 105A.

Canada

BRITISH NORTH AMERICA ACT, 1867

91. It shall be lawful for the Queen, by and with the Advice and Consent of the Senate and the House of Commons, to make Laws for the Peace, Order, and good Government of Canada, in relation to all Matters not coming within the Classes of Subjects by this Act assigned exclusively to the Legislatures of the Provinces, and for greater Certainty, but not so as to restrict the Generality of the foregoing Terms of the Section, it is hereby declared that (notwithstanding anything in this Act) the exclusive Legislative Authority of the Parliament of Canada extends to all Matters coming within the Classes of Subjects next hereinafter enumerated; that is to say: —

1. The Public Debt and Property.
2. The Regulation of Trade and Commerce.
3. The Raising of Money by any Mode or System of Taxation.
4. The Borrowing of Money on the Public Credit.
14. Currency and Coinage.
15. Banking, Incorporation of Banks and the Issue of Paper Money.
16. Savings Banks.
18. Bills of Exchange and Promissory Notes.
19. Interest.
20. Legal Tender.

92. In each Province the Legislature may exclusively make Laws in relation to Matters coming within the Classes of Subjects next hereinafter enumerated, that is to say: —

3. The Borrowing of Money on the sole Credit of the Province.

104. The annual Interest of the Public Debts of the several Provinces of Canada, Nova Scotia, and New Brunswick at the Union shall form the second charge of the Consolidated Revenue Fund of Canada.

107. All Stocks, Cash, Bankers' Balances, and Securities for Money belonging to each Province at the Time of the Union, except as in this Act mentioned, shall be the Property of Canada, and shall be taken in Reduction of the Amount of the respective Debts of the Provinces at the Union.

110. All Assets connected with such Portions of the Public Debt of each Province as are assumed by that Province shall belong to that Province.

111. Canada shall be liable for the Debts and Liabilities of each Province existing at the Union.

APPENDIX III

Germany

BASIC LAW FOR THE FEDERAL REPUBLIC OF GERMANY, 1949

Article 73. The Federation has exclusive legislation on:
4. currency, money and coinage, weights and measures and regulation of time and calendar.

Article 79. Concurrent legislation extends over the following fields:
11. laws relating to the economy (mining, industry, power supply, crafts, trades, commerce, banking and stock exchange, insurance to which civil and not public law applies).

Article 88. The Federation establishes a bank of issues as a federal bank.

Article 115. Funds may be obtained by way of credits only in the case of extraordinary requirements and as a rule only for expenditure for productive purposes and only on the basis of a federal law. The granting of credits and providing of securities as a charge on the Federation, the effect of which extends beyond the fiscal year, may be undertaken only on the basis of a federal law. The amount of the credits or the extent of the obligation for which the Federation assumes liability must be determined in the law.

APPENDIX IV

Switzerland

FEDERAL CONSTITUTION OF THE SWISS CONFEDERATION, 1848, AS AMENDED AND REVISED

Article 31-*quater*. The Confederation is authorized to regulate banks. These regulations must take into account the special function and position of the cantonal banks.[26]

Article 38. The Confederation shall exercise all the rights comprised in the coinage monopoly.

It has the sole right of coining money.

It shall determine the monetary system and may, if necessary, regulate the rate of exchange of foreign money.

Article 39. The right of issuing bank-notes and any other fiduciary money is vested exclusively in the Confederation.

The Confederation may exercise its monopoly of note issue through a state bank under a special administration, or may concede its exercise, subject to the right of redemption, to a central joint-stock bank to be estab-

---

[26] Amended October 1, 1947.

lished, which shall be administered with the assistance and under the control of the Confederation. The principal function of the bank holding the monopoly shall be to regulate the money market in Switzerland and to facilitate payments.

At least two thirds of the net profits of the bank, after payment of interest or reasonable dividend on the endowment or share capital, and deduction of payments to the reserve funds, shall go to the cantons.

The bank and its branches shall be exempt from all cantonal taxation.

The compulsory acceptance of bank-notes and any other form of fiduciary money may only be decreed by the Confederation in case of necessity in time of war.

Federal legislation shall make provision as to the seat of the bank, its basis and organization, and the carrying into effect of this Article in general.

APPENDIX V

United States

FEDERAL CONSTITUTION

ARTICLE I, *Section* 8. The Congress shall have Power To lay and collect Taxes, Duties, Imposts, and Excises, to pay the Debts and provide for the common Defence and general Welfare of the United States; but all Duties, Imposts and Excises shall be uniform throughout the United States;

To borrow money on the credit of the United States; . . .

To coin Money, regulate the Value thereof, and of foreign Coin, and fix the Standard of Weights and Measures;

To provide for the Punishment of counterfeiting the Securities and current Coin of the United States; . . .

Section 10. No State shall . . . coin Money; emit Bills of Credit; make any Thing but gold and silver Coin a Tender in Payment of Debts; pass any . . . Law impairing the Obligation of Contracts . . .

Agriculture

I. INTRODUCTION

It is characteristic of the three federal governments considered here — Australia, Canada, and the United States — that a national agricultural policy had its beginning in the evolution of programs to promote the development of frontier land. In each instance, these nations occupied large continental areas which represented a vast economic potential to be developed by pioneer settlement. Consequently, the role of the federal governments was initially to promote rapid settlement. The more specific problems of integrating this development with the political, social, and economic development of the area was left to the State governments. As the central governments developed programs to promote the economic welfare of the agricultural community, the traditional boundaries between federal and State powers and between private interest and public welfare were disputed and the high courts of those countries were called upon to settle the specific questions of the rights and powers of the various claimants. In all three nations the possibility and fact of court decisions favoring the rights of the States and Provinces over those of the central government limited the initiative of the central government in developing a positive agricultural policy. However, the demands created by two world wars and a major economic depression for a nationally integrated economic policy for all factors in the economy broke down many of these inhibitions. Within recent times positive programs have been established and central governments have laid the foundations of a general economic policy.

In the course of this development it has become clear that a policy for agriculture, to be consistent with any welfare objective, must be coordinated and integrated with general economic policy — a fact that was implied at least in the various federal constitutions which make no special provisions for agriculture. Thus, measures for implementing agricultural policy are created within the constitutional provisions under which this general policy is created and applied. This is not to say that the requirements of a dynamic agricultural economy do not in specific instances require particular measures, but the possibility of carrying out such measures rests in the general powers for economic management. Creating and establishing necessary agricultural policy are thus rooted in the political process and in the interplay of interests and institutions.

This general point of view is relevant vis-à-vis the proposal to establish an agricultural union in Europe. It is apparent in the case of the three nations considered here that the success of the agricultural segment of the economy depends on the integration of agricultural policy with a general program to maintain full employment, promote the efficient development of resources, and increase trade. The agricultural economy exists as a part of the whole, the roots of its health and disease are in the whole economy. To attempt to deal with agriculture as a separate entity would be to treat symptoms rather than causes, and the results would be both costly to the whole economy and ineffective for agriculture. It is true that in a frontier economy a piecemeal approach is possible, but if the history of economic development in the United States is a valid illustration such methods in a modern sophisticated economy are an anachronism. Of necessity a policy for agriculture has become an aspect of the general economic and political policy.

II. THE UNITED STATES

The development of agricultural policy in the United States has been a political process interacting with but not determined by the economic situation. Policy was formulated by the empirical method of integrating and projecting short-run solutions to immediate problems. Since this policy was focused on current issues rather than the general question of the politics of economic development, the overall problem of the relation between the State and federal governments and the independent initiative left to each depended on current needs rather than consistency with a comprehensive design. That this course was possible and reasonably successful is an indication of the capacity of the American federal system to meet the requirements of a dynamic economy.

Historically the role of the federal government has been to assist the development of an agriculture whose primary welfare objective was individual ownership of land. The Jeffersonian doctrine of the individual has long been symbolized by the farmer as the independent American citizen who supplied the necessary Roman virtues for a healthy democracy. A corollary of this doctrine was the necessity to permit a maximum amount of freedom and initiative to the landowner while holding to a minimum the controls of either State or federal government. On the other hand, in the development of the American continent it became necessary to protect small entrepreneurs and to promote opportunities for them. The major example of a federal policy for these objectives is the distribution of public lands in such ways as to encourage settlement by small holders, a policy reaching fullest expression in the Homestead Act of 1862.

After the Civil War the attempts of the federal government to aid agriculture took the form of providing education through the land grant colleges, collecting information by establishing State experiment stations to develop new agricultural methods and processes, and creating the United

States Department of Agriculture in the first instance as a fact-finding and seed-distributing agency in Washington. In dealing with the problem of agricultural discontent in the latter half of the nineteenth century, the role of the government was primarily to provide broad prescriptions such as a monetary policy to solve the problems of the time rather than to attempt a specific attack on questions such as misuse of resources and poverty in agriculture.

A change in attitude which characterizes the present relation of the federal government to agriculture as a segment of the economy began with the establishment of regulatory agencies within the Department of Agriculture. The purpose of the initial regulation was to protect the European market for American meat. It was undertaken as an aspect of the obligation of the federal government to maintain a necessary inflow of European gold. This was expanded to include the concept of disease control among livestock. In the first instance, the power of regulation exercised by the Department of Agriculture was enforced against processors of food rather than farmers. An extension of this doctrine was the application of grading rules and standards devised and applied by representatives of the Department of Agriculture. Particularly with regard to commodities in a perfectly competitive market such as wheat, the development of standards of quality reflecting price differentials was a matter of extreme importance to the producer. Enforcement of market standards has become an important force for a more efficient distribution of agricultural products and contributes in certain segments of agricultural marketing to a more nearly competitive market.

The second area of regulation beginning at this time was the control of domestic livestock movement and inspection to detect contagious diseases with the objective of ultimate slaughter of infected animals. Both State and federal governments play an active role in this area, although the initial impetus and direction came from the federal government. Here two important aspects of agricultural policy are involved. First, this program of disease control was possible only because of government-subsidized research into the causes and control of the disease. A further subsidy paying compensation to owners of livestock slaughtered for sanitary reasons was a necessary additional factor. Second, this program, although a drastic limitation in the first instance on the livestock owner, was clearly in the best interests of all producers in the long run. The inspection of livestock is one drastic control of agricultural activity by both State and federal governments which has had the general support of farmers when provided with the subsidy to make the long-run objective more palatable.

The change in attitude is also shown by the direct concern of the federal government with the actual promotion of agricultural policies for the general welfare. An example of this is the establishment of federally subsidized credit agencies following World War I. The federal government recognized its obligation to use its power to encourage food production during the war. In the readjustment of agriculture following the war and the subsequent severe agricultural depression the solution was assumed to be twofold: one, that of supplying additional credit, and the other, that of promoting more efficient marketing of agricultural products.

Efficiency in this instance was equated with the classical concepts of competition although the methods adopted, such as encouraging marketing cooperatives, aimed at giving farmers a degree of monopolistic control of their markets. The establishment of the Farm Credit Administration by Congress was, among others, a response of the legislature to an executive appeal for a specific solution to the problem as identified and recommended by the bureaucracy. The essence of this governmental attempt to solve the problem of low income in agriculture was, first, to subsidize the interest rate and the administration of the liberalized credit program, and, second, to provide that the ownership and control of the program could be taken over by private individuals once the program was established and the need for subsidy was removed. Thus there was in the program a tacit recognition of the doctrine that the States enjoy all rights except those the Constitution specifically reserved to the federal government.

In this case, as in many to follow, the federal agency made specific provision to relinquish its powers when federal aid was no longer necessary — federal intervention was directly related to the crisis in credit rather than to the problem of long-run relative shortages of capital. This latter problem was left to private enterprise as a developed opportunity. There was no attempt to insure here, nor in most subsequent credit aid programs, that the lending policies for which the agency was established should be continued after the financial control of the federal government had been relinquished. One result of this failure to provide for a continuity of lending policy to meet the capital needs of agriculture was that in each succeeding crisis of agricultural credit it was necessary to create new federal agencies to lend funds on more liberal terms.

More significant results of the agricultural depression of the 1920's from the point of view of federal organization were the direct subsidies to support agricultural prices and farm income at home, and the dumping of farm products abroad. Agricultural prices following the inflation of land values and prices during World War I fell to depression levels sooner than other prices and remained there longer. Consequently, attempts to solve the agricultural depression began in the atmosphere of a continuing general prosperity. The farm bloc in Congress developed a degree of extra-party unity on proposals for agricultural relief and a specialist's concern with a particular problem which had the effect of isolating agriculture as a special case and outside the test of the general interest. Agricultural policy remained in this protected position until the economic depression of the 1930's became general and agricultural policy was of necessity made a part of a total and integrated program for economic improvement.

With this development, the character of agricultural policy as it is related to the distribution of power among federal, State, regional, and other political subdivisions changed substantially. This evolution was conditioned by at least four dominant factors: first, the traditional approach to agriculture as a process of resource development; second, the role of the United States Supreme Court and its evolving concept of the positive role of the federal government; third, the explicit incorporation of agricultural policy into a program of general welfare; and, finally, the proliferation of lines of authority and communication that grew up with the development of an array of action programs directly concerning individual farm operators. These created a new set of relationships among the federal government, the regions, the State, the county, and the community.

In the United States today the basic immediate problems in agricultural policy are, first, the achievement of a more equitable distribution of income in which agriculture receives a higher relative share; second, and associated with this, the problem of resource allocation, a part of the general question of income and welfare, but for analytical purposes, at least, separable from it; and, third, the problem of resource conservation. In one sense this is a special aspect of the preceding issue, but when the objective is the maximization of returns for society in the long run the issues and methods of solution are frequently quite different. There is a fourth problem, namely, that of administering a complex agricultural economy. Here the issue is first that of creating policies and then integrating and coordinating the efforts of the agencies charged with carrying out those policies.

The efforts of government to resolve these problems fall into three broad categories: (1) The payment of subsidies by the government upon the condition that the recipient carry out certain marketing or land-use practices. Examples of such subsidies are (a) non-recourse loans offered by the federal government to producers of certain crops to stabilize prices; (b) grants of fertilizers and other material assistance to promote conservation and land-use adjustment; and (c) technical assistance in planning and carrying out conservation practices and programs to increase economic efficiency. (2) Regulation of private land use by State and federal governments. These include zoning ordinances, land-use regulation by political subdivisions such as soil conservation districts, and statutory requirements applicable to farm leases. (3) Direct administration of lands by State and federal governments. This includes the retirement of submarginal land and the administration of specific resources such as forests, wildlife, and watersheds.[1]

The power of the Congress to legislate on these matters rests in general on Section 8 of Article I of the Constitution and supplementary provisions in several other sections as well as on the Fifth, Tenth, and Fourteenth Amendments later adopted. These can be summarized in the following terms:

[1] Cf. Glick, "The Soil and the Law," in *Soils and Men*, Yearbook of Agriculture 296–318 (1938).

(1) To collect revenues by taxation; (Art. I, §8)
(2) To spend the proceeds of taxation "to pay the debts and provide for the common defense and general welfare of the United States;" (Art. I, §8)
(3) "To regulate commerce with foreign nations, and among the several states, and with the Indian tribes"; (Art. I, §8)
(4) "To make all laws which shall be necessary and proper for carrying into execution the foregoing powers, and all other powers vested by this Constitution in the Government of the United States, or in any department or officer thereof." (Art. I, §8)
(5) To "dispose of and make all needful rules and regulations respecting the territory or other property belonging to the United States." (Art. IV, §3)[2]

While granting these powers, the federal Constitution also places certain limitations upon the exercise of such power. Most important of these is the "due process" clause which provides that no person may be deprived of liberty or property without due process of law. At present, however, this does not represent an absolute limitation on governmental regulation of agriculture since the "police power" permitting the federal government to act to protect and promote public health, safety, morals, or welfare has been successfully invoked to provide an overriding authority. A specific case in point is the decision of the Supreme Court of the United States in the *Nebbia* decision (*Nebbia v. New York,* 291 U.S. 502 (1934)) which sustained a New York statute regulating milk prices and contributed this definition of "due process": "And the guarantee of due process, as has often been held, demands only that the law shall not be unreasonable, arbitrary, or capricious, and that the means selected shall have a real and substantial relation to the object sought to be attained."

A second limitation on the power of the Congress to legislate for agriculture is the fact that the proceeds received from taxation must be spent for those purposes which clearly promote the "general welfare." The interpretation of this provision would seem to be becoming increasingly liberal, and the Supreme Court has permitted the expenditure of tax-derived funds in cases where the benefit to private individuals is incidental to a general welfare purpose that is very broadly defined. Two cases in point are funds for land reclamation and income supplements paid to farmers for carrying out land-use practices that could only be most generously defined as for the general welfare as distinguished from private benefit. However, this limitation on spending power plus that which follows provided the basic issues in one of the most important recent cases before the Supreme Court dealing with agricultural policy. This was *United States v. Butler,* 297 U.S. 1 (1936), in which the Court by a six-to-three decision declared the Agricultural Adjustment Act of 1933 to be unconstitutional. One element in this decision was the fact that a tax paid by processors of agricultural products was re-

[2] *Id.* at 297–298.

turned to the producers by the federal government as a benefit payment. A second point in the decision was that the act violated the Tenth Amendment of the Constitution which provides: "The powers not delegated to the United States by the Constitution, nor prohibited by it to the States, are reserved to the States, respectively, or to the people."

This decision was in a sense the beginning of a new phase of agricultural policy in the United States. The disallowed act was within less than two months replaced by the Soil Conservation and Domestic Allotment Act of 1936 which achieved the same purposes of a wider distribution of income to agriculture but for the somewhat anomalous reason of promoting resource conservation. The subsequent Agricultural Adjustment Act of 1938 continued the theme of conservation as a prime reason for legislative action but more specifically tied the benefit payments to production and marketing practices designed to support farm prices at higher levels. These provisions were based on the constitutional power to tax and spend. A third and supporting device to control agricultural surpluses, the assignment of marketing quotas to individual farmers, depended upon the constitutional grant of power to regulate interstate and foreign commerce.

This use of the "commerce clause" of the Constitution was buttressed by recent decisions of the Supreme Court which interpreted that clause to permit an extension of the power of the Congress to regulate trade. Broad power to regulate interstate commerce had originally been affirmed in 1824 by Chief Justice Marshall's decision in *Gibbons v. Ogden,* 9 Wheat. 2, and most recently in the decision of the court in 1938 sustaining the validity of the National Labor Relations Act (*National Labor Relations Board v. Santa Cruz Fruit Packing Company,* 303 U.S. 453 (1938)). From the point of view of agricultural policy, the critical case was *Wickard v. Filburn,* 317 U.S. 111 (1942). In this instance the Court approved regulations to enforce wheat marketing quotas as provided in the Agricultural Adjustment Act of 1938 on the grounds that such marketing control came within the power of the Congress to regulate commerce among the several States. Thus a new avenue became available to the federal government, and what had been denied in the *Butler* decision was more than returned in *Wickard v. Filburn.* In fact the possibilities of this extension of regulatory power to the Congress have yet to be fully defined.

That the Supreme Court decision in *Wickard v. Filburn* reflects an evolution of the point of view of the Court rather than the discovery of a new constitutional basis for welfare legislation is indicated by two decisions of the Court only one year after the *Butler* decision. In this interval the personnel of the Court had changed somewhat, a factor of some weight in this development. But regardless of the cause, the important fact is that in two cases sustaining the validity of the Social Security Act, *Steward Machine Company v. Davis,* 301 U.S. 548 (1937), and *Helvering v. Davis,* 301 U.S. 619 (1937), the Court affirmed the very broad power of Congress to appropriate proceeds of taxation for purposes of aid to the general welfare. This was essentially a reversal of the position of the Court in the *Butler* case, although in the opinion of the Court the *Butler* decision was not by these later decisions overruled, but rather it was "distinguished."

A fourth limitation on the power of Congress to legislate for agriculture is one which is not explicitly stated, but which has been derived from the Constitution as a whole by the Supreme Court of the United States. This has been defined in the following terms: "The Congress, the President, and the courts are each forbidden to delegate to either of the others any of the powers conferred, and no one of these three may invade the field assigned to either of the others." [3]

In addition to limiting the legislative powers of the Congress the Constitution also restricts the powers of the various States. Again the foremost of these limitations is the due process requirement. The courts have implied from this that the proceeds of taxation may not be expended upon other than a "public purpose." Finally, the States are required to give "equal protection of laws" to all persons within their jurisdiction. These additional limitations on legislative powers are found in most State constitutions:

(1) All but a very few, expressly or by judicially derived implication, prohibit delegation of power from one department of the government to another, and invasion of the respective spheres. (It is important to note that the Federal Constitution does not require separation of powers for the state governments, although it does require such separation for the federal government.)

(2) The constitutions of ten states prohibit either the state or political subdivisions of the state, or both, from engaging in "works of internal improvement"; or impose limitations on such action.

(3) The constitutions of 45 states prohibit the "lending or donating" by the state or political subdivisions, or both, of credit, money, or property to or in aid of private persons.[4]

The relationship between the States and the federal government in developing agricultural legislation can be illustrated by the evolution of the Milk Marketing Agreements program. Under the Agricultural Adjustment Act of 1933 the Secretary of Agriculture was permitted to enter into marketing agreements with processors, associations of producers, and distributors of farm products in interstate or foreign commerce. To police these agreements, which were entered into voluntarily, the Secretary was authorized to issue licenses to the contracting parties, primarily to eliminate trade practices that depressed producer prices, and to force to comply with the Secretary's regulations the minority who would not support the marketing scheme proposed by the industry. At the same time various States, particularly those with large metropolitan milksheds, also established State milk control boards to enforce "orderly" marketing procedures that would

---

[3] Glick, "The Soil and the Law," in *Soils and Men,* Yearbook of Agriculture 298 (1938).
[4] *Ibid.*

stabilize prices paid to "normal" producers. In many cases the objectives of these boards were in fact to regulate interstate shipment of fluid milk to bolster the prices, and to aid local producers.

With the decision of the Supreme Court in the *Panama Refining Company* (*Panama Refining Co. v. Ryan*, 293 U.S. 388 (1934)) and *Schechter* (*A. L. A. Schechter Poultry Corp. v. United States*, 295 U.S. 495 (1935)), cases casting doubt on the use of the licensing power to enforce compliance, the 1935 amendments to the Agricultural Adjustment Act and the Marketing Agreement Act of 1937 substituted Orders of the Secretary of Agriculture for licenses. The powers of State milk control boards, however, were not affected by those decisions, since they were granted by the State legislatures and defined by State courts. The States, however, were challenged in the United States Supreme Court on the grounds that State boards were attempting to fix milk prices illegally. In *Nebbia v. New York*, the United States Supreme Court ruled in favor of the State of New York and in its decision helped to clarify the definition of the relationship between "due process" and "police power."

The passage of the Agricultural Marketing Act of 1937 marked the beginning of a considerable expansion of federally controlled milk markets. Basically this is an enabling act; it permits producers to vote on accepting a marketing agreement. If the support is sufficient and the agreement judged feasible, the Secretary of Agriculture approves it. A Federal Milk Marketing Administration is established for the area to carry out the regulations provided in the agreement. The costs of the programs are financed by the affected industry.

In most cases, federal milk markets are coexistent with State milk control boards, although the tendency has been for the federal agency to exercise a controlling influence largely because of its power to regulate the supply and price of milk in milksheds covering several States. State milk control boards have attempted on occasions of surplus production within the State to exclude shipments from other States, but under the Constitution they have no control of interstate commerce and the devices adopted such as health inspections favoring local producers have little effect in the long run.

Milk handlers brought suit against the Boston Milk Market Administrator in an attempt to have the Agricultural Marketing Act of 1937 declared unconstitutional. The Supreme Court upheld the federal Government in the *Eisenberg* decision (*Milk Control Board v. Eisenberg Farm Products*, 306 U.S. 346 (1939)) and since then the program has continued with little legal interference. In effect, this legislation makes it possible to control a market existing within a State but supplied from an area covering several States. Since federal markets are usually the major markets within a State, the prices and practices established in the federal markets become dominant, and State regulation is becoming a method of maintaining federal market standards in State markets not included under federal control. The particular characteristics that make this legislation possible under the restrictions of the Constitution are that, in the first instance, the agreement is established by the voluntary action of the industry. Second, the legislation itself creates no marketing control; it is rather an enabling act permitting the milk industry to provide itself with a marketing authority to exercise such control. Finally, the Milk Marketing Agreements are by their nature variable and can be adjusted to the particular needs of the areas adopting them. Thus they avoid the rigidity of much federal regulatory legislation. It is important to note that under the federal milk marketing orders, it is the prices to producers not the prices paid by consumers that are regulated. On the other hand, most State legislation establishing milk control boards requires that consumer interest shall be represented in the price decisions of the board. Federal milk markets which managed to keep prices close to the consumers price demand by using a formula reflecting consumer spending power as one of the components of the index to determine the price to be paid to producers. This device seems to be more effective in balancing supply and demand than the hearings provided for producer and consumer interest groups under State laws.

Another device for adjusting economic relations between States, and of considerable importance where the sovereignty of the constituent States is an issue of great weight, is provided under Section 10 of Article I of the Constitution. According to this, two or more States may enter into an agreement or compact if this compact receives the consent of the Congress. Thus far this provision has had little relevance to questions of agricultural policy. However, it has played a part in the development of natural resources, particularly watersheds and river basins. The primary difficulty in this method is securing agreement among the contracting States and then holding them to the agreement. There is the further limitation that such compacts deal with a static situation and do little to encourage future development. However, this fault is not inherent in the device. Finally, the interstate compact has been little used in recent times because of the greater current popularity of an alternative instrument, the valley, basin, or area authority, an agency capable of dealing with interstate resource control and development under the authority of the Congress. The outstanding example of this is the Tennessee Valley Authority.

It is important to emphasize that the constitutional framework briefly described here is capable of development and change even though at times the rate of change seems wholly inadequate to meet present and pressing needs. One reason for this greater flexibility is that unlike the Constitutions of Australia and Canada it does not rest upon a grant of powers from a mother country. Furthermore, particularly with reference to Australia, the amending power is more workable. Perhaps most important is the fact that the requirements of the more complex American economy have brought greater pressures to bear against constitutional blocks to necessary change. In any event, it is within this framework that the present issues of the American agricultural economy are being formulated and developed toward resolution.

It has been recognized within the past two decades that the problem of income distribution is an aspect of public policy in which all segments of the economy not only have an equal stake, but also that the achievement of a satisfactory income level depends on holding a balance of equitable distribution among the various segments of the economy.

Economic policy is rooted in the modern preoccupation with maintaining full employment. Unlike the period of the twenties when the plight of agriculture was considered to be a special case, agricultural income today is as a whole in a relatively favorable balance with incomes in general. However, a modern inheritance from the period when agriculture was a special case is the assumption within certain segments of agriculture that equity is synonymous with equality of income. Hence programs such as that of benefit payments to farmers have had a tendency to become a built-in feature of agricultural policy, with the attendant difficulty that such programs may retard necessary agricultural adjustment and subsidize malallocation of resources and inefficiency at public expense.

Nevertheless, it cannot be denied that there are within agriculture large areas of poverty which infect the economy of whole regions, particularly those with limited capital and a low level of industrial development. Two methods of attack on the problem of income inequity in agriculture are subsidized credit and income supplements.

The primary credit agencies in this area have been two, established by the federal government, the Farm Credit Administration and the Farmers' Home Administration. The first of these has become a supplement to the private banking system, extending mortgage and production credit to solvent farmers who do not have private credit immediately available. It is significant that with war-nourished increases in farm income a growing proportion of these credit functions are carried by the private banking system. It is also relevant to observe that the credit agencies established by the federal government to alleviate the agricultural distress of the 1920's have tended to become increasingly conservative in their lending policies and have largely ignored the possibilities of credit innovation, particularly in the area of intermediate credit to finance adjustments to increase production efficiency such as conservation and development. One cause for this rigidity has been that these agencies were established so that the farm borrowers could replace initial government capital with their own funds as loans were repaid, and as the capital funds have come under the control of private individuals the primary concern of the managers has been to ensure the stability of the institution rather than respond to the new demands of a public need.

The Farmers' Home Administration on the other hand is a public agency primarily designed to promote higher levels of living among farmers whose economic condition excludes them from private credit sources. This agency extends long-term loans to enable tenants to purchase farms, intermediate loans to provide the capital that will make it possible for farmers to establish themselves as successful operators, and short-term production loans. In all cases the borrowers must be financially beyond the aid of private credit. A more important aspect of this credit is the elaborate supervision of the use of the borrowed funds by trained agency personnel. The loan is basically contingent upon the drafting and carrying out of a farm plan which has been agreed upon by the borrower and the Farmers' Home Administration.

During the recent agricultural prosperity this program also has been on the wane, although there remain in agriculture a great many persons existing below the level to which wartime prosperity filtered and lacking the opportunity or knowledge of the possibility of improving their condition. Unfortunately this is a group which also lives in those backwaters that escape public notice. Thus while there is a need for the work of agencies such as the Farmers' Home Administration, the severe conditions of the agricultural depression that called it into being have been solved by the general rise in the price level, if not by governmental efforts, and it has curtailed its activities under the pressure of declining Congressional favor and appropriations.

A second and equally potent factor in cutting down this program is that its most articulate defender was of necessity the agency itself. This has meant weak Congressional support, to which has been added the open hostility of organized agricultural interests, particularly the American Farm Bureau Federation, which has taken the position that this kind of paternalism is inconsistent with an efficient capitalist economy. It could be argued that a federal system enhances the power of organized groups such as the Farm Bureau which is based on State organizations with a powerful leverage on representatives from agricultural areas and inhibits the power of minorities in the various States to get a friendly hearing in Congress.

The second form of income subsidy has been discussed previously in this paper. This is the program of maintaining price support and making payments for carrying out so-called conservation practices. Associated with this is the device of establishing marketing quotas which can be applied only with an affirmative vote of two thirds of the producers, and which is designed to prevent surpluses from choking the price-supported market. The benefits from the conservation program are available to all farmers although the primary recipients of price support aid are the producers of basic commodities such as wheat, corn, and dairy products. This general distribution of aid to farmers plus the fact that local administration is based on farmer committees elected in each farm community has given the program a powerful clientèle which has been able to insure its effective continuation regardless of the party in power in Washington. A second point relevant here and in subsequent discussions of government aid to agriculture is the fact that this clientèle consists almost exclusively of producer interests. This is a particularly serious problem when the drafting of agricultural legislation is the prerogative of a farm bloc in Congress working with a Department of Agriculture representing the same interests. This has frequently been the case in the past with the result that subsidies have aided the general welfare only indirectly by contributing to a generally higher level of income. Attempts to increase the welfare efficiency of these grants by provisions which would have passed on to consumers, in the form of lower prices, or better or more desirable products, the benefits of public support for increased productivity have rarely been successful. Moreover, since many subsidy payments were made to maintain present producers in fixed production patterns, such payments had a marked tendency to prevent necessary production adjustment. The particular marshaling of forces around a Congressional farm bloc supported by producer interest groups and a federal department organized to serve commodity groups left little room for the more general but less well organized forces of consumer interests and the supporters of economic efficiency. On the other hand, the system was effective in bringing to a sharp focus for a solution the problems of a distressed agriculture.

Recently, particularly with the attempts to develop a long-range agricultural policy, the issues have been brought before Congress for more general debate. It may be that the phase in which agricultural policy and legislation were shaped by the Agricultural Committees of the House of Representatives and Senate in comparative isolation has passed with the development of extensive federal programs of aid to agriculture and that the problem of integrating and coordinating them with a general economic policy will force their adjustment to a broader concept of the general welfare. One sign of this possibility is the fact that the Farm Bureau Federation has become a strong supporter of a general non-restrictive foreign trade policy and a more flexible domestic farm price support program.

Another indication of this trend is the extensive development of programs to conserve natural resources. This is within the frame of reference of a private property economy, but through public benefits private owners are encouraged to use the resources under their control to maximize their usefulness for a continuing society. In general this aid takes the form of subsidizing the additional costs such practices require, promoting local organizations such as soil conservation districts to use equipment, technical assistance, and the developments of government-supported research more efficiently, and expansion of educational programs such as that of the Cooperative Agricultural Extension Service which is maintained by funds from federal, State, county, and in some instances private organizations such as the State Farm Bureaus. Resource conservation has become such an important activity that it has been frequently suggested that the relevant bureaus in the Departments of Agriculture and Interior be combined in a Department of Natural Resources.

The major governmental agency in this field is the United States Soil

Conservation Service in the Department of Agriculture. This agency provides technical assistance to local soil conservation districts which are units of government established under State enabling acts. While the governing body of each of these districts is the locally elected board of supervisors operating under the general supervision of a State conservation Committee, the dominant force in the past has been the personnel of the Soil Conservation Service working in the district. However, with the coordination of the work of federal agencies working in agriculture at the county and State levels under orders issued by the Secretary of Agriculture in 1951, the district supervisors are playing a more effective role in determining district policy.

A particular problem in the use of a State enabling act to implement a federal program operating in the State is that of maintaining standards of performance in the State act which meet the requirements of the federal program. A case in point is the role of land-use regulations in State soil conservation district enabling acts. A model law to advise the States in drafting enabling legislation was prepared by the federal Soil Conservation Service. A provision for land-use regulation was included in the model law. Colorado was one of the States which enacted an ordinance permitting land-use regulation in its enabling act. When an attempt was made to enforce this ordinance a group led by absentee landowners successfully petitioned the State legislature to amend the law so that it was for all practical purposes ineffective.

In this instance, the federal Soil Conservation Service decided to abandon its policy of promoting land-use regulation ordinances, and consequently the federal program in the State was not materially affected. Had the Soil Conservation Service wished to do so, it could have withdrawn the assistance it provided for the local soil conservation districts in an effort to force State compliance with its standards. Such a course of action, however, would have been politically infeasible since it would have left the federal agency open to a charge of attempting to coerce a member State. Thus while this general issue has not become an important one in developing a federal land-use policy, the possibility of a serious conflict remains.

From the point of view of a federal system and its relation to agriculture it is significant that certain States, particularly Wisconsin and Michigan, have been important proving grounds for programs which were subsequently adopted on a national level. It should be added that an agency of the federal government, the Tennessee Valley Authority, has played a similar role of testing experimental programs.

In addition to greater opportunity for experimentation a federal system is also supposed to permit the full expression of a wider diversity of interests. However, this doctrine must be accepted with certain modifications when it is applied to agriculture. When a Congressional bloc is formed to represent agriculture, the agricultural interests that receive consideration are those of the dominant interests of the bloc. This monolithic structure tends to be reproduced in the executive department of the government, since the Department of Agriculture is dependent for its appropriations on this Congressional bloc. Furthermore, while agricultural policy may to a large extent originate in the Department, the veto power of this bloc is frequently the dominant factor in shaping the policy that emerges. One explanation for the existence of such a bloc is the fact that in certain States agriculture, and in some cases one commodity or interest group, is a sufficiently strong political force to dominate its Congressional delegation with regard to matters affecting agriculture. As was noted earlier, this may be a temporary phase in the development of a general long-range agricultural policy from a series of particular programs to relieve agricultural distress.

Since for the present at least and certainly in the past the source of political power is the State organization of agricultural interests there has been a strong demand on Congress to insist that agricultural programs place a maximum of authority in State and community groups. Two indications of this have been the successful assault on the regional organization of such agencies as the Agricultural Adjustment Administration, the Farm Security Administration and the Bureau of Agricultural Economics. In each of these instances the agencies were forced to abandon regional offices which, it was argued, bypassed State offices of these agencies and dealt directly with the county and local units of their programs. A second indication is the fact that agencies such as the Production and Marketing Administration and the Soil Conservation Service, the so-called action agencies, have found it desirable to establish at the bases of their programs locally elected governing committees or boards. Perhaps paradoxically, it is for this very fact that these agencies are frequently attacked by interest groups such as the Farm Bureau on the grounds that such local committees become publicly supported rivals to private interest groups and competitors for control of the shaping of agricultural policy. Thus federal agencies are opposed on the one hand for not permitting sufficient local control of the policies that shape their activities, and on the other for creating a strong local clientèle.

The solution to this problem advocated by the Farm Bureau and its ally, the land grant colleges, is that policies should be determined by State agencies within broad terms established by Congress, and these policies should be implemented with funds and necessary technical assistance passed on to the States by federal agencies. As precedent for such a program the grant-in-aid system of maintaining the cooperative Extension Services is cited. In its simplest terms, the reply to this argument has been that such a system could not effectively represent the general welfare and it would be impossible to maintain necessary standards of performance in the various States. It is also dubious that the States would be so effective as innovators of programs to meet changing needs as the federal bureaus. Certainly such a program would make the formulation of a truly general agricultural policy much more difficult.

While these problems are not inherent in a federal constitution and probably could not be resolved by specific constitutional provisions, they are rooted in the traditions of the federal system as it evolved in the United States. The best method for their solution would seem to be not through the route of constitutional amendment but rather through the development of administrative techniques, political invention, and the continued creation of a policy dictated by the general welfare. The specific points on which the federal system in the United States must prove itself today are, first, its capacity to bring to a focus and resolve at the proper level of government — county, State, or federal — the relevant issues of agricultural policies, and, second, to create and maintain within the bureaucracy the power, responsibility, energy, and imagination to carry out assigned policies and lay the foundation for the policies of the future.

III. AUSTRALIA

State governments have played a large role in the agricultural policies of Australia since federation under the Commonwealth of Australia Constitution Act of 1900. This is a continuation of the power vested in them prior to federation. State legislation has been enacted in almost all fields of agricultural policy. The States have maintained the legislative initiative particularly with respect to policy bearing on agricultural development and rehabilitation. The same is true of acts designed to curb disease, pests, and weeds, as well as of policies relating to credit provision and consumer protection. Moreover, State governments were the first to provide agricultural marketing programs. Subsequently, however, these marketing policies were largely nullified by court action. Nevertheless, these programs remain in effect as far as intrastate trade is concerned. In addition, the States have provided educational programs and experimental farms.

The Commonwealth government's major agricultural policies have largely borne on the export trade. Thus boards have been set up to supervise and promote the sale of almost all the major agricultural export products. Regulations with respect to grading and inspection have been established; and international contracts and agreements have been carefully negotiated. The attempt of the Commonwealth government during the thirties to institute a more comprehensive program covering both domestic and export marketing was denied by the courts. Three efforts to revise the Constitution in order to legalize Commonwealth marketing programs in the home market have failed. Aside from its marketing programs, the central government has passed various measures relating to quarantine and disease regulation. Also, it has passed various immigration laws. More important than these policies, however, has been the subsidy and tariff policy designed to stimulate domestic production and exports. Finally, the Commonwealth government has cooperated with State legislatures on a number of measures such as debt relief. In an effort to integrate State and fed-

eral policies the Agricultural Council, consisting of State and Commonwealth Ministers, has been established.

The legal history of both State and Commonwealth agricultural policies
is dominated by conflicts involving Section 92 of the Constitution stating
that interstate trade must be "absolutely" free. At first, it was decided that
this did not apply to the central government but only to the State
governments. In 1936, however, this view was reversed and it was decided
that the clause applied to both central and State governments. On the
whole, the interpretative history of Section 92 seems hopelessly complex.
This impression is reinforced by the number of decisions which have been
reversed, and the number of times High Court Justices have questioned a
previous court opinion. Hence there exists a maze of subtle distinctions
through which legislation, bearing on trade and commerce, must find its
way before it can become effective.

This problem is particularly significant since agricultural products are a
vital element in maintaining the Australian balance of payments. At the
same time, agricultural production has decreased and domestic demand
has increased for most primary commodities. Thus increasing thought has
been directed to agricultural development in recent years. At the same
time, Australia has maintained a very high tariff structure, by which some
agricultural commodities have gained while others have received subsidies.
At the same time, however, some of the major agricultural industries such
as wool have been penalized to the extent that their costs have been inflated.

In general the major problem in Australia has been one of applying capital and manpower, in the right proportions, to agricultural resources that
are in the early stages of development and that are essential to maintain
a satisfactory balance of payments schedule. A complicating factor in this
situation is the conflict between employment and investment opportunity
in the urban and rural sectors of the economy. Especially since the rise of
the Australian trade unions, positive federal policy has been in the direction of promoting conditions favorable to industrial and other urban employment. This has tended to intensify the insistence of the States where
agricultural interests can speak with political authority that the initiative
for developing and carrying out agricultural programs should remain with
the States.

In spite of these pressures, however, the scope of farm problems and the
necessity to maintain a world market for Australian farm products have
required a considerable increase in the role of the Commonwealth government with respect to agriculture. The High Court entered a new phase in
the 1930's and the general drift of constitutional development has been to
tie the Commonwealth more closely together and to augment the power
of the central government. At the same time, the interpretation and construction of the decisions have come to resemble somewhat less those of the
United States and more closely those of the British tradition. On the other
hand, attempts to overcome the restrictions on developing an overall mar-

keting policy embodied in Section 92 of the Constitution Act have all failed. This poses as a major long-run issue in creating a positive Australian agricultural policy the discovery of a solution to constitutional inflexibility.

Since the mid-twenties, government agricultural policy at all levels has been preoccupied with the persisting economic problems of farming areas. Attempts to solve these problems are the basis of policies, marketing regulations as well as programs of agricultural rehabilitation and reorientation. State governments have actively participated in marketing policies. Indeed, the Queensland government gave the initial impetus to the various peacetime schemes with the Queensland Wheat Pool (1920) and the Queensland Primary Products Act (1922). The latter was expanded and revised in the Primary Producers' Organization and Marketing Act (1926). In addition, the Fruit Marketing Organization Act was passed (1923). The gist of these schemes was to provide for a board, consisting of representatives of both producers and State officials, empowered to make all transactions with respect to a particular commodity. Any agricultural group could come into the program provided a certain majority — at one time two thirds — desired to sell its produce collectively. The commodity boards dealt with both intrastate and interstate trade and were alleged to have as their aim the maintenance of orderly marketing conditions. Similar programs were adopted by other State governments. After 1933, however, the State schemes were found *ultra vires* in so far as they applied to interstate trade. Henceforth they had to limit themselves to a few intrastate commodities such as fluid milk.

For those of their industries primarily dependent on export the States devised various schemes explicitly designed to bolster the domestic price by limiting the quantity which could be sold domestically and exporting the remainder at the going world price. To effect these programs the commodity boards of the various States worked in cooperation after several earlier voluntary schemes had broken down. In 1927 the courts voided these policies by finding the Dried Fruit Acts *ultra vires.* As this and similar measures were rejected, the Commonwealth government took an active hand since in the *Macarthur* case, it had been held that Section 92 did not apply to the central authority. Thus, for example, the Commonwealth reestablished the quotas of the Dried Fruit Boards under the Dried Fruit Act. Hence, there was State legislation to deal with the intrastate aspects of marketing and Commonwealth legislation to cover the interstate and export aspects. In 1936, however, the courts reversed the *Macarthur* decision and declared the Commonwealth legislation *ultra vires.* Now only voluntary association remained as a way to implement an overall policy of quotas and restrictions in the volume of domestic sales.

Despite these difficulties in regulating domestic marketing the Commonwealth government maintained a network of marketing boards to deal with the export trade. A Department of Markets was set up in 1925. It and the boards under it administered a variety of acts such as the Canned

Fruits Export Act (1926), the Dried Fruits Export Control Act (1924), the Dairy Produce Export Control Act (1924), the Wine Marketing Act (1929), the Meat Export Control Act (1935), and the Apple and Pear Organization Act (1938). In general, these acts dealt with supervising and organizing overseas marketing, publicity and advertising, obtaining favorable shipping and insurance rates, etc. A levy was imposed to cover the administrative expenses of the various boards. The boards, composed of industry and government representatives, were usually set up at the request of the industry and could again be dissolved at the industry's request. Since no attempt was made to control the home trade, the legality of the scheme was unquestioned.

A further aspect of Commonwealth policy related to tariffs and bounties. By the end of the thirties bounties were paid to many of the major industries. In the case of sugar, imports were barred, prices were fixed in the home market, and bounties were paid to keep the industry solvent. Bounties were also paid for the export of wine and fruit, the domestic production of raw cotton, butter, wheat, and fruit. A manure subsidy was granted primary producers other than wheat growers. In those industries where the domestic price was held above world market levels, import duties were applied.

In addition to the marketing policies, various measures with respect to farm credit were adopted by both central and State governments. By the "Premier's Plan" it was agreed by all governments to reduce the rate of interest. Additional relief from the serious farm debt problems was provided by the various State governments. Although the acts varied slightly, most of them established a tribunal to which farmers could apply before foreclosure. The tribunal could grant a stay, make adjustments in the terms and amount of debt, and give the farmer an opportunity to regain solvency. In hopeless cases foreclosure could be allowed although instances of this were rare. The banks set up similar schemes whereby the farmer was kept going with the hope he could eventually pay the debt. Strict supervision was provided, going so far in South Australia, for instance, as to give advice on cropping and land use. This strict supervision usually proved successful. Eventually more drastic schemes were undertaken and more foreclosures, although still relatively few, followed. In addition, further steps were taken to force creditors to accept reduction in the debt and lower interest. In West Australia, the Land Bank was refurbished after it verged on insolvency in 1934. The Commonwealth government undertook to assist the various Farm Relief Boards by providing additional funds. It raised the money under the Commonwealth Loan Act of 1935, and the States passed the legislation necessary for the application of the funds.

In order to deal more adequately with agricultural policies the various governments in 1934 agreed to set up the Australian Agricultural Council. This Council consisted of the Commonwealth and State Ministers responsible for agricultural policy. An advisory committee — the Standing Committee on Agriculture — was instituted to facilitate cooperative handling of agricultural problems.

When war began in 1939, the Commonwealth government's powers expanded greatly under the National Security Regulations (1939). The various measures adopted included all the now familiar devices of price control, rationing, commodity boards, subsidies, production goals, manpower control, contract purchases with the United Kingdom, fertilizer rationing, machinery priorities, etc. When the National Security Regulations were rescinded at the end of 1946 many of these policies disappeared or were substantially weakened.

During the postwar period most of the Commonwealth's marketing boards have continued their activities, somewhat strengthened over their prewar counterparts. In 1945 at the Empire Wool Conference, the Wool Realization Act was drafted which was later adopted by the Commonwealth government. In addition, the Commonwealth entered the Wheat Industry Stabilization Scheme (1946–1948) and, more recently, has signed the International Wheat Agreement. Moreover, through its marketing boards, the Commonwealth has negotiated the various commodity contracts with the United Kingdom. Finally, the Australian government has participated in the various programs of UNRRA and FAC.

On three occasions since 1930 constitutional amendments, designed to increase central government power in the field of marketing legislation, have been attempted and rejected. The first referendum occurred in 1937; the second in 1944; the third in 1946. At present, therefore, the formal constitutional division of powers remains the same as before the war.

IV. CANADA

In Canada, the British North America Act of 1867 and eight additional acts define the constitutional powers of the Dominion government. This legislation, which reserves to the Provinces what is not specifically awarded to the Dominion government, and the decisions of the Supreme Court, have established a pattern of relatively weak federal control in agricultural policy. The initiative in critical areas remains with the provincial legislatures, although since the War Measures Act, passed in 1914 and again invoked in 1939, the balance of power between the Dominion government and the provincial governments has shifted in favor of Ottawa. By opening the door to government by orders-in-council, the War Measures Act gave powers to the Dominion government to regulate and promote agricultural activity, and although in both World Wars the tide of this power receded from the high-water mark of actual wartime, in each succeeding instance it did not fall back to the original level.

As in the United States, the economic catastrophe of the 1930's resulted in many innovations in agricultural programs, and, because of its obviously greater economic power, the Dominion government played the domi-

nant role in this development.   Again, also as in the United States, the
Supreme Court limited the range of available policy alternatives open to
the Dominion government.   In general terms, the powers of the Dominion
government to regulate production and marketing of agricultural commodities were closely restricted, while the right to subsidize farm prices and
incomes, particularly the wheat cooperatives whose attempts at price fixing
had brought them close to bankruptcy, was, if not explicitly recognized, certainly not withdrawn.   Since the time of the Rowell-Sirois Commission,
which made a post-depression study of the possibilities of constitutional
means of aiding agriculture as one segment of the economy, there has been
a growing tendency to explore ways of increasing the power of the government in Ottawa to play a more active part in developing a positive program
for agricultural resources.

   While Canada has large areas of undeveloped agricultural resources
which pose for the Dominion government major problems of investment
policy, of greater significance is the issue of establishing a more desirable
distribution of income among the various segments of the Canadian economy along with a more efficient use of resources.   Canada, like the United
States, is a nation of large physiographic and economic regions and this
creates particular problems for the central government.   The predominance of agriculture in certain Provinces is overwhelming, while in others it
is relatively unimportant.   If the distribution of income is related to the
principle of the most efficient use of resources, those agricultural areas in
which the return from agricultural resources is relatively low will have a
lower level of living or welfare than the nation as a whole.   An equalization
grant to these poorer areas maintains and in some instances promotes an
inefficient use of resources.   In Canada this issue is compounded by the
presence of two major nationality groups whose cultural differences are
matched by disparities almost as great in economic situation.   On the other
hand it is possible that the sensitivity of the federal system to such group
interests, inefficient though it may be in terms of resource allocation, accounts for lack of crippling friction in the Dominion government.

   During the late twenties and thirties various marketing laws were enacted in an attempt to improve farm income by establishing orderly marketing.   Prior to World War II the government had limited its active price
support program to wheat, but following the war these measures were supplemented by general price support programs.   Peripheral problems in the
area of agriculture such as credit assistance, insurance, and relief also
received increasing attention since the thirties.   A second major objective
of policy was the improvement of production and the rehabilitation of exhausted resources.   The policies of agricultural encouragement and product improvement date from the later years of the nineteenth century; those
relating to land reallocation and reclamation received their primary impetus during the thirties.   The policy of assuming government responsibility for disease and pest control as well as policing malpractices in the sale of

commodities has continued with increasing support since its inception soon after the Dominion was established.

Provincial policies can be summarized under four main heads: first, there are those activities which the Provinces have carried over from their pre-confederation days. Among these were the encouragement of local agricultural societies and educational programs. Since the thirties, however, a second major area of policy has become predominant. As in Dominion legislation this new approach is an attempt to solve problems related to farm income. In this sphere provincial legislation has been closely akin to Dominion policy except that it has necessarily been limited to introprovincial measures. Third, the Provinces have undertaken programs of local development and land utilization frequently in cooperation with the central government. Finally, the Provinces have passed legislation to control disease, pests, and sharp selling practices.

It is fair to say that, taking the post-confederation era as a whole, a sincere effort has been made by the Provinces to cooperate with the Dominion government in matters relating to agricultural policy. On the one hand it has been recognized that the financial strength and power of the Dominion as well as its responsibility for international and interprovincial negotiations and trade enable the central government to achieve substantial benefits for the agricultural community which are far beyond the power of the Provinces. On the other hand the Provinces' ability to deal with certain regional and local problems as well as to give expression to provincial loyalties and ways of life is seldom questioned by the Dominion. There have, of course, been vigorous conflicts and sustained frictions. Perhaps the most serious of these have been instances in which the Provinces have adopted policies ostensibly designed to deal with disease, etc., but which were in fact intended primarily to inhibit interprovincial trade. Difficulties of this sort, for example, followed the recent outbreak of hoof-and-mouth disease. In this case action by a few Provinces worsened the overall economic problem. In the main, however, instances of this have been relatively minor compared to the frequent examples of cooperation.

Except for the first decade after confederation and for war years, provincial constitutional powers generally broadened whereas the Dominion government's powers tended to become more narrow. This was the result of the interpretation laid upon the Constitution by the courts over the years. These developments had their most serious consequences in the thirties when policies designed to ease the farm depression were seriously hampered. The exception to this is legislation affecting exports and tariffs, both clearly within Dominion jurisdiction. The latter is treated as an integral part of general commercial policy rather than agricultural policy. Tariffs on most farm products disappeared early, and Canada has ever since been virtually a free trade country with respect to agricultural commodities. However, there has been serious controversy with respect to manufactured commodities. Agricultural interests have contended that whereas they have had to sell in the face of world competition, they have had to buy in a protected domestic market. This pressure has been a strong factor tending to keep the Canadian tariff structure low, especially for manufactured commodities such as farm machinery. The prime importance of the export question to agricultural policy arises from the historic role of agricultural products in supporting general prosperity and the balance of international payments. Since World War II the growth of a more diversified agriculture, a larger home market, and the development of non-agrarian resources have lessened this dependence on international markets somewhat, but the necessity of agricultural exports remains a fundamental fact to be considered in formulating agricultural and other policies.

The most notable development of agricultural policy has been the Dominion government's invasion of the field of active price support. In the Provinces a wide network of marketing boards had grown up during the war interval. In addition, various credit, conservation, and land-use policies were enacted. The most striking feature of Dominion-provincial policy has been the development of cooperation between the various legislative bodies. This had already been apparent before the war but reached its culmination with the institution of annual conferences between the Dominion and provincial departments of agriculture during the war and continuing until the present. The conferences were designed to devise an integrated program of agricultural production and marketing. During most of this period the tasks of the legislatures were eased greatly by buoyant markets for scarce primary commodities.

Federal government price support policies are embodied in the Agricultural Prices Support Act (1949), amendments to the Canadian Wheat Board Act of 1935, the Agricultural Products Act (1947), and the Agricultural Products Board Act (1951). The first price support Act, which became effective in 1946, empowers the Board set up under it to buy and sell produce to maintain a floor price. The price, however, may vary and is not tied to any rigid formula. The Act has been used extensively to support the prices of apples, potatoes, beans, honey, cheese, eggs, butter, and pork. The Canadian Wheat Board Act was an outgrowth of the Wheat Board Act of the thirties but was more inclusive. The change in policy came in 1943 with the closing of the Winnipeg Grain Exchange and the establishment of a monopoly position for the Wheat Board. The third bill noted was designed to facilitate export contracts with foreign governments, and expired in 1950. The last Act empowers a board to transact business and negotiations with foreign countries, to buy, sell, and store commodities, and to operate in conjunction with the Agricultural Prices Support Board. It should be noted that the two Boards just mentioned do not have jurisdiction over grain dealings which fall within the powers of the Wheat Board.

The Dominion government's marketing program outside the area of price support has been provided for in several acts, the most important of which is the Agricultural Products Marketing Act (1949). This Act in effect attempts to apply marketing regulations similar in scope to those provided in the Natural Products Marketing Act (1934). It empowers the Minister to grant authority to boards, authorized under provincial statutes, to exercise the same powers of supervision and regulation for produce going to interprovincial and export trade as for products moving in intraprovincial trade. It is generally felt that this is the constitutional limit to which the Dominion government can go in this area. The Act has been invoked on several occasions, e.g. in British Columbia for fruit and vegetables, in Nova Scotia for apples. The Agricultural Cooperative Marketing Act (1939) has also been applied during the postwar period to deal with such items as seeds, honey, onions, and potatoes. A number of other acts dealing with market regulation of particular commodities have also been passed, e.g. the Dairy Products Act (1951).

The growth of provincial marketing boards began prior to the war and continued at an increasing pace through, and after, the war. The power and composition of these boards are highly variable. Usually the provincial boards have regional representatives and they may set up local boards. The boards have wide powers to investigate, arbitrate, and settle disputes; they may investigate cost-price relations, financial arrangements, management, grading, orderly marketing devices, and negotiate prices.

The development of bulk-buying schemes and international commodity agreements has placed various new obligations on the Dominion government. For instance, the government has carried out Canadian negotiations in the International Wheat Agreement. In addition, various boards were constituted to negotiate and administer the United Kingdom food contracts such as those for bacon, cheese, and eggs. Many of these boards which derived their initial powers from the War Measures Act were later taken over under the Agricultural Products Act. Both these developments became, in fact, an intricate part of the price support policy. Besides these actions, the government has cooperated fully with UNRRA and FAO in the postwar policies of these organizations.

Farm credit facilities have been expanded by both the Dominion and provincial governments. In 1944, the federal government amended the Bank Act and passed the Farm Improvement Loans Act (1944) whereby chartered banks could lend financial assistance to farms for the purchase of equipment and livestock as well as to make general improvements. Moreover, the operations of the Farm Loan Board have been extended. In addition, the Prairie Grain Producers' Interim Financing Act (1951) was passed providing short-term credit to grain growers. Also, the National Housing Act (1944) contained special provisions for farm housing. Finally, the various Prairie Assistance measures implemented in the thirties were extended. Thus at the present time the federal government is involved in short, intermediate, and long-term credit programs. The Provinces have continued to develop facilities inaugurated before World War II, but have tended to limit themselves to shorter-term credit operations.

Both Dominion and provincial governments have engaged in various conservation and land-use schemes. Under the Prairie Farm Rehabilitation Act, the Dominion government has engaged in extensive projects of water conservation, community pastures, and irrigation. Among the most impressive of these has been the St. Mary-Milk River Project. In addition to activities in the Prairie Provinces, the Dominion has undertaken extensive programs in British Columbia and the Maritimes. Most of these programs have been carried out with provincial cooperation.

Since World War II there has been one major, formal constitutional development. This concerned the abolition of appeals to the Judicial Committee of the Privy Council at Westminster, thus establishing the Supreme Court of Canada as the final court of appeal.

It is difficult to assess constitutional developments during this period, apart from the formal changes, because of the powers granted the Dominion, first under the War Measures Act and, second, under the Transitional Measures Act. The latter has been renewed from year to year. Where these Acts did not apply, the court has returned to the prewar position favoring minimum central controls. This is in line with normal peacetime court precedent to restrict continued application of wartime power. One case worthy of note is the famed *Nolan* case, where the government's power over the postwar control of grain movements, assumed under the Transitional Measures Act, was challenged. The courts, however, upheld the government.

V. CONCLUSION

This brief and incomplete sketch of the relation of agricultural policies and programs to federal government in Australia, Canada, and the United States indicates that any generalization about a federal system in this instance would be invalid. There is ample evidence to support Dicey's dictum that federalism produces legalism. The causative factor in these three cases, however, may be inherent in the situations in which these federal systems exist rather than a necessary condition of federalism. Again there is much to give substance to Laski's charge that the overriding condition of divided powers is the dispersal of responsibility and of the power to act. On the other hand, the ideal of efficiency which is the basis of Laski's objection may be irrelevant in judging the particular processes of economic and political development of large and diverse continental nations such as Australia, Canada, and the United States.

If the three nations are compared there are significant similarities and differences which suggest that the controlling factor in the development of a federal state, so far as agriculture is concerned, is the unique combination of human objectives with each given situation. For example, in all three countries the supreme courts in the past employed the test of legalism to the exclusion of other relevant considerations in ruling on agricultural legislation. However, with the growing sophistication of agricultural policy and its closer relation to the more general policies of maintaining full employment, the tests of relevance and efficiency have become increasingly important. This is most true in the case of the United States and least so in that of Australia, which may be related to the fact that such development is an aspect of the long-run evolution of the federal system. Perhaps more important in accounting for the greater rigidity of the Canadian and Australian courts is the fact that the Constitutions of these two nations stem from a superior power while in the United States the Constitution is paramount.

The question of rigidity of interpretation raises this point: Why, when the constitutional limits prevent necessary legislative action, was the constitution not amended? In the case of Australia the answer would seem to be that the amending process is unduly cumbersome. To a lesser degree this is also true of Canada, although both the provincial and Dominion governments have been able to make necessary adjustments to achieve changing legislative needs within the boundaries of constitutional limits. In the case of the United States, constitutional amendment was suggested at the time of the *Butler* decision, but it was easier to develop other legislative devices to achieve the same objective, and in fact the subsequent interpretations of the Supreme Court reflected a greater awareness of the relevance of need and suitability as necessary criteria.

More serious than either of these objections is the fact that under a federal system it is sometimes difficult to fix responsibility, particularly for failure to act or to develop policy. In the case of agriculture this problem is being solved as a result of the general assumption of responsibility by central governments for economic stability and development. This does not mean that the ultimate solution depends on the subservience of the State to the federal government, but it does rest on a new division of powers and responsibilities consistent with modern federal programs to promote the general welfare. A specific case in point is the problem of adjusting State and local expenditures to a federal fiscal policy program.

On the plus side of the ledger it can be argued that the division of powers in a federal system makes it possible to uncover and deal with a greater range of problems. Certainly it provides for a broader representation of interests. However, such diversity is not necessarily inherent in federalism and consequently needs special attention if it is to be developed.

It is perhaps characteristic of an analysis in which the United States is the largest element that the ultimate argument in favor of federalism would be the pragmatic one. In all three cases the federal system has survived, and if the state of the arts and the standard of living may be taken as criteria it has not blocked growth and development. Furthermore, in spite of the objections raised earlier, it is quite possible that the federal system has been more flexible and sensitive to necessary change than would have been any possible alternative. Certainly there is at present no important movement to make any substantial structural changes in the federal systems as they now exist in Australia, Canada, and the United States. The possibilities of change and development within the systems have made this unnecessary.

APPENDIX I
Australia

Legislative power over agriculture is not specifically mentioned in the Commonwealth of Australia Constitution Act. Thus, the authority is assumed under a number of more general clauses and is shared by both central and State governments.

In Section 90 of the Act, the only "exclusive" powers of the Commonwealth government are named. These are the powers over customs, excise, and bounties "on the production or export of goods." States may, however, grant bounties on the production or export of goods if both houses of the Commonwealth Parliament are agreeable. In Section 92, the Act goes on to state unequivocally that trade between States must be "absolutely" free.

In Section 51 the powers of the Commonwealth government to make laws for the "peace, order and good government of the country" are enumerated. It must be realized that these powers are not "exclusive" but are exercised concurrently by the Commonwealth and the States with the proviso, as enumerated in Section 109, that in cases of conflicting legislation, the Commonwealth's legislation shall prevail. In some cases, however, the nature of the jurisdiction in the subtitles in Section 51 is such as virtually to exclude all but one governmental authority. Among the thirty-nine powers listed in the Section are these: "Trade and commerce with other countries and among the States"; "taxation, but so as not to discriminate between states or parts of states"; "bounties on the production or export of goods, but so that the bounties shall be uniform throughout the Commonwealth"; "immigration and emigration"; "external affairs"; "matters referred to the Commonwealth Parliament by state parliaments" (with qualifications); quarantine; and so on. Sections 92 to 102 attempt to elucidate further the powers over trade and commerce. This authority extends to navigation and shipping, and to state railways; no preference is to be given one "state or any part thereof over another state or any part thereof"; neither shall the Commonwealth "abridge the right of a state to reasonable use of the waters of rivers for conservation or irrigation."

In Chapter V of the Act the powers of the States are listed. Section 107 states that "every power . . . of a Colony which . . . becomes a State, shall, unless it is by this Constitution exclusively vested in the Parliament of the Commonwealth or withdrawn from the Parliament of the State, continue as at the establishment of the Commonwealth, or as at the admission or establishment of the State . . ." Then follows (§108) the "law saving" clause which proclaims that State laws which are in force at the time of union shall continue in force in the State until the Commonwealth Parliament shall take action on that particular matter.

In Chapter III the High Court of Australia is established as the final court of appeal on all constitutional matters. Two possible circumstances, however, are recognized as justifying appeal to the Privy Council in London. In Chapter VIII three possible ways of amending the Constitution are provided. Only one of these has been effective to date. It provides that a proposed amendment becomes law after it has passed both houses of the Commonwealth Parliament and, in a referendum, is upheld, first, by a majority of the electorate of the entire country and, second, by a majority of electors in a majority of the States. These requirements have, in practice, shown themselves to be extremely stiff, and only four proposed amendments have been accepted since 1901.

In summary, then, it can be said that the Constitution Act establishes a situation in which the Commonwealth has exclusive powers over one field of jurisdiction while the States and the Commonwealth exercise joint responsibility over certain other areas. In those other areas conflicting State legislation is overridden by Commonwealth legislation. Finally the residuum of power is reserved for the States. In the main, the Commonwealth's concern with agriculture is derived from its powers over "trade and commerce with other countries and among the states," "customs, excise and bounties," quarantine and immigration. On the other hand, the States maintain their jurisdiction as a result of their control over intrastate trade and their residual powers. It will be apparent at once that the Australian Constitution more closely resembles that of the United States than that of Canada. Moreover, thus far in its history the High Court has resembled the United States Supreme Court both in the concept of its powers and in the nature of reasoning by which it has arrived at its decisions. Indeed, upon occasion it has not been averse to backing up its decisions with reference to opinions rendered by United States Supreme Court Justices (cf. Griffith, C.J. in *D'Emden v. Pedder* (1904)).

With the event of federation coming at about the midpoint of the period 1880–1920, many farm industries were already well established under the aegis of the colonial, and, after 1901, the State governments. Hence the State governments already had well-established agricultural policies and deeply entrenched departments of agriculture. The Constitutional Act clipped the powers of these departments to some extent in so far as they interfered with interstate and export trade. However, primary responsibility for policies relative to production and development, as well as to intrastate trade, remained firmly embedded at the State level. For the first two decades, the Commonwealth government's agricultural program remained limited although there were several attempts to regulate interstate and foreign trade as well as to control quarantine and immigration. The period of World War I was an exception, but the wartime controls lapsed soon after 1918. Economic conditions generally were somewhat erratic over those first two decades. Federation occurred in the middle of the 1892–1908 depression. Prosperity carried through from 1908 until the twenties, when economic difficulties again gradually developed. With respect to the Constitution, the High Court began its interpretative role early and by 1920 had handed down several decisions bearing on agricultural policy. In most instances, as has been the case ever since, the most controversial constitutional clause was Section 92 decreeing that interstate trade shall be "absolutely" free.

The fact that such a broad range of policy was carried out by six State governments acting separately led to a great diversity of programs. One of the more important of these concerned land settlement and immigration. Although each State government administered a separate program, they bore considerable resemblance to each other. Generally there were four categories of acts. The first dealt with the disposition of Crown lands; the second with closer settlement; the third with soldier settlement; and the fourth with advances to settlers. These acts were designed to break up the larger estates and to enable rural areas to absorb substantially more people. The State governments by buying and selling large areas of land entered into the policies very vigorously. On the whole, it seems to be generally agreed that the schemes resulted in a considerable amount of inappropriate land utilization, as well as in the taking of large areas of marginal and submarginal land. Immigration was fostered by the States in conjunction with the Commonwealth government as a supplement to the land programs. Both authorities adhered to a "White Australia" policy, and an overwhelming proportion of the migrants came from Britain. Prior to World War I each State had set up a scheme of assisted immigration. After the war the Commonwealth government became more active and entered, with the States and Great Britain, into the Empire Settlement Act (1922). This was superseded by the "£34 Million Agreement" and other plans. These policies seem to have overreached themselves and lapsed after 1929. Besides these activities, the States promoted schemes of land improvement, particularly irrigation projects. The irrigation programs were carried out in close alliance with the Closer Settlement Acts. One of the earlier irrigation projects was that developed by Victoria on the Murray River.

In addition to these measures the States retained the initiative in legislation bearing on the control of noxious weeds, pests, and disease as well as in the fields of marketing and education. Examples of weed and pest control acts are the Pastures Protection Act (N.S.W., 1902), the Vermin Destruction Act (Vict., 1890), the Dog Act (W.A., 1903). In several instances disease control acts were questioned on the grounds that they interfered with the freedom of interstate commerce; and, indeed, upon occasion the laws were designed with precisely that end in mind. State governments also legislated with respect to the grading of commodities — particularly those entering foreign trade. Moreover, various pieces of legislation were enacted to protect the farmer, such as the Fertilizer and Artificial Manure Acts. In the realm of educational policy, each State set up a variety of agricultural colleges and technical schools. Furthermore experimental farms were established in most States during this period.

The State governments entered the field of farm credit policy relatively early, and by 1920 all States had credit facilities available to farmers. These policies developed simultaneously with the various Settlement Acts and were modeled to some extent on the Landschaften Bank in Germany and the Crédit Foncier in France. The money was lent for 31 years at a rate slightly higher than the government rate. The schemes were usually managed by the State savings banks and proved highly successful.

Prior to World War I the new Commonwealth government had a rather limited agricultural program. About the only acts of importance were the various Sugar Bounty Acts, the Quarantine Act (1908), the Immigration Act (1901), and the Commerce Act (1905) setting up grading requirements for certain export commodities.

With the advent of war the powers of the Commonwealth increased sharply. From 1916 to 1924 wool marketing was under the control of the British-Australian Wool Realization Scheme (Bawra). Prices were fixed and policies were devised to handle carry-overs. In the case of wheat, the government actively encouraged production, made financial advances to farmers, and commandeered the transportation system to provide shipment. These activities were executed by a Wheat Marketing Board set up co-operatively by the Commonwealth and State governments. The Board fixed all prices and bought the entire crop (with some minor exceptions). The States also had local boards or commissions to control local sales. In 1915 the Commonwealth also took complete charge of the sugar industry. Exports were prohibited, imports were controlled, and prices were fixed. In the same year the government began selling all meat to the United Kingdom on a contract basis.

After the war, these emergency measures were dropped and most of the industries concerned returned partially, if not wholly, to the prewar free market system. In 1922 Sir John Higgins suggested that the Central Wool Committee under "Bawra" continue, but the proposal was rejected by the growers and brokers. In the wheat industry, the compulsory pool arrangement of the war was discontinued in 1922. Although there was some pressure on the government to continue the arrangement it refused, and pressure developed for the State governments to set up pools. This was also rejected, with one exception, and the growers then turned to voluntary pool arrangements. The exception, Queensland, however, adopted a compulsory State-controlled pool. In Victoria and New South Wales financial guarantees were given the voluntary pools. The sugar industry had prospered under government controls, and by 1923 the country was virtually self-sufficient. In 1923 the industry was handed over to the Queensland government and an arrangement was made to prohibit sugar imports and maintain domestic prices. It was also agreed that export losses would not be cause for raising the domestic sugar price. After 1920 the meat contracts were also suspended. Thus, by the early twenties the Commonwealth government had divested itself of most of the controls over agriculture which it had acquired during the war.

Despite the general sloughing off of powers in the postwar period, the Commonwealth government took over from the States most of the responsibility for the grading and inspection of export commodities. Prior to 1920, except for the war period, each State had had its own regulations. This proved hopelessly confusing and self-defeating. An order under the Customs Act in 1921 effectively eliminated State regulations in the field. This action was later sustained by the courts.

Another aspect of Commonwealth policy of this period was concerned with bounties and tariffs on agricultural commodities. In 1909, the Bounties Act was passed to encourage production of cotton, tobacco, dried fruits, and other items. Later the Apple Bounty Act was passed to encourage the export of apples. The Sugar Bounty Acts have been mentioned. In addition, in 1921, the government established the Tariff Board.

The twenties also saw one phase of the High Court's history come to an end. During the first two decades the Court was dominated by three members, Justices O'Connor, Griffith, and Barton, whose decisions had the general effect of bolstering the power of the States. In addition, the court imported the American concepts of "implied prohibitions" and "implied limitations." The three men mentioned had participated in the conferences leading up to federation and were inclined to view the Constitution as a compact between the States rather than an instrument by which all Australian governments began anew.

One of the more important decisions during these years relating specifically to agriculture was made in *W. and A. Macarthur Ltd. v. Queensland* (1920). Here it was held that Section 92 of the Constitution stipulating absolutely free trade was binding only on the State governments and not on the Commonwealth government, provided, of course, it remained within its limits in other respects. Thus Queensland's Profit Prevention Act (1920) and its attempt at price fixing were deemed *ultra vires*. On the other hand in *New South Wales v. Commonwealth* (1915) — the Wheat Case — it was held that the wheat expropriation scheme resorted to by New South Wales during World War I was valid. It was said that when the wheat became the property of the King he could dispose of it as he wished. Since this was done for the public safety, it overruled the interstate commerce clause. Following on this decision New South Wales attempted to requisition all pigs but without expropriation. This was, however, declared *ultra vires* in *Feggitt, Jones and Co. Ltd. v. New South Wales*

(1916). In *Duncan v. Queensland* (1916), an Act similar to the one over-ruled for New South Wales was upheld. It was held here that, since the Imperial government had acquired an interest in the cattle, the State could interfere without infringing upon Section 92. With respect to disease regulations, it was decided in 1920 that the Stock Act of New South Wales was not a regulation of interstate commerce. Its aim was rather the protection of animals against diseases in other States.

Since 1920 judicial decisions have been of considerable consequence so far as agricultural policy is concerned. One of the early cases (*Committee of Direction of Fruit Marketing v. Collins* (1925) challenged the Fruit Marketing Act (1923) of Queensland. The Act created a board to control intrastate fruit marketing. The courts upheld the Act since sales other than in the State remained free. A more important case, however, followed (*James v. South Australia* (1927)) in which South Australia's Dried Fruits Act (1924) was held invalid. The Act provided for grading in such a way as to be held to be in violation of Section 92. A year later, however, the Court upheld a pre-federation State quarantine law, which had been invoked by New South Wales although the Court was divided equally (*Ex parte Nelson* (1928)). One further interesting case was *James v. Commonwealth* (1928) where it was held that regulations made by the Committee on the Export of Dried Fruits were invalid since the Committee did not provide representation from all the States and thus violated Section 51 (ii) of the Constitution ("Taxation, but not so as to discriminate between states or parts of states").

The stiffest test for agricultural marketing legislation — the primary aspect of agricultural policy involved in constitutional problems — came in the thirties, and by the end of the decade relatively little of such legislation remained. One of the more important cases was *James v. Cowan* in 1932. In an attempt to control dried fruit marketing, the Commonwealth passed the Dried Fruits Export Control Act (1924), and several States supplemented the legislation. These schemes provided for outright expropriation. The courts found that the acts were in violation of Section 92 since the State laws interfered with interstate trade. This was followed in 1933 by the Peanut Case (*Peanut Board v. Rockhampton Harbour Board*). Here expropriation also had been carried out, allegedly with a view to orderly marketing. Again the courts found the action illegal. (These latter two decisions are quite different from the Wheat Case (1915) referred to earlier. The distinction seems to be that in the latter case expropriation was a matter of public safety and defense, whereas in *James v. Cowan* and the Peanut Case the action was aimed at regulation and restriction.) The Peanut Board had been set up under Queensland law, and, when it was overruled, almost all State marketing legislation bearing on anything but intrastate trade became ineffective. An example of effective intrastate regulation occurred one year later when the courts upheld the expropriation of milk by the Milk

Board in New South Wales on the ground that it did not violate Section 92 (*Crothers v. Sheil* (1933)).

Two noteworthy cases were heard in 1935. In *Crane v. Commonwealth* (1935), the plaintiff claimed the Dried Fruits Exports Control Act gave preferences to certain areas and violated Section 99 of the Constitution. The courts upheld the legislation since they found no evidence of a "tangible advantage obtainable in the course of trading" in one area over another. In the same year the Potato Case was decided (*Tasmania v. Victoria* (1935)). Victoria had absolutely prohibited the import of Tasmanian potatoes because, it was said, Tasmanian potatoes were disease-ridden. The courts, however, felt that the facts of the case clearly showed that the embargo had been invoked to prevent interstate trade, and hence the order was overruled.

In 1936 the Commonwealth government's marketing legislation, which had been enacted after State legislation had been severely curtailed in the Peanut Board Case, was also revoked. In *James v. Commonwealth* (1936) the Privy Council held that Section 92 applied to the Commonwealth as well as the States. This reversed the decision in the *Macarthur* case (1920) and left something of a void in the field of marketing legislation.

Two additional pre-World War II cases should be mentioned. In *Harley v. Walsh* (1937) a regulation by the Victoria government, stipulating that dried fruit bought and sold in Victoria must be packed in a shed under Victorian registry and according to certain standards, was upheld. This decision was questioned later, in *Milk Board (N.S.W.) v. Metropolitan Cream Pty. Ltd.* (1939), by Justice Starke, in so far as it related to Section 92, and by Justice Dixon, in *Parten v. Milk Board* (1949), in so far as it related to excise. In the Milk Board Case (1939), the courts upheld the State milk board which controlled all milk sales despite the fact that milk from Victoria was prevented from entering the State. It was argued that the board aimed at regulation rather than prohibition.

Two decisions have been rendered which relate particularly to State pools. In *Matthews v. Chicory Marketing Board (Vict.)* (1938), the pools were upheld, despite the ruling in the Peanut Case, since the Victoria Act explicitly excluded commodities entering interstate trade. In 1948 there followed the *Field Peas Marketing Board (Tas.) v. Clements Marshall Pty. Ltd.* decision, in which the Court found that the Board's operations were contrary to Section 92 despite a clause somewhat similar to that in the Victoria Chicory Board Act concerning interstate trade.

Since 1949, as H. S. Nicholas reports in *The Australian Constitution*, cases "have been decided on the words of the State Act . . . or on the facts of the case rather than on an interpretation of section 92." He goes on to cite several cases to support this assertion, among them *Carter v. Potato Marketing Board* (1951), wherein trade and commerce between the States was held not to be involved.

APPENDIX II

Canada

"In each province the legislature may make laws in relation to agriculture in the province . . . ; and it is hereby declared that the Parliament of Canada may from time to time make laws in relation to agriculture in all or any of the provinces . . . and any law of the legislature of a province relative to agriculture . . . shall have effect in and for the province as long and as far only as it is not repugnant to any Act of the Parliament of Canada." With this forthright statement the British North America Act 1867 establishes concurrent powers of legislation between the Dominion and provincial governments for agriculture. In cases of conflict it has been established that the federal law prevails.

This same clarity, however, does not extend to various other clauses of the British North America Act. Although these further provisions do not relate specifically or solely to agriculture, most of the constitutional difficulties in which agricultural legislation has been involved have arisen from these later stipulations. In Section 91 of the Act, the Dominion's powers are set forth: "It shall be lawful for the Queen, by and with the Advice and Consent of the Senate and House of Commons, to make Laws for the Peace, Order and Good Government of Canada, in relation to all Matters not coming within the Classes of Subjects by this Act assigned exclusively to the Legislatures of the Provinces; and for greater Certainty, but not so as to restrict the Generality of the foregoing Terms of this Section, it is hereby declared that (notwithstanding anything in this Act) the exclusive Legislative Authority of the Parliament of Canada extends to all Matters coming within the Classes of Subjects hereinafter enumerated." Among the twenty-nine subtitles which follow are: the regulation of Trade and Commerce; Census and Statistics; Interest; Bankruptcy and Insolvency; and the Raising of Money by any Mode or System of Taxation. The section concludes by stating that "any matter coming within any of the classes of subjects enumerated in this section shall not be deemed to come within the class of matters of a local or private nature comprised in the enumeration of the classes of subjects by this Act assigned exclusively to the legislatures of the provinces." In Section 121 it is stated that "all articles of growth, produce or manufacture of any one of the provinces shall be admitted free into each of the other provinces." Finally, the Dominion government is given exclusive control over tariffs.

In Section 92, the "exclusive powers" of the Provinces are enumerated under sixteen subtitles. As the Act has in fact been applied, the most controversial of these has been the power over "Property and Civil Rights in the Province." Other provisions relevant in this context give the Provinces control over "Direct Taxation within the Province in order to . . . [raise]

. . . Revenue for Provincial purposes"; "the Management and Sale of Public Lands belonging to the Province . . ."; "Local Works and Undertakings . . ." with certain exceptions, and "municipal institutions." The final subhead gives the Province power over "Generally all Matters of a merely local or private Nature in the province." Section 93 provides that "for each Province the Legislature may exclusively make Laws in relation to Education" subject to certain limitations none of which are relevant here.

The British North America Act thus formally confers definite spheres of legislative power to both federal and provincial governments with the residuum of power left with the central government. However, as the Rowell-Sirois Report observes, "no amount of care in phrasing the division of powers in a federal scheme will prevent difficulty when the division comes to be applied to the variety and complexity of social relationships." In the course of this interpretative development certain key phrases of the Act reappear. On the side of the central legislature are the powers over the regulation of trade and commerce, peace, order and good government, and residual legislation. In favor of the provincial parliaments are the exclusive powers over property and civil rights and all matters of a merely local or private nature in the province. The broad sweep of these phrases made jurisdictional conflict inevitable and placed upon the courts the task of delineation, reconciliation, and definition. As matters have in fact turned out, the courts have interpreted provincial powers relatively broadly and federal powers rather more narrowly. Thus any possibility which the granting of residual powers to the Dominion government may have opened to the extension of its jurisdiction has been offset to a significant extent by juridical decision.

It is appropriate here to mention the amendment procedure of the Constitution. The British North America Act makes no mention of amendment procedures. Thus there is in Canada no power to alter the distribution of legislative power or to vary the form of government. Amendment can be achieved only by an Act of the British Parliament. As a result, difficulties have arisen when some governments in the country have desired an amendment to which others were opposed.

Four prevailing themes underlie Dominion government agricultural policy during this period. First and foremost of these was the policy of land settlement and the extension of the western frontier. Second, various regulatory measures were enacted. These dealt with such subjects as disease control and quarantine, fraudulent selling practices, and so on. Third, a number of activities were undertaken with a view to improving the grades and standards of agricultural produce. Finally, during the last decade certain marketing controls were developed. The Provinces on their side concerned themselves largely with encouraging agriculture by financing and supervising agricultural societies, assisting livestock shows and exhibitions, and fostering agricultural education. In addition, they engaged, to varying degrees, in immigration activities more or less cooperatively with the central government.

Throughout these years the newly formed nation was exposed to sharp economic fluctuations. The years from 1867 to 1896 saw sustained depression. From 1896 to 1914, however, the wheat boom and the general prosperity in all regions at last made real the glowing promises of confederation and provided the first substantial source of national spirit and pride. On the legal side, agricultural legislation passed during this period by both the Dominion and provincial governments raised few constitutional issues. Nevertheless, the interval was one during which the general interpretative evolution of the Constitution advanced materially.

It would be incorrect to view Canadian agriculture as springing forth and reaching its present stature unaided and unabetted by the state. State assistance to agriculture had early been generally recognized as a legitimate function of government in all those areas which joined the confederation in 1867. Confederation itself to a large extent was brought about by considerations of agricultural expansion and progress. The possibility of a virile Western agricultural economy duplicating the recent boom in the United States, the likelihood that the ensuing general prosperity would bolster lagging provincial finances and stagnant economies, and the prospect of a large free-trade area linked by rail and water transport all encouraged plans to promote a successful agricultural development after confederation. Hence, a Dominion Department of Agriculture was established at once. It immediately plunged into the work of stimulating immigration and settlement. In the Minister's Annual Report of 1870, for instance, agriculture is covered in one paragraph whereas immigration activities take up most of the remaining 160 pages. This disproportion in the reports continues, with agriculture gradually making small advances, until 1888, when the reports of the immigration officers are reduced to a synopsis. Finally in 1892 the immigration section of the report disappears entirely with the transfer of the administration of immigration to the Department of the Interior. This trend closely reflects the actual operations of the Department. The Manitoba Act of 1870, whereby public lands were withheld from provincial control and all "ungranted or waste lands" in the entire Northwest were "administered by the Government of Canada for the purposes of the Dominion," supplemented the central government's overall development program. The Dominion Lands Act (1872), its subsequent liberalization in 1882, and the substantial land grants to the railroads which in turn created even more pressure for immigration, lent further substance to the government's policy.

A listing of some of the major statutes of the period indicates other aspects of Dominion policy. First, there are those acts bearing on disease and consumer protection: the Contagious Diseases Act (1879), Act in Restraint of Fraudulent Sale or Marketing (1894), the Adulteration Act (1884), Act Respecting the Inspection of Meats and Canned Foods (1907), the Destructive Insects and Pest Act (1910). Second, there are the acts designed to encourage and assist production. Foremost of these was the establishment of the Dominion Experimental Farm in 1886 and the demonstration stations in Western Canada in 1915. One of the most notable achievements of the Farm was the development of the Marquis variety of wheat. The government also made a number of grants to agricultural societies and enabled Canadian exhibits to be sent to various expositions such as those in Paris, Australia, and Philadelphia.

A further development in later years was the appearance of the first vestiges of marketing legislation. This policy developed first with respect to dairying but was gradually extended. Among the Acts passed were: General Inspection Act (1874), providing for the grading of grains; Dairy Products Act (1893), establishing the branding of dairy products and preventing the manufacture of imitations; Fruit Market Act (1901); Grain Inspection Act (1904); Canada Grain Act (1912). An additional indication of the growing concern with markets is given by the Minister of Agriculture's Annual Reports. In 1895 the Report referred to the provision of advances to creameries in order to promote the butter market in Britain. In 1896 the Minister discussed the success of an experiment in shipping perishable commodities via refrigerator cars. Later the Comissioner of Agriculture and Dairying was authorized to assist with marketing operations. A markets division was set up and was reported to have checked the condition of cheese on arrival in Britain and found it in a "heated condition" which was "telling against it in the markets." In 1907 an act was passed to foster cold storage warehouses. The report of 1909–1910 noted that the Division — now the Division of Extension of Markets — was formerly concerned only with the export market but now also paid attention to the domestic market.

The major policy lines pursued by the Provinces have already been noted. In some cases the Provinces supplemented Dominion legislation relating to disease and pests. Moreover, attempts were made to legislate against malpractices in local areas — particularly with respect to milk. Subsequently inspectors were appointed to enforce these policies. In many cases provincial interference was concerned mainly with matters of public health. Municipal authorities were used extensively in effecting these policies. In addition to these schemes, the Provinces adopted land policies designed to supplement Dominion legislation and adapt it to local circumstances. Furthermore, in 1873 Ontario established the Ontario Agricultural College; Quebec also developed a variety of government-aided farm schools. In their educational programs the Provinces were assisted by a Dominion grant-in-aid under the Agricultural Instruction Act (1913).

As stated earlier, agricultural legislation was relatively free of constitutional restriction during this period. The one exception was the Canada Grain Act (1912). This act set up a Board of Grain Commissioners empowered to regulate the grain trade in various ways, e.g. by licensing dealers, grading grain, etc. In *Rex v. Eastern Terminal Elevator Company* (1925), the courts found that the Act was aimed at trade regulation and was not a law for the encouragement and support of agriculture. The licensing section was held *ultra vires* on the ground that it interfered with "property and civil rights." The Crown had contended that grain was an important export commodity and so came under its jurisdiction. In an earlier case, *Rex v. Manitoba Grain Company* (1922), the Courts had also found that the Dominion's attempt to extend its grading system to the domestic trade was illegal. Henceforth the Dominion had to limit its efforts to interprovincial trade and to export trade.

Two further cases dealing with agriculture are worth noting. In *Brooks v. Moore* (1906) the courts held that the word "agriculture" should not be limited only to those things which grow and derive their sustenance from the soil. Therefore, the Dominion Animals Contagious Diseases Act was supported on the ground that it related to federal agriculture as well as on the ground that it was legislation relating to a subject of general concern to the whole of Canada. The other ruling upheld the Dominion Livestock Pedigree Act also on the ground that it related to the whole of Canada (*Rex v. Davenport* (1928)).

From 1867 until about 1870 the Dominion government clearly claimed dominance over the Provinces and under John Alexander MacDonald's leadership exercised freely its powers of disallowance. With the advent of the depression in 1873 and the failure of MacDonald's "National Policy," provincial discontent grew rapidly. A conference in 1887 attended by provincial premiers challenged federal predominance, demanded larger subsidies, and a curbing of Dominion disallowance. As a result of the clamor, the central government acquiesced on the powers of disallowance and began the gradual downward revision of the tariff. In *Hodge v. The Queen* (1893) the Privy Council affirmed the equality of provincial and Dominion legislatures in their respective spheres. In *Russell v. The Queen* (1882) the court held that where it could be shown that an act was designed for "the peace, order, and good government of Canada" (for instance the Canada Temperance Act), it was *intra vires* the Dominion Parliament. This decision, however, was virtually overruled by subsequent opinions. One of the most important of these was the Local Prohibition Case decision (1896) where it was held that only in exceptional cases would the "good government" clause overrule the "exclusive" powers assigned to the Provinces. Hence, as the Rowell-Sirois Commission notes, the struggle shifted to a competition between the enumerated heads of Section 91 and those of Section 92. In this contest, the Provinces had the advantage of two sweeping clauses — "property and civil rights," and "matters of a local nature" — as opposed to only one for the Dominion government — "regulation of trade and commerce." The Report also notes that pursuit of the *Russell v. The Queen* decision might have imperiled the federal character of the union. In *Citizens Insurance Company v. Parsons* (1881), the courts had already given an early indication that they would interpret Dominion powers over trade and commerce relatively narrowly, since to do otherwise would virtually extinguish provincial jurisdiction. They held too that the two sections describing provincial and Dominion powers must be read in conjunction with each other. These and other decisions were to cast their shadow over agricultural policy in ensuing years.

The pace of economic, and particularly agricultural, activity varied greatly from 1918 to 1939. The war boom was followed by a slump only to be succeeded, in turn, by record prosperity and, finally, by a staggering depression. During the first decade of this period Dominion government policy aimed at retrenchment and the continuance of prewar regulatory and developmental programs. The various regulatory laws were amended to bring them up to date, and new laws, such as the following were enacted: An Act to Regulate the Sale and Inspection of Commercial Feeding Stuffs . . . (1920); Livestock and Livestock Products Act (1923); Agricultural Pest Control Act (1927); Maple Sugar Act (1930). In line with its policy of return to prewar conditions, the Dominion government in 1920 dissolved the Wheat Board, which had superseded the wartime Board of Grain Supervisors, despite great pressure from the growers to continue the Board. The government contended that a compulsory wheat board with powers over the price and shipment of wheat was beyond its normal peacetime constitutional powers. The pressure for a wheat board subsided after 1923 when the farmers turned attention to the wheat pools.

During this period, the Provinces gained the initiative in agricultural legislation. Their traditional local and regulatory activities were expanded. Each Province now had an agricultural college (New Brunswick and Prince Edward Island excepted) and all engaged in educational activities at a more elementary level. Some of the Provinces instituted a system of agricultural representatives. Much attention was given to the development of new areas and the settlement of areas untouched by the Dominion's programs. In addition, the Provinces supplemented Dominion grading and inspecting legislation with similar legislation covering intraprovincial trade. The two most noteworthy developments were provincial legislation in the almost virgin fields of credit provision and marketing legislation. Each of the larger Provinces had a farm mortgage agency: the British Columbia Agricultural Credit Commission, the Ontario Agricultural Development Board, the Manitoba Farm Loans Association, and the Saskatchewan Farm Loan Board. In addition, legislation was passed in Ontario, Alberta, and Manitoba to encourage the development of rural cooperative credit societies. In Quebec, the Caisse Populaire had been founded as early as 1900. In most cases these facilities were limited to providing short-term credit. In the Prairie Provinces' credit was provided for the wheat pools and, as will be seen, these Provinces eventually became overextended in this area. It remained for British Columbia, however, to usher in new marketing legislation in 1927 with the Produce Marketing Act. This was followed by the Dairy Products

Sales Adjustment Act (1929). Although various other Provinces followed suit, all came to naught when the courts held that the legislation was *ultra vires*.

The first occasion upon which the Dominion government moved significantly from its position of the twenties was when it came to the financial assistance of the wheat pools. With the collapse of the world wheat market in 1929, wheat prices soon fell below the initial payment level and the pools found themselves insolvent. The provincial governments attempted to stem the tide by guaranteeing pool liabilities to the banks. When the task became too burdensome even for them, the Dominion government intervened. Since then, Dominion government support of wheat farming has been frequent. From 1930 to 1934, the government employed the wheat pool arrangement to support the price. In 1935, the Wheat Board was set up under a scheme of voluntary pooling. Although farmers were not compelled to sell to the Board, the Board had to buy all the wheat offered at a fixed initial advance price along with participation certificates, except when specifically exempt as from 1936 to 1938 when the market price exceeded the initial payment. Also by this time the Dominion had managed to extend its powers over the grading and inspection of wheat by a variety of amendments and revisions to the Canada Grain Act which were satisfactory to the courts.

With the annulment of provincial marketing legislation and the persistence of the agricultural depression the Dominion government in 1934 passed the Natural Products Marketing Act. The Act provided for marketing boards, financed by licenses, whose primary purpose was to maintain orderly conditions by market regulation as opposed to price fixing. The courts, however, quashed the Act on constitutional grounds in 1937. After this setback, the Dominion in 1939 passed two acts designed to encourage co-operative marketing: the Agricultural Products Cooperative Marketing Act and the Wheat Cooperative Marketing Act.

When the Natural Products Act was thrown out by the courts, the initiative for marketing legislation passed again to the Provinces. Those provincial marketing boards set up under the Dominion Act such as the Nova Scotia Apple Marketing Board disappeared with the Dominion Act. Nevertheless, several Provinces enacted marketing legislation on their own. In British Columbia, the Natural Products Marketing Act (1934) was designed to deal with intraprovincial marketing. The law was upheld and under it the British Columbia Marketing Board and various boards concerned with particular commodities were established. Somewhat similar legislation was passed in New Brunswick and Ontario. In every case, however, great care had to be taken to limit the various other boards' powers wholly to intraprovincial jurisdiction. Provincial marketing control reached its zenith in control of fluid milk. By 1939 all the Province with the exception of British Columbia had set up milk boards designed to control "the purchase and sale of milk intended for consumption in fluid form."

Both Dominion and Provincial governments actively entered the field of legislation. The Canadian Farm Loan Board, which began operations in 1929, had its operations greatly extended by a 1934 amendment. The Board existed to make long-term loans to farmers on the security of first mortgages. In addition the Farmers' Creditors Arrangement Act was passed. The Act provided for a board of review to "accept proposals from either debtor or creditor for a composition, extension of time or rearrangement of a farmer's indebtedness, or for assignments in bankruptcy." The Board's decisions were binding on both parties. Some credit relief was also provided by the Dominion Government's adoption of a lower interest rate policy after 1933. In 1937 Quebec established its own farm credit system known as the Quebec Farm Credit Bureau. The strongest provincial farm credit legislation, however, came out of Alberta, with the Provincial Debt Adjustment Act (1937). The Act later was found *ultra vires* since it violated Dominion jurisdiction over bankruptcy and interest.

Various other measures aimed at offsetting the effects of the depression were instituted by the federal government during this period. Among these were the Prairie Farm Assistance Act (1939), providing insurance to farmers plagued by crop failures. The Prairie Farm Rehabilitation Program was set up in 1935 to "introduce measures in the affected areas to control these conditions [of drought and soil drifting] and to establish agriculture on a sound economic basis." Attempts were made to promote irrigation, strip farming, tree planting, and to return marginal and submarginal land to pasture. The Provinces cooperated in these various schemes of land reclamation and relief. In 1930 unalienated resources were returned by the Dominion government to the Provinces. Subsequently a financial reimbursement was made by the Dominion government.

Among the more significant legal tenets arising from non-agricultural litigation from 1918 to 1938 was the severe limitation of the "Trade and Commerce" clause to a point where it was questioned if it yielded any separate legislative power at all (*Toronto Electric Commissioners v. Snider* (1925)). Likewise, it was declared that the powers to provide "peace, order, and good government" could be invoked only under the most dire emergency (*Re Board of Commerce Act* (1922)). Up to 1939 only one Privy Council decision acknowledged the ascendancy of this clause (*Fort Francis Pulp and Paper Company v. Manitoba Free Press* (1923)). In all other cases the powers over "property and civil rights" and over "local affairs" remained superior.

Most of the legal problems specifically related to agriculture arose from various pieces of marketing legislation. In 1922 in *Rex v. Manitoba Grain Co.* it was clearly set out that Dominion grading regulations and inspection could apply only to interprovincial and export trade. The next step was the attempt on the part of the Provinces to pass "enabling legislation" whereby it was enacted that in so far as the terms of the particular Dominion bill went beyond Dominion and into provincial fields, the illegal provisions of the Dominion bill were to be a part of provincial law. In other words, the provincial acts were designed to "enable" the Dominion to exercise its powers over intraprovincial as well as other trade. The Provinces generally took the view that the Dominion could better handle these regulatory functions and that it would avoid duplications, conflict, and confusion. At the same time they reserved the power of revoking their acts. Until 1935 this technique was used extensively and a variety of regulatory acts were given general application. Among these were the Livestock and Livestock Products Act, Dairy Industry Act, Fruit, Vegetable and Honey Act, Meat and Canned Foods Act, etc. This type of enabling legislation was usually framed in the same or highly similar language to that of the Dominion act to avoid confusion. Also it attempted to implement future amendments to the Dominion act automatically. In 1935, however, enabling legislation was challenged in *Rex v. Zaslavsky* and the courts held that it amounted to a delegation of powers by one legislature to another and hence was illegal. The aspect of the legislation found particularly objectionable was that giving powers into the future. This decision led to the virtual abandonment of "enabling legislation" and gave rise to "conjoint legislation." By this plan the Provinces passed regulatory legislation very similar to that of the Dominion and appointed the same officials as the Dominion to administer the regulations.

Marketing legislation which went beyond grading and inspection was also revoked by the courts, as indicated earlier. On the one hand, it was decided that the Dominion Natural Products Marketing Act (1937) interfered with local trade. At the same time, it was held that the British Columbia Produce Marketing Act (1927) interfered with interprovincial trade. Subsequently the British Columbia Natural Products Marketing Act (1934) was upheld, but only in so far as it was limited to local trade. Hence, with the single exception of acts relating to wheat, which by this time had managed to overcome most of the constitutional restrictions, government activity in this area was limited. This situation led one brief, which was submitted to the Rowell-Sirois Commission, to declare, "It would appear therefore, that the position after almost 20 years of legislating and referring the constitutionality of various acts of Parliament and the legislative assemblies to the courts finds us exactly where we began, namely, no one knows how to draft workable legislation dealing with the regulation of grading, packing, storing, and marketing of agricultural products, which will come squarely within the respective jurisdictions of the Dominion and the Provinces without the exercise of almost incredible caution."

APPENDIX III

United States

The Constitution of the United States makes no special provision for particular economic activities such as agriculture. Those sections of the Constitution that have been controlling in determining the validity of State and federal legislation designed to affect agriculture apply generally. The following provisions of the federal Constitution form the basis of the decisions of the Supreme Court in cases that have shaped agricultural policy.

The most important powers for effective legislative action are embodied in Article I, Section 8, of the Constitution. Here the powers to collect taxes, pay debts, and provide for the general welfare are set forth. The last power is also stated in the preamble of the Constitution, which has also been used to support legislation to promote the economic welfare of agriculture. This section contains, in addition, the grant of power to the Congress to regulate commerce between the States and "to make all laws which shall be necessary and proper to carrying in execution the foregoing powers, and all other powers vested by this Constitution in the Government of the United States, or in any department or officer thereof." Section 9 of the same article limits the powers of the States to "levy taxes or duties on articles exported from any state." Section 10 of Article I prohibits the States from interfering with interstate commerce.

Article IV, Section 3, states that "the Congress shall have the power to dispose of and make all needful rules and regulations respecting the Territory or other property belonging to the United States; and nothing in this Constitution shall be so construed as to prejudice any claims of the United States, or of any particular state." This provision has become increasingly important as the federal government has used the device of purchase of land and resources to carry out its policy of land-use development and the retirement of marginal lands.

The rights of individuals to private property are protected under the Fifth Amendment, which states that federal legislation may not deprive them ". . . of life, liberty, or property, without due process of law; nor shall private property be taken for public use, without just compensation." A similar restriction is placed on State legislation by the Fourteenth Amendment.

The Tenth Amendment has played a large part in decisions limiting federal power to make laws concerning income distribution and resource allocation in the agricultural field. This amendment states that "the powers not delegated to the United States by the Constitution, nor prohibited by it to the States, are reserved to the States respectively, or to the people." The restrictions implicit in this provision have, in recent times, been overcome by a more liberal interpretation of the powers to regulate commerce granted in Article I, Section 8.

In addition to the limitations and powers granted in the federal Constitution, the several State constitutions follow the same pattern, and particularly in cases where federal programs depend for their execution on State enabling acts, interpretations of State courts become extremely important.

Finally, the implied powers derived by the Supreme Court from the Constitution as a whole, rather than from specific provisions, have played a part in shaping agricultural policy and implementing legislation. The most important of these is that by which the Congress, the President, and the courts are each forbidden to delegate any of the powers conferred on them to either of the others, nor may one invade the field assigned to the others.

The first approach of both the federal and State governments to execute an agricultural policy was to facilitate the settlement of the public domain. On the federal level, at least, there were two issues of general political nature which conditioned the patterns and institutions of land ownership. The first of these was the requirement in the initial land ordinances following peace with Great Britain that restrictions on tenure such as entail and laws of primogeniture be prohibited. Later with the coming to a head of the slavery issue a second general political question was the limitation of slavery as an institution on the public domain surrendered to the States. However, with these general exceptions the first consideration of the legislatures in dealing with the vast area of unsettled land was to encourage settlement as rapidly as possible. A corollary to this principle was the belief that the ultimate return to the nation would be greater if immediate revenue derived from the sale of land were sacrificed to hasten settlement. The first period of federal land policy was one of seeking formulas that would turn public land over to small holders, and the specific device was the continued lowering of the price and relaxation of the conditions for taking up such land.

The Ordinances of 1785 and 1787 established the pattern of liberal tenure laws for the public domain. This was followed by the Pre-emption Act of 1841 which permitted those settlers who had already established themselves on public land before it was offered for sale to buy their farmsteads at the established price at the time the land was opened for public sale. The final triumph of the advocates of rapid settlement was the passage of the Homestead Act of 1862 which permitted entrants to take up 160 acres of government land without cost provided they met the criteria of bona fide settlement. That same year the Morrill Act was passed establishing the land grant colleges. To encourage this development the federal government turned over to the States federal land to be used to help finance these institutions.

From this period on, the problem of disposing of the public domain became largely one of encouraging settlement on the less desirable areas. In 1873 the Timber Culture Act granted 160 acres free to anyone who would plant 40 acres of trees on that quarter section. The concept of the small farm limited to 160 acres was breached by the Desert Land Act of 1877 which permitted a settler to take up 640 acres at $1.25 per acre provided he irrigated it within three years. A year later two Acts widened the gap through which the public domain was parceled out to private owners. The Timber Cutting Act permitted private owners to cut timber on public land for their own use, and the Timber and Stone Act offered for sale at $2.40 per acre non-agricultural land in the public domain. One of the reasons for these efforts to encourage the taking up of the less desirable public land was the fact that the federal government had also made grants of 155 million acres of land to promote the building of railroads through the unsettled West. The railroads had seen to it that the land in their grants was of good enough quality to attract settlers. Consequently, the federal government found itself operating in a land market in which their subsidized competitor was able to make the more attractive offerings.

Reaction against these Acts marked the beginning of a new policy of attempting to conserve land resources in public ownership — a beginning, however, which was greatly prolonged by the fact that the openhanded policy of disposing of the public domain was not to end for some years. This new policy was inaugurated in 1891 with Congressional action. The Timber Cutting Act and the Pre-emption Act of 1841 were repealed. The Desert Land Act was tightened with a provision that to take up land under the Act the prospective settler had to invest three dollars an acre in irrigation works. Finally, the President was permitted to set aside as a public reserve timber lands on the public domain. A move in the opposite direction was made in 1894 when the Carey Act was passed. This Act gave one million acres of the public domain to any State which would promote the settlement and irrigation of arid land. The failure of this Act to produce any significant development of arid lands led to the passage of the Reclamation Act of 1902. By this legislation the Congress provided that money received from the sale of public land should be used to develop resources on undeveloped land in public ownership.

During this whole period there was a growing interest in the conservation of natural resources. The issues were brought to public attention by the White House Conference of Governors in 1908, and as a result of this meeting forty-one States established State departments of conservation. However, at the same time Congress continued to implement its policy of encouraging the settlement of the remaining public domain, although by this time practically all land not requiring supplementary water for agriculture had been taken up. In 1904, four years before the White House Conference, Congress passed the Kincaid Act permitting homesteads of 640 acres in the arid area of western Nebraska. This program was expanded by the enlarged Homestead Act of 1909, which allowed 320-acre homesteads in certain States and territories. To further ease the taking of public land the residence requirement for homesteading was cut from five to three years. Finally in 1916 the Stock Raising Homestead Act became law. With this legislation Congress opened for homesteads of 640 acres land classified as suitable for grazing only.

It would be a mistake to consider the extension of the acreage available for homesteads as nothing more than an attempt to dispose of the public domain as rapidly as possible. Nor did this increase in acreage mean that Congress had abandoned the principle laid down at the outset that federal policy should be designed to favor small ownerships. While a certain amount of Congressional action was response to pressure from powerful landholding groups to favor their interests, a pressure at least as important in influencing the increased size of homesteads was the growing realization that the necessarily extensive land-use patterns of arid areas made large holding necessary to support a single operator, a fact that had been brought to Congressional attention in 1878 in the report on the *Lands of the Arid Region of the United States* by Major John Wesley Powell. In a very real sense the gradual extension of the size of homesteads was a measure of Congressional recognition that a land policy for the humid East could not be indiscriminately applied to the arid West. This was further complicated by the fact that the legal tradition in which land laws were written was derived from the humid area of Western Europe. These came into direct conflict with the Spanish legal tradition which had prevailed in much of the arid area of the United States as a result of the earlier Spanish settlement. The essential problem was that legal and political institutions were not derived from the natural potentials of the area, but were rather superimposed without significant change from a quite different environment.

A more realistic approach to the problem of land development — more realistic in the sense that it was designed to be relevant to the whole situation — began to take shape in the 1920's. In 1923 a federally sponsored land inventory pointed out that the basic issue to be resolved by federal land policy was not the shortage of land, as the conservation movement was claiming, but rather the improper use and development of land. The Reclamation Act of 1902 had placed the federal government in the role of resource development. Federal agencies, particularly the United States Forest Service, which had been established to act as the custodian of the withdrawn federal forest lands, had been carrying out a program of forest land development. But it was not until the 1930's and the great depression of that decade that the federal government fully elaborated a program of government-subsidized land-use development.

The Taylor Grazing Act was passed in 1934. Under this Act the remaining public domain in those States supporting a livestock industry was divided into grazing districts under federal management to preserve the grass cover of the range and make possible the re-establishment of more desirable range pasture.

The most powerful force directing the attention of Congress to a positive resource development program was the economic depression of the 1930's. The evolution of this program began in the disorder of an administrative and legislative emergency but within the next decade the well-defined outlines of a program if not a policy began to appear. The National Industrial Recovery Act of 1933 set up a special fund to purchase private land to be added to timber and other government reservations. These purchases were made through the Public Works Administration, an emergency relief agency. It is clear that in the first instance this was a straight income-distribution measure in which the land-use aspects of the program were a sugar-coating to make it more palatable to those who held such action was beyond the obligation if not the power of the Congress. In 1934 this purchase program was expanded to buy and retire submarginal agricultural land in an effort to reduce surplus production, and the administration was assigned to the Land Policy Section of the Agricultural Adjustment Administration.

Also in 1933 the National Planning Board was established in the Public Works Administration. A year later this became the National Resources Board as a permanent planning agency attached to the executive office of the President. The purpose of this Board was to provide a coordinated plan for resource development, and one of its major efforts was to encourage the various States and local planning boards by assigning a planning consultant to each of the forty-eight states. This Board subsequently became the National Resources Committee, but owing to conflicts over the concept of planning, was discontinued by act of Congress.

Associated with the land retirement program was the Division of Subsistence Homesteads established in the Department of the Interior. The purpose of this agency was to provide for the shift of rural and urban people from overcrowded areas to more favorable sites. In 1935 this was combined with the land purchase program to become the Resettlement Administration in the Department of Agriculture. This latter program which had up until this time been carried out by an executive order was given statutory support by the passage of the Bankhead-Jones Farm Tenancy Act of 1937 which under Title III provided funds and standards for the purchase of private land by federal agencies. Thus federal land policy completed a full circle, beginning with the sale of land to private owners and ending with the purchase of land from such owners to retire or rehabilitate it. At the same time, under the pressures of a major depression, the federal government was forced to develop a land-use and resource policy to be integrated with a general policy of economic stability and development.

A corollary of the federal land program was the development of a series of measures to promote the conservation of natural resources by both the

State and federal governments. The first concrete step in this direction was the creation of the United States Commission of Fish and Fisheries in 1871 as a result of public concern over the decline of fisheries. This was followed by a series of governmental actions to protect the natural resources on the public domain, e.g. the Act of 1891 permitting the President to set aside public lands as forest preserves. In 1905 these became the National Forests, with a change in policy from one of merely holding forest land to one of developing the forest potentials of such land. By 1911 the federal government was purchasing land in eastern States in which there was no public domain to be used as national forests The great expansion of this program came in the 1930's with the establishment of the Soil Erosion Service in the Department of the Interior. In 1935 this became the Soil Conservation Service in the Department of Agriculture under the provisions of the Soil Conservation Act of that year. At first this agency attempted to encourage soil and water conservation on private land by setting up demonstration projects. This policy was later changed to one of providing technical assistance for soil conservation districts established in the various States under State enabling acts. While the general plan of soil conservation districts was first developed in Wisconsin and Michigan, the promotion of the program on a nation-wide scale became the principal objective of the Federal Soil Conservation Service. In 1936, with the passage of the Soil Conservation and Domestic Allotment Act, the Soil Conservation Service was combined with the Agricultural Adjustment Administration. However, the Soil Conservation Service has maintained an autonomous position in the Department of Agriculture in spite of continuing efforts by the Secretary of Agriculture to combine it with other agencies doing similar work in the Department.

While the conservation of agricultural resources remains a basic part of federal agricultural policy it is but part of a general policy to support a prosperous agricultural economy. Initially, in addition to a generous land policy, the major support offered by the federal government was a tariff policy which offered some protection to agriculture. By 1916 the problem of tenancy in agriculture had become sufficiently acute to cause Congress to pass the Federal Farm Loan Act. This Act established the Federal Farm Loan Board which by easing credit for agriculture hoped to maintain and encourage ownership by small holders.

Following World War I the position of agriculture continued to deteriorate particularly because of the overexpansion of agriculture during the war and the subsequent unfavorable cost-price relationships. At the National Agricultural Conference of 1922, President Harding told the farm delegates: ". . . in the last analysis, legislation can do little more than give the farmer the chance to organize and help himself." A somewhat different line was taken in the final report of the conference, which stated: ". . . it is the sense of this committee that the Congress and the President of the United States should take such steps as will immediately reestablish a fair exchange value for all farm products with that of all other com-modities." Thus the doctrine of "equality for agriculture" was enunciated and a series of bills were presented in Congress to deal with the problem of agricultural surplus and to maintain the prices of farm products rela-tive to other prices. One feature of these proposals was to provide a federal subsidy to finance the disposal of this surplus abroad.

In 1929 the farm block succeeded in securing the passage of the Agri-cultural Marketing Act. This was in one sense a *quid pro quo* with the Smoot-Hawley Tariff Act which established a series of high import duties. Under the Agricultural Marketing Act a farm board was created to subsi-dize farm cooperatives to withhold products from the market in the hope of increasing prices. The Act did not make any provisions for limiting pro-duction and the Farm Board was eventually overwhelmed by its holdings of surplus stocks.

With the change in administration in 1933 the Agricultural Adjustment Act was passed in that year. This granted subsidies to maintain prices and did provide for limiting production. When the Act was declared uncon-stitutional in 1936, it was followed by the Soil Conservation and District Allotment Act which attempted to get the same result of parity for agri-culture but the subsidy was paid in the name of promoting soil conserva-tion rather than solely to maintain prices. A year later the Marketing Agreement Act was passed enabling farmers to combine under federal or-ganization to maintain orderly marketing arrangements. Authority to make subagreements was first granted under the Agricultural Adjustment Act of 1933, but was given greater scope under the 1937 Act. This Act has been used primarily to establish milk marketing agreements under federal milk market administrations, although marketing agreements for fruits, vegetables, and nuts have also been developed under this legislation. Since the *Panama Refining Company* (*Panama Refining Co. v. Ryan*, 293 U.S. 388 (1934)) and *Schecter* (*A. L. A. Schechter Poultry Corp. v. United States*, 295 U.S. 495 (1935)) decisions of the United States Supreme Court cast doubt on the use of a licensing provision to control marketing practices, the implementation of the regulation was based on Orders of the Secretary of Agriculture in the amendments to the Agricultural Adjustment Act of 1935 and continued in the Marketing Agreement Act of 1937.

In 1938 a new Agricultural Adjustment Act was passed. This legislation provided for four basic agricultural programs. The first provided subsidies to farmers who carried out certain prescribed practices designed to build and maintain soil fertility. These payments were tied to a system of in-dividual acreage allotments for various crops in an attempt to adjust pro-duction to the capacity of the soil and the demands of the domestic and foreign markets. Farmers exceeding their allotments were penalized. Un-der a separate title of the Act farmers producing corn, wheat, tobacco, cotton, and rice were given non-recourse loans to withhold surplus supplies. As a further aid to the loan program, farmers could by a two-thirds vote apply marketing quotas which were then assigned to each farm. A penalty was assessed for sales in excess of the quotas. As a final price-support measure, the Secretary of Agriculture was authorized to make payments to the producers of the five basic commodities, within the limits of the prescribed funds, which would bring their returns from the sale of their crops to the level they would have received had the price been equal to parity price for a normal crop. Under Section 32 of the 1935 amendment of the Agriculture Adjustment Act of 1933, 30 per cent of the receipts from import duties were segregated to be used to finance the purchase of surplus farm crops. This operation was put under the Federal Surplus Commodities Corporation. The Agricultural Adjustment Act of 1938 continued this Corporation, which undertook to divert surplus supplies through a food stamp plan which made them available to low-income consumers through regular trade channels. Title V of the Agricultural Adjustment Act of 1938 created the Federal Crop Insurance Corporation within the Department of Agriculture to underwrite losses in wheat yields.

Subsequent legislation has followed this general pattern with crop loans, marketing quotas and acreage allotments, and income payments. During World War II additional incentives to producers of essential crops were offered, particularly through the Stegall Amendment which guaranteed prices on certain crops for two years following the end of hostilities. There have been few recent substantial changes in agricultural adjustment legislation, although currently there is an attempt to reduce the level of subsidy payments and eliminate restrictions on production and marketing. Proposals in 1948 and 1950 to shift parity payments to an income basis have been partially accepted, as has a moving average rather than a fixed base to calculate parity levels. An attempt to relate farm income subsidy directly to consumption levels has so far failed to materialize in legislation. Major changes that have occurred have been largely in the area of administration, and reflect the efforts of Congress and of the Department of Agriculture to coordinate and integrate various agricultural progams. One of the more significant changes in this area was the creation of the Commodity Credit Corporation under the Commodity Credit Corporation Act of 1948. This split off a large area of the price support program from the Agricultural Adjustment Administration (later the Production and Marketing Administration). Under this Act the functions of the Commodity Credit Corporation are to stabilize, support, and protect farm income and prices, to assist in maintaining balanced and adequate supplies, and to facilitate the orderly distribution of agricultural commodities. Funds for these activities are derived from the Corporation's own operations and the substantial borrowing power granted to it by Congress.

While the federal government was developing the elaborate machinery to support agricultural prices and income, farmers through their own organizations were attempting to achieve a control of the market through cooperatives. In addition to promoting control of railroad rates and practices, the Granger movement also supported the organization of farm cooperatives as a further device to improve the market position of agriculture. Congress regarded this development favorably and in 1914 excluded farm cooperatives from the antimonopoly provisions of the Clayton Anti-Trust Act, provided they operated without capital stock. Under the Capper-Volstead Act of 1922 to strengthen the farm cooperative movement, this limiting provision was dropped. Subsequent legislation to control monopolistic practices and establish fair trade practices has continued to exempt farm cooperatives from the restrictions applied to other types of marketing firms. As a further aid to cooperatives, under federal tax legislation, they have been exempt from certain tax levies.

A third approach to assisting farm cooperatives was the provision of federal funds to such organizations. The Farm Board established under the Agricultural Marketing Act of 1929 initially regarded its principal function to be the encouragement of cooperative marketing associations and they were made the agencies through which its surplus purchase program was originally carried out. Later, under the authority given in Section 201 (e) of the Emergency Relief and Construction Act of 1932, the Reconstruction Finance Corporation established regional agricultural credit corporations in each of the Federal Land Bank districts. This function was transferred to the Farm Credit Administration created by executive order, May 27, 1933. The functions of this agency were given statutory recognition by the Farm Credit Act passed in June of the same year. Under this legislation twelve district banks and one central bank were established to extend credit to farm cooperatives. Provision was also made in this Act to set up production credit associations which were federally financed local farm credit cooperatives to extend short-term production credit to farmers.

These various credit aids to cooperatives and the stimulus to establishing cooperative credit associations were part of a general federal program of assisting agriculture by providing easier loan funds. The Federal Land Banks were established in 1917 under the Farm Loan Act of 1916 which was designed to provide mortgage credit to agriculture. In 1923 this was supplemented by the Federal Intermediate Credit Act which established in each of the twelve Land Bank districts a bank to rediscount intermediate agricultural paper. The Emergency Farm Mortgage Act of 1932 issued emergency loans to farmers through the Federal Land Banks and additional funds were provided as the agricultural depression continued.

With the establishment of the Farm Credit Administration in 1933 the program of government-administered credit was inaugurated. Unlike the previous credit institutions set up under federal legislation this program was not designed to become a farmer-owned, farmer-controlled institution. By executive order various agencies which ultimately became the Farmers Home Administration provided supervised credit for farmers who were considered to be too great risks for commercial or cooperative banking. This

program was extended by Title I of the Bankhead-Jones Farm Tenancy
Act of 1937, which provided funds for establishing tenants as farm owners.

In a quite different category was the extensive program of federal aid to
agricultural education. The basic legislation in this field is the Morrill
Act of 1862 establishing State colleges of agriculture to be financed by
grants of federal land. Outright grants of funds were subsequently made to
establish similar colleges in those eastern States in which there was no federal domain. When this act was first proposed in 1857 it was vetoed by
President James Buchanan on the grounds that it was too costly and the
use of federal wealth for special interests was unconstitutional. It is significant that the Morrill Act as passed provided that the State legislatures
could prescribe the curricula of the land grant colleges although the expressed purpose of the Act was stated to be to teach "such branches of learn-
ing as related to agriculture and mechanic arts." State legislatures were
slow to provide financial assistance to the land grant colleges and a new
Morrill Act was passed in 1890 to grant additional federal subsidies. This
was increased in 1907 with the passage of the Nelson Amendment.

Twenty-five years after the passage of the first Morrill Act, Congress enacted the Hatch Act (1887) creating, in connection with the land grant
colleges, the agricultural experiment stations. The purpose of these institutions was to improve the condition of agriculture by applying scientific
techniques to the study of farming methods and to develop new crop va-
rieties. To coordinate this research an Office of Experiment Stations was set
up in the United States Department of Agriculture.

With agricultural colleges and firmly established agricultural research institutions in being in the States, the next problem was to extend the benefits of better agricultural information to a larger number of farmers. At
the turn of the century the federal Department of Agriculture was carrying
on demonstration projects in several States, particularly to teach farmers
how to combat the Mexican boll weevil. The General Education Board
of New York City agreed to supplement federal funds to finance additional
agents to work in the States. Later it was decided that the proper organization for such work was on a county basis, and that individual
farmers and businessmen should help subsidize county agricultural agents.
A large part of the success of this work depended on cooperation of the
various land grant colleges. In 1914 Congress passed the Smith-Lever Act
according to which the federal government matches State grants for extension work. Special extension education divisions were set up in the
State colleges to cooperate with a federal extension office in the Department
of Agriculture. From this program has developed the Cooperative Extension Service which provides education and many services to farmers in all
agricultural counties in the United States.

The program of education was further supplemented by the Smith-
Hughes Vocational Education Act of 1917 which granted funds to States
willing to expand their secondary educational systems to include courses

in agriculture, trade, industries, and home economics. To receive such funds a State board of vocational education must submit a program of how the federal funds are to be used for approval by a federal board of vocational education.

The first proposal to establish a federal department of agriculture was made in 1776 by the Second Continental Congress. However, it was not until 1839 that an Agricultural Division was set up in the United States Patent Office to collect agricultural statistics, conduct agricultural investigations, and distribute seeds. In 1862 Congress established a Department of Agriculture under a Commissioner and below Cabinet rank. The powers and duties of the Department were much the same as they were in 1839 although the range had increased greatly. The Department was raised to Cabinet status by Congress in 1889 largely as a result of the continued agitation of farm organizations. From that period the work of the Department expanded greatly. New bureaus were created in the Department, and with the increased use of the police power by the federal government to promote the general welfare, the Department took on a new range of duties. In 1906 the Department assumed the enforcement of the Food and Drug Act which gave it control of the movement of substandard or misbranded products moving in interstate commerce. Because of its earlier and successful work in controlling animal disease and regulating the meat export trade, the Department was given the Meat Inspection Act of 1907 to administer. These new regulatory activities brought the Department directly into the marketing field. One of the important activities in this area became the development and publication of economic data particularly relevant to agriculture. In 1922 the Department began publishing outlook reports for farmers to indicate possible desirable levels of crop planting. This work became associated with other market restriction projects of the period. On the ground that prediction of this sort ultimately did more harm than good Congress specifically forbade the Department of Agriculture to issue further reports of this sort although currently a large volume of price and supply data is issued to farmers either directly or through the land grant colleges and the Cooperative Extension Service.

Until the 1930's agricultural legislation rarely came into direct conflict with constitutional limitations. The area in which the problem arose was chiefly that of the commerce clause of the federal Constitution. Farmers were greatly interested in and their organizations promoted railroad rate regulation measures first in the States and later, when the *Wabash* decision of the Supreme Court (118 U.S. 557 (1876)) effectively stopped State regulation, by the federal government. In this instance, after a series of failures before the United States Supreme Court, the Interstate Commerce Commission largely through the Hepburn Act (1906) and the series of amendments to the Interstate Commerce Act (1887) exercised sufficient control of railroad rates to quiet agrarian protest.

With the development of agricultural policies aimed at reallocation of resources and more favorable income distribution for agriculture, the problem of complying with the Constitution became a major issue. In the *Butler* case (297 U.S. 1 (1936)) the decision went against the developing federal welfare programs, but within a very short time, in *Wickard v. Filburn* (317 U.S. 111 (1942)), the broad interpretation of the commerce clause of the Constitution opened the way to a vast range of possible legislation to control agricultural development and production. Further support to this broad view was found in *Steward Machine Company v. Davis* (301 U.S. 548 (1937)) and *Helvering v. Davis* (301 U.S. 619 (1937)).

The fact that they occurred in wartime may account for the failure to challenge before the Supreme Court the various price and production control measures adopted by Congress. The 1917 Food and Fuel Control Act gave the President the power to use licensing as a control over prices, inventories, buying and selling, and trade practices. In the 1930's the court rulings suggested that the licensing power could not be used to support agricultural prices. Subsequently, under the Emergency Price Control Act of 1942, prices were even more drastically regulated, but without resort to licensing.

Recent agricultural legislation such as the current Agricultural Adjustment Act continues programs the basic tenets of which were established during the period of legislative innovation in the mid-thirties. In addition to the political sophistication which has given greater legislative refinement to current acts, the fact that the Supreme Court has through its liberal interpretation of the commerce clause particularly opened a greater range of legislative possibility has made the question of developing an agricultural policy a live and fruitful one for Congress and agricultural groups.

Labor and Social Security

I. INTRODUCTION

The creation of an economic community in Western Europe embracing no more than the coal, steel, and iron industries is itself bound to produce new problems in the labor field. The attempts by employers, workers, and the several governments to resolve these problems will of necessity, given the new nature of things, be by way of new approaches. Whatever transitional arrangements might exist, ultimately the impact of labor practices and labor legislation in one country on the labor aspects of the economies of other countries will have to be met by something other than the old competition-meeting devices of tariffs and quotas. Pressures for some uniformity of wages, hours, and labor standards are certain to result. From the labor relations point of view, any increase in industrial interdepend ence arising from combined efforts to supply the military needs of the unified military force of Western Europe will mean an increased pressure for some international participation in efforts to resolve labor disputes threatening military production.

A political Community must eventually deal with additional problems over and above those that will be faced by the present economic organization. For example, the extent to which labor will be permitted free movement within the Community will have to be considered both in drafting the Constitution of the Community and in subsequent legislation.

Finally, both during the limited economic cooperation period and in the time of the broader political Community, social insurance coordination will be a major problem, as an adequate treatment of such matters as transferability of credits and subsidization of credits accrued in areas of less liberal social insurance programs will be required by the need for maintaining a high level of worker morale.

What this study proposes to do, accordingly, is to outline the ways in which the problems of the labor and social insurance fields have been met by other constitution-writers, legislators, and executives; to point out the diversity of the approaches, and to demonstrate the reaction of the systems embodying each approach to the stimulus of pressures for action on the part of the federal government in these fields; to suggest on the basis of the experience of these major Western federal systems what general treat-

ment might be accorded labor and social insurance matters in the Constitution of the European Community; and what basic techniques of legislation
or administration the constitutional authors might foresee being adopted in
the practice of the new system.

Necessarily, the theoretical analysis and the more specialized country studies following are oriented to a legal approach, although an effort has been
made to cite some of the factors influencing the genesis of the final legal
form, so far as space limitations have allowed. The evolution of any constitutional, legislative, or administrative pattern is of course provoked by
social activity, by historical events, by technological changes, and by a host
of other factors whose role in the casting of the legal form can never be
fully stated. Nor can anyone think that a knowledge of the cold legal form
is a knowledge of the situation as it exists. In this study we try to emphasize, for example, the role of cooperative arrangements and informal operations in the determination of the actual role of the various levels of government in the labor field. In an intensely human area, a study of forms
is only a beginning, but a study of forms still is of great importance.

Here our study is divided into the traditional areas of labor relations;
wages, hours, and factory inspection; employment agencies and labor
movement; and social insurance.

II. LABOR RELATIONS

The general subject of labor relations in the federal state can be considered conveniently under three headings: first, that treating of the way
in which responsibility is distributed between the federal and state governments, respectively, for dealing with the problems arising out of the modern inclination of workers and employers to form their separate associations
for the advancement of their respective purposes and arising out of the relationships between the employer and the worker given the existence of
these organizations; second, that dealing with the authority of the governments in the system to establish institutions and procedures for the settlement of labor disputes; and third, that dealing with the assignment of
responsibility for special problems of wages, hours and other labor standards, and factory inspection. It happens that in those major federal systems in which labor problems are specifically treated, this is the division
along which the constitutional provisions are usually shaped.

While the entrance of the federal governments in Canada and the United
States into the field of labor affairs has been mostly by way of new interpretations or applications of older powers, the framers of the new federal
constitutions have treated labor subjects directly in the original charter. In
some of the older systems such as the Australian, amendments designed to
facilitate federal activity in the labor field have either been adopted or
have been strongly advocated and, in some cases, barely failed of adoption.

A. *Labor Organization*

In the newer German constitutions, both the Weimar Constitution and the Bonn Basic Law, the organizational aspect of labor affairs is treated under two headings. First, there is a general provision guaranteeing to labor the right of assembly in order to form associations to safeguard and to improve the contractual terms of labor. Second, there are provisions for the organization of enterprises under which authority is given the federal government to issue regulations respecting the organization of the enterprise, and more specifically, the functions of works councils. And while generally in both the Weimar Constitution and the Bonn Basic Law the provisions respecting labor are in the list of concurrent powers, there is one exception in the Weimar Constitution which is not repeated in the Bonn Basic Law. That is in the case of Article 165 where "the regulation of the development and functions of the workers and economic councils" is made an exclusive responsibility of the central government.

In the United States, on the other hand, there is no mention of labor matters in the original Constitution, nor have any amendments dealt with this topic. Instead, as far as concerns the organization of labor, wages, hours, and working conditions, and the handling of disputes, the federal government has relied for the most part on its power over interstate commerce (Art. 1, §8) to justify its extensive activities in this field. The National Labor Relations Act of 1935 (Wagner Act) was adopted under the authority of this grant of power. It sought to protect the organization of workers into unions free of employer influence. Subsequent amendments, notably that of 1947, known as the Labor-Management Relations Act (Taft-Hartley Act), have sought to correct what was considered an excessive prejudice in the first Act in behalf of labor organizations, and have attempted to protect the rights of management in such matters as the obligation of the parties to bargain in good faith. Since its original 1937 decision upholding the Act, the Supreme Court has construed it to extend to labor relations in enterprises engaged in manufacturing or trading activity having a tangible effect upon the flow of interstate commerce, whether that effect is direct or indirect. A long series of court decisions has shown that the Acts apply to all kinds of business activity having even a remote connection with the movement of goods from State to State. The Court's interpretation of the power given to the federal government by the commerce clause has not, of course, removed the State governments completely from the field of labor relations. Encouraged by the federal legislation and Supreme Court decisions, several State legislatures enacted statutes modeled on the federal legislation but applicable to local businesses. For a time the State and federal authorities avoided conflict or duplication by informal agreements under which they allocated their respective fields of action. In cases in which there was doubt as to whether the State or federal government should exercise jurisdiction it was assumed that there was concurrent jurisdiction and that the case could be handled by whichever government was the first to assert its authority. In time, however, and especially after the enactment of the 1947 amendment, conflicts between State and federal legislation, and in State and federal administrative procedure, began to come more frequently into the open. As these conflicts developed, the Supreme Court decided that the federal legislation was an expression of the intent of the Congress to exclude from State regulation all cases covered by the federal Acts and that the practice of exercising concurrent jurisdiction was untenable. The States, it was held, ought not to intervene in any case where the federal authorities had power to act. Since a determination as to whether an unfair labor practice "affects interstate commerce" depends on the facts of the particular case and since no one can tell in advance how the particular case will be decided, this Supreme Court doctrine of federal exclusiveness has created a good many problems for the State agencies in borderline cases. Today they have clear jurisdiction only in such obviously local enterprises as small retail and service establishments, local transit companies, restaurants, theaters, and the like. However, there still exists close cooperation between federal and State conciliation authorities to avoid duplication of functions and to avoid untimely interference by one agency in the mediation efforts of another, particularly where the question of jurisdiction is not clear.

In Australia the existence of a clause in the federal Constitution on interstate trade similar to that in the United States Constitution did not serve, as events proved, to give to the federal government a like power over the organizational relations of employers and employees. There the presence of a further clause giving to the federal authorities the responsibility for establishing conciliation and arbitration machinery led the interpreting judicial bodies to conclude that the constitutional author had intended to limit the activity of the federal government in the labor field to this single role. In effect this has meant that in Australia most labor legislation, and certainly that part of the legislation respecting the organization of workers, has been a consequence of some residuary power of the States. It should of course be recalled that at the time of the writing of the Australian Constitution the American federal government had not yet attempted to use the interstate commerce powers for legislating on the organization of labor, nor was it to do so for many years, and there was therefore as yet no American federal experience by which the framers of the Australian Constitution could be guided in this field as they were guided in so many other respects. All this has meant that the legal position of Australian trade unions as the agents of their members in negotiating conditions of employment is guaranteed by way of the several State Trade Union Acts.

Where industrial disputes arise, whether in the course of collective bargaining looking to a new contractual arrangement with the employer or as a result of a dispute under a contractual agreement already in effect, the unions are protected in their very right to bargain collectively by legislation (whether federal or State as the case might be in the particular dispute) establishing industrial tribunals. The High Court has insisted in the past on the power of the States to control their own industrial affairs and on the power of the Commonwealth to enable its courts to settle by arbitration only industrial disputes extending beyond the limits of any one State, and has held that particular cases must be so construed as to make the existence or the exercise of these two prerogatives as little as possible inconsistent with each other (*Federated Saw Mill Case*, 8 C. L. R. 465 (1909)). But while formal jurisdiction is restrained, the impact of decisions of the federal arbitration tribunal is more pervasive as the industrialization of the country proceeds, with the result that formal jurisdiction is not a good guide to actual effect and import.

In the Canadian system, another device, that of recourse to its authority over the criminal law, has been used as the means for the federal government's moving into matters of labor organization and into the general relationship between organized labor and management. Under Section 91 (27), the Dominion government is charged with exclusive authority over the criminal law. Acting under this authority the Canadian government in 1939, for example, amended the Criminal Code so as to provide that any employer or his agent, whether a private individual or a corporation, was liable to a fine or imprisonment, where appropriate to the personality, for refusing to employ or for dismissing any person on the ground that that person was a member of a trade union or other association of workers which had been founded in a lawful manner for the purpose of advancing their interests and for their protection in the regulation of wages and conditions of work. Protection against intimidation was also granted the worker. The right of trade unions to exist free from the threat of criminal prosecution as conspiracies in restraint of trade, and the right of unions to strike, are similarly protected by the Dominion under its power to legislate with respect to the criminal law. As we shall see later, the Dominion has intervened legislatively in the general area of labor disputes though in so doing it has risked going beyond its constitutional powers. The limits within which the federal government must operate in Canada are those set up by the fact of the assignment to the Provinces in Section 92 of the Constitution of responsibility for civil rights and property. Where the American federal government was able to persuade the Supreme Court that power over interstate commerce gave it authority to protect the organization and operation of a large part of the trade union system against employer interference, the Privy Council has more and more been tending to emphasize the "civil rights and property" clause against the "trade and commerce" clause granting power to the federal government in Section 91 of the Constitution. Of course, under Section 91, the Dominion government is given power with respect to labor relations in fields of legislation directly assigned to it. Accordingly, it has jurisdiction over workers in interpro-

vincial transportation, over seamen, and over employees of private firms
engaged on Dominion public works.

Again, in another circumstance, it has been possible for the Swiss federation to rely upon its power over the national civil code to give to the trade
unions a legal power to represent their members in negotiations with the
employer or his organization even though there might not be a constitutional provision looking especially to such activity by the federal authorities
in the field of labor relations. Until 1908 the Swiss federal government was
in this position and adopted the practice of resorting to its power over the
civil code's provisions. In that year, however, an amendment was adopted
to the provisions of Article 34 of the Constitution, and under its terms
(the old Article 34-*ter*) the federal government was authorized to establish
uniform regulations for the governing of economic activities. Under this
amendment, long unused by the federal government for labor affairs, there
was enacted in 1943 a statute regulating the contractual relationships between employer and employees generally throughout the federation. In
1947 a new Article 34-*ter* was enacted giving the Confederation an even
more specific power to legislate on the relations between employers and
their workers.

B. *Conciliation and Arbitration*

Three schemes commonly used by governments for dealing with threatened or existent disputes are investigation, conciliation, and arbitration in
a judicial or quasi-judicial process. Here too the general rule in the major
federal systems is that jurisdiction over the organization of labor and employer associations and the jurisdiction over peace-making institutions are
divided along the same lines. However, in those areas where judicial systems for settlement of labor disputes exist, the need for a national uniformity of labor law tends to magnify the authority of the federal officers.
It may be noted from the outset that under one provision or another investigation or conciliation machinery exists in all the federal systems. It
may depend, as in the United States, upon the use of a power derived by
extension of an old power. The system of investigation under the 1947
Labor-Management Relations Act relies for its validity upon the Congress's
jurisdiction over commerce among the States. Similarly, the Conciliation
Service, long established by statute, intervenes only in disputes which involve the national interest. In Canada, however, Dominion activity begins
with the assertion of the Dominion's authority over disputes within that
sphere unquestionably assigned the Dominion, involving such matters as
transport among the Provinces, but there is one additional feature which is
unusual and of interest. The 1907 Industrial Disputes Investigation Act
is the basic legislation under which the Dominion system of investigation
and conciliation operates. In the beginning this Act was applied to disputes in the following fields: mining; steam, electric, and other railways;

steamships; telegraph and telephone lines; gas, electric light, water and power works. Later, in 1925, the Dominion government laid claim to several other categories of enterprises by an extension of its constitutional powers which will be of considerable interest in an evaluation of federal government. Among these are works carried on by aliens and foreign corporations; works for the general advantage of Canada; works existing under a charter granted by the Dominion; disputes designated by the Governor General in Council as affecting the public welfare during periods of national emergency. All of these depend on provisions of the Constitution having no direct relationship to labor. Under the 1907 Act, whether on the initiative of the Dominion Minister of Labour, or on the request of either party, a three-member board of conciliation may be appointed to investigate a labor dispute and to report on the points at issue. While this board is making its study any strike or lockout is forbidden. In the industries involved, notice of any contemplated change in the conditions of work or in the working demands of the employees must be made public thirty days in advance of the date they are to be effective. Although the point was not pressed for almost twenty years, in the end the Dominion government found what many observers had long thought to be the case, namely, that the list of industries over which the federal government was seeking to extend its influence was far longer than could be justified under the British North America Act. In 1925 the Privy Council ruled that the Industrial Disputes Investigation Act exceeded the powers of the Dominion. Rather, however, than alter the Act by merely eliminating such offending clauses as that applying to public utilities, which could not be sustained as valid, the Dominion, while making clear its purpose of retaining conciliation control in those industries clearly allotted to it, such as the railways, decided to use the technique of the "enabling legislative device," to retain the conciliation machinery for use in disputes which the Privy Council now held to be under the scope of provincial power. The Canadian "enabling legislative device" involves the enactment of legislation by the Dominion government in an area over which it is recognized by all that the government does not have control: for example, the marketing of fruit. However, the several Provinces are then called upon to enact the Dominion legislation as their own and to declare that in so far as the Dominion legislation and the regulations under it are beyond the powers of the Dominion and within the powers of the Province, these invalid provisions of the Dominion act are to be part of the law of the Province. In some cases the provincial enabling legislation has gone so far as to authorize the Lieutenant-Governor to amend the provincial legislation on his own authority whenever the Dominion Parliament might amend the basic act. Under this arrangement the Industrial Disputes Investigation Act was accepted by all the provinces except Prince Edward Island. Later, however, British Columbia withdrew its participation in the program because of the doubtful validity of the system and the prolonged delays under it. In practice, the Dominion government seems to have followed a policy of not using the Act in disputes of a limited nature unless called upon to do so by the provincial authorities.

In Switzerland the clearly defined power of the federal government over at least a part of the economy was long utilized, under a 1914 law, to require the establishment, but under the administration of the cantonal governments, of conciliation offices to resolve collective disputes that might occur in enterprises falling under the classification of "*fabriques*," that is, larger industrial enterprises. In 1949, following the addition to the Swiss Constitution of the new Article 34-*ter* by which the Confederation's jurisdiction over management-labor relations was expanded, the Confederation enacted legislation making it possible for a Federal Conciliation Office to enter disputes "extending beyond the borders of one canton." The need for reliance on the old distinction between fabriques and other forms of commercial enterprises therefore no longer exists as a limitation to Confederation intervention in labor disputes. Many of the cantons in addition established judicial bodies known variously as labor tribunals, professional tribunals, or Conseils de Prud'hommes, for the purpose of resolving disputes arising out of the interpretation of contracts where enterprises are involved that are not subject to the federal factory law. The Swiss conciliation machinery, it should be noted, is not directed to the resolution of disputes over the terms of a new agreement, but rather concerns itself with collective disputes arising out of the interpretation of existing agreements. Further, where an individual has a grievance arising out of the interpretation of a contract which he cannot transform into a collective grievance, his only resort is to an ordinary civil court. Unlike the Australian system, the conciliation offices possess no powers of compulsion and merely are available to contesting parties on a voluntary basis. However, under the 1949 law, once conciliation proceedings are begun, the parties are bound to preserve industrial order.

More elaborate systems of conciliation and arbitration exist in Australia and in Germany. The Australian is much the less comprehensive of the two because of the more limited constitutional authority granted in this field to the Commonwealth government, at least as interpreted by the Australian High Court. At the time of the 1897–1898 Constitutional Convention, the Liberals, and, to a considerable extent, the Labourites who desired that any federal Constitution adopted should allow for legal recognition of the trade union movement, pressed for the inclusion of what came to be Section 51 (xxxv) of the Constitution. This placitum provided that the Commonwealth Parliament might have power to make laws for the peace, order, and good government of the Commonwealth with respect to "Conciliation and Arbitration for the prevention and settlement of industrial disputes extending beyond the limits of any one state." The High Court of Australia has made clear that the Constitution leaves to each State exclusive control over all phases of industry operating solely within

State limits, and, of course, this must be understood in the sense explained earlier, a much more restricted sense than that attributed to the similar expression in the United States Constitution. And so, the States may make laws imposing any rights, duties, or obligations they deem fit on employees and employers engaged in their respective industries. Under the authority of placitum (xxxv), however, the federal authorities have established a conciliation and arbitration system capped by a judicial agency possessing all the paraphernalia and powers of other constituted courts. Arbitration authorities now have power to call a compulsory conference of parties engaged in a dispute in an effort to have the dispute resolved by the process of conciliation. Should this intervention fail, these arbitration officials may then refer the dispute to the arbitration courts established by the Commonwealth, which are topped by the Conciliation and Arbitration Court, from which appeals may be carried to the High Court of the Commonwealth itself. It appears that a considerable number of the members of the Constitutional Convention were in favor of having placitum (xxxv) apply not only to the settlement of disputes, but to the definition of wages, hours, and working conditions per se. The abortive attempt (abortive because later annulled by judicial review) in 1901 by the Commonwealth Parliament to assign to the Commonwealth authorities complete powers over wages, hours, and conditions of labor was supported by thirty members who were delegates to the 1897–1898 Convention. It might be noted, also, that the proposed assumption of powers in this field was approved unanimously by both houses of the Parliament. The arbitration courts have in time come to be the key agencies for the establishment of basic wage rates in that part of the economy coming under Commonwealth influence by virtue of constitutional provisions, but the point has always been made by the judicial courts that such activity is merely incidental to the arbitration courts' settling of disputes.

Two attempts have been made, one in 1911 and one in 1913, to gain approval by the electorate of a constitutional amendment enlarging the federal power, so as to include wages and conditions of labor and employment in any trade, industry, or calling, but these failed of the required number of votes. Attempts made also in 1911 and 1913 to extend the jurisdiction of the court so as to encompass disputes in relation to employment on or about the railways operating within the States have also failed. Some of the leaders in the attempt to enlarge the scope of the Commonwealth powers so as to have them include jurisdiction over wages, hours, and working conditions, have felt rather deeply on the matter and have offered advice to other federal constitution-makers. Some ten years after the writing of the Australian Constitution, by the National Convention of 1897–1899, the British government sought to profit from the experience of Australia over the first decade of federal constitutional government by asking advice of Australian leaders that might help in the drafting of the proposed constitution for South Africa. Two Australian leaders,

Deakin and Garran, who had been disappointed by the nature of legislation under placitum (xxxv), answered this request by warning of a lesson they thought could be learned explicitly from what had happened under this placitum. "The specific powers," they said, "should be defined in words as general as possible, avoiding as far as possible all conditions, exceptions and limitations."

The most highly structured system of arbitration and conciliation institutions among the major federal powers was without doubt that of the Germany of the Weimar period. Here the nature of the constitutional provisions made it possible for the federal legislature to enact laws covering as much of the labor field as it wished. Section 9 of Article 7, in the list of concurrent powers, granted the federal government legislative powers over "labor law." Acting under its authority the federal government established both systems of conciliation and of arbitration. Under the act of 1923 the federal Parliament directed the establishment of conciliation committees (*Schlichtungsausschüsse*) by the Länder authorities in agreement with the federal Minister of Labor. Authorization was given for the establishment of committees covering two or more States, or a part of a State, or whatever might seem most called for by the peculiar regional economic circumstances. This local autonomy in the first instance in the establishment and operation of conciliation committees was in accord with a general belief among students of labor mediation problems that the presence of mediation officials well acquainted with local problems and special features of local industries is to be desired and, other things permitting, ought to be the guide to the organization of mediation systems. However, in Weimar Germany the "paramount interests" of the federal government were protected by the presence in the conciliation system of federal conciliators appointed by the Minister of Labor either for special areas or for special cases in which the federal government might take an interest. The State committees then usually handled routine matters, and at any time the federal authorities might intervene. The conciliation machinery in Germany, unlike that in some other countries, was concerned only with the resolution of disputes arising out of negotiations over the terms of new collective agreements. Some students thought they saw additional latitude for the committees, but on the whole it is agreed that this was their function. In addition to these disputes there are of course those that arise out of the interpretation of collective agreements already in force. In Weimar Germany the labor courts system was established to deal with these. Here again there was a combination of State and federal government activity. There were labor courts first at the local level, usually covering the district coterminous with that of a labor office. The great bulk of cases was resolved at this level, usually without any formal hearings having taken place, since the courts were instructed under federal regulations to seek amicable, non-judicial settlement of the conflict before actually allowing it to come before the court. There were, however, courts at the State level to hear appeals from these courts of first instance, of which there might be ten or twelve in each State. The personnel of both these courts was appointed by the government of the State. Finally, there was a Federal Labor Court whose personnel was appointed by the federal government. The purpose of this court was to ensure the unity of the labor law. Its members were usually drawn from the highest judicial court, the Reichsgericht itself, except for a number of non-judicial "assessors" (lay judges) drawn from employers and employees. The situation in the case of arbitration and conciliation machinery in Germany at the present time is substantially the same as it was during the Weimar period. By the time the Bonn government was established, all conciliation and labor courts machinery had been established in the Länder of Western Germany under the independent authority of the State governments, who of course had no central German authority to consult, and under the general supervision of the occupation authorities. A Federal Labor Court has now been established for the West German federation and is exercising its primary function of maintaining the labor law's unity.

But it often happens that the best conciliation machinery fails. In the Australian system of arbitration, labor disputes coming within the federal jurisdiction theoretically have no chance to erupt into work stoppages. In Germany, the limited number of disputes coming under the jurisdiction of the labor courts are similarly kept from developing into stoppages. In the other major federal systems, however, there is no means of ensuring that stoppages are permanently averted. In none of the major federal systems, except for the Australian, is there in peacetime a means for permanently averting such a work stoppage. The procedures under the American Taft-Hartley Law of 1947, and those under the Railway Mediation Acts relating to disputes over the terms of a new agreement, are investigative in nature, and can only serve to delay in the hope of a voluntary settlement, but cannot prevent. In some of the American States, the legislatures, acting under their police powers, have made it possible for strikes to be resolved compulsorily in public utilities such as electricity, gas, and waterworks. In Switzerland, the federal government has no peacetime compulsion power in labor disputes.

During periods in which federal governments act under their war powers, whether there is an actual condition of hostilities or not, their powers over labor disputes increase. Judicial interpreting bodies have been very generous in the federations in recognizing the authority of the federal governments to intervene in areas under their war powers where their peacetime powers alone could never have taken them. But as we shall see later on in considering the problem of wages, hours, and working conditions, in at least one of the major federations, the courts have imposed limits even on federal wartime labor powers, and have done something toward establishing principles regulating the wartime enlargement of federal powers. In the United States, the Selective Service Act and other acts enacted under the power of the Congress to declare war and raise armies, have included, during past hostilities, provisions authorizing the President to assume control if necessary of any installation operating directly, or by way of another party who is the primary contractor, on material essential to the war or defense effort. In World War II, the American President under this power went so far as to seize control of a large mail-order house and to eject bodily from office the recalcitrant head of that business organization, although in fact the validity of this particular and rather extreme action was never fully tested in the courts. On several occasions during the Second World War the coal mines were seized by executive order when strikes by the miners threatened production. Even where hostilities have ceased, the existence of a formal state of emergency is sufficient to give the executive certain powers he could not otherwise exercise.

In the American system, the power of the President as commander-in-chief of the armed forces has sufficed in time of war emergency for such seizure, with no need of specific legislation.

In Australia the jurisdiction of the Conciliation and Arbitration Service was extended, beyond the rather limited area authorized it in peacetime, to include installations normally covered by the State arbitration and conciliation boards, where such existed (although not all States have such agencies), but where there was work being carried on which was considered by the Commonwealth government as important to the defense program. In Canada, the Industrial Disputes Investigation Act of 1907 was extended during World War II to all war industries. In 1941 a full-time National War Labour Board was organized which had the jurisdiction to decide authoritatively all issues in labor disputes and to pass on all voluntary wage increases. Strikes in violation of the Industrial Disputes Act, and after 1943 all strikes for unauthorized wage changes, or for changes in wage provisions during the life of a contract, were punishable by fine and imprisonment, and this without regard to their taking place in war industries or not.

During World War II, the Swiss federal government extended somewhat the scope of the operations of the conciliation offices but there was no element of compulsion introduced even during this period. By a decree of May 24, 1940, a federal office of conciliation was established to conciliate disputes over wages and other conditions of work. This office might very well have been set up by the Federal Council in peacetime, but it had not been. However, the authority of all offices of conciliation, federal and cantonal, were extended beyond the "fabrique" limits imposed by the 1914 act, to include any enterprise. This extension was accomplished under the "pleins pouvoirs" (emergency powers) assumed by the federal government at the outbreak of the war.

Governments are faced also with the problem of how to deal with work stoppages occurring in time of peace in industries essential to the well-being of the community, such for example as public utilities. In Australia and Germany some of these at least may of course be thwarted under the routine conciliation and arbitration processes. In Weimar Germany the effect of Article 48 as a possible weapon in labor disputes in vital industries that could not otherwise be dealt with was never determined. In the United States the 1947 Labor-Management Relations Act included provisions making it possible for the executive branch to delay a work stoppage in a critical industry with the aid of the courts; but such delay could at the most be for eighty days, and after that time there was nothing in the terms of the Act to prevent a work stoppage from taking place. Further, it should be noted that the authority under which these provisions of the Act were enacted was the interstate commerce power of the Constitution. There are no such special provisions for peacetime economic emergencies of this nature in Canada or Switzerland.

In Australia emergency legislation permanently enacted or directed at specific industrial disturbances has been used in the past to curb work stoppages. Under the Crimes Act, the Governor-General may declare an industrial disturbance to be so grave as to prejudice interstate or foreign commerce and may then enjoin work stoppages in interstate or foreign transport. In 1949, as an example of a more specific Act, the National Emergency (coal strike) Act was enacted, and under it the use of funds by any union whatever to support the general coal mine strike then in progress was prohibited. The Act expired with the end of the strike.

In the American States, as well as in the Australian, a number of State acts have been passed, of a general nature, to enable State governments to cope with actual or threatened work stoppages in public utility enterprises, either by bringing them to an end privately, or by other means, such as giving the State Executive authority to insure that the minimal needs of the community are met.

There seems to be general agreement among students of Australian federal relations in the labor field that the interpretations of the High Court as to the meaning of the "conciliation and arbitration" clause of the Constitution have resulted in a limitation of federal power to a point beneath the level of adequacy. In other words, there are too many industries where labor difficulties might occur which could in reality affect economic life in other States and which could not be brought under the compass of federal conciliation and arbitration activities. Another criticism is that the High Court has so limited the functional scope of the clause as to render the power of the federal government weak in proportion to the needs of a country undergoing a considerable industrialization. As we shall see in the discussion on wages and hours which follows, the Conciliation and Arbitration Courts have in fact become the instrumentalities for fixing of basic wage and hour standards in Australia. But observers of the system feel that a federal government ought to have some more flexible and direct means of influencing the labor situation. As for Canada, at the time of the adoption of the British North America Act, she was almost completely an agricultural country. At the same time, unlike the American situation in which interpretations of old clauses have satisfied proponents of expanding federal power, the interpreters of the Canadian clauses granting power to the Dominion government, such as the trade and commerce, and the peace, order, and good government clauses, have permitted the clauses granting powers to the Provinces to operate as girdling restrictions on the operations of the Canadian government in economics, forcing not only the federal government, but the Provinces as well, to engage in schemes of circumvention of dubious validity.

Bearing in mind the view of the Australian leaders on the desirability of keeping power-granting clauses of the Constitution as general as possible, and yet recognizing that it may not be practical either economically or politically at this time to entrust extensive operating powers in the field of labor to the governments of the European Community, it would seem that there is considerable merit in the practice under the Weimar Constitution by which the labor function was, in the first place, made a concurrent power, and by which even the execution of such legislation as might be adopted under the federation's power was left in the first instance to the States, thus permitting activity at the local level of administrators, conciliators, and arbitrators who understand the peculiarities of the local economic situation on the whole and the nature of problems in the specialized industries which the area might possess, while still leaving available to federal authorities the possibility of their intervention in disputes involving the interests of several parts of the federation or of the federation as a whole. There is, in other words, room for both unity and diversity, characteristics of a federal system which ought to be characteristics of operations under it as far as possible.

C. *Wages, Hours, and Factory Inspection*

If we allow for a number of exceptions, we can set down as a general rule that in the major federal systems the jurisdiction over wages, hours, and working conditions runs along the same lines as jurisdiction in the field of labor relations. It must be noted, first, that again the constitutional interpretation of the High Court in Australia has not only deprived the federal government there of power over wages and hours which many political leaders and students have thought the Constitutional Convention had given it, but it has prevented any significant activity by the Commonwealth Government in the field of working conditions. There is therefore to be found no federal peacetime legislation in Australia relating to sanitation in factories, or to safeguards against occupational hazards including occupational diseases, except in the limited area of work for the naval and military service, and on works and railways within the federal territories.

The 1906 Excise Tariff Act was declared invalid by the High Court because the Court felt that rather than being an exercise of the Commonwealth's power to tax, it was an attempt to regulate the working conditions and the remuneration of Australian agricultural labor. In a line of reasoning reminiscent of the decision by the United States Supreme Court in the *Hoosac Mills* case, the Court held that the laboring conditions of workers in Australian agriculture were the concern of the States, and the Australian government could not interfere in this domestic concern of the States either by taxation or by any other device. Factory inspection and working conditions have always in peacetime been matters for the States.

The original Australian Constitution authorized a federal conciliation and arbitration court system for resolving labor disputes. In practice one of the principal tasks of this court system has come to be the establishment of a basic wage pattern for enterprises falling under the federal jurisdiction by virtue of their direct influence on interstate industrial operations. But here, too, historically the federal power has been constricted at points by federal decision in favor of State action.

Of course, these historical facts ought not to be permitted to obscure the reality of the present situation in Australia, which is that the ever-greater industrialization and the increasing interdependence of the formerly mutually isolated sections of the country have meant that the power of the federal Conciliation and Arbitration Court to establish basic wages in those enterprises engaged in work having interstate implications has come to be a power to influence the whole Australian wage structure, as the decisions of the federal Court inevitably influence the wage pattern in enterprises which once would have come exclusively under the jurisdiction of State conciliation and arbitration tribunals.

On the other hand, while the provisions of the Swiss Constitution referring to hours legislation by the federal government have in the past limited federal legislation to the fabriques (industrial plants), this is not the case with the provision referring to working conditions which gives to the federal government general authority over all economic enterprises to take measures for the protection of workers against occupational diseases and hazards. In actual practice, the measures for the protection of the worker are under the concurrent jurisdiction of the cantons and the federal government. So long as there is no legislation on a particular matter by the federal government, the cantons may legislate. However, so far as hours legislation is concerned, the situation has not been in practice the same, though the same theory on federal-canton relations would appear to exist. In 1890, for example, the Federal Council declared, in answer to a question put by a workers' delegation, that the prescription of eleven hours as normal for fabriques, which had been established by federal law, might not be modified by the cantons even though the eleven-hour rule had been established in favor of the workers. The Federal Council justified this by saying that the provisions of the federal law established a just balance between the interests of the workers and the employers and that this balance ought to be uniform throughout Switzerland in order to ensure uniform manufacturing conditions. It would appear that the Federal Council took the provisions of Article 34 granting the federal government power over working time in fabriques as an exclusive disposition of power, while the more general provision on conditions of the working place was a power that could be shared. Even in respect to the working time of young people, however, the federal legislature has been willing to allow a certain temporary amount of flexibility to the localities in making the adjustment to meet the provisions of new legislation. In 1940 when the minimum age of employment for children in fabriques was raised from 14 to 15 years, several years were allowed before the act should take effect in cantons which had not yet fixed the compulsory age for school attendance at this figure. Again the Swiss government has resorted in the field of wages to its authority over the civil law to justify its enacting uniform national provisions. The law of 1902 regarding the payment of wages refers not only to fabriques but to all enterprises subjected to the federal law of 1887 on the extension of civil responsibility. There have even been regulations, based on this civil law power, regarding the employment of children under the age of 14 and the night work of women and young people. Such regulations apply not only to fabriques but to all enterprises in the category covered by the statute. Since the adoption of the new Article 34-*ter* as an amendment to the Swiss Constitution in 1947, the power of the Confederation government has been greatly enlarged over such matters as labor standards and factory inspection, but it is too early yet to see what form the new federal activity in this area will take.

In the United States, wage and hour regulation is accomplished under the same power over interstate commerce which is the justification for the government's activity in the protection of workers' rights to organize and to bargain collectively. Since 1938 the federal government has imposed a minimum wage rate and decreed the number of weekly hours beyond which overtime must be paid to the worker. In the field of occupational diseases and hazards, however, the federal government has permitted the extensive legislation of the States to remain as controlling, and no special legislation has been enacted by the Congress in this field. It should be noted, however, that at the administrative level, the federal Department of Labor is active in making available to the States information on occupational diseases and hazards which the States are then free to use as a basis for their own legislation. Among the forms of this information are sample codes drafted by the Department and ready for enactment by the legislature with a minimum of change for local circumstances.

Both Canada and the United States have used their authority to regulate the conditions under which workers are employed by private contractors on federal projects. Under the 1935 Walsh-Healey Act certain minimum standards of wages, hours, and age of workers are required to be met by the contractor. Since 1900 the Dominion government has followed the practice of requiring its contractors to pay "fair" wages to those employed by them on Dominion work. What this has meant in practice is that prevailing wage rates in the area are paid. There has, it might be noted, never been any Dominion legislation fixing a minimum age for employment on Dominion public works. There is also no legislation in Canada limiting hours of work on vessels at sea or on inland waters even though this field is within the competence of the Dominion government. As a general rule, then, the regulation of hours of work and, as we noted earlier, of wages as well, falls mainly on the Provinces, as does the responsibility for supervising conditions under which the workers labor. Not even all of the area of competence authorized by the British North America Act has been covered, as we noted. However, an interesting attempt made by a reformist-minded Canadian federal administration in the mid-1930's to extend the scope of the Dominion's power over wages and hours should be noted. In 1935 the Drew government caused the adherence of Canada to International Labour Office agreements relating to minimum wages, maximum weekly hours of work, and the weekly rest period. After adoption of these treaties by the Parliament, the government proceeded to introduce legislation enacting the provisions of these treaties as federal law, and applying the terms generally throughout the Dominion without any regard for the traditionally accepted delimitation of power in this field between the federal government and the Provinces. The justification advanced by the Drew government was that the treaties must be considered on a par with the British North America Act as sources of legislative power for the federation, since they create international obligations which can be met only under the supervision of the federation. This of course is substantially the line of thought accepted by the United States Supreme Court in the case of *Missouri v. Holland* in which the American federal government was authorized to legislate in the protection of migratory birds by virtue of the existence of a treaty with the British Crown, although it was admitted that under the provisions of the Constitution itself and without the existence of the treaty such legislation would be beyond the Congress's powers. However, the Privy Council did not accept the treaties as sources of new legislative authority, emphasizing the Dominion's changed relationship with the rest of the world since her entrance into direct diplomatic relations with other powers had been permitted by the British government. The Privy Council did not see that the British North America Act covered Canada's treaty-making power in the new situation and the Privy Council could not therefore approve the three acts as valid exercises of Dominion power.

In Weimar Germany, wages and hours were set as a result of collective bargaining, and there was but little exercise of either federal or State power. In the field of conditions of labor, however, there was considerable activity by the governments, particularly the State governments acting under the general supervision of the federal authorities. Conditions of labor were of course within the jurisdiction of both the federal and the State authorities under the Constitution. The factory inspection services established by the States were considered by students to be models of their kind.

In considering Canadian federal legislation on working conditions we can note one exception to the general rule that working conditions are dealt with by the Provinces. And this introduces us for the first time in this study to the participation by a federal government in a labor matter by way of the financial arrangements. This very limited activity came in the field of technical education, with the intent of the Dominion government being the promotion of vocational education and, in the Unemployment and Agricultural Assistance Act of 1937, particularly the employment of "learners" by industry. What the Dominion government did in this case, and what is typical of arrangements made, was to agree to defray 40 per cent of the cost of a 13-week training course for unemployed youth to be conducted in accord with Dominion-approved plans of the Provinces. The course was to fit the youth for immediate work in industry. Again, the Canadian federal government's control over criminal law has been used by it to regulate in a mild way one aspect of employment practices. This is through the enactment of a Lord's Day Act (1906) under which employment was prohibited on Sunday except on work of necessity and mercy. This Act was adopted following the 1903 decision of the Privy Council in which an Ontario Lord's Day Act was invalidated on the grounds that it constituted legislation over the criminal law, reserved to the federal government. The Dominion Act, however, did not attempt to establish a federal inspectorate, but rather was more in the nature of a favor to provincial authorities who desired the legal power to prevent Sunday labor. The responsibility for enforcement of the Act rests with the provincial authorities and the Dominion government may not commence prosecution without the leave of the Attorney-General in the Province in which the offense is alleged to have been committed. This particular action of the Dominion government and the attempt cited earlier to enact legislation in execution of a treaty in a field otherwise closed to that government are typical of the devices to which governments are obliged to resort when political pressures cannot be channeled into acts authorized by existing constitutional provisions.

Some of the changes made in relations between federal and State jurisdictions in the field of legislation dealing with wages and hours and conditions of labor during war periods have already been noted. A few other examples are appropriate at this point. In the United States, the extension of powers over wages was effected in an informal manner during World War II since there was never in that period any control on wages established legislatively. Instead the labor unions had agreed to submit their requests for wage increases to the jurisdiction of a board which would then rule whether their requests were allowable in the light of the price legislation and policy of the federal government. In other words, the federal government did not use the war powers which it undoubtedly possessed to control wages as it had controlled prices. We have already noted the way in which the Canadian, Australian, and Swiss governments extended the functions of arbitration and conciliation agencies and, in the case of Australia and Switzerland, established new ones to deal, with varying degrees of severity, with problems of wages and hours. In Australia attempts were also made by the Commonwealth government to control conditions of work in enterprises not under its jurisdiction in peacetime. In some cases this succeeded. In at least one it did not. An attempt by the government to oblige an employer to install an improved system of lighting in his enterprise was held by the High Court to be an invalid exercise of the Commonwealth's war powers (*Victorian Chamber of Manufactures and the Commonwealth,* 1943, A.L.R. 325). The Court observed that the framers of the Constitution could never have intended that the whole Constitution should be suspended on the simple exercise of one of the powers granted to the Commonwealth government, however vital that power might be. The war power was not an unlimited power, said the Court, and actions taken under it must have some definite and necessary relationship to the war effort. The attempt to dictate lighting in a factory seemed to the Court to be too indirect. In the same way, an attempt of the Commonwealth government to oblige employees of State governments to work on public holidays whatever the nature of their work was invalidated by the Commonwealth High Court (*State of Victoria v. Commonwealth,* 66 C.L.R. 488) (1942).

Again, as with labor relations we see a variety of methods for dividing jurisdiction between federal and State governments in matters of wages, hours, and conditions under which men work. In part the limitations on the federal government are due to the nature of the particular country's economy at the time of the adoption of the Constitution, to the seeming difficulty in amending a Constitution when economic conditions undergo an extensive change, and to interpretations of judicial bodies limiting the power of the federal government; at the same time the various State governments are often not particularly active in legislating in this field, frequently because of a desire to retain the economic advantage the goods of a State possess in trade within the federation by reason of the lower wage which unorganized workers in the State are obliged to accept. Where there are extensive powers given to the federal government, as in the case of the Weimar Constitution, they are not always fully used by the central authorities, by reason of the nature of collective bargaining relations in the country, or else the burden of administering and even legislating in the field is left to the States under general supervision of the federal government in a system in which the constitutional jurisdiction over the problems is concurrent.

D. *Labor Exchanges and the Mobility of Labor*

Of the major federal states, only Germany possesses specific constitutional provisions authorizing the federal government to legislate with respect to labor offices.   In the Weimar Constitution, Article 7, listing the concurrent powers, authorized the federal government to concern itself with such offices.   Likewise in the Bonn Basic Law a provision relating to the federal government's power over labor placement is to be found in Article 74 listing the concurrent powers.   In the other federal systems, that is, the older ones, what activity the federal governments have engaged in with respect to labor placement has been by way of some other power.   The new Canadian Dominion power over unemployment insurance, however, granted in a 1940 amendment to the Constitution, is there so intimately related historically to employment exchanges that the new amendment can almost be said to apply specifically to exchanges as well.   The general characteristic of federal-state relations in this field is that whatever the form of federal activity, the States are in fact everywhere charged with the task of actually operating the labor exchanges, although this is not completely true in the new Canadian system.   It seems to be almost a general rule that once there has been an acceptance throughout a country of the principle of public exchanges, thereafter the whole field is removed from the arena of political dispute and comes to be thought of as a service function in which the role of the federal government is to facilitate the movement of labor from employment in one State to employment in another, and to subsidize the State operation of the labor exchanges.   There is perhaps a certain resistance to federal activity on the part of State politicians anxious to maintain control over appointments to administrative positions in the State employment service, but this is usually outweighed by the inducement value of federal moneys.   There was great resistance for example in Australia to the establishment of a Commonwealth supervision over labor exchanges until the establishment, after the Japanese attack in December, 1941, of a Manpower Directorate administratively independent of the Commonwealth Minister of Labour.

Where there is no direct constitutional provision authorizing federal activity in this field, the usual procedure has been to rely upon the federation's power to appropriate moneys and to establish a grant-in-aid program under which the States accept a general administrative control of varying strictness in exchange for subsidization of a part, usually about half, of the administrative cost of the program.   In the case of Switzerland, where labor offices are all cantonal, the federal decree of October 29, 1909, concerning the federal encouragement of cantonal placement services, appears, on the basis of the accompanying message, to have depended for its validity on the provisions of Article 2 of the Constitution under which the Confederation is entrusted with the responsibility of increasing the common prosperity of the cantons.   In Canada, the old 1918 Public Employment Offices Coordination Act provided for a nation-wide system of public employment offices, with the offices to be established by the Provinces, and the expenses to be subsidized up to 50 per cent in the case of each Province. There was no constitutional reason why the Dominion should not have exerted leadership in the operation of these labor offices by carrying out research, labor market surveys, or performing educational work on behalf of the provincial agencies, but the fact is that the Dominion contented itself with a simple audit control. One exception to this general Dominion passivity was the establishment by the Dominion government of two interprovincial clearing houses which it itself operated at Ottawa and Winnipeg for the purpose of aiding in the distribution to provincial exchanges of information as to available jobs throughout the federation and of surplus labor. In operating these clearing houses, the Dominion government had power to require statistical and other information on employment conditions from any person or firm. In 1940, after the amendment of the British North America Act in that year to give the Dominion power over unemployment insurance, a new Dominion employment service was provided for to aid in the administration of unemployment insurance and also to fulfill the normal functions of labor exchanges. Since that time, the provincial labor exchanges have been closed everywhere except in Quebec. The United States program emphasizes a much greater federal assistance in operations, with special attention to aiding employees of the State exchanges to keep abreast of new ideas in counseling, new trends in industry, and the movement of the economy, especially with regard to long-range employment prospects. There is a stricter control by the American federal government over personnel policies in the local offices, and the establishment of an acceptable merit system by the States is required as a condition for continuation of the grant-in-aid. Otherwise, the offices are State offices affiliated with the United States Employment Service. In Germany, the responsibility for administering the employment exchanges rests now, as it did in Weimar Germany, with the State governments who appoint the personnel of the Labor Offices and see to their financing. However, the federal Minister of Labor has the power to issue administrative regulations, especially with regard to reporting procedures to be followed by the State labor offices.

During wartime, as might be expected, the degree of federal activity over labor exchange centers increases. In the United States, the federal government acting under its war powers assumed direct operational control of the State agencies, and their titles were changed to United States Employment Service offices. After the war's close the operational control of the offices was returned to the States. During the period of federal operation the offices were controlled by all pertinent federal regulations affecting federal agencies. There was no compulsory employment reference during the Second World War in the United States, but the Employment Services did have certain control responsibilities under which skilled workers were prevented from moving about without compelling reason from one plant engaged in vital war work to another so engaged. In Canada during the demobilization period after the first World War, when provincial employment exchanges were not yet as numerous as they were by the time of the

Second World War, the Dominion government, acting under the War Measures Act, authorized the Dominion Minister of Labour to establish employment offices where none was operated by a provincial government. Under this power offices were established in New Brunswick, Nova Scotia, and Prince Edward Island, and an interprovincial clearing house was established at Moncton. We have already noted the establishment of a Commonwealth Employment Service in Australia during the Second World War, and under this service compulsory labor direction did take place, being upheld by the High Court as a valid exercise of the Commonwealth's war powers. Much greater autonomy appears to have been left to the State services than was the case in the United States, but this was not, constitutionally speaking, necessary.

One other item might be mentioned under this heading, as the nature of manpower distribution in Western Europe must necessarily cause some thought to be given to the question of whether an absolutely free movement of labor ought to be permitted in the federal system. In the United States, the Supreme Court has already decided, in the recent case of *Edwards v. California,* 314 U. S. 160 (1941), that the States are forbidden to establish economic criteria for judging whether a citizen of the United States should be permitted to enter a State. Such attempts on the part of a State to exclude the indigent, the Court held in its controlling opinion, constituted unwarranted regulation by the States of interstate commerce and were therefore invalid. Other members of the Court, while agreeing with the decision, thought that a wiser course in declaring the State actions void would have been to declare that free movement from one State to another was a privilege and immunity of United States citizens. The Bonn Basic Law contains the only constitutional provision to be found among the major federal powers which authorizes some control of movement of citizens of the Republic from one State to another. Article 11 declares that "all Germans shall enjoy freedom of movement throughout the federal territory." But then it goes on to modify this by providing that "this right may be restricted only by legislation and only for the cases in which an adequate basis of existence is absent and, as a result, particular burdens would arise for the general public or in which it is necessary for the protection of juveniles from neglect, for combating the danger of epidemics, or in order to prevent criminal acts." It would appear from the existence of a similar provision in the Weimar Constitution (Article 111, that this article in the Bonn Basic Law means that any control over interstate movement of persons should be imposed by the federal government, not by the localities. In the German Imperial Constitution of 1871, however, Article III provided that those regulations which were concerned with the care of the poor and their admission into local parishes (Gemeindeverbände) were not to be affected by the provision that a person belonging to one of the confederated States must be treated in every other State as a native. It would certainly seem that the movement of populations within the Western European federation could be controlled only by the federal government, if the principles of federalism requiring a certain uniformity in such matters are to be maintained. It is conceivable that for a temporary, transitional period, however, entrance might be limited by the States to prevent a swamping of their labor markets by labor moving from surplus labor areas.

As far as labor exchange is concerned and the operation of employment offices, it would seem again, as has been the case with the other labor matters already considered, that a regard for local peculiarities in the labor market and in the nature of the economy requires that some considerable degree of operational control be left to State governments. At the same time, and particularly since the movement of labor is likely to be one of the major problems of a West European federation, a general supervision is indicated in order to facilitate the pooling and the circulation of information on job openings. and labor surpluses, in order to raise the performance level of local officials in such matters as vocational guidance, and in order to raise the administrative efficiency of labor offices to the highest possible level. It would seem therefore that the wisest course is to make jurisdiction over labor exchange and the operation of employment offices a concurrent responsibility of the federal and State governments, while insuring by some provision such as that of Article 72 in the Bonn Basic Law that federal activity does not go beyond the bounds of the requirements of the federation.

III. SOCIAL INSURANCE

We include under "social insurance" these kinds of insurance: sickness; accident; old-age and survivors; invalidity; and unemployment.

The treatment of social insurances in the major federal constitutions is of three types. In some constitutions, specifically the American, there is no mention whatever of social insurance. In others, for example, the Australian, and lately the Canadian, one or a few but not all the forms of social insurance are recognized and jurisdiction over them allotted. Third, in some constitutions, provision is made for all types of social insurance; in the case of Switzerland all five forms are mentions in provisions scattered throughout the constitution; on the other hand, there are constitutions such as Weimar and the Bonn Basic Law, in which social insurance is mentioned as a category in which there is no particular mention of any of the various types of insurance, with one small exception.

As far as legislation and administration of social insurance matters are concerned we may observe that there exist practically as many patterns of division of legislative and administrative responsibility, whether imposed by the Constitution itself or by legislative arrangement, as there are major federal systems. In some cases, such as that of Weimar Germany, the federal government had complete legislative authority over all the branches of social insurance we are considering. But in fact a certain legislative latitude was left in the case of one of these, unemployment insurance, to the States. Again, in some cases the federal government has responsibility legislatively and administratively over a few types of social insurance, but the rest of the types remain the legislative and administrative responsibility of the States, although in a few such cases the federal government aids the States financially.

Division of responsibility between federation and state governments is not everywhere the same. In Canada the old-age pension systems are provincial responsibilities, but the Dominion government aids the Provinces financially; in the United States, the old-age pension scheme is a national scheme of direct federal legislation and administration, while the unemployment scheme, which in Canada is federal, is in the United States a legislative and administrative responsibility of the States, although the federal government aids the States financially. Nowhere are all forms of social insurance constitutionally, legislatively, and administratively either exclusively the responsibility of the States, or exclusively the responsibility of the federal governments. Everywhere the federal government has an unshared jurisdiction over at least one of the fields, even though it may not be a jurisdiction assigned constitutionally. Everywhere the States have some responsibility, if only an administrative one. This is true also in the new Bonn Basic Law (Art. 74 (12)), where jurisdiction over social insurance matters, including unemployment insurance, is a part of the list of concurrent powers. Though there are strong pressures for a unification of the social insurance system, it seems certain that this will not mean complete administrative control by the federal government. Tradition and the uneven economic geography of Germany would run counter to any such proposal.

In the United States, intervention by the federal government in social insurance matters has been sanctioned by the courts as a proper exercise of the Congress's power to tax for the general welfare. The Congress has thus far enacted legislation giving the federal government complete administrative control over a national system of old-age and survivors insurance. There is also legislation regarding unemployment insurance; and the rate of contributions and the general outlines of the system, including such matters as the incidence of the tax, are determined in the Congressional enactment. But for practical purposes, the old-age and survivors insurance is the only completely national program, for in the case of unemployment insurance, it is left to each State to determine such matters as the benefit rate and the conditions of eligibility for benefits, although mandatory guides are imposed by the Congress in some matters. There has been a continual criticism of the lack of a more uniform character to the American unemployment insurance program. But thus far the extremes of regional economic wealth in the United States have seemed to encourage the Congress to allow a considerable latitude to local authorities in maintaining the solvency of their particular programs. While an equalization system similar to that adopted late in the Weimar period has been proposed for the United

States, thus far it has not been given serious attention by the Congress. Another criticism has come out of the loss of credited time suffered by a worker who moves from one state to another. There is no transfer of cred- its from the State of the old employment to the new state, and this situa- tion has prompted proposals for the establishment of such a credit system. Accident and invalidity insurance are left to the States, although there is no reason to believe this is constitutionally necessary. A sickness insur- ance program is now strongly urged by some political leaders in the United States. There are no State programs in the sickness insurance field. The federal government aids States by grants-in-aid to maintain such pro- grams as old-age assistance, for those not covered by the pension scheme; widows and orphans aid; aid to the blind and physically handicapped. These of course are more in the nature of welfare than insurance.

In Canada, the Dominion government's entry into the social insurance field came by way of the indirect financial aid device in the old-age in- surance field. In 1930, without having obtained any constitutional change, the Dominion government undertook to provide to the Provinces 75 per cent of the funds needed for a scheme of non-contributory old-age pensions, with the Provinces administering the service. But when the Dominion de- cided in 1935 to establish a uniform nation-wide system of unemployment insurance and to do this in a direct manner, with a governing Dominion Act and essentially Dominion legislation, and no resort to the indirect, though undoubtedly constitutional, device of the grant-in-aid, the Privy Council decided that the Dominion government had exceeded its powers and that it was infringing on the Provinces' power over civil rights and property. The Privy Council did not seem to doubt the power of the Do- minion to tax, but denied its power to use money so accumulated in the way it had proposed. The Council felt that "in pith and substance the legisla- tion invaded the civil rights within the Province." In 1940 an amendment to the British North America Act was adopted under which the Dominion government was given power over unemployment insurance. Workmen's compensation, which is the principal other form of social insurance common in Canada, is exclusively in the hands of the provinces, and there is no federal function in respect to it. There is, however, a considerable uni- formity about it, with much the same administrative organization in the various Provinces, and with the employer paying the contribution. It should be noted, that, unlike the Canadian practice and the practice fol- lowed generally throughout Europe, the American unemployment insurance system is financed exclusively by employer contributions, with no partici- pation by the employee.

In Australia, the Commonwealth government by specific constitutional provision has from the beginning had power to establish a national pro- gram of old-age and invalidity insurance. In 1946 its power in the social insurance field was broadened by the adoption of an amendment authoriz- ing it to legislate for maternity allowances (although such allowances had been in effect since before the First World War); widows' pensions; child endowment; unemployment; pharmaceutical, sickness, and hospital benefits; medical and dental services; and family allowances. Legislation has since been enacted to cover a number of these, and the whole program is to be financed by contributions to the National Welfare Fund. This places the program more in the insurance category, unlike the old-age and invalidity schemes which were financed out of the general treasury, and were operated on the basis of need, rather than of right.

In Switzerland, the federal government was granted power to legislate in the fields of accident and sickness insurance, old-age and invalidity insurance, and, in 1947, unemployment insurance, by constitutional amendment. However, in order to aid in the cantonal assistance to those sick who are for one reason or another not covered by the federal program, the federal government also provides grant-in-aid assistance. Similar aid is given to the cantons for the operation of their unemployment insurance programs.

The Austrian program of social insurance is so similar to the German that there is no reason to dwell on it, except to point out one problem the federal government has encountered in legislating on it. Under an act of 1921 the compulsory sickness insurance program which had first been enacted in 1888 was extended to cover agricultural workers. However, the State government of Salzburg contested the law on the grounds that the Constitution's placing of legislation over agriculture and forestry in that category for which only the broad legislative principles might be provided by the federal government, with the details to be enacted by provincial legislatures, meant that a uniform sickness insurance program covering industrial workers could not be extended automatically by the federal government to include farm workers. The Constitutional Court in 1924 agreed with this argument and the States were then left to adopt their own legislation in this matter. While the diet of the State of Vienna adopted a duplicate of the federal law, in other States laws were adopted which contained provisions less favorable to agricultural workers than the federal law.

With the adoption of an unemployment insurance law by the German government in 1927, that country completed coverage of the social insurance field as it is considered in this study. In terms of federal-state relations, there was on the whole a strong centralization of both legislative and administrative power in the hands of the federal government. It should be recognized, however, that the self-governing features of much of the German administrative activity in this field, with administration being carried out initially in a multitude of private organizations, reduced governmental activity considerably below what might have been expected in terms of the scope of the program. The special history of unemployment legislation, dating from the demobilization period after the First World War, made administration in this area somewhat unusual and of considerable interest to students seeking ways of establishing a general, if not uniform, social insurance program in a Western European federal system. Under the 1927 statute, benefits were uniform throughout the Reich, but the determination of rates of contribution by the employer and employee were left to the individual States, within limits imposed by the federal government which established an overall federal maximum rate. This maximum was composed of the federally determined contribution rate, proceeds from which went into the federal fund for use as reserve and for equalization purposes; it also was composed of another factor, this being the State-determined contribution rate. This could be whatever the State authorities determined, but it could not be such as to raise the combined federal and State contribution rate above the federal maximum rate. Ultimately this maximum rate was 6½ percent. The federal contribution rate was determined on the basis of requirements for building and maintaining a reserve large enough to guarantee compensation for 600,000 unemployed for three months. Should the individual States find themselves unable to finance benefits because of an economic crisis they could call upon the statutory reserve for aid. The States were controlled by three conditions: one half of any local surplus had to be turned over to the Federal Unemployment Insurance Institute, so keeping the rate of contributions set by the State from being too high; the combined State and federal levy could not exceed the federal maximum rate, also a control on the top level of the State rate; and any State deficit incurred while the State rate was lower than the maximum authorized might not be federally financed, which kept the State authorities from setting the rate too low. Such a scheme was designed to deal with the problem of seasonal unemployment in some areas, particularly rural, and cyclical unemployment in others, such as the industrial, without obliging the respective areas to resort to excessively high contribution rates. The rapid advent of the depression and the subsequent downfall of the Republic made it impossible to test such a scheme in practice, although its general validity seemed clear to most students.

The Western European nations making up the area that might be covered in a federal union all have social insurance systems that are now, particularly since the war, broad in their coverage, if not of equal strength in the rate of benefits. The movement of labor from one part of the union to another, some of it permanent and some for seasonal employment, will mean, in itself, that one of the most vexing long-run problems to face the Western European legislator and administrator will be that of social insurance. Because of the long history of seasonal labor migration, there is already a considerable fund of international European experience in such matters as the transfer of credits, and we may expect that this experience will be called upon to guide the legislators of the union after its establishment. This of course does not even take into account such pressures for a uniform social insurance program as might well be expected to arise throughout the union if in time the psychological unity of the area is strengthened, mobility of citizens becomes easier, and their adaptation to life in new parts of the union easier. In such circumstances, the need for a more uniform or for a completely reciprocal system of social insurance will be felt strongly. At the same time, the varying economic qualities of the several areas which will make up the federal union will dictate the maintenance of a considerable degree of local autonomy in this field. This is particularly true, in addition, when we take into account the long history of some of the social insurance systems, and the diversity of lower-level organization that exists from one part of Western Europe to another. For example, it should not be expected that the long-developed and jealously guarded autonomy of German sickness insurance programs will easily be surrendered in favor of a uniform administrative regulation from the center of a new federal union. The solution seems to be again, as it has been in all the matters with which we have dealt in this study, to assign the jurisdiction over social insurance to both the federal and the State governments in the new union, with only such restrictions on the federal government as will be common to all those powers which are assigned to it as part of a concurrent list.

IV. Summary

In no federation is labor an exclusive function of the federation government. On the other hand, it is nowhere left exclusively in the hands of the States.

In expanding industrial economies the rise of associations of workers and of employers that link together men working or managing industry in places perhaps thousands of miles removed from each other has been accompanied by the growth of political pressures that have been productive of legislation at the national level. In older federations, such as that of the United States, the originally agricultural bias of the economy is still reflected in the lack of any specific Constitutional provisions applying to labor matters or to social insurance. Here the entrance of the federal government into the labor field has been accomplished by appeal to other Constitutional powers possessed by it from the beginning. This has been done against often serious opposition and in the face of arguments holding that the original balance between the central government and the States was being jeopardized. In some federations where legislative attempts to enlarge federal jurisdiction over labor and social insurance matters were negatived by action of the controlling institutional devices, for example, judicial decision in Canada, Australia, and the United States, the efforts of the proponents of such moves were then turned to attempts to modify the constitution. These were not always successful.

In some federations where the federal government is one of assigned powers, the very fact of its having been given a specific labor function in the original constitution, and the very specificity of the grant, have become obstacles to the later enlargement through legislation of the federal government's new powers. This was the case in Australia.

In the more recently established federal systems, such as the German, the original national legislative power over labor and social insurance matters has been made much more extensive by the constitutional authors than in the older systems. But in Germany, the nature of the administrative system differs so from older federal systems that, following the general pattern of extensive local administration of federal functions, the major responsibility for executing federal labor legislation has been vested in the localities, though under the general supervision of federal officers. Of course, the provincial authorities have not been excluded in the first instance from a potential share in legislative responsibility in labor matters, for in Germany the subject of labor is considered, at least to a considerable degree, to be under the concurrent jurisdiction of the federal and provincial governments, though the Bonn Basic Law protects the interests of the State from unwarranted federal usurpation more fully than was the case under the Weimar Constitution.

However, a study of constitutional provisions alone or even of decisions by judicial bodies will not suffice to portray federal-state relations in respect to labor and social insurance matters. The formal division of powers is in many cases modified by arrangements of a cooperative kind that have often come into being and grown without their initiators being aware of the constitutional-structural implications of what they were doing. In the field of labor exchange, federal authorities have established information services to serve as clearing houses for manpower information and as coordinating centers for the operations of agencies themselves, furnishing guidance in such matters as administration, vocational counseling, and other technical fields. In the area of social insurance, even where the federal government has not assumed sole responsibility it has exercised the power it always possesses, to tax and spend, in order to aid State systems of insurance in an effort to attain some uniformity of benefits and provisions among the systems.

A P P E N D I X I

Australia

General Constitutional Provisions

In its original form, the Australian Commonwealth Constitution of 1900–1901 included only two provisions respecting the relation of government, whether Commonwealth or State, to labor problems. These provisions were both part of Section 51 respecting the powers of the Commonwealth Parliament. Placitum (xxiii) provided:

51. The Parliament shall, subject to this Constitution, have power to make laws for the peace, order, and good government of the Commonwealth with respect to:
   (xxiii) Invalid and old-age pensions:

Placitum (xxxv) provided:

Conciliation and arbitration for the prevention and settlement of industrial disputes extending beyond the limits of any one State.

Some political leaders in Australia have felt that the framers of the Constitution were unwise to include such a specific statement of the Commonwealth's powers regarding labor and social insurance, and the High Court has on a number of occasions in fact declared labor legislation of the Commonwealth to be *ultra vires* and has seemed to view the granting of these constitutional powers as limitations on activity by the Commonwealth Parliament in other labor fields. It is nonetheless a fact that use has been made of placitum (xxxv) to extend the functions of Commonwealth instrumentalities far beyond the simple role of mediation or arbitration in labor disputes. For example, the whole Australian wage system, in so far as covered in the orbit of federal activities, depends on decisions of conciliation and arbitration tribunals.

Very recently, the powers of the Commonwealth in the field of social insurance have been expanded by way of constitutional amendment, although it cannot in fact yet be said that the Australian system for providing for the aged, the ill, and the other usual categories constitutes insurance. Indeed, many Australian leaders prefer to think of the establishment of an insurance system of aid to these categories as undesirable and are pointing rather to the organization of a comprehensive scheme of social services which will not be self-financing.

I. Labor Relations

A. *Trade Union and Employers Organizations*

The Australian Constitution contains neither a general clause protecting a right of assembly and association from governmental intervention nor the more specific provision found in some constitutions (such as that of Weimar Germany) protecting the right of workers and employers to organize for the advancement of their respective purposes. It is through the legislation of the individual Australian States that the actual freedom of workers to organize into trade unions, to bargain collectively, and to conduct collective activities in the advancement of their aims is protected from such interference as troubles the labor unions in Britain because of the existence of the ancient common law doctrines of conspiracy and because of the old right of affected employers to bring civil action for damages against trade unions following a strike or other collective action.

Beyond this, however, the Commonwealth government undertakes to protect the individual worker from discrimination against him by the employer for reason of the worker's trade union membership, officeholding, or activity. This protection is afforded under the provisions of the Commonwealth Conciliation and Arbitration Act of 1904, as amended. This Act was passed under the provisions of placitum (xxxv) of Section 51 of the Commonwealth Constitution.

It should be noted further that an additional protection is accorded a member of the trade union by the Act against illegal actions of trade union officers. The Act provides, for example, that any union registered under it with the Commonwealth Conciliation and Arbitration Court must comply in its rules with certain requirements, including. such as govern the time and manner of electing officers, the manner in which meetings are to be called, and the manner in which industrial agreements are to be drawn up on behalf of the association.

The Conciliation and Arbitration Act also protects the organization of employers and provides for registration of such organizations voluntarily before the conciliation and arbitration tribunal. The Conciliation and Arbitration Court has deemed itself vested with a responsibility to encourage the organization of both employers and employees into their respective representative bodies (*Federated Engine Drivers and Firemen's Association v. Broken Hill Pottery Co. Ltd.*, 5 C.A.R. 9 (1911). It is believed by the Court that without such organizations on both sides the system of arbitration and of industrial agreements would be unworkable.

B. *Conciliation and Arbitration*

One of the most serious labor disputes in Australian history was the Maritime (dockers) strike of 1890, and for some four years thereafter Australia experienced a succession of strikes such as had not been seen previously in her history. When the Australian Constitutional Convention met toward the end of that decade, there seems to have been a willingness in all parties, including generally the trade unionists, to accept some scheme for ensuring industrial peace. What resulted was the constitutional provision we have noted and the Conciliation and Arbitration Act, 1904.

The chief objects of the 1904 Act, according to its Section 1, were "to prevent lockouts and strikes in relation to industrial disputes," to encourage the settling of disputes by conciliation, to provide for their determination by arbitration of a judicial body, and "to facilitate and encourage the organization of representative bodies of employers and employees."

Section 6 of the Act, as it stood in its 1928 version, provided specifically: "no person or organization shall, on account of any industrial dispute, do anything in the nature of a lock-out or strike, or continue any lock-out or strike." A heavy financial penalty might be imposed for violation of this provision. In 1930 this absolute prohibition on strikes was repealed, although the arbitration and conciliation tribunal still possesses power to punish those who strike in contravention of its awards.

Under the terms of the early versions of the Act, not only did the Conciliation and Arbitration Court established by the Act have the task of judging disputes brought to it by contending parties or referred to it by public authorities, but it had the positive function of seeking out disputes over which the tribunal might have jurisdiction and of working to end these disputes without judicial intervention. The court's function was therefore not only judicial, but conciliatory as well. In 1947 a major revision was effected in the provisions of the Act with the primary purpose of making possible a more rapid termination of disputes. Conciliation Commissioners had for some years been a part of the system, and now these were given the authority to make final and non-appealable decisions in all matters formerly reserved to the Conciliation and Arbitration Court, such as matters of piecework, or the "privileges, rights and duties of employers and employees," except for the four following categories still reserved to the Court itself (§13, 1947 version of the Act):

(a) standard hours of work in an industry;
(b) basic wage or the principles upon which it is computed;
(c) period which shall be granted as annual leave with pay;
(d) minimum rate of remuneration for adult females in an industry.

The jurisdiction of the Conciliation and Arbitration Court extends, first, to those disputes having a public interest and which extend beyond the limits of a single State. The High Court of the Commonwealth has been quite specific on the requirements which must be met before a dispute can be considered as "extending beyond the limits of any one State." The essential features were laid down in the *Federated Sawmillers* case, 8 C.L.R. 465 (1909):

> It [the term "extending beyond the limits etc.] connotes something in the nature of industrial war existing or threatening extending from one State to another State. . . . There must be a real community of action on the part of the demandants, and some community of action on the part of the parties on whom the demand is made . . . If it is found that large bodies of men in two or more States are in fact acting with one accord, then, if the other elements of an industrial dispute are present, an occasion arises for the exercise of the federal power in question.
>
> The dispute must be actually existing and actually extending beyond the limits of one State before such an occasion can arise. Mere mischief-makers cannot, therefore, by the expenditure of a few shillings in paper, ink, and postage stamps create such an occasion.

Further, until the 1947 version of the Act, the Court might intervene and decide in those industrial disputes "with which any State industrial authority, or the Governor-in-Council of a State in which there is no State industrial authority, requests the Court to deal" (§19 (c), 1928 version). An example of a "State industrial authority" would be the State conciliation and arbitration courts which exist in most of the States and which have jurisdiction over those disputes not coming within the Commonwealth Court's jurisdiction. This provision does not appear in the 1947 version of the Act.

It is of interest to observe that the Act provides that disputes between the workers and the management in an industry carried on by or under the control or authority of a State also are brought within the scope of the functions of the Conciliation Commissioners and the Conciliation and Arbitration Court (§4, 1947 version). This extension of the Act has been upheld in a number of decisions of the Australian High Court, notably *Merchant Service Guild v. Commonwealth S.S. Owners Association,* 28 C.L.R. 436 (1920).

The constitutionally valid operations of the Court have received special protection from the interference of State bodies. Section 27 (1) of the 1947 version of the Act provides:

> If it appears to the [Commonwealth] Court that any State industrial authority is dealing or about to deal with an industrial dispute, with part of an industrial dispute or with a matter which is provided for in an award of the Court or is the subject of proceedings before the Court, the Court may make such order restraining the State authority from dealing with that dispute or any part thereof . . . and thereupon the [State] authority shall, in accordance with that order, cease to proceed in the dispute or part thereof or in that matter.

Section 27 (2) provides further:

> Any award, order or determination of a State industrial authority made in contravention of an order made under this section shall, to the extent of the contravention, be void.

With two sets of judicial authorities operating, and with the standard of jurisdiction being not function but that of a dispute in a geographical area, it often happens that the same employer will be faced by two standards for dealing with his workers or a part of them. In the early days, such a question of the responsibility of the employer who might be faced by two awards respecting his employees, one from the State arbitration tribunal and the other from the Commonwealth Court, was treated by the Australian High Court so that the employer was obliged to abide by both awards simultaneously, yielding in cases of irresolvable conflict by paying the higher wages prescribed. However, in the case of *Clyde Engineering v. Cowburn,* 37 C.L.R. 466 (1926), it was finally held that the test of inconsistency was whether the Commonwealth purported to cover the same field as that claimed by the State award. If it did, then the State award was to yield to the degree inconsistent.

By an amendment of 1911 the jurisdiction of the Commonwealth Court was enlarged to include agricultural and other rural industries, provided always of course that the dispute was one extending beyond the limits of a single State. The word "industry" now includes "any business, trade, manufacture, undertaking, or calling of employers" (Conciliation and Arbitration Act, 1904–1950, §4).

Stated briefly, what the Conciliation and Arbitration Act makes possible is the conciliation, and if need be the determination, under federal auspices of any industrial dispute coming within the federal authority's powers and believed to be of more than a trivial nature, and in which conciliation and arbitration would be in the public interest. The Court however has followed the policy of not forcing upon an employer and employees an award which neither of them wants.

One source of industrial dispute, the jurisdictional conflict between unions, has been largely eliminated through the provision of the Act (§82, 1950 version) providing: "The Registrar [of the Court] shall . . . refuse to register any association as an organization if an organization, to which the members of the association might conveniently belong, has already been registered." In reading this section, it should be borne in mind that the Court also has the task of ensuring that there is compliance in the activities of a registered association with the provisions of the association's charter, and that the charter conforms to the standards mentioned earlier. It should also be borne in mind that registration with the Court gives to the organization distinct advantages over an unregistered organization, including the very right to present a controversy before the Court. Finally, it cannot be forgotten that whatever compulsory powers the Court possesses are applicable only to parties registered with it.

C. *Emergency Peacetime Legislation*

For dealing with labor emergencies in peacetime that are affecting or threatening to affect interstate or foreign transport or the operating of some service provided by the Commonwealth, there exist Sections 30J and 30K of the Commonwealth Crimes Act, 1914, as amended. Section 30J reads: "If at any time the Governor-General is of opinion that there exists a serious industrial disturbance prejudicing or threatening trade or commerce with other countries or among the states he may make a Proclamation to that effect, which Proclamation shall be and remain in operation for the purposes of this situation until it is revoked."

If after such proclamation any person takes part in, continues, or incites a lockout or strike in an enterprise concerned with interstate or foreign transport, he is liable to punishment by imprisonment.

Section 30K applies to incitements of strikes in the public service of the Commonwealth or to the hindering of such service, and provides for punishment of persons violating the section.

D. *Labor Disputes in Wartime*

During World War II, industrial Peace Regulations were issued under the terms of the National Security Act of 1939 which was enacted under the authority of placitum (vi) of Section 51 of the Constitution which provides that the Commonwealth Parliament shall have power with respect to "the naval and military defense of the Commonwealth and of the several

States, and the control of the forces to execute and maintain the laws of the Commonwealth." Under the terms of the Industrial Peace Regulations, December, 1940, the provisions of the Commonwealth Conciliation and Arbitration Act were to be construed so that the Court or the Conciliation Commissioners would no longer be restricted to acting with respect to disputes "which extend beyond the limits of any one state." Rather, Section 5 provided: "The court shall also have cognizance of all industrial disputes — (a) which the Court is satisfied are, or which the Minister certifies to the Court as being proper to be dealt with in the interests of industrial peace and national security." These regulations were continued in force for some years after the war.

E. *Federal-State Coordination of Conciliation and Arbitration Activities*

Since its amendment in 1928, the Conciliation and Arbitration Act has included a provision to stimulate improved Commonwealth-State relations in the area of conciliation and arbitration through the device of conferences looking to coordination. As it stands in the 1947 version of the Act, Section 52 reads:

> Where it appears to the Court or a Conciliation Commissioner to be desirable, in relation to an industrial matter, that a conference should be held with a State Industrial Authority, it or he may, if that Authority is willing, confer with that Authority with a view to securing coordination between any orders or awards made or to be made under this Act and any orders, awards, decisions or determinations made or given or to be made or given by that Authority.

II. WAGES AND HOURS AND FACTORY INSPECTION
A. *Wages and Hours*

The principal governmental device for the regulation of wages and hour conditions in establishments brought under Commonwealth jurisdiction is the judgment or award of the Commonwealth Court of Conciliation and Arbitration in the specific disputes brought before it by contending industrial and trade union representatives. It is also by way of the jurisdiction granted the Commonwealth in Section 51, placitum (xxxv) of the Constitution quoted above, over conciliation and arbitration, that the given enterprises affected by awards of the Court are brought within the frame of Commonwealth functions. In other words, there is no Commonwealth legislation fixing a specific minimum wage, or granting to any body a power to establish a flat minimum wage for Australian industry generally. What happens is that the Conciliation and Arbitration Court makes an award in specific disputes. But the effect of these awards spreads out through all industry, either by reason of the accumulation of awards or because a par-

ticular award is made in a key case. The Court of Conciliation and Arbitration expressed the situation well in its forty-hour week decision in
Printing Industry Employees Union v. Balmoral Press and Ors., decided in
September, 1947, and the words of the Court are applicable to the wage
situation as well as to the hour problem with which the Court was dealing:

> While it is true that the limit of the constitutional power of the
> Court is to settle only the particular disputes before it, within their
> respective ambits, experience has shown that its decision in relation to
> a question of standard hours will, in the long run, lead to uniform
> standard hours throughout Australia. The powers of the Court, there-
> fore, in relation to the fixation of standard hours are in form arbitral,
> but in substance legislative.

In the Act of 1904 power was given the Court to establish a minimum rate
in a given dispute (§40a). But within a few years a new concept, the
basic wage, was introduced by the Court, specifically in the 1907 *Harvester*
judgment of Justice Higgins (*Ex Parte H. V. McKay*, 2 C.A.R. 1). The
basic wage is the lowest wage that may legally be paid to an employee in a
given geographical area. The minimum wage is the lowest wage payable to
employees (workers) in a particular industry. Of course, within a given
area it will be at least as high as the basic wage. Until 1931 it appears that
the Court thought of the basic wage as a family wage, that is, a minimum
amount necessary to provide the reasonable necessaries of life for the family
of an unskilled laborer, the assumption being that such a family consisted
of a father, mother, and three children. The view of the Court seemed to
be then that any enterprise which could not pay this amount ought not to
remain in business. However, since 1931 the Court has operated on the
principle that the basic wage is the highest amount to which the productivity
standard existing in an area will permit the floor of the wage schedule
in an industry to be set, and that as productivity increases, the basic wage
should increase. But in fact, there has been a continued relationship of
the basic wage to the cost-of-living index as well as to the productivity capacity of Australian industry. The real situation therefore is that the Court
seeks to adjust its awards in terms both of purchasing power and the productive capacity of an industry, seeking to give all wage earners a basic wage
with the same purchasing power wherever they may live.

During World War II the enlarged jurisdiction of the Court, discussed
in Section I above, led also in the case of wages to an expansion of the
impact of the Court's awards, with many more workers being brought into
the coverage of the Court's awards.

What has been said of wages above applies equally to hours.

The Conciliation and Arbitration Court sought very early to exercise a
direct effect on general wage standards rather than the indirect effect that
has come to be characteristic. This it sought to do by the "common-rule"
system under which wage prescriptions imposed in a particular case arising

out of a specific dispute would be extended by fiat and without further hearings to other workers not engaged in the dispute but similarly situated as regards geographical location, type of work, skill, and so on. In 1910, the Commonwealth High Court declared this essay invalid (*Australian Boot Trade Employees' Federation v. Whybrow & Co.*, 11 C.L.R. 311). However, the clause in the Act authorizing the Court to operate on the common-rule principle was never actually dropped. In the 1950 version of the Act there is a restatement of the common-rule power by which the legislator sought to avoid the defects of the original provision by relating the common-rule decree to the efforts to avoid industrial disputes:

> The Court or a Conciliation Commissioner may, if it appears to be necessary or expedient for the purpose of preventing or settling an industrial dispute which comes before it or him or of preventing further industrial disputes, declare by an order or award that any term of an order or award shall be a common rule of any industry in connexion with which the dispute arose [§41 (1)].

During World War II the Commonwealth Government also decreed National Security (Female Minimum Rates) Regulations by which it was ordered:

> Notwithstanding anything contained in any law of the Commonwealth or of any State or territory of the Commonwealth or in any award . . . or industrial agreement, the rate of remuneration to which any female employed in any occupation within a vital industry shall be entitled, in respect of the normal weekly hours worked . . . shall be (a). . . . not less than seventy-five per centum of the corresponding minimum male rate [§4A (1)].

B. *Factory Inspection*

In time of peace the responsibility for the prescription of health, sanitation, and safety standards and the inspection of factories to ensure their adherence to these standards is exclusively a State responsibility. During World War II, however, the Commonwealth. Parliament undertook to use the defense provisions of the Constitution, mentioned above, to enact the Women's Employment Regulations under which employers in any enterprise in Australia proposing to employ women to do work usually employed by men or in a task not previously existing were required to obtain the permission of a Commonwealth Board. The Board had power to decide whether women would be so employed, the hours during which they might work, and had power to decree such special safety, health, or welfare conditions respecting their labor as it might choose. The Board had the right (§14) to give permission in the case of factories engaged in munitions (war material) work, notwithstanding anything contained to the contrary in the laws of the State.

It should be observed that an attempt to apply these regulations in the case of women employed in purely governmental activities of the States or local governments was held to be beyond the defense powers of the Commonwealth (*Rex v. Commonwealth Court of Conciliation and Arbitration, ex parte State of Victoria*, 68 C.L.R. 485 (1944)).

Other attempts on the part of the Commonwealth government to intrude in wartime into the factory inspection area normally reserved to the States were made by way of various defense regulations. While many of these Commonwealth regulatory prescriptions were validated by the High Court as logical corollaries of the defense powers, the Court did reject a few attempts, and, in so doing, did begin to sketch something of a line of demarcation beyond which the defense power might not carry the Commonwealth government. In the Holiday Case, for example (*State of Victoria v. Commonwealth*, 66 C.L.R. 488 (1942)), the High Court held that an attempt by the Commonwealth to require all employees of State governments to work on holidays and to work at holiday rates of pay, regardless of the nature of their work and its relation to the defense effort, was unconstitutional. Said the Court:

> If, under the defense power, the Commonwealth can control the pay, hours and duties of all State public servants, it is obvious that the Commonwealth can take complete control of all governmental administration within Australia. The result would be the abolition in all but name of the federal system of government . . . the Constitution cannot be made to disappear because a particular power conferred by the Constitution upon the Commonwealth Parliament is exercised by that Parliament.

Similarly the High Court in the Industrial Lighting Case (*Victorian Chamber of Manufactures and the Commonwealth*, 67 C.L.R. 413 (1943)) made clear that there were limits to which the defense power could be applied in the regulation by the Commonwealth of factory conditions. In a unanimous decision, the Court said through the Chief Justice:

> No doubt good lighting is conducive to industrial efficiency, and industrial efficiency is important for the purpose of the effective prosecution of the war. But the same thing may also be said of any prescription of standards in factory conditions, or in almost any other conditions affecting human life and well-being. For example, the provision of food, clothing, housing and recreation for workers is required for full industrial efficiency. But . . . the existence of war does not result in handing over to the Commonwealth general control of those subjects. The existence of war enables the Commonwealth . . . to deal with war problems and with war-created problems, but it does not produce the result that the Commonwealth Parliament is empowered to legislate upon all subjects whatever.

In a concurring opinion, Justice Williams added that "the defense power is not a paramount power, and the Constitution does not become in time of war a unitary Constitution." He said also that "the emergencies which war creates are of an abnormal character, so that the validity of legislation which invades a domain normally reserved to the States must be judged on a basis that it can only be justified so far as it can conceivably be required to meet a temporary crisis."

C. *Labor Placement*

There are no provisions in the Australian Commonwealth Constitution directly referring to the problem of labor exchange. Prior to World War II all governmental activities respecting the operation of labor exchanges were the exclusive responsibility of the State governments. Public labor exchanges operated in each of the States as State instrumentalities, usually under the direction of the State Department of Labor. In addition such private employment services as did exist (and in some states such as Tasmania there were practically none) were subjected in many cases to licensing and inspection requirements.

It was during World War II and out of the exercise of its defense powers that the Commonwealth government first undertook to establish national direction of public employment services.

A Commonwealth Department of Labour and National Service was established in October, 1940, and on January 31, 1942, the National Security (Manpower) Regulations were issued by which it was intended "to secure that the resources of manpower and woman power in Australia shall be organized and applied in the best possible way to meet the requirements of the Defense Force and the needs of industry in the production of munitions and the maintenance of supplies and services essential to the life of the community" (§3).

The authority for these regulations was the National Security Act, 1939–40, and specifically its Section 13A which provided that the Governor-General might make such regulations as appeared to him necessary and expedient for requiring persons to place themselves, their services, and their property at the disposal of the Commonwealth when the defense of the Commonwealth required.

It was the intention of the Manpower Regulations that in establishing a Commonwealth supervision of the utilization of manpower full use should be made of existing State Employment Exchanges:

The Minister [for Labour and National Service] may, on the recommendation of the Director-General, establish and maintain National Service Offices at such places as he thinks fit, and is hereby authorized to use, in accordance with arrangements made between the Commonwealth and the States for that purpose, as he thinks necessary, the services or officers of any organization, undertaking, or Government Department in any State.

At first reluctant, the States, after the adoption of these Regulations and the appointment as Director-General of Manpower of a former high State official popular with other State officers, made their facilities available to the Commonwealth government.

Under these wartime Regulations the control over employable persons in the Commonwealth was theoretically complete. The Director-General had power, under Section 15 of the Regulations, to "direct any person resident in Australia to engage in employment under the direction and control of the employer specified in the direction, or to perform work or services (whether for a specified employer or not) specified in the direction." There were of course many provisions respecting payment of wages, pension rights, and appeals from directions. The right of management to hire labor freely, while not wholly abridged, was restricted, particularly as respects employment of certain types of skilled workers by non-war industries.

After the war, the Commonwealth Employment Service was established under terms of the Re-Establishment and Employment Act, 1945. It is not clear from the terms of the Act on what constitutional authority it purports to exist, and it appears that there have as yet been no judicial tests of the validity of those sections of the Act establishing the Employment Service. However, the emphasis, in the Act's statement of the purposes for which the Service is being established, on the role the Service should play in the readjustment of former servicemen and of those engaged in industrial occupations intimately related to the war effort to peacetime pursuits, indicates a reliance on the defense powers of the Commonwealth. However this may be, the Commonwealth Employment Service is by no means restricted to aiding only in the readjustment of war personnel. It is given the task in the Act of providing "services and facilities in relation to employment for the benefit of persons seeking to become employed, to change employment or to engage labour, to provide facilities to assist in bringing about and maintaining a high and stable level of employment throughout the Commonwealth."

Commonwealth Employment Offices have been established now throughout Australia, and the official reports of the Commonwealth government state that with the setting up of the Commonwealth Employment Service most of the State Labor Exchange organizations have ceased to function.

Registration with the Commonwealth Employment Service is voluntary on the part of both the employer and the person seeking work. In addition to allocation functions, the Employment Offices have the task of giving occupational advice and vocational guidance to those seeking it.

III. Social Insurance

In its original form the Australian Constitution contained one provision clearly authorizing the Commonwealth government to operate insurance programs in two fields, and another provision which, it was thought by some students, might be used as warrant for the extension of Commonwealth social insurance schemes into other fields.

The first of these provisions was placitum (xxiii) of Section 51, which stated that the Parliament should have power to make laws "for the peace, order, and good government of the Commonwealth with respect to invalid and old age pensions."

The second provision, which has not been applied in the social insurance area, is placitum (xiv) of Section 51, providing that the Commonwealth Parliament should have powers with respect to "insurance, other than state insurance; also state insurance extending beyond the limits of the State concerned."

Commonwealth old-age pensions were introduced in 1909 and invalidity pensions adopted in 1910. In neither case was the pension scheme contributory; in both cases payment of the pension was subject to a means test; aliens were not covered in the scheme, and a long period of residence in the country was required. At the present time, these remain the general features of the old-age and invalidity schemes although these programs are now a part of the Consolidated Social Services of the Commonwealth under the system established in the Social Services Consolidation Act, 1947–1949. As a result the financing of these two programs is modified to accord with the financing of the other programs in the Consolidated Services.

In 1946 the social insurance authority of the Commonwealth was considerably broadened by the adoption of a constitutional amendment in the form of placitum (xxiiiA) to Section 51, reading that the Commonwealth Parliament might enact laws with respect to "the provision of maternity allowances, widows' pensions, unemployment, pharmaceutical, sickness and hospital benefits, medical and dental services (but not so as to authorize any form of civil conscription), benefits to students and family allowances."

Actually, a separate Widows' Pensions program, of a non-contributory nature, and not directly related to the old-age program, had already been adopted in 1942. Here too a means test was required. Similarly, an Unemployment and Sickness Benefits Act had been passed in 1944, a Maternity Allowance Act had been passed as long ago as 1912, and a Child Endowment Act and Pharmaceutical Benefits Act had been adopted in 1941. It was the invalidation by the High Court of the Commonwealth Parliament's attempt to establish a pharmaceutical benefits program on the basis of its authority to appropriate and provide for the expenditure of public money that was the immediate cause for the proposal of the new placitum (xxiiiA).

A. The Financing of the Social Services

Unlike similar programs in other countries, the financing of the social insurance programs mentioned is accomplished by way of a single fund for the whole rather than through separate funds for each program. There is good reason for saying that it is very doubtful if the old-age and invalidity systems and other systems existing before the end of World War II were really, in view of their non-contributory nature, social insurance programs. However, in 1943 the National Welfare Fund Act was adopted by the Commonwealth Parliament. Payments to finance the benefit programs of the social insurance schemes mentioned are made from this consolidated fund. The whole program is financed by a social services contribution levied on individuals at a graduated rate which in 1949 varied from 3*d*. in the pound sterling to £1.6.0. In addition, employers are required to pay a payroll tax in support of the fund. It is clear from the remarks made at the time of the introduction of this bill that its supporters were of the view that a non-contributory program was as much a social insurance program as one in which the worker and the employer, or the worker alone, financed a separate fund for each program. In effect, under the new system, neither the individual parts of the social services program nor the program as a whole is intended to be self-financing, but rather to become, at least in part, a charge upon the community as a whole. In this way, it was felt, the burden on lower-income members of the community would be lighter than if the financing of each individual program were separate and were designed to make that specific program self-supporting, or if an effort were made to have the program as a whole self-supporting. In fact, there is a tendency, particularly on the part of the Labour Party, to avoid use of the term "insurance" and speak rather of "social services."

B. *The Programs*

The old-age and invalidity programs are still substantially as described above. As with the other programs here dealt with, these are treated in the Social Services Consolidation Act, 1947–1949.

Maternity allowances were introduced in 1912. Under this scheme a flat one-time payment of £15 for the first child, and up to £17.10.0 for every child beyond the third, is paid to the mother. There is no means test.

The Child Endowment Program provides that the mother shall receive from the National Welfare Fund the sum of 10 shillings weekly for each child in her family below the age of 16 years, not counting the first child. Again, there is no means test associated with this program. It was begun in 1941.

The comprehensive Unemployment and Sickness Benefits Act was passed in 1944. Its provisions are incorporated in the Social Services Consolidation Act, 1947–1949. Under its terms persons unemployed, willing to work, and seeking work, are granted unemployment benefits of as much as £1.5.0 per week for an indefinite period. The same amounts of money are accordable for an indefinite period as sickness benefits where there has been a loss of salary, wages, or other income because of sickness or accident. Benefits received from Friendly Societies are not held to be income under the Act, and persons receiving such benefits are therefore further subsidized by the Welfare Fund as though they had no income whatever. These benefits are in addition to treatment and supplies which the ill person may receive under the Hospital Benefits Act, 1945–1947, or the Pharmaceutical Benefits Act, 1947.

The services provided under the Hospital Benefits Act, the Pharmaceutical Benefits Act and the Tuberculosis Act, 1945, are administered by the Commonwealth Department of Health. The other services described are administered in the Department of Social Services. However, the Act establishing each of these last three services provided that the funds in each case should come also from the National Welfare Fund.

In the case of the Hospital Benefits Act, 1945, a grant-in-aid scheme is authorized under which, as a result of agreement between the Minister of Health and the individual States, the Commonwealth will help to defray a portion of the cost of hospital care for persons in public and non-public wards in public hospitals. The charges to patients in non-public wards are then to be proportionately reduced, and the State commits itself to permitting the free use of public wards by residents of Australia without subjection of such persons to a means test. Provision is also made in the Act for arrangements with private hospitals.

Under the Tuberculosis Act, 1945, the Minister of Health is authorized to enter into agreements with the States by which the Commonwealth and the respective State provide equal sums for the maintenance of tuberculosis diagnosis and after-care facilities. In addition, the Minister is authorized to grant to certain tuberculosis sufferers a special allowance, over and above the usual sickness allowance, and intended to encourage such sufferers to seek care.

In the case of the Pharmaceutical Benefits Act it was provided that all residents of Australia should be entitled to receive without charge, from a pharmacy approved for the purposes of the Act by the Commonwealth government, and on prescription of a medical practitioner, such medicines as are authorized in a Commonwealth Pharmaceutical Formulary. The pharmacist is then reimbursed by the Commonwealth Minister of Health under terms of an agreement entered into by him with the Commonwealth.

Until the passage in 1946 of the amendment to Section 51 that is now placitum (xxiiiA), the authority for all the services we have here discussed, except of course the old-age and invalidity insurance, was, according to the schedule in the *Official Acts of Parliament*, placitum (xxxix) of Section 51, which gives the Parliament power to legislate in respect to "matters incidental to the execution of any power vested by this Constitution in the Parliament or in either House thereof, or in the Government of the Commonwealth, or in the Federal judicature, or in any department or officer of the Commonwealth."

As we have seen, however, since 1946 there is a specific constitutional prescription for each of the services discussed here.

The responsibility of the States is to fill in any gaps remaining on the execution of the Commonwealth program. For example, there are a great number of people unable for one reason or another to meet the requirements of the old-age and invalidity program. It will be the responsibility of the States to care for as many of these as are not able to provide for themselves.

Finally, there is no Commonwealth workmen's compensation legislation. Such legislation is completely the responsibility of the States. There has been some conjecture over the possible use of placitum (xiv) of Section 51 (insurance) as authority for Commonwealth legislation in this field, but there is considerable doubt in the minds of many authorities that this approach would stand the constitutional test. To date it has not been attempted.

SUMMARY

The Australian practices in the field of labor relations and wages and hours standards are unique among the federal systems. They are practices which have grown up in an unsystematic way over a period of decades. This does not mean that they could not be adopted in their present form by another government. Although they do not eliminate political discussion in this area, it does seem that the peculiar way in which decision-making has been institutionalized here would make for less likelihood of such discussion's resulting in severe political crises. Many of the matters which in other federal systems are determined legislatively are in Australia adjusted in a judicial process with all that that can mean for the allaying of political passions.

In the social services field, there is a mixture of the old and new, means tests on the one hand, and liberal provisions without means tests on the other. The picture presented is one of a system in flux, and in rather violent flux at that.

APPENDIX II

Canada

GENERAL CONSTITUTIONAL PROVISIONS

The Canadian Constitution in the form of its adoption in 1867 as the British North America Act contained no clauses referring to labor or social insurance matters. As the economic life of the Provinces and of the Dominion quickened with the growth of population and the rise of large industrial establishments and a more complicated network of business relationships, political pressures for legislation in these fields began to be exerted on governments at both levels. However, this pressure did not result in the adoption of any amendments to the British North America Act other than one in 1940 by which the Dominion government was authorized to legislate with respect to unemployment insurance. Instead, such Dominion legislation as has been enacted in this area and as has stood the test of judicial review, has depended for its validity on provisions of the original Constitution.

Originally, the provisions of importance in subsequent Dominion labor legislation were included for the most part in Section 91 of the British North America Act:

> 91. It shall be lawful for the Queen, by and with the advice and consent of the Senate and House of Commons, to make laws for the Peace, Order and Good Government of Canada, in relation to all matters not coming within the classes of subjects by this Act assigned exclusively to the legislatures of the Provinces; and for greater certainly, but not so as to restrict the generality of the foregoing terms of this section, it is hereby declared that (notwithstanding anything in this Act) the exclusive legislative authority of the Parliament of Canada extends to all matters coming within the classes of subjects next hereinafter enumerated, that is to say:
>   2. The regulation of trade and commerce.
>   10. Navigation and shipping.
>   27. The Criminal Law, except the Constitution of the Courts of Criminal Jurisdiction, but including the Procedure in Criminal Matters.

In addition, Section 92 (10) provided that certain "local works and undertakings" might be within the control of the Dominion rather than of the Provinces:

> a. Lines of Steam and other Ships, Railways, Canals, Telegraphs and other Works and Undertakings connecting the Province with any other or others of the Provinces, or extending beyond the Limits of the Province.
> b. Lines of Steam Ships between the Province and any British or Foreign Country.
> c. Such Works as, although wholly situate within the Province, are before or after their Execution declared by the Parliament of Canada to be for the general Advantage of Canada or for the Advantage of Two or more of the Provinces.

However, the particular constitutional obstacle to the Dominion's enactment of labor legislation has proved to be Section 92 (13). Section 92 deals with the "exclusive powers of provincial legislatures," and declares:

> In each Province the legislature may exclusively make laws in relation to matters within the classes of subjects hereinafter enumerated:
>   13. Property and Civil Rights in the Province.

I. LABOR RELATIONS

A. *The Right of Organization and Collective Action*

Until 1872, Dominion criminal law provisions striking at conspiracies in restraint of trade had jeopardized the existence of trade unions. In that year, however, the Dominion Parliament enacted the Trade Unions Act by which a trade union was protected from prosecution that might have been brought in the past solely because the union existed. Article 497 of the Criminal Code, enacted by virtue of the Dominion Parliament's authority under Section 91 (27) of the British North America Act, reads: "The purposes of a trade union are not, by reason merely that they are in restraint of trade, unlawful within the meaning of the last preceding section."

But, under the common law a trade union whose existence was protected might nonetheless be subject to criminal penalties for having carried out strike activities which the courts considered as attempts to coerce the employer. The unions, therefore, in 1886 received the protection of an amendment to Section 4 of the 1876 Act regarding trade unions and which is now a part of the Revised Statutes of Canada, 1927, c. 146, §590: "No prosecution shall be maintainable against any person for conspiracy in refusing to work with or for any employer or workman, or for doing any act or causing any act to be done for the purpose of a trade combination, unless such act is an offence punishable by statute." This language has the same effect as the provision of the 1875 English Conspiracy and Protection of Property Act which provides that a combination of workers carrying out an act in furtherance of a trade dispute is not indictable for the act unless an individual person would be indictable under a law for having performed the very same act.

There is a third problem faced under the common law by trade unions regarding which the ability of the Dominion to act would appear to be limited. This is the difficulty which many trade unions would have under the common law in gaining standing before a court, in their suits for enforcement of contract or for other civil actions, because of the existence of statutes and rules in a union with respect to the calling of strikes or the punishment of members, actions which courts might be inclined to consider restraints of trade. The Canadian Trade Unions Act of 1872 sought to protect the unions' position before the courts in such civil cases, at least in the case of unions registering under the act by providing in Section 22: "The purposes of any trade union shall not, by reason merely that they are in restraint of trade, be deemed to be unlawful, so as to render any member of such trade union liable to criminal prosecution for criminal conspiracy or otherwise, or so as to render void or voidable any agreement or trust." It needs to be noted, however, that the number of trade unions which have registered themselves under the act is very small. Furthermore, there are a number of legal scholars who are of the view that for the Dominion to con-

cern itself with the civil rights of unions without regard to the nature of
the industry which they organize and the extent of the Dominion Parliament's jurisdiction over such an industry, is to infringe on the exclusive
right of each Province, granted by Section 92 (13), over "property and
civil rights in the Province." Some of the Provinces have sought to protect
trade unions in this respect through provincial legislation. The Ontario
Rights of Labour Act, 1944 (Labour Laws of Ontario, c. 54 (1)), provided,
for example: "A trade union and the acts thereof shall not be deemed to
be unlawful by reason only that one or more of its objects are in restraint
of trade."

A fourth and final problem existing for trade unions in the common law
portions of Canada is the possibility that under the common law trade
unions may be sued civilly by the employer for damage which he may al-
lege he suffered during the course of a labor stoppage. The Dominion has
never taken any steps to protect the unions against such action, and it is
doubtful that it could, given the nature of the British North America Act
and the existing interpretation of it. However, some of the Provinces have
used their undoubted powers in this field. An example again is the Ontario Rights of Labour Act, 1944, cited above, which provides: "Any act
done by two or more members of a trade union, if done in contemplation
or furtherance of a trade dispute, shall not be actionable unless the act
would be actionable if done without any agreement or combination."

B. *Employer-Worker Relations*

Over and above the problem of the right of organization and its relation
to the common law, attention has been focused in Canada on the degree
to which the Dominion or provincial governments should go in regulating
the powers of the employer to deal with his workers in respect to matters
arising out of their membership in a trade union, or in defining obligations
of the employer and an organization of his workers to each other.

Until the outbreak of World War II, the only Dominion legislation attempting to protect the worker from discrimination by his employer by
reason of the worker's membership or activities in a trade union, was that
enacted in 1939 as an amendment to the Criminal Code (R.S. 1927, c. 36):

> 502A. Any employer or his agent, whether a person, company or
> corporation, who wrongfully and without lawful authority
>   a. refuses to employ or dismisses from his employment any person
>   for the sole reason that such person is a member of a lawful trade
>   union or of a lawful association or combination of workmen or
>   employees formed for the purpose of advancing in a lawful man-
>   ner their interests and organized for their protection in the regu-
>   lation of wages and conditions of work;
>   b. seeks by intimidation, [etc.] to compel workmen or employees to
>   abstain from belonging to such a trade union . . .

    c. conspires, combines, agrees or arranges with any employer or his agent to do any of the things mentioned in the preceding paragraphs:

is guilty of an offence punishable on indictment or on summary conviction before two justices, and liable on conviction, if an individual, to a fine not exceeding one hundred dollars or to three months' imprisonment with or without hard labour, and, if a company or corporation, to a fine not exceeding one thousand dollars.

During World War II, several orders-in-council relevant to the protection of the worker in his relations with his employer were issued under the authority of the War Measures Act, 1914 (R.S. 1927, c. 306). The pertinent provision of the War Measures Act, 1914, reads as follows:

3. The Governor-in-Council may do and authorize such acts and things, and make from time to time such orders and regulations, as he may by reason of the existence of real or apprehended war, invasion or insurrection deem necessary or advisable for the security, defense, peace, order and welfare of Canada; and for greater certainty, but not so as to restrict the generality of the foregoing terms, it is hereby declared that the powers of the Governor-in-Council shall extend to all matters coming within the classes of subjects hereinafter enumerated, that is to say:

    e. trading, exportation, importation, production and manufacture
    f. appropriation, control, forfeiture, and disposition of property and of the use thereof.

An order-in-council of June, 1941, provided that the machinery of the Industrial Disputes Act should be used to inquire into any charge of dismissal of workers in war industries on the ground of union membership.

Later on in the war, on February 17, 1944, another order-in-council was issued, as the Wartime Labour Relations Regulations, which went much further than the 1941 order, and which provided:

4. (1) Every employee shall have the right to be a member of a trade union or employees' organization and to participate in the lawful activities thereof;

(2) Every employer shall have the right to be a member of an employer's organization and to participate in the lawful activities thereof;

19. (1) No employer shall dominate or interfere with the formation or administration of a trade union or employees' organization or contribute financial or other support to it . . .

(2) No employer . . . shall

    (a) refuse to employ any person because he is a member of a trade union or an employees' organization;

    (b) impose any condition in the contract of employment seeking to restrain an employee from exercising his rights under these regulations; or

    (c) seek by intimidation, by dismissal or threat of dismissal, by any other kind of threat . . . to compel an employee to abstain from becoming or continuing to be a member or officer or representative of a trade union or an employees' organization, or from exercising his lawful rights.

Although the preamble to these Regulations recites that they are deemed necessary, "by reason of the war, for the security, defense, peace, order and welfare of Canada [see the opening paragraph of Section 91 of the Constitution] and for the effective prosecution of the war," it should be noted that the Regulations did not by any means apply to all industrial or commercial enterprises in Canada; rather, Section 3 (1) provided that they should apply only in the case of employees:

(a) who are employed upon or in connection with a work, undertaking or business that is ordinarily within the legislative authority of Parliament, including but not so as to restrict the generality of the foregoing,

    (i) . . . navigation and shipping, whether inland or maritime;

    (ii) lines of steam or other ships, railways, canals, telegraphs and other works and undertakings connecting any province with any other or others of the provinces, or extending beyond the limits of the province;

    (iii) lines of steamships between a province and any British or foreign country;

    (iv) ferries between any provinces and any British or foreign country, or between two provinces; and

    (v) such works as, although wholly situate within the province, have been or may be declared by the Parliament of Canada to be for the general advantage of Canada, or for the advantage of two or more of the provinces;

(b) who are employed upon or in connection with a work, undertaking or business that is essential to the efficient prosecution of the war;

(c) or whose relations with their employers in matters covered by these regulations are ordinarily within the exclusive legislative jurisdiction of a provincial legislature to regulate and to whom these regulations have been applied by the provincial legislature in respect of their relations with their employers;

Of course, the Regulations applied equally to the employers of workers covered.

The provisions of Section 3 (1) (c) alone should be noted carefully as they constitute one of the examples of the "enabling legislative device" scheme to which the Dominion and provincial parliaments have resorted in an effort to achieve uniformity in a field in which the Dominion Parliament is not competent to legislate, or at any rate is not competent to legislate so as to cover the whole of the field. As we shall see later, this scheme was applied after the declaration in 1925 by the Judicial Committee of the Privy Council at London that the 1907 Industrial Disputes Investigation Act was *ultra vires* the Dominion Parliament. The Wartime Labour Relations Regulations expired with the ending of the War.

It was not long thereafter, however, that the Industrial Relations and Disputes Investigation Act of June 30, 1948, was enacted. This Act is the primary existing Dominion labor relations legislation. For the purpose of this section, we can note that the provisions of the 1948 Act, with respect to the rights and duties of the employer and worker, are substantially those we have enumerated above as existing as part of the Wartime Labour Relations Regulations.

The 1948 Act was declared by Section 53 (1) to apply to persons employed in industries making up the same list as enumerated above in the Wartime Labour Relations Regulations, except that the clause relating to enterprises engaged in war work was not included.

Provisions similar to those of the Dominion's 1948 Act and regarding the rights of workers, and in some cases of employers, are to be found in some of the Provinces and cover industries subject to provincial control. It should be noted that the Dominion 1948 Act, in its Section 62 (1), provides for machinery to encourage the establishment of a joint Dominion-Provincial administration of labor legislation, of which more is said in the section on labor disputes immediately following.

C. *Labor Disputes*

The Dominion Parliament has entered the field of labor disputes in three ways: (a) by establishing voluntary conciliation machinery; (b) by providing, for use in cases where conciliation does not succeed, for arbitration boards having powers to require the attendance and testimony of witnesses, but not having power to enforce recommendations; (c) by providing in the case of serious disputes in enterprises or industries important to the economy, for a period of delay in any strike or lockout action, and for publication of the facts in a case.

In the Conciliation Act, 1900, the Dominion Parliament sought to make available to the Dominion government machinery for aiding disputing parties to reach an agreement through the intervention of a neutral person. The Act was intended to apply to disputes in any industry whatever in which the Dominion government might think it wise to proffer its good offices. Therefore, the Parliament could not introduce any compulsory features into this Act. After the Act became a part of the Conciliation and Labour Act, 1906 (R.S. 1927, c. 96, §1), it provided, *inter alia*:

> *Section* 6. Where a dispute exists between an employer or any class of employers and workmen, or between different classes of workmen, the Minister may if he thinks fit, exercise all or any of the following powers, namely:
>> b. take such steps as to him seem expedient for the purpose of enabling the parties to the dispute to meet together, by themselves or their representatives, under the presidency of a chairman mutually agreed upon or nominated by him or some other

person or body, with a view to the amicable settlement of the dispute.

    d. on the application of both parties to this dispute, appoint an arbitrator or arbitrators.

  Section 9. It shall be the duty of the conciliator to promote conditions favorable to a settlement, by endeavoring to allay distrust, to remove causes of friction, to promote good feeling, to restore confidence, and to encourage the parties to come together and themselves effect a settlement, and also to promote agreements between employers and employees with a view to the submission of disputes to conciliation or arbitration before resorting to strikes or lockouts.

The second half of the Conciliation and Labour Act of 1906 was what had been the Railway Disputes Act of 1903. This section applied not only to the railways under the jurisdiction of the Dominion but to any railway if it was threatened in its efficient operations by an industrial dispute so that, in the words of Section 14 of the Act, "a railway lockout or strike has been or is likely to be caused, or the regular and safe transportation of mails, passengers or freight has been or is likely to be interrupted, or the safety of any person employed on a railway train or car has been or is likely to be endangered."

In the case of railway disputes, where conciliation failed, the Minister of Labour might appoint an arbitration board. The most this board could do was to investigate, by means of compulsory presentation of witnesses and papers if necessary, and then, in the words of Section 20, "[consider] what would be reasonable and proper to be done by both or either of the parties with a view to putting an end to the difference, and to preventing its recurrence . . ." The report and recommendations of the arbitration board were to be published and made available to the press.

In 1907 the Industrial Disputes Investigation Act was passed by the Dominion Parliament. This Act did not affect the Conciliation and Labour Act, 1906, but rather added one additional compulsory feature to the conciliation and investigation process. Under the terms of the IDI Act, a "cooling-off" period was required during the investigative process. Under Section 57 of the Act, the employers and employees in an industry covered by the terms of the Act were obliged to give thirty days' notice of intent to change or to seek to change "conditions of employment with respect to wages and hours." Thereupon, either side might petition the Minister of Labour, certifying the possibility of work stoppage on its part should no agreement be reached and asking for a three-man board of arbitration to be established. Section 63A of the Act as amended provided: "Where in any industry any strike or lockout has occurred or seems to the Minister imminent and, in the public interest it seems to the Minister expedient, the Minister on application of any municipality interested . . . or of his own motion may . . . constitute a Board of Conciliation and Investigation." In the end, however, all the board could do was to investigate and publish its findings. It might compel the appearance of witnesses and the presentation of papers, but beyond this there was no compulsion.

Two problems growing out of the federal nature of the Canadian system presented themselves in the Act. First, there was the question of whether the Act's terms could apply in the case of a dispute involving a utility owned by a municipality. The second, and related problem, arose out of the Act's attempted coverage. Section 2 (c) of the Act provided that it should apply to any individual employer, company or corporation, "employing ten or more persons and owning or operating any mining property, agency of transportation or communication, or public service utility, including . . . railways, whether operated by steam, electricity or other motive powers, steamships, telegraph and telephone lines, gas, electric light, water and power works . . ."

As early as 1911 the right of the Dominion to intervene in disputes involving the employees and the management of electric power works was questioned. But it was not until 1926 that the views of the Privy Council were obtained on the constitutionality of the Act. At that time the Privy Council took issue with the Parliament on the Act's attemped coverage. In interpreting the Act, the members of the Judicial Committee of the Privy Council had this significant statement to make about the relation of Section 91 and Section 92 of the British North America Act to each other:

> The Dominion Parliament has, under the initial words of S. 91, a general power to make laws for Canada. But these laws are not to relate to classes of subjects assigned to the Provinces by S. 92, unless their enactment falls under the heads specifically assigned to the Dominion Parliament by the enumeration in S. 91. When there is a question as to which legislative authority has the power to pass an Act, the first question must therefore be whether the subject falls within S. 92. Even if it does, the further question must be answered, whether it falls also under an enumerated head in S. 91. If so, the Dominion has the paramount power of legislation in relation to it. If the subject falls within neither of the sets of enumerated heads, then the Dominion may have power to legislate under the general words at the beginning of S. 91.
> [*Toronto Electric Commissioners v. Snider et al.*, [1925] A.C. 396]

The Dominion sought to justify the constitutionality of the Act by referring it to subsection 27 of Section 91 respecting the Dominion's power over the criminal law. This was disposed of by the members of the Judicial Committee of the Privy Council by their assertion that the right to create penal sanctions does not give the Dominion the power to convert legislation which would otherwise infringe on the Provinces' power into valid enactments. In sum, the Privy Council held that such an Act could quite validly have been enacted by any of the provincial legislatures; that in fact such legislation did exist in some of the Provinces; that the very failure of the Act to deal more severely than it did with what it said were emergencies

belied the Act's stated purpose of safeguarding the economy against crises
of labor relations; and that the Act was a usurpation of the Provinces'
rights over "property and civil rights."

The Act was thereupon amended in 1925 to eliminate reference to gas,
electric light, water and power works. Dominion authority over interprovincial means of transport and communications was reasserted, as was
authority over works which the Dominion Parliament had declared to
be "for the general advantage of Canada or for the advantage of two or
more provinces" (§3a (vii)).

Finally, the Act made use of the "enabling device" technique to extend
its scope to other enterprises solely within the provincial authority. Section
3d applied the Act to "any dispute which is within the exclusive legislative
jurisdiction of any province and which by the legislation of the province
is made subject to the provisions of this Act." In other words, Provinces
might enact legislation providing that industries such as their local
utilities should fall under the control of the administrative agencies established by the IDI Act. By 1937 the legislatures of Nova Scotia, New
Brunswick, Quebec, Ontario, Manitoba, Saskatchewan, Alberta, and British
Columbia had enacted such enabling legislation, though in 1937 British Columbia repealed its adherence to the program in favor of its own Act. The
Industrial Disputes Investigation Act has now been repealed by the 1948
Industrial Relations and Disputes Investigation Act.

The War Labour Relations Regulations mentioned earlier also dealt with
labor disputes. Strikes or lockouts during the period of time covered by
a collective agreement were forbidden. Where an agreement had expired,
a cooling-off period was enforced during which investigation and publication procedures were to be followed. In the end, however, after all these
prescriptions had been adhered to, and still no settlement had been
reached, a strike or lockout could take place.

The Industrial Relations and Disputes Investigation Act of 1948 seeks
to reduce the number of strikes and lockouts by forbidding them during
the period of a contract's life, by continuing substantially the conciliation,
investigation, and publication features of the 1907 Act, as amended, and
by prohibiting strikes and lockouts in any event until all the steps in this
procedure have been taken futilely. In the end, however, a strike or lockout may take place, and there are no further legislative enactments to deal
with strike or lockout situations beyond the point reached by the 1948 Act.

The 1948 Act extends to the same list of industries as the old IDI Act
covered after its amendment following the 1925 Privy Council decision in
Toronto Electric Commissioners v. Snider et al., [1925] A.C. 396. The
new Act does add jurisdiction over the air transport industry and radio
broadcasting stations. The provisions of the 1925 amendment relating to
Dominion-Provincial cooperation are retained in Section 62 of the new
Act.

II. WAGES AND HOURS AND FACTORY INSPECTION

In peacetime the regulation of wages and hours of work has been exercised exclusively by the Provinces, except in the limited area of Dominion projects or enterprises engaged in the production of goods for the Dominion government.

In the early 1880's the Dominion government considered pressing for the enactment of Dominion factory legislation, and in fact in 1883 a bill was introduced with the aim of controlling the minimum age of child labor and the length of the working week of young people, and it was proposed to justify this action under the authority possessed by the Dominion over the criminal law. After long discussion in Parliament, it appears to have been concluded generally that control of wages, hours and factory conditions rested with the Provinces under the terms of Section 92 (13), regarding "property and civil rights" in the Provinces. The probability that this view was that which might have been suggested later in judicial proceedings is indicated by the attitude of the Privy Council in the 1925 *Toronto Electric Commissioners* case mentioned earlier. At any rate the Dominion government did not pursue its efforts with respect to these child labor controls, and so recognized the strength of those arguing that such legislation would affect the civil rights in the Provinces because they would impair the contractual rights of the employer and worker.

An interesting effort was made by a Dominion reform government under the premiership of Mr. Drew in the mid-1930's to gain jurisdiction over wages, hours and weekly-rest provisions through the device of having the Dominion government execute its obligations under the provisions of three International Labor Office conventions to which the Dominion government had adhered. The Dominion government maintained that the Conventions created obligations which could be met only by the Dominion government although it was admitted that the Dominion otherwise had no power under the British North America Act to operate in these fields. In a decision in the case of *Attorney-General of Canada v. Attorney-General of Ontario, Reference Re Weekly Rest in Industrial Undertakings Act, Minimum Wages Act, and Limitation of Hours Act* [1937] A.C. 326, the Privy Council said that labor laws regulating wages, working hours and rest days in industrial undertakings and which are enacted by the Dominion Parliament in accordance with conventions adopted by the International Labor Office under the Treaty of Versailles are not legislation "necessary or proper for performing obligations arising under treaties between the Empire and foreign countries" within the powers of the Dominion under Section 132 of the British North America Act, nor within the Dominion's powers under Section 81 "to make laws for the peace, order, and good government of Canada," such legislation being exclusively within the competence of the Provinces under its powers as to "property and civil rights."

It should be noted, however, that in every Province there has been extensive legislation in the fields of wages, hours, and factory inspection, except that there has been no wage legislation in Prince Edward Island.

In 1938 there was organized the Canadian Association of Administrators of Labour Legislation. This Association has as members the Dominion Department of Labour and every provincial department, board or commission administering any labor law. The aim of the Association is to stimulate reciprocal knowledge of provincial labor legislation and conditions with a view to the raising of labor standards through legislation and the arrival of some uniformity. A recent subject of concern to the Association has been the establishment of a uniform minimum employment age. It is still too early, particularly in view of the intervention of the war years, when little was done by the Association, to evaluate its effectiveness.

The Dominion has used its power over the criminal law to enact Sunday labor legislation which thus becomes a form of control. The Lord's Day Act goes back to 1906 and attempts to regulate Sunday labor by making a crime any activity for gain on Sunday except such as might be classified as work of necessity or mercy.

In addition, the Dominion's power over its own contracts and over its own projects affords it one means of control over labor conditions. The controlling legislation in this field is the Fair Wages and Hours of Labour Act respecting public works. The policy of imposing standards in contract provisions with private persons entering into commercial relations with the Dominion government actually goes back, however, to 1900 with the enactment by the House of Commons of a Fair Wages Resolution. From that time the Governor-in-Council has issued orders respecting the incorporation of labor details in public contracts. Generally speaking, fair wages are held in the orders to be those prevailing in the area. In addition, employers have been required to conform to such requirements as publishing and posting wage schedules, and keeping proper books and records for examination by government officers (Fair Wages and Hours of Labour Act, 1935, §6). As far as hours of labor are concerned, a 44-hour week is the standard set down by the Act itself.

During wartime the Dominion's authority over wages and hours in all enterprises in Canada may approach totality. Under the War Measures Act, 1914, there was established in World War II a series of measures resulting in a direct or indirect control of wages by the Dominion authorities. In November, 1939, the terms of the Industrial Disputes Investigation Act of 1907 as amended were extended to disputes between employers and workers in war industries, including munitions, supplies and defense projects. In December, 1940, an order-in-council was issued (P.C. 3495) establishing criteria for the maintenance of wartime wage controls in all industries engaged in war work. These criteria took as standard the wage situation in Canada between 1926 and 1929 and sought to ensure that workers should

not fall below this standard. It further agreed that some cost-of-living bo-
nuses might be authorized by those arbitration boards set up under the IDI
Act's provisions.

A more general control over wages extending beyond the war industries
was inaugurated by the Dominion government by an order-in-council of
July 10, 1942 (Wartime Wages Control Order, Order-in-Council P.C.
5963), applying to all wage payments in Canada, and providing for a National War Labour Board and Regional Boards to approve all wage
changes proposed to be effected. The Boards further had power even to
direct an employer to increase wages. The order-in-council of July, 1942,
and subsequent orders provided also that "an employee who strikes or takes
part in a strike to obtain an increase in wages . . . or to obtain a decision
from or influence a decision of a War Labour Board or in protest . . .
against such direction," might be fined and imprisoned for up to
three months. For a time the effect of Dominion operations under these
wartime orders was to suspend the activities of the provincial minimum-
wage boards, but, later on, these provincial boards were used to assist in the
furtherance of the Dominion wage-control program.

III. Labor Placement

Until the First World War governmental activity with respect to public
employment exchanges was provincial exclusively. In 1918, however, the
Dominion enacted legislation of the grant-in-aid variety, the Employment
Offices Coordination Act, 1918, under which the public employment offices
remained in control and administration of the Provinces but were subsidized in part by the Dominion government. The Dominion Minister of
Labour was authorized by Section 3 of the Act to:

  a. aid and encourage the organization of employment offices and pro-
     mote uniformity among them;
  b. establish one or more clearing houses for the interchange of informa-
     tion between employment offices concerning the transfer of labor;
  c. compile and distribute information on prevailing conditions of em-
     ployment.

The Minister of Labour was authorized to aid each Province, in operating
its employment service, to the extent of subsidizing one half of the costs of
operation, provided that the Province agreed to cooperate with the Minister.
A significant section, 5 (2), provided: ". . . The Minister may in any year
set aside from the moneys allotted to a province such sum as may seem
desirable for the maintenance of employment offices where none are operated by the provincial government." The Ministry operated two interprovincial offices for the clearing of information, at Ottawa and Winnipeg.

In 1940, the Amendment to the British North America Act noted previously and which referred to the Dominion's activity in the field of unem-

ployment insurance was adopted. Shortly thereafter the Dominion Parliament enacted the Unemployment Insurance Act, 1940 (Statutes of 1940, c. 44). On the theory that the unemployment insurance amendment granted powers to the Dominion to establish whatever system was needed to administer an unemployment insurance program and to seek to end the burden on the program by aiding the unemployed to find work, the Dominion in this 1940 Act altered its relation to public employment exchanges by establishing its own system of such exchanges:

Section 88. (1) The Commission shall organize and maintain an employment service for Canada and in respect of that service shall be responsible to the Minister.

(3) The Employment Service shall in relation to unemployment insurance, perform such duties under this act as may be prescribed by the Commission, and undertake such other services as the Commission in the exercise of its power may prescribe.

The degree to which the Dominion government may go in requiring employer cooperation in its employment exchange program is indicated in the National Employment Service Regulations, 1949.

Section 3. If an employer who needs to engage an employee in insurable employment other than an employee to be engaged pursuant to his seniority rights does not engage such employee within twenty-four hours after the time when the employment becomes available, he shall forthwith after the said twenty-four hours have elapsed notify the local employment office of such requirement, stating the place when and the occupation for which the employee is required, a description of the duties to be performed . . . [4 Canada, Statutory Orders and Regulations, Consolidation 1949, 4012]

Although the 1940 law provided in Section 107 that "The Law for Coordination of the Placement Offices can be abrogated by the Governor-in-Council," the 1918 law was not repealed outright. There was no reason therefore under law why the provincial offices should not have remained open. But, in fact, as expected, they closed everywhere, except in Quebec where the Province itself operates twelve employment offices. A regional Dominion office exists there in Montreal. The 1918 law was repealed by proclamation, January 19, 1943.

During World War II, the Dominion government, acting under the War Measures Act, adopted National Selective Service Civilian regulations, making possible strict control of manpower movement. The Act was to be administered locally by National Selective Service officers at the Employment and Selective Service Offices made available by the Unemployment Insurance Commission. The National Selective Service Officer could, under the regulations, require employers to seek labor through the employment offices, prevent their advertising for labor, order persons 16 to 65 years old to report to the Employment Office for interview, require an unemployed person to accept suitable employment, request any employed person to change to more important work on seven days' notice, and direct persons in some age groups to apply for specific employment. At the end of the . war these regulations went out of effect.

IV. SOCIAL INSURANCE

Of the five commonly recognized forms of social insurance — sickness, accident, old-age and survivors, invalidity, and unemployment — all are treated in one way or another by some governmental unit in Canada, but only in the case of old-age insurance and unemployment insurance does the Dominion government become engaged in a program.

Accident insurance legislation, first enacted in Ontario in 1914, is now in force in every province except Prince Edward Island. It is considered by authorities to be more nearly uniform in its legislative provisions and administration than any of the other forms of insurance. The burden of contributing to the accident insurance fund in each Province lies on the employer except in British Columbia where the cost of medical care, as distinguished from compensation for time lost, is supported by contributions from employees as well as employers. The old common law rules respecting employee negligence, the responsibility of the fellow servant, and the assumption of risks, by which the employer had been able to avoid responsibility in many cases in the past, no longer apply. Invalidity arising out of accidents is usually dealt with in accident insurance legislation.

Sickness insurance legislation exists in a number of the Provinces, in some cases unimplemented, and of varying coverage and design from Province to Province. There is no federal activity in this field.

Old-age insurance was the first of the social insurance fields to be entered by the Dominion government. The first form of Dominion activity in the old-age insurance field (and actually an insurance program, while the other form of Dominion activity is in reality an old-age assistance program) is the Government Annuities Act. This Act was passed in 1907 by the Dominion Parliament "in the public interest that habits of thrift be promoted and that the people of Canada be encouraged and aided thereto so that provision may be made for old age." The annuities program is essentially one of governmentally encouraged savings by individuals depositing money at will into a fund, usually over a period of several decades under the incentive of a voluntary schedule suggested by the government. The money saved then lies in the care of the Dominion government, accumulating interest at the rate of 4 per cent compounded annually. At age 55-65, as the insured desires, an annuity of from $120 to $1200 is paid to him for life, and under certain circumstances after his death to his survivors. Rates of contribution are very low and it is certainly doubtful that they could be matched by private insurance firms. Default in payment of contributions does not jeopardize the insured, but merely results in an ultimately lower annuity. There is no medical examination, and entrance is possible from childhood through to any age, with provision for persons more than 55 years of age, if they desire, to deposit a lump sum of money into the fund and receive monthly benefits at once. In recent years, there has been an increasing number of group insurance contracts entered into under the program. Often an employer will agree contractually with the union representing his workers to enter into an annuity contract with the government on behalf of the workers and to pay the cost of contributions. The whole program is administered by the Dominion Minister of Labour and in most cases contact is directly between the government and the insured, except for some group insurance cases.

The Old-Age Pension Act was first passed in 1927 and provided for Dominion participation on the grant-in-aid basis. The Act, as amended, provided that on conclusion of an agreement with a Province the Dominion Government might defray out of its funds 75 per cent of the net sum paid out during the preceding quarter by the Province for pensions under a Provincial old-age pension act, provided that the Province's act and the regulations under it are approved by the Dominion Government. And there follows a list of standards to which provincial legislation must conform, all of which might be summarized by saying that the insurance is non-contributory and as of need to British subjects at least 70 years old and long resident in Canada. The Provinces make up from their own finances the remainder of the old-age payment, and pay the administrative costs of the program. As suggested earlier, this is not a real insurance program.

While the Old-Age Pensions Act is a grants-in-aid program with basic administrative responsibility resting with the Provinces, the unemployment insurance program is nationally legislated and administered. The Employment and Social Insurance Act of 1935, the Dominion's first legislation in the field, was declared invalid by the Judicial Committee of the Privy Council in the case of *Attorney-General of Canada v. Attorney-General of Ontario, Reference Re Employment and Social Insurance Act, 1935* (1937) A.C. 326. The Act had cited the social welfare provisions of the Versailles Treaty and Canada's obligations under them toward her wage earners, and had stated that the peace, order, and good government of Canada required insurance against unemployment, as did the maintenance of interprovincial and international trade. A Dominion employment service such as that later established under the 1940 Act was provided for, and a system of unemployment insurance benefits financed by contributions of the worker, employer and the government. The Privy Council held that in pith and substance the Act was an insurance act affecting the civil rights of the employers and employed in each Province and as such was invalid, and could not be supported on the suggestion of a special emergency or as legislation coming under the public debt or the taxation provisions of the British North America Act, subsections 1 and 3 respectively of Section 91. Even though the Dominion had collected a fund by means of taxation, the Privy Council said, it did not follow that legislation disposing of that money was within the competence of the Dominion.

In 1940 the Canadian Constitution was amended as noted previously so that subsection 2A was added to Section 91 and the Dominion Government was given power to legislate with respect to "unemployment insurance." In the same year the Unemployment Insurance Act of 1940 was adopted. This established a national system of unemployment insurance to be administered by the Commission of Unemployment Insurance. The Act now covers workmen earning not more than $2400, unless paid on an hourly, daily, or weekly basis, in all industries except agricultural and forestry and allied fields; stevedoring; domestic service; non-profit hospitals; municipal services; and teaching.

According to Section 17 (1), "The funds required for providing insurance benefits and for making any other payments which under this Act are to be made out of the Unemployment Insurance Fund, established under this part of this Act, shall be derived partly from moneys provided by Parliament, partly from contributions by employed persons and partly from contributions by employers of those persons." Contributions are based on a schedule attached to the Act and usually the employer and employee contributions are the same, each about 1½ per cent of the wage. Workers' contributions are deducted from their pay by the employer and forwarded to the Unemployment Insurance Fund (*Caisse d'Assurance-Chômage*).

APPENDIX III

Germany

I. LABOR RELATIONS

A. *Worker and Employer Organizations*

The Weimar Constitution of 1919 provided special protection to the organization of labor and employer organizations. Over and above the provisions of Article 124, respecting the forming of associations, was the greater security of Article 159: "Liberty of association for the preservation and improvement of labor and industry is guaranteed to everybody and for all types of work. Any agreement or measure which attempts to restrict or obstruct this liberty is unlawful." In addition Article 165 provided: "Workers and employees are entitled to cooperate on an equal basis with employers in the regulation of conditions of work and wages and in the general economic development of productive forces. Legal recognition is given to the associations of both parties and to their agreements." Legislatively the existence of workers' and employers' organizations was recognized during the Weimar period in such laws as the Wage Contract Law (*Tarifvertragsordnung*) of 1928 (RGBl. I, p. 47) by which collective agreements between workers' and employers' groups might be extended to include other workers and enterprises; or the Law on Labor Exchange and Unemployment Insurance (Gesetz über Arbeitsvermittlung und Arbeitslosenversicherung) of 1927 (RGBl. I, p. 187), in which these organizations were recognized as the sources for lists of persons from which employer and worker representatives might be chosen by State authorities to sit on the administrative committees of the Labor Office (*Verwaltungsausschüsse des Arbeitsamts*). A similar provision appeared in the Law on Works Councils (*Betriebsrätegesetz*) of February 4, 1920, which also took notice of the existence of employer and worker organizations: "8. The present law does not affect the right of economic associations of workers and employers to represent the interests of their members."

In the Bonn Basic Law of 1949, the right of workers and employers to organize into their respective organizations is recognized in Article 9, which brings together into one article labor provisions found in several places in the Weimar Constitution:

(1) All Germans shall have the right to form associations and societies.
(3) The right to form associations to safeguard and improve working conditions shall be guaranteed to everyone and to all professions. Agreements which restrict or hinder this right shall be null and void; measures directed to this end shall be illegal.

In addition to the recognition of worker and employer organizations as entities existing under the right of workers and employers to self-association, the Weimar Constitution provided also for positive action to be taken by the Reich government exclusively, for the establishing of a system of labor and economic councils. These councils were part of the scheme of industrial and economic government which the Weimar Constitution proposed should be established, with a nation-wide Economic Council to aid the political legislature in the enactment of economic legislation. The last paragraph of Article 165 of the Weimar Constitution reads as follows: "The regulations on the organization and the responsibilities of the Councils of Labor and Industry and on their relationships to other self-governing bodies are left exclusively to the Reich."

It was under the provisions of this Article that the 1920 Works Councils Law (*Betriebsrätegesetz*) was enacted by the Reich Parliament. During the Weimar period there was no state activity respecting works councils. The Works Councils Law provided that in each factory having more than twenty persons employed there should be established under detailed provisions of the law and its implementing ordinances a council to represent the economic, social and personnel interests of the workers. Although it was anticipated that ultimately these councils would have a legally protected share in the management of the enterprises, such provisions of law were not brought into being during the Weimar period. As it was, then, these works councils stood alongside the trade unions as representatives of the workers, and in practice it was the responsibility of these councils to implement at the factory level the collective agreements negotiated over the area of a whole industry by the trade unions and the employers associations.

After the surrender of Germany in 1945, there was no constitutionally based federal German authority in existence until the establishment of the Bonn Republic in 1949. During the four year interval, State governments were organized throughout Western Germany, and these had all enacted their own constitutions by the time the Bonn Basic Law was adopted. With no federal government in existence, the pressure for legislation in economic affairs which might otherwise have been directed toward the central government was instead directed on the Länder. The existence of this pressure is evident in the postwar Western German Länder constitutions and legislation. For example, in the Hesse Constitution of 1946, Article 37 provides:

> With the cooperation of the trade unions, the employees, workers and officials in all enterprises and public agencies have common representative bodies which must be elected by general, equal, free, direct and secret ballot of the persons employed.
>
> The duty of the works councils is to exercise the right of participation in the solution of social, personnel and economic problems of the enterprise on equal terms with management and in collaboration with the trade unions.

Article 47 of the Constitution of the Free Hanseatic City of Bremen has a similar provision, as does Article 22 of the Constitution of Württemberg-Baden.

Before the Assembly which drafted the Bonn Basic Law had even met, implementing legislation for these codetermination (*Mitbestimmungs*) articles had been enacted by the Land legislatures, notably in Württemberg-Baden and in Hesse where much of the legislation (particularly that respecting economic codetermination by the workers' representatives) was suspended by order of the American Military Government on the grounds that the Basic Law was then being prepared, that this would determine the powers to be reserved to the several States and powers to be delegated to the central government, and that, in the words of the American Military Governor, General Clay, "it would be a serious mistake to prejudge this basic law now by resolving separately in several states their separate economic patterns."

Political considerations, strengthened by the existence of what their proponents considered unsurrenderable rights granted by legislatures and the constitutions in the Länder insured that in the Bonn Basic Law the section relating to the government of economic enterprises should be part of the list of concurrent powers. Article 74, therefore, reads:

> Concurrent legislation shall extend to the following fields:
> (12) labor law, including the legal organization of enterprises, protection of workers and provision of employment, as well as social insurance, including unemployment insurance.

Article 70 of the Basic Law provides that "the Länder shall have the right of legislation in so far as this Basic Law does not accord legislative powers to the Federation."

Further, Article 72 reads as follows:

(1) In the field of concurrent legislation, the Länder shall have power of legislation so long and so far as the Federation makes no use of its legislative rights.

But then, unlike the Weimar Constitution, the Basic Law proceeds to set down the criteria to regulate the enactments of federal legislation in a concurrent field:

(2) The Federation shall have legislative rights in this field in so far as a necessity for regulation by federal law exists because:
1. A matter cannot be effectively regulated by the legislation of individual Länder, or
2. The regulation of a matter by a Land law could prejudice the interests of the other Länder or of the Länder as a whole, or
3. The preservation of legal or economic unity demands it, in particular the preservation of uniformity of living conditions extending beyond the territory of an individual Land.

A federal codetermination law, the Law on Codetermination in the Boards of Trustees and the Governing Boards of the Mining Industry and of the Iron and Steel Producing Industries, was passed on May 21, 1951. Prior to that time, early in 1950, the American Military Government had lifted its suspension of the provisions of the Hesse and Württemberg-Baden laws referred to above. This means that at the moment, while there is serious pressure being put on the West German federal government for a codetermination law covering all West German industry, workers in Hesse and Württemberg-Baden have the power of taking part in decision-making along with management in social, economic, and personnel questions. The Hesse law, for example, is very broad, and refers to "all business enterprises" (Art. 2, par. 1).

It is clear that to the present time historical and political circumstances have facilitated a devolution of responsibility in this general area of worker representation and worker participation in the government of the economy from the highly centralized condition which existed during the Weimar Republic period.

B. *Labor Disputes*

During the Weimar period the responsibility for legislation in the matter of labor disputes rested with the federal government which enacted laws under the authority of Article 7, paragraph (9), which read:

The Reich has the legislative power over:
9. labor law, insurance, protective labor legislation for workers and employees, and labor offices.

However, much of the responsibility in executing this federal legislation rested with the Länder. Such State participation in the execution of federal enactments was a feature of other than the labor field in Weimar Germany, and was a practice carried over from the Empire period, and given sanction in the Weimar Constitution in Article 14: "The laws of the Reich are executed by the authorities of the Länder, unless the laws of the Reich state otherwise." A clear distinction is made in German labor theory and labor law between conciliation (*Schlichtung*) and the judicial process as instruments for the resolving or determination of disputes. Conciliation operations of the government arise out of disputes between two economic parties over the terms of an agreement being negotiated. Judicial process is essentially reserved for the determination of disputes arising out of an existing agreement. It should be noted, however, that labor courts also had jurisdiction over other disputes, notably those arising out of activities under the Works Council Law.

During the Weimar period, the basic federal document respecting the conciliation service was the Decree on Conciliation Procedure of October 30, 1923 (RGBl. I, pp. 1043, 1080). This Verordnung essentially prescribed that the responsibility for the establishment of conciliation offices should rest with the Länder. However, the Reich Minister of Labor himself appointed some sixteen officers to represent him for particular parts of Germany or for special cases in which the Reich government might take an interest. Finally, the Minister of Labor himself was the ultimate conciliation authority, and was vested by law with powers of compulsion to effect agreement in certain specified instances.

Article 1, Section 1 of the Decree provided:

1. In the place of the former Conciliation Committees, the Supreme Administrative Authority of the Land establishes new Conciliation Committees in consultation with the Reich Minister of Labor. Their seat and jurisdictional district shall be determined with utmost consideration for economic ties. The establishment of common Conciliation Committees for several Länder or for parts of several Länder is permitted.
2. After the Highest Administrative Authorities of the Länder in question have been given the opportunity to voice their opinions, the Minister of Labor appoints conciliators for larger economic regions. He may also appoint a special conciliator for a specific case.
7. The Reich Minister of Labor may issue general rules for the activities of the Conciliation Committees and of the Conciliators. In their decisions in individual cases, the Conciliation Committees and Conciliators are independent and not bound by instructions.
9. The expenses for the Conciliators are carried by the Reich. The expenses for the Conciliation Committees are carried by the Land by which they are established.

The Minister, of course, might inspect the operations of the Land Conciliation Service.

While, on the whole, the conciliation process is voluntary as far as acceptance of final terms is concerned, the Labor court proceedings, concerned with the interpretation of existing agreements, are in the end judicial in nature, although it is by law incumbent on Labor Court judges to seek a pretrial voluntary agreement of the contesting parties, and statistics give evidence of the effectiveness of this mediation. In the end, however, if a dispute does come to trial, the decision is as binding as that of any other judicial body.

The basic legislation on Labor Courts was the Labor Law of December 23, 1926 (RGBl. I, p. 507). Under its provisions courts of first instance generally were established "for the jurisdictional district of a Municipal Court [Amtsgericht] as independent courts by the Ministry of Justice of the Land in consultation with the highest administrative agency for the social administration after the economic association of employers and employees had been heard" (§ 14). To a considerable extent, however, Labor Courts possessed jurisdiction in the area of a labor office district somewhat larger than the district of a Municipal Court [Amtsgericht].

Above these labor courts of the first instance were courts of appeal at the Land level. The federal law prescribed that the Land labor court should be established "at the Superior Courts [Landgerichte] by the judicial administration of the Land in consultation with the highest Land agency for the social administration after the economic associations of the employers and employees had been heard . . ." (§33).

Finally, there was the Reich Labor Court which had the task of maintaining the unity of Labor Law.

At each level the court was composed of a presiding judge with legal training, and an equal number of lay judges representing employers and employees. They were drawn from panels approved by employers' and workers' organizations, set up for this purpose, and they served on an honorary basis.

The lack of a central German government for some years after World War II influenced the nature of State constitutional and legislative provisions in the case of labor disputes as in other instances.

By the time the Bonn government was established, the Western State governments had almost universally established conciliation systems with the same scope of activity as had been assigned conciliation systems before 1933. No element of compulsion now exists. A particular impetus to the establishing of such systems in the States came from Control Council Law No. 35 of August 20, 1946 which prescribed, in Article IV, that "the Conciliation Committees shall be established by each German Provincial or Land Labor Authority."

In the same way, as a result of Control Council Law No. 21, of March

30, 1946, there were established in all the German States, local and Land labor courts.

Under the Bonn government, a West German Supreme Labor Court is now in existence. It is to be expected that a West German conciliation service will operate for some disputes of special interest to the federal government, but as yet there has been no authority given the federal Minister to intervene in labor disputes as the Weimar federal Minister did before 1933, or to make binding awards in case of grave social and economic necessity.

II. Wages and Hours and Factory Inspection

Some legal regulations affecting labor in its wage, hour, and working conditions relationship with the employer are dealt with in German civil law, such as the legislation of August 18, 1896, contained in the Civil Code or the Trade Regulations Statute (Gewerbeordnung) for the German Reich of July 26, 1900. These and other similar laws dealt with such matters as the rights of workers in respect to the form in which their wages were paid them, and particularly the right to wages in legal currency; in respect to Sunday and holiday work; in respect to health and sanitary requirements in the factory and the conditions governing the work of apprentices and journeymen.

In addition, during the Weimar period, special attention was given by the federal government to the promulgation of regulations respecting hours of work. The expansive character of these regulations is indicated in the first article of the Regulation on Hours of Work in Industry of November 23, 1918 (RGBl. I, p. 1334): "The Regulation applies to all workers in all industrial and trade enterprises including the mining industry, in the enterprises of the Reich, the Land, communities and community compounds (Gemeindeverbände), even when they are not conducted for profit, as well as in agricultural industrial accessory enterprises."

The responsibility for the enforcement of such wage and hour prescriptions as existed in federal laws or ordinances lay with the Factory Inspection Service (Gewerbeaufsichtsamt).

An example of the way in which federal law left room for local discretion in labor matters is given in the provisions of the Trade Regulations respecting Sunday and holiday labor, which provide: "The Land governments determine, with due regard to the local and confessional conditions, which days shall be considered as legal holidays."

However, the truly essential wage and hour prescriptions in Germany during the Weimar period were those adopted in collective agreements between organizations of employers and organizations of workers. Such agreements were permitted to contravene federal legislation respecting wages, hours, and working conditions so long as such changes were to the advantage of the worker (Wage Agreement Law of December 23, 1918, as amended (RGBl. I, p. 1456)).

During the Weimar period, the Reich Minister of Labor was given authority, under certain conditions prescribed by law, to extend the validity of a collective agreement to include workers and employers not parties to the agreement. This "common rule" system was provided for in the Wage Agreement Law (see especially the version of March 1, 1928, RGBl. I, p. 47):

> *Section* 2. The Reich Minister of Labor may declare as generally binding Collective Wage Agreements which assumed predominant importance in the molding of conditions of labor in the district of the Wage Agreement.
>
> *Section* 3. The aforementioned declaration of paragraph 2 by the Reich Minister of Labor is made only upon petition. The petition may be filed by either contracting party of the Collective Wage Agreement and by associations of employers or employees whose members would be affected by such a declaration of the Reich Minister of Labor.

Of course, in the Weimar period, the Minister was not restricted in his application of a collective agreement to larger areas or additional enterprises by any considerations for the rights of the Länder. Control over wages and hours was practically exclusively in the hands of the federation during this time.

Since the war, such wage controls as have existed have been enforced by the Länder, primarily through the Factory Inspection Services (*Gewerbeaufsichtsämter*). In the early part of the occupation, military authorities prescribed general wage conditions, usually on a "freeze" basis. It should be noted, however, that, almost universally, the new constitutions of the German States include provisions respecting the power of the State to legislate in the field of wages. Since the new West German federal government possesses wage powers as part of the list of concurrent powers, as, of course, was the case in the Weimar period, it is possible that, given the amount of Länder activity in wage controls which has been taking place since the end of the war, there may be a devolution in the legislative aspects of wage controls. However, it should be noted that, with the end of the wage freeze following the currency reform of June, 1948, in the Western Zones, wages have been determined almost exclusively by collective negotiation of workers and employers. It is still too early to see whether the common-rule system will be established on the federal level.

A Factory Inspection Service (*Gewerbeaufsichtsamt*) existed in each of the Länder during the Weimar period. It was usually under the supervision of the Land Labor Ministry or Department, of which there was one in seventeen of the States, and in all the largest ones. While wage and hour controls and supervision of labor relations were exclusively federal matters, factory inspection and the establishment and enforcement of safety and health standards were concurrent responsibilities of the federal and State governments.

While the federal government relied on such legislation as Title VII of the Trade Regulations Statute (*Gewerbeordnung*) of 1891 (Protective Labor Law (*Arbeiterschutzgesetz*)), the States might stipulate supplementary conditions.

Not only did the Factory Inspection Services concern themselves with health and safety, but by means of various enactments they were given charge of supervising adherence to regulations as to hours of labor, hours of closing, wages prescriptions provided in the civil law, and the treatment of apprentices, journeymen, other young people, and women.

Since the end of World War II, the Factory Inspection Services have continued as State instrumentalities. During the period of food rationing in Germany following the war, they were used also for determining the relative difficulty of work being done, for ration-card purposes.

III. LABOR EXCHANGE

It will be recalled that Article 7, paragraph 9, of the Constitution authorized the Weimar Republic to enact legislation for the establishment and operation of "labor bureaus."

A comprehensive, Germany-wide system of labor offices was established under this authority in 1927 by the Law on Labor Exchanges and Unemployment Insurance (*Gesetz über Arbeitsvermittlung und Arbeitslosenversicherung*) of July 16, 1927 (RGBl. I, p. 187). In each Land there was to be established a Land labor office, and a number of subordinate labor offices. These agencies were to administer the Reich program for the voluntary placement of workers, for vocational counseling, and for unemployment insurance.

Section 34 (2) of that law provided: "The Presidents of the Land Labor Offices and their permanent representatives are appointed by the Reichspräsident [president of the German Reich] in consultation with the *Reichsanstalt* [the supervising federal organ] and the Supreme Land Authorities." Heads of the lower labor offices were appointed by the Reichsanstalt für Arbeitsvermittlung und Arbeitslosenversicherung (Reich Institute for Labor Placement and Unemployment Insurance).

Private employment exchanges were abolished in 1931.

Supervision of the labor offices from the federal level was the task of the Reichsanstalt. Directives from it concerned, among other things, the organizational form of the offices, and reporting procedures. Inspection of labor office facilities and operations was also a part of the Reichsanstalt's responsibility. It was also the responsibility of the Reichsanstalt to keep labor offices abreast of influences likely to affect the labor market. Beyond this, however, the labor offices operated under the supervision of the Land government, and specifically of the Land Labor Ministry or department, where such existed. In this way, local officials were able to control such important features of labor office operation as the encouragement of skilled worker training programs patterned to suit local needs, and to integrate labor office activities more effectively into the pattern of State programs, for example, of public construction, or forestry care, or agricultural improvements. Some of the labor offices particularly well-managed became the centers of the community's economic activity, serving as friendly, neutral grounds on which labor and management were able to meet, and on which both could work with local and State officials in the furtherance of community programs. In many ways the labor office system was the best example of federal-Land cooperation during the Weimar period.

Until the Hitler period, labor registration and placement were voluntary.

After World War II, the labor offices were reopened and operated under the supervision of Land Labor Ministries. With the establishment of the federal West German government, it appears likely that a return to the pre-1933 form of relationship between the federal and Länder authorities will be accomplished without difficulty.

IV. SOCIAL INSURANCE

In Germany, social insurance legislation embraces sickness (1883), accident (1884), old-age, widows, and survivors (1889) and invalidity (1911), and unemployment (1927) insurance.

The Länder have not played a legislative role in recent decades in any of the social insurance fields. Administratively, however, there was a close relationship between the social insurance system and the State and local governments.

The basic code for all the social insurances except unemployment has been the Reich Social Insurance Law (*Reichsversicherungsordnung*) of July 19, 1911, as amended (RGBl. 1911, p. 509). Under this code, provision was made for the social insurance carriers (*Träger der Reichsversicherung*), the self-governing local associations through which the insured and his employer made their contact with the particular social insurance system. There were some 4400 of these democratically governed associations in Germany during the Weimar period in the sickness insurance field alone. Some of these were at the factory level, some covered members of a guild, some were merely fraternal, others were regional in nature, embracing those persons not covered in any other society. Every insured person in the sickness insurance field was a member of some sickness insurance group; and similarly for some of the other social insurance fields covered by the Reich Social Insurance Law (*Reichsversicherungsordnung* (RVO)).

Provision was also made in the RVO for a series of supervisory agencies, the Reich Central Insurance Office (*Reichsversicherungsamt*), district offices (*Oberversicherungsämter*), and the local offices (*Versicherungsämter*). In addition, the various levels of *Versichungsämter* served as appeals bodies in cases of disputes over claims.

The Versicherungsämter were regularly departments of the Kreis (county) governments, and were part of the office of the mayor in the urban districts or of the county official in the rural districts. Section 36 of the RVO spells out the details respecting the organization of the local and district offices (the latter, incidentally, are at the subprovincial level):

(1) At every lower administrative body a department for Reich Insurance, a local insurance office [*Versicherungsamt*] shall be established. The highest administrative authority may decide that a common local insurance agency shall be established at one of these agencies for the districts of several lower administrative bodies.

(2) The governments of several Länder may agree to establish for their boundaries or parts thereof a common insurance office at a lower administrative body.

Sections 59 and 80, respectively, provided that the operating costs of the local and district insurance agencies should fall on the Land.

The financing of the insurance systems covered by the RVO was shared by the insured and his employer, Section 381 (1) of the RVO providing, for example, in the case of sickness insurance: "The compulsory insured members pay two thirds, their employers pay one third of the premiums."

The degree of autonomy which was very often left to the local associations is indicated in the sickness-insurance provisions relating to guild sickness associations. Section 381 (2) of the Reich Insurance Law says: "The Bylaws of the Guild Insurance Associations may provide that employers and employees each carry one half of the premiums." The exact amount to be paid by each insured person was left to the individual fund, although there was an upper wage percentage limit, which might be somewhat modified by the supervisory insurance offices.

On the whole, there were only limited federal and State subsidies to the sickness insurance fund. Old-age, invalidity, and survivors insurance received a subsidy of some 400–500 million Reichsmarks per year for its workers' section. The unemployment and accident insurance funds were not subsidized by the governments.

Financing of the accident insurance system was an exclusive responsibility of the employers who insured themselves in various Accident Insurance Associations (*Unfallversicherungskassen*). The premiums paid by an employer were based on the amount of annual wages paid his workers and the risk-class into which his firm fell.

The old-age, survivors, and invalidity systems are administered through Land Insurance Institute (in the case of laborers) and the Reich Insurance Agency (in the case of salaried employees), which, again, are under the supervision of the Reichsversicherungsamt.

V. The Unemployment Insurance Program

State participation in the unemployment insurance program was principally by way of the determination of the amount of the State-imposed unemployment insurance tax which should be levied. This amount varied from time to time depending upon the current and anticipated benefit load. The exact amount of the State tax was determined by the executive committee of the Land labor office. Section 151 (1) of the Law on Employment Services and Unemployment Insurance of July 16, 1927 (RGBl. I, p. 187) provides: "The State's share [*Landesanteil*] is determined by the administrative committee of the Land Labor Office for its district according to its needs." Section 151 (4) provides: "The share of the Land together with the share of the Reich shall not exceed the maximum amount fixed by the Reich."

The proceeds from the federal levy were forwarded to the Reichsanstalt für Arbeitsvermittlung by the labor offices (§154) and were used by it to support a regular federal subsidy to poorer districts, and the maintenance of a statutory reserve for general emergencies, large enough to guarantee the compensation of 600,000 unemployed for three months (§159 (2)).

The amount of the State levy might be set as the State officers willed, except that (1) the State tax might not be so high that when added to the federal tax the federally imposed limit would be exceeded; (2) one half of any surplus accumulated by a State office should be forwarded to the Reich Central Office (*Reichsanstalt*); and (3) if the State fund fell into a deficit while the State levy was lower than the maximum possible, no federal subsidies would be granted for that month.

Actually, this equalization program, by which the burden of unemployment was shared and the wealthier States aided the poorer with the federal government as the balancing agent, never was fully put into effect, but its features have aroused interest among social insurance experts inside and outside Germany, particularly in the United States.

Finally, it should be noted that benefits on the whole were the same throughout Germany for the same class of worker, except that after 1929 it was provided, by a change in the law, that in any event the benefits ought not to exceed the local average wage. The benefits rates are enacted in Sections 105–107 of the 1927 Act.

The Reich Social Insurance Law (*Reichsversicherungsordnung*) now has persisted in substantially unmodified form through three major constitutional crises in recent German history, except that the "leadership principle" temporarily supplanted democratic administration of the insurance carriers during the Hitler period.

However, it should be noted that there were constitutional provisions in the Weimar Constitution, in the list of concurrent powers, respecting social insurance. Article 7, paragraph 9, we have quoted earlier. A further provision was Article 161: "For the preservation of health and of the ability to work, for the protection of motherhood, and for providing against the economic consequences of old age, infirmity, and the vicissitudes of life, a comprehensive insurance system will be established by the Reich with the influential cooperation of the insured."

In the Bonn Basic Law, the only social insurance reference was in Article 74, paragraph 12, to which we have referred, and which again is in the list of concurrent powers.

The land constitutional conventions held during the period between the end of World War II and the establishment of the Bonn government generally made reference to social insurance. For example, the Hesse Constitution, in a very long article (Art. 35) provided: "A system of Social Insurance must be created which will serve all the people. It must be systematically developed. The insured are entitled to administer their own system. Their administrative bodies shall be elected by secret, general, free and equal ballot."

During this postwar period the Land labor ministries assumed the functions of the Reich Insurance Office and the Reich Ministry of Labor.

Since the establishment of the Bonn government, plans have been effected for restoring a federal control, but it is not yet clear how broad this control will be. The independent position of the States in the period since the surrender has strengthened the position of the supporters of greater State autonomy in the social insurance field, although in fact there has been practically no State legislation of any permanent importance under these provisions of the State constitutions. It is to be expected, however, that while some movement toward greater State autonomy in legislation and administration may take place, the existence of prospective federal subsidies will serve to moderate this tendency, so that in the end, whatever reorganization may take place, within each social insurance field, federal-state relations will continue substantially as they were during the Weimar period.

APPENDIX IV

Switzerland

I. LABOR RELATIONS

A. The Collective Organizations of Workers and Employers

The right of the workers, and of the employers as well, to organize for their mutual welfare is guaranteed throughout the Confederation by Article 56 of the Constitution: "The citizens have the right to form associations, provided that neither the aims of these associations nor their means is unlawful or endangers the state."

The right of workers to bargain collectively with their employers for the establishment of common terms of employment has been recognized from the beginning of the modern Confederation of 1874 in the Law of Contracts (Arts. 322, 323). This Law is enacted by the federation under the authority of Article 64 of the Constitution, which reads:

1. Legislation on the civil contractual capacity, on all matters of law which deal with commerce and personal property, the law of contracts, including the law of commerce and laws on promissory notes, belong to the Confederation.
2. The Confederation has the right to legislate also on other matters of civil law.

Article 322 of the Law of Contracts of March 30, 1911 (Recueil Officiel des Lois Fédérales, 1911, p. 321) provides: "Regulations relating to conditions of labor may be prescribed by the employers and the interested workers through contracts entered into by the employers or employers' organizations and by the workers or their workers' associations." These regulations are valid as to all enterprises in Switzerland, whether their operations be cantonal or national, whether they are large enterprises or artisan shops, or commercial activities.

The power of the federal authorities to intervene legislatively in this field was further secured by the very important and broad constitutional amendment of 1947 which provided, *inter alia*:

Article 34-ter.
  (1) The Confederation has the right to legislate:
     b. On the relationships between employers and employees or workers, specifically on a general regulation on questions which affect the enterprise and the profession.

It should be noted that considerable attention is given in both Swiss federal and cantonal law to organizations established by employers to further their socio-political and economic ends; in many instances in cantonal law, the views of the employers' associations on proposed administrative regulations regarding the economy must be received by the executive before promulgation of the regulations.

B. *Labor Disputes: Conciliation and Arbitration*

Until the amendment of 1947 to Article 34, the federal government relied for its authority in intervening in industrial disputes on the provisions of the first paragraph of Article 34: "The Confederation has the right to prescribe general regulations with regard to child labor in industrial plants, on the hours of work which may be required from adults . . ."

The Federal Law on Labor in Industrial Plants of June 18, 1914, provided in its Article 30: "In order to regulate amicably the differences of a collective type between industrialists and the workers on conditions of labor and on the interpretation and execution of collective contracts or contract-types, the cantons shall establish permanent conciliation offices, giving due attention to the various industries." The law provided further that the federal authorities should have the power of approving the mode of organization of the cantonal offices. In addition, Article 32 stated that "in a case of conflict which spreads over the limits of one canton, the Federal Council nominates the conciliation office. It can also designate a cantonal office to take charge of the conciliation."

The jurisdiction of the conciliation offices could extend under the 1914 law only to disputes involving those enterprises considered under Swiss law to be industrial plants (*fabriques*), that is, enterprises which could not be put into the category of arts and crafts shops, or simple trading establishments. The concept evoked by the English term "factory" would appear to be equivalent to the concept involved in the Swiss "fabriques." The 1914 law spoke of a *fabrique* as "an establishment that employs a number of workers outside their homes, either on the premises of the establishment and in yards pertaining thereto, or on outside work connected with the industrial production" (Art. 1 (2)). In practice, during the period when the 1914 law controlled, the determination of what was and what was not a fabrique was very much influenced in the case of each canton by what cantonal law considered a fabrique to be. Agriculture was always excluded; usually home industry or home work also. In some cases, as in Uri, a minimum number of workers was required.

Such disputes as could not be embraced by the jurisdiction of the 1914 law might become the care of the cantonal conciliation offices, existing in almost every canton before 1914, and after then required to be established by that law.

As a result of the 1947 amendment, which left the first paragraph of Article 34 intact, but which radically altered the old Article 34-*ter* to allow for the enactment by the Confederation of general legislation in the field of labor relations in any industry whatever, a new statute, specially concerned with the federal conciliation office was adopted in 1949. This statute ignored the previous distinction between fabriques and other establishments, and chose to restrict federal intervention in disputes to those extending beyond the limits of one canton, though there is no reason evident why the Confederation could not proceed to govern all labor relations if it chose to do so. This law of February 12, 1949 (Recueil Officiel des Lois Fédérales, 1949, p. 1398), the Federal Law on the Federal Conciliation Office for the Conciliation of Collective Labor Differences (*Bundesgesetz über die eidgenössische Einigungsstelle zur Beilegung von kollektiven Arbeitsstreitigkeiten*) provided, *inter alia*:

Article 1.

    (1) To conciliate between employers and employees in collective differences on the labor relationship which extend beyond the boundaries of one canton, the Federal Council [Bundesrat] may authorize the Federal Department of Economics to appoint a Federal Conciliation Office in a given case.

(3) The appointment of a Conciliation Office takes place only upon petition of interested parties if attempts at conciliation through direct negotiations between the parties have been unsuccessful, and only if there exists no contractual conciliation or arbitration office which operates on a footing of equality.

Article 6.

(1) The employers and employees in question, and their organizations, are under obligation to preserve the peace and to refrain from all aggressive measures during the conciliation or arbitration procedure. This obligation to preserve the peace begins with the moment at which the parties have been notified of the establishment of the conciliation or arbitration office, and it lasts 45 days. This period can be extended by a unanimous decision of the conciliation or arbitration office.

It should be noted that for each dispute in which the federal authorities intervene there is established a board of five members, including a chairman, two neutrals and one member each proposed by the respective parties to the dispute. (Recueil Officiel des Lois Fédérales, 1949, p. 1403).

II. Wages and Hours and Factory Inspection

Until the amendment to Article 34-*ter* in 1947, the Swiss federal government was on the whole restricted in its activities over wages and hours to control over fabriques. However, the Confederation's power with respect to the civil law was also a source of federal jurisdiction.

The fixing of wage standards by law or governmental fiat takes three forms in Switzerland. First, there is the prescribing of a minimum wage by legislation for a given industry, where such law is to all intents and purposes the simple expression of the legislator's will. The number of cases in which a wage standard has been fixed in such a way is small. Either the federation or the cantons may legislate in this area. An example of such regulation is the Confederation's ordinance of 1943 "fixing minimum wages for the hand-knitting home industry."

Second, there is the standard contract system, under which wage and hour standards and prescriptions for working conditions are enacted by the legislation of the federation or of the cantons under the authority of Article 324 of the Law of Contracts, which reads:

The Federal Council and the authorities designated by the cantons can, after consultation with the interested professional organizations or with the public utilities associations, issue standard contracts for various kinds of labor contracts and for apprenticeship training; the contents of these contracts are presumed to express the will of the parties if there exists no written contract to the contrary.

Before World War II this ideal or standard type contract scheme was not very widely used. Since the war there have been a number of instances in which such a contract has been applied. By a decree of the Federal Council of March 28, 1947, for example, a contract-type was enacted for medical assistants; on April 16, 1947, for hospital attendants and other similar patient aides; in March, 1946, for dental technicians. Such decrees provided for length of working time, vacations, amount of pay, and accident insurance benefits. Cantons also have power to decree such contract-types. In 1918, for example, in Fribourg, where the cantonal Conciliation Office has been given power to put such contracts into force, there was one established for masons at work in the city of Fribourg.

One of the most significant developments in Swiss governmental wage and hour regulation since World War I has been the growing movement for the legitimatizing and extension of the common-rule system. Under this arrangement, increasing in popularity in many of the federal systems and in other states as well, contracts concluded through collective negotiation for a part of an industry are made valid by governmental ordinance for the whole of that industry. In Switzerland, as elsewhere, this general rule was modified by the addition of a number of restrictions, but the basic idea remains. An act was passed by the Federal Assembly in 1918 to give the federal government authority, under certain conditions, to extend the validity of collective agreements to enterprises not covered by the original agreement but this act was rejected by a referendum. It was not until the authorization was given in a decree of October 1, 1941, effected under the Federal Council's "full power" (*pleins pouvoirs*), that the common-rule system was established in Switzerland. Both the federal government and the cantons were authorized to effect the extension of agreements. In 1943 the emergency decree was replaced by a regular federal decree which has since been extended several times. Between 1942 and 1949, 153 agreements were given general applicability by the Federal Council and 185 by the cantons. Under the decree of June 23, 1943 (Recueil Officiel des Lois Fédérales, 1943, p. 853), the division of competence between the federal government and the cantons was divided thus:

II, *Article* 3.
   (1) If the clauses which shall be made compulsory are applicable only in one canton or in part of a canton, the right to declare them generally compulsory rests with the cantonal government.
   (2) The Federal Council is competent in all other cases. It determines, whenever necessary, if and in what respect the terms which had been declared generally compulsory by the cantons shall be annulled.

In 1939 an amendment to the Constitution respecting compulsory extension of agreements had been passed by the Federal Assembly, but with the outbreak of war, no attempt was made to carry the ratification process further. Finally, the change was accepted in the referendum of 1947 as a part of the completely new Article 34-*ter*. The pertinent sections provide as follows:

Article 34-ter.

(1) The Confederation has the right to legislate:

    c. on the general compulsory function of collective labor contracts or other agreements between organizations of employers and employees or workers in order that peaceful working conditions will be preserved.

A further clause, protective of the rights of the cantons, provides:

(2) The general compulsory function envisaged in (c) can be declared only in matters connected with work relationships between employers and workers, under the condition, however, that the intended regulations take sufficient consideration of regional differences, of legitimate interests of minorities, and respect equality before the law and freedom of association.

Under Article 34, the Confederation has always had the power of regulating wages and hours of work in fabriques. Since 1919, when the 1914 Law on Industrial Enterprises was amended, the normal work week in fabriques has been prescribed as 48 hours. Beyond this, the law of 1919 provided, workers were to receive a 25 per cent overtime premium. In addition, a law of March 6, 1929 regulated work weeks for workers on railroads, in post offices, in trucking, and in those enterprises engaged under contract for the federal government. The Law on Industrial Enterprises of 1914 also provided for weekly rest in the plants covered, and especially prohibited work on Sundays, with only rare exceptions.

Since 1931 workers in commerce, traffic, and restaurant establishments and in certain other industrial establishments have been guaranteed 24 successive hours rest in any one week, by a federal law.

Workers in other than the enterprises mentioned above have had to rely on cantonal protection, which has been far from complete, or on the provisions of collective agreements.

To what extent the federal government will rely for legislation in the field of wages and hours on the provisions of the new Article 34-*ter*, 1 (a), giving the Confederation power to legislate "on the protection of employees and workers," remains to be seen.

Article 34 (1) of the 1874 Constitution gave the Federal Government power to legislate with respect to "the protection to be accorded to workers in unsanitary or dangerous industries." By 1877, legislation had already been enacted providing for a federal inspection service in fabriques (Law on Industrial Plants of 1877), which was reorganized under the 1914 law on fabriques already mentioned. The country is divided into four inspectorates under the control of the Federal Council. As a general rule, inspectors visit a factory once each year. The 1914 law is concerned with the protection of the worker against accidents and industrial or other illnesses, effective general sanitation and lighting, clean personal sanitation facilities, adequate heating, and the establishing of suitable conveniences, such as canteens (Art. 5).

The 1914 law provided also that factories under the inspection of the federal system might also be inspected by cantonal offices (e.g., Art. 7). Such inspection is concerned mostly with such matters as fire control and related items.

III. LABOR EXCHANGES

Historically, public employment exchanges in Switzerland have been administered by the cantons. Since 1909, however, there have been both federal assistance and supervision. The Federal Decree of the Federal Assembly regarding "the encouragement of Employment Services by the Confederation" was enacted on October 29, 1909. Although itself citing no authority, the law had been preceded in its enactment by a message from the Federal Council referring to Article 2 of the Constitution which reads: "The Confederation has as its aim to preserve internal peace and order, to protect liberty and the rights of the citizens and to increase their general prosperity."

While being granted subsidies provided for by the law, the cantons were required to adhere to certain conditions in the operation of their offices: the service must be free; it must be impartial, and representatives of both labor and management must be represented on an advisory board; in case of a strike or lockout creating job openings, workers seeking positions must be informed of the existence of such a labor disturbance; budgetary and fiscal reports must be submitted to the federal Department of Public Economics, as well as a copy of the service's statutes and regulations.

Cantons were not required under the 1909 law to establish exchanges, nor were they required to accept federal discipline or subsidies, though of course once the subsidies were accepted, the discipline needed to be as well. However, the Ordinance of November 11, 1924, issued by the Federal Council, made establishment of cantonal labor exchanges and their adherence to federal supervision obligatory. The ordinance pointed to several instruments for its justification, including the 1909 law, but in particular to the International Labor Convention signed at Washington in 1919 and ratified by Switzerland in 1922, as well as Article 102 (1), 8, of the Swiss Constitution, which reads:

Article 102.
> (1) The power and the obligations of the Federal Council within
>   the limits of this Constitution are specifically the following:
>   8. It watches over the external interests of the Confederation,
>   specifically on its international relations, and it is in general in charge of external relations.

Article 4 of this 1924 Ordinance decreed that the cantonal services should meet four conditions, these encompassing for all practical purposes those cited above as being required by the 1909 Federal Decree. The federal Department of Public Economics was also made responsible for coordinating the work of the public services and the still-existing private services (Art. 6).

As it stands now, since its adoption in completely revised form in 1947, Article 34-*ter* of the Constitution includes the following provision:

Article 34-ter.
  (1) The Confederation has the right to legislate:
    e. On labor exchanges

Acting under this authority, the Federal Assembly on June 22, 1951 enacted the Federal Law on Employment Services. The public labor exchanges continue to be cantonal, and federal assistance and supervision remain. The functions of the offices are described as labor placement and labor counseling. The federal authorities are authorized to take other measures so as to aid, for example, in the temporary or permanent transfer of workers between professions and regions.

Private exchanges operated for profit are subjected under the law's terms to the supervision of the cantonal authorities.

The federation authorities are authorized to defray between 10 and 30 per cent of the costs of personnel and materiel in the local labor offices, in cluding their rental charges, their furnishing, and their maintenance.

The federal authorities are also authorized to aid employment services operated jointly by employers and employees (*services paritaires*), where the operations of a service cover the whole country and where its offices are open to the public. Aid may reach 30 per cent of the agency's cost of personnel and materiel.

An interesting instance of intercantonal cooperation to protect their workers in placement in foreign countries is the still-existing concordat of 1875 between the cantons of Fribourg, Vaud, Neuchâtel, and Geneva (Recueil Officiel des Lois, 1 N.S. §796). This concordat was adopted by the cantons and approved by the Federal Council under the provisions of Article 7 (2) of the Federal Constitution, giving the cantons "the right to conclude amongst themselves conventions on matters of legislation, administration, and justice." The concordat essentially bound the participating cantons to a strict police surveillance of placement agencies engaged in placing domestics, nurses, teachers, and governesses abroad.

IV. Social Insurance

With the adoption of the new Article 34-*ter* in 1947, all the traditional forms of social insurance — sickness, accident, old-age, widows, and survivors, invalidity, and unemployment — now find mention in the Swiss Constitution. Though there are federal legislation and federal administrative machinery for all the five forms of insurance, none of the insurance programs is administered wholly by the federal government, nor is federal law the sole controlling law. Legislative determinations of many important features, such as the question of compulsion in coverage for sickness insurance, are left to the cantons. Administration is often in the hands of private associations, or of the cantons.

A. *Sickness Insurance*

In reading the legislative history of Swiss sickness insurance one needs to bear in mind that voluntary sickness insurance associations were common among the working population before the Confederation initiated its legislation, and that many of these associations were organized under the compulsion of cantonal governments. The constitutional amendment of 1890, Article 34-*bis,* recognized this situation in declaring: "(1) The Confederation shall introduce by means of legislation sickness and accident insurance whereby it will give consideration to existing associations for assistance." The rejection of the first federal legislation under this amendment in a 1900 referendum appears to have been caused by a belief on the part of many citizens that the proposed legislation did not accord sufficient protection to the private associations as against the public ones which the cantons might establish, or the factory associations that might come into being. But even the 1900 law did not attempt to establish a uniform national system of contributions, benefits, or administration.

Finally, in 1911, the Federal Law of Insurance in Case of Sickness and Accidents was adopted. (Recueil Officiel des Lois Fédérales, 1912, p. 351). The form of federal activity in the sickness insurance field is reflected in Article 1:

(1) The Confederation encourages sickness insurance by granting, in accordance with the present law, subsidies to sickness insurance associations.

(2) All the sickness insurance associations which satisfy the provisions of the present law are entitled to federal subsidies; they can organize themselves as they please in so far as the law does not contain regulations to the contrary.

No federal benefit rate was established, and there was no uniform contribution rate. Each approved association was to be granted subsidies on a per capita basis. Whether pharmaceutical benefits were to be available was left to the decisions of the particular association. It would have to meet such costs with no additional federal aid.

The decisions as to whether or not sickness insurance should be made compulsory was left to the individual cantons (Art. 2). The cantons might also establish public associations (*Caisses*), giving due regard to existing insurance associations.

The choice of the doctor was prescribed by the law as being left to the patient from among qualified medical men in the area, but the associations were charged with insuring that there was no fraud. Among the federal prescriptions imposed by the law were these:

1. The right of free transfer from one association to another when the insured is obliged, because of the statutes of one society, to leave it as a result of his change of residence, profession, or employment, or if the society is dissolved or is no longer recognized.
2. Societies may restrict membership on the basis of religion, political affiliation, profession, or place of work (Art. 3 (6)), but no person can be refused entrance to a society if in his area there is no society whose qualifications of this nature he can meet (Art. 5 (2)).
3. Associations desiring federal approval, and the consequent federal subsidies, must present their statutes and other instruments regulating the rights and obligations of their members for the approval of the Federal Council (Art. 4).

B. *Accident Insurance*

Before the passage of Article 34-*bis* in 1890 and the subsequent law of 1911, responsibility for compensation in the case of industrial accidents was regulated under the civil law. The law of July 1, 1875 had established criteria for civilly assigning responsibility on railroads, steamboats, and later, under the laws of 1894 and 1905, in the postal service.

However, the most significant legislation prior to that of 1911 was Article 5 of the Act of March 23, 1877 on Work in Industrial Plants. This article provided for the judicial determination of responsibility, with the guiding principle being that of employer responsibility for accidents and industrial illness except in case of acts of God, criminal acts, or contributory negligence on the part of the worker or a fellow servant. As a result of this legislation, numerous mutual associations were established by employers for their protection against accident claims.

What the Act of 1911 (Recueil Systématique des Lois et Ordonnances, 1848–1947, 283) did was to transfer the insurance from the person of the employer directly to the person of the worker, although it continues to be the employer who pays the premium. This Act of 1911, a part of the general act which also deals with sickness insurance, is the existing guiding legislation on accident insurance. It established a national program, administered by a National Swiss Accident Insurance Association in Lucerne, although in some circumstances the Caisse Nationale may call on a local sickness association to administer medical and other services to an injured worker.

Compulsorily insured are workers on railroads, steam vessels, and in the postal service; the building industry; trucking, and hauling by water; telephone and telegraph repair work; workers on heavy construction work on such installations as railroads, bridges, roads, and tunnels.   In addition, the Federal Council was authorized to extend the compulsory features to include personnel in work involving the transmission of electrical energy; in industrial enterprises engaged in work considered especially dangerous or unhealthy; and on public works.

Workers in industries not covered may insure themselves voluntarily, and in some cases with part of the premium being subsidized by the Caisse Nationale.

Insurance benefits for invalidity arising out of accidents or industrial illness in covered employment are provided for in Article 76.

C. *Old-Age and Survivors Insurance*

Until 1925 there was no federal activity in the field of old-age and survivors insurance. To that time, social insurance provisions in the Constitution referred only to sickness and accident insurance. However in some of the cantons, e.g. Vaud and Neuchâtel, there were voluntary old-age insurance plans established by the cantons, while in others, e.g. Glaris and Bâle-Ville, the plans were compulsory at least for some residents. In 1925, Article 34-*quater* was added to the Constitution, reading in part thus:

(1) The Confederation shall establish by legislative means insurance for old age and survivors insurance: it can ultimately introduce invalidity insurance.

(2) The insurance plans shall be carried out with the cooperation of the cantons; public or private insurance associations may be drawn into the plan.

An attempt to implement this constitutional provision in 1931 was rejected in a referendum, and so, until 1947, there was still no federal old-age insurance. In the meantime, however, needy aged and survivors were aided by a federal old-age assistance program in the form of subsidies to cantons to be used under certain conditions in cantonal assistance programs. One of these conditions was that cantons must not provide old-age assistance in the form of a charity arrangement. Preference was to be given those aged who had not received public charity in the past.

In 1947, the Law on Old-Age and Survivors Insurance of December 20, 1946, was approved in a referendum (Recueil Officiel des Lois Fédérales, 1947, p. 843). A program of uniform benefits is provided. The financing of the program is from three sources: (1) employees' contributions of a percentage of their salary (2 per cent); (2) employers' contributions matching these — or a self-employed contribution of 4 per cent; (3) federal and cantonal subsidies of the required remainder, with the federal subsidy being financed by a tobacco tax.

As in the case of the sickness insurance program, those insured in the old-age and survivors scheme participate by way of membership in private or cantonal associations, to which they and their employers pay contributions, and which supervise their receipt of benefits. The administration of the law is the responsibility of the Federal Council aided by a Commission on Old-Age and Survivors Insurance, in which are represented (Art. 73), in equal numbers, the insured, Swiss economic associations, old-age insurance associations (caisses) recognized by the Federal Council, the Confederation, and the cantons.

D. *Invalidity Insurance*

Except for the provisions, already referred to, in the Sickness and Accident Insurance Law, there is no federal legislation on invalidity insurance, and that portion of Article 34-*quater* which has already been quoted and under which the Confederation was given power to legislate in this field remains unused.

E. *Unemployment Insurance*

The form which governmental activity takes in Switzerland in respect to unemployment insurance is very much influenced by the fact that from 1880 to the First World War the basic insurance scheme for the alleviation of the effects of unemployment was that effected through organizations of workers created for that purpose. There were, in addition, cantonal funds established in a few instances, as at Berne and St. Gall. During World War I, the federal government began to aid these established funds. The funds, in exchange for the subsidies, were required to adhere to certain regulations respecting the amount of benefits and the duration of benefit-time. Federal subsidies were not granted to a fund unless cantonal and communal aid was given simultaneously.

The 1947 amendment to Article 34-*ter* for the first time provided a specific constitutional basis for federal activities in the unemployment insurance field in these terms:

> (1) The Confederation has the right to legislate:
>   e. . . . on unemployment insurance and aid to the unemployed;

With the further provision:

> (3) The unemployment insurance rests with the public and private associations which may be organized as syndicates on the basis of equality. The right to establish public associations and to declare unemployment insurance generally compulsory rests with the cantons.

The Law on Unemployment Insurance of June 22, 1951 (Recueil Officiel des Lois Fédérales, 1951, p. 1167), conforms with these provisions. The 1951 law decrees that the private (including those in which employers and workers cooperate), public, and trade union funds (caisses) established especially and solely for unemployment insurance purposes (Art. 6 (2)), shall be the basic administrative agencies for the unemployment insurance program. The Office of Industry, of Arts and Crafts, and of Labors, accords petitioning funds recognition and ensures that their activities are conducted according to law.

Article 3 provides: "The Confederation supervises the execution of the present law and sees to it that it is uniformly applied by the cantons and the recognized insurance association."

Article 4 repeats the constitutional provision regarding the exclusive power of the cantons to establish public funds and then empowers the cantons to issue the necessary regulations for the compulsory insurance, and specifically to force the employers to deduct the worker's withholding contributions.

The treasuries are built up in the first instance from contributions of the worker. The amount of the individual's contribution may vary from fund to fund, depending on the decision taken by the members of the fund, and their peculiar financial circumstances, and among the members of a fund depending on their wages. At least 12 francs a year must be paid by each insured person; that much the federal law requires. It might be noted, too, that 500 members are required before a fund can be given recognition.

Further revenues come to the fund from investments, from federal subsidies, and from the cantonal subsidies, which must equal the federal.

Benefit rates are according to a uniform scale throughout Switzerland. The amount of the federal subsidies to each fund is adjusted to insure that the benefit scale can be maintained by the particular fund.

The Federal Council is empowered to provide for cases where workers move from one fund to another because of movement from one area or one job to another (Art. 18 (3)).

F. *Summary*

It is clear that the general principles of Swiss federal activity are encouragement of the coverage of all persons in the country, general supervision of operations under criteria based on legislatively established standards, subsidization of programs financed primarily by the insured, and administration of each program in the first instance by democratically governed, local associations of the insured which are allowed considerable discretion regarding the fields to be covered and the amount of benefits, and which are vested with the responsibility for insuring the honest, efficient operation of their particular program. It is a combination of federal incentive and aid with local freedom to adjust to local inclinations and needs.

A P P E N D I X   V

United States

I. LABOR RELATIONS

A. *Union Organization and Collective Bargaining*

The entry of the federal government into this field is a development of the present century. Until some twenty years ago, no one questioned the power of the states to regulate union organization and the strike and picketing activities of such organizations even in the case of businesses which covered several States or which received goods in interstate commerce. Until then, the organization of labor unions and such activities as strikes and boycotts in pursuance of their aims were subject to the control of State courts and legislatures.

Although there were early indications that any combination of working men would be held by courts to be a criminal conspiracy, by 1880 it was well established that employees might form labor unions without criminal liability and might engage in limited strikes. However, the possibility of striking was severely limited in fact until 1930 because of the readiness of both the State and the federal courts to issue injunctions under the common law for the purpose of ending a strike. Even peaceful picketing was often held an unlawful means of carrying on a strike, and such common labor goals as the organization of a shop, collective bargaining, and the closed shop were often held to be unlawful objectives. The union which was found to have carried on an unlawful strike was liable in damages, and its further activities might even be enjoined.

Under certain circumstances, it was possible for an employer to obtain a labor injunction in the federal courts. Article III of the Constitution and the enabling legislation empower the federal courts to hear suits between citizens of different States. Many American corporations are chartered by States other than those in which they do business. Consequently a corporation chartered in one State could obtain an injunction in cases where the strike against it was carried on by employees living in another State. In 1933 Congress enacted the Norris-LaGuardia Act (47 Stat. 70), under its power over the lower federal courts, and effectively prevented the federal courts from issuing injunctions against strikes or picketing by labor unions during a dispute except where there was fraud or violence. This Act recited its intention of protecting the normal activities of workers in the formation of unions and in acting together to further their interests as members of a union, and from being regarded as constituting a conspiracy. Since the statute is a regulation of the jurisdiction of the federal courts, it does not affect the legality of strikes and picketing under State law.   Nevertheless, enactment of the Norris-LaGuardia Act gave new impetus to State legislation and a considerable number of statutes modeled after it have been enacted.

In the case of national legislation, the right to organize and to strike is guaranteed by a number of acts, but especially by the National Labor Relations Act of 1935 and the Labor-Management Relations Act of 1947 which is an amendment to the act of 1935.

These acts are based on the power given to Congress in Article I, Section 8, of the Constitution: "The Congress shall have Power . . . [3] To regulate Commerce with foreign Nations, and among the several States, and with the Indian Tribes."

In the National Labor Relations Act (Wagner Act), the following statement of policy and justification is found:

> The denial by employers of the right of employees to organize and the refusal by employers to accept the procedure of collective bargaining lead to strikes and other forms of industrial strife or unrest, which have the intent or the necessary effect of burdening or obstructing commerce by (a) impairing the efficiency, safety, or operation of the instrumentalities of commerce; (b) occurring in the current of commerce; (c) materially affecting, restraining, or controlling the flow of raw materials or manufactured or processed goods from or into the channels of commerce; or (d) causing diminution of employment and wages in such volume as substantially to impair or disrupt the market for goods flowing from or into the channels of commerce [49 Stat. 449].

The 1947 Act (Taft-Hartley Act) has much the same clauses for justification of its constitutionality, but in addition emphasizes the reciprocal duties of the labor unions toward the employer.

Decisions of the federal Supreme Court before 1937 had held that the "interstate commerce" power might not be used by the Congress to control the conditions under which goods were manufactured, even though the raw materials for the manufacture thereof might be obtained from other States, and the goods might be sold in other than the producing State.   See, for example, *Hammer v. Dagenhart* (247 U.S. 251 (1918)), where the attempt of Congress to control child labor under the interstate commerce clause was invalidated.   There the Supreme Court held that the power to regulate interstate commerce is the power to prescribe the rule by which the commerce is to be governed, in other words, to control the means by which it is carried on.   But, the Supreme Court said, the manufacture of goods is not commerce, nor does the fact that they are intended for, and afterwards are shipped in, interstate commerce, make their production a part of that commerce and so subject to the control of Congress.   Control over local trade and manufacture was a reserve of the States' police powers.

In 1937, however, in the case of *United States v. Jones & Laughlin Steel Corporation* (301 U.S. 1), in which the constitutionality of the National Labor Relations Act was being challenged, the Supreme Court held that Congress did have the constitutional authority, arising out of its power to "protect" interstate commerce, to safeguard the right of the employees in a manufacturing plant to self-organization and to the free choice of their representatives for collective bargaining.

Among the companies to which, in one case or another, the 1935 and 1947 Acts have been held to apply, are those engaged in the manufacture of building materials, clothing and textiles, electrical and radio equipment, flour and feed mills, food packers and manufacturers, furniture, iron and steel, lumber and logging, wood products, meat packers, dairies, newspapers, public utilities. Of course the case of each company involved in litigation under the Act is studied in itself in terms of its relationship to interstate commerce to determine whether the Acts do really apply.

Until 1947 the States were free to regulate all strikes, picketing and other concerted labor activities except, perhaps, those directed at railroads and other interstate carriers. Until 1937 this condition was the result, partially, of the constitutional doctrine mentioned above under which the power of the federal government in this field under the interstate commerce clause was severely restricted by the Supreme Court. After 1937 the jurisdiction of the federal government was expanded, as noted, but the jurisdiction of the States was not necessarily affected. Only after 1947 did two developments occur which resulted in a substantial diminution of State power in this field. In that year the federal Congress enacted the Taft-Hartley Act which outlaws certain concerted activities on the part of labor organizations. Second, the Supreme Court held that the federal statute guaranteeing employees in industries subject to federal control the right to engage in union organization, collective bargaining, and "concerted activities for the purposes of collective bargaining and other mutual aid or protection," prevented the States from interfering with strikes and picketing by such employees because rights created by federal legislation are "the supreme law of the land."

B. *Labor Disputes*

In time of peace, federal intervention in labor affairs was limited before the 1947 Labor-Management Relations Act to the work of a Conciliation Service in the Department of Labor. There were no compulsion, no investigation, and no public reporting. As a result, the Service was able to operate well beyond what before 1937 were the limits of federal competence. The 1947 Act directs the Federal Mediation and Conciliation Service to proffer its services in any labor dispute in any industry affecting commerce whenever in its judgment such dispute threatens to cause what the Act calls a "substantial" interruption of commerce, but the Service is directed to avoid intervention in disputes having only a minor effect on interstate commerce if State or other conciliation services are available. Again, there is neither compulsion nor investigation, nor fact-finding (29 U.S. Code §173).

Additional legislation exists for use in disputes in peacetime that threaten to imperil the "national health or safety" (29 U.S. Code §176), but in the end in every case the parties are free to carry their dispute to the strike or lockout stage and no further intervention by the federal government is possible under existing legislation. Legislation respecting railway labor disputes extends back in one form or another to 1888. At present the legislation in force is the Railway Labor Disputes Act of 1926 which provides for a special National Mediation Board for railroad disputes to attempt to adjust differences through conciliation. Parties may be persuaded to agree to binding arbitration. Where the parties refuse arbitration, the President may, as a last resort, appoint a fact-finding board to study the situation and make its statement of the facts and its recommendations in a public report. During the long period required for all these steps, no strike or lockout may be undertaken.

For other than railway disputes affecting the national health or safety the 1947 Labor-Management Relations Act provides a system under which the executive may appeal to federal courts for an injunction to be kept in force a possible 80 days, in which time investigation and publication of the facts in the dispute, but with no recommendations to be made by the investigating body, are to be carried out and other mediatory attempts made.

Conciliation services exist in most States. In addition, a number of States now have legislation providing for State intervention in disputes in public utility enterprises, e.g. electric power, gas, public transportation. Usually such laws permit some form of compulsion on the initiative of the executive to maintain service to the public. In some cases, seizure of the enterprise by the State executive is authorized. In other cases, intervention may take the form simply of requiring the parties to the dispute to submit the matters at issue to compulsory arbitration by an arbitration board. The intervention by States into public utility labor disputes would seem to have been generally acceptable to the United States Supreme Court since its approval more than thirty-five years ago of the validity of national legislation respecting wages and hours standards in interstate transportation (*Wilson v. New*, 243 U.S. 332 (1917)). And, although the Supreme Court has not been faced with the problem in recent years, it would also seem that its new policy of permitting broad intervention by the State and federal governments in the relations between management and labor, and in the operation of enterprises, e.g. State minimum wage legislation, would permit compulsory State arbitration in other than public utility enterprises. When, in 1925, the Court was considering a Kansas statute establishing a Court of Industrial Relations for disposing compulsorily of disputes "in all industries affected with a public interest," it held that the industrial relations court might not deal with disputes in such an industry as meat packing, on the grounds that the "public interest" in such an industry was not a direct one (*Wolff Packing Co. v. Kansas Court of Industrial Relations*, 262 U.S. 522 (1923) and 267 U.S. 552 (1925)). This view would now seem to be outmoded.

During wartime the President, acting under his powers as commander-in-chief, possesses broad powers to act in industrial disputes affecting the conduct of the war, and the Congress has broader powers to legislate in these circumstances than it does possess or than it chooses to exercise in peacetime disputes in interstate commerce.

Article II, Section 2, of the Constitution provides that "the President shall be commander-in-chief of the Army and Navy of the United States."

Article I, Sec. 8, (11) provides that Congress shall have power "to declare war"; (12) "to raise and support armies"; (13) and "to provide and maintain a navy." During World War II, in January, 1942, the President, acting under his powers as commander-in-chief and citing the existence of authority under general war statutes, established a National War Labor Board having the power to resolve by compulsion all disputes "which might interrupt work which contributes to the prosecution of the war" (Executive Order No. 9017, January 12, 1942. In the few instances in which there was persevering resistance to a determining order of the Board, the Board appealed to the President, who in a number of cases used his war powers to seize the factories involved, after which the Board order was effected; the orders of the Board itself were not judicially enforceable.

The Board was given statutory sanction by an Act of Congress of June, 1943 (War Labor Disputes Act, 57 Stat. 163), which substantially reaffirmed the powers of the Board as they had existed under the Executive Order of January, 1942. The Act reaffirmed the Presidential power to seize industrial or other facilities necessary for the war effort if and when he found that strikes or other labor disturbances were interrupting the operation of such facilities. It was under the terms of this seizure section that the President seized struck coal mines as late as May, 1946, but while hostilities were still technically continuing, and caused his representatives to negotiate with representatives of the miners concerning the terms and conditions of employment. As late as the Spring of 1952 many of the nation's railroads were in the control of the federal government under a continuing war power, even though all peace treaties had by then been signed, the six-month period of grace (beyond the treaty-ratification date) provided in the Act of 1943 not having yet elapsed.

II. Wages, Hours, and Working Conditions

The federal government enters the area of wage and hour regulation under the interstate commerce power and to the same degree that it does in the case of labor conflicts.

Before 1941, when the Fair Labor Standards Act of 1938 (52 Stat. 1060) was held constitutional, several attempts of the federal government to impose minimum wage and maximum hour standards had been overturned by the Supreme Court. Under the National Industrial Recovery Act of 1933 (48 Stat. 195) there was provision for a scheme of wages and hours controls (including a modified form of "common rule" arrangement) in the case of industries engaged in interstate or foreign commerce. The agreements made within an industry between employees and management could be made applicable by the President to the whole industry, even to those plants whose managements were not signatories to the agreement. Or the President, in the absence of an approved agreement, might himself establish these standards and apply them to a whole industry or to an industry within an area. The whole NIRA act was invalidated by the decision of the Supreme Court in 1935 in *A.L.A. Schechter Poultry Corp. v. United States* (295 U.S. 495). These particular provisions savoring of the common rule, the Court thought, constituted the result of an unlawful delegation by the Congress of its legislative powers to private individuals. In addition, the Court denied that the Congress could even legislate in respect to wages and hours in production industries.

Another attempt to establish a common-rule system was voided by the federal Supreme Court in *Carter v. Carter Coal Co.* (298 U.S. 238) in 1936. The Bituminous Coal Conservation Act of 1935 (Guffey Act) had sought to have the wages and hours standards agreed to by collective bargaining in a particular coal-producing district extended to all workers and plants in that district provided that in the original agreements one half of the workers and two thirds of the coal mined were affected.

After the Supreme Court's change of orientation in the spring of 1937, the prospects for the Court's acceptance of a direct federal minimum wage and maximum hour statute increased. The Fair Labor Standards Act was passed in 1938. This act, in addition to regulating child labor and establishing hours or work standards, required the payment of a minimum wage of 25 cents per hour (75 cents after January, 1950) to all workers in interstate commerce industries. In 1949 the Act was amended so as to exempt most agricultural workers, some fishery workers, and a few other categories. The Act was held valid in *United States v. Darby Lumber Co.* (312 U.S. 100 (1941)).

It may be interesting to note that in the days prior to the Supreme Court's shift in attitude toward the interstate commerce clause, when various devices were being suggested for effecting nation-wide standards of wages and hours, Massachusetts and New Hampshire sought, by doing so between themselves, to encourage the signing of interstate compacts to be approved by the respective legislatures and the Congress which would specify the minimal conditions of labor, and make these uniform throughout the country. Such resorts are no longer necessary.

These compacts were also intended as a means of circumventing the persistent overturn by the federal Supreme Court in the early 1930's of State minimum wage legislation. The Court long had held that for a State legislation to prescribe minimum wages was to interfere with the right of the employer and employee to negotiate freely to an agreement. Such interference, it was held, was a violation of the "contract clause" of the federal Constitution, Article III, Section 10, which provided that no State should pass any "law impairing the obligation of contracts." In the circumstances, such an attitude toward the State attempts at minimum wage legislation, and toward federal attempts at control over these matters, meant that there could in fact be no minimum wage legislation at all, since the commerce clause could not cover the federal power, and the contract clause limited the power of the States. The Court's line of reasoning until 1937 is well illustrated in *Morehead v. Tipaldo* (298 U.S. 587), handed down in 1936. There the State was held forbidden to intervene in any way in the bargaining process. *Morehead v. Tipaldo* was, however, overturned in the very next year, and the present policy of the Court to uphold State minimum wage legislation was inaugurated in *West Coast Hotel v. Parrish* (300 U.S. 379 (1937)). In that case, the Court said: "If the protection of women is a legitimate exercise of state power . . . the legislature of the state was clearly entitled to consider the situation of women in employment, the fact that they are in the class receiving the least pay, [and] that their bargaining power is relatively weak . . ."

It is still the case today, however, that there is no minimum wage legislation in several States.

It might be noted that where there is minimum wage legislation in a State, and where the State-prescribed minimum is higher than the one prescribed by the federal statute, then, in accordance with Section 18 of the federal Act, the State standard prevails.

Occupations not covered by the federal statute today are, *inter alia*, laundries, cleaning establishments, canneries, restaurants, hotels, beauty parlors, farms, and households.

An interesting attempt by the federal government to aid States in their individual efforts to improve the conditions of their workers was made in the Ashhurst-Sumners Act of 1935 (49 Stat. 494). When a number of States enacted legislation forbidding the sale within their borders of prison-made goods, the federal government added its weight to the States' efforts by resorting to the interstate commerce power to prevent the transportation of such goods from one State into a State forbidding their sale. This use of the interstate commerce power was validated by the Supreme Court early in 1937 (*Kentucky Whip and Collar Co. v. Illinois Central Railroad*, 299 U.S. 334), on the eve of its dramatic change of view by which a greater participation of the federal government in the whole field of labor relations was made possible.

The power of Congress to regulate the conditions under which purchases of government supplies are to be made (see *Ellis v. United States*, 206 U.S. 246 (1907), where the right of the federal government as well as of the State governments to lay down the conditions under which they shall receive materials from private sources for use in public works was upheld as an inherent power of any governing power) is used by the Congress to prescribe the minimum wages to be paid workers by those holding contracts to produce material for the use of the government. In the Public Contracts Act of 1936 (49 Stat. 2036), known as the Walsh-Healey Act, the Congress required that contractors pay not less than the prevailing minimum wages in their localities, and provided further, and importantly, that the determination of what were the prevailing minimum wages should be made by the federal Secretary of Labor.

In time of war, again, the power of the Congress over wages becomes much broader than in peacetime, and the interstate commerce limits are ignored. In the recent war, for example, the National War Labor Board, as we noted earlier, was given blanket power by the President, acting under his war powers, to determine any labor dispute. In so doing it obviously would be determining wage and hour conditions in the enterprise affected. In July, 1942, the Board adopted a standard, for instance, to which it adhered more or less during the rest of the war. Under this "Little Steel formula," wage increases of not more than 15 per cent above the particular January, 1941, wage earnings were to be allowed.

Later, in October, 1942, the Wage and Salary Stabilization Act (56 Stat. 765) was passed as an amendment to the Emergency Price Control Act of that year. In the Wage Act the President was directed to take measures to stabilize wages affecting the cost of living (as well as prices and salaries) at the levels of September 15, 1942, though the President was authorized to make adjustments to correct inequities. The Act of course applied to any wages received in any employment wherever located, and fines and prison sentences were provided for the payment or receipt of wages or salaries in violation of the President's orders. The powers of State rate-fixing agencies having supervision over public utility companies were not affected, however, except that notice of an intended request for rise in rates had to be given the National War Labor Board by the utility to afford the Board an opportunity to intervene before the State regulating body. Nor were State or local governments prevented from increasing the wages and salaries of their employees. The Executive Order of October, 1942, for example, referred only to "employers or corporations."

As in the case of legislative and executive orders on labor disputes, there was for a short time (shorter than in the case of the disputes) after the actual end of hostilities in World War II a continued control exercised over wages and salaries by the federal government. But this was ended by the abolition of all wage controls in 1947.

III. Labor Placement

Except for a United States Employment Service created in 1907 to aid in the placing of immigrants on farms, there were, until the depression years, practically no public employment exchanges operated by any government in the United States. Exchanges were privately owned.

By 1933 the pressure of demands from workers seeking inexpensive job-placement aid which would look impartially and honestly to the needs of both employer and worker had resulted in the establishment of public employment offices in a number of States. With the passage of the National Cooperative Employment Service Act (48 Stat. 113), known as the Wagner-Peyser Act, the federal executive was authorized to aid States already having public agencies considered of acceptable standard and willing to receive the aid on terms prescribed; it was authorized also to establish federal offices where there were no public agencies. Section 3a, for example, read:

> It shall be the duty and the province of the Bureau to promote and
> develop a national system of employment offices for [those] who are
> legally qualified to engage in gainful occupations . . . to maintain a
> farm placement service, to maintain a public employment service for
> the District of Columbia, and . . . to assist in establishing and main-
> taining systems of public employment offices in the several states and the
> political subdivisions thereof . . . The Bureau shall also assist in co-
> ordinating the public employment offices throughout the country and
> in increasing their usefulness by developing the prescribed minimum
> standards of efficiency, assisting them in meeting problems peculiar to
> their localities, promoting uniformity in their administrative and statis-
> tical procedure, furnishing and publishing information as to oppor-
> tunities for employment and other information of value in the operation
> of the system, and maintaining a system of clearing labor between the
> several states.

Funds were to be apportioned under the Act to the States in the proportion of the population of each State to the total United States population. Reports to the United States Employment Service were required from each State agency receiving grants. Among the standards imposed on the States are those requiring that the hiring and administration of personnel staffing the offices be accomplished through a satisfactory merit system.

This Act remains the basis of the relations between the United States and the States in the operation of the employment services. At present the United States operates its exchanges in nine States not having their own.

During World War II the facilities and personnel of the State offices were assumed by the United States Employment Service (see Executive Orders No. 8990 of December 23, 1941, and No. 9008 of January 2, 1942, regarding the personnel), under the federal war powers. In 1946 by special action of the Congress, these offices were returned to the States, and their personnel as well (60 Stat. 679). The emphasis during the war was on the use of the federal agencies as clearing houses to facilitate the movement of workers from one part of the nation to another. Controls on movement from job to job were relatively weak, compared to those in existence in other countries. There was no compulsory direction, or even registration.

Workers who had held certain jobs requiring skill and being considered essential to the war effort could leave such jobs, but before gaining employment in another place they might be required to obtain a clearance from the first employer.

IV. SOCIAL INSURANCE

A. *Old-Age Insurance and Survivors Benefits, and Old-Age Assistance*

The only social insurance program of the federal government which is completely and solely administered by it without the participation of the States in any way is the old-age insurance (benefits) program. This was established under the Federal Social Security Act of 1935 (49 Stat. 620). The Act was amended to provide for survivors' insurance in 1939 (53 Stat. 1360), and was further amended in 1950 to increase the number of employment fields covered, so that now the self-employed, domestics, and some agricultural workers are included (Public Law No. 734, 81st Cong., 2d Sess. (1950)). Under the terms of the 1935 Act, as amended, there was established under federal control an Old-Age Reserve Account, to be built up from the payment of a wages tax paid in equal amounts by both employer and employee, being a fixed percentage of the worker's wage. From this Account, old-age and survivors benefits are paid on the basis of right to those meeting age requirements, in the case of the aged and the youthful survivors, except that persons earning more than a certain amount of wages or salary are not for that period of time permitted to be recipients of benefits. There is no means test.

The constitutionality of the old-age and survivors insurance system, as well as of the unemployment insurance program, was challenged before the federal Supreme Court in 1937, but unsuccessfully. The Congress justified enactment of this legislation on the grounds of its power under Article 1, Section 8 (1), of the Constitution: "The Congress shall have Power To lay and collect Taxes, Duties, Imposts and Excises, to pay the Debts and provide for the common Defence and general Welfare of the United States . . ." The Congress contended that it had power to tax wages for the financing of an old-age and unemployment insurance program as a part of its power to tax for the general welfare.

Early in 1936 the federal Supreme Court had handed down a decision in *United States v. Butler* (297 U.S. 1), the Hoosac Mills case, which would seem to have foredoomed the old-age and unemployment insurance schemes to being declared unconstitutional. In *United States v. Butler* the Court invalidated a tax on the processing of farm commodities proceeds from which were to have gone to finance a program of agricultural production control and farm benefits. There the Court made these points:

A tax, in the general understanding of the term, and as used in the Constitution, signifies an exaction for the support of the government.

The word has never been thought to connote the expropriation of money from one group for the benefit of another.

[In the Child Labor Tax Case, *Bailey v. Drexel Furniture,* 259 U.S. 20, the Supreme Court had held in 1922 that the Congress could not control child labor by taxing its products in discrimination from products of adult labor not taxed.]

The power of taxation, which is expressly granted, may of course be adopted as a means to carry into operation another power also expressly granted. But resort to the taxing power to effectuate an end which is not legitimate, not within the scope of the Constitution, is obviously inadmissible.

However, in *Helvering v. Davis* (301 U.S. 619), decided in 1937, the old-age pension program was upheld. In a similar decision, *Steward Machine Co. v. Davis* (301 U.S. 548), on the same day, the validity of the unemployment insurance system was upheld. Said the Court in *Helvering v. Davis:*

Congress may spend money in aid of the "general welfare." . . . [yet] the line must still be drawn between one welfare and another, between particular and general. Where this shall be placed cannot be known through a formula in advance of the event. There is a middle ground or penumbra in which discretion is large. The discretion, however, is not confined to the courts. The discretion belongs to Congress, unless the choice is clearly wrong, a display of arbitrary power, not an exercise of judgment . . .

Congress did not improvise a judgment when it found that the award of old-age pension benefits would be conducive to the general welfare . . . The fate of workers over 65, when thrown out of work, is little less than desperate . . . The problem is plainly national in area and dimensions. Moreover, laws of the separate states cannot deal with it effectively. Congress, at least, had a basis for that belief. State and local governments are often lacking in the resources that are necessary to finance an adequate program of security for the aged. States and local governments are at times reluctant to increase so heavily the burden of taxation to be borne by their residents for fear of placing themselves in a position of economic disadvantage as compared with their neighbors or competitors . . . A system of old-age insurance has special dangers of its own, if put in force in one state and rejected in another. The existence of such a system is a bait to the needy and dependent elsewhere, encouraging them to migrate and seek a haven of repose. Only a power that is national can serve the interests of all.

The old-age assistance programs in the American system are State-sponsored and State-administered. The federal government subsidizes them to a certain extent under the usual terms of the American grant-in-aid system, giving a certain administrative control to the federal government. Old-age assistance is given as of need, and is non-contributory on the part of the potential recipient. Provision for federal subsidization was made in the 1935 Social Security Act, which sought to aid those who were already aged and so could not fall under the federal insurance scheme, and those aged who might be in need and who might not have been engaged in their lifetimes in employment covered by the old-age insurance tax and benefit program. Under a 1948 amendment, the federal government provides to each State subsidies to pay three quarters of the first $20 given by the State to a needy aged person each month, and one half of the remaining amount provided by the State, except that the federal government will not subsidize that portion of a monthly assistance payment in excess of $50.

Monthly payments vary greatly throughout the Union. In the State of Washington in 1948 they averaged $53; in Mississippi, $18.80.

It should be noted that States receiving federal subsidies may not, in respect to old-age assistance programs, require excessive residence periods; no more than 5 years' residence in the State out of the last 9 may be demanded, nor more than one year's continuous residence immediately before application.

B. *Unemployment Insurance*

The unemployment insurance program is basically a State responsibility, both legislatively and administratively. However, under the 1935 Social Security Act it was provided that every employer of eight or more persons, in whatever industry, should pay to the federal government a tax amounting to 1 per cent of his workers' wages, at the beginning, over and above the tax paid by him to share the financing of the old-age benefit program (§901). But it was further provided in the Act that if there was an unemployment fund under the law of his State to which he contributed tax moneys, then he might credit this contribution against the contribution required by the federal government, up to 90 per cent of the amount of the federal contribution (§902), the remaining 10 per cent being required by the federal government for the administration of its own program.

The federal aid to the States is proportionate on the basis of population and "such other factors" as the Federal Social Security Board may find relevant. Before aid is given to a State, its administrative organization for unemployment compensation and its legislation must meet certain requirements imposed by the statute, such, for example, as that no one shall be denied unemployment compensation for having refused to accept proffered employment if such employment is the result of a position's being vacant because of a strike, lockout, or other labor dispute (§903, a, 5).

There is no reciprocity among the States under the present unemployment insurance system, either as provided by federal legislation or interstate agreement. This means that there is no transfer of credit time accumulated by a worker in one State to the unemployment insurance system of another State should the worker move to a new employment.

There are now State unemployment compensation programs in every State. However, even when there were some States which did not have their own program, the federal government did not intervene in such a State to establish a national program. The unemployment insurance tax on employers in those States simply went *in toto* to the federal Treasury.

Except in the cases of Alabama and New Jersey, no States at present require employee contributions to the unemployment insurance fund, though at one time nine states required such contributions.

C. *Accident Insurance*

There is no federal program respecting accident insurance, except of course that there are arrangements providing for cases of accident among employees of the federal government itself. Industrial accident insurance is solely a State responsibility.

D. *Disability (Invalidity) Insurance*

In 1946, under an amendment to the Railroad Unemployment Insurance Act of 1938 (52 Stat. 1094), railroad workers were given a limited-time coverage for disability not arising in the course of their employment (60 Stat. 735).

Also in 1936 the Social Security Act of 1935 was amended to permit States which collect employee contributions (now Alabama and New Jersey) under unemployment insurance programs to use these funds for disability insurance (60 Stat. 991).

E. *Health Insurance*

There are no governmental health insurance programs in the United States, either at the national or State levels.

F. *Intergovernmental Immunity*

Employees of States or local governments are not covered by the federal old-age benefits program (Public Law No. 734, 81st Cong., 2d Sess. §204). For purposes of the unemployment insurance program of the federal government, States or local governments are not employers. Similarly, for State social insurance programs, the federal government is not an employer.

G. *Closing Statement*

Experience indicates that the States generally require the leadership of the federal government before taking action for the establishment of social insurance programs. The accident insurance system is an exception. The particular form of state-federal cooperation or participation in a program is the result of programs existing when the federal government system is adopted. Since there were already some State unemployment insurance systems and State labor exchanges in existence when federal legislation on these subjects was adopted, the federal government chose to subsidize and to coordinate the existing systems and such of those as the States might later adopt, being prepared in the case of the labor exchanges to establish its own offices on default of the States. There were practically no programs of old-age insurance in the States when the federal government adopted its program. This was one of the considerations, among many, influencing the adoption of a federal program.

With the adoption of a broader concept by the Supreme Court of the federal government's powers under the interstate commerce clause, the relations between the federal authority and the States in the fields of labor relations and wages and hours have tended to come closer to the ideal of a system within which national needs can be met, while local flexibility to deal with peculiar local situations will not be sacrificed, and the interests of both spheres can be guaranteed rather than being the consequence of generosity or tolerance on the part of one of the parties.

Personal Rights

I. INTRODUCTION

One lesson above all can be inferred from the experience of the federal systems considered in this study: that the decision to provide some protection for personal rights is the beginning, not the end of the problem's difficulties. Well-meant and sonorous generalities on the subject may serve a useful purpose in that they fix and define a society's libertarian ideals. But the essence of the personal rights problem is the issue of enforcement — how shall the machinery for protecting rights be organized? To what agencies of government shall the task be assigned? To what extent can a claim of personal rights be asserted against the other legitimate interests of society? The questions of how, by whom, and to what degree rights are secured is both more troublesome and more important than the identification of the rights themselves.

Three variant approaches to the rights problem on the level of constitutional structure can be distinguished at the outset, and each approach is exemplified by one or more of the federalisms considered. (1) A nation may choose to rest its main dependence on custom and on extraconstitutional understandings that personal rights will be respected. (2) The attempt may be made to distribute powers in such a way that the authority to affect rights is inherently limited by the constitutional structure. (3) It may be decided to incorporate in the constitution specific limitations on governmental power in the form of a bill or declaration of rights. The bulk of the pages that follow are devoted to consideration of the third solution, for reasons that will appear. However, the first and second approaches merit brief preliminary treatment.

A. Protection of Rights by Custom and Extraconstitutional Understanding

The dependence on extraconstitutional understanding for securing rights is, of course, characteristic of the English constitutional tradition. The British Parliament is nominally supreme and unfettered by constitutional restrictions. Such documents of the British "constitution" as the "Bill of Rights" and the "Act of Settlement" restrict Parliament only in the moral sense, and the legislature is legally free at any time to suspend or abolish these limitations. In fact, however, these and other restrictions on government are so hallowed by a long tradition of observance that the scope of rights actually respected is very wide, and it is almost unthinkable that Parliament would encroach on the liberties which the tradition regards as basic. Moreover, in addition to such fundamental documents as those referred to, English custom recognizes that the usages established by courts in molding the common law have established a network of unalienable rights for the individual.

This English tradition was inherited by Australia and Canada and has profoundly influenced their approach to the personal rights problem. Although both countries have, unlike England, a body of organic law which can be legitimately described as a written constitution, neither Australia nor Canada has imposed many specific bill-of-rights limitations on the power of government. The minor exceptions to this generalization deserve to be noted. Section 116 of the Australian Constitution asserts that the Commonwealth "shall not make any law for establishing any religion, or for imposing any religious observance, or for prohibiting the free exercise of any religion," and this provision has presented the Australian courts with problems of interpretation analogous to those discussed later in this study in connection with the enforcement of bills of rights. In 1941, the Commonwealth declared as a measure of national defense that the religious sect of Jehovah's Witnesses was an unlawful association, since its members refused to submit to secular authority. The High Court held the government's defense regulations invalid and, although the holding did not rest on Section 116, the Court was forced to deal with arguments arising under that section. In the Canadian Constitution Section 93 guarantees certain rights of particular religious groups to separate schools, and Section 133 guarantees the right to use either the English or French language in most public proceedings. These provisions were incorporated to take account of the misgivings of the inhabitants of Quebec who are ethnically separate from the rest of the nation. Nevertheless, the exceptions merely underline the fact that Australia and Canada have in general eschewed the bill-of-rights solution and have placed heavy reliance on customary observances as a guarantee of rights protection. As in Britain, the assumption is made that government will respect the basic documents of English constitutional history and will be morally bound by the common law tradition. (In the Canadian Province of Quebec the civil law rules, but the effect is much the same.)

This English-derived approach to the personal rights problem is supported by arguments which are by no means negligible. As Alexander Hamilton pointed out in *The Federalist* when the American Constitution was under consideration, the ultimate protection for all liberties is a libertarian spirit in the nation as a whole; legal devices are futile unless the popular will generally supports them. And it has been argued that the English approach serves to cultivate this spirit by reminding the people that their liberties are in their own hands. Yet these arguments lose some of their force when applied to a nation that is not small and homogeneous like England, but large and composed of diverse elements, organized on a federal pattern. And their force is still further lessened when we apply them to a political entity that is new and untried. A national spirit favorable to civil liberty may be ineffective to curb localized attacks on specific freedoms; and the veneration which many Englishmen feel for their ancient usages may be missing in a nation that has no national past. Both Australia and Canadà have sometimes had cause to question whether the approach they inherited from the English motherland is fully adequate for their somewhat different needs. In Canada, especially since the Second World War, arguments for the adoption of a bill of rights are heard with increasing frequency. It is pointed out that many of her citizens are products of countries in which the English constitutional usages are unknown and that some of these countries have no developed tradition of constitutional freedom. The problem is in part therefore educative, and the vague and complicated pattern of English custom is not very useful as an educational aid. As a result of such considerations, the legislature in the Canadian Province of Saskatchewan adopted a Bill of Rights in 1947; and while this document is not constitutionally binding on the legislature, its enactment does signify that in some quarters there is dissatisfaction with the "use and wont" of orthodox English tradition.

B. *Protection of Rights by the Constitutional Distribution of Powers*

It is obvious that the distribution of powers between the national government and the States in a federal system can have an important bearing on the protection of personal rights. If the central government is endowed with certain powers, then the member States may be correspondingly restricted in their capacity to legislate against rights in that field; and conversely the existence of certain powers in the States may impede the encroaching tendencies of the national government. The five systems studied have approached this issue of distribution of power in varied ways.

At one extreme is Australia, whose Constitution was framed in the light of a strong spirit of local autonomy. The Australian States who joined in the federation of 1900 saw the need for providing some common authority to deal with issues of national defense, economic relationships, immigration, and a few other inherently national questions. They had no intention of depriving the States of any powers other than those which were strictly necessary for the effective operation of a national government. The result is that the government of the Commonwealth is sharply restricted in its power to pass laws affecting rights, while the States to a large extent are inhibited only by their own sense of self-restraint. The Commonwealth is said to exercise only "enumerated powers" and all other powers are reserved to the States. And the tendency has been for the States to guard their powers jealously and for the courts to construe the powers of the national government narrowly. Even the power to provide for national defense, which has been given wider construction than the other Commonwealth powers, is sharply confined. The National Security Regulations, which were involved in the attack on Jehovah's Witnesses mentioned above, were held invalid in their entirety as outside the scope of the Commonwealth's delegated powers, even though the nation was at war. And an attempt to dissolve the Communist Party in 1950 was also held *ultra vires* in spite of the fact that the government urged its necessity in the name of national defense. The States, on the other hand, could have passed such a law without hindrance.

The United States, like Australia, nominally provided in its Constitution for a national government which would exercise only the powers delegated to it, while the residue of power was reserved to the States. In fact, the American system was to a large degree the Australian model so far as this point was concerned. An important part of the tradition which Thomas Jefferson passed on to the American republic was a faith that government would be less likely to encroach on rights if it were kept "close to the people," and it followed that liberties were safest if the power to affect them was in the hands of the States. In the Articles of Confederation, which represented the first attempt at American union, the national government was rendered almost impotent, and the States were left unconfined. The Constitution of 1789 attempted to preserve a modified version of this distribution pattern. But constitutional evolution has drastically altered this original conception, and it can hardly be said that the national government's authority is today very seriously restricted by the distribution of powers. Under such enumerated authority as the commerce and war powers, the American national government can reach almost any subject it might desire to reach. The fact is that the federal compact's distribution of powers sets more limitations on the States than it does on the national government, a curious reversal of the expectations of those who framed and ratified the document. It has been held, for example, that the States may not require the segregation of races on busses moving in interstate commerce, since this encroaches on the national power to regulate interstate trade.

In Canada, the situation is rather complex. Constitutional theory prescribes that the provincial governments exercise enumerated, and therefore limited, powers, while the residue of governmental powers resides in the Dominion government. As the organic law puts it, the Provinces have power to legislate with respect to property and civil rights, while the national government has, in addition to other powers, the authority to provide for the criminal law. But it is often extremely difficult to draw a line between these powers and therefore difficult to see just where the authority to affect rights may lie. And the picture is further complicated by the fact that Canadian courts have, in spite of constitutional theory, tended to construe the powers of the Provinces broadly and the powers of the Dominion government narrowly, so that it is only partially accurate to say that the balance of constitutional power to affect rights rests with the central government.

Nevertheless the broad fact remains that the distribution of powers does inhibit the Provinces to some degree when they seek to invade personal rights. The national power over the criminal law precludes the Provinces from setting very effective limitations on civil liberties. The Provinces have been denied the right to restrict the freedom of the press on the ground that such restriction is a matter for the Dominion alone, and it can be assumed that the reasoning applies to other freedoms regarded as essential.

The Swiss approach to the problem of distributed powers is constitutionally speaking much like that of the United States. The Swiss Constitution resembles the American both in theory and practice on this point; as in the United States, a Confederation government whose powers were originally limited by enumeration has expanded its range greatly through custom and interpretation. Both the Confederation and cantonal governments therefore possess wide authority to legislate in ways affecting personal rights either adversely or favorably.

The German Constitutions, both of Weimar and of the German Federal Republic, represent the opposite extreme from Australia on the issue of divided powers. Both the Federal government and the Länder have power to pass laws affecting rights in various ways, but the supremacy of federal law over laws of the member States is undisputed, and this means that the central government has, in the personal rights field, more power and more responsibility relative to the constituent States than in any of the other federal systems considered.

In summary: in one of the systems considered (Australia) the major authority to pass laws affecting rights either adversely or favorably is retained by the States; in one (Germany) the largest share of power in this field is clearly held by the national government; while in the remaining three (Canada, United States, Switzerland) the authority is divided or concurrent, with the balance, if any, falling in favor of the national government. Experience would seem to suggest that the distribution of powers in a federal system can be helpful in protecting rights from government encroachment, but two caveats are in order. For one thing, it seems clear that the distribution of powers is not itself a sufficient protection, since by definition the powers denied to one level of government are granted to the other, and there is no assurance, in spite of the Jeffersonian tradition, that the States will be more scrupulous about protecting rights than the national government. For another thing, it is extremely difficult under modern conditions to hedge government with the restrictions that seemed reasonable enough in earlier days, if government is to accomplish its modern tasks. Hence the strict construction of enumerated powers is likely to be abandoned through interpretation, as in the United States, or to become a serious handicap to effective operation, as some feel is the case in Australia. The conclusion seems warranted that the distribution of powers is at best a limited device for the protection of basic liberties.

C. Protection of Rights Through a Bill of Rights

In the modern era it has become almost matter of course to prescribe in a formal bill or declaration of rights the liberties that are deemed worthy of protection. The idea of such a declaration, setting definite restrictions on the power of government, has its origins deep in the past, but it came to full flower in the eighteenth century under the stimulus of the American and French Revolutions. In the United States, the struggle for independence had given rise to a strong prejudice against unlimited government, and the separation from England inaugurated a great outburst of rights declarations among the now sovereign States. Practically all of the State constitutions framed in the period following the Declaration of Independence contained statements of rights which the government was forbidden to encroach, and some of them were very elaborate. The Constitutional Convention at Philadelphia in 1787, however, produced a constitutional document which did not contain a formal statement of rights and which nominally therefore left most of the fundamental rights unprotected by specific prohibitions. Apparently, the framers believed that it was unnecessary to enumerate the restrictions on the new national government because, under the doctrine of delegated powers, its authority was already sufficiently restricted. And the States, it was felt, could be left free to protect rights by declarations in their own constitutions. This reasoning, however persuasive it may have seemed to the delegates to the convention, was unconvincing to the people at large; and the Constitution was ratified only on the understanding that a bill of rights would be presented at the earliest opportunity. In 1791, therefore, the Congress adopted the first ten Amendments to the federal Constitution, setting forth as guaranteed against the federal government most of the rights which had been characteristic of the analogous provisions in the constitutions of the States. Although the American Constitution contains other specific prohibitions on the power of government to affect rights, these Amendments have in particular come to symbolize the American libertarian tradition.

By the time Switzerland adopted her modern Constitution in 1874, the custom of incorporating a specific statement of rights had become almost axiomatic. Although the rights protected are not listed in a separate portion of the Constitution as they are in the American organic law, but are rather scattered throughout the document, Switzerland has placed its main reliance on the concept of specific prohibitions. The Swiss approach is thus closely similar to the American, and in fact the American constitutional experience had an important influence on the framers of the Swiss system. Germany has incorporated formal statements of rights both in the Weimar and in the Bonn Constitutions.

The wide acceptance of the notion that a formal bill of rights is a near-necessity in an effective constitutional government undoubtedly arises in part from the conviction that neither custom nor the distribution of powers can provide fundamental rights with the protection their importance merits. The unique English situation is simply not exportable, and other nations have generally felt that their governments need the constant reminder which a bill of rights provides, while their people need the reassurance which it can supply. But, as has already been suggested, the decision to adopt a bill of rights is only the first step towards the protection of basic liberties. Many problems remain: the nature of the rights which shall be chosen for special protection; the range of their application; the extent to which they are subordinated to the other interests of society; and finally, and above all, the machinery of enforcement which transmutes them from pious declarations into positive and enforceable rules of governmental conduct. The remainder of this study is devoted to consideration of those problems.

II. The Scope and Content of a Declaration of Rights

A. *The Scope of Protection*

A primary and important question to be asked concerning any bill of rights is the question as to the range of its applicability. How adequately does it cover the necessary ground? To whom are its prohibitions addressed? In this connection, two points must be made.

In the first place, it is of some importance to note that, in general, bills of rights have been conceived as protecting freedom against government and not against other individuals or groups within the society. It is assumed, sometimes correctly and sometimes not, that the ordinary processes of law should be enough to protect rights against these non-governmental encroachments. The idea is, of course, that the threatened person will be protected by the police or that he can defend his rights by bringing action against the offender. This assumption is by no means always a valid one, but it perhaps serves to explain the reason that specific constitutional provisions on this subject have been regarded as somewhat pointless: in general protection from other individuals requires positive action by the government in the form of police or court action authorized by legislation. And if the government neglects to act, then it is difficult to see how a provision in a bill of rights could be used to compel it to do so. A bill of rights can operate negatively to *prevent* a government from doing something that is forbidden. But as a positive mandate it cannot, by its nature, function as anything more than a moral admonition.

Nevertheless some limited attempts have been made to include in formal statements of rights certain proscriptions against private action. The Swiss, Australian, and Canadian Constitutions are generally silent on the subject, although the suggestion has been made in Canada that certain "crimes against liberty" should be made punishable by Dominion legislation. The Dominion government has this power, of course, by virtue of its control over the criminal law, and the Confederation government in Switzerland has a like authority; but no constitutional provision even purports to require that they use it for this purpose. The federation under the Bonn Constitution possesses similar power, and West Germany has constitutionally singled out some rights against private action, such as the right against involuntary servitude and the right against "abuse of economic power." The issue of how these rights can be enforced against individuals remains unanswered, but there may be some advantage in emphasizing their importance by giving them constitutional status.

In the United States, the national government can legislate to protect rights only within the sphere of its delegated powers, and the result is that it cannot in general extend its grasp to punish individuals who encroach on liberties of others. This gap in the system of rights protection is a fairly serious one, and it has sometimes meant that local minorities are unprotected unless the States are willing to protect them. However, the Fifteenth Amendment to the federal Constitution does prohibit involuntary servitude, and this has been construed to permit the national government to punish those who hold another in service against his will. Private transgressions on other rights — such as the right to vote and the right to bodily security — have also been approached somewhat obliquely by a federal "Civil Rights Act" which provides criminal punishment for a State official who deprives an individual of rights secured by the federal Constitution.

It would seem to be especially important that a federal system, embodying as it does divergent groups, make clear provision for federal authority to ensure protection of the individual against private action. And the case for recognizing such authority in the bill of rights is a strong one, since it may serve to quiet the apprehensions of minorities. Of course, it must be recognized that no bill of rights can guarantee that the government will take the positive action that is authorized by such a provision. But the existence of the power is an almost indispensable concomitant of an effective system of rights protection.

In the second place, it is important to consider whether the bill of rights is operative against both the central government and the States, or whether its prohibitions are directed to only one of the levels of government in a federal system. Here practice has differed rather markedly. The few "bill of rights provisions" of the Canadian Constitution are applicable to both the Dominion and the provincial legislatures. In Australia, the religious freedom provision inhibits only the Commonwealth government. In Switzerland, all the personal rights provisions of the Constitution are nominally binding as against both the Confederation and the cantons, and this is true under the Bonn Constitution of Germany as well.

The American situation is somewhat complicated. The original Bill of Rights protected liberties only against invasion by the national government.

The States were forbidden by restrictions in the main body of the Constitution to pass certain kinds of laws which the framers regarded as particularly reprehensible, but otherwise they were technically free to encroach on rights at will. Of course, as has been noted above, the States restricted themselves in their own constitutions, and sometimes the standard they imposed was more rigorous than the standard prescribed by the national Constitution for the federal government. But the fact remains that the uniform national requirements imposed upon them by the original constitutional arrangement were comparatively few. However, the course of subsequent history has substantially altered this arrangement. In 1868, the Fourteenth Amendment provided that no State might deprive any person of "life, liberty, or property" without "due process" of law, and court interpretation has given this prohibition a content similar, though not identical to, the national Bill of Rights. The result is that the federal Constitution protects a wide range of liberty against either State or national action. For reasons which are discussed later, the national government is held to a somewhat stricter standard when "procedural rights" are involved, while the States seem to be somewhat more sharply circumscribed than the national government when they deal with "substantive rights." But the difference is one of emphasis, and the generalization holds that the national Constitution binds both the States and the nation.

B. The Rights Protected

For the purposes of clarity, it is necessary to distinguish between several concepts that are often subsumed under the general term "rights." The word is often used to include the following: (1) The "substantive rights" of the individual, of which freedom of speech is perhaps the best example. These are the rights which are cherished by the individual for their own sake — the rights that make life livable. (2) "Procedural rights" having to do with arrest and trial, such as the right to counsel in a criminal case, or freedom from "unreasonable search and seizure." These rights pertain, not so much to *what* government does, which is the chief concern of the first category, but to the *way* in which the government goes about achieving certain substantive results. (3) What might be called "positive rights" owing from government, such as the right to economic security.

1. SUBSTANTIVE RIGHTS

The constitutions considered recognize a large number of substantive liberties, and the attempt here is not to exhaust the enumeration, but to single out those which seem to be regarded as universally important or which are of special interest. The only substantive right which is recognized in some form as constitutionally secured by all systems is religious freedom. The Australian and Canadian provisions on this subject have already been touched on. In Canada, it should be observed, the organic law is concerned not so much with protecting the substantive rights of individuals, but the substantive rights of religious *groups*.

In the United States, substantive rights protected by the federal Constitution include, in addition to religious freedom, liberty of press, assembly, and petition. The First Amendment also includes a prohibition against any law "respecting an establishment of religion," and recent decisions of the Supreme Court have made it reasonably clear that this inhibition applies to the States as well as the national government. The Fifth and Fourteenth Amendments also forbid the nation and the States respectively to deprive any person of life, liberty or property "without due process of law," and these clauses have been interpreted as providing substantive as well as procedural protection to property owners, and as securing certain economic rights such as "freedom of contract." The Fourteenth Amendment also denies the States the authority to pass discriminatory legislation. Liberty of movement and trade throughout the federal territory is insured by interpreting the commerce clause (which in terms merely grants the national government authority over "commerce among the States") as if it prohibited State restrictions in the field.

The substantive rights protected by the Swiss Constitution include the freedom of commerce and industry, a provision which reflected (as did the United States Supreme Court's interpretation of the due process clause) the assumptions of a laissez-faire, liberal economy. It is interesting to observe that in both Switzerland and the United States these laissez-faire inhibitions of the Constitution have been whittled away, in Switzerland by formal amendment, in the United States by court interpretation. Not only freedom of religion, but also the concomitant right of secularism are specifically recognized in the Swiss Constitution. Freedom of press, petition, and assembly are also expressly guaranteed. The Swiss Constitution likewise ensures equality of treatment for all persons throughout the federal territory.

Substantive liberties were set forth in some detail by the Weimar Constitution of Germany, and this practice was continued in the Bonn Constitution. A large number of substantive liberties are constitutionally secured and are defined with somewhat more exactness than is the case in any of the other constitutions considered. More or less unique provisions include the right of conscientious objection to military service (in the United States this has not been regarded as a constitutional right, although one might expect it to have been inferred from the guarantee of freedom of religion), the right of academic freedom, the right to the free development of the personality, and the equality of the sexes.

2. PROCEDURAL RIGHTS

Neither Canada nor Australia recognizes procedural rights in their Constitutions, and these rights are therefore nominally unprotected against legislative abridgment. Nevertheless, it should be emphasized that both nations inherit the English common law tradition, and that tradition lays heavy emphasis on procedural rights. The courts of these countries therefore regard themselves as morally bound by the basic documents of British constitutional history, and such ancient writs as habeas corpus are available to accused persons as a matter of course. Moreover, the influence of custom and usage is perhaps more effective in the area of procedural rights than in any other; the inhabitant of either country is hedged about with various protections which, though not technically inviolable, are solid and certain.

The United States, of course, shares this tradition to some degree, but has also made elaborate specific provision for procedural rights. The constitutions of the several States impose a host of procedural restrictions on the State governments. Amendments Four through Eight of the federal Constitution enumerate a number of procedural rights guaranteed against abridgment by the national government, and others are set forth in the body of the Constitution. They include the right to be arrested only upon sworn warrant, the right to privacy against arbitrary search by officers, the right to a fair jury trial with the assistance of counsel, and the right against excessive or cruel punishment. Arbitrary detention is correctible by the writs of habeas corpus, which cannot be suspended except under extraordinary conditions.

In addition to the enumerated rights against the national government, various restrictions of the national Constitution are applicable to the States. Some of these are defined in the body of the Constitution, but the great source of procedural protection against the States is the due process clause of the Fourteenth Amendment. Under existing precedents of the Supreme Court, this clause enforces against the States a body of procedural rights similar, though not identical, to those secured by the Bill of Rights against national action. The Supreme Court has attempted to make a very careful distinction between the standards binding the federal government and those binding the States. In general, it can be said that the procedural rights regarded by the Supreme Court as basic to a free society are protected against State infringement, but that the rights thought to be of debatable or secondary importance can be abridged by the States if they choose and if their own constitutions permit. The States, in short, enjoy a greater degree of flexibility in prescribing for law enforcement and criminal procedures than does the federal government. This principle of distinction undoubtedly reflects in part a traditional American notion that the States should be left free to experiment within limits, that they are the "laboratories" of the federal system.

In Switzerland, only scattered procedural rights are set forth in the Constitution. But, as in Australia and Canada, the courts are bound in procedural matters by legislative enactment and by the national legal tradition — in this case, of course, the civil law. In the Bonn Constitution, on the other hand, Germany has adopted several procedural provisions similar to the American Bill of Rights enumeration, and has made them binding on both the federation and Länder governments. Included, for example, are a provision against what Anglo-American law calls "ex post facto" legislation, against search without warrant, against ill-treatment of detained persons, and so on.

In summary, procedural rights are protected in three of the systems (Australia, Canada, Switzerland) largely by legislation and by the national legal tradition. Only two countries (the United States and Germany) have seen fit to spell out procedural rights as constitutional limitations. In the Bonn Constitution these rights are presumably equally binding on all parties to the federal system, but in the United States the national government is held to a stricter procedural standard than the States.

3. POSITIVE RIGHTS

Positive rights, in the sense defined, are not constitutionally recognized in Australia, Canada, or the United States. Switzerland has imposed on the cantons a requirement that they provide free universal education, and the Confederation is constitutionally committed to providing for the economic security of the people. The Weimar Constitution laid stress on such positive rights as the right to work, but the Bonn Constitution touches such matters only by implication. In none of the systems here considered was any attempt made to define positive rights in constitutional terms on a very wide scale. Apparently they are regarded as rights which are meaningless except as they are politically attainable, and this may indeed be the common sense of the matter. Positive rights are recognized by all the systems in practice, but it is not easy to define them in legal terms and their moral effectiveness is at best conjectural. The Preamble of the United States Constitution, which admittedly has no legal effect, but which contains such phrases as "to promote the general welfare" amongst its statement of purposes, may serve the function of a positive rights declaration about as meaningfully as is practically possible.

C. Limitations on Enumerated Rights

Of the three systems which have adopted bills of rights or their equivalent, all three recognize that the liberties are not absolute. In general, Switzerland and Germany have tried to express this notion of qualification by specific constitutional language. Both provide that certain guaranteed rights shall not be "abused," while the Bonn Constitution qualifies the qualification by providing that legislation must not affect the right "in its basic content." The United States Constitution seems to impose many of its limitations in unqualified terms — "Congress shall make no law . . . abridging the freedom of speech." Nevertheless, in practice the United States Constitution has been interpreted as if it contained the modifying language found in the organic laws of Switzerland and Germany. This further underlines a point made earlier in this study — that the statement of rights is the beginning not the end of difficulty in this field. It seems very doubtful that explicit language can prescribe the extent of rights protection with any effective precision. American experience with the "clear and present danger rule" merely illustrates the proposition that the distinction between freedom and license must always be made and that it is impossible to make it precisely.

The extent to which a right may be regarded as yielding to other and "higher" societal concerns is therefore a problem that must be worked out gradually, since it involves the balancing of the social interest in freedom against the other interests of the community. Not infrequently two "rights" will conflict with one another, as when the freedom of the press to criticize the conduct of public affairs is directed against a court proceeding, thus endangering the right of fair trial. Sometimes a right must be modified when a public emergency subordinates all other concerns to the preservation of the state. Under Article 48 of the Weimar Constitution this concept of emergency could be gravely abused and sometimes was. Yet all modern governments must recognize that an emergency may cast a shadow on rights which are otherwise inviolable. A Chief Justice of the United States Supreme Court once said that "the power to wage war is the power to wage war successfully," an explicit recognition of the principle that a bill of rights is not a rigid dogma but a practical instrument of government.

III. The Machinery of Rights Protection

The method by which rights are secured is, as has already been suggested, the major problem which faces a federal republic once it is decided that certain enumerated rights merit protection. Indeed, the declaration of rights becomes almost meaningless unless some practical method for giving it effect is provided, and the bill of rights may even become a detriment to the concept of constitutional government itself. The American States in the 1780's included bills of rights in their constitutions, but many of them neglected to establish a method for making the rights effective, and the legislatures transgressed the supposedly unalienable rights at will. The result was that the whole concept of limited government was seriously endangered, and some observers felt that the existence of the bills of rights merely served to underline the fact that the powers of the legislature were in practice unlimited.

A. Protection by Executive Action

Executive action to protect rights can be and sometimes has been taken effectively within a certain limited range in the federal systems studied.

Ultimately of course the executive power of the national government stands behind the constitutional commands of the other branches of that government, and it is obvious that neither the legislature nor the courts can make their mandates effective unless executive support is potentially available. President Andrew Jackson of the United States was once reported to have said about a particular matter: "John Marshall [the Chief Justice] has made his decision; now let him enforce it." And whether the President said this or not, the legend serves to confirm the truism that executive support for rights is indispensable. But it is under ordinary circumstances enough that the threat of executive action is available, and the power is actually called into being very seldom. The American Constitution authorizes the President to intervene to restore order in the States when he is requested to do so by the State government, and while this power has not gone unused, it is regarded as an extraordinary measure. Executive authority has also been employed to enforce the constitutional prohibition against peonage and to carry out the Civil Rights Acts referred to above; that is, federal police officials have investigated transgressions on the rights so protected and have laid the basis for criminal action against the offending persons. In Germany, the federal government is endowed with specific authority to control the execution of laws by the Länder so as to ensure conformity to the federal pattern, and this authority is an important potential source of personal rights protection. All in all, however, it is probably true that executive action to protect rights is chiefly useful as an auxiliary to other methods. Certainly it has not in practice been employed very extensively in any of the systems considered.

B. *Enforcement by Popular Referendum*

In one form or another, the method of popular control has played a part in protecting rights in some systems, and it deserves brief mention. Obviously the amending process is itself a potential instrument for rights protection, and insofar as this process is controlled by the vote of the people it therefore offers the possibility of a popular check on governmental acts. In the United States, the federal Constitution can be amended by a two-thirds vote of both houses of Congress and the approval of three fourths of the States. The Thirteenth, Fourteenth, and Fifteenth Amendments were adopted in the period following the Civil War to secure the rights of Negroes; and the Nineteenth Amendment guaranteed women the right to vote. The Australian Constitution provides for amendment by parliamentary resolution followed by popular referendum; and in 1950 the voters refused to ratify a proposal that would have given the Commonwealth government the authority to outlaw the Communist Party. But the amending method in any constitutional system is likely to be slow-moving and cumbersome, and, while it may be of great significance in asserting the popular will on an occasional important issue, it can hardly be depended upon to protect the rights of individuals against a multiplicity of day-to-day encroachments by government.

Switzerland has carried the method of popular referendum farther than any other system, providing for a referendum on federal laws when demanded by 30,000 active citizens from eight cantons. This unique provision theoretically ensures that the ultimate guardianship of personal right will remain in the hands of the people. However, a majority of the two Councils of the Confederation government can circumvent this requirement by declaring certain laws or resolutions "urgent" and therefore exempt from popular veto. The federal government employed this technique so often in the years following the Second World War that a referendum was finally adopted in 1949 drastically limiting the duration of the "emergency" legislation enacted in the preceding period. Whether this specific decision was wise or not, it had the effect of reminding the central government that the constitutional limitations must be taken seriously and that the popular will stands ready to assert itself to protect rights. Nevertheless, it must be said that even at best the method of popular referendum performs the function of protecting rights imperfectly. It lacks both the efficiency and the flexibility that are necessary to a successful system of rights enforcement.

C. *Protection by Courts*

The deficiencies of other techniques for protection of rights point up the advantages of employing courts to enforce the rights prescribed by the constitution. The judicial process is adapted by nature to deal with rights problems, not in terms of broad generalities, but in terms of the complexities of each individual situation. This attribute of courts is of great importance, since, as has been suggested above, the major problem in connection with personal rights is not their initial promulgation but their practical application. No matter how carefully the constitution may spell out the content and incidence of its personal liberty guarantees, it cannot anticipate the multitude of problems that may arise as they are implemented. "The process of judicial inclusion and exclusion" is uniquely designed to deal with these problems, to provide the combination of security and flexibility that an operating constitutional system requires.

THE PROBLEM OF JUDICIAL REVIEW

Even though it is conceded that courts are an indispensable agent in protecting rights, it is still legitimate to inquire whether they must be granted the ultimate authority to disallow acts of all other government branches — the power of judicial review. All of the systems studied provide in some degree for the enforcement of rights by litigation in tribunals maintained by the national government, but not all confide to the courts the final word as to constitutionality. In Australia, the Commonwealth courts exercise this power in a limited way, enforcing the few substantive guarantees of the Constitution and determining whether or not acts of the Commonwealth or State governments are *ultra vires* under the constitutional distribution of powers.

The Canadian situation is similar to that of Australia. The courts, though prescribed by the Provinces, are staffed by national authority and are regarded as having the power to invalidate the unconstitutional acts of either Dominion or provincial governments. But because the specific guarantees of personal liberty are so few, judicial review in the full sense of the word is not very extensive. The Quebec legislature in 1937 enacted a "padlock law" which authorized the provincial government to lock up buildings used in the distribution of Communist literature, and the courts refused to invalidate the law, since nothing in the Constitution forbade it. On the other hand, an act of the Alberta legislature restricting freedom of the press on a broad scale was held *ultra vires* on the basis that the Province had encroached on Dominion authority.

In Switzerland, personal rights are nominally secured against both the cantons and the federal government, but in fact the Constitution grants the right of court appeal only against cantonal laws. The laws of the Confederation legislature are specifically exempt from judicial review, which means that the only recourse against an unconstitutional act of the national government is the popular referendum considered above. Switzerland deliberately chose, in erecting her constitutional system, to depart from the American model on this point of judicial review, preferring to retain the power of constitutional interpretation for the Federal Assembly.

In Germany, under the Weimar Constitution the power of judicial review over laws of the Länder was explicitly established, and the Supreme Court assumed, as early as 1925, that it had the power to disallow unconstitutional national laws as well. This potential authority to protect personal rights against all government encroachments was, however, seriously qualified by the government's power to pass emergency decrees. The Bonn Constitution explicitly provides that basic rights "shall be binding as directly valid law" and grants to the Federal Constitutional Court the power of judicial review over the governments of both the federation and the Länder.

The United States is, of course, the nation in which judicial review has been longest and most firmly established, and it merits some special attention on that account. The American Supreme Court reviews acts of either national or State authority and possesses the power to nullify any law or order which violates basic constitutional rights. And a similar power is exercised by the courts of the States under the State constitutions. The Supreme Court is not explicitly granted the power of judicial review by the federal Constitution; although the framers seem to have assumed that the power would be exercised, they neglected to provide for it in terms. However, the Court itself early took the initiative in asserting the authority to review both State and federal acts, arguing that the guarantees of basic rights would be meaningless unless the judiciary were empowered to protect them against all other branches of government.

In a sense then the American Supreme Court is literally "supreme," since it speaks with final authority on matters that are brought before it. But its supremacy can easily be exaggerated, and the scope of its supervisory power is less than it may at first seem. For one thing, its appellate jurisdiction (which is by far the most important aspect of its authority) is entirely controlled by Congressional act. For another thing, the Supreme Court will consider issues of constitutionality only when they are presented in the course of actual litigation. The Court does not issue advisory opinions, nor will it review "moot" cases in which there is no actual controversy between the parties. This feature of the Court's procedure has important relevance to its effectiveness as a protector of personal rights. It means, of course, that no conclusive decision as to the constitutionality of government action will be made unless some affected person is willing and able to go through the somewhat elaborate process of contesting the law through the lower tribunals and up to the Supreme Court. American statute books undoubtedly contain laws which transgress basic rights and may well be unconstitutional but which have never been invalidated because no one has ever presented the constitutional issue properly in the course of litigation. On the other hand, the Court's insistence on dealing with genuine cases means that the Court need not guess whether a particular law will infringe basic rights. By examining the law in the context of actual practice the Court can tell exactly how it affects liberty and can better judge its conformity to the requirements of the Constitution. A federal sedition law passed in 1940 penalized membership in organizations which advocate the overthrow of the government by violence. The Supreme Court held it valid as applied to certain leaders of the Communist Party who were indicted in 1948, but reserved the right to reach a different conclusion in different times and circumstances, a holding which illustrates the flexibility of the judicial method.

A person desiring to assert his constitutional rights must show then that those rights have been adversely affected. If they have been so affected, he can set up a claim of constitutional right in the course of legal proceedings and seek a determination as to whether his claim is justified. The claim can be made against any branch of the government. If, for example, an executive act touching his rights is unconstitutional, the injured party can ask a court to enjoin the official concerned. In some circumstances, he can ask that a court order the official to take action restoring his right. If he is being held in confinement by the police in violation of his constitutional rights, he can petition for a writ of habeas corpus. All of these actions are begun in lower federal or State courts which make the preliminary judgment on the validity of the claim; but they are appealable to higher courts and, in certain circumstances, to the Supreme Court itself. The lower courts, both of the States and of the nation, are themselves bound to observe the Constitution, and their holdings are reviewable just as are the acts of an executive official. And a similar process is followed if a litigant claims that a law itself is invalid as a violation of his constitutional rights. If his rights are in fact affected, he can ask the courts to hold it void and can press his claim upward by appeal if the lower court fails to grant him relief.

The protection of rights by courts, even when supported by the institution of judicial review, is not a perfect method by any means. It leaves the initiative for defense of rights to the individual litigant which means that chance sometimes determines whether a question involving rights will be raised. Since litigation is often costly and onerous, the affected person may sometimes choose to let an invasion of his rights go uncontested. Moreover, judical review itself is capable of abuse. Critics have argued that the courts in the United States have often been so concerned to protect rights that they have intolerably hampered the effective operation of government. And it has been said that the American preoccupation with judicial defense of rights has led legislators to feel that they need not trouble themselves on the subject, since the courts will have the last word in any event. Yet it must be concluded, in spite of faults, that a strong and independent judiciary is almost indispensable to the effective preservation of fundamental liberties. The procedures of courts are well calculated to take account of the almost infinite variety of day-to-day problems presented by a bill of rights and to consider these problems in their context. While judges are no more likely to be perfect than other men, it is true, as Hamilton pointed out long ago, that they are less dangerous when entrusted with power simply because they lack the facilities for abusing it. Since they are dependent on the executive and legislature for the enforcement of their decrees, they can never become an independent threat to the liberties of the people. And while judicial review may sometimes have hampered government in the United States, it has also served to keep the populace awake to threats against their fundamental rights.

IV. CONCLUSION

The case for including some statement of legally enforceable rights in a federal constitution is almost irresistible. The divergencies of custom and culture that are likely to be found in such a state suggest both the need and the difficulty of framing such a declaration. The need is obvious. Particularist fears of encroachment by national authority must be put to rest, and while a bill of rights cannot accomplish that objective, it can further it. It is a commonplace of American history that the federal Constitution was ratified only after its proponents had agreed to add a bill of rights at the earliest possible moment. The argument that the scope of the national government's power was already sufficiently limited by the nature of the grant was rebutted by history, and the record is not dissimilar in the other federal nations considered. It is almost equally important to the success of a federal venture that the member States be controlled by some minimum standard in the field of rights, simply because agreement on the fundamentals of human freedom is one of the great unifying factors in human affairs.

At the same time, it must be acknowledged that the difficulties in framing such a declaration for a federal state are many. If it is to have either legal or moral effect, the statement must consist of more than sonorous generalities; yet its provisions must be acceptable to the divergent members of the system. The problem of enforcement, to which so much attention has been given above, is undoubtedly the most serious issue. Protection by courts, though an imperfect method, is reasonably effective, and it has, as the American experience suggests, the merit of flexibility. American courts, operating within the broad provisions of the federal Constitution, have been able to move slowly and judiciously towards the ideal of national uniformity, recognizing the necessity for imposing different standards on States and nation when that necessity exists. But this method almost inevitably implies some form of judicial review over both national and State acts. It may be argued, as it was in *The Federalist* papers, that such power, if it must be granted at all, is best entrusted to courts, since their positive powers are so drastically limited. But it must be admitted that judicial review has not always been a satisfactory institution even in the United States, and its limitations, as well as its virtues for the protection of basic rights, must be carefully considered.

If it is decided to place heavy reliance for the protection of rights on courts armed with the power of judicial review, it becomes centrally important to make the jurisdiction and authority of the highest court explicit. The Comité d'Etudes pour la Constitution Européenne has, of course, resolved to recommend the Convention for the Protection of Human Rights and Fundamental Freedom and Protocol of the Council of Europe as the basic bill of rights of the European Community. This is an important step forward, but it would seem desirable to make it clear that the ultimate responsibility and authority for enforcing those rights within the Community is confided to its own high court and not to any court established by the Council of Europe.

A P P E N D I X   I

Australia

I. THE PLACE OF PERSONAL RIGHTS IN THE CONSTITUTION

The American Bill of Rights, expressing the thought of the eighteenth century and its experience with arbitrary government, and even the Canadian Constitution, reflecting problems arising from a large and localized cultural minority, both deal more explicitly with civil liberties than does the younger Australian Constitution. The federal Commonwealth of Australia, organized in 1900 under the Commonwealth Constitution Act, was proclaimed on January 1, 1901. It followed the British system "in establishing a parliamentary executive based on the Cabinet principle, and in leaving basic individual liberties to be secured by the common law, and also through and by, rather than by formal limitations and prohibitions upon, the Parliament . . . The protection of the individual's rights is left to the common law and the good sense and justice of a Parliament democratically elected, and required to go to the constituencies every three years at the longest." [1] However, besides the common law tradition and the reliance on the democratic process, two more explicit constitutional principles are relevant to the area of civil liberties in Australia: first, the Constitution Act contains a few specific limitations on the exercise of governmental authority in favor of individual freedom; second, the Commonwealth government is one of enumerated powers and its limited competence is a protection for the rights of the individual as well as for those of the States.

II. The Rights of the Australian Constitution

Individual liberties or rights are explicitly protected by three sections of the Constitution: a limited guarantee of freedom of religion (§116); [2] a requirement that any acquisition of property authorized by Commonwealth terms should be on "just terms" (§51 (xxxi)); a declaration that interstate trade shall be absolutely free (§92). [3]

Section 116 of the Constitution forbids the Commonwealth to make "any law for establishing any religion, or for imposing any religious observance, or for prohibiting the free exercise of any religion, and no religious test shall be required as a qualification for any office or public trust under the Commonwealth." There is no comparable provision in the State constitutions, except (since 1934) in Tasmania, where the guarantee is expressly made "subject to public order and morality."

Interpretations of Section 116 have had to define where inviolability of belief ends and the requirements of public order begin. Where the requirements of public order included compulsory military training, the High Court in 1912 held that such training — under the Defense Act — did not "prohibit the free exercise of any religion."

The decision of the High Court in 1943 in *Adelaide Company of Jehovah's Witnesses v. The Commonwealth*, [4] however, appears to Professor Bailey to have gone "perhaps further in the recognition of the regulation of public order and safety than decisions on the First Amendment." This case held that the National Security (Subversive Associations) Regulations, while

---

[1] Bailey, "Fifty Years of the Australian Constitution," 25 Aust. L.J. 326 (1951).

[2] Interpretation of Section 116 has followed to a large extent that of the First Amendment to the United States Constitution, according to Professor Bailey.

[3] For a discussion see Appendix I to Study 6, Commerce, Transportation and Customs.

[4] 67 C.L.R. 116 (1943).

invalid on other grounds, did not in their application to the Jehovah's Witnesses[5] contravene Section 116. The purpose of the Regulations had been not only to dissolve associations whose continued existence was regarded as prejudicial to the defense of the Commonwealth but also to prohibit the advocacy of any tenet or doctrine held by a dissolved association. These were wartime regulations, and the attempt to enact similar peacetime — or, rather, cold war time — legislation against the Communist Party has been invalidated.

Apart from the specific constitutional restrictions, the Commonwealth government is limited by the extent of its constitutional grant of power. Having no express grant of power over the criminal law, its competence in the civil liberties field is restricted to such matters as can be claimed as incidental to one of its expressly granted powers. Thus legislation against sedition has been upheld as incidental to the defense power (*The King v. Sharkey*) although the extent of authority under this power has been held to depend on the nature of the emergency existing at the time.

The positive limitation on the Commonwealth from its restricted grant of power is evinced by the *Communist Party Dissolution* case.[6] The Communist Party Dissolution Act of 1950 went beyond the previous cases dealing with sedition by defining a "communist" as a person who supports or advocates the objectives, policies, teachings, principles, or practice of communism as expounded by Marx and Lenin (§4), and, secondly, by declaring the Australian Communist Party to be an unlawful association, dissolving it, and providing for the vesting of its property in a receiver. Further sections dealt with the definition and dissolution of Communist-dominated and/or-affiliated associations; with the ineligibility of a communist for office as a member of a body corporate or of an industrial organization deemed vital to the security and defense of Australia; and with the procedure for the legal accomplishment of the purposes described.[7]

Once the Act had been passed, challenged, and brought up to the Court, the Commonwealth claimed authorization for it primarily under subsections (vi) and (xxxix) of Section 51 of the Constitution, i.e., the defense power and the "general implementation" power, respectively.[8] Six Justices adjudged the Act invalid. Chief Justice Latham dissented.

As it has been interpreted, the extent of the Commonwealth authority under the defense power depends on whether and what kind of emergency exists.[9] The maxim that "those who are responsible for the national security must be the sole judges of what the national security requires" cannot — the High Court holds — be the maxim in a federation and certainly has

---

[5] "There appears to be no parallel in Australia for the drastic step taken by the authorities in Quebec [against the Jehovah's Witnesses]." 24 Australian Law Journal 68 (1950).

[6] 83 C.L.R. 1 (1951).

[7] 24 Austr. L.J. 485 (1950).

[8] The development of the defense power is briefly spelled out by Professor Bailey in "Fifty Years of the Australian Constitution," 25 Aust. L.J. 314 (1951).

[9] See also the preamble to the Act.

not been the wartime law of Australia. The Parliament has the power to do anything which the Court is satisfied has a sufficient connection with the defense of Australia, but what is actually required for defense must expand and contract according to the dangers to Australia's security that exist from time to time.

In the Communist Party Dissolution Case, "the judgment of the Parliament and the Government was that, what Dixon, J., summarized as 'the past acts, the tenets and opinions and the present . . . tendencies' of the Communist Party, of certain other bodies of persons, and of members of the Australian Communist Party and other communists, constituted, in the circumstances that existed in 1950, a danger to the defense of Australia of such a nature as to require measures of the character described. The question for the Court was whether the Constitution permitted it to accept that judgment in the circumstances that prevailed in October, 1950, as it had done in the wartime cases in 1918 and 1942. By majority, the court's answer to this question was in the negative. . . .

". . . The court's judgment [was] that in dangers short of war, the defense power is necessarily short of its wartime scope, and [that] . . . the Court and not the Parliament or the Government, must be the final judge both of the existence of the degree of danger and of the necessity of the measures adopted to meet it." [10]

What the Commonwealth cannot itself do except in time of war or national emergency (as recognized by judicial notice), i.e. legislate in regard to unincorporated voluntary associations, could be accomplished either by (1) State legislation or (2) referral by the States of this power to the Commonwealth under Section 51 (xxxvii) of the Constitution. But the States have shown no haste to accept the Prime Minister's invitation to refer what there is little certainty they will ever get back; and they do not appear to wish to enter this field themselves. The third alternative is a popular referendum to obtain consent for a constitutional alteration which will give the Commonwealth the power now denied it by the Court.[11]

III. The Machinery of Protection

As evident from the above, the legal protection of civil liberties is based on the High Court's power both of interpreting the common and statute law and of declaring statutes *ultra vires*. In the field of civil liberties, this power of judicial review is primarily a protection against Commonwealth action — the States having retained the powers not granted to the central government. But, as stated at the outset, the primary protection of the individual rests not in the legal protection derived from the power of the courts but in the democratic process and the political traditions of the people.

[10] Bailey, "Fifty Years of the Australian Constitution," 25 Aust. L.J. 314, 321 (1951).
[11] Beasley, "Australia's Communist Party Dissolution Act," 29 Can. B. Rev. 51 (1951).

A P P E N D I X   I I

Canada

I. The Place of Personal Rights in the Constitution

As in Australia, the primary protection of personal rights in Canada rests in the common law tradition and in the political ethos of the people. However, as the Dominion has from its inception contained a cohesive national and religious minority, the British North America Act makes more explicit provision for certain minority rights than the corresponding constituent for Australia. Finally, rights also receive protection from the division of competence between the Dominion and provincial governments although, in distinction to Australia, this operates as a source of protection against the provincial rather than the central government.

II. The Rights of the Canadian Constitution

The specific protections of the British North America Act concern the use of English and French as official languages and, more important, Section 93 provides that though the Provinces have exclusive legislative authority over education "nothing in any such law shall prejudicially affect any Right or Privilege with respect to Denominational Schools" existing at the time of the union.

In respect to personal rights, the important constitutional provisions defining the division of competence between Dominion and provincial governments are Section 92 (13) and Section 91 (27). The former makes "property and civil rights" the exclusive concern of the provincial governments while the latter vests exclusive responsibility for the Criminal Law in the central government. Provincial punitive authority — "The Imposition of Punishment by Fine, Penalty, or Imprisonment" — exists only for enforcing "any Law of the Province made in relation to any Matter coming within any of the Classes of Subjects enumerated in this Section" (§92 (15)). Common law, statute, national and provincial law are all enforced in the provincial courts. In Quebec, the customary French civil law continues, but English criminal law applies throughout the whole country and is systematized in the criminal code enacted by the national Parliament. This power to define the criminal law enables the national government to counteract sectional hysteria and make for some uniformity of rights and liberties throughout the country, but it has evaded this responsibility in some instances, and has itself transgressed in others.

Through their authority over "property and civil rights," the provincial legislatures have some power to modify the inherited common law rights.

The Alberta Press Bill Case[12] would, however, indicate that rights such as freedom of discussion are solely under national jurisdiction.[13]   But the national government cannot extend its authority by attempting — in the guise of enacting a criminal law — to "appropriate to itself exclusively a field of jurisdiction in which, apart from such a procedure it could exert no legal authority." [14]

However, the national government can, through the criminal law, exert considerable weight in protecting individual liberties.   Freedom of worship exists, for example, because "no province could prevent it and the federal parliament has not made any religion a crime." [15]

Freedom of association likewise comes within the ambit of the criminal law.   All associations which do not amount to seditious conspiracies and unlawful assemblies as defined by the criminal code are permitted.   No Province can legislate against them, except by regulating the use of parks and public places so as to avoid nuisances and preserve order.   "Freedom of speech and of the press belong likewise in this category, even though a province may legitimately protect the individual's character against defamation." [16]

The right of free access to information is protected at least from criminal interference by Section 136 of the Code.   It is a crime for anyone knowingly to publish false news "whereby injury or mischief is or is likely to be occasioned to any public interest." [17]   A more general declaration of law is difficult to imagine, and, as might be expected, this section has been rarely used.[18]

Censorship of printed matter is conducted by a national agency, the Customs.   This censorship is "secret, continuous, and seemingly unchecked by any independent authority." [19]   With few exceptions, moreover, all imported books are taxed.   Domestic publications can be effectively censored through national control of the mails or through the laws against immoral literature.

Where a freedom is federally protected, the Provinces cannot attack it obliquely by appearing to act under an enumerated power.   "No legislature is permitted to do indirectly what it may not do directly." [20]

The right to work, included in the United Nations Declaration of Human Rights, involves considerably more positive state intervention than do the rights already mentioned.   It also involves questions of economic policy

---

[12] [1939] A.C. 117.   This was a landmark case, declaring *ultra vires* an Alberta statute obliging newspapers to disclose the source of their news and compelling them to publish statements issued by the government to correct previous articles.

[13] Dawson, *The Government of Canada* 78 (1947).

[14] *Id*. at 105.

[15] Scott, "Dominion Jurisdiction over Human Rights and Fundamental Freedoms," 27 Can. B. Rev. 509, 520 (1949).

[16] *Ibid*.

[17] *Id*. at 525.

[18] *Ibid*.

[19] *Id*. at 524.

[20] *Id*. at 520.

which cannot be discussed here. Where, however, the right to work is challenged by private or public discriminatory tactics, it may be less questionable to discuss relevant legislation or judicial interpretation under the heading of "civil liberties."

The most serious precedent for discrimination appears to lie in the possible denial to Communists of entrance to a profession and to unions of use of public labor relations boards. The attempt legally to drive Communists out of the labor movement has taken the form of denying certification by a labor relations board to an applicant union on the ground that the union's leadership is Communist. The certification of or refusal to recertify Communist-dominated unions — on the theory that they are not really trade unions within the meaning of the Industrial Relations and Disputes Investigation Act — is the policy now of the Canada and Quebec Labour Relations Boards but not of any of the others. There is no Province-by-Province conception and administration.

For civil liberties, the important questions are: how inclusively is a communist defined by statute, and who has the final say as to the constitutionality or public policy aspects of the definition? With labor relations falling within their authority, the Provinces are free to pass any legislation (so long as no criminal penalties are attached) in regard to refusal to certify without any fear of violating a constitutional prohibition about personal rights or of exceeding the authority of their enumerated powers.

Freedom of opinion has been restricted by the law of sedition but the difficulty seems to be that no real distinction has been made between what type of written or oral statement constitutes a menace and what type is merely distasteful to the majority in a particular area. The criminal law is national but the courts applying it and the juries are subject to local influence. Unless the distinction between seditious and merely distasteful is made clearly — and nationally — there will be sectional differences and injustices as to what really constitutes sedition.

The greatest number of subversives appear to have sought out the Province of Quebec. Strikers, Jehovah's Witnesses, and anticlericals in general find themselves charged with sedition. The Jehovah's Witnesses, who have contributed so much to American constitutional development, are especially successful in antagonizing Quebec patriots. The most recent — and perhaps most important — case is *Boucher v. The King*.[21] This case arose from a classic situation: Jehovah's Witness style of proselytizing outraging Catholic sentiments.

The final Supreme Court decision in favor of the defendant Jehovah's Witness was mainly concerned with the common law definition of sedition. Justice Kellock stated:

> To say that advocacy of any belief becomes seditious libel if the publisher has reason to believe that he will be set upon by those with whom

[21] [1951] S.C.R. 265.

his views are unpopular (and therefore promotes violence) is without support in principle or authority, and would be to elevate mob violence to a place of supremacy. The law breakers are those who resort to violence rather than those who exercise the right of free speech. . . .[22]

This appears to widen considerably the range of free speech as defined by Justice Walsh in the Quebec case of *Rex v. Brodie:*

. . . though it is the right of a British subject to exhibit the imbecility of the Government; this must be done *without violating feelings.* There is no sedition in just censure or . . . in fair criticism. Theoretical political discussions, comparisons of forms of government are permissible.[23]

III. THE MACHINERY OF PROTECTION

The legal protection of personal rights in Canada rests on the Supreme Court's powers of interpreting the common law and of declaring Dominion and provincial legislation *ultra vires.* The Dominion government's power of vetoing provincial legislation — "disallowance" — could also be mentioned, but it has been of almost no significance recently. (See Appendix II to Study 2, The Federal Executive.) There has been considerable demand for the inclusion of a bill of rights in the Constitution, based on the apprehension that the political tradition is not a sufficient protection for fundamental rights. The argument is based on the fact that the Court's present authority over legislation is too restricted, especially as in times of emergency the Dominion's power under the "peace, order, and good government" clause appears to be virtually unlimited. Likewise provincial infringement on personal rights has gone, especially in Quebec, to considerable lengths, and is constitutionally limited only by the Dominion's exclusive jurisdiction over the criminal law. The concept of a bill of rights is, however, sharply at variance with the traditional concept of Parliamentary sovereignty and stands little chance of acceptance.

APPENDIX III

Germany

I. THE PLACE OF PERSONAL RIGHTS IN THE CONSTITUTION

The Imperial Constitution treated the basic rights of the individual in a very summary fashion. It expressly listed only a few and merely referred to the others in general terms, thereby establishing no more than a pre-

---

[22] *Id.* at 302.
[23] How, "The Case for a Canadian Bill of Rights," 26 Can. B. Rev. 791 (1948).

sumption that the latter might be included under the constitutional guarantee extended to the former.

The Weimar Constitution laid down a comprehensive and detailed program of basic rights and duties in the political, social, cultural, and economic field. It thus went beyond the realm of historic rights of the individual. Examples of this were the right to rest from labor on Sundays and state holidays (Art. 139), or the right to work (Art. 163). With few exceptions, however, the Weimar basic rights were not directly valid as subjective rights attainable through the ordinary process of justice, but were conceived rather as guiding principles for the legislator.

The Basic Law of the German Federal Republic (hereafter called the Bonn Constitution) mainly confined itself again to the historic basic rights and, apart from two provisions, it does not contain regulations of the social sphere. According to the Basic Law the rights of the individual emanate from the dignity of man (Art. 1) as the most important principle of a democratic state. Particular emphasis is given to this fact by regulating these rights in the opening articles of the Constitution. Independent of any statutory provisions growing out of these articles, they create immediate rights and duties and enable everybody, in case of complaint, to enforce these rights and duties through ordinary action in the courts.

II. The Rights of the German Constitution

A. The Imperial Constitution of 1871

Under the Imperial Constitution, on the basis of common denizenship (*Indigenat*) all Germans were assured of equality before, and protection by, the law. They were accordingly entitled to permanent residence, pursuit of business, public offices, acquisition of land, citizenship, and "the enjoyment of all other civil rights." The latter general phrase may be taken to refer to the claim to protection against foreign countries (Art. 3), to the protection of intellectual property, the freedom of the press and of societies (Art. 4), as well as to the right to petition (Art. 23).

B. Weimar and Bonn Constitutions of 1919 and 1949

Benefiting from the experience of the Weimar Republic the Bonn Constitution embodies many features of its predecessor. The basic freedoms may best be divided in positive and negative rights.

1. POSITIVE RIGHTS OF THE INDIVIDUAL

The former commit the state to positive action and efforts by way of granting protection and assuming responsibility for welfare.

The politically persecuted enjoy the right of asylum (Art. 16, II). Marriage, family, and motherhood have a special claim to the protection and care of the state and the community (Art. 6; Weimar, Art. 119). Further-more, the entire educational system is placed under state supervision (Art. 7; Weimar, Art. 144).

2. NEGATIVE RIGHTS OF THE INDIVIDUAL

The negative basic rights consist of rights to certain freedoms, rights of equality and rights of inviolability. They commit the state to non-inter-ference, and together they define the sphere of personal freedom.

The first group includes the freedom of movement throughout the federal territory (Art. 11), the freedoms of opinion, of press, and from censorship (Art. 5), as well as the rights to assemble (Art. 8) and to form associations or societies (Art. 9, I and II). Another provision grants the right to form combinations to safeguard and improve economic conditions. Agreements which seek to restrict this right are void and measures designed to this end are illegal (Art. 9, III). Everybody has the right to petition (Art. 17; Weimar, Art. 126) and the freedom of choice as to occupation, place of work, and training, and no one may be subjected to compulsory work ex-cept within an established general public service applicable to all (Art. 12).

In regulating the freedoms of belief and conscience (Arts. 4, 33), the rights of parents (Arts. 6, 7), and the question of religious instruction, the Basic Law very largely draws on the Weimar Constitution by providing that "Articles 136, 137, 138, 139, and 141 of the German Constitution of 1919 be an integral part of this Basic Law." It adds, however, the significant provisions for conscientious objectors (Art. 4, III).

It then completes the list of freedoms by guaranteeing non-interference with reading, art, science, and research, emphasizing, however, that this shall not absolve from loyalty to the Constitution (Art. 5, III). It corre-lates this to the right to set up private schools, though the latter is subject to detailed statutory limitations (Art. 7).

The second list comprises the rights to equality. All men are equal before the law (Art. 3, I). Every German in every Land of the federal republic has the same civil rights and duties, including equal access to pub-lic offices independent of religious confession (Art. 33). These provisions as well as those governing the equality of sexes (Art. 3, II) and of legitimate and illegitimate children (Art. 6, V) are reinforced by two powerful non-discrimination clauses (Arts. 3, III, and 33, III).

The last group is devoted to the rights of inviolability. The Basic Law established in great detail for everybody the right to the free development of his personality, the right to life and physical inviolability (Art. 2), and the freedom from extradition (Art. 16, II). The provisions guaranteeing the rights to property and inheritance as well as the freedom from forcible expropriation (Art. 14) deliberately leave the door open to socialization (Art. 15). The right to inviolability of the home (Art. 13) is temporarily restricted owing to postwar housing shortage but may otherwise be interfered with only by statute or official warrant. Similar clearly defined statutory requirements apply to secrecy of mail, post, and telecommunication (Art. 10).

Finally, no one may be deprived of his German citizenship against his will except by law and provided the person concerned is not thereby rendered stateless (Art. 16).

III. THE MACHINERY OF PROTECTION

The Imperial Constitution though it lacked a specific guarantee of the basic rights provided that any members of the federation which failed to fulfill their constitutional federal duties could be held thereto by way of execution (Art. 19). This execution was to be decided upon by the Bundesrat and carried out by the Emperor. It was the duty of the Bundesrat to receive substantiated complaints concerning denial of justice, or delay in the process of law (Art. 77). No distinction was made between the amendment of basic rights and that of other articles of the Constitution (Art. 78).

The lack of weight and protection of the basic rights as guaranteed by the Weimar Constitution is apparent — as confirmed by constitutional experience of the interwar period — primarily on grounds of two conspicuous features which it embodies.

The frequent qualifications attached to the basic rights that a statute or law was to regulate the actual scope of application did not stipulate, except in a few cases, whether this was to be done by federal statute or by laws of the respective Land.

Furthermore, the ill-fated Article 48 gave dictatorial emergency powers to the Reichspräsident which entitled him to suspend from operation, wholly or partly, seven of the most important basic rights guaranteed by the Constitution (Arts. 114, 115, 117, 118, 123, 124, and 153). And "in case of danger from delay" even a Land government could take within its territory measures of this nature.

The Bonn Constitution, on the other hand, avoided these ambiguities and dangers. Instead, its basic rights establish immediate legal validity and are, therefore, binding on legislature, executive, and judiciary alike (Art. 1, III).

Insofar as a basic law is subject to restriction by a statutory provision attached to the article (e.g. some of the rights of inviolability), the restricting law must apply in general and not solely to an individual case. "Furthermore, the law must name the basic right, indicating the Article" of the Constitution. "In no case may a basic right be affected in its basic content" (Art. 19, I and II).

Every citizen has a legal claim to demand compliance on the part of all public authorities with the obligations created by the basic rights. Should any person's rights be infringed, he may appeal to the courts (Art. 19, iv).

Thereby the basic rights are no longer abstract guiding lines for the legislator but of immediate practical importance to the individual.

The basic rights according to their general and "supranational" nature are due to everybody, including foreigners, unless the Constitution explicitly limits their application to citizens of the Federal Republic (e.g. Arts. 8, I; 9, I; 11, I; and 12). They also apply to juridical persons within the country insofar as, according to their nature, they may be applied to such persons (Art. 19, III). A significant addition to the list of basic rights is made by the provision (Art. 18) that whoever abuses the freedoms and rights of the Constitution, in order to attack the free, democratic basic order, forfeits the rights of Articles 5, I and III, 8, 9, 10, 14, and 16, II. The forfeiture and its extent is subject to a ruling by the Federal Constitutional Court.

Under the Imperial Constitution the Empire had the power of legislation and supervision of all matters concerning basic rights, but it conceded to Bavaria the right to make its own regulations as to the relationships of domicile and settlement (Art. 5, I).

The Weimar Constitution distinguished between such basic rights as to which the Reich claimed exclusive legislative power (Art. 6) and such as to which it shared this power with other legislative bodies (Art. 7). Though the guiding principle was that "Reich law supersedes Land law" (Art. 13), there was provided for the case of doubts about compatibilities between federal and Land laws that the competent Reich or Land central authority could appeal to a supreme judicial court for interpretation and decision.

The Bonn Constitution permits the Länder to maintain the basic rights which their constitutions may contain but only insofar as they conform to Articles 1-18 of the federal Basic Law, and without prejudicing the principle that federal law supersedes Land law (Art. 142). This provision is of significance because in some Land constitutions there exist special guarantees for the protection of basic rights (Bavarian Constitution, Art. 120: Whoever feels that his constitutional rights are being infringed may appeal directly to the Constitutional Court).

The responsibility of legislation and supervision of basic rights, however, clearly lies with the federal authority, as it had also been the case, though less clearly, under the two preceding German Constitutions.

A P P E N D I X   I V

Switzerland

I. THE PLACE OF PERSONAL RIGHTS IN THE CONSTITUTION

There is no one section in the Swiss Constitution of 1874 devoted to a declaration of rights, but guarantees are scattered through the first chapter. Its predecessor, the Constitution of 1848, had contained an impressive catalogue of basic rights and, apart from minor modifications, the new Constitution reaffirmed their validity for the whole federal territory. It added only two further guarantees, freedom of commerce and industry (Art. 31) and liberty of conscience and belief (Art. 49), because in some cantonal constitutions these were either omitted or insufficiently provided for.

On the other hand, the federal Constitution fails to guarantee such important rights as the inviolability of the person and the home because these had been firmly established and unconditionally recognized by all cantons in the past. In the same way as the Constitution tacitly assumes certain federal competences, it also contains tacit guarantees of certain basic rights. From the very nature of these constitutional liberties as the basis of a liberal system of values it follows that the federal Constitution guarantees *every* individual freedom of practical import, and not only those which are expressly mentioned. This does not apply, of course, where the legislature refused to grant certain aspects of an individual freedom, as in the case of teaching (Art. 27).

II. THE RIGHTS OF THE SWISS CONSTITUTION
A. *Freedom of Settlement*

The competency for the freedom of settlement rests with the cantons, except in cases which concern foreigners (Art. 69, III). This cantonal competency is, however, restricted insofar as under certain conditions the federation has power to grant this right independently (Art. 45). The federal Constitution distinguishes two kinds of settlement: the actual or permanent residence and the rights of temporary residence. The former, as especially the political rights derived from it, are determined by the Constitution, while the regulation of the latter is subject to federal legislation (Art. 47). This freedom derives its significance from the federal structure of the country, and is, as such, not one of the "traditional" basic rights.

It contains the freedom of movement and emigration, and grants to the citizen, once settled at his place of residence, all cantonal and communal rights (Art. 43, IV).

B. *Freedom of Commerce and Industry*

The liberal theory of free and equal competition was given expression through a guarantee of the freedom of commerce and industry (Art. 31), granting to this right more extensive scope than has been done in any other national constitution. With the gradual departure from the laissez-faire economy this was to lead inevitably to a deep tension between the federal Constitution and legal reality, since the federal authority was not vested with the constitutional competency of controlling the economy. These measures therefore ran counter to the provision of Article 3 and could only be given legal validity through emergency legislation, until in

1947 the so-called "new economy articles" were inserted into the Constitution (Arts. 31, I-V, 32, and 34, III).

C. *Freedom of Religion*

The experience gathered during the "Kulturkampf" between the federation and the Vatican gave birth to the constitutional guarantee of religious freedom. The much debated provisions relating to religion in the Constitution (Arts. 49 to 54) which, apart from guaranteeing individual freedom, also determine the relationship of church and state, are based on four guiding principles:

(1) the guarantee of individual freedom of conscience and belief together with the freedom of worship,
(2) the maintenance of peace between religious bodies,
(3) the secularization of matters which so far had been partly or wholly under the influence of the church (school, marriage, funeral, jurisdiction, etc.),
(4) the restriction of certain specific religious institutions (bishoprics, monasteries, orders).

Insofar as these establish rights for the individual citizen, they stand under the special protection of the federal tribunal.

D. *Freedom of the Press*

The freedom of the press extends to Swiss citizens and foreigners alike (Art. 55). As the principal expression of the freedom of opinion this provision is closely related to the secrecy of mail and telecommunication (Art. 36) and to the freedoms of writing, publishing, broadcasting, arts, and sciences. Any limitations which the cantons may consider necessary are subject to previous examination and authorization by the Bundesrat.

E. *Freedom of Association*

The right to form associations (Art. 56) is guaranteed by the federation provided that their objects and methods are not unlawful or dangerous to the state. The cantons are entitled to make the necessary laws for the prevention of abuses of this right.

Though not expressly granted by the Constitution, the freedom of assembly may be inferred from this provision. Other articles of the Constitution which prohibit certain kinds of associations (Arts. 51, 52) are, of course, not prejudiced thereby.

F. *Freedom of Petition*

The freedom of petition (Art. 57) can be claimed by Swiss citizens and foreigners alike regardless of residence. It includes juridical persons and is also extended to civil servants and other officials. Besides individual petitions, the law permits collective petitions, and apart from the written petition the individual may claim the right to be heard.

The authorities, however, are not obliged to reply to, or act upon, the petition, which considerably diminishes its value compared with the legal constitutional appeal, on the one hand, or popular initiative, on the other.

G. *Freedom of Languages*

A further freedom particularly characteristic for Switzerland is that of the four national languages. Although it is not expressly guaranteed like other basic rights, it is by its nature an inherent and integral part of most of these. From the fact that the four languages are recognized as national languages (Art. 116), a guarantee of their use and maintenance may be inferred. In addition, Article 4 must apply here in the same way as to other basic liberties.

H. *Other Rights and Freedoms*

To extend and clarify the scope of application of some of the constitutional rights mentioned above, the Constitution contains various further provisions.

Education is compulsory and, in public schools, free of charge (Art. 27). There is to be no discrimination whatever, no corporal punishment (Art. 65).

The state has the positive duty to protect the intellectual property (Art. 64), to provide for welfare and economic security (Art. 31A) and against unemployment (Art. 31D). Marriage and motherhood are under the special care of state and community (Art. 34D). The right of asylum is only referred to (Art. 69B, d) and the rights to citizenship and nationality are specially regulated (Art. 44).

I. *Rights of Equality*

The fundamental principle underlying these freedoms is that all Swiss are equal before the law. This is supplemented by the declaration that there shall be no subjects or privileges of rank, birth, person, or family (Art. 4), and that everybody is entitled to equal treatment throughout the federal territory (Art. 60). This principle of equality is directly addressed to the legislature and thereby dominates the whole legal order.

As such it is also the basis of political equality. Article 4 must therefore be understood as embodying the principle of general and equal, active and passive, election rights, as well as that of general and equal access to public office. It is worth noting, however, that the exclusion of women from many political rights appears to be considered compatible with these provisions of the Constitution.

III. The Machinery of Protection

The rights and freedoms of the individual under the Swiss Constitution are absolute rights in the sense that they are binding upon the legislature, executive, and judiciary of cantons and federation alike. They have direct and immediate legal validity and constitute rights which the individual may claim at any time or place. They also extend to juridical persons insofar as by their nature they are applicable to these. This concerns particularly the freedoms of commerce and industry (Art. 31), of worship and pursuit of cultural interests (Art. 50, I), and that of petition (Art. 57). Federal legislation prescribes the limits within which a Swiss citizen may be deprived of his political rights (Art. 66).

A serious weakness, however, may be found in the fact that the basic rights, as far as the highest federal organs are concerned, remain *leges imperfectae,* because they do not afford any legal remedy against acts of the federal executive. The Swiss law grants such right of complaint about the violation of constitutional rights only against cantonal acts.

The exclusion of federal laws, or generally binding federal resolutions, or treaties, from the federal tribunal's sphere of competency and power of review is specially emphasized (Art. 113). However, by protecting the individual's constitutional rights against the cantons, the tribunal as a federal organ gives practical meaning to the guarantees granted by the state (Art. 5).

The institutions of "direct democracy" in Switzerland have proved a protection rather than a danger to civil liberties as the results of the various referenda clearly show. On the other hand, it is precisely because these popular decisions were often negative that the federal authorities had to resort more and more to the dangerous practice of emergency legislation (Art. 89). Some of these emergency decisions have ventured outside the framework of the Constitution and severely restricted certain basic rights, particularly the freedom of commerce and industry, and the right to equality before the law. Others established new competences for the federal authority, unknown to the Constitution, and thereby curtailed the sphere of cantonal independence. The danger to basic rights that is inherent in this practice cannot be denied, particularly since in Switzerland there is no judge who can act as guardian of the Constitution against federal power.

Restrictions upon basic rights by either canton or federation if necessary for the maintenance of public order and security must be justified by substantive legal provisions. This is, for instance, specially required for restrictions on the exercise of economic freedoms (Art. 32) and on the freedoms of press and association (Arts. 55 and 56).

APPENDIX V

United States

I. THE PLACE OF PERSONAL RIGHTS IN THE CONSTITUTION

The Constitution of the United States was composed in the light of three dominant considerations: the desire to establish a national government which would be adequate to serve the interests of the Union as a whole; the desire to make sure that the autonomy of the States would be impaired as little as possible; and the desire to prevent governmental power from being used to infringe on the rights of the people. The national government was granted substantial control over such subjects as interstate commerce and foreign relations, but it was understood that all authority not specifically granted to the central government was reserved to the States. Apparently, the framers of the original document felt that this principle of limitation by enumeration would forestall national encroachment on private rights, while the populations of the several States could be counted upon to guard against infringement by the State governments. The specific guarantees of rights in the original Constitution were, therefore, few.

However, when the proposed Constitution was presented for approval by State conventions the omission of a bill of rights was seen to be a serious error, since it almost prevented ratification. In several States an affirmative vote was secured only by promising that the new government would immediately propose amendments in the form of a bill of rights so as to define more carefully the boundaries of the national authority. This promise was fulfilled in the first Congress which drew up the first ten Amendments — the "Bill of Rights" — and submitted them to the States for ratification. The persistence of the idea that the people themselves would prevent the State governments from encroaching on freedom was reflected in the fact that the Bill of Rights left those governments as untrammeled as before.

Soon after the new republic commenced operations, it became evident that the critics of the proposed Constitution had been right in their fears that the principle of enumerated powers would not suffice to confine the powers of the national government. The concept was advanced that the Congress could exercise not only the powers specifically granted to it, but also such powers as were "convenient or appropriate" for carrying out those which were enumerated; and, as this interpretation was accepted, it became apparent that the decision to adopt the supplementary protections of the Bill of Rights had been a wise one.

The States were not subjected to the proscriptions of the Bill of Rights until many years later. After the Civil War, the victorious North determined that the States must be deprived of the power to infringe the rights of the newly emancipated Negroes, and the Thirteenth, Fourteenth, and Fifteenth Amendments were added to the federal Constitution. The Thirteenth outlawed involuntary servitude; and the Fifteenth forbade the States to abridge the right of franchise on the grounds of race or color. The Fourteenth, however, was in the long run the most important of the three, since it became the basis for applying the provisions of the Bill of Rights as limitations on the State governments. Its commands that no State shall deprive any person of "due process of law" or "equal protection of the laws" have been construed as inhibiting the States from impinging on basic liberties.

II. THE RIGHTS OF THE AMERICAN CONSTITUTION

In general, the American Constitution is concerned with two categories of personal rights: "substantive rights," such as freedom of speech and of property, i.e. limitations on the actual objectives of governmental action; and "procedural rights," such as the right of fair trial, i.e. limitations, not on the end of legislation, but on its method. These are explicitly regarded by the American Constitution as rights held against government, and with the single exception of the Thirteenth Amendment (which applies to individuals as well as governments) the organic law makes no attempt to secure rights against the action of other individuals or private groups. Indeed, it is usually assumed that the Constitution forbids the national government to take action to protect individuals against private infringement on their rights, since this authority is not to be found among the enumerated or implied powers. The States, of course, do possess this authority, but no constitutional provision requires that they exercise it. As for "positive rights," such as the "right to work" or the right to old-age security, these too are left to the discretion of the national or State governments and are unmentioned by the Constitution.

A. Substantive Rights

Among the significant substantive rights recognized by the American Constitution, four categories deserve special notice:

1. FREEDOM OF EXPRESSION

Expression in the broad sense may be said to include freedom of speech and press, freedom of assembly and association, and the right to petition the government for redress of grievances. All of these rights are specifically or impliedly recognized in the First Amendment to the Constitution as limitations on the national government, and all the State constitutions also include language which imposes similar limitations on the State governments. In any case, as has been mentioned above, the due process clause of the

Fourteenth Amendment to the federal Constitution limits the power of the States to affect these substantive liberties.

2. FREEDOM OF RELIGION

The First Amendment forbids Congress to make any law "respecting an establishment of religion, or prohibiting the free exercise thereof." Under the due process clause similar limitations apply to the States. There has been much controversy as to whether the "establishment clause" prohibits all state aid to religion or merely prohibits the creation of a state church. Recent decisions would seem to indicate that the answer falls somewhere between these extremes, although it seems quite plain that direct government financial support to churches as such is forbidden.

3. POLITICAL RIGHTS: THE RIGHT TO VOTE

Under the Constitution, the States are granted the authority to prescribe voting qualifications, and the organic law limits them only in that they may not abridge the franchise on certain grounds or discriminate arbitrarily in denying it. The Fifteenth Amendment forbids abridgment of the right to vote on account of "race, color or previous condition of servitude," and the Nineteenth Amendment prohibits denial of the right on account of sex. Arbitrary discrimination between classes of voters on other grounds may also be regarded as invalid on the ground that it denies the Fourteenth Amendment's guarantee of equal protection of the laws.

4. THE RIGHT OF PROPERTY

Property rights are specifically protected by Article I, Section 10, which forbids the States to pass laws impairing the obligation of contracts, and by the Fifth Amendment, which prohibits the national government from taking private property for public use without "just compensation." But the most important source of property rights protection has been the due process clause, which applies to both the national government and the States through the Fifth and Fourteenth Amendments respectively. This clause has been construed in the past to restrict legislation touching property rights, not only as to its procedures, but also as to its objective. And for a time it protected the right of property owners to such incidents of ownership as "beneficial use and enjoyment" and "freedom of contract." For example, in 1923, it was held that the due process clause outlawed governmental attempts to establish a minimum wage, since such laws were arbitrary interferences with the wage contract. However, in recent years the right of the property owner has been regarded less solicitously, and a substantive interpretation of the due process clause in relation to economic regulation seems to have been abandoned.

B. *Procedural Rights*

These rights secured by the American Constitution can be considered under two general headings:

1. FREEDOM FROM ARBITRARY ACTION BY GOVERNMENTAL OFFICIALS

As far as action by officials of the national government is concerned, the scope of this right is largely defined by the Fourth Amendment and by the provision of Article I, Section 9, that "the privilege of the writ of *habeas corpus* shall not be suspended" except in times of rebellion or invasion. The Fourth Amendment forbids search of premises without warrant and arrest without warrant, and it has been held that the Fifth Amendment requires the exclusion from the subsequent trial of evidence which is obtained by unlawful search. The writ of habeas corpus is one of the ancient safeguards of Anglo-American law, and it is noteworthy that the framers of the Constitution assumed that it would be available even without explicit constitutional authorization. In general its effect is to require that a person held in confinement be brought before a tribunal or released. Finally, brutal treatment of prisoners by officials is to some extent mitigated by the judicial rule, based on the Fifth Amendment, that evidence obtained by force cannot be used against the accused person.

2. THE RIGHT TO A FAIR TRIAL

Most of the procedural guarantees of the first eight Amendments have to do with the judicatory methods permissible in the courts of the federal government. The rights ensured include: indictment by grand jury on a criminal charge; jury trial of all criminal causes and of civil suits for more than twenty dollars; assistance of counsel in criminal cases; compulsory process for obtaining defense witnesses; and the right to confront the witnesses for the prosecution. A man cannot be compelled to give evidence against himself, nor be tried twice for the same offense, nor be denied bail unreasonably. "Bills of attainder" (laws which inflict punishment without judicial trial) and "ex post facto laws" (laws which make conduct criminal which was not criminal at the time performed, or vary the punishment for an act after its performance) are prohibited in Article I to both the State and federal governments. Article III also defines "treason" very carefully and strictly.

The procedural requirements of the federal Bill of Rights are not directly binding on the State governments, but the States are forbidden by the due process clause of the Fourteenth Amendment from denying certain procedural rights. The States must provide counsel for the accused under some circumstances; and forced confessions cannot be used as evidence in State courts. However, the States may dispense with grand jury indictment and even with jury trial; and they are not forbidden to try a person twice under some circumstances or to require that he take the witness stand in his own defense. In general, the rule is that the States may not abridge the procedural rights which are essential to a system of ordered liberty, but are free to experiment within a wider range than is the federal government.

C. *Limitations on Constitutional Rights*

While the First Amendment speaks in unqualified terms ("Congress shall make *no* law . . ."), in fact it has always been assumed that such rights as freedom of speech can be abridged if the public need requires it, and the problem has been to draw an acceptable line between personal rights and public necessity. In general, it can be said that the freedoms of the First Amendment can be abridged if their exercise clearly threatens a fairly serious danger to the public. It is obvious that this evaluation will vary in different circumstances, and practice suggests that a state of emergency will be regarded as warranting a rather widespread abridgment of rights which in other times may be inviolable. This generalization applies, not only to the substantive liberties of the First Amendment, but to procedural rights as well. Of course, the provision for suspension of habeas corpus clearly recognizes the bearing emergency may have on the rights of the citizen.

III. The Machinery of Protection

The United States has relied very heavily, almost exclusively, on courts for the protection of fundamental rights. And the courts, both of the State and the nation, have been from the first supported in their performance of this task by the power of judicial review. While no clause of the federal Constitution expressly grants the judiciary this power, there is fairly general agreement among historians that the framers expected it to be exercised by the judges appointed under Article III. The Supreme Court under John Marshall early claimed the right of judicial review as an indispensable feature of constitutional government, and despite some opposition the power became clearly and indisputably established. The result is that any act of another branch of government, either State or federal, which infringes on the right of some individual can be challenged by that individual on the ground that it violates the Constitution. The person raising the challenge must be one whose rights are genuinely affected (the federal courts will not consider issues of constitutionality except in the course of an actual case), but if they are he can obtain a hearing on the point in some court. The State courts and the lower federal courts are themselves bound to uphold the Constitution, and it may be that the question of constitutional right will be settled at the lower court level. If it is not, the individual may under certain circumstances carry his appeal to the Supreme Court itself.

The process of claiming a right may take several forms. If a person is arrested or sued in either a State or federal court, he can set up his claim of constitutional right as part of his defense. In certain circumstances when his rights are threatened by impending governmental action, he can ask a court to restrain the official concerned or to order the official to abide by the command of the Constitution. Under some conditions he can bring suit against the official who has deprived him of a right owing to him under the Constitution. All these approaches are regulated by legislation and by judicial rules of extremely elaborate character. Congress possesses full and undisputed authority over the appellate jurisdiction of the Supreme Court, so that, while judicial review is firmly established as an adjunct to the system of constitutional rights, the determination of its scope and incidence is ultimately in the control of the legislative body.

STUDY 12

Citizenship and Immigration

I. INTRODUCTION

The individuals in a federation have a dual relationship, as citizens of both the federation and a member State. Within their respective areas of competence, both the federation and the member States create rights and obligations for such individuals. Accordingly, in the fields of federal power the citizens of the member States, upon the creation of the federation, become directly subject to the central authority.

This dual relationship raises a number of problems. Who is to possess the new status of citizenship in the federation? If this is left for determination by each State, different rules might be adopted by each. This would be unsatisfactory since the States have a common interest in who is admitted to the body politic of the federation. If the federation determines who are to be its citizens, shall this affect citizenship in the member States? If the States retain complete control of determining who their citizens shall be, the necessary interstate relationships may be prejudiced.

The question of immigration is also closely bound up with these questions of citizenship. There is a common interest among the member States in the number and type of people admitted to the territory of the federation, who may thereafter become citizens or who may remain alien groups. Moreover, where there is freedom of movement among the member States, each State has an interest in who is admitted to, or excluded from, any part of the federation.

The status of citizenship is a relationship of rights and obligations between an individual and a government, and it is necessary to consider what this relationship shall be in the case of citizens of the States and the federation respectively. What are the incidents of federal and State citizenship? These incidents are of course closely connected with the distribution of powers between the States and the federation. This consideration leads to the further question of what the relationship among the States should be with regard to their respective citizens; what interstate privileges should be provided?

All these questions require consideration in the preparation of a federal constitution, and may require treatment in its provisions. All of them have arisen in the experiences of some or all of the federal systems of Australia, Canada, Germany, Switzerland, and the United States, and many of them are dealt with in the constitutions of these systems. This study discusses the experiences and constitutional provisions of these countries with regard to these questions, and seeks to draw conclusions which may be helpful in considering these aspects of the structure of a new federation.

II. REGULATION OF CITIZENSHIP OF THE FEDERATION

All the federal systems studied have provided for the concept of federal citizenship. Upon formation of the federation, federal citizenship has devolved upon all persons then possessing citizenship under the laws applicable in the member States.[1] In all the federal systems, the federation has subsequently exercised power to determine who are to be its citizens, through regulation of both acquisition and loss of its citizenship. This constitutional grant of power to the federation has been based on recognition that independent control of federal citizenship by the member States would produce unsatisfactory variations in regulations, and that all the States have an interest in who is admitted to the body politic of the federation. In some cases, the constitution itself has included certain rules regarding citizenship.

Federal citizenship may, in general, be acquired either by naturalization or by birth or marriage. Federal control of naturalization involves not only the granting of citizenship, but also the prevention or regulation of any distinctions between rights of naturalized citizens and those who are native-born; the latter point is discussed below in connection with the incidents of citizenship. In all the contemporary federal systems studied, except Switzerland, the federation alone exercises control of the granting of citizenship through naturalization.[2] Although the Australian Constitution permits the States to regulate naturalization to an extent consistent with federal regulations, federal legislation enacted very early in the federation's history has excluded State action. For a short transitional period prior to this federal legislation, however, the Australian States exercised power over naturalization, and naturalization then granted in any State was effective throughout the federation.

In Switzerland, the member States retained control of naturalization from the creation of the Confederation until adoption of the Constitution of 1874. The unsatisfactory standards for granting citizenship applied by some localities, as well as the diversity of cantonal laws, led to inclusion in the Constitution of 1874 of a grant to the Confederation of power to regulate nat-

---

[1] Prior to the formation of the American, Swiss, and Imperial German federations, the member States of each had created their own nationality. Canada and Australia were formed, however, by unions of British colonies, in all of which there had existed only the status of British subjects. The term "federal citizens," where used with reference to Canada or Australia, includes both the citizens of those countries and other British subjects within their territories. The status of British subjects has significance throughout the British Commonwealth.

[2] Even in the loose union of the British Commonwealth, the member countries have found it necessary to standardize, to a great extent, their laws on naturalization.

uralization. Under the resulting federal legislation, the important requirements for naturalization are imposed by the Confederation; however, the cantons are authorized to prescribe supplementary rules applicable to aliens living within their borders. These cantonal rules have been limited mainly to requirements of local residence and the payment of fees by applicants for naturalization, although some cantons have provided further restrictions. An alien who meets both federal and cantonal requirements is recognized as a Swiss citizen throughout Switzerland. Under the Imperial German and Weimar Constitutions, there was a similar arrangement. The federal legislature exercised its power with regard to citizenship to specify requirements for naturalization, but the member States were given discretion to deny citizenship even though persons met those requirements.

Acquisition of federal citizenship by birth or marriage is also regulated by the federation, or by the constitution itself, in all the federal systems studied. No federation has delegated any power in this respect to the member States. In Switzerland, this power has derived from the general federal power with respect to fields of civil law. The United States Constitution expressly provides that all persons born in the United States, and subject to its jurisdiction, shall be American citizens. This provision was added by amendment following the Civil War, in order to assure the primacy of federal citizenship. The Fourteenth Amendment disposed of the contention that federal citizenship was held only through the mediacy of State citizenship; that contention had been made by some of the member States in connection with their resistance to the exercise of federal powers. Thus, both the United States and Switzerland have found it necessary to make constitutional changes in order to eliminate or control State powers with respect to federal citizenship.

Federal control of citizenship has also proved necessary in order to reduce the number of aliens resident within the country, by reducing the requirements for citizenship, where this is in the interest of the federation. Thus, Switzerland, faced with an alarming increase in the proportion of resident aliens prior to World War I, amended its Constitution expressly to permit federal legislation conferring Swiss citizenship upon certain persons born in Switzerland who would otherwise be aliens. A similar problem is faced by any federation which admits large numbers of immigrants or refugees, and their presence provides an added reason for central regulation of federal citizenship. The German Basic Law thus provides expressly that refugees of German stock, and their spouses and descendants, shall be Germans, subject to regulation by legislation; and the exclusive power to enact such legislation is granted to the federation.

Of the federal systems studied, the Swiss Constitution and the German Imperial and Weimar Constitutions have made federal citizenship derive, in theory, from State citizenship. This theory has not, however, interfered with federal regulation of federal citizenship, but has meant only that the federation regulates State as well as federal citizenship. Under the German

Imperial and Weimar Constitutions federal citizenship could be possessed without State citizenship by certain groups, such as German citizens in the colonies. In the United States, although citizens of the federation are ordinarily State citizens as well, American citizens who are residents of the District of Columbia or of a territory or dependency, or who reside abroad, possess no State citizenship.

Loss of federal citizenship, by denaturalization, renunciation, or deprivation, is likewise regulated by the federation in all these countries. In Switzerland, until 1928, the Confederation had no power to deprive persons of their citizenship, but it was found necessary then to adopt a constitutional amendment granting such a federal power. The German Basic Law, although stating the principle that no one may be deprived of German citizenship, provides that loss of citizenship may take place in accordance with federal law. The need for federal regulation of this matter stems from the common interest in depriving of citizenship persons who have shown that they do not deserve its privileges or who have severed their connections with the federation.

III. REGULATION OF CITIZENSHIP OF THE MEMBER STATES

There is some variation among the federal systems studied in the manner of regulation of citizenship of the member States. In Canada and Australia, no such concept exists. This results mainly from the circumstances at the time of creation of those federations; in the British colonies which then united, there was only the single status of British subject. In all the federations studied, State citizenship is conferred only on persons who are citizens of the federation. Moreover, only the Swiss cantons and the member States of the German Empire and Weimar Republic have exercised a significant control of their citizenship.

In Switzerland and Imperial and Weimar Germany, the member States, under federal law, have imposed requirements for acquisition of their citizenship, but might grant it only to persons also satisfying requirements set by the federation. Once the State requirements have been met, the individual becomes a citizen not only of the State but also, automatically, of the federation. The Swiss cantons may also regulate acquisition of their citizenship by the citizens of other cantons (who are of course federal citizens). Under the German Constitutions, the citizen of any State had the right to become a citizen of any other State upon satisfying conditions fixed by federal law.

Under the Fourteenth Amendment to the United States Constitution mentioned above, a citizen of the federation becomes automatically a citizen of the member State in which he resides, and a change in State citizenship results from the mere change in residence. Thus, State citizenship is in fact regulated by the federation, through its power to regulate federal citizenship, although the States exercise some control by prescribing requirements for residence.

The Weimar Constitution gave to the federation exclusive power to regulate citizenship of the member States, as well as citizenship of the federation. As noted above, however, this power was exercised to permit the States to regulate their citizenship to some extent. Under the German Basic Law, the federation and the member States are granted concurrent powers with respect to citizenship of the latter; this means, however, that the States may only issue regulations which are not inconsistent with federal measures.

IV. IMMIGRATION

Policies concerning immigration into the federation bear a close relation to those regarding the granting of its citizenship. Regulation of immigrants is also a matter of common interest to all the member States because of the movement of persons throughout the territory of the federation. In fact, the need for central control of immigration was one of the factors leading to federation in Australia.

Immigration into the territory of the federation, and expulsion from its territory, are subject to federal control in all the federal systems studied. In most cases this power has been granted specifically by the constitution to the federation, but in the United States it has been held to arise from the federal power with respect to commerce and foreign affairs. During the early history of the United States, immigration was regulated by the member States which, because of their competition to attract immigrants, failed to take adequate measures of control. This led to federal control, which is now held to be exclusive. In Canada and Australia, the member States, as well as the federation, have power under the constitution to legislate with respect to immigration into their territories, but State regulations may not be inconsistent with federal laws. Foreign immigration throughout Australia and Canada is now, in fact, controlled by the federal government. However, the States are closely consulted by the federal authorities of both countries concerning immigration policies.

The problem of immigration includes not only the admission of persons, but also their subsequent treatment, since, for example, federal policies with respect to admission may be frustrated by local treatment of immigrants. Each State has, however, a special interest in the immigrants who settle within its territory. This is recognized by the Swiss Constitution which grants to the cantons the power to regulate the "sojourn and settlement" of aliens, in accordance with general federal regulation and subject to more direct federal control in certain respects. In some of the federal systems, protection against discriminatory treatment of immigrants by local measures may be provided by constitutional guarantees of equality before the law.

Moreover, federal power with respect to "immigration" or "aliens" enables the federation to exercise some control over the treatment of the immigrants after their entry. However, the relation between this federal power and the various State powers has been difficult to define. This relationship has been a particular source of federal-state conflict in Canada; the Canadian Constitution grants the federation "exclusive" power with regard to aliens, and a potential constitutional question is therefore raised whenever provincial legislation affects aliens. Therefore, close federal-provincial cooperation has been very important for the success of large-scale immigration programs. In both Australia and Canada, the member States play a large part in the settlement of immigrants, and in such matters as citizenship training. In Australia, federal-State cooperation has, on some occasions, taken the form of formal agreements between the federation and member States regarding immigration programs.

Special provisions regarding immigration are found in the constitutions of some of the federal systems. The German Basic Law guarantees the right of asylum to persons persecuted for political reasons. The United States Constitution limited the federal power to interfere with State measures regarding the "migration or importation" of persons during a specified period after adoption of the Constitution; this provision was included as a concession to the States interested in continuation of the slave trade. In Australia, the federation is granted power by the Constitution to control the "influx of criminals."

A special aspect of the problem of immigration is the reception and treatment of refugees. The German Basic Law is the only constitution in which it has been considered necessary to deal specifically with the problem of refugees. In addition to providing the right of political asylum, the Basic Law grants to both the federation and the member States the power to legislate with respect to refugees and expellees, but measures taken by the States may not be inconsistent with federal regulations. Federal legislation has sought to equalize the burden of supporting and integrating large numbers of refugees, and agreements regarding refugee affairs have been concluded between the federation and member States. (As noted above, the Basic Law also defines as "Germans" refugees and expellees of German stock, and their spouses and descendants.) In the constitutions of the other federal systems, the problem of refugees has not been separated from the general question of immigration.

V. INCIDENTS OF CITIZENSHIP

A. *Federal Citizenship*

1. SOURCES OF RIGHTS AND OBLIGATIONS

The rights and obligations of federal citizenship are derived from two sources, the constitution of the federation and the statutes enacted by the federation and the member States within their respected spheres of power.

Of the constitutions considered, those of Australia and Canada contain very few provisions regarding the incidents of citizenship, and this has been left mainly to the legislatures. The United States Constitution provides for some of the basic political rights of citizens and protects them against action by the States, and the Swiss Constitution goes somewhat further in defining the incidents of citizenship. The German Constitutions of the Weimar Republic and the Federal Republic have, to a considerably greater extent, provided for the rights and obligations of federal citizenship.

Within the limits of the constitutional provisions regarding the incidents of citizenship, the federations and their member States have also created rights and duties of federal citizenship in the exercise of their respective powers under the constitution. Ordinarily, of course, this has been done by the federation, rather than the States. But the States frequently have also enacted such measures; for example, in the United States, Australia, and Canada, the States, which define eligibility for voting, have made this right depend on federal citizenship.

2. NATURE OF RIGHTS AND OBLIGATIONS

a. *Political rights.* Federal citizenship is, in all the federal systems studied, the basis for political rights with respect to the federation and, in many cases, with respect to the member States as well. In all these systems, only federal citizens may vote for, or be elected to, federal offices. Federal citizenship has been the basis also for the right to vote in State elections in Australia, Canada, and the United States, and under the Weimar Constitution and German Basic Law. In the United States, although the voting right is regulated by the States (which have granted it on the basis of federal citizenship), the Constitution protects federal citizens against deprivation of this right on the ground of race, color, or sex. The United States Constitution also establishes the right of federal citizens to be citizens of the State in which they reside, and protects them against abridgment by the States of the privileges and immunities of federal citizenship granted them in the Constitution or federal laws. The Swiss and Weimar Constitutions, and the German Basic Law, make federal citizenship the basis for the right to form political associations, and under the two German Constitutions it is also made the basis for the right of assembly.

b. *Personal rights.*[3] Personal rights, such as freedom of speech and religion, often have not been made dependent on citizenship, but rather, where guaranteed by the constitution, have been extended to all persons within the jurisdiction of the federation. Under the United States Constitution and federal laws these rights are, in principle, granted to all persons within the country's jurisdiction, although distinctions are made in certain respects

---

[3] The treatment of personal rights in the federal systems studied, and the distinctions which they make between the rights of citizens and those of aliens, are discussed at length in Study 11, Personal Rights.

between the rights of citizens and aliens. Among the provisions on personal rights contained in the Swiss Constitution, a reference to citizenship is included in the guarantee of equality before the law. The Weimar Constitution limited to citizens its guarantees of equality before the law, freedom of expression, and inviolability of the dwelling; and the Basic Law guarantees only to Germans the right to choose their trade or profession. These limitations have not excluded extension of these rights to non-citizens by legislation. Moreover, both Constitutions have guaranteed other personal rights to both citizens and aliens.

c. *Other rights and obligations.* In addition to political and personal rights, other rights, as well as obligations, are made incidents of federal citizenship by constitution or statute. The most important of these rights is that of protection abroad, which in most cases has been created by federal legislation in the exercise of federal power with respect to foreign affairs. The Weimar and Imperial Constitutions expressly made this a right of German citizenship. In addition, under all three German federations, citizens have been guaranteed against extradition to foreign countries.

The most important of these obligations is the duty to perform military service, which is made an incident of federal citizenship by the Swiss and German Imperial Constitutions, and by legislation in the United States, Australia, and Canada. The Weimar Constitution created the more general obligations of all citizens to perform personal services for the state, and to contribute to public burdens, as required by law.

Federal legislation has also, in some cases, made citizenship a requirement for such privileges as command of federally licensed vessels, exploitation of federally owned natural resources, and obtaining federal pensions or similar benefits.

3. EQUALITY OF NATURALIZED CITIZENS

A fundamental principle of many of the federal systems studied is that, in general, the incidents of citizenship are the same, whether citizenship is acquired by birth or by naturalization. A few exceptions have been made, however, even in those countries which observe the principle in general. Under the United States Constitution, only a "natural-born citizen" or a citizen at the time of adoption of the Constitution may be President or Vice-President, and citizenship may be lost more easily by a naturalized citizen than by one who is native-born. The Swiss Constitution guarantees equal rights for naturalized citizens, except with regard to certain properties owned by the local communities. Naturalized citizens in Australia and Canada receive some protection against discriminatory measures of the member States from the principle that such measures may be an invalid interference with the federal power over naturalization; however, the length to which this principle may be extended to invalidate State regulations is not clear. In Canada, the federal naturalization law also guarantees the equality of naturalized citizens. Nevertheless, the Canadian Provinces have discriminated against naturalized citizens in a few respects, and have been able to restrict the rights of racial groups composed largely of naturalized citizens.

B. *State Citizenship*

Rights and privileges of State citizenship may be determined by the member States within the limits of their competence. Thus, political rights with respect to the States have in some cases been made incidents of State citizenship. And, in Switzerland, the relief of the poor is made a right of local citizens by cantonal law. Federal laws may also create incidents of State citizenship. In Switzerland, the federal naturalization law provides that federal citizenship is acquired when one obtains cantonal nationality; in addition, the cantons are granted by federal law certain rights with respect to litigation involving their citizens. Both the Imperial and Weimar Constitutions of Germany also made federal citizenship, in theory, a derivative of State citizenship.

To a limited extent, the constitution is also a source of incidents of State citizenship in some of the federal systems studied. Thus, the United States Constitution provides that suits between citizens of different States may be brought in federal courts. The creation of incidents of State citizenship by the constitution has also been a means of giving some assurance of appropriate State representation in federal matters. Under the Swiss Constitution, only one member of the Federal Executive Council may be chosen from the citizens of each canton, and the Weimar Constitution provided that officials entrusted with direct national administration in the States should, as a rule, be citizens of such States.

In Canada and Australia, where the concept of State citizenship does not exist, and in such countries as the United States, where that concept is not much used, a requirement of residence has been made the basis for applicability of many State measures, such as those regarding suffrage, election to office, and taxation. However, residence has not been made a legal status comparable to citizenship, since its definition often varies according to the purpose of the legislation involved, and since its acquisition and loss are not regulated by formal provisions of the type which govern citizenship.

C. *Interstate Privileges of Citizenship*

Among the most important incidents of citizenship in a federal system are the rights which it grants to persons with respect to member States of which they are not citizens. These rights are provided in the constitutions of all the federal systems studied except Canada, in the form of rights of either federal or State citizenship. The United States Constitution makes these interstate privileges a right of State citizenship, by providing that:

"The citizens of each State shall be entitled to all privileges and immunities of citizens in the several States." However, this does not prevent the States from imposing a requirement of residence for the granting of certain privileges, such as the issuance of hunting permits. Under the Australian and Swiss Constitutions, similar protection is granted on the basis of federal citizenship. The federal citizen is guaranteed by the Swiss Constitution that, whatever his cantonal citizenship, he will not be discriminated against by any canton or community in which he is domiciled (except in regard to certain local matters). This protection against discrimination is further ensured by a constitutional provision requiring the cantons to grant to all federal citizens the same treatment as their own citizens in legislation and judicial proceedings. Each canton has, however, retained control of granting its citizenship to the citizens of other cantons. All three German Constitutions have also protected German citizens against discrimination by the member States.

All the federal systems considered permit freedom of movement among, and settlement in, their member States, although various constitutional means of protecting this freedom have been applied. In Switzerland, and under the German Constitutions, federal citizens have been granted a constitutional right to settle anywhere in the country. Attempts by the American States to restrict movement of persons have been held invalid as an interference with the federal power over interstate commerce (and the freedom of movement is therefore, in this respect, not limited to citizens). In Canada, similar attempts by the Provinces, when aimed at the movement of naturalized citizens or of aliens lawfully admitted to Canada, have been struck down on the ground of interference with the federal power over naturalization and immigration. The Australian Constitution's guarantee of freedom of "trade, commerce and intercourse among the States" has been a barrier to limitations on movement throughout the country.

VI. CONCLUSION

The practices and experience of the federal systems studied with regard to citizenship and immigration may be summarized, in their most important respects, as follows.

(1) All these systems have created the status of federal citizenship. By their constitutions and by law, this status is made the basis for certain political and other rights and obligations. Federal citizenship does not supersede State citizenship; the citizen owes a double allegiance, to the new federal community and to his own member State.

(2) The federation has been granted power to control acquisition and loss of federal citizenship, including power over naturalization of aliens. Thus, the standards of citizenship can be kept uniform and consistent with the common welfare. In some cases, the federation has prescribed only the basic requirements for naturalization, permitting the States to add con-

ditions which they consider appropriate for their particular circumstances. However, in such cases, the federation has had the power to intervene if the States' provisions become too diverse or if otherwise necessary to protect the common interest. Some constitutions contain fundamental principles concerning acquisition of citizenship by birth, or equality of naturalized and natural-born citizens. Upon formation of the federation, all citizens of the member States have become federal citizens.

(3) The constitution provides some means of coordinating federal and State citizenship. In the United States, the Constitution prescribes essentially the same standards for both. In several other federal systems, the constitution makes federal citizenship depend on State citizenship, but confers on the federation power to regulate both types of citizenship. In practice, however, these federations have fixed the basic requirements for citizenship, leaving the States free to add supplementary requirements for the acquisition of State, and hence federal, citizenship. None of the federal systems studied has permitted persons to possess State citizenship without federal citizenship. This situation would have a divisive influence. In some of the federations it has been possible to be a federal citizen without also being a citizen of a State, but the number of persons in this category has been quite small.

(4) The federation has been granted power to control the entry of immigrants (including refugees) into the federation, and their expulsion from its territory. In several cases, the constitution has granted to the federation and the member States concurrent powers with respect to immigration and aliens, giving the federation, however, power to displace State regulations. Thus, the States might continue to regulate the entry and settlement of immigrants and refugees until the federation finds it desirable to take steps to unify or control these measures. In practice, in such systems, the federation and the member States have cooperated in the settlement of immigrants and their treatment after entry.

(5) The constitutions of the federal systems studied have provided for those rights and obligations of citizenship which it has been considered desirable to exempt from change by the ordinary legislative processes. These have included the fundamental political rights and personal rights (although many of the latter have usually been extended, not only to citizens, but to all persons within the jurisdiction of the federation). Such basic obligations as the duty of military service have also been included in some constitutions.

(6) Almost all the constitutions studied have specifically prohibited unreasonable discrimination by any member State against citizens of other States or of the federation. This has not barred the States from making reasonable distinctions, in the application of their regulations, between their citizens or residents and other persons. However, a constitutional guarantee such as this has been necessary to support the freedom of intercourse which is necessary in a federal system. Some constitutions have included

a specific guarantee of freedom of movement among, and settlement in, the member States, subject only to regulation by the federation, and have provided assurance that citizens of one State might easily acquire the citizenship of another State.

A P P E N D I X   I

Australia

INTRODUCTION

An understanding of the characteristics of the Australian law as to citizenship and alienage requires an appreciation of the results of the status of that country as, successively, an unfederated congeries of British colonies, a federated colony, and a self-governing country of the British commonwealth of Nations. As in Canada,[4] prior to federation, the law of nationality in each of the colonies later to be federated was the law of the United Kingdom, subject only to the exception that there was, at least in New South Wales, a local form of naturalization effective only within the colony concerned. This position was changed by federation only in the sense that local naturalization thereafter became the concern of the federal (Commonwealth)[5] authorities rather than that of the States (the former individual colonies). The federal Parliament, a new creation of course, was empowered to make laws with respect to "naturalization and aliens." [6] But both the existing legislation of the States and their existing legislative powers were maintained. The local naturalization legislation of the States thus continued to stand until the federal Parliament legislated on that topic two years after its creation. Thereafter, the States were unable to legislate repugnantly to the federal statute.[7] However, notwithstanding federation, the general law of nationality continued to be that of the United Kingdom and the only non-alien status known was that of a British subject. This situation continued after the enactment and the adoption in Australia of the United Kingdom British Nationality and Status of Aliens Act, 1914, with the difference only that under that Act Australia, through the federal government, acquired power to issue certificates of naturalization valid extraterri-

---

[4] See Appendix II. Because of their membership in the British Empire or Commonwealth of Nations, and because of the similarity, in certain respects, of their political development, Australia and Canada have had much similar experience in the development of their law of nationality and citizenship. The details of this development in Canada are set forth in Appendix II, to which reference is made, and are therefore not repeated in the present appendix.

[5] Upon federation, Australia adopted the designation of "Commonwealth." The Australian Commonwealth, however, should not be confused with the (British) Commonwealth of Nations, of which it is a member.

[6] Australian Constitution, §51 (xix).

[7] *Id.* §§107–109.

torially as well as within Australia. A distinct Australian citizenship arose only with the (Australian federal) Nationality and Citizenship Act, 1948, which forms part of the scheme of Commonwealth citizenship and thus provides not only for citizenship of persons connected with Australia, but also that every Australian citizen continues to be a British subject and that every citizen of any other country belonging to or associated with the Commonwealth of Nations shall be a British subject in Australia.

In Australia, as in Canada, the absence until recently of any concept of separate citizenship, and the basing of that concept, when ultimately achieved, upon the continuing association of the country with the Commonwealth of Nations, have colored the character of immigration legislation. Difficulty in immigration control was one of the motives for federation. It is not surprising, therefore, to find that the Constitution gives to the federal Parliament power to make laws with respect to immigration and emigration.[8] But the States continue to possess power to legislate consistently with federal law in the same field. And immigration restrictions are based not upon any distinction between citizen and alien but cut across the categories of British subjects and aliens, and of Australian citizens and noncitizens.

Likewise, in the matter of the law governing the status of aliens, it has to be realized that in Australia, at first of necessity and, after the Statute of Westminster, 1931, as a result of the absence of comprehensive legislation, the relevant law has been that of the United Kingdom. The federal Parliament was given the power, as has been seen, to legislate concerning "aliens." This did not necessarily include power to deal with alienage generally, and the status of aliens still largely depends upon the law of the United Kingdom as extended to Australia before that country acquired complete legislative sovereignty.

The Australian federation has, however, differed from the time of its creation from the Canadian in one material respect. For, even before the Statute of Westminster, Australia had power to alter its Constitution,[9] subject only to the Governor-General's power of disallowance. But the amendment process requires endorsement of action by the federal Parliament by the majority of the federal electorate in a majority of the States, so that the central legislature is unable in practice to disturb the balance of powers as between itself and the States without the consent of the latter.

I. CITIZENSHIP

The federal legislation introduced shortly after federation, while providing that anyone previously naturalized under the laws of any of the colonies

[8] *Id.* §51 (xxvii).
[9] *Id.* §128.

which became the States should be deemed to have been naturalized under federal law, excluded for the future any local naturalization in the States. But, as has been explained already, until the adoption of the United Kingdom Act of 1914, even federal naturalization had no effect outside Australia. Moreover, naturalization under that Act elsewhere in the British Commonwealth was effective in Australia. This position is materially changed by the Nationality and Citizenship Act, 1948. Nevertheless, persons who are Australian citizens under that Act are concurrently British subjects both inside and outside Australia, and citizens of other countries of, or associated with, the Commonwealth of Nations are British subjects in Australia.

The principles upon which Australian citizenship are acquired are very similar to those governing acquisition of citizenship of the United Kingdom and which used to govern the former common status of British subjects. Birth in Australia thus confers such citizenship. As to persons born outside Australia, they acquire citizenship only if born of a father or, in the case of a child born out of wedlock, a mother, who is an Australian citizen at the time of birth, and if the birth is registered at an Australian consulate. Moreover, if the birth is in another country of the Commonwealth, citizenship is not acquired if, under the local law, citizenship of the country concerned vests in that person. Australian law thus leans heavily on the scheme of citizenship within the status of British subject. The provisions regarding naturalization are exactly as in Canada, the requirement of "first papers" being likewise waived in the case of an applicant who is already a British subject in virtue of some other citizenship. The provisions as to loss of Australian citizenship are also broadly the same as those governing Canadian citizenship.

Australian citizenship is strictly a federal creation. There is no separate State citizenship.

II. IMMIGRATION

As explained, the primary legislative competence with respect to immigration is federal, and a federal enactment of 1901 has excluded the possibility of any supplementary legislation by the States. This enactment proceeds on the basis that a British subject, even though born in Australia, may be excluded or deported equally with an alien.[10] It has been administered in accordance with a firm policy of racial discrimination. But Australia has recognized to a greater extent than Canada the right of permanent residents of the country to return thereto.

Just as in Canada, despite the federal legislative monopoly, there has been considerable cooperation between central and local organs of govern-

[10] See Rex v. MacFarlane, 32 C.L.R. 518 (1923); Donohoe v. Wong Sau, 36 C.L.R. 404 (1925); Potter v. Minahan, 7 C.L.R. 277 (1908).

ment in Australia with respect to the settlement and care of immigrants, once they are admitted. This has indeed been the subject of formal agreements between federal and State governments.[11]

III. Distinction Between Citizens and Aliens

The basis of the law of alienage in Australia is, as explained, the law of the United Kingdom; and a British subject, even after the introduction of Australian citizenship, is not an alien in that country. Election to the federal Parliament and the federal franchise are confined to British subjects.[12] Federal legislation enacted before the introduction of Australian citizenship restricts the operation of social security measures and liability to military service to British subjects.[13] Australian residence is also required of a British subject under federal legislation before he may qualify for certain social benefits. Despite the introduction of Australian citizenship, a passport may be issued in Australia to a British subject who is not an Australian citizen.[14] Emergency legislation, which incidentally extended liability to military service to some categories of aliens, has discriminated in some respects between natural-born and naturalized persons, contrary to the general tenor of United Kingdom law.[15]

As has been seen, there is no State citizenship. The Constitution, moreover, contains a clause guaranteeing equal treatment in any State to British subjects resident in any other State.[16] There is also a clause guaranteeing that "trade, commerce, and intercourse among the States . . . shall be absolutely free." [17] Nevertheless, the States have occasionally practiced successfully a policy of racial discrimination,[18] and have distinguished for certain purposes, notably taxation, between domiciliaries and others.[19]

[11] See Migrant Settlement Agreement Act, 31 Australian Commonwealth Acts, 1933, p. 239.

[12] Constitution, §§16, 34; Commonwealth Electoral Act, 1949, §§3, 5.

[13] Commonwealth Public Service Act, 1922, §33; Social Services Consolidation Act, 1947, §§19, 62; Defence Act, 1903–1934, §§59, 125. During World War II, however, aliens who were nationals of Allied countries were also liable for military service. National Security (Aliens Service) Regulations, Stat. Rules, 1942, No. 39, Reg. 6, as amended. See Polites v. The Commonwealth, 70 C.L.R. 60 (1945).

[14] Passports Act, 1948, §4.

[15] National Security Act, 1939, §5 (1) (f).

[16] Sec. 117 of the Constitution provides: "A subject of the Queen, resident in any State, shall not be subject in any other State to any disability or discrimination which would not be equally applicable to him if he were a subject of the Queen resident in such other State."

[17] §92. Rex v. Smithers, 16 C.L.R. 99 (1912), declared unconstitutional a State statute prohibiting entry into the State of certain classes of criminals.

[18] See Bailey, "The Legal Position of Foreigners in Australia," in Mackenzie (ed.), *The Legal Control of Aliens in Pacific Countries* 41 et seq. (1937).

[19] See Davies & Jones v. Western Australia, 2 C.L.R. 29 (1904), which upheld a State law permitting "persons bona fide residents of and domiciled in" the State to pay succession duties at half rates.

CONCLUSION

Apart from certain trivial distinctions based on domicile, State law plays no part in connection with questions of citizenship, immigration, or status of aliens in Australia. These are all federal matters, federal law being strongly influenced by Australia's former status as a British dependency and her continuing membership of the Commonwealth of Nations.

APPENDIX II

Canada

INTRODUCTION

The exact nature of Canadian citizenship cannot be appreciated save in the light of the circumstance that it has only recently been created and that before its creation a British subject belonging to the United Kingdom and a British subject belonging to Canada were virtually indistinguishable in the nationality law both of Canada and the United Kingdom. Even now a Canadian citizen is not an alien according to the law of each of nine other communities of the Commonwealth, nor is a citizen of any one of these communities an alien in Canada. Who is a Canadian citizen is indeed determined now according to the law of Canada exclusively, but the applicable rules result from a tacit bargain with the other Commonwealth communities and have a more stable character than the doctrine of parliamentary sovereignty would alone involve.

The precise form of Canadian restrictions upon immigration cannot, either, be understood except in the light of the circumstance that, all British subjects from all parts of the Commonwealth or Empire being formally equal before the law of Canada, mere alienage did not alone constitute a criterion for discrimination. If it was decided, as indeed it was, to exclude certain races, this could not be done by drawing a distinction between citizen and alien, because every British subject was a citizen whatever his race or place of origin.

These propositions may be said to flow from the fact that Canada was originally a dependency of the United Kingdom and still remains linked by constitutional laws and conventions, in addition to or in substitution for international legal ties, both with the latter country and with others of its emancipated and unemancipated dependencies. The federation which is a feature of legal organization of Canada was set up before that country obtained international independence, and it was an essential element in the division of powers between central and provincial legislatures that its maintenance remained under the guarantee of a third party, the Parliament of the United Kingdom, and that its interpretation was the responsibility of a non-Canadian court, the Privy Council, applying for the purpose the principles of English rather than the Canadian law. The original existence of these external safeguards explains many of the peculiar features of the Canadian Constitution. However, these safeguards have largely or wholly disappeared; the appeal to the Privy Council has thus been swept away. Although the *status quo* as respects the division of competence between Dominion and Provinces of the British North America Act, 1867, is for the time being preserved, the Statute of Westminster, 1931, leaves it unclear whether the Dominion legislature could not procure a restriction of the powers of the Provinces by calling upon the United Kingdom Parliament to legislate to that end.[20] It is possible, however, that this is the case and that the provincial spheres may be invaded by constitutional amendments to which their consent is not requisite. It has therefore always to be borne in mind that the exact character of the Canadian federal scheme is to some extent fortuitous and not necessarily permanent.

I. CITIZENSHIP

The only exception to the former unity of English and Canadian law respecting nationality was that, both in the Provinces before federation and in the Dominion thereafter, local naturalization was possible, as it was in other British colonies and protectorates.[21] Such naturalization had no effect outside the colony where it was granted,[22] but naturalization in the United Kingdom was of necessity acknowledged in any colony. The alteration of the law of nationality in relation to any matter other than naturalization was not within the power of either the Dominion or the Provinces. The law of local naturalization was, however, consolidated in 1868,[23] the year following the federation, pursuant to the exclusive competence over naturalization given to the Dominion Parliament in Section 91 of the British North America Act. The procedure prescribed followed the American rather than the United Kingdom model, the function of naturalization being confided to the courts rather than to the legislature. Naturalization was apparently granted under this system with the greatest freedom and the minimum of inquiry.[24] This, however, was changed when in 1914 the British Nationality and Status of Aliens Act was enacted in the United Kingdom and subsequently adopted or re-enacted throughout the Commonwealth. This legislation both changed the pre-existing general nationality law (for instance, by restricting the acquisition of nationality *jure sanguinis* to the first foreign-born generation) and provided for an

[20] This position is not altered by the British North America Act, No. 2, 1949, which, while conferring power on the Dominion Parliament to amend portions of the British North America Act, does not apply in relation to the list of provincial legislative powers in Section 92 thereof.

[21] See Mervyn Jones, *British Nationality* (1937).

[22] Markwald v. Attorney-General, [1920] 1 Ch. 348.

[23] 31 Vict., c. 66 (Canada).

[24] Cf. Re Cimonian, [1915] 23 D.L.R. 363, per Meredith, C.J.C.P., at 368.

Imperial certificate of naturalization, to be issued by the executive in each community of the Commonwealth on approximately the same terms, but to be effective in every such community. It thus materially changed the law of Canada, first by changing the general nationality law, and secondly, by producing a sweeping away of the former system of local, curial naturalization. For the latter was substituted federal executive naturalization still preceded, however, by curial investigation, effective not only in Canada but elsewhere in the Commonwealth or Empire. The Act of 1914 did not, however, exclude the possibility of continued local naturalization, though it is apprehended that it did not persist in Canada.

The Act of 1914 was amended in 1918 and again in 1922, and these amendments duly went into force in Canada. Incidentally, in 1921 the Dominion legislated for the purpose of defining Canadian "nationals" in connection with elections of Judges of the Permanent Court of International Justice, but specifically without prejudice to the common status of British subjects in Canada and elsewhere. The breach between Canadian and United Kingdom nationality law began in connection with the question of the nationality of married women. In 1933, the Act of 1914 was amended in the United Kingdom so as to restore partially the original common law rule that marriage had no effect on nationality. Canada, however, had anticipated the general change by legislation in 1931. By that date the Statute of Westminster had become law, but it remains perhaps an open question whether the legislation passed was *intra vires* the Dominion Parliament. Moreover, though the parallel legislation of 1933 in the United Kingdom (followed in 1935 in New Zealand, and in 1938 in Australia) partially restored the earlier unity, it is arguable that the variety of legislative techniques employed left gaps, even between Canada and the United Kingdom.[25] If disunity followed the enactments of 1931 and 1933, it was increased by the United Kingdom Act of 1943, which amended further the original Act of 1914, but which was not immediately followed in Canada. By that date, too, a movement had grown up in favor of the use of the term "Canadian citizen," derived from the Immigration Act,[26] to describe British subjects of Canadian origin or association, together with a feeling that it was undignified for the definition of such a citizen to be found only in the immigration laws. Accordingly, the scheme of Canadian nationality law was recast in the Canadian Citizenship Act, 1946.[27] But no doubt one motive for the legislation was a desire to hurry on a general change of Commonwealth nationality law and when, as a result of the Canadian action, a common scheme of Commonwealth citizenship was worked out, the Act of 1946 was considerably modified to take account of that scheme. It remains of the essence of Canadian nationality law that that law takes account of Canada's membership in the Commonwealth.

[25] Cf. Kennedy, *Constitution of Canada* 484–488 (2d ed. 1937).
[26] Discussed below.
[27] 10 Geo. VI, c. 15.

The present law is to be found in the Canadian Citizenship Act, 1946, as extensively amended by the similarly entitled enactment of 1950.[28] This legislation provides:

(a) A natural-born Canadian citizen is a person born in Canada or aboard a Canadian-registered ship (other than the child of an alien diplomatic envoy); a foundling found in Canada; or a person born elsewhere whose father, or, in the case of a child born out of wedlock, whose mother, was a Canadian citizen at the time of the birth, provided that such birth is registered at a Canadian consulate within two years of its occurrence or such longer time as may be specially prescribed. While, therefore, the *jus soli* operates to confer Canadian nationality even upon the child of a prohibited immigrant born in Canada, Canadian citizenship is never acquired exclusively *jure sanguinis;* a foreign birth must be appropriately registered before parentage can confer citizenship. Moreover, a natural-born Canadian citizen who is born outside Canada loses his status as such at majority unless he executes a declaration of retention and also divests himself of any other citizenship, be it of another community of the Commonwealth merely or a foreign nationality, which he may simultaneously possess. This extraordinarily restrictive provision was even narrower as originally formulated in 1946, when it extended only to the foreign-born children of Canadian citizens themselves born, naturalized, or permanently resident in Canada. Its tenor illustrates forcibly the assumption of the Canadian legislature that the lacunae will be supplied by the law of the United Kingdom so that excluded persons, while they may not be Canadian citizens, may yet sometimes remain British subjects.

(b) A Canadian citizen other than natural-born is in effect a naturalized citizen. The provisions as to naturalization are much as they were before the latest legislation in Canada and as they continue to be elsewhere in the Commonwealth. That is to say, naturalization is a matter of executive discretion and the prerequisites therefor are five years' residence following lawful immigration, an intention to continue to reside, good character, and an adequate knowledge of French or English. But Canada clings to the device of "first papers" adopted from the law of the United States, where it has now been abandoned. Moreover, the factual requirements have to be proved in judicial rather than administrative proceedings. British subjects not being already Canadian citizens are exempt from the requirement of "first papers," as are the spouses of citizens.

If, however, the conditions for naturalization have not been materially changed by the new legislation, note must be taken of the manner in which they were formerly administered. For it appears that in practice even after 1914 no inquiry was made as to the adequacy of the languages of applicants for naturalization, nor any judicial inquiry as to character.[29] It

[28] 14 Geo. VI, c. 29.
[29] Cf. Hancock, "Naturalization in Canada," in Mackenzie (ed.), *The Legal Control of Aliens in Pacific Countries* (1937).

seems also that the administrative discretion was so exercised as to virtually exclude the naturalization of Orientals.[30]

(c) The provisions as to loss of Canadian citizenship are particularly stringent. Voluntary acquisition of the citizenship of another country, whether within the Commonwealth or without, thus produces loss of citizenship. A naturalized citizen in general expatriates himself automatically by six years' residence abroad. The obtaining of naturalization by fraud, trading with the enemy, and disaffection towards the Crown are among the discretionary grounds for revocation of naturalization. A dual citizen may renounce his Canadian citizenship.

To describe the content of the Canadian Citizenship Act, as amended, is not, however, to set out the whole law of nationality in Canada. For, in the first place, it must be noticed that a person who is a British subject by the law of some other part of the Commonwealth is also a British subject by the law of Canada. This circumstance will not necessarily enable such a person to enter Canada. But, once he is there and while he remains there, his rights are not materially different from those of Canadian citizens. This follows from the fact that most legislation on personal rights and status antedates the scheme of Canadian citizenship and assumes as its basis the former common structure of British nationality law. Nevertheless, the rights of British subjects and even of Canadian citizens are not necessarily equal and are not so in fact. For, in the second place, provincial legislation has to be taken into account. Canadian citizenship, as has been said, is the creature of the Dominion Parliament; it is federal citizenship. The continuing equal status of British subjects other than Canadian citizens is likewise the result of federal legislation. The provinces have no power to legislate with respect to either nationality generally or to naturalization. This would not, presumably, preclude the creation of an intranational provincial citizenship. But no steps to this end have been taken and there is no common concept of provincial citizenship comparable to even the vestigial State citizenship within the United States. On the other hand, the Provinces have exclusive legislative competence with respect to "property and civil rights" within each Province[31] and competence concurrently with the Dominion Parliament in relation to immigration. As will be shown in the next section, this has enabled them to pursue something approaching a separatist and discriminatory policy.

Summing up, therefore, the history of the development of Canadian nationality law, it may be said: (1) that before federation there was a common nationality law in the separate Provinces coupled with separate naturalization laws which, however, could produce only exclusively local citizenship; (2) that after federation and until the British Nationality and Status of Aliens Act, 1914, there was a general nationality law common to the whole Dominion and other British territories, coupled with a Dominion

[30] *Ibid.* See also Angus, "Canadian Immigration," in the same volume.
[31] B.N.A. Act, 1867, §92 (13).

local naturalization process, effective throughout the Canadian Provinces, but without extraterritorial effect; (3) that after the Act of 1914 the situation remained the same except that the Dominion acquired power to issue naturalization certificates with extraterritorial effect; and (4) that since 1946 a separate Dominion citizenship has existed the scheme of which is, however, framed on a basis of Canada's continuing membership of the Commonwealth, with the result that the rules respecting the acquisition and loss of Canadian citizenship are somewhat narrower but are compensated for by the wider terms of the legislation of other parts of the Commonwealth and by the circumstance that a citizen of any other part of the Commonwealth is a British subject by the law of Canada. And, by way of conclusion, it may be re-emphasized that since federation the Provinces have had no competence in connection with either nationality or naturalization and that no common conception of provincial citizenship exists.

II. IMMIGRATION

Section 95 of the British North America Act, 1867, gives to each Province power to make laws in relation to "immigration into the Province." But it also authorizes the Dominion Parliament to legislate with respect to "Immigration into any or all of the Provinces" and provides that provincial legislation shall have effect "as long and as far only as it is not repugnant to any Act of the Parliament of Canada." Even as thus stated, the concurrent competence of the Provinces is not unlimited, as the Governor-General in council may disallow a provincial enactment (as was done in the case of a British Columbia statute prohibiting Chinese immigration in 1884 [32]) or the Lieutenant Governor of the Province may reserve such a measure for the signification of the Governor-General's pleasure. As a last resort the treaty power might be used to curb provincial legislation.[33] The result is that immigration has largely been controlled by the federation, subject to the qualification that until 1910 immigration from the United Kingdom was not under the supervision of any Canadian authority whatever.[34] However, the federal immigration legislation has been primarily directed to the establishment of categories of prohibited immigrants and to the setting up of a federal ministry for dealing with immigration in general under delegated legislation of a detailed sort. The main characteristic of the rules directly affecting immigrants is that they are extremely stringent. They discriminate specifically against the Chinese, a treaty settlement of the parallel question having been achieved with Japan.[35] They make little or no distinction between aliens and non-aliens, because of the

[32] See Angus, "Canadian Immigration," in Mackenzie (ed.), *The Legal Control of Aliens in Pacific Countries* 58 n. 6 (1937).
[33] *Id.* at 59; Attorney-General for British Columbia v. Attorney-General for Canada, [1924] A.C. 203.
[34] Kennedy, *Constitution of Canada* 346 (2d ed. 1937).
[35] Angus, *op. cit. supra* note 32, at page 6.

circumstance that, as explained, Canada had no citizenship properly so called of its own until recently. But since 1910 there has been employed in other contexts the concept of "Canadian citizenship" (meaning persons born in Canada and British subjects of Canadian domicile) and "Canadian domicile" (meaning the quality of being a lawful immigrant and having resided in Canada for five years with the intent permanently to reside) to distinguish between persons entitled to readmisission to the country and others. The power of deportation has been freely used even against British subjects and persons born in Canada. The Privy Council has held such exercise to be *intra vires* the powers of the Dominion Parliament even when coupled with deprivation of the status of a British subject within Canada.[36] Possibly Canada will not, or will not be able to, resort to measures of this sort so freely in the future. For they have been justifiable in the past only because of the willingness of the government of the United Kingdom to receive as British subjects persons excluded from Canada, e.g. persons naturalized in Canada, never being resident in the United Kingdom.[37] Moreover, deprivation of the status of a British subject within Canada did not, under the former law, operate elsewhere in British territory. But since the inception of the Commonwealth citizenship scheme such deprivation must normally mean that the person concerned ceases to be a British subject anywhere, and the policy of the United Kingdom will presumably be modified to take account of this. Another feature of Canadian immigration legislation of note is the existence in it of latently discriminatory provisions, e.g. the prohibition of immigrants' arriving in Canada otherwise than by continuous journey from the country of which they are natives or naturalized citizens.[38] This particular measure was directed against Indians.

The attempts of the Provinces to legislate more restrictively than the Dominion in the matter of immigration have in general been unsuccessful. As has been said, an early British Columbia enactment prohibiting Chinese immigration was disallowed though, as has been seen also, the historical consequence seems merely to have been the adoption of an identical enactment by the federation as a whole.[39] Similarly, a British Columbia statute prohibiting the entry of immigrants not knowing a European language has been held invalid as repugnant to federal legislation.[40] Again, it may be remarked that the statute here in question was directed against Indians and its fate has to be appreciated in the light of certain federal subordinate legislation to the same end which has survived.

Immigrants to Canada have been bound in the nature of things to settle in the Provinces and the latter have had much to do with their settlement

---

[36] Cooperative Commission on Japanese Canadians v. Attorney-General of Canada, [1947] A.C. 87.

[37] See H. H. Wrong, *Some Observations on the Operation of Certain Clauses of the Canadian Immigration Act* (1929).

[38] See Angus, *op. cit. supra* note 32, at pages 65–66.

[39] Chinese Immigration Act, R.S.C. 1927, c. 95.

[40] In re Narain Singh, [1908] 13 B.C. 477.

and care. A high degree of cooperation between federal and provincial authorities has thus come about in this regard. But this would not seem to detract from the general conclusion that, despite the existence of a concurrent but non-repugnant legislative competence in the Provinces, the control of immigration in Canada has been primarily a federal concern. Because of Canada's position in the Commonwealth such control has been exercised not so much on the basis of a distinction between aliens and non-aliens as on racial grounds.

III. Distinction Between Citizens and Aliens

Legislation with respect to aliens is exclusively a federal function under the Canadian Constitution. Nevertheless, as a matter of history, the general incidents of alienage in Canada have flowed not so much from federal enactments as from the former extension of the law of the United Kingdom to Canada. The rules that an alien may hold real or personal property as freely as a subject or a citizen, but that he may not hold public office or own a Canadian ship or share thereof, are traceable to this source, though it would seem that the relation of the alien to the rights to vote and be voted for in public elections depends for the most part on Canadian legislation.[41]

In general, the bulk of federal legislation discriminating between aliens and non-aliens is small. Aliens are excluded from participating in federal elections,[42] either as candidates or voters, from service in the armed forces, and from responsible positions in ships' crews.[43] But measures to this effect date from the time when the only non-alien nationality known in Canada was the wider British nationality, and they remained unamended despite the introduction of Canadian citizenship, to the scheme of which it was in any case, as has been explained, an essential addendum that citizens of other communities of the Commonwealth should continue to enjoy the status of British subjects in Canada. The distinctions of the immigration laws are not drawn, as has also been explained, essentially between Canadian citizens and others, but employ distinctions of race or fitness cutting across the categories of Canadian citizens, British subjects, and aliens. There are, however, no constitutional guarantees against discrimination between aliens and citizens. But this is as much attributable to the circumstances that Canada has no complete written constitution and that declarations of rights are foreign to Canadian legal and political tradition as to anything else.

Provincial legislation may not deal primarily with aliens and may be declared *ultra vires* by the courts as infringing the Dominion's powers if it does. But, in the area of the common status of British subjects, the Prov-

[41] See, as to the federal Senate, however, the British North America Act, 1867, §23 (2).
[42] Canada Election Act, 1948, §§14, 19.
[43] Canada Shipping Act, 1934, §6; *id.*, 1948, §118; *id.*, 1950, §419.

inces have been no more concerned to attempt to distinguish between alien and non-alien than has the federation. They have, however, resorted to legislation discriminatory against members of Asian races, whether British subjects or not. Thus, acting under the British North America Act, which gives each Province power to provide for its franchise, British Columbia has excluded from the electorate not only aliens but most Asian British subjects and also North American Indians. Both aliens and Asians have also been excluded from provincial public office. Similar discrimination has been practiced in relation to admission to certain professions and trades, issuance of government fishing licenses, and to government contracts. Labor legislation has likewise been highly discriminatory in actual effect. On occasion parts of this mass of legislation have been challenged in the courts as unconstitutional, sometimes with success.[44] But carefully drafted provincial measures can be and are highly discriminatory, without there being any means of redress for an aggrieved person. Very often the discriminatory purpose requires, in order to be effective, to be carefully concealed. In that connection, the denial to the provinces of any power to control aliens requires special consideration. For it is clear that they have sometimes been forced to discriminate against classes of Canadian citizens, or British subjects, because of lack of competence to deal with aliens alone.[45]

CONCLUSION

By way of conclusion it may be said that naturalization is an exclusive federal concern in both law and practice in Canada; that immigration, though capable of being dealt with concurrently by the Provinces in law, has in practice also been a federal matter; and that the drawing of distinctions between aliens and non-aliens is also a federal matter; but that the lack of any concurrent competence in this sphere has reinforced a tendency toward racial discrimination in provincial legislation. At the same time, these conclusions are meaningless save in the light of Canadian history. Until very recently Canada's federal structure was under the guarantee of a non-Canadian third party, and the distribution of powers between central and local units was at least theoretically capable of being changed only by that third party. Now the central organs of the federation would appear to be, at least theoretically, capable of curtailing the spheres of the Provinces at will. Similarly, until very recently, Canada had no concept of citizenship of its own; a Canadian was merely a British subject. Immigration law and the law respecting public rights could not therefore be based on distinctions of nationality. Finally, though it has achieved full legislative sovereignty and an independent concept of citizenship, Canada remains a

---

[44] Union Colliery Co. of British Columbia v. Bryder, [1899] A.C. 580.

[45] See, generally, Angus, "The Legal Status in British Columbia of Residents of Oriental Race and their Descendants," in Mackenzie (ed.), *The Legal Control of Aliens in Pacific Countries* (1937).

member of the Commonwealth, and that circumstance materially influences the present structure of her laws as to nationality, immigration, and the status of aliens. Indeed, insofar as nationality and the status of aliens are concerned, the relevant "central" and "local" organs to be looked to in the Canadian federation are sometimes not so much the Dominion and the Provinces as the United Kingdom and the Dominion.

APPENDIX III

Germany

I. REGULATION OF FEDERAL AND STATE CITIZENSHIP

A. *The Imperial Constitution*

The Imperial Constitution of 1871 provided for a common citizenship (or "denizenship," *Indigenat*) throughout the Empire which was granted to the citizens of all member States, and gave to the Empire power to regulate citizenship (Art. 4 (1)). Imperial citizenship was, in principle, a derivative of State citizenship. Acquisition or loss of State citizenship resulted automatically in acquisition or loss of Imperial citizenship, and only in exceptional cases (e.g. German citizens in the colonies) could the latter be possessed without the former. Under Article 3 of the Constitution, a citizen of one State was entitled to obtain the citizenship of any other State.

The first Imperial legislation on citizenship was a continuation of a law enacted under the North German Confederation which preceded the Constitution of 1871. This legislation was succeeded by an Imperial Law of August 22, 1913 (*Reichs- und Staatsangehörigkeitsgesetz*) and was based on the principle that citizenship of the Empire was derived from citizenship of the States; therefore, the law regulated both State and Imperial citizenship. It incorporated the principle of *jus sanguinis,* and provided that all legitimate children of a German father were German citizens; illegitimate children acquired the citizenship of their mother. German citizenship was acquired by an alien woman upon marriage to a German citizen, and by aliens employed as officials by the Empire or by a State or community. Naturalization was left mainly to the member States. Although minimum requirements for naturalization were specified in the Imperial law (regarding, e.g., age, domicile, and character), the States were free to exercise their discretion in granting citizenship to aliens satisfying these requirements. When a State granted its citizenship to an alien, he became automatically an Imperial citizen as well. The States could not, however, grant their citizenship to persons who did not meet the requirements of the Imperial law.

Under the Imperial legislation, citizenship might be lost by a German woman upon her marriage to an alien, by renunciation (subject to reservations regarding military service), or upon acquisition of a foreign citizenship (unless German domicile was retained or official dispensation was obtained). Citizenship might be revoked for failure to return to Germany in time of war, or upon entry into the service of a foreign government (unless permission was granted by the State authorities). The States might also request the Imperial government for permission to deprive persons of their citizenship in certain circumstances, which could lead to deprivation of State citizenship alone, or Imperial citizenship as well.

Imperial legislation gave German citizens the right of release from the citizenship of one State upon acquisition of another State citizenship. And a State was required to grant its citizenship to any German citizen if he satisfied certain requirements, such as domicile, which were specified in the Imperial law and uniform throughout Germany; the States might waive these requirements if they wished, however.

B. The Weimar Constitution

Under the Weimar Constitution, federal citizenship was also, in theory, derived from the citizenship of the member States; Article 110 (1) provided that every citizen of a State was also a citizen of the federation. The federation was, however, granted exclusive legislative power with regard to both federal and State citizenship (Art. 6), and Article 110 (1) provided that "citizenship in the Federation and in the States is acquired and lost in accordance with the provisions of federal law." However, the law of 1913 was continued in force, and, under this law, the member States continued to have discretion to deny citizenship to aliens even if they satisfied the federal requirements, and to have power to request the federal government for permission to deprive persons of their citizenship. The provisions concerning change of State citizenship by German citizens also continued in force.[46]

C. The Basic Law of 1949

The Basic Law grants to the federation exclusive power to legislate with regard to federal citizenship (Art. 73 (2)). Federal citizenship is not dependent upon citizenship of the Länder. In Article 116 (1), the Basic Law defines "Germans" to include all persons possessing German nationality, and any person received in Germany (as it existed on December 31, 1937) as a refugee or expellee of German stock (or a spouse or descendant of such a person). In addition, persons deprived of German citizenship between 1933 and 1945 for racial, religious, or political reasons will be regranted German citizenship upon application; such persons will not be regarded as

---

[46] Under the Nazi regime, by a law of 1934, State citizenship was abolished. This was an aspect of the transformation from a federal to a unitary state.

having lost their citizenship if they have a domicile in Germany, unless they have expressed a contrary desire (Art. 116 (2)). The Basic Law provides further (Art. 16 (1)) that no one may be deprived of German citizenship, and that loss of citizenship may arise only pursuant to a law. Thus, the provisions of the law of 1913 regarding deprivation of citizenship no longer apply. Subject to these constitutional provisions, the law of 1913 has been continued in force. Although the member States continue to administer the naturalization of aliens, they no longer have discretion to deny citizenship to aliens who satisfy the federal requirements.

Under the Basic Law, citizenship of the Länder is subject to concurrent legislative power of the federation and the Länder (Art. 74 (8)). This means, however, that the Länder may legislate only to an extent not inconsistent with federal law. In fact, only three of the Länder have provided for Land citizenship,[47] and none of these has enacted legislation concerning its regulation.

II. IMMIGRATION AND REFUGEES

Under all three German federal Constitutions, the federation has had exclusive power to control immigration. The Imperial Constitution (Art. 4 (1)) gave the Empire power to legislate concerning "freedom of travel" and "police supervision of foreigners and strangers." Although, under the Imperial Constitution, the States had power to refuse their citizenship to immigrants, they were not authorized to exclude immigrants from their territory. Under the Weimar Constitution, the federation alone had power to legislate regarding immigration (Art. 6 (3)), and the Basic Law also grants this power to the federation exclusively (Art. 73 (3)).

The Basic Law contains additional provisions affecting immigration. These deal with the special problem of refugees. Article 16 (2) of the Basic Law provides that "Persons persecuted for political reasons enjoy the right of asylum." And, under Article 75 (6), the federation and the member States have concurrent legislative powers concerning "the affairs of refugees and expellees." Under this provision, however, State legislation may not be inconsistent with federal laws, and by the Equalization of Burdens Law (Lastenausgleichgesetz) of 1951 the federation assumed responsibility for all refugees of German stock. However, there was no central regulation of the distribution and settlement of refugees in Western Germany during the period of their main influx. Some States have therefore received many more refugees than others. After formation of the Federal Republic, federal-state agreements were concluded to help to correct this maldistribution, but they were not effective. Therefore, to equalize the burden of caring for refugees, the federation has required financial contributions by the States which have received few refugees to those which

[47] See Articles 6 and 8, Constitution of Bavaria; Article 3, Constitution of Baden; and Article 6, Constitution of Württemberg-Hohenzollern.

have received many. Although the federal legislation concerning refugees has controlling authority, the regulation of their distribution, settlement, employment, and care has been left largely to the States. As mentioned above, all refugees or expellees of German stock, and their spouses and descendants, are granted German citizenship by Article 116 (1) of the Basic Law.

III. INCIDENTS OF CITIZENSHIP

Naturalized German citizens are granted the same rights and have the same obligations as natural-born citizens. This equality has been protected under all three German Constitutions by guarantees of equality before the law.

A. *The Imperial Constitution*

Article 3 of the Imperial Constitution provided that a citizen of any member State was a citizen of the Empire and entitled to be treated in any other State in the same manner as its citizens; he was entitled to "permanent residence, pursuit of business, public offices, acquisition of citizenship, and enjoyment of all other civil rights," to the same extent as citizens of the State, and likewise to equal treatment in "the administration of justice and the protection of the law." (This guarantee did not apply, however, to relief of the poor or membership in local community associations.) The emphasis was thus upon State citizenship as the source of rights, although Article 3 provided further that the enumerated rights could not be denied to a German citizen by the State of which he was a citizen or by any other State. Additional protection from State discrimination against non-citizens or non-residents was provided by Article 4 (1), which granted the Empire power to legislate concerning "freedom of travel" and "relationships of domicile and settlement."

German citizens were also guaranteed the protection of the Empire in regard to foreign countries (Art. 3), and were subject to military service (Art. 59). The Constitution contained no additional provisions regarding incidents of citizenship, but further rights were provided by Imperial law. Among these was the right of German citizens to vote for, and be elected to, the Imperial legislature (but to be eligible for election they must also have been citizens of a State for at least a year). In addition, by law, no citizen could be expelled or extradited to a foreign country, and all citizens were entitled to travel and reside in any part of the Empire.

B. *The Weimar Constitution*

Some political rights of citizenship were provided by the Weimar Constitution. Article 41 specified that only Germans were eligible for the Fed-

eral Presidency, and Article 17 provided that all German citizens should
have the right to vote for representatives in State and community elections
(but State law might require up to one year of local residence as a condition for suffrage in community elections). The right to vote in federal
elections was regulated by federal law, which made this also a right of
German citizenship. Articles 123, 124, and 126 of the Constitution granted
to Germans the right to assemble peaceably, to form associations, and to
petition the government; and Article 128 provided that all German citizens should have equal access to public office, in accordance with provisions
of law.

The Weimar Constitution contained a number of provisions concerning
personal rights, several of which were guaranteed only to Germans. Thus,
equality before the law (Art. 109), inviolability of the dwelling (Art.
115), and freedom of expression (Art. 118) were granted by the Constitution to Germans alone. In some cases, however, these rights were extended
by federal law to non-Germans; for example, a federal law granted freedom
of the press to both aliens and Germans. Other constitutional provisions
on personal rights (e.g., freedom of the person, Art. 114; secrecy of correspondence, Art. 117) applied to aliens as well as Germans, and Article 135
guaranteed freedom of religion to "all inhabitants of the Reich."

By Article 110 (2), the Weimar Constitution granted to every German
the same rights in any State as the citizens of the State. Article 111 gave
all Germans freedom of travel and residence throughout Germany, subject,
however, to regulation by the exclusive legislative power of the federation
(Art. 6 (3)). In addition, under Article 112, Germans were granted the
right to emigrate (also subject to regulation by federal law) and to claim
the protection of the federation against foreign countries; and no German
might be extradited to a foreign country.

The Weimar Constitution gave to all German citizens the obligation to perform personal services for the federation, Land, or local community, and to contribute to all public burdens in proportion to their
means, according to provisions of law (Art. 133, 134).

The only incidents of State citizenship contained in the Weimar Constitution were provided by Article 110 (1), which made federal citizenship
derive, in theory, from State citizenship; and by Article 16, which required
that "the officials entrusted with the direct federal administration in the
States shall, as a rule, be citizens of the State in which they serve."

C. *The Basic Law*

Under the federal electoral law, only German citizens may vote in federal
elections (i.e. elections for the Bundestag). Eligibility for election to the
Bundestag is also regulated by federal law, which provides that anyone who
has held German citizenship for one year or more is eligible for election.
Under Article 33 (2) of the Basic Law, all Germans have equal access to

every public office, and Article 54 (1) provides that every German is eligible for the office of Federal President. The Basic Law also guarantees to all Germans the right of peaceable assembly and the right to form associations (Art. 8, 9).

In contrast to the Weimar Constitution, the Basic Law's guarantees of equality before the law (Art. 3 (1)), freedom of expression (Art. 5), and inviolability of the home (Art. 13) are not limited to Germans, but apply to aliens as well.

The Basic Law, in Article 33 (1), gives to every German the same "civil rights and duties" in every Land, thus preventing discrimination by the Länder against non-residents. However, this does not prevent the Länder from imposing a requirement of residence for participation in Land elections, or from distinguishing between residents and non-residents in matters relating to housing shortages or unemployment. Germans are likewise guaranteed freedom of movement throughout the territory of the German Federal Republic, subject to regulation by federal law in certain circumstances (Art. 11).

Other rights of a German under the Basic Law include freedom to choose a trade or profession and a place of work and training (Art. 12), the right not to lose his citizenship against his will if he would thereby become stateless (Art. 16 (1)), and the right not to be extradited to a foreign country (Art. 16 (2)).

A P P E N D I X   I V

Switzerland

INTRODUCTION

Every Swiss has three different citizenships: citizenship of the Confederation, citizenship of a canton, and citizenship of a local community (*Gemeinde*). There is no federal citizenship without cantonal citizenship, and no cantonal citizenship without community citizenship. Cantonal and community citizenships are, however, coordinated with federal citizenship by federal law.

Upon formation of the Swiss Confederation, the citizens of the cantons became citizens of the Confederation as well. The Swiss Constitution has gone through several stages in the development of its basic provisions regarding regulation of citizenship. The federal Constitution of 1848 provided that "Every citizen of a canton is a Swiss citizen" (Art. 42), and that "No canton may deprive a citizen of his citizenship" (Art. 43). The power to regulate the acquisition and the loss of citizenship was left to the cantons and communities.

The federal Constitution of 1874 took over the two quoted provisions in its Articles 43 and 44. In addition, in Article 44, paragraph 2, it provided:

"Federal legislation' shall determine the conditions upon which aliens may be naturalized and those upon which Swiss citizens may renounce their nationality in order to obtain naturalization in a foreign country." One of the reasons for the grant of power over naturalization to the Confederation was the practice, carried on by several communities before 1874, of selling their citizenship (and with it cantonal and federal citizenship as well) to aliens living abroad. This federal power was exercised in 1876 by the enactment of a "law on naturalization and on the renunciation of Swiss citizenship" which was renewed in 1903.

Federal control of citizenship was further extended by adoption of the Swiss Civil Code in 1907, which regulated the acquisition of citizenship by birth and by marriage. This legislation was enacted under the general authority of the Confederation in fields of civil law (Constitution, Art. 64).

In 1928, Article 44 of the federal Constitution was amended to its present form in which it grants a more general federal power by providing that "Federal legislation shall determine the rules applicable to the acquisition or loss of Swiss citizenship." The amendment of 1928 also repealed the provision that a Swiss citizen may not be deprived of his citizenship. Despite this amendment, the law of 1903 on naturalization and renunciation remained in force. However, the Federal Assembly recently adopted a new law "on the acquisition and the loss of Swiss citizenship," to replace the law of 1903. This law will become effective, unless a popular referendum is demanded before December 29, 1952.

I. REGULATION OF CITIZENSHIP

A. *Acquisition of Citizenship*

1. BY BIRTH OR MARRIAGE

As noted above, the acquisition of citizenship by birth or marriage is regulated entirely by federal law.

Under the Civil Code, legitimate children of a Swiss citizen obtain, by birth, the federal, cantonal, and community citizenships of their father (Art. 270). Illegitimate children have the citizenships of their mother, unless paternity is acknowledged or judicially determined. In all these cases the place of birth is of no consequence, according to the doctrine of *jus sanguinis*.[48]

In addition to these provisions of the Civil Code, the Federal Court has

---

[48] Article 44, par. 3, of the federal Constitution, as amended in 1928, contains a provision which approaches the *jus soli*. It states: "Federal legislation may enact that a child born of alien parents is a Swiss national by birth when the mother was of Swiss origin by filiation and if the parents are domiciled in Switzerland at the moment of the child's birth." Federal legislation, however, has never exercised this power. Enactment of this amendment was caused by a desire to reduce the proportion of aliens among the population of Switzerland, which had reached 15 per cent in 1910. (This proportion diminished considerably, however, in the years following World War I.)

ruled that a legitimate child of an alien father and a Swiss mother has Swiss citizenship if he does not acquire another citizenship by birth. This rule is included in the new law of 1952 (Art. 5).

The wife of a Swiss citizen obtains the federal, cantonal, and community citizenships of her husband upon marriage (Civil Code, Art. 161). She cannot refuse his citizenship, and it is not altered by divorce (Art. 149).

2. BY NATURALIZATION

Since adoption of the federal Constitution of 1874, the regulation of acquisition of citizenship by naturalization has been a federal power, which has been implemented by federal legislation. The federal law of 1903, as well as that of 1952, sets forth the rules on naturalization of aliens. Under these provisions, an alien who satisfies specified conditions regarding domicile and the like obtains federal permission to acquire cantonal and community citizenship. This permission, however, does not give him a right to citizenship, but indicates only that the Confederation raises no objections to his naturalization. Under the federal law, it remains for the cantons and local communities to grant him their citizenship. The cantons or, if provided by cantonal law, the local communities may impose further conditions. When an alien obtains cantonal and community citizenship, he becomes automatically a citizen of the Confederation; the wife and minor children are naturalized automatically with the husband or father. The cantons may not, however, grant their citizenship to an alien without federal permission. Moreover, all the important requirements for citizenship are imposed by the federal law; although, in addition, the cantons collect duties from applicants for naturalization, may require a longer period of domicile than does the federal law, and some impose other requirements as well (such as an adequate means of support, important in view of the cantonal regulation of poor relief, mentioned below).

In addition to the foregoing procedure, the federal law of 1952 provides for a "privileged naturalization" which permits the alien children of a Swiss-born mother to acquire Swiss citizenship upon simpler conditions than those generally applicable. The federal legislation also provides a simplified procedure for the renaturalization of former Swiss citizens, where citizenship was lost for certain specified reasons (such as marriage of a Swiss woman to an alien); this legislation has been enacted under the authority of Article 44, paragraph 4, of the federal Constitution which provides that "Federal legislation shall lay down the rules governing the reestablishment of citizenship."

Swiss citizens have a right to settle anywhere in Switzerland, and may acquire more than one cantonal or community citizenship. The power to regulate the acquisition of cantonal and community citizenships by Swiss citizens of other cantons or communities is left completely to the cantons.

Generally, the conditions for the acquisition of cantonal or community citizenship are less severe for Swiss citizens than for aliens.

The question of the immigration of aliens is closely connected with their naturalization, and, under Article 69, paragraph 1, of the federal Constitution, "The Confederation has the right to legislate regarding the entry and exit, sojourn and establishment of aliens." By Article 69, paragraph 2, the cantons are granted power to decide concerning the sojourn and settlement of aliens, in accordance with general federal legislation and subject to final decision by the Confederation in regard to certain questions. Article 70 empowers the Confederation to expel aliens who endanger the internal or external security.

B. *Loss of Citizenship*

The federal Constitution of 1874 provided for the regulation by federal legislation of the loss of citizenship by renunciation. By the constitutional amendment of 1928, the federal power was extended to permit regulation of the loss of citizenship generally. The loss of federal citizenship results, in all cases, in the loss of cantonal and community citizenships as well.

In general, federal legislation provides that citizenship is lost by renunciation, or by a Swiss woman who marries an alien; and the naturalization of an alien may be annulled if it was procured by false statements or by concealment of important facts.[49] In addition, the constitutional amendment of 1928 permits federal legislation to provide for the deprivation of Swiss citizenship; previously, the federal Constitution of 1874 had stated that a Swiss could not be deprived of his citizenship. Provisions for the deprivation of Swiss citizenship were not adopted, however, until 1941. Then, an emergency decree of the Federal Council prescribed that a person of dual nationality could be deprived of his Swiss citizenship if his behavior prejudiced the interests and the reputation of Switzerland. The same provision has been included in the law of 1952 (Art. 48).

Under the law of 1952, citizenship may also be lost, in certain circumstances, through birth abroad. Strict application of the principle of *jus sanguinis* has permitted descendants of Swiss citizens to claim Swiss citizenship, even though they have lived abroad for several generations and have lost any connection with Switzerland. This was unsatisfactory, especially before and during World War II. For this reason, Article 10 of the law of 1952 provides that a Swiss citizen who is born abroad, and whose father was also born abroad, loses his citizenship at the age of 22 unless he declares to a Swiss official that he desires to retain it.

[49] See Articles 7 and 12 of the law of 1903, and Articles 9, 41, and 42 of the law of 1952.

II. INCIDENTS OF CITIZENSHIP

In almost all respects, all Swiss citizens possess the same rights, regardless of how they acquired citizenship. This is provided by Article 44, paragraph 5, of the federal Constitution, which states: "Naturalized persons enjoy the same rights as other citizens with the only exception that they have no right to such property which is exclusively communal and corporative unless cantonal legislation provides otherwise."

A. *Community Citizenship*

Community citizenship has lost a great part of its importance. At present, its most important incident is poor relief. The poor obtain assistance from the local community of which they are citizens. During the last decades, however, several cantons have enacted regulations according to which the duty of poor relief is transferred to the communities of domicile.

The citizens of a community may have the sole right to vote in matters relating exclusively to the community citizenship, except as otherwise provided by cantonal laws. In addition, and subject also to cantonal law, the citizens of a community may have the exclusive right to share in the proceeds of certain community properties (which, however, are no longer common); under Article 44, paragraph 5, of the federal Constitution, naturalized citizens may also be excluded from sharing in these proceeds. With these exceptions, a community may not discriminate in favor of its own citizens and against those of its domiciliaries who are citizens of other communities. This is provided by Article 43, paragraph 4, of the federal Constitution, which states: "A Swiss citizen enjoys at his place of domicile all rights of a citizen of the canton, together with all rights of a citizen of the local community. Participation in the property of the local corporations as well as the voting right in [matters relating to such property or to community citizenship] . . . are, however, excepted from these provisions except as cantonal legislation determines otherwise."

In a few exceptional cases, enumerated in Article 45 of the federal Constitution, the cantons and local communities have the right to expel citizens of other cantons or communities. In such cases, the community of citizenship is the only place where the expelled person can settle.

In addition, the Swiss Civil Code grants to the local communities certain rights of intervention against the marriage of its citizens and in affiliation cases and cases of guardianship of its citizens (Arts. 106, 108, 256, 261, 378, 396).

B. *Cantonal Citizenship*

The most important aspect of cantonal citizenship is that an alien can only become a Swiss citizen when he acquires cantonal citizenship.

The Civil Code gives the canton of origin certain rights in a few cases in which their citizens are involved (alteration of name, Art. 30; questions of succession, Arts. 472, 550). Before the Civil Code came into force in 1912, cantonal citizenship had an important role in conflict of laws cases, in which the status of a person was governed by the law of the canton of origin.

Article 96 of the federal Constitution provides that "not more than one member of the Federal Council may be chosen from the same canton." This means that not more than one *citizen* of the same canton can be elected to the Federal Council. If a person has more than one citizenship, the place in which he has his domicile is the decisive one; and if he is not a citizen of the canton of his domicile, the citizenship most recently acquired governs (see *Garantiegesetz* of December 23, 1851, Art. 5).

Article 43, paragraph 4, of the federal Constitution, quoted above, prohibits the cantons, as well as the communities, from discriminating in favor of their citizens and against those of its domiciliaries who are citizens of other cantons.

C. *Federal Citizenship*

Federal citizenship is the most important. It carries with it the obligation to perform military service (Constitution, Art. 18), and is the basis for diplomatic protection abroad. It is also the basis for political rights, including the right to take part in federal, cantonal, and community elections and referenda, to form associations, to be elected to the Federal Assembly or the Executive Council, and to be selected for the Federal Court (Arts. 43, 56, 75, 96, and 108).

The Swiss citizen is guaranteed by Article 43, paragraph 4, of the federal Constitution (quoted above) that, whatever his cantonal or community citizenship, he will not be discriminated against by any canton or community in which he is domiciled (except in regard to voting on certain community matters and sharing in the proceeds of community properties). A further guarantee of his equal treatment is contained in Article 60 of the federal Constitution, which provides: "Every canton is bound to accord to all Swiss citizens the same treatment as to its own citizens in regard to legislation and judicial proceedings." In addition, Article 45 of the Constitution grants to every Swiss citizen the right to settle anywhere in Switzerland, and Article 4 provides that all Swiss are equal before the law.

A P P E N D I X   V

United States

A person who owes allegiance to the United States is classified either as a citizen of the United States, or a national without citizenship in the case of inhabitants of certain American dependencies. Moreover, citizens of the United States are also citizens of the member State where they reside.

I. FEDERAL CITIZENSHIP AND NATIONALITY

A. *Acquisition of Citizenship*

1. BY BIRTH

The Constitution, as adopted in 1789, referred to United States citizens in several of its provisions but contained no definition of the term. Upon the coming into force of the Constitution all persons who were, at the time, recognized as citizens of the member States were considered also to be citizens of the new federation. Thereafter, citizenship in the United States was considered to result from birth therein, following the English common law doctrine of *jus soli.* Exceptions were made in the case of Negroes (both slaves and freedmen) and aboriginal Indians, who were excluded from citizenship, even though born in the United States, on the ground that traditionally they were not a part of the body politic.[50] Moreover, a strong faction contended that United States citizenship was possessed only through the mediacy of State citizenship. This contention was a part of the general dispute over the powers of the federation in certain fields which some of the States considered reserved to them; the advocates of each side of this question urged that the citizen's primary allegiance was to the governmental body whose powers they favored.

The Fourteenth Amendment was added to the Constitution in 1868, following the Civil War, and provides, in Section 1: "All persons born or naturalized in the United States, and subject to the jurisdiction thereof, are citizens of the United States and of the State wherein they reside. . . ." This provision of the Fourteenth Amendment makes it unnecessary for one to be a citizen of a member State in order to be a citizen of the federation. It was enacted principally to provide for the primacy of federal citizenship and to assure that Negroes would be regarded as citizens if they were born in the United States. It also had the effect of granting citizenship to children born in the United States to alien parents, even though those parents, under naturalization laws, were ineligible for citizenship.[51] The Fourteenth Amendment did not, however, extend the privilege of citizenship to aboriginal Indians born in the United States, who were considered not to be "subject to the jurisdiction" of the United States because of the continuance of their tribal jurisdictions.[52] Moreover, persons born in dependencies of the United States are not citizens by virtue of the Fourteenth Amendment; such places are not part of the United States within the meaning of that Amendment (although the territories of Hawaii and Alaska are considered

---

[50] Dred Scott v. Sanford, 19 How. 393 (1856).
[51] United States v. Wong Kim Ark, 169 U.S. 649 (1898).
[52] Elk v. Wilkins, 112 U.S. 94 (1894).

part of the United States), and the status of their inhabitants is regulated by Congress.

Federal legislation, however, has conferred the rights of citizenship at birth upon certain classes of persons, in addition to those covered by the Fourteenth Amendment. These classes include aboriginal Indians, certain persons born outside the United States to American parents, and persons born in certain American dependencies.[53] The power of Congress to enact such provisions stems from its power to provide for naturalization of citizens (discussed below) and, in the case of inhabitants of dependencies, from its power to ". . . make all needful Rules and Regulations respecting the Territory or other Property belonging to the United States . . ." (U.S. Const. Art. IV, §3).

2. BY NATURALIZATION

The Constitution provides in Article I, Section 8, that "The Congress shall have Power . . . To establish a uniform Rule of Naturalization . . ." This power was held at an early date to be exclusive of any authority of the member States in this field.[54] Before the Constitution came into force, during the period of the Articles of Confederation, naturalization was a function of the States, and several of them had enacted naturalization laws. This diverse treatment of an important field was considered by the drafters of the Constitution to be unsatisfactory; especially since there were to be complete freedom of movement within the Federation and other interstate privileges,[55] the federal legislature alone should determine who was to be admitted to membership in the body politic.

Closely related to the problem of naturalization is that of immigration, and the federal government exercises exclusive power in this field as well, by virtue of its constitutional powers with regard to commerce and foreign affairs. Throughout much of the early history of the United States, however, immigration was regulated by the States, in large part as a matter of necessity because of the lack of federal action. These regulations were, in many instances, held by the courts to be outside the competence of the States, but the States continued their attempts to regulate immigration until the federal government eventually enacted adequate measures. The necessity for uniform federal action was demonstrated by experience with the diverse efforts of the States; although they wished to prevent entry of unfit persons, the States were in competition to attract immigrants to satisfy their great labor needs, and the result of this competition was inadequate regulation.[56]

[53] See §§101 (a) and 301 (a) of the Immigration and Nationality Act of 1952.

[54] Chirac v. Chirac, 2 Wheat. 259 (1817).

[55] See, for example, Article IV, Section 2, of the Constitution: "The Citizens of each State shall be entitled to all Privileges and Immunities of Citizens in the several States."

[56] As a result of a compromise, the Constitution postponed for the first twenty years the power of Congress to regulate the importation of slaves (Art. I, §9).

Pursuant to these powers over naturalization and immigration, Congress has passed a number of laws providing for immigration, deportation, and naturalization. This legislation has set standards and quotas for immigration and has provided for naturalization (both on an individual basis and sometimes, as in the case of aboriginal Indians and inhabitants of certain dependencies, on a collective basis). In addition, the federation, under these powers and its power with regard to foreign affairs, has concluded immigration and naturalization treaties with many countries. Although the States play no constitutional role in forming policies with regard to immigration and naturalization, their regional interests have great influence over those policies; such factors as the need for labor in industrial areas or other localities, and apprehension on the West Coast about large-scale immigration of Orientals, have at one time or another been reflected in federal laws.

B. *Loss of Citizenship*

1. EXPATRIATION

The United States recognized at an early date the right of individuals to divest themselves of American citizenship through expatriation. The circumstances in which expatriation is effected are defined by federal law. Loss of citizenship may, for example, result from formal renunciation, treason, desertion from the armed forces, entry into the armed forces or civil service of a foreign country, or a protracted stay in a foreign country.[57] The original theory underlying such provisions was that loss of citizenship was the reasonable consequence of a voluntary act by the individual, rather than a penalty.[58] Some of the present grounds for loss of citizenship appear, however, to depart from that theory.

2. DENATURALIZATION

A naturalized citizen may lose his citizenship through expatriation and, in addition, his naturalization may be revoked on the ground that it was procured by fraud or other illegal action. By federal law, certain types of action by a naturalized citizen subsequent to naturalization create a presumption of such fraud.[59] The process of denaturalization is also subject to exclusive regulation by Congress, as a corollary of its power with regard to naturalization.

C. *Nationals of the Federation Who Are Not Citizens*

The status of inhabitants of American overseas dependencies is regulated by Congress pursuant to its power to make regulations with respect to ter-

[57] See Immigration and Nationality Act of 1952, §§349–352.
[58] Mackenzie v. Hare, 239 U.S. 299 (1915).
[59] Immigration and Nationality Act of 1952, §340.

ritories belonging to the United States (U.S. Const. Art. IV, §3, quoted above). This power has been exercised to make the inhabitants of most dependencies citizens of the United States at birth. In the case of the inhabitants of a few small dependencies, however, Congress has created a distinct category, making them "nationals, but not citizens, of the United States at birth." [60] This category of non-citizen nationals is very small.

II. CITIZENSHIP IN THE MEMBER STATES

As indicated above, the Fourteenth Amendment makes citizenship in the State of his residence a right of every United States citizen. Thus there are no concepts of acquisition of State citizenship by birth or naturalization; a United States citizen who takes up residence in a State, whether at birth or subsequently, becomes automatically a citizen of that State. One may therefore change his State citizenship by changing his residence; and, in fact, by moving his residence abroad, or to the federal District of Columbia or Alaska or Hawaii, he may deprive himself of citizenship in any State without prejudicing his United States citizenship. Moreover, the States may not restrict the movement of persons into or from their territories.[61] Thus, State citizenship is regulated principally by the federal government through its regulation of federal citizenship. However, the States may exercise some control by prescribing requirements for residence.

III. INCIDENTS OF FEDERAL CITIZENSHIP

A principle of American law has been that citizens who acquire that status by birth and by naturalization shall have identical rights, excepting only that under Article II, Section 1, and the Twelfth Amendment of the Constitution no one but a "natural-born citizen, or a citizen of the United States at the time of the adoption of this Constitution" may be President or Vice-President. Recent federal legislation distinguishes between naturalized and natural-born citizens, however, in defining grounds for loss of citizenship. It also provides for revocation of naturalization on the basis of acts done after citizenship was acquired, thus further distinguishing the naturalized citizen.

The incidents of federal citizenship, as compared with State citizenship, reflect of course the constitutional powers of the federation as compared with those of the States. That is, the federal government can exercise its powers under the Constitution to create rights and duties of federal citizenship relating to the fields of its powers. Thus, since the federation has competence in foreign affairs and it alone is an entity in international law, protection abroad by the federation and federal regulation of foreign travel are incidents of federal citizenship. Other rights, such as the exploitation

[60] *Id.* §308.
[61] Edwards v. California, 314 U.S. 160 (1941); Crandall v. Nevada, 6 Wall. 35 (1868).

of mineral deposits owned by the United States and the command of vessels licensed by the United States, also depend upon federal citizenship.[62] Similarly, federal citizenship imposes the obligation of military service under federal conscription laws.[63]

In addition, the Constitution specifically prescribes certain privileges which arise from federal citizenship: Article II, Section 1, and the Twelfth Amendment provide that only a native-born citizen of the United States may be President or Vice-President; Article I, Section 2, provides that only persons who have been citizens of the United States for seven years may be elected to the lower house of the federal legislature; and Article I, Section 3, requires nine years of citizenship in the United States for members of the upper house. In addition, of course, the Fourteenth Amendment gives to each United States citizen the right of citizenship in the State in which he resides.

The right to vote in federal and State elections is not a constitutional right of United States citizens. Within certain constitutional limits, described below, qualifications for voting are prescribed by the States, which have, however, in general, made it a right of federal citizenship.[64] Nevertheless, at various times, certain groups of citizens (e.g. women) have been excluded from voting while aliens intending to become citizens have been permitted to vote. The Constitution does, however, protect United States citizens against denial of the privilege of voting on certain grounds. Thus, the Fifteenth Amendment provides: "The right of citizens of the United States to vote shall not be denied or abridged by the United States or by any State on account of race, color, or previous condition of servitude." The Nineteenth Amendment contains similar safeguards against denial of the voting rights of United States citizens on account of sex. In addition, Section 2 of the Fourteenth Amendment provides that Congress may reduce a State's representation in the lower chamber of the federal legislature, in proportion to the number of "male inhabitants of such a State, being twenty-one years of age, and citizens of the United States" whose right to vote is denied or abridged "except for participation in rebellion, or other crime"; this power has never been exercised by Congress, however.

The Constitution includes one further reference to federal citizenship. The Fourteenth Amendment provides: ". . . No State shall make or enforce any law which shall abridge the privileges or immunities of citizens of the United States; . . ." This clause has not had an important effect on the definition and protection of rights of federal citizenship, because of an

---

[62] See 22 U.S. Code, §§212, 224; 30 U.S. Code, §22; 46 U.S. Code, §262.

[63] See, e.g., Universal Military Training Act of 1948, 50 U.S. Code, App., §454. See also Blackmer v. United States, 284 U.S. 421 (1931).

[64] See, e.g., the Constitution of the State of Ohio, Art. V, §1: "Every citizen of the United States, of the age of twenty-one years, who shall have been a resident of the State one year next preceding the election . . . shall . . . be entitled to vote at all elections." Other State regulatory laws often require that persons conducting certain activities must be United States citizens.

early decision of the Supreme Court interpreting the "privileges and immunities" of federal citizenship to be those specifically conferred by the Constitution, federal laws, or treaties.[65]

The important provisions of the Constitution protecting the individual against action by the federal government (the "Bill of Rights," i.e. the first ten Amendments of the Constitution) or by State governments (principally the "due process" and "equal protection" clauses of the Fourteenth Amendment) are not by their terms limited to the protection of citizens either of the federation or of the States. These provisions speak largely in terms of protection of "the people" or "any person" or "the accused." Accordingly, these rights and privileges are not limited to citizens, but accrue to all within the jurisdiction of the United States. Nevertheless, distinctions have been made in certain respects between the rights of citizens and of aliens under these provisions but these distinctions are discussed at length in another study.[66]

IV. INCIDENTS OF STATE CITIZENSHIP

Just as the federal government may exercise its powers under the Constitution to create rights and duties of federal citizenship, so may the States create incidents of State citizenship in the exercise of their constitutional powers. In practice, however, the applicability of most State legislation is not based on State citizenship, but rather on residence within the State or presence within the State's jurisdiction.[67] In exercising their power to prescribe qualifications for voting (discussed above), the States have created rights of federal citizenship, combined, however, with State residence.

The federal Constitution does, however, expressly create some incidents of State citizenship. Article III, Section 2, provides that the judicial power of the United States shall extend to "controversies . . . between citizens of different States." More important, Article IV, Section 2, provides: "The Citizens of each State shall be entitled to all Privileges and Immunities of Citizens in the several States." Although various meanings have been attributed to this clause, the Supreme Court has established that its effect is simply to prevent any State from discriminating unreasonably in favor of its citizens and against those of another State. However, there are certain privileges for which a State may require previous residence, thus discriminating against the citizens of other States, as, for example, the privilege of voting.

---

[65] Slaughterhouse Cases, 16 Wall. 36 (1872). Attempts have been made, however, to extend the meaning of this clause to protect other fundamental rights. See Hague v. Committee for Industrial Organization, 307 U.S. 496 (1938); Edwards v. California, 314 U.S. 160, 177 (1941).

[66] See Study 11, Personal Rights.

[67] See, e.g., Article I, Section 11, of the Constitution of the State of New York, providing that ". . . No person shall, because of race, color, creed or religion, be subjected to any discrimination in regard to his civil rights by any other person. . . ."

S T U D Y   1 3

Defense of the Constitutional Order[*]

I. INTRODUCTION

Like all forms of constitutional government, federal systems rest on the assumption that the exercise of political authority ought, under normal conditions, to be subject to certain legal restrictions. Situations may arise, however, where the survival of the constitution itself requires measures which, to a greater or lesser degree, are incompatible with the maintenance of these restrictions. If the existing constitutional order is to be preserved under these circumstances, the constitutional framework of the federation must either explicity anticipate the need for emergency action, or else be given enough inherent flexibility to enable the government to deal with emergencies by means of extraordinary devices. The question, in either case, is to provide for the temporary relaxation of constitutional restraints without permanently impairing the norms of constitutional government. This is the problem of "emergency powers," on the solution of which the maintenance of constitutional order under federalism to a large extent depends.

The crises which have required the exercise of emergency powers are of five main types. Three of these — war, economic depression, and secession — are considered in other studies of this series.[1] It is to the remaining two types of emergency — insurrection and subversion — that the present study is addressed.[2] These two threats to the constitutional order are of course closely related to secession. They represent a deliberate refusal on the part of certain members of a constitutional society to accept the legitimate procedures of that society as binding upon their own present or future action. But these two threats differ from secession in that the disaffected members

---

[*] Professor F. W. Watkins of Yale University assisted greatly in the completion of this study, by reviewing and revising the final draft.

[1] Wartime emergency powers are discussed in Study 4, Defense; the response to economic catastrophe is treated in Study 6, Commerce, Transportation, and Customs; and secession is analyzed in Study 15, Admission of New States.

[2] The reader will nevertheless notice that constitutional precedents drawn from the first three sorts of emergency are included in the Appendices to the present study, even though they are not discussed in the body of the text. Two considerations underlie this seeming discrepancy: (1) the paucity of precedents directly dealing with insurrection and/or subversion in several of the federations under study; (2) the fact that the three studies cited in the preceding footnote are only peripherally concerned with emergency powers, and that for reasons of space emergency precedents were omitted from the Appendices thereto.

are not necessarily interested in securing independence for a particular member State or for any other geographical region; they may equally well be striving to change the constitutional order within the whole of the existing federal system. Movements of secession, moreover, may be content to operate through the existing procedures of constitutional legitimacy, whereas insurrection and subversion are, by definition, an attempt to act in violation of those procedures. Unwillingness to abide by the established processes of constitutional government, no matter whether that unwillingness is or is not coupled with a desire for secession, gives rise to very special problems within any constitutional system and thus, a fortiori, within any federal system. Those problems are the subject of the present study.

II. CIVIL DISORDER AND INSURRECTION

Civil disorder and insurrection are, along with foreign invasion, the typical crisis situations for which the basic emergency institutions of modern constitutional government were initially created, and with which they are best able to deal. It is true that emergencies of this sort do not necessarily call for the use of emergency powers. Under all forms of government, including federal systems, forcible resistance to the legitimately constituted authorities is a criminal act, and may properly be met with ordinary police action. The degree and extent of resistance is often such, however, that normal police measures are inadequate to ensure the prompt restoration of public order. Under these circumstances, the propriety of emergency action is universally recognized in modern constitutional states, including those which are federal in character. Since the executive is the branch of government primarily responsible for law enforcement, the resulting arrangements normally take the form of a temporary increase in the powers of the executive.

The executives of modern constitutional states are subject to two or, in the case of federal systems, to three main types of legal restraint. (1) In their relations with ordinary citizens, they are limited by the principle of civil liberties, which may differ considerably from country to country, but which serve, in any truly constitutional country, to guarantee the citizen a substantial range of immunity to governmental interference. (2) In their relations with other branches of the government, they are limited by the principle of the separation of powers, which is less elaborately developed in some countries than in others, but which regularly reserves certain functions for an independent judiciary and others for the legislature. (3) In federal systems they are also limited by the principle of federalism itself, with its constitutionally guaranteed distribution of functions between federal and local agencies of government. Respect for all three types of limitations is essential to the normal functioning of all present-day federal systems and all three may have to be suspended in times of serious emergency.

The most frequent form of emergency action consists in the partial or total suspension of civil liberties. For the more rapid suppression of civil disorders, the executive authorities of most constitutional countries have on occasion found it necessary to forbid public assemblies, to suppress newspapers, to confiscate private property, and in various other ways to violate practically all the rights normally guaranteed to private citizens. No constitutional system would be complete without some sort of provision for emergency measures of this kind.

Since the maintenance of the rule of law is a normal executive function, it is often possible for a constitutional executive to deal with internal disorder and insurrection without encroaching on the functions of other branches of government. In particularly severe emergencies, however, the need for such encroachments may occur. Usually this takes the form of an executive assumption of judicial functions. Courts-martial and other extraordinary tribunals designed for the summary trial and punishment of offenders have often been found to be a necessary device for the restoration of order in seriously disturbed areas. The executive assumption of legislative functions is less usual in crises of this sort, but even so it is by no means unknown. At the outbreak of the American Civil War, for example, President Lincoln found it necessary, at a time when it was not yet possible for Congress to assemble, to authorize an increase in the military establishment of the United States, a step ordinarily requiring Congressional action.[3] Provision for temporary suspensions of the normal separation of powers must be reckoned, therefore, as one of the significant aspects of the problem of emergency powers in any constitutional state.

In federal systems, the normal distribution of functions between federal and local authorities may likewise have to be disregarded for the more effective repression of internal disorder and insurrection. Primary responsibility for the maintenance of public order rests, in most federal countries, on the local governments, which regularly have police forces, and often armies, of their own. There is always a possibility, however, that a local government may be faced with a crisis too severe to be met by its own unaided resources. It is also possible that a local government may itself decide to rise in insurrection against the federal constitution, and direct its military police forces to the furtherance of that end. In either case, the maintenance of the established constitutional order may depend on the intervention of federal authority to supplement or even, for the duration of the crisis, to supplant the regular local authorities. To provide for such forms of federal intervention, without permanently impairing the federal principle itself, is one of the more difficult problems implicit in any attempt to create a federal constitution.

For the purpose of dealing with all these problems of emergency action, modern constitutional states have developed two main types of institutions, the state of siege and martial rule. Martial rule, the basic emergency device of common law countries, is the more flexible of the two. It is based on

[3] See Appendix V, pp. 708–709.

the proposition that, when the rule of law is seriously interrupted, it is the right and duty of all citizens (which means, in practice, the executive authorities) to take all necessary measures to bring it back into effective operation. Since reasonable necessity is the only standard of judgment, it follows that there is no form of emergency action which may not, under certain circumstances, be justified as a legitimate exercise of martial rule.

The state of siege, which in one form or another is incorporated in the constitutional systems of all civil law countries, differs from martial rule in that it tries to define in advance the legally permissible consequences of emergency action. The right to suspend civil liberties is usually limited, for example, to certain enumerated provisions of the constitution; the composition and powers of emergency tribunals are explicitly defined; and in various other ways an attempt is made to confine the use of emergency powers within definite legal channels. In the interests of effective action, however, the powers thus granted always have to be quite broadly defined, and the actual scope of the resulting powers does not in fact differ, to any significant degree, from that exercised in common law countries in the name of martial rule. In both cases, an adequate legal basis is provided for all the various types of emergency measures needed to surmount the crises of civil disorder and insurrection.

The only type of emergency action not fully covered by the state of siege or martial rule is the elimination of restraints based on the separation of powers. Although provision is regularly made for the executive assumption of judicial functions, there is no similar provision for the assumption of legislative functions. In this respect the provisions of the Weimar Constitution of Germany were exceptional. The right granted under Article 48 to undertake "all necessary measures" for the restoration of public safety and order was interpreted as justifying not only the exercise of those powers normally associated with the state of siege, but also the issuance of legislative decrees by authority of the executive. Ordinarily, however, the state of siege and martial rule are both regarded as involving no grant of legislative authority. In those rare cases, therefore, when the effective handling of an insurrectionary crisis calls for emergency legislative action, such action must be justified on other grounds. One method is for the executive to usurp the powers of the legislature for the time being, relying on subsequent ratification by the legislature itself to give retroactive legality to the proceedings. This was the device used by President Lincoln in the previously mentioned crisis at the outbreak of the American Civil War.[4] Another method is for the legislature to pass an enabling act empowering the executive to issue legislative decrees under certain emergency conditions. But these provisions for the establishment of emergency powers in the legislative field, though vitally important in connection with many types of emergency, such as foreign warfare or economic crisis, are of relatively little use in cases of civil disorder and insurrection, where legislative measures are rarely re-

---

[4] See Appendix V, note 71.

quired. It would, therefore, be inappropriate to go into the matter further in this study.

So far we have been considering those aspects of the state of siege and martial rule which are common to all constitutional states, whether federal or unitary in character. It remains to inquire into the more specific question of their operation in modern federal systems. Since both of these emergency institutions were first developed in countries (France and England respectively) which enjoyed a unitary rather than a federal form of government, it might be supposed that they would have required substantial modification in order to meet the needs of countries based on a very different allocation of powers. The fact is, however, that little effort has ever been made to adjust them to the specific conditions of federal government. Although the powers of local units are, in normal times, rather jealously safeguarded in federal systems, final responsibility for the maintenance of public order is everywhere vested in the federal rather than in the local authorities. Through the operation of the state of siege and martial rule, federal executives are thus enabled, in times of emergency, to act in all essential respects as the executive of a unitary state.

It is true that, in all federal systems, initial responsibility for the maintenance of public order, and hence for the application of emergency measures, is in the hands of the local authorities. This is true both of countries with a common law tradition, like the United States, Canada, and Australia, and of civil law countries, like Switzerland and Germany. In many federal constitutions, moreover, the importance of local initiative in these matters is underlined by the inclusion in the federal constitution of provisions specifically empowering the local authorities to call on the federal government for aid whenever their own resources for the restoration of public order seem inadequate to the purpose. Specific articles to this effect are to be found in the constitutions of the United States,[5] Australia,[6] and Switzerland.[7] In Canada a comparable provision is incorporated in the Militia Act.[8] From all this it might be supposed that, in modern federal states, the maintenance of public order is regarded primarily as a local rather than as a federal function.

Overriding all these concessions to the federal principle, however, is the fact that final responsibility for the exercise of emergency powers rests with the federal executive, and that these powers may, if necessary, be used to suspend the functions of local governments and transfer them to federal authorities. Although local governments are often specifically authorized to request the aid of the federal government, the latter has complete discretion in deciding whether or not to accede to this request. In no federal constitution, moreover, is there any provision requiring the federal govern-

[5] Art. IV, §4.
[6] Art. 119.
[7] Arts. 15, 16.
[8] 1904, 4 Edw. VII, c. 23, §1.

ment to wait for an invitation from the local authorities before intervening in local affairs. With the possible exception of the present West German Constitution, which fails, at least explicitly, to provide the federal government with any special powers for the maintenance of public order, all federal states recognize that the prevention of civil disorder and insurrection is a legitimate federal function, and that the powers of local government are wholly subordinate to that end. This principle is most clearly spelled out, perhaps, in the Swiss Constitution, whereas in others, like the American or the Canadian, it is left to be inferred from more general provisions,[9] but the results are in either case the same. The practical importance of the matter is demonstrated, moreover, by the actual experience of all those federal states which have had, in recent times, to undergo serious insurrectionary crises. During the American Civil War, for example, the powers of martial rule had to be used repeatedly, not only in the seceding States but also in some of the border States, to maintain peace and order against the will of lukewarm or disloyal State authorities. The early years of the Weimar Republic were likewise characterized by a number of insurrectionary crises in which, because of the unreliability or disloyalty of various local governments, the maintenance of public order could be achieved only by the emergency transfer of local functions to federal commissioners, a proceeding which was held to be justified under the provisions of Article 48. The theory and practice of modern federal systems all go to show, therefore, that provision for the temporary suspension of local authority is one of the more indispensable features of the state of siege and martial rule.

Altogether it may be said that the executives of modern federal states are amply provided with powers to deal with the crises of civil disorder and insurrection. These powers are, of course, subject to abuses, which, if unchecked, would destroy that balance of federal and local functions which lies at the very basis of any federal system. Armed with the tremendous powers inherent in the state of siege and martial rule, federal executives may well be tempted to use an actual or imaginary breach of the public order as an occasion to deprive local authorities, with whom they may be in disagreement, of their normal constitutional rights. An extreme instance of this type of abuse is to be found in the last year of the Weimar Republic, when Chancellor von Papen invoked his emergency powers under Article 48 to depose the Socialist government of Prussia in favor of a federal commissioner. Although the ostensible justification of this move was the alleged unwillingness or inability of that government to repress civil disorders within its territories, the actual purpose was to enable the Chancellor to assume control over the Prussian delegation to the Reichsrat, and thus to further his own plans for the subversion of the Weimar Republic. Clearly

[9] In the United States, for example, the existence of a federal power of martial rule is never directly mentioned in the Constitution, but may be inferred from the provision relating to the suspension of habeas corpus (which would be meaningless in the absence of such a power). The significance of this provision is discussed in Section IV below.

the vesting of broad emergency powers in the hands of the central authorities is not without danger to the maintenance of any federal system of government. But the value of these emergency powers as a defense against civil
disorder and insurrection is so great that the founders of modern federal
states have regularly found it necessary to include them among their constitutional arrangements. The problem is not to weaken these essential
institutions, but to provide adequate guarantees against their possible abuse.
The constitutional devices available for this purpose are the subject of
Section IV of this study, which deals with limitations on the exercise of
emergency powers.

III. Subversion

Subversion may be defined as a course of action designed mediately or
immediately to change an established constitutional order by unconstitutional means. Civil disorder and insurrection may be, and often are, the
means adopted for the attainment of this end. When subversion is accompanied by overt acts of this sort, it gives rise to the sort of problems considered in the preceding section of this study. Subversive purposes may well
be accomplished, however, without any such incidents.[10] In many South
American republics, for example, constitutions have not infrequently been
subverted by the illegal actions of presidents and other legitimate authorities
who, being in effective control of the military and police forces of the state,
were able to avoid all forcible conflict with the defenders of public order.
The last stages of Hitler's rise to power in Germany, though accompanied
by many acts of illegal violence, provide yet another instance of this particular type of subversion. Even when insurrection is ultimately intended,
moreover, it is usually preceded by a longer or shorter preparatory period,
during which the subversive movement may find it prudent to refrain from
any overt act of insurrection, or from any other illegal acts which could
legitimately be regarded as constituting a state of civil disorder. The problem of constitutional defense against movements of this sort is the subject
of the present section of this study.

The simplest cases are those where subversion approaches most nearly to
the conditions of civil disorder and insurrection. According to the usual
principles of criminal law, conspiracy to commit a crime is in itself a
criminal act. When there is a clear and present danger, therefore, that sub-

---

[10] Conversely it is perhaps worth noting at this point that civil disorder and insurrection
are not necessarily subversive in character. Thus floods and other natural disasters often
lead to lootings and other illegal acts which constitute a state of civil disorder, and consequently justify the imposition of martial law or the state of siege, without being associated
with any political purpose whatsoever. The same is true of other forcible challenges to
legitimate authority, such as bread riots, which may be deliberate and concerted enough
to constitute insurrection without envisaging any permanent change in the existing constitution of the state.

version will lead to civil disorder and insurrection, and when it further appears that this danger cannot be met by ordinary police measures, emergency measures under the state of siege or martial rule may properly be invoked. Although actual instances of this, as of insurrection itself, are comparatively rare in the history of most modern federal systems, they are by no means unknown. The events in Germany preceding the Beer Hall Putsch of 1923 are perhaps the best example. Having reason, in the face of an impending insurrectionary crisis, to doubt the loyalty both of the right-wing Bavarian government and of the left-wing Saxon government, the federal Cabinet did not wait for the outbreak of actual violence, but used its powers under Article 48 to appoint federal commissioners, as a precautionary measure, in both of these regions. Although the unreliability of the army made this federal intervention relatively ineffective in Bavaria, the federal commissioner in Saxony was able, through the use of his emergency powers, to secure the dissolution of the "proletarian hundreds," paramilitary formations largely under the control of Communists, and to take other effective measures to avert the danger of a revolutionary outbreak in that region. This helped the Weimar Constitution to survive the last of the many insurrectionary threats directed against it in the earlier years of its existence. Like measures undoubtedly would and should be taken under like circumstances by governments responsible for the maintenance of public order in any federal system.

Necessary as it may be, however, the use of emergency powers for the prevention of potential breakdowns of the public peace is clearly much more liable to abuse than is the use of such powers for the repression of actual violence. It is true that civil disorder and insurrection themselves can never be distinguished from lesser breaches of the peace by any precise line, and the von Papen case shows that the resulting uncertainties may serve as an invitation to subversive action on the part of legally constituted authorities. But the fact that there can be no civil disorder or insurrection without at least *some* overt acts of resistance to the rule of law has the advantage of providing a relatively objective though insufficient criterion for determining the propriety of emergency action in cases of this sort.

When emergency measures, on the other hand, are applied in situations where there has been as yet no overt breach of the public peace, it is very much harder to determine the necessity, and hence the legality, of resorting to the use of emergency powers. Three questions are involved in such a crisis: (1) How great is the insurrectionary intent of the people who have yet to engage in insurrectionary action? (2) What is the probability that this intent will be translated into action? (3) Will the action constitute a serious threat to the maintenance of public order? To answer such questions correctly is no easy matter. As a general rule, the likelihood of reaching a correct estimate of the situation will tend to increase in proportion as the danger of insurrection becomes more imminent. That is why the concept of "clear and present danger" is so often used to define the legally permissible occasions for the use of emergency powers.[11]   But the determination of what constitutes a clear and present danger, to an even greater extent than the determination of what constitutes an actual state of civil disorder and insurrection, is open to uncertainties, and thus to abuses which, if left unchecked, might well lead to the destruction of any federal system.

There is yet another obstacle, moreover, to the use of emergency powers against subversion: in this context they tend to be especially ineffective. The state of siege and martial rule were originally intended, as the names themselves imply, for crises of a military or quasi-military character, involving a direct trial of strength between opposing forces.   Since crises of this sort are normally settled one way or another in a relatively short period of time, it is possible to deal with them by means which frankly deviate from the norms of constitutional action, in the expectation that this deviation, being strictly temporary, will involve no permanent change in the normal constitutional order.   But subversion conforms to this classic pattern only in so far as it is committed to the use of insurrectionary methods.   A subversive movement which has already engaged its forces in overt conflict with the forces of the state, or which is completing its preparations for such an engagement, may often suffer a decisive setback through the use of emergency powers.   But a subversive movement which is not committed to immediate insurrectionary action may well lie low during the period when emergency powers are invoked, and then resume its subversive activities on precisely the same scale as before.   In other words, subversion, unless closely associated with insurrection, tends to give rise to long-range rather than short-range problems.   For that reason any attempt to counteract it by the use of temporary emergency powers is bound to be comparatively ineffectual.

A striking illustration of this fact is to be found in the experience of the Weimar Republic.   During the earlier years of its existence, when insurrection was the typical means of subversion employed by enemies of the Constitution, the emergency powers available under Article 48 proved to be a highly effective resource for the maintenance of constitutional order.   From 1924 onwards, however, the Communists and Nazis both decided that there was little hope of successful insurrection in the immediately foreseeable future.   They, therefore, devoted their energies to subverting the Constitu-

[11] While the concept of impending crisis is recognized in all constitutional states, the term "clear and present danger" is identified with the United States.   For the clearest enunciation of the "clear and present danger" rule, see Schenck v. United States, 249 U.S. 47 (1919), at 52, where Justice Holmes, delivering the opinion of the Court, said, "The question in every case is whether the words used are used in such circumstances and are of such a nature as to create a clear and present danger that they will bring about the substantive evils that [the State] has a right to prevent. It is a question of proximity and degree."   See also the opinion of Chief Justice Vinson in Dennis v. United States, 341 U.S. 494 (1951), at 510, quoting Judge Learned Hand "In each case [courts] must ask whether the gravity of the 'evil,' discounted by its improbability, justifies such invasion of free speech as is necessary to avoid the danger."

tion by other means. Their primary tactic was to build up a massive popular and parliamentary following, and to use the resulting powers to paralyze and discredit the institutions of constitutional democracy. In support of this enterprise they indulged in street fights, disorderly interruptions of public meetings, assassinations of party opponents, and other forms of illegal violence. These breaches of the peace, though seriously disruptive of the normal functioning of constitutional government, were never insurrectionary in purpose, and were seldom sufficiently concentrated in any one time or place to constitute a full-fledged state of civil disorder. With the advent of the depression, these various activities, legal and illegal, became a serious threat to the maintenance of the Weimar Constitution. From 1932 onwards the established authorities found it necessary once again to bolster their position by frequent invocations of Article 48. This time, however, the experiment was largely unsuccessful. It is true that the powers of emergency legislation did for a time enable them to stave off the crisis of parliamentary paralysis which resulted from the increasingly powerful position of extremist parties in the Reichstag. But as a means of counteracting the illegal violence of these parties, Article 48 was comparatively disappointing. Emergency measures would be invoked from time to time to prohibit the wearing of party uniforms, to forbid the holding of public meetings, and otherwise to inhibit the disorderly activities which were doing so much to discredit the Republic. Since they were temporary, however, these measures did more to advertise the weakness of the government than to produce any lasting improvement in its position. When emergency measures were used against them, the subversive parties suffered no decisive setback, and they were able to resume their activities with unimpaired vigor as soon as those measures were withdrawn. Emergency powers, when they finally fell into the hands of a Hitler or a von Papen, were still destined to prove themselves an efficient means for the subversion of the Weimar Constitution. As means for the defense of that Constitution against subversion, they were a good deal less effective.

If temporary measures are inadequate to deal with the problem of subversion, it would seem to follow that the proper remedy should be sought by way of permanent legislation. This conclusion has not infrequently been reached by the supporters of constitutional government. As a result of increasing awareness of the dangers implicit in modern subversive techniques, legislative attempts to deal with those dangers have been particularly numerous and widespread in the present postwar era. The resulting laws have frequently gone beyond the concept that legal responsibilities are determined by individual actions, and have assigned collective responsibility to organizations deemed subversive in character and purpose, without regard to the question of whether or not their activities constitute a clear and present danger to the maintenance of constitutional order. The most conspicuous example of this tendency is to be found in the Basic Law of the German Federal Republic, which proscribes all organizations and parties whose internal structure, declared policy, and open behavior fail to conform with democratic principles.[12] In Switzerland, where the Communist Party had already been dissolved several years previously,[13] the Criminal Code was amended in 1949 to specify in general terms that participation in associations "dangerous to the state" should constitute a punishable act.[14] Even where participation in subversive movements is not entirely prohibited, moreover, people are often, on the grounds of such participation, subjected to special disabilities of a more drastic sort. The American Internal Security Act of 1950,[15] for example, requires certain types of associations and individuals to register with a Subversive Activities Control Board. These are only a few of the many instances which might be adduced to illustrate the current tendency to resort to novel forms of legislation for the control of subversive movements.

Under a federal system of government, the enactment of anti-subversive legislation gives rise to special problems. In view of their responsibility for the maintenance of public order in their own territories, it is only natural that local governments should claim the right to legislate in this field. Many Swiss cantons, American States,[16] and other local units have accordingly passed laws which parallel and, in some cases, are even more severe than the corresponding federal measures. The Communist Party, for example, was outlawed in several Swiss cantons some time before it was outlawed in the Confederation as a whole. Such adaptations to local circumstances are wholly in accord with the spirit and practice of federal government. Because of the close connection between federal and local parties, however, there is always a possibility that the exercise of parallel responsibilities in this field may give rise to serious conflicts of policy. A rightist federal government might decide, for example, to outlaw a left-wing party which was participating in, and essential to the survival of, a leftist local government, or vice versa. In a case of this sort, the will of the federal authorities would generally prevail, on the principle that the federal government has overall responsibility for the maintenance of public order. Such situations have not in fact arisen in connection with any of the recent experiments in anti-subversive legislation.[17] This is largely to be explained by the happy circumstance that extremist parties are not at present a major factor in the political life, federal or local, of any important federal system. But in a

[12] Art. 9 (2).

[13] *Recueil Officiel*, vol. 56, pt. II, p. 1931 (Nov. 26, 1940).

[14] Tit. 13, §3, Art. 275 (1937), as amended by Art. 5.10.50, Message F.F. (1949).

[15] 64 Stat. 987 (1950–1951).

[16] See Gellhorn (ed.), *The States and Subversion* (1952).

[17] At one time there was some reason to believe that a federal-local conflict might result from the passage of the Padlock Law in the Province of Quebec (see Appendix II). This Act, which gave the provincial government extensive powers to suppress activities which it might at its discretion declare subversive, was feared by some left-wing members of the Liberal Party, which controlled the Dominion government, as a threat to the future political activities of their own and left-wing parties, in Dominion no less than in provincial elections. The Dominion government, though possessing the right to disallow provincial legislation, refused to intervene, so the issue was avoided.

federal country where this condition did not prevail, unrestricted federal powers of anti-subversive legislation might well lead to a serious impairment of the independence of local politics, and thus produce a significant change in the balance of federal and local powers.

This is but one example of the many problems which are created in constitutional democracies by legislation of this sort. These problems have little to do, however, with the question of emergency action with which we have been dealing. It is true that the right to enact anti-subversive legislation is sometimes claimed on grounds of unusual emergency. When statutes which would otherwise be unconstitutional are justified on this basis, the problem of testing the validity of that justification does, of course, arise. This problem comes within the proper scope of this study, and is considered in the next section. But the essential difficulty presented by subversion, and the essential reason for countering it by legislative rather than by executive action, lie precisely in the fact that it cannot very well be handled on a temporary basis. The result is that anti-subversive legislation, even when it is originally justified as an emergency measure, is apt to become not a temporary but a permanent or at least long-range matter.[18] In response to changing conditions, every constitutional system must provide some procedures of legislative or constitutional change. The development of new techniques of subversion may well call for a long-range revision of the statutory and constitutional rules which prescribe the legitimate conditions of party competition in modern democracies. Whether these revisions are made in such a way as to minimize subversion without unduly impairing the effectiveness of democratic politics will depend on the adequacy of the legislative and amending procedures of democratic constitutions, on the political prudence of democratic statesmen and electorates, and on many other considerations involving all the basic issues of modern constitutional government. These questions, though vitally connected with the problem of subversion, are clearly beyond the scope of the present study.

IV. Limitations on the Exercise of Emergency Powers

In the preceding sections of this study we have considered the nature and extent of the emergency powers granted in modern federal systems for the purpose of dealing with (1) civil disorder and insurrection, and (2) subversion. Although these powers have proved generally valuable, especially in the first connection, we have already had occasion to indicate that they are also liable to abuses which, if left unchecked, might well lead to the usurpation rather than to the preservation of constitutional government. Emergency action involves, by definition, the temporary suspension of con-

---

[18] In the United States, for example, the Espionage Act of 1917 (40 Stat. 75 (1917)) and the Alien Registration Act of 1940 (54 Stat. 675 (1940)), though originally passed in response to emergency conditions, still continue to provide a part of the basis for current proceedings against subversive activities.

stitutional restraints normally thought necessary to the maintenance of constitutional order. This can be justified only as long as, and to the extent that, normal methods are actually inadequate to the requirements of a crisis situation. The existence and duration of an emergency, and the extent and severity of the measures needed to overcome it, are matters incapable of precise legal formulation. Thus the justification of emergency action must always be a matter primarily of political judgment and discretion. But judgment is always liable to distortion through self-interest. If constitutional executives or legislatures were able, on the pretext of emergency, to exercise unlimited discretion in the assumption of powers normally denied to them, self-interest would often tempt them to discover imaginary crises, or to exaggerate the extent and severity of real ones. This situation, which if carried far enough would make a farce of any system of constitutional restraints, can be avoided only by subjecting the exercise of emergency powers to the judgment of some relatively independent and disinterested authority. All modern constitutional governments, including federal systems, have recognized the necessity of limiting emergency powers in this way. The nature and adequacy of these arrangements is the subject of the present section of the study.

The state of siege and martial rule, the two most important emergency institutions of modern times, are both designed to increase the powers of the executive branch of government. The responsibility for the limitation of these particular forms of emergency action lies with the legislative and judicial branches, since they are the only agents which, under modern constitutions, retain some measure of independence from the executive. Experience has shown that an executive does not, in emergency situations, always exercise adequate self-restraint. Legislatures and courts are both relied upon for this purpose in all federal systems. As between civil law and common law countries, however, there is a substantial difference in the relative degree of importance ascribed to judicial as contrasted with legislative restraints.

In the English-speaking world, including such federal systems as Canada, Australia, and the United States, primary responsibility for the prevention of abuses in the application of martial rule is vested in the judicial authorities. The legislature does, of course, have a general right and duty to prevent the executive from violating the principles of constitutional order. Through impeachment, as in the United States, or through the principle of parliamentary responsibility, as in the Commonwealth countries, it would be possible to secure the removal of a government which, in the opinion of the legislature, was abusing any of its powers, including the power of martial rule. The legislative authorities in these countries are not required, however, to take any special responsibility for the proper exercise of these emergency powers, and judicial action is left as the regular means of preventing possible abuses. It is a basic principle of the common law that all persons, including executive officials, are equally subject to the rule of law. When the executive presumes, therefore, to disregard normal legal restraints in the name of martial rule, it is the right of any party whose interests have been adversely affected to bring legal proceedings against the executive.[19] When such a case arises, the court must decide whether the circumstances were such as to justify the executive, under the rule of reasonable necessity, in acting as he did. It is true that, for the duration of an actual emergency, this normal responsibility for the limitation of martial rule may be transferred from the judicial to the legislative authorities. The device used for this purpose is an act suspending the writ of habeas corpus, a device authorized by the American Constitution,[20] and recognized in one form or another in all common law countries. Since this writ is the most important procedural device available for the initiation of legal proceedings against executive officers, the effect of suspending it is to deprive the courts of most occasions for judging the propriety of emergency action, and to leave the legislature for the time being as the sole agency capable of limiting its abuse. But martial rule often takes place without a suspension of the writ, and even if a suspending act is passed, the consequence is to postpone rather than to prevent the exercise of judicial authority in these matters. Once the period of suspension is over, executive actions which took place during that period may once again become a proper subject for legal proceedings against the executive. In the long run, therefore, anyone who presumes to exercise special powers in the name of martial rule does so in the knowledge that he may have to face the responsibility of proving, to the satisfaction of a judge and jury, that his acts were reasonably necessary. This is the main device employed in common law countries to prevent the abuse of these powers.

In civil law countries, on the other hand, limitations on the exercise of the state of siege are almost wholly legislative in character. It is true that judicial controls are not wholly lacking. Since, as we have seen, the powers available under the state of siege, as contrasted with martial rule, are often specifically enumerated, it follows that actions taken on this basis may be challenged, quite apart from any question of reasonable necessity, on the grounds that they are *ultra vires*. This may serve, in certain circumstances, to impose judicial restraints on the abuse of emergency powers. When von Papen, for example, tried on the basis of Article 48 not only to replace the Prussian government with a federal commissioner, but also to appoint Prussian representatives to the Reichsrat, he was foiled in this latter objective

---

[19] This right may be subject to certain limitations in the United States. See Mississippi v. Johnson, 4 Wall. 75 (1867); Georgia v. Stanton, 4 Wall. 50 (1867); and Youngstown Sheet and Tube Co. v. Sawyer, 343 U.S. 579 (1952).

[20] The Constitution authorizes the suspension of the writ of habeas corpus. But while the provision is found in Article I, which deals with the legislature, it is not listed among the powers expressly delegated to the Congress, Section 8, but is rather to be found in Section 9, clause 2.

by a court decision which declared that the right to make appointments of this sort was beyond the limits of the authority granted by that Article.[21] But the state of siege has of necessity to be defined so broadly that emergency measures are rarely *ultra vires*. To determine whether those measures are really necessary, and thus constitutionally defensible, calls for judgment as to the actual circumstances of the case, and civil law judges, unlike their common law counterparts, are generally loath to challenge the judgment of executive authorities in matters of this kind.[22] Thus the German court which refused to allow von Papen to pack the Reichsrat at the same time did not question his appointment of a federal commissioner for Prussia, an act which, although *intra vires,* could hardly have been defended under the existing circumstances as a necessary or proper measure for the defense of public order in Germany. The resulting weakness of judicial checks in civil law countries is counterbalanced, however, by a correspondingly greater emphasis on legislative checks. Just as in common law countries the principle of responsibility, or some other constitutional device, is generally available to give the legislature a large measure of control over all executive actions, including those dictated by the requirements of emergency situations. But quite apart from these general powers of supervision and control, the legislatures of civil law countries are regularly given particular powers and responsibilities. The basic principle underlying this institution is that it is a legislative rather than an executive device. If a crisis arises while the legislature is in session, the legislature itself is normally required to declare the state of siege. On other occasions the executive is allowed to act on its own initiative, but usually with the proviso that it must promptly convene the legislature and secure its approval. In Switzerland, for example, the Federal Council may take emergency measures when the Federal Assembly is not sitting, but must convene the Assembly at once if the number of troops involved is more than 2000, or if they remain mobilized for more than three weeks.[23] The emergency provisions of the Weimar Constitution were less carefully safeguarded in that the powers granted under Article 48 could at all times be invoked on the initiative of the executive, and required no subsequent ratification by the legislature. Even there, however, the executive was required to report to the Reichstag all measures taken on this basis, within a specified period of time, and to withdraw them on demand. This reliance on legislative sanctions to prevent abuses of the state of siege is typical of civil law countries.

The problem of emergency legislation, in so far as it is relevant to the present study,[24] is comparatively simple, and is handled in much the same

[21] *Preussen gegen das Deutsche Reich* 25 Oktober, 1932. Entscheidungen des Reichsgerichts in Zivilsachen. 138 Band, mit Anhang Entscheidungen des Staatsgerichtshofs. p. 1 ff. Berlin and Leipsiz, 1933.
[22] Because of the Continental concept of legislative supremacy, broadly drawn emergency powers tend to limit the determinative and interpretative functions of the courts.
[23] Constitution, Art. 102, par. 11.
[24] The most difficult problems of emergency legislation arise when the breakdown of

way both in civil law and in common law countries. In modern federal systems, powers of legislation are not absolute, but are subject to constitutional restraints. When a federal or local legislature tries, therefore, to enact anti-subversive laws, it may find that its proposals are in violation of the bill of rights, that they lie outside the field of competence assigned to this particular legislature in the federal-local distribution of powers, or that they are in some other way contrary to established constitutional principles. Under these circumstances it must either put those proposals through in the form of a constitutional amendment, or else justify them on the basis of emergency powers implicitly or explicitly granted under the existing constitution. Since legislatures, like executives, may be tempted to use actual or supposed emergencies as a pretext for the undue enlargement of their own powers, it follows that their judgment ought likewise to be subject to limitation by some independent authority. This need is recognized in all federal systems, and the authority everywhere designated for this purpose is the judiciary. Of all the countries considered in this study, Switzerland is the only one which fails to permit the judicial review of federal legislation, and all, including Switzerland, provide for the judicial review of local legislation. The Basic Law of the German Federal Republic is unusual in that it specifically authorizes the Federal Constitutional Court to determine whether or not parties and organizations are subversive, and thus subject to dissolution.[25] This power has recently been successfully invoked against a neo-Nazi party.[26] In most countries, however, the right of the courts to intervene in such matters is not specific, but is merely an incident of the more general right to test the constitutionality of all legislation. The High Court of Australia, for example, promptly invalidated the Communist Party Dissolution Act of 1950[27] on the ground that, in the absence of any grave national emergency, the Act could not be justified as a valid exercise of the defense power.[28] This is a typical example of the way in which courts may operate to check the discretion of legislatures in matters of emergency legislation.

From this brief survey the fact emerges that limitations on the exercise of emergency powers are an important part of the constitutional arrangements of modern federal systems. There is room for serious doubt, however, as to the adequacy of these limitations. This is particularly true with regard

---

normal legislative procedures encourages the executive to assume legislative functions, either on the basis of powers delegated to him by the legislature itself, or, as in the case of Weimar Germany, on the basis of a prerogative power to issue emergency decrees on his own responsibility. Whether these executive invasions of the legislative sphere ought to be allowed, and if so under what conditions and safeguards, is a highly controversial issue of modern constitutional government. The problem chiefly arises, however, in connection with foreign warfare or economic depression, and has little to do with the subject of this study.

[25] II, Art. 21 (2).
[26] See Appendix III, note 57.
[27] 48 Australian Commonwealth Acts, No. 16 (1950).
[28] Communist Party of Australia v. Commonwealth, 83 C.L.R. 1 (1951).

to the methods used to prevent abuse of the state of siege and martial rule. The difficulty is that, in the search for an independent authority to limit the emergency powers of executives, the tendency has been to rely either on the legislative or on the judicial branch of government, and that neither is fully capable by itself of ensuring the desired results. Because of the well-established tradition of judicial independence, judges are relatively immune to executive pressures, which makes them quite satisfactory as independent agents for the control of executive actions. Unfortunately the nature of their authority prevents that control from being very effective. Judges have no occasion to consider the propriety of martial rule until a case involving some specific exercise of that power has been brought before them. Even if there has been no suspension of the writ of habeas corpus, the slowness of judicial proceedings is such that it may be months or even years before a final decision is reached. It is not atypical that *Ex parte Milligan*,[29] the most important case arising out of the use of martial rule during the American Civil War, was not settled until a year after the war itself was over. Control exercised so long after the event is by no means wholly effective as a restraint on executive action. In this respect the state of siege, with its insistence on the legislative inauguration or ratification of emergency powers, is clearly superior. The drawback here is that, under the conditions of modern constitutional government, legislatures are closely associated with executives, and are thus much less well qualified than judiciaries to provide a truly independent judgment of executive conduct.[30] In countries like Germany, which follow the principle of parliamentary responsibility, the normal expectation is that the Cabinet will consist of leaders of the party or coalition of parties which has a majority in the legislature. Even where this principle is not followed, as in Switzerland, a similar correspondence of party alignments is by no means unlikely. In situations where the application of emergency powers is serviceable to party interests, it is rather unrealistic to rely on legislatures to prevent executives from abusing those powers. A more nearly adequate arrangement for the limitation of emergency powers would be to combine both systems, requiring the executive to secure prior authorization or prompt ratification from the legislature, as in the state of siege, for the declaration of any state of emergency, and at the same time subjecting its actions to the possibility of subsequent judicial condemnation, as in martial rule. But no such experiment has yet been made in any federal system, nor indeed in any other form of constitutional state.

In view of the obvious loopholes in all current arrangements for the limitation of emergency powers, it might be supposed that federal governments would often be tempted to use those powers to limit or nullify the authority of local governments. And the experience of the Weimar Republic, under the chancellorships of von Papen and Hitler, does indeed show that institu-

---

[29] 4 Wall. 2 (1866).
[30] But see Youngstown Sheet and Tube Co. v. Sawyer, 343 U.S. 579 (1952).

tions designed to enable a federal constitution to withstand crisis conditions are capable of being employed to subvert that selfsame constitution. It should be remembered, however, that this took place under highly exceptional circumstances, at a time when a majority of the German people had already demonstrated, by their vote in free elections, that they were opposed to the continuation of constitutional government. Under such conditions the breakdown of emergency institutions is by no means surprising. But in other federal countries, and even in Weimar Germany during the greater part of its existence, theoretical weaknesses in the limitation of emergency powers have led to no such abuses. The reason for this is that, quite apart from the question of legal limitations, a truly federal system of government tends by its very nature to produce important political safeguards against the abuse of emergency powers. Political parties which have to fight both local and federal elections, and which have to appeal to voters whose political interests and loyalties are local as well as federal, are bound to grow wary of any line of action which is likely to be seriously unacceptable to any considerable section of the community. Federal governments, even when, as in Canada or in the United States, they are in the hands of a single party, are too dependent on local party organizations to risk offending local sentiments. The result is that, even when they are vested with almost unlimited powers of emergency action, they are usually unable or unwilling to use them as a basis for unnecessary interferences with the authority of local governments. The strength of these political safeguards goes far to explain why modern federal systems have been so little concerned to remedy weaknesses in their legal arrangements for the limitation of emergency powers.

V. Conclusions

The major problem posed by this study is that of safeguarding the principles of a constitution at times when emergency situations make it necessary to limit some of those principles. The experiences of constitutional states point to four requirements which, if satisfied, tend to provide basic technical barriers against usurpation of power during emergency periods. These requirements are:

(1) That the assumption of emergency powers be strictly legitimate in character — it must have its origin in and its authority must be derived from the legitimate constitutional source of power.

(2) The assumption of power must be for a relatively short period of time.

(3) Final authority to determine the need for emergency power must never rest with the agency which assumes the power.

(4) There must be an independent agency to determine whether or not acts perpetrated under an assumption of emergency powers were in defense of the constitution.

These safeguards are logical and necessary in view of the decentralization of power sought in a constitutional state. Along with a people attached to the principle of constitutionalism and habitually accepting the rules which the constitution prescribes, these formal restraints are the framework within which constitutional states may successfully meet emergency situations.

APPENDIX I

Australia

I. THE DETERMINATION OF AN EMERGENCY

The determination that an emergency exists is a judicial as well as an executive and legislative act in Australia. It is an executive act because, under the Constitution of the federation, the executive is the commander-in-chief of the armed forces and retains the responsibility for the formal declaration of war. It is a legislative act, for it is the federal Parliament which in Sections 51 and 119 of the Constitution is given the power to ensure internal peace and to make laws "for the peace, order and good government of the Commonwealth with respect to the naval and military defense of the Commonwealth and of the several states." It is also a judicial act, because despite the Court's statement that the content of the authority always remains the same, the scope of activity permitted to both federation and States has varied widely under the Court's determination of the seriousness of the crisis with which the country is faced.

Thus, while one can be relatively certain that in time of war almost any legislation or regulation pursuant to it, which bears in some way on the defense effort, will satisfy the judiciary, a formal declaration of war is not sufficient to bring the permitted exercise of power to its full scope. Nor, as was indicated by the Court's decision in a 1951 case dealing with the suppression of the Communist Party,[31] is a mere declaration by the legislature that an emergency exists (see below). Further, after the conclusion of a conflict, it is for the courts rather than the legislature to make the final determination as to when the authority granted under the defense power contracts to normal peacetime dimensions.

II. MILITARY EMERGENCY

The Constitution provides that the Commonwealth shall protect every State against domestic violence upon the application of the executive government of the State.[32] The provision, however, has been invoked only once, by the State of Queensland in 1913, and it would seem that it is for

---

[31] Communist Party of Australia v. Commonwealth, 83 C.L.R. 1 (1951).
[32] §119.

the Commonwealth Cabinet itself to determine whether help is actually required.

In time of war, as indicated, the defense power takes on its full scope and with rare exceptions the regulations made pursuant to a few very general delegations of power by Parliament have always been upheld by the High Court, referred to hereinafter as "the Court."

The delegation of legislative authority has not presented any significant constitutional problem in Australia and, in fact, during World War II virtually the whole of the defense power was delegated to the Governor-General in Council, for he was granted power to make regulations "for securing the public safety and the defense of the Commonwealth." [33] During the war only a few major pieces of legislation were passed in this field, the National Security Act[34] and the Trading with the Enemy Act.[35] All lesser matters were dealt with by executive regulation. The executive was also given authority under the National Security Act to abrogate certain other acts. The government, among other things, fixed wages in all defense industries[36] and exercised complete control over commerce[37] and industrial production,[38] regulating output and shipment as essential to defense. Furthermore, the Court permitted it to establish price controls as well as direct controls of profits.[39]

The defense power, however, is not unlimited. The Court invalidated an attempt to set quotas for admissions to certain graduate schools[40] as well as certain regulations prescribing improved standards of industrial lighting,[41] because it held that neither of these matters had any direct bearing on the total war effort. Further, the Court, in the *Jehovah's Witnesses* case,[42] declared *ultra vires* a government regulation which had claimed the power to outlaw as subversive all doctrines advocated by an organization itself found to be so.

Secondly, the Court has held that none of the restrictions placed upon the federal government by the Constitution can be transcended.[43] Nor may functions specifically assigned to the States be assumed by the federal government. This limitation, however, has proven to be relatively unimpor-

[33] 1 Manual of National Security Legislation 3, 1943, 4th ed.
[34] 1939–1943, complete in 41 Australian Commonwealth Acts, 1943, p. 108, No. 38 of 1943.
[35] No. 14 of 1939, 37 *id.* at 59, as amended by No. 33 of 1940, 38 *id.* at 55.
[36] 1 Manual Nat. Secur. Legis. 1944, 5th ed., Nat. Secur. (Economic Organization) Regs., at pp. 282–284.
[37] 1 Manual Nat. Secur. Legis. 1944, 5th ed., Nat. Secur. (Land Transport) Regs., p. 573.
[38] 1 Manual Nat. Secur. Legis. 1943, 3d ed., Nat. Secur. (General) Regs., Part V, Reg. 59, p. 404.
[39] Arnold v. Hunt, 67 C.L.R. 429 (1943), upholding 1 Manual Nat. Secur. Legis. 1944, 5th ed., Nat. Secur. (Prices) Regs., p. 773.
[40] University of Sydney; ex parte Drummond, 67 C.L.R. 95 (1943).
[41] Victorian Chamber of Manufacturers v. Commonwealth, 67 C.L.R. 413 (1943).
[42] Adelaide Company of Jehovah's Witnesses v. Commonwealth, 67 C.L.R. 116 (1943).
[43] Adelaide Company of Jehovah's Witnesses v. Commonwealth, 67 C.L.R. 116 (1943), at 152.

tant. Section 92 of the Constitution, moreover, states that trade, commerce and intercourse among the States "shall be absolutely free," and during time of peace this restriction has been interpreted as imposing serious limitations upon both federal and State power. While the Court did invoke Section 92 in time of war to strike down a federal regulation[44] which *specifically* prohibited interstate railway travel and other travel except as licensed, it permitted other general regulations concerning interstate commerce on the grounds that these only affected it incidentally and were specifically directed to defense problems.

III. EMERGENCY POWERS IN TIME OF PEACE

The Commonwealth has never attempted to invoke the concept of emergency in dealing with purely economic problems, despite the fact that constitutional restrictions placed rather stringent limitations upon the means which could be used to combat the depression of the early 1930's. However, the defense power has been used to justify the continuation in postwar periods of exercises of power not otherwise within the defined powers of the federal government. World War I decisions in this area were few and inconclusive, and it has only been since the end of World War II, particularly since the Defense Act[45] (transitional provisions), that the Court has explored this realm with greater thoroughness.

Immediately following the war, the Court, adhering to the cited interpretation, upheld price and wage controls. In fact so broad was the power permitted that some interpreted it as an indication that the defense power might provide the back door to regulations otherwise prohibited. On the other hand, in a number of cases decided in 1949, the Court invalidated a whole series of regulations, including gas rationing and manpower control.

While the Court suggested that price control, for example, might have been valid at least *through* 1948, both gas rationing and the regulation of women's wages were held invalid *as of 1948*.[46] In other words, the Court felt that while "the recent war has produced some changes in every part of our lives, this fact does not mean that the whole life of man is to be regarded as a war consequence."

In peacetime it is generally accepted that the defense power extends to such matters as regulating the production of items for stockpiling or putting facilities acquired in time of war to civilian production for purposes of maintaining industrial capacity. How much further the government may go is a debatable question. In the Defense Preparations Act of 1951[47] it invoked the concept of emergency to justify the broad grant of regulatory

---

[44] See Andrews v. Howell, 65 C.L.R. 255 (1941), which arose under National Security (Land Transport) Regulations, Stat. Rules 1942, No. 149, as amended by Rules 1943, Nos. 28 and 88.

[45] No. 77 of 1948, 44 Australian Commonwealth Acts, 1948, p. 240.

[46] Hume v. Higgins, 78 C.L.R. 116 (1949).

[47] Australian Commonwealth Acts, 1951.

power included therein. While no litigation has been forthcoming under this act, the case of the *Communist Party of Australia v. Commonwealth*[48] may shed some light on this question. The Act of 1950 dissolving the Party[49] is the most recent attempt to combat subversion on a large scale but it also constitutes an interesting test case for the constitutional powers granted for, and the limitations imposed upon, such action.

The Act empowered the Governor-General to extend the application of the Act to any organization that was either affiliated with, or advocated the principles and objectives of, communism. Attempting to carry on the activities of a dissolved body was made a criminal offense and declared prejudicial to national security. Any person found to have been a communist after 1948 was disqualified from public office as well as employment in any industrial organization.

Upon actions brought in the highest Commonwealth Court by the Party and several trade unions, the Act was declared unconstitutional as not within the powers of the federal Parliament. A constitutional amendment specifically authorizing the Act was rejected in a popular referendum.

Since the Australian Constitution contains virtually no express guarantees of civil liberties in so many words, the only question was whether the Act would be sustained under any of the powers conferred on Parliament by the Constitution. Primary emphasis was placed on the defense power, with incidental reliance on the power to aid the executive in the defense of the Constitution and on the implied power of self-preservation. It was held that in the absence of a grave national emergency, neither the legislative findings recited in the preamble declaring communist activities a danger, nor the Governor-General's findings that certain bodies or persons were prejudicial to security, could alone establish the necessary relationship of the Act to the defense power, since a contrary opinion of the Court would allow a government to "recite itself" into power. Evidence as to activities of some communists could not warrant the application of the Act to others identified merely by communist aims. The Court's decision may be due to an understandable tendency, in the absence of a formal bill of rights, to construe granted powers so strictly that measures conflicting with traditional concepts of "due process" could be invalidated as dangerous to the constitutional order.

APPENDIX II

Canada

Since the subject of constitutional defense in the Dominion of Canada much resembles, in its main aspects, that of Australia, we can confine our-

[48] 83 C.L.R. 1 (1951).
[49] Communist Party Dissolution Act, 48 Australian Commonwealth Acts, No. 16 (1950).

698 STUDIES IN FEDERALISM

selves to a few observations on the essential characteristics. Since there is no clear-cut bill of rights in the British North America Act of 1867 (the Canadian Constitution),[50] the Parliament of Canada is in a position to engage in the widest range of activities directed toward the defense of the constitutional order, limited only by its conscience and the will of the electorate. Although in general the constituent Provinces of the Canadian federation have been more successful than the States of Australia in maintaining their independence against centripetal tendencies, in matters of threats to their constitutional order they largely rely on federal initiative and protection.

As under the Australian Constitution, heavy reliance is placed upon the defense power to ensure the protection of the Constitution of Canada. The only provision of the Constitution relating to this problem is Article 91, granting to the Dominion Parliament the authority to make laws for the "peace, order and good government" of Canada. It gives almost exclusive legislative power to the Dominion in relation to "militia, military and naval services, and defense." The scope and limits of this power have never been authoritatively defined, for it has seldom been invoked. It may well be asked whether it might not have been invoked in these cases where Dominion legislation was instead held to rest entirely on an "emergency" conception of the general power conferred in Article 91.

While the courts have rejected attempts by the Dominion government to legislate, using this clause as justification, on certain important economic matters in peacetime, its adequacy as a constitutional basis for handling cases of potential or actual subversion has never been either successfully challenged or conclusively sustained.

The pre-1914 Militia Act[51] gave to the governments of the Provinces the power to appeal to the federal government for aid against insurrection. This act has been interpreted in such a way as to include separatist movements aiming at secession because the latter subject was not dealt with in the Constitution.

The basis of war emergency legislation passed under Section 91 was the War Measures Act of 1914.[52] Though the orders issued under this Act were invoked at the end of the war, the Act itself was never repealed and it came into force again upon the outbreak of World War II. The War Measures Act provides that the provisions of Section 6 of this Act are to be in force only during war, invasion, or insurrection, real or apprehended. Issuance of a government proclamation is conclusive evidence that these exist until such time as a second proclamation declares them to exist no longer. By this section of the Act the Governor in Council is to have power to do and authorize such acts, and to make such orders and regulations, as he may deem necessary or advisable for the security, defense, peace, order, and welfare of Canada.

---

[50] 30 & 31 Vict., c. 3, p. 3.
[51] 1904, 4 Edw. VII, c. 23, §1.
[52] 5 Geo. V, 1915 2d Sess., c. 2, §1, as amended by R.S. 1927, c. 206, p. 4085.

These powers are to extend, among other matters, to trading, exportation, importation, production, manufacture, and also to appropriation, control, forfeiture, and disposition of property.

The Act grants the broadest of powers to the government, such as those of detaining or deporting suspected individuals and establishing censorship over all published materials. Under its authority the government of Canada, during World War II, suspended the Communist Party and several Fascist groups, expelled Canadian citizens of Japanese ancestry from the western coastal region, and arrested several individuals who had delivered speeches considered subversive.

More recently, the much-debated Padlock Law of the Province of Quebec[53] grants considerable powers, including that of closing premises of business or publication, to the provincial government, for action against activities and organizations which are communist or bolshevist in purpose. The relevant sections of this Act read as follows:

> Section 3. It shall be illegal for any person, who possesses or occupies a house within the province, to use it or allow any person to make use of it to propagate communism or bolshevism by any means whatsoever.
> Section 12. It shall be unlawful to print, to publish in any manner whatsoever, or to distribute in the province any newspaper, periodical, pamphlet, circular, document or writing whatsoever propagating or tending to propagate communism or bolshevism.

During the present period of cold war, in which the War Measures Act is not operative, the Canadian Parliament has passed a series of enabling acts granting to the government authority broader than its usual powers, but narrower than those of the War Measures Act. The Emergency Powers Act of 1951,[54] for example, specifically prohibits the executive from arresting, detaining, or deporting anyone except pending judicial trial, and from imposing any censorship or other control over written material.

APPENDIX III

Germany

I. THE IMPERIAL CONSTITUTION OF 1871

The chief emergency institution of Imperial Germany was the *Kriegszustand*, or state of war, a standard form of constitutional emergency modeled directly on the French state of siege, although with certain alterations in keeping with the more autocratic character of the Empire. A similar device was to be found in the various State constitutions, the *Belagerungszustand*,

[53] Act Respecting Communist Propaganda, 1937, 1 Geo. VI, c. 2, p. 41.
[54] 15 Geo. VI, c. 5, p. 47.

or state of siege. Article 68 of the Imperial Constitution, which the Emperor was authorized to invoke whenever he felt that "public safety was in danger," had as its primary function the overcoming of the natural limits of a federal government in time of military crisis. An imperial statute was to be passed to regulate the conditions and effects of such declarations. Until then, a Prussian statute of 1851[55] was to be the basis for its application.

No imperial statute was ever enacted and this Prussian law continued in force until the collapse of the Empire. It regulated carefully the form of the proclamation, the suspension of certain rights, and various other effects of the state of war such as the transfer of executive power from civil to military authorities and the establishment of military courts for the trial of specified crimes. The initiation of such measures was at the discretion of the Emperor, acting not as Head of the State but as commander-in-chief of the armed forces. In the forty years before 1914 there were but two occasions for the state of war, but its extensive use during World War I, particularly against left-wing elements, made it increasingly controversial.

II. THE WEIMAR CONSTITUTION OF 1919

The five years following the birth of the Weimar Republic brought the government and people no relief from the economic distress and unemployment, from the inclination to secession of many areas and elements in the Reich, or from occupation of German soil. In anticipation of nation-wide disorder of this kind the framers of the Weimar Constitution inserted the ill-fated Article 48. It is clear, however, that the Republic could not have survived the first troubled years without this emergency provision. The relevant provisions of the article read as follows:

> If public safety and order in the German Reich is materially disturbed or endangered, the President may take necessary measures to restore public safety and order, intervening if necessary with the aid of the armed forces. To this end he may temporarily suspend in whole or in part the fundamental rights established by Articles 114 [personal liberty], 115 [inviolability of dwelling], 118 [freedom of opinion], 123 [freedom of assembly], 124 [freedom of association], 153 [private property].
> The President must immediately inform the Reichstag of all measures adopted by authority of the first or second paragraphs of this article. These measures are to be revoked upon demand of the Reichstag.

For the non-responsible Emperor was substituted the President and the Chancellor, including his responsible Cabinet, and indeed (by Arts. 48, III, and 54) the Reichstag. Moreover, in any action to be taken under Article 48, the military authorities were subordinate to the ordinary civil officials of the Reich government. These were the two liberalizing alterations of the old state of war. On the other hand, by expressly reading the Prussian stat-

---

[55] Gesetz-Sammlung für die Königlichen Preussischen Staaten, No. 26, p. 451 (1851).

ute of 1851 into its Article 68, the old Constitution had limited and qualified the use of the *Kriegszustand* more closely than did Weimar in Article 48 the use of its broad emergency powers. Yet, because President, Ministry, and Reichstag were joint participants in its exercise, the state of emergency and war under the Weimar Constitution had become a civil and republican institution.

Within the scope of the present study we cannot recount the frequent resort had to it, its use as a state of siege in early insurrections and as an enabling act in economic crises; we must concern ourselves with its general place in the constitutional scheme and the efficacy of the limitations imposed upon its use.

The success of Article 48 in *suppressing attempted insurrections* can perhaps best be judged by the fact that both the right and the left abandoned, after the unsuccessful Nazi Beer Hall *Putsch* of 1923, their attempts to seize power by force. Not that force ceased to be used as a weapon but it was used as an instrument for terrorizing the voters in order to obtain parliamentary control through the ballot box.

In the early twenties vigorous steps were taken for the "protection of the Republic"; for example, the government ordered the suspension of newspapers which were actively urging the assassination of political opponents. Regulations forbidding the use of uniforms and suspending the right of public meeting were promulgated in the early thirties but the former was soon rescinded by the von Papen Ministry.

The definition of what could be regarded as "necessary measures" or as a "serious disturbance of public safety and order" was left to the President, the Chancellor and his Cabinet. Owing to the absence of a qualifying law the government could act on the authority of Article 48 alone and indeed did so over a much wider field than originally intended by the constitution-makers. The President issued numerous legal ordinances for the regulation of financial, economic, and social matters, first during the inflation, then under the administration of Chancellor Bruening and the subsequent Presidential Cabinets. Of course, such decrees could be, and several times were, altered or annulled by a subsequent Reichstag statute, but only twice in thirteen years were formal requests made by the Reichstag for the revocation of such ordinances.

In the exercise of these exceptional powers, as in every action, the German President was liable to removal from office for abuse of power and trust. It could be effected by a popular vote on the proposal of two thirds of the Reichstag (Art. 43). Furthermore, he could be impeached before the Staatsgerichtshof by two thirds of the Reichstag "for having culpably violated the constitution or a law of the Reich" (Art. 59). Finally he could be prosecuted criminally with the consent of the Reichstag.

Therefore, it is obvious that the vigilance of the Reichstag was the chief, if not the only, barrier provided in the Constitution against the misuse of Article 48. From the constitutional requirement of ministerial responsibility, and from the Reichstag's right to disapprove or amend any measure adopted by the President, it may be concluded that the representatives of the people were intended to provide the most important limitation on the employment of extraordinary powers. Article 25 of the Constitution, however, entrusted the President with the power to dissolve the Reichstag at any time. In the case of Hitler this provision meant the disappearance of all effective checks upon the President and his Cabinet, with the result that techniques designed and evolved for the defense of the Constitution of the Republic were, in the end, to play a considerable part in its destruction.

III. THE BASIC LAW OF 1949

The Basic Law of the German Federal Republic is more cautious than the Weimar Constitution in its provision for defense of the constitutional order in time of emergency although it goes further than any other federal constitution in providing means for dealing with subversive elements. The constitution-makers were anxious to avoid the granting of any power that might be turned into, or used as, a basis for unrestrained emergency law-making by the executive (*Notverordnungsrecht*) as had been done under the Weimar Republic. A special problem faced them, because of the particular form they had given the parliamentary system. For what was to be done if the federal Chancellor could not muster a majority in Parliament and if Parliament in turn were unable to agree on the election of another Chancellor—for example, if the combined opposition were strong enough to obstruct successfully the working of the government but not sufficient to form a workable majority (Art. 68)? The President may, upon the request of the government and with approval of the Bundesrat, declare a state of legislative emergency for a bill which the Bundestag rejects despite the fact that the government has declared it to be urgent. The same applies if it rejects the bill although the Chancellor has combined with it the motion for a vote of confidence. If the Bundestag again throws out the bill or does not pass it within four weeks after its resubmission during the declaration of the state of emergency the bill is deemed adopted if the Bundesrat approves it (Art. 81, II). Thus, every emergency law requires approval of the Bundesrat. The latter's approval in these cases replaces that of its popularly elected counterpart. Therefore, in the provisions of the Basic Law, the *federal principle overrides the popular national principle*.

To forestall the possibility of abuse, this power has been limited in two ways: the state of legislative emergency may not continue for more than six months within the term of office of a federal Chancellor, and it may be declared only once in any one Chancellor's term of office. The Basic Law may neither be amended nor wholly or partially repealed or suspended by emergency laws (Art. 81, IV).

These provisions are narrowly limited in scope and designed primarily as a means to cope with certain types of parliamentary deadlocks. In order to protect the constitutional order of a modern state against the many possible threats from within, other effective and far-reaching safeguards are needed.

The Basic Law embodies several provisions to this end. Neither the Imperial nor the Weimar Constitution contained any mention of political parties and their role. The Basic Law specifically recognized them as vital factors in the formation of the political will of the people and clearly defines their rights and duties (Art. 21). Their internal organization must conform to democratic principles. Parties, groups, or associations which, according to their aims and the behavior of their members, seek to impair or abolish the free and democratic basic order or to jeopardize the existence of the federal Republic are unconstitutional. To prevent abuse in the application and interpretation of this important clause, the power to decide questions of unconstitutionality is vested in the Federal Constitutional Court.[56]

Furthermore, the Basic Law provides that associations, the object and activities of which are directed against the constitutional order, shall be prohibited (Art. 9). Whoever abuses the freedom of association for the attainment of such ends will forfeit this and certain other basic rights. Here again, the forfeiture and its extent are to be pronounced by the Federal Constitutional Court (Art. 18). These functions of the new Constitutional Court (which by no means constitute an exhaustive list) clearly show the great authority entrusted to it as guardian of the basic foundations of the Constitution (the federal principle, the democratic principle, and the principle of the rule of law).

The efficacy of these provisions was put to the test for the first time in the recent decision by which the Court declared the neo-Nazi party SRP (Sozialistische Reichspartei) unconstitutional.[57] The party was found guilty under Articles 9 (2), 18, and 21, on the strength of overwhelming evidence. This decision eliminated West German parliamentary seats held by Socialist Reich members, confiscated the party's property, and forbade the formation of a substitute organization. Execution of this decision is entrusted to the Ministries of the Interior of the Länder.

The federal legislature played an important part in strengthening these provisions of the Basic Law. It considerably extended the scope of application of the criminal code by the significant amendment of August 11, 1951. Thereby a large number of treasonable, subversive, or otherwise dangerous conspiracies and activities by individuals or groups of individuals against the foundation of the constitutional order of the Federal Republic were brought within the reach of the criminal code (§§80–101, StGB). Such conspiracies and activities include the dissemination of subversive information and acts designed to bring the Federal Republic, or any part thereof, under foreign influence or control, to foster the secession of any part of the area

[56] II, Art. 21 (2).
[57] Entscheidungen des Bundesverfassungsgerichts (1953), Urteil vom 23 Oktober 1952 (1 BvB 1/51): Feststellung der Verfassungswidrigkeit der Sozialistischen Reichspartei.

of the Federal Republic, or to impair the fundamental principles of the democratic system of government (§88).

There is, as stated, a serious lack of other essential emergency powers, for no power of declaring war is granted by the Basic Law, and the useful but dangerous category of "war powers" is therefore of dubious constitutional status. Since insurrection or rebellion, as a state of factual threat in the constitutional order, is also not specifically recognized in the Constitution, the Basic Law must be considered very weak in this vital respect. It must be remembered, however, that the Basic Law was adopted at a time when the occupying powers claimed a practically unlimited emergency power under the Occupation Statute, and that the federal and Land governments retained the usual police powers. Under the Contractual Agreements, the occupying powers are surrendering many of their emergency prerogatives, and reliance must be placed even more upon the general police powers of the German federal and Land governments themselves.

APPENDIX IV

Switzerland

I. POWERS FOR MILITARY EMERGENCY

The maintenance of public order and internal security within the limits of the cantonal territories is a duty of the cantonal governments. In addition, the federal Constitution provides in Article 19, paragraph 4:

> The cantons exercise control over military forces in their territory save in so far as this right is limited by the Constitution or by federal legislation.

If a canton is not able to maintain order and security, the Confederation has the right of *intervention*. Article 16 prescribes:

> In case of internal troubles or when danger threatens from another canton, the government of the canton threatened must immediately notify the Federal Council, in order that the latter may take the necessary measures within the limits of its power (Article 102, pars. 3, 10, and 11) or convene the Federal Assembly. In case of urgency the cantonal government, while immediately notifying the Federal Council, may call for the assistance of the other cantons which are bound to render the same [par. 1].
>
> When the cantonal government is not in a position to summon assistance, the competent federal authority may intervene on its own initiative, and is bound to do so if the disorders endanger the safety of Switzerland [par. 2].

The power of intervention is entrusted to the Federal Assembly (Art. 85, par. 7), but Article 102, paragraph 11 provides:

In case of urgency arising when the Federal Assembly is not in session, the Federal Council has authority to call out troops and employ them as it may think necessary, provided that it must convene the Assembly immediately if the number of troops called out exceeds two thousand or if they remain mobilized for more than three weeks.

There have been only a few cases of federal interventions since 1848. They all arose from political troubles of mainly local concern. In all the cases the Federal Council nominated a federal commissioner and empowered him to take all the measures necessary for restoring the public order.

In Switzerland, federal laws, decrees, and decisions are generally executed by cantonal rather than by federal authorities. The Federal Council, however, exercises supervision over the cantonal authorities in so far as federal matters are concerned. If a canton refuses to execute federal legislation or decisions or if it otherwise acts against federal law, the Federal Assembly may order coercive measures and, if necessary, employ military forces (Art. 85, par. 8, Federal Execution). The Confederation has never yet been forced to take such measures.

II. Powers for Economic Emergency

The economic emergencies of the two World Wars and of the depression of the 1930's required federal measures for the maintenance of economic and social security. The Constitution, however, did not provide for such measures, and the federal authorities therefore undertook extraconstitutional emergency measures. At the beginning of the two World Wars, in 1914[58] and in 1939,[59] the Federal Assembly enabled the Federal Council, by a broad grant of power, to take all the measures necessary for the security, independence, neutrality, and economic interests of Switzerland. The Federal Council, accordingly, enacted a great number of decrees concerning rationing, the control of prices, rents and wages, and various kinds of social aid. In the depression of the 1930's, the Federal Assembly itself enacted a great deal of legislation, particularly on unemployment relief.[60] Article 89 of the Constitution (in the version then in force) enabled the Assembly to declare its decrees urgent, that is, to put them into force without having submitted them to the popular referendum. Many of these emergency measures violated cantonal or individual rights, but since there is no judicial review of federal legislation, the courts could not invalidate such acts.

Two constitutional amendments, one in 1947 and one in 1949, changed the basis of federal powers in this field. The first one (concerning Articles 31, 31-bis, 31-ter, 31-quater, 31-quinquies, 32, 34-ter) greatly broadened federal powers in the field of economic and social legislation. It provides for extensive aid to agriculture and to branches of industry suffering economic

[58] Arrêté du 3 août 1914 (R.O., 1914, p. 347).
[59] Arrêté du 30 août 1939.
[60] See Malézieux, *Les Pleins Pouvoirs en Suisse* 43 (1942).

difficulties, and authorizes measures to ensure preparedness in time of war and to deal with unemployment. The second amendment (Article 89-*bis*), introduced by a popular initiative, revised the provisions on emergency decrees of the Federal Assembly. The Federal Assembly still may declare its decrees urgent if a delay would be prejudicial, but, if the duration of the decree is longer than one year, 30,000 citizens or eight cantons now may require its submission to popular referendum. The amendment further provides that the Federal Assembly may also enact urgent decrees which are not based on federal constitutional powers. Such decrees, however, become invalid if they are not confirmed by the people and the cantons within one year. Emergency decrees of this latter kind may, of course, deal with any subject matter.

III. Powers to Deal with Subversion and Cold War Emergency

The Swiss Criminal Code of 1937[61] severely punishes all crimes against the state and the national defense, for example, treason. An amendment of the Swiss Criminal Code in 1949[62] introduced some new provisions for a more effective prosecution of subversive activities. In particular, subversive propaganda and participation in associations dangerous to the state have been made punishable. The Military Criminal Code deals more especially with crimes against national defense and military security.

In addition to criminal prosecution, the federal as well as the cantonal governments may, under their police powers, prevent dangerous activities, such as subversive meetings, associations, or publications. Civil liberties are only guaranteed within the limits of public order and security. Thus, for example, the right to form associations is guaranteed by the Constitution only in so far as "the objects and methods of such associations are not unlawful and dangerous to the state" (Art. 56). In the years preceding World War II, several cantons prohibited the Communist Party. The Federal Court (which may invalidate cantonal acts) upheld the prohibitions in view of Article 56. In 1940 the Federal Council dissolved the Communist Party throughout Switzerland.[63] In recent years the Federal Council has, in a few cases, prohibited the public appearance of foreign leaders of the Communist Party or other extremist groups. Under the emergency laws of the two World Wars[64] some measures of the federal authorities, such as their severe censorship of the press, limited civil liberties more strictly than is authorized by the Constitution.

[61] Tit. 13, §3, Art. 275 (1937).
[62] Art. 5.10.50, Message F.F. (1949).
[63] Recueil officiel, vol. 56, pt. II, p. 1931 (Nov. 26, 1940).
[64] See notes 58 and 59, above.

APPENDIX V

United States

The Constitution of the United States marks out separate spheres of action for the federal and State governments and provides for a division of power between a national legislature and a national executive elected independently of each other. A long list of provisions explicitly limits the actions of both the national and State governments in certain areas relating to civil liberties.[65]

The responsibility for interpreting the document and for determining the constitutionality of political acts has fallen to a supreme judicial tribunal. The flexibility this Supreme Court has demonstrated in applying the Constitution to changing circumstances has shown that the meaning of its provisions tends to shift in the light of new experience of crisis situations.

Before going into detail it may be well to recall that the Bill of Rights, federalism, and the separation of powers are the three main constitutional barriers to the easy establishment of emergency government in the United States. The Constitution is no unsurmountable barrier to the often cited law of self-preservation, particularly since there are grants of powers scattered throughout the provisions of Articles I, II, and IV, upon which almost all known instances and institutions of federal emergency government could probably be based. However, the other parts of the Constitution are not to be overlooked. It is important to remember that the Bill of Rights stands as a barrier against legislative encroachment on the rights therein asserted, and that legislation by any but the normal process is not specifically provided for. It should also be remembered that in several instances the due process clauses of the Fifth and Fourteenth Amendments have been held by the Supreme court to be decisive barriers to administrative and legislative action.

I. POWERS TO DEAL WITH INSURRECTION

The federal government has never lacked the constitutional authority to provide for the internal security of the nation. Although the line has never been precisely drawn between the respective constitutional powers of President and Congress in the employment of the nation's armed forces, it is chiefly through legislative delegation and executive initiative that the President occupies an important position today. He is empowered "to call forth the militia of any or all of the states, and to employ such parts of the land and naval forces as he may deem necessary to enforce the faithful execution of the laws." This establishes the executive branch of the government in a powerful position to act in an emergency.

[65] Amendments I-X, XIII-XV, XIX.

The institution of martial law, and indeed federal martial law, which like the State variety is patterned on the English institution, is implicit in the Constitution though not provided in express terms. The provision for the suspension of the writ of habeas corpus, a process historically associated with martial law, is evidence that its use was contemplated. While martial law in the United States has been primarily a device of the State governments, it is equally important for the federation as a whole. The realities of government seem to place the use of this device almost exclusively in the hands of the President, rather than of the Congress, particularly in view of his constitutional powers as commander-in-chief and executor of the laws which permit him to determine not only the advent of a national emergency but, in some cases, also its termination.[66] Martial law is for the federal government, however, a recourse which can usually be justified only by actual war, civil or foreign.

Presidential ascendancy in any condition of emergency is built squarely upon two foundations: (1) the President's initiative in claiming extraordinary authority without prior Congressional sanction, and (2) explicit grants to him by Congress of emergency powers. Even if the Constitution is rigid, the executive power therein defined most certainly is not, and although much of the President's power to act decisively in emergencies has been granted by Congress, some Presidents have laid claim to "implied" powers which, they have asserted, must be inherent in the Presidential office.[67] The separation of powers has proved in many ways to be less of an obstacle than might have been expected. Congress itself has recognized that only the executive can act effectively in an emergency which includes responsibility for the use of the armed forces in a "police action" where vital American interests are considered to be at stake, although Congress has subsequently always scrutinized the Presidential action. In the exercise of emergency powers the executive has effectively denied civil liberties to groups of American citizens despite the fact that they had not engaged in overt acts detrimental to the republic. The evacuation of Japanese-Americans from coastal areas during World War II and the Supreme Court's upholding of the constitutionality of the step [68] are evidence of the scope of Presidential discretion; here again, however, Presidential action was supported by legislation in Congress.[69]

In times of less severe crisis there do appear to be limits beyond which the executive cannot go alone. In the recent Steel Case[70] the Court's decision invalidated the President's seizure of the steel industry on the ground that

[66] Note President Lincoln's actions regarding the suspension of the writ of habeas corpus and the subsequent ratification of this action by Congress (12 Stat. 755 (1863)); also that it was the President who determined the duration of the suspension (13 Stat. 734 (1863)).

[67] See the government's contention in Youngstown Sheet and Tube Co. v. Sawyer, 343 U.S. 579 (1952).

[68] Korematsu v. United States, 323 U.S. 214 (1944).

[69] 56 Stat. 173 (1942).

[70] Youngstown Sheet and Tube Co. v. Sawyer, 343 U.S. 579 (1952).

this was not authorized by law and exceeded his implied powers as chief executive and commander-in-chief. The opinion also emphasized that Congress had previously rejected proposed legislation authorizing action such as that taken by the President.

In spite of Buchanan's assertion that as President he had no right to coerce a State to remain in the Union, Lincoln was ready to use military force to prevent secession by resorting to measures directly contrary to the constitutional and statutory limitations on his powers. Congress, faced by a *fait accompli* that was in its nature irrevocable, registered approval of "all acts, proclamations, and orders of the President" in an act of 1861.[71] Moreover, the Supreme Court, asked later in the *Prize Cases*[72] to determine the legality of the Presidential measures, gave its direct sanction to Lincoln's extraordinary exercise of war power, saying even that the subsequent Congressional ratification was unnecessary. What the Supreme Court held was simply this: The President has the constitutional power, under such circumstances as he shall deem imperative, to brand as belligerents the inhabitants of any area in general insurrection. In other words, he has an almost unrestrained right to act toward insurrectionary citizens as if they were enemies of the United States, and thus place them outside the protection of the Constitution. In the United States precedents in the matter of Presidential emergency power under the Constitution have been built more by accepted Presidential action than by Court pronouncements.

If the President's power to act alone is broad, that which is granted him by Congressional statute is also of considerable scope. Congress has rarely failed to go along with Presidential requests for emergency war powers.

The Selective Service Act of 1917,[73] the Emergency Shipping Fund[74] and Lever[75] Acts, and the Overman Act of 1918[76] placed large segments of the economy under executive control for the first time. None of these was successfully challenged in the courts, except for certain minor provisions of the Lever Act. As Justice Black said in discussing legislation which authorized the President virtually to take over the entire shipbuilding industry, ". . . Congress can draft men for battle service. Its power to draft business organizations . . . can be no less."

Hardly any limits were set to the President's power to create a proliferation of agencies to administer the various aspects of the American effort in World War I. While the national economy was brought under the control of the administration, the administration was under the legal control of the President. His authority acted as a driving force in all these agencies, and none was ever set up against his will. Some of them functioned without any statutory foundation.

[71] 12 Stat. 326 (1861). See also 12 Stat. 755 (1863).
[72] 2 Black 635 (1863).
[73] 40 Stat. 76 (1917).
[74] 40 Stat. 182 (1917).
[75] 40 Stat. 276 (1917).
[76] 40 Stat. 556 (1918).

Even larger grants of power were involved in prosecuting World War II.[77] Some statutory authority for emergency action already existed, either specifically provided for by peacetime statutes, or left on the books as a residue of previous conflicts, and more was added upon request.[78]

II. POWERS TO DEAL WITH SUBVERSION

The growing tendency of the government to resort to exceptional powers as a measure of protection against subversion is leading to a considerable degree of legislative intrusion into almost every field of public life.

For many years a law had been in force fixing punishment to forcible opposition to the execution of an Act of Congress, but a mere conspiracy for that purpose was not criminal until the passage of the Act of 1861.[79] The statute was interpreted as including seditious conspiracy for the overthrow of the government as well as agreements, whether by few or many, whether public or private, forcibly to resist, or even delay, the execution of any law of the United States. Despite this legislation considerable freedom of expression was allowed throughout the years of the Civil War, and indeed almost more so than in World War I.

President Wilson made it clear that he was opposed to military trial of sedition and espionage cases as unconstitutional and bad policy. Congress, this time, took the initiative. The various treason laws in force at the outbreak of war were supplemented and reinforced by the Espionage Act of 1917[80] and the stringent sedition law amendment thereto, as well as by statutes such as the Selective Service Act[81] and the Trading with the Enemy Act.[82] They made it a penal offense not only to aid the enemy in any way but also to "willfully utter, print, write, or publish any disloyal, scurrilous, or abusive language" about the American form of government, the Constitution, the President, or the flag, bringing these "into contempt or disrespect." It was through governmental prosecution in the federal courts that these sweeping measures were enforced and disloyalty or sedition punished. All demands for censorship were defeated because the existing statutes were considered adequate for this purpose.

With a new crisis approaching, the existing laws against treason, sedition, and subversion were no longer considered adequate and, therefore, were supplemented by the Alien Registration Act of 1940.[83] This statute, necessitated by the fear and discovery of extensive fascist activities and propaganda among minority groups in the United States, went further than its prede-

[77] See First War Powers Act, 55 Stat. 838 (1941); Emergency Price Control Act, 56 Stat. 23 (1942); War Labor Disputes Act, 57 Stat. 163 (1943).
[78] For further details, see Appendix V of Study 4, Defense.
[79] 12 Stat. 284 (1861).
[80] 40 Stat. 75 (1917).
[81] 40 Stat. 76 (1917).
[82] 40 Stat. 411 (1917).
[83] 54 Stat. 670 (1940).

cessor and was aimed directly at subversive influences in advocating, leading, or advising the necessity or desirability of overthrowing the government by force, violence, or assassination of certain individuals. These conspiracies were considered to have created such a "clear and present danger" as to justify their suppression.

Congressional investigating committees have for a long time been another device to protect the constitutional order against maladministration or threats from within. Judiciously handled, this important weapon of Congressional control would go a long way toward rendering any emergency administration more effective and responsible.

The most recent measure, the Internal Security Act of 1950,[84] gives fresh application to the registration device. Though this type of law may not lead organizations to register themselves with the authorities, it may open the way to prosecution for non-registration. The Act attempts to cover those subversive activities which cannot be reached by the Alien Registration Act and the Smith Act,[85] each of which deals with wrongs in terms of advocating the overthrow of the government. By enunciating the theory of governmental power in terms of self-protection of the state, it curtails some of the basic constitutional freedoms. The test by which proscribed acts are to be judged seems to be that of "clear and present danger" (§4a). This obviously involves considerable difficulties for application and enforcement of the Act. Under the Smith Act, the prosecution has but to show that there has been willful advocacy to overthrow the government by force and violence.[86] The Internal Security Act of 1950, however, requires the prosecution to prove that at a particular time the intent of the conspiracy was to implant in the United States a *foreign*-controlled dictatorship. The statute delegates to the Subversive Activities Control Board not only the duty to decide inclusion or exclusion within the Act, but also an exercise of discretion which may be beyond the scope of a non-Congressional and non-judicial body.

[84] 64 Stat. 987 (1950).
[85] The Smith Act was passed in 1940 as part of the Alien Registration Act and consists substantially of certain portions of the Espionage Act of 1917. See Dennis v. United States, 341 U.S. 494 (1951); and see Dunne v. United States, 138 F.2d 137 (8th Cir. 1943), *cert. denied,* 320 U.S. 790 (1943).
[86] See Cases cited in note 85, above.

STUDY 14

Overseas Territories

I. INTRODUCTION

Federal systems distribute power between central and local authorities. Overseas and other dependent territories are usually primarily administered from the metropolitan center. Their government represents the will of the administering power, not that of the people of the territory. Thus, they are not equal members of the federation, and they occupy a somewhat anomalous position in the federal system. Yet, four of the federations studied here, with Switzerland the only exception, have or at least had in the past dependencies. Some of these possessions belonged to the member States before the federation was established. Others were acquired by the federation itself. In no case, after the establishment of the federation, did member States maintain control over dependencies for more than a period of transition.

Among the members of the European Community are some of the most important colonial powers, past and present. Consequently, their reservoir of experience with dependencies is clearly greater than that of the federal systems studied here. Still, the latter had some experiences and faced certain situations significantly different from those of the members of the European Community. Although the unequal nature of relations between the metropolitan power and the dependency makes the former act in many ways similar to a unitary state, there would seem to be, in the nature of the federation, ways of handling diversity and habits of distributing power likely to influence in a subtle and complex fashion the policies of the federal metropolitan power toward its dependencies. But perhaps the colonial origin and the long democratic tradition of the three English-speaking federations have been more important factors in that respect than their federal nature. Imperial Germany, while a federal system, pursued colonial policies not unlike those of other European powers which were unitary states.

Since World War II, on the other hand, European colonial powers have tended to move in the direction of a federal restructuring of their imperial systems. Their experience, although relatively recent, is bound to influence the decisions of the European Community at least as much as the record of older federal systems.

This study examines the practices of Australia, Canada, and the United States concerning their overseas and other dependent territories. The experience of Germany from 1884 to 1919 is also considered, where relevant, but it occupies only a minor part, as the German colonial record offers little of special importance to a study of federalist policies and practices.

The first part of this study examines the place of overseas territories and other dependencies in federal systems and the directions in which such dependencies move, away from purely colonial administration.

The second part of this study reviews how federations acquired dependencies, from their member States or from outside the federal system, by the various methods known in international law.

The third part of this study is concerned with the government of overseas territories and other dependencies of federal systems.

II. NATURE AND STATUS OF FEDERAL DEPENDENCIES

The title of this study relies on geographic criteria. The term "overseas territories" is currently much used, but it lacks the precision of more technical concepts. Although all non-self-governing territories connected with members of the European Community are overseas, some such extra-European lands are an integral part of the metropolitan country, from a constitutional point of view. And in the case of the federations studied here some of their dependencies were, and still are, not overseas but contiguous, continental.

A. *Territories Heading Toward Full Membership in the Federation*

When the thirteen American colonies joined in a Confederation in 1776 and declared their independence, some of them had claims to western territories which were at that time hardly distinguishable from colonial interests. By 1912, with the admission of New Mexico and Arizona into the Union, the process had been completed by which territories forming a contiguous mass of land with the existing States matured into full members of the Union. All remaining dependencies of the United States were insular possessions, with the exception of Alaska, separated from the United States by the Canadian Northwest. At present, one of these overseas territories, Hawaii, is in the process of becoming the forty-ninth member of the Union. On March 10, 1953, the House of Representatives passed a bill (H.R. 3575) providing statehood for Hawaii and after passage by the Senate Hawaii will then be the first overseas territory to become a full member of the American federal system.

In the case of Canada, Rupert's Land and the Northwest Territory were transferred to the Dominion by Imperial order-in-council in June, 1870. Out of these federal territories, governed by the Dominion government, Alberta and Saskatchewan were set up in 1905 as Provinces, becoming equal members of the federation.

B. *Territories Heading Toward Independence*

The United States acquired a dominion beyond the seas when Hawaii passed formally under the jurisdiction of the United States in August, 1898. A few months later, by the treaty of peace signed in Paris on December 10, 1898, Spain ceded to the United States the Philippine Islands, Guam, and Puerto Rico. It might be significant for the flexibility of a federal system that each of these three dependencies has followed a different line of development in the past decades.

The Philippines achieved independence on July 4, 1946. This was already anticipated by the first commission sent out to investigate conditions in the Philippines, in January, 1899, by President McKinley. Significantly it reported that the Filipinos were not ready for independence, due to their "lack of education and political experience, combined with their racial and linguistic diversities." But concern with independence was already present. The Jones Act of August 29, 1916,[1] contained an important declaration of policy in its preamble, which stated that it was and had always been "the purpose of the people of the United States to withdraw their sovereignty over the Philippine Islands and to recognize their independence as soon as a capable government can be established therein."

The Tydings-McDuffie Act of March 24, 1934,[2] the result of pressures and counterpressures too complex to be related here, but in which special economic interests played their part, started the Philippines on the road to independence. A constitution was adopted in 1935 and a period of transition of ten years was to lead to complete independence by July 4, 1946. This was achieved despite the intervening war and Japanese occupation. During the transition period the new political entity was known as the Commonwealth of the Philippines.

No other dependency of any of the federal systems studied here has followed a similar path.

C. *The Special Case of Puerto Rico*

On July 25, 1952, the Commonwealth of Puerto Rico came into existence. Its status is different both from that of Hawaii, soon to be a full member of the American federal system, and from that of the Philippines, which are no longer either governed by or a part of the federation. In Puerto Rico, federal authorities and agencies operate as fully as in the forty-eight States, but the Puerto Ricans lack full Congressional representation and are excluded from the Presidential elections. Yet their new achieved status has great symbolic effect, as it is the result of a compact with the United States

[1] 39 Stat. 545–556.
[2] 48 Stat. 456–465.

and they now govern themselves under an instrument of their own fashioning.[3]

Public Law No. 600 of 1950,[4] basis of the new relationship between the Commonwealth of Puerto Rico and the United States, is explicitly based on the assumption that the fundamental relation between Puerto Rico and the United States will remain unchanged. The 1952 Constitution of Puerto Rico affirms in its preamble that the Commonwealth is created "within our union with the United States of America." When the General Assembly of the United Nations debated, in November, 1953, the question whether Puerto Rico has ceased to be a non-self-governing territory, the American delegate stated in the name of the President of the United States that he would support in Congress a request by the Puerto Rican Legislature for full independence, following which the United Nations confirmed that Puerto Rico can no longer be considered a dependency.

The new status of Puerto Rico is not only an unprecedented development within the constitutional structure of the United States, but it is also a novelty within the history of Western constitutionalism in its entirety. Algeria, with which it can in some way be compared, has a much more limited sphere of autonomy, but also greater participation in the government of metropolitan France.

The status of Puerto Rico creates a new dimension of the federal principle, in that it places the old principle of "unity with diversity" on a new basis. It thus conceivably provides a striking model for future developments in the sphere of the liberation of colonial peoples who do not wish or may not be able to organize themselves as independent political communities.[5]

D. *Other Dependencies of Federal Systems*

Territories which are not heading toward independence, statehood, or commonwealth, have to be lumped together into a residual category. This would include other insular possessions of the United States like Guam, American Samoa, and the Virgin Islands, too small in territory and population to expect a different status in the foreseeable future. It would also include wide but almost uninhabited areas like the Canadian Northwest Territories and the Yukon, and the Australian Northern Territory and Antarctic Territory. It would also include a territory like Papua-New Guinea, relatively large in population and territory, but culturally unlikely to become a civilized self-governing political entity in the next few generations. Part of the latter territory, administered as a unit by federal Australian authorities, is a trust territory held from the United Nations, and so is the

[3] Emerson, "Puerto Rico and American Policy Toward Dependent Areas," 285 The Annals, 9 (1953).

[4] 64 Stat. 319.

[5] Friedrich, "The World Significance of the New Constitution," in *Puerto Rico: A Study in Democratic Development, The Annals,* January, 1953.

American Trust Territory of the Pacific. Both represent a special case, as under international law they cannot become integral parts of the administering federations.

E. *Conclusion*

If the various dependencies mentioned above were to be administered by unitary states and not by federal systems, it is unlikely that their government would be significantly different in form, although differences in spirit along the lines mentioned above might appear to a shrewd observer.

In a unitary state, in which the executive branch of the government is centralized, the lack of local self-government in dependent territories may be less striking than in a federal system which has a good deal of local self-government, whereas the unitary state might provide more easily for representation of dependencies in the central legislature than a federal system in which such representation raises sensitive problems of balance between the component parts of the Union.

III. TRANSMISSION AND ACQUISITION OF TITLE OVER DEPENDENCIES

Of the five federations studied, three had no problems concerning the treatment of overseas territories and other dependencies at the time of the establishment of the federation. The other two, the United States and Australia, had to reach decisions about the dependencies of their member States. They exemplify two different situations, namely, reluctance to transmit title to the federation, in the case of the United States, and eagerness to get other members of the federal system to share the burdens of colonial rule, in the Australian case.

A. *Member States Wanting to Maintain Title over Dependencies*

The problem of dependent territories was a major source of difficulty in the crucial years of loose union preceding the adoption of the Constitution of the United States in 1787. The elimination of this obstacle to a more perfect union, during the period of the Continental Congress, facilitated the work of the Federal Convention assembled at Philadelphia.

In the summer of 1776 the committee appointed "to prepare and digest the form of a confederation" faced, as one of the three most important questions, whether the States which laid claim to large tracts of unsettled land in the West were to be permitted to utilize those lands for their own expansion or profit, or be required to place them in the common stock for the behoof of the Union. While Virginia stood stoutly upon the position that it "owns to the South Sea," Maryland took the position that "no Colony has a right to go to the South Sea." No agreement was reached, for almost four years.

After repeated discussions and negotiations, public opinion had matured early in 1780 to the point that observers recorded "a violent inclination in most of the states to appropriate all the western lands to the use of the United States." In February, 1780, the New York legislature passed an act designed "especially to accelerate the federal alliance" by relinquishing for the benefit of the United States some part of its western lands. This led to renewed discussions in Congress in September, 1780, in the hope that other States would follow the example of New York. On October 10, 1780, it was resolved:

That the unappropriated lands that may be added or relinquished to the United States, by any particular state . . . shall be disposed of for the common benefit of the United States and be settled and formed into distinct republican states, which shall become members of the federal union, and have the same rights of sovereignty, freedom and independence, as the other states . . .

This proposition, offered by the Virginia delegates, established one of the basic principles of American expansion across the continent. The same month, Connecticut came forward with a cession of territory, and in January, 1781, the Virginia assembly passed an act ceding to the United States the territory northwest of the Ohio River.

These belated concessions to Maryland's demands, as well as a word of admonition from the French minister, Luzerne, to whom Maryland had applied for aid in defending the Chesapeake Bay against the British sea power, succeeded. Early in February, 1781, the assembly of Maryland authorized the State's delegate in Congress to subscribe the Articles of Confederation and the final ratification solemnly took place on March 1.

From 1781 to 1784, although at wide intervals, Congress debated if the cessions of Virginia, New York, and Connecticut should be accepted with the conditions named in the cessions, or if those States should be asked to make their cessions conform to the recommendations of Congress of October 10, 1780. Eventually, in 1784, Virginia's deed of cession was accepted and an act, drafted by a committee of which Jefferson was chairman, outlined a plan for territorial government which became the core of the system adopted in the famous ordinance of July 13, 1787. At that time the Philadelphia Convention was already assembled, but the drafters of the Constitution were spared the solution of one thorny problem.

B. *Member States Willing to Transmit Title to the Federation*

While in the case of the United States those members of the federal system which had territorial possessions wanted to keep them to themselves, as the lands seemed of great promise, in the case of Australia the opposite appears to have been the case. Dependencies, arid or savage lands, were burdens that the administering States were quite willing to see carried by the federal system as a whole.

According to Lord Bryce, one of the earliest events which evoked a Pan-Australian feeling and indicated objects fit to be secured by a united Australian government, was the opposition in 1883 of Lord Derby, then Secretary of State for the Colonies, to the occupation of the neighboring island of New Guinea, which Australian opinion desired to see British. Yet several years passed, after the inauguration of the Commonwealth of Australia, before that part of New Guinea which had meanwhile been occupied by Queensland was taken over by the federation.

Reluctantly, and only after the Australian colonies had assumed financial responsibilities, a British protectorate over that part of New Guinea which became known as the Territory of Papua was proclaimed in November, 1884. Under the New Guinea and Pacific Jurisdiction and Contribution Act, 1884, the Australian colonies, New Zealand, and Fiji agreed to contribute varying amounts, to a total of £15,000 a year, to meet the expenses of establishing control over Papua. But the special commissioner appointed by the Colonial Office encountered difficulties in collecting the agreed revenue. South Australia withdrew after a year. Fiji was soon excused. Then Western Australia, Tasmania, and New Zealand dropped out.

Three colonies, New South Wales, Victoria, and Queensland, were left to carry the burden. In 1887 their representatives convened in London to arrange the conditions under which annexation of the protectorate should take place. While Queensland was to perform and proclaim the annexation, the other two interested colonies pledged to reimburse Queensland for two thirds of the annual administrative expenses of Papua. Thus the territory became a dependency of Queensland.

After the proclamation of the Commonwealth, in 1901, Australia granted the territory an annual subsidy, although it remained under the control of the Governor of Queensland for some time. Finally, in 1905, the Australian Parliament passed legislation placing the territory under exclusively federal control, and after September 1, 1906, the Territory of Papua was administered by a Lieutenant-Governor. The delay was not due to reluctance on the part of the federation to assume responsibility, but to the fact that the time of statesmen and of parliamentarians was fully occupied in considering and passing laws for the amalgamation of the various colonies into one Commonwealth. In the rush of business, New Guinea was relegated to a secondary place.

The vast and arid Northern Territory of Australia is another interesting case. Covering 523,620 square miles, or 17.5 per cent of the whole continental area, it had only 4850 inhabitants, or .07 per cent of the total population, at the 1933 census. It was handed over by the State of South Australia to the Commonwealth in 1911. After an attempt to subdivide it into two parts, it has been administered since 1931 as one Commonwealth territory. Deficits of £4 million were taken over from South Australia by the Commonwealth in 1911, and the total cost of the territory to the federation amounted to £9 million by 1926. Clearly it has been advantageous to the State of South Australia to shift the burden of responsibility for this dependency to the whole.

The Northern Territory Acceptance Act, 1910, and the Northern Territory (Administration) Act, 1910, passed by the Commonwealth Parliament in accordance with Section 122 of the Constitution, continued in effect in the Northern Territory, as laws of the Commonwealth, the laws of South Australia, including those concerning taxation.[6]

A smaller territory, Norfolk Island, a dependency of New South Wales since 1856, was similarly accepted as a territory of Australia in 1913, twelve years after the establishment of the Commonwealth.

Yet there is an exception. In 1926 Western Australia refused an offer to be relieved of the burden of the northwestern part of her territory, which is in many ways similar to the contiguous Northern Territory, ceded by South Australia.

C. *Continued Administration by a Member State of a Federal System*

As indicated above, the Territory of Papua remained under the administration of Queensland from the inauguration of the Commonwealth of Australia on January 1, 1901, until September 1, 1906. This would be one of the very few cases in which temporarily a member State continued to administer dependencies after the establishment of a federal system.

The other such case is the one, also mentioned above, of Norfolk Island, administered by the Governor of New South Wales, as a dependency of the latter state, until 1913.

The Northern Territory was not a dependency but an integral part of South Australia until it was taken over by the Commonwealth and administered as a federal territory, in 1910.

A special case is that of Labrador, which from 1927 to 1949 was considered a dependency of Newfoundland. Its very small population made permanent governmental agencies unnecessary, but it was administered from the capital of Newfoundland, St. John's. After the union between Canada and Newfoundland, Labrador became an integral part of what is, since 1949, the tenth Province of the Dominion. Therefore, the territory, which had been, until 1927, the object of a dispute between Canada and Newfoundland, neither became federal territory nor did it remain the dependency of the State.

The record indicates that in the two federal systems the members of which had dependencies at the time of the formation of the new community, control over such dependencies, whether contiguous or overseas territories, was eventually assumed by the central government, both in situations where it was advantageous and in situations where it was burdensome to do so.

[6] Cf. Buchanan v. Commonwealth, [1913] 16 C.L.R. 315; 19 A.L.R. 251.

D. *Territorial Acquisitions by Federal Systems*

Four of the five federations studied acquired dependencies after they came into existence. In so doing their actions were not different from those of unitary states facing similar problems. Acquisition of new territories, which were not incorporated, but administered as dependencies, was carried out by the central government, which has in all federations major or even exclusive control over foreign affairs. The government of the new acquisition then became an extension of federal powers, often military at first, then civilian.

In the case of the federations studied here, the earliest such acquisition was the Louisiana Purchase, the Sesquicentennial of which was celebrated in 1953 in the United States. War with Mexico leading to the Treaty of Guadalupe Hidalgo of February 2, 1848, resulted in the cession of Texas, New Mexico (including Arizona), and Upper California. Purchase from Russia in 1867 brought Alaska under American sovereignty. The burst of imperialism of 1898 added overseas territories which have since followed destinies as different as those of the Philippines, Puerto Rico, Hawaii, and Guam. This by no means exhaustive list of American territorial acquisitions shows that the United States used a diversity of methods recognized by international law, in acquiring dependencies.

Of the two federations which belong to the British Commonwealth, Canada acquired territories only by having placed under the authority of the Dominion lands which were already under the British Crown, but had previously been held by the Hudson's Bay Company under its charter of 1670 and by license of 1821. Australia acquired possessions by occupation, as in the case of Papua, by proclamation, namely the Antarctic Territory in 1936, and by Mandate Agreements with the League of Nations, followed by Trusteeship Agreements with the United Nations, in the case of the former German colonies, New Guinea and Nauru.

The German Reich had no overseas territories before 1871, but acquired extended possessions in Africa and the Pacific after 1884 by the usual diplomatic devices of imperialism, signing protectorate agreements with native chiefs.

IV. GOVERNMENT OF OVERSEAS TERRITORIES AND OTHER DEPENDENCIES

A. *Constitutional Provisions*

The Constitutions of Australia, Canada, and the United States all include provisions authorizing the federation to provide for the government of dependent territories and for the admission of new member States. In addition, those of Australia and Canada authorize the federation to provide for the representation of such territories in the federal legislature; in the United

States, this power has been exercised by Congress despite the absence of a specific constitutional grant. The Australian Constitution further refers to the surrender of territories by the States to the federation.

In the Constitution of the United States, Article IV, Section 3, provides:

> The Congress shall have Power to dispose of and make all needful Rules and Regulations respecting the Territory or other Property belonging to the United States . . .

No similar provision appeared in the first of the acts of the Imperial Parliament which form the Constitution of Canada. The British North America Act of 1871 filled this gap, in Section 4:

> The Parliament of Canada may from Time to Time make Provision for the Administration, Peace, Order and good Government of any Territory not for the Time being included in any Province.

To this, the British North America Act of 1886 added in Section 1:

> The Parliament of Canada may, from Time to Time, make Provisions for the Representation in the Senate and House of Commons of Canada, or in either of them, of any Territories which for the Time being form Part of the Dominion of Canada, but are not included in any Province thereof.

The Australian Constitution, drawing on American and Canadian experience, defined the powers of the Commonwealth in Section 122:

> The Parliament may make laws for the government of any territory surrendered by any State and accepted by the Commonwealth, or of any territory placed by the Queen under the authority of and accepted by the Commonwealth, or otherwise acquired by the Commonwealth, and may allow the representation of such territory in either House of the Parliament to the extent and on the terms which it thinks fit.

As the texts clearly indicate, the federation has much broader powers with regard to its dependencies than over its member States. The German *Schutzgebietsgesetz* of 1900 gave wide powers of colonial government to the Emperor, in the absence of specific provisions in the 1871 Constitution.

B. *Legislative Powers*

Constitutional provisions give the federal legislature large powers over dependencies, as indicated by the respective paragraphs quoted above. Whereas, in the case of full members of the federal system, legislative powers are divided between the central legislature and the State legislatures, some of the dependencies do not participate at all in the legislative process. The

extreme case would be that of a territory without a legislature of its own
and with no representation in the federal legislature, like the German
colonies before 1919. Such was also, until recently, the case of Papua-New
Guinea, where a Legislative Council, including three elected members, was
formally inaugurated on November 26, 1951. The Territory has no representative in the Parliament of the Commonwealth.

More frequent now is the case of territories which have an elected legislature, or a partly elected and partly appointed legislative council, but are
not in any fashion represented in the federal Parliament. The Virgin Islands and Guam, among American overseas territories, would fall in this
category. It would also include all Australian dependencies with the exception of the Northern Territory, as well as the Canadian Northwest
Territories.

A step further toward equal status in the federation is the existence of
a voteless representative in the federal legislature. Alaska, Hawaii, and
Puerto Rico are represented in Congress by elected Resident Commissioners,
voteless but influential on matters concerning their territory. The Philippines had such a representative before independence. In addition these
territories have elected legislatures with wide authority over a variety of
local matters.

The Australian Northern Territory sends one representative to the federal
Parliament, but he has a vote only on issues concerning his electorate. In
1947 a Legislative Council was set up, with eight appointed and six elected
members. It participates therefore somewhat more than the American
territories represented by Resident Commissioners or Delegates, in the federal legislative process, but has a less representative territorial legislature.

Finally the Yukon together with parts of the Northwest Territories forms
an electoral district for the Canadian Parliament. Its elected representative
is a full and equal member of the Dominion's House of Commons.

If Hawaii achieves statehood during the current session of the United
States Congress, it will then elect, in 1954, two United States Senators and
one or two members of the United States House of Representatives, while
the bicameral legislature of the Territory will continue to function in the
new State with its present structure, but without the possibility for the
United States Congress to change or abolish it by amending the Hawaiian
organic act. While legally the United States Congress can now interfere
drastically in the government of a territory like Hawaii, in fact in the whole
history of the Territory it has never even vetoed laws enacted by the
territorial legislature. That this is not an exception is suggested by another
case. The Governor of Puerto Rico wrote on January 17, 1953, in an official letter to the President of the United States: "In the entire fifty-four
years' history of United States administration of Puerto Rico, Congress did
not in any instance exercise its power to annul or amend an Act of the
Puerto Rican legislature.[7]

[7] Information transmitted by the United States to the United Nations, March 20, 1953.

C. *Executive Powers*

Even in dependencies which are quite advanced on the road toward self-government, having a fully elected legislature, the executive power is responsible to and an expression of the will of the metropolitan government. As it does not express the will of the people and is not responsible to the local electorate, such territorial executive is clearly not a form of representative government.

In many ways, not the least from a symbolic point of view, a very important distinction appears when the appointed governor is a native or at least a resident of the territory. In the case of Hawaii, the Governor must have been a resident of the Territory for at least three years preceding his appointment. In Puerto Rico, the first important step toward the present new status of Commonwealth was the appointment, in 1946, of a native as Governor of Puerto Rico, who in addition had previously been the elected Resident Commissioner in Washington. But in most cases the governor is the symbol of "alien rule" in the dependency.

In the special case of the Commonwealth of Puerto Rico, the Governor is popularly elected and the heads of all executive departments are appointed by the Governor, with the advice and consent of the Puerto Rican Senate. Neither the President of the United States nor the United States Senate participate in any way in the appointment of any official of the government of the Commonwealth.

D. *Judiciary Powers*

In three cases studied, the court of last resort for the overseas territory or dependency is the supreme court of the federal system. In Imperial Germany the colonial judiciary was not part of the Reich's system. In most cases, the judicial, like the executive, branch of the government is responsible to the federal government rather than to the people of the territory.

Federations generally have two judicial systems, one for cases under State law, the other for federal cases. While this is in accordance with the logic of the federal system, there are, of course, instances of concurrent jurisdiction and other deviations from a rigorously logical pattern. In the case of dependencies, some approximate fairly closely the state-federal patterns, while others have institutions for which the explanation is historical rather than logical.

Among American dependencies, the Philippines had and Hawaii and Puerto Rico have each its system of courts with a supreme court at the top and lesser courts in appropriate numbers and grades. Hawaii and Puerto Rico have each, in addition, a United States district court to try cases under the Constitution or laws of the United States. In Alaska and the Virgin Islands similar United States courts handle both federal and local cases. There was no United States court in the Philippines; local courts enforced applicable federal laws. Cases involving United States law and major cases of other kinds could be appealed from the highest local courts to federal circuit courts of appeals in the United States or to the United States Supreme Court, depending upon circumstances.[8]

In the Philippines, Justices of the Supreme Court were appointed, like all federal judges, by the President of the United States with the consent of the Senate, judges of the courts of first instance by the Governor. In Hawaii, justices of the supreme and circuit courts are appointed by the President of the United States, whereas district judges are named by the Chief Justice of the Territory.

Public Law No. 600, of 1950, the Puerto Rican Federal Relations Act, preserved, among others, the sections of the Organic Act of 1917 which refer to the Federal District Court in Puerto Rico and the relations between the insular and federal judicial systems. United States statutory laws apply in Puerto Rico as in the United States, except tax laws. The 1952 Constitution provides in Article V, Section 3, that "the Supreme Court shall be the court of last resort in Puerto Rico," and in Section 8 that "judges shall be appointed by the Governor with the advice and consent of the Senate." But this refers only to the local judiciary and leaves intact Puerto Rico's place in the federal system.

In the Northern Territory of Australia the federal judiciary has a special position, as the supreme court of the Commonwealth, the High Court of Australia, has held that the Supreme Court of the Northern Territory is not a federal court within the meaning of the Constitution, but a special court created by Parliament in the exercise of its powers under Section 122 of the Constitution.

E. Defense and Foreign Affairs

Since defense and foreign affairs are among the main *raisons d'être* of a federal system, they are usually responsibilities of the federal government, even if member States in some cases have their own military establishments and diplomatic representation. With regard to dependent territories, even protectorates which presumably enjoy a good deal of self-government entrust their foreign relations and defense to the metropolitan power.

Some non-self-governing territories have been in the past members of the League of Nations and some still are members of various specialized agencies of the United Nations. No such instance exists in the case of the federal systems studied here. Their overseas territories and dependencies are all represented in international affairs by the federal government.

While the military forces of the German Reich from 1871 to 1919 were provided by the member States, the colonial army was specially recruited and maintained by the Reich itself, under the authority of the Colonial Office.

[8] Cf. Pratt, *America's Colonial Experiment* 165–166 (1950).

In the Canadian territories even local police functions are entrusted to the federal Royal Canadian Mounted Police.

F. *Public Finances and Customs*

"No taxation without representation" has become an important tenet of Western political doctrine and as such is used to justify claims for equal status by various dependent territories. Perhaps the most convincing argument for Hawaii and Alaska statehood has been the fact that the two territories are subject to federal taxation. At the recent hearings on statehood for Hawaii, the Territory's Delegate pointed out that it "consistently pays into the United States Treasury considerably larger amounts than the Federal government, excluding expenditures for national defense, has spent in the Territory." [9]

Before the United States government decided, on January 19, 1953, to cease to transmit information on Puerto Rico to the United Nations under Article 73(e) of the Charter, the question was raised if Puerto Rico had really ceased to be a non-self-governing territory. Although it clearly did not enjoy "representation without discrimination in the central legislative organs," namely in the Congress of the United States, under Resolution 567 (VI) of the United Nations such representation appears as an important criterion in determining which territories come under the provision of Article 73 of the Charter. Although the argument was not used by the government of the United States, previously it had been suggested that Puerto Rico's lack of representation in Congress could be justified on the ground that it is not subject to federal taxation and therefore this is not a case of "taxation without representation." [10]

Puerto Rico's exemption from federal income taxes and the fact that it secures return to its treasury of custom duties collected under the United States tariff can only be explained historically. Neither Alaska nor Hawaii benefits from similar advantages, nor do the Virgin Islands; all three dependencies pay taxes collected under federal internal revenue laws and the sums obtained are not returned to the insular treasury.

In more typically colonial territories, like American Samoa or Papua-New Guinea, local government is in part supported by a poll tax levied on every adult male.

Dependencies are usually within the tariff wall of the metropolitan power or at least a preferential system is established. As Canada does not have overseas territories, a unitary tariff and customs administration applies to Provinces and territories alike. On the other hand each German colony had

[9] House Subcommittee on Territories and Insular Possessions, Hearings on H.R. 21, etc., 83d Cong., 1st Sess. 61 (1953).

[10] Cf. Emerson, "Puerto Rico and American Policy Toward Dependent Areas," 285 *The Annals* 4 (1953). See also March 20, 1953, Memorandum by the Government of the United States concerning Puerto Rico.

its own tariff, and no preferential system was created. The United States illustrates a variety of problems of some interest to the present discussion.

American Samoa is the only American dependency to which a preferential system could not be extended, under an 1899 tripartite treaty. A duty was collected on imports from the United States, equal to the duty paid by imports from foreign shores.

The Panama Canal Zone is technically not a United States possession and is treated as foreign soil in respect to the tariff. Goods imported into the United States from the Zone pay the regular tariff rates. Imports into the Zone for the use of the administration and its employees pay no duty regardless of origin.

All the other territories commanded, after the Payne-Aldrich Tariff Act of 1909, a free market in the United States. Imports from abroad paid the regular metropolitan duties in Alaska, Hawaii, and Puerto Rico, duties fixed by the Philippine government in the Philippines, and by the naval administration in Guam and Samoa.

In Puerto Rico the tariff rates on foreign imports are the same as in the United States, but customs collections are covered into Puerto Rico's Treasury, not into the Treasury of the United States. The arrangement can be interpreted as a customs union between Puerto Rico and the United States, on the basis of the United States tariff.[11]

The present elected Governor and political leader of Puerto Rico, Luis Muñoz-Marín, has explained that a study of the history of Philippine emancipation convinced him that free trade between Puerto Rico and the United States could not be continued if Puerto Rico were an independent nation, due to the existence of most-favored-nation clauses in trade treaties to which the United States is a party. This determined him to "devise creatively a realistically free form of political status which would not be at war with the solution of the economic problems of Puerto Rico and yet would protect the dignity of our people within our association with the American Union."[12]

According to the trade provisions of the Tydings-McDuffie Act of 1934, the Philippines were to be treated in every way as a foreign country after achieving independence on July 4, 1946. The Philippine Trade Act of 1946 [13] provided for complete free trade between the United States and the Philippines until July 3, 1954, but set quotas upon American importations from the Philippines of sugar, cordage, rice, cigars, tobacco, coconut oil, and shell or pearl buttons. The quotas were to be reduced 5 per cent annually, reaching zero in 1974. For sugar, tariff duties of 5 per cent of the regular rates were to be applied, increasing by 5 per cent annually, to reach the full rate in 1974. Thus the Philippine Trade Act of 1946 allows an adjustment period of twenty years.

[11] Fernos-Isern, "From Colony to Commonwealth," 285 *The Annals* 22 (1953).
[12] Muñoz-Marín, "Development Through Democracy," 285 *The Annals* 5 (1953).
[13] 60 Stat. 141–159.

G. *Citizenship*

Under the organic acts of the two territories, citizens of Alaska and Hawaii were declared to be citizens of the United States. Citizenship was extended to Puerto Ricans in 1917 and they remain citizens of the United States under the new Commonwealth. Citizenship was granted to the Virgin Islanders in 1927 and to the inhabitants of Guam in 1950. The 1902 organic act for the Philippines declared the inhabitants of the islands who had been Spanish subjects on April 11, 1899, and who continued to reside there, to be citizens of the Philippine Islands. Abroad they were entitled to the protection of the United States as "nationals." Citizens of all territories and possessions of the United States are not treated as "aliens" as the term is defined by immigration laws and are free to come to the United States or to move from one territory to another. After the institution of the Commonwealth, in 1935, the Filipinos were legally aliens. Free immigration is another very important advantage maintained by Puerto Rico under its 1952 Constitution.

The Australian Nationality and Citizenship Act, 1948, which repealed all previous Commonwealth legislation on this subject, automatically gave Australian citizenship, among other categories, to persons who were British subjects and were born in New Guinea. Thus Papuan aborigines are now Australian citizens.

Canada raises no special problems, as her dependencies are within the continental limits of the Dominion, and under the Canadian Citizenship Act of 1947 all persons born in the Dominion are natural-born Canadians.

German colonies were not considered part of the territory of the Reich, under the 1871 Constitution, and citizenship was only granted to inhabitants of the colonies in special instances.

V. CONCLUSION

It is rather difficult to apply directly the experience of the federal systems studied in the preceding pages to the problems of the European Community. In surveying briefly the overseas territories of the members of the European Community, Appendix V to this study illustrates the complexity of problems and situations involved. In the case of the three English-speaking federations examined, major dependencies were ultimately incorporated into the federal system, following their settlement by sufficient numbers of immigrants. Their colonial dependencies are few. They are administered by the metropolitan power in ways not really different from those of unitary states possessing colonies. That the spirit of a federal system induces greater respect and understanding for diversity is a plausible assumption, but the point cannot be demonstrated in truly convincing fashion.

Perhaps the main conclusion of this study would be that, whatever the advantages or disadvantages for them, federal systems had to assume full responsibility for dependencies. Even where such considerations were less pressing than in the situations facing the European Community, the federal systems' tasks regarding foreign affairs and defense made federal colonial administration an unavoidable consequence. Burdens and advantages had to be shared by the federal system as a whole.

From this study one can conclude that the major problems with respect to overseas territories in a European Political Community will concern: (1) defense and foreign affairs, (2) trade and economic development, (3) administration and financial support.

If the member States retain responsibility for the defense of their present dependencies, inconsistencies may arise between State policies and the defense policies of the Community. And, in view of the scope of modern defense activities, these may involve inconsistencies in fiscal, economic, and foreign policies. On the other hand, where the burden of defense of a dependency is considerable, the other member States of the Community may be reluctant to share it.

Closely related to the problem of defense is that of participation in trade with and economic development of dependent territories, for sharing the burden of defense may move the member States to claim a share in trade and development. Even where defense constitutes no appreciable problem, it may be felt that the area of the Community's common market should include overseas territories.

The third principal problem concerning the status of overseas territories in a European Community is the responsibility for their administration and for the necessary financial support. This is of course tied in with the two questions discussed above, for the authority which has responsibility for defense of a territory, or which shares in its trade and development, will want assurance against inconsistent measures of local government. Conversely, where a territory represents a financial liability, the authority, State or federal, which bears that liability will feel entitled to a strong voice in trade and development policies.

A P P E N D I X I

Australia

When the Commonwealth of Australia was inaugurated on January 1, 1901 (by an Act of the British Parliament of July 9, 1900, 63 & 64 Vict. 1, c. 12), some of the six member States of the federation possessed dependent territories both within and outside the Australian continent. Since then, all such territories have been placed under the authority of the Commonwealth, with the exception of Lord Howe Island, which forms an electoral district of New South Wales and whose inhabitants pay the taxes of that State.

Section 122 of the Australian Constitution defines the powers of the Commonwealth regarding dependent territories. It provides:

> The Parliament may make laws for the government of any territory surrendered by any State and accepted by the Commonwealth, or of any territory placed by the Queen under the authority of and accepted by the Commonwealth, or otherwise acquired by the Commonwealth, and may allow the representation of such territory in either House of the Parliament to the extent and on the terms which it thinks fit.

With the exception of the Australian Capital Territory, which is administered by the Minister for the Interior, all territories are administered by the Department of Territories in Canberra. Traditionally, one distinguishes between "internal" and "external" territories.

I. INTERNAL TERRITORIES

The territories referred to in Section 122 which are located within the geographic limits of the Australian continent are considered "internal," or, more recently, "territories of the Commonwealth." The Australian Capital Territory, created for the special purpose of providing a "neutral" seat for the federal government, is one such "internal" territory. The other "internal" territory, the vast and arid Northern Territory, is an interesting example of shift of control from a State to a federation. It covers 523,620 square miles, or 17.5 per cent of the continental area, but had an estimated population of only 15,500 whites in 1951 and some 13,960 full-blood and half-caste aborigines in 1950.

Incorporated in the colony of New South Wales in 1825, the Northern Territory was annexed by Royal Letters Patent to the province of South Australia in 1863. It was handed over by the State of South Australia to the Commonwealth in 1911. In connection with this transfer, deficits of £4 million were taken over from South Australia by the Commonwealth in 1911, and the total cost of the Northern Territory to the federation amounted to £9 million by 1926. Despite the advantages which accrued to the State of South Australia from the transfer of responsibility for this dependency to the federation, the State of Western Australia refused a federal offer in 1926 to be relieved of the burden of the northwestern part of its territory, similar in character to the Northern Territory.

The Northern Territory Acceptance Act, 1910, and the Northern Territory (Administration) Act, 1910, passed by the Commonwealth Parliament in accordance with Section 122 of the Constitution, continued in effect in the Northern Territory the laws of South Australia, including those concerning taxation (cf. *Buchanan v. Commonwealth,* [1913] 16 C.L.R. 315, 19 A.L.R. 251). All such laws can be altered or repealed by laws of the Commonwealth and are subject to ordinances of the Governor-General.

An ordinance of the Governor-General, No. 6 of 1913, instituted the

"Public Service of the Northern Territory," controlled by the Governor-General in Council, under the powers of the Crown. It was not affected by the Commonwealth Public Service Act, 1902–1918 (cf. *Trower v. Commonwealth*, [1924] 34 C.L.R. 587). The federal judiciary in the Northern Territory is likewise distinct from the regular federal court system. The High Court of Australia has held that the Supreme Court of the Northern Territory is not a federal court within the meaning of the Constitution, but a special court created by Parliament in the exercise of its powers under Section 122 of the Constitution (cf. *Porter v. The King; Ex parte Chin Man Yee*, [1926] 37 C.L.R. 432).

The objections of the inhabitants of the Northern Territory to the authoritarian type of government instituted there by the Commonwealth led to an investigation by a Royal Commission in 1920. With the increase in territorial population following World War II, the Northern Territory (Administration) Act of 1931 was amended in 1947 to establish a Legislative Council with power to enact ordinances for the Territory, subject to the assent of the federal Administrator.

II. EXTERNAL TERRITORIES

The "external territories" of Australia, outside the continent, are: Papua, Norfolk Island, the Australian Antarctic Territory, Ashmore and Cartier Islands, Nauru, the Territory of New Guinea, and the Cocos Islands. Some of these territories were acquired by the Commonwealth, in accordance with its powers under Section 122 of the Constitution, without having been previously under the jurisdiction of any of the member States.

Norfolk Island, a distinct and separate settlement under the jurisdiction of New South Wales since 1856, was made a dependency under the Governor of that colony in 1896 and continued to be administered as such until the passage of the Norfolk Island Act, 1913, when it was accepted by the federal Parliament as a territory of Australia. It was at first administered by the Territories Branch of the Prime Minister's Department, through an Administrator assisted, since 1935, by an Advisory Council of eight members elected by the inhabitants of the Island. At present it is under the control of the Department of Territories.

Nauru, a small insular phosphate mine, was a possession of Germany from 1888 till 1919. Since that time it has been administered by Australia on behalf of Australia, Great Britain, and New Zealand, pursuant to a mandate of the League of Nations, followed by a Trusteeship Agreement with the United Nations.

Australia asserted dominion over some 2,472,000 square miles, nearly half of the Antarctic Continent, through the Antarctic Territory Acceptance Act, 1933, brought into force by proclamation of the Governor-General in 1936.

The Cocos Islands, situated in the Indian Ocean, are also administered by Australia. Their transfer, for strategic reasons, from the government of Singapore, was announced in June, 1951.

The most important Australian dependency, in terms of population, is the eastern part of the island of New Guinea, the acquisition of which is described in some detail below. At present the two parts of this possession, the Territory of Papua and the Trust Territory of New Guinea, are governed as an Administrative Union under the Papua and New Guinea Act, 1949, which came into force on July 1, 1949. The Act declares the intention of the Commonwealth Parliament to maintain the identity and status of the Territory of Papua as a possession of the Crown and the identity and status of the Territory of New Guinea as a Trust Territory. It provides, however, for a common Executive Council appointed by the Governor-General of Australia and a common Legislative Council to consist of the Administrator, sixteen members who are civil servants ("official" members), and twelve members representing the white and native population ("non-official" members). Only three of the "non-official" members are elected, the natives being excluded from the electorate. The Legislative Council was formally inaugurated on November 26, 1951.

The territory of New Guinea was a German dependency prior to the First World War, and has been administered by Australia since that time pursuant to a mandate from the League of Nations and, since 1946, a Trusteeship Agreement with the United Nations. The New Guinea Act of September 30, 1920, provided the fundamental law of the territory. Various laws of the Commonwealth, the State of Queensland, and Great Britain, and ordinances of the Territory of Papua, were extended to the territory of New Guinea. The Trusteeship Agreement of 1946 authorized the Commonwealth "to bring the Territory into a customs, fiscal or administrative union or federation with other dependent territories under its jurisdiction or control" (Art. 5). Such a union with Papua was carried out by the Act of 1949 mentioned above.

Papua, the other part of the Administrative Union created by the 1949 Act, has an interesting history as a former dependency of the State of Queensland which came under federal control only several years after the inauguration of the Commonwealth of Australia. In 1883, Queensland took possession, in the name of the British Crown, of the portion of the island of New Guinea which became known as Papua. Following the Treaty of Berlin in 1886, which adjusted British and German colonial claims in the island of New Guinea, this territory was annexed by the Crown as the "Possession of British New Guinea."

Under an agreement then reached by Great Britain with the three colonies of New South Wales, Victoria, and Queensland, which had previously shared financial responsibility for the territory, a sum not to exceed £15,000 annually was to be provided by Queensland for the expenses of its administration. However, New South Wales and Victoria were each to reimburse Queensland for one third of the annual payment (see British New Guinea

(Queensland) Act of 1887). Queensland thus assumed direct legislative and financial responsibility. An Administrator, recommended by Queensland, was sent to Port Moresby, capital of British New Guinea. The laws of Queensland were adopted, so far as they were appropriate for the territory. Ordinance No. VII of 1902 of British New Guinea, for instance, provided that the Queensland criminal code should be the law of British New Guinea.

After the proclamation of the Commonwealth of Australia in 1901, a financial subsidy of £30,000 annually was granted to the territory by Australia. However, until March 6, 1902, British New Guinea was a Crown colony under an Administrator subject to the control of the Governor of Queensland (cf. *Strachan v. Commonwealth*, [1906] 4 C.L.R. 455, 13 A.L.R. 631). In 1902, British New Guinea was placed under the authority of the Commonwealth, and the Governor-General of Australia was granted the powers and duties formerly entrusted to the Governor of Queensland until laws for the government of the territory were enacted by the Australian Parliament. The Papua Act (Commonwealth) of 1905 placed the possession of British New Guinea under federal control, altered its name to "The Territory of Papua," and provided for government by a Lieutenant-Governor assisted by Executive and Legislative Councils.

From 1907 to 1945 the Commonwealth has disbursed approximately £1,500,000 in annual grants for the administration of Papua. For 1949–1950 a direct grant of £4,183,121 was made by the Commonwealth of Australia toward the cost of administration of the Territory of Papua and New Guinea of which £2,281,140 was allocated directly to the Trust Territory of New Guinea and the balance of £1,901,981 directly to the Territory of Papua (cf. UN Document T/C.1/L.12, 8, June 1951).

Under the Papua Act of 1905 the Lieutenant-Governor appoints all necessary judges, magistrates, and other officers of the territory, in the name of the Governor-General of Australia. The Legislative Council has, under the same Act, power to make ordinances for the peace, order, and good government of the territory. Under the Public Service Ordinance of 1907 the Lieutenant-Governor, with the advice of the Executive Council, can make, alter or repeal rules and regulations for the good order and conduct of the Public Service of the Territory (cf. *Faithorn v. Territory of Papua*, [1938] 60 C.L.R. 772, 12 A.L.J. 260). Certain ordinances of the territory, among them those concerning divorce, disposal of Crown or native lands, native labor, and immigration, must be submitted to the Governor-General of the Commonwealth, who may disallow them.

Papua and Norfolk Island are significant examples of colonial possessions over which control was retained for several years by a State which had entered a federal union. Eventually, despite the fact that it represented a financial burden to the whole, the federation assumed responsibility for these territories. A careful examination of the record indicates that the delay in transferring jurisdiction was due to the pressure of other matters on the federal legislature, not to hesitations to accept the colonial burden.

A P P E N D I X   I I

Canada

None of the Canadian Provinces possessed any dependencies when the Dominion of Canada came into existence on July 1, 1867. Now there are, however, two territories not included in any Province and under direct federal control: the Northwest Territories, which had a population of only 12,028 in 1941, of which 2284 were whites, 4334 Indians, and 5404 Eskimos; and the Yukon Territory, which had only 4914 inhabitants of all races in 1941. In addition, Labrador, today an integral part of Newfoundland, was a dependency of the latter until 1949. Labrador had a population of only 5528 in 1945. The dependencies of Canada are not colonial in character, but are territories which, for geographic, climatic, and demographic reasons, are unlikely to become Provinces of the federation in the foreseeable future.

I. The Northwest Territories and the Yukon

The Northwest Territories and the Yukon Territory originated from the area granted by the British Crown to the Hudson's Bay Company under its charter of 1670. However, their present boundaries are not the same as those of "Rupert's Land," the original name of the Company's territory, which included in 1670 all the land drained by rivers flowing into the Hudson Bay and the Arctic Ocean, and of the old "North-Western Territory," the western Indian country held by the Company by license of 1821 and renewed for twenty-one years in 1838. These are the territories which the Imperial government transferred to the Dominion of Canada by order-in-council in 1870.

In the first of the British North America Acts, 1867 to 1949, which form the "Constitution" of Canada, the British Parliament was authorized to provide for the admission of

> Rupert's Land and the North-Western Territory, or either of them, into the Union, on such Terms and Conditions in each Case as are in the Addresses expressed and as the Queen thinks fit to approve, subject to the Provisions of this Act . . . [30 & 31 Vict., c. 3, §146].

In 1870 the Province of Manitoba was created out of the North-Western Territory, the rest of which, with Rupert's Land, passed under Dominion control, after two centuries of administration by the Hudson's Bay Company. The British North America Act of 1871 (34 & 35 Vict., c. 28) confirmed the power of the Dominion Parliament to create new Provinces from these territories, and stated:

> 4. The Parliament of Canada may from time to time make provision for the administration, peace, order, and good government of any territory not for the time being included in any Province.

This provision gives exclusive legislative authority over dependencies to the federal government of the Dominion. To these provisions, the British North America Act of 1886 (49 & 50 Vict., c. 35) added provisions for the representation of the territories:

> 1. The Parliament of Canada may from time to time make provision for the representation in the Senate and House of Commons of Canada, or in either of them, of any territories which for the time being form part of the Dominion of Canada, but are not included in any province thereof.

The Yukon Territory was created by act of the Dominion Parliament in 1898 (St. Can., 61 Vict., c. 6) after the Klondike gold rush of 1896. In 1901 it had a vigorous population of 27,219 and was given a local government with a capital at Dawson, residence of the appointed Commissioner and of a Territorial Council of three elected members. The Yukon Territory was also given representation by one member in the Dominion House of Commons. However, the population had dwindled to 4157 by 1921 and has increased little since then.

During the years 1897–1905 immigration into the Canadian Northwest increased considerably and led to the demand for provincial autonomy. In 1905 two acts of the Dominion Parliament (St. Can., 4 & 5 Edw. VII, c. 3 and c. 42 §3) created the Provinces of Saskatchewan and Alberta. A collateral measure delimited the remaining portion of the old North-west Territories and provided for its future government under a Commissioner and a Council.

Federal control over the territories was reorganized by the North West Territories Act (R.S.C. 1927, c. 142) and the Yukon Act (R.S.C. 1927, c. 215). The first provided for a territorial government with its seat at Ottawa, composed of the Commissioner of the Northwest Territories, the Deputy-Commissioner and five councilors, all appointed by the Governor-General in Council. The Commissioner was given power to enact ordinances under instructions from the Governor-General in Council or the Minister of Mines and Resources.

The Yukon Act of 1927 did not change the general structure of local government in the territory, but in 1947 the electoral district of the Yukon, for the Dominion Parliament, was enlarged to include part of the Northwest Territories, and an amendment to the Yukon Act, passed in 1951, increased the territorial legislative council to five members.

In the federal government the Land and Forests Branch of the Department of Mines and Resources was responsible for the territories until the Department of Resources and Development was constituted in January, 1950 (13 Geo. 6, c. 18). The Northern Administration and Lands Branch of the new Department deals with local government in the Northwest Territories and the Yukon, and administers the land, mineral, timber, and other resources of the more than 1,500,000 square miles of these territories. Law enforcement in the territories is carried out by the federal Royal Canadian Mounted Police.

II. LABRADOR

Labrador has usually been described as a dependency of Newfoundland, although a Report of the Lords of the Judicial Committee of the Privy Council in the Matter of the Boundary between the Dominion of Canada and the Colony of Newfoundland in the Labrador Peninsula decided in 1927 that the coast of Labrador and the island of Newfoundland were equal parts of a colonial unit within the British Commonwealth (see Joint Appendix to the Report 1019). Interest in Labrador has recently increased greatly following discovery of important natural resources and because of its strategic military importance.

Labrador was annexed to Newfoundland when it was first acquired by the British, but was later transferred to Lower Canada. It was reannexed to Newfoundland in 1809 (Newfoundland Act, 1809, 49 Geo. III, c. 27 (Imp.)), and was placed under the supervision of the Governor of the Island. Subsequent government Commissions were issued by the British Crown to the "Governor and Commander-in-chief of the Island of Newfoundland and its dependencies," including the coast of Labrador (see Letters Patent, 1876, 2 Joint Appendix 754).

In 1832, when the colony of Newfoundland was permitted to become self-governing, its local assembly represented only the island of Newfoundland (see 4 Joint Appendix 1954). The inhabitants of Labrador remained subject to Newfoundland laws despite the fact they were not represented in its legislature (see 3 Joint Appendix 1489, 1496, 1505). Labrador had still not received representation in the Newfoundland legislature by 1934 when the local Newfoundland government was dissolved in favor of government by Royal Commission (see House of Assembly Act, 1932 (Newf.)). From 1934 to 1949, the Letters Patent of the Governor and the Commission referred, as before, to the "Island of Newfoundland and its dependencies" (see Letters Patent, 1934, in Newfoundland Statutes for 1934).

When steps were taken in 1945 by the British Parliament to authorize Newfoundland to elect a national convention to determine her future form of government, provision was made for election of one representative from Labrador in addition to 37 representatives from districts in Newfoundland.

On July 22, 1948, Newfoundland decided by referendum to join Canada. This union was consummated on March 31, 1949, when Newfoundland became the tenth Province of Canada. The act of union clarified the position of Labrador, which became, with the island of Newfoundland and adjacent islands, an integral part of the Province of Newfoundland (Terms of Union, §2, contained in Schedule to B.N.A. Act, 1949, 12 & 13 Geo. VI, c. 22). Labrador was granted participation in both the federal and provincial governments, becoming part of a federal electoral district (Terms of Union, §6 (1)) and a separate electoral district for provincial elections (Terms of Union, §15 (2)).

A P P E N D I X   I I I

Germany

When the German Empire was proclaimed on January 18, 1871, no German State had overseas territories. All such territories subsequently acquired came under direct federal control. From 1884, when the first German protectorate, over Southwest Africa, was proclaimed, until 1919 when Germany lost her colonies, which then became mandates under the League of Nations, colonial government was a direct expression of the Kaiser's Imperial sovereignity, and the German Chancellor was the chief executive responsible for colonial administration.

At first, German colonial affairs were administered by the political division of the Foreign Office, as the Empire assumed only the external protection of the colonies which were to be administered by chartered companies. By April, 1890, a special colonial division was established in the Foreign Office, but the Chancellor of the Reich was still directly responsible for colonial affairs.

A Colonial Office was created in May, 1907. The territory of Kiaochow (China) remained under the administration of the Navy. The Colonial Office had four divisions, three concerned with the civilian administration of the colonies, while the fourth was the Military Command of the special colonial troops *(Schutztruppen)*. These units were an independent part of the German Empire's Wehrmacht, distinct from the Imperial Army and Navy, having been created by Imperial law in 1896.

In the colonies, the special units were at the disposal of the Governor, but the Commanding Officer could report directly to the Chancellor of the Empire, in case of conflict. Among civilian members of the colonial service, German law distinguished between *Reichsbeamte,* officers of the Colonial Office, and *Kolonialbeamte,* responsible to the Emperor not in his capacity as sovereign of the Reich but as sovereign *(Schutzherr)* of the colony.

The colonies were not considered part of the territory of the Reich, in the sense of Article 1 of the Constitution of 1871, although Germany assumed full sovereignty, expressed through legislative, executive, and judiciary powers. The name *Schutzgebiete* was not considered an indication of a mere protectorate relationship, but only a survival of the early period of colonial expansion: German Southwest Africa, the Cameroons, Togo, German East Africa, German New Guinea, Samoa, and Kiaochow were considered, in law as well as in fact, colonies of the German Reich.

According to German legal doctrine, the inhabitants of the colonies were not citizens of the Reich, because they did not live on Reich territory but on territory under the sovereignty of the Reich. As such they were entitled to German protection, but citizenship could only be extended in special cases, in conformity with federal legislation.

The *Schutzgebietsgesetz* of September 10, 1900 (RGBl. S. 812), a federal law applying to all German colonies, attributed legislative powers to the Emperor, in the name of the Reich, without participation of the Bundesrat and Reichstag. The Imperial Constitution did not extend to the colonies. The sovereign power of the Emperor was considered unlimited with regard to the native population, while the *Schutzgebietsgesetz* defined more strictly the legal status of European residents in the colonies, to which German federal legislation applied. Judiciary powers were mainly administered on the principles of consular jurisdiction, with various local modifications, while the executive was organized as indicated above, under the authority of the Chancellor and of the Secretary of State for Colonies.

Public finances were organized on an autonomous basis for each colony, while the Reich assumed financial responsiblity for the expenditures of the *Schutztruppen* stationed in the colonies and in general for their external defense. Despite such general financial principles, federal subventions were often necessary especially in economically very backward areas like New Guinea.

The German Reich did not establish a preferential system with its colonies. Parts of the German African colonies were free trade zones under the international agreements concerning the Congo Basin, parts of the Pacific colonies under other international agreements. Each colony had its own tariff, for fiscal as well as protectionist purposes.

A P P E N D I X   I V

United States

In 1780 there was no "territory of the United States." In theory the Crown title to ungranted land passed to the individual States of the Union. Between 1781 and 1785 these States ceded the title and jurisdiction to the nation. The federal Constitution gave Congress the power "to dispose of, and make all needful rules and regulations respecting the territory belonging to the United States."

Westward expansion increased the number of States to forty-eight by 1912. The aborigines were partly absorbed, partly pushed back to reservations, colonial enclaves in the territory of the Union. "Manifest destiny" was much more a drive toward occupation of land than a desire to rule alien peoples. Overseas colonial expansion, comparable to the earlier similar phenomenon in Europe, began only toward the end of the nineteenth century. Strategic considerations outweighed, in 1898, reluctance toward rule over territories which were not expected to become eventually full and equal members of the federal Union, if America's burst of imperialism need be explained at all in rational terms.

In analyzing the acquisition and government of American dependencies, one distinguishes usually between so-called "incorporated" territories, preparing for statehood, and "unincorporated" territories which are not expected to achieve statehood.

I. DEPENDENT TERRITORIES PREPARING FOR STATEHOOD

A. *Territorial Claims of Member States*

During the period before adoption of the American Constitution in 1789, a number of the thirteen American colonies asserted overlapping and conflicting claims to the immense adjacent western lands extending to the Mississippi. Prior to the American Declaration of Independence in 1776, these claims had been cut off by the British Crown by the Proclamation of 1763 and by the Quebec Act of 1774. After independence, however, the conflicting claims of seven States were renewed and were serious enough to delay for more than three years (until 1781) the coming into effect of the Articles of Confederation, which preceded the Constitution. The Articles included a clause declaring that no State should be deprived of territory for the benefit of the United States. However, the States eventually ceded to the Union their claims to western territories. This was largely because the State of Maryland refused to ratify the Articles until satisfied that such cession would take place.

The definitive Treaty of Peace between England and the United States, signed at Paris, September 3, 1783, granted to the United States the vast tract of country lying between the thirteen States and the Mississippi. By then, the idea had prevailed that these lands should be ceded by the States to the Union. It had also been accepted that the western territory would in time be constituted into distinct States to be taken into the Union on the basis of equality with existing States.

B. *Territorial Governments*

The federal Ordinance of July 13, 1787, provided a government for the territory ceded by the States to the Union which lay northwest of the Ohio River. This Ordinance was the prototype for territorial governments subsequently organized. The Ordinance of 1787 established a temporary government of this territory by Congressionally approved agents until its population numbered 5000 adult free males, at which time a representative legislature was to be established. It also provided for the formation within the territory of three to five new States, and tentatively established their boundaries. These States were to be created as soon as there were 60,000 free inhabitants within their boundaries. The Ordinance of 1787 also established religious freedom within the territories, prohibited slavery, and guaranteed the fundamental individual liberties and just treatment of the Indians.

Out of this territory, the States of Indiana, Illinois, Wisconsin, Michigan, Ohio, and part of Minnesota were subsequently created. As the United States expanded to the Pacific, altogether twenty-nine States of the Union passed through the territorial stage in much the same manner. Until 1873 such territories were administered by the Department of State; since then they have been under the Department of the Interior.

At present, only Hawaii, organized by Congress on June 14, 1900, and Alaska, organized on August 24, 1912, are dependencies of the United States having the status of "incorporated" territories. Alaska, the first acquisition of non-contiguous territory, belonged to the United States for seventeen years, from 1867 to 1884, before even a temporary form of government was provided. The Americans who settled there conducted their affairs in accordance with the laws, social customs, and business practices of the continental States or territories from which they had come. Purchased from Russia under the Treaty of March 30, 1867, for $7,200,000, Alaska was constituted a "civil and judicial district" by an act of Congress of May 17, 1884, with a governor and a judiciary appointed by the President. The organic act made the general laws of Oregon applicable to the "district of Alaska." By designating Alaska a "district" rather than a "territory," Congress made clear its intention not to create the pre-statehood status which had come to be associated with the latter (see *Ex parte Morgan*, 20 Fed. 304, 305 (1883)). Moreover, the Act stated: "There shall be no legislative assembly in said district, nor shall any Delegate be sent to Congress therefrom."

The situation soon changed, however. The Klondike gold rush of 1896–1898 broke down the existing governmental machinery, and parts of Alaska had to be placed temporarily under military rule. The growing white population persuaded Congress in 1906 to give the people of Alaska the right to elect a non-voting delegate to the House of Representatives. The present Organic Act for Alaska, enacted in 1912, specifically extended the Constitution of the United States to Alaska, which was advanced to full territorial status, with a legislature of two houses given authority over a wide variety of local matters. A bill providing for the admission of Alaska to the Union was passed by the lower house of Congress in 1950, following a plebiscite held in Alaska in 1946 which favored statehood by approximately 3 to 2. Although this bill was not passed by the Senate, the 1952 platforms of both major American parties either "urged immediate statehood" or "favored statehood" for Alaska.

The evolution of Hawaii toward statehood is at present in a somewhat more advanced stage than that of Alaska. The House of Representatives passed in March, 1953, a bill providing statehood for Hawaii. If passed by the Senate, Hawaii will achieve statehood during 1954. The 1952 platforms of both major political parties had "urged" or "favored" immediate statehood for Hawaii. A republic, with a constitution adopted in 1894, Hawaii was annexed to the United States by Joint Resolution of Congress of July 7, 1898, which left the existing municipal legislation and governmental structure in effect. The Organic Act of 1900 provided that all those who had been citizens of the Republic of Hawaii on August 12, 1898, became citizens of the United States and of the Territory of Hawaii; all citizens of the United States who resided in Hawaii on that date or who had subsequently resided there for one year became citizens of this Territory. Only citizens of the Territory could be appointed by the President of the United States to territorial office. The bicameral territorial legislature retained large powers, and the Territory was to be represented in the House of Representatives of the United States by a popularly elected delegate. The Hawaiian delegate, like the delegate from Alaska, participates without vote in the debates of the House of Representatives.

During the 1950 Senate Committee hearings on statehood for Hawaii, it was suggested that Hawaii be made a part of the State of California, but it was strongly felt by members of the Senate Committee on Interior and Insular Affairs that it would be "entirely impracticable for a State to administer a Territory," and that this was clearly a task to be left to the Federal government until achievement of statehood.

II. DEPENDENT TERRITORIES NOT PREPARING FOR STATEHOOD

By the treaty of peace signed in Paris on December 10, 1898, following the war between Spain and the United States, Spain ceded to the United States the Philippine Islands, Guam, Puerto Rico, "and other islands now under Spanish sovereignty in the West Indies." Grave doubts were expressed at this time concerning the power of the United States to hold and govern colonies. It was argued that under the Constitution there was no place for a colonial system based "upon the fundamental idea that the people of immense areas of territory can be held as subjects never to become citizens." In the famous *Dred Scott* decision (19 How. 393 (1857)), Chief Justice Taney had written the dictum at pages 446–450: "There is certainly no power given by the Constitution to Federal Government to establish or maintain colonies bordering on the United States or at a distance, to be ruled and governed at its own pleasure; nor to enlarge its territorial limits in any way, except by the admission of new States."

After approval of the treaty with Spain, however, a Senate resolution of

1899 declared that it was "not intended to incorporate the inhabitants of the Philippine Islands into citizenship of the United States" nor "to permanently annex said islands as an integral part of the territory of the United States." This resolution was never acted upon by the House and gained no legal standing, but the subsequent history of the Philippines, which finally achieved independence in 1946, proves that the tendency of American policy remained oriented toward this goal.

The new acquisitions of the United States soon raised problems of constitutional law which had to be solved by the Supreme Court. Was the United States Constitution applicable in the new possessions? In the "Insular Cases" of 1901, the Court decided that, although Puerto Rico was not a foreign country, neither was it in the full sense a domestic territory. Therefore, a tariff on goods imported into the continental United States from Puerto Rico was valid despite the constitutional requirements that all duties be uniform throughout the United States (*De Lima v. Bidwell, Downes v. Bidwell,* 182 U.S. 1, 244 (1901)).

In an unincorporated possession such as Puerto Rico, only certain "fundamental" constitutional guarantees apply, such as freedom of religion, freedom of speech and of the press, immunity from unreasonable searches and seizures and from cruel and unusual punishments, free access to the courts, and the protection against deprivation of life, liberty, or property without due process of law (cf. *Balzac v. People of Puerto Rico,* 258 U.S. 298, 312–313 (1922)).

The unincorporated possessions of the United States include, in addition to those acquired from Spain, American Samoa (acquired under an American-British-German treaty of 1899) and the Virgin Islands (purchased from Denmark in 1916–1917). The "use, occupation and control" of the Panama Canal Zone was obtained by the treaty of 1903 with the Republic of Panama, and the Trust Territory of the Pacific Islands (Northern Marianas, Western Carolines, Eastern Carolines, and Marshalls) was placed under American administration by agreement with the United Nations Security Council of July 18, 1947.

Within the federal government, administrative responsibility for most overseas possessions has been exercised by the Department of the Interior. Within the Department, a Division of Territories and Island Possessions was created by executive order of the President in 1934, although without clearly defined powers. In 1950, the Division was raised to the status of an Office of Territories. The tendency of American colonial administration has been an increasing shift from military to civilian government. At present only the Panama Canal Zone is under the control of the Department of the Army. The Virgin Islands, which had been under the control of the Navy Department since 1917, were transferred to the Department of the Interior in 1931. Guam was transferred from the Navy Department to the Department of the Interior by executive order on August 1, 1950, but was returned to the Navy Department late in 1952. American

Samoa and the Trust Territory were likewise transferred on July 1, 1951. Puerto Rico, which had been administered since 1909 by a Bureau of Insular Affairs in the War Department, was transferred to the newly created Division of Territories and Island Possessions in 1934.

In 1952, Puerto Rico acquired a status *sui generis:* of self-governing Commonwealth "within our union with the United States." Puerto Rico had been under United States military government from 1898 to 1900. Then it received a mixed system of government with an elected house of delegates, checked by an upper house and governor appointed by the United States government. An elective upper house and American citizenship were obtained in 1917. A federal law of August 5, 1947, gave Puerto Rico an elective governorship, and the first popular election for governor took place on November 3, 1948. On July 3, 1950, Congress enacted a law which empowered the people of Puerto Rico, if they so determined by plebiscite, to elect a constitutional convention. A Constitution was adopted by the people of Puerto Rico on March 3, 1952, and approved with some modifications by Congress in 1952. On July 24, 1952, the Commonwealth of Puerto Rico came into existence, with a Constitution vesting full authority and responsibility for local self-government in the people of the island. The relations of the Commonwealth with the United States are governed by the Puerto Rican Federal Relations Act (Public Law No. 600, 81st Cong., 2d Sess. (1950)), which continues the provisions of the Organic Act of 1917 insofar as they were not superseded by the Constitution of 1952. Section 3 deals with matters of tariff and customs. In Section 5, the Act declares citizens of Puerto Rico to be citizens of the Unites States. Section 6 provides that expenses for defense, barracks, harbors, lighthouses, and wharves shall be undertaken by the United States, while all other expenses shall be paid out of Puerto Rican revenue. Section 9 extends United States statutes not locally inapplicable to Puerto Rico, except United States internal revenue laws.

The remaining American overseas possessions are very small in size and population: Guam, with a population of 85,000, of which only some 30,-000 are natives; American Samoa, with its few thousand native inhabitants; the Virgin Islands, with a population of 30,000 only recently increasing; the scattered population of the Trust Territory; and the population of United States government employees of the Panama Canal Zone. These possessions therefore raise questions very different from those of large and densely settled territories. Their importance is primarily strategic, and they all lie outside the tariff wall of the United States.

APPENDIX V

Dependencies of Members of the European Community

The overseas territories of the countries associated in the development of a European Political Community may be classified in several groups:

(1) Territories forming an integral part of the metropolitan country, such as the French overseas departments. Although these territories are not dependencies, their geographical remoteness from Europe may raise some problems similar to those concerning dependencies.

(2) Territories, such as the Indo-Chinese states, the Netherlands Antilles and Surinam, having a considerable measure of local self-government, but association with a metropolitan power in a relationship which leaves that power primarily responsible for at least defense and foreign affairs. Any change in the status of such territories would presumably require their consent, especially where, as in the case of Tunisia and Morocco, their present status is based on treaty.

(3) Territories in the status of colonial dependencies.

(4) Territories which are the subjects of United Nations trusteeship agreements. Any change in their status would presumably require a change in such agreements, involving of course the consent of the United Nations.

I. Belgium

Belgium's central African empire is composed of the colony of the Congo and the trust territory of Ruanda-Urundi. The Congo became a Belgian colony in 1908, but, as the Congo Free State, it was associated with Belgium in a union under the Belgian king from 1885 to 1908. In 1893 a provision concerning colonial government was added to Article 1 of the Constitution of Belgium, in anticipation of the transfer of the Congo to colonial status. This provision stipulated: "The colonies, possessions beyond the seas, or protectorates which Belgium may acquire shall be governed by special laws. The Belgian forces required for their defense shall be recruited only by voluntary enlistment."

During World War I, Belgian troops occupied the northwestern part of German East Africa, which the Allied Supreme Council allocated to Belgium in the form of a mandate over the territory of Ruanda-Urundi on August 21, 1919. On December 13, 1946, the General Assembly of the United Nations approved a trusteeship agreement with Belgium for this territory.

The basic law of the Belgian Congo is the *Charte Coloniale* of October

18, 1908. The colony has a "distinct personality" from the metropolis and is under special laws (Art. 1). The King legislates for the Congo by decree, at the proposal of the Minister for Colonies (Art. 7). A Colonial Council of fourteen members, of whom eight are appointed by the King and six by Parliament, has advisory powers in legislative matters (Art. 24). The Governor-General of the Congo may also issue legislation in the form of ordinances, but such ordinances must be approved by royal decree in order to remain in force more than six months. The Governor-General may also suspend temporarily the execution of a decree. Foreign relations are handled by the Belgian Ministry of Foreign Affairs (Art. 28).

The executive power in the Congo is exercised by the King through the Ministry of Colonies, except in regard to foreign relations for which the Ministry of Foreign Affairs is responsible. The Governor-General of the colony, as representative of the sovereign and supreme commander, has very wide executive powers. The Minister of Colonies provides the link between the government of the metropolis and the government of the colony. The administration of the Congo was reorganized by decree on July 1, 1947.

The judiciary of the Congo is entirely independent of the Governor-General.

Belgian administration of the Congo is regulated in some respects by the Treaty of Saint-Germain-en-Laye of 1919, which modified the Act of Berlin of 1885 and the Act of Brussels of 1890, and permits Belgium to establish a non-discriminatory tariff for the Congo and to control navigation. Previously, the Act of Berlin had established free trade and the Act of Brussels had fixed a 10 per cent ad valorem ceiling on import duties. Belgian and foreign goods are now taxed at the same rate and the ships of all nations are treated equally.

The acquisition of interests in land in the Congo is closely controlled. Tracts of rural land up to 500 hectares can be granted by the provincial governors, under conditions established by royal decree. However, Article 15 of the Charte Coloniale provides that cessions of more than 500 hectares of land require a special agreement between the colony and the landholder, which is submitted to the Colonial Council for its advisory opinion and approved by royal decree. Cessions involving more than 10,000 hectares and concessions of rights for more than 25,000 hectares for over thirty years have to be approved by decree after tabling the agreements for thirty days in both houses of the Belgian Parliament. Mining rights in all land are set apart and belong to the colony (decree of June 8, 1888). Exploration and exploitation of minerals must be authorized by decree.

In 1950 the Ministry of Colonies developed a Ten-Year Plan for the Economic and Social Development of the Congo, which was approved by the Belgian Parliament. A Permanent Commission for the Economic Coordination of Belgium and its Overseas Territories was created by ministerial order on June 25, 1951.

The 1946 Trusteeship Agreement with the United Nations authorizes

Belgium "to constitute Ruanda-Urundi into a customs, fiscal or administrative union or federation with adjacent territories under its sovereignty" (Art. 5). The territory is administered by a Vice-Governor General, under the control of the Governor-General of the Belgian Congo. A coordinated but distinct Ten-Year Plan for the Economic and Social Development of Ruanda-Urundi was published in 1951.

II. THE FRENCH UNION

French overseas expansion which began in the time of Richelieu in the seventeenth century created a large empire, of which only fragments were left at the end of the Napoleonic wars. The treaty of March 30, 1814, confirmed French possession of Martinique, Guadeloupe, Reunion Island, French Guiana, trading posts in Senegal, five cities in India, and St. Pierre and Miquelon. The second imperial drive started with the occupation of Algeria in 1830, and brought under the French flag large parts of Africa, Indo-China, and various islands in the Pacific.

Since the end of World War II the terms "empire," "colony," and "protectorate" have been discarded in describing the territories having constitutional links with France, and the terms "union," "overseas territory," and "associated state" have replaced them. These territories, together with metropolitan France, make up the French Union, whose structure and composition are described in the French Constitution of 1946 (Art. 60–82).

A. *Composition of the French Union*

The composition of the French Union is described in Article 60 of the French Constitution of 1946, which provides: "The French Union shall be composed, on the one hand, of the French Republic which comprises metropolitan France and the overseas departments and territories, and on the other hand, of the associated territories and states."

Overseas Departments. The "overseas departments" mentioned in Article 60 are an integral part of the French Republic. The four oldest French colonies, Martinique, Guadeloupe, Reunion Island, and French Guiana, became French departments by a law of March 19, 1946; the word "overseas" with reference to them has only geographic, not legal, meaning. They are administered like all other parts of metropolitan France.

Northern Algeria is divided into three departments, Algiers, Constantine, and Oran, which are also considered overseas departments in the sense of Article 60. Algeria, as a whole, is administered by a Governor-General, under the authority of the Ministry of the Interior. In the election of representatives to the French Parliament a restricted franchise is given to the native Moslem population of the Algerian departments.

Overseas Territories. The "overseas territories," within the meaning of Article 60, are those areas under colonial administration through the

Ministry for Overseas Territories (the former Ministry of Colonies). The
most important territories are in Africa, including French West Africa,
French Equatorial Africa, French Somaliland, Madagascar, and the
Comoro Archipelago. In other parts of the world, these territories include
St. Pierre and Miquelon, the French settlements in India, New Caledonia
and its dependencies, the Wallis Islands, the French Settlements in Oceania,
the New Hebrides (Anglo-French condominium), and some smaller islands.

Associated Territories. The "associated territories" are those parts of the
former German colonies, Togoland and Cameroon, which in 1919 became
French mandates under the League of Nations, and for which Trusteeship
Agreements between France and the United Nations were approved by the
General Assembly of the United Nations on December 13, 1946. From an
administrative point of view these areas can be placed in the same category
with French overseas territories, but from a constitutional standpoint they
are not part of the French Republic. However, the Trusteeship Agreements permit administration by France "in accordance with its own laws, as
an integral part of its territory."

Associated States. Finally, the "associated states" are the three Indo-
Chinese states of Laos, Cambodia, and Vietnam, and the two North African
states of Tunisia and Morocco. The French Cabinet includes a Minister for
Associated States.

B. *Structure of the French Union*

The structure of the French Union is outlined in the Constitution of
1946. Its complexity, due to the historical, geographic, and cultural
diversity of its components, creates special problems. These are clearly reflected in the Preamble of the Constitution of 1946, which asserts:

> The French Union is composed of nations and peoples who wish to
> place in common or coordinate their resources and their efforts in order
> to develop their respective civilizations, increase their welfare, and se-
> cure their security.
>
> Faithful to her traditional mission, France proposes to guide the peo-
> ples for whom she has assumed responsibility toward freedom to govern
> themselves and democratic administration of their own affairs . . .

1. ORGANS OF THE FRENCH UNION

Article 63 to 66 of the Constitution of the French Republic establish as
organs of the French Union: the President, the High Council, and the Assembly. The President is the President of the French Republic. The
High Council is to be composed of a delegation from the French government and of representatives accredited by each associated state to the President of the Union. The High Council convened for the first time on November 20, 1951. Representatives of the French Republic and of Laos,

Cambodia, and Vietnam participated. In plenary session, the Assembly of the French Union would contain 120 representatives from metropolitan France and 120 from overseas. It has held sessions in Versailles since December, 1947, with a reduced membership. The role of the organs of the French Union is consultative.

2. RELATIONS BETWEEN FRANCE AND THE OVERSEAS MEMBERS OF THE FRENCH UNION

The relationship between France and the overseas departments and territories and associated territories is defined by French law, subject to a number of constitutional provisions which are mentioned below. The position of the associated states in the French Union is determined for each of them, under Article 61 of the Constitution of 1946, by the instrument which defines its relationship with France. Instruments defining the relationship between the Indo-Chinese states and France, in the form of agreements between each of the states and France, have been signed and were approved by a French law of February 2, 1950. On July 3, 1953, the Government of the French Republic issued a "solemn declaration" in which it stated that "there is every reason to complete the independence and sovereignty of the Associated States of Indo-China by ensuring, in agreement with each of the three interested Governments, the transfer of powers that she had still retained in the interests of the States themselves, because of the perilous circumstances resulting from the state of war." At the end of the November, 1953, session of the Council of the French Union, President Vincent Auriol described the Indo-Chinese states as independent, sovereign, free and equal with France, and the French Union as a "fraternal association." New treaties defining the relationship of the Indo-Chinese states with France should be forthcoming. It remains to be seen whether they will fit into the framework of the 1946 Constitution. Tunisia's relationship with France is defined by the treaty of Le Bardo of 1881, by which a French protectorate was established. Similarly, Morocco's relationship with France is defined by the treaty of protectorate signed by the Sultan in 1912.

Defense. Under the Constitution of 1946, the French Republic assumes responsibility for defense of the entire Union. Article 62 provides:

> The members of the French Union shall place in common all their resources to guarantee the defense of the whole Union.
>
> The government of the Republic shall assume the coordination of these resources and the direction of such policy as will prepare and ensure this defense.

Foreign Affairs. The French Republic also exercises power with respect to foreign affairs on behalf of the entire Union. In the case of the associated states, this is based on arrangements between each state and the Republic (as are the other aspects of the relations between those states and the

Republic). The states of Laos, Cambodia, and Vietnam, however, have diplomatic representation in some countries and, in 1952, were sponsored by France for membership in the United Nations.

Legislative Power. In the overseas departments the legislative regime is the same as that of the metropolitan departments, save for exceptions determined by law (Art. 73). The legislative power in respect of the overseas territories and associated territories is exercised by the French Parliament with regard to general law, civil liberties, and political and administrative organization. In all other matters French law applies only by virtue of an express provision, or if it has been extended by decree, after consultation with the Assembly of the French Union. Special measures for each territory can be decreed by the President in Council, after consultation with the Assembly of the French Union (Art. 72). The overseas territories and associated territories elect, by restricted franchise, a total of 38 deputies to the French National Assembly and 44 senators to the Council of the Republic (Art. 79). In addition, under Article 77, an elected assembly is to be established in each territory, with its competences prescribed by French law. These assemblies, as well as the Assembly of the French Union, are to be consulted regarding the internal organization of the overseas territories (Art. 74).

The legislative power in the associated states is allocated in the instruments defining their relationships with France, under Article 61 of the Constitution. In Tunisia and Morocco legislation by decree has been most common; decisions of the Bey or of the Sultan come into force only upon their enactment by the French Resident General.

Public Finance. The overseas departments, other than those of Algeria, are assimilated financially to metropolitan France. In the overseas territories and associated territories there has been a trend toward budgetary autonomy, but no separate treasuries are maintained. Where possible, contributions toward local defense expenditures have been required of the territories, but increasingly heavy expenditures have made necessary contributions by France to various of its colonies. Taxation is less heavy and simpler than in metropolitan France. A head tax is used in most territories.

Algeria (including the Algerian departments), Morocco, and Tunisia each have an autonomous budget and treasury. The system of taxation is based on both Islamic and French principles. France takes charge directly of expenditures for defense, but draws contributions from the local treasuries. In Indo-China the system of public finance has been disorganized by the civil war, which is also one of the heaviest burdens on the French Treasury.

Trade and Development. France has a far-reaching preferential system with the overseas members of the French Union, although Laos, Cambodia, and Vietnam, which form a customs union, have been increasingly autonomous since 1946. Since 1948, France's exports to the overseas members of the Union increased in relation to its imports, until, in 1950, her favorable trade balance with them was about $400,000,000, and in 1951 $680,000,000. This indicates the extent to which France has supported these overseas areas.

A French law of April 30, 1946, requested the Ministry of Overseas Territories to work out Ten-Year Development Plans for each territory. In addition, an Investment Fund for Economic and Social Development (F.I.D.E.S.) has been established.

Citizenship. The Constitution of 1946 extends French citizenship to the overseas territories, and also creates a distinct "citizenship of the French Union" which is common to French citizens and citizens of the associated states (Arts. 80, 81).

III. ITALY

Italy's acquisition of colonies began in 1885 when, after the withdrawal of the British from the Sudan, Italy took possession of part of the western coast of the Red Sea which was called Eritrea. By 1912 Italy had an African empire of 780,000 square miles (Libya, Eritrea, and Somaliland), but much of this area was desert and its total population was less than two million. By Article 23 of the Treaty of Peace between the Allied and Associated Powers and Italy, signed in Paris on February 10, 1947, Italy renounced "all right and title to the Italian territorial possessions in Africa."

The Constitution of the Italian Republic of December 22, 1947, contains no provision with regard to dependent territories.

At present, Italy has again temporarily acquired an overseas dependency. Somaliland became, on April 1, 1950, an Italian trust territory for a period of ten years. The peace treaty of 1947 provided that final disposal of former Italian colonies should be determined jointly by the governments of the Soviet Union, United Kingdom, United States, and France, within one year from the coming into force of the treaty. This was not done, and the General Assembly of the United Nations, in Resolution 289 (IV) of November 21, 1949, instructed the Trusteeship Council to draft an agreement for Italian trusteeship over Somaliland. The Trusteeship Agreement with Italy was adopted by the Trusteeship Council on January 27, 1950. Article 24 of the Agreement stipulates: "The present Agreement shall cease to be in force ten years after the date of the approval of the Trusteeship Agreement by the General Assembly at the conclusion of which the Territory shall become an independent sovereign State."

The General Assembly approved the Trusteeship Agreement on December 2, 1950.

IV. THE NETHERLANDS

The status of the overseas territories of the Netherlands Empire, as it existed prior to World War II, has been changed greatly since the war, and the only territory still remaining in a genuine colonial relationship with the Netherlands is Western New Guinea. These changes are reflected by several recent amendments to the Netherlands Constitution. Within the Netherlands government, the Ministry for Colonies was replaced in 1945 by the *Ministerie van Overzeese Gebiedsdelen,* now called *Department Voor Uniezaken en Overzeese Rijksdelen.*

The Constitution of August 24, 1815, reissued on January 22, 1947, states in its first two Articles:

1. The Kingdom of the Netherlands comprises the territory of the Netherlands, Indonesia, Surinam and Netherlands Antilles.
2. The Constitution shall be binding only for the Realm in Europe in so far as the contrary does not appear therefrom.

On September 3, 1948, Articles 207–210 of the Constitution were modified, in an attempt to adjust to the rapid changes that were taking place in the Dutch colonial empire. Article 208 provided, among other things:

2. A Union shall be formed in which shall participate as equal states the Kingdom denoted in the fifth clause and the United States of Indonesia.
5. The Netherlands, Surinam and the Netherlands Antilles form a Kingdom . . . Within the Union, the Netherlands can maintain direct relations with the United States of Indonesia . . .
6. The United States of Indonesia shall be federatively composed of mutually equal partner states.

A. *Relations with Indonesia*

On December 27, 1949, the Netherlands formally transferred sovereignty over the whole of the former Netherlands East Indies, except Western New Guinea, to the new Republic of the United States of Indonesia. The "Charter of the Transfer of Sovereignty" provides in Article 1, paragraph 1: "The Kingdom of the Netherlands unconditionally and irrevocably transfers complete sovereignty over Indonesia to the Republic of the United States of Indonesia and thereby recognizes said Republic of the United States of Indonesia as an independent and sovereign state."

The Provisional Constitution of the Republic of Indonesia of August 15, 1950 does not mention the relationship with the Netherlands. It is therefore difficult to characterize the union mentioned in Article 208 of the Netherlands Constitution. There is a Netherlands High Commissioner in Jakarta and an Indonesian High Commissioner in The Hague, but their functions are those of ambassadors of one sovereign nation to another. The organs of the Union (*De Nederlands — Indonesische Unie*) are a Conference of Ministers, Commissions, a Permanent Secretariat, and an Arbitral Court of the Union.

B. *Surinam and the Netherlands Antilles*

The constitutional amendments of 1948 inaugurated for Surinam (Dutch Guiana) and the Netherlands Antilles (Curaçao, Aruba, Buen Ayre, St. Eustatius, Saba, and part of St. Martin) a new type of relationship with the Netherlands. In an Explanatory Note to the United Nations of August, 1951, the Netherlands government announced that it would no longer transmit to the United Nations information concerning these two territories under Article 73 (e) of the United Nations Charter, since they were no longer to be considered non-self-governing territories. The note explained that the new arrangements regarding these territories were aimed at "fully enabling the territories to manage their domestic affairs by means of their national organs" and that "it was intended to give the term 'domestic affairs' as wide a meaning as possible." In November, 1953, the General Assembly of the United Nations expressed the opinion that Surinam and the Netherlands Antilles have not ceased to be non-self-governing territories in the sense of Article 73 of the United Nations Charter.

Responsibility for domestic affairs in Surinam and the Antilles is no longer exercised by a Governor appointed by the Queen of the Netherlands, but is now discharged by the governments of the two territories. Each of these governments consists of a Governing Council responsible to the local legislature, and a Governor whose relationship to the legislature is similar to that of a Cabinet form of government. The legislature is popularly elected.

The constitutional reforms for the two territories were introduced by so-called Interim Orders of Government, which came into effect for Surinam on January 20, 1950, and for the Netherlands Antilles on February 7, 1951. The two texts are similar in most important matters. They define the scope of the domestic affairs over which the local governments have jurisdiction, and specifically exclude from this category international questions relating to the Kingdom as a whole and the mutual relations of the parts of the Kingdom. Article 2, paragraph 2, of the Interim Order of Government of the Netherlands Antilles excludes from domestic affairs, among other matters:

(a) anything concerning the maintenance of the independence and the defense of the Kingdom . . .

(b) anything concerning the treaties and other agreements concluded with foreign powers and international organizations and the rights and obligations arising from the laws of nations in general . . .

(h) the supervision of the general conditions concerning the admittance, residence, and expulsion of Netherlanders . . .

(j) consultation regarding questions of an international character in the matter of currency and finance, banking and foreign exchange policy . . .

Expenditures for matters which are not defined as "domestic affairs" can only be charged to the governments of the two territories by legislation of the Netherlands Parliament after consultation with the territory's government. Each territory has a General Representative at The Hague, who takes part in ministerial consultations and has an advisory voice in matters effecting his territory. The territories are consulted concerning legislation which will become binding upon them before the bill is introduced in the Netherlands Parliament. The *Departement Voor Uniezaken en Overzeese Rijksdelen* in the Netherlands government includes an *Afdeling* for the affairs of Surinam and the Antilles.

C. *Dutch New Guinea*

The western part of New Guinea, one of the most backward regions of the world, is administered directly by Dutch officials. There is no local representation, even in an advisory capacity, except at the regional level. Strong claims to Western New Guinea have been voiced by the Republic of Indonesia. Negotiations about the future of the territory, which the Indonesians call Irian, took place at The Hague in December, 1950, ending in deadlock. The Netherlands has recently taken moves toward a development program for Western New Guinea. In the *Departement Voor Uniezaken en Overzeese Rijksdelen an Afdeling* is exclusively concerned with this colony.

Admission of New States, Territorial Adjustments, and Secession

I. THE PROBLEM

The problem of admission of new States, regrouping of territory, and the secession of States has been one of the major problems of federations in the past and is likely to be of great importance for the contemplated European political community. Some federations tend to be exclusive, that is, restricted for instance to one continent or to people with a common language. The European political community is exclusive in the sense that it is restricted to a continent — Europe. The main criterion for admission would, therefore, be the determination that the applicant is a European state.

The question under consideration here is what provisions or procedures should the original members provide for future applicants. We may assume that the future European political community will have to face this problem immediately after its foundation, since the six states preparing federal union consider themselves as the hard core for a future larger European federation.

Some federations of the past show certain traits which might be useful for the development of a procedure for the admission of new States. The United States, which is frequently cited as a comparison, expanded across the continent by the admission of new States. Yet only two of these States previously existed as independent states.

In the case of the federation of Germany, in the latter part of the nineteenth century, the binding force was the German national movement struggling for the creation of a nation-state to include all German-speaking people.

The British Commonwealth of Nations, another possible comparison, has developed over a considerable period of time and is neither a league, federation, nor a state, but a community of States in which the absence of a rigid legal basis of association is compensated for by bonds of common origin, history, legal tradition and solidarity of interest.

The planned European political community, by contrast, is a federation, at the commencement, of six nations, Belgium, France, Germany, Italy, Luxembourg and the Netherlands, with centuries of independent national existence, no common language and no force comparable to German nationalism, or even the common bonds of the Commonwealth, to bind them together.

The European states not in the political community are divided into three groups; first, constitutional states, mostly members of the Council of Europe; secondly, totalitarian states under Soviet dominance; and thirdly, other nondemocratic states.

The constitutional states which, with the six countries about to form the European community, are members of the Council of Europe are Great Britain, Ireland, Denmark, Norway, Sweden, Iceland, Greece, Turkey and the Saar. These states, as well as Austria and Switzerland, may be considered as prospective members of the European community, and may well seek to join the European political community at a future date.

But Europe extends, in the geographical sense at least, from the Urals to the Atlantic Ocean, and most of the countries under Soviet domination and the Soviet Union itself, as well as Yugoslavia, Spain and Portugal, are also potential candidates and may desire to join the European community should they become constitutional states. This possibly might create problems concerning the stability of the political system of states to be admitted to the European federation.

New members of existing federations were usually small units incorporated into a larger body; territories, colonies or provinces developing into federal states, not powerful states with influence equal to or similar to several smaller member States, if not to the federation itself, as would be the case if, for instance, Great Britain should decide to join the European political community.

Among existing federal systems, the United States has shown the greatest readiness to admit new States, and the constitutional provisions under which this has been effected therefore deserve the closest scrutiny. For while the differences are, of course, enormous, between admitting to statehood territories which are just emerging "from the wilderness," and admitting fully developed national states with a long and deep-rooted tradition, from a strictly constitutional viewpoint this difference appears to be of less importance.

The problem of territorial adjustments within the federation is also common to all federal structures, and most federal constitutions contain some definite provisions for dealing with them so that the interest of all members may be properly balanced against the particular interest of the State or States more immediately concerned.

This balance is especially valuable in the case of territorial conflict between States at the time of union. The Saar conflict, even though it is hoped that it may be settled before federation, is one such problem. A similar question is presented by the territorial claims of members to territories outside the political community, such as the claim of the Federal Republic of Germany that it potentially includes the new Soviet-dominated

"German Democratic Republic" or the demand of Italy that the Free
Territory of Trieste be returned to her. While the first case could be settled by an advance adoption of a constitutional procedure, the latter could
alternatively be treated as the admission of a new State or as territorial
adjustment.

Other issues of this kind are bound to arise from time to time and are
apt to cause serious difficulty if no procedure for dealing with them is
written into the constitution.

Finally, the issue of secession, usually not openly faced by federal states,
and even avoided by leagues such as the United Nations, presents itself
with considerable urgency in the case of a federal system compounded of
firmly established national states.

The whole problem of admission and secession might be considered as a
procedure for peaceful expansion or contraction of a federal body. It will
be examined in the narrow constitutional sense, but it is important to realize that the demands for admission or secession do not depend mainly on
the constitutional provisions for them. The constitution can only facilitate
or hamper admission or secession but the attractiveness or advantages of
federation are certainly the main factor in effecting applications for membership. Disregard of sectional or other interests might, in turn, cause secession. Provision for secession might also be a factor in overcoming the
reluctance of a state, joining the federation, to renounce permanently part
of the exercise of its sovereignty, and might hence be advisable even
though it does not conform with the spirit of a federation.

II. Admission of States to Federations

A. *Constitutional Provisions*

In the admission of new States to a federation we must distinguish between three cases — first, the admission of dependent territories *within* the
federation to equal status of statehood; second, the expansion of the federation by transfer of sovereignty from a mother country to a dominion;
and third, the expansion of the federal territory by the admission of independent states.

In the case of granting statehood to federal territories, the act is fully
within the domestic jurisdiction of the state concerned. The federal state
therefore, through its executive or legislative branch, determines the conditions for granting full statehood to a territory formerly administered by the
federation itself.

In the case of transfer of sovereignty, the negotiations are carried on
between the federal union and the mother country. Usually the consent
of the legislature of the federal state and the colony concerned is also required, although the transfer of sovereignty can be made by executive
agreement between the mother country and dominion only. It has also

become customary to ask for a plebiscite as popular confirmation before a change of sovereignty is agreed upon.

The cases of independent states joining federations are very few and usually the independence of the state has existed for a short period only. Some racial or national connection frequently exists between the admitted state and other States of the union.

Without distinguishing between these three cases a special procedure for the admission of new States is provided in the American Constitution and in the Commonwealth of Australia Constitution Act. In both cases the legislature alone has the power to admit new States. In the British North America Act, Canada has the right to send addresses from the Canadian Parliament to the Crown requesting the admission of a new Province. The Act also provides that should any of the colonies of Great Britain be admitted, an address from the legislature of that colony to the Crown is also necessary.

The Basic Law of the German Federal Republic does not provide for a specific admission procedure but clearly states that the founders of the federation are acting also on behalf of those Germans to whom participation was denied. The German people are called upon to "accomplish, by free self-determination, the unity and freedom of Germany."

Moreover the Basic Law, after enumerating the States forming the federation, provides in Article 23 that it shall be put into force for other parts of Germany on their accession. However, to distinguish Western German constitutionalism from the totalitarian order in Eastern Germany, the Basic Law requires of all Länder in the federation, or joining it in the future, a constitutional order which must conform to the principles of the republican, democratic and social state based on the rule of law.

Any part of Germany could therefore join the federation if its internal organization was a constitutional government based on free elections and it was ready to observe civil rights.

B. *Admission in Practice*

1. ADMISSION OF INDEPENDENT STATES

In only two cases has an independent state been admitted to a federation. The United States admitted Vermont in 1791 as the fourteenth State, and Texas, after a ten-year period of independence, was admitted in 1845. These States however had a common boundary with the federation and a common language.

Vermont declared its independence from Great Britain in 1777 and established an independent state government. It retained its independence from Great Britain and the United States with the aid of a militia for fourteen years. On March 4, 1791 its application for admission to the United States was approved and it became the fourteenth State of the United States. Vermont, however, had to return some towns to the State of New Hampshire, and also to pay $30,000, a considerable sum at that date, to the State of New York, in order to effect renunciation of the territorial claims of New York against Vermont.

The admission of Texas originated with an annexation resolution passed by both houses of the American Congress on March 3, 1845. This resolution consented to the convocation of a convention in Texas for the purpose of adopting a State constitution. Furthermore the resolution of Congress stipulated certain conditions which the new constitution of Texas had to meet. After its adoption the Texas Constitution was to be delivered to the President of the United States, who would then submit it to Congress for final approval on or before January 1, 1846.

The terms of admission were prescribed by Congress without any prior consultation with the executive branch of the American government or negotiations and discussion with representatives of the Republic of Texas. Those terms stipulated:

1. "The government of Texas must be Republican in form";

2. The federal government would adjust all boundary disputes between Texas and other governments;

3. Texas must cede all "public edifices, fortifications, barracks, ports and harbors, navy and navy yards, docks, magazines, arms, armaments and means pertaining to public defense";

4. Texas retains "all the public funds, debts, taxes, and dues of any kind which may belong to or be due or owing the said republic. . . ." Texas also retains the "vacant and unappropriated land lying within its limits, to be applied to the payments of the debts and liabilities" of the republic;

5. The liabilities and debts of Texas cannot become a charge on the United States;

6. Texas may be subdivided into new states "of convenient size, not exceeding four in number, in addition to said state of Texas . . . with the consent of Texas" providing they have sufficient population;

7. Texas shall have two representatives in Congress until the next apportionment takes place.

Congress offered no special inducements to the Texans, and President Polk urged them to accept all of the terms laid down by the Congress. However, Polk, who strongly favored admission, did, through his representative in the smaller republic, encourage the Texans to ask the American Congress for a fair sum of money to pay for the transfer of any public lands to the United States. The President of Texas called a special session of the Texan Congress which promptly adopted the American resolution. A special convention to adopt a State constitution was then called. On July 7, 1845, the convention, meeting in Austin, formally requested the President of the United States to send troops and military installations to Texas. A State constitution was adopted which was soon ratified by popular vote, and which was then sent to the American President for submission to the American Congress. Texas was admitted in December according to the terms first set forth in the annexation resolution passed in March, but not without opposition in both countries.

2. ADMISSION OF DEPENDENT TERRITORIES WITHIN THE FEDERATION TO FULL STATEHOOD

Over a period of 112 years, from the admission of the territory south of the Ohio River as the State of Tennessee in 1796 to the admission of the territories of New Mexico and Arizona in 1912, twenty-nine American States have been carved out of the territorial domain of the United States. The procedure for admitting these territories has usually followed the same pattern:

(a) The United States Congress passed a specific enabling act under which the citizens of the territory chose delegates to a territorial constitutional convention;

(b) After the constitution was completed it was submitted to the people of the territory for their ratification;

(c) The authorities of the territory then formally applied for admission to full status in the Union;

(d) If the constitution of the new State was acceptable to the Congress, the latter authorized admission to the Union, prescribing the date of admission.

Most territories accepted as States have been admitted with little difficulty. The reasons for this are few and simple. Incorporated territories in the United States are prepared for statehood as a matter of policy. Most of the leaders and settlers of all territories admitted to statehood have been Americans. All of the territories admitted to the United States, with the exception of California, have been contiguous to the rest of the nation.

The argument most often used by opponents to admission of the territories was insufficiency of population. Illinois, Florida, Oregon, Kansas, Nevada, Nebraska, Colorado, Montana, Idaho, and Wyoming all had less population at the time of admission than was required by the prevailing apportionment formula used to determine representation in the House of Representatives to give them one representative. There were, however, some difficult cases.

The difficulties and the controversies raised by the questions of admitting Missouri (1812) and California (1850) into the American Union were caused by the issue of slavery.

When in 1818 and 1819 popular and legislative petitions were presented to Congress from Missouri requesting statehood, a bitter sectional controversy over the question of extension or prohibition of slavery in the territories and new States ensued. After a protracted wrangle, a set of compromises was worked out so as not to disturb the balance between free and slave States.

The admission of California similarly presented difficulties because of the slavery controversy in the United States. It, too, was resolved by a complex compromise.

The admission of the slave State of Missouri and of the free State of California are examples of admissions won by compromise in a time of extreme tension and division within the American federation itself.

A similar development took place in Canada where territorial areas administered from the capital were admitted to equal status as Provinces of the Dominion. Parts of the Northwestern Territories and of Rupert's Land were divided into the Provinces of Manitoba, Alberta, and Saskatchewan and admitted as Provinces over a period of thirty-five years, 1870–1905. The main provisions for status as full Province were, usually, the procedure to be followed in the first election, the retention by Canada of public land, and an agreement on the number of representatives in the Canadian Parliament for the new Province.

The admission of each of these Provinces was preceded by intensive negotiation and financial settlements normally favorable to the Province. In Canada, as distinct from the United States, the Dominion government usually took the initiative in elevating a dependent territory to the status of a full Province. In the United States, the territory usually applied to Congress for admission as full State.

The United States still has two territories, Hawaii and Alaska, which are waiting to be admitted as States. In both cases a bill admitting the two areas as States was passed in 1950 by the House of Representatives but shelved by the Senate of the United States on February 27, 1952, despite inclusion of statehood for Hawaii and Alaska in the platform of both political parties and support by the President of the United States.

Hawaii was an independent republic from 1894 to 1898, after the deposition of the Queen had ended the monarchy. On July 6, 1898, Hawaii was annexed by the United States following concurring resolutions of the United States Congress and the Hawaiian legislature, but was not granted statehood. On June 14, 1900, it was made a territory by the United States Congress as the first step towards statehood. The reasons advanced in favor of statehood for Hawaii are manifold. Hawaii's population of over 500,-000 is larger than six States of the Union. It is also greater than the population of any territory previously admitted to statehood, with the exception of Oklahoma. The Hawaiians, inhabitants of an incorporated territory, are citizens of the United States, pay federal income tax and are subject to military duty. At present more federal taxes are collected in the islands than in ten of the States. Hawaii has an elected legislature and in 1948 a referendum on the question of statehood was carried by 74,538 votes to 46,514. Moreover, in the continental United States all farm, labor and veterans' organizations as well as the political parties support Hawaii's bid for statehood.

The opposition to admission of Hawaii is based mainly on the change of voting strength in the Senate where Hawaii would gain two seats. It is also argued that the racial stock of Hawaii — about one third of Japanese origin — is too varied and too different from that of most citizens in the United States. Some say the population of Hawaii is too small. Others feel that the population growth of Hawaii is too great. It is also argued that the admission of the incorporated territory of Hawaii would lead to demands for the admission of the unincorporated territories of the Virgin Islands, Guam and Puerto Rico. Others maintain that Hawaii would be an economic liability. But the strongest and most conclusive opposition comes from Senators from the South who evidently fear an additional two votes in the Senate for measures which they consider inimical to the interests of the region which they represent.

Alaska, like Hawaii, has accepted a constitution and voted 9630 to 6822 for statehood in 1946. Alaska, a sparsely settled region four times the size of the State of Texas, has been a possession of the United States since 1867. It presents problems different from those of Hawaii. It is argued that too much of Alaskan territory remains unsurveyed. In rebuttal the advocates of statehood point out that large parts of New Mexico, Oregon and Nebraska were not surveyed when they were admitted to the Union. Another objection is that only a small portion of Alaska is suitable for settlement, but proponents of statehood maintain that even if only ten per cent of the territory were suitable for habitation, that would still be an area larger than thirty American States. Opponents show that 99.4 per cent of the land is under federal control. Supporters of statehood answer that the vast majority of the lands in California were federally owned at the time of its admission. The principal argument against admission has been that the population of Alaska — 100,000 — is too small. And once again the most effective opposition to Alaskan statehood has come from Senators from the South, fearful that two additional votes in the Senate might hurt the South. On February 27, 1952, the Senate by a vote of 45 to 44 adopted the motion, brought forward by a Southern Senator, to return the Alaska statehood bill to committee with instructions to study the possibility of making Alaska and Hawaii "commonwealths" by constitutional amendment.

It has also been suggested by legislators and academicians that both Alaska and Hawaii be incorporated into some State of the Union — California or Oregon in the case of Hawaii, or perhaps Washington in the case of Alaska — but no serious political agitation has resulted from such suggestions.

Canada and Australia have territories which show developments towards statehood similar to those of Alaska. These too are large and thinly populated and, at the present time, administered by the central government.

The Northwest Territories of Canada have an area of 1,300,000 square miles and about 15,000 inhabitants. They are administered by a commissioner, deputy commissioner and five councillors. With a future increase in population it may be expected that a legislature will be established and eventual status as a Province secured.

The Northern Territory of Australia, with a population of less than 11,000 and an area of 500,000 square miles, has been administered since 1947 by an administrator and a council consisting of seven officials and six elected members. The right to elect members was not granted until 1947, as a first step towards self-government.

Of the six federal states under consideration, only Switzerland does not provide for admission of new States, nor has it evidenced any desire to do so. At the end of the First World War when the Austro-Hungarian Empire disintegrated, Vorarlberg attempted to join the Swiss federation and to cut its ties with the provisional government of the Republic of Austria. In an official plebiscite on May 11, 1919, 80.75 per cent of the voters favored joining Switzerland while only 19.25 per cent voiced opposition. Although there was public support in Switzerland for the admission of Vorarlberg, the government of Switzerland reserved its position and in the Treaty of Saint Germain the question was decided by the Allies in favor of Austria. When the new Austrian Constitution entered into force on October 1, 1920, agitation continued but with no support from Swiss authorities and around 1922 the movement died.

The Swiss federation, with a century-old tradition of neutrality, acted very cautiously concerning the admission of Vorarlberg primarily because responsible leaders felt that any acquisition of territory even with the over-whelming consent of the people might create tension in the future between Austria or even Germany and Switzerland. This could only endanger the continuance of Swiss neutrality and the security of Switzerland.

Furthermore, the admission of the German-speaking State of Vorarlberg was opposed by the French-speaking Swiss who feared a change in the balance of cultural groups in Switzerland.

The Swiss federation, a small state surrounded by powerful neighbors, found it therefore wiser to refuse to admit any new State to safeguard its external security and its internal cultural balance.

3. ADMISSION OF FORMER COLONIAL AREAS AS PROVINCES

The Dominion of Canada has admitted colonies as Provinces after transfer of sovereignty from Great Britain to the Dominion of Canada. Prince Edward Island, British Columbia, and Newfoundland were self-governing colonies with territories contiguous to Canada and with predominantly English-speaking populations. The historical pattern for the admission of these colonies has been similar:

The British North America Act of 1867 laid down conditions for representation in the Canadian Parliament. At first the colonies refused to join in the formation of the Dominion. Subsequently negotiations were held between representatives of the colonies and the Dominion, leading to an agreement on the terms of admission. Acts were then passed by the Canadian Parliament and accepted by the colonial parliaments. These granted terms which were extremely favorable to the colonies.

III. REGROUPING OR DIVIDING OF STATES
A. *Constitutional Provisions*

Regrouping or dividing of States usually forms part of a federal constitution although in practice once the federation is established regrouping of States is unusual. Unsolved territorial problems at the time of federation are provided for in most of the federal constitutions, and solved shortly after the organization of the federation. Territorial adjustments after the transitory period are unlikely since the approval of the legislatures of the State concerned and of the federation itself is necessary and no legislature is likely to approve the ceding of territory.

Five federal constitutions provide procedures for the alteration of State boundaries, and only the Swiss Constitution is silent on this point. Constitutional provisions for change of State boundaries provide, except in special cases, for the authorization of both the federal legislature and the State legislature affected.

The Constitution of Australia is the only one which makes provisions for the transfer of territory held by a State to the federal government, although such transfers have taken place in the United States. Only in Australia is it necessary to get "the approval of the majority of the electors of the State voting upon the question" in addition to the approval of the federal and State legislatures.

Special provisions for regrouping of States were made in Austria by the federal Constitution of October, 1920, and in Germany by the Bonn Constitution of the German Federal Republic of 1949.

The Austrian Constitution provided for the separation of Vienna from Lower Austria and the establishment of Vienna as a State (Land) of Austria. This was effected with little difficulty on December 29, 1921.

The provisions in the German Basic Law were the consequence of the fact that new Länder had been created during the Allied occupation of Germany, without due regard to historical or traditional ties but mainly on the basis of strategic considerations and political expediency.

In the Basic Law, provision was made for the citizens of those Länder whose Land was joined to another Land after May 8, 1945, without a plebiscite, to demand by popular initiative to change the relationship within one year after the coming into force of the Basic Law. Since no procedure was outlined for the recognition of the initiative, presumably initiative procedures could be established by federal law. The Basic Law of West Germany is also the only constitution which sets constitutional criteria for the alteration of boundaries. "Regional unity, historical and cultural connections,

economic expediency and social structure" are the standards which are set
for the reorganization of the States.

Another special provision was made for the "reorganization of the territory comprising the Länder Baden, Württemberg-Baden, and Württemburg-
Hohenzollern . . . by agreement of the Länder concerned." The importance of the reorganization of these Länder was recognized by an additional
provision stipulating that "should an agreement not be reached the reorganization shall be regulated by federal legislation which must provide for
a referendum."

B. *The Alteration of Boundaries in Practice*

Changes of the boundaries of States have been effected in Germany and
Austria to satisfy territorial claims existing at the time of federation. In
the case of Germany, the change was made with the help of federal intervention after one of three States concerned refused to sign any agreement.

Agitation for territorial changes in other federal states has succeeded
mainly in obtaining either economic concessions from the federation or in
increasing the influence of the region concerned on legislation affecting
their area.

Of the six federations under consideration territorial reorganization has
been a major problem only in Germany after 1945. Because the State
boundaries established by Allied Military Government and confirmed in
the German Basic Law were artificial, the Allied governments encouraged
the German Minister Presidents to reach an agreement on territorial reorganization along more suitable lines. But the Minister Presidents were
unable to agree to change or to contemplate the immediate change of any
boundaries with the exception of the three states in the southwest area.
These three were Württemberg-Baden (the northern halves of which were
formerly Württemberg and Baden), Württemberg-Hohenzollern (formerly
the southern half of Württemberg combined with the small former Prussian
enclave of Hohenzollern), and South Baden.

Since alteration of these boundaries, according to the Basic Law, could
take place only with the agreement of the Länder concerned, negotiations
toward that end were held in the summer of 1950, but ended in failure.
After considerable agitation, including a referendum for *advisory* purposes
and a decision by the Supreme Constitutional Court, a federal plebiscite
was finally held on December 9. The vote was 69.7 per cent in favor of
fusion. In the areas outside of Baden the vote for fusion was well over
90 per cent. In South Baden, 62.2 per cent of those voting favored restoration, and North Baden voted 57.1 per cent for fusion; however, the popular vote for both parts of Baden was 52.2 per cent for restoration. The
partisans of the restoration of Baden blamed their defeat in North Baden
on the influx of evacuees from other parts of Germany now under Soviet

control and from the Sudetenland, amounting to about 8 per cent of the voting population.

There are three cases of territorial reorganization in the United States. The three American States of Kentucky, Maine, and West Virginia were all carved out of other States before being admitted to the Union.

In 1776 the State of Virginia established the county of Kentucky in answer to requests made by settlers in that region. By 1784 a population increase in the area, and the increasing fear of Indian attacks combined with the inability of Virginia to provide assistance necessary to meet those attacks, precipitated a series of nine conventions held in Kentucky between 1784 and 1790. The tenth convention, held in 1792, adopted a State constitution in which Virginia acquiesced, and which served as the basis for an application to the American Union as a full-fledged State.

In 1692 the province of Maine was made a part of the royal colony of Massachusetts. During the seventeenth and early eighteenth centuries it was traded back and forth between the English and the French three times. Finally, it was delivered permanently to the English, and, following the War of Independence, to the State of Massachusetts.

It soon developed that commercial Massachusetts had little in common with the frontiersmen to the north, who were anxious for cheap money, low tariffs, low taxation, and no expenditures for internal improvements. Ill feeling between the population in the two areas was further engendered when Bostonians speculated in Maine lands, creating an artificial scarcity in land at a time when the Napoleonic Wars raised market prices of agricultural products.

Demands in Maine for independent statehood grew until Boston was unable to resist any longer. In 1820 the settlers of Maine, nearly 300,000 strong, adopted a State constitution which was accepted by the American Congress, and Maine was admitted to statehood.

The State of West Virginia was created by the Civil War. But the tendency of separation from Virginia had begun in the 1830's when, following the War of 1812, there was an awakened interest in the trans-Allegheny region in industry, internal improvements, and banking. The northwestern part of Virginia developed a regional feeling not shared by the planters to the east and south. Still reforms in State government and the unifying effect of abolitionist activity helped hold the State together.

But the secession ordinance passed by the Virginians in 1862 was too much for the northwest, which seized the opportunity to assert its regional sentiment by declaring its loyalty to the Union. A new State capital was set up at Wheeling and on June 20, 1863, after the adoption of a State constitution, and in accordance with a Congressional enabling act passed in December, 1862, West Virginia was admitted to the Union.

In Australia movements for division of States developed in Queensland and in New South Wales. However, these movements were appeased by the granting of economic concessions.

IV. SECESSION OF STATES

No federal constitution makes provision for secession. Even such loose organizations as the British Empire do not expressly grant the right of secession.

It is true, however, that some of the States which ratified the Australian and the American Constitutions assumed that the right of withdrawal remained intact. The States of Virginia, Rhode Island, and New York all reserved such a right in their ratification resolutions.

Such theory as exists has been developed principally in the United States, and is based fundamentally upon the argument which Thomas Jefferson made in his Kentucky Resolution of 1798 protesting the Alien and Sedition Acts. Jefferson argued: "The powers of the general government are delegated by the States, who alone are truly sovereign; and must be exercised in subordination to the States, who alone possess supreme dominion."

The theory was given its fullest treatment by John Calhoun in his doctrine of nullification. Nullification was based first upon the Jeffersonian idea that the federal Constitution was a compact among States which are and remain sovereign, and, second, upon the postulate that a State convention, as an expression of State sovereignty, could determine whether an act of Congress was constitutional or not. The State legislature in South Carolina invoked the doctrine against the tariff acts of 1828 and 1834.

New England Federalists, angered by Jefferson's purchase of Louisiana and by the restrictive Embargo Act, actively planned a confederacy composed of New England and New York. Nothing came of the activity, however, and talk of separation subsided until the War of 1812, when leaders of the Federalist Party once again met in convention called at the invitation of the Massachusetts legislature in 1814 for the purpose of considering constitutional amendments to limit the power of the national government to impose commercial embargoes, declare war, admit new States, and to do other things. There is little doubt that the object of the secret Hartford Convention was dissolution of the Union, and the formation of a New England confederacy, in case their proposed reforms failed. The end of the war quieted their agitation.

The issue of slavery brought talk of secession from slaveowners and abolitionists. John Quincy Adams believed the free States would secede if Texas were admitted to the Union. And Southern leaders threatened secession if slavery were excluded from the Mexican cession. The controversy was temporarily dispelled when several Southern States meeting in convention agreed to accept the Compromise of 1850 already referred to.

After the election of Lincoln, the legislature of South Carolina called a State convention which unanimously passed a secession ordinance on December 20, 1861, dissolving "the union now subsisting between South Carolina and other States." The convention appointed commissioners to other Southern States and to Washington. Six other States similarly called conventions which passed secession ordinances — Mississippi, Florida, Alabama, Georgia, Louisiana, and Texas. Representatives of these States met at Montgomery, Alabama, on February 4, 1862, to organize the Southern Confederacy. Virginia, Arkansas, Tennessee, and North Carolina, after some hesitation, followed suit. The Southern secession has been the only large-scale secession in any federal government, and its story is too long to be told here. The question of the "right" of secession was settled after the victory of the North in the Civil War. In cases decided after the war, the United States Supreme Court denied the right of secession by declaring that "the Constitution, in all its provisions, looks to an indestructible Union composed of indestructible States." The various Southern States were made to comply with certain requirements before their readmission to the Union. The officers of those States which had seceded were obliged to sign oaths denying participation in the rebellion, and State legislatures in the seceded States were obliged to ratify the Fourteenth Amendment.

In Australia, an attempt at secession by Western Australia was denied by a joint select committee of the United Kingdom Parliament, although the people of Western Australia favored secession in a plebiscite by 138,-653 to 70,706 in 1933.

The decision of the select committee of the United Kingdom Parliament not to receive this petition in effect denies the right of secession in either Australia or Canada.

The Swiss federation not only does not conceive of secession but was founded after a successful war against an attempt of some cantons to secede from the league which preceded the federation of 1848.

The Basic Law of West Germany also does not mention secession, but allows the federation in Article 37 to interfere in any State if that State should not fulfill its obligation towards the federation. The federal government needs only the approval of the upper chamber (Bundesrat) for such intervention. Secession would, of course, be considered an extreme case of lack of fulfillment of the duties towards the federation and there seems little doubt that the federal government or its commissioners would have the right "to give orders to all Länder and their authorities" as provided in the Basic Law.

V. CONCLUSION

A. *Admission of States*

In the six federal constitutions under consideration, new States can be admitted by a simple majority vote, i.e., by a law passed in the federal legislature admitting a new State.

This procedure is a flexible one and facilitates the admission of States; it prevents a majority being frustrated by a minority. It is difficult to see how the admission procedures could be rendered more flexible.

Prior to the law admitting the new State, either negotiations between the executive of the federation and bona fide representatives of the new member nominated by its government or legislature, take place, or the federal legislature passes a law defining the conditions of admission.

The main condition for admission is the constitutional order of the new State. Should no constitution exist, a constitutional convention is summoned and the acceptance of a constitution is usually a condition for admission.

For constitutional states, there are usually four criteria for admission, which are examined during the negotiations or by the legislature. They are: first, the character of the constitution concerned; secondly, representation in the federal legislature, if not determined by the federal constitution; thirdly, financial settlement, such as transfers of property, debts and negotiations of tariff; fourthly, a resolution of the legislature accepting the federal constitution and requesting admission. In many cases a plebiscite favorable to union is also required.

Of all the federations, the United States has been most inclined to admit new States. Canada, whose constitution was influenced by that of the United States, has also favored admission of new States. Both of these federations have tended to expand from the Atlantic to the Pacific by the admission of new States, while they accept their common border as limitation for expansion north and south. Australia, with a Constitution in many ways similar, covered one large continent from its inception, and has therefore no need to admit any new States.

The Federal Republic of Germany accepts as a self-evident fact that it is the hard core of the future German Republic and is willing and expects to admit all German Länder now under totalitarian control as soon as they have a constitutional government free from Soviet dominance. The preamble of the Basic Law specifically promises admission to all Germans to whom participation was denied and asks all Germans to accomplish by free self-determination the unity and freedom of Germany.

Austria and Switzerland are two federations which seem disinclined to admit any new State or to expand the territorial limits of the present federation.

Based on these six federations we might conclude that federations will admit new States willingly by a majority vote if the admission does not interfere with national security or endanger peaceful relations with their neighbors.

Opposition to admission of new States is frequently based on the expected change in the voting situation in the upper house or senate. In some of the upper chambers such as those of the United States and Switzerland all States have an equal number of seats, which gives new States a considerable influence on legislation and might disturb the balance among religious, political or cultural forces.

A new federation might therefore decide that admission of States should not be effected by a majority vote only but by a two-thirds vote or some other qualified voting system. It might also require that one half, or even two thirds, of the States should ratify the admission of a new State. There is hardly any doubt that too restrictive an admission procedure would be incompatible with the establishment of a federation. Even leagues, such as the United Nations and the League of Nations, insisted on admission by a two-thirds vote and not on unanimity, nor on ratification by all states.

The advantage of a two-thirds vote of the legislature compared to a simple majority vote would be the protection of a minority of States, against the admission of blocks of States.

The experience in the United States with the difficulties encountered time and again over admission of new States demonstrates that a large minority can protect itself through its weighted voting strength in the second chamber even when an easy method for the admission of States is prescribed. It is doubtful whether a small minority should be permitted to frustrate the needs and wishes of a substantial majority in the federation and the State desiring admission.

It is possible to include in one constitution a different and more restrictive method for the admission of some independent states than for the admission of others; one might also differentiate between the admission of existing States and federal territories. The advantage of this would be to adopt a general policy of "promised statehood" to federal territories, while making it necessary to get wider approval within the federation for the admission of other States. The United States, in effect, promises statehood when it incorporates territories, as it has done thirty-one times. By not incorporating territories such as Guam and Puerto Rico, the federal government indicates that such territories will not be considered for statehood.

Each constitution is in itself an elaborate set of conditions by which States applying for statehood must pledge to abide. However, the Swiss, the American, and the German Constitutions include specific brief criteria for membership in the federation. In both cases the criteria are very general, and add little to the conditions which must be met by adoption of the entire federal constitution.

What has been the effect on admissions of the criteria listed in the Swiss, American, and German Constitutions? In the American case each State is required constitutionally to have a republican form of government — no more. Recent debates in the Congress in connection with Puerto Rico would indicate that this term connotes a constitutional, democratic regime including a bill of rights. The Swiss requirements are similarly general except for one which stipulates that all cantonal constitutions must be amendable by an absolute majority of the people of the canton. Since the Swiss have admitted no States there is no way of judging the effect of these criteria for membership on admission. In the case of Germany, the criteria are, of course, intended to denote the difference between the constitutionalism of the West and the totalitarianism of the Soviet Eastern satellite.

In practice federal legislatures define the terms of admission. These terms will vary from time to time with the policies which prevail in the national legislature and the national executive. Before admission, Nebraska was told it could not discriminate against colored persons; Missouri was told it could not discriminate against colored citizens of other States; Utah was told to strike from its constitution a provision for the recall of judges; more recently, issues of economic policy (socialism) have been a factor.

The advantage of limiting or omitting criteria for membership in the constitution is that the federal legislature will then be left free to establish terms of admission which suit the needs of the case. The listing of general criteria might be helpful as a guide in judging the validity of an application for admission, but might also be harmful as a roadblock in keeping out a State which federal policy and public opinion want in the federation.

B. *Territorial Readjustments*

All federal constitutions which deal with the problem provide that the alteration of boundaries within the federation shall be the joint responsibility of the federal legislature and the legislatures of the States affected by the change — with the exception of special provisions for the German Southwest State and for Vienna and Lower Austria.

In practice, most of the States have been able to resist attempts to divide their territory. In cases where readjustment of territory did take place, it was a case of settlement of a territorial conflict which existed at the time of federation, or the development of a territory previously sparsely populated. In the case of Western Germany, federal action was necessary in order to overcome the resistance of one of the three States involved in the readjustment of territory.

Conceivably alteration of boundaries could take place as a result of federal action alone or State action alone. But it is difficult to see any advantage in such an arrangement since people in all States are directly affected by any alteration of boundaries which affect the distribution of representation in the federal legislature, as any territorial adjustments between States must do.

Allowing the federation or the States by themselves to decide upon territorial adjustments would make the procedure easier than that adopted in any existing federal constitution. The advantage of an easy solution is that economic and political needs can more readily be met by quick action. The disadvantage, alluded to above, is that units of government directly affected will be deprived of an opportunity to participate in the decision.

A more restrictive method for the regrouping of States could be adopted. The unanimous consent of all States or the passage of a constitutional amendment or a two-thirds vote of the federal legislature might be required. The advantage of a more restrictive method would lie in the protection which small States might desire at the outset of federation, or which States with unique and separate cultures might demand. The disadvantage of a restrictive method lies in the difficulty with which the federation will be faced in altering boundaries to meet changes in economy, population growth, migration, and other facts wrought by time.

C. *Secession*

Federal states do not provide for secession. In practice, all attempts at secession in federations have been fought by the central organs through propaganda, economic measures, or even by military action. The Swiss Confederation successfully fought an attempt at secession before even adopting a federal constitution.

The advantage of adopting an article providing for secession is usually limited to the initial period of the federation, since some States might be induced to adhere to the federation only if they are ensured the right to secede.

The disadvantage is that the threat of secession by a major member might paralyze effective federal action and endanger the whole federation.

It seems therefore highly questionable whether a federation ought to provide the right of secession. The federation, to be effective, has to be granted specific irrevocable powers and cannot be subject to the right of States to challenge the legitimacy of federal laws.

Even a loose organization of States, such as the British Commonwealth, or a league such as the United Nations, does not explicitly grant the right to secede.

The disadvantages of allowing the right of withdrawal are obvious. Such a provision gives each State an ultimate veto power over the federation's policies. It also renders incapable of solution many problems, if each member State has to calculate in what situation it would be left if a particular other member State seceded. This sort of calculation would raise havoc with many crucial economic policies. Nor is it even wise to leave the issue open. Experience in the United States, and to a very limited extent in Australia, shows that ambiguity over the question of secession only serves to exacerbate tensions rather than to relieve them, and to thwart efforts toward a mutually collaborative solution of the problems which cause discontent. Characteristically, France sought guarantees from Great Britain and the United States against the withdrawal of Germany from the European Defense Community.

It is certainly questionable whether the "right" of secession is compatible with federal government. The creation of a federal state involves a permanent commitment to collaborate according to the terms set forth in the constitution. That the terms include the right not to collaborate is self-contradictory. Each federal constitution provides that federal law is supreme in its own sphere and operates directly on individuals. States cannot be made the judge of the legitimacy of federal law if there is to be federal government.

APPENDIX I

Australia

I. ADMISSION

Constitutional Provisions

121. The Parliament may admit to the Commonwealth or establish new States, and may upon such admission or establishment make or impose such terms and conditions, including the extent of representation in either House of Parliament, as it thinks fit.

II. REGROUPING

A. *Constitutional Provisions*

111. The Parliament of a State may surrender any part of the State to the Commonwealth; and upon such surrender, and the acceptance thereof by the Commonwealth, such part of the State shall become subject to the exclusive jurisdiction of the Commonwealth.

123. The Parliament of the Commonwealth may, with the consent of the Parliament of a State, and the approval of the majority of the electors of the State voting upon the question, increase, diminish, or otherwise alter the limits of the State, upon such terms and conditions as may be agreed on, and may, with the like consent, make provision respecting the effect and operation of any increase or diminution or alteration of territory in relation to any State affected.

124. A new State may be formed by separation of territory from a State, but only with the consent of the Parliaments of the States affected.

B. *Regrouping in Practice*

No alteration of boundaries has ever taken place, but political agitation for the creation of new States has taken place in the States of Queensland and New South Wales, most particularly in rural areas.

1. QUEENSLAND

1. Pioneers in the north and west of Queensland complained of the lack of roads, railways, port construction and of tariffs.

2. The sugar industry backed the separatist movement in Queensland on account of the threatened end of the immigration of colored labor.

3. After federation in 1900, the separatist movement decreased; the sugar industry lost interest in secession and after the advent of the Labour Party to power the government paid increasing attention to northern developments and extended local government in that area.

4. A residue of separatist feeling is still in existence. In 1949 State election party leaders appealed to it and the Labour Prime Minister promised to recommend creation of a new State as soon as it was financially feasible.

2. NEW SOUTH WALES

1. Separatist agitation has existed since 1900 in the areas of the Northern Rivers, Riverina and the Monaro.

2. In 1915 it became stronger mainly on account of insufficient expenditure on railways, roads and port facilities, and it reached its peak in 1916 when New South Wales rejected a proposal by Victoria to build new railroads into Riverina.

3. Continuous support of separation from New South Wales exists in the rural communities, especially in the Farmers' and Settlers' Associations and the Graziers' Association, and finds its political expression in the New South Wales Country Party. It is opposed by the Labour Party. The movement played a part in the 1950 election but appeared to be motivated more by attempts to influence the government in favor of more expenditure in that area than by a real desire for separation.

III. SECESSION

Secession from the Commonwealth of Australia was attempted by Western Australia in 1933. It was approved by popular vote, but the petition was rejected by a committee of Parliament in London.

1. WESTERN AUSTRALIA

1. Western Australia was induced to join the federation in 1900 in some measure by the favorable vote given by the population of the gold fields, mostly arrived recently from other States. Western Australia also retained the right to enact its own customs duties for a period of five years.

2. A Royal Commission of Finances in Western Australia found, in 1925, that economic disabilities had been imposed upon the State by the federation. The majority favored tariff autonomy, the minority, secession.

3. The Dominion League, a secessionist organization, was formed during the depression years by the farm interests to combat alleged favor by the federation to manufacturers' interest and the urban population. Two national parties, the Nationalists and Country Party, advocated secession

partly as election strategy and in 1933 the State Parliament voted to submit the question of secession to popular vote. The plebiscite favored secession by a vote of 138,653 to 70,706, despite efforts by Commonwealth leaders to defeat the Secessionists. However, the antisecessionist Labour Party won the election by a large vote.

4. The Labour Premier forwarded a secession petition drafted by a committee to a joint select committee of the United Kingdom Parliament. The select committee declared that the petition was not receivable, in effect denying the right of secession in either Australia or Canada.

5. The major considerations for decline of secessionist sentiment since 1933 are: first, that the antisecessionists were not vindictive; second, that the secessionist vote was a protest vote against neglect by the Commonwealth, and, finally, that economic conditions in the State did improve.

APPENDIX II

Austria

I. ADMISSION

There is no general constitutional provision in the Austrian Constitution pertaining to admission. However, there is a special one referring to the admission of Burgenland in the Constitutional Law of October 1, 1920, Concerning the Transition to the Constitution of the Federal State, II, Section 12:

1. As soon as it has manifested its intention, Burgenland shall be incorporated in the Federal State as an autonomous state having equal rights with the other states.
2. Detailed regulations concerning the status of Burgenland in the Federal State as an autonomous state, having equal rights with other states, shall be prescribed by special federal constitutional law.

II. REGROUPING

A. Constitutional Provisions

FEDERAL CONSTITUTION, OCTOBER, 1920

Article 3. (2) Alteration of federal boundaries, affecting also the boundaries of a state, as well as alteration of the state boundaries within the federal territory may take place — except as provided by peace treaties — only by concurrent constitutional laws of the Federal State and the state affected thereby.

Article 114. A separate state of Vienna may be formed by concurrent laws of the municipal council of Vienna and the Landtag of the state of Lower Austria.

B. *Regrouping in Practice*

The separation of Vienna from Lower Austria, made possible by the constitutional provision quoted directly above, was accomplished with little difficulty on December 29, 1921.

III. SECESSION

Separatist Attempts in Austria

In the period following World War I some of the Austrian States took action to separate from the federal republic. (See also the Appendix on Switzerland, below, for an account of the case of Vorarlberg.) The history of the separatist activity may be summed up as follows:

1. Before the adoption of the Constitution the legislatures of Salzburg and Tirol voted for union with Germany: Tirol for an economic union and Salzburg for a direct union with Bavaria;

2. Tirol held a plebiscite in April, 1921, on the question of union; nine tenths of the qualified voters participated, and 98.8 per cent of these voted for union;

3. The diet of Salzburg passed a resolution calling for such a plebiscite;

4. Referenda were also scheduled by Styria and Upper Austria on the question of union with Germany;

5. France, intervening for the Entente, threatened to withdraw credit from Austria if the plebiscites were held;

6. The federal diet passed legislation designed to forestall the State plebiscites by calling for a federal referendum on the question; but

7. Although the States did not hold their plebiscites as scheduled the federal government did not designate a date for the holding of its referendum, which, in fact, was never held.

A P P E N D I X   I I I

Canada

I. ADMISSION

A. *Constitutional Provisions*

146. It shall be lawful for the Queen, by and with the advice of Her Majesty's Most Honourable Privy Council, on addresses from the Houses of the Parliament of Canada, and from the Houses of the respective Legislatures of the Colonies or Provinces of Newfoundland, Prince Edward Island, and British Columbia, to admit those colonies or provinces, or any of them into the Union, and on address from the Houses of Parliament of Canada to admit Rupert's Land and the North-

Western Territory, or either of them, into the Union, on such terms and conditions in each case as are in the address expressed and as the Queen thinks fit to approve, subject to the provisions of this Act; and the provisions of any Order in Council in that behalf shall have effect as if they had been enacted by the Parliament of the United Kingdom of Great Britain and Ireland.

147. In the case of the admission of Newfoundland and Prince Edward Island or either of them, each shall be entitled to representation, in the Senate of Canada, of four members, and (notwithstanding anything in this Act, in case of the admission of Newfoundland the normal number of Senators shall be Seventy-six and their maximum number shall be Eighty-two; but Prince Edward Island when admitted shall be deemed to be comprised in the third of the Three Divisions into which Canada, in relation to the constitution of the Senate, [is] divided by this Act, and accordingly, after the admission of Prince Edward Island, whether Newfoundland is admitted or not, the representation of Nova Scotia and New Brunswick in the Senate shall, as vacancies occur, be reduced from Twelve to Ten members respectively, and the representation of each of those Provinces shall not be increased at any time beyond Ten, except under the Provisions of this Act, for the appointment of Three or Six additional Senators under the direction of the Queen.

After the creation and admission of the Province of Manitoba by the Manitoba Act of 1870 (33 Vict., c. 3) some doubts were raised about the power of the Canadian Parliament to establish Provinces in the territories admitted, Rupert's Land and the North-Western Territory (Rupert's Land Act, 1870, 31 & 32 Vict., c. 105). The doubts were quieted by the passage of an amendment to the British North America Act, part of which stated:

> The Parliament of Canada may from time to time establish new Provinces in any territories forming for the time being part of the Dominion of Canada, but not included in any province thereof, and may, at the time of such establishment make provision for the constitution and administration of any such Province, and for its representation in the said Parliament [An Act Respecting the Establishment of Provinces in the Dominion of Canada, §2, B.N.A. Act as amended, 34 & 35 Vict., c. 28].

B. *Admissions in Practice*

Admissions to the federal Dominion have taken place in the following order: Manitoba (1870), British Columbia (1871), Prince Edward Island (1873), Alberta and Saskatchewan (1905), and Newfoundland (1949).

1. ADMISSION OF TERRITORIES

Manitoba, Alberta, and Saskatchewan were all created out of the federal domain.

(a) Illustrative legislation

The Manitoba Act of 1870 (33 Vict., c. 3), like the acts which admitted the territories of Alberta and Saskatchewan, provided for the following:

1. A definition of the boundaries of the new Province;
2. An assignment of representatives to the new Province;
3. The creation of electoral districts, with a provision for readjustment according to census;
4. The outline of the governmental structure of the new Province;
5. The procedures to be followed in the first election, the legislation of customs laws, and other matters;
6. The setting up of a separate school system for religious groups;
7. The retention by Canada of public lands;
8. The recognition of existing land titles; and
9. The governance of the territory of Rupert's Land and the North-West not included in the new Province.

(b) Manitoba

Prince Rupert's Land and the North-Western Territories were granted by Royal Charter to the Hudson's Bay Company. In July, 1868, the English Parliament passed an enabling act granting the Crown the right to transfer the land rights from the Hudson's Bay Company to Canada by the Queen's Order-in-Council. Dominion representatives in London completed the negotiations and an agreement on the terms of transfer was made. The Canadian Parliament accepted those terms and passed an act admitting the territories into the Dominion. Two years later, in the Manitoba Act, that portion of the territory known as Manitoba was admitted as a Province.

The following difficulties arose:

1. Negotiations for the transfer of the area had taken place entirely without consulting representatives of the local population, of which the métis were the largest and most cohesive group. They were afraid of being swamped by an alien tide from the East, and of being governed in a way inimical to their traditions.
2. The métis were prepared to fight to keep the Lieutenant Governor appointed by the Dominion out of Manitoba. Under the leadership of Louis Riel, the anti-Canadian forces formed a national committee, which constituted the *de facto* government of the settlement, executing at least one important pro-Canadian.
3. The Canadian government dispatched a combined force of British regulars and Canadian militia under Colonel Garnet Wolsley to put down resistance and to assert Canadian authority, which was done in August, 1870.
4. The Dominion government granted the demands of the Manitoba emissaries for immediate provincial status on terms extremely favorable to the

inhabitants of the settlement. The Act of Manitoba, which defined the boundaries of the Province, included the following terms:

(a) Representation all out of proportion to numbers. The Act provided for two Senators from Manitoba and four representatives;

(b) A provision for a separate school system for the métis;

(c) Canadian retention of public lands, but the recognition of existing land titles and a provision giving special grants to half-breeds.

(c) Alberta and Saskatchewan

The territories outside of Manitoba were governed according to the Rupert's Land Act of 1869. Gradually the population in these areas grew until in 1897 the Parliament of Canada passed legislation, effective July 20, 1905, establishing territorial government for what later became Alberta and Saskatchewan. The terms of admission were favorable to the entering territories. They included:

(a) A generous subsidy for the admitted Provinces;

(b) The division of properties and the assets of the North-Western Territories between Alberta and Saskatchewan;

(c) A provision in the Acts respecting the establishment of separate schools which any class of persons had at the date of the passing of the Acts.

2. ADMISSION OF DEPENDENT AREAS (COLONIES)

Three self-governing colonies, Prince Edward Island, British Columbia and Newfoundland, were admitted to Canada by special procedure. These colonies were neither part of the territorial domain of Canada nor independent states, but dependent territories.

The historical pattern for the admission of these three colonies has been the same:

(a) Early refusal of the colonies to join in the formation of the Dominion;

(b) Subsequent negotiations between representatives of the colonies and the Dominion, leading to agreement on the terms of admission;

(c) The passage of an act by the Canadian Parliament, accepted by the colonial parliaments, and granting terms which were extremely favorable to the colonies.

(a) British Columbia

1. At the time of federation, some popular sentiment among the 10,000 white inhabitants of this colony was probably in favor of having British Columbia join Canada, but the governor of the colony, Seymour, and the Legislative Council, were opposed to federation. In 1868 the Council refused to adopt articles intended to define the terms of union and to pray for admission.

2. After sentiment for union with Canada grew, the Legislative Council passed a resolution in February, 1869, urging the British government "not to take any decisive steps towards the present consummation of such a Union."

3. When Governor Seymour, the main opponent of the union, died in June, 1869, a new governor was appointed, who was instructed to do what could be done to promote union. The new Legislative Council, which met in March, 1870, adopted resolutions defining terms of admissions and a delegation was sent with them to Ottawa. The Canadian authorities agreed to the terms demanded, some of the important ones being:

(a) The federal assumption of the provincial debt;

(b) Full representation in the Dominion Parliament;

(c) The granting of an annual federal subsidy of $35,000 and of an annual payment of 80 cents per head of the population of 60,000, both to be made half-yearly in advance;

(d) A pledge by the Dominion to begin construction of a railway within two years, to be completed within ten, from the Pacific toward the Rocky Mountains and from points east of the Rocky Mountains to connect the seaboard of British Columbia with the railway system of Canada;

(e) The maintenance of existing customs tariff and excise duties in force in British Columbia until the railway from the Pacific Coast and the system of railways in the rest of Canada are connected;

(f) The maintenance by the Dominion of mail service by steam communication between Victoria and San Francisco fortnightly and twice a week between Victoria and Olympia;

(g) The assumption by the Dominion of the trusteeship and management of the Indians and their land, and a pledge by the Dominion to maintain a policy as liberal as that hitherto pursued by the British Columbia government;

(h) The granting by the Dominion of suitable pensions to government servants in the colony whose incomes were diminished by the union.

(b) Prince Edward Island

Anti-union sentiment was very strong in Prince Edward Island. The colonial legislature asked the Crown to refuse assent to any union with Canada; it refused to send delegates to a conference which planned federal union (1866–1867); it opposed overtures for maritime union with Nova Scotia; and finally it even rebuffed American and Nova Scotian missions seeking the exchange of fishing and trade privileges.

In 1873, however, Prince Edward Island was incorporated after it failed to finance the building of an island railway. The terms were:

(a) The assumption by the Dominion of all provincial debts;

(b) The granting of six representatives to the Island with a population of 94,021;

(c) The payment of an annual subsidy of $30,000 and the annual grant of 80 cents per head of the Island population;

(d) The allowance to the colony of a debt equal to $50 per head of its population;

(e) The assumption by the Dominion of expenses for such things as provincial fisheries and provincial penitentiary;

On these and many other advantageous terms Prince Edward Island was formally admitted to the Union by the Queen's Order-in-Council.

(c) Newfoundland

Newfoundland alone of the North American colonies remained outside Canada until 1949.

In 1896 the government which was favorable to the union was defeated, and the financial support given to Newfoundland was not considered sufficient; mail-steamship service was considered insufficient and finally interference with prosperous fish trade with the United States was feared.

In the mid-nineties, when a deputation from Newfoundland wished to discuss union, the Canadian government refused to burden itself with the debt of Newfoundland.

The changed strategic situation with the advent of the air age resulted in Canada's willingness to accept Newfoundland after the Second World War.

II. REGROUPING

Constitutional Provision

The British North America Act as amended in 1871 by an Act Respecting the Establishment of the Provinces in the Dominion of Canada, June 29, 1871 (34 & 35 Vict., c. 28), provides in Section 3 that the Parliament of Canada may alter the limits of any Province created out of Canadian territory upon terms and conditions agreed to by the legislature of such Province.

APPENDIX IV

Germany

I. ADMISSION

Constitutional Provisions

This Basic Law of the Federal Republic of Germany to give a new order to political life for a transitional period.

It acted also on behalf of those Germans to whom participation was denied.

The entire German people is called upon to accomplish by free self-determination, the unity and freedom of Germany (Excerpt from Preamble of the Basic Law).

Article 23. For the time being, this Basic Law shall apply in the territory of the Länder Baden, Bavaria, Bremen, Greater Berlin, Hamburg, Hesse, Lower Saxony, North Rhine-Westphalia, Rhineland-Palatinate, Schleswig-Holstein, Württemberg-Baden and Württemberg-Hohenzollern. *It shall be put into force for other parts of Germany on their accession.*

Article 28. (1) The constitutional order in the Länder must conform to the principles of the republican, democratic and social state based on the rule of law [*Rechtsstaat*] within the meaning of this Basic Law.

II. REGROUPING
A. *General Constitutional Provisions*

Article 29. (1) The federal territory shall be reorganized by a federal law with due regard to regional unity, historical and cultural connections, economic expedience and social structure. The reorganization shall create Länder which by their size and potentiality are able to fulfill efficiently the functions incumbent upon them.

(2) In areas which, in the reorganization of Länder after 8 May 1945, joined another Land without plebiscite, a certain change in the decision made concerning this subject may be demanded by popular initiative within one year after the coming into force of the Basic Law. The popular initiative shall require the consent of one-tenth of the population qualified to vote in Landtag elections. Should the popular initiative take place, the Federal Government must, in the draft law regarding the reorganization, include a provision determining to which Land the area concerned shall belong.

(3) After adoption of the Law, in each area which it is intended should join another Land, that part of the law which concerns this area must be submitted to a referendum. If a popular initiative takes place in accordance with paragraph (2), a referendum must always be carried out in the area concerned.

(4) Insofar as thereby the law is rejected in at least one area, it must be reintroduced in the Bundestag. After re-enactment, it shall require accordingly acceptance by referendum in the entire federal territory.

(5) In a referendum, the majority of the votes cast shall decide.

(6) The procedure shall be regulated by federal law. The reorganization shall be regulated before the expiring of three years after the promulgation of the Basic Law and, should it be necessary in consequence of accession of another part of Germany, within two years after such accession.

(7) The procedure regarding any other change in the existing territory of the Länder shall be regulated by federal law, which shall require ap-

proval of the Bundesrat and of the majority of the members of the Bundestag.

B. *Special Constitutional Provision*

Article 118. The reorganization of the territory comprising Länder Baden, Württemberg-Baden, and Württemberg-Hohenzollern may be accomplished, by agreement between the Länder concerned, in a manner deviating from the provisions of Article 29. Should an agreement not be reached, the reorganization shall be regulated by federal legislation which must provide for a referendum.

C. *Regrouping in Practice*

The history of the creation of the German Southwest State was as follows:

1. Inclusion in the Basic Law of Article 118 calling for the reorganization of Länder Baden, Württemberg-Baden, and Württemberg-Hohenzollern by agreement between the Länder themselves, or, failing such agreement, by the federal government.

2. Negotiations between the Länder resulting in 1950 in a decision to hold an advisory referendum on the subject.

3. On September 24, 1950, the referendum was held. The voters were asked if they favored either the restoration of the States along boundary lines as they were before the occupation or the creation of a new Southwest German State combining all three States. The results of the vote showed over-all sympathy for fusion, but resistance in Baden, especially in South Baden.

4. The federal government passed legislation for the reorganization of the Länder since the Länder had failed to act themselves. The legislation provided for a referendum in the three States on the question of the formation of a Southwest German State.

5. The question to be asked at the referendum posed the alternatives of fusion or restoration. The political campaign which developed was active and widespread through the States, fusionist sentiment centering in Württemberg-Baden, and restoration feeling centering in South Baden.

6. The President of South Baden challenged the constitutionality of the federal reorganization law, and the Federal Constitutional Court issued an injunction until that question could be decided, postponing the referendum.

7. The Court decided that in essential respects the federal reorganization legislation was constitutional, and on December 9, 1951, the plebiscite was held.

8. For the purposes of the referendum the area of the three States was divided into four electoral districts. All districts, except South Baden, voted for fusion. For the "union of the three States" to succeed, it was

necessary for a majority in at least three districts as well as a majority of the entire population of the three States to vote for fusion; 58.7 per cent of the eligible 4,207,791 voters turned out. Of these, 69.7 per cent voted for the Southwest State. The voting by districts was as follows (in percentages):

- a. South Baden   62.2 for restoration
- b. Baden part of Württemberg-Baden   57.5 for fusion
- c. Württemberg-Hohenzollern   91.4 for fusion
- d. Württemberg part of Württemberg-Baden 93.5 for fusion

A new State of seven million people living in 13,800 square miles was thus created.

The plebiscite which decided the creation of the Southwest State showed, however, that more than 50 per cent of the people in both parts of Baden voted against it. Partisans for restoration of Baden contend that, despite the influx of so-called evacuees from all parts of Germany, the population of all of Baden rejected the new State. Their attacks had been directed against the provision that three of the four election districts had to favor the union, and they had demanded that the vote of all of Baden and all of Württemberg should be counted separately.

The first government after the creation of the Southwest State was formed without participation of the Christian Democratic Union, the major opponent of the union and even without participation of prominent Badeners from other parties.

III. Secession

Constitutional Provisions

No provisions for secession are contained in the German Basic Law. However, the federation has special power in case of nonfulfillment of obligations towards the federation. Secession would be considered the extreme case of disobedience towards the federal government.

Article 37. (1) If a Land fails to fulfill its obligations towards the Federation under the Basic Law or any other federal law, the Federal Government may, with the approval of the Bundesrat, take the necessary measures to force the Land by way of federal compulsion to fulfill its duties.

(2) In order to carry out federal compulsion, the Federal Government or its commissioner shall have the right to give orders to all Länder and their authorities.

A P P E N D I X V

Switzerland

I. Admission

A. *Criteria for Membership*

Although there is no provision in the Swiss Constitution which deals with admissions, there is one which lists requirements for cantonal constitutions. These three requirements are:

1. They must contain no provision contrary to those of the federal Constitution;

2. They must assure the exercise of political rights according to republican — representative or democratic — forms of government;

3. They must have been accepted by, and be susceptible of amendment at the demand of, the absolute majority of the people (Art. 6, pars. 1, 2, 3).

B. *Attempt by Vorarlberg to Join the Swiss Federation*

At the time of the abdication of Charles VI as Emperor of Austria on November 11, 1918, the legal tie existing since 1713 between Vorarlberg and the Hapsburgs, the ruling power of Austria, disappeared, and Vorarlberg attempted to join the Swiss federation instead of adhering to the Austrian Republic.

The following is a summary of the events.

1. On October 21, 1918, the provisional National Assembly of Austria asked for the voluntary adherence of all Länder to Austria.

2. In Vorarlberg a provisional assembly was formed under the leadership of Jodor Fink, deputy of the Upper House, and Franz Loser, deputy of the Parliament, by the three major political parties. This assembly decided, on November 3, 1918, to remain within the framework of the German-Austrian state, a provisional state depending on the recognition of the Allied Peace Conference at Saint Germain.

3. On account of the weakness of the new Austrian Republic, a movement to join the Swiss federation gained strength in Vorarlberg. This movement was based on geographical and economic links with Switzerland, the similarity of dialect and most local institutions. An unofficial plebiscite was organized by the movement's two leaders, Riedmann and Pirker, and the provisional assembly of Vorarlberg was asked to discuss the matter.

4. In the official plebiscite approved by the assembly, and held on May 11, 1919, 45,566 (80.75 per cent) of the voters voted for union with Switzerland and 11,029 (19.25 per cent) against. Only in three communities, Bludenz, Hittisau, and Bolgenach, was the proposal to join Switzerland defeated.

5. The dissolution of the provisional tie with the Austrian Republic could only be effected by the consent of the Allies and by agreement between the Swiss Federation and Austria. Although there was popular support in Switzerland, especially by the newspapers, the federal authorities maintained an attitude of reserve since they realized that the final decision had to be made by the Allies at the Peace Conference in Saint Germain. Moreover, the French-speaking Swiss were opposed to the admission of a German-speaking State which might disturb the linguistic equilibrium.

6. On May 13, 1919, the Governor (*Landeshauptmann*), Dr. Ender, traveled as the representative of Vorarlberg with the Austrian delegation to Paris. However, the leader of the Austrian delegation, Chancellor Renner, indicated that the question of Vorarlberg should be discussed later. A telegram to Clémenceau from the leaders of the movement to join Switzerland brought about a discussion in the Territorial Commission at Saint Germain. A paragraph was to be included in the Peace Treaty permitting Vorarlberg to join Switzerland if Austria could reach an agreement with the Swiss federation. The Austrian delegation successfully resisted this attempt to change the territorial limits of Austria, and this paragraph was omitted from the Peace Treaty.

7. On September 10, 1919, the Peace Treaty was signed and the Austrian border with Switzerland was confirmed by the Allies. On December 17, 1919, in Paris, and on October 1, 1920, in the League of Nations in Geneva, Vorarlberg attempted to obtain another hearing for their case of union with Switzerland, but failed. On October 1, 1920, the new Austrian Constitution came into force and Vorarlberg remained a State in the Austrian federation.

A P P E N D I X   V I

United States

I. ADMISSION

A. *Constitutional Provisions*

ARTICLE IV, *Section* 3. New States may be admitted by the Congress into this Union . . .

ARTICLE IV, *Section* 4. The United States shall guarantee to every State in this Union a Republican Form of Government . . .

B. *Admissions in Practice*

1. GENERAL

The procedure for admitting all States has followed a common pattern. Territories generally have been subjected to (a), (b), ·(c), and (d) of the procedure outlined immediately below. The other States admitted have usually not been subjected to (a).

(a) The United States Congress passes a specific enabling act under which the citizens of the territory are to choose delegates to a constitutional convention;

(b) The constitution is then submitted to the people of the area for ratification;

(c) The authorities of the area apply for admission to the Union;

(d) If the State constitution is acceptable, Congress passes a resolution admitting the area to statehood.

C. *Illustrative Contemporary Legislation*

A bill to enable Hawaii to be admitted as a State which was passed by the House of Representatives on March 3, 1950, would do the following things (H.R. 49, 81st Cong., 2d Sess.):

1. Authorize a State constitutional convention to be held in the territory;

2. Outline the manner of election of delegates to the convention;

3. Establish the qualifications for voting for delegates to the convention;

4. Provide the manner for the adoption of a State constitution;

5. Outline special requirements to be included in the constitution, particularly with reference to the distribution of public lands;

6. Provide a method of ratification for the constitution;

7. Require the approval of the constitution by the President of the United States;

8. Provide for representation in Congress;

9. Authorize the expenses of the convention and the elections to be held;

10. Establish the State of Hawaii as a judicial district within the Ninth Judicial Circuit;

11. Establish jurisdiction for the United States district court for the district;

12. Authorize appointment of court officials, etc.

13. Provide for the extension of existing laws of the Territory of Hawaii after its admission as a State;

14. Retain jurisdiction of the United States over military, naval, and Coast Guard property, the Hawaii National Park, and other lands, and;

15. Repeal existing legislation in conflict with H.R. 49.

D. *Important Cases at Law*

1. *United States v. Texas*, 339 U.S. 699 (1950). In this case the United States Supreme Court decided that the status of Texas as an independent nation prior to admission to the Union did not entitle Texas to ownership of the lands underneath her coastal waters because Texas was admitted

to the Union by Congressional resolution "on an equal footing with the original States in all respects whatsoever" (9 Stat. 198).

2. *Virginia v. West Virginia,* 220 U.S. 1 (1911). In this case the Supreme Court decided that West Virginia was obligated to pay a portion of the total debt of the State of Virginia at the time of the separation of the two States.

E. *Five Cases of Admission*

1. MISSOURI

The petition for Missouri's admission was presented to Congress between 1818 and 1819 when a bitter sectional controversy over slavery was in progress. The House bill, prohibiting the further introduction of slaves into Missouri and ensuring that the children of slaves should be freed at the age of 25, was rejected by the Senate. Maine, applying for admission at the same time, was admitted as a free State by the House in December, 1819. The Senate, however, combined the two bills without mention of slavery.

The struggle between House and Senate ended in a compromise by admitting Maine as a free State, Missouri as a slave State, and prohibiting slavery in the territories north of the 36′ 30°N. Latitude line.

2. CALIFORNIA

California was ceded to the United States after the Mexican War by the Treaty of Guadalupe Hidalgo, February 2, 1848.

To avoid the slavery issue, California, on its own initiative, adopted a State constitution ratified by popular vote on November 13, 1849. Congress admitted California on June 17, 1850, to statehood, as part of a larger compromise on the slavery issue. The conditions were the following:

The admission act acknowledged that the California constitution was republican and laid down three further terms of admission:

(a) California was to be admitted on equal footing with other States;

(b) California was never to "interfere with the primary disposal of the soil within same [California] by the United States," and never tax the lands which belonged to the United States;

(c) California was to be given two representatives until the next apportionment.

3. OREGON

When a bill to admit the State of Oregon was introduced in Congress in May, 1858, an enabling act having previously been passed to permit the people of the territory to form a constitutional government, the population of the area was only 52,000. Since the current apportionment formula required a population of 80,000 for one representative, many legislators from larger States protested against the admission of Oregon. Senators from New York and Virginia inveighed against the insufficient population of the territory to no avail. Their arguments were largely ignored and Oregon easily admitted.

4. NEBRASKA

In Nebraska the discussion over admission was only slightly more complicated. At a time when the apportionment ratio was 127,000 to one representative, the territory of Nebraska had a population somewhat over 28,000. Despite this fact an enabling act was passed by the Congress, a convention was held in the territory to draft a constitution, and the latter was ratified by popular vote, 3938 to 3838.

Opponents of admission referred to the smallness of the vote, and to the fact two companies of federal troops from Iowa had fraudulently voted in the referendum. Since the companies voted 134 to 24 in favor of the Nebraska constitution, the issue was of consequence. Another and more important objection to admission was that the proposed constitution disenfranchised colored voters.

The question of fraud was largely ignored. When one Senator complained that more people lived in his county than in the entire territory of Nebraska, his complaint went unanswered. Only the problem of treatment of colored people — the very same problem which made extremely difficult the admission of other States in the Union — remained a formidable obstacle to admission.

In this case the Senate insisted that Nebraska pledge there would be no discrimination by the State on account of race or color. The House of Representatives did not agree with the Senate's stipulation, and passed an amendment which left the matter open to the Nebraska legislature. President Johnson vetoed a compromise measure, maintaining that the Congress had no right to prescribe the conditions of franchise to a State, but his veto was overwhelmingly overruled, and Nebraska was admitted according to the terms laid down by Congress.

5. WYOMING

Wyoming was another State which met opposition in gaining admission because of its small population. At a time when the apportionment ratio was 151,000 to one representative, Wyoming had a population of 60,000. Because of this insufficiency of population, the Fiftieth Congress in 1889 failed to act on an enabling bill proposed in the Senate. However, after a majority of the boards of county commissioners in the territory petitioned the Governor to issue a proclamation for a constitutional convention, that convention was called and adopted a constitution which was ratified by popular vote 6272 to 1923. Once again it was argued that Wyoming had fewer voters than lived in this county or that county, but the Congress, as it has consistently done, admitted the territory regardless of its population.

II. REGROUPING OF STATES

A. *Constitutional Provisions*

ARTICLE IV, *Section* 3. . . . no new State shall be formed or erected within the Jurisdiction of any other State; nor shall any State be formed by the Junction of two or more States, or parts of States, without the Consent of the Legislatures of the States concerned as well as of the Congress.

B. *Regrouping in Practice*

Three times portions of a State have broken away from that State to form a new state subsequently admitted to the Union.

1. KENTUCKY

In 1792 the settlers of Kentucky County in Virginia adopted a State constitution which Virginia acquiesced in, and which the Congress accepted.

2. MAINE

In 1820 the inhabitants of Maine, after a long period of agitation, requested separation from Massachusetts, and statehood in the American Union, which were both granted.

3. WEST VIRGINIA

Because of the decision by Virginia to secede from the Union in 1861, West Virginia, settled by fewer slaveholders and by inhabitants more closely identified with the interests of the trans-Allegheny region than the lower South, set up a State government of its own, and was admitted to the Union.

III. SECESSION

Several American states have seceded from the Union. They were all Southern States and all seceded in 1860–1861. Each passed a special secession ordinance in a specially called convention. The assertion of the right of secession by these States and the denial of that right by the national government resulted in the Civil War.

The States which seceded were South Carolina, Mississippi, Florida, Alabama, Georgia, Louisiana, Texas, Tennessee, Arkansas, Virginia, and North Carolina.

In *Texas v. White* (7 Wall. 700 (1869)), the Supreme Court settled the constitutional question of the right of secession, as it had in fact been settled by the Civil War, by asserting:

> When, therefore, Texas became one of the United States, she entered into an indissoluble relation. All the obligations of perpetual union and all the guarantees of republican government in the Union, attached at once to the State. The act which consummated her admission into Union was something more than a compact; it was the incorporation of a new member into the political body. And it was complete and final . . . . There was no place for reconsideration or revocation, except through revolution or consent of the States.

Amendment of the Constitution

I. GENERAL CHARACTERISTICS OF THE AMENDMENT PROCESS

The central problem in devising a procedure for constitutional change is to reconcile two principles: the need for preventing ill-considered change, and the need to allow desirable and substantially supported amendments to be made. The necessity of provision for change is recognized by the inclusion in all constitutions of procedures for their amendment. The necessity for thorough consideration and general support of change is recognized by various methods which make the amending process more difficult than the enactment of ordinary legislation. These methods fall into three general classes: (1) the use of separate steps for initiation and ratification of amendments; (2) the requirement of acceptance by an extraordinary majority at some point in the amendment procedure; and (3) the requirement of ratification by popular referendum.

In most cases the process of amendment involves separate steps for initiation and ratification, providing a period for public deliberation midway in the procedure. Separate steps for initiation and ratification are required under the Constitutions of Australia, Switzerland, and the United States, and were provided for in certain cases by the Weimar Constitution. Under the Basic Law of the German Federal Republic, however, amendment is a single-stage process of the federal legislature. Amendment by action of the federal legislature alone was also provided for in the Weimar Constitution and the German Imperial Constitution; and, in certain limited cases, the Canadian organic act provides for its amendment by means of ordinary laws of the Dominion legislature.

A second characteristic of several amendment procedures is the requirement of an extraordinary majority at some step in the process. With the limited exception of the Canadian organic act, those constitutions which permit constitutional amendment by action of the legislature alone require an extraordinary legislative majority for the passage of amendments. Thus, both the Weimar Constitution and the German Basic Law require two-thirds votes of the federal legislature, and, under the German Imperial Constitution, an extraordinary majority of the upper legislative chamber was required. The United States Constitution requires an extraordinary majority for both steps in the amending process; a vote of two thirds of each house of Congress for initiation, and approval by three fourths of the States for ratification.

Where the device of an extraordinary majority is not employed in the amendment process, as in Switzerland and Australia, a popular referendum has been provided for. Thus, the procedure for initiation of constitutional amendment in Australia requires only a majority in the federal Parliament; for ratification, the approval of a majority of the electors throughout Australia, and also in a majority of the States, is required. The Swiss procedure is identical with the Australian, except that the Swiss Constitution provides as well for initiation of proposals by popular initiative.

II. AGENCIES OF AMENDMENT

A. *Role of the Federal Legislature*

Some federal systems have empowered the federal legislature to adopt constitutional amendments by its action alone. Thus, under the German Basic Law, the Weimar Constitution, and the German Imperial Constitution, amendments could be adopted by action of the federal legislature alone. In Canada, amendment may be adopted by an ordinary federal law, in the limited areas which are not still formally amended by the United Kingdom Parliament. The simplicity of the amendment process where only the legislature need act made it possible, under the Weimar Constitution, to use this power to deal with emergencies by the adoption of measures temporarily amending the Constitution.

In the other federal systems studied, the legislature plays a prominent, although not the only, part in the amendment process. Amendments are initiated by the federal legislature in the United States (upon a two-thirds vote of each house) and Australia (upon vote of an absolute majority), and may be initiated in Switzerland in the form of federal legislation. Under the Swiss Constitution the Federal Assembly may also submit counterproposals to amendments proposed by popular initiative, or recommend rejection of such proposals. The federal legislature does not take part in the ratification of amendments in any of these countries. In the United States, however, Congress selects the ratification procedure to be used, i.e. whether by the legislatures of, or conventions in, three fourths of the States.

In several cases a distinction has been made between the roles of the two legislative chambers in the amendment process. In Australia and Canada the principal role falls to the lower chamber, since the Cabinet systems of those countries have led to dominance by that chamber. Under the Weimar Constitution, the upper chamber could not block an amendment adopted by the lower chamber, but could compel its submission to popular referendum. In the United States and Switzerland, and under the German Basic Law, the roles of the two chambers are equal.

B. *Role of the Member States*

The only Constitution allowing participation of the State legislatures in the amendment process is that of the United States, which provides that ratification of proposals for amendment may be effected by the legislatures of three fourths of the States. This provision for ratification has not proved to be a great obstacle, as only five of the twenty-seven proposals presented to the States for ratification have not been approved. In addition, the United States Constitution provides, as an alternative method of initiation of amendments, for the calling of a convention to propose amendments upon the application of the legislatures of two thirds of the States. Although this method of initiation has never been employed, the possibility of its use has, on occasion, influenced the federal legislature (the usual initiating body) to propose amendments.

The States also fill a significant role in the amendment process under the German Constitutions, where delegates to the upper federal legislative chamber are appointed and instructed by the State governments, and the upper chamber has an important part in adopting amendments. In most cases, under the other constitutional systems studied, members of the upper chamber represent State interests but are popularly elected and are not subject to instructions. In these systems, protection of State interests through the action of the federal legislature is therefore not so great, and of course depends further on the role of the upper chamber in the amendment process.

The Constitutions of Switzerland and Australia both accord some recognition to State interests at the stage of ratification of amendments by requiring that proposed amendments be approved, at a referendum, by a majority of the voters in a majority of the States, as well as by a majority of the voters throughout the country. This additional requirement of the approval of a majority of the voters in a majority of the States has not proved to be an obstacle to proposals for amendment. In only one case under the Swiss Constitution and in only three cases under the Australian Constitution, apparently, have proposals obtained approval of a majority throughout the country but failed to secure a majority in most of the States. A variant of this Swiss and Australian system is provided, in effect, by an alternative method of ratification under the United States Constitution; if the federal legislature so decides, ratification may be accomplished by approval of conventions in three fourths of the States, rather than by approval of the State legislatures. In the single case where the convention method was selected, delegates to the conventions were popularly elected and, in almost all States, were pledged to their views by their electors, so that this system amounted to a referendum in each State.

Some of the constitutions studied expressly require the consent of the States concerned to certain amendments affecting their rights secured by the constitution. This was the case, for example, under the German Constitution of 1871, and the United States Constitution stipulates that no State, without its consent, shall be deprived of its equal suffrage in the Senate. Similarly, the Australian Constitution declares that no amendment diminishing the proportionate representation of any State in either house of the federal Parliament, or the minimum number of representatives of a State in the lower house, or altering the limits of the States, shall be adopted except with the approval of a majority of the electors in the State concerned.[1]

In the current attempts to revise the procedure for amendment of the Canadian organic act, there has been an attempt to classify the sections of the Constitution according to their relative importance to the Provinces, and to prescribe different procedures for amendment according to that importance. It has been agreed in principle by representatives of the Dominion and provincial governments that those sections of the constitution which concern the Dominion only should be capable of being amended by act of the Dominion Parliament alone; while those sections concerning the Provinces only should require action by their legislatures alone. The amendment of provisions which concern equally the Dominion and the Provinces should require the approval of the Dominion Parliament and of a proportion (perhaps two thirds) of the provincial legislatures. Agreement has not been reached, however, on the classification of the various sections of the Constitution.

C. Direct Popular Participation

Several constitutions provide for initiation of amendments upon demand of a specified number of the voters, or provide for their ratification by popular vote. The Swiss Constitution, under an amendment adopted in 1891, allows direct popular proposal of constitutional amendments through popular initiative, that is, on the demand of 50,000 Swiss voters. About one third of the proposals initiated in Switzerland since 1848 have been introduced by popular initiative, but less than one fifth of these have been adopted (as compared with nineteen of twenty-two proposals initiated by the legislature since 1918). The Weimar Constitution allowed amendments to be proposed on the petition of one tenth of the persons qualified to vote. The Constitution of the United States establishes, as an alternative mode of initiation of amendments, that Congress shall, on the application of the legislatures of two thirds of the States, call a convention for the purpose of proposing amendments; but as this provision has never been used it is not clear whether the members of the convention would be popularly elected.

The Swiss and Australian Constitutions provide for popular referendum as the sole method of ratification of proposals for amendment. The experiences of the two countries with this method have been very different, however. Of twenty-four proposals submitted to referendum in Australia in

<hr>

[1] See also the discussion of special arrangements between the federation and the member States for constitutional adjustment, at page 797.

about fifty years, only four have been adopted; in Switzerland about half of the more than a hundred proposals for amendment since 1848 have been adopted.

The Weimar Constitution also required a popular referendum for ratification, on demand of the upper legislative chamber, where the lower chamber adopted a proposed constitutional amendment in spite of the former's objections. The Weimar Constitution provided as well that proposals for amendment originated by popular initiative should be submitted to popular referendum, unless in the meantime they had been passed unaltered by the lower chamber.

The United States Constitution established, as an alternative mode of ratification, that proposals for amendment may be ratified by conventions in three fourths of the States. As noted above, this method, on the single occasion when it was used, amounted in effect to a popular referendum in each State.

The objection most frequently raised against direct popular participation in the amendment process, whether at the initiation or at the ratification stage, is that the drafting and appraising of proposals for amendment are too difficult and technical to be entrusted directly to the electorate. The Swiss Constitution partially meets such objections, so far as they relate to the initiation of proposals, by allowing the Federal Assembly to present counterproposals to the electorate along with the proposals originating by popular initiative. The proposal and counterproposal are then submitted to referendum. Only seven of thirty-nine proposals for amendment originating by popular initiative have been accepted in Switzerland at the referenda which have been held upon them; whereas, out of nine cases in which the Assembly submitted counterproposals, they were accepted by referenda in seven instances. In a number of cases, the sponsors of the original popular initiative proposal seem to have withdrawn their proposal in favor of the Federal Assembly's counterproposal. Similarly, in Switzerland, where a proposal originating by popular initiative is couched in general terms (rather than in the form of a draft of an amendment) the actual drafting of the proposal for submission to referendum is done by the Federal Assembly.

III. Variations in Amendment Procedure According to Subject Matter

Several constitutions provide for a variation in the amendment procedure according to the subject matter of the proposed amendment. Under the agreed principles for revision of the Canadian amending procedure discussed above, for example, the constitutional provisions relating to fundamental rights could be amended only by acts of the federal legislature and of all the provincial legislatures, while a less difficult procedure would be used for other amendments. Some constitutions have placed certain sections beyond the possibility of amendment or repeal. The variation in the amendment procedure in the case of provisions of particular concern to the member States has been discussed above.

A. *Prohibition of Amendment*

It has been suggested that there is an implied limitation, under a federal constitution, against any amendment interfering with the federal system, as such, or with the continued existence of the States. Of the constitutions surveyed, however, only the German Basic Law contains any provisions of this sort. It prohibits any amendment affecting the organization of the federation into Länder or the basic cooperation of the Länder in legislation. It also prohibits any amendment affecting the basic rights defined in the Basic Law or the organization of Germany as a democratic and social federal state, operating under a limited constitution, and with a separation of powers.

The United States Constitution prohibited amendment of certain of its terms during a specified number of years following its adoption. Those terms embodied compromises between the slaveholding and non-slaveholding States concerning the federal power with regard to slavery, and prohibition of their amendment represented a further concession to the latter States.

B. *Choice of Alternative Amendment Procedures*

Where the amendment procedure provides for selection of alternative methods for initiation and ratification, there may be variation in treatment according to which section of the constitution is to be dealt with. For example, the United States Constitution permits Congress to determine whether ratification of a proposed amendment shall take place upon approval by the legislatures of three fourths of the States or by conventions (amounting to referenda) in three fourths of the States. Thus, where Congress considers it desirable to have direct popular participation in ratification it may provide for the convention procedure.

C. *General Revision of the Constitution*

Only the Swiss Constitution makes express provision for its general revision, and establishes a special procedure for that purpose. Apart from Switzerland, where a total revision of the Constitution was effected in 1874 (and has been proposed on three occasions), none of the countries surveyed has attempted to revise its constitution as a whole. There have, however, been recurrent public suggestions in Canada and Australia to that end.

IV. Other Methods of Constitutional Adjustment

A. *Temporary or Transitional Provisions*

It is now a general practice to include in federal constitutions so-called "temporary" or "transitional" provisions. These provisions are normally concerned with the adjustment between the federal and state governments of such questions as finance, taxation, customs and excise duties, and the transfer of staff and property, consequent upon the formation of the federal union. Unless such provisions are specifically declared to continue in force only for a defined term of years after the formation of the federation, their termination usually occurs when some agency, normally the federal legislature, has taken certain action defined in the provisions themselves; in most cases this action consists merely of the federal legislature's declaring the provisions to be terminated. The employment of temporary provisions seems a useful device in tiding a new federal system over its early stages, especially when those provisions are subject to the control of the federal legislature so that they can be readily deleted from the constitution when their usefulness is past. The Canadian, Australian, and Swiss Constitutions, and the Weimar Constitution and German Basic Law, all include provisions of this nature.

B. *Emergency Provisions*[2]

The Swiss and German Constitutions contain provisions permitting the federal legislatures or the federal executive, in periods of emergency, in effect to suspend all or part of the Constitution. Under an amendment adopted in 1949, the Swiss Federal Assembly may enact "urgent" legislation which is not subject to popular referendum (as other legislation may be) and need not be based on the Constitution. Such legislation may continue in force for only one year, however, unless adopted by popular referendum in the same manner as other constitutional amendments.

Under the Weimar Constitution, the President was authorized to take "such measures as are necessary," including use of the armed forces or temporary suspension of the fundamental constitutional rights, in the event of a serious threat to public safety and order. Any measures taken by him under this power, however, had to be canceled upon the demand of the lower house of the federal legislature. The German Basic Law also contains an emergency provision; where the lower house of the federal legislature rejects a bill which the Cabinet considers necessary, the President may, on the request of the Cabinet and with the consent of the upper house, declare a "legislative emergency" in which the bill may come into force upon action of the upper house alone. However, legislation so enacted may not itself amend the Basic Law, and a Cabinet may exercise this power only once during its existence.

[2] Such provisions are also considered in other studies, in particular Study 13, Defense of the Constitutional Order.

C. *Special Arrangements Between the Federation and the Member States*

The Australian Constitution includes a special provision permitting alteration of the system of distribution of powers between the federation and the member States. It provides, in addition to the other federal legislative powers, that the federal legislature may enact laws with respect to matters referred to it by any State legislature; such laws shall apply, however, only in those States whose legislatures concur in the reference. In practice, with regard to most matters, the effective grant of such powers to the federation would require the agreement of all State legislatures. For this reason, this constitutional provision has been applied infrequently, though unsuccessfully pressed during World War II with a view to conferring on the federal legislature additional powers to deal with reconstruction following the war.

Another somewhat similar provision of the Australian Constitution authorizes agreements between the federation and the member States with regard to the public debts of the latter, and states that such agreements shall be binding "notwithstanding anything contained" in the Constitution.

The agreed principles for revision of the procedure for amendment of the Canadian Constitution include an arrangement by which amendments concerning only the Dominion and one or more, but less than all, of the Provinces might be adopted upon approval by the Dominion Parliament and the legislatures of the Provinces concerned.

D. *Custom*

Custom and interpretation have also had significant roles in constitutional adjustment. In considering the effectiveness of the formal procedures for constitutional amendment in the countries surveyed, it is necessary therefore to study the operation of these factors, as well as the working of the formal procedures. The constitutional instruments of Australia and Canada, for example, were in their juridical origins statutes of the United Kingdom Parliament, and at the time of their passage the United Kingdom Parliament still retained unlimited law-making power in relation to both countries. With the progressive development of customs governing the relationship of the United Kingdom and the self-governing Dominions, the principle developed that the law-making power of the United Kingdom Parliament should not be exercised in relation to the Dominions except at their request. This principle was made positive law by the United Kingdom Parliament's passage in 1931 of the Statute of Westminster.

Custom has also played a part in the United States; for example, in the principle, generally accepted for many years, that a President should serve only two terms of office. This principle has, since World War II, been adopted as a formal amendment to the United States Constitution.

E. *Judicial Interpretation*

Judicial interpretation has been an important means of constitutional adjustment in the United States, Canada, and Australia, especially in relation to those sections of the Constitution dealing with the division of legislative powers between the federal government and the member States.[3] The expansion of the federal legislative power under the United States Constitution, which supported the social and economic legislation of the 1930's, was accomplished not by formal amendment but by judicial interpretation. Likewise, the grants of legislative power to the federal governments of Canada and Australia have been substantially modified by the operation of judicial review. The trend in Canada has been to cut down the Dominion legislative powers in favor of the Provinces; while the trend in Australia, by contrast, has been considerably to enlarge federal powers, usually in the name of the defense power.

This judicial process operates as a supplement to the amending procedure, permitting a more gradual development of constitutional principles. In addition, judicial interpretation of the constitution permits controlled expansion of government powers in order to meet the requirements of emergency periods, as in the United States during the economic depression of the 1930's and in Australia during World War II, and thus provides a substitute for the emergency provisions discussed above.

V. CONCLUSION

The objective in framing a constitution is to lay down basic principles, expected to be of considerable permanence, for the regulation of the institutions of the federation. Accordingly, the procedure for constitutional amendment should assure that these basic principles are changed only after thorough consideration and with substantial support. At the same time, if a constitution is too rigid in the face of demands for change, there will be strong pressures for resort to informal methods of constitutional adjustment.

Constitutional safeguards against amendments which may be unwise or not widely approved have been described above. These are, notably, separate steps for initiation and ratification, the requirement of extraordinary majorities, the use of popular referendum, or a combination of these devices.

The requirement of separate steps for initiation and ratification, with different agencies participating, is employed in all the federal systems studied except those of Germany[4] (and, in limited cases, Canada). This method is less rapid than enactment by the legislature alone (as under the

---

[3] The role of the judiciary in constitutional interpretation is considered at length in Study 3, The Federal Judiciary.

[4] Indeed, the procedure under the German Constitutions is a special case, in view of the composition of their upper chambers. Since these have been composed of instructed State delegates, an amendment, in fact, required approval of the States as well as of the federal lower chamber.

German Constitutions) but affords a better opportunity and incentive for thorough consideration of proposals during and between the two steps. Three possible agencies may participate in the two stages of the amendment process: the federal legislature, the member States, and the general electorate.

The initiation of amendments appears to be appropriate for the federal legislature as the representative of all State and regional interests. Experience with use of the popular initiative has largely been limited to Switzerland, but the high proportion of rejections of popular proposals there seems to suggest doubt as to the value of this method. If the popular initiative is employed, however, it seems wise, in the light of Swiss experience, to permit the federal legislature to present counterproposals for consideration by the ratifying body. Initiation of amendments directly by the member States has not been provided in any of the constitutions studied, and appears to be too unwieldy a method to be practical, since it requires fairly uniform and simultaneous action by several different bodies in initiating proposals. If the federal legislature may initiate amendments, that would seem sufficient to ensure the formal proposal of any measures having substantial support among the electorate or among the States.

The agency of ratification can be either the member States, through action of their legislatures, or the general electorate through referendum. The Australian and Swiss experience with the use of popular referendum for ratification has been strikingly different. This system has blocked adoption of most proposals for amendment in Australia, whereas in Switzerland about half the proposals have been ratified. An adequate analysis of these divergent results would have to take into consideration the subject matter of the amendments and proposals involved. But it seems fair to conclude that successful use of the popular referendum for ratification depends in large part on sustained experience with direct popular action as part of the working machinery of the constitution (as in Switzerland). Ratification by the State legislatures, on the other hand, assures consideration of proposals by experienced representative bodies, and provides adequate protection for State interests.

Ratification could properly require the approval of an extraordinary majority of the member States, but unanimity would be much too rigid as a general provision. Some variation of the amendment procedure may be justified, however, according to the subject matter of the proposed amendment. In particular, the unanimous agreement of the States might be required for amendment of those sections of the constitution which regulate State representation in the federal legislature, or for amendment of certain provisions during a specified period following its adoption. Such restrictions may help achieve adoption of the constitution by the States. The federal legislature should be authorized to provide for some regulation of the ratification procedure, as by specifying a period within which the States must approve a proposed amendment.

The formal means of constitutional amendment may be supplemented by several formal and informal methods of constitutional adjustment, one or more of which have been employed by each of the federal systems studied. One such method which has been widely used is the provision for repeal of "temporary" or "transitional" sections of the constitution by action of the federal legislature alone. These sections are designed to help a new federal system through its early stages, by continuing temporarily certain functions of the States until the federation is ready to assume them. Another method of constitutional adjustment, provided for in the Australian Constitution, permits arrangements between the member States and the federation for the latter to exercise certain powers not otherwise granted to it. This procedure may be useful as a simplified means of granting to the federation power to deal with temporary or special problems or with matters of concern to only a few of the member States.

Finally, the processes of custom and of judicial interpretation of the constitution are important supplements to the formal amendment procedure. The process of interpretation makes possible the controlled expansion of government powers in times of crisis, and thus helps to avoid the need for special constitutional provisions for emergency powers.

APPENDIX I

Australia

I. The Constitutional Background

The basic constitutional instrument of Australia is the Commonwealth of Australia Constitution Act, which in its juridical origin is a statute of the United Kingdom Parliament passed in 1900. In fact, however, the federation of the six British Colonies in Australia was preceded by a series of Constitutional Conventions extending over a period of years, and the Constitution Act as finally passed by the United Kingdom Parliament is substantially in accordance with a draft agreed upon by representatives of the six Australian colonies and subsequently approved by popular vote in each colony.

II. Constitutional Provisions on Amendment

The main procedure for amendment of the Constitution is that provided under Section 128 of the Constitution, which states:

This Constitution shall not be altered except in the following manner:

The proposed law for the alteration thereof must be passed by an absolute majority of each House of the Parliament, and not less than two nor more than six months after its passage through both Houses the proposed law shall be submitted in each State to the electors qualified to vote for the election of members of the House of Representatives.

But if either House passes any such proposed law by an absolute majority, and the other House rejects or fails to pass it, . . . and if after an interval of three months the first-mentioned House . . . again passes the proposed law by an absolute majority . . . the Governor-General may submit the proposed law . . . to the electors of each State qualified to vote for the election of the House of Representatives. . . .

And if in a majority of the States a majority of the electors voting approve the proposed law, and if a majority of all the electors voting also approve the proposed law, it shall be presented to the Governor-General for the Queen's assent.

Two further modes of constitutional adjustment are provided in the Constitution. Certain so-called "Temporary Provisions" of the Constitution are prefaced by the words: "until the [Federal] Parliament otherwise provides." These sections are mainly concerned with such matters as electoral laws and customs and excise duties, and frequently preserve the relevant State laws until such time as the Commonwealth chooses to act.

Further, Section 51 (XXXVII) of the Constitution grants to the Parliament of the Commonwealth the power to make laws with respect to:

Matters referred to the Parliament of the Commonwealth by the Parliament or Parliaments of any State or States, but so that the law shall extend only to those States by whose Parliaments the matter is referred, or which afterwards adopt the law.

It seems clear that, except for matters of local interest, it would be necessary, for the reference of any power, to obtain the agreement of all the States. In practice, the difficulty of securing unanimity among the States has proved almost insuperable, and this mode of adjustment has therefore been resorted to but rarely. The most important occasion on which it was attempted to put this provision to use was during World War II, when the representatives of all six States agreed to refer a list of fourteen legislative powers (to be used in postwar reconstruction) to the Commonwealth. The plan broke down, however, when it came to obtaining the necessary legislative action by the State Parliaments. Owing to lack of use, the limits of Section 51 (XXXVII) have not been definitively mapped out; it is not clear, for example, whether a reference once made to the Commonwealth by a State can be revoked, at least before the legislative power referred has been acted on by the Commonwealth.

One method of amendment not mentioned in the Constitution is available, in theory. Since the Constitution originated as a statute of the United Kingdom Parliament, that Parliament should, in theory, be able to enact amendments. Even at the time the Constitution was being drafted, however, it was agreed that this power of amendment by the United Kingdom

Parliament was only a theoretical one. With the progressive development of the conventions and practice governing the relationship of the United Kingdom to her former colonies, and particularly since the Statute of Westminster of 1931, the powers of the United Kingdom Parliament in this regard are probably at an end.

III. LIMITS OF ACTION UNDER SECTION 128

The final paragraph of Section 128 defines certain limitations of the scope of action under that section:

> No alteration diminishing the proportionate representation of any State in either House of the Parliament, or the minimum number of representatives of a State in the House of Representatives, or increasing, diminishing, or otherwise altering the limits of the State, or in any manner affecting the provisions of the Constitution in relation thereto, shall become law unless the majority of the electors voting in that State approve the proposed law.

It is not clear whether an amendment, in accordance with the procedure under Section 128, seeking to eliminate the final paragraph of that section, would be valid; or whether, even if it might be valid, such an amendment would itself require the approval of the electors in all of the States, rather than merely in a majority of States as is the general requirement under Section 128.

A further possible limitation, of a specialized nature, arises from Section 105 A of the Constitution. This section authorizes agreements between the Commonwealth and the States with respect to the public debts of the latter, including the taking over of such debts by the Commonwealth and the borrowing of money by the States. The suggested limitation is contained in subsection (5) of Section 105 A, which states that any such agreement shall be binding upon the Commonwealth and States parties thereto "notwithstanding anything contained in this Constitution."

IV. PRACTICE UNDER SECTION 128

Section 128 provides that, in the event a proposal for amendment is agreed to by only one house of Parliament, the proposal may be submitted directly to popular referendum by the Governor-General. This portion of Section 128 has arisen only once — in 1914, when it was established that the Governor-General must defer to the advice of the federal Cabinet as to whether or not the proposal shall be permitted to go to a referendum. This means that a proposal would probably not be submitted for referendum unless it had been approved by the House of Representatives, the body to which the Cabinet is responsible.

Twelve referenda have been held to date under Section 128, beginning in 1906. Sometimes these referenda have contained several separate proposals for constitutional amendment and sometimes only one proposal. The referendum of May, 1913, for example, contained six separate proposals. On the other hand, where a referendum contains only one proposal, it may be of a very sweeping nature; the referendum of August, 1944, contained only one proposal, but this in effect involved the conferring of fourteen additional heads of legislative power on the Commonwealth government. In the twelve referenda that have been held to date, a total of twenty-four separate proposals have been presented to the electors.

Of the twenty-four proposals, only four have been adopted as constitutional amendments. Only two of these were of major importance: the State Debts proposal of 1928, which inserted Section 105A into the Constitution (supra), and the proposal of 1946 which provided for federal legislative power over social services. In three cases, proposals have been approved by a majority of the electorate throughout Australia, but failed as constitutional amendments because of failure to secure also majorities in a majority (four) of the six States. In no case has a majority of States approved but a proposal failed because of not securing a majority throughout Australia.

APPENDIX II

Canada

I. PROCEDURE FOR AMENDMENT OF THE BRITISH NORTH AMERICA ACT

A. Constitutional Provisions

The basic constitutional instrument of Canada is the British North America Act of 1867 which, in its juridical origin, is a statute of the United Kingdom Parliament.

The British North America Act, as originally enacted, contained no provision for its own amendment. There seems to have been no discussion of this point in 1867, probably due to the view that, as it was a British statute, it could only be amended by the British Parliament. In fact, the amendments to the Act that have been made since 1867 have been effected through acts of the United Kingdom Parliament. In 1949, however, an amendment, passed by the United Kingdom Parliament, conferred upon the Dominion Parliament a power to amend "the Constitution of Canada" with respect to certain limited matters; that is, to legislate regarding:

The amendment from time to time of the Constitution of Canada, except as regards matters coming within the classes of subjects by this Act assigned exclusively to the Legislatures of the Provinces, or as regards rights or privileges by this or any other Constitutional Act granted or secured to the Legislature or the Government of a Province, or to any class of persons with respect to schools or as regards the use of the English or the French language, or as regards the requirements that there shall be a session of the Parliament of Canada at least once each year, and that no House of Commons shall continue for more than five years from the day of the return of the Writs for choosing the House; provided, however, that a House of Commons may in time of real or apprehended war, invasion, or insurrection be continued by the Parliament of Canada, if such continuation is not opposed by the votes of more than one-third of the members of such House.

It will be noted that the technique of amendment here provided is expressed in the form of a general federal legislative power, subject to certain defined exceptions. The ordinary process of legislation is all that is required.

In all other respects the procedure for amendment remains as it was before, that is, by statute of the United Kingdom Parliament.

B. *The Role of the United Kingdom Parliament*

Certain rules have developed by convention and statute concerning the role of the United Kingdom Parliament in amendment of the British North America Act. First, it is clear that the United Kingdom Parliament will act only at the request of Canada. This limitation on the theoretically unlimited law-making power of the United Kingdom Parliament in relation to Canada operated from the outset as a convention of British constitutional law, and was formalized by the passage by the United Kingdom Parliament in 1931 of the Statute of Westminster.

In practice, the request to the United Kingdom Parliament from Canada takes the form of an address to the Crown by the two houses of the Dominion Parliament. The United Kingdom Parliament is bound to act on such a request. The amending statute is now drafted in Canada, and the only changes made by the United Kingdom in recent years have been purely verbal. The United Kingdom Parliament, it seems clear, will not pass amendments to the British North America Act on the initiative of the Provinces of Canada.

C. *The Role of the Dominion and Provinces*

The federal government has, on several occasions, consulted the Provinces before transmitting requests to the United Kingdom Parliament for the amendment of the British North America Act. The first occasion seems to have been in the case of the amendment of 1907 which followed a Dominion-Provincial conference for consideration of the proposed amendment. Again, in 1930, the approval of the interested Provinces was obtained by the Dominion before an amendment was requested; and in 1940, in the case of an amendment granting the Dominion Parliament powers relating to unemployment insurance, the Dominion obtained the approval of the ministries of all the Provinces before transmitting its "request" to the United Kingdom Parliament. The other amendments, however, including the amendment of 1949 which conferred a limited power of amendment upon the Dominion Parliament, were requested by the Dominion Government without prior consultation with the Provinces.

Past practice thus suggests there is no customary obligation that the Dominion consult the Provinces, or obtain their approval, in all cases with regard to proposed amendments. Some text-writers have asserted, however, that there is such a duty, especially toward the Provinces concerned with the amendment. There is also disagreement as to the manner by which provincial agreement should be expressed. Practices in these respects therefore reflect, in each case, the influence of political forces in the Dominion Parliament.

II. SUGGESTED CHANGES FOR THE PROCEDURE FOR AMENDING THE BRITISH NORTH AMERICA ACT

For the last generation there has been considerable discussion of the question of providing machinery for the amendment of the British North America Act within Canada itself, without the necessity of recourse to the United Kingdom Parliament. In 1950 the Dominion government called a conference of the Dominion and the Provinces to consider the problem of devising such an amending procedure to cover those matters not falling within the scope of the limited amending power conferred on the Dominion Parliament by the amendment to the Act made in 1949. The conference agreed on a series of categories into which the various provisions of the British North America Act should be fitted. These categories would require different procedures for their amendment, depending on the importance of the subject matter to the Dominion and to each Province. The categories adopted by the conference were as follows:

(1) Provisions which concern the Dominion Parliament only; amendment to be by Act of the Dominion Parliament.

(2) Provisions which concern the Provincial legislatures only; amendment to be by Act of the Provincial legislatures.

(3) Provisions which concern the Dominion Parliament and one or more, but not all, of the Provincial legislatures; amendment to be by Act of the Dominion Parliament and an Act of the legislature of each of the Provinces affected.

(4) Provisions which concern the Dominion Parliament and all of the Provincial legislatures; amendment to be by Act of the Dominion Parliament and Acts of such majority of the Provincial legislatures and upon such additional conditions, if any, as may be decided upon.

(5) Provisions concerning fundamental rights (as for instance, but

without restriction, education, language, solemnization of marriage, administration of justice, provincial property in lands, mines, and other natural resources) and the amendment of the amending procedures; amendment to be by Act of the Dominion Parliament and Acts of the legislatures of all the Provinces.

(6) Provisions which should be repealed.

The Conference also recommended that the process of amendment with respect to categories (3) to (6) should be capable of being initiated by one or more of the provincial legislatures or by the Dominion Parliament.

Once these categories had been agreed upon, a Dominion-Provincial committee was established to seek agreement on classification of the various provisions of the British North America Act. There was in fact a large measure of agreement as to the classification of nearly one hundred sections of the Act, but many of these were unimportant. There was also much difficulty concerning the mode of amending provisions in category (4), in particular as to what majority of provincial legislatures should be required. So far, these difficulties have not been resolved.

APPENDIX III

Germany

I. THE FEDERAL CONSTITUTION OF 1871

The federal Constitution of 1871 could be amended by the ordinary process of legislation, the only restrictions being that an amendment was considered as rejected if fourteen votes (of a total of fifty-eight) were cast against it in the upper federal legislative chamber (the Bundesrat), and that rights secured to particular States could only be modified with the consent of the States affected. These restrictions were of considerable effect. The delegates to the Bundesrat from each member State were required to vote as a unit, and were appointed and instructed by the governments of the States. Therefore, Prussia alone (with seventeen votes), or a combination of as few as three of the larger States, or even a combination of the small States having only one vote each, was able to veto an amendment. Only twelve explicit constitutional amendments seemed to have been passed throughout the history of the Constitution of 1871.

II. THE WEIMAR CONSTITUTION

A. *Provisions on Amendment*

The main provision on the amendment of the Weimar Constitution, Article 76, allowed amendment by action of the legislature alone. However, approval of amendments by the Reichstag (lower chamber) was effective only if two thirds of the members were present, and if two thirds of those present voted in favor of the amendment. Approval of amendments by the Reichsrat (upper chamber) also required two thirds of the votes taken. As under the Constitution of 1871, delegates to the Reichsrat were appointed by the governments of the member States; in general, the delegates from each State therefore voted as a bloc according to the instructions of their government.

If the Reichstag approved an amendment to the Constitution in spite of an objection by the Reichsrat, the amendment became effective unless, within two weeks, the Reichsrat demanded a referendum (Art. 76). But a referendum could nullify an enactment of the Reichstag only if a majority of those qualified to vote took part in the election (Art. 75), and if the enactment was rejected by a majority of those voting. This provision for amendment by action of the legislature alone made it possible, where sufficient support in the legislature could be mustered, to take emergency action through rapid, temporary measures amending the Constitution. This method was employed on several occasions to deal with economic and other crises. The measures enacted took the form principally of "enabling acts" granting to the executive broad powers for a limited period.

Amendments also could be introduced by popular initiative. The popular initiative, as defined in Article 73 of the Constitution, required a petition by one tenth of the qualified voters. The proposed amendment was then submitted to referendum for ratification, unless the proposal had in the meantime been passed unaltered by the Reichstag. Article 76 specified that, in the case of referendum on an amendment of the Constitution proposed by popular initiative, the consent of a majority of those qualified to vote was necessary.

B. *Provisions on Emergency Measures*

Article 48 of the Constitution provided (*inter alia*):

> The Reich President may, if the public safety and order in the German Reich are seriously disturbed or endangered, take such measures as are necessary to restore public safety and order. If necessary, he may intervene with the help of the armed forces.

Article 48 also authorized the President "temporarily" to suspend, either partially or wholly, certain fundamental rights established in the Constitution. The President, however, was to inform the Reichstag without delay of all measures taken under the Article, and, on demand by the Reichstag, the measures were to be repealed.

This power was employed many times to deal with domestic disorders and economic crises. It was in fact the source of governmental power during the last years of the Republic, and was, finally, one of the means by which the Republic was destroyed.

III. The Basic Law of 1949

A. *Provisions on Amendment*

Article 79, Sections (1) and (2), of the Basic Law provide as follows:

(1) The Basic Law may be amended only by a law which expressly alters or adds to the text of the Basic Law.

(2) Such a law shall require the approval of two-thirds of the members of the Bundestag and two-thirds of the votes of the Bundesrat.

Delegates to the Bundesrat are appointed by the governments of the Länder, and are therefore instructed by their governments. The delegates from each Land are required to vote as a unit.

Article 79, Section (3), limits the amending power by providing:

(3) An amendment to this Basic Law by which the organization of the Federation into Länder, the basic cooperation of the Länder in legislation, or the basic principles laid down in Articles 1 and 20 are affected, shall be inadmissible.

In regard to these limitations, Article 1 provides:

(1) The dignity of man shall be inviolable. To respect and protect it shall be the duty of all state authority.

(2) The German people therefore acknowledges inviolable and inalienable human rights as the basis of every human community, of peace and of justice in the world.

(3) The following basic rights shall be binding as directly valid law on legislation, administration and judiciary.

The basic rights referred to in Section (3) of Article 1 are those contained in Articles 2 to 19. It seems probable, therefore, that the whole of Part I of the Basic Law, that is, Articles 1 to 19 inclusive, is withdrawn from amendment under Article 79.

Article 20, whose principles also are placed beyond the power of amendment under Article 79, provides:

(1) The Federal Republic of Germany is a democratic and social federal state.

(2) All state authority emanates from the people. It shall be exercised by the people in elections and plebiscites and by means of separate legislative, executive, and judicial organs.

(3) Legislation shall be limited by the constitution; the executive and the administration of justice by legislation and the law.

B. *Provisions on Emergency Measures*

Article 81 of the Basic Law contains provisions designed to meet the case of disagreement between the Cabinet and the Bundestag. Under certain circumstances, the Federal President may, on the request of the Cabinet and with the approval of the Bundesrat, declare a state of legislative emergency, if the Bundestag rejects a bill despite the fact that the Cabinet has declared it to be urgent. Under such circumstances, Article 81 allows the adoption of the bill on the approval of the Bundesrat alone. However, Article 81 (4) states that the Basic Law may neither be amended nor wholly or partially repealed or suspended by a law enacted in accordance with these provisions of Article 81.

APPENDIX IV
Switzerland

I. CONSTITUTIONAL PROVISIONS ON AMENDMENT

The provisions governing the amendment of the Swiss Constitution are contained in Chapter III, Articles 118 to 123, of the Constitution. Minor changes were made in the provisions for amendment in 1874, when the Swiss Constitution itself underwent a total revision. A major change in those provisions was effected in 1891, when the popular initiative was adopted for the first time as a mode of introducing constitutional amendments.

The Constitution may be amended either by total revision or partial revision (Art. 118).

Total Revision. A proposal for total revision may be introduced in the forms laid down in respect to federal legislation (Art. 119). If both chambers of the Federal Assembly are in agreement upon the desirability of making a total revision, they may proceed to draft a new constitution. If the two chambers disagree, or if 50,000 voters demand a total revision, the question whether there should be such a revision is submitted to a popular referendum; in either of these cases, if a majority of the voters at the referendum favor the total revision, members of both chambers of the Federal Assembly are elected anew for the purpose of drafting a new constitution (Art. 120).

When the two chambers of the Federal Assembly have decided on a draft of a new constitution, that draft must be submitted to a referendum. The new constitution comes into force if, at this referendum, it is accepted by the majority of those voting, and by the majority of the cantons. In this latter respect, the result of the popular vote in each canton is considered as the vote of that canton (Art. 123).

Partial Revision. A proposal for partial revision may be introduced either by the popular initiative of 50,000 voters or in the forms laid down in respect to federal legislation (Art. 121). Each proposal for amendment must be the subject of a separate initiative demand (Art. 121).

The initiative demand may take the form either of a proposal couched in general terms or of a bill complete in all details. Article 121 lays down the procedure to be followed by the Federal Assembly with respect to either type of initiative proposal:

. . . When the demand is couched in general terms, the federal chambers, if they approve thereof, will proceed to undertake the partial revision in the sense indicated, and will submit the draft for acceptance or rejection by the people and the cantons. If, on the contrary, they do not approve the demand, the question of partial revision shall be submitted to the vote of the people; if a majority of the Swiss citizens taking part in the vote pronounce in the affirmative, the Federal Assembly will proceed to undertake the revision in conformity with the popular decision.

When a demand is presented in the form of a bill complete in all details, and the Federal Assembly approves thereof, the bill shall be submitted for acceptance or rejection by the people and the cantons. If the Federal Assembly is not in agreement, it may draw up a separate bill or recommend to the people the rejection of the bill proposed, and submit to the vote its counterdraft or its proposal for rejection at the same time as the bill presented by popular initiative.

A proposal for partial revision of the Constitution, whether it has originated by means of the popular initiative or in the forms laid down in respect to federal legislation, must be submitted in its final draft form to a referendum. The amendment comes into force if it is accepted by the majority of those voting at the referendum, and by the majority of the cantons.

II. EMERGENCY PROVISIONS FOR TRANSITORY AMENDMENT

In 1949 there was added to the federal Constitution a provision (Art. 89-*bis*) authorizing a majority of the members of both chambers of the Federal Assembly to enact urgent decrees. Such decrees are not subject to referendum (as other legislation may be) and need not be based on the Constitution. However, urgent decrees which are not based on the Constitution become invalid after one year unless adopted by the people and the cantons. Thus, the Federal Assembly can, in effect, enact amendments of the Constitution for this limited period. This provision is an outcome of the emergency periods of the two World Wars. During both wars the Federal Assembly and Executive Council found it necessary to exercise more extensive powers than provided for in the Constitution. After World War II, Article 89-*bis* was proposed by popular initiative, in order to limit the federal emergency power.

III. Practice Under the Provisions for Amendment of the Constitution[5]

Three proposals for total revision have been made since 1848 and have reached the referendum stage, in 1872, 1874, and 1935. Only one of these proposals was adopted, that of 1874.

Since 1848 there have been 55 proposals for partial revision originating in the form of federal legislation; of these proposals, 38 have been accepted by subsequent referenda, and 17 rejected. In the period 1848 to 1891 there were 17 such proposals, of which only seven were accepted; from 1891 to 1918, there were 16 such proposals, of which 12 were accepted; from 1918 to the present, of 22 such proposals, 19 have been accepted. The clear trend here in favor of proposals initiated by the Federal Assembly seems to point, *inter alia,* to an increasing tendency on the part of the Federal Assembly not to introduce measures for constitutional amendment until there is a reasonable consensus of public opinion in support of them.

Since 1891 (when provision for the popular initiative was first added to the Constitution), 39 proposals for partial revision have originated by popular initiative. Seven of these proposals have been accepted and 32 rejected. There have been, since 1891, nine counterproposals submitted to referendum by the Federal Assembly in reply to proposals originating by popular initiative. Seven of these counterproposals have been adopted, and two rejected. In regard to a number of the counterproposals, indeed, it appears that prior to the referendum the sponsors of the original initiative proposal withdrew their proposal in favor of the government counterproposal.

As to the double requirement in Article 123 that a proposed amendment, to be adopted at the referendum, must secure both a majority of the vote throughout Switzerland, and a majority of the vote in a majority of the cantons, there appears to have been only one case where a proposal has secured a majority of the overall popular vote but failed also to carry a majority of the cantons. (In two cases, however, proposals carried a majority of the cantons but failed to carry a majority of the overall popular vote.) It seems, therefore, that this requirement has not operated to limit the adoption of constitutional amendments.

[5] The figures given go up to July, 1951.

APPENDIX V
United States

I. CONSTITUTIONAL PROVISIONS ON AMENDMENT

The Constitution provides a two-stage procedure for its amendment, with separate steps for initiation and ratification. Thus, Article V of the Constitution states:

> The Congress, whenever two thirds of both Houses shall deem it necessary, shall propose Amendments to this Constitution, or, on the Application of the Legislatures of two thirds of the several States, shall call a Convention for proposing Amendments, which, in either Case, shall be valid to all Intents and Purposes, as Part of this Constitution, when ratified by the Legislatures of three fourths of the several States, or by Conventions in three fourths thereof, as the one or the other Mode of Ratification may be proposed by the Congress; . . .

Two express limitations on the power of amending the Constitution are also set out in Article V. The first is that:

> . . . no Amendment which may be made prior to the Year One thousand eight hundred and eight shall in any Manner affect the first and fourth Clauses in the Ninth Section of the first Article.

The clauses referred to restricted the powers of Congress to interfere with the importation or maintenance of slaves. This limitation of the power to amend those clauses was inserted to meet further the apprehensions of the slaveholding States concerning attempts to abolish or limit slavery.

The second express limitation on the amending power is the proviso in Article V that "no State, without its Consent, shall be deprived of its equal Suffrage in the Senate."

II. PRACTICE UNDER THE CONSTITUTIONAL PROVISIONS

The amendments to the Constitution that have been made fall into four distinct time periods. The first twelve Amendments were all adopted in the very early period of the Constitution, the first ten Amendments (the Bill of Rights) in fact being proposed as a unit in 1789 pursuant to a general understanding existing at the time of the ratification of the Constitution. More than sixty years then elapsed before the Constitution was amended again; the Thirteenth, Fourteenth, and Fifteenth Amendments were proposed and adopted in the immediate aftermath of the Civil War. Nearly half a century passed before another change was introduced into the Constitution, but in the period from 1909 to 1933 six Amendments were adopted. Finally, one further Amendment has been adopted since World War II.

A. *Initiation of Amendments*

Article V of the Constitution provides alternative means for the initiation of amendments; that is, either by vote of two thirds of each house of the federal legislature, or, on the application of the legislatures of two thirds of the States, by a convention called by Congress for that purpose. The initiation of constitutional amendments has, in practice, been made in all cases by Congress. These proposals by Congress need not be submitted to the President for his approval, as in the case of other measures enacted by Congress, since adoption of a proposal for amendment is considered an act unconnected with the ordinary business of legislation.[6] From 1789 until the present, twenty-seven proposals for amendment have been initiated by Congress.

The second method of initiating amendments has never been employed, since the required number of State legislatures have never applied for the calling of a convention. It is therefore not clear to what extent the applications by the State legislatures must be uniform in purpose, or whether, if a convention were called, its deliberations could be limited by Congress or by the requesting States. On some occasions a lesser number of States than two thirds have applied for a convention, and in at least one instance Congress has initiated an amendment, previously rejected by it, only after the States seemed about to recruit the two thirds of their number required for the calling of a convention. The amendment involved in this case provided changes in the method of electing members of the upper house of Congress and had been resisted strongly by members of that house.

B. *Ratification of Amendments*

Article V also provides alternative methods for the ratification of amendments; ratification may be accomplished by vote of the legislatures of three fourths of the States, or by conventions in three fourths of the States. The choice of method is wholly within the discretion of Congress,[7] which has designated the latter method only for the ratification of the Twenty-first Amendment (which repealed an earlier Amendment prohibiting alcoholic beverages). In designating the convention method in this instance, Congress specified only that ratification should be by popularly elected conventions, chosen for that purpose; the details were left to the States. In most of the States, the votes of the convention delegates were pledged to their electors, so that this procedure approximated very closely to a popular referendum, with a majority in three fourths of the States being required.

All other proposals for amendment have been submitted by Congress to the

[6] Hollingsworth v. Virginia, 3 Dall. 378 (U.S. 1798).

[7] United States v. Sprague, 282 U.S. 716 (1931). In this case it was unsuccessfully contended that ratification of the Amendment in question, providing for prohibition of alcoholic beverages, should have been by popularly elected conventions, since it dealt with "a matter affecting the liberty of the citizen."

State legislatures for ratification. A proposed amendment thus submitted remains open for ratification by the State legislatures during a reasonable period after its proposal. The duration of this period is for determination by Congress, which may specify a period of years within which ratification by three fourths of the State legislatures must be completed.[8] In the case of several of the amendments most recently initiated by Congress, it has specified the period of seven years for this purpose. Once a State has notified the federal government of ratification of a proposed amendment by its legislature, withdrawal of its ratification has not been permitted; however, the courts have refused to interfere with notification by a State of ratification of a proposal previously rejected by it.[9] Ratification of amendments is a special power conferred on the State legislatures by the Constitution, and therefore cannot be restricted by limitations sought to be imposed on their legislature by the people of a State, such as a requirement of a referendum on ratification.[10] It thus seems clear that the governor of a State could not veto an act of ratification by its legislature, regardless of his powers under the constitution of the State.

In the twenty-seven instances in which Congress has initiated amendments, ratification has followed in all but five cases. Three of these cases were in the very early period of the Constitution and were of comparatively minor importance. The fourth was an intimate part of the antecedents of the Civil War, being designed to prevent interference with slavery; but it was superseded by other amendments to the Constitution adopted immediately after the Civil War. The fifth instance was the Child Labor Amendment proposal of 1924 which was pending for seventeen years before being rendered unnecessary by a constitutional interpretation of the Supreme Court. The time required for ratification by the States, after proposal of an amendment by Congress, has not been great. Seven amendments have required less than one year for ratification, while the longest period required was four years.

III. OTHER METHODS OF CONSTITUTIONAL ADJUSTMENT

Substantial modifications in constitutional law have been made through changes in interpretation of the Constitution by the Supreme Court. In one instance, referred to above, a proposal for amendment of the Constitution, which was pending for seventeen years, was rendered unnecessary by a change in the Court's interpretation of the powers of Congress. This role of the Court has in many cases made possible a gradual modification of constitutional principles, through judicial interpretation, conforming to changes in the needs of government and in public opinion.

Custom has also played a part in developing rules of governmental and

[8] Dillon v. Gloss, 256 U.S. 368 (1920); Coleman v. Miller 307 U.S. 433 (1939).
[9] Coleman v. Miller, 307 U.S. 433 (1939).
[10] Hawke v. Smith, 253 U.S. 221 (1919). Cf. Coleman v. Miller, 307 U.S. 433, at 446 (1939).

political practice. For example, prior to President Franklin Roosevelt's re-election to a third term in office in 1940, it had been generally accepted in principle, and always followed in practice, that no one should serve more than two terms as President. This custom was enacted as part of the Constitution by the recent adoption of the Twenty-second Amendment. Custom has also greatly modified the method which the Constitution established for election of a President. The Constitution provides for his election by an electoral college composed of members selected in each State, who were intended to meet in their respective States as deliberative bodies to debate and vote individually for a President. For many years this practice was followed. With the development of national political parties, however, the President has in fact been selected by popular vote from among candidates nominated by the parties, and the members of the electoral college in each State are virtually bound merely to record the decision of the majority of voters in that State.

Appendices

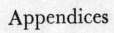

Appendices

APPENDIX I

Draft Resolutions of the Study Committee for the European Constitution

Brussels, November, 1952

Adopted by the Committee for the European Constitution

FIRST RESOLUTION
PREAMBLE AND GENERAL PROPOSALS

A. The Assembly shall decide to incorporate in the Statute a preamble which shall conform to the following principles:

With the present Statute an indissoluble European Community shall be established (constituted).

This Community which has grown out of the initiative of the Member States of the European Coal and Steel Community and of the European Defense Community shall be concluded between their peoples.

By establishing a close union between these peoples, it shall have as its goal to guarantee their common well-being, the existence and the exterior security of the Member States, and to safeguard their constitutional order, their democratic institutions and their fundamental liberties.

B. The Assembly shall decide to incorporate in the Statute general provisions which shall conform to the following principles:

1. The Community shall have juridical personality. It shall enjoy the necessary juridical personality both in its international relationships and in the territories of the Member States.
2. According to the provisions of the Statute and the laws of the Community, the institutions of the Community shall assume the irrevocable task of fulfilling the functions prescribed in the Statute and those which may later be assigned to the Community under the procedure of the Statute.
3. All those powers exercised by the Member States which have not been expressly transferred to the Community shall remain within the competence of the States.

    This shall hold true e.g., with respect to the powers of the States in the religious, cultural, and educational fields.
4. The Member States shall not be able to take any measure which may counteract or impede in any manner whatsoever the actions of the Community. In any contested litigation they shall not be able to take the law into their own hands, but they shall be under obligation to submit the differences to the Supreme Court of the Community.
5. All the citizens of the Member States shall be citizens of the Community. They shall enjoy the political rights prescribed and determined in the Statute.

6. The Statute shall come into force at the moment when it has been ratified by all the signatory States.

   The Community shall begin to exist on that day.

7. Each Member State shall be under obligation to respect the rights of man as they are defined in the Declaration of Human Rights, signed in Rome, November 4, 1950, and in the additional Protocol, signed in Paris, March 20, 1952.

   On the request of the constitutional authorities of a Member State, the Community shall come to its aid in order to maintain constitutional order, democratic institutions or the fundamental rights of man.

   If the Government of the Community should come to the conclusion that the constitutional order, the democratic institutions or the fundamental liberties of man are gravely violated in a Member State and that its constitutional authorities cannot or do not want to re-establish the same, the Community shall take action in the name and place of these authorities until the situation shall have become normal. In this case, the measures taken by the Government of the Community shall be submitted without delay to the Parliament of the Community for confirmation.

8. Any European State may request to accede to the Statute. This request shall be decided upon by the Parliament of the Community by two-thirds of the votes cast.

   The accession to the Community shall become effective when the instrument of accession has been deposited with the President of the Government of the Community.

   It shall be preceded by the conclusion of an agreement which shall regulate the conditions under which the acceding State will participate, e.g., its representation in the organs of the Community.

9. No change of frontiers between Member States shall be allowed to take place, except with the concurrent consent of the constitutional authorities of the respective States and the Parliament of the Community.

SECOND RESOLUTION

THE GOVERNMENT OF THE COMMUNITY

The Assembly shall decide to incorporate in the Statute of the Community articles which concern the direction of its common affairs. These shall conform to the following principles:

1. The conduct of the affairs which the Statute transferred to the Community, as well as the organization and administration which are necessary for their effectuation, shall be entrusted to a Government of six to twelve members. This Government shall take its decisions collectively and shall be responsible collectively.

2. The Government shall exercise its functions according to the Statute and to the laws of the Community.

   Only in so far as it carries out the decisions of the Parliament of the Community shall it have the power to impose taxes or to make expenditures.

   With the exception of the administration of defense, administrative measures shall, in principle, be delegated to the national administrations. The Community shall have, however, the right to establish its own administration in those cases in which it has been so authorized by Parliament.

   Whenever the execution of laws has been entrusted to the administrative services of the Member States, the Government of the Community shall have the right to control the execution by all necessary means of investigation. It may, for instance, require reports, make inquiries on the spot, take testimony, and scrutinize files.

In order to ensure the harmonious functioning of the administration of the Community and of the national administrations, the Government of the Community shall have the power to establish councils, administrative committees and mixed advisory boards.

3. The members of the Government shall be appointed for four years by the Parliament of the Community from the eligible European citizens.

The members whose term has expired may be reappointed.

Not more than one-fourth of its members shall be of the same nationality.

In case of death, resignation or dismissal, of one or more members these shall be replaced for the duration of the term.

4. The members of the Government shall exercise their functions in the general interest of the Community. They shall be completely independent of any national government. They shall be excluded from any other professional activity, whether paid or unpaid. Before taking office, they shall swear that they will uphold the Statute and the laws of the Community.

All the officers of the Government shall swear to a similar oath before assuming their functions.

5. The Government shall present to Parliament an annual report on the general state of the Community, a budget for the coming year, and a financial account for the closing year.

Its members shall have the right to attend the sessions of Parliament, to address the Assembly, and to initiate laws, resolutions and amendments.

6. Parliament shall elect the President and the Vice-President of the Government from the members of the Government. The election shall be made for two years and may be renewed.

The President shall represent the Community, he shall be the Supreme Commander of the Armed Forces of the Community and he shall coordinate the work of the Government.

7. The Government shall be able to take action only when the majority of its members are present (one-half plus one of its members). It shall take its decisions by a majority vote of its members. The Government shall distribute its tasks and its administrative departments among its members.

8. The Chamber of Deputies shall have the power to propose to the Senate the dismissal of one or more members of the Government for violation of the Statute or of the laws of the Community.

The decision of the Senate shall be taken by a two-thirds vote.

9. The functions of the High Authority of the European Coal and Steel Community and of the Board of Commissioners of the European Defense Community as well as those of other executive organs of any other future specialized authorities shall be assumed by the Government of the Community.

It shall belong to the jurisdiction of the Parliament of the Community to regulate the respective relationships of these bodies.

THIRD RESOLUTION
PARLIAMENT OF THE COMMUNITY

The Assembly shall decide to incorporate in the Statute of the Community articles concerning the Parliament of the Community which shall conform to the following principles:

1. The Parliament of the Community shall be composed of two Chambers: The Chamber of Deputies [Peoples' Chamber] and the Senate.

2. The Chamber of Deputies shall be composed of citizens of the Community who shall be at least twenty-five years of age. They shall be elected by universal and direct suffrage and by secret ballot by the citizens of the Community who have the right to vote in their respective countries.

The election shall take place every four years, the .... day of the .... In any event, the election of the First Chamber shall take place three months after the Statute has come into force.

It shall belong to the jurisdiction of each Member State to determine the voluntary or compulsory right to vote in the election for the Chamber of Deputies. The exercise of the functions of a Member of the Chamber of Deputies of the Community shall be incompatible with that of the functions of a Member of a National Parliament.

When the two mandates have been cumulated, the elected Member must make his option between the two. An exception shall be made, however, for the first European legislature.

The exercise of the functions of a Member of the Chamber of Deputies shall be incompatible with that of the Member of the Senate of the Community.

3. The election laws for the Chamber of Deputies shall be enacted by the Parliament of the Community. Until these laws have been enacted, the Assembly shall enact an election law for the first election, according to the following principles:

The Deputies shall be elected by a system of uninominal voting at the ratio of one Deputy for 500,000 inhabitants or a fraction of 500,000 inhabitants. Each State, however, shall have at least two Deputies.

The electoral college of the Community shall be divided into electoral districts which shall correspond to a territory, if possible continuous, and each belonging to one and the same Member State. The districts shall be determined by the Assembly in collaboration with the Governments of the Member States on the basis of their last official census.

The districts may be modified by the Parliament of the Community after each general census of the population.

4. The Senate shall be composed of citizens of the Community who shall be at least thirty-five years of age. They shall be elected by the Parliaments of each Member State according to the procedure regulated by each of them.

The election shall take place every four years, seven days or later after the results of the elections for the Chamber of Deputies have been publicly announced.

Each National Parliament shall elect a number of Senators equal to that which is provided in the Assembly of the European Defense Community for each Member.

The Senators of the Community may be members of national Parliaments or Governments.

5. The Members of the Parliament of the Community shall not vote as a national delegation (unit). They shall vote individually according to their own conscience, without any instructions.

They shall enjoy the traditional parliamentary immunities.

6. The Parliament shall discuss and vote the laws and taxes of the Community, adopt the budgets, and declare, in case of aggression, a state of war, confirm peace treaties, and appoint the Government.

Unless otherwise indicated in the Statute, each of the two Chambers shall make its decision by a simple majority of the votes cast.

Each of the two Chambers shall be entitled to make inquiries into the activities of each organ of the Community.

International treaties shall be negotiated by the Government of the Community. They shall be submitted for the approval of Parliament under the same conditions as are laws. They shall be ratified by the President of the Government in the name of the Community.

7. The right of initiative in regard to matters of law and taxes shall lie with the Government and with the Members of the two Chambers.

8. Within the limits of the competence of the Community its legislation takes precedence over that of the Member States.

9. The projected budget of the Community shall be submitted annually to the Chamber of Deputies and then to the Senate. Parliament may accept, modify or refuse it.

Parliament shall also examine the financial account for the past year.

10. The members of the Government shall be elected by the joint Chambers.

Each Member of Parliament may present one or more candidates. These must have declared their acceptance.

Those candidates who receive the largest number of votes or who get at least the simple majority of the votes cast shall have been elected as Members of the Government.

The foregoing rules shall apply likewise to the election of the President and Vice-President.

11. Each of the two Chambers shall elect its bureau and enact its rules of procedure.

12. The functions of the Council of Ministers, of the General Assembly of the European Coal and Steel Community, and of the European Defense Community shall be assumed by the Government and the Parliament of the Community.

It belongs to the duties of the Parliament of the Community to take the necessary steps which will assure the execution of this measure.

FOURTH RESOLUTION
THE JUDICIARY POWER OF THE COMMUNITY

The Assembly shall decide to incorporate in the Statute of the Community articles concerning the judiciary power which shall conform to the following principles:

1. The judiciary functions of the Community shall be exercised by a Supreme Court and by other courts which may be established by law.

2. The Supreme Court shall ensure the rule of law in the interpretation and application of the Statute and of the laws of the Community.

It shall be both Constitutional Court and Supreme Court of Appeals. (Cour de Cassation.)

3. It shall therefore be competent:
   (a) in case of conflict between the Statute and the laws or public acts of the Community;
   (b) in case of conflict between the Statute and the laws or public acts of Member States;
   (c) in case of differences between Member States or in differences in which the Community is a party;
   (d) when diplomatic prerogatives and immunities have been violated;
   (e) It is finally competent in the field of civil, penal, and public law which belong to the competence of the Community and which have been assigned to it by law.

The Parliament of the Community shall regulate by law the right to bring a case before the Court.

In the cases of (a) and (b), this right shall be given to each affected citizen, to each Member State and to each organ of the Community or to a specified part of any one of these.

4. The Parliament of the Community shall have the right to establish under the jurisdiction of the Supreme Court other courts for the purpose of guaranteeing respect for the laws of the Community. The distribution of jurisdiction between the Supreme Court and the other courts shall be established by law.

5. The Judges of the Community shall be appointed for life. They cannot be dismissed except after a procedure which proves a serious transgression of a disciplinary nature or physical incapacity. The rules for retirement at a certain age shall be determined by law.

The Judges shall receive a salary determined by law, and the salary of a Judge shall not be reduced during the duration of his functions.

6. The Supreme Court shall be composed of . . . . members. Its organization, its procedure, and its relationships with the Courts of the Community and those of the Member States shall be established by law.

7. The Government of the Community shall appoint the members of the Supreme Court. It shall be obligatory that one-third be chosen from a list submitted by the Law Faculties, and one-third from a list submitted by the highest judicial organs of the Member States.

8. The functions of the Court of the European Coal and Steel Community and of the European Defense Community shall be assumed by the Supreme Court and by the other courts of the Community.

It belongs to the duties of the Parliament of the Community to regulate the manner in which these functions shall be assumed.

FIFTH RESOLUTION

COMPETENCE OF THE COMMUNITY IN MATTERS OF COAL AND STEEL

The Assembly shall decide to incorporate in the Statute of the Community articles concerning the competence of the Community in matters of coal and steel. These articles shall conform to the following principles:

1. Articles 1 to 6 of the Treaty instituting the European Coal and Steel Community and the other provisions of the Treaty concerning the general powers of the Community in matters of coal and steel shall be incorporated in the Statute with the necessary changes of terms involved.

2. The rest of the Treaty and the Convention concerning the transitional provisions shall be considered as binding laws of the Community, with the exception of these provisions which have been modified by the Statute.

At the end of the transitional period the Parliament shall have the right to complete, modify or abrogate provisions of the Treaty.

SIXTH RESOLUTION

COMPETENCE OF THE COMMUNITY IN MATTERS OF DEFENSE

The Assembly shall decide to incorporate in the Statute articles concerning defense which shall conform to the following principles:

1. The Community shall be responsible for the security and defense of the populations and territories of the Member States against any aggression or threat of aggression.

2. The defense of the non-European territories which belong to the Member States

or which are associated with them shall, at the present stage, not belong to the competence of the Community.

With the consent of the interested non-European territory, provided that it has the right of decision in this matter, a Member State may, however, ask that the defense of this territory be assured by the Community. It shall then become the duty of the Government of the Community to negotiate the conditions for the acceptance of this request and for the Parliament of the Community to decide upon them with a two-thirds majority.

3. In order to attain the aims indicated in Paragraph 1 above, the Community shall have the power to take all measures for the purpose to recruit, instruct, equip, arm, supply and employ Armed Forces.

In case of military mobilization, of war, or any other kind of international conflict, the Community shall take all extraordinary measures to organize the economy of the Community in such a manner that it is able to meet the situation.

In case of serious international tension which has been so acknowledged by the Government, Parliament may with a two-thirds majority authorize the Government to take the extraordinary steps mentioned in the preceding paragraph.

4. The Member States shall be allowed to possess and employ:
   (a) armed national police forces and gendarmes who are exclusively charged with the maintenance of internal order;
   (b) national Armed Forces which are necessary for the defense of their non-European territories to the extent to which the conditions mentioned in Paragraph 2, Subsection 2, should not be fulfilled;
   (c) national Armed Forces in fulfillment of international commitments which the States in question assumed prior to the coming into force of the Statute and which have not been taken over directly by the Community;
   (d) national armed contingents which are assigned in each State to the personal protection of the Chief of State.

5. The production of war matériel, of import and export of war matériel coming from or destined for third States, measures which are of primary concern to the installations destined for the production of war matériel and the production of prototypes, and technical research concerning war matériel shall be forbidden, except by authorization of the Community.

6. The Community shall have the right to request from its citizens military service in its Armed Forces under the conditions laid down by law.

The citizens shall be subject to the jurisdiction of military tribunals which shall be established in the European Armed Forces.

If, prior to the formation of the Community, the Constitution or the law of a Member State gave to its citizens rights as conscientious objectors, these rights shall not be abrogated by the Community.

7. The law on recruitment enacted by the Community shall take cognizance of the military needs of the Member States as indicated in Paragraph 4.

8. The President of the Government shall be the Supreme Commander of the Armed Forces of the Community. The Government shall appoint the officers, mobilize the Armed Forces, issue fighting orders, and authorize the signing of an armistice.

9. The Treaty instituting the European Defense Community shall be considered as law of the Community with the exception of the provisions modified by the Statute.

SEVENTH RESOLUTION

COMPETENCE OF THE COMMUNITY IN MATTERS OF FOREIGN AFFAIRS

The Assembly shall decide to incorporate in the Statute of the Community articles concerning the foreign affairs of the Community which shall conform to the following principles:

1. All relationships with third States or with international organizations in matters which have been transferred to the Community shall lie within the competence of the Community.

   The Community shall have, e.g., the power to conclude treaties, to declare war, to conclude the peace, and to take part in international agreements or to enter international organizations which have defensive aims.

   The Community shall have the right to accredit and receive diplomatic representatives.

2. The Member States shall retain their authority in specific international relations, including the right of diplomatic representation, in all those matters which lie within their competence.

   They shall have the right to delegate to the Community the power to conclude in their name treaties which concern these matters.

   The Member States shall not be allowed to sign or ratify treaties which are contrary to the general policies of the Community if the latter informs the Member State in question of its opposition and of the reasons for it.

3. As long as no later amendment to the Statute provides otherwise, the Member States of the Community shall come to an agreement with one another in order to determine the modalities of their respective representations in international organizations and the coordination of their diplomatic services.

   With the consent of NATO an Appendix to the Statute shall stipulate that the Community will be substituted for the Member States in their relations to NATO.

4. Treaties or parts of treaties which have previously been concluded by Member States with third States and which concern matters within the competence of the Community shall remain in force according to the principles of international law. They cannot be renewed, however, after their expiration.

   Member States shall be under obligation to inform the co-signers of the treaties of their new status as Member of the Community and to ask them to proceed by common agreement toward the abrogation or revision of these treaties.

   If, on the other hand, the Community should make a treaty with a third State on matters within the competence of the Community, the Member States shall presume that existing treaties on like matters between that State and Member States have been automatically abrogated.

EIGHTH RESOLUTION

COMPETENCE OF THE COMMUNITY IN FINANCIAL MATTERS

The Assembly shall decide to incorporate in the Statute of the Community articles concerning the financial affairs of the Community which shall conform to the following principles:

1. In order to make it possible for the Community to fulfill the tasks assigned to it, the Community shall have the power to impose and collect direct and in-

direct taxes, to take up loans, to buy, own and sell personal property and real estate in the territory of the Member States.

2. The right to impose and collect taxes shall by no means be limited by the above provision.

   In order to harmonize the fiscal system of the Community and those of the Member States consultations shall be held between the competent organs of the respective parties prior to the adoption of a new tax.

3. The fiscal legislation of the Community shall not discriminate against any of their taxpayers by virtue of the fact they are members of one or the other Member State.

4. The tax systems and the contributions laid down in the Treaty on the European Coal and Steel Community and in the European Defense Community shall remain in force during the first fiscal year of the Community.

   The budget shall contain the necessary expenditures to set up the institutions of the Community during that period. For the following period which shall not exceed three years, the Community shall have the right to impose by law contributions on the Member States. These contributions shall be gradually replaced by direct or indirect taxes of the Community.

5. The Community shall have the power to give subsidies to Member States in order to realize its aims.

6. The budgetary expenditures shall be controlled by an Auditor (*controleur financier*).

   The verification of the accounts shall be done by an Office of the Comptroller (Accounting Department).

   The Auditor and the members of the Office of the Comptroller (Accounting Department) shall be appointed by Parliament.

NINTH RESOLUTION
REVISION OF THE STATUTE

The Assembly shall decide to incorporate in the Statute of the Community articles concerning the procedure for the amendment of the Constitution which shall conform to the following principles:

1. The Parliament of the Community shall have the power to adopt Amendments which modify or supplement the Statute:
   (a) on its own initiative;
   (b) on the request of the Government of the Community;
   (c) on the desire expressed by a national government or Parliament.

2. The Amendments which have thus been adopted shall come into force under the following conditions:
   (a) During a period of ten years from the coming into force of the Statute there shall be required for all Amendments except that mentioned in (c) thereafter the consent of all the Member States, expressed according to their constitutional requirements.
   (b) With the beginning of the eleventh year, Amendments shall receive the consent of two-thirds of the Member States, arrived at in the above stated manner.
   (c) From the beginning of the first legislature of the Community, those Amendments which refer to the necessary power of the Community for the establishment of a common market shall require the consent of two-thirds of the Member States, arrived at in the above stated manner.

The above provisions shall not affect the case mentioned in Resolution 6, Paragraph 3.

APPENDIX II

Draft Treaty Embodying the Statute of the European Community

PREAMBLE

WE, THE PEOPLES OF THE FEDERAL REPUBLIC OF GERMANY, THE KINGDOM OF BELGIUM, THE FRENCH REPUBLIC, THE ITALIAN REPUBLIC, THE GRAND DUCHY OF LUXEMBOURG AND THE KINGDOM OF THE NETHERLANDS,

CONSIDERING that world peace may be safeguarded only by creative efforts equal to the dangers which menace it;

CONVINCED that the contribution which a living, united free Europe can bring to civilization and to the preservation of our common spiritual heritage is indispensable to the maintenance of peaceful relations;

DESIROUS of assisting through the expansion of our production in improving the standard of living and furthering the works of peace;

DETERMINED to safeguard by our common action the dignity, freedom and fundamental equality of men of every condition, race or creed;

RESOLVED to substitute for our historic rivalries a fusion of our essential interests by creating institutions capable of giving guidance to our future common destiny;

DETERMINED to invite other European peoples, inspired with the same ideal, to join with us in our endeavour;

HAVE DECIDED to create a European Community.

Wherefore our respective Governments, through their Plenipotentiaries, meeting in the city of ...., with powers found in good and due form, have adopted the present Treaty.

PART I

The European Community

ARTICLE 1

The present Treaty sets up a EUROPEAN COMMUNITY of a supra-national character.

The Community is founded upon a union of peoples and States, upon respect for their personality and upon equal rights and duties for all. It shall be indissoluble.

ARTICLE 2

The Community has the following mission and general aims:
— to contribute towards the protection of human rights and fundamental freedoms in Member States;
— to co-operate with the other free nations in ensuring the security of Member States against all aggression;
— to ensure the co-ordination of the foreign policy of Member States in questions likely to involve the existence, the security or the prosperity of the Community;
— to promote, in harmony with the general economy of Member States, the economic expansion, the development of employment and the improvement of the standard of living in Member States, by means, in particular, of the progressive establishment of a common market, transitional or other measures being taken to ensure that no fundamental and persistent disturbance is thereby caused to the economy of Member States;
— to contribute towards the endeavours of Member States to achieve the general objectives laid down in the Statute of the Council of Europe, the European Convention for Economic Co-operation, and the North Atlantic Treaty, in co-operation with the other States parties thereto.

ARTICLE 3

The provisions of Part 1 of the Convention for the Protection of Human Rights and Fundamental Freedoms signed in Rome on 4th November 1950, together with those of the protocol signed in Paris on 20th March 1952, are an integral part of the present Statute.

ARTICLE 4

The Community shall have juridical personality.
In international relationships the Community shall enjoy the juridical personality necessary to the exercise of its functions and the attainment of its ends.
In each of the Member States the Community shall enjoy the most extensive juridical personality which is recognized for legal persons of the nationality of the country in question. Specifically, it may acquire, or transfer, immovable and movable assets and may sue and be sued in its own name.
The Community shall possess, in the territories of the Member States, such immunities and privileges as are necessary to the fulfilment of its task, under conditions determined in the Protocol appended to the present Treaty.

ARTICLE 5

The Community, together with the European Coal and Steel Community and the European Defence Community, shall constitute a single legal entity, within which certain organs may retain such administrative and financial autonomy as is necessary to the accomplishment of the tasks assigned by the treaties instituting the European Coal and Steel Community and the European Defence Community.

ARTICLE 6

The Community shall exercise all such powers and competence as are conferred upon it by the present Statute or by subsequent enactment.

The provisions defining the powers and competence conferred upon the Community by the present Treaty shall be restrictively interpreted.

ARTICLE 7

The Community shall carry out its functions in close co-operation with the national civil services, through their respective governments, and with any international organization having objectives similar to its own.

ARTICLE 8

The Community shall enact legislation defining the fundamental principles of the general status of its officials.

PART II

The Institutions of the Community

ARTICLE 9

The institutions of the Community shall be:
— Parliament;
— the European Executive Council;
— the Council of National Ministers;
— the Court of Justice, hereinafter termed "the Court";
— the Economic and Social Council.

Chapter I

PARLIAMENT

ARTICLE 10

Parliament shall enact legislation and make recommendations and proposals. It shall also approve the budget and pass a bill approving the accounts* of the Community. It shall exercise such powers of supervision as are conferred upon it by the present Statute.

ARTICLE 11

Parliament shall be composed of two Chambers which, unless the present Statute otherwise provides, shall have the same powers and competence.

The first Chamber, entitled the Peoples' Chamber, shall be composed of deputies representing the peoples united in the Community.

The second Chamber, entitled the Senate, shall be composed of senators representing the people of each State.

* La loi des comptes.

ARTICLE 12

Deputies and senators shall vote as individuals and in person.

They may not accept any mandate as to the way in which they shall cast their votes.

ARTICLE 13

Deputies shall be elected by universal, equal and direct suffrage, by secret ballot open to both men and women.

The Community shall enact legislation defining the principles of the electoral system.

ARTICLE 14

The Peoples' Chamber shall be elected for five years, subject to the provisions of Article 31, paragraphs 4 and 5.

ARTICLE 15

The peoples united in the Community shall be represented in the Peoples' Chamber in accordance with the following conditions:

1. The number of deputies elected from the territory of a Member State may not be less than 12 nor more than 70.

2. An equal number of deputies shall be elected from the territories of Germany, France and Italy. Additional representation shall, however, be granted to the French Republic in order to take into account its overseas departments and territories, under conditions to be laid down by French legislation.

An equal number of deputies shall be elected from the territories of Belgium and the Netherlands.

3. The number of deputies elected from the territories of the Member States shall be as follows:

Germany 63
Belgium 30
France 70
Italy 63
Luxembourg 12
Netherlands 30

ARTICLE 16

1. Senators shall be elected by the national Parliaments for five years in accordance with the procedure determined by each Member State.

2. A senator shall commence his term of office at the opening of the session of the Senate next following his election.

ARTICLE 17

The number of senators shall be as follows:

Germany 21
Belgium 10
France 21
Italy 21

Luxembourg 4
Netherlands 10

ARTICLE 18

Each Chamber of Parliament shall verify the regularity of the election of its Members.

ARTICLE 19

The Community shall enact legislation determining the conditions of eligibility for membership of Parliament.

ARTICLE 20

1. Membership of the European Parliament shall not be confined to members of national Parliaments.
2. A combination of the office of a senator with that of a deputy shall be prohibited.
3. The exercise of the functions of a Member of Parliament of the Community shall be incompatible with that of the functions of a Member of the Council of National Ministers and of a Member of the Economic and Social Council.
4. The exercise of the functions of a Member of Parliament of the Community shall be incompatible with the holding of judicial office on behalf of the Community, with permanent functions remunerated by the Community or with directorial functions in an enterprise or organization directly controlled by the Community.
5. The Community may enact legislation laying down other rules as to incompatibility.

ARTICLE 21

Parliament shall hold two ordinary sessions annually. It shall assemble regularly on the second Tuesday in May and the last Tuesday in October.

An extraordinary session of either Chamber may be convened by its President, either on his own initiative, or at the request of a quarter of the Members of the Chamber concerned, or of the European Executive Council.

ARTICLE 22

Each Chamber shall elect its President and its Bureau from among its own Members, by secret ballot. It shall decide upon its Rules of Procedure by majority vote of its Members.

The records of the proceedings of each Chamber shall be published in accordance with the conditions laid down in its Rules of Procedure.

ARTICLE 23

1. Members of Parliament and of the European Executive Council shall have the right to initiate legislation.
2. Members of Parliament shall have the right of amendment and interpellation. They may put oral or written questions to the European Executive Council, which shall be required to answer them.

3. Each Chamber shall receive and examine any petitions which may be addressed to it. Such petitions may not be presented in person.

4. Each Chamber shall have the right to institute inquiries. The Community shall enact legislation governing the exercise of this right.

ARTICLE 24

1. Members of the European Executive Council may attend all meetings of each of the Chambers. They shall be heard if they so request. They may take part in the work of the Committees.

2. Members of the Council of National Ministers may attend all meetings of each of the Chambers. The President of the Council of National Ministers, or a member of the Council specially appointed to represent him, may be heard on behalf of the Council by each of the Chambers, either at the request of the latter, or on his own initiative.

ARTICLE 25

1. No restriction shall be placed upon the travel of Members of Parliament proceeding to or coming from the place of meeting of Parliament.

As concerns customs and exchange control, Members of Parliament shall be granted the privileges accorded to accredited Heads of diplomatic Missions; they shall be exempted from the visa regulations in force in Member States.

2. During their term of office, Members of Parliament shall enjoy exemption from all measures of detention and from any legal prosecution.

Such immunity may not be invoked when Members are found committing, attempting to commit, or just having committed an offence.

Each Chamber of Parliament may waive the immunity of its Members.

3. Members of Parliament shall enjoy absolute immunity from legal action in respect of opinions or votes expressed by them in the exercise of their functions. They shall continue to enjoy this immunity after the expiry of their term of office.

ARTICLE 26

Each Chamber shall lay down in its Rules of Procedure the manner in which it will exercise its powers and competence.

Chapter II

THE EUROPEAN EXECUTIVE COUNCIL

ARTICLE 27

The European Executive Council shall undertake the general administration of the Community. It shall have no powers other than those conferred upon it by the present Statute.

ARTICLE 28

1. The Senate shall elect the President of the European Executive Council in secret ballot, by majority vote of its Members.

2. The President shall appoint the other Members of the European Executive Council.

3. The European Executive Council shall not include more than two Members of the same nationality.

4. The Members of the European Executive Council shall have the title of Ministers of the European Community.

ARTICLE 29

Only nationals of Member States may be Members of the European Executive Council.

ARTICLE 30

1. The office of a member of the European Executive Council shall be incompatible with that of a member of the Government of a participating State, of a judge or solicitor-general in the Court or of a member of the Economic and Social Council.

2. Members of the European Executive Council may not exercise any paid function.

They may belong neither to the management nor the Board of Directors of any enterprise conducted for profit.

ARTICLE 31

1. The European Executive Council shall assume its functions as soon as its composition has been published in the Official Journal of the Community. It shall forthwith request the Peoples' Chamber and the Senate for their vote of confidence, which shall be given by each Chamber by majority vote of its members.

2. The European Executive Council shall remain in office until the end of the life of the current Peoples' Chamber. It shall resign from office notwithstanding, if a vote of no confidence is passed against it by the Peoples' Chamber or the Senate. It shall also be required to resign if the Peoples' Chamber or the Senate refuses to grant its request for a vote of confidence.

3. The Senate shall be deemed to have passed a vote of no confidence in the European Executive Council if it elects a new President, under the provisions of the first paragraph of Article 28.

The Peoples' Chamber shall pass a vote of no confidence in the European Executive Council by a three-fifths majority vote of its members.

Subject to the provisions of paragraph 1 of the present article, the withholding of a vote of confidence, if it is to be effective, must take place under the same conditions as a vote of no confidence.

4. If a motion of no confidence, or alternatively the withholding of a vote of confidence which has been requested of the Peoples' Chamber by the European Executive Council, is voted by a majority of less than three-fifths of the members of the Chamber, it shall be at discretion of the European Executive Council either to resign or to declare the Chamber dissolved.

Such dissolution may not be ordered until after the expiry of a period of five clear days. The instrument of dissolution shall include convocation of the electoral body of the Peoples' Chamber within a period of forty days, and of the Chamber within two months.

The withholding of a vote confidence by the Peoples' Chamber shall not, however, entail the option of dissolving the Chamber in the case mentioned in paragraph 1 of the present Article.

5. The right of the European Executive Council to order the dissolution of the Peoples' Chamber in implementation of the preceding paragraph shall lapse if, within the period determined in that paragraph, the Senate passes a vote of no confidence in the European Executive Council under the conditions laid down in paragraph 3 of the present Article.

6. The President of the European Executive Council shall tender the resignation of the Council to the President of the Senate. The retiring Council shall conduct current business until its successor takes up office.

7. The members of the European Executive Council shall resign in a body if and when the President ceases to exercise his functions.

ARTICLE 32

The President of the European Executive Council may dismiss or replace any Member of that Council subject to the approval of the Peoples' Chamber and the Senate.

ARTICLE 33

In order to fulfil the tasks entrusted to it, and in accordance with the conditions laid down in the present Statute, the European Executive Council shall take decisions, make recommendations or express opinions.

Decisions shall be binding in all aspects.

Recommendations shall have binding effect as regards the aims specified therein, but shall leave the means of implementation to the Authorities to whom the recommendation is addressed.

Opinions shall not be binding.

ARTICLE 34

The President of the European Executive Council shall represent the Community in international relations.

Chapter III

THE COUNCIL OF NATIONAL MINISTERS

ARTICLE 35

The Council of National Ministers shall exercise its powers and competence in the cases specified and in the manner indicated in the present Statute with a view to harmonising the action of the European Executive Council with that of the Governments of Member States.

The Council of National Ministers and the European Executive Council shall exchange information and consult each other.

ARTICLE 36

The Council of National Ministers shall be composed of representatives of the Member States. Each State shall delegate a member of its Government as a representative.

The Chairmanship shall be taken by each of the Members of the Council in turn for a period of three months, in accordance with the alphabetical order of the names of the Member States.

ARTICLE 37

The Council of National Ministers shall be convened by its Chairman at the request of a Member State or of the European Executive Council.

The Council of National Ministers shall communicate with each Member State through the Minister representing the latter.

Chapter IV

THE COURT

ARTICLE 38

1. The Court shall ensure the rule of law in the interpretation and application of the present Statute and of the laws and regulations of the Community.

2. The Court of the Community shall be identical with the Court of the European Coal and Steel Community and of the European Defence Community, thus ensuring unity of jurisprudence.

3. Other courts set up by existing or subsequent treaties shall assist the Court in the exercise of its functions.

ARTICLE 39

1. The number of judges shall not exceed fifteen.

They shall be selected from a double list by the European Executive Council, acting with the approval of the Senate. Each Member State may put forward three candidates; the national groups of the Permanent Arbitration Court in each Member State shall be entitled to exercise a similar right.

2. The candidates must be of the highest moral character, and must either possess the qualifications required, under their national legislation, for the exercise of the highest judicial functions, or be jurists of unquestionable ability.

3. Judges shall be appointed for nine years and shall be re-eligible. Nevertheless, the first seven judges shall cease to exercise their functions at the expiry of the period for which provision is made in the treaty instituting the European Coal and Steel Community.

4. The Court shall have exclusive jurisdiction in disciplinary proceedings against its own members.

5. The judges shall be independent and subject only to the law.

ARTICLE 40

1. The texts relating to the competence of the Court and the organisation of the judicial system shall be supplemented and modified in accordance with Articles 112 or 113. Nevertheless, should such modification entail an alteration in the powers and competence of the Community vis-à-vis the Member States, the provisions of Article 111 shall be applicable.

2. Notwithstanding the provisions in the preceding paragraph, the Court shall lay down its own Rules of Procedure.

ARTICLE 41

1. The Court shall in its own right take cognisance of disputes arising out of the application or interpretation of the present Statute or of a law of the Community, to which the parties are
— either Member States among themselves,
— or one or more Member States and the Community.
2. The Court shall take cognisance, through the machinery provided for the hearing of appeals, of the judgments or decisions delivered by the judicial organs of the Community, all of which are subordinate to it.

ARTICLE 42

1. The Court shall take cognisance in first and final instance of all appeals formally lodged against the Community, except when provision is made to the contrary in the present Statute or in a law of the Community conferring this competence on another Court.
2. The Court shall pass judgment on disputes arising from the application of the Treaties instituting the European Coal and Steel Community and the European Defence Community in accordance with the provisions of those Treaties.

ARTICLE 43

The Court shall have jurisdiction to pass judgment on appeals for annulment on grounds of lack of competence, substantial procedural violations, violation of the Statute or of any regulation concerning its application, or abuse of power, where such appeals are lodged by any interested party against the decisions or recommendations of the European Executive Council or of the administrative authorities subordinate thereto.

ARTICLE 44

The Court shall have sole jurisdiction to decide on the validity of decisions or recommendations of the European Executive Council and of deliberations of the Council of National Ministers, in cases where such validity is contested in litigation before a national Court.

ARTICLE 45

1. Any dispute arising from a decision or measure taken by one of the Institutions of the Community, which affects the rights recognised in the Convention for the Protection of Human Rights and Fundamental Freedoms, shall be referred to the Court.
2. If an appeal is lodged with the Court under the conditions mentioned in the preceding paragraph by a natural or legal person, such appeal shall be deemed to be lodged in accordance with the terms of Article 26 of the Convention for the Protection of Human Rights and Fundamental Freedoms.
3. After the establishment of the legal machinery for which provision is made in the Convention for the Protection of Human Rights and Fundamental Freedoms, should any dispute arise which involves a question of principle as to the interpretation or extent of the obligations resulting from the said Convention and which consequently affects all the Parties thereto, the Court shall renounce judgment, if necessary, until the question of principle has been settled by the judicial organs for which provision is made in the Convention.

ARTICLE 46

The Member States undertake not to avail themselves of any mutual declarations or conventions existing among them to submit any difference arising out of the interpretation or application of the present Treaty to a method of settlement other than those provided for herein.

ARTICLE 47

The Court may also, by virtue of the present Statute or a law of the Community, be empowered to act as an Arbitration Court.

ARTICLE 48

The judicial organs of the Community and those of Member States shall assist each other in the exercise of their functions.

ARTICLE 49

Appeals lodged with the Court shall have no suspensory effect. Notwithstanding this provision the Court may, if it considers that circumstances so demand, order a stay of execution of the decision or recommendation which is the subject of the appeal.

The Court may also order any other interim measures which it deems necessary.

Chapter V

THE ECONOMIC AND SOCIAL COUNCIL

ARTICLE 50

The Economic and Social Council shall assist the European Executive Council and Parliament in an advisory capacity.

It shall deliver opinions to each of the Chambers of Parliament and the European Executive Council, if they so request. It may also transmit resolutions to them.

ARTICLE 51

The Community shall enact legislation establishing the membership, competence and *modus operandi* of the Economic and Social Council.

If an Economic and Social Council is set up by the Council of Europe, agreements shall be concluded to enable the Economic and Social Council of the Community to constitute a section of the Council thus created, and to take part in its deliberations. Where necessary, however, the Economic and Social Council of the Community shall be separately consulted.

Chapter VI

LEGISLATION

ARTICLE 52

1. The passing of legislation shall require the assent of each of the two Chambers in succession by simple majority.

2. After the adoption of a bill by the two Chambers, a second deliberation shall be held automatically in the Peoples' Chamber and in the Senate if requested by one quarter of the Members of the Senate within three clear days.

The second deliberation shall begin ten clear days after the request has been made.

A second deliberation in accordance with this procedure may not be requested more than once on the same bill.

3. A bill shall be considered as finally passed into law after it has been approved at a second deliberation, or, if no admissible request for a second deliberation has been made, at the expiry of the period of three clear days laid down in §2 of the present Article.

4. Laws shall be promulgated by the President of the European Executive Council within a period of eight clear days from the day on which they are finally voted in accordance with the provisions of §3.

Before the expiry of this period the President of the European Executive Council may request Parliament to hold a new debate.

5. Laws shall be published in the Official Journal of the Community. They shall have executive effect at such time and under such conditions as shall be laid down in legislation enacted by the Community.

ARTICLE 53

The European Executive Council may issue regulations to ensure the implementation of the laws of the Community.

The European Executive Council and the Authorities of each Member State shall be charged, as they are each and severally affected, with the execution of the Community's legislation and of the regulations of the European Executive Council.

ARTICLE 54

Under the conditions and within the limits in which it is entitled to legislate, Parliament may also make recommendations which shall be binding as regards the aims specified therein, but shall leave the means of implementation to the Authorities to whom the recommendation is addressed.

Recommendations shall be adopted and promulgated in accordance with the procedure laid down in Article 52 for legislation of the Community.

PART III

Powers and Competence

Chapter I

GENERAL RIGHT OF INITIATIVE

ARTICLE 55

The Community may make proposals to the Member States with the object of attaining the general aims defined in Article 2.

Such proposals shall be made by the European Executive Council, either on its own initiative or as a result of a motion by Parliament or by one of the Chambers.

The European Executive Council may request Member States for information on the action which they have taken in regard to the proposals of the Community.

Chapter II

INTEGRATION OF THE EUROPEAN COAL AND STEEL COMMUNITY AND OF THE DEFENCE COMMUNITY

ARTICLE 56

The Community shall, with due regard to the provisions of Article 5, exercise the powers and competence of the European Coal and Steel Community and those of the European Defence Community.

ARTICLE 57

Subject to the provisions of Articles 5 and 56, the provisions of the Treaties instituting the European Coal and Steel Community and the European Defence Community shall remain in force, except in the cases provided for in Articles 39, 58 to 65, 109 and 116, and in the Protocol on the privileges and immunities of the Community.

ARTICLE 58

The decisions which the High Authority or the Board of Commissioners are authorized to take by virtue of the first paragraph of Article 95 of the Treaty instituting the European Coal and Steel Community and Article 124 of the Treaty instituting the European Defence Community must be submitted to Parliament for prior approval.

In urgent cases the measures taken shall be immediately submitted to Parliament for subsequent ratification.

ARTICLE 59

The integration of the European Coal and Steel Community and the European Defence Community shall be accomplished progressively during a period of adaptation not exceeding two years from the date of the constitution of the Peoples' Chamber.

ARTICLE 60

1. As soon as the Peoples' Chamber has come into being, the Common Assembly of the European Coal and Steel Community and the European Defence Community shall be replaced by the Parliament of the Community, which shall exercise the powers and competence of the former, except as laid down in the transitional provision embodied in sub-paragraph (ii) of paragraph 1 of Article 62.

2. When the present Treaty comes into force:

— The Council of National Ministers shall replace the special Councils of Ministers of the European Coal and Steel Community and the European Defence Community and shall exercise their powers and competence.

— The judicial powers provided for in the present Statute shall be exercised by the Court of Justice of the European Coal and Steel Community and of the European Defence Community.

ARTICLE 61

During the period laid down in Article 59, the High Authority of the European Coal and Steel Community and the Board of Commissioners* of the European Defence Community shall discharge their functions under the supervision and responsibility of the European Executive Council.

ARTICLE 62

1. During the period laid down in Article 59:

(i) The President of the High Authority of the European Coal and Steel Community and the President of the Board of Commissioners of the European Defence Community shall sit "ex officio" on the European Executive Council with the right to vote:

(ii) The President of the High Authority of the European Coal and Steel Community shall retain the status resulting from the treaty instituting the European Coal and Steel Community.

The responsibility envisaged in Article 24 of that treaty may be questioned only before the Senate.

2. As soon as the first European Executive Council takes office, the Board of Commissioners of the European Defence Community shall be responsible to Parliament under the same conditions as the European Executive Council.

ARTICLE 63

At the expiry of the period laid down in Article 59, and with due regard to the provisions of Articles 5 and 56:

1. The European Executive Council shall be substituted for the Board of Commissioners of the European Defence Community and shall exercise the powers and competence thereof;

* "Commissariat."

2. The High Authority of the European Coal and Steel Community shall continue to exist as an administrative body having the character of a board. Its members shall be appointed by the European Executive Council on proposals submitted by the Governments of the Member States. It shall discharge its functions under the direction and supervision of the European Executive Council.

ARTICLE 64

1. The budgetary and financial provisions of the treaty instituting the European Coal and Steel Community shall remain in force during the period laid down in Article 59.

2. Nevertheless, with effect from the date on which the Peoples' Chamber comes into being the budget of expenditure of the European Defence Community shall be voted by Parliament, under the conditions laid down in Article 76 of the present Treaty.

3. At the expiry of the period laid down in Article 59, the whole of the regulations embodied in Articles 75 to 81 shall come into force, subject to the proviso that the allotment of receipts resulting from the implementation of the Treaties instituting the European Coal and Steel Community shall be maintained.

ARTICLE 65

The European Executive Council, during the period laid down in Article 59, shall take such decisions as are necessary to ensure the implementation of Articles 5 and 56.

Should these measures involve the amendment of one or more provisions of the treaties instituting the European Coal and Steel Community and the European Defence Community, other than those already modified by the present Treaty, in particular by Articles 5, 56 and 59 to 64, such amendments shall be made in accordance with the provisions of Articles 110 to 115.

ARTICLE 66

Such provisions of the present Treaty as relate to the European Defence Community shall be applicable when both the present Treaty and the treaty instituting the European Defence Community shall have come into force.

Chapter III

INTERNATIONAL RELATIONS

ARTICLE 67

1. Within the limits of the powers and competence conferred upon it, the Community may conclude treaties or international agreements or accede thereto.

2. The Community may conclude treaties or agreements of association with third States, under the conditions prescribed in Articles 90 to 92.

ARTICLE 68

The European Executive Council shall negotiate and conclude treaties or international agreements on behalf of the Community.

Where such treaties or agreements relate to matters in which the present Statute provides for the assent of another institution of the Community, the European Executive Council may ratify them only when authorized so to do by the other institution concerned, acting in accordance with the procedure and conditions laid down for the exercise of its competence.

ARTICLE 69

In order to achieve the general aims laid down in Article 2, the Community shall ensure that the foreign policies of Member States are co-ordinated.

For this purpose the European Executive Council may be empowered, by unanimous decision of the Council of National Ministers, to act as common representative of the Member States.

ARTICLE 70

For the purposes defined in the previous article:

1. Representatives of Member States in the Council of National Ministers shall exchange information and institute a procedure for mutual and permanent consultation on all questions which affect the interests of the Community.

2. The European Executive Council may make proposals for this purpose to the Council of National Ministers. It shall have the right to be heard at all meetings of the Council of National Ministers when these proposals are examined.

3. Parliament, acting through the European Executive Council, may address proposals to the Council of National Ministers or to the Governments of Member States on all matters affecting the interests of the Community.

The European Executive Council may, at the request of Parliament, invite the Council of National Ministers or the governments in question to make known what action has been taken on these proposals.

ARTICLE 71

The Community shall:

1. institute a procedure for consultations among the Member States, so that a common attitude may be adopted at any international conferences where the interests of the Community may be involved;

2. prepare a draft pact for the peaceful settlement of any disputes which may arise between the Member States and which do not come within the competence of the Court;

3. establish the procedure for conciliation and arbitration required for the implementation of Article 73;

4. draft other treaties or agreements among the Member States or between certain individual Member States.

The European Executive Council shall invite the Member States to implement such treaties or agreements in accordance with their usual constitutional procedure.

ARTICLE 72

Member States may not conclude treaties or international agreements which run counter to commitments entered into by the Community or adhere to such treaties or agreements.

ARTICLE 73

Member States shall inform the European Executive Council of any draft treaties or agreements which they are in process of negotiating, or of any initiative taken by them which affects the Community.

If the European Executive Council considers that any such draft or initiative is likely to impede the implementation of the present Statute or to affect the interests of the Community, and if no agreement with the State in question can be reached, the dispute shall, subject to any other procedure provided for in the present Statute, be submitted to conciliation or, if this is unsuccessful, to arbitration.

ARTICLE 74

The Community shall, to the extent required for the achievement of its aims and within the limits of its powers and competence, have the right to accredit and receive diplomatic representatives.

Chapter IV

FINANCIAL PROVISIONS

ARTICLE 75

1. The budget shall embrace the total receipts and expenditure of the Community. It shall be divided into Chapters.
2. The Community shall enact legislation defining the methods of presentation and implementation of the budget, together with the methods by which this implementation shall be supervised.

ARTICLE 76

1. The budget shall be proposed by the European Executive Council, subject to the provisions of Articles 78, 79 and 80.
2. The budget shall be voted annually by Parliament. Parliament may exercise its right of amendment only within the limits of the grand total of the proposed expenditure. It may not add new Chapters involving additional expenditure.
3. If the budget is not approved by Parliament before the beginning of the financial year, the European Executive Council may prolong the budget of the preceding year for a quarter at a time, until the new budget shall have been adopted. In that case, the provisions of Article 81, relating to the transfer of credits from one chapter to another, shall not be applicable.

ARTICLE 77

The financial resources of the Community shall be derived from:
— its own receipts, which include taxes, loans and various products of the Community;
— the contributions paid by Member States.

ARTICLE 78

1. The methods of determining the assessment, the rates of taxation and the manner in which the Community's taxes are levied shall be laid down by the European

Executive Council in the form of bills, with the unanimous concurrence of the Council of National Ministers. Such bills shall be submitted to Parliament for approval. Their provisions shall be promulgated as legislation of the Community.

2. There shall be no exemption from taxes levied by the Community.

ARTICLE 79

No loan may be issued without the approval of Parliament, except such loans as fall due within less than one year when necessary to provide for the annual balancing of accounts by the Treasury.

ARTICLE 80

The basis for determining the contributions of Member States and the rate of contribution shall be unanimously decided by the Council of National Ministers, on the proposal of the European Executive Council.

ARTICLE 81

1. The European Executive Council shall implement the provisions of the budget, in accordance with the provisions of the legislation envisaged in Article 75. It may not transfer credits from one Chapter to another, unless authorised by Parliament so to do.

2. Not later than six months after the end of the financial year, the European Executive Council shall submit to Parliament a bill approving the accounts for that financial year.

Chapter V

ECONOMIC POWERS

ARTICLE 82

The Community, while unholding the principles defined in Articles 2, 3 and 4 of the Treaty instituting the European Coal and Steel Community, shall establish progressively a common market among the Member States, based on the free movement of goods, capital and persons.

In order to achieve the aim mentioned in the preceding paragraph, the Community shall foster the co-ordination of the policy of the Member States in monetary, credit and financial matters.

The Community shall have the power to take the measures rendered necessary by Articles 84 to 87.

ARTICLE 83

From the date on which the present Treaty becomes effective, nationals of Member States who have completed their service in the European defence forces shall have freedom of movement within the Community and freedom to choose their domicile in the territory of any Member State under the same conditions as are applicable to nationals of that State.

The same facilities shall be afforded to nationals of Member States born after the present Treaty has come into force.

ARTICLE 84

1. The Community may not exercise the powers conferred upon it by Article 82 until one year after the present Treaty has come into force.

2. At the expiry of the period mentioned in the preceding paragraph, and during a period of five years thereafter, the measures to be taken in application of Article 82 shall be embodied in proposals drawn up by the European Executive Council, with the unanimous concurrence of the Council of National Ministers who may consult, if need be, their respective national Parliaments before delivering an opinion. Such proposals shall be submitted to the Parliament of the Community for approval. The provisions which they contain shall be enacted as legislation of the Community.

3. At the expiry of this period of five years, the measures to be taken in application of Article 82 shall be embodied in proposals drawn up by the European Executive Council, with the concurrence of the Council of National Ministers. Such proposals shall be submitted for approval to the Peoples' Chamber, voting by simple majority and to the Senate, voting by two-thirds majority. The provisions which they contain shall be enacted as legislation of the Community. .

ARTICLE 85

1. In order to facilitate the progressive establishment of the common market envisaged in Article 82 a European Re-adaptation Fund shall be instituted, to enable assistance to be given where necessary to enterprises and workers, on lines similar to those laid down in Article 56 of the treaty instituting the European Coal and Steel Community.

Applications for assistance may also be made by the Governments of Member States.

2. The Fund shall be financed by:

(i) contributions from the Member States,

(ii) loans raised by the Community,

(iii) an annual levy at a rate not exceeding 5% of the value of orders placed in execution of the programmes referred to in Article 101 of the treaty instituting the European Defence Community.

The rate of the levy, within the limits defined above, and its assessment and collection shall be laid down in legislation to be enacted by the Community.

3. The Fund shall be administered by the European Executive Council under the supervision of Parliament.

The Economic and Social Council may be consulted on the administration and operation of the Fund.

ARTICLE 86

One or more Member States may appeal to the Arbitration tribunal provided for in Article 73 or, prior to the date on which such tribunal is set up, to the Court, against the measures taken by the Community in implementation of paragraph 3 of Article 84, if they deem that such measures might cause fundamental and persistent disturbances to their economy.

The existence or imminence of such disturbances shall be confirmed, at the request of the Member State or States concerned, by the Court or Arbitration Tribunal. Until such time as the competent institution of the Community shall have taken appropriate steps to eliminate the disturbances, the Court or Arbitration Tribunal shall, at the request of the same State or States and in so far as that State or States are concerned, suspend application of the measures in question.

The Court or the Arbitration Tribunal shall pass summary judgment, notify the President of each Chamber that the appeal has been lodged, and state what decision it has taken.

ARTICLE 87

Member States shall consult the European Executive Council before concluding among themselves agreements likely to restrict the movement of labour and commodities, or before taking any measures, particularly in the monetary field, which might have similar effects.

Should the European Executive Council find that such agreements or measures conflict with the aims of the present Treaty, in particular those defined in Article 82, or that they are likely to cause fundamental and persistent disturbances to the economy of the other Member States or to entail the application of the measures specified in Article 67 of the treaty instituting the European Coal and Steel Community, it may, with the assent of the Council of National Ministers, address appropriate proposals to the Member States concerned.

Chapter VI

SPECIALIZED AUTHORITIES

ARTICLE 88

Within the framework of the mission and general aims laid down in Article 2, the Community may set up, or sponsor the creation of, administrative bodies, institutions, public services or services in the European public interest, or self-governing and financially independent organizations, centralized or decentralized; it may also exercise supervision over them.

Organizations of the Community for which provision is made in the preceding paragraph may be governed by any form of public or private law, or be subject to national or Community legislation.

In order to fulfil the tasks entrusted to it, the Community may also make use of existing services.

The Community shall enact legislation in implementation of the present Article.

ARTICLE 89

The Community may represent its Member States in any Specialized Authority or Community to which all such Member States belong.

PART IV

Association

ARTICLE 90

The Community may conclude treaties or agreements of association in order to establish, in certain fields, close co-operation, involving reciprocal rights and obligations, with such third States as guarantee the protection of the human rights and fundamental freedoms mentioned in Article 3.

Such treaties or agreements may be concluded either with a European non-member State or, in accordance with the provisions of its Constitution, with an overseas

State, having constitutional links either with a Member State or with a State which is already associated with the Community.

Should such treaty or agreement of association necessitate a revision of the present Statute, such revision shall be made in accordance with the provisions of Article 116.

ARTICLE 91

A treaty of association may provide *inter alia* for:

1. Participation in the Council of National Ministers of representatives of the Governments of the associated States, and participation in the Senate of representatives of the peoples of the associated States, either with full or with partial rights;

2. the creation of permanent joint committees on the governmental or parliamentary level;

3. the obligation to exchange information and undertake mutual consultation.

ARTICLE 92

The treaty of association shall provide for procedure to uphold the rule of law in the interpretation and application of the treaty of association.

The Court of the Community may be empowered by the treaty of association to settle differences between the Community and an associated State.

The Court and the other judicial organs of the Community may also be given competence to take cognizance of certain litigation concerning nationals of an associated State.

In such cases, and in accordance with the methods defined in the treaty of association, judges appointed by the associated State may sit in the judicial organs of the Community.

ARTICLE 93

The members of the European Executive Council, those of the Council of National Ministers and the representatives of the associated States shall periodically meet in conference.

PART V

Inauguration of the Institutions
of the Community

ARTICLE 94

The first Senate shall be constituted within a month after the present Treaty has come into force.

It shall be convened by the President of the Common Assembly of the European Coal and Steel Community.

ARTICLE 95 *

The Senate shall fix the date of the elections to the Peoples' Chamber. They shall take place within six months after the present Treaty comes into force.

* After voting on this Article, the Assembly agreed to the recommendation of the Constitutional Committee "that the expenses of the first election to the Peoples' Chamber be

ARTICLE 96

1. Until such time as the legislation envisaged in Article 13 has come into force, elections to the Peoples' Chamber shall take place in the territory of each Member State on a basis of proportional representation, the use of the "combined list" (apparentement) system being optional.

The procedure to be followed in each State shall be laid down by national legislation. Regulations concerning the electoral law, in particular the right of franchise, the electoral list, the organization and counting of votes, shall be laid down by legislation in each Member State.

2. Until such time as:

(i) the law on eligibility mentioned in Article 19;

(ii) the law on incompatibility mentioned in paragraph 5 of Article 20,

have come into force, the regulations concerning eligibility and incompatibility shall be laid down by the legislation of each Member State, subject to the reservation that paragraphs 1, 2, 3 and 4 of Article 20 shall be applied forthwith.

ARTICLE 97

The President of the Senate shall convene the Peoples' Chamber and the Senate within the fortnight following the date of the elections which shall be determined in accordance with the provisions of Article 95.

ARTICLE 98

As soon as the Peoples' Chamber has been constituted, the Senate shall elect the President of the European Executive Council.

ARTICLE 99

The Council of National Ministers shall meet as soon as the European Executive Council has taken up office.

PART VI

General Provisions

ARTICLE 100

1. The seat of the various Institutions of the Community shall be determined by Parliament within a period of one year from the date on which the Peoples' Chamber comes into being.

2. Each Chamber shall vote by a two-thirds majority of its Members.

3. As an appendix to the law which they adopt, a Protocol shall be issued by the European Executive Council, placing the location or locations selected under the exclusive jurisdiction of the Community. Before this law is voted, the Protocol

borne by the Community, subject to such precautions and safeguards as the Community shall stipulate."

must be agreed between the European Executive Council and the Government or Governments of the State or States whose territory is affected.

4. Pending the decision for which provision is made in paragraph 1 of the present Article, the Institutions of the Community shall have their provisional seat at Strasbourg.

ARTICLE 101

1. Unless any Member State concerned makes a declaration to the contrary before signature of the Treaty, the provisions of the Statute shall apply to all territories under the jurisdiction of each State.

2. Laws, recommendations and all other decisions of the Community, together with the treaties concluded by the latter, shall not be applicable to non-European territories except with such adaptations as may be laid down by the Member State under whose jurisdiction they fall.

3. The provisions of the Statute may be extended in whole or in part, by means of separate protocols, to the territories mentioned in the declaration provided for in paragraph 1, and also to States, countries or territories for whose international relations a Member State or an Associated State is responsible.

ARTICLE 102 *

ARTICLE 103

When a Member State regains jurisdiction over a territory which formed part of that State on 31st December 1937, the present Statute shall *ipso facto* become applicable to the said territory.

Any adjustments to the composition of the Peoples' Chamber which might result from this situation shall be made by means of the procedure provided in Article 112.

ARTICLE 104

Member States may request the European Executive Council for assistance in maintaining constitutional order and democratic institutions within their territory.

* This Article was referred, with the relevant Amendments, to the Special Council of Ministers of the European Coal and Steel Community.

The European Executive Council, with the unanimous concurrence of the Council of National Ministers, shall lay down the conditions under which the Community shall be empowered to intervene on its own initiative. The relevant provisions shall take the form of a bill to be submitted to Parliament for approval within one year from the date of the coming into being of the Peoples' Chamber. They shall be enacted as legislation of the Community.

ARTICLE 105

The Member States pledge themselves to take all measures necessary to implement the laws, regulations, decisions and recommendations of the Community and to assist the Community in the accomplishment of its mission.

The Member States further undertake to refrain from any measure incompatible with the provisions of the present Statute.

ARTICLE 106

The decisions of the European Executive Council and the judgements of the Court shall have executive force in the territory of the Member States.

Enforcement in the territory of the Member States shall be ensured through the normal legal channels of each State. It shall be preceded by the customary executive formula employed in the State within whose territory the decision is to be enforced, there being no intervention by the national authorities other than a verification of the authenticity of the decision. This formality shall be entrusted to a Minister appointed for the purpose by each Government.

ARTICLE 107

Liaison between the Institutions of the Community and the Council of Europe shall be ensured in accordance with the provisions of the Protocol appended to the present Treaty.

ARTICLE 108

1. In the present Treaty the words "the present Treaty" shall be interpreted to mean the clauses of the Treaty and its appendices.

2. In the present Treaty, the words "the present Statute" shall be interpreted to mean the clauses of the present Treaty as defined in the preceding paragraph, together with the provisions of the treaty instituting the European Coal and Steel Community and of the treaty instituting the European Defence Community, to the extent that these have not been modified by the present Treaty.

ARTICLE 109

The 3rd and 4th paragraphs of Article 95 and Article 96 of the Treaty instituting the European Coal and Steel Community, and Articles 125 and 126 of the Treaty instituting the European Defence Community are abrogated.

ARTICLE 110

The European Executive Council, either of the two Chambers, and each of the Member States may make proposals for the amendment of the present Statute.

Proposals for amendment made by one of the Chambers or by a Member State shall be transmitted to the European Executive Council which shall set in motion the procedure for which provision is made in Articles 111 to 115 of the present Statute.

ARTICLE 111

Amendments to the provisions of the present Statute involving a modification of the powers and competence of the Community vis-à-vis the Member States, or a modification of the definition of human rights and fundamental freedoms guaranteed by the present Statute, shall be made by means of the following procedure:

The European Executive Council shall decide on a draft amendment to the Statute, with the unanimous concurrence of the Council of National Ministers.

The draft amendment shall be submitted for approval to the Parliament of the Community and to the Parliaments of the Member States.

The amendment shall be promulgated by the European Executive Council.

ARTICLE 112

Amendments to the provisions of the present Statute involving an alteration in the relations between the Institutions of the Community, or in the division of powers and competence among them, or amendments tending to affect the guarantees provided for the States in the composition or working procedure of these Institutions, shall be made in accordance with the following procedure:

The European Executive Council shall decide on a draft amendment of the Statute, which shall be submitted to the Council of National Ministers for unanimous approval.

The draft amendment shall be submitted for approval to the Parliament of the Community.

The amendment shall be promulgated by the European Executive Council.

ARTICLE 113

Amendments to the provisions of the present Statute other than those referred to in Articles 111 and 112 shall be made in accordance with the following procedure:

The European Executive Council shall decide on a draft amendment to the Statute.

The draft amendment shall be submitted for approval to the Parliament of the Community.

The amendment shall be promulgated by the European Executive Council.

ARTICLE 114

The Court shall adjudicate in any dispute concerning the procedure to be followed on a proposal for amendment, if requested to do so by an institution of the Community or a Member State.

ARTICLE 115

Amendments to the provisions of the Treaty instituting the European Defence Community, which might affect mutual aid agreements between the Member States of the European Defence Community and the United Kingdom, on the one hand, and the Member States of the European Defence Community and States parties to the North Atlantic Treaty, on the other hand, shall not become effective until agreement has been reached with the interested States.

ARTICLE 116

1. Accession to the Community shall be open to the Member States of the Council of Europe and to any other European State which guarantees the protection of human rights and fundamental freedoms mentioned in Article 3.

2. Any State desirous of acceding to the present Statute shall address its request to the European Executive Council. The latter shall inform the Council of National Ministers and the Parliament of the Community accordingly.

3. Accession shall form the subject of an instrument of accession which shall form a Protocol to the present Statute. This instrument, which shall contain the necessary amendments to the Statute, shall be drawn up by the European Executive Council with the concurrence of the Council of National Ministers. It shall be submitted to the Parliament of the Community for approval.

4. The instrument of accession shall come into force as soon as the European Executive Council has promulgated it and the State concerned has deposited its instrument of ratification with the European Executive Council.

5. The provisions of Article 98 of the treaty instituting the European Coal and Steel Community and of Article 129 of the treaty instituting the European Defence Community are abrogated.

ARTICLE 117

The present Treaty, drawn up in a single original copy, shall be provisionally deposited in the archives of .... which shall transmit a certified copy thereof to the governments of each of the other signatory States.

The present Treaty shall be ratified. The instruments of ratification shall be deposited with ...., which shall notify the Governments of the other Member States accordingly.

The present Treaty shall come into force on the day when the instrument of ratification shall be deposited by the penultimate State to fulfil this formality.

Within one year after the present Treaty shall have come into force, ... shall deposit the present Treaty, together with the instruments of ratification, in the archives of the European Executive Council.

When the Council of National Ministers has taken up office, it shall arrange for the preparation of authoritative texts of the present Treaty in the languages other than that of the original copy.

Should there be any divergence, the text of the original copy shall prevail.

In witness whereof the undersigned Plenipotentiaries have placed their signatures and seals at the end of the present Treaty.

Bibliography

Bibliography

FEDERALISM IN GENERAL

ADARKAR, B. P. *The Principles and Problems of Federal Finance* (1933).

ANDERSON, WILLIAM. *Federalism and Intergovernmental Relations* (A Budget of Suggestions for Research), Public Administration Service (1946).

DENNEWITZ, BODO. *Der Föderalismus: Sein Wesen und seine Geschichte* (1947).

FLEINER, FRITZ. *Entstehung und Wandlung moderner Staatstheorien in der Schweiz* (1916).

FRANTZ, CONSTANTIN. *Der Föderalismus als das leitende Prinzip für die soziale, staatliche und internationale Organisation unter besonderer Bezugnahme auf Deutschland, kritisch untersucht und konstruktiv dargestellt* (1879).

FREEMAN, EDWARD A. *A History of Federal Government in Greece and Italy* (1893).

GMELIN, HANS. "Unitarismus und Föderalismus," *in Handwörterbuch der Rechtswissenschaft*, VI. Bd. S. 220 et seq. Hrsg. von Fritz Stier-Somlo (1929).

GREAVES, HAROLD RICHARD. *Federal Union in Practice* (1940).

HART, ALBERT BUSHNELL. *Introduction to the Study of Federal Government* (1891).

JELLINEK, GEORG. *Die Lehre von den Staatenverbindungen* (1882).

JERUSALEM, FRANZ. *Die Staatsidee des Föderalismus* (Recht und Staat 142–143) (1949).

KÄGI, WERNER. "Vom Sinn des Föderalismus." Gedanken zur Verfassungspolitik, in "Die Schweiz" (Ein nationales Jahrbuch), S. 44 *et seq.* (1944).

KARVE, D. B. *Federations, a Study in Comparative Politics* (1932).

KUNZ, JOSEPH L. *Die Staatenverbindungen* (1929).

LAFORET, GEORG. *Föderalismus und Gesellschaftsordnung* (1947).

MACMAHON, ARTHUR W. (ed.), *Federalism Mature and Emergent* (to be published).

MESSMER, GEORGE. *Föderalismus und Demokratie.* Studien zur Staatslehre und Rechtsphilosophie, Hrsg. von Giacometti und Schindler, Heft I (1946).

MOGI, SOBEI. *The Problem of Federalism* (1931).

NAWIASKY, HANS. *Der Bundesstaat als Rechtsbegriff* (1920).

NÜRNBERGER. "Wesen und Wandel des Föderalismus," in Festschrift für Gerhard Ritter (1949).

SHIRRAS, G. F. *Federal Finance in Peace and War* (1944).

STOKE, H. W. *The Foreign Relations of the Federal State* (1931).

TREITSCHKE, HEINRICH VON. "Bundesstaat und Einheitsstaat (1864)" in Historische und politische Aufsätze, II (1886).

WESTERKAMP, JUSTUS B. *Staatenbund und Bundesstaat.* Untersuchungen über die Praxis und das Recht der modernen Bünde (1892).

WHEARE, KENNETH CLINTON. *Federal Government* (2d ed., 1951).

WORKS DEALING WITH FEDERALISM WITHIN A BROADER FRAMEWORK

DUGUIT, L. *Eléments de Droit Constitutionnel Comparé Français et Comparé* (8th ed. 1927–28).

ESMEIN, A. *Traité de Droit Constitutionnel* (5 vols., 2d ed. 1921–25).

FINER, H. *The Theory and Practice of Modern Government* (rev. ed. 1949).
FRIEDRICH, C. J. *Constitutional Government and Democracy* (rev. ed. 1950).
HELLER, H. *Staatslehre* (1934).
JELLINEK, G. *Die Staatsidee des Föderalismus* (Recht und Staat 142–143, 1929).
SMEND, R. *Verfassung und Verfassungsrecht* (1928).

AUSTRALIA

I. HISTORY AND FRAMING OF THE FEDERAL CONSTITUTION

Melbourne Conference of 1890. *Official Record of the Proceedings and Debates of the Australasian Federal Conference, 1890, held in Parliament House, Melbourne* (1890).
Sydney Conference of 1891. *Official Record of the Proceedings and Debates of the National Australasian Convention held in the Parliament House, Sydney, in 1891* (1891).
Convention of 1897–98. *Official Report of the National Australasian Convention Debates* (1897).
———. *Official Record of the Debates of the Australasian Federal Convention, Second Session* (1897). *Third Session* (1898).
DEAKIN, ALFRED. *The Federal Story* (Brookes ed. 1944).
HUNT, ERLING M. *American Precedents in Australian Federation* (1930).

II. THE EVOLUTION AND WORKING OF THE FEDERAL CONSTITUTION

BLAND, F. A. *Government in Australia* (2d ed. 1944).
CRAMP, KARL R. *The State and Federal Constitutions of Australia* (1914).
DRUMMOND, D. H. *Australia's Changing Constitution* (1946).
EGERTON, HUGH EDWARD. *Federations and Unions Within the British Empire* (1924).
GREENWOOD, G. *The Future of Australian Federation* (1946).
HOLMAN, W. H. *The Australian Constitution* (1928).
KERR, DONALD. *The Law of the Australian Constitution* (1925).
MAUGHAN, DAVID, and Others. *Constitutional Revision in Australia* (1944).
NICHOLAS, H. S. *The Australian Constitution* (2d ed. 1952).
PATON, G. (ed.). *The Law of the Commonwealth of Australia* (vol. 2 of the series, The British Commonwealth) (1952).
QUICK, SIR JOHN. *The Legislative Powers of the Commonwealth and the States of Australia* (1919).
QUICK, SIR JOHN, and GARRAN, ROBERT RANDOLPH. *The Annotated Constitution of the Australian Commonwealth* (1901).
SAWER, G. *The Australian Constitution* (1946). (Pocket book)
———. *Australian Government Today* (1948).
———. *Casebook on Australian Constitutional Law* (1948).

III. MONOGRAPHS ON FEDERALISM

BAKER, SIR RICHARD CHAFFEE. *The Executive in a Federation* (1897).
CRISP, L. F. *Parliamentary Government in the Commonwealth of Australia* (1949).
WYNES, F. ANSTEY. *Legislative and Executive Powers in Australia* (1936).

AUSTRIA

I. HISTORY AND FRAMING OF THE FEDERAL CONSTITUTION

ADAMOVICH, LUDWIG. *Grundriss des österreichischen Verfassungsrechts* (4th ed. 1947).
FROEHLICH, GEORG. *Die "Verfassung 1934" des Bundesstaates Österreich* (1936).
SEIPEL, IGNAZ. *Der Kampf um die österreichische Verfassung* (1930).

II. THE EVOLUTION AND WORKING OF THE FEDERAL CONSTITUTION

ADAMOVICH, LUDWIG. *Grundriss des österreichischen Verfassungsrecht* (4th ed. 1947).
——. *Grundriss des österreichischen Verwaltungsrechts* (4th ed. 1948).
FROEHLICH, GEORG. *Die "Verfassung 1934" des Bundesstaates Österreich* (1936).
MERKL, ADOLF. *Die Verfassung der Republik Deutschösterreich* (1919).

III. MONOGRAPHS ON FEDERALISM

ADAMOVICH, LUDWIG. *Die Prüfung der Gesetze und Verordnungen durch den österreichischen Verfassungsgerichtshof* (1924).
KULISCH, M. "Die verfassungsgesetzliche Bezeichnung Österreichs als Bundesstaat," in *Prager wissenschaftliche Vierteljahrsschrift*, Heft II-III (1925).
MERKL, ADOLF. "Der Föderalismus im österreichischen Verfassungsleben," in *Kultur und Politik*, 1. Jahrgang, p. 398.
——. "Zum rechtstechnischen Problem der bundesstaatlichen Kompetenzverteilung," in Zeitschrift für offentliches Recht, 2. Jahrgang, p. 336.

CANADA

I. HISTORY AND FRAMING OF THE FEDERAL CONSTITUTION

Debates on Confederation in the Legislature of the Province of Canada (1865).
ROGERS, M. N. "The Compact Theory of Confederation," *Proceedings, Canadian Political Science Association* (1931).
WHITELAW, W. M. *The Maritimes and Canada before Confederation* (1934).

II. THE EVOLUTION AND WORKING OF THE FEDERAL CONSTITUTION

BOURINOT, JOHN G. *Federal Government in Canada* (1889).
CLOKIE, H. M. *Canadian Government and Politics* (1944).
——. "Judicial Review, Federalism and the Canadian Constitution," Canadian Journal of Economics and Political Science (Nov. 1942).
DAWSON, R. M. G. *The Government of Canada* (1947).
EGERTON, H. E., and GRANT, W. K. *Canadian Constitutional Development* (1907).
EGGLESTON, W. "The Road to Nationhood," *Dominion-Provincial Relations* (1946).
KENNEDY, W. P. M. *The Constitution of Canada* (1938).
——. *The Nature of Canadian Federalism* (1921).
LASKIN, B. *Canadian Constitutional Law* (1951).
——. *Cases on Canadian Constitutional Law* (1951).
LEFROY, A. H. F. *Canada's Federal System* (1913).
PARRY, C. *British Nationality* (1951).
ROWAN, D. C. "Recent Developments in Canadian Federalism," Canadian Journal of Economics and Political Science (Feb. 1952).

Report of the Royal Commission on Dominion-Provincial Relations (Rowell-Sirois report) (1938).
"Nationhood and the Constitution," 29 Canadian Bar Review No. 10 (Dec. 1951) (symposium).

III. MONOGRAPHS ON FEDERALISM

BUCK, A. E. *Financing Canadian Government* (1949).
CORRY, J. A. *Difficulties of Divided Jurisdiction* (Study submitted to the Rowell-Sirois Commission).
CREIGHTON, D. C. *British North America at Confederation* (Study submitted to the Rowell-Sirois Commission).
GOUIN, L. M., and CLAYTON, B. *Legislative Expedients and Devices adopted by the Dominion and the Provinces* (Study submitted to the Rowell-Sirois Commission).
GRAUER, A. E. *Public Assistance and Social Insurance* (Rowell-Sirois Commission, 1940).
MACGREGOR, D. C., and Others. *National Income* (Rowell-Sirois Commission, 1940).
MACKINTOSH. *The Economic Background of Dominion-Provincial Relations* (Rowell-Sirois Commission, 1940).
MINVILLE, ESDRAS. *Labour Legislation and Social Services in the Province of Quebec* (Rowell-Sirois Commission, 1940).

GERMANY

Constitution of the Empire

I. HISTORY AND FRAMING OF THE FEDERAL CONSTITUTION

ARNDT, ADOLF. *Das Staatsrecht des deutschen Reiches* (1901).
BERGSTRASSER, L. "Geschichte der Reichsverfassung," in Archiv des öffentlichen Rechts, Beilageheft III (1914).
BEZOLD, E. (ed.). *Materialien der Deutschen Reichs-Verfassung* (3 vols. 1873).
BINDING, KARL. *Staatsgrundgesetze,* Deutsche (Sammlung) (1892–1907).
BRANDENBURG, E. *Der Eintritt der Süddeutschen Staaten in den Norddeutschen Bund* (1910).
———. *Die Reichsgründung* (2 vol. 1916).
———. "Die Verhandlungen über die Gründung des Deutschen Reichs 1870," in Historische Vierteljahrsschrift, Jahrgang 15, p. 493 (1912).
———. *Untersuchungen und Akenstuecke zur Geschichte der Reichsgründung* (1916).
BUSCH, W. *Die Kämpfe um Reichsverfassung und Kaisertum 1870 bis 1871* (1906).
———. "Württemberg und Bayern in den Einheitsverhandlungen 1870," in Historische Zeitschrift, vol. 109, p. 161 (1912).
DUPUY-DUTEMPS, JEAN. *La constitution fédérale de l'Allemagne de 1815 à 1866,* Diss. (1939).
FORSTHOFF, ERNST. *Deutsche Verfassungsgeschichte der Neuzeit* (1940).
HARTUNG, FRITZ. *Deutsche Verfassungsgeschichte vom 15. Jahrhundert bis zur Gegenwart* (1922).
MARTITZ, FERDINAND VON. *Betrachtungen über die Verfassung des Norddeutschen Bundes* (1868).
PREUSS, HUGO. *Gemeinde, Staat, Reich als Gebietskörperschaften* (1889).
PROEBST, MAX. *Vergleichende Darstellung der Bundesorgane des Deutschen Reiches und der Schweiz* (1912).

RONNE, LUDWIG VON. *Das Staatsrecht des Deutschen Reiches,* 2. Aufl., 2 Bände (1876–1877).

SCHNORR, GERHARD. "Die Stellung der Ländervertretungen im System der deutschen Verfassungen seit 1815. Ein Beitrag zur Entwicklung des deutschen Föderalismus," in Archiv des öffentlichen Rechts, 76 Bd. 3. Heft (1950–1951).

STENGEL, FLEISCHMANN. *Wörterbuch des Deutschen Staats- und Verwaltungsrechts Bd. 1 bis 3* (1911–1914).

STENGEL, KARL FREIHERR VON. "Staatenbund und Bundesstaat," in Schmollers Jahrbuch XXII, S. 707 *et seq.* 1098 *et seq.* (1898).

STOLZE, W. *Die Gründung des Deutschen Reichs im Jahre 1870* (1912).

TRIEPEL, HEINRICH. "Zur Vorgeschichte der Norddeutschen Bundesverfassung" in Festschrift Otto Gierke zum siebzigsten Geburtstag, p. 589 (1911).

TRIEPEL, HEINRICH (ed.). *Quellensammlung zum deutschen Reichsstaatsrecht* (2d ed. 1907).

WAITZ, G. *Deutsche Verfassungsgeschichte* (1st to 3d ed. 1844–1880).

ZEUMER, K. (ed.). *Quellensammlung zur Geschichte der Deutschen Reichsverfassung in Mittelalter und Neuzeit,* (2d ed. 1913).

II. THE EVOLUTION AND WORKING OF THE FEDERAL CONSTITUTION

ANDREN, GEORG. *Federalismen i den tyska riksorganisationen 1871–1914* (1920).

ANSCHÜTZ, GERHARD. "Deutsches Staatsrecht," in von Holtzehdorff-Kohlers Enzyklopädie IV, 2. Aufl. (1914).

EMERSON, RUPERT. *State and Sovereignty in Modern Germany* (1923).

HANEL, ALBERT. *Deutsches Staatsrecht,* 1. Bd. (1892).

LABAND, PAUL. *Das Staatsrecht des Deutschen Reiches* (1st ed., I–III: 1,2, 1876–1882; 2nd ed. I–IV, 1911–1914).

——. *Deutsches Reichsstaatsrecht,* 7. Aufl. bearb. von Otto Mayer (1919).

——. "Die geschichtliche Entwicklung der Reichsverfassung seit der Reichsgründung, in Jahrbuch des öffentlichen Rechts der Gegenwart vol. I, p. 1 (1907).

——. *Die Wandlungen der deutschen Reichsverfassung* (1895).

——. *Handbuch der Politik,* Bd. 1–2 (1912–1913).

LOENING, E. *Grundzüge der Verfassung des Deutschen Reichs* (4th ed. 1913).

MEYER, G. *Lehrbuch des Deutschen Staatsrechts* (7th ed. by Anschütz, I, II, 1914, 1917).

——. *Staatsrechtliche Erörterungen über die deutsche Reichsverfassung* (1872).

MOHL, R. VON. *Das deutsche Reichsstaatsrecht* (1873).

REHM, HERMANN. *Unitarismus und Föderalismus in der Deutschen Reichsverfassung* (1898).

ROSENBERG, A. *Staat, Souveränität und Bundesstaat,* in Annalen des Deutschen Reiches, Nr. 4 und 5 (1905).

SEYDEL, MAX VON. *Commentar zur Verfassungs-Urkunde für das Deutsche Reich* (2d ed. 1897).

TRIEPEL, HEINRICH. "Die Kompetenzen das Bundesstaates und die geschriebne Verfassung," in Festgabe für Paul Laband (1908).

——. *Unitarismus und Föderalismus im Deutschen Reich* (1907).

——. *Völkerrecht und Landesrecht* (1899).

TRIEPS, AUGUST. *Das deutsche Reich und die deutschen Bundesstaaten in ihren rechtlichen Beziehungen* (1890).

III. MONOGRAPHS ON FEDERALISM

DIENSFERTIG, J. *Die rechtliche Mitwirkung des Bundesrats und des Reichstags auf dem Gebiete der auswärtigen Angelegenheiten des Deutschen Reiches,* Diss. (1908).

FICHT, GEORG VON. *Das Aufsichtsrecht der Reichsgewalt über die Einzelstaaten*, Diss. (1907).

FISCHER, R. *Das Recht des Deutschen Kaisers* (1895).

FLEISCHER, M. "Die Züständigkeit des deutschen Bundesrates für Erledigung von öffentlichrechtlichen Streitigkeiten," in Abhandlungen aus dem Staats- und Verwaltungsrecht, vol. 9 (Brie ed. 1914).

HAFF, K. "Neue Probleme des Körperschaftsrechts und speziell des Bundesstaates," in Archiv des öffentlichen Rechts, vol. 37, p. 352 (1917).

HERWEGEN, A. *Reichsverfassung und Bundesrat*, Diss. (1902).

HIRSCHBERG, W. *Haben die Abweichungen der Reichsverfassung von der Verfassung des Norddeutschen Bundes das föderative oder das unitarische Element gestärkt?* Diss. (1912).

JACOBI, ERWIN. *Der Rechtsbestand der deutschen Bundesstaaten* (1917).

KLIEMKE, E. *Die staatsrechtliche Natur und Stellung des Bundesrates* (1894).

KOCH, E. *Der deutsche Bundesrat des geltenden Rechtes und die früheren deutschen Verfassungsentwüffe*, Diss. (1897).

LABAND, PAUL. "Der Bundesrat," in Deutsche Juristen-Zeitung, Jahrgang 16, p. 1 (1911).

————. *Die Wandlungen der deutschen Reichsverfassung* (1895).

LIPHARDT, ERNST. *Sind die deutschen Bundesstaaten noch souveräne Staaten?* Diss. (1906).

LUX, K. *Der Bundesrat und seine Befugnisse* (1913).

MAYER, O. "Republikanischer und monarchischer Bundesstaat," in Archiv für öffentliches Recht, vol. 18, p. 337 (1903).

MEENTZEN, W. *Artikel 78 der Verfassung des Deutschen Reichs in Theorie und Praxis*, Diss. (1893).

MEIER, H. *Die Instruktion und Verantwortlichkeit der deutschen Bundesratsbevollmächtigten*, Diss. (1893).

MEYER, O. "Republikanischer und monarchischer Bundesstaat," in Archiv für öffentliches Recht, Bd. 18 (1903).

MULLER, F. *Begriff und Rechte des deutschen Bundesrates*, Diss. (1908).

MULLER, M. *Die rechtliche Stellung der Bundesratsmitglieder*, Diss. (1909).

NAUMANN, FRIEDRICH. *Demokratie und Kaisertum* (1900).

OESCHEY, R. "Wandlungen der Bundesstaaten und Artikel 6 der Reichsverfassung," in Archiv des öffentlichen Rechts, vol. 38, p. 185 (1918).

PREUSS, HUGO. *Das deutsche Volk und die Politik* (1915).

QUERFURTH, K. *Die rechtliche Stellung der Mitglieder des Bundesrates*, Diss. (1908).

RAUSCHENBERGER, W. *Der Anteil des Bundesrates an der Reichsgesetzgebung*, Diss. (1906).

SAUTER, K. *Das Recht des Bundesrats, besonders nach Artikel 7 der Reichsverfassung* (1909).

SCHUCKING, WALTER. "Neue Ziele der staatlichen Entwicklung," in Festschrift für Eneccerus (1913).

SEYDEL, MAX VON. "Der Bundesstaatsbegriff." Aus: Zeitschrift für die gesamten Staatswissenschaften. Abgedruckt in Staatsrechtliche und politische Abhandlungen (1893).

SIBEN, A. *Die richterlichen Funktionen des Bundesrates*, Diss. (1909).

SIMON, M. *Ursprung und Entwicklung der Staatenhauses in der deutschen Reichsverfassung* (1898).

TESCHEMACHER, H. *Reichsfinanzreform und innere Reichspolitik 1906–1913* (1915).

TRIEPEL, HEINRICH. *Die Reichsaufsicht* (1917).

VOGELS, A. *Die staatsrechtliche Stellung der Bundesratsbevollmächtigten* (1911).

WEBER, MAX. "Deutschlands künftige Staatsform." Flugschriften der Frankfurter Zeitung, Heft 2 (1918).

———. "Parlament und Regierung im neugeordneten Deutschland" in Die innere Politik, hrsg. von Hellmann (1918).

WESTPHAL, M. Der Einfluss der Landtage in den deutschen Einzelstaaten auf die Instruktion der Bundesratsbevollmächtigten, Diss. (1910).

Weimar Constitution

I. HISTORY AND FRAMING OF THE CONSTITUTION

Anlagen zu den Stenographischen Berichten der Verhandlungen der Verfassunggebenden Deutschen Nationalversammlung.

Mündlicher Bericht des 8. Ausschusses (Verfassungsausschuss) über den Entwurf einer Verfassung des Deutschen Reiches.

Stenographische Berichte der Verhandlungen der Verfassunggebenden Deutschen Nationalversammlung.

ANSCHÜTZ, GERHARD. "Drei Leitgedanken der Weimarer Reichsverfassung." Recht und Staat in Geschichte und Gegenwart, Heft 26 (1923).

ANSCHÜTZ, GERHARD, and Others. "Handbuch der Politik," Bd. 3–5 (1921–1922), Bd. 6 1926).

APELT, F. "Das Werden der neuen Reichsverfassung," in Juristische Wochenschrift (1910).

EBERS, G. J. Die Verfassung des deutschen Reiches (1919).

HEILFRON, E. Die deutsche Nationalversammlung im Jahre 1919.

HUSEN, PAULUS VAN. Die staatsrechtliche Organisation von der Revolution 1918 bis zum Zusammentritt der Nationalsammlung, Diss. (1920).

JELLINEK, WALTER. "Revolution und Reichsverfassung." Bericht über die Zeit vom 9. November 1918 bis 31. Dezember 1919, in Jahrbuch des öffentlichen Rechts der Gegenwart, Bd. IX (1920).

MEYER, O., and ANSCHÜTZ, GERHARD. "Lehrbuch des Deutschen Staatsrechts," 7. Aufl. (1919).

NAWIASKY, HANS. Die Grundegedanken der Reichsverfassung (1920).

PREUSS, HUGO. "Der Entwurf der deutschen Reichsverfassung, und Denkschrift zum Reichsverfassungsentwurf," in Reichsanzeiger No. 15, 20 (January, 1919).

———. Reich und Länder; Bruchstücke eines Kommentars zur Verfassung des Deutschen Reiches, hrsg. von Anschütz (1928).

REDSLOB, ROBERT. Die parlamentarische Regierung in ihrer Wahren und in ihrer unechten Form (1918).

STIER-SOMLO, FRITZ. Die Verfassungsurkunde der Vereinigten Staaten von Deutschland (1919).

II. THE EVOLUTION AND WORKING OF THE CONSTITUTION

ANSCHÜTZ, GERHARD. Die Verfassung des Deutschen Reiches, 3. Bearbeitung, 13. Aufl. (1930), 14. Aufl. (1933).

ANSCHÜTZ, GERHARD, and THOMA, RICHARD. Handbuch des Deutschen Staatsrechts. Das öffentliche Recht der Gegenwart, Bd. 28–29, 1.–2. Bd. (1930–1932).

APELT, WILLIBALT. Geschichte der Weimarer Verfassung (1946).

ARNDT, ADOLF. "Die Verfassung des Deutschen Reiches vom 11. August 1919," Kommentar (1927).

BILFINGER, KARL. Der Einfluss der Einzelstaaten auf die Bildung des Reichswillens (1923).

BLACHLY, FREDERICK F., and OATMAN, MIRIAM E. The Government and Administration of Germany (1928).

BUHLER, OTTMAR. "Finanzgewalt im Wandel der Verfassungen," in Festschrift für
    Richard Thoma (1950).
CARRE DE MALBERG, R. *La question du caractère étatique des pays allemands et
    l'article 76 de la constitution de Weimar* (1924).
DE GRAIS-PETERS, HUE. *Handbuch der Verfassung und Verwaltung in Preussen und
    dem Deutschen Reiche,* 25. Aufl. (1930).
FREYTAGH-LORINGHOVEN, AXEL FREIHERR VON. *Die Weimarer Verfassung in Lehre
    und Wirklichkeit* (1924).
GIESE, FRIEDRICH. *Die Verfassung des Deutschen Reiches* (1926).
HATSCHECK, JULIUS. *Deutsches und Preussisches Staatsrecht,* 2 Bände, 2 Aufl. (1930).
MEISSNER, C. *Das Staatsrecht des Reiches und der Länder,* 2 Aufl. (1923).
POETZSCH-HEFFTER, FRITZ. "Handkommentar der Reichsverfassung vom 11. August
    1919." Ein Handbuch für Verfassungsrecht und Verfassungspolitik, 3. Aufl.
    (1928).
STIER-SOMLO, FRITZ. *Deutsches Reichs- und Landesstaatsrecht* (1924).
VERMEIL, EDMOND. *L'Allemagne contemporaine 1919–1924, sa structure et son
    évolution politique, économique et social* (1925).
————. *La constitution de Weimar et la Principe de la démocratie allemande—
    Essay d'histoire et de psychologie politique* (1923).

III. MONOGRAPHS ON FEDERALISM

ANSCHÜTZ, GERHARD. *Das Preussische-Deutsche Problem* (1922).
ANSCHÜTZ, GERHARD, and Others. "Der deutsche Föderalismus." Die Diktatur des
    Reichspräsidenten. Referate von Gerhard Anschütz, Karl Bilfinger, Carl Schmitt
    und Erwin Jacobi. Veröffentlichungen der Vereinigung der deutschen Staats-
    rechtslehrer, Heft 1 (1924).
APELT, WILLIBALT. "Staatstheoretische Bemerkungen zur Reichsreform," in Festgabe
    für Richard Schmidt, Bd. 1 (1932).
————. *Vom Bundesstaat zum Regionalstaat.* Betrachtungen zur Gesamtentwicklung
    über den endgültigen Reichswirtschaftsrat (1927).
BECKER, WALTER. *Föderalistische Tendenzen im deutschen Staatsleben seit dem
    Umsturze der Bismarck'schen Verfassung.* Eine politisch-staatsrechtliche Studie
    (1928).
BEYERLE, KONRAD. "Föderalismus." Festschrift für Felix Porsch (1923).
————. *Föderalistische Reichspolitik* (1924).
————. "Reich und Länder," in Volk und Reich der Deutschen, Bd. 2 (1929).
BRAASCH, HEINRICH. *Die Reichsaufsicht,* Diss. (1926).
BRAUN, OTTO. *Deutscher Einheitsstaat oder Föderativsystem* (1927).
BRECHT, ARNOLD. *Föderalismus, Regionalismus und die Teilung Preussens.* Deutsche
    Ubersetzung aus dem Amerikanischen: Federalism and Regionalism in Ger-
    many (1949).
COHN, RUDOLPH. *Die Reichsaufsicht über die Länder* (1921).
EVERLING, FRIEDRICH. *Der Unitarismus als Reichszerstörer* (1927).
FICK, F. *Reichseinheit oder Föderalismus* (1924).
FICKER, HANS G. "Vertragliche Beziehungen zwischen Gesamtstaat und Einzelstaat im
    Deutschen Reich." Abhandlungen aus dem Staats- und Verwaltungsrecht, Heft
    38 (1926).
FRANTZ, CONSTANTIN. *Deutschland und der Föderalismus* (1921).
FRIELINGHAUS, OTTO. *Der dezentralisierte Einheitsstaat* (1928).
HALLER, JOHANNES. *Bundesstaat oder Einheitsstaat?* (1928).
————. *Partikularismus und Nationalstaat* (1926).

HELD, JOSEF. *Der Reichsrat, seine Geschichte, seine Rechte und seine Stellung nach der Reichsverfassung vom 11 August 1919* (1926).

HENSEL, ALBERT. *Der Finanzausgleich im Bundesstaat in seiner staatsrechtlichen Bedeutung* (1922).

HEYLAND, CARL. *Zur Lehre von der staatsrechtlichen Stellung der Reichsratsmitglieder nach dem deutschen Reichsund Landesstaatsrecht* (1927).

HEYMANN, E. *Reichsexekution und Ausnahmezustand,* Diss. (1923).

HOEPKER-ASCHOFF, HERMANN. *Deutscher Einheitsstaat* (1928).

HOLTZ, DIETRICH. *Verfassungs- und Verwaltungsreform in Reich und Ländern* (1928). Nachtrag: Reichsreform (1932).

JACOBI, ERWIN. *Einheitsstaat oder Bundesstaat* (1919).

KITZ, WILHELM. *Reichsland Preussen.* Ein Beitrag zur Verfassungs- und Verwaltungsreform (1927).

KOCH-WESER, ERICH. *Einheitsstaat und Selbstverwaltung* (1928).

———. *Vom Kleinstaat zum grossen Reich und zum Einheitsstaat* (1929).

KONIG, CHRISTIAN. *Die süddeutschen Staaten und das Problem der Reichsreform,* Diss. (1929).

LASSAR, HERHARD. "Reichseigene Verwaltung unter der Weimarer Verfassung," in Jahrbuch des öffentlichen Rechts der Gegenwalt, Bd. XIV (1926).

LOHMAYER, H. C. *Zentralismus oder Selbstverwaltung* (1928).

MARKULL, WILHELM. *Kommentar zum Gesetz über den Finanzausgleich zwischen Reich, Ländern und Gemeinden* (1923).

MOOSMANN, HANS B. *Die Reichsexekution nach der Weimarer Verfassung* (1925).

NAWIASKY, HANS. "Die Bestimmungen der Reichsverfassung über die Gebietsgewalt der Länder," in Hirths Annalen des Deutschen Reiches, Jg. 1919 und 1920.

———. *Grundprobleme der Reichsverfassung,* Bd. 1, Das Reich als Bundesstaat (1928).

———. *Grundsätzliche Betrachtungen über die finanzielle Auseinandersetzung zwischen Reich und Ländern.* Vorgelegt dem Verfassungsausschuss der Länderkonferenz (1929).

PETERS, HANS. *Zentralisation und Dezentralisation* (1928).

POPITZ, JOHANNES. *Der künftige Finanzausgleich zwischen Reich, Ländern und Gemeinden.* Gutachten, erstattet der Studiengesellschaft für den Finanzausgleich (1932).

PREUSS, HUGO. *Artikel 18 der Reichsverfassung.* Seine Entstehung und Bedeutung (1922).

———. *Verfassungspolitische Entwicklungen in Deutschland und Westeuropa.* Historische Grundlegung zu einem Staatsrecht der Deutschen Republik (Nachlass hrsg. von Hedwig Hintze) (1927).

PRION, P. *Die Abgeltung von Ansprüchen gegen das Reich,* Diss. (1926).

REICH UND LÄNDER. *Vorschläge, Begründungen, Gesetzentwürfe.* Bund zur Erneuerung des Reiches (1928).

REICH UND LÄNDER. *Zeitschrift für die Entwicklung der Verfassung und Verwaltung in Deutschland,* 4.Jg. (1930).

RITTER, ERWIN. *Freie Reichsländer* (1927).

SCHADE, HANS. *Das Vetorecht in der Gesetzgebung unter besonderer Berücksichtigung des deutschen Reichsverfassungsrechts* (1929).

SCHMIDT, RICHARD. "Der preussische Einheitsstaat und der deutsche Bundesstaat." Gedanken zur Revision des Artikel 18 der Reichsverfassung und des Gesetzes zur Ausführung der Neugliederungsbestimmungen, in Zeitschrift für Politik, Bd. 16, S. 201 *et seq.* (1926–1927).

SCHMITTMANN, BENEDICT. *Grosspreussen oder deutscher Volksstaat* (1930).

SCHNORR, GERHARD. "Die Stellung der Ländervertretungen im System der Deutschen

Verfassungen seit 1815." Ein Beitrag zur Entwicklung des deutschen Föderalismus, in Archiv des öffentlichen Rechts, 76. Bd. 3. Heft (1950–1951).

STIER-SOMLO, FRITZ. "Zur Frage des Unitarismus und Föderalismus im deutschen
Reich," in Zeitschrift für die gesamte Staatswissenschaft, vol. 79.

THOMA, RICHARD. "Die Problematik des deutschen Länderstaates, in Die Justiz Bd.
3, S. 1 *et seq.* (1927–1928).

TRIEPEL, HEINRICH. "Der Föderalismus und die Revision der Weimarer Reichsverfassung," in Zeitschrift für Politik, Bd. 14, S. 193 *et seq.* (1924–1925).

VOGEL, WALTHER. "Deutsche Reichsgliederung und Reichsreform," in Vergangenheit
und Gegenwart (1932).

———. *Festgabe der Berliner Juristenfakulät für Wilhelm Kahl* (1923).

Bonn Constitution

I. HISTORY AND FRAMING OF THE CONSTITUTION

ABRAHAM and Others. *Kommentar zum Bonner Grundgesetz* (Bonner Kommentar)
(1950).

DOEMMING, and Others. "Entstehungsgeschichte der Artikel des Grundgesetzes."
Jahrbuch des öffentlichen Rechts der Gegenwart. N.F. Bd. 1, Hrsg. von Leib-
holz und von v. Mangoldt (1951).

GERLOFF, WILHELM. *Die Finanzgewalt im Bundesstaat* (1948).

GIESE, FRIEDRICH. *Grundgesetz für die Bundesrepublik Deutschland.* Textaugs. mit
Erläuterungen, 3. Aufl. (1953).

GLUM, FRIEDRICH. *Der künftige deutsche Bundesstaat* (1949).

MANGOLDT, HERMANN VON. *Das Bonner Grundgesetz.* Kommentar, 1. bis 5. Lie-
ferung (1950–1953).

MAUNZ, THEODOR. *Deutsches Staatsrecht.* 2. Aufl. (1952).

MENZEL, WALTER. "Die politische und staatliche Ordnung der Bundesrepublik
Deutschland," in Recht-Staat-Wirtschaft, Bd. 2 (1950).

NAWIASKY, HANS. *Die Grundgedanken des Grundgesetzes für die Bundesrepublik
Deutschland* (1950).

PETERS, HANS. "Deutscher Föderalismus." Zeit- und Streitfrange, Heft 4 (1947).

———. *Die problematik der deutschen Demokratie* (1948).

SCHEUNER, ULRICH. "Grundfragen des modernen Staates," in Recht-Staat-Wirtschaft,
Bd. 3 (1951).

SCHNORR, GERHARD. "Die Stellung der Ländervertretungen im System der deutschen
Verfassungen seit 1815." Ein Beitrag zur Entwicklung des deutschen Föderalismus, in Archiv des öffentlichen Rechts, 76 Bd., 3. Heft (1950–1951).

STELTZER, THEODOR. "Der deutsche Föderalismus," in Von deutscher Politik (1949).

II. THE EVOLUTION AND WORKING OF THE CONSTITUTION

SCHAFER, HANS. "Bundesaufsicht und Bundeszwang," in Archiv des öffentlichen
Rechts, Bd. 78 (1952).

III. MONOGRAPHS ON FEDERALISM

APELT, WILLIBALT. "Zum Begriff Föderalismus," in Festschrift für Erich Kaufmann
(1950).

BRILL, HERMANN. "Der Typ des künftigen deutschen Bundeslandes," in Die Bundes-
länder (1950).

BUHLER, OTTMAR. "Finanzgewalt im Wandel der Verfassungen," in Festschrift für
Richard Thoma (1950).

FISCHER-MENSHAUSEN, HERBERT. "Die Abgrenzung der Finanzverantwortung zwischen Bund und Ländern," in Die öffentliche Verwaltung, Jg. 5 (1952).
GREWE, WILHELM. "Antinomien des Föderalismus." Recht und Zeit. Heft 3 (1948).
JERUSALEM, FRANZ. "Die Staatsidee des Föderalismus," in Festschrift für Laforet (1952).
———. "Zentralismus und Föderalismus," in Festschrift für Laforet (1952).
MAIER, HEDWIG. Deutscher und meopäischer Föderalismus (1948).

SWITZERLAND

I. HISTORY AND FRAMING OF THE FEDERAL CONSTITUTION

BLUNTSCHLI, JOHANN CASPER. Geschichte des schweiberischen Bundesrechtes von dem ersten ewigen Bunde bis auf die Gegenwart, Zürich 1848–1859, 2 Bände, 2. Aufl. (1875).
BONJOUR, EDGAR. Die Gründung des schweizerischen Bundesstaats (1948).
BOSSARD, DAMIEN. Das Verhältnis zwischen Bundesversammlung und Bundesrat. Eine Studie über das Prinzip der Gewalttrennung im schweizerischen Bundesstaatsrecht, Diss. (1909).
FLEINER, FRITZ. Die Gründung des schweizerischen Bundesstaates im Jahr 1848, ausgewählte Schriften und Reden (1941).
———. Entstehung und Wandlung moderner Staatstheorien in der Schweiz (1916).
NABHOLZ, HANS. Comment et pourquoi la Confédération Suisse est-elle devenue Etat fédératif en 1848 (1947).
———. Die Entstehung des Bundesstaats wirtschaftlich betrachtet (1944).
RAPPARD, WILLIAM E. La Constitution Fédérale de la Suisse, 1848–1948 (1948).
———. L'individu et l'Etat dans l'évolution constitutionelle de la Suisse (1936).
SCHOLLENBERGER, JOHANN JAKOB. Die schweizerische Eidgenossenschaft.
ZACHARIA, HEINRICH ALBERT. Die schweizerische Eidgenossenschaft, der Bund und die Bundesrevision. Eine staats- und bundesrechtliche Erörterung (1848).

II. THE EVOLUTION AND WORKING OF THE FEDERAL CONSTITUTION

BIRCHMEIER, W. Handbuch des Bundesgesetzes über die Organisation der Bundesrechtsplege vom lt. Dez. 1943 (1950).
BROOKS, ROBERT C. Government and Politics of Switzerland (1927).
BUNSEN, HERMAN. Die Dynamik der Schweizerischen Demokraties (1937).
BURCKHARDT, WALTER. Kommentar der schweizerischen Bundesverfassung vom 19. Mai 1874 (1905), 3. Aufl. (1931).
CRON, P. Die Geschäftsordnung der schweizerischen Bundesversammlung (1946).
EICHENBERGER, K. Die oberste Gewalt im Bunde (1949).
FLEINER, FRITZ. Schweizerisches Bundesstaatsrecht (1923).
———. Unitarismus und Föderalismus in der Schweiz und in den Vereinigten Staaten von Amerika (1941).
———. Zentralismus und Föderalismus in der Schweiz (1918).
GIACOMETTI, ZACCARIA. Das öffentliche Recht der schweize rischen Eidgenossenschaft, 2 Aufl. (1938).
———. Das Staatsrecht der schweizerische Kanton (1941).
———. Verfassungsrecht und Verfassungspraxis in der schweizerischen Eidgenossenschaft. Festgabe für Fritz Fleiner (1937).
GIACOMETTI, ZACCARIA, and FLEINER, FRITZ. Schweizerisches Bundesstaatsrecht (1949).
HEFTI, M. Rechsstellung und Tätigkeit der Vollmachtenkommissionen der Schweizer-

868 BIBLIOGRAPHY

ischen Bundesversammlung im zweiten Weltkrieg und in der Nachkriegs-zeit (1951).

————. "Des rapports entre le droit civil fédéral et le droit public cantonal."

HUBER, HANS. "Die Garantie der individuellen Verfassungsrechte," 55 n.F. *Zeits. f. Schweiz. Recht* (1935).

IMBODEN, MAX. "Erfahrungen auf dem Gebiet der Verwaltungsrechtsprechung in Bund und Kantonen," 66 n.F. *Zeits. f. Schweiz. Recht* (1947).

KÄGI, WERNER. *Die Verfassung als rechtliche Grundordnung des Staates.* Unter-suchungen über die Entwicklungstendenzen im modernen Verfassungsrecht (1947).

KIRCHHOFER. "Die Verwaltungsrechtspflege beim Bundesgericht," 49 n.F. *Zeits. f. Schweiz. Recht* 79 (1930).

NAWIASKY, HANS. *Aufbau und Begriff der Eidgenossenschaft,* (Veröffentlichungen der Handelschochschule St. Gallen, Reihe A, Heft 11 (1937).

NEF, H. "Sinn und Schultz verfassungsmässiger Gesetzgebung und rechtmässiger Verwaltung im Bunde," 69 n.F. *Zeits. f. Schweiz. Recht.* 133a (1950).

PANCHAUD, A. "Les garanties de la constitutionnalité et de la légalité en droit féd-éral," 69 n.F. *Zeits. f. Schweiz. Recht* (1950).

RAPPARD, WILLIAM E. *Die Bundesverfassung,* (1948).

————. *La Constitution Fédérale de la Suisse, 1848–1948* (1948).

————. *The Government of Switzerland* (1936).

SCHOLLENBERGER, JOHANN JAKOB. *Das Bundesstaatsrecht der Schweiz,* 2. Aufl. (1920).

VINCENT, JOHN MARTIN. *State and Federal Government in Switzerland* (1891).

III. MONOGRAPHS ON FEDERALISM

BERCHEN, RENE VAN. *De la chambre unique au système becaméral* (1924).

BRUGGER, FRIEDRICH. *Die Kompetenzverteilung zwischen dem Bund und den Kan-tonen,* Diss. (1922).

FEHR, GEROLD. *Die Wahl der Regierung in Bund und Kantonen,* Diss. (1945).

GLENK, T. *Das Subventionswesen im Bund.* Diss. (1912).

GUHL, T. *Bundesgesetz, Bundesbeschluss und Verordnung nach schweizerischem Staatsrecht* (1908).

HIS, EDUARD. *Amerikanische Einflüsse im schweizerischen Verfassungsrecht* (1920).

HUBER, HANS. *Der Kompetenzkonflikt zwischen dem Bund und den Kantonen,* Diss. (1926).

IMBODEN, MAX. *Bundesrecht, kantonales Recht.* Ein Beitrag zur Lehre vom Bundes-staat unter Verarbeitung der schweizerischer Staatsrechtspraxis, Diss. (1940).

KÄGI, WERNER. *Persönliche Freiheit, Demokratie und Föderalismus,* in Die Freiheit des Bürgers im schweizerischen Recht. Festgabe zur Hundertjahresfeier der Bundesverfassung (1948).

————. *Vom Sinn des Föderalismus.* Gedanken zur Verfassungspolitik, in Die Schweiz (Ein nationales Jahrbuch) (1944).

LAUBER, OTTO. *Der Bundesstaatsbegriff,* Diss. (1910).

NAEF, WERNER. *Föderalismus und Demokratie in der Schweiz.*

NAWIASKY, HANS. *Staatstypen der Gegenwart.* (Veröffentlichungen der Handel-schochschule St. Gallen, Heft 9) (1934).

ORELLI, KONRAD. "Das Verhältnis von Demokratie und Gewaltenteilung und seine Wandlung insbesondere im schweizerischen Bunde" in (Züricher Beiträge zur Rechtswissenschaft, n.F. Heft 125) (1947).

OSWALD, WILHELM. *Die Gewaltentrennung im schweizerischen Staatsrecht,* in Zeit-schrift für Schweizerisches Recht, n.F., Heft 62 (1943).

BIBLIOGRAPHY

869

RAPPARD, WILLIAM E. *Federalism in Switzerland,* in Parliamentary Affairs (1951).
———. Les expériences politiques de la Confédération suisse, in Le fédéralisme: Problèmes et Méthodes. Edité par l'UNESCO (1952).
RASCHLE, H. *Oberste Gewalt im Bund und Aussenpolitik,* in Schweizenischte Monatshefte (May, 1925).
RUTTIMANN, JAKOB. *Das nordamerikanische Bundesstaatsrecht, verglichen mit den politischen Einrichtungen der Schweiz,* (1867–1876).
SCHINDLER, DIETRICH. *Die Rechtsbeziehungen zwischen Bund und Kantonen im Heereswesen* (1916).
———. *Verfassungsrecht und soziale Struktur* (1932).
SEEGER, Z. R. *Das Gesetzgebungsverfahren in der Schweizerischen Bundesversammlung,* Diss. (1915).
STRAULI, H. *Die·Kompetenzausscheidung zwischen Bund und Kantonen auf dem Gebiete der Gesetzgebung,* Diss. (1933).
TRIPP, M. L. *Der schweizerische und der amerikanische Bundesstaat,* trans. by Hans Huber (1942).
TROXLER, I. P. V. *Die Verfassung der Vereinigten Staaten Nordamerikas als Musterbild der schweizerischen Bundesform* (1948).
VEITH, M. *Der rechtliche Einfluss der Kantone auf die Bundesgewalt nach schweizerischem Staatsrecht,* Diss. (1902).
WALDKIRCH, E. O. VON. *Die Mitwirkung des Volkes bei der Rechtsetzung nach dem Staatsrecht der Schweizerischen Eidgenossenschaft und ihrer Kantone* (1918).
———. *Die Notverordnungen in schweizerischen Bundesstaatsrecht,* Diss. (1915).

UNITED STATES

I. HISTORY AND FRAMING OF THE FEDERAL CONSTITUTION

ELLIOT, J. (ed.). *The Debates in the Several State Conventions on the Adoption of the Constitution* (1901).
FARRAND, MAX (ed.). *The Records of the Federal Convention* (1911).
———. *The Framing of the Constitution* (1913).
MADISON, HAMILTON, JAY. *The Federalist* (1788).
VAN DOREN, CARL. *The Great Rehearsal* (1948).
WARREN, CHARLES. *The Making of the Constitution* (1928).

II. THE EVOLUTION AND WORKING OF THE FEDERAL CONSTITUTION

BEARD, CHARLES A. *American Government and Politics* (10th ed. 1952).
BROGAN, D. W. *The American Political System* (1943).
BRYCE, JAMES. *The American Commonwealth* (1926).
BUCHANAN, J. "An Analogy in Support of the World Court," 30 Journal of American Judicature Society 130 (1946).
BUNN, C. *United States Courts* (5th ed. 1949).
BURNETT, E. *The Continental Congress* (1941).
CHEEVER, D. S. and HAVILAND, H. *American Foreign Policy and the Separation of Powers* (1952).
CLARK, JANE. *The Rise of a New Federalism* (1938).
CORWIN, EDWARD S. *The Constitution and What It Means Today* (10th ed. 1948).
DOBIE, A. *Handbook of Federal Jurisdiction* (1928).
DOBIE, A., and LADD, M. *Cases on Federal Jurisdiction and Procedure* (2d ed. 1950).
DOWLING, NOEL T. *Cases on Constitutional Law* (4th ed. 1950).

FAIRCHILD, H. P. *Immigration* (rev. ed. 1925).

FRANK, J. "The Appointment of Supreme Court Justices," [1941] Wisconsin Law Review 172, 342, 461.

FRANKFURTER, FELIX. "A Note on Advisory Opinions," 37 Harvard Law Review 1002 (1924).

———. "Advisory Opinions," *Encyclopaedia of Social Sciences.*

———. "Distribution of Judicial Power Between United States and State Courts," 13 Cornell Law Quarterly 499 (1928).

———. "Supreme Court," *Encyclopaedia of Social Sciences.*

FRANKFURTER, FELIX, and LANDIS, JAMES M. *The Business of the Supreme Court* (rev. ed. 1938).

FRANKFURTER, FELIX, and SHULMAN, HARRY. *Cases on Federal Jurisdiction and Procedure* (rev. ed. 1937).

FREUND, PAUL A. *On Understanding the Supreme Court* (1949).

———. "The Supreme Court of the United States," 29 Canadian Bar Review 1090 (1951).

HAYNES, G. *The Senate of the United States: Its History and Practice* (2 vols. 1938).

HOLCOMBE, A. N. *Our More Perfect Union: From Eighteenth Century Principles to Twentieth Century Practice* (1950).

HUGHES, CHARLES E. *The Supreme Court of the United States* (1928).

JACKSON, ROBERT H. "Full Faith and Credit: The Lawyers' Clause of the Constitution," 45 Columbia Law Review 1 (1945).

———. *The Struggle for Judicial Supremacy* (1941).

McCORMICK, C., and CHADBOURN, J. *Cases on Federal Courts* (2d ed. 1950).

MUNRO, WILLIAM B. *The National Government of the United States* (5th ed. 1947).

PRATT, J. W. *America's Colonial Experiment* (1950).

"Puerto Rico: A Study in International Development," 285 Annals of the American Society of Political Social Science (Jan. 1953).

Report of Secretary of State on Citizenship, Expatriation and Protection Abroad, H. R. Dec. No. 326, 53d Cong., 2d Sess. (1906).

ROGERS, L. *The American Senate* (1926).

ROSS, G. "Full Faith and Credit in a Federal System," 20 Minnesota Law Review 140 (1936).

ROSSITER, C. *Constitutional Dictatorship* (1948).

———. *The Supreme Court and the Commander-in-Chief* (1951).

ROTTSCHAEFER, L. HENRY. *The Constitution and Socio-Economic Change* (1948).

SHOLLEY, JOHN B. *Cases on Constitutional Law* (1951).

SWISHER, C. B. *The Growth of Constitutional Power in the United States* (1946).

WARREN, CHARLES. *The Supreme Court in United States History* (rev. ed., 2 vols. 1926).

WHITE, LEONARD D. *Trends in Public Administration* (1933).

WIENER, F. B. *A Practical Manual of Martial Law* (1940).

———. "The Militia Clause of the Constitution," 54 Harvard Law Review 181 (1940).

WILLOUGHBY, W. F. *Principles of Legislative Organization and Administration* (1934).

WRIGHT, BENJAMIN F. *The Growth of American Constitutional Law* (1942).

ZINK, H. *Government and Politics in the United States* (1951).

Selected Essays in Constitutional Law (4 vols., Association of American Law Schools, 1938).

Selected Essays on Constitutional Law (Harvard Law Review, 1952).

"A Symposium on Current Constitutional Problems," 4 Vanderbilt Law Review 399 (1951).

Index

Index

conciliation and arbitration, 502, 527, 546, 559, 569. *See also* Conciliation and arbitration
conditions. *See* Factory inspection; Hours; Wages
conscription, 220
conventions, 271, 294, 298, 550, 574
courts, 144, 504, 561
disputes, 502, 527, 530, 546, 559, 569, 583
exchange, 516, 535, 552, 564, 574, 588
federal power, 499, 525, 540, 556, 568, 581
Germany, 556
I.L.O. *See* International Labour Organization
interstate commerce, 499, 581
judiciary, 510, 526, 557, 569, 581
mobility, 516
organization of unions, 499, 526, 542, 556, 568, 581
relations, 325, 498, 515, 526, 542, 556, 568, 581
states, 499, 504, 511, 529, 551, 558, 574, 581
strikes, 507, 581
Switzerland, 568
United States, 581
Labor, Department of
Australia, 535
Canada, 551
United States, 512
Labor Management Relations Act (Taft-Hartley), 499, 502, 509, 582
Labor Relations Act (Wagner Act), 326, 449, 499, 582
Labor Relations Board, 326
Labrador, 735
Land Banks (United States), 493
Land Central Banks (Germany), 428
Land grant colleges, 444, 457, 486
Land, public, 444, 471, 486
Land use, 456, 467, 486
Länder, 94, 141, 209
Language. *See also* Multi-lingualism
qualification, 76, 93, 99
right to, 617, 627
Laski, Harold, 467
Law
civil, 605, 617, 689
common, 132, 170, 543, 581, 596, 614, 617, 688
conflicts, 112, 164, 171
due process, 171, 448, 604, 630

ex post facto, 632
international, 112, 164, 171, 266
rule of, 678, 689
uniformity, 112, 131, 139, 145, 156, 163, 170
League of Nations
mandates, German, 736
membership, 241
Legislation
agriculture, 447, 451, 458, 460, 471, 478, 489, 495
citizenship, 647, 653, 657
emergency, 181, 184, 530, 684
enabling. *See* Enabling acts
executive, 13, 83, 104
fiscal, 14, 375
initiation of. *See* Bills
labor, 510, 526, 541, 557, 569, 581
legislature, 12, 32, 45, 52, 59
social security, 519
taxation, 32, 40
Legislature. *See also* Lower house; Upper house
admission of states, 756, 766, 775
amendment of constitution. *See* Amendment of constitution
Australia, 29
Canada, 36
committees, 32, 39, 52, 59, 92, 711
deadlock, 21, 33, 41, 45, 52, 56, 60, 69, 71, 702
defense, 184, 189, 222
dissolution, 11, 15, 32, 37, 44, 50, 69, 82, 87, 95
election, 4, 30, 37, 43, 50
emergency powers, 679, 688, 703
executive, 10, 16, 23, 31, 38, 44, 58, 69, 82, 97, 103
finance, 375
foreign affairs, 239, 245, 247, 255, 267, 274, 277, 284, 289
Germany, 41
judiciary, 48, 54, 122
qualifications for membership, 31, 37, 44, 51, 57
salaries, 7, 30, 37, 51
Switzerland, 49
taxation, 32, 392, 396, 403, 408
treaties, 19, 33, 40, 60, 247, 258, 264, 269, 278, 287
tenure, 6, 29, 37, 43, 50, 56
territories, 721
United States, 55
voting, 8, 36, 42, 58